Y0-BXG-079

INTERMEDIATE ACCOUNTING

VOLUME ONE

THIRD EDITION

Thomas H. Beechy
Schulich School of Business
York University

Joan E.D. Conrod
Faculty of Management
Dalhousie University

Toronto • Montréal • Boston • Burr Ridge, IL • Dubuque, IA • Madison, WI • New York
San Francisco • St. Louis • Bangkok • Bogotá • Caracas • Kuala Lumpur • Lisbon • London
Madrid • Mexico City • Milan • New Delhi • Santiago • Seoul • Singapore • Sydney • Taipei

The McGraw-Hill Companies

McGraw-Hill Ryerson

Intermediate Accounting, Volume 1
Third Edition

ISBN: 0-07-093031-7

1 2 3 4 5 6 7 8 9 10 TCP 0 9 8 7 6 5

Printed and bound in Canada

Sponsoring Editor: Tom Gale
Marketing Manager: Kim Verhaeghe
Developmental Editors: Brook Nymark/Suzanne Simpson Millar
Production Coordinator: Paula Brown
Supervising Editor: Anne Nellis
Copy Editor: Karen Rolfe
Cover Design: Sharon Lucas
Interior Designer: Dianna Little
Composition: ArtPlus Design & Communications
Printer: Transcontinental Printing Inc.

Library and Archives Canada Cataloguing in Publication

Beechy, Thomas H., 1937-
Intermediate accounting / Thomas H. Beechy, Joan E.D. Conrod. — 3rd ed.

Includes bibliographical references and index.
ISBN 0-07-093031-7 (v. 1).—ISBN 0-07-093035-X (v. 2)

1. Accounting—Textbooks. I. Conrod, Joan E. D. (Joan Elizabeth Davison), 1956- II. Title.

HF5635.B466 2005 657'.044 C2004-906030-9

About the Authors

Thomas H. Beechy

Thomas H. Beechy is a Professor Emeritus of Accounting at the Schulich School of Business, York University. For many years, he was also the Associate Dean of the school. He currently holds the additional titles of Executive Director of International Relations, Assistant Dean—Special Projects, and BBA/iBBA Program Director. Professor Beechy holds degrees from George Washington University (BA), Northwestern University (MBA), and Washington University (DBA). He has been active in research and publication for almost 40 years, having published six books, including *Canadian Advanced Financial Accounting*, and numerous articles in major accounting journals. Professor Beechy has been a leader in Canadian accounting education, emphasizing the importance of case analysis in developing students' professional judgement and accounting skills. He has been an active researcher and advocate in both business and non-profit financial reporting, and has been particularly active in international accounting circles.

Joan E.D. Conrod

Joan E.D. Conrod is a Professor of Accounting in the Faculty of Management at Dalhousie University. She recently received the 2004 Atlantic Canada Leaders in Management Education Award from PriceWaterhouseCoopersLLP. This award recognizes her teaching excellence and her contributions to management practice. Joan's teaching excellence has also been recognized through awards such as the Dalhousie University Alumni Award for Teaching Excellence and the AAU Distinguished Teacher Award. She was awarded her FCA from the Nova Scotia Institute of Chartered Accountants in 1999. Joan is an active member of the University community and has served on many committees, including Dalhousie University Senate and the Board of Governors. She is a past president of the Canadian Academic Accounting Association. Joan has a lengthy history of involvement in professional accounting education. She has taught financial and managerial accounting courses to CA students across Canada, but particularly in Atlantic Canada, for 20 years. She has served on CA education committees at the local, regional, and national levels. Her publications include the text *Intermediate Accounting*, with Tom Beechy, *Financial Accounting 3* for CGA-Canada, and a variety of case material and other publications.

Brief Table of Contents—Volume 1

Table of Contents—Volume 1

Preface

What is intermediate accounting all about? There is a vast body of knowledge that must be mastered before you can account for the activities of an enterprise. Intermediate accounting is the nuts-and-bolts course where it all happens. Although a few topics are covered in greater depth in advanced accounting courses, virtually every important topic is included in an intermediate accounting course. Mastery of the content of intermediate accounting is crucial for anyone who hopes to either use or prepare accounting information.

Accounting in general involves a blend of technical know-how and professional judgement. So that's what *Intermediate Accounting* appropriately dwells on: technical knowledge and professional judgement, covering the range of corporate reporting topics.

In selecting material to include in this book, we have taken a fresh look at the realities of Canadian business practice. Accounting practices and policies have been in the public eye as never before, with both fraud and judgement issues causing material restatements. It's the perfect time to focus on judgement in accounting policy choice. In addition, there has been a tremendous explosion in accounting standards recently, and this text reflects many new standards. It also has a uniquely Canadian agenda.

Here's what this book reflects:

TECHNICAL KNOWLEDGE

Accountants have to be able to account for things! There is a base level of expertise that must become part of every accountant's body of knowledge: how to defer a cost, capitalize a lease, account for a pension, or prepare a cash flow statement. Accounting is very quantitative, and it takes lots of practice. Some of the transactions that we must account for are very complex. Their accounting treatment is equally complex. An affinity for numbers is important.

PROFESSIONAL JUDGEMENT

Judgement, it is often said, is the hallmark of a profession. There are often different ways to account for the same transaction. Professional accountants have to become good at sizing up the circumstances and establishing the appropriate accounting policy for those circumstances. Once an accounting policy has been established, there are usually estimates that must be made before the numbers can be recorded. Accounting estimates also require the exercise of professional judgement. Professional judgement is not acquired overnight. It is nurtured and slowly grows over a lifetime. In this book, we begin the development process by explicitly examining the variables that companies consider when evaluating their options, and the criteria accountants use to make choices.

NON-GAAP SITUATIONS

For a variety of reasons, businesses often have to follow generally accepted accounting principles. However, companies can and do prepare reports based on accounting policies that are tailored for their unique circumstances and the specific decisions that are to be made based on the financial statements. Therefore, accountants cannot wear GAAP like a pair of blinders. Accountants have to be aware of accounting alternatives, and the circumstances under which such policies are needed. This book provides practice in this area.

A CANADIAN AGENDA

Issues that receive the most attention in this book are those that are relevant in a Canadian context. Many times, the topics covered in other intermediate texts are determined by U.S. standards and priorities because those books are adaptations of U.S. texts. However, there are some significant differences between Canadian and U.S. businesses and business environments that dictate a different emphasis and coverage. We hope you appreciate the redirected emphasis!

AN INTERNATIONAL VIEW

Of course, following a Canadian agenda does not mean that we're blind to what is happening in the rest of the world. This book informs you about major developments around the world, and other acceptable accounting practices. In particular, most chapters explain the differences between Canadian practice and the policies recommended by the International Accounting Standards Committee.

A LIVELY WRITING STYLE

We've consistently heard from students who use this book that the material is fresh and easy to read. Difficult? Sometimes. Boring? Never!

KEY FEATURES

Introduction

Each chapter has an introduction that explains the objectives of the chapter in narrative form.

Concept Review

Throughout each chapter, there are periodic pauses for the student to stop and think through the answers to basic questions covering the previously explained material. This helps comprehension and focus! If you have trouble determining the correct response to the concept review questions, the answers can be found in the Study Guide and on the book's website.

Summary of Key Points

At the end of each chapter, a summary of key points lists the key ideas explained in the chapter. This is meant to reinforce the chapter material.

Key Terms and the Glossary

At the end of each chapter there is a list of new terms used in the chapter. These terms are explained in the chapter, and are also defined in the glossary, which is available on the Online Learning Centre.

International Perspective

Most chapters include a review of international accounting policies, and differences that are found both internationally and in different countries. While the U.S. position is very important to us here in Canada, and is discussed when appropriate, there are many other countries around the world worth watching!

Integration of Cash Flow Material throughout the Text

The cash flow statement (CFS) is reviewed in Chapter 5, following coverage of the income statement and balance sheet. Students can thus learn how to do the statement early in the course. Following this chapter, though, the cash flow implications of various complex transactions are reviewed in each relevant chapter. There is cash flow assignment material in most chapters of the book. For those instructors who like to emphasize cash flow material at the end of the course, an appendix has been added to the final chapter that summarizes cash flow statement issues and provides a comprehensive example. This is reinforced with assignment material in the last chapter.

Cases

More than 80 cases are included in *Intermediate Accounting*, and there is at least one new case in every chapter in the third edition. The cases typically are not single-subject, paragraph-long "think pieces," but rather are meant to portray circumstances evocative of real life. Students have to put themselves into the situation and grapple with the facts and real users and uses to arrive at appropriate accounting policies for the circumstances. A blend of professional judgement and technical skills is needed to respond to a case. Case coverage is not limited to "one chapter" bites, but integrates material learned to date. For those trying to build a base of professionalism, the use of cases consistently over the term is highly recommended. Cases can be assigned for class debriefing, class presentations, or written assignments.

Assignment Material

There is an extensive range of assignment material at the end of each chapter. The assignments give students the opportunity to learn by doing.

We have selected a few assignments from each chapter and put their solutions in the Study Guide and on the book's website; students can practise on their own. These selected assignments are highlighted by an icon in the margin. Excel templates for selected assignments have been developed; these assignments are marked with an icon in the margin.

Stars in the margins at the end of each chapter indicate length, with one star being the shortest assignment, and three stars being the longest assignment.

Integrative Problems

From time to time in the book, there are integrative problems that formally deal with accounting topics covered in five or six chapters. These problems are a great pre-test review!

Ethics Material

Ethics material has been incorporated into case material. Essentially, when an accountant makes a recommendation on a contentious choice of accounting policy, ethics are tested. We decided against putting in smaller ethics "vignettes," as it is always painfully obvious that the accountant is meant to take the high path and demonstrate good ethics. We feel that our students exercise more true-to-life ethical judgement when they have to make a tough judgement call and recommend an accounting policy that is "good" for one group but "bad" for another. Ethical overtones are highlighted in the case solutions to help instructors draw them out in discussion and evaluation.

The Accounting Cycle

The basic debit and credit of the accounting world is hardly a topic for an intermediate accounting course. It represents the baby steps, and we're trying to learn how to run, or at least jog. For many students, this material was covered in a high school course or an introductory accounting course. Others, who avoided the course in high school and/or who took a conceptually oriented introductory course in college or university, may need grounding in this area. Therefore, we have included the accounting cycle as an appendix to Volume I, to allow maximum flexibility to instructors. Some courses may formally devote time to this appendix, and others may use it as a reference only.

TOPICAL HIGHLIGHTS OF THE TEXT

Chapters 1 and 2

The book starts with a review of the GAAP (and non-GAAP) world, and establishes the common reporting motivations of companies and financial statement users, as well as the basic concepts of accounting. This is fundamental material underlying professional judgement, and it reflects new AcSB pronouncements on the hierarchy of generally accepted accounting principles.

Chapters 3 and 4

These chapters review the income statement, retained earnings statement, balance sheet, and disclosure notes. New to the third edition is an explanation of the new statement of comprehensive income. Real-life examples show the degree of diversity that exists and how little information some companies provide in their financial statements. The chapters highlight the judgemental issues inherent in the statements and disclosures.

Chapter 5

The CFS is dealt with in sequence, as a primary financial statement. Again, coverage begins with a real-life example, to analyze the nature of information presented and the judgemental issues involved. The chapter deals with the mechanics of statement preparation, using both a format-free approach, and a journal-entry-based worksheet. The T-account method is reviewed in an appendix. CFS issues are reviewed in every subsequent chapter of the text, and include CFS assignment material. We summarize text topics that impact on the CFS in an appendix to Chapter 21, for those who wish to reinforce this topic as a stand-alone topic later in the course.

Chapter 6

Revenue and expense recognition are surely the most judgemental areas of accounting policy choice in the GAAP world. For the third edition of the book, we have combined the topics of revenue and expense recognition into one chapter to fully integrate these policy choices. The emphasis of the text material is on the financial statement impact of these policies on net assets. There is extensive discussion of the criteria to be applied to determine appropriate revenue recognition policy, and the numeric implications. Expense recognition is critically reviewed, both from a theoretical and practical perspective.

Chapter 7

Issues related to monetary balances—cash, receivables, and payables—are gathered and reviewed together. Important topics such as foreign currency translation (a must, in this age of globalization) and the new rules governing the transfer of receivables are incorporated. Material covering the mathematical basics of present and future value is now available on the Online Learning Centre, as is a more extensive set of compound interest tables.

Chapter 8

Inventory issues are dealt with in this chapter. The chapter includes the basics of policy decision in this critical area, as well as the mechanics of inventory costing methods, lower of cost or market writedowns, and inventory estimation techniques.

Chapters 9 and 10

Accounting for capital assets, both tangible and intangible, follows a common pattern. These chapters systematically look at acquisition, amortization, impairment, and disposal. We explain and illustrate the new accounting standards relating to asset retirement obligations, held-for-sale assets, and asset impairments.

Chapter 11

Welcome to the new world of accounting for investments! This chapter has been extensively rewritten to reflect the AcSB material that is expected to be approved for implementation in 2006. We think our students should be on the cutting edge of these standards, which are consistent with U.S. and IASC pronouncements. Accounting for held-to-maturity, trading, available-for-sale, significant influence, and control investees is covered. Both policy and numeric issues are thoroughly explored. The chapter includes a number of very useful summary diagrams and schedules to clarify the roadmap through this new territory. The material was classroom tested on Intermediate Accounting students during development, and is as clear and comprehensive as it gets! The "old rules," effective until the end of 2005, are available in material posted on the Online Learning Centre.

Chapters 12 and 13

These chapters deal with straightforward debt and shareholders' equity issues. The debt chapter looks at the always-challenging long-term debt issues, including material on effective and straight-line interest calculations. The financial instrument rules are integrated into these chapters. The new requirement for reporting other comprehensive income, including certain types of unrealized foreign currency gains/losses, is fully explained.

Chapter 14

Classification of debt versus equity, and appropriate treatment of hybrid financial instruments, are the topics in this chapter. Students learn how to determine the substance of a financial instrument, rather than its legal form, and account for it accordingly. Revised accounting standards for convertible debt are fully reflected in the material. Students also learn the nature of derivative instruments and why they are reported at fair value. The chapter then turns to accounting for stock options and provides an overview of the various circumstances in which options are granted. The two basic accounting paths, recognition and disclosure, are established. The chapter has complete coverage of the AcSB rules for employee stock options.

Chapters 15 and 16

Accounting for income tax remains two separate chapters, to acknowledge that many instructors prefer to spend two blocks of time on this most challenging area. The Chapter 15 material has been extensively rewritten to establish a three-step process for typical situations. The focus of Chapter 16 remains accounting for the tax effect of losses—carrybacks and carryforwards. This is difficult material for students, but the Chapter 16 problems incorporate the prior chapter material, and allow solid reinforcement of the steps associated with tax accounting.

Chapter 17

The leases material has been consolidated into one chapter, with appropriate focus on the lessee. Most companies lease something as a lessee, and thus lessee accounting is very commonly encountered in practice. Both the judgemental issues of lease classification and the complex calculations are extensively reviewed in this chapter, with examples.

Lessors, on the other hand, are rare. They tend to be quite specialized entities—financial intermediaries. Since lessors comprise a specialized industry, accounting by lessors is presented in a chapter appendix. The appendix includes an overview of the major aspects of lessor accounting and how it contrasts with lessee accounting. The appendix may be omitted if the instructor does not wish to deal with this specialized industry.

Chapter 18

Pensions and other post-retirement benefits are complex, long-term arrangements with employees. Accounting issues are also complex and have been structured in a worksheet format to improve clarity and comprehension. The worksheet has been carefully explained to help students—and instructors—get comfortable with this topic.

Chapter 19

Earnings per share material includes explanation of basic and diluted EPS. The procedural steps associated with organizing a complex EPS question are emphasized, to provide more comfort and support in this complicated area.

Chapter 20

Accounting policy changes and error corrections require restatement of one or more prior years' financial statements. Restatement is surely a current topic, given the number of fraud-based restatements reported in the public press over the last few years. This chapter deals with the theory and mechanics related to such restatement, reflecting new AcSB standards.

Chapter 21

The text concludes with a review of financial statement analysis, and emphasizes the importance of accounting policy choice and disclosure in the analysis of published financial statements. There is an extensive case illustration, based on a real Canadian company, that demonstrates the importance of accounting policy choice. This chapter also includes an appendix on the cash flow statement. The appendix summarizes the impact on the CFS of various transactions, and includes a comprehensive example. This appendix is meant to reinforce the CFS for instructors who like to deal with the statement as a stand-alone topic that reviews many topics within Intermediate Accounting.

Accuracy

The text has been extensively reviewed and proofread prior to publication. All assignment materials have been solved independently by individual "technical checkers" in addition to the authors. Nevertheless, it is inevitable that a few errors remain, for which we accept full responsibility. If you find errors, please e-mail the authors at j.conrod@dal.ca or tbeechy@schulich.yorku.ca. There are thousands of calculations in this text—it's a daunting task to bring them to the degree of accuracy we'd like to be famous for. Your help will be greatly appreciated.

SUPERIOR SERVICE

Service takes on a whole new meaning with McGraw-Hill Ryerson and *Intermediate Accounting*. More than just bringing you the textbook, we have consistently raised the bar in terms of innovation and educational research—both in accounting and in education in general. These investments in learning and the education community have helped us to understand the needs of students and educators across the country, and allowed us to foster the growth of truly innovative, integrated learning.

- Your **Integrated Learning Sales Specialist** is a McGraw-Hill Ryerson representative who has the experience, product knowledge, training, and support to help you assess and integrate any of the below-noted products, technology, and services into your course for optimum teaching and learning performance. Whether it's using our test bank software, helping your students improve their grades, or putting your entire course online, your *i*Learning Sales Specialist is there to help you do it. Contact your local *i*Learning Sales Specialist today to learn how to maximize all of McGraw-Hill Ryerson's resources!

- ***i*Learning Services Program**
  McGraw-Hill Ryerson offers a unique *i*Services package designed for Canadian faculty. Our mission is to equip providers of higher education with superior tools and resources required for excellence in teaching. For additional information visit **http://www.mcgrawhill.ca/highereducation/iservices**.

SUPPLEMENTS

For the Instructor

Supplements include

- **Instructor's Resource CD-ROM.** A one-stop convenient source of supplemental material.
  - **Instructor's Manual.** For each chapter you will find a brief topical outline that indicates the topics to discuss in class and an assignment guide that provides at a glance the topical content of each exercise, problem, and case.
  - **Computerized Test Bank.** With an abundance of objective questions, multiple-choice questions, and short exercises, this supplement is a valuable resource for instructors when preparing quizzes and examinations.
  - **Solutions manual.** This comprehensive manual provides solutions to all cases, questions, assignments, and comprehensive problems.
  - **PowerPoint® Slides.** This slide presentation can be used to review chapter concepts.
  - **Spreadsheet Application Software for specific problems (SPATS).** This feature provides an introduction to basic computerized accounting. In-text icons identify problems that can be solved using Excel® templates, which reside on the Online Learning Centre.
- **Solutions Transparencies.**

For the Student

- **Study Guide with Check Figures.** [0-07-094280-3] The study guide allows students to measure progress through a wealth of self-test material (with solutions) and a summary of chapter key points. The study guide also includes the solutions to designated assignment material, marked with an icon in the text. These solutions are also available on the Online Learning Centre.
- **Spreadsheet Application Software for specific problems (SPATS).** This feature provides an introduction to basic computerized accounting. In-text icons identify problems that can be solved using Excel® templates, which reside on the Online Learning Centre.

TECHNOLOGY SOLUTIONS

Online Learning Centre

Updated for the third edition, McGraw-Hill Ryerson offers you an online resource that combines the best content with the flexibility and power of the Internet. By connecting to the "real world" through the Online Learning Centre (OLC), you will enjoy a dynamic and rich source of current information that will help you get more from your course and improve your chances for success, both in accounting and in the future.

Organized by chapter, the Beechy/Conrod *Intermediate Accounting* OLC provides an impressive array of helpful learning features, including

- Solutions to selected text assignments;
- Summaries of each chapter;
- Self-assessment quizzes;
- A glossary of all key terms in the text;
- SPATS downloads to help solve selected in-text assignments;
- Compound Interest Tables; and
- Appendix: Interest—Concepts of Future and Present Value.

For the Student

ONLINE QUIZZES Do you know the material? You can reference the Glossary or consult the Key Terms for each chapter. Need some practice? Cases and short-answer questions are contained for every chapter. If that isn't enough, test your knowledge with the multiple-choice and true/false quizzes to maximize the effect of the time spent reviewing text concepts. They are auto-graded with feedback, and you have the option to send results directly to your instructor.

WEBLINKS This section references various websites, including all company websites mentioned in the text.

INTERNET APPLICATION QUESTIONS Go online to learn how companies use the Internet in their day-to-day activities. Answer questions based on current organization websites and strategies.

Your Internet companion to the most exciting education tools on the Web!
The Online Learning Centre can be found at www.mcgrawhill.ca/college/beechy.

For the Instructor

The OLC includes a password protected website for instructors. All key supplements are downloadable for instant access. The site is password protected to preserve the integrity of the material.

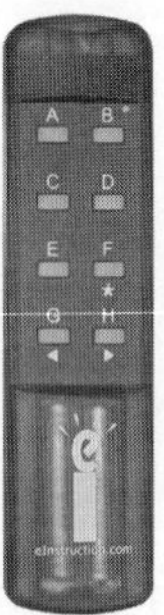

eInstruction's Classroom Performance System (CPS)

Bring interactivity into the classroom or lecture hall.

CPS by eInstruction is a student response system using wireless connectivity. It gives instructors and students immediate feedback from the entire class. The response pads are remotes that are easy to use and engage students.

- CPS helps you to increase student preparation, interactivity and active learning so you can receive immediate feedback and know what students understand.
- CPS allows you to administer quizzes and tests, and provide immediate grading.
- With CPS you can create lecture questions that can be multiple-choice, true/false and subjective. You can even create questions on-the-fly as well as conduct group activities.
- CPS not only allows you to evaluate classroom attendance, activity, and grading for your course as a whole, but CPSOnline allows you to provide students with an immediate study guide. All results and scores can easily be imported into Excel and can be used with various classroom management systems.

CPS ready content is available for use with the Beechy/Conrod, *Intermediate Accounting*, Third Edition. Please contact your *i*Learning Sales Specialist for more information on how you can integrate CPS into your accounting classroom.

PAGEOUT Create your own course web page for free—quickly and easily. Your professionally designed website links directly to OLC material, allows you to post a class syllabus, offers an online gradebook, and much more! No knowledge of HTML is required. Visit www.pageout.net

PRIMIS ONLINE Professors can now create their unique, custom eBook or printed text online. With Primis Online you can select, view, review your table of contents, fill out your customer cover and shipping information, and then have the opportunity to approve a complimentary sample book! Once you have approved your sample eBook or printed book, your students can purchase it—either through McGraw-Hill's Primis eBookstore or your local campus bookstore. Start creating your own customized text through Primis Online by going to www.mcgrawhill.ca/highereduction/primis+online.

WEBCT/BLACKBOARD This text is available in two of the most popular delivery platforms, WebCT and Blackboard. These platforms provide instructors with user-friendly, flexible teaching tools.

Acknowledgements

The text would not have been possible without the contributions of a great many people. We recognize and appreciate all of their efforts.

Our thanks and gratitude are extended to the outstanding anonymous faculty reviewers who provided criticism and constructive suggestions on the text material. It hasn't been possible to incorporate all the (sometimes conflicting!) suggestions, but the quality of this book has improved thanks to the people who reviewed it:

Talal AL-Hayale	University of Windsor
Teresa Anderson	University of Ottawa
Ann Bigelow	University of Western Ontario
Walt Burton	Okanagan University College
David Carter	University of Waterloo
Sandra L. Daga	University of Toronto—Scarborough
Elizabeth Farrell	York University
David Fleming	George Brown College
Leo Gallant	St. Francis Xavier University
Darrell Herauf	Carleton University
Shari Mann	University of Waterloo
Stephen Priddle	Carleton University
Doug Ringrose	Grant MacEwan College
Johan de Rooy	University of British Columbia
Wendy Roscoe	Concordia University
Catherine Seguin	University of Toronto—Mississauga
Claire G. St. Pierre	CGA-Canada

We are grateful to our dedicated team of problem checkers, including Jeff Christian, C.A.; Cheryl Nachtigal; Chris Arsenault, C.A.; Paolo Lorenzoni; Martino Calvaruso; Ann Bigelow; and Catalina Huzum, who have exhaustively checked the accuracy of the assignment material.

To numerous other colleagues and users whose constructive comments and suggestions have led to improvements, our thanks. We also appreciate the permissions granted by the following organizations for use of their problem and case material:

- The Canadian Institute of Chartered Accountants
- The Certified General Accountants' Association of Canada
- The Society of Management Accountants
- The Ontario Institute of Chartered Accountants
- The Atlantic School of Chartered Accountancy
- The American Institute of Certified Public Accountants

We are grateful to the people at McGraw-Hill Ryerson who guided this manuscript through its development process. In particular, we are extremely grateful for the strong and continuous support of Joseph Gladstone, who is responsible for many improvements over three editions. We also appreciate the support of Tom Gale and his people at McGraw-Hill Ryerson, most notably Nicole Lukach, Executive Sponsoring Editor. We also thank Brook Nymark and Suzanne Simpson Millar, who have done their best to keep us motivated and productive. Our production team, including Anne Nellis and freelance editor Karen Rolfe, has contributed in significant ways to this final product.

On a personal level, we would like to thank our friends and family members for their support and encouragement throughout the lengthy process of bringing this book to fruition: especially, in Halifax, Peter Conrod and Warren and Carmita Fetterly, and in Toronto, Calvin Luong and Brian McBurney.

Thomas H. Beechy
Schulich School of Business
York University
Toronto

Joan E.D. Conrod
Faculty of Management
Dalhousie University
Halifax

CHAPTER 1

The Environment of Accounting

INTRODUCTION

The purpose of financial accounting is to communicate information, and information is useful only if it can be used to make decisions. It is possible, therefore, to characterize accounting as being a *behavioural* discipline; every financial reporting choice that an accountant makes has the potential power to influence someone's or some group's behaviour.

This chapter will discuss the environment of financial accounting, including various forms of organization and the factors that influence and constrain financial reporting. In particular, we will discuss the question of what constitutes generally accepted accounting principles (GAAP) and the possible alternatives to GAAP.

Accounting is full of choices. To present an organization's financial results, management must make many choices from possible accounting policies. Management must also make a continuing series of estimates that affect every single amount reported on the financial statements. There is no single correct answer in accounting; the "answer" depends on a series of accounting *policy* choices, accounting *measurements*, and accounting *estimates*.

In every company, accounting choices are guided primarily by that company's own objectives of financial reporting—what information do users want, and what are the motivations of management? This chapter will discuss the most common financial reporting objectives for businesses. The rest of the book will regularly refer to these objectives when discussing the criteria that affect management's choices in dealing with specific accounting issues. Therefore, *the discussion of reporting objectives in this chapter should not be skimmed over.*

In this book, we will emphasize the nature of the choice process. We also will emphasize the variations in reported results that arise as the result of different choices.

This chapter discusses reporting objectives. In Chapter 2, we will discuss additional criteria used to make accounting choices, as well as the nature of professional judgement.

THE DIFFERENCE BETWEEN ACCOUNTING AND BOOKKEEPING

Before proceeding with a discussion of the environment of accounting, it is important to make a distinction between *accounting* and *bookkeeping*. Bookkeeping is a *recording* process, much of which has been automated in recent decades through the widespread use of computers, even in quite small organizations. The role of the bookkeeper has declined as computers have taken over most of the routine processing of financial data.

The accountant is responsible for telling the computer what to do. The responsibility is not for the programming, of course, but is for deciding how to classify and record transactions, how to disclose those transactions in the financial statements, how to measure the value of assets and liabilities and their related revenues and expenses, and what additional disclosures are appropriate. An accountant must never lose sight of the fact that financial statements are the end product of a large number of accounting *policy decisions* and *measurement estimates* by management (often with the advice of accountants), many of which are based on expectations about future events. Accounting involves many subjective choices. It is not the mechanical task of bookkeeping.

THE REALM OF FINANCIAL ACCOUNTING

financial accounting
methods used to report an organization's financial condition and results of operations to internal and external parties

Financial accounting is concerned with the way an organization communicates financial information about the economic activities of an enterprise to its stakeholders. Stakeholders can be both internal and external. The primary internal stakeholder is management, while the primary external stakeholder depends on the nature of the organization. For a large, public corporation, the primary external stakeholder group may be the shareholders. For a small private corporation in which the shareholder is also management, the only *external* stakeholder may be the Canada Revenue Agency (CRA), which assesses income taxes.

Financial accounting is the realm of accounting that is concerned primarily with producing financial statements that report on the economic well-being of an organization and on the flow of its resources. Financial accounting applies to all types of organizations, including

- Businesses
  - Proprietorships
  - Partnerships
  - Corporations
- Non-profit organizations[1]
  - Charitable
    - Incorporated
    - Unincorporated
  - Non-charitable
    - Incorporated
    - Unincorporated
- Governments
  - Senior governments (federal, provincial, and territorial)
  - Municipal governments (and school boards)

[1] There are several terms in widespread use to denote organizations of this type. The most common term in general use is *non-profit*. However, some people prefer the term *not-for-profit*, presumably to prevent naïve users from thinking that "non-profit" means for-profit companies that are operating at a loss. Indeed, the *CICA Handbook* uses "not-for-profit." In this text, we will use the more common "non-profit."

Non-Business Organizations

Not all organizations are business enterprises. Many are non-profit organizations, which may or may not be charitable organizations. Charitable organizations are those that the CRA has ruled are engaged in charitable activities and that therefore are authorized to issue tax receipts to donors. Donors can use the tax receipts to reduce their income taxes, via a tax credit. There are over 100,000 charitable organizations in Canada, roughly half of which are churches or religious charities.

The number of non-charitable non-profit organizations is unknown, but it must be in the hundreds of thousands. Think of all of the student organizations (clubs, volunteer organizations, student governments, etc.) in any college or university. Some are very small, but others may be quite large and have control of substantial amounts of money. Political parties are non-charitable non-profit organizations, as are labour unions and industry trade associations.

Non-profit organizations may or may not be incorporated. If a non-profit organization is incorporated, it is a *corporation without share capital.* There are no shareholders in a non-profit corporation. A non-profit corporation may have capital on its balance sheet, but that capital is not the result of the issuance of shares. Instead, capital is the result of donations or accumulated operating surpluses.

The third type of organization is *governments.* Governments at all levels must prepare financial statements, but the rules guiding the preparation of governmental statements vary considerably from those guiding businesses. There is a completely separate standard-setting body, the Public Sector Accounting and Auditing Board, that strives to improve the financial reporting of governments. Furthermore, there is a difference in financial reporting for senior governments (the federal, provincial, and territorial governments) and for municipalities. Municipal accounting varies according to the laws of the provinces.

Financial Statements

The financial accounting system produces reports both at a point in time (*point* statement) and for a period of time (*flow* statements). The point statement is usually known as the balance sheet, regardless of the type of organization, while flow statements vary depending on the type of organization. Organizations normally prepare at least three flow statements:

1. statement of operations
2. statement of changes in capital
3. cash flow statement

Other flow statements may be prepared as the nature of the company, industry, or organizational segment requires. For example,

- Companies with foreign currency transactions or foreign operations may need to prepare a statement of "other comprehensive income" (discussed in Chapter 3).
- Mutual funds and investment companies normally prepare a statement of changes in net assets and a statement of changes in the investment portfolio.
- Many non-profit organizations prepare a statement of changes in fund balances.
- Governments may prepare a statement of changes in capital assets (especially when capital assets are not included on the balance sheet).

The statement of operations for a business is known as the *income statement* or *statement of earnings.* In business corporations, the statement of changes in capital is known as the *statement of changes in retained earnings*; but in proprietorships and partnerships, owners' equity is not subdivided into contributed capital and retained earnings, and therefore the statement is called simply the *statement of changes in capital.* In many corporate businesses, the first two flow statements are combined into a single statement, known in corporations as a *statement of income* (or *earnings*) *and retained earnings.* Proprietorships and partnerships may prepare a combined *statement of income and capital.*

Non-profit organizations prepare financial statements that bear a somewhat superficial resemblance to those of a business, both point statements and flow statements. Unlike business organizations, however, non-profits are not seeking a profit and their flow statements often differ sharply from those of businesses. The operating statement usually focuses on the flow of resources rather than on the measurement of net income. The difference in focus is the result of the needs of the users, who usually are the financial supporters of the organization (e.g., members, donors, government ministries) and who want to know what the organization has done with the money with which the managers were entrusted.

Small organizations (particularly non-profit organizations) may use a very simplified statement that serves as both an operating statement and a cash flow statement. Proprietorships may prepare an income statement but no balance sheet because the business assets are co-mingled with the owner's assets; the CRA does not require proprietorships and partnerships to present a balance sheet because the income is taxed directly to the proprietor or partners; only corporations are separate legal entities and are taxed as such.

Accounting for Business Organizations

In this book, we focus exclusively on business organizations, primarily corporations. Indeed, several chapters are applicable *only* to corporations (for example, the chapters on shareholders' equity, earnings per share, and income taxes). Non-profit and governmental reporting is generally covered in advanced accounting texts, even though both non-business types of organizations are pervasive in our society and economy.[2]

Management accounting is concerned with preparing and analyzing information for the exclusive use of management for decision-making, planning, employee motivation, and internal performance evaluation. The level of detail is much greater, and the basis of accountability may differ from that presented in the organization's financial statements. Management accounting deals primarily with segments of an organization and management's specific decision-making needs. The users of management accounting information are known with certainty, and thus the information can be tailored to suit their specific needs. In financial accounting, however, there often are multiple users. The various users often have conflicting objectives, and the financial statements must be prepared on a basis that optimizes the trade-offs between the various users' needs.

CONCEPT REVIEW

1. What is the essential difference between a bookkeeper and an accountant?
2. What is the general realm of financial accounting? How does financial accounting differ from management accounting?
3. What are non-business organizations?
4. Describe the difference between point statements and flow statements. Give examples of each.

PUBLIC VERSUS PRIVATE CORPORATIONS

A *public corporation* is one that issues securities (either debt or equity, or both) to the public. The securities can then be traded on the open market, usually through an *organized exchange* such as the Toronto Stock Exchange. Public corporations must be *registered* with the securities commissions in each province in which their securities are traded and must comply with the reporting requirements of the securities commissions.

[2] For example, Statistics Canada data show that approximately 17% of employed persons are working for a non-profit organization; another 7% work for some level of government or governmental body. Together, about 25% of the Canadian workforce is employed by non-business organizations.

A *private corporation* is one that does not issue securities to the public. This does not mean that a private corporation has no external sources of capital. Some of Canada's largest corporations are private corporations (e.g., McCain Foods Ltd. or Bata Shoes, both with annual revenues in excess of $4 billion), but they obtain capital through **private placements** of debt or equity instruments. As their securities are not publicly traded, they are not under the jurisdiction of the provincial securities acts and securities regulators. The suppliers of capital to a private corporation are assumed to be either insiders or sophisticated investors who do not need the special protection given to members of the general public who may buy shares on the open market.

private placements (privately placed securities)
securities that are issued to individuals or organizations (e.g., pension funds, insurance companies) without being listed with a securities commission for public trading.

A type of private corporation with special accounting implications is a Canadian corporation that is a wholly owned subsidiary of a foreign parent corporation. For example, General Motors of Canada Ltd. and Ford Motor Company of Canada Ltd., two of the three largest corporations in Canada, are wholly owned by their U.S. parent company and thus are private corporations.

Accounting Implications

The ownership of a corporation has important accounting ramifications. Public corporations must be audited and their reporting generally must conform to generally accepted accounting principles (GAAP). As the remainder of this text will repeatedly point out, however, GAAP may not be very restrictive because there is a great deal of reporting flexibility in some parts of GAAP.

All corporations are governed by the business corporations act in the province in which they are incorporated or by the *Canadian Business Corporations Act* (CBCA) for federally incorporated corporations. The business corporations acts usually state that an audit is required for corporations that are above a specified size threshold (e.g., in the CBCA, $10 million in gross revenue or $5 million in total assets). However, exemptions from the audit requirement are readily available if all the shareholders agree to waive the audit. Effectively, therefore, there is no audit requirement for private corporations.

Wholly owned subsidiaries of foreign parents probably will be audited, because the parent is likely to be a public company in its home country (most commonly, the United States). But private corporations, whether domestically owned or foreign-owned, are not required to issue their financial statements to the public. Since the primary user of the statements will be the foreign parent (and the statements will be consolidated with the parent's statements), the subsidiary may use the parent's home country GAAP instead of Canadian GAAP.

Control Blocks

Even when a Canadian corporation is public, it may be controlled by a small number of shareholders who have the majority of the voting shares. A small number of related or affiliated shareholders who hold a majority of the voting shares is called a **control block**. It is common Canadian practice for a public corporation to issue two or more classes of shares, one with multiple votes and another with few or no voting rights. Shares that have limited voting power are called **restricted shares**. Restricted shares are used as a means of raising public capital without losing the power of the control block.

control block
a small number of related or affiliated shareholders collectively having a majority of voting shares of a corporation

restricted shares
shares with limited or no voting rights

In the *Financial Post*'s annual listing of Canada's 500 largest corporations, known as the *FP500*, approximately half of the companies are public. Of the public companies, however, well over half have control blocks. Only about 20% of the companies in the *FP500* list are "widely held" public companies. This 20% actually overstates the importance of widely held public companies in Canada, because the list does not include a large number of private companies for which no data is available. For example, Bata Shoes is the world's largest shoe company and has annual revenues of about $4 billion, but the company never appears on lists of the largest Canadian corporations.

The implication of the existence of control blocks for Canadian financial reporting is that the accounting approach is unlikely to be dominated by a concern for the public shareholder, as is often the case in the United States. Instead, the reporting objectives of the controlling shareholder may well take precedence over those of the public investor.

CONCEPT REVIEW

1. What is the difference between a public corporation and a private corporation? Which type is dominant in the Canadian economy?
2. How can private corporations obtain capital from outside investors without becoming public companies?
3. What is a control block?

WHAT IS GAAP?

generally accepted accounting principles (GAAP)
body of accounting practices built up over time for use in preparing external accounting statements

The body of **generally accepted accounting principles (GAAP)** is just what the name implies—accounting principles that have become "generally accepted" in practice. General acceptance can come via two routes:

1. historical accounting practices that have become widely accepted over time; and
2. authoritative pronouncements by accounting standard-setting bodies.

Historical Accounting Practices

Historical accounting practices have been developed by businesses and have stood the test of time. Over many decades, preparers (i.e., managers, with advice from professional accountants) have devised measurement and reporting approaches that users accepted as being reasonable and that auditors have accepted as well. The vast bulk of today's accounting practices evolved this way.

Historical practices also include accounting practices followed by the so-called specialized industries such as real property development, agriculture, and financial services (e.g., insurance, banking, investment funds). Specialized industries account for a majority of the economic activity of Canada.

Many historical practices have found their way into the *CICA Handbook*. The AcSB's recommendations on many items of measurement and disclosure are simply a codification of past practice. Indeed, the broad basic practices of historical cost valuation and of expense and revenue recognition owe their origins to historical practice.

Authoritative Pronouncements

In contrast, **authoritative pronouncements** are accounting standards established by accounting standard-setting bodies that may sharply deviate from general practice. Canada's standard-setting body is the CICA's Accounting Standards Board (AcSB). In the United States, the standard-setter is the independent Financial Accounting Standards Board (FASB). Internationally, the accounting standard-setter is the International Accounting Standards Board (IASB), an independent group based in London that we will discuss in a later section.

GAAP is constantly evolving. The business environment is one of continuous innovation, and accountants must develop ways of accounting for new types of transactions and events. Accounting standards develop only after a new business practice has developed. Therefore, authoritative standards usually are not new practices or principles. Generally speaking, standard-setters try to narrow the range of accounting practices for any particular type of transaction or economic event. The recommended practice almost always existed in practice prior to issuance of the standard, although the practice may have been used in a different country. The standard-setting goal is to improve comparability between different companies that have the same types of transactions or that experience the same types of economic events.

The term "authoritative standards" sounds very official and precise. However, the application of almost all authoritative standards requires the exercise of professional judgement.

Many standards effectively eliminate all but one acceptable accounting policy for a particular event. Nevertheless, most standards still require accounting estimates and may also require other types of judgement, such as timing of recognition or the extent of note disclosure. The need for professional judgement is always present in accounting. We cannot rely on "standards" as an excuse to stop thinking.

Hierarchy of Standards

The various sources of GAAP do not have equal status; some take precedence over others. In Section 1100 of the *CICA Handbook*, the AcSB clarifies the relative status of different sources of GAAP to help preparers find their way through the maze that constitutes GAAP. In addition, the AcSB also clearly wants to rein in some of the more flagrant flights of fancy among preparers who might seize on remote aspects of GAAP to justify rather bizarre accounting policies.

The AcSB defines GAAP as the "broad principles and conventions of general application as well as procedures that determine accepted accounting practices at a particular time" (*CICA* 1100.02(b)). GAAP sources are be grouped into two categories:

- primary sources, consisting of pronouncements of the AcSB; and
- other sources.

PRIMARY SOURCES The primary sources of GAAP are the various standards, guidelines, EIC abstracts, and supporting materials issued by the AcSB. Within this group, there is a hierarchy—some sources take precedence over others. In *descending* order of authority, the primary sources are (*CICA* 1100.02(c))

1. The accounting sections of the *CICA Handbook*, including the appendices;
2. Accounting Guidelines, including appendices;
3. EIC abstracts;
4. AcSB documents that describe the background information and basis for conclusions for *CICA Handbook* accounting recommendations and *Accounting Guidelines*;
5. Illustrative material for the preceding sources, issued separately from the related accounting recommendations, *Accounting Guidelines*, or EIC abstracts; and
6. *Implementation guides* authorized by the AcSB.

The dominant source is the *CICA Handbook*. When managers of a GAAP-reporting company are selecting accounting policies, they cannot choose a source as being "authoritative" if it conflicts with one or more recommendations in the *CICA Handbook*.

The *CICA Handbook* sections often contain appendices, which have been approved by the AcSB and therefore carry the same authority as the recommendations in sections (*CICA* 1100.18).

The various sections of the *CICA Handbook* contain both italicized and non-italicized paragraphs. The italicized paragraphs are the recommendations themselves, the non-italicized paragraphs provide additional explanation or background. *Italicized and non-italicized paragraphs are of equal importance* (*CICA* 1100.13).

accounting guidelines
pronouncements issued by the Steering Committee of the Accounting Board concerning significant accounting issues.

The second source of GAAP within the primary sources are Accounting Guidelines issued by the AcSB. **Accounting Guidelines** reflect the Board's opinion on specific accounting issues and are issued very rarely. Guidelines are secondary to the recommendations of the *CICA Handbook* because they have not gone through the due process required for introducing new recommendations into the *CICA Handbook*. The "Introduction to Accounting Guidelines" states that

> Guidelines express the opinions of the Board and do not have the authority of Recommendations issued by the Board.

The third primary source is the *Emerging Issues Committee (EIC)*. The EIC is part of the standard-setting section of the *CICA*. The Committee meets regularly and issues opinions on accounting issues where current practice is unclear and guidance has been requested by

EXHIBIT 1-1

HIERARCHY OF GAAP

Primary sources (in descending order of authority):

- Accounting sections of the *CICA Handbook*;
- *Accounting Guidelines* issued by the Accounting Standards Board;
- Abstracts of Issues Discussed by the Emerging Issues Committee (EIC Abstracts);
- *Background Information and Basis for Conclusions* documents issued by the AcSB in conjunction with *CICA Handbook* recommendations or *Accounting Guidelines*;
- Illustrative material for all of the above sources that is issued by the AcSB; and
- Implementation Guides authorized by the AcSB, but not issued directly by the AcSB.

Other (secondary) sources (not in order of authority, but as relevant in the particular circumstances):

- FASB accounting standards (U.S.);
- International accounting standards;
- Implementation guides issued independent of the AcSB, particularly those specifically relating to the Canadian environment;
- Draft materials for primary sources (above), such as exposure drafts, statements of principles, and discussion documents;
- Research reports and research studies issued by the CICA or other groups;
- Accounting textbooks, journals, and articles that are relevant to the Canadian environment; and
- Established practice, whether written or unwritten, that is consistent with the application of professional judgment using the basic financial accounting concepts of *CICA Handbook* Section 1000.

accountants and/or managers. The EIC issues brief statements called *Abstracts of Issues Discussed (EIC Abstracts)* that describe the issue, the nature of the EIC's discussion, and the Committee's conclusion. Many of the issues involve interpretation of *CICA Handbook* sections in ambiguous or complex situations.

The fourth primary source is a type of AcSB document called *Background Information and Basis for Conclusions.* On occasion, the AcSB issues one of these background documents when the Board introduces a new or significantly revised *CICA Handbook* section. Background documents explain the research that the Board undertook when it examined an issue, including references to standards in other jurisdictions, particularly those of the U.S. FASB and international standards (IAS). The Board explains the reasons for its recommendations. Since these documents explain the reasoning of the Board more fully than the *CICA Handbook* sections, they become a primary source, particularly when there is some doubt about the relevant application of a standard in a specific situation.

The fifth primary source is illustrative material issued by the Board. These illustrations are not part of the *CICA Handbook* section, but are specially issued to provide additional illustrations of how a particular section should be applied. Illustrative material shows how an accounting standard might be applied in particular situations (*CICA* 1100.19). The material may also summarize certain aspects of the standard, including decision trees and other helpful guidance.

Finally, the sixth primary source consists of *implementation guides* authorized by the Board to help preparers apply complex sections of the *CICA Handbook* such as post-retirement benefits or financial instruments. There is a subtle distinction between the fifth and sixth sources. The fifth source is illustrative material *issued* by the Board. The sixth source is illustrative material that has been *authorized* by the Board, but that has been prepared by the CICA accounting standards staff and not approved directly by the Board.

OTHER SOURCES Essentially, *other sources* consist of anything that is relevant in a particular situation. These might also be called *secondary* sources, in contrast to AcSB-issued primary sources. Managers may turn to secondary sources when the primary sources of GAAP do not deal with the reporting of a specific transaction or combination of transactions (*CICA* 1100.06). Whenever secondary sources are used, the accounting policies and disclosures must be

1. consistent with the primary sources of GAAP; and
2. developed through the exercise of professional judgement and the application of financial accounting concept as described in Section 1000 of the *CICA Handbook* (*CICA* 1100.04).

Secondary sources should be evaluated on the basis of four criteria (*CICA* 1100.07):

1. *The specificity of the source.* A source that deals with the specific situation confronted by management is more relevant than a more general source.
2. *The authority of the issuer or author.* Other authoritative bodies such as the FASB and the IASB are viewed as better sources than opinions of others in the same jurisdiction.
3. *The continued relevance of the source.* Generally speaking, recent sources are better than possibly outdated sources.
4. *The development process for the source.* A source that is just the opinion of one person or one group is less relevant than a source that has been developed through a process of consultation with other interested individuals and groups.

Clearly, an important secondary source is the body of standards issued by the FASB and the IASB. These two standard-setters are the main points of reference for the AcSB when it develops or revises accounting standards. The goal of the AcSB is to harmonize Canadian standards with the FASB first, and the IASB second. Therefore, when adequate guidance is not provided by the primary Canadian sources, the logical next step is to turn to the FASB and the IASB.

However, there is no hierarchy within the secondary sources. FASB and IASB standards are relevant only if they satisfy the four criteria cited above. If they do not fit the Canadian situation, then they are irrelevant.

Another secondary source is implementation guidance issued by organizations other than the AcSB. Such guidance may be issued in book form by independent authors or groups, or in loose-leaf form by professional accounting reference services. Since the Board has not authorized these guides, they have less authority than the Board-authorized implementation guides included in the primary sources.

The AcSB issues exposure drafts, research studies, and background studies. Not all of these documents end up being formulated into accounting standards. However, the discussions in these documents may be used as a secondary source, *if* they do not conflict with final standards issued by the Board. The Board does not always follow the recommendations of its research reports and exposure drafts when it issues a final standard, so caution is necessary.

Additional secondary sources include accounting textbooks, accounting journals, independent research studies, and articles that describe specific approaches. Canadian-sourced materials are preferable to non-Canadian publications, which most likely will not consider the Canadian environment.

In all instances where secondary "other" sources are used, the resulting accounting policies must (1) be consistent with the primary sources of GAAP and (2) be developed through the exercise of professional judgement and application of basic accounting concepts. The mere fact that an existing practice has been in use in a particular industry does not make it acceptable as GAAP if the practice is inconsistent with primary sources and with basic accounting concepts (*CICA* 1100.31).

The AcSB expresses the role of professional judgement quite clearly:

> No rule of general application can be phrased to suit all circumstances or combinations of circumstances that may arise. As a result, matters may arise that are not specifically addressed in the primary sources of GAAP. It is necessary to refer to other sources when the primary sources do not deal with the accounting and reporting in financial statements of transactions or events encountered by the entity or when additional guidance is needed to apply a primary source to specific circumstances (*CICA* 1100.06).

Summary

GAAP is a historically accepted body of principles that has been developed over a long period of time. Many of the historical principles have been codified into written accounting standards in Canada, by inclusion as recommendations in the *CICA Handbook*. Often, inclusion in the *CICA Handbook* has meant a narrowing of the range of acceptable practices so that different companies report similar transactions and events in a similar manner.

In recent years, the AcSB has significantly altered existing Canadian GAAP by introducing new sections (or modifying existing sections) in accordance with evolving U.S. or international practice. International harmonization is a stated goal of the AcSB. We will discuss international standards a little later in this chapter.

The hierarchy of GAAP sources goes from the official pronouncements of the AcSB at the highest level to written and unwritten practice and sources at the lowest level. If a company is required to follow GAAP, then a practice that is cited in a lower-level source cannot be used to override a source at a higher level.

Applicability of GAAP

As we mentioned earlier, corporations that have issued securities to the public are required to follow GAAP. GAAP is defined by the provincial securities acts as following the recommendations of the *CICA Handbook*.

Private corporations have other options:

1. foreign parent company accounting policies
2. differential reporting
3. disclosed basis of accounting

We have already discussed the fact that wholly owned subsidiaries of foreign parent corporations may be required by their parent to prepare financial statements in accordance with the parent's home-country GAAP (most often, the United States). We will discuss the second and third options in the following sections.

DIFFERENTIAL REPORTING For many years, the accounting profession has discussed an issue commonly known as *Big GAAP/Little GAAP*. GAAP has become more and more complex in response to the increasing complexity of business activities. As accounting complexity increased, many accountants questioned the usefulness of full-scale GAAP for small, private enterprises. Serious questions were raised about whether the cost and complexity of some aspects of GAAP were worth the benefit for small businesses and the users of their financial statements. Therefore, many people suggested that there should be a different GAAP (or a subset of existing GAAP) for small enterprises.

Although the discussion usually focused on small versus large enterprises, the more appropriate distinction is *public versus private* companies. Some public companies are quite small, while some private companies are very large.

A major concern of standard-setters is to develop GAAP that are suitable for public corporations. Public company shareholders do not have access to the company's internal accounting records and therefore must rely exclusively on financial statements prepared by the company's management.

Some AcSB-recommended accounting policies are very complex and require a great deal of work to prepare. Additional work means additional cost. In a public company, the cost is borne by the company to better inform the shareholders. In a private company, however, the shareholders normally are able to demand additional information beyond that disclosed in the company's financial statements. The range of financial statement users and uses is more restricted in a private company. Indeed, it is quite possible that the shareholders of a private company are better served by simpler information rather than by the more complex information often required by the *CICA Handbook.*

The AcSB released a research report on this issue in 1999.[3] As a result of this research, the AcSB issued Section 1300 of the *CICA Handbook* that established differential reporting for private corporations. Under the **differential reporting** recommendations, a corporation can choose not to apply certain recommendations of the *CICA Handbook* if

differential reporting

financial reporting in which qualifying private companies may use a limited number of simplified accounting options that are not available to publicly traded enterprises; part of Canadian GAAP

- the company has no shares or other securities that are publicly traded; and
- the company is not otherwise publicly accountable, such as a rate-regulated enterprise or a financial institution; and
- its shareholders agree unanimously with use of the alternative differential reporting options.

In other words, private companies can use the differential reporting option with the blessing of the *CICA Handbook.*

The specific areas in which a private company can deviate from some *CICA Handbook* recommendations are

- Annual impairment tests for goodwill (Chapter 10);
- the reporting method used for subsidiaries, joint ventures, and other long-term strategic investments (Chapter 11)—cost or equity reporting can be used;
- disclosure and presentation of the fair value of financial instruments (Chapters 12 and 14)—fair value disclosure can be reduced;
- reporting of certain types of redeemable preferred shares (Chapter 14)—equity classification can be used instead of liability classification;
- income taxes (Chapter 15)—interperiod income tax allocation (i.e., future income taxes) need not be used; and
- share capital disclosures (Chapter 13)—less detailed disclosure is required.

The parenthetical chapter references refer to later discussions in this book.

A company does not have to take an all-or-nothing approach to differential reporting. Management can elect to use differential reporting for one or more specific items while still using public-company GAAP for the remainder.

DISCLOSED BASIS OF ACCOUNTING The preceding pages described GAAP, the standard-setting process, and the influence of external standards. The general thrust of the *CICA Handbook* is accounting policy for public companies.

Private companies are not bound by GAAP, unless an external user (such as a major lender) requires that GAAP be used. While many private companies do use GAAP, many others deviate from GAAP in one or more respects. The deviation is usually in order to make the statements more useful for specific users or to coincide with the income tax treatment of specific items. Many such deviations fall within the exemptions permitted under differential reporting, as discussed in the preceding section.

disclosed basis of accounting (DBA)

a basis of financial reporting that differs in some respects from generally accepted accounting practices. The accounting practices that the organization is using are *disclosed* in a note to the financial statements

When non-GAAP accounting policies are used, the company is said to be reporting on a **disclosed basis of accounting** (DBA). The *CICA Handbook* recommends that

> A clear and concise description of the significant accounting policies of an enterprise should be included as an integral part of the financial statements.
> (*CICA* 1505.04)

[3] Canadian Institute of Chartered Accountants, *Financial Reporting by Small Business Enterprises* (Toronto: *CICA*, May 1999).

The description of DBA will normally be included in the accounting policy note to the financial statements, and the auditor's opinion (if any) will refer to the fact that the financial statements have been prepared in accordance with the accounting principles described in the accounting policy note (instead of containing the auditor's usual reference to GAAP).

A company may prepare statements to satisfy contractual requirements, such as a major bank loan. If the contractual requirements are those of a public company, then statements prepared on a disclosed basis of accounting are *special purpose* statements rather than the *general purpose* statements that the *CICA Handbook* recommendations apply to. In private corporations, partnerships, or proprietorships, the only external users may be for contractual requirements (e.g., lenders or shareholders). In such cases, the DBA statements are the only externally issued statements and there is no need to issue general purpose statements to the public at large.

CONCEPT REVIEW

1. Are all Canadian generally accepted accounting policies found in the *CICA Handbook*? Explain.
2. Do the EIC Abstracts of Issues Discussed have the same authority as recommendations in the *CICA Handbook*?
3. What companies are permitted to use differential reporting?
4. Why would a company use a disclosed basis of accounting instead of GAAP?

Additional Influences on Accounting Policies

CANADA REVENUE AGENCY Canada Revenue Agency (CRA) is an agency of the federal government established to interpret and enforce the nation's federal tax laws. To do so, CRA has adopted procedures and reporting requirements whose primary purpose is to collect money. At times, the government also uses tax law to attain specific social or economic objectives considered important by Parliament, such as encouraging investment in research and development.

The general aim of the *Income Tax Act* is to collect revenue. In general, the act provides for taxation when cash is flowing, so that revenues are usually taxed when they have been substantively realized and costs are deducted from taxable revenue when they are incurred. Taxation principles tend to emphasize cash flows because those flows normally can be measured quite clearly. The computation of taxable income abhors estimates and discourages interperiod allocations, both of which are dear to the hearts of Canadian accountants. There are exceptions to the cash flow emphasis in assessing taxable income, of course. For example, the taxation of revenue often is affected by the revenue recognition policy used by the business, which may differ significantly from the revenue cash flow.

Expenses may be recognized for tax purposes in a way that is quite different from their accounting treatment. This is particularly true for costs that are subject to a defer-and-amortize approach for accounting purposes, such as development costs, pension costs, long-term leases, and goodwill. Capital assets are subject to Capital Cost Allowance for tax purposes, which is completely unrelated to depreciation or amortization expense for financial reporting purposes.

CRA does not require a corporation (or the owners of proprietorships and partnerships) to use the same reporting principles for tax as for accounting, or vice versa. However, corporations must attach their annual financial statements to the tax return. In addition, one of the basic parts of the corporate income tax form is a required reconciliation of reported pre-tax accounting income to reported taxable income. The corporation must make it clear just what accounting differences caused any discrepancy between the net earnings reported to its shareholders and the taxable income reported to CRA. This is the principle of *exception reporting* as applied to the taxable income calculation.

Since a corporate tax return must include the corporation's financial statements and a reconciliation of income, there is a tendency for companies to consider adopting the same accounting treatment for both tax and financial reporting purposes. The influence of tax considerations is particularly strong in private corporations when there are few (if any) external users.

When corporations adopt the same accounting practices for financial reporting as for tax reporting, this is known as *book-tax conformity*. Many accountants believe that disclosure of variations between tax and book reporting on the tax return acts as a "red flag" for the CRA and invites a tax audit. Two tax experts also observe

> Firms also adopt book-tax conformity to increase the probability that the courts will uphold the method chosen as appropriate for tax purposes. According to a 1992 decision ... the accounting method used in the financial statements will generally prevail unless another method results in a "truer picture of a taxpayer's revenue, which more fairly and accurately portrays income, and which matches revenue and expenditure"[4]

Therefore, although there is no requirement in Canada (unlike some other countries, such as Germany and Japan) that tax reporting be identical to financial reporting, tax treatment of items may have an impact on financial reporting. The impact is most likely to be observed for revenue; CRA generally takes a dim view of a corporation's recognizing revenue in the income statement while deferring revenue recognition for tax purposes.

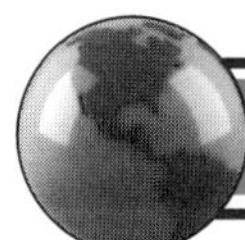

International Perspective

INFLUENCE OF ACCOUNTING STANDARDS OF OTHER COUNTRIES

The accounting standards of other countries can have a profound impact through two forms of accounting imperialism. Historically, accounting has tended to follow both (1) political influence and (2) capital flows. Throughout the British Commonwealth, for example, there is a strong influence from U.K. accounting. Similarly, the former colonies of France tend to use accounting principles that found their origin in the French system of accounting. These groups of similar accounting practices among politically related (or formerly related) countries are called *families* of accounting standards.

Political connections are an historical influence, but capital-exporting nations have often been able to export their accounting principles along with their capital and override previously existing political accounting heritage. Canada is part of the British Commonwealth and Canadian accounting has its roots in England and Scotland. However, the dominance of U.S. investors (both corporate and individual) as providers of capital for Canadian enterprises soon resulted in Canadian accounting veering away from the U.K. model and becoming part of the U.S. family of accounting practice. While there are significant differences in accounting between the United States and Canada, the accounting practices of the two countries are more similar than any other two developed countries in the world.

Given the relative dominance of U.S. capital in Canada, it should be no surprise that there is continual pressure to *harmonize* Canadian accounting with that of the United States. The pressure is due to several factors, including the following:

- Uniform U.S.–Canada accounting standards would simplify life for the large number of U.S. subsidiaries operating in Canada.
- Canadian-owned corporations that raise capital in the United States would be relieved of the obligation to report under two different sets of accounting standards.

[4] Alan MacNaughton and Amin Mawani, "Tax Minimization Versus Good Tax Planning," *CA Magazine* (January–February 1997), p. 41.

- Securities commissions in the two countries could share the regulatory burden (and reduce their costs) because approval of a public company's financial statement in one country could automatically be transferred to the other country.
- International audit firms could transfer staff between the two countries without the need for local retraining.

The idea behind accounting harmonization is that two or more countries work together to eliminate differences in their accounting approaches when there is no underlying economic or environmental reason to use different approaches. Historically, the harmonization process between the United States and Canada took the form of the AcSB's deciding whether or not to adopt U.S. accounting standards.

Recently, there has been much closer coordination between the AcSB and the FASB. The AcSB's explicit policy is to bring Canadian accounting standards into line with U.S. standards. That does not mean that the Canadian standards are exactly the same as the U.S. standards. The AcSB may vary the Canadian version of specific standards in order to reflect differences in Canada's reporting and business environment. A Canadian standard may permit a wider range of reporting options, but still include the option that the FASB prefers. In that way, Canadian companies that report in the United States can comply simultaneously with U.S. and Canadian GAAP. On the other hand, companies that do not need to comply with U.S. GAAP may be less restricted in their choice of accounting policies. Nevertheless, AcSB's immediate goal is harmonization with the United States.[5]

In the longer run, the goal is to harmonize Canadian standards with international standards, as developed by the International Accounting Standards Board (IASB). We will discuss international standards a little later in this chapter. First, however, we will briefly discuss the standard-setting process in Canada.

ACCOUNTING STANDARD-SETTING IN CANADA

Source of AcSB Authority

The AcSB establishes accounting standards in Canada. As we explained above, the AcSB issues accounting recommendations that are incorporated into the *CICA Handbook*, which constitutes the primary authority for Canadian GAAP. The AcSB also occasionally issues Accounting Guidelines, serves as the source of authority for the Emerging Issues Committee, and authorizes other pronouncements that also are primary sources for GAAP.

The AcSB is a creation of the CICA's Board of Directors. There is no direct legal authority for the AcSB to set standards for Canadian companies. However, the federal and provincial corporations acts require that auditors report in accordance with GAAP. The regulations for the *Canadian Business Corporations Act* (CBCA) define compliance with GAAP to mean compliance with the recommendations of the *CICA Handbook*. Provincial corporations acts (or the regulations thereto) generally are consistent with the CBCA regulations. As a result, the *CICA Handbook* has achieved quasi-legal status.

Canadian standard-setting is unique among developed countries because standard-setting authority resides in a single professional organization, exclusively in the private domain. In other countries, standards are determined by a quasi-public agency that operates with the support and participation of representatives from more diverse backgrounds. A prime (and nearby) example is the Financial Accounting Standards Board (FASB) in the United States. The FASB is supported both by professional accounting bodies (e.g., the American Institute of CPAs) and by a powerful government body (the Securities and Exchange Commission), but the FASB is independent of both.

---

[5] Canadian Institute of Chartered Accountants, *Task Force on Standard Setting: Final Report* (Toronto: CICA, 1998).

Membership

The AcSB consists of a maximum of nine members. The chair is a full-time paid position, while the other members are unpaid volunteers. The members serve three-year terms, with staggered end dates. Members can serve for a maximum of two terms.

The eight volunteers have different backgrounds and employment, and yet they also tend to have a strong commonality of interest—almost all are CAs, and most have an interest in large corporations either as preparers, auditors, or users (e.g., bankers, investment dealers, trust fund managers) of public company financial statements.

In addition to its voting members, the board has three non-voting members from the CICA staff: (1) the Vice-President, Standards, (2) the Director, Accounting Standards, and (3) the CICA representative on the International Accounting Standards Board. The work of the AcSB is supported by a small staff of six principals who do the research and writing on behalf of the board.

Due Process

When the AcSB identifies a reporting issue that is a likely agenda topic, the Board instructs the staff to prepare a *Project Proposal.* The project proposal analyzes the topic to see if there really is a significant issue and to sketch the probable scope and objectives of the project. When the project proposal is complete, it is reviewed by the Board and accepted or rejected as a full agenda item. Acceptance requires a two-thirds majority.

After the Board approves the project proposal, the staff continues to work on the project with the goal of preparing an *Exposure Draft* (ED) of a proposed standard. Sometimes a special task force of experts is created to help the staff and the AcSB wrestle with a complex topic.

An Exposure Draft must be approved by two-thirds of the AcSB members. After approval, it is released for public comment via the CICA website. The public has a limited amount of time (usually three months) to make comments on the Exposure Draft.

Exposure Draft comments are analyzed by the staff and reviewed by the AcSB members. The AcSB may approve minor modifications in the proposed standard without seeking additional public comment. If the Board decides to make significant changes in the proposal, the AcSB may issue a *Re-exposure Draft.*

Approval of the final standard requires yet another two-thirds vote of the AcSB members, in writing.

After approval, the new standard is posted on the website of the *CICA Handbook*, sent as a monthly update to subscribers of the CD-ROM version, and sent quarterly to users of the paper version.

The process of standard-setting has accelerated considerably in recent years. Rapidly evolving changes in the international business environment have forced the AcSB to accelerate a lengthy process. Increasingly, we are seeing new accounting standards proposed and adopted within a year or less. Much of the acceleration is in order to stay in step with international and U.S. standard-setting activity.

Contrast with U.S. GAAP

Some accountants, analysts, securities dealers, and managers have suggested that Canada should simply follow U.S. GAAP as promulgated by the Financial Accounting Standards Board. After all, since the countries are so closely tied economically, why shouldn't they share a common set of accounting principles?

This question most frequently arises around the time that major cross-border public companies release their financial results. If a Canadian public company has securities traded in the United States but uses Canadian GAAP, the company must recalculate its reported results in accordance with U.S. GAAP. Obviously there is a cost to such restatement, but perhaps the most significant "cost" is confusion on the part of the readers. For example, in its 2003 annual report, BCE Inc. reported the following net income amounts (in millions of Canadian dollars):

BCE	2003	2002	2001
Net income (loss) under Canadian GAAP	1,815	2,407	436
Net income (loss) under U.S. GAAP	1,636	(4,649)	612

Under Canadian GAAP, the company earned a profit in every year. Under U.S. GAAP, the company had a $4.6 billion loss in 2002. In 2001, however, U.S. GAAP earnings were higher than earnings under Canadian GAAP. Which are the "right" numbers?

There is no one right answer in accounting (although there are a lot of wrong answers). Accounting differences arise because of differing legal, economic, and institutional environments. Although Canada and the United States may look a lot alike, there are significant differences between them that have led accounting development down somewhat differing paths:

- The legal environment in Canada is much less conducive to legal action to address perceived misdeeds. The fear of lawsuits in the United States has led to detailed accounting rule-making rather than relying on professional judgement in accounting. If an accountant or auditor "follows the rules," he or she is much less likely to be sued successfully.
- The greater reliance on professional judgement in Canadian standards makes it easier to respond to innovative business practices. A rule orientation breaks down when businesses devise a business practice that isn't covered by the existing rules; there is no end to continual rule revisions.
- The accounting profession in the United States is much larger, much more spread out geographically, and less unified as a professional body. This also reinforces the rules approach.
- Canada is largely a private-company economy; public companies are not nearly as prevalent as in the United States. Therefore, financing methods are quite different, with banks and institutional investors (e.g., pension funds) playing a much larger role. When companies get into financial distress, the legal environment in Canada places a relatively higher emphasis on creditor protection and less on shareholder protection.
- The nature of economic activity is quite different. The United States has large manufacturing and mercantile sectors, while Canada is mainly a resource and service-based economy. This alters the relative importance of various types of accounting standards.

International Accounting Standards (IAS); International Financial Reporting Standards (IFRS): accounting standards developed and issued by the International Accounting Standards Board for use by companies with securities traded in international financial markets. IAS were issued prior to 2001; standards issued in later years are designated as IFRS.

Despite the differences, standard-setters in Canada have been striving to reduce the reporting differences between the two countries. Harmonization certainly makes life easier for companies that report in both countries, but there are fewer than 200 such companies as compared to hundreds of thousands of companies that report within Canada alone. Because the adoption of ever more complicated standards is of doubtful benefit to the majority of companies in Canada, the AcSB has adopted the principle of differential reporting, as we discussed earlier.

The harmonization process lies behind the rapid change in accounting standards in recent years. Harmonization is not only with U.S. standards, but also with international standards, the topic of the next section.

INTERNATIONAL FINANCIAL REPORTING STANDARDS

Many multinational companies have securities listed and traded in more than one national market. The shares of Daimler-Chrysler and Siemens, for example, are listed on many stock exchanges around the world. In order to facilitate international capital markets, a substantial body of accounting standards has been developed. International standards are developed by the International Accounting Standards Board (IASB), which was reorganized in 2001. International standards that were initially issued before the reorganization are known as **International Accounting Standards (IAS)**. Standards issued after the reorganization are known as **International Financial Reporting Standards (IFRS)**. The difference is one of name, not substance. The current structure of the IASB is as follows:

- The *IASC Foundation*, incorporated in Delaware (U.S.A.), is responsible for the overall strategy and effectiveness of the IASC. The Foundation has 19 trustees, of which six are from North America (including five from the United States), seven from Europe, four from the Asia-Pacific region, one from South America, and one from Africa. The trustees appoint the members of the IASB.

- The *International Accounting Standard Board*, located in London, England, is solely responsible for issuing International Financial Reporting Standards (IFRS). The Board has 14 members, seven of whom are direct liaisons with seven national standard-setting bodies (the United Kingdom, the United States, Canada, Australia, Germany, France, and Japan).
- *The Standards Advisory Council* (SAC) has approximately 45 members who are "knowledgeable about the problems and impact of financial reporting or possess an expertise of value to IASB."[6] The SAC meets with the IASB at least three times a year to advise the Board on agenda decisions, priorities, and other matters.
- The *Standing Interpretations Committee* provides technical updates for interpreting International Accounting Standards.

The IASC was not created by any legal authority. It began, in 1973, as a volunteer organization to strive for greater consistency in accounting standards among developed nations. Prior to 2001, IASC members were professional accounting bodies in individual countries, not standard-setting bodies and certainly not the countries' governments. For example, the U.S. member was the American Institute of Certified Public Accountants (AICPA), not the FASB nor the SEC nor the federal government.

The IASC began with 10 members, dominated by English-speaking countries (the United Kingdom, the United States, Canada, Australia, and New Zealand), by developed countries, and by western countries, Japan being the only Asian country. The number of member countries grew to almost 100 by 2000, the last year of the "old" structure. But the IASC Board, which had 13 members, carried out the real work of the IASC. The Board had a core of virtually permanent members: the United Kingdom, United States, Canada, Australia, Germany, France, and Japan—the same group of countries that have permanent liaison members in the new Board structure.

The old IASC issued a substantial series of International Accounting Standards (IAS). These standards bear a strong similarity to the accounting recommendations of the *CICA Handbook* in style, length, and substance. The similarity is not accidental—the CICA has worked closely with the IASC for 30 years.

The newly constituted IASB will issue International Financial Reporting Standards (IFRS) to differentiate them from the earlier IAS. However, the IASB will assume jurisdiction over the preceding IAS. By definition, IFRS will include the earlier IAS. Indeed, the IASB is continuing to issue revisions of existing IAS.

The IASB has no authority to require companies to use international standards; financial reporting requirements are the jurisdiction of the securities exchanges and securities regulators in each country. Nevertheless, international standards already are in widespread use:

- The vast majority of stock exchanges around the world accept financial statements based on international standards for *foreign* listed companies—that is, from companies based in a country other than the exchange's home country. These exchanges include most of the world's major exchanges, including Tokyo, London, Frankfurt, Hong Kong, Buenos Aries, and Paris.
- Companies based in the European Community will be *required* to use international standards for their *consolidated* financial statements by 2005. Many European companies already prepare their consolidated statements using international standards. Separate-entity statements (that is, unconsolidated) will continue to be prepared using the home country's GAAP in order to comply with national tax and corporations laws.

The few major exchanges that do not yet accept financial statements based on international standards are those of the United States, Canada, and Chile. However, the Ontario Securities Commission and the U.S. Securities and Exchange Commission currently are considering accepting international standards for foreign registrants. The New York Stock Exchange already accepts international reporting for foreign companies, provided that the company's statements provide a reconciliation to U.S. GAAP. Canada is not that advanced.

---

[6] *IASB Insight*, March 2001, p. 4.

IFRS in Canada

Canada's capital market is fairly small, especially in comparison with the world's leading exchanges in New York, Tokyo, London, and Frankfurt. A non-Canadian company can issue financial statements in Canada that use its home country GAAP, but the financial results must be reconciled to Canadian GAAP. Some observers argue that current rules discourage foreign issuers from extending major new stock offerings to Canada.[7]

In March 2001, the Canadian Securities Administrators (representing the several provincial regulators) issued a Discussion Paper seeking public comment on the advantages and disadvantages of accepting financial statements based on IFRS without reconciliation to Canadian GAAP.[8] The discussion paper points out that, except in British Columbia, there is no statutory requirement that companies using non-Canadian GAAP must reconcile their reported results to Canadian GAAP. The reconciliation requirement has been a traditional practice of the securities commissions rather than a practice mandated by law.

The discussion paper cites comparability issues that may arise from having three sets of GAAP in circulation in the country—Canadian, U.S., and IFRS—but also recognizes that major Canadian companies already are being compared to foreign companies that do not prepare Canadian GAAP statements.

While the securities commissions deliberate on the acceptability of IFRS, the AcSB is moving rapidly toward bringing Canadian GAAP more in line with international standards—a process once known as "uniformity," then as "harmonization," and now as "convergence." Indeed, the AcSB is a bit schizophrenic, in that it wishes to attain convergence with both FASB and international standards, but the two are not the same. Historically, Canadian standards were quite close to IFRS. As the IASB has undertaken new issues, the AcSB has moved in step, frequently issuing new standards that are identical to new IASB standards (e.g., financial instruments). In other issues, the AcSB has moved to adopt U.S. standards (e.g., earnings per share, income tax accounting, business combinations).

Historically, the FASB paid little attention to the activities of the IASB. In recent years, however, the FASB has played an increasingly important role in the IASB. The IASB wants SEC blessing for its body of standards, and SEC blessing may require greater convergence with FASB standards. This is worrisome to some observers, because FASB standards are the particular result of the U.S. economic, business, legal, and political environment.

Nevertheless, it is clear that the U.S. standards will continue to have an increasing impact on Canadian GAAP. The AcSB has a clear objective of convergence with the United States, which will benefit Canadian companies that are registered with the SEC and that currently must either (1) report in Canadian GAAP with reconciliation to U.S. GAAP, or (2) report in U.S. GAAP with reconciliation to Canadian GAAP.[9]

OBJECTIVES OF FINANCIAL REPORTING

Managers and accountants must make many judgemental decisions. They must (1) choose appropriate accounting policies, (2) make suitable accounting estimates, and (3) decide what information to disclose in both the statements and the notes. To exercise judgement, the accountant must have *criteria* against which to measure the suitability of alternatives. The fundamental criteria for deciding on policies, estimates, and disclosures are the **objectives of financial reporting** for the specific reporting enterprise or organization.

objectives of financial reporting
the various users' needs and managers' motivations that are the basic criteria for choices from among different possible accounting policies, accounting estimates, and note disclosures

[7] In 2002, only 3% of the 1,287 listings on the Toronto Stock Exchange were of non-Canadian companies, compared to 20% foreign companies on the New York Stock Exchange, 18% in London, and 23% in Frankfurt. Source: Website of the World Federation of Exchanges at www.fibv.com.

[8] "Financial Reporting in Canada's Capital Markets," Canadian Securities Administrators Discussion Paper 52-401, March 2001. Available on the OSC website at www.ocs.gov.on.ca.

[9] The New York Stock Exchange website showed 78 listed Canadian companies in late 2003. There were an additional 79 companies listed on NASDAQ.

The purpose of financial statements is to communicate information to one or more groups or types of users. To be useful to the users, the financial statements must convey information that is useful for their decision purposes. These decision purposes may vary widely, and the information that is suitable for one purpose may not be suitable for another purpose.

Financial statements often have direct economic impacts for either the enterprise or its stakeholders, or both. For example,

- Reported earnings may be used as the basis for employee profit-sharing and/or management bonuses.
- Accounting methods may increase or decrease a corporation's income tax liability.
- The reported level of accounts receivable and inventories affects the level of financing provided by a bank through an operating line of credit.
- Reported earnings and reported net asset value affect the permitted return in regulated industries, such as cable companies and pipelines.
- Various reported numbers in the financial statements may trigger a default on loan requirements, known as *covenants.*
- In partnerships, co-operatives, and mutual insurance companies, the reported financial results affect the financial rewards of the partners, members, and policyholders.

In addition, many of the decisions that users must make are *evaluative* decisions that may not have immediate economic impacts, but that do affect the users' perceptions of the reporting enterprise and affect their relations with (or stake in) the enterprise:

- Lenders evaluate the cash flow potential of a borrower in order to assess the ability of the borrower to service the loan (that is, to pay the interest and principal as they come due).
- Income tax authorities evaluate the financial statements to see whether the information that a corporation is reporting to its owners is compatible with (but not necessarily the same as) the information it is reporting to the CRA.
- Individual donors, charitable foundations, and government ministries assess a non-profit agency's use of donated funds.
- Employees evaluate an employer's ability to pay higher compensation (or the validity of employer requests for reductions in compensation).
- Shareholders assess management's ability to conduct the affairs of the enterprise.
- Security analysts evaluate public companies' performance and issue recommendations to buy, hold, or sell shares.
- Regulators evaluate a regulated enterprise to see if the enterprise's earnings are reasonable.

The *CICA Handbook* contains the following statement regarding the objectives of financial statements:

> The objective of financial statements is to communicate information that is useful to investors, members, contributors, creditors and other users in making their resource allocation decisions and/or assessing management stewardship.
>
> (*CICA* 1000.15)

As a generic statement of objectives, the AcSB's statement is satisfactory. However, by lumping all users together into a single group (and all decisions into a single category), the definition provides no guidance for accountants to use in exercising their professional judgement. Therefore, we must look beyond the AcSB's definition. The following sections discuss some of the more common objectives of financial reporting.

Bear in mind that, as we discussed in previous sections, relatively few Canadian enterprises are widely held, public companies. To be able to recommend suitable accounting policies, a professional accountant must be able to discern the financial reporting objectives that affect each individual enterprise. Otherwise, there is no basis for choosing one accounting policy instead of another.

Assessing and Predicting Cash Flows

A financial reporting objective that has received much attention in both the professional and academic accounting literature is that of *cash flow prediction*:

> Investors and creditors of profit oriented enterprises are interested, for the purpose of making resource allocation decisions, in predicting the ability of the entity to earn income and generate cash flows in the future to meet its obligations and to generate a return on investment. (*CICA* 1000.12)

Bankers and creditors need to assess a business's ability to generate enough cash through its normal operations to be able to pay interest and to repay the principal. The shareholders of public companies may also be interested in cash flow prediction because, in theory, share value is derived from the present value of the perpetual stream of future dividend payments. To the extent that earnings are retained (instead of being paid out as dividends), the reinvested earnings increase the asset base and should generate increased cash flow (and increased dividends) in the future.

There is a subtle difference between the assessment of current cash flows and the prediction of future cash flows. In assessing current cash flows, the financial statement user wants to know the cash inflows and outflows of the enterprise in the current period. Normally, the user places particular emphasis on the cash flow from operations to assess the entity's ability to generate cash. The availability of other sources of financing is also important, as is the disposition of those funds: *How much cash is the company generating or raising externally, and what is the company doing with that money?*

Improvements in the presentation of the cash flow statement have helped this objective in recent years, although much remains hidden from view. In particular, details of cash flow from operations are buried in very broad summary figures, and it is not easy to discern anything beyond gross cash flow from operations. As we will see in later chapters, accounting policy decisions can affect the amount reported as cash flow from operations, and companies have been known to select accounting policies that have the effect of increasing the *apparent* cash flow from operations.

Cash flow *prediction* from historically oriented financial statements involves taking the current cash flow and extrapolating it into future years. Assumptions must be made in order to do this, and accounting can help this process by measuring and/or disclosing the company's commitments to future cash flows (for example, forthcoming lease and loan payments).

As all accountants are fully aware, the measurement of operating cash flow differs from the measurement of earnings. In the long run, however, they are the same. Revenues and expenses arise from cash flows, but differ from the actual cash flows to the extent that accountants engage in the processes of *accrual accounting* and *interperiod allocation* in order to estimate earnings. Financial analysts and bankers, too, are aware of the difference.

Creditors and analysts who attempt to assess and predict future cash flows tend to prefer earnings measures that are supported by operating cash flows. For this reason, analysts often use the reported *cash flow from operations* to calculate *cash flow per share* for public companies. They compare the operating cash flow per share with the earnings per share, and conclude that if there is a high degree of correlation between the two measures, the company has high quality earnings. If there is a wide disparity between the two, then the company is said to have low quality earnings. Sometimes a company will report positive earnings but negative cash flow from operations; this phenomenon is not viewed kindly by analysts.

IMPACT OF CASH FLOW PREDICTION ON FINANCIAL REPORTING What impact does an objective of cash flow prediction have on financial reporting? The consequences of adopting cash flow prediction as a primary reporting objective include the following:

- *Accounting policies are chosen that tend to reduce interperiod allocations.* For example, revenue is recognized when cash is received. Similarly, costs that could be deferred and amortized (e.g., start-up costs) will be expensed instead, so that the impact on earnings (as an expense) will coincide with the cash flow.

- *Full disclosure of future cash flow commitments is given in the notes.* There is a great deal of leeway permitted in disclosing future commitments of various kinds. Under a cash flow reporting objective, the choice is to provide liberal disclosure of future cash flows, and particularly to signal forthcoming changes in cash flows (positive or negative).

When cash flow assessment and prediction is the primary objective, financial reporting policies are chosen that provide the clearest indication of the cash flows underlying reported earnings. Accrual accounting and interperiod allocation are still used, but their use is restricted to those instances in which there is little or no choice, such as amortization of capital assets for profit-oriented enterprises. Non-profit organizations, on the other hand, may use no interperiod allocations, even for capital assets, because cash flow assessment may be the overriding objective of financial reporting.

Income Tax Minimization

A very common objective, particularly for private companies, is that of *income tax minimization.* Since there is a time value of money, why pay taxes this year if they can be delayed until next year? The cash saved by reducing the income tax bill can be invested to earn a return, or can be used to service debt or pay dividends. A company has a lot of better things to do with its money than pay income taxes, if the payment is unnecessary.

Note that we are not talking about *cheating* on the income tax. There is flexibility in the timing of reporting certain revenues and expenses on the corporate tax return. To some extent, a company can affect the amount of tax that it pays through its selection of accounting policies. The use of legitimate options for reducing a company's current taxable income is known as *tax minimization* or *tax avoidance.* In contrast, deliberate misstatement on the tax return is tax evasion, which is fraud.

If a company wishes to minimize the amount of taxes that it pays, it will adopt accounting policies that tend to

- Delay the recognition of revenue to the extent permitted by the *Income Tax Act*, particularly for long earnings cycles, and
- Speed up the payment of expenses that can legitimately be deducted for tax purposes.

A common example of legitimate minimization of *personal* income taxes is the rush of Canadians at the end of February each year to invest in RRSPs. By investing up to the permitted level within 60 days following the taxation year, individuals reduce their income tax bill. The motivation is so strong that customers borrow from their banks in order to make the investment. The same principle applies to businesses' motivation to speed up expense payment to reduce their income tax.

Why wouldn't every company attempt to reduce its income tax bill? The reason is that if the company adopts accounting policies that reduce taxable income, those policies will also reduce reported net income:

> This might be a problem for managers whose compensation is tied to book income. A lower book income may also lead to a poorer performance evaluation and hence reduced promotion possibilities for managers. Furthermore, many executive compensation packages include significant amounts of stock options. Anything that lowers the firm's stock price will lower the value of those options. Many managers believe that a firm's stock price is determined more by its book income than by its cash flows.[10]

As a result of the impact on reported earnings, income tax minimization is more likely to be an objective for private corporations and, to a lesser extent, for public corporations that have a strong family control block. The owner-managers of these types of corporations have independent sources of information about the company, and their bankers usually are

---

[10] Alan MacNaughton and Amin Mawani, "Tax Minimization versus Good Tax Planning," *CA Magazine* (January–February 1997), p. 40.

kept closely informed about the activities of the corporation. A tax minimization objective is in the best interests of bankers and creditors, but they must recognize that reported earnings under a tax minimization objective will *look* poorer, but the cash flow will actually be better. In contrast, public corporations are likely to place less emphasis on tax minimization because their managers are more concerned about external stakeholder perceptions of the company's earnings ability.

Some aspects of taxation are independent of their accounting treatment. For example, the *Income Tax Act* provides for capital cost allowance for capital assets; accounting depreciation is irrelevant to determining taxable income. Similarly, the tax deduction for an employer's liability for an employee pension plan is linked to the cash flow, and does not depend on the accounting treatment. For these types of expenses, adopting an *income tax minimization* objective will have no accounting choice implications.

Contract Compliance

External users often use financial statements as the basis for assessing whether an enterprise has complied with contract provisions. The most common type of financial statement contracting is for debt, particularly with bank loans and with issues of bonds (both publicly issued and privately placed). Debt contracts or agreements usually have provisions that require companies to maintain a certain level of performance, such as

- a maximum debt-to-equity ratio
- a maximum percentage of dividend payout
- a minimum times-interest-earned ratio
- a minimum level of shareholders' equity

covenants or maintenance tests
contract requirements that specify a minimum level of organization performance, usually in debt contracts

These provisions are known as **covenants** or **maintenance tests**. If a company fails to meet the covenants, the lender (or trustee, in the case of publicly issued bonds) has the right to call the loan and force immediate repayment. Since the debtor seldom will be able to satisfy the call for repayment, the company is forced into reorganization or receivership.

shareholders' agreements
A contract signed by shareholders that stipulates the rights and restrictions that govern shareholder behaviour. Shareholders' agreements are normal in a private corporation.

Shareholders' agreements in private corporations also usually contain provisions that affect the valuation of shares if a shareholder decides to sell her or his shares. Sales of shares in a private corporation can be made only through private contracting with a third party, or by selling the shares back to the corporation. Often shareholders' agreements include a requirement that shares offered for sale must first be offered to the other existing shareholders, who have the *right of first refusal*. If existing shareholders do not agree to buy the shares, then the selling shareholder can approach other interested investors.

Since there is no public market for the shares of private corporations, there is no easily identifiable market price. The market price is normally determined on the basis of the financial statements. In theory, the value of shares is a function of future earnings (and cash flow) and of the fair value of the corporation's net assets. In practice, most shareholders' agreements stipulate that the price is based on historical earnings and on net asset book values.[11]

Accounting policy choices and accounting estimates can have a significant effect on the ratios used in debt agreements and for share valuation in shareholders' agreements. GAAP provides quite a bit of flexibility in accounting policy choice, and accounting policy choices can have a substantial impact on financial statement ratios. Therefore, some debt agreements (particularly in private placements) stipulate the accounting policies that will be used in calculating the ratios in order to restrict management's ability to select policies that will enhance the ratios.

Similarly, the share valuation components of shareholders' agreements often contain specific provisions concerning the valuation of net assets. These provisions are not constrained by GAAP, and therefore may be more suitable to the needs of the shareholders for a fair valuation of their shares than would a GAAP-based valuation.

---

[11] Jeffrey Kantor, *Valuation of Unlisted Shares* (Toronto: CCH Canadian Limited, 1988), p. 224.

Stewardship

A question commonly asked by business investors, taxpayers, and donors to charitable organizations is: "What did they do with my money?" A *steward* is a person who is responsible for managing an enterprise on behalf of someone else. The word originally applied to the person who managed large household estates on behalf of the owners. Stewardship reporting, therefore, focuses on showing the financial statement reader just how the resources entrusted to management's care were managed. Transparency is important; full disclosure should exist, not confused by a large number of allocations that obscure the operating results for the year.

The stewardship objective is most clearly dominant in reporting for non-profit organizations, where donors and members need to see how managers used the resources at their disposal for the period. In profit-oriented enterprises, the objective of stewardship is reflected in full disclosure, revealing in the notes to the financial statements much information on the company's financial position, disclosure that often is well in excess of the recommendations of the *CICA Handbook.* The role of stewardship is especially clear in the case of mutual fund reporting, where the investment activity of the organization is fully documented in order to satisfy investors' natural inquisitiveness about the nature of the fund's investments and the level of investment activity during the year.

Performance Evaluation

Financial statement readers often use the statements to evaluate management performance. The common use of bonus schemes based on reported earnings as means of compensating managers attests to the widespread use of financial statements for this purpose.

Performance evaluation is a concern not only of external users, but also of managers themselves. Managers are users of financial statements in order to (1) evaluate their own performance and (2) evaluate the performance of the managers of subsidiaries and other related companies in a corporate family of companies.

In order to be useful for performance evaluation, financial statements should reflect the basis on which management decisions are made, at least to the extent possible. For example, suppose that a cruise line builds and introduces a new ship. There are substantial costs involved in staffing and training a new staff. The costs are incurred because a properly trained staff is essential to successful operation of the ship. If performance evaluation is a reporting objective, these costs are deferred and amortized in order to be matched against the revenue that they are intended to enhance. If cash flow prediction were the dominant objective instead, then the costs would be expensed when incurred.

Managers are fully aware of the performance evaluation objective of financial statements, and the managers of widely held public companies are apt to be quite sensitive to the earnings impacts of accounting policy choices. Therefore, managers have strong motivations to select accounting policies that will enhance their apparent performance. The issue of management motivations in financial accounting policy selection is important and is the subject of the next section.

MANAGEMENT MOTIVATIONS

While the needs of external financial statement users are vital to developing appropriate financial reporting objectives *for each specific enterprise,* managers have motivations of their own that influence their selection of accounting policies and their accounting estimates. These motivations often conflict with users' objectives and may dominate the accounting choice process if the users lack the power to enforce the dominance of their objectives. This section will briefly discuss the most common management motivations.

Income Maximization or Minimization

Maximization of net income is one of the most common motivations of managers. This motive stems from three powerful concerns:

1. To make it easier to comply with debt covenants, and to provide a margin of safety between the covenant requirements and the reported numbers (to keep lenders from getting edgy);
2. To positively influence users' judgement in evaluating the performance of management (to help them keep their jobs and to enhance their public standing); and
3. To enhance managers' compensation, in the many corporations wherein management compensation is tied either to net income or to stock price performance (or both).

These concerns are particularly relevant for the managers of public companies, because ownership is dispersed and there is a general concern on the part of the shareholders and the Board of Directors about the share price. Managers believe, not without reason, that share prices are affected by reported earnings. There is ample evidence to show that investors in an efficient public market are able to "see through" accounting manipulations that are intended to maximize earnings. However, this ability may be only short run. In the long run, the information that is necessary to make adjustments for accounting policy differences often disappears from view, and there is no evidence that shareholders are able to "see through" complex earnings maximization objectives.

As well, the wide distribution of shares of a widely held public company makes it infeasible for the managers to point out that their "true" performance may be better than that indicated by earnings numbers that are prepared with the objective (for example) of minimizing income taxes.

BIG BATH Sometimes, a corporation will elect to *maximize a loss* in one year as part of an ongoing strategy to *maximize earnings.* The philosophy is that if there will be an operating loss anyway, they might as well take advantage of the opportunity to load as many losses into that year as possible (known as "taking a big bath" or a "big hit"). It is not at all unusual to see a corporation (in a bad year) announcing changes to accounting estimates that increase the total loss, including substantial writedowns of investments and capital assets. If a company writes down its capital assets (tangible or intangible), there remains less amortization to charge in future years, thereby enhancing *future* earnings. Another ploy is to make a substantial provision (charged to expense) for restructuring costs or for the costs of discontinued operations. If these costs turn out to have been overestimated (justified by the principle of *conservatism*), the company will recognize a *gain* in future periods.

MINIMIZING EARNINGS Instead of *maximizing* reported earnings, management may wish to *minimize* reported earnings as an ongoing endeavour. In addition to the possible objective of minimizing income taxes, management may strive to reduce earnings for any of the following reasons:

- to avoid public embarrassment by reporting earnings that may be viewed by the public as "excessive";
- to avoid attracting competitors into a very profitable business;
- to discourage hostile takeover bids;
- to avoid the scrutiny of regulators or politicians; or
- to discourage large wage claims by employees (or to justify management initiatives for wage reductions and cutbacks).

Accounting policies that *maximize* earnings include early revenue recognition and delayed expense recognition (including a defer-and-amortize approach to the widest possible array of costs). Accounting policies for *minimizing* earnings are just the opposite: delay revenue recognition and expense every cost in sight as soon as possible.

Income-Smoothing

Managers often seem to be fond of showing a smooth record of earnings, free of disturbing peaks and valleys. Widely fluctuating earnings are an indication of business risk, and managers often do not want investors or creditors to perceive the company as being risky.

Income can be smoothed by taking advantage of the many opportunities available (within GAAP) for spreading both revenues and costs over several periods. The defer-and-amortize approach beloved by many managers and supported by the *CICA Handbook* is a reflection of wide acceptance of the income-smoothing motivation.

Accounting estimates also provide a great opportunity for income-smoothing. By edging various accounting estimates up or down within the feasible range, management often can significantly affect the net income amount. Remember that net income is a residual that is only a small proportion of the overall level of activity of the business. It doesn't take much change in the amount of accruals, the estimate of bad debts, or the writedown of inventory to smooth this residual. The impact of accounting estimates is invisible to the external user. There is no need for management to disclose the vast majority of accounting estimates; their impact is simply impounded in the numbers to which they relate.

Minimum Compliance

Minimum compliance refers to the motivation of managers to reveal the least amount of information that is possible within the recommendations of the *CICA Handbook*, and still comply with GAAP.

Minimum compliance may be a motivation for managers in a public company because management does not wish to give outsiders any more information about the company than is absolutely necessary. Managers may wish to maintain confidentiality about their business activities in order to keep competitors in the dark.

Minimum compliance is usually equated with *minimum cost* of providing accounting information. However, the buyers and sellers of public companies' shares may value a company's shares at a lower level if they feel that the company is being less than forthcoming about its operations and financial position. Minimum compliance may save accounting and auditing costs, but may bear a cost in reduced share prices.

In a private company, management and the shareholders have access to whatever information they need, and the general financial statements may be used only to accompany the tax return. The information needs of bankers and other lenders may be served by special purpose reports. In these circumstances, the company is likely also to use accounting policies that coincide (to the extent possible) with the policies used for income tax purposes. Depreciation on fixed assets, for example, will be calculated on the same basis as for capital cost allowance for tax purposes; inventory costs will be calculated on the same basis for accounting and tax purposes; costs that are deductible immediately for income tax purposes will be expensed immediately on the income statement, and so forth.

Expanded Disclosure

The opposite to minimum compliance may be called **expanded disclosure**. Management may wish to disclose a great deal of information that it is not required to disclose under GAAP. The motivation for expanded disclosure may be simply to indicate that the company and its management are "good citizens" who have nothing to hide and wish to provide the most informative financial statements possible. Sometimes expanded disclosure is motivated by the expected concerns of specific stakeholders.

For example, a company that might be accused of polluting the environment may choose to disclose its environmental record and its efforts to curb pollution and/or clean up an already-polluted environment. By providing additional disclosure, management may hope to forestall criticism of the company's pollution-control efforts.

In other situations, the company may be complying voluntarily with the disclosure expectations of current or expected future stakeholders outside Canada. For instance, a company that expects to do significant business (or raise significant capital) in Europe may provide supplemental disclosure on its employment record and employment benefits, as well as on environmental and ethical aspects of its business. Such disclosure is expected of responsible companies in Europe, even though these types of disclosures are not a normal part of Canadian reporting practice.

Finally, a company may provide expanded voluntary disclosures in order to reassure the capital markets that the company is a good investment. Although financial projections (e.g., of management's forecast of future earnings) are not provided in annual financial statements, information on product demand may be provided in the notes or in management's discussion and analysis; examples include information such as the value of current contracts for a service company or the order backlog for a manufacturer.

OBJECTIVES VERSUS MOTIVATIONS

Users' objectives and managers' motivations often conflict. Managers are aware of users' objectives, and therefore managers may attempt to present the best picture of the corporation's operations and financial position. The resolution of this conflict depends on general concepts of fair presentation and often presents an ethical dilemma for management, the company's accountants, and auditors (if any). Prioritizing conflicting objectives is part of the exercise of professional judgement that is discussed further in Chapter 2.

CONCEPT REVIEW

1. Why is it important to establish the financial reporting objectives for a company?
2. Give an example of how the reporting objectives of a public company may differ from those of a private corporation.
3. How might a shareholders' agreement influence a company's financial reporting objectives?
4. Why might the objectives of financial statement users conflict with the motivations of managers?

SUMMARY OF KEY POINTS

1. Financial accounting is concerned with the preparation of financial statements that report on the financial position and results of operations for an entity as a whole.
2. Financial accounting encompasses all types of organizations (profit-seeking, non-profit, and governmental) and all types of ownership (proprietorships, partnerships, share corporations).
3. A corporation that issues securities (debt or equity) to the general public is a *public corporation* that must abide by the regulations of the securities commissions in the jurisdiction(s) in which its securities are traded.
4. Public corporations generally must comply with generally accepted accounting principles in their financial reporting.
5. The vast majority of corporations in Canada are private corporations. About half of the corporations listed in the *FP500* are private. Many large private corporations are wholly owned subsidiaries of non-Canadian parents; the others are family-owned. Of large public Canadian corporations, most have a control block that is in individual or family hands.
6. If all of the shareholders agree, a private corporation that does not have public accountability may use *differential reporting*. Differential reporting is permitted by the *CICA Handbook* for a few specific topics. Differential reporting is intended to improve the benefit/cost relationship for corporations with few financial statement users.
7. Private corporations that use other than generally accepted accounting principles and do not use differential reporting may prepare their financial statements on a disclosed basis of accounting.

8. The *CICA Handbook* identifies two levels of authority for GAAP: (1) *primary* sources, which consist of AcSB-issued recommendations, guidelines, EIC abstracts, and related background and illustrative material; and (2) *other* (or secondary) sources, including standards issued by the FASB and the IASB, implementation guides issued by groups other than the AcSB, research studies, and other materials that reflect the Canadian reporting environment. Secondary sources are appropriate only if their application is based on the accounting concepts in *CICA Handbook* Section 1000 and reflect the exercise of professional judgement.

9. Accounting standards in the United States have an impact on those in Canada. However, the different professional, legal, and economic environment in Canada makes U.S. accounting standards not directly applicable to Canadian enterprise.

10. The *Income Tax Act* and the regulations and policies of the CRA are *not* a part of GAAP. However, income taxation does have an impact on the accounting policies used by corporations because the accounting policies may affect the amount of tax paid. A copy of a corporation's financial statements (unconsolidated) must be appended to its tax return, and all differences between taxable income and accounting income must be reconciled in a supporting schedule to the tax return, the T2(S1).

11. International accounting standards are widely accepted on international stock exchanges for the financial reporting of foreign companies. European companies are required to use international standards for consolidated statements by 2005. Canada and the United States do not accept international standards on their exchanges, but both countries are considering accepting them.

12. It is impossible to impose a single, dominant objective on financial reporting. The objectives of financial reporting must be determined with reference to the organization's environment and its stakeholders, and with regard to the users' decisions that the financial statements are intended to facilitate.

13. A financial reporting objective that is often appropriate for lenders, creditors, and shareholders is cash flow prediction. Financial stakeholders need to be able to predict a corporation's ability to generate cash flow from operations to service debt or to pay dividends. Under a cash flow objective, revenues and expenses are recognized in a way that corresponds (on an accrual basis) with cash flow.

14. Another very common objective is that of income tax minimization, especially for private corporations. Public corporations are less likely to have this as a primary objective, however, because they may be more concerned about the perceptions of other users of the statements than about saving taxes in the short run. An income tax minimization objective leads to delayed revenue recognition and faster expense recognition.

15. Financial statement readers often use the statements to assess the corporation's adherence to contract requirements, such as those in loan agreements and shareholders' agreements.

16. A major objective is that of performance evaluation. Statements that are prepared to facilitate the evaluation of management's performance will use reporting policies that coincide as closely as possible to the basis for management's operating decisions.

17. Managers are the preparers of financial statements. Managers often have motivations that stem from their desire to influence the decisions of external users, particularly those of public companies. Managers may be tempted to adopt accounting policies and make accounting estimates that tend to maximize reported earnings, minimize earnings, smooth earnings, or show compliance with contract provisions such as loan covenants.

18. The motivations of preparers often conflict with the financial reporting objectives that are appropriate for external users in a particular situation. Accountants must use their professional judgement to try to reconcile such conflicts ethically and to avoid issuing financial statements that contain biased measurements.

KEY TERMS

QUESTIONS

Q1-1 Describe three types of organizations for which financial statements must be prepared.

Q1-2 What is the difference between public and private companies? What are the accounting implications of this difference?

Q1-3 What is a control block? What are the accounting policy implications?

Q1-4 Define generally accepted accounting principles, including their sources.

Q1-5 What body sets standards in Canada? What organizations have given authority to these standards?

Q1-6 What are the primary sources of GAAP? Explain.

Q1-7 What is differential reporting?

Q1-8 Briefly explain the steps followed by the AcSB to develop an accounting standard.

Q1-9 What is the role of the Emerging Issues Committee?

Q1-10 Name the two major factors that influence the spread of accounting policies from one country to another. What force is most noticeable in Canada?

Q1-11 Why should Canadian standards be similar to those found in the United States? What are the arguments against this phenomenon?

Q1-12 What is the IASB? Describe the status of IASB standards.

Q1-13 Explain the importance of IASB standards to stock exchanges around the world.

Q1-14 What is a disclosed basis of accounting? Explain.

Q1-15 What are the objectives of general purpose financial statements? What common specific objectives may a set of financial statements be tailored to serve?

Q1-16 How can financial statements have an economic impact on an organization?

Q1-17 If a set of financial statements were meant to portray the cash flows of an organization, what kinds of accounting policies would likely be chosen?

Q1-18 What accounting policies would best serve the reporting objective of tax minimization?

Q1-19 What is a covenant? What kinds of accounting policies would be common among companies with severe restrictive covenants?

Q1-20 Describe how the motivations of managers are different than those of shareholders. What accounting policies might be commonly found if managers receive bonuses based on net income?

Q1-21 What is income-smoothing? What is a "big bath"?

Q1-22 What would characterize a set of financial statements designed to provide minimum compliance?

CASE 1-1
Metropolitan Transit Incorporated

Metropolitan Transit Inc. (MTI) is a privately owned corporation that runs a bus service between the city of Metropolis and the suburb of Sprawl. The company is owned by Mr. Victor Li and his father. Victor is the CEO and president of the company.

The company has long-term mortgages on most of its bus fleet. The mortgages are held by the Royal Dominion Bank of Nova Scotia.

The bus service is run under a franchise granted by the town council of Sprawl. The franchise is for 10 years and is renewable by mutual agreement of MTI and Sprawl town council at the end of the 10-year period.

MTI is eligible for subsidies from Sprawl if the company is unable to achieve a rate of return on total assets of at least 12% per year. The subsidy is equal to the difference between MTI's reported net income and the 12% target.

As a private for-profit corporation, MTI is subject to federal and provincial taxation.

Required:
Explain the probable financial reporting objectives for Metropolitan Transit Inc. Rank the probable objectives from most important to least important, and explain the reasons for your ranking.

CASE 1-2
John Plowit

You, CA, a sole practitioner, are sitting in your office when your most important agricultural client, John Plowit, walks in. Mr Plowit runs a large dairy farm.

"I'm sorry to barge in like this, but I've just been to see my banker. He suggested that I ask you to explain to me some matters that affect my statements. You will recall that I needed to renew my loans this year. The new bank manager wants some changes made to my statements before he will process my loan application.

"The banker wants me to switch from a cash basis of accounting to an accrual basis. The cash basis provides me with the information I need to evaluate my performance for the year—after all, what I make in a year is the cash left in the bank once the harvest is sold.

"And I use these statements only for my banker and to pay tax! I know the tax department will accept either the cash or accrual basis.

"Also, the bank wants me to value all my cattle at their market value. Why do they want me to group all my cattle together when they aren't the same? Some are used for breeding and some just for milk. Personally, I don't see the sense in valuing them at market when most of them won't be sold or replaced for a very long time.

"I realize that I must provide the type of information that the bank manager wants, but I am very interested in understanding why. After all, I'm the one who has to pay for all of this!"

Required:
Respond to Mr. Plowit. (CICA, adapted)

CASE 1-3
Chan & Baaz

Sandy Chan and Philip Baaz have operated an import and sales partnership for 15 years. They import a variety of food products into Canada and distribute them through small grocery stores and some chains in southern Ontario. At times, they have made up to $150,000 per year (profits and losses are split evenly); however, the lingering recession has hurt their business, and profits were $80,000 last year. Philip Baaz, in his late 50s and financially secure, has decided to retire. Tired of Canadian winters, he has retired to Mexico and left the partnership in Sandy Chan's hands.

Sandy Chan is in his mid-40s, and through a series of personal tribulations, is nowhere near as financially secure as his partner. He does not have the resources to buy out Baaz personally, and there is no cash in the partnership at the moment. Assets consist of receivables and inventory. A significant downsizing would be required to buy out Baaz with a payment from the partnership right now. Baaz, however, is in no hurry for his money. The partners have agreed that for the rest of this year, Chan will operate the business alone, and profits will be split evenly. At year-end, Baaz will leave the partnership and take back a five-year note payable for the book value of the balance in his partnership account, which would include his share of current-year profits. While Baaz would not have helped generate this year's profits, this allocation was agreed to be fair due to his past contributions.

At the end of the year, you have arrived to prepare the financial statements for the year. You are a professional accountant. The partnership has been your client for 15 years (since the partnership was formed), and you are on excellent terms with the partners and their staff. You have met with the bookkeeper and obtained the following information:

- The partnership has always established an allowance for doubtful accounts based on specific identification of problem accounts, since Chan and Baaz had personal contact with their customers. This year, the allowance has been based on a percentage of sales—at a rate that is double the historical trend. The bookkeeper has assured you that most receivables are current, but "there's a recession on and we expect some problems to crop up."
- During the year, a sizable amount of inventory acquired during the last two years was written off. The bookkeeper explained that the product was not perishable, and it was still in the warehouse. The product was very slow moving, and Chan had given up trying to sell it.
- A personal computer and laser printer were acquired for office use late in the year. Consistent with prior policy, a full year's amortization was booked in the year of acquisition. Previous office equipment has been amortized using the straight-line method, but the computer is being amortized on a 40% declining balance scheme "because of the risk of technological obsolescence."

You have a meeting scheduled with Chan this afternoon to discuss accounting policies and operating results; Baaz is still in Mexico.

Required:

Write a brief report on which to base your discussion with Chan. Describe how Chan and Baaz have different reporting objectives. Outline the issues and alternatives, then write an analysis of each issue and your recommendation.

(CGA-Canada, adapted)

ASSIGNMENTS

A1-1 Chapter Overview: Indicate whether each of the following statements is true or false.

1. The presence of restrictive bond covenants, specifying minimum times-interest-earned ratios, means that an organization will have a tendency to pick discretionary accounting policies that minimize income. (Note: Times-interest-earned is calculated as income before interest and taxes, divided by interest.)
2. External decision-makers have direct access to the information generated by the internal operations of a company.
3. All generally accepted accounting principles are the result of a designated rule-making body.
4. The primary objective of financial accounting is to report on stewardship.
5. Company earnings goals are often tailored to a smooth pattern of earnings growth.
6. GAAP must be followed for all financial accounting reports.
7. The presence of a control block can have an impact on a company's choice of accounting policies.
8. GAAP includes practices that have evolved and gained acceptance over time, even when not codified in writing.
9. IASB standards must be followed by countries that do not develop their own standards in order to facilitate access to international capital markets.
10. The EIC provides technical guidance to the AcSB on matters of broad importance and scope.

A1-2 Chapter Overview: Indicate whether each statement is true or false.

1. Financial accounting focuses primarily on the needs of creditors.
2. Accounting imperialism manifests itself in Canada through the prevalence of U.K. accounting practices, reflecting Canada's roots in the British Commonwealth.
3. The standard-setting process followed by the AcSB allows for due process input by the user and preparer communities before a standard is promulgated.
4. Canada and the United States have similar legal, economic, and financing structures, so that accounting standards should be the same for the two countries.
5. Performance evaluation is well served by accounting policies that delay revenue recognition and recognize expenses close to the time that they are incurred.
6. A company that wishes to report smooth earnings is attempting to appear less risky to financial statement users.
7. Entities whose financial reports are meant to address cash flow objectives are primarily concerned with minimizing cash flows.
8. The Accounting Standards Board's due process, used to establish new accounting standards in Canada, is slow and therefore ineffective.
9. IASB standards have no legal status on their own.
10. A public company may use a DBA for external public financial reporting.

A1-3 Neutrality and Standard-Setting: A speaker at a recent conference stated: "Many groups, including governments, financial institutions, investors, and corporations in various industries, argue that their interests are affected by present and proposed accounting pronouncements. The sometimes contradictory interests of these groups are recognized by the accounting profession in the standard-setting process. However, accounting is neutral and is not influenced by the self-interest of any one group."

Required:

Write a report that discusses the issues raised. (CICA, adapted)

---

* These stars indicate length, with one star being the shortest assignment, and three stars being the longest assignment.

A1-4 Acronyms: The language of accounting is littered with acronyms, abbreviations for common organizations or phrases. These are listed on the left in the section that follows. To the right are commonly used abbreviations. Match the phrase or organization with its abbreviation.

Phrase or Organization	Abbreviation
1. International Accounting Standards Board	A. AcSB
2. Emerging Issues Committee	B. GAAP
3. Ontario Securities Commission	C. IFRS
4. Accounting Standards Board	D. CICA
5. Financial Accounting Standards Board	E. SEC
6. Canadian Institute of Chartered Accountants	F. CBCA
7. Securities and Exchange Commission	G. DBA
8. Canada Business Corporations Act	H. OSC
9. Disclosed Basis of Accounting	I. IASB
10. Generally Accepted Accounting Principles	J. FASB
11. International Financial Reporting Standards	K. EIC

A1-5 Accounting Choices: The practice of accounting requires many choices. Making informed and reasonable choices is the exercise of *professional judgement.* Professional judgement must be used for

a. accounting policies
b. accounting estimates

For each of the accounting decisions listed below, indicate whether the required choice is one of policy, measurement, or estimate:

1. The useful life of a newly acquired building
2. The types of overhead cost to include in the cost of manufactured inventory
3. The amount of bad debt expense for the year
4. Depreciation method to use for trucks (e.g., straight line or declining balance)
5. The future costs to be incurred in a planned restructuring of an operating division (e.g., employee severance payments, relocation costs, the costs of rearranging a factory's physical layout)
6. The costs to be capitalized as part of the total cost of buying and installing new equipment;
7. Inventory cost flow assumption (e.g., FIFO or average cost)
8. The Canadian dollar equivalent of funds held in a Mexican bank account in Mexican pesos

A1-6 Effect of Accounting Policies: A company has two debt covenants in place:

a. Maximum debt-to-equity ratio
   - Current and long-term liabilities, excluding future income taxes, are divided by total shareholders' equity
b. Minimum times-interest-earned ratio
   - Income before interest and taxes is divided by total interest expense

For each of the accounting policy choices listed below, indicate which ratio(s), if any, would be affected, and whether the policy would increase or decrease the ratio.

1. Depreciation method is straight line, rather than declining balance.
2. Costs that could either be deferred and written off or expensed immediately are expensed immediately.
3. Interest expense could be measured using straight-line amortization for the debt discount; alternatively, the effective interest rate method could be used. The straight-line method results in lower interest expense in the early years, and is the chosen policy.
4. An issue of preferred shares that has the characteristics of debt (guaranteed cash flows to the investor), is reclassified as debt, from the equity section.

5. Warranty expense is accrued as sales are made, rather than expensing it as warranty claims are paid.
6. Revenue is recorded as goods are delivered, rather than when cash is later collected.

A1-7 Accounting Principles: At the completion of the annual audit of the financial statements of Alt Corporation, the president of the company asked about the meaning of the phrase "generally accepted accounting principles," which appears in the audit report accompanying the financial statements.

You have been asked to respond in writing to the president's question. You have decided to respond by considering the following:

a. What is the meaning of the term "accounting principles" as used in audit reports (excluding what "generally accepted" means)?
b. How does one determine whether an accounting principle is generally accepted?
c. Diversity in accounting practice will, and should, always exist among companies despite efforts to improve comparability. Discuss arguments that support this statement.

(AICPA, adapted)

A1-8 Differential Reporting: For each of the situations below, indicate whether the company can use the differential reporting provisions of the *CICA Handbook*:

1. The owner-manager of Bon Nuit Limited wishes to use the "taxes payable" method of reporting income tax expense. In all other respects, Bon Nuit will follow the recommendations of the *CICA Handbook*. The owner-manager is the only shareholder.
2. The management of Wahn-Ahn Inc., a private B.C. corporation, wishes to issue unconsolidated financial statements, as provided by the differential reporting provisions. The owners of 90% of Wahn-Ahn's shares have agreed.
3. Both shareholders of Gute Nacht Corporation have agreed with management's intent to report the company's land and buildings on the balance sheet at appraised market value instead of cost.
4. Buouno Notte Financial Corporation is a private corporation wholly owned by a public holding company based in Winnipeg. The company wishes to avail itself of all the differential reporting provisions specified by the *CICA Handbook*. The shareholder (i.e., the holding company) approves.

A1-9 Disclosed Basis of Accounting: For each of the situations below, indicate whether the company can use the disclosed basis of accounting instead of Canadian GAAP for the purpose indicated:

1. A master stone mason operates a small business building retaining walls, constructing formal garden planting areas, refacing deteriorating buildings, and so forth. The mason is the sole shareholder, and prepares financial statements only for his own use and for submitting to Canada Revenue Agency in support of his corporate income tax return.
2. The Canadian subsidiary of a U.K. carpet manufacturer wishes to use U.K. GAAP instead of Canadian GAAP. The subsidiary is wholly owned by the U.K. parent.
3. A developing company, listed on the Canadian Venture Exchange, wants to use tailored accounting policies instead of Canadian GAAP for reporting to its shareholders.
4. A large publicly owned airline corporation is soliciting substantial new investment from private Canadian investors. One potential investor has requested that the corporation submit to him special private financial statements that do not follow certain recommendations of the *CICA Handbook*.
5. The Canadian subsidiary of a People's Republic of China–based manufacturer wishes to use its parent company's accounting policies, based on Chinese GAAP. The subsidiary has restricted non-voting shares listed on the Toronto Stock Exchange.

A1-10 Authoritative Sources of GAAP: The Thistle Whistle Corporation is a private company incorporated in Alberta. The company's banker insists that the company submit audited financial statements "in accordance with GAAP" in order to maintain a line of credit that is essential to the company's financial health. The company has recently developed a new method of selling its products that involves the Internet, brokers, out-of-country warehouses, and various intermediary offshore bankers. Management has been recognizing revenue as soon as possible, but the company's auditors have indicated that they are not pleased with the revenue recognition method Thistle is using.

The *CICA Handbook* recommendations are silent on Thistle's particular type of transaction, but Thistle's desired accounting policy does not seem to fit the *CICA Handbook's* general requirements for revenue recognition. However, the company's controller has gone to other sources of GAAP and has found the following:

a. An Internet industry guide, published by an Internet trade association, that encourages early revenue recognition and indirectly supports Thistle's position.
b. An exposure draft in another country that suggests Thistle's method as one possible option.
c. A private report from a Canadian accounting consultant that states that Thistle's proposed methodology "recognizes the full earnings potential of Thistle's innovative ways of doing business."
d. An article in a U.S. financial analysis magazine that cites Thistle's revenue recognition policy as a particularly creative way of accounting.

There is no EIC Abstract that deals with this issue, nor has the AcSB issued an Accounting Guideline on the subject.

Required:
Write a report to the controller of Thistle to explain whether the authoritative support for Thistle's revenue recognition policy is adequate.

A1-11 Accounting Authority: Oswald is a private Canadian corporation. Its Canadian bankers require the company to submit annual audited financial statements, prepared in accordance with Canadian GAAP. Oswald Oracles Ltd. has overseas operations that involve many complex financial instruments, and many aspects of accounting for financial instruments are still unresolved. The financial instruments accounting proposals of Canada, the United States, and the IASB take differing approaches. Generally, there is much authoritative guidance on disclosure, but little on *measurement.* To measure its financial instruments, Oswald wishes to use current market values. In making its argument to the auditors, Oswald's managers point to several authoritative sources:

- In the United States, GAAP requires certain types of financial instruments to be reported at market value on the balance sheet.
- Years ago, the CICA published a research study that proposed that market value be used for investments (including financial instruments), although the recommendations of the study were never implemented by the AcSB.
- The IASB has published a discussion paper that proposes that all financial instruments be valued at current market value.

Oswald managers concede that the traditional practice in Canada has been to report financial instruments at book value, which in the case of long-term instruments means the discounted present value using the effective interest rate at the date that the instrument was created. However, the managers argue that the profession clearly is moving in the direction of market valuation, and Oswald would simply be a leader in applying the market value approach.

Required:
Evaluate the various sources that Oswald managers are citing in support of their proposed practice. What practice should the auditors require Oswald to use?

A1-12 GAAP Hierarchy: Listed below are several sources of GAAP:

1. Implementation guides issued by authority of the AcSB
2. *Statements of Financial Accounting Standards* issued by the FASB (U.S.)
3. Research reports issued by the Certified General Accountants Association of Canada
4. Historical practice, as cited in a widely used Canadian *Intermediate Accounting* textbook
5. *International Accounting Standards* issued by the IASB
6. Non-italicized paragraphs in the *CICA Handbook*
7. Published industry accounting guides
8. *EIC Abstracts*
9. Prevalent industry practice
10. Illustrative examples accompanying the appendices in accounting guidelines

Required:

Using the item number, rearrange the list in order of authority, from the highest authority to the lowest. For each item in the list, indicate whether it is a primary source or an other source.

A1-13 Canadian versus U.S. Standards: There are many similarities, but also some significant differences, between Canadian and U.S. standards. Explain the factors that support common standards, and the factors that support differences between accounting standards of the two countries.

A1-14 International Harmonization of Accounting Standards: What would Canada gain from achieving a greater harmonization (less diversity) in world-wide accounting standards? Write a brief essay to support your opinion. Include a description of the IASB in your response.

A1-15 Standard-Setting Process: The accounting profession has a long history of developing accounting standards that are part of generally accepted accounting principles (GAAP). Listed below are some stages in the due process that creates accounting standards. Indicate the order of the steps, and match each step with a description of the activity.

Order Description	Step	Activity
	1. Re-exposure Draft	A. Circulated to accountants and interested users
	2. Analyze public comments	B. Identify accounting problems and issues
	3. Revisions	C. Modifications recirculated for feedback
	4. Project proposal	D. Comments from specific individuals on the ED
	5. Exposure Draft	E. Final product
	6. *CICA Handbook* section	F. Changes based on written feedback

A1-16 Accounting Policy Disagreement: You have been hired as the assistant in the finance department of a medium-sized publicly traded firm. Realizing the importance of accounting to your new duties, you have recently completed an introductory course in financial accounting. In this course, you learned that research costs are expensed during the period they are incurred. You also recall, however, that accountants believe in matching the costs of a given activity with the revenues resulting from that activity.

Recently your firm has developed an important breakthrough in electronic copying equipment. The research cost has been considerable. If this cost were capitalized this year and written off against expected future revenues from the new machine that will eventually be developed, this year's earnings per share would increase by 10% rather than show a modest decline.

Your superior clearly favours capitalization because the firm's CEO wants to continue a 20-quarter record of increasing earnings per share figures. She has asked your opinion based on your recent exposure to accounting standards. A meeting with your superior is set for tomorrow morning.

In the meantime, you have researched your firm's past practice in this area and you have reread the accounting standard, Section 3450 of the *CICA Handbook*. Although your firm has not previously experienced the level of research expenses associated with the present project, past practice in your firm has been to expense these costs. Your reading of the accounting standard confirms what you recall from class—namely, that these expenditures should be expensed.

Unfortunately, your superior is anxious to take the alternative position and has been known to be intolerant of views differing from her own. How would you handle the meeting the next day?

A1-17 Non-GAAP Situations: A manager of a medium-sized, private company recently complained, "I'm confused! I always thought that companies had to comply with GAAP. Now I hear that there are many companies that don't use GAAP, and other circumstances where GAAP is not really appropriate."

Required:

Explain the status of GAAP to this manager. Be sure to distinguish between general purpose and special purpose financial statements.

A1-18 Accounting Policies and Reporting Objectives: Entities may have a variety of corporate reporting objectives specific to their circumstances, such as

a. Assessing and predicting cash flows;
b. Income tax minimization;
c. Contract compliance (in this case, debt covenants that specify minimum levels of shareholders' equity); and
d. Performance evaluation of managers.

For each of the accounting policies listed below, indicate which of the objectives of corporate reporting is best served. Each policy may serve more than one objective.

1. Capitalize and amortize costs.
2. Provide full disclosure of five-year cash flow for loan repayments.
3. Defer expenses to match them against revenue generated from the activity.
4. Recognize revenue as cash is collected.
5. Defer revenue as long as possible.
6. Recognize revenues as effort is spent.
7. Recognize expenses close to the time that they are paid for.

A1-19 Objectives of Financial Reporting: The *CICA Handbook* sets out the objectives of general purpose financial statements, but companies and their managers have objectives that relate to their specific circumstances. Explain how these objectives impact on the choice of accounting policy and when differential reporting may be appropriate.

A1-20 Policy Choice: Marcon Properties Ltd. is a diversified company that owns approximately 60 retail properties, which they have operated as discount department stores. These stores are small, stand-alone properties that Marcon owns outright, although most properties are heavily mortgaged. In 20X1, the company decided, due to increasing losses from retail operations, that all discount department stores should be closed and properties converted to rental units. This process was successfully started in 20X1, with 22 of 60 properties signed to long-term rental agreements with tenants. It is now the end of 20X1, and all retail operations have ceased. There are 38 properties currently sitting vacant. Marcon believes that it can successfully lease the remaining properties over the next nine to 23 months.

An accounting policy issue has come up, in relation to the vacant properties, for the 20X1 fiscal year, namely, whether the properties should be depreciated during the period that they sit vacant prior to rental. Those in favour of recording depreciation point out that the properties continue to deteriorate during the period in which they are idle, and that depreciation is meant to allow for obsolescence, not just wear and tear. Those who favour suspension of depreciation point out that depreciation should be matched with the rental revenue that the properties will generate in the future.

Marcon is reporting a positive net income in 20X1, generated from a variety of other activities.

Required:

Explain which accounting policy you would expect to be adopted in the following independent circumstances. Note that in some circumstances, the company will be indifferent as to the policy chosen.

1. Marcon has a team of senior managers who are compensated with a cash bonus based on a percentage of annual net income. Senior managers will pick the policy.
2. Marcon is financed 60% through debt and 40% through equity, and has debt covenants that specify minimum debt-to-equity and return on assets (net income divided by total assets.)
3. Marcon is managed by its major shareholders, who wish to minimize income tax payments.
4. Marcon is a public company and wants to show a smooth earnings trend.
5. Marcon has a team of senior managers who are compensated with a cash bonus based on a percentage of annual income. Assume for this part only that the company will report a loss in 20X1 from other sources, and managers will not receive any bonus this year.
6. Marcon's controlling shareholders are not directly involved in the business and they wish to use the financial statements as a method to evaluate the stewardship and performance of managers.

CHAPTER 2

Criteria for Accounting Choices

INTRODUCTION

This chapter lays out the common criteria that accountants use to develop financial statements that external decision-makers can use with reasonable levels of reliability. Accounting policy choice is often a matter of professional judgement, and there is reasonable evidence to indicate that choice is difficult and contentious.

Major American companies such as Enron, CMS Energy, Dynergy, Tyco, Reliant Resources, Computer Associates, Network Associates, Global Crossing, Trump, Xerox, Worldcom and Lucent have had to restate their financial statements because of accounting policy issues. There have been hundreds of other examples, spilling over into Canadian and international financial markets. Some of these restatements were the result of fraud, and some reflect changing economic conditions. However, some reflect basic disagreements about how a given set of economic circumstances should be reflected in the financial statements. Why do such disagreements occur?

As we discussed in the last chapter, establishing users and user needs is integral to the choice of accounting policies on a situation-by-situation basis. After all, accounting information is used by particular individuals to make decisions. If the information can't be used to support decisions, it is worthless.

Furthermore, accounting policy should not be chosen to manipulate or misrepresent a particular situation because such information would then be biased and misleading. Deliberately presenting misleading information in the financial statements is highly unethical, to say the least, and may be fraudulent. Accountants have a vested interest in maintaining the credibility of financial statements, despite some considerable temptation for short-term gain in certain situations!

Accounting standard-setters have an even more difficult task than those in charge of picking accounting policies for a particular company. Standard-setters must establish accounting policy that is acceptable for a wide variety of situations, and a wide variety of companies. Where do they start? The standard-setting process was reviewed in Chapter 1, and its reliance on due process, which allows many diverse views to be heard, was noted. But again, where do standard-setters turn after listening to all the arguments? Clearly, it can't be a majority rule situation, or lobbyists would dominate.

To guide standard-setters, and accountants using professional judgement to deal with policy issues, there are underlying concepts and principles of accounting. This chapter lays out the underlying assumptions of our accounting model, and discusses the qualitative criteria needed to provide useful information. The chapter reviews recognition and measurement criteria. The elements of the financial statements are established in theoretical terms. The critical role of professional judgement, based on set criteria rather than uninformed opinion or bias, is emphasized.

SORTING OUT ACCOUNTING "PRINCIPLES"

The body of generally accepted accounting principles is a rather motley collection. If one was to ask someone in business to give examples of accounting principles, he or she would likely come up with a list that includes concepts such as historical cost, consistency, matching, going concern, and objectivity. The general body of accounting "principles," however, actually consists of three different types of concepts: **underlying assumptions**, **measurement conventions**, and **qualitative criteria**. They may be distinguished as follows:

- **Underlying assumptions** (or **postulates**) are the basic foundation upon which generally accepted accounting rests. For example, the accounting principle (or *concept*) of going concern is an *underlying assumption*.
- **Measurement methods** (or **measurement conventions**) are the various ways in which financial position and the results of operations can be reported. These are the *accounting choices* that management of every organization must make. The accounting principles of historical cost and matching are examples of measurement conventions, both of which are based on the underlying assumption of going concern.
- **Qualitative criteria** (or **qualitative characteristics**) are the criteria that, *in conjunction with the organization's reporting objectives*, are used to evaluate the possible measurement options and choose the most appropriate accounting policies *for the given situation*. The principles of consistency and objectivity are examples of *qualitative criteria*.

Measurement conventions (or *methods*) are *how* transactions and events are measured and reported; qualitative criteria (or characteristics) are *why* they are measured that way, provided that the underlying assumptions are valid in the particular situation.

For example, historical cost is a widely used measurement method in which assets are reported at their acquisition cost. Historical cost (a *measurement method*) is so commonly used because it is perceived as being more objective (a *qualitative criterion*) than possible alternative measurement methods. But the use of historical cost depends on the reporting enterprise's continuity as a going concern (an *underlying assumption*).

To set standards and to understand the accounting choice process, it is necessary to clearly differentiate between underlying assumptions, measurement methods, and qualitative characteristics. Otherwise, one becomes hopelessly entangled in fuzzy conceptualization that fails to recognize implicit assumptions.

For example, *historical cost* is not a fundamental concept of financial accounting, but *objectivity* is. Without a high degree of objectivity, accounting reports would have no credibility and accounting would not serve its most basic societal mission of conveying information. But there are many situations in which historical cost is not the appropriate measurement method, situations in which market value is both highly objective and more *relevant* (which is another qualitative criterion).

Structure of Policy Choice

To construct financial statements for a particular enterprise, it is necessary first to establish the facts of the business and its operating and economic environment, then to determine the objectives of financial reporting, and finally to develop the statements by using situation-appropriate accounting policies to measure the elements of the financial statements.

This process can be illustrated by the pyramid shown in Exhibit 2-1. The financial statements themselves are the apex of the process; the foundation is the objectives, facts, and constraints for the reporting enterprise. The objectives, facts, and constraints were introduced in Chapter 1; this chapter will focus on the three levels of principles that build upon the objectives, facts, and constraints. Exhibit 2-1 can be used to organize a very complex structure for both standard-setting and application.

EXHIBIT 2-1

STRUCTURE OF THE ACCOUNTING CHOICE PROCESS

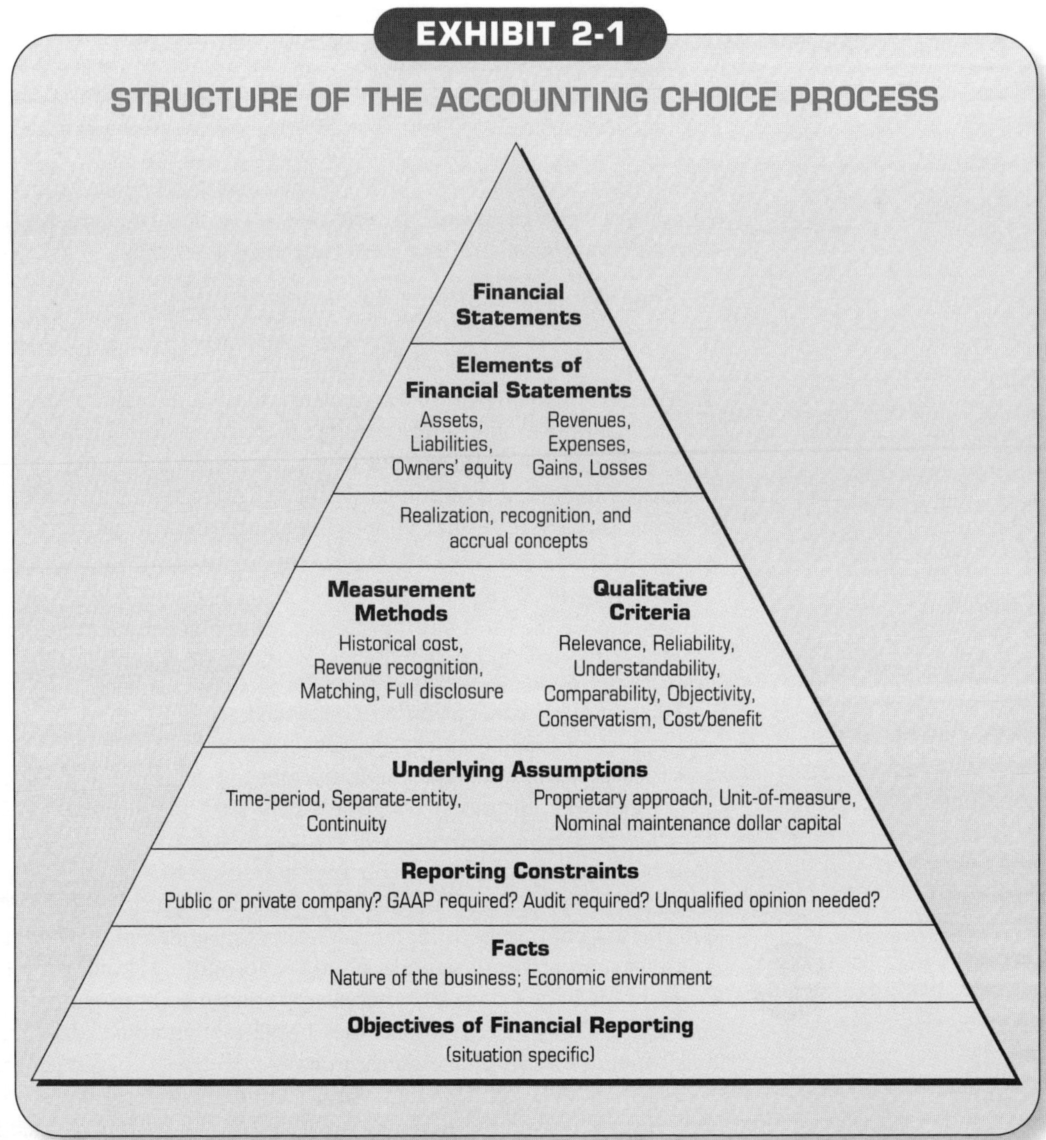

THE AcSB'S FINANCIAL STATEMENT CONCEPTS

The *CICA Handbook* establishes certain "Financial Statement Concepts" in Section 1000. The purpose and scope of this section is

> ... to describe the concepts underlying the development and use of accounting principles in general purpose financial statements ... Such financial statements are designed to meet the common information needs of external users for financial information about an entity. (*CICA* 1000.01)

Section 1000 is sometimes characterized as the AcSB's *conceptual framework*, but these words are not used in the section. The AcSB's financial statement concepts (FSC) constitute an attempt to put in writing the theoretical basis that the AcSB has used to support solutions to financial reporting problems. The AcSB's conceptual framework is strongly reflected in the tone of its published standards, although some *CICA Handbook* sections predate the framework. To understand the logic underlying the AcSB's standards, it is most helpful to understand the FSCs and the logic behind them.

General Purpose Statements

The financial statement concepts contained in Section 1000 pertain to general purpose financial statements. *General purpose* statements are those prepared for distribution to a wide, undefined public. Thus, statements prepared for a *specific* use, or user group, may well have attributes different than those described in the FSCs. Since one of the primary purposes of the FSCs is to help standard-setters determine appropriate policies for wide application, their focus on generalities is appropriate. *But it also means that there are exceptions to the applicability of the concepts and conclusions!*

The *CICA Handbook* section begins by establishing a perspective on financial reporting and the limitations of information that can be reported therein. The process of financial reporting includes more than just financial statements; for public companies, it includes other information in the annual report as well as information included in prospectuses. The FSCs relate only to the statements themselves. Remember, too, that an enterprise can communicate financial results through various media. For example, press releases and statements made in interviews result in fast, widespread dissemination of information as does information posted on a company's website.

The financial statements themselves are limited to financial information about transactions and events. The information is based on past transactions, not future events, although many estimates are required about future transactions and events. As well, the basic business environment itself is acknowledged:

> In the Canadian economic environment, the production of goods and the provision of services are, to a significant extent, carried out by investor-owned business enterprises in the private sector and to a lesser extent by government-owned business enterprises. Debt and equity markets and financial institutions act as exchange mechanisms for investment resources used by these enterprises.
>
> (*CICA* 1000.07)

The Environment

The nature of the environment has a profound effect on the entire conceptual framework. If the business environment were different, the choices made in the FSC would not be appropriate:

> In a country like India, for example, private investors play a much less important part in the economy than they do in [North America]; government and other public agencies play a larger part. The financial reporting needs of the public sector are more important there, and the objectives of financial reporting in those countries should reflect those needs.[1]

Remember, too, that if the environment changes, we must expect the FSCs to change as well, and that what is generally applicable for the business community as a whole may not be appropriate for one firm in its own unique environment.

Limits of the FSC

The FSCs define the elements of financial statements (e.g., assets, liabilities, revenues, expenses) and describe basic recognition and measurement criteria. Only some of the underlying assumptions (e.g., financial capital maintenance, going concern) and a few of the qualitative criteria are discussed in Section 1000. Therefore, Section 1000 cannot be described as a comprehensive theoretical framework, nor was it intended to be one. The AcSB's stated objective for the section is more modest:

> The Committee expects this Section to be used by preparers of financial statements and accounting practitioners in exercising their professional judgement as

---

[1] David Solomons, "The FASB's Conceptual Framework: An Evaluation," *Journal of Accountancy* (June 1986), p. 118.

> to the application of generally accepted accounting principles and in establishing accounting policies in areas in which accounting principles are developing.
> (*CICA* 1000.02)

The remaining sections of this chapter discuss the conceptual bases of accounting and the criteria by which accounting choices are made *in a particular situation*. Chapter 1 described the reality of the corporate sector in Canada: only about one-fifth of the 800 largest Canadian corporations are widely held public companies. Therefore, we do not confine ourselves to reporting by public companies only; to do so would be to ignore the structural reality of the Canadian economy. References will be made to the AcSB's financial statement concepts when appropriate, but the discussion is not restricted to those concepts that are included in Section 1000 of the *CICA Handbook*.

ETHICAL PROFESSIONAL JUDGEMENT IN ACCOUNTING

professional judgement
the ability of a professional to make appropriate choices based on established criteria, recognizing facts and circumstances surrounding the specific choices to be made

The process of making (or recommending) choices in accounting is the process of exercising **professional judgement**. Professional judgement is pervasive in accounting, and the *CICA Handbook* makes frequent references to the exercise of professional judgement. Indeed, one of the differentiating characteristics of most AcSB accounting standards, in contrast to their FASB cousins south of the border, is that they place a great deal of reliance on professional judgement in preference to stipulating rigid rules. As well, the need for judgement is pervasive in the many aspects of accounting that are not dealt with specifically in the *CICA Handbook*. As we examine various specific accounting topics throughout this text, we will emphasize their judgemental aspects.

Accountants must act *ethically*, and exercise judgement to be fair to all stakeholders. In any specific situation, an accountant exercises ethical professional judgement by taking into account many factors:

- The users of the financial statements, and their *specific* information needs;
- The motivations of managers;
- The organization's operations, e.g., the type of ownership, the sources of financing, the nature of its operating or earnings cycle, etc.; and
- Its reporting constraints, if any, e.g., audit requirements, reporting to securities regulators, constraints imposed by foreign owners, etc.

Alternative measurement methods, both accounting *policies* and accounting *estimates*, are considered in light of the forgoing factors, and a selection of appropriate policies is made with reference to the qualitative criteria, after making sure that the underlying assumptions are valid.

We will return to a discussion of ethical professional judgement and the way that accounting policy choices are made at the end of this chapter. But first, we must examine the three types of accounting principles: (1) underlying assumptions, (2) qualitative criteria, and (3) measurement conventions.

CONCEPT REVIEW

1. What is the difference between the accounting principles known as measurement methods and those known as qualitative criteria?
2. What are general purpose financial statements?
3. What factors must a professional accountant take into account in order to exercise ethical professional judgement?

UNDERLYING ASSUMPTIONS

Underlying assumptions provide a foundation for accounting policy choice, as shown in Exhibit 2-1. Six basic assumptions significantly affect the recording, measuring, and reporting of accounting information.[2] They are

1. *Time-period assumption*—meaningful information can be assembled and reported for a time period that is less than the enterprise's life span.
2. *Separate-entity assumption*—the enterprise can be accounted for and reported independent of its owners and other stakeholders.
3. *Continuity assumption*—the enterprise will continue in operation for a reasonable future period; also known as the *going-concern assumption.*
4. *Proprietary assumption*—the results of the enterprise's operations should be reported from the viewpoint of its owners.
5. *Unit-of-measure assumption*—the results of the enterprise's operations can meaningfully be measured in monetary terms.
6. *Nominal dollar capital maintenance assumption*—the enterprise has generated a profit if its revenues are higher than the historical cost of the resources used.

These six assumptions underlie GAAP. There are times when one or more of the assumptions is not valid, in which case GAAP is not appropriate. GAAP might be useless or highly misleading if used when the assumptions are not valid.

Time-Period Assumption

The operating results of any business enterprise cannot be known with certainty until the company has completed its life span and ceased doing business. In the meantime, external decision-makers require timely accounting information to satisfy their analytical needs. To meet their needs, the **time-period assumption** requires that changes in a business's financial position be reported over a series of shorter time periods.

Although the reporting period varies, one year is the standard. Some companies use a calendar year, and others use a fiscal year-end that coincides with the low point in business activity over a 12-month period. Some businesses (e.g., retail, movie chains) report on a 52-week basis (53 weeks every few years) because their activity cycle is weekly. In addition, companies also report summarized financial information on an interim basis, usually quarterly for public reporting or monthly for internal purposes.

The time-period assumption recognizes that decision-makers need timely financial information. However, recognition of accruals and deferrals is necessary for reporting information that reasonably represents the operations of the enterprise. *Accruals* and *deferrals* are associated with **accrual-basis accounting**.

accrual-basis accounting
a basis of accounting that reflects transactions as they occur rather than when cash flows occur

ACCRUALS AND DEFERRALS **Accruals** are the accounting recognition of assets and liabilities that have not yet been *realized* as a cash flow; **deferrals** refer to the delayed recognition of costs and receipts that have been *realized* through cash flows but have not yet contributed to the earnings process as expenses and revenues.

The traditional one year time-period assumption may not be appropriate for limited-life enterprises that will last longer than one year. While financial statements may be prepared at the end of a year (for income tax purposes, for example), the statements will be meaningless if both the revenue-generation and expense-incurring activities are in mid-

[2] An early, and still very relevant, study of the underlying assumptions of accounting was published by the American Institute of Certified Public Accountants as their *Research Study No. 1*: Maurice Moonitz, *The Basic Postulates of Accounting* (NY: AICPA, 1961).

stream, with no obvious basis for estimation. For example, the statements of junior mining companies that are still in the process of exploring or developing their sites do little more than convey the amount expended (and capitalized) to date. The attempted measurement of annual operating results in the income statement is of little predictive or evaluative use; the value of the company and its earnings ability will not be known until the exploration and development process is completed.

Separate-Entity Assumption

Accounting deals with specific, identifiable business entities, each considered an accounting unit separate and apart from its owners and from other entities. A corporation is an entity that is legally quite distinct from its owners, even if the corporation is a private family corporation or has a single shareholder. No matter how closely the corporation and its owners are intertwined, they are legally separate.

For taxation purposes as well, a corporation is considered to be distinct from its owners. This is true even though many of the financial interactions between a private corporation and its shareholder(s) are strongly affected by tax considerations. Both the legal and tax views of a corporation as a distinct entity are easily translated into accounting terms; a corporation is accounted for as an entity distinct from its owners.

Partnerships and sole proprietorships do not share the legal and tax status of separate entities; in law and in taxation, they are viewed as an extension of their owners. Partners and proprietors are fully liable for the debts of the business, and the personal assets of the owners cannot legally be isolated from the business.

Indeed, partners and proprietors often attempt to isolate their personal assets by transferring the legal title to their houses and cars to their spouses, children, or trusts while retaining "constructive enjoyment" of the assets. This attempt is not always successful; bankruptcy courts may rule that such transfers are invalid and seize the transferred assets to settle debts of the business. Similarly, the profits of partnerships and proprietorships are taxed directly to the owners, as personal earnings.

For accounting purposes, however, there must be an underlying assumption that a non-corporate business is distinct from its owners; otherwise, accounting for the business would be impossible. Under the **separate-entity assumption**, all accounting records and reports are developed from the viewpoint of a single entity, whether it is a proprietorship, a partnership, or a corporation. The assumption is that an individual's transactions are distinguishable from those of the business he or she might own. For example, the personal residence of a business owner is not considered an asset of the business even though the residence and the business are owned by the same person.

separate-entity assumption
accounting information that reflects the assumption that a business and its owners are separate economic entities

Even when accounting for private corporations, the accountant must be aware of the relationship between the corporation and its owner(s), and must take care to portray this relationship realistically. For example, loans by a controlling shareholder to the corporation are, in substance, equity infusions. Bankers routinely insist that such loans be subordinated (or made secondary) to their own loans and classify the corporation's liability to its owner as equity when they perform their analysis of the company. The accountant must strive to disclose the nature of the shareholder loan so that any external user is able to understand that there is a special relationship between the creditor and the debtor.

Continuity Assumption

The **continuity assumption** is also known as the **going-concern assumption**. Under the continuity assumption, the business entity is expected not to liquidate but to continue operations for a reasonable future period. That is, it will stay in business for a period of time sufficient to carry out contemplated operations, contracts, and commitments. Note that this is not an assumption of perpetual life, but rather an assumption that the business will continue in operation long enough to recover (or use up) its assets and repay its outstanding liabilities.

This non-liquidation assumption provides a conceptual basis for many of the measurement methods used in accounting. For example, the historical cost concept assumes that the business's capital assets will be used up over their lifetime, which gives rise to the process of interperiod allocation, due to the underlying continuity assumption.

Similarly, the continuity assumption underlies the classifications used in accounting. Assets and liabilities, for example, are classified as either current or long term on the basis of this assumption. If continuity is not assumed, the distinction between current and long-term loses its significance; all assets and liabilities become current.

EXCEPTIONS TO THE CONTINUITY ASSUMPTION If the continuity of a business enterprise is in doubt, then many commonly used measurement methods are not appropriate. Two instances in which the continuity assumption is not valid are (1) when a business is a limited-life venture, or (2) when a business is in financial difficulty and is expected to be shut down or liquidated.

As an example of the first instance, consider a summer carnival or fair that is organized by an entrepreneur in a resort area. The fair is a one-time event, even if it may be repeated in future years. The future repetition is a separate business decision and a separate venture, and not a continuation of a going concern. In such a situation, the principle of interperiod allocation is rendered nonsensical. There will not be more than one period, and therefore the concept of interperiod allocation of revenues and expenses becomes irrelevant; what matters is the short-term cash flows from revenue and expenditure.

In the second instance, the business may be intended to continue but is unable to do so due to continuing losses. The owners, creditors, and bankruptcy trustees decide that the only remedy is to terminate the business. In a liquidation scenario, the historical cost of the assets is irrelevant and useless; conventional accounting, based on the continuity assumption, is not appropriate. Such circumstances call instead for the use of *liquidation accounting*, which values assets and liabilities at estimated net realizable amounts (liquidation values).

Proprietary Assumption

One of the fundamental assumptions of Canadian (and U.S.) business accounting is the **proprietary assumption** (or proprietary concept). The proprietary concept is one of two possible approaches that can be used in accounting:

- The **proprietary concept**: an organization's financial condition and results of operations are reported from the point of view of the owners, or proprietors in an economic sense. Net income is calculated by regarding all other claims on the assets as liabilities and all payments other than those to the owners as being expenses. An important aspect of the proprietary concept is that the dominant construct is the *residual*, both owners' equity in the balance sheet and net income in the income statement.
- The **entity concept**: the owners are just one of many participants in the enterprise. The net value added by the enterprise (that is, the revenue minus the purchases of goods and services from third parties) is distributed to the various *factors of production* (in economic terms), consisting of providers of capital (both interest on debt and dividends on equity), labour (i.e., wages and salaries and benefits), and government (in taxes and fees for services), with any residual representing reinvestment in the enterprise. The owners constitute just one group among many.

The proprietary concept is applied to accounting for all types of *business* organizations; it has nothing to do with the *form* of organization, such as proprietorship, partnership, or corporation. *All* businesses are accounted for with this concept. Since most of GAAP is based on the assumption that the reporting enterprise is a business, the proprietary concept is the assumption that underlies many accounting principles; thus it is known as the *proprietary assumption.*

In Canada (and the United States), the entity concept underlies macroeconomic accounting; that is, the construction of the national income and GNP accounts. In some other countries, however, the entity concept is either permitted or required for businesses. Some developing countries require corporations to report on the entity basis because this is the only reporting basis that permits public policy-makers to discern whether a guest corporation is contributing to the national economy or is "milking" the economy for the benefit of foreigners. The information conveyed in a value-added report is not visible in a traditional, North American-style income statement.

For example, pick up any published corporate annual report in Canada and try to figure out from the income statement how much the corporation contributed to the economy in the form of wages—it simply cannot be done because there is no separate disclosure of wages! Nor is it possible even to figure out the net economic *value added* by the corporation. Value added is the basis of the Canadian goods and services tax (GST), and therefore the government is in a position to know, at least in gross terms, the net contribution that a business makes to the Canadian economy. However, a business's value added is not public information in Canada, nor is it used by the government for public policy determination.

Unit-of-Measure Assumption

The **unit-of-measure assumption** means that the results of a business's economic activities can be reported in terms of a standard monetary unit throughout the financial statements. Simply stated, the assumption is that it is possible to meaningfully prepare financial statements for an enterprise because everything of relevance can be measured using the dollar as the unit of measure. Money amounts are thus the language of accounting: the common unit of measure enables dissimilar items such as the cost of a ton of coal and the amount of an account payable to be aggregated into a single total.

Unfortunately, the use of a standard monetary unit for measurement purposes poses a dilemma. If financial statements are to be meaningful, they must include all (or at least most) of the relevant information to enable a user to make informed decisions. The unit-of-measure assumption implies that *if it can't be measured, it can't be reported.* And, by extension, that *if it can't be reported, it can't be used for decision-making by external users.* This assumption means that many important aspects of a modern business's operations cannot be embodied in the financial statements, such as

- the value of customer goodwill
- the impact of operations on the environment
- the value of intellectual and human capital

In modern industrial corporations, the environmental impact of the business's operations is very important, not only for society but also for the shareholders and other direct stakeholders. But accounting is unable to incorporate environmental impacts into the statements because they do not fit the underlying assumptions of accounting, including the unit-of-measure concept.

Canada is primarily a service-based economy. The value of any successful bank, insurance company, or software company is dependent on the *intellectual capital* of its employees. If key employees leave, they take their intellectual capital with them. The value of this capital to the corporation is crucial, but there is no way (as yet conceived) to put a dollar value to this capital and thus to include it in the financial statements.

Nominal Dollar Capital Maintenance Assumption

The monetary unit of measure is often compared to a ruler, by which the dimensions of a business and its operations are measured. But unlike a ruler, which is always the same length, the relative value of a currency changes over time. The relative value of a currency can be measured in two ways:

1. in relation to the value of other currencies (its *exchange rate*), or
2. in relation to the amount of goods and services that it will buy (its *purchasing power*).

These two relative values are themselves related. As the general purchasing power of a currency declines, its value in relation to currencies that have constant purchasing power also declines. A decline in the general level of purchasing power is a condition of *inflation.*

purchasing power parity

over time, different relative values of currencies will adjust in the currency markets to reflect relative purchasing power; reflects level of country's inflation

Over time, the relative values of currencies of different nations will adjust to maintain their relative purchasing powers; this is known as maintaining **purchasing power parity.**

STABLE DOLLAR Accounting is performed under the assumption that every dollar of revenue and expense has the same stable value, regardless of whether the dollar was a 1935 dollar, a 1970 dollar, or a 2004 dollar. Dollars of different vintages are accounted for without regard to the fact that some have greater purchasing power than others. Profits and losses are determined by assuming that the value of the dollar does not change over time. Of course, the assumption of an absolutely stable dollar is not correct, but it is used because North American inflation has been relatively modest. Over time, however, even modest annual rates of inflation can cause large changes in purchasing power. For example, the purchasing power of the 2004 Canadian dollar was only about one-fifth of the purchasing power of the 1970 dollar.

nominal dollar capital maintenance

the concept that income results only after preserving financial capital in dollars; the closing amount of net financial assets must exceed the amount at the start before income is present

CAPITAL MAINTENANCE If the operations of a business result in a profit, an increase results in the (nominal dollar) amount of owners' equity, before dividends. If the company suffers a net loss, the dollar amount of owners' equity will decline and recorded invested capital will not be maintained. This is called **nominal dollar capital maintenance** (or **maintenance of nominal dollar financial capital**); financial measurements are in nominal dollars only, without regard to the purchasing power of the dollars. If a unit of inventory is sold, the profit is measured as the difference between the sales price and the historical cost of the item, in nominal dollars.

Although nominal dollar capital maintenance is often viewed by U.S. and Canadian accountants as being part of the natural order of the universe, such is not the case. Countries that have sustained high rates of inflation have developed a different approach to determining whether a business's capital base has been maintained, enhanced, or eroded.

In countries with high levels of inflation (sometimes at a rate of 100% per year or more), a business is deemed to have earned a profit only if it has generated enough earnings to *maintain the purchasing power of the owners' equity.* Countries that account on this basis include Mexico, Brazil, Argentina, and Israel. Maintaining the purchasing power of the owners' investment is called **constant dollar capital maintenance.** When an item of inventory is sold, profit is measured as the difference between the sales proceeds and the historical cost of the item after the historical cost is *adjusted for changes in the general price level since its acquisition.*

For example, assume that $1,000 of inventory is held for one year and then sold for $1,400. The profit of $400 is recorded as income, and retained earnings will increase by this amount, under nominal dollar capital maintenance. However, assume that inflation during the period was 10%. The inflation-adjusted cost of the inventory would be $1,100 (the cost of $1,000 multiplied by 110%) and only $300 of profit has been earned in constant dollars. The $400 nominal figure was overstated, once inflation was brought into the picture.

This way of looking at profit performance seems very different. However, the accounting model can adapt very quickly to an inflation-adjusted model. Such a change would be necessary if our Canadian economic environment shifted to higher inflation and nominal dollars were no longer as stable.

CONCEPT REVIEW

1. Why may the separate entity assumption be artificial for a small corporation with a single shareholder?
2. When might the continuity assumption not be valid?
3. Describe the alternative to the proprietary concept.
4. Which underlying assumption is not appropriate in a country that suffers triple-digit annual inflation?

QUALITATIVE CRITERIA

Qualitative criteria are needed to established accounting policies, as demonstrated in Exhibit 2-1. The first widely distributed effort at defining the qualitative criteria of accounting measurements was published in 1966 by the American Accounting Association (AAA), which is a large association of (primarily) U.S. university and college professors of accounting. The report, *A Statement of Basic Accounting Theory*, did not explicitly use the term "qualitative criteria," but recommended four basic "standards for accounting information" and five "guidelines for communicating accounting information" that have since come to be known as qualitative criteria.

Successive years saw many similar attempts to create a definitive set of qualitative criteria. Most of the work took place in the United States. The FASB published a set of criteria, along with a chart that suggests a hierarchy of criteria, in 1980.[3] This criteria set seems to be the basis that the AcSB used for the criteria that are described in Section 1000 of the *CICA Handbook*.

Although the FASB effort is the most widely known, perhaps the best attempt was part of a CICA Research Study that was also published in 1980, *Corporate Reporting: Its Future Evolution*.[4] The CICA study identified 20 different qualitative criteria, as compared to about a dozen in the FASB statement. However, the real contribution of the CICA study is not in the number of identified criteria, but rather in explicitly recognizing the conflicts that exist between some of the criteria.

In the following pages, we will examine the most important qualitative criteria:

- relevance
- reliability
- understandability
- comparability
- objectivity
- conservatism
- cost/benefit

Different sources sometimes use different names for the same criterion, but these are the names used by both the AcSB and the FASB.

EXHIBIT 2-2

TRADE-OFF BETWEEN RELEVANCE AND RELIABILITY

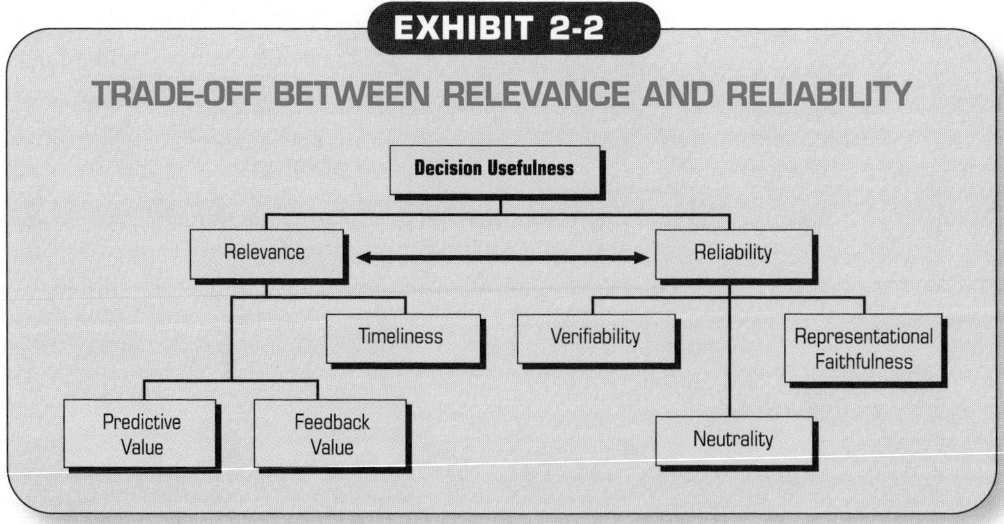

Source: Excerpt from "A Hierarchy of Accounting Qualities," *Statement of Financial Accounting Concepts No. 2: Qualitative Characteristics of Accounting Information* (FASB: May 1980), p. 15.

[3] Financial Accounting Standards Board, *Statement of Financial Accounting Concepts No. 2: Qualitative Characteristics of Accounting Information* (May 1980).

[4] Qualitative characteristics are discussed in Chapter 7 of the study. The report was written by Professor Edward Stamp, FCA, but authorship officially is credited to a Study Group. Unfortunately, the report seems to have sunk without a trace in the consciousness of Canadian professional accountants.

Relevance

relevance
information that is useful or influential for decision-makers; such information is timely and has predictive value and feedback value

Theoretically, **relevance** is the most important qualitative characteristic because it means that accounting information is decision-useful. Relevance relates to the objectives of financial reporting. Chapter 1 pointed out that the accounting choices that are made when cash flow prediction is the primary reporting objective are not necessarily the same choices that are made when performance evaluation is the primary objective. The concept refers to the capacity of accounting information to make a difference to the external decision-makers who use financial reports.

Qualities that contribute to relevance are

1. *Timeliness.* Accounting information should be reported soon enough for it to be useful for decision-making. Like the news of the world, stale financial information has less impact than fresh information. Lack of timeliness reduces relevance.
2. *Predictive value.* Accounting information should be helpful to external decision-makers by increasing their ability to make predictions about the outcome of future events. Decision-makers working from accounting information that has little or no predictive value are merely speculating intuitively.
3. *Feedback value.* Accounting information should be helpful to external decision-makers who are confirming past predictions or making updates, adjustments, or corrections to predictions.

Reliability

reliability
information that can be depended upon as accurate; reliable information is representationally faithful, verifiable, and free from bias

The other criteria of decision usefulness is **reliability**. Information is reliable if users can depend on it as a sufficiently accurate measure of what it is intended to measure. Reliability is closely related to the general concept of usefulness, but has additional subcomponents.

Reliability conflicts with *relevance.* While both relevance and reliability are needed to established decision usefulness, some of the potentially most useful information may be very unreliable. This conflict is illustrated in Exhibit 2-2. For example, relevant information such as the value of intellectual capital or market values for intangible capital assets may not be recorded.

To ensure reliability, accounting information must be free from error and bias and faithfully represent what it claims to represent. It must not mislead or deceive. There are three components to reliability:

1. Representational faithfulness (including substance over form)
2. Verifiability
3. Freedom from bias (or neutrality)

validity
information reported accurately reflects actual events and transactions

REPRESENTATIONAL FAITHFULNESS This attribute is also sometimes called **validity**.[5] Information must give a faithful picture of the facts and circumstances involved, as a city map should accurately represent the layout of the city that it represents.

In accounting, the balance sheet is considered to be a "statement of financial position," but it represents the financial position of the organization faithfully only if it really does portray all of the assets and liabilities of the business. If our accounting conventions and measurement models do not show all of the assets or liabilities, then the balance sheet does not represent faithfully the financial position of the business.

[5] In the CICA's 1980 *Corporate Reporting* study, this characteristic is known as isomorphism. *Isomorphism* is a well-established concept in science that indicates a similarity between two different forms or constructs.

An important aspect of representational faithfulness is **substance over form**. Accounting information should represent what it purports to represent and should report the economic substance of transactions, not just their form or surface appearance.

As an example of accountants' efforts to portray substance over form, consider a company that rents, or leases, a computer system. The form of the contract is a rental agreement, which would seem to suggest that payments made by the company should simply be reported as rent expense with no other financial statement impact. However, suppose that the accountant discovers that this company decided to lease the computer instead of buying one outright with money borrowed from a bank. The lease term covers the full expected useful life of the computer, cannot be cancelled by the company, and provides a full return of the cost of the computer, plus a profit margin (in the form of interest) to the lessor. Now it appears as though, *in substance*, the company has acquired property rights over the computer, far more than a simple rental contract would imply. In substance, the company owns full rights to the use of the asset and is financing it with a lease agreement. Thus, to reflect *substance over form*, the asset and the obligation should be shown on the balance sheet of the lessee, and the income statement should reflect both depreciation of the computer and interest on the liability.

VERIFIABILITY If knowledgeable and independent observers can apply an accounting measurement and obtain essentially the same result, the measurement is said to be *verifiable*. This is considered by the AcSB to be a component of reliability, but many accountants and auditors view verifiability as the essence of *objectivity*. Verification implies that independent measures *using the same measurement methods* would reach substantially the same conclusion. Verifiability of a measurement does not, however, mean that the measurement was necessarily objective or non-arbitrary, but only that its computation can be reproduced or replicated.

FREEDOM FROM BIAS Accounting information is biased if the measurements result in consistent overstatements or understatements of the items being measured. Preparers of financial reports should not attempt to induce a predetermined outcome or a particular mode of behaviour. For example, a set of financial statements should not be made to look "rosy" to influence potential investors to purchase a company's shares.

The *CICA Handbook* uses the term "neutrality" to indicate the characteristic of *freedom from bias*. However, the concept of *neutrality* is sometimes taken to mean that reported accounting information should be neutral in its impact and should not influence economic decisions. If accounting information has no impact on economic decisions, then it is essentially useless. But accounting information should not provide the motivation for dysfunctional economic decisions (i.e., those that are contrary to the best economic interests of the enterprise). Management often makes decisions that are influenced by the financial reporting implications of those decisions. For example,

> ... the provision of information that is both relevant and objective will tend to eliminate problems of bias. Yet it may creep in if there is a desire on the part of management to influence user decisions in favour of the company. For example, the adoption of accounting practices that help to smooth out fluctuations in periodic income measures will bias users into a belief that the risk attached to the company's operations is less than it really is.[6]

Understandability

Information must be understandable to be useful to users in their decision-making process. Understandability does not mean that all information has to be reduced to the lowest common level or simplified so that the least sophisticated investor should understand it. Investors

---

[6] *Corporate Reporting: Its Future Evolution* (CICA, 1980), p. 60.

and creditors should have a reasonable understanding of business and economic activities, as well as some understanding of accounting. These users are expected to study the information with reasonable diligence. User groups include those who provide advice to investors and creditors; users who lack expertise are assumed to be properly advised.

Comparability

comparability
the relationship between two pieces of information; data that has been prepared using the same accounting policies for a corporation over time, or for different corporations in order that they can be logically compared

The *CICA Handbook* states that "**comparability** is a characteristic of the relationship between two pieces of information rather than of a particular piece of information by itself." (*CICA* 1000.22)

There are two aspects of comparability—**consistency**, which entails using the same accounting policies from year to year within a firm, and **uniformity**, which means that companies with similar transactions and similar circumstances use the same accounting treatments.

Consistency involves applying accounting concepts and principles from period to period in the same manner. There is a presumption that an accounting principle once used should not be changed. However, if consistency is carried too far, it adversely affects relevance. A change to a preferred accounting principle is permitted, even though this would impair consistency. This apparent conflict is usually resolved by retroactive restatement of financial statements to reflect the new policy and supplemental note disclosure.

Objectivity: The "Missing" Criterion

Objectivity is one of the most-used concepts in accounting, and yet it is not even mentioned in the AcSB's Financial Accounting Concepts section. The reason is that *objectivity* often has different implicit meanings for different people. Objectivity can be viewed as being one or a combination of the following characteristics:

- **Quantifiability**, the ability to attach a number to an event or transaction. For example, the impact of some events, like some contingent losses, cannot be measured with any degree of reliability and any attempt to measure them is said not to be objective.
- **Verifiability**, or the ability of independent accountants to replicate the results of an accounting measurement, discussed previously as a component of *reliability*.
- **Freedom from bias**, the absence of intentional or unintentional misstatement or skewing of an accounting measurement. This also is a component of *reliability*.
- **Non-arbitrariness**, the basing of accounting measurements on observable values.

verifiability
independent persons using a specific measurement method would reach substantially the same results; an attribute of reliability

Because of the wide variety of possible interpretations of *objectivity*, most discussions of qualitative criteria avoid using the word completely.

Conservatism

conservatism
the principle that when two accounting methods are acceptable, the one having the less favourable effect on net income and net assets is preferable

A curious feature of the AcSB's list of qualitative characteristics is that the Board includes **conservatism**. Most discussions of the qualities of accounting information consider conservatism to be a measurement convention. The AcSB characterizes conservatism as follows:

> When uncertainty exists, estimates of a conservative nature attempt to ensure that assets, revenues and gains are not overstated and, conversely, that liabilities, expenses and losses are not understated. However, conservatism does not encompass the deliberate understatement of assets, revenues and gains or the deliberate overstatement of liabilities, expenses and losses. (*CICA* 1000.21)

Conservatism is a tricky animal. Conservative measurements in one period almost inevitably have offsetting effects in one or more later periods. If assets are "conservatively" measured by understating assets, then expenses are accordingly reduced when those assets are transferred to the income statement when the assets are used (or amortized). Reducing expenses has the effect of increasing net income, which is not conservative.

Managements has been known to use conservatism to justify asset writedowns, even though the obvious result of the writedowns would be to enhance future earnings, i.e., part of a "big bath." Auditors, required to use skepticism, would often be uncomfortable arguing against the "conservative" writedown. In recognition of this problem, the second sentence of the above quotation is an attempt by the AcSB to discourage the deliberate understatement of assets or overstatement of liabilities.

Conservatism originated in the late 19th century, when the balance sheet was viewed as the most important statement (and often the only statement given to shareholders). The "conservative" valuation of assets and liabilities made some sense in that environment. But as increased emphasis was placed on the income statement in the mid-20th century, conservatism became a tool for manipulation rather than a practice intended to protect investors.

In modern accounting, conservatism might best be characterized as follows:

> "Conservatism" is a reaction to uncertainty and represents in essence merely a counsel of caution. The proper role of conservatism in accounting is to insure that the uncertainties and risks inherent in any given business situation are given adequate consideration.[7]

The Trade-off between Cost and Benefit

The concept of **cost/benefit effectiveness** holds that any accounting measurement or disclosure should result in greater benefits to the users than it costs to prepare and present. Benefits should exceed costs.

In standard-setting, this is a very difficult concept to implement, since the benefits of an accounting standard are very vague while the costs of compliance are very real. Furthermore, the costs are borne by the companies while the benefits are usually enjoyed by the external users. The cost/benefit perceptions of the AcSB and of the preparers of financial statements do not always coincide, with the result that some of the AcSB's recommendations have less than full compliance, even by public companies.

For private companies that are not bound by the GAAP constraint for public companies, the cost/benefit trade-off is very pragmatic. In particular, if there are no external users of a private company's financial statements (other than the CRA), then there is no benefit to be derived from incurring higher accounting costs. Commonly, such companies will use accounting methods that coincide with their tax treatment even though they are not GAAP. Examples include calculating depreciation/amortization expense on the same basis as CCA, and recognizing revenue on the same basis for accounting as for tax purposes.

The AcSB formally allows **differential reporting** for non-public enterprises whose shareholders unanimously approve. Differential reporting allows these companies to follow simpler accounting policies (that typically follow cash flow) in a few key areas. For example, these companies can simply expense income tax as paid, instead of using the more complex accrual method. This would be considered GAAP for the enterprise.

Other Trade-Offs

As discussed at the beginning of this section, there is often a trade-off between qualitative characteristics, but especially between relevance and reliability. Reliability may have to be reduced to increase the degree of relevance, or vice versa. For example, if financial statements were delayed until all the future events that affect them were to come to pass, they would be far more reliable. Uncollectable accounts, warranty reserves, and useful lives of depreciable assets would not have to be estimated. On the other hand, the timeliness of the financial statements would suffer, and thus the statements would lack relevance. Thus, a degree of reliability is sacrificed to gain relevance. The relative importance of the characteristics changes from situation to situation and calls for the exercise of professional judgement.

---

[7] Maurice Moonitz, *The Basic Postulates of Accounting* (AICPA, 1961), p. 47.

The extent of trade-offs is, in itself, subjective. This is particularly apparent in the standard-setting process, where there often is a vigorous debate amongst the participants about what is relevant and what is measurable. The concerns of the auditing profession often show up in the presence of standards that seem to emphasize verifiability. The historical cost measurement convention often also seems to override what many observers perceive to be the relevance of other highly objective measurements.

CONCEPT REVIEW

1. Why does the criterion of relevance relate to financial reporting objectives?
2. Does the criterion of understandability mean that anyone should be able to understand the financial statements?
3. What are the three components of reliability?
4. What are the four characteristics of objectivity?
5. Why must there often be trade-offs between different qualitative criteria?

ELEMENTS OF FINANCIAL STATEMENTS AND RECOGNITION

elements
the building blocks of financial statements, e.g., assets, liabilities, revenues, expenses

Periodic financial statements are the primary medium used to communicate accounting information about a business enterprise. The building blocks of financial statements are called **elements**. Elements are the classes of items that financial statements should contain and they are affected by accounting policy choice, as indicated in Exhibit 2-1. There are seven elements, as shown in Exhibit 2-3. The first three elements (assets, liabilities, and equity/net assets) relate directly to the balance sheet; the next four elements (revenues, expenses, gains, and losses) relate directly to the income statement. The definitions of these seven elements are particularly important because they provide the basis for deciding whether or not to recognize the results of a transaction or event in the financial statements.

Recognition

An element will be recognized or included in the accounts when

- The item meets the definition of an element.
- The item has an appropriate basis of measurement, and a reasonable estimate can be made of the amount.
- For assets and liabilities, it is probable that the economic benefits will be received or given up, i.e., realized.

Measurability is important. If an item cannot be measured, it cannot be recognized, even if it has a high probability of being realized.

It is entirely possible that an item that meets the first two recognition criteria will not be recognized because of failure of the last criterion—probability of realization. Suppose a company was suing a supplier for $125,000 for damages incurred when faulty materials provided by the supplier were used in a production process. The future economic benefit, or asset, can be measured at $125,000, or a lower amount if the parties are likely to settle. The difficulty arises when assessing the probability of the receipt of the economic benefit, as the lawsuit may not be successful. It may be proven that the company ordered the wrong materials or used them incorrectly. For this reason, such items are disclosed in the notes to the financial statements as contingencies and are not recognized until the result of the court decision is known and the probability of collection assessed.

EXHIBIT 2-3

ELEMENTS OF FINANCIAL STATEMENTS

Elements	Transaction Characteristics
Balance Sheet (discussed in Chapter 4)	
1. Assets are economic resources controlled by an entity as a result of past transactions or events from which future economic benefits may be obtained.	**1.** To qualify as assets, the resources involved must **a.** have future economic benefits; **b.** be under the entity's current control; and **c.** result from past transactions.
2. Liabilities are obligations of an entity arising from past transactions or events, the settlement of which will result in the transfer or use of assets, provision of services, or other yielding of economic benefits in the future.	**2.** To qualify as liabilities, obligations must **a.** require future transfer of assets or economic benefits; **b.** be an unavoidable current obligation; and **c.** result from past transactions.
3. Owners' equity/net assets is the ownership interest in the assets of an entity after deducting its liabilities. While equity in total is a residual, it includes specific categories of items, for example, types of share capital, other contributed capital, and retained earnings.	**3.** The dollar amounts reported represent the residual interest in the assets after deducting the liabilities. In addition, the equity element is used to report capital transactions.
Income Statement (discussed in Chapter 3)	
4. Revenues are increases in economic resources, either by way of **(a)** inflows or enhancements of assets or **(b)** reductions of liabilities, resulting from the ordinary activities of an entity, Normally from the sale of goods, the rendering of services, or the use by others of entity resources yielding rent, interest, royalties, or dividends.	**4.** An essential characteristic of a revenue transaction is that it arises from the company's ordinary earning activities, and not from **(a)** capital transactions, **(b)** the settlement of monetary liabilities, or **(c)** the sale of capital assets or investment assets.
5. Expenses are decreases in economic resources, either by way of **(a)** outflows or reductions of assets or **(b)** incurrences of liabilities, resulting from the ordinary revenue-earning activities of an entity.	**5.** The essential characteristic of an expense is that it must be incurred in conjunction with the company's revenue-generating process. Expenditures that do not qualify as expenses are treated either as assets (future economic benefit to be derived), as losses (no economic benefit), or as distributions to owners.
6. Gains are increases in net assets from peripheral or incidental transactions and events affecting an entity and from all other transactions, events, and circumstances affecting an entity that are given accounting recognition except those that result from revenues or equity contributions.	**6.** The transaction must not be one that meets the characteristics of **(a)** a revenue-producing transaction or **(b)** a capital transaction (e.g., capital infusion by the owners).
7. Losses are decreases in equity from peripheral or incidental transactions and events affecting an entity and from all other transactions, events, and circumstances affecting an entity that are given accounting recognition except those that result from expenses or distributions of equity.	**7.** The transaction must not be one that meets the characteristics of **(a)** an expense transaction or **(b)** a capital transaction (e.g., dividends or other distributions to owners).

Source: CICA Handbook, Section 1000, "Financial Statement Concepts."

ASSETS AND LIABILITIES Assets and liabilities are central to the definitions, since all other definitions are *derived from* asset and liability definitions. That is, owners' equity equals assets less liabilities. Revenues are defined as increases in assets or decreases in liabilities; expenses are decreases in assets or increases in liabilities. Obviously, the AcSB's definitions place emphasis on the balance sheet and the assets and liabilities that comprise it.

So, what are assets? According to the AcSB, assets have three essential characteristics:

1. they embody a future benefit, involving a capacity to contribute to future net cash flows;
2. the entity must be able to control access to the benefit; and
3. the asset must be the result of a past transaction or event.

Similarly, consider the three characteristics of liabilities:

1. they embody a duty or a responsibility to others that will involve a future transfer or use of assets, or other economic benefits, or rendering service, at a specific time or after a specific event;
2. the entity has little or no discretion to avoid the obligation; and
3. the liability must be the result of a past transaction or event.

NECESSARY CONDITIONS The definitions of both of these two elements (i.e., assets and liabilities) include three components and embody three time frames:

1. An asset must be entitled to a *future benefit* (e.g., through a direct future cash flow or through its use in generating a future cash flow), and a liability must entail a future sacrifice (either a payment of cash or performance of service).
2. The reporting enterprise has a clear *present right* to the asset or obligation for the liability.
3. The asset or liability arose as the result of a *past transaction* or event.

SUFFICIENT CONDITIONS While these three components are *necessary* conditions for recognizing an asset or a liability, they are not *sufficient* conditions. There still are transactions and events that seem to fit the definitions and yet are not recognized as assets and liabilities in the accounts.

For example, suppose that a company signs a three-year contract to hire a special consultant; the contract is non-cancellable. Should the company recognize a liability? The conditions for recognition do seem to be satisfied: (1) the contract will require a cash outflow over the next three years; (2) there is a present obligation that is unavoidable; and (3) the transaction has already occurred. However, such a contract is *not* recognized in business accounting because the consultant has not yet rendered the services for which she was hired. There is a distinction drawn between a recognizable asset or liability on the one hand, and a **commitment** on the other hand. A commitment, even if irrevocable, does not normally result in recognition of a liability or asset.

commitment
a promise, either written or oral, that obligates an entity to provide a future service or deliver an asset at some future time

From a practical standpoint, a useful way of approaching the question of whether a transaction or event has given rise to a recognizable asset or liability is to ask: "What do I do with the offset?" If the commitment to the consultant were recognized as a liability, there would have to be an offsetting debit. There are only two choices for the debit: an asset or an expense. Clearly, the expense has not been incurred yet, because the service has not yet been rendered nor has the contract time passed. Therefore, the only choice for an offset is an asset. But what is the asset? It would have to be the future benefit to be derived from the costs that have not yet been incurred. The prospect of recognizing an asset for costs to be incurred in the future for services not yet rendered is a prospect that most accountants would find objectionable. Therefore, the commitment would be viewed as an **executory contract**—a contract wherein neither party has yet fulfilled the requirements of the contract—and would not be recognized.

The important aspect of these AcSB definitions of assets and liabilities is that they are far from iron-clad. Accountants still must make decisions on whether or not to recognize the future effects of past transactions and events as assets or liabilities.

INCOME STATEMENT ELEMENTS The AcSB's definitions of the income statement elements—revenues, expenses, gains, and losses—are related to changes in net assets (i.e., total assets minus total liabilities):

- Revenues are increases in net assets, either by way of inflows or enhancements of assets or reductions of liabilities, resulting from the ordinary activities of the enterprise.
- Expenses are decreases in net assets, either by way of outflows or reductions of assets or incurrences of liabilities, resulting from an enterprise's ordinary revenue-generating or service-delivery activities.
- Gains are increases in net assets from peripheral or incidental transactions.
- Losses are decreases in net assets from peripheral or incidental transactions.

The only difference between revenues and gains and between expenses and losses is the nature of the activity that gave rise to them. Revenues and expenses relate to the ordinary operating activities of the enterprise; gains and losses relate to non-operating activities.

The "ordinary" versus "peripheral" criterion is rather vague. For example, some movie theatre chains regularly report "gains" from the sale of theatre properties in their income statements. But if an enterprise operates hundreds of movie screens, then isn't the purchase and sale of theatre properties an ordinary business activity rather than a peripheral activity? The key is that the business of a theatre chain is not that of buying and selling theatres; such an activity is essential to the health of the company, but it is *incidental* to the primary business activity of exhibiting movies. Revenue should include only the proceeds from the sale of tickets and popcorn and the delivery of other routine services and products, and not from the sale of the capital assets.

Recognition and Realization

Recognition is the process of measuring and including an item in the financial statements. A recognized item is given a title and numerical value. Recognition applies to all financial statement elements in all accounting entities. *Disclosure* (information in the notes to the financial statements) is not the same as recognition; when a financial statement element is recognized, it is reported on the face of the financial statements.

Realization is the process of converting an asset, liability, or commitment into a cash flow. A receivable is said to be *realized* when it is collected, revenues are *realized* when received, expenses and liabilities are *realized* when the cash payment occurs.

Once realization has occurred, recognition *must* occur because there has been a cash flow impact that cannot be ignored in the accounts. For example,

- A customer makes a deposit (or pays in advance) for goods yet to be produced and delivered; since the cash has been received (realized), it must be recognized. Since revenue will not yet have been earned, the offsetting credit is to recognize unearned revenue.
- A company pays a retainer to a lawyer who will be acting on the company's behalf in the next fiscal year; the cash outflow triggers recognition of a prepaid expense.

However, recognition often occurs *prior* to realization. For example,

- An accounts receivable is recognized when a service has been performed for a client; realization occurs when the client pays the account. The offset is to recognize revenue.
- A liability for a purchase of inventory is recognized when the goods are received; realization occurs when the creditor is paid. The offset is to recognize inventory as an asset.
- A change in the value of cash held in U.S. dollars is recognized at the balance sheet date; realization occurs only when the U.S. dollars are converted to Canadian dollars. The offset is to a gain or loss account, depending on the direction of the change in value.

- The liability for a purchase of new equipment is recognized; the liability is offset by an increase in an asset account (i.e., equipment).
- Unpaid wages are accrued at the end of a fiscal period; a liability is recognized. The liability is offset by a debit to an expense account.

THE ACCRUAL CONCEPT When we recognize the effects of transactions and events prior to their realization, we are using the *accrual concept*. The accrual concept says that we recognize assets when we have the right to receive their benefits, and we recognize liabilities when we take on the obligation to deliver cash (or other assets) or services in the future. The International Accounting Standards Committee, for example, states that

> Under the accrual basis of accounting, transactions and other events are recognized when they occur (and not as cash or its equivalent is received or paid) and they are recorded in the accounting records and reported in the financial statements of the periods to which they relate.[8]

Accrual means that assets and liabilities are recognized when the rights and obligations pertaining thereto are established; accrual does *not* refer to the subsequent transfer of amounts from the balance sheet to the income statement, which is a secondary form of recognition. For example,

- Inventory is purchased on account. The liability is *accrued* as an account payable, and the asset is recorded as inventory. Both an asset and a related liability are recognized. This is an application of the accrual concept because the transaction is recorded prior to its cash flow impact. When the inventory is sold, its cost is transferred to cost of goods sold, which is recognition of an expense. However, this subsequent expense recognition is not an application of the accrual concept; the liability had already been accrued. The temporary classification of the cost of the inventory as an asset, which then is transferred to an expense, is the result of *matching*, not of accrual.
- Equipment is purchased by giving a 20% cash down payment and giving a promissory note for the remaining 80%. The full cost of the equipment is *recognized* as an asset, including the 80% portion of the cost represented by the liability that is *accrued*. The equipment is recorded as an asset; it is expected to have a four-year useful life. For each of the next four years, 25% of the cost is transferred to the income statement as depreciation, thereby recognizing depreciation expense in each year. The recognition of depreciation is *not* an accrual; it is an *interperiod allocation* (which also is a function of *matching*).

In matching and interperiod allocation, amounts originally recognized as assets are transferred to (or *recognized* as) expense, and amounts recorded as liabilities are transferred to the income statement as revenue (or as reduction of expense). Interperiod allocation (e.g., amortization) is *not* part of the accrual concept:

> [Accrual] is a broader concept than the matching concept which simply requires expense to be recognized in the same period as the associated revenue is recognized as income.[9]

Before leaving the concepts of realization and recognition, we must stress that accounting recognition always relates to realized cash flows—past, present, and future. The recognition issue is always one of fitting the actual (or predicted) cash flows into

---

[8] International Accounting Standards Committee, International Accounting Standard IAS 1, *Presentation of Financial Statements* (1997), paragraph 26.

[9] IASC, *Draft Statement of Principles for Presentation of Financial Statements* (1995), paragraph 28.

time periods through a complex system of accruals and interperiod allocations. If actual cash flows deviate from those that we presumed in recognizing revenues and expenses, then we must adjust our accounts. *At no time can accounting recognize financial statement elements that are not based on actual or predicted cash flows!*

CONCEPT REVIEW

1. What are the seven elements of financial statements?
2. What is the difference between realization and accounting recognition?
3. What is the difference between accrual and interperiod allocation?

MEASUREMENT METHODS

Measurement is the process of determining the amount at which an item is recognized in the financial statements. It is integral to accounting choice, as illustrated in Exhibit 2-1. Although measurement underlies the financial statement elements, we described the elements first to make the measurement discussion more meaningful. If there is no appropriate basis of measurement, a transaction fails the second recognition criterion, as previously defined.

Measurement methods encompass not only the process of attaching a number to a construct such as a specific asset or a liability, but also the process of income measurement as it is conventionally practised in Canadian accounting. The process of income measurement involves the initial measurement and the disposition of that measurement as it moves through the financial statements. There are four pervasive measurement conventions:

1. historical cost
2. revenue recognition
3. matching
4. full disclosure

Historical Cost Method

There are many alternative measurement bases, including historical cost, price level adjusted historical cost, replacement cost, current sales value, net realizable value, and the sum of the cash flows an item will generate over its life, discounted at an appropriate rate. The FSCs state that, *generally*, historical cost should be used as a measurement base.

Our GAAP model is described as an historical cost model, yet there are many examples in it of other valuation bases—obsolete inventory carried at market value when this amount is less than cost, long-term liabilities with interest rates lower than market rates recorded on the date of issuance at discounted amounts, inventories of agricultural products and precious metals carried at market values, and so on. The implication of the FSCs is that this *ad hoc* basis will continue and that we will continue to see a variety of measurement bases, although historical cost will dominate.

historical cost convention
economic transactions are recorded using the cost (historic cost) of the transaction

Normally applied in conjunction with asset acquisitions, the **historical cost convention** specifies that the actual acquisition cost be used for initial accounting recognition purposes. The cost principle assumes that assets are acquired in business transactions conducted at arm's length—that is, transactions between a buyer and a seller are at the fair value prevailing at the time of the transaction.

If an asset is acquired via some means other than cash, the cost of the asset is based on the *value of the consideration given*. **Consideration** is whatever the buyer gives the seller. For non-cash transactions conducted at arm's length, the cost principle assumes that the fair value of the resources *given up* in a transaction provides reliable evidence for the valuation of the item acquired. This may be the amount of money paid, market value of common shares issued, or the present value of debt assumed in the transaction. It is often useful to refer to both the market value of the assets or securities given up, if any, and the market value of the assets received. Usually one of these values is more reliable than the other, and provides a basis for valuation.

The cost principle provides guidance primarily at the initial acquisition date. Once acquired, the original cost basis of long-lived assets is then subject to depreciation, depletion, amortization, or writedown in conformity with the matching principle, discussed later in this section. Write-ups of appreciated asset values are generally not permitted within GAAP.

Revenue Recognition

Revenue recognition requires the recognition and reporting of revenues when all three of the recognition criteria—definition, measurability, and probability—are met.

Revenue has been defined as inflows of cash or other enhancements of a business's assets, settlements of its liabilities, or a combination of the two. Such inflows must be derived from delivering or producing goods, rendering service, or performing other activities that constitute a company's ongoing business operations over a specific period of time. More generally, revenue is measured as the market value of the resources received or the *fair value* of the product or service given, whichever is the more reliably determinable. This broader definition comes into play in conjunction with non-cash or *barter* transactions (that is, direct exchanges of goods and services).

The revenue recognition convention pertains only to accrual-basis accounting, and not to cash-basis accounting. Therefore, completed transactions for the sale of goods or services on credit usually are recognized as revenue for the period in which the sale or service occurs rather than in the period in which the cash is eventually collected. Furthermore, related expenses are matched to these revenues.

Traditionally, four conditions have to be met to satisfy the revenue recognition convention:

1. All significant acts required of the seller have been performed.
2. Consideration is measurable.
3. Collection is reasonably assured.
4. The risks and rewards of ownership have passed to the buyer.

These conditions are easily applied to traditional trading activities, wherein a company buys and sells inventory or manufactures items for sale. Many sectors of the Canadian economy do not fit into these traditional modes of business, and multiperiod earnings cycles are common. Transactions that do not quite fit into the four conditions above include instalment sales, long-term construction contracts, sales of land with minimal down payments, software development contracts, long-term leases, and sales of franchises that require a certain level of performance on the part of the purchaser as a condition of sale. In these transactions and in others, there are significant uncertainties concerning one or more of the listed criteria. In long earnings cycles, the first condition is particularly troublesome. If *all* significant acts must be performed before revenue can be recognized, there would be no such thing as percentage-of-completion accounting, instalment-basis revenue recognition, loan interest revenue, and so forth. Instead, revenue would be recognized only when all of the effort has been expended and the earnings process is complete.

The AcSB has a somewhat more modest statement of when revenue recognition is appropriate:

> Revenues are generally recognized when performance is achieved and reasonable assurance regarding measurement and collectibility of the consideration exists.
> (*CICA* 1000.47)

Note the AcSB's use of the major qualifier "generally," and note that performance is not modified by "all" or "complete." The interpretation of what constitutes *performance* is a major issue in financial reporting for many companies, one that is subject to many different interpretations. As well, *measurability* is an elusive concept in revenue recognition. The issue of revenue recognition is one of the most pervasive and most difficult in the practice of accounting. Chapter 6 is devoted exclusively to a discussion of this important issue.

Matching

matching
the recognition of expenses in the same time period that the revenues (generated by incurring the expenses) are recognized

Matching refers to the timing of recognition of revenues and expenses in the income statement. Under this concept, all expenses incurred in earning revenue should be recognized in the same period that the revenue is recognized. For example,

- If revenue is carried over (deferred) for recognition in a future period, any related expenses should also be carried over or deferred, since they are incurred in earning that revenue.
- If revenue is recognized in the current period but there are expenditures yet to be incurred in future periods, the expenses are recognized and a liability is created (e.g., the estimated provision for warranty costs).
- If costs are incurred to enhance the general revenue-generating ability of the company in future periods and the future benefits are measurable, the costs are capitalized and amortized.

Matching is widely considered useful for evaluating the ability of a company to generate net income and thus for performance evaluation. After all, if revenue is recognized, then surely all of the expenses related to earning that revenue should also be recognized in the same period.

The problem is that most costs are not *directly* related to revenue. Some costs are directly related to revenues, such as inventory costs for goods sold and labour costs in a service contract. But even in those "direct" costs, there is considerable flexibility in measurement. For most types of cost, expenses are only indirectly related to specific revenue-generating activity. These indirect costs are often called *overhead*, and they constitute a majority of the costs of most companies.

As a result, most matching is not directly to revenue, but is instead to *time periods*. Examples are the expenditures for administration and for promotional activities. These items are **period costs**—they are recognized as expenses during the period in which they are incurred. Another type of example is that of investments in long-lived assets. Amortization seldom is allocated on the basis of revenues but instead is usually allocated over an estimated useful life or, in the case of intangible assets, often over an arbitrary number of years.

Adjusting entries may be required at the end of the accounting period to update revenues and expenses in step with recognized sales revenue. Examples include wage expense earned but not paid, estimated uncollectible accounts receivable, estimated warranty expense, and interest expense accrued but not paid.

ILLUSTRATION To illustrate the matching principle, assume a home appliance is sold for cash with a 100% warranty on parts and labour in effect for the first 12 months from date of sale. The revenue from the sale is recognized immediately, as are the directly related costs involved in manufacturing and assembling the unit and the shipping and direct selling expenses incurred. Furthermore, the expenses involved in honouring the warranty should also be recognized in the same period as the sales revenue, even though the actual warranty cost may not be known until the next year. At the end of the year in which the sale occurs, the warranty expense should be estimated, recorded on the books, and recognized for financial statement reporting purposes. In this way, the warranty expense is matched with the revenue to which it is related even though the cash may be expended at a later time. Depreciation on the equipment used in manufacturing the appliance is allocated to the period, but the depreciation is not directly related to (or affected by the amount of) the revenue.

A simple table is helpful in summarizing the accounting disposition of costs and expenses in accordance with the matching principle and the definitions of elements:

Time frame of benefit:	Expenditure should be:
Future verifiable economic benefits	Recorded as an asset
Current economic benefits	Recorded as an expense
No economic benefits	Recorded as a loss

The timing of expense recognition and the measurement of the cost is another matter for professional judgement. There is hardly an expense item in the income statement that is not the subject of several interrelated judgements and estimates. Chapter 6 discusses the issue of expense recognition at some length, and most of the other chapters in this book deal with expense recognition in the context of specific accounting issues, such as inventories, capital assets, leases, pensions, income taxes, and so forth.

Full Disclosure

Full disclosure means that the financial statements should report all *relevant* information bearing on the economic affairs of a business enterprise. The aim of full disclosure is to provide external users with the accounting information they need to make informed investment and credit decisions. Full disclosure requires, among other things, that the accounting policies followed be explained in the notes to the financial statements.

Although the common expression is "full disclosure," perhaps a more realistic expression is "adequate disclosure." Obviously, not all information that may be relevant to a financial statement user can be disclosed. Instead, the objective is to disclose enough supplemental information to keep from misleading the users of the statements who are likely to be using the statements to predict cash flows or to evaluate the earnings ability of the company.

A useful guide to deciding what to disclose is as follows:[10]

- Disclose items not in the regular or normal activities of the business.
- Disclose items reflecting changes in expectations.
- Disclose that which a statute or contract requires to be disclosed.
- Disclose new activities or major changes in old ones.

The emphasis in this list is on disclosing what causes changes in expectations for an external reader of the financial statements. Such disclosure will reduce the likelihood of a user being misled by assuming that the company will continue in the future much as it has in the past.

THE EXERCISE OF ETHICAL PROFESSIONAL JUDGEMENT

Chapter 1 gave examples of the many accounting choices that are affected by the financial reporting objectives *in any particular situation*. Reporting objectives (and motivations) do vary, and choices of accounting policies and accounting estimates are significantly affected by whether the primary reporting objective is, for example, income tax minimization, cash flow prediction, or net income maximization.

Early in this chapter, we pointed out that the ability to make appropriate choices in accounting is ethical professional judgement. Professional judgement permeates the work of a professional accountant, and it involves an ability to build accounting measurements that take into account

- the objectives of financial reporting in each particular situation,
- the facts of the business environment and operations, and
- the organization's reporting constraints (if any).

[10] Maurice Moonitz, *The Basic Postulates of Accounting* (AICPA, 1961), pp. 48–49.

The result of properly applied ethical professional judgement is fair financial information. Failure of ethical professional judgement may result in false or misleading information. Let's follow the steps required to apply professional judgement in an ethical fashion. The building blocks for accounting choice were illustrated in Exhibit 2-1 in the form of a pyramid.

1. At the base of the pyramid, on which all else is built, are the objectives of financial reporting. There usually are multiple objectives, and the objectives must be ethically and appropriately prioritized in order to be able to resolve conflicts between them when decisions about specific accounting policies or estimates must be made.
2. The facts of the organization's operations and its economic environment must be determined in order to understand just what is to be measured. Fraud may interfere with fact-finding and an accountant must be very careful here.
3. Next, the reporting constraints must be determined. Is the reporting enterprise a public company, bound by the reporting constraints of the securities commissions? Is it a private company that uses the financial statements only for its owner(s) and for income tax purposes? Is an audit required? If an audit is required (or desired by management), is a "clean" audit opinion necessarily needed? Does the company qualify for *differential reporting*? Can the enterprise report on the basis of disclosed (or tailored) accounting policies rather than GAAP?
4. The underlying assumptions must be tested. In preparing the financial statements for the vast majority of Canadian business organizations, the normal underlying assumptions of continuity, nominal dollar capital maintenance, proprietary approach, etc., are quite valid. But they cannot be taken for granted, and their appropriateness in the specific reporting situation must be evaluated.
5. Once the objectives have been discerned and prioritized, the facts and constraints determined, and the underlying assumptions evaluated, only then should the accounting policies or measurement choices be considered.
6. The measurement choices must be consistent with the objectives, facts, and constraints. The measurement choices are further tempered by the qualitative criteria, especially in the realm of recognition. When should revenues be recognized? When should costs incurred or committed be recognized? When costs are recognized, should they be recognized as assets or as expenses? If they are recognized as assets, when should they be transferred to expense (as a secondary recognition)? There are many ethical decisions to be made.
7. The measurement and recognition criteria lead to the financial statement elements, which then are classified in a manner that is appropriate to the industry and consistent with the operational activities of the enterprise. The result is, finally, the financial statements themselves. To be appropriate for the specific reporting situation, the final financial statements must satisfy the specific reporting objectives that are at the foundation of the whole pyramid.
8. The ethical requirements are met if the financial statements are a fair representation of the underlying business activity.

FINANCIAL STATEMENTS Financial statements are not uniform. They vary considerably by industry and type of company. Although there are *common* forms of balance sheets and income statements, there actually is no *standard* format. The AcSB does not prescribe a format for the balance sheet and income statement; only the disclosure of certain types of assets, liabilities, revenues, and expenses is recommended in the *CICA Handbook*. The balance sheet of a life insurance company looks very different from the balance sheet of a steel company; the income statement of a mutual fund is very different from that of a retailer. The next two chapters will discuss the form and organization of the income statement and the balance sheet, and will point out many of the industry differences that arise in practice.

The cash flow statement does have an AcSB-prescribed format, but the accounting choices that go into measurement of the financial statement elements can have an impact on the way cash flows are reported in the cash flow statement, as we will see in Chapter 5.

CONCEPT REVIEW

1. When should revenue be recognized, in the view of the AcSB?
2. How is the concept of matching usually applied to period costs?
3. Are there standardized formats for Canadian balance sheets and income statements?

SUMMARY OF KEY POINTS

1. Accounting "principles" consist of three different sets of concepts: (1) underlying assumptions, (2) measurement methods, and (3) qualitative criteria.
2. *Underlying assumptions* include the basic postulates that make accounting measurements possible (such as the *separate-entity assumption*, the *unit-of-measure concept*, and the *time-period assumption*), but they also include underlying measurement assumptions that usually, but not always, are true in a given reporting situation. These measurement assumptions include the *continuity assumption*, the *proprietary assumption*, and the *nominal dollar capital maintenance concept.*
3. *Qualitative criteria* are the criteria that are used in conjunction with an enterprise's financial reporting objectives to determine the most appropriate measurement methods to use in that particular reporting situation. Qualitative criteria include relevance, reliability, objectivity, understandability, conservatism, and the cost/benefit tradeoff.
4. The most important qualitative criterion is that of *relevance*; relevance should be determined with reference to the users of the financial statements and the resultant financial reporting objectives. Relevance is enhanced if information is timely, and has predictive and feedback value.
5. Some qualitative criteria conflict with each other. For example, the most *relevant* measurement in a particular situation may not be sufficiently *reliable* to permit its use.
6. *Reliability* is a general concept that has several components, including verifiability, freedom from bias, and representational faithfulness.
7. The role of *conservatism* in accounting is to ensure that the uncertainties and risks inherent in measuring the effects of any given business situation are given adequate consideration. Conservatism may not be used as a justification for overstating liabilities or understating assets.
8. *Measurement methods* are the various ways that the results of transactions and events can be reported in the financial statements. There is a group of widely used measurement methods that can be called *measurement conventions*, but they are not universally applicable. Measurement conventions include historical cost, the revenue recognition convention, matching, and full disclosure.
9. The *elements of financial statements* are the seven types of accounts that appear on the balance sheet and income statement: assets, liabilities, owners' equity, revenues, expenses, gains, and losses.
10. Initial accounting *recognition* occurs when the effects or results of a transaction or event are first measured and assigned to an account or *element.* Subsequent recognition occurs when an amount previously recognized is transferred from one element to another, such as by recognizing an expense that previously had been recognized as an asset.
11. Recognition of an asset or liability requires that three time references be present: a *future* benefit or sacrifice and a *present* right or obligation, arising from a *past* transaction or event.
12. *Realization* occurs when a cash flow occurs. Realization often occurs after recognition, but can never occur prior to recognition because the cash flow forces recognition if it has not occurred previously.

13. The accrual concept relates to the recognition of receivables when the right to receive cash arises, and to the recognition of liabilities when the obligation is created. Accrual does not refer to subsequent secondary recognition through matching and interperiod allocations.

14. Accounting is full of choices. Financial statements are constructed from the financial statement elements that have been recognized using measurement methods that optimize the qualitative characteristics and that are based on the appropriate underlying assumptions. The organization's reporting constraints as well as the facts of its business and environment all impact on the choice of accounting policy. The result is information that best satisfies the objectives of financial reporting in any given situation. This series of related decisions constitutes *ethical professional judgement in accounting.*

KEY TERMS

accrual-basis accounting, 43
accruals, 43
commitment, 55
comparability, 51
conservatism, 51
consideration, 58
consistency, 51
constant dollar capital maintenance, 47
continuity assumption, 44
cost/benefit effectiveness, 52
deferrals, 43
differential reporting, 52
elements, 53
entity concept, 45
executory contract, 55
freedom from bias, 51
full disclosure, 61
going-concern assumption, 44
historical cost convention, 58
maintenance of nominal dollar financial control, 47
matching, 60
measurement conventions, 39
nominal dollar capital maintenance, 47
non-arbitrariness, 51
period costs, 60
professional judgement, 42
proprietary assumption, 45
purchasing power parity, 47
qualitative criteria, 39
quantifiability, 51
realization, 56
recognition, 56
relevance, 49
reliability, 49
separate-entity assumption, 44
substance over form, 50
time-period assumption, 43
underlying assumption, 39
uniformity, 51
unit-of-measure assumption, 46
validity, 49
verifiability, 51

QUESTIONS

Q2-1 Identify the three different building blocks that comprise accounting principles.

Q2-2 Does the *CICA Handbook's* Section 1000, Financial Statement Concepts, include an explanation of all accounting principles? Explain.

Q2-3 What topics are covered in the *CICA Handbook's* Section 1000, Financial Statement Concepts?

Q2-4 Identify and describe the six underlying assumptions included in accounting principles.

Q2-5 Explain why the time-period assumption causes accruals and deferrals in accounting.

Q2-6 Does the separate-entity assumption follow the tax and legal status of a corporation? A sole proprietorship?

Q2-7 Relate the continuity assumption to use of historical cost in financial statement measurements of assets.

Q2-8 How are owners viewed under the proprietary assumption as compared to the entity assumption?

Q2-9 Financial statements record goodwill only when it has been purchased in a business combination. How does this relate to the units-of-measure assumption and the historical cost convention?

Q2-10 Which assumption or principle discussed in this chapter is most affected by the phenomenon of inflation? Give reasons for your choice.

Q2-11 List and describe the significant qualitative criteria that are part of accounting principles.

Q2-12 Explain the trade-off that occurs between relevance and reliability.

Q2-13 "If the financial statements are to be understandable to users, they must be reduced to a very simple level for the benefit of those who are less sophisticated." Is this true? Explain.

Q2-14 Describe the characteristics that make information (a) relevant and (b) reliable.

Q2-15 Describe how consistency and uniformity promote comparability.

Q2-16 When a company evaluates an accounting policy with reference to its cost/benefit effectiveness, what benefits are under consideration? What are the costs?

Q2-17 What are the recognition criteria?

Q2-18 The definitions of assets and liabilities involve a consideration of the past, present, and future. Explain.

Q2-19 Why is it said that the definitions of assets and liabilities are central to the financial statement element definitions?

Q2-20 Explain why executory contracts are not recognized in the financial statements.

Q2-21 What is the difference between a revenue and a gain?

Q2-22 Contrast recognition and realization. Why can realization not precede recognition?

Q2-23 Explain the historical cost convention. Why is it used in the basic financial statements instead of current replacement value?

Q2-24 What criteria must be met before revenue can be recognized?

Q2-25 What is the purpose of full, or at least adequate, disclosure?

Q2-26 Describe the role of ethical professional judgement in the choice of accounting policies. What are the influencing factors?

CASE 2-1
FutureLink Cable Incorporated

FutureLink Cable Inc. (FutureLink) is a communications provider offering data transmission and data services to businesses and consumers. Brian MacInnis has been head accountant for three years, and is more than satisfied with the salary and stock option package that lured him away from a competitor. Stock options, awarded at each year-end, are especially attractive, as the stock price has increased significantly each year up to this year.

This year, the financial picture has been of considerable concern. Stock price has been depressed, largely because of a slowdown in the economy that has affected FutureLink's revenue stream. Internal projections indicate that customer volume is down between 15% and 20%. The FutureLink management team is focusing efforts on cost containment for the remainder of the year, hoping that reduced costs will allow the company to almost make its publicly announced projected income levels. This might avoid further erosion of stock price. Costs are being cut to the bone, and layoffs have been announced. FutureLink has had cash flow challenges, which are about to be addressed through a new $50 million credit facility with a chartered bank.

Brian is examining the budget, and accounting policies, for line costs. FutureLink rents capacity on data transmission lines owned by other companies at an annual cost of approximately $48 million. This rent is paid regardless of the actual use of the line. The payment has been expensed as time passes, but Brian is no longer sure that this accounting policy is appropriate. In the past, most of the daily capacity rented was used by FutureLink customers. In the current year, usage is closer to 75%. FutureLink cannot reduce the level of capacity rented, as the company would then not be assured of additional capacity once volumes recover. It would not be possible to replace this capacity in a cost-effective manner, and thus FutureLink is committed to the existing level of payment.

Brian is considering whether it would be appropriate to defer the line costs in proportion to the unused capacity in the current period (i.e., 25%). Deferred line costs would be a capital asset, amortized over a relatively short period of five years, commencing when volumes returned to normal. Brian believes this treatment is justified because future periods will benefit from access to the full rented capacity, and this capacity would be necessary to handle the larger number of customers. Brian, along with other members of top management, is convinced that the reduction in volume is temporary, although there has been additional competition in the past year.

Deferral of approximately $12 million in line costs will go a long way toward eliminating the current shortfall in earnings. Brian knows this will be a huge relief to the senior management team, and it might help expedite the $50 million loan and improve stock price.

Required:

Write a report evaluating the proposed change in policy. Include your recommendations to Brian.

Case 2-2
96824 Alberta Limited

96824 Alberta Limited is an Alberta corporation. Its shares are owned, in equal amounts, by the three Buchari brothers. The company was a thriving import business, started by the father of these men, and left to them upon his death. The import business continued to be very profitable until the operation was sold in 20X6 to a multinational conglomerate. The conglomerate paid over $80 million, in cash and shares, for the company.

96824 Alberta Limited now exists as an investment company, holding cash and shares. All other assets and liabilities were transferred as part of the transfer of operations. The bulk of these assets will shortly be distributed to the brothers and various trusts and private companies that they own.

The shareholders have agreed to leave $6 million in 96824 Alberta Limited to make certain investments together. This $6 million investment will be levered through borrowing. Any borrowing will be personally guaranteed by the three brothers (if and when required by the lender) and will be secured by the company's investments.

Profits and losses will be split evenly, as the shares are owned evenly. 96824 Alberta Limited could distribute profits as dividend distributions, but the three shareholders are not anxious for such a payout. They have agreed to reinvest profits.

The brothers are interested in the following types of investments:

1. Real estate in currently depressed markets that are likely, in their opinion, to rebound in the next 5 to 10 years.
2. Shares in high-tech companies.
3. Shares in biotechnology companies.
4. Shares in mining companies (gold and oil are both possibilities.)

Some investments would be in publicly listed companies, but the remainder would be privately placed and probably would be illiquid because of the potential scarcity of other investors.

You have acted as an independent financial advisor to the family for some time. The brothers have agreed that the financial statements need not follow GAAP for investment accounting. However, they are disagreeing about how to value investments in the financial statements, and have asked for your opinion. One alternative is to value the investments at cost and recognize gains and losses only when the investments are sold. The other alternative is to measure investments at market values and measure gains and losses as market values shift. Measurement of market value is obviously difficult for certain investments. You have specifically been asked to address this issue in your report. Of course, investments can go down in value as well as up—the implications of using a strict cost method in such a case must also be explained.

Creditors and the shareholders are the primary financial statement users. The primary financial statements will not be used for income tax purposes, as separate statements will be provided for the CRA.

Required:

Prepare a report that explains both alternatives to value the investments. Your report should conclude with your recommendation.

CASE 2-3
SpaceSat Limited

SpaceSat Limited (SSL), a Canadian public company established in 1972, is involved in global telecommunication transmissions. SSL has over $1.4 billion in assets, financed by $900 million in liabilities and $500 million in equity. As a federally regulated monopoly in the public spotlight, the company adheres to high standards of disclosure and accountability. SSL owns satellite and underground (and under-ocean) cable communication networks. Access to these facilities is rented to North American customers, including broadcasters, telephone companies, and banking institutions. SSL also has extensive computer facilities, specializing in the development of technology associated with data transmission. Operating revenue for the most recent fiscal year was $420 million. Net income of $26 million provided a reasonable (but not spectacular) return on equity. Income has been stable.

Recently, concern has arisen regarding SSL's abandoned satellites. When satellites reach the end of their technologically useful life, state-of-the-art replacement satellites are launched; the old satellites are either shot out of orbit and into deep space or shut down and "abandoned" in orbit, where they remain indefinitely. There is a risk of the orbit becoming unstable and the satellite crashing to earth. Because of this risk, and the increasing volume of "space junk," there is talk internationally, and within the Canadian government, of requiring owners to properly dispose of abandoned space equipment. No one is quite sure how this could be accomplished. Alternatives include destruction by explosion, retrieval by a shuttle, creation of a "junkyard" on the moon, and so on. All of these alternatives seem far-fetched and extremely expensive. Technology does not exist to achieve many of these alternatives, and the ultimate method of disposal would necessitate extensive research.

SSL is uncertain as to whether it should record, or even disclose, a liability for its abandoned satellites. Legal liability is not established, and at present there is no feasible disposal method. Satellite abandonment is current industry practice; everyone does it. Furthermore, estimates of disposal cost would be based on significant assumptions. It seems clear that any solution will require large initial expenditures.

SSL's Chief Financial Officer has asked the controller's office to prepare a brief report that examines SSL's reporting alternatives for this situation and provides a recommendation. As assistant controller, you have been assigned the task. You have decided to structure your report around a discussion of the recognition criteria, and whether this item meets these criteria.

Required:

Prepare the report. (CGA-Canada, adapted)

CASE 2-4
G Limited

G Limited (GL) is a private company, incorporated 20 years ago under federal legislation. GL was audited for the first time in the year ended 31 December 20X1 by an auditor who issued a qualified audit opinion on the basis that GL did not record depreciation. During the current year, the vice-president, Finance, has indicated that the company wishes to have an unqualified (or "clean") opinion for the year ended 31 December 20X2, as he anticipates that the company will become a public company in the near future. Management believes that a pattern of smooth earnings will be the most attractive to potential shareholders.

The vice-president, Finance, has provided CA with the following list of contentious accounting issues facing the company:

1. GL has not, in the past, recorded depreciation on its capital assets. The president's feelings about this subject were noted in last year's report to the shareholders as follows: "Our capital assets are increasing in value, not decreasing. In my opinion, the recording of a fictitious expense like depreciation makes our financial statements unreliable and less useful to investors and creditors."
2. During 20X2, GL was sued by a customer who incorporated one of GL's components in manufactured products that were subsequently returned by its customers due to the failure of the GL component. GL refutes this claim. The amount in dispute is $250,000. Correspondence indicates that a settlement of $100,000 would be acceptable to the customer; GL has not agreed to this. Court proceedings will commence early in 20X3. The claim has not been recorded in GL's books.
3. GL incurred expenditures of approximately $400,000 related to refining an existing product, which is now expected to have a significantly longer life and thus increased sales. GL plans to defer this cost and amortize it over a period of 10 years. The product life cycle has rarely been longer than five years in this line, but management is optimistic in this particular case that the product will have a sales life of 10 years.
4. During the year, GL sold a building at a gain of $200,000. The $1.4 million sales price has been included in sales, while the $1.2 million net book value has been included in cost of goods sold.
5. GL issued preferred shares to investors, who also owned common shares, during 20X2. The preferred shares must be redeemed, or bought back, at their $100 stated value per share, in the year 2X12. The dividends are cumulative, which means that if they are not paid in a given year, dividends in arrears must be made up before common dividends are paid. If there are dividends in arrears on the redemption date, these must be paid at that time. GL plans to classify this preferred share issue consistent with its legal form, in the equity section of the balance sheet.
6. GL plans to prepare minimal note disclosures, as has been its practice in the past in order to reduce the time and effort that the accounting staff have to devote to preparation of the annual report.

Required:

Adopt the role of CA and evaluate the list of contentious accounting policies, referring to accounting principles when appropriate.

(CICA, adapted)

ASSIGNMENTS

* 

A2-1 Underlying Assumptions: Indicate whether each of the following statements is true or false:

1. The continuity assumption states that a business entity will last forever.
2. Nominal dollar capital maintenance takes inflation into account before profits are recognized.
3. The unit of measure assumption is the justification for ignoring inflation in the financial statements.
4. The time-period assumption requires accrual and deferrals.
5. The continuity assumption justifies the use of historical cost in the financial statements.
6. The separate-entity assumption equates the tax, legal, and accounting status of companies.
7. The separate-entity assumption equates the tax, legal, and accounting status of partnerships.
8. Owners are viewed as central in the proprietary assumption.
9. Nominal dollar capital maintenance requires financial capital to be preserved before profits are recognized.
10. Quantification is a key element of the unit-of-measure assumption.

A 2-2 Explanation of underlying assumptions: Explain each of the following statements:

1. The value assigned to land, purchased 10 years ago, would change if the going-concern assumption was not applied.
2. Since the balance sheet of a sole proprietorship excludes the personal assets of the proprietor, it reflects the separate-entity assumption but not the assets that a creditor could demand to meet proprietorship obligations.
3. Accrued accounts receivable and deferred revenues indicate the application of the time-period assumption.
4. Many important assets are excluded from the balance sheet of biotechnology companies because of the unit-of-measure assumption.
5. Dividends to shareholders are reported on the retained earnings statement, and are not reported as expenses on the income statement, because financial statements reflect the proprietary assumption.

A2-3 Definitions of Assumptions, Qualitative Criteria, and Measurement Conventions: The following assumptions, qualitative criteria, and measurement conventions are lettered for response purposes:

A. Time period
B. Separate entity
C. Unit of measure
D. Relevance
E. Cost/benefit effectiveness
F. Comparability
G. Revenue recognition
H. Nominal dollar capital maintenance
I. Reliability
J. Historical cost
K. Conservatism
L. Proprietary
M. Continuity
N. Matching
O. Full disclosure

The following list of key phrases is directly related to the preceding list. Match these phrases with the list by entering the appropriate letter to the left.

	Key Phrase
______	1. Going-concern basis
______	2. Preserve invested capital before recognizing profits
______	3. Preparation cost versus value of benefit to the user

* These stars indicate length, with one star being the shortest assignment, and three stars being the longest assignment.

_____ 4. Common denominator—the yardstick
_____ 5. Report all relevant information
_____ 6. Focus on owners in reporting and measurement decisions
_____ 7. Capable of making a difference to the decision being made
_____ 8. Risks and rewards have transferred
_____ 9. Skepticism in the face of uncertainty
_____ 10. Free from error or bias
_____ 11. Reporting periods—usually one year
_____ 12. Uniform and consistent
_____ 13. Separate and apart from its owners and other entities
_____ 14. Cash-equivalent expenditures to acquire
_____ 15. Recognize expenses incurred in earning the period's revenues

A2-4 Definitions—Relevance and Reliability: Relevance and reliability are two important qualitative characteristics of accounting information. Each has three characteristics. Provide a brief definition of each of the following eight items using the following format:

Characteristic	Brief Definition
A. Relevance	
1. Timeliness	
2. Predictive value	
3. Feedback value	
B. Reliability	
1. Representational faithfulness	
2. Verifiability	
3. Freedom from bias (or neutrality)	

A2-5 Relevance versus Reliability: Tannino Limited is a private investment company that manages investments for a group of about 30 wealthy individuals. The company is owned and managed by two experienced investment managers, each of whom own 50% of the shares. The company merges all of its clients' money into a single investment fund. A majority of the investments are in publicly traded companies, but a significant portion is invested in real estate and in private companies as (quite speculative) venture capital. The company is preparing its financial statements for its first fiscal year ended 31 December 20X4. GAAP is not a constraint. The two owner-managers are discussing the proper method of reporting the company's investment portfolio. On the one hand, they wish to present the most useful and relevant information to their investors, as well as to the bank that provides some debt financing. On the other hand, they are concerned about the reliability of the reported asset values for various parts of the investment portfolio.

Required:

Discuss the trade-off between relevance and reliability for reporting the asset value of the various types of investments: publicly traded securities, real estate, and venture capital. Your discussion must be relevant to Tannino Limited's specific situation.

A2-6 Relevance and Reliability: Relevance is characterized by the presence of the qualities of timeliness, predictive value, and feedback value. Reliability is characterized by the presence of the qualities of representational faithfulness, verifiability, and freedom from bias. For each of the following, indicate the quality demonstrated:

1. The value assigned to equipment is checked by referring to the original invoice.
2. Predictions concerning this year's income, issued 12 months ago, are compared to the actual results to assess the accuracy of the prediction.
3. Past trends are used to forecast this year's sales.

4. An outside expert is retained to review estimates of warranty liability.
5. Adjustments are made to financial statements that both increase and decrease net income, despite the manager's preference to report lower net income.
6. Financial statements are issued four weeks after the year-end, even though this requires the use of estimates for some elements.
7. Preferred shares that have to be repaid on a given date are classified as a liability despite their legal status as equity.
8. The company releases estimates of operating results for the coming year, based on their budgets.
9. Cash received in advance of work done is recorded as a liability, unearned revenue.

A2-7 Questions on Principles: Is each of the following statements true or false?

1. Acknowledging the needs of users and the decisions that will be made based on the financial statements when picking accounting policies means that information cannot be free from bias.
2. Accounting standards require uniformity, which is necessary to achieve comparability.
3. Financial statement readers are well served by conservative financial statements that understate income and assets.
4. Neutrality in accounting means that the information reported is neither biased in favour of a particular party nor designed to achieve a particular outcome.
5. Relevancy is defined as information that is current, or up to date.
6. Relevance and reliability are necessary for recognition.
7. Realization is necessary for recognition to occur.
8. All items (resulting from a transaction) must be recognized if they meet the definition of a financial statement element.
9. Reliability is promoted if accounting information is representationally faithful to the underlying economic events.
10. Useful information may lack objectivity.

A2-8 Application of Principles: The following list of statements pose conceptual issues:

1. The business entity is considered to be separate and apart from its owners for accounting purposes.
2. A transaction is always recorded in such a way as to reflect its legal form.
3. It is permissible for a company to use straight-line depreciation, even though the rest of the industry uses declining balance, because the company feels that straight-line better reflects the pattern of benefits received from these assets.
4. All details of transactions must be disclosed in the notes to the financial statements.
5. The lower of cost or market method must be used in valuing inventories.
6. The cost principle relates only to the income statement.
7. Revenue should be recognized only when the cash is received.
8. Accruals and deferrals are necessary because of the separate-entity assumption.
9. Revenue should be recognized as late as possible and expenses as early as possible.

Required:

1. Indicate whether each statement is correct or incorrect.
2. Identify the principle(s) posed.
3. Provide a brief discussion of its (their) implications.

A2-9 Realization versus Recognition: For each of the following transactions, indicate the point at which (1) the transaction is recognized and (2) the financial statement element is realized.

1. Expected warranty claims on products sold are accrued as the sales are made. Cash payments for warranty claims are made in the subsequent fiscal year.
2. Inventory is bought on 1 August, on credit. It is paid for on 12 September.
3. A customer orders a custom-built machine, and pays when the order is placed on 20 February. The machine is delivered on 10 March.
4. A customer buys a product as a cash sale, on 1 July.
5. Interest is accrued daily, and collected at the end of six months.
6. A sale on credit is completed, and the product delivered, on 1 February. Payment is received on 1 March.

A2-10 Recognition of Elements: In each of the following situations, identify the element or elements, if any, that would appear in financial statements. If no element is recognized, give the reason.

1. Unpaid electricity bill
2. A reputation for quality products
3. A patent on a new invention developed by a firm
4. Unissued common shares of a company that will likely be issued for cash next year
5. A good credit rating
6. The reputation for not paying accounts payable on time
7. University degrees held by employees
8. Cash received from a customer for work to be done next year

A2-11 Elements of Financial Statements: Financial statement elements have specific definitions. To the right, some important aspects of the definitions are listed. Match the aspects with the elements by entering appropriate letters in the blanks. More than one letter can be placed in a blank.

Elements of Financial Statements		Important Aspect of the Definition of the Element
A. Assets	___	1. Using up of assets or incurrence of liabilities
B. Liabilities	___	2. Probable future economic benefits obtained by an entity
C. Owners' equity/net assets	___	3. Enhancement of assets or settlements of liabilities
D. Revenues	___	4. Residual interest in the assets after deducting liabilities
E. Expenses	___	5. Increases in net assets from peripheral or incidental activities
F. Gains	___	6. From peripheral or incidental transactions of the entity
G. Losses	___	7. Future sacrifices arising from past transactions
H. None of the above	___	8. Results from the entity's ongoing major or central operation

A2-12 Accrual Accounting: Under accrual accounting, the effects of transactions and events are reflected in the financial statements relatively independently of the underlying cash flow. Accruals and deferrals are created as a result. Give an example of each of the following:

1. An accrued account receivable is recognized.
2. An accrued liability is recorded.
3. Prepaid expenses are increased.
4. Unearned revenue is recorded.
5. Unearned revenue is decreased.

A2-13 Questions on Principles: For each of the following circumstances, give the letter item(s) indicating the accounting principle involved:

A. Comparability
B. Conservatism
C. Continuity
D. Cost/benefit effectiveness
E. Full disclosure
F. Historical cost
G. Matching
H. Nominal dollar capital maintenance
I. Proprietary
J. Relevance
K. Reliability
L. Revenue recognition
M. Separate entity
N. Time period
O. Unit of measure

1. Goodwill is recorded in the accounts only when it arises from the purchase of another entity.
2. A note describing the company's possible liability in a lawsuit is included with the financial statements even though no formal liability exists at the balance sheet date.
3. Owners are considered the primary focus of the financial statements; others who have a significant stake in the profitability of the company, such as lenders or employees, are not given equal status.
4. The personal assets of partners are excluded from the partnership balance sheet, even though pledged as security for partnership loans.
5. A retail store uses estimates rather than a complete physical count of its inventory for purposes of preparing monthly financial statements.
6. Marketable securities are valued at market value, when market value is lower than cost.
7. An entity reports a $50 profit after buying a unit of inventory for $100 and selling it for $150, even though the cost to replace the unit has escalated to $112, due to inflation.
8. An advance deposit on a sale contract is reported as unearned revenue.
9. A company spends $50,000 to promote a new location. The costs are deferred on the balance sheet, and will be expensed over a period of five years.
10. Accounting policies chosen for revenue recognition are the same as those of the entity's major competitors.
11. Capital assets are amortized over their useful lives.

A2-14 Identification of Accounting Principles: In the following cases, indicate the principle that applies to each case and state whether it was followed or violated.

Case A. Loran Company used FIFO in 20X2; LIFO in 20X3; and FIFO in 20X4.

Case B. A tract of land was acquired on credit by signing a $55,000, one-year, non-interest-bearing note. The asset account was debited for $55,000. The going rate of interest was 10%.

Case C. Loran Company always issues its annual financial report nine months after the end of the annual reporting period.

Case D. Loran Company recognizes all sales revenues on the cash basis.

Case E. Loran Company records interest expense only on the payment dates.

Case F. Loran Company includes among its financial statement elements an apartment building owned and operated by the owner of the company.

Case G. Loran Company never uses notes or supplemental schedules as a part of its financial reports.

A2-15 Recognition: Some of the following items may not be recognized or recorded in a company's financial statements. Indicate the likely recognition problem.

1. Recording employee morale as an asset.
2. The company's major competitor has gone out of business, resulting in a flood of new customers.
3. Recording a liability (and expense) for cleaning up chemical dumps.

4. The company's share price has increased from $6.41 to $13.50 on the TSE. Therefore, unissued shares are worth more.

A2-16 Recognition and Elements: Indicate how each of the following items would be recognized in a company's financial statements for 20X3, and what elements would be recognized. For any items that would not be recognized, explain the reason for non-recognition.

1. The estimated future cost of restoring a mining site to its original condition.
2. A non-revocable commitment to buy equipment early in the following year.
3. The right to use an international industrial trademark over the next five years, purchased from a Taiwanese computer manufacturer.
4. The value of customer lists built up over time.
5. Increases in the value of funds held overseas in U.S. dollars.

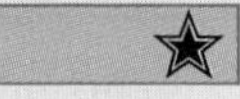

A2-17 Revenue Recognition: Which of the following events would normally involve revenue recognition, assuming use of accrual accounting and revenue recognition on delivery:

1. Collection of cash from a customer 30 days after the product is delivered.
2. Collection of cash from a customer 30 days before the product is delivered.
3. Delivery of a magazine as part of a 12-month subscription.
4. Land that cost $40,000 is known to have a value of $67,000.
5. A financial institution loans $100,000 to a client; interest is due after 12 months; the financial institution is preparing financial statements two months after the loan was granted.
6. Goods are delivered to a customer with an invoice price of $26,000; the customer is notoriously slow in paying.

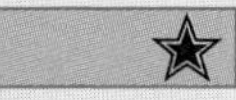

A2-18 Application of Principles: During an audit of L.R.T. Company, the following situations were found to exist:

a. The company uses the straight-line method of measuring depreciation on manufacturing machinery, even though it knows that a method based on actual usage would provide better matching, more accurate income determination, and thus better information for financial statement users. The straight-line method is significantly cheaper to calculate, because of the level of data needed to implement a usage method.
b. For inventory purposes, L.R.T. switched from FIFO to LIFO to FIFO for the same items during a five-year period.
c. L.R.T. does not provide information about future contracts, called the "order backlog" in its financial statements, even though this disclosure is quite common in the industry.
d. L.R.T. follows a policy of depreciating plant and equipment on the straight-line basis over a period of time that is 50% longer than the most reliable useful life estimate.
e. Interest is reported at the end of each fiscal year as the net amount of interest expense less interest revenue.

Required:

1. Identify and briefly explain the accounting principle that is directly involved in each situation.
2. Indicate what, if anything, the company should do in the future by way of any change in accounting policy.

A2-19 Application of Principles: An inspection of the annual financial statements and the accounting records revealed that the George L. Massey Hardware Company had violated some aspect of accounting principles. The following transactions were involved:

a. Merchandise purchased for resale was recorded as a debit to inventory for the invoice price of $80,000 (accounts payable was credited for the same amount); terms were 2/10, n/30. Ten days later, the account was paid at the net amount due, $78,400 ($80,000 less the 2% discount for paying within 10 days). The $1,600 discount was credited to an other revenue account. The goods purchased were still in inventory at $80,000 at year-end.

b. Depreciation expense of $227,000 was recorded as a debit to retained earnings and was deducted directly from retained earnings on the balance sheet.

c. Usual and ordinary repairs on operational assets were recorded as follows: debit operational assets, $150,000; credit cash, $150,000.

d. The company sustained a $96,000 storm damage loss during the current year (no insurance). The loss was recorded and reported as follows:

Income statement: Extraordinary item—storm loss	$24,000
Balance sheet (assets): Deferred charge—storm loss	$72,000

e. Accounts receivable of $95,000 were reported on the balance sheet; this amount included a $42,000 loan to the company president. The maturity date of the loan was not specified.

Required:

1. For each transaction, identify the inappropriate treatment and the principle(s) violated.
2. Give the entry that should have been made or the appropriate reporting.

A2-20 Conservatism and Consistency: Prestan Stores, a specialty retailer, has just purchased a new Canadair jet aircraft for its senior officers' travel needs. The treasurer wants to depreciate the plane for financial accounting purposes using an accelerated method because, she argues, the lower income numbers will be more conservative and this, in turn, will generate shareholder confidence in the firm. The controller, however, argues that the firm uses the straight-line method on other assets, so using an accelerated method to depreciate the plane's cost would violate the consistency of the firm's depreciation policy.

Required:

Which, if either, officer's argument is correct? Write a brief memo to the president of Prestan Stores explaining your reasons.

A2-21 Conservatism versus Reliability: Canada Regional Telephone Corporation (CRTC) had been a regulated company. Early in 20X1, the government passed legislation that required CRTC to allow other competing companies to use CRTC cable for retail telephone and high-speed computer services. Competing companies had to pay a reasonable fee, of course; access was not free. The controller of CRTC proposes to reduce the carrying value of all of the company's property and equipment to about 15% of its previous book value. "Who knows what the value of our property and equipment will be in coming years," the controller argues, "when we can't get the fair return that we had been promised by the government when we built this network. We might as well get most of it off the books now, so we won't be burdened with high amortization in future years."

Required:

Discuss the controller's proposal. What principles are involved?

A2-22 Implementation of Principles: The following summarized transactions were recorded as indicated for Carleton Builders Limited during the current year.

a. The company originally sold and issued 100,000 common shares. During the current year, 94,000 of these shares were outstanding and 6,000 were repurchased from the shareholders and retired. Near the end of the current year, the Board of Directors declared and paid a cash dividend of $8 per share. The dividend was recorded as follows:

Retained earnings	800,000	
Cash		752,000
Dividend income ($8 × 6,000)		48,000

b. Carleton Builders Limited purchased a machine that had a fair value of $90,000, although there were few comparable transactions to back this up. The company paid for the machine in full by issuing 10,000 common shares (market price $8.50). The purchase was recorded as follows:

Machine	90,000	
Share capital		85,000
Gain on acquisition		5,000

c. Carleton needed a small structure for temporary storage. A contractor quoted a price of $769,000. The company decided to build the structure itself. The cost was $542,000, and construction required three months. The following entry was made:

Buildings—warehouse	769,000	
Cash		542,000
Revenue—self-construction		227,000

d. Carleton owns a plant located on a river that floods every few years. As a result, the company suffers a flood loss regularly. During the current year, the flood was severe, causing an uninsured loss of $97,000, which was the amount spent to repair the flood damage. The following entry was made:

Retained earnings, flood loss	97,000	
Cash		97,000

e. On 28 December, the company collected $76,000 cash in advance for merchandise to be available and shipped during February of the next accounting year (the accounting period ends 31 December). This transaction was recorded on 28 December as follows:

Cash	76,000	
Sales revenue		76,000

Required:

1. For each transaction, determine which accounting principle (if any) was violated.
2. Explain the nature of the violation.
3. In each instance, indicate how the transaction should have been originally recorded.

A2-23 Implementation of Principles: R. H. Hall has drawn up a financial statement on 31 December 20X2, employing valuation procedures as follows:

Cash	$40,000	Includes cash in the bank, $35,000, and customers' cheques that could not be cashed (insufficient funds) but that Hall feels will ultimately be recoverable, $5,000.
Marketable securities	$90,000	Represents the cost of securities. At 31 December 20X2, the market value was $81,200.
Intangible assets	$36,000	Recorded in 20X2 when a competitor offered to pay Hall this amount if Hall would move and let the competitor take over Hall's space. Hall entered into the lease when the company was formed. It still has five years to run at a "bargain" rental that is 7% of net sales.
Sundry payables	$ 1	Recorded as a result of a lawsuit of $20,000 against Hall for breach of contract; Hall has offered to pay $5,000 in settlement of the lawsuit, but this has been rejected; it is the opinion of Hall's attorney that the lawsuit can be settled by payment of $10,000.

Required:

1. Indicate what change, if any, you would make in reporting each of the preceding items.
2. In each case, discuss the accounting principle involved.

A2-24 Implementation of Principles: Analyze each of the following situations and indicate which accounting principle or principles, as described in the chapter, is in evidence.

Case A. The financial statements of Raychem Corporation included the following note: "During the current year, plant assets were written down by $8,000,000. This writedown will reduce future expenses. Depreciation and other expenses in future years will be lower, and as a result this will benefit profits of future years."

Case B. During an audit of the Silvona Company, certain liabilities such as taxes appear to be overstated. Also, some quasi-obsolete inventory items seem to be undervalued, and the tendency is to expense rather than capitalize as many items as possible. Management states that "the company has always taken a very conservative view of the business and its future prospects." Management suggests that it does not wish to weaken the company by reporting any more earnings or paying any more dividends than are absolutely necessary because it does not expect business to continue to be good. Management points out that the lower valuations for assets and so on do not lose anything for the company but do create reserves for "hard times."

Case C. There was no comment or explanation of the fact that ABC Company changed its inventory method from FIFO to LIFO at the beginning of the current reporting period. A large changeover difference was involved, and there was no retroactive restatement.

Case D. Current assets amounted to $314,000 and current liabilities, $205,000; the balance sheet of Nelta Corp. reported a single amount "Working capital, $109,000."

Case E. In 20X1, the Tryler Corporation switched its inventory method for financial reporting from LIFO to FIFO. Tryler publicly explained, "Our major competitors have consistently used the FIFO method. Therefore, the reported loss for 20X1 and the restated profit for 20X0 are on a comparable basis as to inventory valuation with competitors." The impact on opening balances is not material.

A2-25 Recognition Criteria: In each case below, discuss issues surrounding recognition of the element in the financial statements.

Case A. Airlines offer frequent-flyer mileage credits to customers. Currently there exists a huge resource of potential trips the public could sign up for at the airlines' expense. Most airlines allow passengers to use mileage credits only for unused capacity—otherwise empty seats. Industry experts estimate that the incremental cost of putting a passenger on a plane is around only $15—the cost of the meal and a little extra fuel for the additional weight. If the passenger were to use mileage credits to "bump" a full-fare passenger, then there is obviously a significant opportunity cost associated with the trip. The element to be recognized is the liability to frequent flyers but airlines grapple with alternative values for the liability.

Case B. The value of Coca-Cola's trademark has been estimated in excess of $1 billion. Yet even though Coca-Cola reports over $4 billion of goodwill and other intangible assets, none of this reported value is due to the Coca-Cola trademark, which is unrecognized despite its considerable commercial value.

Case C. Waste Disposal Limited is being sued to force it to clean up pollution in over 60 sites; this information is reported in the notes to the company's annual report, but no amount is accrued in the financial statements. The extent of the future cleanup costs is reported to be "substantial."

CHAPTER 3

The Income Statement and the Retained Earnings Statement

INTRODUCTION

The income statement (or statement of earnings) is the primary source of information for a company's current profit performance. Investors, lenders, analysts, and other financial statement readers use this and other information in predicting the amount, timing, and uncertainty of the firm's future income and cash flows. This predictive value of the income statement is one of the reasons it is so relevant. The income statement also plays an important role in providing feedback: how good were predictions of prior years' earnings?

Another important use of the income statement is for performance evaluation. The primary financial statement for evaluating the performance of managers (both internally and by external stakeholders) is the income statement. Of course, the income statement must be interpreted within the company's economic, industrial, and competitive environment. Nevertheless, profit is considered to be the main indicator of management's performance.

Investors look at the return on and risk of their investment. The level of earnings is viewed as the **return**, while the volatility of earnings is viewed as one measure of **risk**. Management is so often concerned about maximizing and smoothing net income because managers hope that by maximizing net income they can improve investors' perception of return, while by smoothing net income, they hope to lower investors' perception of risk.

Our purpose in this chapter is to develop an understanding of the information contained in the income statement, how that information is presented, and how it might be used. Measurement and recognition issues are critical, but those issues will be discussed in the following chapters. This chapter focuses on the display of revenues, expenses, gains, and losses after they have been recorded. Accounting standards require that certain items of information be reported on the income statement. In general, however, the level of information provided on the income statement is left to the discretion of management.

In this chapter, we will begin by discussing the alternative presentation formats. We then will discuss extraordinary items, discontinued operations, and other required disclosures that are specifically mandated by accounting standards. We then turn our attention to *other comprehensive income*, a very recent addition to the accounting vocabulary. The chapter will end with a discussion of the retained earnings statement.

NATURE OF INCOME

Change in Retained Earnings

The income statement links a company's beginning and ending balance sheets for a given accounting period. Under the proprietary concept of accounting (discussed in Chapter 2), the income statement explains changes in owners' equity caused by operations and certain other activities during the period. When there is no new investment or disinvestment by owners (or other minor technical changes), the change in owners' equity from the beginning to the end of the period equals net income. Exhibit 3-1 illustrates this point.

EXHIBIT 3-1

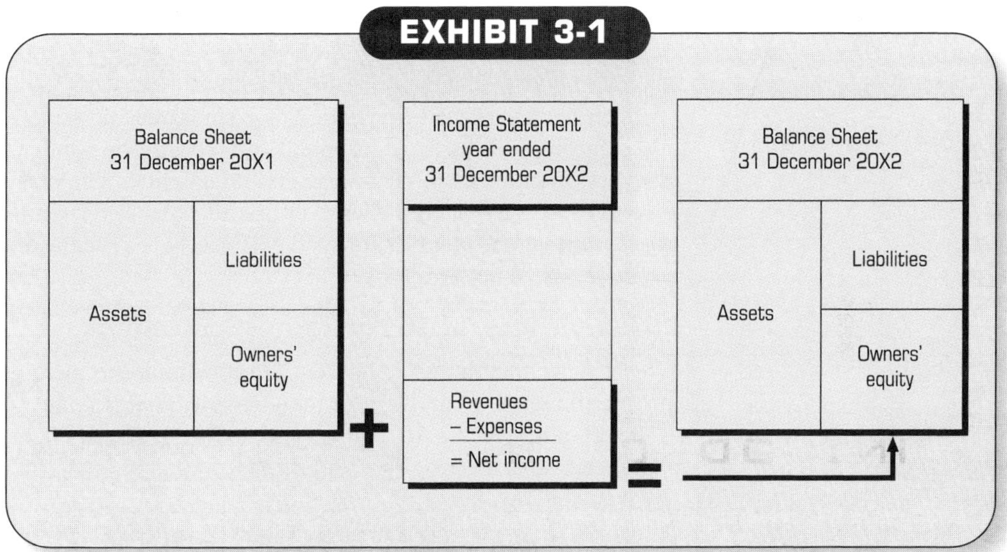

Economic Income versus Accounting Income

The term "income" means different things to different people. For example, an economist defines a *change in wealth*, whether realized or not, as income. Suppose that a company owns a parcel of land for which it paid $10,000 several years ago. A new highway has just been built next to the property, and several individuals have offered to pay $125,000 to $150,000 for the land. The firm has not yet agreed to sell. The economist would say that an increase in wealth has occurred because the land is worth more than historic cost. The wealth increase is called **economic income**, and it is based on an *events approach* rather than on completed transactions.

economic income
an increase in the wealth of a corporation; a measure of income based on events rather than transactions

Using the historical cost measurement principle, an accountant usually would not recognize such an increase in wealth as income. Only if the land is sold to another party in an arm's-length transaction would the accountant recognize the increase in wealth as income. This is **accounting income**, based on the *transactions approach.*

accounting income
an increase in the reported wealth of a corporation based on actual transactions completed; a measure of income based on the accounting model

There are three general problems with the transactions approach to reporting income:

1. The transactions approach may result in the exclusion of important information. The transactions approach captures some information, but not all information that may be relevant for a particular user or decision. For example, the relevant market value of the land in the above example is excluded from recognition in the financial statements, but is of considerable interest to a bank that uses the land as collateral for a loan.

2. Not all transactions are treated equally. Some treatments are more subjective than others. Accounting policies determine which transactions are recorded and how their impacts are measured. Management makes choices about the *accounting policies* to be used, which significantly affect the amount of reported net income. As well, most *accounting estimates*

are determined by management. Even within given measurement rules, the flexibility provided by accounting estimates significantly affects reported net income. The events approach is often criticized as being subjective, and yet the choices of which transactions to measure and how to measure the results of those transactions (and their subsequent disposition or recognition, such as an asset versus an expense) may also be highly subjective.

3. With the knowledge of which transactions will be measured (and how they will be measured), management can enter into transactions (or avoid transactions) with the primary purpose of affecting the reported results. In the land example cited above, management could decide to sell the land to a related party in order to trigger recognition of a gain, while still retaining substantive control over the land (or buying it back from the related party after a short period of time).

Revenue and expense recognition are key concepts in accounting. The concepts determine when and how revenues, gains, expenses, and losses are recorded. Determining the proper treatment for a particular transaction or event is often difficult. Indeed, a large part of the study of accounting addresses measurement and recognition issues as they apply to revenues, gains, expenses, and losses, as well as to assets and liabilities. Chapter 2 discussed the general nature of recognition criteria. Because revenue and expense recognition is such a significant aspect of accounting, Chapter 6 is devoted exclusively to revenue and expense recognition.

Inclusiveness of the Income Statement

Which items affecting shareholders' equity should be included in the computation of net income and reported in the income statement? That is, what items, if any, should be recorded as direct adjustments to equity and excluded from income? There are two extreme approaches to answering these questions.

CURRENT OPERATING PERFORMANCE At one extreme is the current operating performance approach. Advocates of this approach maintain that only items that are part of the *ordinary recurring operations* of the firm should be included in earnings. Other items such as gains and losses that relate to prior periods or to unusual or non-recurring activities are recorded as direct adjustments to retained earnings.

Advocates of this approach believe that users of financial statements attach a particular significance to the figure labelled "net income" and that it should have maximum power for predicting operating income. If users are not able to analyze the income statement and make adjustments for those items that are unrelated to the company's current period operating performance, the predictive power of the income statement will suffer.

ALL-INCLUSIVE APPROACH At the other extreme is the all-inclusive approach, in which all transactions affecting the net increase or decrease in equity during the period are included in the determination of net income, except contributions by or distributions to owners.

Advocates of this approach believe that items such as those related to the extraordinary activities and events related to prior years are all part of the earnings history of the firm and that exclusion of such items from the income statement increases the probability that they will be overlooked in a review of the operating results for a period of years. They also point out the dangers of possible manipulation of the annual earnings figure if preparers of financial statements are permitted to omit certain items in determining net income. Advocates of the all-inclusive approach believe that full disclosure in the income statement of the nature of various transactions enables income statement users to assess fully the importance of each item and its effect on operating results and cash flows.

CURRENT PRACTICE Accounting standards in Canada and in most other countries generally reflect an approach that is closer to the all-inclusive approach. Virtually all items affecting equity (other than investment by or distributions to owners) are included in net income; the AcSB has eliminated the possibility of charging or crediting items directly to retained earnings.

CONCEPT REVIEW

1. Explain the relationship between the income statement and the balance sheet.
2. What is the difference between an events approach and a transactions approach to measuring income? Which approach is the dominant one in accounting practice?

GENERAL PRESENTATION FORMAT

Canadian, U.S., and international accounting standards require that a company show three specific subtotals on its income statement, when applicable:

- Income before discontinued operations and extraordinary items (often referred to as *income from continuing operations*);
- Income before extraordinary items (that is, discontinued operations after adding and subtracting extraordinary gains and losses, if any); and
- Net income (after adding and subtracting gains and losses from extraordinary items).

Of course, if the company has no discontinued operations and/or extraordinary items, then the first and/or second subtotal will not be applicable.

In addition to extraordinary items and discontinued operations, the *CICA Handbook* requires that a few specific items be disclosed (*CICA* 1520.03). The most important mandatory disclosures are

- revenues recognized
- investment income
- amortization expense
- research and development expense
- interest expense
- income tax expense
- earnings per share

Although *disclosure* of these items of revenue and expense is required, the *format* of presentation usually is not prescribed. Earnings per share (EPS) must be shown on the face of the income statement, but the other amounts can be disclosed either on the face of the income statement or in the disclosure notes.

The list above is notable for the narrow range of required disclosures. The *CICA Handbook* does not require disclosure of items such as cost of goods sold or major categories of expense—these are only "desirable" disclosures (*CICA* 1520.04).

To present the components of income from continuing operations, companies may use a variety of formats ranging from *single-step* to extensive multiple-step. The following two sections describe these two ends of the continuum of income statement presentation. Most companies use presentations that fall between these two extremes.

Single-Step Format

The single-step format uses only two broad classifications for presenting income from continuing operations: (1) a section showing revenues and gains and (2) a section showing expenses and losses. Income from continuing operations is computed in one step, without intermediate subtotals.

Petro-Canada (Exhibit 3-2) uses a modified version of the single-step method. The company groups all of the revenues together and all of the expenses together, except income tax. The company then shows a subtotal for *earnings before income taxes.* In a "pure" single-step statement, income tax expense would be listed as just another expense, with no subtotal for earnings before income taxes.

EXHIBIT 3-2

PETRO-CANADA
CONSOLIDATED STATEMENT OF EARNINGS

(stated in millions of Canadian dollars)

For the years ended December 31,	**2003**	2002	2001
Revenue			
Operating	**$12,209**	$9,917	$8,582
Investment and other income	**12**	—	154
	12,221	9,917	8,736
Expenses			
Crude oil and product purchases	**5,098**	4,556	4,687
Operating, marketing and general	**2,407**	2,036	1,670
Exploration	**271**	301	245
Depreciation, depletion and amortization	**1,539**	957	568
Foreign currency translation	**(251)**	52	102
Interest	**182**	187	135
	9,246	8,089	7,407
Earnings before income taxes	**2,975**	1,828	1,329
Provision for income taxes			
Current	**1,247**	959	528
Future	**59**	(105)	(45)
	1,306	854	483
Net earnings	**$ 1,669**	$ 974	$ 846
Earnings per share (dollars)			
Basic	**$ 6.30**	$ 3.71	$ 3.19
Diluted	**$ 6.23**	$ 3.67	$ 3.16

CONSOLIDATED STATEMENT OF RETAINED EARNINGS

(stated in millions of Canadian dollars)

For the years ended December 31,	**2003**	2002	2001
Retained Earnings at Beginning of Year	**$ 2,380**	$ 1,511	$ 771
Net earnings	**1,669**	974	846
Dividends on common shares	**(106)**	(105)	(106)
Retained Earnings at End of Year	**$ 3,943**	$2,380	$ 1,511

References to disclosure notes have been deleted.

The company discloses the required items of income and expense on the face of its income statement, including operating revenue, investment income, amortization (i.e., "depreciation, depletion, and amortization"), interest expense, and income tax expense. The company reports major categories of expense, but shows no amount labelled as cost of goods sold. Earnings per share also are shown on the face of the statement, following net earnings.

Notice that the word "income" does not appear in either the statement heading or the body of the statement. Instead, the company's preferred term is "earnings." *Financial Reporting in Canada 2003* reports that there is an almost equal split between the use of "earnings" and "income" by Canadian companies, with a slight edge in favour of "earnings."

Petro-Canada reports three years' earnings rather than the two years normally required in Canada because the company also reports to the Securities and Exchange Commission (SEC) in the United States. The SEC requires a three-year presentation on the income statement.

Petro-Canada's retained earnings statement is shown at the bottom of Exhibit 3-2. It is easy to see the transfer of annual net earnings into the retained earnings (e.g., $1,669 million for 2003), as described by the diagram in Exhibit 3-1.

Multiple-Step Format

Exhibit 3-3 presents the income statement for Dofasco Inc., a large steel producer. Dofasco uses a classified income statement. This format is known as *multiple-step*, to differentiate it from the *single-step* format.

A multiple-step income statement shows several subtotals before arriving at operating income. The most common characteristic of multiple-step statements is that they usually have separate categories for (1) operating revenues and expenses and (2) non-operating revenues and expenses.

For example, Dofasco shows interest income and interest expense following the subtotal for operating income. In comparison, Petro-Canada shows investment income along with operating revenue, and lists interest expense along with operating expenses. Dofasco shows four subtotals before arriving at net income:

- Gross income (also known as *gross margin* or *gross profit*);
- Operating income;
- Income before income taxes; and
- Income after income taxes but before minority interest (not labelled on the statement).

None of these subtotals is required by the *CICA Handbook*.

Minority interest pertains to non-wholly owned subsidiaries; remember that these are *consolidated* statements. Consolidated statements include all of the revenues and expenses of all of the parent's subsidiaries, but some subsidiaries may have shareholders other than the parent company. Minority interest in earnings is the portion of the consolidated earnings attributable to the outside, third-party shareholders. The minority interests' share of earnings must be subtracted from consolidated net income in order to determine the earnings available to the parent company's shareholders. We will discuss this further in Chapter 11.

The various categories of revenue and expense that appear on a multiple-step statement are as follows. Not every multiple-step income statement will include all of these sections. There is no prescribed format for the income statement, except that there must be an earnings subtotal both before discontinued operations and before extraordinary items, if either of those types of items exist.

OPERATING REVENUES The revenues that normally appear at the beginning of a multiple-step statement are operating revenues only. In a multiple-step statement, investment and other income show up later in the statement.

COST OF SALES The second section shows the cost of the goods sold or services provided. Subtracting cost of sales from operating revenues gives gross margin. Gross margin sometimes is called "net revenue" because gross margin indicates how much of the revenue is left over after the product (or service) costs are paid. Some analysts like to see a high gross margin as a percentage of revenue because a company with a high margin may have more flexibility in dealing with economic downturns.

However, many costs can be allocated either to cost of sales or to operating expenses—the next section of the statement. An outside reader has no way of knowing what specific costs the company includes in cost of sales. Does cost of sales represent mainly variable costs, or is there a large component of fixed overhead? Inventory costs are supposed to include some overhead costs (discussed in Chapter 8), but much is left to the discretion of management.

EXHIBIT 3-3

DOFASCO
CONSOLIDATED STATEMENTS OF INCOME
(in millions)

For the years ended December 31	**2003**	2002
Income		
Sales	**$3,554.9**	$3,583.7
Cost of sales (before the following item)	**2,962.3**	2,885.8
Employees' profit sharing	**32.9**	50.7
	2,995.2	2,936.5
Gross income	**559.7**	647.2
Depreciation and amortization	**251.8**	274.8
Impairment of long-lived assets	**—**	118.5
Operating income	**307.9**	253.9
Interest on long-term debt	**48.6**	57.4
Investment and other income	**(6.1)**	(6.9)
Foreign exchange loss	**32.4**	4.1
Loss on disposal of QCM	**27.9**	—
Income before income taxes	**205.1**	199.3
Income tax expense	**85.7**	69.1
	119.4	130.2
Minority interest	**1.0**	7.4
Net income	**$ 118.4**	$ 122.8

References to disclosure notes and earnings per share information have been deleted.

OPERATING EXPENSES The next section shows the operating expenses that are not included in cost of sales. Dofasco shows only two items in this category: (1) depreciation and amortization and (2) impairment of long-lived assets (i.e., a writedown). Apparently, Dofasco includes virtually all of its operating expenses in cost of sales.

More commonly, this section shows substantial amounts for very broad categories of expense, such as "General, selling, and administrative expense." As with cost of sales, companies do not disclose the components of this item, such as labour costs, materials costs, selling commissions, and so forth.

OPERATING INCOME FROM CONTINUING OPERATIONS This subtotal gives an indication of the ability of the company to generate earnings from its continuing operations excluding (1) income and expense from investing and financing activities, (2) income taxes, and (3) the results of discontinued operations.

OTHER INCOME AND EXPENSE The next section on Dofasco's income statement shows non-operating income and expense. This section normally shows investment income and interest expense, as well as foreign exchange gains and losses. "Loss on disposal of QCM" is an example of an *unusual item*. We will discuss unusual items later in the chapter.

INCOME TAX The contents of this section are rather obvious—both current and future income tax expense or benefits are recognized.

DISCONTINUED OPERATIONS This section includes the results for any parts of the business that either were discontinued during the year or that the Board of Directors has decided to discontinue, either by sale or by shutting them down. The discontinued operations section includes the revenues and expenses for the operation for the year, as well as any asset writedowns.

The objective of reporting discontinued operations separately is to make it clear to users that the revenues and expenses relating to these operations will not contribute to earnings in future periods.

Later in this chapter, we will discuss discontinued operations more extensively.

EXTRAORDINARY ITEMS Neither Petro-Canada nor Dofasco has extraordinary items. It is very rare to report an extraordinary item under Canadian GAAP. We will discuss extraordinary items more extensively later in the chapter.

Which Format?

The single-step format has the advantage of simplicity. A single-step statement contains the same information as a multiple-step income statement, and users can rearrange components of the statement to suit their needs.

The multiple-step format is potentially more informative to decision-makers because it highlights important relationships and intermediate subtotals in the report. Advocates of the multiple-step format believe that there are important relationships in revenue and expense data and that the income statement is more useful when these relationships are explicitly shown.

In practice, few Canadian companies use a pure single-step statement. Almost 40% provide one intermediate subtotal, similar to the almost-single-step statement of Petro-Canada (Exhibit 3-2). Only about 10% of surveyed public companies in *Financial Reporting in Canada 2003* show all three subtotals of gross margin, operating income, and pre-tax income. Therefore, the vast majority of companies use a format that falls between the extremes of pure single-step and fully classified multiple-step statements.

Finally, remember that a subtotal for gross margin can be reported only if the company discloses its cost of sales. About 40% of companies report cost of sales, and only a minority of those companies deduct cost of sales from revenues. When a company does disclose cost of sales, it most likely will show cost of sales as a separate item within other expenses—an approach consistent with single-step format.

Minimum Disclosure

Exhibits 3-2 and 3-3 show income statements that contain some detail in the expense and revenue categories, but also involve a lot of grouping. For example, in Exhibit 3-3 Dofasco reports a single expense category—cost of sales—that accounts for 83% of sales and 86% of total expenses. The company discloses no additional quantitative detail about the components of that one substantial item. Would you like to know how much of Dofasco's expenses comprise labour costs? You won't find out from the financial statements.

Dofasco is not unusual in this respect. Income statements seldom disclose much useful information about the operating revenues and expenses of a company.

Management has a lot of flexibility in presenting revenue, expense, gain, and loss items in the income statement. Grouping reduces the length and complexity of the statement, but it may also reduce its predictive value and the information content of the statement. Grouping also hides sensitive information from competitors.

Since there is no requirement that major items of expense be reported, an income statement prepared on the basis of minimum disclosure need not be continuous. Exhibit 3-4 illustrates an income statement that contains only required disclosures. Cara Operations will be best known to readers for Swiss Chalet chicken, Harvey's hamburgers, and airline food. After reporting system sales and gross revenue, Cara draws a line and starts again with "Earnings before the following." The "following" items are simply all of the disclosures pertaining to Cara's operations that are required by the *CICA Handbook.*

CONCEPT REVIEW

1. What income statement sections are required by recommendations in the *CICA Handbook*?
2. How might interest expense on long-term debt be presented differently in a single-step versus a multiple-step income statement?
3. What distinguishes expense items that are reported as operating expense from those that are reported as other expense?
4. How is the all-inclusive approach to the income statement different from the current operating performance approach? Which approach best reflects Canadian practice?

OTHER FORMAT CHOICES

There is a great deal of flexibility in format issues for the income statement, leaving companies leeway to pick policies that suit their individual circumstances and that best serve their user groups and themselves.

TITLE The income statement is also known as the *earnings statement* or *statement of operations.* In this text, we will most often use the term *income statement.* When a parent company and its subsidiaries are combined for the report, the statement is identified as a *consolidated income statement.*

FISCAL YEAR-END A company must choose a fiscal year-end. Normally, companies try to pick a point that represents the low point in their seasonal pattern. This is to ensure that year-end adjustments and the annual report do not have to be prepared during their busy season. However, there are other factors to consider. For example, having the same year-end as other companies in the industry facilitates comparisons. Companies that are part of a corporate group prefer to have the same year-end as their parent to allow consolidation. Some industries are governed by legislation that mandates a certain year-end. For example, the federal *Bank Act* requires banks to use a 31 October year-end. Most businesses pick the calendar year as a fiscal year.

REPORTING PERIOD LENGTH AND COMPOSITION Another basic issue to decide is the length of the reporting period. Annual reports are the norm, as companies are expected to use a 12-month period. The 12-month period facilitates preparation of required annual reports to shareholders and securities commissions.

The operating cycle of some companies leads them to end their fiscal period at the end of a *week* instead of the end of a month. For example, Cara's fiscal year-ends on the last Sunday in March (Exhibit 3-4). Such companies are usually in the retail trade or are suppliers to retail companies. In earlier times, many such businesses were closed on Sundays and therefore the weekend provided a natural time to "take stock" and to close the books. These companies typically define their reporting period as 52 weeks. Every so often, the company must include 53 weeks in the reporting period so as to avoid moving its year-end far from a particular target date.

Companies often also issue financial statements for shorter periods, most often quarterly. Public companies are required by securities commissions to issue quarterly statements to their shareholders.

REPORTING CURRENCY Companies must also determine the reporting currency used to report to shareholders. Normally, one would assume that a Canadian company, reporting with Canadian GAAP, would report in Canadian dollars. This is the norm, but it is not required. Although Canadian GAAP usually will be followed, any reporting currency can be used.

Why would a Canadian company choose to report in, say, U.S. dollars? The primary reason is that most of the company's business is conducted in United States dollars. U.S. dollars may be used by companies that have the bulk of their operations in the United States (e.g., Cineplex Odeon, Inco, Seagram's) or whose product is priced worldwide in United States dollars (e.g., gold mining companies, paper products companies).

EXHIBIT 3-4

CARA OPERATIONS LIMITED

CONSOLIDATED STATEMENTS OF EARNINGS AND RETAINED EARNINGS

(In thousands of dollars, except earnings per share data)

For the years ended March 30, 2003 and March 31, 2002	**2003**	2002
System Sales	**$ 1,769,597**	$ 1,548,745
Gross Revenue	**$ 1,133,202**	$ 1,036,749
Earnings before the following:	**$ 128,600**	$ 109,108
Amortization of property, plant and equipment	**49,204**	41,830
Amortization of intangible assets	**941**	1,230
	78,455	66,048
Interest expense net of investment income	**(6,735)**	(5,487)
Gain on sale of business	**21,697**	—
Provision for Air Canada	**(15,362)**	—
Stock-based compensation expense—Kelsey's	**(8,382)**	—
Equity investments	**824**	887
Earnings before income taxes and non-controlling shareholders' interest	**70,497**	61,448
Provision for income taxes	**21,396**	23,434
Non-controlling shareholders' interest	**2,043**	2,360
Net earnings for the year	**47,058**	35,654

References to disclosure notes have been deleted.

Bear in mind, though, that reporting in U.S. dollars doesn't mean reporting in U.S. GAAP. Canadian-based public companies that report in U.S. dollars normally still use Canadian GAAP.

SELECTION OF GAAP The vast majority of Canadian companies report in accordance with Canadian GAAP. This is even true for many companies that report in U.S. dollars. One such company is Stratos Global Corporation. Note 2 to Stratos Global Corporation's 2003 financial statements explains that

> The Corporation and each of its subsidiaries use the U.S. dollar as its currency of measurement and reporting as a substantial portion of the Corporation's ongoing business is conducted in U.S. dollars.

There are a few large Canadian companies that report in U.S. GAAP. Such companies inevitably also report in U.S. dollars. A company may choose to use U.S. accounting standards because the vast majority of its share trading takes place on U.S. exchanges. For example, The Seagram Company Limited says in its financial statements that

> ... more than 50% of the Company's shares are held by U.S. residents. As a result, the Company has prepared its consolidated financial statements in accordance with U.S. generally accepted accounting principles.

A mutual recognition agreement between the Ontario Securities Commission and the SEC enables Canadian companies to report in U.S. GAAP, although they must then provide a reconciliation to Canadian GAAP in the disclosure notes.

ROUNDING Unrounded figures give an illusion of exactitude that is not appropriate. Reported accounting numbers are the result of many accounting policy decisions and estimates, and the numbers would be quite different under different policies and different, equally valid, estimates and assumptions. Rounding helps to emphasize the approximate nature of the numbers.

The extent of rounding depends on the size of the company. A company with revenues and assets in the billions will round to the nearest million dollars at least, but many round to the nearest billion. Smaller companies will round to the nearest thousand.

LANGUAGE What is the language of the user group? Obviously, financial statements are written for that group, in their language. Companies that are incorporated in Quebec must publish their statements in French, but many other Canadian public companies publish French versions of their annual reports (and Quebec companies publish English versions). Some present the English and French version together in the same report, but the majority provide a separate French version on request.

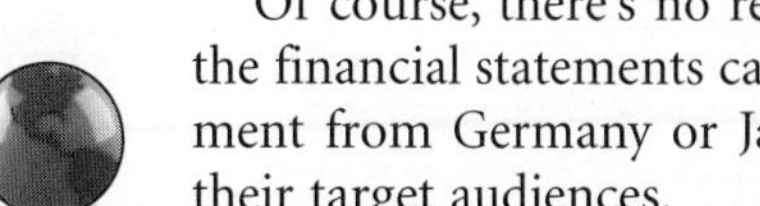

Of course, there's no reason for limiting financial statements to English and French—the financial statements can be prepared in any language. Some companies, seeking investment from Germany or Japan, prepare reports that are in the appropriate languages for their target audiences.

The fact that a company translates its financial statements into other languages does not mean that the statements have been adjusted to reflect GAAP in that language's home country. For example, some Canadian companies translate their financial statements into Japanese for the convenience of Japanese investors and business partners, but the statements still reflect Canadian GAAP and not Japanese GAAP. On the other hand, many Japanese companies translate their financial statements into English. Here one must be careful; some of the Japanese companies report in U.S. GAAP (even in Japan), while others use Japanese GAAP in their English-language statements. Users must be careful to ascertain the GAAP choices made by the company.

COMPARATIVE DATA Accounting numbers are meaningless unless they can be compared to some other numbers. The most obvious comparison for a company is to look at how it did this year compared to the preceding year. Trends in financial information are much more revealing than information for only one period. In recognition of this fact, paragraphs 1400.12–13 of the *CICA Handbook* recommend that comparative figures be presented *when they are meaningful.* In most situations, comparative statements are meaningful. Presentation of one year's comparative information is the norm, although some companies present two years' comparative results on the income statement to comply with the U.S. SEC regulation requiring this expanded disclosure.

Public companies also often provide a longer-term comparison of selected numbers, usually on a five-year basis. Five-year comparative numbers usually include operating earnings, net income, earnings per share, and total assets, among others.

DETAIL The *CICA Handbook* specifies certain items that have to be separately disclosed on the income statement, as we have seen. Other items may be grouped, or separately disclosed. The extent of this grouping is a major policy decision for the company. How much detail should be included on the income statement? Typically, disclosures meet little more than the minimum standards. We'll come back to discuss this policy decision in a few pages, when we review the minimum recommended income statement disclosures.

CONCEPT REVIEW

1. Why might a company have a year-end other than December 31?
2. When might a Canadian company choose to prepare its financial statements in U.S. dollars?
3. Why are comparative statements usually presented, instead of just the current year's amounts?

SPECIAL ASPECTS OF THE INCOME STATEMENT

In the preceding sections we have discussed the general format of the income statement. We also have described relevant reporting requirements for GAAP-constrained financial statements, including the *CICA Handbook* recommendations for disclosing certain items of revenue and expense.

However, some aspects still need further explanation, especially

- intraperiod income tax allocation
- discontinued operations
- extraordinary items
- unusual items

The following sections will discuss these special aspects of income reporting.

intraperiod tax allocation
allocating the income tax expense within the period to various subclassifications on the income statement and retained earnings statements

interperiod tax allocation
allocating the tax paid to appropriate reporting periods based on accounting recognition of individual revenue and expense items

Intraperiod Tax Allocation

If an item is shown net of *related tax*, it means that the tax consequences of the item have been determined and the reported amount is shown after these tax effects have been adjusted for. Determining this amount is the process of **intraperiod tax allocation.** *Intra* means that the allocation is within the period and within the income statement and retained earnings statement. **Interperiod tax allocation** is the allocation of tax expense to different reporting periods, covered in depth in Chapter 15.

To demonstrate *intraperiod* tax allocation, consider the following situation for the Calgary Storage Company. Sales for 20X1 total $1 million, and expenses before income taxes total $700,000. During 20X1, the company experiences an extraordinary loss of $200,000 when an earthquake destroys several of the company's uninsured warehouses. Assume that the income tax rate is 40% and that the $200,000 earthquake loss is deductible for income tax purposes. Calgary Storage Company's income statement with and without intraperiod tax allocation is as shown in Exhibit 3-5.

EXHIBIT 3-5

CALGARY STORAGE COMPANY
INCOME STATEMENT

For the year ended December 31, 20X1	Without Intraperiod Tax Allocation	With Intraperiod Tax Allocation
Sales	$1,000,000	$1,000,000
Expenses	700,000	700,000
Income from operations	300,000	300,000
Income tax expense:		
On operations ($300,000 × 40%)	—	120,000
On taxable income ($100,000 × 40%)	40,000	—
Income before extraordinary loss	260,000	180,000
Extraordinary item:		
Loss from earthquake damage:		
Gross amount	(200,000)	(200,000)
Tax reduction	—	80,000
Net extraordinary item	(200,000)	(120,000)
Net income	$ 60,000	$ 60,000

In the column without intraperiod tax allocation, the tax expense is shown at the actual amount that will be paid, or 40% of the $100,000 taxable income (revenues of $1 million less expenses of $700,000 and less the loss of $200,000). In the column with intraperiod tax allocation, the tax effects of the two activities (operations and the earthquake loss) are shown separately. Thus, the income tax expense that would be paid if there were no loss from the earthquake would be 40% of $300,000, or $120,000. The tax effect of the earthquake loss reduces income tax for the period by 40% of the loss, or $80,000. The $80,000 tax savings resulting from the loss is subtracted from the gross loss of $200,000 to arrive at the after-tax amount of $120,000.

In Exhibit 3-5, the tax impact of the extraordinary item is shown directly on the face of the statement for illustrative purposes, but usually only the net amount of $120,000 would be shown. The tax effect is usually disclosed in a note rather than on the face of the income statement, if it is disclosed at all.

Canadian accounting standards require intraperiod tax allocation, as illustrated, for discontinued operations and extraordinary items. Intraperiod tax allocation also applies to the *cumulative effect of a retroactive change in accounting policy*, shown on the retained earnings statement. Accounting policy changes are discussed later in the chapter.

Discontinued Operations

Sometimes a company decides to discontinue part of its operations. Often, the decision is due to insufficient profitability for that operation. At other times, the operation is successful, but the company wishes to sell it either to gain cash or because management is narrowing the range of businesses that the company is engaged in.

There are two broad alternative approaches to discontinuance. The company can dispose of an operation by either

- Shutting down the operation, laying off the employees, and selling any salvageable assets; or
- Selling the operation as an operating unit (i.e., as a going concern) to the highest bidder, thereby transferring the operation to the buyer intact and as a functioning unit.

In the year that a company decides to dispose of an operation, the revenues, expenses, losses, and gains relating to that unit are removed from the general operations on the income statement and reclassified separately as *discontinued operations.* One of the functions of the income statement is to provide a basis for investors and others to predict future earnings. Investors need to be told if a significant part of the company's revenues and earnings will not continue into the future. Therefore, operating results of a discontinued operation are segregated so that financial statement users will not expect the revenues and earnings relating to this unit to continue into the future. The segregation happens not only in the year that the discontinuance decision is made, but also for the prior year's comparative income statement.

Similarly, the assets and liabilities of the discontinued operation are segregated on the balance sheet. The assets of a discontinued operation become *held-for-sale* assets. Amortization is discontinued, and the assets are revalued at their fair value.

DEFINITION OF A DISCONTINUED OPERATION Many corporations restructure their business operations by shutting down factories or distribution centres, or by dropping products or eliminating product lines. When a company decides to exit from some part of its operations, the first financial reporting issue is whether termination of that part of the business fits the *CICA Handbook* definition of a "discontinued operation."

The *CICA Handbook* defines a **discontinued operation** as "a component of an enterprise ... that can be clearly distinguished, operationally and for financial reporting purposes, from the rest of the enterprise" (*CICA* 3475.28). A discontinued operation can be a subsidiary or an operating division; it can either comprise an asset group or be "operations without long-lived assets" (*CICA* 3475.28). The important aspect is that the operation be *separable* from the rest of the enterprise. That is, the operation must not be so integrated with the continuing operations that its revenues and assets cannot be separately identified.

For example, suppose that a U.S. automobile manufacturer decides to shut down a factory in Ontario. Certainly, for the people working in that plant, shutting down appears to be the discontinuance of an operation. However, for financial reporting purposes, the Ontario factory is just one of a larger group of factories producing the same or similar products. The individual factory does not have its own revenue stream from outsiders. Therefore, shutting down one factory in the group does not fit the definition of *discontinued operations* for financial reporting.

Instead, however, suppose that the automobile manufacturer also manufactures buses. The manufacturer decides to shut down its entire bus-manufacturing operation. The bus business is a separate division of the larger company, with separate responsibility and reporting lines within the company and with separately measurable revenues and expenses. In that case, the bus operation is a *discontinued operation* for accounting purposes.

EFFECTIVE DATE OF DISCONTINUANCE An operation is reported as *discontinued* when management has moved decisively to cease operations by either selling the operation or shutting it down. It is not necessary that the operation actually be discontinued during the reporting period. The *CICA Handbook* says that six criteria must be satisfied before an operation (or an asset) can be categorized as *held for sale* (*CICA* 3475.08):

1. Management commits itself (usually by action of the Board of Directors) to a plan to sell.
2. The operation is available for immediate sale.
3. A buyer is actively being sought, or a plan to shut down the operation has begun.
4. A sale or shutdown is probable and is expected to be completed within one year.
5. The price being solicited for a sale is reasonable.
6. It is unlikely that significant changes to the plan will occur or that the plan will be withdrawn.

These criteria are much tighter than pre-2004 requirements for reporting discontinued operations. The objective of the new criteria is to make sure that management really is serious about discontinuing the operation, and not acting on a whim that might be reversed in the next year. Management must take clear action for discontinuance. In the past, companies sometimes reported a significant loss from discontinued operations in one period and then reversed the loss (creating a gain) in the following period. Such whimsical action led to suspicions of income manipulation or smoothing, otherwise known by the euphemism *income management.* The AcSB clearly wishes to discourage such manipulation, intentional or accidental.

The AcSB provides two additional requirements for reporting a *discontinued operation* (*CICA* 3475.27):

1. The operations and cash flows of the operations will be eliminated from the future reported results of the company after the disposal transaction.
2. The selling company will not have any significant continuing involvement in the future operations of the discontinued operations.

These two additional requirements prevent management from "discontinuing" an operation in a legal sense but still benefiting from the operation. This is an example of applying form over substance.

An operation is reported as discontinued when management has made the decision and has begun the process of selling it or shutting it down. It is quite likely that a plan of discontinuance will be begun in one fiscal year and finished in the next. Almost certainly, any discontinuance plan will extend over more than one quarterly reporting period. Therefore, an operation that is reported as discontinued may, in fact, still be in operation at the end of the fiscal period. *Discontinued* should not be taken too literally. Remember that there is a one-year future time horizon. An operation that can feasibly be sold or shut down within the next year can still be reported as discontinued.

REPORTING DISCONTINUED OPERATIONS As discussed earlier in this chapter, "the results of discontinued operations, less applicable income taxes, should be reported as a separate element of income or loss before extraordinary items" (*CICA* 3475.30). There are three broad components of the amount reported as gain or loss on discontinued operations:

- The net profit or loss from operating the discontinued operation to the date of disposal or the end of the reporting period, if the disposal is not complete by year-end;
- Writedowns of asset carrying value to *fair value less cost to sell*; and
- For completed sales or shutdowns of an operation, the gain or loss on disposal to the extent not previously recognized.

All amounts are *net of related income taxes*, as we explained under *intraperiod tax allocation* earlier in this chapter.

We will discuss the measurement of writedowns when we get to Chapter 10. The measurement criteria for disposing of a discontinued operation are the same as for disposing of an asset or a group of assets. For now, just bear in mind that the gain or loss on disposal is a combination of the current year's operating revenues and expenses plus the gains and losses on disposal, including any appropriate reduction of assets' book value to their net realizable value. A reduction to fair value is known as an *impairment loss*.

There is an important restriction on the amount of gain or loss that can be reported—"future losses associated with the operations of a discontinued operation are not accrued" (*CICA* 3475.31). Prior to 2003, companies often had forecast future losses and included those anticipated losses as part of the loss of the discontinued operation. Now, future losses will be recognized in the period in which they occur. Advance recognition of such losses gave management another tool for income management, a tool that the AcSB has now removed.

On the balance sheet, the accounting basis of the assets is changed. The assets change their status to become *held-for-sale* assets. This is a significant change in status:

> A long-lived asset classified as held for sale should be measured at the lower of its carrying amount or fair value less cost to sell. A long-lived asset should not be amortized while it is classified as held for sale. Interest and other expenses attributable to the liabilities of a disposal group ... should continue to be accrued. (*CICA* 3475.13)

The balance sheet reporting effects are

- Amortization ceases, effective on the date of the discontinuance decision;
- Current assets are carried on the balance sheet at fair value;
- Capital assets (tangible and intangible) are carried at lower of cost or fair value; and
- Liabilities continue to accrue.

DISCLOSURE The AcSB recommends several note disclosures of the circumstances and amounts relating to discontinued operations (*CICA* 3475.37). The main items to be disclosed are

- A description of the facts and circumstances leading to the disposal or expected disposal, along with the expected manner and timing of the disposal;
- The carrying amount of the major classes of assets and liabilities included in the discontinued operations;
- The impairment loss that is included in the net gain or loss for discontinued operations; and
- The amounts of revenue and of pre-tax profit (loss) reported in discontinued operations.

The last two items are amounts that may be reported on the face of the income statement. If they are reported on the face of the income statement, they don't also have to be disclosed in the notes.

If the disposal is not finalized during the current fiscal year, there will be additional revenues, expenses, gains, and losses between the beginning of the following year and the date that the disposal is completed. Those amounts will be recognized in that following period, when they are realized, and not anticipated by any accruals in the year that the decision to discontinue was made (*CICA* 3475.31–.32). Subsequent-year adjustments must be reported separately as *discontinued operations* and not "hidden" in other revenues and expenses.

ILLUSTRATION The Board of Directors of Pacific & Eastern Corporation (PEC), a large consumer products company, approved a plan to sell its Automatic Transmission Diagnostic Centres division at a Board meeting on 30 August 20X1. The company engaged professional business valuators to appraise the fair value of the division's assets and solicited competitive bids from prospective buyers for the division. PEC engaged the consultancy firm of Artur Yonge to assist with the bidding and selling process. At 31 December 20X1, the following information is available:

- From 1 January 20X1 through 30 August 20X1, the division earned $7 million before tax.
- From 1 September through 31 December 20X1, the division earned an additional $2 million before tax.
- The evaluators estimate that the fair value of the division's net assets is $40 million; this is $5 million less than the $45 million carrying value on PEC's books.
- The bidding process closes on 31 January 20X2. Final negotiations and preparation for sale are expected to extend to at least the end of April, after which date PEC expects to have no continued interest in the division.
- PEC managers estimate that due to uncertainty surrounding the fate of the division, the division will probably lose $4 million between 1 January 20X2 and the closing date of the sale.
- PEC managers expect to receive a total purchase price of at least $50 million when the deal is finalized.
- PEC will have to pay a 5% commission to Artur Yonge on any sale.
- PEC's marginal income tax rate is 30%.

The disposal of this division qualifies for reporting as a *discontinued operation* in 20X1 because the sale has been properly authorized, the division is a separate and separable division of the company, a plan is in place to actively sell the division, PEC will have no interest in the cash flows or operations after the sale, and the other criteria cited above appear to have been met.

The next issue is what amount should be reported in the discontinued operations section of PEC's 20X1 income statement. The total reported amount will be $1,400,000, comprising the following components:

Earnings from operations for 20X1, before income tax ($7 mil. + $2 mil.)	$9,000,000
Reduction in carrying value of the assets to estimated fair value	(5,000,000)
5% commission to be paid on the estimated asset fair value of $40 million (that is, the estimated *cost to sell*)	(2,000,000)
Income tax expense related to all of the above [($9m − $5m − $2m) × 30%]	(600,000)
Total gain (loss) on discontinued operations, net of tax, 20X1	$1,400,000

The gain of $1,400,000 is the division's profit, adjusted for the asset impairment and the cost to sell the division. The anticipated operating loss for 20X2 is not included, nor is the estimated gain or loss arising from the final sale.

Suppose that in 20X2, the division is finally and irrevocably sold to an Australian company for $53 million, minus the 5% commission and minus estimated additional income tax expense of $3 million. The net amount to be shown in PEC's 20X2 income statement is:

Sales price, gross	$53,000,000
Less carrying value of assets sold (net of cost to sell, recognized in 20×1)	(40,000,000)
Sales commission not previously recognized [($53 mil. – $40 mil.) × 5%]	(650,000)
Income tax expense not previously recognized	(3,000,000)
Gain on discontinued operation, 20×2	$9,350,000

Extraordinary Items

Classification of an item as extraordinary is sometimes a tough call. The "attractive" thing about extraordinary items from the perspective of the company is their segregation on the income statement, preceded by a subtotal that clearly encourages users to focus on the "pre-extraordinary item" amount as the continuing amount. It's sort of an official blessing on the one-time nature of the item.

CRITERIA FOR EXTRAORDINARY ITEMS Section 3480 of the *CICA Handbook* identifies extraordinary items as those resulting from transactions or events that have *all* of the following three characteristics:

1. They are not expected to occur frequently over several years.
2. They do not typify the normal business activities of the entity.
3. They do not depend primarily on decisions or determinations by management or owners.

The following examples are extraordinary items:

- Government expropriation of land and buildings for a highway.
- The destruction of a large portion of a wheat crop by a tornado.
- An explosion in a nearby nuclear reactor resulting in high-level radioactive emissions.

Gains or losses resulting from the risks inherent in an entity's *normal business activities* are not considered extraordinary. The environment in which the firm operates should be considered when determining whether an underlying event or transaction is abnormally and significantly different from the ordinary and typical activities of the business. A firm's environment includes such factors as the characteristics of the industry or industries in which it operates, the geographical location of its operations, and the nature and extent of governmental regulations. An event or transaction may be unusual for one firm, but not for another, because of differences in their respective environments. For example, the following two transactions are similar, but the first is to be treated as extraordinary while the second is not:

- *Extraordinary.* A wheat farmer's crops are destroyed by a hailstorm. Severe damage from hailstorms in the locality where the wheat farmer operates are rare.
- *Ordinary.* An apple grower's crop is damaged by frost. Frost damage occurs every three or four years.

The first situation is considered extraordinary because, given the environment in which the wheat farmer operates, hailstorms are very infrequent. In the second situation, taking into account the environment in which the company operates, the criterion of infrequency of occurrence would not be met. The history of losses by frost damage provides evidence that such damage may reasonably be expected to recur in the foreseeable future.

Section 3480 specifically identifies the following events that should *not* be considered as extraordinary because they are expected during the customary and continuing business activities of a firm

- Losses and provisions for losses with respect to bad debts and inventories;
- Gains and losses from fluctuations in foreign exchange rates;
- Adjustments with respect to contract prices;
- Gains and losses from writedown or sale of property, plant, equipment, or other investments; and
- Income tax reductions on utilization of prior period losses or reversal of previously recorded tax benefits. (Such reductions were once considered extraordinary and were a common example of an extraordinary item.)

A very important criterion for classifying a gain or loss as an extraordinary item is that the gain or loss *does not depend primarily on the decisions of managers or owners.* A transaction would be considered to be outside the control of managers or owners if their decisions would not influence the transaction. For example, consider the following situations:

- A manufacturing concern sells the only land it owns. While this is an infrequent and unusual item, it results from a decision of managers or owners and thus any resulting gain or loss is considered not extraordinary.
- An airplane owned by the company is destroyed by a terrorist act. The event is infrequent, unusual, and not the result of a decision of managers or owners; any gain or loss, net of insurance proceeds, is an extraordinary item.
- A lawsuit is settled out of court. The settlement is clearly an action of management or owners, but the settlement itself is a secondary event and should not dictate classification. The nature of the event causing the lawsuit must dictate whether or not the item is extraordinary.

Probably the largest single extraordinary item ever reported by a Canadian company was the $2.95 *billion* charge taken by BCE Inc. in 1997. The charge was to write down the carrying value of its telecommunication assets to reflect their lower recoverable value in a deregulated environment. Asset writedowns usually do not qualify as extraordinary items, but the BCE writedown did qualify because deregulation was beyond the control of management.

Sometimes, extraordinary items are described as "acts of God or government." It's a useful decision rule to remember—events such as tornadoes, fires, floods, expropriations, and so on, if not frequent, are normally the best examples of extraordinary items. Another decision rule is that extraordinary items are *rare.*

As illustrated in our Calgary Storage Company example (Exhibit 3-5), extraordinary items are reported in the income statement under a separate classification and are net of any income tax effect. If subject to income tax, an extraordinary gain increases income tax and an extraordinary loss reduces income tax. In both cases, the extraordinary gain or loss is adjusted for its tax effects and reported net of tax. Extraordinary items are usually explained in disclosure notes.

Recent examples of extraordinary items found in practice include losses caused by

- Damage caused by a major ice storm;
- Robbery of an armoured car, and
- A provincial government's cancellation of a previously approved mining project, necessitating a write-off of all investment to date plus an estimate of site restoration costs.

Unusual Items

Some events or transactions are not extraordinary but should be disclosed separately on the income statement to emphasize their nature as unusual or infrequent. The *CICA Handbook* suggests that companies *should* disclose items

> that do not have all of the characteristics of extraordinary items but result from transactions or events that are not expected to occur frequently over several years, or do not typify normal business activities of the entity. (*CICA* 1520.03(l))

Unusual items should *not* be shown net of income tax.

For example, assume a timber company has a material writedown of its pulp and paper inventory and timber resources (a capital asset) due to prevailing low prices in the timber industry. The writedown, an impairment of value, has been determined by management but caused by outside events—low market prices. It is certainly infrequent, since the company reports that it is the first time in the company's 40-year history that such a writedown has been necessary. However, risks associated with price fluctuations in a natural resource market are surely a *typical business risk* in the timber industry. The item is not extraordinary.

Classification of an item as "unusual" is quite open to management discretion: Any item deemed "unusual" may be reported in this fashion. Common examples of losses or expenses given separate disclosure include restructuring costs, writedown of capital assets and investments, and severance payments. Common types of gains that are given separate disclosure are gains on disposal of an investment and gains on sale of capital assets.

The Dofasco income statement (Exhibit 3-3) shows an unusual item, "Loss on disposal of QCM," as the last item before "Income before income taxes." A disclosure note explains that this loss arose from the capital restructuring of Quebec Cartier Mining Company, a joint venture of Dofasco and a Brazilian company. The loss is not something that would arise regularly, but it is not extraordinary because it relates to the operations of the business and was the result of decisions of management. The loss does not qualify as a discontinued operation because, as Dofasco states

basic earnings per share
net income for a period minus dividend entitlements of senior shares, divided by the weighted average of common shares outstanding during that same period. *See also* diluted earnings per share.

> ... the disposition does not qualify for treatment as a discontinued operation under the new *CICA Handbook* Section 3475 "Disposal of Long-lived Assets and Discontinued Operations," effective for disposals after May 1, 2003, because of the nature of the Corporation's continuing involvement in the operations of QCM.

The loss of $27.9 million is an unusual item, but it must be reported as an operating expense because it is neither an extraordinary item nor a discontinued operation.

EARNINGS PER SHARE

Public companies are required to report earnings per share. Earnings per share (EPS) is a summary figure that is often quoted by analysts and investors as the primary (and sometimes only) indication of a company's earnings record. Investors find EPS useful because it relates the income of the company to a single common share and automatically adjusts for changes in the number of shares outstanding from year to year. EPS numbers are very widely quoted in the financial press. Financial analysts and investment services often present EPS graphs.

The computation of EPS is governed by Section 3500 of the *CICA Handbook*, which is one of only three sections in the *CICA Handbook* that apply only to public companies. Public companies are required to report earnings per share for both (1) income before discontinued operations and extraordinary items, and (2) net income. Refer to the Petro-Canada income statement in Exhibit 3-2, which shows EPS at the bottom of the statement. Companies must show EPS on the face of the income statement.

diluted earnings per share
similar to basic earnings per share, but the weighted average number of shares is adjusted to reflect all of the shares that would be outstanding if the common share entitlements of dilutive convertible senior securities and stock options were issued. The numerator also is adjusted to reflect the potential impact of conversions.

Basic earnings per share is computed by dividing reported income available to the holders of common shares by the weighted average number of common shares outstanding during the year. For computation of EPS on common shares, income must be reduced by any preferred share dividend claims since such dividends are not available to common share owners and have not been subtracted in computing income.

Diluted earnings per share shows how earnings per share would change in the event that all common shares promised under the terms of existing option agreements, conversion privileges on bonds or preferred shares, etc., were actually issued. We'll study earnings per share in depth in Chapter 19.

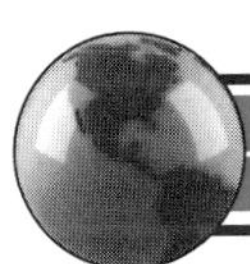

International Perspective

The financial reporting requirements in virtually every country include an income statement of one form or another. The measurement basis and specific measurement rules vary, but there is always some attempt to measure the results of operations.

The International Accounting Standards Board recommends a list of income statement disclosures in IAS 1 that looks a lot like the AcSB recommendations. But the IAS recommends "an analysis of expenses" either by type of expense or by function within the enterprise (para. 77). The AcSB makes no such recommendation, as we have seen.

Income statements in some countries' reporting environments may be even less revealing than those in Canada. Some statements are terse, with very few accounts being reported. In the extreme, an income statement consists of the single net earnings line or of the three lines: earnings before taxes, tax expense, and net earnings. Australian statements usually start with "operating profit before interest, tax, depreciation, and amortization," and then proceed to deduct each of interest, tax, depreciation, and amortization step by step. However, total revenue is usually disclosed in a note.

The biggest difficulty a reader has with international financial income statements is understanding what an item means and how it was measured. Although Australia, Canada, the United States, and the United Kingdom identify items as "unusual or infrequent" (these items are called "exceptional" in the United Kingdom, and "abnormal" in Australia) and "extraordinary," the reporting requirements in most countries do not make these distinctions. Moreover, very few countries other than Canada and the United States require separate reporting of discontinued operations, although the practice is beginning to spread, thanks largely to efforts by the IASB.

Some countries have higher disclosure standards, or require disclosure of a longer list of specific items. France, for example, has a fairly detailed list of income statement items, including wages and salaries. Germany also requires disclosure of employment costs and materials costs.

However, the income statements of many European countries may include a wide variety of provisions and reserves that have no counterpart in Canada or the United States. Germany and Austria have a number of profit reserves that are required by law—an officially sanctioned smoothing technique!

In many countries, the accounting measurement rules are greatly influenced by tax law. For example, an item that is deducted for tax reporting may be required to be expensed in the financial statements. A firm might take a large tax deduction for an item such as bad debt expense, for example, and this same amount would have to be reported on the income statement even though it is an overestimate of the actual expense. Such reporting could mislead the reader who assumes that bad debt expense means the same thing in the foreign financial statement as in a Canadian financial statement.

When reading an income statement generated outside Canada, it is important to remember that even though it may appear very much like a statement prepared under Canadian GAAP, the terms and labels may have quite different meanings. It is important to understand how revenues, expenses, gains, and losses are defined in the environment in which the statement was prepared before trying to interpret the information in the statement.

CONCEPT REVIEW

1. What are the three basic subsections of an income statement required by Canadian GAAP?
2. Explain what intraperiod income tax allocation is.
3. Why is separate disclosure of discontinued operations important to users?
4. What are the three criteria that a gain or loss must satisfy before it can be classified as extraordinary?

COMPREHENSIVE INCOME

Beginning in 2006, Canadian GAAP requires companies to report *comprehensive income.* Comprehensive income has two components:

1. net income
2. other comprehensive income

A company should present a separate statement of comprehensive income that shows (1) *net income* and (2) the components of *other comprehensive income.* "Other comprehensive income" is not a mandatory title (*CICA* 1530.09). Some companies call it "other changes in shareholders' equity."

Net income is determined via the income statement. *The concept of comprehensive income makes no change in the measurement of net income and the presentation of the income statement.*

However, changes in the reporting of financial instruments and of held-for-sale assets have led to a need for a new classification. In addition, another type of accounting adjustment had always been excluded from net income and been reported as a separate component of shareholders' equity. Starting in 2006, these adjustments are reported as components *of other comprehensive income.* **Other comprehensive income** includes only those items specifically identified by the *CICA Handbook*:

other comprehensive income
amounts that are not included in determining net income but that also do not represent investment or disinvestment by owners; examples include unrealized gains and losses on held-for-sale assets

- Unrealized gains and losses on held-for-sale assets;
- Unrealized gains and losses from translating the financial statements of foreign subsidiaries; and
- Unrealized gains and losses on cash flow hedges relating to anticipated transactions.

Obviously, all three components involve unrealized gains/losses. We will briefly discuss each of these items.

Held-for-Sale Assets

Reporting unrealized changes in value is not new. For example, *mutual funds* are companies that take individual investors' money and invest the money in a portfolio of stocks and bonds. Individual mutual fund investors must be able to see the value of their holdings in the mutual fund. Therefore, mutual funds are required by law to report their investments at market value, updated every day.

When the investments are revalued each day, the company recognizes an unrealized gain or loss. This gain or loss is *recognized*, but is not included in income because it has not yet been *realized.* Therefore, the cumulative unrealized gains and losses are carried in a separate component of shareholders' equity. When investments are sold (and the gain or loss is thereby realized), the realized gain or loss is removed from the separate component of shareholders' equity and is transferred to the income statement.

The mutual fund industry is a type of specialized industry. Mutual fund accounting is not ordinarily included in intermediate accounting courses, because mainstream accounting courses cover only accounting concepts and principles that can be widely applied. However, the principles underlying mutual fund accounting now are becoming more widespread. As the accounting profession worldwide moves to market valuation for financial instruments (including derivative instruments), unrealized gains and losses are arising in many ordinary companies. *Unrealized* gains and losses must be kept separate from *realized* gains and losses, and the concept of other comprehensive income is designed to deal with this problem.

Translation Gain/Loss

Many corporations have foreign operations. When these foreign subsidiaries operate reasonably autonomously, they are called "self-sustaining foreign operations." Foreign operations normally keep their accounts in a foreign currency. To consolidate the subsidiary in the Canadian parent's financial statements, the subsidiary's financial statements must be translated into Canadian dollars. The conversion process inevitably leads to an imbalance, which is "plugged" by an amount called the "translation gain or loss." This amount is an accounting phenomenon. It has no economic significance, but it must be included in the consolidated financial statements or the balance sheet won't balance. The solution to this problem has been to put the cumulative translation gain or loss into a separate component of shareholders' equity. Now, instead, the translation gain/loss will be reported as a component of other comprehensive income.

We discuss foreign operations a bit more in Chapter 11. Intensive study of foreign operations is reserved for advanced accounting courses.

Cash Flow Hedges

Often a company will make a commitment that is denominated in a foreign currency. The commitment might be to acquire an asset at a price that is expressed in a foreign currency, such as U.S. dollars, euros, or Japanese yen. Alternately, the commitment may be to deliver goods or services in the future at a price fixed in a foreign currency. Either way, the Canadian company is subject to foreign exchange risk.

For example, suppose that a company contracts to buy advanced electronic equipment from Japan. The price of the equipment is ¥7.5 million. If the exchange rate is C$1.00 = ¥75 at the time of the commitment, the commitment is worth C$100,000. But suppose that the exchange changes before the equipment is delivered and paid for. If the exchange rate drops to C$1.00 = ¥68, the company will have to pay C$110,294, a cost increase of 10%.

To protect against foreign exchange risk, most companies will use a derivative instrument, usually a "forward contract," which is an agreement with a bank that has the effect of offsetting the risk. If the value of the commitment goes up, then the value of the forward contract goes down, and vice versa. The gain on one offsets the loss on the other.

Changes in the value of the commitment will be *realized* only when the contract is complete and payment has been made. Therefore, the *unrealized* gain or loss on the derivative instrument must be deferred and matched against the realized gain/loss on the transaction.

As we will discuss in Chapter 14, all derivative instruments are reported at fair value on the balance sheet. However, because the cash flow for commitment has not yet occurred, the unrealized gains/losses on the cash flow hedge are not included in net income, but instead are reported as a part of other comprehensive income.

Accounting for hedges is definitely a topic for advanced accounting! We will not go into hedging further in this book. But you should have a general understanding of the nature of cash flow hedges for anticipated transactions, and why the gains and losses are included in other comprehensive income.

Reporting Example

Since the comprehensive income concept is new to Canada, we cannot provide a Canadian example. Instead, we will turn to a well-known U.S. company to illustrate the general approach. Exhibit 3-6 presents the income statement, the statement of comprehensive income, and part of the statement of shareholders' equity for Nike Inc. Nike is a well-known manufacturer of athletic shoes and other sports equipment, clothing, and accessories. We have modified the presentation slightly in order to avoid confusion about the differences between Canadian and U.S. GAAP.

The income statement, at the top of the Exhibit, is perfectly straightforward.[1] It shows a final net income figure of $474 million. The middle section of the Exhibit shows Nike's Statement of Comprehensive Income. The company has two components in this category:

1. Unrealized changes in foreign currency translation, relating to foreign subsidiaries; and
2. Changes in the market value of derivative instruments.

[1] As an aside, referring to the discussion earlier in this chapter, it is worth noting just how brief the Nike income statement is for a company that has revenues of almost U.S.$11 *billion*.

EXHIBIT 3-6

NIKE INCORPORATED
CONSOLIDATED STATEMENT OF INCOME

(In millions of U.S. dollars; presentation modified slightly from the original)

Year ended May 31, 2003	
Revenues	$ 10,697.0
Cost of sales	6,313.6
Gross margin	4,383.4
Selling and administrative	3,137.6
Interest expense	42.9
Other expense, net	346.0
Operating and other income/expense	3,526.5
Income before income taxes	856.9
Income taxes	382.9
Net income	$ **474.0**

STATEMENT OF COMPREHENSIVE INCOME

Net income	$ 474.0
Other comprehensive income (loss):	
Change in cumulative translation adjustment (net of tax)	127.4
Net unrealized gain (loss) on hedge derivatives (net of tax)	(311.9)
Reclassification to net income of previously unrealized gains (losses) on hedge derivatives (net of tax)	137.2
Other comprehensive income (loss)	**(47.3)**
Total comprehensive income	$ **426.7**

CONSOLIDATED STATEMENT OF SHAREHOLDERS' EQUITY [PARTIAL]

	Accumulated Other Comprehensive Income (Loss)	Retained Earnings	Total
Balance at May 31, 2002	$ (192.4)	$3,495.0	$3,302.6
Repurchase of Class B Common Stock		(186.2)	(186.2)
Dividends on Common Stock ($.54 per share)		(142.7)	(142.7)
Forfeiture of shares from employees		(0.9)	(0.9)
Changes from transactions with shareholders		(329.8)	(329.8)
Net income		**474.0**	**474.0**
Foreign currency translation	127.4		127.4
Adjustment for fair value of hedge derivatives (net)	(174.7)		(174.7)
Comprehensive income	**(47.3)**	**474.0**	**426.7**
Balance at May 31, 2003	$ (239.7)	$3,639.2	$3,399.5

The statement has two entries relating to the second component. The first (a loss of $311.9 million) is the unrealized loss that arose in 2003. The second (an addition of $137.2 million) is the amount of previously unrealized gains that were realized in 2003 and therefore moved to the income statement.

The bottom section of the Exhibit shows the shareholders' equity reconciliation for retained earnings and for other comprehensive income. Notice that only the net income of $474 million goes into retained earnings. The other items that affect retained earnings are transactions with shareholders: share repurchase, dividends, and forfeitures of shares by employee-shareholders.

The components of other comprehensive income are placed in the separate column for accumulated other comprehensive income. In that column, the adjustment for fair value of hedge derivatives is the combination of two separate lines on the Statement of Comprehensive Income: $(311.9) + 137.2 = $(174.7).

The items in the two columns are combined only in the final column. (In Nike's original presentation, the amounts of paid-in capital also are added into the total column.)

International Convergence

Comprehensive income is the result of convergence efforts. Convergence is the attempt to harmonize U.S. GAAP, Canadian GAAP, and international GAAP. The FASB was the first to establish the concept of comprehensive income. The goal was to find a place to put items that did not seem to fit into net income but that the FASB was reluctant to allow into retained earnings. Historically, the FASB has refused to let companies "hide" things by burying them in retained earnings. These items included the correction of errors and other adjustments. For example, the cumulative impact of changes in accounting standards was included in net income in the United States but in retained earnings in other countries (including Canada). Restatement of prior years' financial statements was not permitted.

On the international scene, the IASB has been moving steadily toward market values for a wide variety of assets and liabilities, especially financial instruments. The trend clearly is to "mark-to-market," in which assets and liabilities are revalued at every balance sheet date. As well, the IASB was concerned that writedowns (and, in some countries, write-ups) of assets for "impairment" were not really realized and should be reported separately from the primary measurement of transaction-based net income. Therefore, the IASB also moved toward a separate reporting of value changes. The IASB calls them "other changes in equity" rather than "comprehensive income," but the result is the same.

In Canada, the AcSB has an explicit objective of harmonizing Canadian GAAP with U.S. and international GAAP as much as possible. *CICA Handbook* Section 1530 is not identical to either the U.S. or international GAAP, but it is harmonized with both. A company that reports into the United States but uses Canadian GAAP will not have to restate for comprehensive income for U.S. purposes. A company can report the same comprehensive income numbers in the United States and Canada and be in compliance with both countries' accounting standards.

CONCEPT REVIEW

1. What are the components of other comprehensive income?
2. How should comprehensive income be reported in a company's financial statements?
3. What is "convergence"?

RETAINED EARNINGS STATEMENT

A statement of retained earnings is one of the four basic financial statements, which ties together the income statement and the balance sheet by showing the changes that occurred in retained earnings for the year. The purpose of the retained earnings statement is to report all changes in retained earnings during the accounting period, to reconcile the beginning and ending balances of retained earnings, and to provide a connecting link between the income statement and the balance sheet. The ending balance of retained earnings is reported on the balance sheet as one element of shareholders' equity.

For many companies, the only changes in retained earnings are (1) net income for the year and (2) dividends declared. Because of the simplicity of the retained earnings statement, it often is appended to the income statement. When a company does combine the retained earnings statement with the income statement, the combined statement's title must reveal that fact, such as by titling it the *Statement of Income and Retained Earnings.*

Instead of a retained earnings statement, some companies instead present a statement of shareholders' equity, which shows changes in all shareholders' equity accounts, using a column for each shareholders' equity account. The columns will be for (1) common shares, (2) other paid-in capital (if any), (3) other comprehensive income, and (4) retained earnings, plus a column for *total.* Nike uses this type of format, two columns of which are shown in Exhibit 3-6.

The five major components of a statement of retained earnings are

1. Net income or loss for the period;
2. Dividends;
3. Error corrections;
4. Cumulative effect of retroactive changes in accounting policy; and
5. Other changes: capital transactions, appropriations, and restrictions.

Exhibit 3-7 shows the retained earnings statement for Shoppers Drug Mart. This example shows three of the five possible components of a retained earnings statement—everything except dividends and error corrections:

- Two adjustments as the result of changed accounting standards;
- Net earnings of $257,670,000 for the year; and
- One capital transaction for 2003 and 2002.

Shoppers paid no dividends in either 2003 or 2002.

Retained earnings statements can be combined with the income statement to become a single combined *statement of income and retained earnings*, or a similar title. The use of the combined format seems to be slowly declining—less than 20% of public companies use the combined format.

EXHIBIT 3-7

SHOPPERS DRUG MART CORPORATION

CONSOLIDATED STATEMENTS OF RETAINED EARNINGS

(In thousands of dollars)

53 weeks ended January 3, 2004 and 52 weeks ended December 28, 2002	**2003**	2002
Retained earnings, beginning of period as reported	**$ 177,716**	$ 15,726
Impact of new accounting standards		
– Foreign currency translation	—	(43,770)
– Stock-based compensation	—	(478)
Net earnings	**257,670**	208,584
Premium on share capital purchased for cancellation	**(82)**	(2,346)
Retained earnings, end of period	**$ 435,304**	$ 177,716

Retroactive Effect of a Change in Accounting Policy

When an accounting policy is changed, the comparability of the financial statements is reduced unless all comparative numbers, including prior years' net incomes, are restated using the newly adopted principle. This change in prior years' income also changes opening retained earnings as previously reported.

Consider the following example. A company's management decides to change from accelerated to straight-line amortization for its capital assets and has made the change to comply with industry practice. The difference between the accumulated amortization under the accelerated method previously used and the amortization that would have accumulated if the straight-line method had been used in all previous periods is $60,000. That is, amortization expense has been $60,000 more using the accelerated method than would have been recorded using straight-line amortization. Assume an income tax rate of 30%. The cumulative effect of the change in accounting policy, net of applicable income taxes, is $60,000 × 70%, or $42,000. The entry to record the effect of the change in accounting policy is as follows:

Accumulated amortization—machinery	60,000	
Retained earnings—cumulative effect of change in accounting principle		42,000
Future income tax liability		18,000

The tax amount is deferred because the change is made for accounting purposes only—the tax return (and taxes payable) is not changed. We discuss this type of tax effect in Chapter 15.

The effect of a retroactive change in accounting policy is shown on the retained earnings statement as follows:

Opening retained earnings, as previously reported (assumed)	$400,000
Effect of change in accounting policy (net of tax)	42,000
Opening retained earnings, as restated	$442,000

Prior financial statements are changed so that only straight-line amortization is shown on the income statements, which obviously would change prior years' net income for all comparative years shown. Appropriate note disclosure would also be prepared.

Accounting policy changes are not always applied with full retroactive restatement. They may also be applied prospectively. Prospective treatment means that the new policy is used for current periods and future periods, but past periods are left as is, with a resulting loss of consistency. This is allowable when specific new accounting standards specifically permit prospective treatment. Prospective treatment is also used as a practical matter when it is simply not possible to reconstruct data for prior periods.

For example, the current *CICA Handbook* recommendations for measuring the gain (loss) on discontinued operations came into effect for disposal decisions made on or after 1 May 2003. The new recommendations are quite different from those in previous years. However, a company does not need to go back and change anything related to discontinued operations that were begun prior to May 2003, even if the disposal was not completed by May 2003. Application of the new recommendations is *prospective* rather than retroactive.

In other circumstances, the company can determine the impact of the change in accounting policy on opening balances in total, but cannot reconstruct the detail needed to restate individual prior years. This will result in an adjustment to opening retained earnings, as illustrated, but no restatement of previous income statements. Again, practicalities force the use of less desirable disclosure of the effect of the new policy on prior years.

It's worth noting that changes in accounting *estimates* are never applied retroactively: the new estimate is used for this year, and future years, but previous income statements are not changed and retained earnings is not touched.

Error Corrections

Errors happen. They usually arise from classifying amounts and transactions incorrectly. Error corrections are not the same as changes in accounting estimates. For example, we may discover in 20X6 that our estimate of net realizable value of year-end 20X4 inventory was far too optimistic; much more should have been written down as obsolete. When we discover that fact, we are not finding an error. Accounting estimates are almost always wrong, because they are estimates about the future, not facts. Subsequent adjustments for past accounting estimates are included in revenues and expenses for the current period; they are not errors.

Usually, errors are accidental. However, some "errors" can be viewed as intentional; management may have been trying to affect reported results by intentionally misclassifying some transactions. Prosecutors allege that major public companies (such as WorldCom, Enron, Live Entertainment, Philip Services, and Tyco) deliberately misstated their financial results. In accounting terms the cause of the errors is irrelevant. All errors are corrected in the same manner, whether they occurred innocently or not-so-innocently.

When errors are discovered, they must be corrected. This sometimes involves restating the financial statements of prior years, and thus changing prior income, which is summarized in retained earnings. Proper disclosure of these changes is accomplished by making an adjustment to opening retained earnings for the cumulative impact of the change to prior income, net of tax. Opening retained earnings *as restated* are presented. Then, the comparative financial statements are adjusted to give effect to the error correction. In effect, the transaction is backed out of the current income statement and into the appropriate prior year. A description of the error and its effect on the financial statements must be included in the disclosure notes.

To illustrate the recording of a retroactive adjustment for an error correction, assume that a machine that cost the Bailey Retail Company $10,000 (with a 10-year estimated useful life and no residual value) was purchased on 1 January 20X2. Further, assume that the total cost was erroneously debited to an expense account in 20X2. The error was discovered 29 December 20×5. A correcting entry would be required in 20X5. Assuming that any income tax effects are recorded separately, the entry is as follows:

29 December 20X5:		
Machinery	10,000	
Amortization expense, straight-line (for 20X5)	1,000	
Accumulated amortization (20X2 through 20X5)		4,000
Retained earnings, error correction		7,000

The $7,000 retroactive adjustment corrects the 1 January 20X5 retained earnings balance on a pre-tax basis. The balance is understated $7,000 before tax:

Understatement of 20X2 income ($10,000 – $1,000)	$9,000
Overstatement of 20X3 and 20X4 income ($1,000 × 2)	(2,000)
Net pre-tax understatement	$ 7,000

Assuming that the same error was also made on the income tax return, the entry to record the income tax effect of the error, assuming a 30% income tax rate, would be as follows:

Retained earnings, error correction ($7,000 × 30%)	2,100	
Income tax payable		2,100

Appropriate reporting on the retained earnings statement is illustrated in Exhibit 3-8. Amounts other than the error correction are assumed.

EXHIBIT 3-8

BAILEY RETAIL COMPANY
RETAINED EARNINGS STATEMENT

(stated in thousands of Canadian dollars)

For the year ended December 31, 20X5	
Retained earnings, 1 January 20X5, as previously reported	$378,800
Correction of error (net of income tax of $2,100) (Note 6)	4,900
Retained earnings, 1 January 20X5, as restated	383,700
Net income	81,200
Cash dividends declared and paid during 20X5	(30,000)
Retained earnings, 31 December 20X5 (Note 7)	$434,900

Note 6. Error correction—During the year, the company discovered that a capital expenditure made in 20X2 was incorrectly expensed. This error caused net income of that period to be understated and that of subsequent periods to be overstated. The adjustment of $4,900 (a $7,000 credit less income tax of $2,100) corrects the error.

Note 7. Restrictions—Of the $434,900 ending balance in retained earnings, $280,000 is restricted from dividend availability under the terms of the bond indenture. When the bonds are retired, the restriction will be removed.

Capital Transactions

The retained earnings statement contains other increases and decreases in equity caused by capital transactions. Most capital transactions are share transactions. Since a corporation is dealing with itself (its owners) in share transactions, gains and losses caused by these transactions are not shown on the income statement because they are not arm's-length transactions. Gains normally create contributed capital—separate shareholders' equity accounts—and losses reduce retained earnings. We'll study these more carefully in Chapter 13.

Other charges to retained earnings result from share issue expenses incurred on the issuance of new shares, taxes resulting from a change in control or triggered by dividend payments to shareholders, and adjustments to retained earnings caused by a reorganization.

Most other countries are more permissive about charging items directly to retained earnings. When looking at a non-Canadian set of financial statements, the reader should not ignore the retained earnings statement; sometimes it contains interesting expenses or losses that don't appear on the income statement!

APPROPRIATIONS OF AND RESTRICTIONS ON RETAINED EARNINGS Appropriations of and restrictions on retained earnings limit the availability of retained earnings to support dividends.

Restrictions result from legal requirements, such as a statutory requirement that retained earnings be restricted for dividend purposes by the cost of any treasury stock held, or contractual agreements, such as a bond agreement (i.e., indenture) requiring that retained earnings of a specified amount be withheld from dividend purposes until the bonds are retired.

Restrictions on retained earnings are especially common in non-profit organizations, such as social service agencies, hospitals, universities, etc. Restrictions indicate that some of the funds shown on the asset side of the balance sheet are available only for special purposes, such as for specific research activities or for constructing new buildings.

Appropriations of retained earnings result from formal decisions by the corporation to set aside, or to *appropriate*, a specific amount of retained earnings (temporarily or permanently). The effect of an appropriation is to remove the specified amount of retained earnings from dividend availability. For example, corporations often set up appropriations such as "retained earnings appropriated for future plant expansion." Appropriations are created by the Board of Directors, and they also can be reduced or eliminated by the Board.

The primary purpose of restrictions and appropriations is to inform statement users that a portion of retained earnings is set aside for a specific purpose (usually long term) and that these amounts are therefore not available for dividend declarations.

Exhibit 3-8 illustrates a restriction of $280,000 on the retained earnings of Bailey Retail Company. The unrestricted balance of retained earnings is $154,900 ($434,900 − $280,000 = $154,900). Details regarding restrictions and appropriations are usually reported in a note, as illustrated in Exhibit 3-8.

CONCEPT REVIEW

1. What types of items will appear on the retained earnings statement?
2. Explain the difference between a restriction and an appropriation of retained earnings.
3. What is the normal approach to accounting for a change in accounting policy?
4. How are errors in prior years corrected? How does this differ from the way we correct the results of accounting estimates made in prior years?
5. Why aren't gains and losses from capital transactions reported on the income statement?

SUMMARY OF KEY POINTS

1. Accounting income is the result of recording transactions in accordance with established measurement rules. Accounting income suffers from its reliance on *transactions*, which ignore economic events that indicate wealth increases. Accounting income may also be affected by the nature of accounting policies chosen, which determines the quality of earnings.
2. Companies must report *comprehensive income*, which has two components: (1) net income, and (2) *other comprehensive income*. Other comprehensive income (which can be called by other names, such as "other changes in shareholders' equity") includes unrealized gains and losses on held-for-sale assets, translation gains/losses on foreign operations, and unrealized gains/losses on cash flow hedges of anticipated future transactions.
3. Many format issues are not governed by accounting pronouncements, and the company must make choices to create an income statement that is useful to financial statement users. Minimum disclosures are recommended by the *CICA Handbook*; additional note disclosures and format decisions are important for full disclosure.
4. Two general formats for presenting income statement information not specifically regulated by accounting pronouncements are the single-step and the multiple-step formats.
5. The single-step format uses only two broad classifications in its presentation: (1) a revenues and gains section and (2) an expenses and losses section. Total expenses and losses are deducted from total revenues and gains in a single computation to determine the net income (earnings) amount.
6. A multiple-step income statement presents several intermediate subtotals, designed to emphasize important relationships in the various revenue and expense categories.
7. The gains or losses resulting from the sale or abandonment of a business segment, whose activities represent a separate major line of business or class of customer, must be reported, net of income tax effects, as a separate component of income, positioned after income from continuing operations and before extraordinary items.

8. Extraordinary items result from transactions or events that are infrequent, not normal business activities, and do not result from the decisions or actions of management. They are required to be reported, net of income tax effects, as a separate component of income, positioned after income from continuing operations.
9. Unusual or infrequent items should be shown separately on the income statement, before tax.
10. Earnings per share amounts relate earnings to common shares outstanding.
11. The statement of retained earnings reports all changes in retained earnings during the period, including net income or loss, dividends declared, capital transactions, and adjustments for changes in accounting policies.
12. Error corrections that affect the financial statements of prior periods are recorded (net of tax) as a change to opening retained earnings, and comparative statements are restated.
13. A change in accounting principle is normally applied retroactively, with the cumulative effect of the change shown as an adjustment to opening retained earnings. Comparative financial statements should be restated. If this treatment is not feasible, only the cumulative effect is shown on the retained earnings statement. In certain circumstances, the change in principle is reflected prospectively. An accounting estimate is always changed prospectively.

KEY TERMS

REVIEW PROBLEM

The following pre-tax amounts are taken from the adjusted trial balance of Killian Corporation at 31 December 20X5, the end of Killian's fiscal year:

Account	Amount
Sales revenue	$ 1,000,000
Service revenue	200,000
Interest revenue	30,000
Gain on sale of capital asset	100,000
Cost of goods sold	600,000
Selling, general, and administrative expense	150,000
Depreciation expense	50,000
Interest expense	20,000
Loss on sale of long-term investment	10,000
Extraordinary item, loss from earthquake damage	200,000
Cumulative effect of change in accounting policy (gain)	50,000
Impairment loss on business segment assets	60,000
Loss on operation of discontinued business segment	10,000

Other information:

a. The income tax rate is 40% on all items.
b. There were 100,000 common shares outstanding throughout the year. No preferred shares are outstanding.
c. Assume that the capital cost allowance deductible for tax purposes is equal to the depreciation expense shown on the income statement.

Required:

1. Prepare a single-step income statement in good form.
2. Prepare a multiple-step income statement in good form.

REVIEW PROBLEM—SOLUTION

1. Single-step income statement:

KILLIAN CORPORATION
INCOME STATEMENT
for the year ended 31 December 20X5

Revenues and gains:	
Sales revenue	$1,000,000
Service revenue	200,000
Interest revenue	30,000
Gain on sale of operational asset	100,000
Total revenue and gains	1,330,000
Expenses and losses:	
Cost of goods sold	600,000
Selling, general, and administrative expenses	150,000
Depreciation	50,000
Interest expense	20,000
Loss on sale of long-term investment	10,000
Income tax expense [see computations below]	200,000
Total expenses and losses	1,030,000
Income from continuing operations	300,000
Discontinued operations:	
Loss from discontinued operations, net of tax of $28,000	(42,000)
Income before extraordinary item	258,000
Extraordinary item:	
Loss from earthquake damage, net of tax benefit of $80,000	(120,000)
Net income	$ 138,000
Earnings per share:	
Income from continuing operations	$ 3.00
Net income	$ 1.38

Computation of income tax expense:

Total revenues		$1,330,000
Expenses before income taxes:		
Cost of goods sold	$600,000	
Selling, general, and administrative expenses	150,000	
Capital cost allowance (equal to depreciation)	50,000	
Interest expense	20,000	
Loss on sale of long-term investment	10,000	830,000
Taxable income		500,000
Tax rate		40%
Income tax expense		$ 200,000

The discontinued operations and extraordinary item are reported net of tax, reflecting intraperiod allocation, and therefore are not included in the computation of income tax expense. The cumulative effect of a change in accounting policy is shown on the retained earnings statement.

2. Multiple-step income statement:

KILLIAN CORPORATION

INCOME STATEMENT

for the year ended 31 December 20X5

Sales revenue		$1,000,000
Cost of goods sold		600,000
Gross margin		400,000
Operating expenses:		
Selling, general, and administrative expenses	$150,000	
Depreciation expense	50,000	200,000
Income from operations		200,000
Other revenues and gains:		
Service revenue	200,000	
Interest revenue	30,000	
Gain on sale of operational asset	100,000	330,000
Other expenses and losses:		
Interest expense	20,000	
Loss on sale of long-term investment	10,000	30,000
Net other items		300,000
Income from continuing operations before income tax		500,000
Income tax expense		200,000
Income from continuing operations		300,000
Discontinued operations:		
Loss from discontinued operations, net of tax of $28,000		(42,000)
Income before extraordinary item		258,000
Extraordinary item:		
Loss from earthquake damage, net of tax effects of $80,000		(120,000)
Net income		$ 138,000
Earnings per share:		
Income from continuing operations		$ 3.00
Net income		$ 1.38

Alternative arrangements of the information above the income from continuing operations line are allowed for both single- and multiple-step formats. In particular, the other revenues and other expenses are commonly combined into a single category of other revenues and expenses instead of being shown in two categories.

The presentation of the items below income from continuing operations should be the same for both single-step and multiple-step statements.

QUESTIONS

Q3-1 Briefly explain how the income statement is a connecting link between the beginning and ending balance sheets.

Q3-2 What is the difference between economic income and accounting income?

Q3-3 How does comprehensive income differ from net income?

Q3-4 Where does cumulative other comprehensive income appear on the balance sheet?

Q3-5 Preferences of user groups dictate some policy choices regarding income statement display. Explain two of these areas.

Q3-6 What factors determine the choice of a fiscal year-end?

Q3-7 Why might a Canadian company prepare its financial statements in U.S. dollars?

Q3-8 Explain how cost of goods sold is reported on a single-step income statement and on a multiple-step income statement.

Q3-9 Briefly define intraperiod tax allocation.

Q3-10 Regis Publishing Corporation computed total income tax expense for 20X5 of $16,640. The following pre-tax amounts were used: (a) income before extraordinary loss, $60,000; (b) extraordinary loss, $12,000; and (c) correction of a prior year's error, $4,000 (a credit on the retained earnings statement). The average income tax rate on all items was 32%. Compute the intraperiod income tax allocation amounts.

Q3-11 What is a discontinued operation? How is it reported in the income statement?

Q3-12 A company has a segment that it decides to sell, effective 1 September, after incurring operating losses of $45,000 to date in the fiscal year. The segment, with net assets of $310,000, was sold for $240,000 on 1 November, after incurring further operating losses of $30,000. Assume a tax rate of 40%. What amounts would be disclosed in the income statement?

Q3-13 List the items that *must* be disclosed on the income statement in relation to continuing operations. Why would companies choose to disclose more than minimum requirements?

Q3-14 Define an extraordinary item. How should extraordinary items be reported on (a) a single-step and (b) a multiple-step income statement?

Q3-15 How are items that are unusual or infrequent reported on the income statement?

Q3-16 Extraordinary items are sometimes described as "Acts of God or government." Why is this a useful rule of thumb?

Q3-17 Define earnings per share (EPS). Why is it required as an integral part of the income statement?

Q3-18 What types of items are reported on a statement of retained earnings?

Q3-19 A company has a machine that cost $21,000 when acquired at the beginning of year 1. It had a 10-year useful life and a $1,000 residual value. Toward the end of year five, the company discovered that, in error, the machine had been expensed when acquired. Straight-line depreciation is appropriate. What adjustment to opening retained earnings is appropriate in year five?

Q3-20 Describe how a change in accounting policy is reflected in the financial statements. Describe two alternative, less desirable approaches and state when each can be used.

Q3-21 What is meant by appropriations or restrictions on retained earnings? How are such items usually reported?

Q3-22 What are capital transactions and why are they reported on the retained earnings statement?

CASE 3-1

Travel Incorporated

Travel Incorporated (TI) is a holding company that has wholly owned interests in the travel and entertainment industry. The company has four separate operating divisions—(1) a scheduled airline, operating mainly in Western Canada and the United States; (2) a hotel management company that manages hotels throughout North America; (3) a real estate division that owns and operates many commercial developments in Canada, including some of the hotels; and (4) a travel services company that sells vacation packages at both retail and wholesale.

Each division operates through one or more separate corporations and is subject to federal and provincial income tax. TI is the sole shareholder in all of its subsidiaries. The senior executives of each of the operating divisions report directly to the senior executives of TI.

TI is listed on the Toronto Stock Exchange and is subject to the reporting requirements of the exchange and of the Ontario Securities Commission. TI prepares consolidated financial statements. TI's income tax rate is 25%.

In 20X5, TI had major transactions affecting two of its four divisions:

Sale of the real estate division

On 15 June 20X5, TI's Board of Directors decided that the company's shares were undervalued in relation to the underlying value of the various divisions. The low valuation was largely attributable to continuing losses in the airline division. Therefore, the Board decided to sell the real estate development company in order to capture the "true" value of that division for the benefit of TI shareholders.

On 23 November 20X5, after conclusion of a 60-day open bidding period, the Board accepted a purchase proposal from Lincoln Goodview Ltd. (LGL). LGL agreed to acquire all of IT's shares in the real estate division for cash consideration of $450 million. LGL will acquire all of the division's assets and assume all debt related to the division's real estate properties. The purchase price is $450 million, based on the fair value of the division's assets less the present value of the related debt that LGL will assume. The transaction is contingent upon the completion of LGL's due diligence review of the division's books. LGL's due diligence is expected to be completed in February 20X6. In the meantime, TI will continue to operate the division and will receive all profits until the sale is finalized, which is expected to occur in February 20X6.

The net book value of the division's real estate asset portfolio was $1,670 million on 23 November 20X5. The appraised fair value on 23 November was $2,240 million. At 31 December 20X5, the fair value of the portfolio is $2,450. The fair value of the related debt was $1,430 on 23 November and $1,420 on 31 December.

In 20X5, the division had total revenues of $300 million and net income of $50 million. Of those amounts, $130 million of revenue and $28 million of net income were earned prior to 15 June.

Forced sale of bus operations

In 20X2, the TI airline division established a long-distance bus operation, BlueSky, to complement its air service. The intent was to provide a seamless transportation experience for airline passengers who were travelling to smaller cities and towns in Alberta. Because TI sold tickets that included both the airline and BlueSky segments of each passenger's voyage, the bus operation was organized as part of the airlines operations. The company did not allocate revenue to airline and bus; BlueSky was operated as a cost centre.

A competing bus company complained that the air-bus combination was in restraint of trade. The regulator agreed. In early January 20X5, TI was ordered by transportation regulators to divest itself of its bus operation within 12 months.

Therefore, TI's airline division sold the bus operations to Trillium Express, an Ontario bus company. The transaction was completed on 17 July 20X5. Trillium Express paid $25 million for the net assets of BlueSky. At the time of the sale, the net book value of BlueSky's net assets was $33 million.

Required:

What are the reporting implications of these two transactions? Explain how each would be shown on TI's consolidated statements for the year ending 31 December 20X5. Be specific.

CASE 3-2
Cashgo Limited

CashGo Limited is a food distributor and retailer in Eastern Canada. The company also owns both a bakery and a dairy, each of which has significant sales through other market channels in addition to CashGo's stores. CashGo is a private company; all of the shares are owned by the founder's family. The company has not needed external share capital as the company is quite profitable and the banks are eager to provide debt financing as needed. The banks require CashGo to give them annual audited financial statements, prepared in accordance with Canadian GAAP.

The CashGo CFO currently is overseeing the preparation of the company's consolidated financial statements for 20X7. There have been many changes to the recommendations of the *CICA Handbook*, not all of which the CFO is sure that she understands. She has come to you for advice on how to report the results of some of the company's 20X7 transactions and events. She also would appreciate receiving draft statements of income, comprehensive income, and retained earnings. CashGo does not wish to provide any more detail in the statements than is necessary to comply with current reporting requirements.

Specific concerns:

1. In the final quarter of 20X7, the Halifax region suffered a major hurricane, which knocked out the electricity in the Halifax region for several days. Hurricanes are extremely uncommon in Nova Scotia. A great quantity of frozen and other perishable foods was spoiled and had to be discarded. The loss amounted to $11 million. The inventory was not insured against this type of loss.

2. CashGo is a private company. In 20X7, the company elected to use the differential reporting option on income taxes, applied retroactively. The cumulative adjustment for prior years was to eliminate the $46 million credit balance of future income taxes. CashGo has tentatively classified this amount as "Gain on income tax reversals."

3. Early in 20X7, the company invested $24 million of excess cash in a portfolio of marketable securities that are available for sale. The company sold some of these securities in November for $14 million; the original cost was $9 million. The remaining securities have a market value of $18 million at year-end 20X7.

4. A major customer of the dairy division went bankrupt in 20X7. The customer owed CashGo $6 million. As an unsecured creditor, CashGo is unlikely to receive any payment on this receivable; therefore, the receivable was written off. CashGo has never before experienced a bad debt of this magnitude.

5. As part of a structuring of retail operations, the company closed a significant number of smaller stores during the year and sold the buildings and land for a gain of $12 million. This was partially offset by $8.5 million in severance costs paid to the employees. The company will continue its restructuring in 20X8 at an estimated net cost of $7 million.

6. CashGo has a U.S. subsidiary that operates a food distribution centre in New England. The subsidiary operates autonomously. CashGo translates the subsidiary's U.S.-dollar financial statements into Canadian dollars in order to consolidate the subsidiary. The mechanical result of the translation is an annual gain or loss. A 20X7 translation loss of $6 million arose when the subsidiary's statements were converted to Canadian dollars.

Additional information:
The CashGo year-end 20X7 trial balance shows the following amounts, *not including amounts explained above:*

millions of Canadian dollars	Debit	Credit
Sales revenue—Retail		$ 390
Sales revenue—Wholesale		251
Sales revenue—Dairy division		45
Sales revenue—Bakery division		65
Sales revenue—U.S.		67
Bank interest paid	$ 12	
Amortization expense	96	
General advertising expense	21	
Investment income		3
Operating expenses—Retail	194	
Operating expenses—Wholesale	256	
Operating expenses—Dairy	20	
Operating expenses—Bakery	23	
Operating expenses—U.S. subsidiary	46	
General corporate administrative expense	33	
Income tax expense	44	
Retained earnings, 31 December 20X6		359
Dividends paid, 20X7	48	

Required:

1. Advise the CFO on the proper treatment of each of her six specific concerns, with explanation.
2. Prepare the draft statements as requested.

CASE 3-3
KIDSaWARE

KIDSaWARE (KW) is a retailer of children's clothing that has been in operation for over 30 years. The stores are located in central Canada—Ontario and Quebec.

Four years ago, KW bought all of the shares of Prairie Kids (PK), an existing chain of retail children's clothing stores that operated throughout Western Canada. PK was suffering from severe competition, particularly from Wal-Mart. KW had just had a successful initial public offering and believed that it could return PK to profitability by injecting fresh capital to modernize the stores, coordinating PK's marketing with KW, and introducing KW merchandise into PK stores.

PK was maintained as a separate corporate entity. The PK store managers reported to the PK district managers, as before, and the district managers reported to the sales manager of KW. All corporate affairs were conducted through KW's head office in Brampton, Ontario.

On 17 September 20X1, however, the KW Board of Directors decided that the PK venture was not successful, and the Board decided to put PK up for sale. KW paid a broker $100,000 to find a buyer for PK. If an acquiror could not be found, PK would be shut down.

In January 20X2, the broker did find a potential buyer. The buyer would agree to acquire PK on 15 March, paying $0.15 per share for 100% of PK shares, plus assuming the outstanding debt and all future lease commitments (see Exhibit 1). Because the potential buyer has no direct experience with children's wear, a condition of the sale is that KW management continue to be involved in managing PK until the end of the next fiscal year—that is, through the Christmas 20X2 selling season.

Meanwhile, the audit committee has been presented with a draft of the KW income statement (Exhibit 2) that treats the PK disposal as a discontinued operation. KW's fiscal year ends on 31 January 20X2.

Required:

1. Assume that the disposal of PK qualifies as a discontinued operation. Is the draft KW presentation correct? If not, how should it be reported?
2. Assume instead that the disposal does not qualify as a discontinued operation, but that PK has become a held-for-sale asset as the result of the Board meeting on 17 September 2001. How would the potential disposal of PK be reported?
3. Does PK qualify for reporting as a discontinued operation, under the requirements of Section 3470 of the *CICA Handbook*? Explain. (CICA, adapted)

EXHIBIT 1

PRAIRIE KIDS INCORPORATED
BALANCE SHEET (Unaudited)

(stated in thousands of Canadian dollars)

January 31, 20X2	Book Values	Estimated Liquidation Values
Assets		
Accounts receivable	$ 584	$ 584
Inventory	10,846	3,841
Prepaid expenses	2,870	NIL
Capital assets	22,869	5,717
Total assets	$ 37,169	
Liabilities		
Bank indebtedness	$ 8,051	$ 8,051
Accounts payable and accrued liabilities	18,389	18,389
Long-term debt	4,936	4,936
Deferred lease inducements	854	
	32,230	
Shareholders' equity		
Common shares (8,342,000 shares issued and outstanding)	17,573	
Deficit	(12,634)	
	4,939	
Total liabilities and shareholders' equity	$ 37,169	

Note 1. The rent expense for the year is $7,147. The minimum rental payments for the leases of the premises are as follows:

20X3	$7,253
20X4	$7,012
20X5	$6,889
20X6	$6,599
20X7	$6,156
20X8–2012	$32,035

The rental payments for the store premises are guaranteed by KW. The rent guarantee is limited to three years of minimum rental payments.

EXHIBIT 2

INCOME STATEMENTS (Unaudited)

(stated in thousands of Canadian dollars)

For the year ended January 31, 20X2	KW Consolidated	PK
Sales	$ 258,420	$ 48,421
Cost of sales and store, warehouse, and administrative expenses	(233,122)	(51,209)
Other expenses	(11,859)	(3,088)
Earnings before income taxes and discontinued operations	13,439	(5,876)
Income taxes (current and future)	(4,829)	
Earnings (loss) from continuing operations	8,547	(5,876)
Loss from discontinued operations*	(9,664)	
Net loss	$ (1,117)	$ (5,876)

* *The loss from discontinued operations was calculated, in thousands of dollars, as:*

Loss from PKI's operations		$ (5,876)
Sale of 8,342,000 shares at $0.15 per share	$ 1,251	
Broker's fee	(100)	
Book value of PKI's net assets	(4,939)	
Loss on disposal at $0.15 per share	$ (3,788)	(3,788)
Loss from discontinued operations		$ (9,664)

CASE 3-4
Delta Limited

Delta Limited (Delta) is incorporated under the *Canada Business Corporations Act.* At the end of 20X1 the Board of Directors decided to sell the printing and binding division of the company and concentrate its efforts in its book publishing division. An offer was received for the assets and liabilities of the printing and binding division, and the sale became effective in late January 20X2. The net assets were sold at a gain. Delta's financial year ends on 31 December.

For the past 20 years Delta had been a public company, with preferred shares listed on a Canadian stock exchange. Its bonds were also publicly traded. On receipt of the offer for the assets and liabilities of the printing and binding division, the Board began rethinking certain aspects of the status of the company. After several meetings, the Board decided that Delta would become a private company, and would therefore call in its bonds for redemption and its preferred shares for cancellation. The necessary legal negotiations were commenced with the provincial securities commissions, the Department of Consumer and Corporate Affairs, the stock exchange, and the holders of the bonds and preferred shares.

The Board decided to change the company's status from public to private because the company would gain greater privacy and tax benefits, and it would be easier to reach agreement on the company's future direction. During their discussions on the change in status, some Board members argued that the financial disclosure required of private companies is less extensive than that required of public companies. In their opinion, not only is the distribution of the financial statements of a private company (such as Delta would become) restricted to a relatively small group, but the financial information that must be disclosed is less extensive. While readily acknowledging that the change in status would restrict the distribution of Delta's financial statements, other directors maintained that disclosure requirements will not change significantly.

The bonds were redeemed in January 20X2. The preferred shares were bought on the open market in several transactions during January and February and were cancelled in February 20X2. On 7 March 20X2, Delta became a private company. Financing for the redemptions came partially from company resources, and partly from increased borrowing, secured by the personal guarantee of the majority shareholder and a first charge on real estate assets of the company.

During January 20X2, the majority shareholder, Mr. Richards, bought out all the minority holders of Delta's common shares.

It is now April 20X2. The Board has engaged you, CA, to help Delta adjust efficiently and effectively to being a private company in the book publishing industry. Board members want you to prepare a report that includes your recommendations on financial accounting and related matters. You have assembled the information shown in Exhibit 1.

Required:

Prepare the report requested by the Board.

EXHIBIT 1

DELTA, LIMITED
INFORMATION ASSEMBLED BY CA

Audited financial statements for the year ended 31 December 20X1 were made available to interested parties in February 20X2. An annual meeting has not yet been scheduled for the calendar year 20X2; the previous annual meeting was held in May 20X1.

1. The legal costs incurred in dealing with the various governmental and stock exchange officials amounted to $70,000.
2. The bonds had to be redeemed at a 2% premium that amounted to $80,000.
3. Some of the preferred shares were bought on the open market in early January 20X2 at a price that was $60,000 more than their recorded book value. The remaining preferred shares, also purchased on the open market, were bought at a price that was $75,000 above their book value.
4. The buyer of the printing and binding division agreed to hire most of Delta's production employees, but not the office staff. Thus, Delta had to offer early retirement or a severance package to these individuals. The cost of this package amounted to $200,000.
5. Other expenses related to the sale of the division amounted to $154,600.
6. The sale of the printing and binding division has reduced Delta's assets to about $3 million, and annual revenues from $15 million to $6 million. This is below the size threshold for mandatory financial statement audit established in legislation.
7. In January 20X2, prior to its sale, the printing and binding division's revenue was $820,000, and cost of goods sold was $430,000. The division incurred other expenses of $170,000.
8. The book publishing division has used the following accounting policies in the years to 31 December 20X1:
   a. Revenue is recognized when books are shipped to book stores. Each store is allowed to return up to 20% of purchases made in the past 12 months. Sales returns are recorded when made.
   b. Inventory is valued at the lower of printing and binding cost or net realizable value.
   c. Amortization is charged in the accounts on a straight-line basis.
   d. Bonuses to employees and royalties to authors are expensed in the year that they are paid, which is normally the year after the period to which they relate.

(CICA, adapted)

CASE 3-5
Keysource Corporation

Keysource Corporation is a small software development company formed by three MBA graduates in the 1980s. In the early years, it specialized in the design and development of new software products. It had several successful years and went public on the strength of its track record. However, the company experienced difficulty in replicating early successes.

Software development requires that a large investment be made upfront, and the success of the final product is hard to predict. Keysource had several spectacular "losers" in the years following its initial public offering. The company shifted its focus to become a marketer of software products developed by other companies or individuals. For example, if an individual wrote a new computer game, Keysource would sign an agreement to produce and market the product, with the author receiving royalties.

Keysource pursued a number of other expansion policies as well, the most important of which was to acquire other small software companies that had either good product lists or excellent marketing departments and channels. Thus, the company grew by leaps and bounds, although its financial results continued to be quite volatile. The company is well known for its choice of accounting policies that maximize income.

In 20X4, the company reported results as follows, (in thousands of Canadian dollars)

	20X4	20X3	20X2
Revenues	$121,287	$109,704	$119,519
Net income (loss)	21,145	(57,250)	(4,983)
Assets	90,815	79,334	128,474
Shareholders' equity (deficit)	37,485	(8,632)	61,933

The company frequently has experienced financial difficulties due to the large initial investment required for each new software product. Nevertheless, Keysource so far has managed to find additional investment to continue operations.

It is now 20X5, and the company is cautiously optimistic about its operating results for the 20X5 year. Three matters have come up that are the subject of dispute between the company and its auditors. The company has asked you, an independent accountant, to provide your opinion as a means to settling the impasse.

1. In 20X0, Keysource obtained a long-term loan from Mr. David Ling, a wealthy Hong Kong industrialist, at a rate of prime plus 6%. To secure the loan, Mr. Ling asked for, and was given, a first charge on the shares of Keysource held personally by the president. No shares could be sold by the president as a result of the conditions of the assignment. The loan had a 20-year term, although the interest rate was to be adjusted every five years. In 20X5, Keysource found another lender, whose interest rate was lower and whose terms were far less onerous. Accordingly, they offered Mr. Ling a payout, which he accepted. However, in return for release of the claim against the president's personal shareholdings, Mr. Ling requested, and received, an additional payment of $200,000.

   The company has requested that this $200,000 payment be recorded as a capital charge, debited directly to retained earnings, because (1) it was related to a share transaction and was not incurred in day-to-day operations and (2) was related to the personal assets of the shareholder/president, and not company assets. The auditor claims that the $200,000 is a cost of refinancing and should be recorded on the income statement, consistent with the all-inclusive concept of income.

2. In 20X4, Keysource accrued an expense of $2,400,000 in expectation of a settlement of a copyright infringement suit. In 20X5, pursuant to a judgement issued by the Supreme Court of Australia, Keysource paid the plaintiffs $3,658,000, including legal fees. The management of Keysource claims that the amount accrued in 20X4 was in error, and the additional $1,258,000 paid should be treated as an error correction, adjusted to 20X5 opening retained earnings and reflected on the 20X4 comparative financial statements.

3. In September 20X5, Keysource sold an operating unit called "Lansa" to a related party, one of the members of the Board of Directors. The operating unit was engaged in the business of customizing software for the aircraft industry. The net assets of the operation had a net book value of ($178,000)—that is, liabilities associated with the division exceeded assets by $178,000—on the date of sale. The proceeds of disposition were $650,000. Proceeds were to be paid through the forgiveness of a $250,000 account payable from Keysource to the purchaser, plus four $100,000 instalments due over the next four years. Keysource wished to record the $828,000 gain as "other revenue" in 20X5; the auditors prefer to recognize the gain as proceeds are realized.
4. At the end of 20X5, management decided that its policy of amortizing software development costs over three years was erroneous. Therefore, the Board of Directors approved a new policy of extending amortization over five years. The cumulative effect of correcting this error is to increase cumulative earnings by $7 million. Management proposes to show this correction as an unusual gain on the income statement. The offset to the gain will be an increase in the net amount (that is, after amortization) of deferred software development costs on the balance sheet.

Required:

Evaluate the accounting policies, as requested by the Keysource board.

(ASCA, adapted)

ASSIGNMENTS

* 

A3-1 Interpreting the Components of Income: Excerpts from the Stanley Produce Company comparative income statements for the years 20X2 through 20X4 are as follows:

(stated in millions of Canadian dollars)

	20X4	20X3	20X2
Income from continuing operations, after tax	$30	$25	$20
Discontinued operations:			
Income from operations of discontinued segment, net of tax	0	10	15
Gain on disposal of discontinued segment, net of tax	50	0	0
Extraordinary items:			
Loss from earthquake damage, net of tax	0	(40)	0
Gain on expropriation of property	0	0	35
Net income (loss)	$80	$ (5)	$70

Required:

1. Stanley Produce has experienced volatile earnings over the three-year period shown. Do you expect this to continue? Why or why not?
2. Net income increased from a loss of $5 million in 20X3 to a profit of $80 million in 20X4. Suppose the company's common share price increased only approximately 20% during the same period. Why might this be the case? Relate the 20% increase in share price to the components of net income.
3. Would you expect net income in 20X5 to be more or less than the amount reported in 20X4? More specifically, assuming no new unusual, non-recurring items, what amount would you estimate net income to be in 20X5?

* These stars indicate length, with one star being the shortest assignment, and three stars being the longest assignment.

A3-2 Accounting Income versus Economic Income: On 1 January 20X1, Tyler Trading Company was incorporated by Jim Tyler, who owned all the common shares. His original investment was $100,000. Transactions over the subsequent three years were as follows:

2 January 20X1	Purchased 10 cars for resale at $10,000 each.
30 June 20X1	Sold six cars for total proceeds of $90,000.
31 December 20X1	Remaining four cars have an estimated sales value of $48,000.
15 July 20X2	Bought three cars for resale at $20,000 each.
3 October 20X2	Sold four cars from 20X1 purchase for total proceeds of $50,000.
31 December 20X2	Cars from 20X2 purchase have an estimated sales value of $84,000.
30 November 20X3	Sold all three cars bought in 20X2 for total proceeds of $106,000.

Required:

1. Calculate accounting income, based on transactions, for 20X1, 20X2, and 20X3.
2. Calculate economic income, based on events or changes in value, for 20X1, 20X2, and 20X3.
3. Compare total accounting income with total economic income and explain your findings.
4. In what ways is accounting income superior to economic income? In what ways is economic income superior? Use the accounting principles from Chapter 2 to explain.

A3-3 Formats of Income Statement, Extraordinary Item: The following selected items were taken from the adjusted trial balance of Amick Manufacturing Corporation at 31 December 20X5:

Sales revenue	$500,000
Cost of goods sold (including amortization, $32,000)	300,000
Dividends received on investment in shares	6,500
Interest expense	4,200
Extraordinary item: earthquake loss (pre-tax)	50,000
Distribution expenses	65,000
General and administrative expenses	48,000
Restructuring expense	23,000
Accounts receivable	136,500
Interest revenue	2,500
Income tax, assuming an average 25% tax rate	?

Required:

1. Prepare a single-step income statement.
2. Prepare a multiple-step income statement.

A3-4 Formats of Income Statement, Extraordinary Item: The Sandvik Cement Company's records provided the following information at 31 December 20X5 (the end of the accounting period):

Sales revenue	$95,000
Rental revenue	35,000
Gain on sale of short-term investments	14,000
Distribution expense	18,000
General and administrative expense	12,000
Depreciation expense	9,000
Interest expense	4,000

Income tax expense (30% rate on all items)	?
Earthquake loss on building (pre-tax)	25,000
Gain on sale of equipment (pre-tax)	15,000
Loss on flood damage (pre-tax)	20,000
Loss on sale of warehouse (pre-tax)	3,000
Cost of goods sold	45,000

Required:

1. Prepare a single-step income statement. State any assumptions made.
2. Prepare a multiple-step income statement.

★★

Ex

A3-5 Formats of Income Statement, Extraordinary Item, Discontinued Operations: The following items were taken from the adjusted trial balance of the Bigler Manufacturing Corporation on 31 December 20X5. Assume an average 30% income tax on all items (including the divestiture loss). The accounting period ends 31 December. All amounts given are pre-tax.

Sales revenue	$745,200
Rent revenue	2,400
Interest revenue	900
Gain on sale of capital assets	2,000
Distribution expenses	136,000
General and administrative expenses	110,000
Interest expense	1,500
Depreciation for the period	6,000
Court-ordered divestiture loss	22,000
Cost of goods sold	330,000
Operating loss of discontinued operation to disposal date	28,000
Loss on sale of assets of discontinued operation	10,000

Required:

1. Prepare a single-step income statement.
2. Prepare a multiple-step income statement.

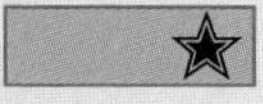

A3-6 Income Statement Format, Tax Allocation: Listed below, in alphabetical order, are selected account balances at 31 December 20X3 for Irving Limited, a Newfoundland public company.

Accounts receivable	$ 47,000
Accumulated amortization	82,000
Administrative expenses	113,000
Advances from customers	17,000
Amortization expense	18,000
Common shares, 10,000 issued and outstanding	50,000
Cost of goods sold	186,000
Dividends declared	14,000
Dividends payable	5,000
Extraordinary gain	18,000
Interest expense	3,000
Gain on disposal of equipment	4,000
Investment revenue	5,000
Loss from discontinued operations	20,000
Sales discounts and allowances	14,000
Sales, gross	513,000
Selling expenses	51,000

The income tax rate on all types of income is 40%.

Required:

Prepare a multiple-step income statement in good form for the year ended 31 December 20X3.

(CGA-Canada, adapted)

A3-7 Minimum Disclosure: MLP Ltd. wishes to present an income statement that complies with minimum required disclosure requirements of the *CICA Handbook*. Data related to the 20X2 income statement is presented below.

Sales revenue	$2,600,000
Investment revenue	12,300
Rent revenue	7,000
Royalty revenue	102,000
Cost of goods sold	860,000
Selling expenses	235,000
General and administrative expenses	210,000
Salaries and wages, sales	420,000
Salaries and wages, administration	236,000
Personnel and placement expense	55,000
Travel expenses	86,000
Amortization expense	120,000
Asset impairment	300,000
Interest expense	13,000
Income tax expense (tax rate is 30%)	?
Extraordinary gain (pre-tax)	30,000

Required:

Prepare an income statement, based on the above information, that discloses only the minimum required by the *CICA Handbook*.

A3-8 Formats of Income Statement, Extraordinary Item: The following pre-tax information was taken from the adjusted trial balance of Turkey Hill Foods Corporation at 31 December 20X5, the end of the accounting period:

Sales revenue	$957,000
Sales returns	7,000
Gain on sale of equipment	8,000
Depreciation expense	25,000
Distribution expense	140,000
General and administrative expense	92,300
Rent revenue	18,000
Investment revenue	7,000
Gain on sale of land	6,000
Interest expense	9,000
Gain on expropriation of property	80,000
Loss on sale of long-term investments	10,000
Cost of goods sold	550,000
Loss due to leaky roof	4,000
Earthquake damage loss	30,000

All items listed above are before tax; the tax rate is 30% on all items. There are 40,000 common shares outstanding.

Required:

1. Prepare a single-step income statement. State any assumptions you make.
2. Prepare a multiple-step income statement.
3. Calculate the EPS disclosures that would be included on the income statement. Include one EPS figure for net income, and one for income before extraordinary items.

A3-9 Formats of Income Statement, Extraordinary Item: The following information was taken from the adjusted trial balance of Montreal Retail Corporation at 31 December 20X6, the end of the accounting period:

Cost of goods sold	$102,000
Accounts payable	121,400
Sales revenue	405,000
Accumulated depreciation	139,500
Sales returns	5,000
Unearned revenue	2,000
Depreciation expense (70% administrative expense, 30% distribution expense)	50,000
Rent revenue	4,000
Interest expense	6,000
Investment revenue	2,500
Distribution expenses (exclusive of depreciation)	105,500
General and administrative expenses (exclusive of depreciation)	46,000
Royalty revenue	6,000
Loss on sale of long-term investments	3,600
Income tax expense	?
Flood loss (extraordinary)	10,000

Assume an average 35% income tax rate on all items, including gains and losses on assets sold and extraordinary items.

Required:

1. Prepare a single-step income statement.
2. Prepare a multiple-step income statement.

A3-10 Minimum Disclosure: Review the data given for A3-9, above. Assume that the company wished to publish an income statement that provides only the minimum required disclosures outlined in the *CICA Handbook.*

Required:

1. Draft a single-step income statement that provides only the minimum required disclosures. Lump all revenues and expenses that need not be shown separately into "other revenues" and "operating expenses," respectively.
2. Explain why the company might prefer minimal disclosures, referring to material explained in Chapters 1 and 2.

A3-11 Classification of Elements on the Income Statement: Fifteen items are listed to the left below that may or may not affect the income statement. Income statement classifications are listed by letter to the right. Match each transaction with the appropriate letter to indicate the usual classification that should be used.

Answer	Selected Transactions	Income Statement Element Classifications
____	1. Sales of goods and services	A. Expenses
____	2. Prepaid insurance premium	B. Extraordinary gain
____	3. Loss on disposal of service trucks	C. Extraordinary loss
____	4. Cost of goods sold	D. Gains (ordinary)
____	5. Value of services rendered	E. Loss (ordinary)
____	6. Gain (unusual but not infrequent)	F. Revenues
____	7. Rent collected in advance	G. Unusual gain
____	8. Cash dividends received on an investment in African diamond mine	H. Unusual loss
		I. None of the above

Answer	Selected Transactions	Income Statement Element Classifications
_____	9. Wages liability (unpaid but recorded)	
_____	10. Cost of successful oil wells in a foreign country that are taken over (expropriated) by that country's government without compensation	
_____	11. Fire loss (infrequent)	
_____	12. Loss due to a very rare freeze that destroys the fruit trees in the Okanagan Valley	
_____	13. Gain on sale of long-term investments not held for resale	
_____	14. Cash dividend declared and paid	
_____	15. Loss due to explosion that completely destroys the factory	

A3-12 Comprehensive Income, Intraperiod Tax Allocation: Recolite Corporation is based in Halifax. For 20X4, the company's accounting records show the following items:

a. A $400,000 loss from hurricane damage. Hurricanes are very rare in Nova Scotia.
b. Total sales revenue of $2,600,000, including $400,000 in the Decolite division, which the company is in the process of selling.
c. Interest expense on long-term debt of $65,000.
d. Gain on sale of marketable securities of $55,000.
e. Operating expenses of $2,100,000, including depreciation and amortization of $500,000. Of this total, $390,000 of expenses (including $75,000 in depreciation and amortization) was incurred in the Decolite division.
f. The company wrote down tangible capital assets by $35,000 during the year, to reduce the Decolite division's assets to their estimated recoverable value.
g. The company has long-term debt that is denominated in U.S. dollars. Due to the weakening of the U.S. dollar during 20X4, the company has an unrealized gain of $20,000.
h. The company has a subsidiary in France. The euro strengthened during the year, with the result that Recolite has an unrealized gain of $15,000 on its net investment in the subsidiary.
i. Recolite's income tax expense for 20X4 is $110,000. This amount is net of a tax recovery of $30,000 on the Decolite division and a $120,000 tax benefit from the hurricane damage.

Required:

Prepare a statement of comprehensive income, including both net income and other comprehensive income, if any.

A3-13 Comprehensive Income: Quebecor World Inc. is the world's largest commercial print media services company. The company is listed on both the Toronto Stock Exchange and the New York Stock Exchange. The company reported the following items in its 2003 financial statements (in millions of U.S. dollars, except per-share amounts – Dr/(Cr)):

a. Cost of sales	$ 5,188.8
b. Loss on extinguishment of long-term debt	30.2
c. Minority interest in earnings	3.1
d. Gain on sale of investments	(3.9)
e. Cumulative effect of changes in accounting policies (net of taxes)	(6.3)
f. Depreciation and amortization	335.9
g. Income tax expense	39.1
h. Impairment of assets	54.4
i. Revenues	6,391.5
j. Translation adjustment for self-sustaining foreign operation	(96.4)
k. Earnings per share	$(136.00)

Required:
Identify whether each of the items above would be included in (1) the income statement, (2) statement of changes in other comprehensive income, or (3) statement of retained earnings.

A3-14 Comprehensive Income: Shaw Communications Inc. reported the following items in its comparative consolidated financial statements for the fiscal year ending 31 August 2003:

a. Gain on sale of cable systems	$ 3,339
b. Amortization of intangible assets	(39,099)
c. Foreign exchange gain on hedged long-term debt	136,975
d. Gain on redemption of debentures	119,521
e. Unrealized gain on available-for-sale securities, net of tax	1,361
f. Debt restructuring costs	(10,634)
g. Adjustment for change in accounting policy	(10,410)
h. Adjustment to fair value of derivatives	(224,341)
i. Loss on sale and writedown of assets	(124,674)
j. Unrealized foreign exchange gain on translation of self-sustaining foreign operations	(1,031)
k. Writedown of investments	(15,000)

Required:
For each item, identify whether Shaw should include the item in determining net income or should report it as a component of other comprehensive income.

A3-15 Combined Income and Retained Earnings Statement: The following amounts were taken from the accounting records of Curtis Recyclers Corporation at 31 December 20X5, the end of the annual accounting period:

Sales revenue	$340,000
Service revenue	64,000
Cost of goods sold	170,000
Distribution and administrative expenses	67,000
Depreciation expense	19,000
Investment revenue	6,000
Interest expense	4,000
Loss on sale of long-term investment (pre-tax)	10,000
Earthquake damage loss	14,000
Cash dividends declared	8,000
Correction of error from prior period, pre-tax (a debit)	12,000
Balance, retained earnings, 1 January 20X5	80,300

a. Common shares, 30,000 shares outstanding.
b. Restriction on retained earnings, $50,000 regarding a bond payable indenture.
c. Assume an average 35% income tax rate on all items.

Required:
Prepare a combined single-step income and retained earnings statement, including tax allocation and EPS for income before extraordinary items and net income. Show computations. Restrictions to retained earnings should be disclosed in a note. State any necessary assumptions.

A3-16 Tax Allocation—Income Statement and Retained Earnings Statement: The records of Cayuga Corporation for 20X4 provided the following *pre-tax* data:

Income Statement—20X4	
Income before extraordinary items	$120,000*
Extraordinary item: Loss from earthquake damage	30,000*
Pre-tax income	$150,000
Statement of Retained Earnings—20X4	
Beginning balance, previously reported	$225,000
Less: Correction of accounting error	(45,000)*
Corrected balance	210,000
Add: Net income, 20X4	90,000
Less: Dividends declared and paid during 20X4	(60,000)
Ending balance	$240,000

* *Subject to a 40% income tax effect.*

Required:

Complete the above statements in good form on an after-tax basis (that is, apply intraperiod tax allocation). Assume all income statement items are fully taxable or tax deductible.

A3-17 Income Statement, Retained Earnings Statement, Tax Allocation: The following pre-tax amounts were taken from the adjusted trial balance of Avoca Automobile Corporation at 31 December 20X5, the end of the annual accounting period:

Sales revenue	$520,000
Cost of goods sold	160,000
Operating expenses	172,000
Gain on expropriation of property	40,000
Writedown of capital assets to reflect impairment of value	44,000
Retained earnings, balance 1 January 20X5	1,060,000
Effect of a change in accounting principles, applied retroactively (a credit)	100,000
Dividends declared and paid	60,000
Dividends declared and not paid	50,000
Restriction of retained earnings due to loan covenant (Amount is included in opening balance of $1,160,000)	100,000
Common shares, no-par, shares outstanding, 20,500 shares	

Required:

1. Prepare a single-step income statement. Assume an average 30% tax rate on all items. Include EPS disclosures.
2. Prepare a statement of retained earnings. Disclose the restriction in a note.

A3-18 Income Statement, Retained Earnings Statement, Tax Allocation: Following is a list of account balances for Blue Boy Limited for the year ended 31 December 20X2:

Amortization expense	$ (363,000)
Change in accounting policy	(166,000)
Common shares (weighted average shares outstanding: 32,500)	25,000
Cost of goods sold	(7,220,000)
Dividends declared	(30,000)
Extraordinary gain	102,000
Income tax expense*	(37,000)
Loss from discontinued operations	(245,000)
Operating expenses	(1,219,000)
Retained earnings, 1 January 20X2	979,000
Sales	9,124,000

* *Income tax expense can be allocated to the following items:*

Change in accounting policy	$ 40,000
Extraordinary gain	(25,000)
Loss from discontinued operations	63,000
Continuing operations	(115,000)
Total	$ (37,000)

Required:

For the year ended 31 December 20X2, prepare in good form:

1. A multiple-step income statement.
2. A statement of retained earnings.

(CGA-Canada)

A3-19 Error Correction: On 23 November 20X7, when engaged in preparing for the 20X7 fiscal year-end, the chief accountant of Harper Limited discovered two accounting errors in the 20X5 statements:

a. Inventory purchases of $2.1 million had inadvertently been charged to Equipment, a capital asset account, and had been amortized by 10% for 20X5. The accounting amortization rate is the same as the CCA rate for tax purposes. The ending and beginning inventories had been properly stated. Therefore, the mistake caused cost of sales to be understated by $2.1 million and pre-tax earnings to be overstated by the same amount.
b. A government ministry had paid $3.2 million in partial settlement of an amount due for a large contract. The contract revenue had already been recognized. However, the payment was accidentally credited to contract revenue instead of to accounts payable, and was included in taxable income.

Harper's income tax rate is 32%.

Required:

1. Calculate the earnings correction that Harper must show in the 20X7 financial statements. Where will these amounts be disclosed?
2. Prepare a general journal entry to record the correction of each error.

A3-20 Error Correction: It is 31 December 20X5, and Manley Delivery Company is preparing adjusting entries at the end of the accounting year. The company owns two trucks of different types. The following situations confront the company accountant:

a. Truck 1 cost $7,700 on 1 January 20X3. It should be depreciated on a straight-line basis over an estimated useful life of 10 years with a $700 residual value. At 31 December 20X5, the accountant discovered that, in error, the truck was never depreciated.

b. Truck 2 cost $4,550 on 1 January 20X2. In error, the $4,550 expenditure was expensed in 20X2. The truck should be depreciated on a straight-line basis over an estimated useful life of seven years with a $350 residual value.

Required:

1. For each truck, give the required entry to record 20X5 depreciation expense at 31 December 20X5. Show computations.
2. Assume that there was a balance of $50,000 in opening retained earnings on 1 January 20X5. Present the top portion of the 20X5 retained earnings statement. Assume a tax rate of 25%.

A3-21 Change in Policy, Retained Earnings Statement: The Hannam Company decided to change from the declining-balance method of depreciation to the straight-line method effective 1 January 20X5. The following information was provided:

Year	Net Income as Reported	Excess of Declining Balance Depreciation over Straight-Line Depreciation
20X1*	$(40,000)	$10,000
20X2	110,000	30,000
20X3	107,000	25,000
20X4	140,000	14,000

* *First year of operations.*

The company has a 31 December year-end. The tax rate is 40%. No dividends were declared until 20X5; $35,000 of dividends were declared and paid in December of 20X5. Income for 20X5, calculated using the new accounting policy, was $210,000.

Required:

Assuming that the change in policy was implemented retroactively, present the 20X5 retained earnings statement.

A3-22 Discontinued Operations, Recording and Reporting: On 1 August 20X5, Fischer Company decided to discontinue the operations of its services division. The services division is not a separate corporation, but it is a separable operation, financially and operationally. On 22 September 20X5, Fischer closed a deal to sell the division to Printemp Limited. Printemp will assume responsibility for the current liabilities (e.g., accounts payable and accrued liabilities) that pertain to the division. The facts pertaining to the sale are as follows:

Divisional assets, book values at 1 August 20X5 (cost of $950,000, less accumulated depreciation of $335,000)	$615,000
Division assets, estimated fair values at 1 August 20X5	450,000
Liabilities assumed by purchaser; fair value = book value	120,000
Purchase price paid by Printemp Ltd.	$420,000
Division revenue:	
1 January–1 August 20X5	560,000
2 August–22 September 20X5	135,000
Division profit (before taxes):	
1 January–1 August 20X5	38,000
2 August–22 September 20X5	12,000
Commission fee paid to the business brokerage that facilitated the sale	80,000
Fischer Corp. marginal income tax rate	30%

On 31 December 20X5, the after-tax income from all income from all operations, including the services division, was $400,000.

Required:

1. Give the entry or entries to record the sale of the services division.
2. Complete the 20X5 income statement, starting with income from continuing operations, after tax.
3. Explain what other disclosures and/or reclassifications are necessary in the 20X5 comparative financial statements and notes.

A3-23 Discontinued Operations: Salmonese Inc. is a food processing company that operates divisions in several type of food, such as cereals, frozen fish, chocolate candy, jams and jellies, and dessert mixes. However, on 13 September 20X1, the Board of Directors voted to put the candy division up for sale. The division's operating results had been declining for the past several years due to intense competition from large international players such as Nestlé and Cadbury.

The Board hired the consulting firm KMGP to conduct a search for potential buyers. The consulting fee was to be 4% of the value of any sale transaction.

By 31 December 20X1, KMGP had found a highly interested buyer for the candy division, and serious negotiations were underway. The potential buyer was a food conglomerate based in Brazil; the company offered to buy the division for $3.6 million cash.

On 25 February 20X2, after further negotiations with the potential buyer, the Salmonese Board accepted an enhanced Brazilian offer to buy the division for $3.8 million. The Salmonese shareholders approved the sale on 5 March 20X2. The transfer of ownership took place on 31 March 20X2.

Salmonese's income tax rate is 30%. Other information is as follows (before tax, in millions of dollars):

	13 September 20X1		31 December 20X1
	Book Value	Fair Value	Fair Value
Candy division's net assets:			
Current assets	$ 0.6	0.5	0.4
Property, plant, and equipment (net)	4.3	3.0	3.2
Current liabilities	0.9	0.9	1.0
Net earnings (loss) of the candy division, 1 January to 31 December 20X1			$0.3
Net earnings (loss) of the candy division, 1 January to 31 March 20X2			$(0.5)

Required:

Prepare the journal entries that are appropriate at 13 September 20X1, 31 December 20X1, 25 February 20X2, 5 March 20X2, and 31 March 20X2.

A3-24 Disposal of Business Segment: NSC Ltd. has a 31 May fiscal year-end. NSC disposed of its Information Systems Group (ISG) on 31 January 20X3. ISG had a net loss (after taxes) of $37,700,000 in 20X3, to the date of disposal. The division was sold for $475,600,000 in cash plus future royalties through 31 May 20X4, which were guaranteed to be $30,000,000. The minimum guaranteed royalties were included in the computation of the 20X3 gain on the sale of the division. Actual royalties received in 20X4 were $35,500,000. Excerpts from comparative income statements found in the 31 May 20X4 financial statements are as follows:

Year ended 31 May	($ millions) 20X4	20X3
Earnings (loss) from continuing operations	$ (29.3)	$ (205.5)
Discontinued operations:		
Gain on sale of discontinued operation (net of incomes taxes of $1.2 in 20X4 and $34.0 in 20X3)	4.3	182.3
Net income (loss)	$ (25.0)	$ (23.2)

Required:

1. Determine the net book value of ISG at the date of disposal.
2. Why does NSC report a gain on the sale of the discontinued operation of $4,300,000 in the year ending 31 May 20X4?
3. NSC reports an after-tax loss from discontinued operations of $37,700,000 for the year ending 31 May 20X3. Over what period was the loss accrued?

A3-25 Discontinued Operations, Unusual Item: In December 20X4, the Board of Directors of Mead Corporation approved a plan to curtail the development of the company's imaging products division. As a result, the company recognized an asset impairment loss before tax totalling $77,000,000. The imaging products division had incurred before-tax losses of $50,000,000 in 20X3 and $41,700,000 in 20X4.

In addition, during 20X4, the company retired an issue of bonds early. These bonds had a carrying value of $200,000,000 and were retired at a cost of $185,000,000, resulting in a pre-tax gain of $15,000,000. The company had never had such a transaction before.

The tax rate on all the above items is Mead Corporation's average income tax rate of 34%.

Assume that earnings from other sources, before income taxes, were $392,500,000 in 20X3 and $168,900,000 in 20X4. This does not include the bond retirement transaction. The average number of common shares outstanding was 65,100,000 shares in 20X3 and 62,200,000 shares in 20X4. Mead Corporation has no preferred shares outstanding.

Required:

Prepare the income statements for Mead Corporation for 20X3 and 20X4, beginning with income from continuing operations. Include appropriate earnings per share computations.

A3-26 Financial Statement Classification: Listed below are some financial statement classifications coded with letters and, below them, selected transactions and account titles. For each transaction or account title, enter in the space provided a code letter to indicate the usual classification. Comment on doubtful items.

Code	Financial Statement Classification
	Income Statement
A	Revenue, or ordinary gain
B	Expense, or ordinary loss
C	Unusual gain or loss
D	Extraordinary item
	Statement of Retained Earnings
E	An addition to or deduction from beginning balance
F	Addition to retained earnings
G	Deduction from retained earnings
	Disclosure Notes
H	Note to the financial statements
	Balance Sheet
I	Appropriately classified balance sheet account

Response	Transaction or Account Title
______	1. Estimated warranties payable
______	2. Allowance for doubtful accounts
______	3. Gain on sale of equipment
______	4. Hurricane damages in Quebec City
______	5. Payment of $30,000 additional income tax assessment on prior year's income
______	6. Earthquake damages in Edmonton
______	7. Distribution expenses
______	8. Total amount of cash and credit sales for the period
______	9. Gain on disposal of long-term investments in shares (non-recurring)
______	10. Net income for the period
______	11. Insurance gain on fire—insurance proceeds exceed the book value of the assets destroyed
______	12. Cash dividends declared and paid
______	13. Rent collected on office space temporarily leased
______	14. Interest paid during the year plus interest accrued on liabilities
______	15. Dividends received on shares held as an investment
______	16. Damages paid as a result of a lawsuit by an individual injured while shopping in the company's store; the litigation lasted three years
______	17. Loss due to expropriation of a plant in a foreign country
______	18. A $100,000 bad debt is to be written off—the receivable had been outstanding for five years. The company estimates bad debts each year and has an allowance for bad debts
______	19. Adjustment due to correction of an error during current year; the error was made two years earlier
______	20. On 31 December of the current year, paid rent expense in advance for the next year
______	21. Cost of goods sold
______	22. Interest collected on 30 November of the current year from a customer on a 90-day note receivable, dated 1 September of the current year
______	23. Year-end bonus of $50,000 paid to employees for performance during the year
______	24. Cumulative effect of a change in accounting policy
______	25. A meteor destroys manufacturing facilities ($5 million book value, no insurance)

A3-27 Analytical—Discuss Statement Classification: The following transactions have been encountered in practice. Assume that all amounts are material.

a. A company discovered that, in error, a payment to the employee's pension fund was all that was expensed last year; the appropriate calculation of expense was $20,000 higher than the payment.

b. A company suffered a casualty loss (a fire) amounting to $500,000. The company has had three fires in the last 10 years, but this was significantly more than any such loss experienced before by the company.

c. A company paid $175,000 damages assessed by the courts as a result of an injury to a customer on the company premises three years earlier.

d. A company sold a significant capital asset and reported a gain of $70,000.

e. A major supplier of raw materials to a company experienced a prolonged strike. As a result, the company reported a loss of $150,000. This is the first such loss; however, the company has three major suppliers, and strikes are not unusual in the industry.

f. A company owns several large blocks of common shares of other corporations. The shares have been held for a number of years and are viewed as long-term investments. During the past year, 20% of the shares were sold to meet an unusual cash demand. Additional disposals are not anticipated.

g. A timber company wrote down inventory and natural resources (a capital asset) after five years of low pulp and paper prices on world markets. The amount was material, it was the first such writedown in the company's history, and it is not expected to recur.

Required:

1. Classify each of the above transactions. Explain the basis for your decision in each situation.
2. Without reference to the above transactions, define the following: unusual gains and losses, extraordinary gains and losses, and error corrections. Explain how the effects of each should be reported.

A3-28 Change in Accounting Policy, Retained Earnings Statement: Moncton Developments Limited was formed in 20X2. During the year ended 31 December 20X4, the company changed its method of accounting for product development expenses from expensing such items to capitalizing them and amortizing them over the period of expected benefit. The 20X4 statements have been prepared using the old policy. Preliminary statements appear as follows:

MONCTON DEVELOPMENTS LIMITED
STATEMENT OF INCOME AND RETAINED EARNINGS

For the year ended 31 December 20X4

Sales	$2,400,000
Costs and expenses (including product development)	1,482,000
Amortization	70,000
Income before tax	848,000
Tax expense	339,200
Net income	508,800
Retained earnings, opening	690,000
	1,198,800
Dividends ($1 per share)	50,000
Retained earnings, closing	$1,148,800
EPS	$10.18

The following pre-tax information was gathered:

	20X4	20X3	20X2
Net income, old policy	$508,800	$540,000	$210,000
Product development costs	200,000	150,000	250,000
Amortization, prior to change	70,000	70,000	60,000
Amortization, after change*	118,000	110,000	90,000

* *Using new policy.*

Required:

1. Prepare a revised 20X4 income and retained earnings statement, giving appropriate treatment to the change in accounting policy. All amounts are taxable at 40%. Include note disclosure.
2. If insufficient information is available to treat the accounting policy change as in (1), what other options does the company have? Describe the impact of the alternatives on the financial statements.

A3-29 Correction of Income and Retained Earnings Statements: The following statements were prepared for Nepal Corporation by the company's new bookkeeper:

NEPAL CORPORATION
PROFIT SHEET
(stated in thousands of Canadian dollars)

31 December 20X8	
Revenues:	
Sales income	$ 1,010
Gain on expropriation of land	130
	1,140
Expenses:	
Amortization	70
Cost of goods sold	600
Income tax	67
Other	270
	1,007
Profit	$ 133

NEPAL CORPORATION
RETAINED EARNINGS
(stated in thousands of Canadian dollars)

31 December 20X8	
Balance, beginning of year	$ 500
Add: Profit	133
Deduct: Severance pay	(200)
Dividends	(30)
Balance, end of year	$ 403

Additional information (all amounts are in thousands of dollars):

a. In December 20X8, the local government expropriated some land (original cost of $70) from Nepal Corporation. The land was needed to provide thoroughfare for a major road bypass around the city. Under the terms of the expropriation, the government paid $130 to Nepal and took possession of the land.
b. Goods costing $42 that were purchased from Finland Company and paid for in November 20X8 were sold in the last week of 20X8 and appropriately recorded as sales of $50. The goods were included in the physical count of goods in Nepal's warehouse on 31 December 20X8, because the goods were on the loading dock waiting to be picked up by the customer.
c. Nepal pays income tax at a rate of 40% on all income except for the gain on the expropriation of the land that is taxed at a rate of 30%. Assume that all revenues, expenses, gains, and losses, are taxable or deductible for income tax purposes.
d. Details of amounts recorded in "other expenses" were as follows:

Loss on closure of transportation division	$ 300
Miscellaneous	10
Outstanding cheques	(40)
	$ 270

The transportation division had been losing money for the last three years. Management decided to shut down the division to avoid future losses.

The bank reconciliation at the end of December showed outstanding cheques of $40. The new bookkeeper thought that these amounts should not be reported as expenses since these cheques had not yet cleared the bank. Therefore, he processed an entry to debit cash and credit other expenses. On 1 January 20X9, he recorded another entry to debit other expenses and credit cash.

e. In 20X8, Nepal laid off five employees who no longer had the skills required to work for the company. In order to avoid a wrongful dismissal lawsuit, the company paid the employees $40 each as severance pay. In turn, the employees agreed not to take any legal action against the company.
f. The company paid $30 to a major shareholder for management services rendered. Since the payment was made to a shareholder, the bookkeeper recorded it as dividends paid.

Required:

1. Briefly explain whether the gain on land expropriation should be shown as an extraordinary item.
2. Prepare, in good form, a multi-step income statement for Nepal for 20X8. Correct any deficiencies and/or errors contained in the draft statements prepared by the new bookkeeper.

(CGA-Canada, adapted)

A3-30 Income Statement, Choice of Accounting Policies: You have been asked to prepare the financial statements for Ali Corporation for the year ended 31 December 20X4. The company began operations in early 20X4. The following information is available about its business activities during the year:

a. On January 2, Ali issued no par common shares for $600,000.
b. On January 3, machinery was purchased for $510,000 cash. It was estimated to have a useful life of 10 years and a residual value of $80,000. Management is considering using either the straight-line amortization method or the declining-balance method at twice the straight-line rate.
c. On January 4, Ali purchased 20% ownership in a long-term investment, ABC Company, for $90,000. During the year, ABC paid dividends of $7,000 and earned net income of $16,000. Ali can use either the cost method or the equity method of accounting for its investment in ABC.
d. Inventory purchases for the year were, in order of acquisition:

Units	Unit Cost	Total Cost
100,000	$4.20	$ 420,000
160,000	4.25	680,000
60,000	4.30	258,000
35,000	4.40	154,000
355,000		$1,512,000

Ali uses a periodic inventory system. There were 50,000 units in ending inventory on 31 December. Management is considering using LIFO, FIFO, or weighted average as the inventory accounting method.

e. Sales during the year were $3,000,000, of which 90% were on account and 10% for cash.
f. Management has estimated that approximately 1% of sales on account will be uncollectible. During the year, $2,070,000 was collected on accounts receivable. When management scrutinizes the year-end outstanding accounts, it estimates that approximately 6% of the accounts will prove to be uncollectible.
g. Additional operating expenses for the year were $1,100,000.

h. On 31 December, the company paid a $10,000 cash dividend on common shares.

i. On 31 December, accounts payable pertaining to operating expenses and inventory purchases totalled $307,000.

j. The cash balance on 31 December was $205,000.

Required:

1. Choosing from the alternative accounting policies described above, prepare a single-step income statement for the year ended 31 December 20X4 that will produce the lowest net income.
2. What are the ethical implications to be considered when selecting from among alternative accounting policies?

(CGA-Canada, adapted)

A3-31 Comprehensive Format: The following trial balance of the Puget Petroleum Corporation at 31 December 20X5 has been prepared and is correct, except that income tax expense has not been allocated.

PUGET PETROLEUM CORPORATION
TRIAL BALANCE

31 December 20X5	Debit	Credit
Cash	$ 636,000	
Accounts receivable (net)	1,695,000	
Inventory	2,185,000	
Property, plant, and equipment (net)	8,660,000	
Accounts payable and accrued liabilities		$ 1,856,000
Income tax payable		399,000
Future income tax		285,000
Common shares, 215,000 shares outstanding		5,975,000
Retained earnings, 1 January 20X5		3,350,000
Net sales, regular*		10,750,000
Net sales, plastics division		2,200,000
Cost of sales, regular	5,920,000	
Cost of sales, plastics division	1,650,000	
Selling and administrative expenses, regular	2,600,000	
Selling and administrative expense, plastics division	660,000	
Interest income, regular		65,000
Error correction		200,000
Depreciation adjustment from accounting change	350,000	
Gain on disposal of plastics division		150,000
Income tax expense	874,000	
Totals	$25,230,000	$25,230,000

* *Accounts identified as regular include all but plastics division for that account.*

Other financial data for the year ended 31 December 20X5:

a. *Income tax expense:*

Tax payments	$475,000
Accrued	399,000
Total charged to income tax expense	$874,000

Tax rate on all types of income: 40%. The $874,000 does not reflect intraperiod income tax allocation, which is required for financial statement purposes.

b. The *error correction* involves a revenue item not recorded in 20X3, the year in which it was earned.
c. *Discontinued operations.* On 31 October 20X5, Puget sold its plastics division for $2,950,000, when the carrying amount was $2,800,000. For financial statement reporting, this sale was considered a disposal of a segment of a business. The disposal date was 31 October 20X5.
d. *Change in depreciation method.* On 1 January 20X5, Puget changed to the declining-balance method from the straight-line method of depreciation to conform to industry practice. The pre-tax cumulative effect of this accounting change was determined to be a charge of $350,000. There was no change in depreciation method for income tax purposes.

Required:

Using the multiple-step format, prepare an income statement for Puget for the year ended 31 December 20X5 (separate disclosure of depreciation and interest expense is not required). Also, prepare a retained earnings statement. All components of income tax expense should be appropriately shown.

(AICPA, adapted)

A3-32 Comprehensive Format: In its 20X3 annual report, MBL Limited identified the following accounts and amounts ($ thousands):

	52 weeks ended:	
	25 Jan. 20X3	**26 Jan. 20X2**
Sales	$ 132,742	$ 178,318
Selling and promotion expenses	39,089	51,653
Opening retained earnings	?	11,560
Discontinued operations—loss on disposal of real estate division*	2,250	—
Franchise revenue	3,000	3,817
Settlement with ex-senior executive	1,959	—
Loss on closure of selected retail operations	—	1,384
Provision for income taxes (recovery)	(443)	(4,400)
Purchase of common shares—excess of redemption price over original proceeds	—	15
General and administration expenses	15,491	17,246
Discontinued operations—loss from operations of real estate division*	196	13
Cost of goods sold	85,959	122,593

* *net of relevant taxes*

Common shares outstanding: 9,875

Required:

Prepare a multiple-step format income statement and a retained earnings statement in good form.

CHAPTER 4

The Balance Sheet and Disclosure Notes

INTRODUCTION

The **balance sheet** is a summary statement of the assets and liabilities of an organization at a single point in time. It is like a financial photograph. But every photograph is *static*—it may yield a detailed and seemingly precise portrait, and yet a photograph taken a little earlier or a little later may appear quite different.

The balance sheet reports critical information to shareholders, creditors, and other financial statement users concerning the financial position of the company. The relative balances of assets, liabilities, and invested and retained equity are reported. "Balance sheet" may seem to be a rather meaningless title for an important financial statement. Some people prefer to call this statement a "statement of financial position," which is perfectly acceptable. However, "balance sheet" is the most common name simply because it emphasizes a very important aspect of this statement—it balances! That is,

Assets = Liabilities + Owner's Equity

The amounts shown on the balance sheet are a combination of historical costs, partially amortized historical costs, discounted present values, fair values, and residuals. However, many of a company's most important assets (and liabilities, to a lesser extent) are not shown on the balance sheet at all. Examples include the value of trademarks, customer goodwill, and intellectual capital. Essentially, the balance sheet is a combination of three types of accounts:

1. Accounts that show the amounts of cash, and amounts owed *to* the company or owed *by* the company (known as **monetary items**).
2. Accounts that represent costs that are being held for recognition in income in future periods (known as **non-monetary items**).
3. Residual accounts that indicate the extent to which the recorded assets exceed the recorded liabilities.

This chapter presents an overview of the balance sheet. We will examine its purpose, format, composition, and major components. We will discuss each of the major account categories on the balance sheet. Each of these categories will be discussed much more extensively in following chapters.

Finally, the chapter will discuss *disclosure notes*, those many pages of explanatory notes that follow the formal financial statements in any company's annual report.

SAMPLE BALANCE SHEETS

monetary items
assets or liabilities whose face value is fixed or determinable in terms of dollars; for example, accounts receivable, accounts payable, and bonds payable

Exhibits 4-1 through 4-4 show the balance sheets for four quite different Canadian corporations. We did not choose these companies at random; each balance sheet was chosen to emphasize particular reporting aspects. Read through them now and reflect on their similarities and differences. We will comment on certain aspects of these sample balance sheets as we go through the chapter.

The first example, Exhibit 4-1, is the balance sheet of the Saskatchewan Wheat Pool. This company was created by special legislation of the Saskatchewan government. The company has two types of shareholders: (1) farmer members who hold the voting shares but receive no dividends and (2) public shareholders who hold non-voting shares but may receive dividends if declared.

The components of the Saskatchewan Wheat Pool's balance sheet are common. Assets consist of receivables, inventories, capital assets, and other assets. *Other assets* include intangible assets such as goodwill and deferred charges such as capitalized start-up costs. Notice that the company has no cash; it relies on bank financing for its daily operating expenses. The company's chequing account is in a deficit (or *overdraft*) position, as indicated by "bank indebtedness" at the top of the current liabilities. The next liability, short-term borrowings, shows the amount of bank operating loans that are outstanding at the end of the year. Most elements are summarized—for example, many kinds of inventory are combined into a single aggregate number.

Bombardier Inc., Exhibit 4-2, is active in a number of different industry sectors. The company is involved in transportation, aerospace, defence, financial services, and real estate. There are no subtotals on this balance sheet, which is dominated by finance and other receivables, inventories, and capital assets.

The Royal Bank of Canada is one of Canada's largest financial institutions. The balance sheet in Exhibit 4-3 is peppered with subtotals, and some fairly exotic assets and liabilities. For the most part, however, its assets are cash, investments, and loans to clients. Liabilities are customer deposits. Notice that this $377 billion company has only $18.8 billion in shareholders' equity; banks are highly levered, which means they have lots of debt in their financial structures. The financial statements of banks must be prepared in accordance with the accounting requirements of the Superintendant of Financial Institutions Canada. Banks have to prepare a fairly rigidly defined set of financial statements so that regulators can be effective; GAAP is defined by these specific accounting requirements in this industry.

EXHIBIT 4-1

SASKATCHEWAN WHEAT POOL
CONSOLIDATED BALANCE SHEETS

(stated in thousands of Canadian dollars)

As at July 31	2002	2001
Assets		
Current assets		
Cash	$ –	$ 25,759
Note receivable	–	5,000
Short-term investments	27,132	19,718
Accounts receivable	127,132	241,410
Inventories	191,843	271,920
Prepaid expenses	10,235	13,055
	356,342	576,862
Investments	10,275	13,838
Property, Plant and Equipment	638,417	797,951
Other Long-Term Assets	202,346	186,485
	$1,207,380	$1,575,136
Liabilities and shareholders' equity		
Current liabilities		
Bank indebtedness	$ 30,952	$ 32,239
Short-term borrowings	2,967	8,080
Members' demand loan	24,624	35,204
Accounts payable	207,970	216,890
Long-term debt due within one year	17,321	156,514
	283,834	448,927
Long-Term Debt	456,224	549,225
Other Long-Term Liabilities	62,766	75,685
Non-Controlling Interest	1,286	5,863
	804,110	1,079,700
Shareholders' equity		
Share capital	457,692	457,699
Retained Earnings (Deficit)	(54,422)	37,737
	403,270	495,436
	$1,207,380	$1,575,136

References to disclosure notes have been deleted.

Finally, Exhibit 4-4 shows the balance sheet of Shaw Communications Incorporated, active in cable TV Internet access, and satellite services. Notice that capital assets are a major part of the company's asset structure—all those cable installations! But Shaw's largest single asset is *intangible*—broadcast licenses, representing 57% of assets ($4,877,256 ÷ $8,513,001). This balance sheet is more conventional in that it provides subtotals for current assets and liabilities.

What policy choices do these very different companies face when preparing a balance sheet? We saw in the previous chapter that income statement preparation is quite judgemental—now it's time to take a long look at the balance sheet.

EXHIBIT 4-2

BOMBARDIER INCORPORATED
CONSOLIDATED BALANCE SHEET
(stated in millions of Canadian dollars)

as at January 31	2003	2002
Assets		
Cash and cash equivalents	$ 1,043.0	$ 462.8
Receivable	2,349.2	1,902.1
Finance receivable	7,013.3	6,398.3
Assets under operating leases	1,350.9	1,831.2
Inventories	5,821.6	6,176.7
Property, plant and equipment	5,871.0	5,618.3
Goodwill	3,244.9	2,712.9
Other assets	2,315.5	2,140.4
	$29,009.4	$27,242.7
Liabilities		
Short-term borrowings	$ 2,563.6	$ 3,037.0
Advances to/from Bombardier	–	–
Accounts payable and accrued liabilities	9,575.0	8,057.4
Advances and progress billings in excess of related costs	3,816.0	3,291.5
Long-term debt	8,815.1	7,857.7
Other liabilities	1,498.7	1,663.0
	26,268.4	23,906.6
Shareholders' equity	2,741.0	3,336.1
	$29,009.4	$27,242.7

References to disclosure notes have been deleted.

PURPOSE AND LIMITATIONS

The Purpose of the Balance Sheet

The balance sheet *will reflect the unamortized cost of the company's major groups of assets, and the sources used to finance those assets.* If you want to know how Shaw's capital structure is organized, the balance sheet provides this information: long-term debt is 41% of total assets ($3,469,637 ÷ $8,513,001), up from 34% ($3,010,348 ÷ $8,794,956) in the prior year.

The balance sheet can also provide some insight into the *risk profile* of a business and its *financial flexibility.* Are the company's assets old and fully amortized or relatively new? Is the organization in a position to finance new activities with relative ease without incurring excessive debt? These are important questions that the balance sheet helps address. The Saskatchewan Wheat Pool reports lower total assets in 2002, with large reductions in accounts receivable and inventory. At the same time, its cash position has declined and accounts payable have not been materially reduced. Retained earnings has become a deficit. Clearly, the financial position of this company has deteriorated.

While the balance sheet provides some information about actions and strategy over the year, the cash flow statement contains more information about the investing and financing activities of the company; we'll take a look at that statement in Chapter 5.

The balance sheet also reflects *liquidity,* often evaluated with reference to **working capital** (current assets less current liabilities). Working capital may also be evaluated by using more restrictive measures that exclude non-monetary current assets such as inventories.

EXHIBIT 4-3

ROYAL BANK OF CANADA
CONSOLIDATED BALANCE SHEET

(stated in millions of Canadian dollars)

As at October 31	2002	2001
Assets		
Cash resources		
Cash and due from banks	$ 2,534	$ 1,792
Interest-bearing deposits with banks	18,789	15,743
	21,323	17,535
Securities		
Trading account	68,328	58,192
Investment account	25,078	21,877
Loan substitute	394	438
	93,800	80,507
Assets purchased under reverse repurchase agreements	35,831	35,870
Loans		
Residential mortgage	72,840	67,442
Personal	31,956	32,511
Credit card	4,914	4,283
Business and government	61,751	67,152
	171,461	171,388
Allowance for loan losses	(2,203)	(2,278)
	169,258	169,110
Other		
Customers' liability under acceptances	8,051	9,923
Derivative-related amounts	30,258	27,240
Premises and equipment	1,653	1,602
Goodwill	5,004	4,919
Other intangibles	665	619
Other assets	11,113	11,935
	56,744	56,238
	$376,956	$359,260
Liabilities and shareholders' equity		
Deposits		
Personal	$ 101,892	$ 101,381
Business and government	119,591	107,141
Bank	22,003	24,925
	243,486	233,447
Other		
Acceptance	8,051	9,923
Obligations related to securities sold short	19,110	16,443
Obligations related to assets sold under repurchase agreements	21,109	20,864
Derivative-related amounts	32,137	28,646
Other liabilities	26,197	23,780
	106,604	99,656
Subordinated debentures	6,614	6,513
Non-controlling interest in subsidiaries	1,469	1,479
Shareholders' equity		
Capital stock		
Preferred	**1,545**	2,024
Common	**7,057**	6,973
Retained earnings	**10,181**	9,168
	18,783	18,165
	$376,956	$359,260

References to disclosure notes have been deleted.

EXHIBIT 4-4

SHAW COMMUNICATIONS INCORPORATED
CONSOLIDATED BALANCE SHEET

(thousands of Canadian dollars)

As at August 31	2002	2001
Assets		
Current		
Accounts receivable	$ 187,505	$ 189,612
Income taxes recoverable	–	6,267
Inventories	128,811	110,375
Prepaids and other	28,177	24,669
Assets held for sale	–	89,500
	344,493	420,423
Investments and other assets	133,602	550,707
Property, plant and equipment	2,777,697	2,507,923
Deferred charges	234,088	277,780
Intangibles		
Broadcast licenses	4,877,256	5,038,123
Goodwill	145,865	–
	$8,513,001	$8,794,956
Liabilities and shareholders' equity		
Current		
Bank indebtedness	$ 2,303	$ 1,789
Accounts payable and accrued liabilities	511,106	565,961
Income taxes payable	10,631	–
Unearned revenue	88,226	72,593
	612,266	640,343
Long-term debt	3,469,637	3,010,348
Deferred credits	634,735	651,425
Future income taxes	1,006,845	1,196,933
	5,723,483	5,499,049
Commitments and contingencies		
Shareholders' equity		
Share capital		
Class A shares	2,493	2,499
Class B shares	2,107,367	2,106,569
Equity instruments	908,472	1,073,678
Retained earnings (deficit)	(230,327)	111,830
Cumulative translation adjustment	1,513	1,331
	2,789,518	3,295,907
	$8,513,001	$8,794,956

References to disclosure notes have been deleted.

Liquidity is evidence of a company's ability to pay short-term debts from its current assets as well as to meet short-term and long-term obligations. Creditors are obviously interested in assessing liquidity. Beyond this, equity investors are interested in liquidity because it affects dividend payments. Unions examine liquidity to establish bargaining positions. Employees are concerned with the company's continuing ability to pay wages. Liquidity is a major concern to many financial statement users.

return on equity ratio
measure of the historical after-tax return to shareholders for the period; focus is on the common equity; income available to common shareholders is compared to common equity

return on assets ratio
the measure of income before interest expense earned in relation to the assets employed by an entity

The balance sheet also provides data needed to determine *rates of return*, including **return on equity (ROE)**, **return on assets (ROA)**, and a variety of other ratios. Of course, the income statement has to provide the earnings information used to calculate these ratios. Return figures are very important to financial statement users, both lenders and equity investors, as they help determine the company's credit rating and share price. The figures used in ratio calculations will depend on the accounting policies chosen by the company, however, and therefore must be interpreted with caution.

Limitations of the Balance Sheet

A balance sheet based on GAAP has limitations as a result of several aspects of applying generally accepted accounting principles:

AMOUNTS SHOWN ON THE BALANCE SHEET ARE THE RESULT OF THE COMPANY'S REPORTING POLICIES Even within the constraints of GAAP, alternative accounting policies are acceptable. Virtually every amount shown on the balance sheet is the result of a company's chosen accounting policies; different policies will result in different balance sheet amounts. For example, a company's choice of amortization policy (e.g., *straight line or declining balance*) will significantly affect the amounts shown for net capital assets, and thereby the amounts shown for total assets and for net assets (i.e., owners' equity).

THE TYPICAL BALANCE SHEET ALSO INCLUDES MANY ESTIMATED AMOUNTS The amounts reported on the balance sheet are affected not only by accounting *policies*, but also by accounting *estimates*. For example, the amounts shown for capital assets will be affected not only by the application of a given amortization policy (such as straight line), but also by the estimates used in applying the policy, such as each asset's useful life and estimated salvage value. Other examples of estimates include the estimated loss from uncollectible receivables and the estimated liability arising from warranties. The impacts of estimates are difficult, sometimes impossible, to figure out. As we will see, companies must disclose the nature of measurement uncertainty that could affect financial statement elements.

BALANCE SHEET VALUES ARE NOT CURRENT VALUES AND ARE NOT INTENDED FOR VALUATION PURPOSES The balance sheet reports historical cost, which is not always a relevant attribute. Investors and creditors may be far more interested in market values. Market value (or fair value) reporting is not a generally accepted practice in Canada except for certain types of investments, and therefore a company that reports market values in its balance sheet may not be able to receive a clean audit opinion. In a set of GAAP statements, market values can be disclosed, but generally are not. Companies may choose to prepare non-GAAP statements when market value is significantly different than cost and important decisions have to be based on market value, not cost. (Note that certain types of financial institutions are required to use market value for reporting.)

The amounts reported for major asset categories such as plant and equipment may be significantly different than cost, given even a modest level of price changes. Individual companies are affected by this problem differently, depending on the date and rate of capital acquisitions and the level of specific price changes for the types of capital assets they use. Uncritical comparisons between companies can therefore be very misleading.

The cost-based balance sheet can have particularly little relationship to market values when a company's assets are primarily intangible. At least tangible capital assets are valued at their fair value on the date of acquisition; the often negligible *cost* of many *internally generated* intangible assets is not even close to their fair value at acquisition. For example, a patent is often recorded only at the legal cost involved in registration. Return figures and ratio comparisons are questionable in these circumstances.

CERTAIN ASSETS AND LIABILITIES SIMPLY DO NOT APPEAR ON THE BALANCE SHEET Remember the recognition criteria that must be met for an element to be recognized: an item must be an element, be measurable, and cash flows must be probable. If recognition criteria are not met, elements are not recognized. Assets that do not appear on the balance sheet include intangible assets acquired at no ascertainable cost, such as the abilities and morale of the workforce, customer loyalty, or brand names. These assets have future benefit—usually future revenue cash flows—but cannot be recognized either because the future cash flows are not measurable or because the future cash flows are not probable. As another example, research costs fail recognition criteria at acquisition and must be expensed.

Significant tangible assets may not appear on the balance sheet because they are rented or leased rather than being owned. Only certain types of lease arrangements are recognized on the balance sheet; most are not. An airline, for example, may lease most or all of its aircraft, with the result that none of the planes appear on its balance sheet. Clearly, however, the airline has to have the planes in order to operate—they are necessary capital assets, but are not recorded. Again, these financial statement elements are excluded from the financial statements because they do not meet the recognition criteria. Measurement is usually the problem—things that cannot be quantified are not recorded.

On the liability side, omitted items include some types of leases, hazardous waste cleanups whose cost cannot be estimated, and unrecorded commitments, such as purchase commitments. Again, these financial statement elements are excluded from the financial statements because they do not meet the recognition criteria. Measurement is usually the problem—things that cannot be quantified are not recorded.

NUMBERS ARE CONSOLIDATED A company can be in one business or be diversified. The Saskatchewan Wheat Pool, for example, operates in one industry. On the other hand, Bombardier operates in four major sectors, which are quite different. If users are relying on balance sheet information to portray relationships, those relationships may well be different for each individual sector.

Adding the data together is problematic, as it may mask important information. Bombardier, for example, presents two additional balance sheets (not reproduced here) beside its consolidated balance sheet—one for its manufacturing operations, and one for the real estate and financial services sector. Many companies rely on disaggregated, or segmented, information to get around this dilemma; we'll talk about these disclosures later in this chapter.

Consolidated statements also do not tell creditors what assets are available to satisfy their claims. A creditor, whether a trade supplier or a lender, has recourse only to the assets owned by the legal entity to which credit has been extended. Assets held by other corporations within the consolidated accounting entity cannot be claimed. It is not unusual for one corporation in a consolidated group to go bankrupt while other corporations in the group remain solvent. The creditors of the bankrupt corporation would be out of luck, if they based their lending decisions only on consolidated statements!

FORMATTING CHOICES

Many presentation issues are open to choice by the company. We reviewed some choice issues in the last chapter, such as choice of year-end, reporting currency, language, etc. Some additional issues are unique to the balance sheet.

Form of Presentation

The **financing form** follows the classic accounting identity, A = L + OE. This format emphasizes the means used to finance the organization's assets. Funds must be raised from creditors (liabilities) or from owners (owners' equity), often by retaining the organization's earnings. Alternatively, the basic accounting identity can be rearranged to reflect the owners' viewpoint, in the **net assets form**. Thus, A − L = OE. That is, net assets, or assets less liabilities, are totalled on the balance sheet to a number that is equal to owners' equity.

According to *Financial Reporting in Canada 2002*, the financing form is the dominant choice, used by virtually all of the 200 surveyed public companies. Two versions exist—one lists assets at the top of the statement, followed vertically by liabilities and then equities. This is called the *report format*, which is used by 97% of the surveyed public companies. Alternatively, assets can be listed on the left of the statement and liabilities and equities on the right. This is called the *account format*.

The Saskatchewan Wheat Pool balance sheet in Exhibit 4-1 has a total for assets and another for liabilities plus equities, so it is in the financing form. It lists assets, then liabilities, then equities down the statement, so it is in report format. The other examples are also in financing form and report format.

Classification and Aggregation

To make accounting information as understandable and usable by decision-makers as possible, items are grouped and arranged in the balance sheet according to certain guidelines. Some of these groupings are non-judgemental, as companies have little choice but to comply with generally accepted practice—users have certain expectations, after all. Other display decisions are very subjective.

In Canadian practice, assets typically are classified and presented in *decreasing order of liquidity*, or convertibility into cash. Those items nearest to cash, that is, those that can be readily converted to cash at any time without restriction, are ranked first. Assets with the least liquidity, or least likely to be converted to cash, are listed last.

Liabilities are generally classified and presented based on *time to maturity*. Thus, obligations currently due are listed first, and those carrying the most distant maturity dates are listed last.

Owners' equity items are classified and presented in *order of permanence*. Thus, paid-in capital accounts, which typically change the least, should be listed first. Equity accounts used to report accumulated earnings and profit distributions are listed last.

current ratio

current assets divided by current liabilities; one measure of short-term solvency

CURRENT ASSETS AND LIABILITIES The most common groupings on the balance sheet are current assets and current liabilities; the net amount of current assets minus current liabilities is called "working capital." Minimum working capital ratios (e.g., a minimum **current ratio**) are often stipulated in loan agreements. It's easier for financial statement users to look at working capital when the company provides the current asset and current liability subtotals.

While most companies group current assets and liabilities, not all follow this practice. For example, Bombardier presents an unclassified balance sheet, claiming that each of its major sectors of activity has its own operating cycle and therefore that the aggregated totals lack meaning. Banks are not required to segregate assets as current or non-current according to the accounting requirements of the Superintendent of Financial Institutions Canada.

Current assets include cash and other assets that are reasonably expected to be realized in cash or to be sold or consumed during the normal operating cycle of the business or within one year from the balance sheet date, whichever is longer. The normal **operating cycle** of a business is the average length of time from the expenditure of cash for inventory, to sale, to accounts receivable, and finally back to cash. This is sometimes called the cash-to-cash cycle. Almost all companies use one year as the time period for classifying items as current or long term because either the operating cycle is less than one year or the length of the operating cycle may be difficult to measure reliably.

Judgement is required in defining the "normal operating cycle" and elements "reasonably expected to be realized in cash." When there is uncertainty, management may be inclined to classify certain items as current assets in order to produce a positive effect on working capital. For example, an investment in debt or equity securities of another company could be classified as a current or non-current asset, depending on the intended holding period and on the likely saleability of the securities. The placement of this asset on a company's balance sheet could be based on the actual intention of management or, alternatively and inappropriately, on management's desire to show its accounts in a better light; this is a problem both for the auditors and for external decision-makers.

Current liabilities are those obligations that are due within one year or one operating cycle, whichever is longer. Current liabilities include the typical range of accounts payable, including accrued amounts, payroll, taxes, and so on. Also included is unearned revenue, which is an obligation to provide service, not cash. The current portion of long-term debt is an important element of current liabilities.

EXHIBIT 4-5

TYPICAL BALANCE SHEET CLASSIFICATIONS

The classification and presentation order below are representative of current reporting practice and terminology.

A. ASSETS

1. **Current assets**
   - **a.** Cash
   - **b.** Short-term investments
   - **c.** Receivables
   - **d.** Inventories
   - **e.** Prepayments (also called prepaid expenses)
   - **f.** Other current assets
2. **Non-current assets**
   - **a.** Investments and funds
   - **b.** Tangible capital assets (also called property, plant, and equipment, or fixed assets)
   - **c.** Intangible capital assets
   - **d.** Long-term prepayments or deferred charges
   - **e.** Other assets

B. LIABILITIES

1. **Current liabilities** (including the current portion of long-term liabilities)
2. **Long-term liabilities** (including share equity elements that have the characteristics of debt)
3. **Future income tax**
4. **Long-term deferred credits**

C. NON-CONTROLLING INTEREST IN SUBSIDIARIES

D. SHAREHOLDERS' EQUITY

1. **Contributed (or paid-in) capital**
   - **a.** Share capital
   - **b.** Debt elements that have the characteristics of equity
   - **c.** Other contributed (or paid-in) capital
2. **Retained earnings**
3. **Other equity items** (primarily deferred investment and foreign exchange gains and losses)

OTHER CLASSIFICATIONS Other classifications on the balance sheet are basically the major asset, liability, and equity items—investments, tangible and intangible capital assets, long-term debt, and so on. Classifications are strongly influenced by the unique characteristics of each industry and each business enterprise. You can readily see by comparing Exhibit 4-2 and Exhibit 4-3 that the balance sheet of a manufacturing company reflects different classifications from those of a bank.

In these classifications, there is some choice, while some accounting policy established by standards and industry norms. "Typical" balance sheet categories are listed in Exhibit 4-5. Next, we'll investigate each of these categories individually, looking at their presentation on the balance sheet and disclosure notes.

CONCEPT REVIEW

1. Why may a company's major assets not appear on the balance sheet?
2. What interpretive problems arise from the fact that the financial statements of public companies are consolidated?
3. What is the definition of "current" for current assets and current liabilities?

SPECIFIC BALANCE SHEET ITEMS

Most of this book is devoted to examining financial statement elements; their recognition, valuation, and required disclosures. This chapter provides a review of many of the facets of the balance sheet that you learned in introductory accounting, and it also introduces some additional subtleties of which you may not be aware. This overview of balance sheet items can't replace the detailed study that lies ahead of you. Instead, try to gain an appreciation for the overall nature of balance sheet accounts and disclosures.

Assets

In most industries, assets are classified into a minimum of two categories: (1) current assets, and (2) other assets, including capital assets, both tangible and intangible. Other categories are used if there are enough items to warrant a separate category instead of including them under the other assets classification. The major categories and the items included therein are described below. Later chapters discuss each type of asset in more detail.

Current Assets

CASH Cash available for operating activities is a current asset. Accounts held for designated purposes (e.g., bond sinking funds) are long term. Some companies lump **cash equivalents** with the cash figure (see the Bombardier balance sheet, Exhibit 4-2). Cash equivalents are specifically defined as short-term (usually no longer than three months), interest-bearing investments, providing little risk of market value fluctuations.

SHORT-TERM INVESTMENTS These investments must be *both* readily marketable *and* intended to be held only for the short term. Investments in debt securities, such as Canadian government treasury bills *(T-bills)*, money market funds, and commercial paper are **short-term investments**. As noted, some short-term investments are cash equivalents that companies group with the cash account. Others are shown separately as short-term investments. Short-term investments also include corporate equity securities. Any significant amounts of short-term investments in debt or in equity securities should be listed separately among the current assets.

financial instrument
any contract that gives rise to both a financial asset of one party and a financial liability or equity instrument to the other party

Short-term investments are reported at their current market value. This is a recent change in Canadian GAAP, as valuation at cost, or the lower of cost and market, was the norm to the end of 2006. These investments are **financial instruments**, and, as such, information concerning their terms and conditions, interest rates, credit risk, and market values should be disclosed. Financial instruments and related disclosures are discussed later in this chapter.

accounts receivable
cash due to a corporation from customers because of purchases of goods or services on credit

RECEIVABLES **Accounts receivable**, and notes receivable, should be reported net of estimated uncollectible amounts. Any receivables pledged as security for an obligation of the firm should be disclosed. Receivables are also financial instruments, and appropriate disclosures are required.

inventories
goods held for resale (finished goods) or use in operations (supplies)

INVENTORIES **Inventories** usually are reported at the lower of cost or market (LCM). In addition, the valuation basis and the completion stage should be indicated (e.g., raw materials, work in process, or finished goods). In some sectors of the economy, inventories are valued at market value or net realizable value. Examples include most commodities (e.g., precious metals, copper, many agricultural products) and securities held by investment companies (e.g., mutual funds). Inventories may also be reported at cost plus profits recognized when revenue is recognized throughout the earnings process, such as in long-term construction projects.

PREPAYMENTS Prepayments, or prepaid expenses, are cash outlays made in advance of receipt of service. Rent paid in May for the month of June is an example. A short-term prepayment should be classified as a current asset, whereas a long-term prepayment should be classified as a non-current asset. Prepaid expenses are current assets because an investment is made by paying cash in advance, thereby reducing cash outlays for the coming reporting period.

OTHER CURRENT ASSETS Are there any other assets being held that are expected to produce cash in the next fiscal year? If so, they are part of current assets. For example, if the capital assets of a discontinued division are sold after the balance sheet date but before the date the financial statements are issued (a **subsequent event**), the assets are appropriately included in current assets.

subsequent events
events that occur after the year-end but before the financial statements are issued; may be recorded or disclosed depending on nature

Non-Current Assets

Assets are non-current if

1. Assets will not be used up in the next operating cycle or in one year, whichever is longer, or
2. Management plans to retain the assets beyond the next year or operating cycle, whichever is longer.

TANGIBLE CAPITAL ASSETS **Tangible capital assets** include all property, plant, equipment, and resources that are used in the company's production or service process, either directly or indirectly. The category does not include property that is held for resale. Historically, tangible capital assets have been called **fixed assets** because of their relative permanence, or by the more descriptive term property, plant, and equipment (PP&E). A wide variety of terminology is found in practice.

Tangible capital assets include both (1) items that are amortized, such as buildings, machinery, and fixtures, mineral deposits and timber stands, and (2) items that are not subject to amortization, such as land. Tangible capital assets also include certain leased assets if the lease arrangement is deemed to be a method of financing a permanent acquisition of the facilities.

The balance sheet or the related notes should report additional information on capital assets, including the following:

- Balances of major classes of capital assets.
- Accumulated amortization, by major class of capital assets.
- A description of the methods used in computing amortization for the major classes of capital assets.

Tangible capital assets are usually shown on the balance sheet at their original cash equivalent cost less any accumulated amortization (or depreciation) to date.

INTANGIBLE CAPITAL ASSETS Intangible capital assets are long-lived assets that lack physical substance. Examples of intangible assets include brand names, copyrights, franchises, licences, patents, software, subscription lists, and trademarks. These assets usually are reported as a separate element in the balance sheet, although sometimes companies will combine the tangible and intangible capital assets on the balance sheet and provide a breakdown in the notes.

By convention, amortization is deducted directly from the intangible asset account instead of being recorded in a contra account (i.e., *accumulated amortization*) as is done with tangible capital assets. Intangible assets are shown net of accumulated amortization on the balance sheet and in the notes. The accumulated amount of amortization usually is disclosed in the notes or elsewhere in the financial statements.

Some important intangible assets are not on company balance sheets at all. This is because intangibles are usually capitalized *only* when they are purchased as part of the acquisition of another firm or when expenditures such as legal fees are made in regard to them.

INVESTMENTS AND FUNDS Accounting for investments is in a state of flux as this text is written, since new classification rules will be effective at the end of 2006. The new rules will require the following for investments:

- *Long-term investments in the share capital or debt instruments of another company that are available for sale but not intended for sale in the year.* Such investments should be recorded at fair market value. (Cost was the norm for these investments to the end of 2005.)
- *Long-term investments in the bonds of another company that will be held to maturity.* Any unamortized premium is added to the investment, and any unamortized discount is subtracted.
- *Investments in subsidiaries, including long-term receivables from subsidiaries.* If the statements are consolidated, these accounts are eliminated.
- *Investments in the shares of another company where significant influence is present.* Such investments are carried at cost plus unremitted earnings, using the equity method.
- *Funds set aside for long-term future use, such as bond sinking funds, expansion funds, share retirement funds, and long-term savings deposits.* Funds are shown at the accumulated amount in the fund—contributions plus interest earned to date.
- *Investments in tangible capital assets, such as land and buildings, that represent excess capacity and that are not being used in operations.* These assets are sometimes left in the tangible asset section, but segregated. Although capital investments are usually shown at their original cost less amortization, they may be recorded at market value if market value is lower than cost and the impairment of value is judged (by management) to be permanent.

The basis of valuation being used for long-term investments should be disclosed. Major classifications of long-term investments should be disclosed separately. Extensive disclosure is required for many kinds of investments.

LONG-TERM DEFERRED CHARGES Deferred charges may be the result of the prepayment of long-term expenses. These expenses have *reliably determinable* future economic benefits useful in earning future revenues. On this basis, they are viewed as assets until they are used. The only conceptual difference between a prepaid expense (classified as a current asset) and a deferred charge is the length of time over which the amount is amortized.

Also included in the deferred charges category are such things as organization costs, machinery rearrangement costs, bond issue costs, and pension costs paid in advance. Deferred charges are sometimes included in the other assets category, but should be disclosed separately. They are items that have economic benefit and qualify for deferral because they will benefit future periods.

The nature of these items, their valuation base, and the method and period of amortization should be disclosed.

OTHER ASSETS The other assets classification is used for assets that are not easily included under alternative asset classifications. Examples include long-term receivables from company officers and assets of discontinued operations held for eventual sale. Long-term investments, special funds, and long-term deferred charges often are lumped together (though separately listed) under the category of other assets. Companies should not use the classification of "other" to hide or disguise certain assets. The nature of, and valuation basis for, these assets should be disclosed. If a reported asset has no future economic benefit, it must be written off and reported in the income statement as a loss.

Liabilities

CURRENT LIABILITIES The current liabilities section of the balance sheet includes all obligations of the company that are due within one year or one operating cycle, whichever period is longer. Commonly found elements include

- Accounts payable for goods and services that enter into the operating cycle of the business (sometimes called "trade payables").
- Special short-term liabilities (i.e., payables) for non-operating items and services.
- Short-term notes payable.

- Short-term bank debt.
- Current maturities of long-term liabilities (including the current portion of capital lease obligations).
- Unearned revenue (such as rent collected in advance) that will be earned within the next year or operating cycle, whichever is longer.
- Accrued expenses for payroll, interest, and taxes.
- Future income taxes relating to current assets and current liabilities.

LONG-TERM LIABILITIES A long-term (non-current) liability is an obligation that is due beyond the next operating cycle or during the next reporting year, whichever is longer. All liabilities not appropriately classified as current liabilities are reported as long term. Typical **long-term liabilities** are bonds payable, long-term notes payable, pension liabilities, deferred long-term revenues (advances from customers), and long-term capital lease obligations. Most long-term liabilities are recorded at the exchange value of the assets or services received.

Long-term liabilities also will include any financial instrument (or the portion of a complex instrument) that has the legal characteristics of debt, even though the instrument may be described by the company as share equity. Financial instruments are discussed a little later in the chapter under "Specific Significant Disclosures."

Note disclosures for long-term debt can be extensive, especially if the debt issue contains unusual features. Disclosure of terms and conditions includes the interest rate, maturity date, sinking fund requirements, redemption and conversion provisions, security, and loan covenants, if applicable. Effective interest rates and fair values should be disclosed. Finally, the aggregate payments (cash flow) required over each of the next five years should be disclosed.

INCOME TAX Income tax is paid on the basis of revenues and expenses that comprise *taxable income*. Revenue and expenses on the income statement may be different, due to the timing of recognition. Income tax *expense* is based on those revenues and expenses that will be included in taxable income, even if they will be included in future years. Therefore, income tax expense consists of two components:

1. Tax payable to the government for the current year, known as "current income tax," and
2. Tax that pertains to revenues and expenses that were recognized on the income statement in the current period but have a future tax impact, known as "future income taxes."

Future income tax is segregated into current and long-term portions. Future income tax relates to current assets or liabilities classified as current. The remainder is classified as long term.

The future income tax accounts can have either a debit or credit balance. A debit balance in the long-term account is shown under other assets. A credit balance is shown as a long-term liability. Credit balances are more common than debit balances.

Future income tax, as defined by the *CICA Handbook*, is measured using the *accrual method* and, if it has a credit balance, it is a liability. However, it is qualitatively different from other liabilities in that there is no creditor and no amount actually owing at the balance sheet date. Therefore, many companies show it as a separate item following long-term debt or, if the balance is relatively small, in other liabilities.

The current Canadian practice is the same as U.S. practice and is in agreement with International Accounting Standards. However, many major countries still use an alternate measurement policy, called the "deferral method." Under this method, a long-term credit balance of *deferred income taxes* is shown below the liabilities section and before shareholders' equity.

LONG-TERM DEFERRED CREDITS Deferred credits can arise from several sources. One example occurs in pension accounting, when the expense recorded is greater than the payments made to date. Another example is revenue that has been received (i.e., as a deposit) but that will not become earned revenue within the next year.

NON-CONTROLLING INTEREST IN SUBSIDIARIES Financial statements of public companies are almost always *consolidated* statements. Consolidated statements include all of the assets and liabilities of the parent and its subsidiaries. However, sometimes the parent does not own 100% of the subsidiary. The amount not owned by the parent is called the *non-controlling interest.*

In order to make the parent's consolidated balance sheet actually balance, it is necessary to include an amount on the right side of the balance sheet to recognize the proportionate part of the subsidiary's net assets that are not owned by the parent. For example, suppose one company controls 80% of the shares of another company. The parent will combine 100% of the subsidiary's assets with the parent's assets even though the parent holds only an 80% equity interest. The 20% equity of the outside shareholders must be reported on the right side of the balance sheet to make it balance.

Non-controlling interest (sometimes called *minority interest*) is not usually shown as a liability because the parent company doesn't owe anything to the outside investors. Non-controlling interests are not shown as shareholder's equity because they represent outsiders' direct share interest in a subsidiary, and do not represent the equity of the parent's owners. Therefore, this amount traditionally has been shown *between* liabilities and shareholders' equity.

Royal Bank (Exhibit 4-3) shows non-controlling interest after liabilities and before shareholders' equity. In contrast, the Saskatchewan Wheat Pool (Exhibit 4-1) adds non-controlling interest into the total liabilities.

Shareholders' Equity

Shareholders' equity is a residual interest, but includes three basic components:

1. contributed (or paid-in) capital
2. retained earnings
3. other comprehensive income

CONTRIBUTED CAPITAL Because of legal requirements, contributed capital is subclassified to reflect detailed sources. For corporations, the most commonly reported subclassifications are

a. share capital.
b. contributed surplus.

The breakdown between these two subclassifications is generally of little significance; they tend to be defined more by legal specifications than by substantive accounting measurement. In some jurisdictions, the amount of share capital is designated as *legal capital* or *stated capital*, but with little legal consequence.

SHARE CAPITAL Share capital is the paid-in value or par value of the issued or outstanding preferred and common shares of the corporation. This amount is not available for dividend declarations.

Each share class should be reported at its paid-in amount, or, in the case of par value shares, at par value. Par value shares are found only in a few provincial jurisdictions in Canada, but may be found in other jurisdictions (e.g., in the United States, United Kingdom, and Hong Kong). Details of the terms and conditions of each class of share capital must be reported separately, including the number of shares authorized, issued, outstanding, and subscribed; also disclosed are conversion features, callability, preferences, dividend rates, and any other special features. Changes in share capital accounts during the period must be disclosed, along with outstanding options.

Share capital also will include any financial instrument (or the portion of a complex instrument) that might be described by the company as debt but that lacks the legal characteristics of debt. Financial instruments are discussed a little later in the chapter under "Specific Significant Disclosures."

CONTRIBUTED SURPLUS Contributed surplus arises from such transactions as the retirement of shares for less than the original investment made and capital arising from donations or recapitalizations. Details and changes during the period should be disclosed.

For corporations that issue par value shares, contributed surplus also includes an account called "contributed capital in excess of par." If shares are issued for an amount in excess of par value, additional contributed capital is created. Details and changes during the period should be disclosed.

RETAINED EARNINGS Retained earnings is essentially a corporation's accumulated net earnings since the company's inception less dividends paid out. In many corporations, retained earnings is the largest amount in the owners' equity section. A negative balance in retained earnings is called a **deficit** and usually arises when a company experiences continuing operating losses.

Retained earnings may be subdivided into two or more accounts through an appropriation or restriction. The additional accounts are shown on the balance sheet or the total can be included on the balance sheet and the appropriation can be disclosed.

Such items create other comprehensive income, an equity item. There are two main sources of other comprehensive income, foreign exchange amounts and unrealized investment appreciation.

OTHER COMPREHENSIVE INCOME Standard-setters occasionally designate an item to be excluded from income and retained earnings.

For example, assume that a company has a subsidiary in Mexico that keeps its records and operates in pesos. At year-end, the financial statements of the subsidiary are translated from the peso to the Canadian dollar so that the subsidiary can be consolidated. Since different exchange rates are used for different financial statement elements according to the accounting rules, an overall exchange gain or loss results to balance the statements. For independent subsidiaries, the cumulative amount of the gain or loss is isolated as a separate component of equity. It will be recognized on the income statement only if the subsidiary is sold or liquidated. In Exhibit 4-4, Shaw Communications reports a credit balance of $1.5 million in this category in its shareholders' equity at fiscal year-end 2002.

Beginning after 2006, certain investments are valued at fair market value, and the unrealized difference between cost and market value is also isolated in equity until realization. We will explore these issues in depth in Chapter 11.

Offsetting Assets and Liabilities

offset (netting)
showing one account less another at their net balance in the financial statements; allowed only if the legal right to offset exists and the entity plans to settle on a net basis

Normally, assets and liabilities should not be offset against one another. Offsetting is a procedure by which a liability is subtracted from an asset or vice versa and the resulting net amount is disclosed. Such practice circumvents full disclosure and could permit a business to show more favourable ratios. Offsetting is permissible only when

- A legal right to offset exists, *and*
- The entity plans to settle the items on a net basis or at least simultaneously.

For instance, it would be permissible to offset a $5,000 overdraft in one bank account against another account reflecting $8,000 on deposit in that same bank, since the bank can legally offset the two deposit accounts. In contrast, it is not acceptable to offset a sinking fund investment account against its related long-term loan, as the company does not have the legal right to offset without creditor acceptance.

disclosure notes
explanatory notes to the financial statements that include information on accounting policy and description of financial statement elements, recognized and unrecognized

CONCEPT REVIEW

1. What is the difference between tangible and intangible capital assets?
2. In what order are assets normally presented on a Canadian company's balance sheet?
3. What types of credit balances are reported on the balance sheet between liabilities and shareholders' equity in international and Canadian practice?

DISCLOSURE NOTES

Disclosure notes are an integral part of the financial statements and must be presented if the statements are to be complete. If the statements are audited, so are the notes. Disclosure notes can adhere to minimal disclosure requirements or be far more extensive; this is management's decision based on corporate reporting objectives and the needs of user groups. Unlike the purely quantitative financial statements, information in disclosure notes can be provided in qualitative terms. Readers can then make their own assessment of the potential quantitative ramifications of the information presented. Notes are sometimes complex and highly technical.

General Classification of Disclosure Notes

In general, notes can fulfill many functions:[1]

1. *Provide accounting policy information that allows users to evaluate data, including the ability to compare data to other companies' and between years.* Section 1505 of the *CICA Handbook*, "Disclosure of Accounting Policies," recommends disclosure of accounting policies used by the firm. The information may be presented as the first note to the financial statements, or in a separate summary of significant accounting policies. Accounting policies include specific accounting principles and the methods of applying these principles. Disclosure should explain important judgements that involve

   - a selection from acceptable alternatives
   - principles and methods specific to the industry in which the company operates

   The specific items found in this disclosure note will vary from firm to firm. Summaries of significant accounting policies often include descriptions of policies for

   - basis of consolidation
   - accounting policies for investments
   - revenue and expense recognition
   - inventory valuation
   - property, plant, and equipment (i.e., amortization policy)
   - intangible assets (valuation and amortization policies)
   - deferred charges
   - deferred credits
   - income tax
   - foreign exchange

   Changes in policy and significant changes in estimate must also be described in disclosure notes, along with the impact on earnings and net assets, if ascertainable.

2. *Describe recognized items.* Some items that have been recognized in the financial statements should be described, especially those that are unusual in nature or not expected to continue. The notes in this regard contribute to the predictive power of the financial statements. Sometimes, though, even the *nature* of a recognized item is mysterious and must be described. For example, the Royal Bank's "Assets purchased under reverse repurchase agreements" are, the notes tell us, "short-term purchases of securities under agreements to resell." That is, the Royal Bank has purchased, or invested in, a note or other security from a company and the company or a third party has agreed to repurchase, or redeem, the investment at a particular time at a particular price. This is another form of lending.

   Another type of note that describes a recognized item provides *disaggregation.* Some things are added together on the balance sheet to reduce clutter, but more detail has to be provided to comply with accounting standards or to convey important information to users. For example, the Saskatchewan Wheat Pool reports the following breakdown of its aggregated inventory balance sheet amount, in thousands of dollars, in the notes:

---

[1] This general categorization of notes is adapted from the work of Mary Barth and Christine Murphy, in "Required Financial Statement Disclosures: Purposes, Subject, Number and Trends," *Accounting Horizons* (December 1994), pp. 1–22.

6. Inventories

	2000	1999
Grain inventory	82,412	68,682
Agri-products	74,618	99,961
Agri-food processing inventory	16,890	73,426
Livestock production and marketing inventory	17,155	28,021
Other inventory	768	1,830
	$ 191,843	$271,920

3. *Describe unrecognized items.* Liabilities such as contingent liabilities that are not probable, or are probable but not measurable, do not qualify for recognition. It is left to the notes to describe the situation, letting the users assess risks for themselves.

   Other examples of unrecognized items include dividends in arrears, liabilities for environmental cleanups, and so on. For example, Bombardier discloses that

> In connection with the sale of aircraft, Bombardier provides credit guarantees in the form of guarantees of lease payments as well as services related to the remarketing of aircraft. These guarantees are issued for the benefit of certain customers or providers of financing to customers. The maximum credit risk as of January 31, 2003 from these guarantees, maturing in different periods up to 2022, was $1,049.4 million. Substantially all financial support involving potential credit risk lies with commercial airline customers. The credit risk relating to two commercial airline customers accounted for 33% of the total maximum credit risk at January 31, 2003.

Shaw Communications discloses in its notes that the company has

- Various long-term commitments for the maintenance of satellite transponders, lease of transmission facilities and premises, and
- Committed to purchase and/or lease a number of ku-band transponders.

4. *Provide information regarding future cash flows.* Financial statements are often used to predict future cash flows; often specific information regarding future cash flows is required by accounting standards, or the company deems such disclosure desirable. Companies must disclose principal payments due for the next five years for long-term debt, minimum lease payments for a five-year period, and so on. Bombardier reports, in $ millions:

> The repayment requirements on the long-term debt during the next five fiscal years are as follows:

2004	$ 1.992.2
2005	897.3
2006	573.0
2007	1,503.0
2008	1,120.0

5. *Provide alternate measurement bases for recognized and unrecognized amounts.* Does the company think that historic costs are irrelevant and market values important? Are they constrained to GAAP for some reason and thus are reporting cost? Not to worry—market value can be disclosed. In fact, companies are required to disclose market values, however defined, for many items. Shaw Communications discloses in its notes the market value of certain long-term investments. Shaw's investment in Motorola Inc. is reported at $8,925 (thousand) but has a market value of $33,858 (thousand).

6. *Provide measures to help investors assess return on investment.* Preferred share dividend rates and effective yields on debt all help investors assess their return on investment.

Specific Significant Disclosures

There are several disclosure requirements that are significant enough to warrant separate discussion, either because they are new or are relatively complex.

FINANCIAL INSTRUMENTS **Financial instruments** have special disclosure and presentation requirements. Financial instruments include

- *Financial assets:* basically *cash* or *contractual rights to receive cash*, or *equity investments* in other firms. Thus, in addition to cash, all types of receivables, loans, and investments in shares are financial assets.
- *Financial liabilities:* those that establish a contractual obligation to *deliver cash*, and encompass most liabilities as we know them, except obligations to provide services, such as warranty liabilities and unearned revenues. (Financial assets and liabilities also include more complicated risk management tools, including swap and option agreements.)
- *Equity instruments:* those that confer a residual interest in net assets of an entity.

The thrust of the AcSB's recommendations is to classify each financial instrument in accordance with its substance. For example, suppose that a company issues preferred shares that carry a legal obligation both to pay the annual dividend and to redeem the share at the investor's request. *Legal obligation to pay* is the defining characteristic of a liability. Therefore, the preferred shares should be reported in the balance sheet as a liability (its substance) instead of as equity (its nominal form).

Some financial instruments have features that reflect characteristics of both debt and equity. In that case, the instrument may need to be broken apart (for financial reporting purposes) into its component parts. For example, suppose that a company has convertible bonds with a legal obligation for the issuer to pay the annual interest, but the investors can request common shares to "repay" the principal at maturity if they wish. The interest flow is a legal obligation, and therefore constitutes debt. The principal amount is debt, but has an option on equity, however. For financial reporting purposes, the two components of the instrument will be segregated on the balance sheet—the debt portion is clearly long-term debt, while the value of the option is owners' equity.

A company must disclose the characteristics of its financial instruments:

1. *Terms and conditions.* Details regarding the contractual terms for all financial assets, liabilities, and equity instruments should be contained in the disclosure notes. This includes principal amounts, dates of maturity or repricing, stated interest rates, and any other information that is relevant to predicting future cash flow related to the item. If the financial instrument is complicated, this disclosure can be extensive.
2. *Interest rate.* The effective interest rate should be disclosed for financial assets and liabilities. Thus, if the stated interest rate is different from the market rate, the true return or cost to the company must be clearly disclosed. Also required are maturity or repricing dates.
3. *Credit risk.* Financial assets, both accounts and loans receivable, carry credit risk. The maximum credit risk exposure and significant concentrations of credit risk should be disclosed.
4. *Fair value.* The fair value of each class of financial asset and liability should be disclosed, unless fair value is impossible to determine. In these circumstances, data related to fair value should be disclosed in as much detail as possible.

If you compare these disclosures to the general classification of disclosure notes above, you'll find that they are quite similar: information regarding cash flows, alternate valuation, rates of return, and so on. The financial instruments disclosures are interesting in that they extend fair value disclosures to broad classes of balance sheet items. The financial instrument disclosures also apply to items that are currently unrecognized on the financial statements, such as options and swap agreements. The Royal Bank includes two pages of densely packed notes outlining specifics related to derivative financial instruments, and a further 1.5 pages laying out the estimated fair value of financial instruments.

SEGMENT DISCLOSURES Consolidated financial information may mask important trends, risks, and opportunities for a diversified company. Therefore, *public companies* are required to disaggregate their reported results by geographical region and by business segment.

The AcSB has provided guidelines for reporting segmented information in Section 1701 of the *CICA Handbook*. Every public company must identify its various operating segments—enough segments to explain 75% of its total revenue. Sometimes this is easier said than done. Is an integrated oil company in exploration, refining, and distribution industries, or just in the oil industry? The company must report selected information such as revenues, profits, and assets for each segment. In addition, information about the geographic spread of its operations and customer base must be disclosed.

The company must reconcile the disaggregated data back to the numbers reported on the primary financial statements, to avoid confusion. The segment disclosures can be quite long and complex if the company is involved in a large number of segments.

Bombardier discloses three business segments—aerospace, recreational products, and transportation. The segmented disclosures indicate, for example, that aerospace accounts for 47% of revenues, and 65% of assets, but reported a loss before tax of $1.3 million. Other segments earned a positive $0.5 million. Bombardier also discloses its revenue and assets for 14 specific countries and four regional groups in other countries. Canada accounts for 67% of assets but only 6% of revenue!

RELATED PARTY TRANSACTIONS When a firm engages in a transaction where one of the parties has the ability to influence the actions and policies of the other, the transaction is termed a **related party transaction**. Such transactions cannot be assumed to be at arm's length because the conditions necessary for a competitive, free-market interaction are not likely to be present. Related parties include management, individuals, and/or corporations with significant shareholdings; other corporations with common major shareholders; family members of related parties; etc. There can be a large number of related parties!

Accounting standards require that related party transactions be recorded at *carrying value*, which is the *book value of the transferor*. Cost would be carrying value for inventory, net book value for capital assets, and so on. Carrying value is considered appropriate because no transaction of substance has taken place—a different related party simply owns the asset in question. However, related party transactions must be recorded at the *exchange value* (usually fair market value) if the transaction is made in the normal course of business. That is, a regular sale of inventory that happened to be to a sister company would be recorded at the exchange value, not carrying value. The exchange amount is also used to value the transaction if the transaction is monetary (that is, if money changes hands), the change of ownership interest is substantive, and the exchange amount can be verified with reference to independent evidence.

Unfortunately, financial statement users tend to assume that all transactions are recorded at fair market value, and the presence of related party transactions may make the financial statements difficult to interpret. Accordingly, the following disclosures are recommended for these transactions:

- The nature of the relationship(s) involved.
- A description of the nature of the transactions, including the dollar amounts, and the measurement basis used.
- Any amounts due to or from related parties as of the balance sheet date, and the terms and conditions.
- Any contingencies or contractual obligations with related parties.

The disclosure of related party transactions is intended to alert financial statement readers to the existence of these relationships, either individual or corporate. The disclosures do not include any measurement of the fair value of transactions (as opposed to the recorded value of the transactions), and therefore there is little opportunity for readers to judge the impact of the non-arm's length transactions on the reporting enterprise's financial statements.

contingency
an event that will occur only if another event occurs; as a liability, may be recorded or disclosed depending on its nature

CONTINGENCIES A **contingency** is an event or transaction that will occur only if some other event happens. For example, a civil lawsuit poses a contingent gain for the plaintiff and a contingent loss for the defendant. However, the parties will not know whether they have a gain or a loss until the court reaches a decision. Generally speaking, a contingent loss should be accrued in the financial statements when both of the following conditions are met:

1. It is likely that a future event will confirm that an asset has been impaired or a liability incurred at the date of the financial statements.
2. The amount of the loss can be reasonably estimated.

Few situations meet both conditions and therefore few contingent losses are recognized in the financial statements. If a loss is probable or estimable but not both, or if there is at least a reasonable possibility that a liability may have been incurred, the nature of the contingency must be disclosed in a note along with an estimate of the possible loss or the range of the possible loss if an estimate can be made. Most companies refrain from estimating any expected loss, arguing that

- The situation does not meet the required reasonable probability level, *and*
- It is not possible to estimate the loss.

Companies are particularly reluctant to disclose potential losses arising from litigation because such disclosure might provide the appearance of wrongdoing. The desire not to release information that might be unfavourable to the company coupled with the vagueness of such words as "it is likely that a future event will confirm" allows many contingencies to go unreported. Shaw Communications, for example, mentions that the company and its subsidiaries are involved in litigation arising from the normal course and conduct of business. The company then states that "such matters cannot be predicted with certainty" and that "management does not consider the Company's exposure litigation to be material to these financial statements."

Although contingent *gains* are also possible, the accounting profession has adopted a conservative position of non-recognition. Contingent gains may be disclosed in notes, but only if there is a high probability of realization. Many instances of this take-the-loss-but-defer-the-gain approach are found throughout accounting standards.

Measurement Uncertainty

Estimates are required for many financial statement elements. Examples of estimated values include such things as warranty liabilities, the likelihood of contingencies, environmental cleanup obligations, and the extent of possible asset impairment based on future cash flows. The list is long.

While financial statement readers are generally aware of the pervasive nature of estimates, it is appropriate to call attention to **measurement uncertainty**. Section 1508 of the *CICA Handbook* requires that the nature of a measurement uncertainty be disclosed, and that

> the extent of a measurement uncertainty that is material should be disclosed when it is reasonably possible that the recognized amount could change by a material amount in the near term (*CICA* 1508.07)

Disclosing the nature and extent of measurement uncertainty would involve a description of the estimated amount, the amount recorded, and an indication of possible dollar change that is possible. Disclosure might also include key assumptions, ranges, and the sensitivity of the range to changes in assumptions.

For example, assume that a company had fully guaranteed a $100,000 loan of an associated company that was now in financial distress. The associated company will likely be able to partially repay the loan, and the guarantor believes that it will have to pay $45,000 under the guarantee. This $45,000 amount is recorded on the guarantor's books. To disclose measurement uncertainty, the notes would indicate the amount recorded, and the maximum liability under the guarantee.

But what if the amount estimated is a lawsuit? Assume that a company is being sued for $100,000, but is willing to settle for $45,000, and thus records this amount. Negotiations surrounding a possible settlement are ongoing; the settlement might be less or more than

$45,000, or the case might still go to court. To avoid disclosure of the company's position to the plaintiff, the $45,000 accrual is grouped with other liabilities on the balance sheet. However, if the amount accrued is then specifically disclosed in a measurement uncertainty note, the plaintiff would be privy to information that would hurt the company's bargaining position in negotiations, and thus jeopardize the legitimate interests of the company's other stakeholders. In these circumstances, the standard allows that the amount recorded need not be specifically identified.

GOING CONCERN The financial statements are prepared using the continuity assumption, as we learned in Chapter 2. This assumption establishes that the business is expected to continue in operations for a reasonable period of time, and is not expected to liquidate. There are situations in which this assumption is not valid. For example, a company may have operated at a loss for several years in a row, eroding its equity base. Management may be unable to arrange operating financing with a financial institution, or new long-term debt with institutional lenders. Financing may not be available to allow continued operations. Alternatively, an adverse outcome from a contingency may suddenly call the viability of the company into question. If the operation is not a going concern, then historical costs are not appropriate for valuation, and all assets and liabilities have to be valued and classified based on immediate liquidation.

But what about the times when a company appears *perhaps* headed for financial distress, but is not quite ready to, or forced to, liquidate? Companies do not usually go directly from financial health to liquidation. There are often years of an intermediate level of poor financial position. This deteriorating financial position is, of course, obvious from analysis of the financial statements. At some stage, these companies "cross the line" and the situation becomes urgent.

In the later intermediate stages, clear disclosure of the seriousness of the situation is important. If clear and adequate disclosure is present, then the financial statements can still be produced on a going-concern basis. These financial statements will comply with generally accepted accounting principles. Such a disclosure note is usually the first (or perhaps second) disclosure note, given prominent position so it cannot be missed.

Of course, inclusion of this note is a difficult decision, as disclosure of this nature can be self-fulfilling. Some creditors will take this as a cue to further tighten up on credit terms, which may hasten financial distress. Careful management of stakeholders is critical.

The Saskatchewan Wheat Pool reports the following in its disclosure notes:

Basis of presentation

These consolidated financial statements have been prepared in accordance with Canadian generally accepted accounting principles applicable to a going concern, which assumes that the company will continue in operations for the foreseeable future and will be able to realize its assets and discharge its liabilities in the normal course of business.

The note goes on to describe the drought conditions that led to poor financial results over the last two years, and the resulting cash flow difficulties of the company. The note describes the credit facilities agreed to with bankers after the end of the fiscal year, but also reports on essential negotiations to restructure medium-term notes payable. The note concludes

> If the going concern assumption was not appropriate for these financial statements, then adjustments would be necessary in the carrying value of assets and liabilities, the reported net loss and the balance sheet classifications used.

SUBSEQUENT EVENTS What happens if the company unexpectedly sells a division soon after the end of the fiscal year? It's not an event of the past fiscal year, but shouldn't it be part of the report? Users have probably learned about this significant event through the financial press, or other sources, as news travels fast. The financial statements must retain their credibility and relevance by reflecting up-to-date information.

Therefore, disclosure comprises significant events that take place *after the end of the fiscal year*, but *before the date that the statements are completed.* The date of the auditor's report is usually used as a cut-off date. (This cut-off date will be extended to the date that the financial statements are authorized for use, in the terms of a recent exposure draft.)

Examples of subsequent events that are disclosed, are

- A decline in the market value of an investment after the balance sheet date.
- An event that results in a loss, such as fire or flood.
- Issuance of debt or equity instruments that changed the common shares, or potential common shares, outstanding.
- Announcing or commencing a restructuring.

Some events that take place *after* the year-end actually reflect economic conditions existing at the year-end; *these events are recognized in the accounts.* For example, if a customer unexpectedly announces bankruptcy after the year-end, the accounts receivable relating to that customer at the year-end would be written down under the reasoning that the customer was actually insolvent at the end of the fiscal year, but this fact did not become known to the company until after the year-end. Other examples of information to be recorded include the settlement of a court case related to events that took place before the balance sheet date, and evidence uncovered of asset impairment existing at the balance sheet date. Such events can be taken into account *in retrospect*, as part of the accounting estimation process that occurs at every financial reporting date.

International Perspective

In Canada and the United States, we show the assets first, followed by the liabilities and owners' equity. This is the practice in some other countries, such as Japan, Australia, Sweden, and Switzerland. In most other industrialized counties, however, the order is reversed.

Germany, the United Kingdom, France, Austria, Spain, and the Netherlands all begin the listing of assets with fixed assets; within fixed assets, intangibles are listed first. Liquid short-term assets are at the bottom of the listing. This approach is also the one prescribed by *The Fourth Directive*, the European Union regulation concerning the reporting of individual company financial statements. On the right side, shareholders' equity is the usual starting point, although some countries permit liabilities to be shown first.

The specific items included in the balance sheet also vary from country to country. The predominant practice in the United Kingdom, for example, is not to record goodwill as an asset. Accounting for leased assets and lease obligations also varies greatly across countries. For example, leased assets are not recorded as assets in France or Japan. In Germany, it is legally required that corporations establish "reserves" in their owners' equity based on an allocation of profit.

Finally, the valuation basis used in preparing the balance sheet in many international environments differs from Canadian GAAP. For example, fixed assets such as property, plant, and equipment can be revalued using current prices in Belgium, Finland, and the Netherlands. Mexican companies must report their inventories and fixed assets either at replacement cost or in constant pesos (that is, adjusted for changes in the general price level). Argentina and Brazil also use price-level adjustments.

It is very difficult to make comparisons between Canadian balance sheets and those prepared in international settings because the principles underlying their preparation differ greatly between countries. Financial statements, including the notes, must be read with care, and can be adequately interpreted only with knowledge of the reporting framework and economic environment in the company's home country. Balance sheets that look alike on the surface may well hide significant differences beneath!

THE AUDITOR'S REPORT

When financial statements are audited (e.g., for public companies), the auditor's report is presented along with the financial statements. The audit report expresses the auditor's professional opinion on the company's financial statement presentation.

EXHIBIT 4-6

AUDITORS' REPORT

To the Shareholders of Shaw Communications Inc. [1]

[2] We have audited the consolidated balance sheets of Shaw Communications Inc. as at August 31, 2002 and 2001 and the consolidated statements of income (loss) and retained earnings (deficit) and cash flows for each of the years in the three-year period ended August 31, 2002. These financial statements are the responsibility of the Company's management. Our responsibility is to express an opinion on these financial statements based on our audits.

[3] We conducted our audits in accordance with Canadian generally accepted auditing standards. Those standards require that we plan and perform an audit to obtain reasonable assurance whether the financial statements are free of material misstatement. An audit includes examining, on a test basis, evidence supporting the amounts and disclosures in the financial statements. An audit also includes assessing the accounting principles used and significant estimates made by management, as well as evaluating the overall financial statement presentation.

[4] In our opinion, these consolidated financial statements present fairly, in all material respects, the financial position of the Company as at August 31, 2002 and 2001 and the results of its operations and its cash flows for each of the years in the three-year period ended August 31, 2002 [5] in accordance with Canadian generally accepted accounting principles.

As discussed in note 1 to the consolidated financial statements, in 2002 the Company changed its method of accounting for "Goodwill and Other Intangible Assets."

(signed)
Ernst & Young LLP [6]
Calgary, Canada
October 11, 2002 [7]

The auditors have sole responsibility for all opinions expressed in the auditor's report, while company management has the primary responsibility for the financial statements, including the supporting notes. Compilation and presentation of the accounting information and all supporting text contained in a company's financial statements is company management's concern and responsibility; the auditors, in rendering their opinion, affirm or disaffirm what management has compiled and presented.

Seven required elements in the auditor's report have special significance. They are identified by number in Exhibit 4-6, the auditor's report for Shaw Communications.

1. Salutation. (The auditor is hired by, and reports to, the shareholders.)
2. Identification of the statements examined.
3. Statement of scope of the examination.
4. Opinion.
5. Reference to fair presentation in conformity with generally accepted accounting principles.

6. Signature of the independent auditor.
7. Date.

When an audit is finished, the auditors are required to draft an opinion paragraph that communicates their professional opinion about the company's financial statements. The auditors can render one of four opinions, although an unqualified opinion is most common.

1. *Unqualified opinion.* An unqualified opinion is given when the auditor concludes that the statements fairly present the results of operations, financial position, and cash flows in compliance with GAAP and provide reasonable assurance that the financial statements are free of material misstatement. Shaw Communication's audit report is unqualified, as is necessary for any company listed on the TSE.
2. *Qualified opinion.* A qualified opinion is given when the auditor takes limited exception to the client's financial statements in a way that does not invalidate the statements as a whole. A qualified opinion must explain the reasons for the exception and its effect on the financial statements.
3. *Adverse opinion.* An adverse opinion is given when the financial statements do not fairly present the results of operations, financial position, and changes in financial position. An adverse opinion means that the statements, taken as a whole, are not presented in accordance with GAAP. Adverse opinions are rare.
4. *Disclaimer of opinion.* When the auditors have not been able to obtain sufficient evidence, they must state that they are unable to express an opinion (i.e., they issue a disclaimer). The disclaimer must provide the reasons the auditor did not give an opinion.

A major purpose of the auditor's report is to give reasonable assurance to the reader that the financial statements conform to GAAP. However, an audit report does not assure the reader that the numbers in the financial statements are the "right" numbers for the reader's purpose. As the preceding chapters have emphasized (and the following chapters will illustrate), management's selection of "acceptable" accounting practices and estimates will strongly colour the resultant financial statements. The auditor's report states only that the accounting policies chosen by the company are within the set deemed generally acceptable. Different choices would have given different reported results, but may have been generally acceptable.

MANAGEMENT DISCUSSION AND ANALYSIS

As part of their annual report, public companies are required to include a section called Management Discussion and Analysis (MD&A). The provincial securities commissions, under the provisions of National Instrument 44-101, effective December 2000, require an MD&A. Prior to this date, certain provinces required the MD&A, while others did not.

The MD&A is not a part of the financial statements, and is not covered by the audit report. The MD&A is meant to give investors insight into management's interpretation of current financial results and plans for the future. An effective MD&A will present an analysis of both past results and future prospects, so that the investor can assess the company's operations and prospects. According to the securities commission rules, information must be presented in the following areas:

1. A general review of the financial statements, as well as areas of risk and uncertainty.
2. Quarterly information; usually the past eight quarters are presented to allow analysis of trends.
3. Liquidity and capital resources, analyzed by management, including a forward look at capital expenditures commitments, requirements for operations, and resources to meet these requirements.
4. Results of operations, analyzed by management to identify trends.

The CICA, in support of MD&A reporting, issued extensive general guidance on the preparation and disclosure of the MD&A in November 2002. General disclosure principles are established as follows:

1. The MD&A should enable readers to view the company through the eyes of management.
2. The MD&A should complement as well as supplement financial statements.
3. The MD&A should be reliable, complete, and fairly balanced, providing material relevant information for decision-making.
4. The MD&A should have a forward-looking orientation.
5. The MD&A should focus on management's strategy for generating value for investors over time.
6. The MD&A should be written in plain language, with candor and without exaggeration, and embody the qualities of understandability, relevance, comparability and consistency over reporting periods.[2]

The CICA provides guidance as to appropriate disclosures, establishing an extensive disclosure framework. These pronouncements also include guidelines for continuous disclosure and outline the responsibilities of management, the Board of Directors, and the Audit Committee with respect to the MD&A.

It is clear that the MD&A must be prepared with a view to relevant information. In the past, MD&A disclosures relating to future plans have been criticized for being quite vague and therefore of limited use to investors. Companies have been reluctant to divulge future plans because positive expectations may not be fulfilled and negative projections may cause an overreaction in the stock market. Nonetheless, companies must begin to meet reporting expectations in this area.

CONCEPT REVIEW

1. In general, what functions are served by disclosure notes?
2. Why might financial statement users want to see segmented information? What companies are required to disclose segmented information?
3. Define a related party transaction.
4. What two conditions must be fulfilled in order for a contingent liability to be recognized on the balance sheet instead of just being disclosed in a note?
5. What is measurement uncertainty?
6. What disclosure is needed if a firm is a questionable going concern?
7. What is the purpose of the management discussion and analysis (MD&A)? Which companies are required to present an MD&A?

SUMMARY OF KEY POINTS

1. The balance sheet provides information about an entity's assets, liabilities, and equities. The balance sheet, taken together with other financial statements, allows financial statement users to assess financial position, risk profile, financial flexibility, liquidity, and rates of return.
2. The balance sheet reports primarily cost, not fair value, which may reduce its relevance for certain decisions. The values reported are the result of the company's reporting policies. The balance sheet also contains many estimates, excludes assets and liabilities that the GAAP model deems unrecognizable, and consolidates financial data from possibly very different industry segments. Financial statement users must proceed with caution.

[2] *Management's Discussion and Analysis*, The Canadian Institute of Chartered Accountants, Toronto, Canada, 2002, Part 2.

3. Classification of balance sheet items is governed by accounting standards and industry norms and characteristics, but has room for judgement. Most, but not all, balance sheets classify current assets and current liabilities to facilitate evaluation of short-term liquidity. Other classifications follow the major asset, liability, and equity groups. Elements are often very summarized on the balance sheet.
4. Various balance sheet categories have specific display and disclosure requirements in order to meet accounting standards and users' expectations.
5. Disclosure notes provide information regarding accounting policies, describe recognized and unrecognized items, and provide information regarding future cash flows, alternate valuation information, and rates of return.
6. A company should make appropriate disclosures of terms and conditions, interest rates, credit risk, and fair values of its financial instruments.
7. Important disclosures include segment disclosures, related-party transaction data, subsequent events, contingencies, and measurement uncertainty. If a company's future is in doubt such that the continuity assumption might not apply, going-concern disclosures are needed.

KEY TERMS

REVIEW PROBLEM

The post-closing balance sheet accounts of Ibsen Icons Incorporated at 31 December 20X3 are as follows:

Account	Debit	Credit
Cash (overdraft)		$ 3,500
Accounts payable		15,000
Future income tax liability—long term		30,000
Common shares		40,000
Preferred shares		24,000
Long-term investment in common shares of Grieg Graphics Inc.	$ 14,000	
Accounts receivable	19,000	
Loan from shareholder, due 1 July 20X9		40,000
Leasehold improvements (net of amortization)	30,000	
Land	120,000	
Furniture and equipment (at cost)	90,000	
Accumulated amortization, furniture and equipment		30,000
Retained earnings		74,000
Deferred revenue		6,500
Instalment notes receivable	7,000	
Goodwill	9,000	
Appropriation for restructuring costs		20,000
Prepaid expenses	3,500	

Account	Debit	Credit
Marketable securities	3,000	
Note payable to bank, due 15 October 20X4		25,000
Allowance for doubtful accounts		2,000
Supplies inventory	14,500	

Required:
Prepare a classified balance sheet in good form, using the financing form and the report format.

REVIEW PROBLEM—SOLUTION

IBSEN ICONS INCORPORATED
BALANCE SHEET
As of 31 December 20X3

Assets			
Current assets:			
Marketable securities		$ 3,000	
Instalment notes receivable		7,000	
Accounts receivable	$19,000		
Less: allowance for doubtful accounts	2,000	17,000	
Supplies inventory		14,500	
Prepaid expenses		3,500	$ 45,000
Investments:			
Investment in Grieg Graphics Inc.			14,000
Capital assets:			
Furniture and equipment	90,000		
Less: accumulated amortization	30,000	60,000	
Leasehold improvements (net)		30,000	
Land		120,000	
Goodwill		9,000	219,000
Total assets			$278,000
Liabilities and shareholders' equity			
Liabilities:			
Current liabilities:			
Bank overdraft		$ 3,500	
Note payable to bank, due 15 October 20X4		25,000	
Accounts payable		15,000	
Deferred revenue		6,500	$ 50,000
Long-term liabilities:			
Loan from shareholder, due 1 July 20X9		40,000	
Future income tax liability		30,000	70,000
Total liabilities			120,000
Shareholders' equity:			
Contributed capital:			
Common shares		40,000	
Preferred shares		24,000	64,000
Retained earnings:			
Appropriated for restructuring costs		20,000	
Unappropriated		74,000	94,000
Total shareholders' equity			158,000
Total liabilities and shareholders' equity			$278,000

Capital assets could be separated into tangible and intangible categories. Deferred revenue and instalment notes receivable are assumed to be within normal business practice for this company and therefore are classified as current.

QUESTIONS

Q4-1 What is the primary purpose of a balance sheet?

Q4-2 What valuations are reported on the balance sheet?

Q4-3 Describe the limitations of the balance sheet.

Q4-4 What is the difference between the net assets and financing form of the balance sheet? The report and account format? What format is the most common in practice?

Q4-5 Describe the usual order of balance sheet accounts.

Q4-6 Define current assets, current liabilities, and working capital. Must these subtotals be disclosed on the balance sheet?

Q4-7 List the areas of choice in balance sheet presentation.

Q4-8 What items are included in the balance sheet category of cash?

Q4-9 When is an asset non-current?

Q4-10 What does the "investments and funds" caption cover in a balance sheet?

Q4-11 What are capital assets? Distinguish between tangible and intangible capital assets.

Q4-12 Comment on the difficulties associated with evaluating the balance sheet of an entity whose primary assets are intangible.

Q4-13 Why is the caption "other assets" sometimes necessary? Name two items that might be reported under this classification.

Q4-14 Explain the term "deferred charge."

Q4-15 Distinguish between current and non-current liabilities. Under what conditions would a previously long-term liability amount be reclassified as a current liability?

Q4-16 What disclosure should accompany a long-term liability? Why is this disclosure important?

Q4-17 What is the nature of future income tax such that this item is classified as a liability? Why is the account classification subject to question?

Q4-18 Explain the term "non-controlling interest."

Q4-19 Is it proper to offset current liabilities against current assets? Explain.

Q4-20 What is owners' equity? What are the main components of owners' equity?

Q4-21 When is debt reclassified as owners' equity?

Q4-22 List the primary types of disclosure notes. Give two examples of each type.

Q4-23 Define financial instruments and identify the four areas of disclosure that are described for financial instruments.

Q4-24 When is a contingency recognized versus disclosed?

Q4-25 When is a subsequent event recognized versus disclosed?

Q4-26 What is the purpose of segment disclosures?

Q4-27 Why might the presence of large volumes of related party transactions make it difficult to evaluate a company based on its financial statements?

Q4-28 What is measurement uncertainty? Why must it be disclosed?

Q4-29 Why is going-concern disclosure sometimes viewed as self-fulfilling?

Q4-30 Identify some of the differences between balance sheets around the world.

Q4-31 What is the auditors' report? What are its basic components? Why is it especially important to the statement user?

CASE 4-1
Orion Investments

Orion Investments is a multi-million dollar, multinational public holding company. Orion specializes in acquisitions of undercapitalized companies and those in financial distress. After suitable reorganization and/or capital investment, these investees may be retained as long-term investments, or resold if market conditions appear appropriate.

You have recently joined Orion as a financial analyst in the mergers and acquisitions group. You are working on the file of Brown Company, one of 16 potential acquisition targets being followed by your group.

Brown is an integrated oilfield service company involved in drilling activities in the Calgary area. The company rents drilling equipment to oil exploration companies; provides crews to staff drill sites; and offers a wide range of testing, maintenance and well site services. Brown also manufactures polycrystalline diamond drill bits and various other specialty drilling components.

For the fiscal year ended 31 December 20X2, Brown reported total assets of $2,380 (million), consisting primarily of tangible capital assets (55%), intangible capital assets (goodwill from acquisitions, 18%) and accounts receivable (18%). 20X2 net assets (shareholders' equity) was $1,210 (million), increased from the $1,105 reported in 20X1. Financing is through current payables to suppliers, operating lines of credit from the bank, and a modest amount of long-term debt.

Your current task is to evaluate several disclosure notes provided by Brown, and potentially recalculate net assets. In doing so, you may also comment on the quality and usefulness of note disclosures, and how they reflect on the management team of Brown Company.

Required:

Prepare a report to complete the assigned analysis. Brown has a 40% tax rate.

EXHIBIT 1

BROWN COMPANY
SELECTED DISCLOSURE NOTES

Measurement uncertainty

The preparation of financial statement in conformity with Canadian GAAP requires the Company's management to make estimates and assumptions about future events that affect the amounts reported in the financial statements and related notes. Actual results may differ from those estimates.

Contingencies

In 20X2, the CRA issued Notices of Reassessment to the Company reconfirming a 20X0 reassessment that required the Company to report, as 20X0 taxable revenue, work done in December 20X0 but not billed until January 20X1. The Company's practice, which is consistent and is in accordance with U.S. industry norms, is to record revenue on a billed basis.

The Company believes it has reported its tax position appropriately, and has filed a Notice of Objection with the CRA. No provision has been made in the accounts for additional income tax, if any, which may be determined to be payable.

The amounts in dispute are as follows (in millions):

	Net revenue	*Income tax interest & penalties*
20X0 and prior	$ 20.6	$ 9.9
20X1	1.2	0.6
20X2	2.3	1.1
	$ 24.1	$ 11.6

The provisions of the *Income Tax Act* require the Company to deposit one-half of the amounts in dispute with the CRA. The amount on deposit with the CRA amounts to $5.5 million and is reported as a long-term deferred charge by Brown.

Subsequent event

On January 21, 20X3, an ice storm of unprecedented proportions damaged certain of the Company's drilling equipment, at risk because of an exposed field location. Equipment with a net book value of $389 (million) as of 31 December 20X2 was destroyed. The Company self-insures for such risks.

Related party transactions

The Company has agreements with a company controlled by the chairman of the Board for the provision of business development and consulting services. The Company has a marketing agreement with a company controlled by a family member of the chairman of the Board that covers certain products manufactured by the Company. All products in three specific lines are sold to this related company, which then assumes the risks and rewards of resale to third parties. All the above-mentioned transactions are measured at the exchange values, which are amounts established and agreed to by the related parties.

Transaction volumes are as follows (millions):

	20X2	20X1
Sales	$566	$459
Consulting services	2.2	1.8
Accounts receivable	$239	$176
Accounts payable	0.8	0.5

During the year ended 31 December 20X2, the Company purchased land and improvements for a proposed plant facility from a company controlled by the executive vice-president for $175 million.

CASE 4-2
The Bakery Limited

The Bakery Limited operates a string of coffee and baked goods shops in Calgary and Edmonton. Its strategy is to establish central bakery operations, with individual outlets and grocery store outlets around each central hub. One bakery can service the needs of about 12 outlets.

The company's shares are held by Bob DiPasco (55%) and two of his friends, George Delaney (18%) and Susan Perchenko (18%). All three sit on the Board of Directors. DiPasco is active in the company as the president and general manager, but the other two shareholders are more passive investors. The remaining shares are held by the managers who operate the various central bakery locations. These shares were sold to the managers, at book value, after five years of service. Book value is defined as the total recorded shareholders' equity, then divided by the number of shares outstanding to get a per-share amount. Shares are subject to a repurchase agreement, and must be bought back from the managers by the company, also at book value, if managers leave the employment of The Bakery.

The Bakery has had respectable operating results, but struggled in early 20X5 because of a liquidity crunch caused by renovation needs and operating losses. The company had to significantly upgrade eight locations, and financing was an issue. During renovations, sales volumes declined, and were slow to recover in two areas.

To solve the liquidity problem, DiPasco invested additional amounts in the company, but he was unable to meet all the cash needs of the company. Delaney and Perchenko agreed to invest $400,000, in the form of a convertible debenture. The debenture requires annual interest, and repayment at the end of the 10th year. However, if an interest payment is missed, or if the current ratio (current assets divided by current liabilities) of the company falls below 0.7, the debenture can be converted into common shares. This would involve issuance of enough common shares that DiPasco would no longer be the majority shareholder.

It is now January 20X6. The preliminary balance sheet for 20X5 has been prepared (see Exhibit 1). You, the company controller, have a meeting with DiPasco tomorrow morning to review the preliminary financial statements. Before the meeting, you must review the balance sheet for accuracy, and revise if necessary. DiPasco has asked for other comments you consider relevant.

Required:

Prepare a memo and revised balance sheet as a basis for discussion.

EXHIBIT 1

THE BAKERY LIMITED

BALANCE SHEET

31 December	20X5	20X4
Assets		
Current assets		
Cash	$ 29,689	$ 96,403
Accounts receivable (Note 1)	67,845	43,060
Marketable securities	36,956	36,956
(at cost, which approximates market value)		
Inventory (Note 2)	80,844	53,902
Prepaid expenses and deposits	3,554	19,851
	218,888	250,172
Capital assets (Note 3)	1,134,895	549,023
Intangible assets (Note 4)	10,237	10,680
	$1,364,020	$809,875
Liabilities and shareholders' equity		
Current liabilities		
Bank loan (Note 5)	$ 211,590	$ 22,233
Accounts payable and accrued liabilities (note 6)	51,253	22,104
	262,843	44,337
Long-term debt (Note 7)	180,625	195,979
Subordinated debentures	400,000	—
Advances from related parties	—	58,479
	843,468	298,795

Shareholders' equity		
Share capital	953,767	549,138
Deficit	(433,215)	(38,058)
	520,552	511,080
Commitments (Note 8)	$1,364,020	$809,875

Additional information:

Note 1

Accounts receivable include trade accounts receivable from various grocery and convenience stores. Payments have been slower in 20X5 than in previous years. The accounts receivable are shown net of an allowance for doubtful accounts of $3,500 but up to $7,500 of the accounts might be uncollectible. Accounts receivable also includes $12,500 from DiPasco, for share capital. That is, share capital and accounts receivable were increased by $12,500. DiPasco will pay this amount in the next 30 days.

Note 2

Inventory is valued at FIFO, and consists of bakery supplies. Inventory has increased over the past year because flour prices are expected to increase and The Bakery has been stockpiling goods while prices remain low.

Note 3

Capital assets are carried at cost, and depreciated over their useful lives using straight-line depreciation.

	Cost	Accumulated depreciation	Net book value
Equipment	$ 628,037	$ 54,000	$ 574,037
Leasehold improvements	570,493	42,898	527,595
Computer software and hardware	26,348	13,792	12,556
Signage	15,220	2,488	12,732
Automobiles	11,702	3,727	7,975
	$1,251,800	$ 116,905	$1,134,895

Note 4

The intangible asset is the registered name of the company and its major product lines. Costs deferred are the legal costs to register the trademark and to prosecute a (successful) legal case against another operation using the same name(s). Amortization is straight line over the useful life. Cost is $11,575, and accumulated amortization is $1,338.

Note 5

The bank loan bears an interest rate of prime plus 1% and is secured by a first charge on accounts receivable, inventory, and capital assets. The bank loan can be called for repayment by the bank at any time, with 30 days' notice. The Bakery has had demand loans since inception, and considers these loans to be a permanent part of its capital structure. The bank has never called a loan granted to The Bakery. Of these loans, $150,000 relates to a purchase of equipment in 20X5.

Note 6

Accounts payable are to suppliers for merchandise. One supplier is owed $7,200, but the supplier has also been a long-term customer of The Bakery. The supplier owed The Bakery $5,600 at year-end. Both accounts receivable and accounts payable were reduced by the inter-company amount, $5,600. After the year-end, the supplier paid the $5,600 amount owing.

Note 7
Long-term debt bears an interest rate of 7.5% and requires annual interest and $5,000 of principal repayments. All payments have been made on schedule. The debt is secured by a second charge on tangible capital property of the company. One covenant states that $20,000 must be maintained at all times on deposit with the lender, as security. This $20,000 is included in cash on the balance sheet, but kept as required in a separate bank account.

Note 8
The Bakery agreed to buy $10,000 of bakery products from a supplier in order to secure supply at a reasonable price. These goods were supposed to be delivered on 15 January 20X6 but were actually delivered on 28 December 20X5. The invoice is not due for payment until 20 February 20X6. This inventory has not been recorded in the financial statements.

CASE 4-3
Autopart Manufacturing Limited

Autopart Manufacturing Limited, incorporated 15 years ago, has grown to be a successful competitor in the cost- and quality-conscious autopart manufacturing market. Autopart specializes in relatively standard replacement parts sold under store, or house, brand labels in hardware stores. Since people are now owning cars longer than ever before (now an average of 8.5 years). The auto repair business is a growth sector of the economy.

You've obtained the balance sheet of Autopart Manufacturing Limited, and have analyzed the basic financial structure of the company. You're thinking of investing in Autopart's common shares, but looking at the balance sheet has reminded you of the definitions of financial statement elements. You've decided to see how well the balance sheet items conform to the definitions. In particular, it's important to explain to yourself exactly why each item is an asset, liability, or equity item. The balance sheet is shown in Exhibit 1, and the notes to the financial statements in Exhibit 2.

EXHIBIT 1

AUTOPART MANUFACTURING LIMITED
CONSOLIDATED BALANCE SHEET

(stated in thousands of Canadian dollars)

31 December	20X1	20X0
Assets		
Current assets		
Cash and short-term investments	$ 9,800	$ 4,390
Accounts receivable	12,464	12,570
Inventories (Note 1)	15,730	14,400
Capital assets		
Property, plant, and equipment (net) (Note 2)	21,529	19,200
Goodwill (Note 3)	5,100	4,750
Licences (Note 4)	1,640	1,490
Other assets		
Future contract costs (Note 5)	1,950	2,300
	$68,213	$59,100

Liabilities and shareholders' equity		
Current liabilities:		
Accounts payable and accrued liabilities	$ 11,384	$15,875
Current portion of long-term debt	450	475
Other	615	655
Long-term liabilities (Note 6)	27,190	10,580
Commitments payable (Note 7)	—	1,900
Prepaid contract (Note 8)	1,650	2,900
Future income tax (Note 9)	950	890
Shareholders' equity (Note 10)	25,974	25,825
	$68,213	$59,100

EXHIBIT 2

NOTES TO THE FINANCIAL STATEMENTS

($ thousands)

As of 31 December

Note 1. Inventories	**20X1**	**20X0**
Raw materials	$ 6,700	$ 6,300
Finished goods	7,700	7,200
Supplies	400	380
Returnable containers	930	520
	$15,730	$14,400

Note 2. Property, Plant, and Equipment (Net)

	Cost	**Accumulated Amortization**	**Net Balance, 31 Dec. 20X1**
Land	$ 990	$ —	$ 990
Buildings	5,910	696	5,214
Machinery and equipment			
Owned	11,480	2,600	8,880
Leased	3,720	200	3,520
Furniture and fixtures	2,600	310	2,290
Transportation equipment	1,120	485	635
	$25,820	$4,291	$21,529

Note 3. Goodwill

During the year ended 31 December 20X1, the company acquired 100% of the shares of Benn Mufflers Limited for $1,240 in cash. Benn Mufflers Limited had tangible assets, at fair value, of $890 on the acquisition date, and goodwill of $350 arose. The opening balance in the goodwill account is from a series of similar acquisitions over the past 12 years.

Note 4. Licences

The company manufactures certain autoparts under licence. Licences are acquired for cash at the beginning of the licence period, usually five years.

Note 5. Future Contract Costs

The company enters into three-year contracts with retailers, guaranteeing the company a market and specific shelf space for its goods. Payments are made to the retailers to secure these multi-year contracts. The payments are amortized against sales over the term of the related contracts.

Note 6. Long-Term Liabilities

	20X1
Term bank loans, 8%, maturing in 20X9	$ 17,830
Mortgages, 7–10%, maturing 20X3–20X6	6,910
Capital leases, 8.5%–14.3%, maturing 20X3–20X9	2,900
	$ 27,640
Less: current portion	450
	$ 27,190

Note 7. Commitments Payable
In 20X0, the company set up a provision of $1,900 for potential losses relating to a guarantee provided for Carburetor King Limited, an associated company. Autoparts had guaranteed a bank loan of Carburetor King, and it appeared in 20X0 that financial difficulties within that company would trigger a payment by Autoparts under the guarantee. In 20X1, Carburetor King was sold and reorganized, and Autoparts was released from its guarantee after a payment of $400,000.

Note 8. Prepaid Contract
Certain customers in long-term contracts with the company prepay a portion of the estimated total contract value. This prepayment is taken into income over the life of the contract, in proportion to deliveries.

Note 9. Future Income Tax
Certain expenses, primarily depreciation, are reported in different periods for income tax and financial statement reporting purposes. The result is a future tax liability.

Note 10. Shareholders' Equity

	20X1
Common shares, unlimited shares authorized, 26,837 shares issued	$ 14,499
Contributed capital from share retirement	49
Retained earnings	11,426
	$25,974

ASSIGNMENTS

A4-1 Balance Sheet Formats: Hobbit Enterprises Inc. had the following post-closing trial balance on 31 December 20X4:

	Debit	Credit
Cash	$ 28,000	
Accounts receivable	52,000	
Inventories	80,000	
Equipment	400,000	
Accumulated amortization		$240,000
Patents	100,000	
Long-term investments	140,000	
Accounts payable		60,000
Long-term notes payable		200,000
Common shares		180,000
Retained earnings		120,000
	$800,000	$800,000

Required:

1. Prepare the balance sheet for Hobbit Enterprises by using
   - Financing form—report format.
   - Financing form—account format.
2. Explain how the balance sheet would be different if the net assets form was used.

A4-2 Balance Sheet Formats: The following list of accounts and balances pertains to Barbecon Corporation on 31 December 20X5, the end of the company's annual accounting period:

Accounts payable	$ 28,000
Accounts receivable	37,000
Accumulated amortization—furniture and fixtures	10,000
Advances from customers (pertaining to goods that Barbecon will supply in 20X6)	6,000
Allowance for doubtful accounts	1,800
Bond sinking fund	90,000
Bonds payable (14%, due 1 January 20X18)	150,000
Cash	26,000
Common shares	30,000
Franchise (net)	86,000
Furniture and fixtures	70,000
Merchandise inventory	48,400
Contributed capital—donation	60,000
Premium on bonds payable	4,000
Prepaid rent	8,400
Retained earnings (to be determined)	?

Required:

Prepare a balance sheet using the following formats:

1. Financing form—report form.
2. Net assets form—report form.

A4-3 Classification on the Balance Sheet: A typical balance sheet has the following classifications:

A. Current assets
B. Investments and funds
C. Tangible capital assets (property, plant, and equipment)
D. Intangible assets
E. Other assets
F. Deferred charges
G. Current liabilities
H. Long-term liabilities
I. Share capital (common or preferred)
J. Additional contributed capital
K. Debt elements that have the characteristics of equity
L. Retained earnings

_– C_ 1. Accumulated depreciation
_____ 2. Bonds payable (due in 10 years)
_____ 3. Accounts payable (trade)
_____ 4. Investment in shares of X Company (long term)
_____ 5. Plant site (in use)
_____ 6. Restriction or appropriation of retained earnings
_____ 7. Office supplies inventory
_____ 8. Loan to company president (collection not expected for two years)
_____ 9. Accumulated income less accumulated dividends

_____ 10. Unamortized bond discount (on bonds payable; a debit balance)
_____ 11. Bond sinking fund (to retire long-term bonds)
_____ 12. Prepaid insurance
_____ 13. Accounts receivable (trade)
_____ 14. Short-term investment
_____ 15. Allowance for doubtful accounts
_____ 16. Building (in use)
_____ 17. Bonds payable (principal payments may be made by issuing common shares at the investor's request)
_____ 18. Interest revenue earned but not collected
_____ 19. Patent
_____ 20. Land, held for investment
_____ 21. Land, idle

Required:

Use the code letters above to indicate the usual classification for each balance sheet item listed. If an item is a contra amount (i.e., a deduction) under a caption, place a minus sign before the lettered response. The first item is completed for you as an example.

★★ **A4-4 Classification on the Balance Sheet:** Typical balance sheet classifications along with a letter for each classification are as follows:

A. Current assets
B. Investments and funds
C. Tangible capital assets (property, plant, and equipment)
D. Intangible assets
E. Other assets
F. Deferred charges
G. Current liabilities
H. Long-term liabilities
I. Debt elements that are equity
J. Contributed capital, share capital, and other
K. Retained earnings

Typical balance sheet items are as follows:

_____ 1. Cash
_____ 2. Cash set aside to meet long-term purchase commitment
_____ 3. Land (used as plant site)
_____ 4. Accrued salaries
_____ 5. Investment in the common shares of another company (long term; not a controlling interest)
_____ 6. Inventory of damaged goods
_____ 7. Idle plant
_____ 8. Assets of discontinued operations held for resale
_____ 9. Preferred shares that have guaranteed redemption for cash
_____ 10. Goodwill
_____ 11. Natural resource (e.g., a timber tract)
_____ 12. Allowance for doubtful accounts
_____ 13. Investment in bonds of another company
_____ 14. Organization costs
_____ 15. Discount on bonds payable
_____ 16. Service revenue collected in advance
_____ 17. Accrued interest payable
_____ 18. Accumulated amortization on patent
_____ 19. Prepaid rent
_____ 20. Short-term investment (common shares)
_____ 21. Rent revenue collected but not earned
_____ 22. Net amount of accumulated revenues, gains, expenses, losses, and dividends

_____ 23. Trade accounts payable
_____ 24. Current maturity of long-term debt
_____ 25. Long-term debt that may be convertible to common shares
_____ 26. Bond issue costs
_____ 27. Special cash fund accumulated to build plant five years hence
_____ 28. Bonds issued—to be repaid within six months out of bond sinking fund
_____ 29. Long-term investment in rental building
_____ 30. Copyright
_____ 31. Accumulated amortization
_____ 32. Deferred plant rearrangement costs
_____ 33. Franchise
_____ 34. Revenue earned but not collected
_____ 35. Premium on bonds payable (unamortized)
_____ 36. Common shares (no-par)
_____ 37. Petty cash fund
_____ 38. Deficit
_____ 39. Contributed capital on share retirement
_____ 40. Earnings retained in the business

Required:

Enter the appropriate letter for each item to indicate its usual classification on the balance sheet. When it is a contra item (i.e., a deduction), place a minus sign before the lettered response.

(AICPA, adapted)

A4-5 Classification on the Balance Sheet: Serious Company is a magazine publisher. The company has the following categories on the balance sheet:

A. Current assets
B. Investments
C. Property, plant, and equipment
D. Intangible assets
E. Other assets
F. Current liabilities
G. Long-term liabilities
H. Share capital
I. Contributed capital
J. Retained earnings

_____ 1. Unearned magazine subscriptions received
_____ 2. Discount on bonds payable, due in 20X6
_____ 3. Bonds payable with an initial term of 20 years, but now due next year
_____ 4. Advances to suppliers
_____ 5. Preferred shares issued
_____ 6. Rare coins
_____ 7. Future income tax
_____ 8. Salaries that the company budget shows will be earned and paid next year
_____ 9. Allowance for decline in market value of inventory
_____ 10. Operating expenses for the current year
_____ 11. Machinery retired and held for resale
_____ 12. Account receivable from company president; to be repaid in two years' time

Required:

Indicate where each of the following items would be classified. If the item is not on the balance sheet, enter an X.

A4-6 Classification on the Balance Sheet: Indicate where the following items would be found in an appropriately classified balance sheet. Be specific. An item might not appear on the balance sheet, or it might be split between two different categories. The first item is done for you as an example.

1. Loans payable — Long-term liability, but short term if due in one operating cycle
2. Discount on bonds payable ______
3. Rent collected in advance ______
4. Future (deferred) income tax caused by capital assets ______
5. Cash account that must be used to retire long-term bonds payable (sinking fund)
6. Common shares of our company ______
7. Land held for speculative purposes ______
8. Interest receivable ______
9. Common shares of another corporation held as a long-term investment ______
10. Long-term pension amounts paid in advance ______
11. Allowance for doubtful accounts ______

A4-7 Determining Values in the Balance Sheet: The consolidated balance sheet of Mutron Lock Incorporated, is shown below.

MUTRON LOCK INCORPORATED
CONSOLIDATED BALANCE SHEET

As of 31 December 20X5

Assets		
Current assets		
Cash and cash equivalents		$ 10,195
Marketable securities		a
Accounts receivable	$153,682	
Allowance for doubtful accounts	b	147,421
Inventories		201,753
Prepaid expenses		8,902
Total current assets		c
Capital assets		
Land		12,482
Building (net)		d
Equipment and machinery	195,467	
Accumulated depreciation	(103,675)	91,792
Total capital assets		261,056
Investments		14,873
Other assets		7,926
Total assets		$661,774

Liabilities and Shareholders' Equity	
Current liabilities	
Accounts payable	$ 85,476
Notes payable	e
Income taxes payable	6,421
Current portion of long-term debt	4,893
Accrued expenses	5,654
Total current liabilities	110,763
Long-term debt	122,004
Future income taxes	f
Non-controlling interest	35,136
Total liabilities	g
Shareholders' equity	
Preferred shares, no-par value (authorized 10,000 shares, issued 2,400 shares for $14,281)	h
Common shares, no-par value (authorized 400,000 shares, issued 20,000 shares)	i
Total contributed capital	j
Retained earnings	206,471
Total shareholders' equity	347,668
Total liabilities and shareholders' equity	$ k

Required:

1. For each of the items (a) through (k) in the balance sheet above, calculate the amount that should appear for that item.
2. What kinds of notes would be commonly found for each balance sheet item; select from the following list.
   i. Financial instruments: disclosure of terms and conditions.
   ii. Financial instruments: disclosure of interest rates, including effective rates.
   iii. Financial instruments: disclosure of credit risk.
   iv. Financial instruments: disclosure of fair value, by class.
   v. Breakdown of accounts aggregated to arrive at a balance sheet total.
   vi. Disclosure of accounting policy.
   vii. Details of changes during the period.

★★

A4-8 Setting up the Balance Sheet: Below is a typical chart of accounts (in alphabetical order) for Altar Paving Corporation for 20X5.

Accounts payable
Accounts receivable
Accrued expenses
Accumulated amortization, all intangible assets
Accumulated depreciation, all tangible assets
Allowance for decline in value of marketable securities
Allowance for doubtful accounts
Amortization expense
Bad debt expense
Bonds payable
Bond sinking fund
Buildings
Cash
Common shares
Contributed capital from share retirement
Cost of goods sold
Depreciation expense
Discount on bonds payable
Dividends payable
Equipment
Finished goods
Future income tax liability
Gain on sale of marketable securities
General and administrative expense
Goodwill
Income tax expense
Income tax payable
Interest payable
Investment in common shares, not intended for resale

Land
Licences
Loss on sale of land
Marketable securities
Miscellaneous expense
Overhead
Patents
Prepaid expense
Purchases
Raw materials
Restricted cash for long-term debt retirement
Retained earnings
Sales revenue
Travel and entertainment expense
Wages expense
Wages payable
Work in process

Required:
Prepare a blank, classified balance sheet in proper form using the financing format. Include all balance sheet accounts—do not summarize.

A4-9 Valuation on the Balance Sheet: The first list below shows the measurement or valuation approaches commonly used for reporting individual items on the balance sheet. The second list indicates some items from a typical balance sheet of a corporation.

A. Amount payable or receivable when due (usually no interest is involved because of the short term)
B. Lower of cost or market
C. Original cost when acquired
D. Fair market value at date of the balance sheet
E. Original cost less accumulated amortization
F. Amount received on sale or issuance
G. Face amount of the obligation adjusted for unamortized premium or discount
H. Accumulated income less accumulated losses and dividends
I. None of the above (when this response is used, explain the valuation approach usually used)

Valuation	Balance Sheet Items
B	1. Land (held as an investment)
____	2. Merchandise inventory, FIFO
____	3. Short-term investments
____	4. Accounts receivable (trade)
____	5. Long-term investment in bonds of another company held to maturity (purchased at a discount; the discount is a credit balance)
____	6. Land used as a plant site (in use)
____	7. Plant and equipment (in use)
____	8. Patent (in use)
____	9. Accounts payable (trade)
____	10. Bonds payable (sold at a premium; the premium is a credit balance)
____	11. Common shares, no par
____	12. Prepaid expenses
____	13. Retained earnings
____	14. Land (future plant site; not in use)
____	15. Idle plant (awaiting disposal)
____	16. Natural resource (in use)

Required:
Use the letters given in the first list to indicate the usual measurement method (or valuation method) commonly used in the balance sheet for each item in the second list. Comment on any doubtful items. Some letters may be used more than once or not at all. The first item is completed for you as an example.

A4-10 Prepare a Classified Balance Sheet; Compare Aggregation Levels: The ledger of the Manitoba Manufacturing Company reflects the following balances, after the books were closed on 31 December 20X5. One adjustment has yet to be made (see below).

Accounts payable	$64,100
Accounts receivable	70,400
Accrued expenses (credit)	2,400
Bonds payable, 14%	400,000
Share capital, 700 shares	400,000
Cash	39,000
Retained earnings (to be determined)	?
Factory equipment	645,900
Finished goods	50,400
Investments	145,500
Office equipment	138,500
Raw materials	30,100
Reserve for bad debts	3,900
Reserve for amortization	137,700
Rent expense paid in advance	16,000
Sinking fund	74,400
Land held for future plant site	96,000
Note receivable	21,700
Work in process	10,900

Other information:
Two-thirds of the depreciation relates to factory equipment and one-third to office equipment. Of the balance in the investments account, $20,000 will be converted to cash in the immediate future; the remainder represents a long-term investment. Rent paid in advance is for the next year. The note receivable is a loan made to the company president on 1 October 20X5, and is due in 20X7, when the principal amount ($21,700) plus 6% interest per annum will be paid to the company. No interest has been accrued on the loan in the above listing. The sinking fund is being accumulated to retire the bonds at maturity.

Required:

1. Prepare a balance sheet using typical format (financing; report format), classifications, and proper terminology. Include all accounts directly on the balance sheet; do not aggregate.
2. Prepare a balance sheet that uses highly aggregated disclosures.
3. Comment on the differences between the two balance sheets. Why might a user prefer one over the other?

A4-11 Prepare a Balance Sheet: The following trial balance was prepared by Vantage Electronics Corporation as of 31 December 20X5. The adjusting entries for 20X5 have been made, except for any specifically noted.

Other information:
You find that certain errors and omissions are reflected in the trial balance below:

a. The $15,000 balance in accounts receivable represents the entire amount owed to the company; of this amount, $12,400 is from trade customers and 5% of that amount is estimated to be uncollectible. The remaining amount owed to the company represents a long-term advance to its president.
b. Inventories include $1,000 of goods incorrectly valued at double their cost (i.e., reported at $2,000). No correction has been recorded. Office supplies on hand of $500 are also included in the balance of inventories.
c. When the equipment and building were purchased new on 1 January 20X0 (i.e., six years earlier), they had estimated lives of 10 and 25 years, respectively. They have been amortized using the straight-line method on the assumption of zero residual value, and depreciation has been credited directly to the asset accounts. Amortization has been recorded for 20X5.

VANTAGE ELECTRONICS
TRIAL BALANCE

31 December 20X5		
Cash	$15,000	
Accounts receivable	15,000	
Inventories	17,000	
Equipment	22,400	
Land	6,400	
Building	7,600	
Deferred charges	1,100	
Accounts payable		$ 5,500
Note payable, 10%		8,000
Share capital, no par, 2,500 shares outstanding		38,500
Retained earnings		32,500
Totals	$84,500	$84,500

d. The balance in the land account includes a $1,000 payment made as a deposit on the purchase of an adjoining tract. The option to buy it has not yet been exercised and probably will not be exercised during the coming year.

e. The interest-bearing note dated 1 April 20X5 matures 31 March 20X6. Interest on it has not been recorded for 20X5.

Required:

1. Prepare a balance sheet with appropriate captions and subcaptions. Use preferred terminology and the financing report form format. Show the computation of the ending balance in retained earnings.
2. How would your balance sheet be different if the net assets form were used? The account format? Explain, do not illustrate.

A4-12 Prepare Balance Sheet, Analytical Questions: The data on the following page is from the accounts of Fleury Corporation on 31 December 20X5, the end of the current reporting year.

Required:

1. Prepare a complete balance sheet. Assume that all amounts are correct, and round to the nearest thousand dollars. Use the account titles as given.
2. Refer to your response to requirement (1) and respond to the following:
   a. Give the amount of working capital.
   b. By what percent was the building amortized?
   c. How much of the company is financed by debt, and how much by equity?
   d. What are the more important assets of the company?

Cash	$ 116,000
Accounts receivable, trade	337,000
Short-term investment in marketable securities	440,000
Inventory of merchandise, FIFO	1,295,000
Prepaid expense (short term)	11,000
Bond sinking fund (to pay bonds at maturity)	147,000
Advances to suppliers (short term)	24,000
Dividends (cash) declared during 20X5	120,000
Rent receivable	34,000
Investment in shares of Life Systems Corporation (long term, at market)	322,000

Unamortized discount on bonds payable	42,000	
Loans to employees (company president; payment date uncertain)	225,000	
Land (building site in use)	3,300,000	
Building	7,450,000	
Equipment	3,236,000	
Franchise (used in operations) (net)	610,000	
Deferred equipment rearrangement cost (long term)	74,000	
Total debits	$17,783,000	
Mortgage payable (due 20X9 14%)		$ 6,500,000
Accounts payable, trade		426,000
Dividends (cash) payable (payable 1 March 20X6)		10,000
Deferred rent revenue		63,000
Future income tax		544,000
Accumulated amortization, building		4,210,000
Accumulated amortization, equipment		420,000
Allowance for doubtful accounts		32,000
Bonds payable (12.5%, maturity 20X13)		2,200,000
Common shares (50,000 shares outstanding)		1,400,000
Preferred shares (8,000 shares outstanding)		400,000
Retained earnings, 1 January 20X5		1,190,000
Net income for 20X5		388,000
Total credits		$17,783,000

A4-13 Analyzing Data and Reporting on the Balance Sheet: Akeman Seed Corporation is preparing its balance sheet at 31 December 20X5. The following items are under consideration:

a. Note payable, long term, $80,000. This note will be paid in instalments. The first instalment, $10,000, will be paid 1 August 20X6.

b. Bonds payable, 12%, $200,000; at 31 December 20X5, unamortized premium amounted to $6,000.

c. Bond sinking fund, $40,000; this fund is being accumulated to retire the bonds at maturity.

d. Rent revenue collected in advance for the first quarter of 20X6, $6,000.

e. After the balance sheet date, but prior to issuance of the 20X5 balance sheet, one-third of the merchandise inventory was destroyed by flood (13 January 20X6); estimated loss, $150,000.

f. Bonds payable, $475,000. At maturity, the investor may choose to receive cash or common shares. Interest must be paid annually.

g. Redeemable preferred shares, $250,000. At maturity, the company has to repay investors the stated value of the shares plus dividends in arrears, if any.

Required:

Show by illustration, with appropriate captions, how each of these items should be reported on the 31 December 20X5 balance sheet. If amounts are not quantifiable, describe the appropriate reporting that would be followed when numbers are available.

A4-14 Redraft a Deficient Balance Sheet: Rutgers e-Terminal Limited is a private corporation that is wholly owned by Mr. Adonis Rutgers. Mr. Rutgers also personally owns 40% of the common shares of a company named Princeton Corporation. A further 20% of the common shares are held by Rutgers e-Terminal Limited. The bookkeeper for Rutgers e-Terminal prepared the following balance sheet:

RUTGERS E-TERMINAL LIMITED
FINANCIAL SITUATION

For the year ending 31 December 20X3

Short-term assets		
Cash on hand	$ 300	
Cash in the Royal Dominion chequing account	15,200	
Overdraft in the ScotiaTrust chequing account	−3,800	
Accounts receivable (includes credit balances of $22,000)	52,600	
Automobile held for resale (fully depreciated—estimated market value)	20,000	
Supplies on hand	1,500	
Inventory for sale	37,900	
Final month's rent on office space (lease expires in 20X7)	3,000	
Investment in shares of Princeton Corporation	110,000	
		$236,700
Long-term assets		
Furniture	40,000	
Warehouse	500,000	
Prepaid expenses	4,500	
Note receivable from customer (issued 5 March 20X1, due on Mr. Rutger's demand)	30,000	
Loan receivable from shareholder	120,000	694,500
Total financial assets		$931,200
Liabilities		
Payable to suppliers	$175,300	
Estimated amounts due for future expenses	50,000	
Reserve for depreciation on furniture	10,000	
Reserve for depreciation on warehouse	75,000	
Mortgage due to the Montreal National Bank	380,000	
Common shares of Rutgers e-Terminal held by Mr. Rutgers	150,000	
Accumulated surplus	90,900	
Total financial liabilities		$931,200

Required:
Prepare a corrected classified balance sheet, using appropriate terminology.

★★★

A4-15 Criticize and Redraft a Deficient Balance Sheet: The most recent balance sheet of Blackstone Tire Corporation appears below:

BLACKSTONE TIRE CORPORATION
BALANCE SHEET

For the year ended 31 December 20X5

Assets	
Current	
Cash	$ 23,000
Short-term investments	10,000
Accounts receivable	15,000
Merchandise	31,000
Supplies	5,000
Shares of Wilmont Co. (not a controlling interest)	17,000
	$101,000

Investments			
Loan to shareholder			82,500
Tangible:			
Building and land ($10,000)	$86,000		
Less: reserve for depreciation	40,000	46,000	
Equipment	$20,000		
Less: reserve for depreciation	15,000	5,000	51,000
Deferred			
Prepaid expenses			5,000
Total			$239,500
Debt and Capital			
Current			
Accounts payable		$16,000	
Reserve for future, deferred income tax		17,000	
Customers' accounts receivable with credit balance		100	$ 33,100
Fixed (interest paid at year-end):			
Bonds payable, 8.5%, due 20X9		45,000	
Mortgage, 11%		12,000	57,000
Reserve for bad debts			900
Capital			
Preferred shares, authorized and outstanding, 6,000 redeemable shares. Must be repaid in 20X9		50,000	
Common shares, authorized 10,000 shares, no par		67,000	
Earned surplus		22,500	
Donated capital		9,000	148,500
Total			$239,500

Required:

1. List and explain in writing your criticisms of the above statement.
2. Prepare a complete balance sheet as far as possible; use appropriate format, captions, and terminology.

A4-16 Income Statement and the Balance Sheet, Format, Disclosures: The adjusted trial balance and other related data for Amana Cement Corporation, at 31 December 20X5, are given below. Although the company uses some obsolete terminology, the amounts are correct.

AMANA CEMENT CORPORATION
ADJUSTED TRIAL BALANCE
31 December 20X5

Debit Balance Accounts	
Cash	$ 38,600
Land (used for building site)	129,000
Cost of goods sold	150,000
Short-term securities (shares of Sanders Co.)	42,000
Goodwill	120,000
Merchandise inventory	29,000
Office supplies inventory	2,000
Patent	7,000

Operating expenses	55,000
Income tax expense	17,500
Bond discount (unamortized)	7,500
Prepaid insurance	900
Building (at cost)	150,000
Land (held for speculation)	75,000
Accrued interest receivable	300
Accounts receivable (trade)	22,700
Note receivable, 10% (long-term investment)	30,000
Subscriber lists (net)	9,000
Deferred plant rearrangement costs	26,000
Dividends, paid during 20X5	15,000
Correction of error from prior year—no income tax effect	15,000
	$941,500

Credit Balance Accounts

Reserve for bad debts	$ 1,100
Accounts payable (trade)	15,000
Revenues	275,000
Deferred income tax	47,500
Note payable (short term)	12,000
Common shares, no par, authorized 50,000 shares, 10,000 shares outstanding	100,000
Reserve for depreciation, building	90,000
Retained earnings, 1 January 20X5	188,500
Accrued wages	2,100
Non-controlling interest (balance sheet account)	10,000
Reserve for patent amortization	4,000
Cash advance from customer	3,000
Accrued property taxes	800
Note payable (long term)	16,000
Rent revenue collected in advance	1,500
Bonds payable, 11% ($25,000 due 1 June 20X6)	175,000
	$941,500

Additional information (no accounting errors are involved):

a. Cost and market value of the short-term marketable securities is $44,000.
b. Merchandise inventory is based on FIFO, lower of cost or market.
c. The patent is being amortized (written off) over a 10-year period. The amortization for 20X5 has already been recorded.
d. Operating expenses as given include amortization and interest expense, and revenues include interest and investment revenues.
e. The "cash advance from customer" was for a special order that will not be completed and shipped until March 20X6; the sales price has not been definitely established because it is to be based on cost (no revenue should be recognized for 20X5).

Required:

1. Prepare a single-step income statement and a separate retained earnings statement. Include EPS disclosures. (In this situation, EPS is net income divided by common shares outstanding.)
2. Prepare a balance sheet. Use preferred terminology, captions, and subcaptions.
3. Indicate the likely note disclosure for balance sheet items.

A4-17 Income Statement and Balance Sheet—Disclosure: The adjusted trial balance for Decca Industries Corporation at 31 December 20X5 is given below in no particular order. Debits and credits are not indicated; however, debits equal credits. All amounts are correct.

Work-in-process inventory	$ 87,000
Accrued interest on notes payable	3,000
Accrued interest receivable	3,600
Accrued interest on short-term investments	3,000
Common shares, no par, authorized 100,000 shares, issued 120,000	450,000
Cash in bank	90,000
Trademarks (amortized cost)	4,200
Land held for speculation	81,000
Supplies inventory	1,800
Goodwill	54,000
Raw materials inventory	39,000
Bond sinking fund	30,000
Accrued property taxes	4,200
Accounts receivable (trade)	87,000
Accrued wages	6,300
Mortgage payable (due in three years)	30,000
Building	390,000
Cash equivalent short-term investments, at market value	5,700
Organization expenses (amortized cost)	23,400
Deposits (cash collected from customers on sales orders to be delivered next quarter: no revenue yet recognized)	3,000
Long-term investment in bonds of Royal Corp. (at amortized cost)	150,000
Patents (amortized cost)	42,000
Reserve for depreciation, office equipment	4,800
Reserve for depreciation, building	15,000
Cash on hand for change	1,200
Preferred shares, $1, no par, authorized 40,000 shares, issued 18,000 shares, non-cumulative, non-convertible	204,000
Pre-collected rent income	2,700
Finished goods inventory	129,000
Notes receivable (short term)	12,000
Bonds payable, 12% (due in six years)	105,000
Future income tax liability	45,000
Accounts payable (trade)	51,000
Reserve for bad credits	4,200
Notes payable (short term)	21,600
Office equipment	75,000
Land (used as building site)	24,000
Short-term investments (at market)	46,500
Retained earnings (1 January 20X5)	69,600
Cash dividends, declared and paid during 20X5	60,000
Revenues during 20X5	1,500,000
Cost of goods sold for 20X5	900,000
Expenses for 20X5 (including interest, amortization, and income tax)	300,000
Income taxes payable	120,000

Required:

1. Prepare a single-step income statement; use preferred terminology. Include EPS disclosure; to compute EPS, deduct $18,000 from net income as an allocation to non-convertible preferred shares and then divide by the common shares outstanding.
2. Prepare a complete balance sheet; use preferred terminology, format, captions, and subcaptions. Indicate likely note disclosure.
3. Assume that between 31 December 20X5, and issuance of the financial statements, a flood damaged the finished goods inventory in an amount estimated to be $60,000. How should this event be reflected in the 20X5 financial statements?

A4-18 Note Disclosures: Note disclosures provide the following information:

1. Provide accounting policy information (information to evaluate data and make comparisons).
2. Describe recognized items.
3. Describe unrecognized items.
4. Provide information regarding future cash flows.
5. Provide alternative measurement information.
6. Help assess return on investment.

Typical notes include:

__2__ a. Description of income statement item, discontinued operations.
_____ b. Revenue recognition policy.
_____ c. Breakdown of balance sheet total for other assets.
_____ d. Description of contingent loss that is not measurable.
_____ e. Amortization policy and amounts of accumulated amortization by asset class.
_____ f. Inventory note—breakdown of inventory into component parts and description of valuation method.
_____ g. Preferred share dividend rate.
_____ h. Description of subsequent event not relating to conditions before balance sheet date.
_____ i. Information on key operating segments of the business.
_____ j. Description of related-party transactions.
_____ k. Long-term debt note—interest rates, terms to maturity, five-year cash flow, market value.
_____ l. Details of outstanding stock options (not recorded in the financial statements).
_____ m. Fair value of debt.
_____ n. Consolidation policy.

Required:

For each note (a) to (n) above, indicate the type(s) of disclosure (numbers (1) to (6)) provided. A note may provide more than one type of disclosure. The first one is done for you as an example.

A4-19 Contingencies: Unlimited Possibilities Limited (UPL) is finalizing the financial statements for 20X5. The company's managers are uncertain how each of the following events and situations should be reported:

a. The company introduced a major new product in the last quarter of the year. Initial sales were $5 million in 20X5. The product carries a two-year replacement guarantee. By the end of 20X5, 0.5% of the units sold had been returned for replacement, at a total cost to UPL of $10,000. Management estimates that return will continue at that rate for the next two quarters, and then taper off over the remainder of the guarantee period.

b. The company owns a lot adjacent to its building that once was the site of a gasoline station. UPL bought the land from the prior owners three years ago, and uses the lot for employee parking. The company has applied to the city for permission to use the lot for expanding its current building, but the city will not issue a building permit until the land is decontaminated. The estimated cost of cleaning the soil ranges from $500,000 to $1,500,000—the exact cost will not be known until the pavement has been removed and full soil testing is possible, which will not occur for at least four months.
c. UPL is the guarantor on a $10 million bank loan that was obtained by another company controlled by the same shareholders who control UPL. The other company has more liabilities than assets, and its cash flow from operations is declining rather alarmingly.
d. UPL has a subsidiary in Japan. UPL has reached agreement to sell the Japanese subsidiary to a Taiwanese company, subject to approval by regulators in Japan. Approval is expected, but it will be at least six months before the outcome will be known for sure. When the sale closes, UPL will realize a profit of $20 million as the purchase price is $20 million higher than the subsidiary's net book value.
e. A minority shareholder alleges that UPL's controlling shareholders entered into transactions that had the effect of reducing the minority shareholder's equity in the company. (In securities legislation this type of action is known as "shareholder oppression.") The minority shareholder filed a complaint with the provincial securities commission, claiming damages of $50 million. The securities commission ruled in favour of the minority shareholder. UPL is appealing the case and UPL's lawyers are confident that the court will overturn the ruling in approximately one year.

Required:
Discuss the appropriate reporting for each of these items on UPL's 20X5 financial statements.

A4-20 Subsequent Events: The auditor has completed her work on the financial statements of Leslie Kwok Incorporated (LKI) for the year ended 31 December 20X7, but the statements have not yet been issued. The auditor signed the audit opinion on 23 March 20X8. The following transactions and events occurred after 31 December 20X7:

a. On 27 January, LKI entered into a long-term lease for a private airplane for the company president and CEO. The lease requires payments of U.S.$75,000 per month for 60 months.
b. On 28 January, LKI acquired all of the shares of Phan Limited by issuing LKI shares in exchange. The acquisition more than doubled the size of KLI, and the former shareholders of Phan now have a majority of the votes in KLI.
c. On 15 February, the Board of Directors of KLI decided to discontinue a major segment of the company's business due to continuing losses and a change of strategy.
d. The Royal Toronto Bank of Montreal extended a $50 million line of credit to KLI on 5 March.
e. One of the company's major customers declared bankruptcy on 22 March. The customer accounted for 27% of KLI's revenue in 20X7.
f. On 31 March, LKI reached an agreement with a major institutional investor to issue $500 million in secured debentures through a private placement.
g. A new Board of Directors was elected on 7 April.
h. On 10 April, the new directors cancelled the lease on the private airplane. The contract calls for a cancellation penalty of U.S.$1 million.

Required:
Discuss how each item should be reported in KLI's 20X7 financial statements as a *subsequent event*, if at all.

A4-21 Contingencies, Subsequent Events: Zero Growth Limited has completed financial statements for the year ended 31 December 20X6. The financial statements have yet to be finalized or issued. The following events and transactions have occurred:

a. The office building housing administrative staff burned to the ground on 15 January 20X7.

b. On 15 November 20X6, a customer sued the company for $1,000,000 based on a claim of negligence leading to personal injury; Zero Growth is actively defending the suit and claims it is unfounded. Nothing has yet been recorded in the 20X6 financial statements in relation to this event.
c. On 1 February 20X7, Zero Growth received a $49,700 income tax reassessment for 20X5.
d. On 20 December 20X6, Zero Growth applied for a bank loan to replace an existing line of credit. The loan was granted on 2 January 20X7. Nothing was recorded in the 20X6 financial statements in relation to this event.
e. Zero Growth has reinterpreted a legal agreement entitling it to commission revenue for the sale of a client's products. Zero Growth's interpretation would entitle it to an extra $60,000 over and above amounts recognized in 20X6. The amount has not been recorded in the accounts. The client was billed for this amount in 20X6 but has disagreed with Zero Growth on the contract interpretation. Both parties have consulted their lawyers; resolution of the issue is not expected soon.
f. On 1 March 20X7, Zero Growth issued common shares for cash.

Required:
Discuss the appropriate accounting treatment for the contingencies and subsequent events described.

A4-22 Financial Instruments: Financial instruments may require disclosure of

1. Terms and conditions
2. Interest rates
3. Credit risk
4. Fair value

Consider the following balance sheet elements:

A. Accounts receivable
B. Inventory
C. Unearned revenue
D. Bank loan payable
E. Preferred shares
F. Machinery and equipment
G. Loans receivable
H. Bonds payable

Required:
1. Which of the above items are financial instruments? Specify whether the item is a financial asset, financial liability, or equity instrument.
2. For the items designated as financial instruments in requirement (1), specify which of the listed disclosures, above, are required.

A4-23 Financial Instruments: The AcSB recommends that financial instruments be classified by their nature, as debt (with required cash payment) or equity (a residual interest). When a financial instrument has characteristics of both debt and equity, the carrying value of the instrument should be separated into its debt and equity components for reporting in the financial statements. Kreiz Corporation issued the following financial instruments in the current year, 20X3:

a. Preferred shares that carry a dividend of $100 per share. On 1 January 20X9, the holder can require Kreiz to redeem the shares at a price of $750. There are 100,000 shares issued and outstanding.
b. Bonds payable with a term of 10 years, with required annual interest payments. At maturity, the investor may elect to receive cash or a specified number of common shares of Kreiz.

Required:
Discuss how each of these financial instruments should be reported on Kreitz's balance sheet at the end of 20X3.

A4-24 Special Disclosures: Respond to the specific questions in each of the three cases, below.

Case A. The following disclosure note is from the 31 October 20X2 financial statements of GreenWorld Limited, a mining company:

> The preparation of the financial statements in conformity with generally accepted accounting principles requires management to make estimates and assumptions that affect the reported amounts of assets and liabilities and disclosure of contingent assets and liabilities at the date of the financial statements and the reported amounts of revenues and expenses during the reporting period. The most significant estimates are related to the physical and economic lives and the recoverability of mining assets, mineral reserves, site restoration and related obligations, commodity contracts and financial instruments, and income taxes. Actual results could differ from those estimates.

Required:

1. What is the purpose of this disclosure note?
2. How could this note be made more meaningful to the financial statement user?
3. List four other financial statement elements (not listed above) that are affected by estimates.

Case B. The following disclosure note is from the 31 December 20X2 financial statements of UMM Limited, a software company:

> UMM has entered into an agreement with Vitech Ltd, a shareholder, with respect to acquiring certain rights to Vitech's software, technology, services, and other benefits. In the current year, UMM acquired $200 (million) of specific software products from Vitech. These assets were recorded at the transaction price, which represents fair market value as determined by an independent appraisal. UMM has expensed $68 (million) in services received from Vitech in 20X2. Sales in 20X2 to Vitech amounted to $151 (million). These transactions were conducted in the normal course of business at prices established and agreed to by both parties.

Required:

1. What is the purpose of this disclosure note?
2. In general, what makes two parties related?
3. What measurement attribute has been used to record software assets, and revenues and expenses between these related parties? Comment.
4. What evidence has UMM gathered to support the value for software purchased?

Case C. The following disclosure note is from the 31 December 20X2 financial statements of Zing Limited, property developer:

> On 7 January 20X3, the Corporation contracted to acquire 60 residential housing units from a third party for a purchase price of $2.8 million, cash. On 24 January 20X3, the Company issued 240,000 stock options to senior officers of the company. These options have a three-year vesting period, with one-third vesting on each anniversary date.

Required:

1. What is the purpose of this disclosure note?
2. Why are these events disclosed rather than recorded in the financial statements?

A4-25 Special Disclosures: Respond to the specific questions in each of the three cases, below.

Case A. The following disclosure note is from the 30 April 20X2 financial statements of Miller Mining Limited:

> The Company has negative working capital and significant obligations with respect to long-term debt in the first quarter of 20X3. This serious financial position has been caused by consistently low commodity process for the base metals mined by the Company. These financial statements have been prepared in accordance with Canadian generally accepted accounting principles applicable to a going concern, which assumes that the company will continue in operations for the foreseeable future and will be able to realize its assets and discharge its liabilities in the normal course of business. The Company must complete negotiations with major creditors and potential new investors in the immediate future to ensure its viability.

Required:

1. What is the purpose of this disclosure note?
2. What will be the outcome if the Company is unsuccessful in negotiations with creditors and investors?
3. What items on the financial statement will change, and how will they change, if negotiations are not successful?

Case B. The following disclosure note is from the 31 December 20X4 financial statements of Riconda Limited:

> The Company operates one operating segment, that being the design, manufacture, and sale of graphics and multimedia products for personal computers and consumer electronic devices.

	20X2	20X1	20X0
Sales			
Canada	$ 23,104	$ 31,119	$ 41,175
United States	325,464	424,472	425,000
Europe	247,795	396,805	412,855
Asia-Pacific	441,446	430,669	307,320
Consolidated sales	$1,037,809	$1,283,065	$1,186,350
Product Sales			
Components	$ 481,083	$ 499,859	$ 390,238
Boards	548,053	778,015	796,112
Other	8,673	5,191	—
Consolidated sales	$1,037,809	$1,283,065	$1,186,350
Capital and Intangible Assets			
Canada	$ 54,162	$ 42,494	$ 36,590
United States	297,417	421,955	31,341
Europe	5,071	5,364	5,410
Asia-Pacific	706	919	1,051
Consolidated capital and intangible assets	$ 357,356	$ 470,732	$ 74,392

Required:

1. What is the purpose of this disclosure note?
2. Evaluate the information presented. What does it tell you about the Company's operations?
3. Review the requirements for segmented disclosures. What information is lacking in the note presented above? Why?

Case C. The following disclosure note is from the 31 December 20X3 financial statements of Limpid Limited:

> All of the Company's sales take place with the parent company, Limpid U.S. Limited. Sales are recorded at the exchange value, which is negotiated by and agreed to by both parties. At year-end, Limpid U.S. owed the Company $540 million with respect to these sales. This amount is in the normal course of business and subject to payment in 60 days.

Required:

1. What is the purpose of this disclosure note?
2. What value is used to record the sale transactions? What conclusions would you draw about the company's income statement as a result of this information?
3. How could fair market value be determined in these circumstances?

A4-26 Balance Sheet Interpretation: The balance sheet of Karmax Ltd. discloses the following assets:

KARMAX LIMITED
EXTRACTS FROM THE BALANCE SHEET

(stated in thousands of Canadian dollars)

At year ended 31 December 20X6		
Assets		
Current assets		
Cash	$ 710	
Short-term investments	416	
Accounts receivable	1,011	
Inventory	2,600	
Prepaid expenses	410	
Total current assets		$ 5,147
Tangible capital assets, net		14,755
Intangible capital assets, net		984
Long-term investments		1,077
Total assets		$21,963

The following information has been established in relation to market values (amounts in $ thousands):

	Market value	Source
Short-term investments	$416	Quoted stock market price
Inventory	$4,190	Karmax price list
Tangible capital assets	$20,000–$25,000	Real estate appraisal
Long-term investment	$3,000	(Note 1)
Intangible capital assets	$10,000	(Note 2)

Note 1
The long-term investment is an investment in the common shares of a company owned and operated by the two sons of Karmax's major shareholder. The Karmax investment is 25% of the outstanding shares. The long-term investment is accounted for using the equity method. The sons' company has never sold shares to a non-family investor, and the Karmax shareholder provided this estimate of value.

Note 2
Karmax holds patents on a successful consumer product, licensed to various manufacturers. Significant annual royalties are earned; the recorded balance sheet value consists of legal fees paid during patent infringement cases. The $10 million estimate of market value is based on discounted future cash flow.

Required:

Prepare a brief report that contains

1. An analysis of the reliability of the various market value estimates as a good predictor of future cash flows.
2. An assessment of the usefulness of the (primarily historical cost) balance sheet to
   a. A banker making a lending decision.
   b. An investor evaluating return on investment.

A4-27 Balance Sheet Interpretation: The following balance sheet reports the financial position of a junior Canadian gold-mining company (amounts in $ thousands):

Assets		
Current assets		
Cash and cash equivalents	$ 8,260	
Accounts receivable, less allowance for doubtful accounts	20,338	
Taxes recoverable	200	
Inventories	20,800	
Prepaid expenses	500	
Investments (cost is equal to market value)	1,830	$ 51,928
Plant, equipment, and mine development costs, net		95,000
Goodwill		2,000
Total assets		$148,928
Liabilities and shareholders' equity		
Current liabilities		
Accounts payable and accrued liabilities	$ 6,550	
Royalties payable	560	$ 7,110
Future liability for site restoration costs		2,280
Convertible bonds		12,000
Future income taxes payable		1,830
Non-controlling interest		1,080
Shareholders' equity		
Convertible bonds	1,128	
Share capital	100,000	
Retained earnings	23,000	
Cumulative exchange adjustment	500	
		124,628
Total liabilities and shareholders' equity		$148,928

Required:

1. Explain the meaning of the following accounts:
   a. Mine development costs.
   b. Goodwill.
   c. Future liability for site restoration costs.
   d. Future income tax.
   e. Non-controlling interest.
   f. Convertible bonds.
   g. Cumulative exchange adjustment.
2. What items on the above balance sheet would mostly likely be estimated? Explain.
3. For what assets would you expect the market value and book value to be the most different? Explain.
4. As a potential shareholder, what additional information would be relevant to any decision to acquire shares in this company? Why is this information not presented with the audited financial statements?

CHAPTER 5

The Cash Flow Statement

INTRODUCTION

The purpose of the cash flow statement is to reveal the various types of cash flows within the company. Cash flows relate to (1) operating activities, (2) investing in (or selling) assets, and (3) issuing or redeeming debt and equity financial instruments. Users can see more than just the net effect on the balance sheet accounts—they can see where the cash came from and where it went. As well, the cash flow statement discloses the amount of cash (as distinct from income) that flows from operations, and also the reasons for the difference between net income and cash flow from operations.

Most users of financial statements are interested in cash flows because, in the long run, users base their own projections of cash flow on those of the company. For example, investors are interested in the amount that is available to pay out in dividends, bankers need to know how a company expects to generate cash to pay its loans, employees need to know the company's "ability to pay" when negotiating wages, salaries, and fringe benefits, and so forth.

The AcSB has identified cash flow prediction as a principal objective of financial reporting. The starting point of cash flow prediction is the analysis of historical cash flows. Therefore, the objective of the cash flow statement is to disclose the historical cash flows of the enterprise during the reporting period.

This chapter discusses the preparation and interpretation of the cash flow statement. As we discuss individual categories of assets, liabilities, and shareholders' equity in following chapters, we also will point out the cash flow impact of that topic.

EVOLUTION OF THE CASH FLOW STATEMENT

cash flow statement
an accounting statement describing the uses and sources of cash for a specific period of time

The cash flow statement has changed more over the past 20 years than any other financial statement. Even the title of **cash flow statement** is fairly recent. Previously, the generic name for the statement was the *statement of changes in financial position.* Earlier names included the *where-got, where-gone statement,* the *statement of source and application of funds,* and the more general *funds flow statement.*

The original focus of the statement was on changes in non-current assets, non-current liabilities, and owners' equity. The underlying assumption was that changes in the current assets and current liabilities were reflected in the income statement through revenues and expenses. Often, the statement was little more than a listing of the changes in long-term assets, liabilities, and shareholders' equity, with the *net* change in working capital (current assets minus current liabilities) as the balancing amount.

The statement was often perceived to be an analysis of working capital itself, although that was not the intended purpose. The statement did present a section labelled *funds provided by operations,* and this was widely interpreted as cash flow from operations. However, when "funds" are defined as net working capital, the amount is affected by accounting policies chosen for all of the current assets, including inventories. This led to an anomalous situation when companies that reported a positive funds flow from operations went into receivership; working capital was increasing because inventories were increasing and receivable collection periods were lengthening, but actual cash flow was down.

In 1985, the AcSB substantially revised Section 1540 to eliminate the working capital approach and focus instead on cash flows. The overall focus of the statement thereby shifted from the historical approach of analyzing long-term assets, long-term liabilities, and owners' equities to that of analyzing cash flows, regardless of the nature of the flows.

In 1996, the AcSB proposed to further modify Section 1540 to bring it in line with International Accounting Standard (IAS) 7. IAS 7 was endorsed in 1993 by the International Organization of Securities Commissions and, in 1994, by the U.S. Securities and Exchange Commission as an alternative to existing FASB standards.

The exposure draft was accepted by the AcSB with only minor changes, and was introduced into the *CICA Handbook* in 1998. This latest revision is an effort at international harmonization, and increases the emphasis on cash flow as the basic measurement approach for the statement, rather than changes in assets and liabilities. In essence, the new standard is the culmination of a long process of moving from a statement of changes in non-current assets and liabilities to a true cash flow statement: *if a transaction doesn't involve cash, then it doesn't go on the cash flow statement!*

CASH FLOW REPORTING

Cash versus Accrual

Under the accrual basis, financial assets and liabilities (that is, receivables and payables) are recorded when the reporting enterprise has a right to receive cash or the obligation to pay cash, rather than later when the cash flows actually occur. It is due to the accrual basis that balance sheets show accounts receivable and payable and accrued revenues and expenses.

revenue
the inflow of assets, the reduction of liabilities, or both from transactions involving the corporation's normal business activities

expense
decreases in economic resources resulting from ordinary revenue-generating on service delivery activities

Interperiod allocations refer to the revenue and expense recognition policies that a company uses to measure net income. A transaction may give rise to a liability, for example, and recording that liability is an application of the accrual basis. The second decision is when to recognize the cost in net income. The cost that gave rise to the liability could be recorded as an expense immediately, or could be deferred until a later period (such as for prepaid expenses or inventories), or capitalized and amortized (such as long-lived assets that are depreciated or amortized). Interperiod allocation also occurs for revenue, especially when the earnings cycle extends over two or more accounting periods.

It is important to keep in mind the difference between **receipts** and **disbursements** and between **revenues** and **expenses**:

- Receipts and disbursements are *cash inflows* and *outflows.* They can be for any purpose, whether to generate operating earnings, change the asset structure, or increase or decrease liabilities.

- Revenues and expenses relate to receipts and disbursements because without the cash flow, there can be no revenue or expense. But revenues and expenses are derived from only *some* cash flows and relate only to net income determination. For example, receipts from a share issue are not revenues, and payments to retire bonds are not expenses. Only a subset of cash flows ever becomes a revenue or expense.
- Because of the accrual concept, a cash receipt or disbursement that gives rise to a revenue or expense may occur in a different period than that in which the revenue or expense is recognized.

On the cash flow statement, the effects of both accruals and interperiod allocations (such as amortization) are eliminated, leaving only the cash receipts and cash disbursements.

As we have seen in previous chapters (and will see in later chapters as well), preparers of financial statements must make many accounting policy choices. The various combinations of choices will affect net income, perhaps very significantly. Cash flow, however, is not affected by accounting policy choices. Cash flow is not "pure," though. Actual cash flows may be altered by management to some extent, such as by making discretionary pension funding contributions or by delaying payment of some obligations, but these are not accounting *policy* choices. Furthermore, accounting policy choices can affect the *way* in which cash flows are reported in the cash flow statement. Indeed, it is quite possible for management to make some accounting choices specifically to affect the reporting of a certain type of transaction on the cash flow statement.

Definition of "Cash"

cash
an asset; the amount of money on hand and in the bank

It might appear that **cash** is cash; it seems to be an unambiguous term. It is not quite so simple, however. In its purest form, cash is currency, but companies do not keep large amounts of currency on hand except for daily operating purposes in cash registers or petty cash funds. In financial circles, cash is better described as the amount of funds that can be accessed by the company at any time, or on demand. In Canada, this is the amount that is held in the company's **current account(s)** with the bank. The current account is the chequing account, except that unlike personal chequing accounts, deposited cheques are not held for collection and the company's cheques are less likely to be returned NSF ("not sufficient funds") if the account is temporarily overdrawn.

Cash is a non-productive asset, and therefore companies strive to keep their immediately accessible cash balance at a minimum. Instead of carrying large cash balances, companies place their cash in term deposits, guaranteed investment certificates, certificates of deposit, or other money market instruments so that they can earn interest. For purposes of the cash flow statement, therefore, cash includes cash on hand, cash on deposit, and highly liquid short-term investments. These are known as cash and **cash equivalents**. IAS 7 and Section 1540 recommend that "for an investment to qualify as a cash equivalent it must be readily convertible to a known amount of cash and be subject to an insignificant risk of changes in value" (*CICA* 1540.08). Three months is suggested as the maximum maturity period. Investments in shares are explicitly excluded.

cash equivalents
one of the components of cash on the cash flow statement; highly liquid, short-term (e.g., three-month term) investments

overdraft
a negative bank balance reported as a current liability; usually part of cash on the cash flow statement

OVERDRAFTS AND LINES OF CREDIT Corporations often are authorized by their banks to have an **overdraft**, which is a negative balance in their chequing account. For example, suppose that a company begins the year with a balance of $10,000 in its current account. By the end of the year, the cash balance is completely used up and the company has written $15,000 more cheques than it has cash. The current account will have a negative balance or an overdraft of $15,000. The change in cash for the year is not simply the decline in cash from $10,000 to zero, but is the change from a $10,000 asset to a $15,000 liability—a decrease of $25,000.

Bank overdrafts form an integral part of an enterprise's cash management. Bank overdrafts are included as a component of cash and cash equivalents when the bank balance fluctuates from positive to negative on a regular basis. That is, if the current account is always overdrawn, it is in substance a bank loan and not a cash equivalent. The current account must be regularly positive and then overdrawn to qualify as "cash." Furthermore, the overdrafts have to be repayable at any time that the bank demands payment (*CICA* 1540.10).

Another important part of cash management is a line of credit. A **line of credit** is a pre-approved borrowing limit that the company has negotiated with the bank in advance. Lines of credit often are used to cover seasonal fluctuations in cash flows. However, lines of credit and other types of short-time bank loans normally are viewed as financing activities and are excluded from cash and cash equivalents.

The components of cash and cash equivalents (including overdrafts) must be disclosed, and the net change that is reported in the cash flow statement should be reconciled to the equivalent items in the balance sheet (*CICA* 1540.48).

Classification of Cash Flows

Once upon a time, the cash flow statement was organized into two sections: (1) sources of cash and (2) uses of cash; the defining characteristic was whether the cash was coming in or going out. Since 1985, though, the recommended classification is on the basis of the type of cash flow:

- **Operating activities** are the principal revenue-producing activities of the enterprise and the related expenditures. The cash inflow from operations is measured as the cash received from customers or clients, plus other revenue-generating activities such as finance revenue. The cash outflows are those disbursements that are incurred to earn the inflow, such as cash paid for inventories, wages and salaries, and overhead costs.
- **Investing activities** are those activities that relate to the asset structure of the company, other than current operating assets such as inventory and accounts receivable. The acquisition and disposal of tangible and intangible capital assets and investments in other assets that are *not* included in cash equivalents are included in this section.
- **Financing activities** relate to liabilities (other than operating liabilities, such as accounts payable) and owners' equity. Cash flows that increase or decrease the size or composition of the non-operating accounts on the right side of the balance sheet are reported in this section.

Exhibit 5-1 lists some of the transactions that fall into each category.

Interest income and expense offer a particular classification challenge. Interest income and interest expense that have been included in determining net income should remain as part of operating cash flow, *but separately disclosed* (*CICA* 1540.34). Interest payments that are *not* included in net income would be classified "according to their nature" (*CICA* 1540.35). For example, interest that has been capitalized will be reported as part of the investment in the related asset.

Similarly, accountants have had difficulty agreeing on the appropriate classification of dividends in the cash flow statement. In current practice, dividends *received* and reported in net income should be reported as an operating cash flow. Dividends received from controlled or significantly influenced affiliates are not included in net income and therefore should be reported in the investing activities section.

Dividends *paid* are not included in net income and therefore should not be included in operating cash flow. Instead, dividend payments are separately disclosed, usually as a financing activity (that is, as a payment to providers of equity capital) (*CICA* 1540.35).

EXHIBIT 5-1

EXAMPLES OF CASH FLOWS BY CATEGORY

OPERATING CASH FLOWS

Inflows	Outflows
Receipts from customers Advance deposits from customers Income tax refunds Interest received on customers' notes or accounts Dividends and interest received from investments and included in determining net income	Payments to suppliers Wages and salaries to employees Income tax payments Other tax payments Interest paid on bank debt or bonds outstanding and included in determining net income

INVESTING CASH FLOWS

Inflows	Outflows
Cash received from sale of capital assets Cash from sale of debt or equity investments Collection of principal on loans to others Interest and dividends received on investments and not included in determining net income	Payments for purchase of capital assets Cash flows capitalized as intangible assets, such as: • development costs • start-up costs • capitalized interest • exploration costs Purchase of debt or equity securities of others Loans extended to others

FINANCING CASH FLOWS

Inflows	Outflows
Net proceeds of issuing debt or equity securities Cash proceeds received from bank loans	Payment of principal on bonds or bank loans Purchase of the entity's own shares Interest paid on bonds not included in determining net income Dividends paid to shareholders

Sample Cash Flow Statement

Exhibit 5-2 shows the 2003 cash flow statement for Research in Motion (RIM). You should observe a few important aspects of this statement:

1. For all three categories, the cash flows can be either positive or negative. For example, financing activities include both cash outflows for buyback of common shares and the proceeds from issuing new share capital.

2. The positive and negative flows are *not* netted. For example, as shown, RIM had a cash inflow of $345,983 thousand in 2003 from sale of marketable securities, and also had a cash outflow of $41,900 thousand to acquire marketable securities.

EXHIBIT 5-2

RESEARCH IN MOTION LIMITED
CONSOLIDATED STATEMENTS OF CASH FLOWS

(United States dollars, in thousands)

	March 1 2003	For the Years Ended March 2 2002	February 28 2001
Cash flows from operating activities			
Net loss	$(148,664)	$(28,479)	$(6,211)
Items not requiring an outlay of cash:			
Amortization	31,600	17,740	9,123
Future income taxes	28,598	(16,921)	5,011
Loss on writedown of capital assets	502	–	–
Gain on foreign currency translation of long term debt	(359)	–	–
Writedown of investments	–	5,350	14,750
Foreign exchange gain (loss)	20	4	(8)
	(88,303)	(22,306)	22,665
Net changes in non-cash working capital items			
Trade receivables	1,958	7,607	(23,029)
Other receivables	1,473	7,918	(7,859)
Inventory	6,202	30,567	(31,192)
Prepaid expenses and other	(525)	(3,467)	(17,730)
Accounts payable and accrued liabilities	24,614	(499)	34,859
Accrued litigation and related expenses	50,702	–	–
Income taxes payable	2,106	(1,018)	2,027
Deferred revenue	4,563	(1,097)	4,593
	91,093	40,011	(38,331)
	2,790	17,705	(15,666)
Cash flows from financing activities			
Issuance of share capital and warrants	1,155	1,491	615,551
Financing costs, net of income tax benefits	–	–	(30,462)
Buyback of common shares	(24,502)	(5,525)	–
Repayment of debt	(614)	(303)	(185)
	(23,961)	(4,337)	584,904
Cash flows from investing activities			
Acquisition of long-term portfolio investments	(190,030)	–	–
Acquisition of capital assets	(39,670)	(73,917)	(59,058)
Acquisition of intangible assets	(30,997)	(7,106)	(6,503)
Acquisition of subsidiaries	(21,990)	(9,709)	–
Acquisition of marketable securities	(41,900)	(925,885)	(388,672)
Proceeds on sale and maturity of marketable securities	345,983	834,907	393,683
	21,396	(181,710)	(60,550)
Foreign exchange effect on cash and cash equivalent	(20)	(4)	8
Net increase (decrease) in cash and cash equivalents for the year	205	(168,346)	508,696
Cash and cash equivalents, beginning of year	340,476	508,822	126
Cash and cash equivalents, end of year	$340,681	$340,476	$508,822

3. The cash provided by operations is calculated indirectly, by starting with net income and then taking out all of the things that did *not* require cash. This is the most common approach—we will discuss an alternative a little later in the chapter.

RIM does not report the cash flows for interest or tax on the face of the statement. Instead, this disclosure is reported in the notes.

Notice also that RIM provides two years of comparative data, and reports in U.S. dollars. Both of these reporting choices serve the U.S. stock markets, as RIM is listed on the New York Stock Exchange.

CONCEPT REVIEW

1. What are the three categories of cash flows that should be reported on a company's cash flow statement?
2. How does *cash from operations* differ from *net income*?
3. What is the definition of *cash* for purposes of the cash flow statement?
4. How should interest and dividends received and paid be reported in the cash flow statement?

PREPARING THE CASH FLOW STATEMENT

Basic Approach to Preparation

The balance sheet, income statement, and retained earnings statement are all prepared from the trial balance. Preparation of these statements can be manual or, more commonly, by computerized systems. The classification of the balance of each account is unambiguously pre-specified in the programming, and the statements (other than the cash flow statement) emerge more or less automatically from the system.

ANALYZING CASH FLOW However, the cash flow statement is not a statement that is an automatic output from account balances. Instead, it is a statement that is prepared by *analyzing* account balances and changes in balances. It is not enough, for example, to know by how much the cash balance has changed over the course of an accounting period; one must analyze the sources of the accounting entries in the cash account. Standard computerized accounting systems normally cannot do that, and therefore the cash flow statement is usually a hand-prepared statement.

If we want to prepare a statement that explains all of the cash flows, it seems logical to start by analyzing the sources of the flows in and out of the cash account(s). The entries to the general ledger cash account are usually summary entries from subsidiary records such as specialized journals or cumulative transaction records. For example, we can see how much cash was received from customers by summarizing the debits to the cash account from the accounts receivable department and/or from the summary posting of the daily cash receipts; we can see how much was paid to employees for wages and salaries by looking at the payroll accounts, etc.

Direct analysis of the cash accounts is difficult and time consuming. Therefore, the normal approach is to describe the cash activities by analyzing the changes in all of the *non-cash and cash equivalents* accounts. Since the basic, indisputable characteristic of the balance sheet is that it *balances*, we can determine cash flows by looking at the causes of the changes in all of the other accounts *except* cash and cash equivalents. For example, we can quickly determine how much cash was received from customers by looking at the total sales revenue figure (on the income statement) and adjusting that accrual-basis amount by the change in trade accounts receivable for the period. If the balance in accounts receivable went up, then we received less cash than we recognized in sales for the period; if the accounts receivable balance went down, then we received more cash than we recognized in sales.

A Simple Example

The data for preparing the cash flow statement for Simple Limited by the indirect preparation approach is shown in Exhibit 5-3. The cash account shows a change from $20 at the beginning of the year to $35 at the end, for a net increase of $15. However, there also is a short-term investment account. Assuming that this account is a *cash equivalent,* it must be included with cash. In that case the net change in the balance of cash and cash equivalents from the end of 20X4 to the end of 20X5 is a *decrease* of $35:

	Ending	Beginning	Change	
Cash balance	$35	$20	$ 15	increase
Short-term investments	20	70	(50)	decrease
Total	$55	$90		
Net increase (decrease) in cash and cash equivalents			$(35)	decrease

EXHIBIT 5-3

SIMPLE LIMITED
BALANCE SHEETS

(in thousands) 31 December	20X5	20X4
Current assets:		
Cash	$ 35	$ 20
Short-term investments	20	70
Accounts receivable	110	125
Inventory	100	135
	$ 265	$ 350
Fixed assets:		
Plant and equipment	1,100	1,000
Accumulated amortization	(250)	(300)
	850	700
Total assets	$ 1,115	$ 1,050
Current liabilities:		
Bank loan	$ 65	$ 50
Accounts payable	100	125
	165	175
Long-term note payable	300	330
Shareholders' equity:		
Common shares	100	100
Retained earnings	550	445
	650	545
Total liabilities and shareholders' equity	$1,115	$1,050

EXHIBIT 5-3 (cont'd)

SIMPLE LIMITED
STATEMENT OF INCOME AND RETAINED EARNINGS

Year ended 31 December 20X5

Revenue:	
Sales revenue	$2,000
Gain on sale of equipment	70
	2,070
Operating expenses:	
Cost of goods sold	1,100
Other expenses	640
	1,740
Net income	330
Retained earnings, 1 January	445
Dividends paid on common shares	(225)
Retained earnings, 31 December	$ 550

Additional information:

i. Other operating expenses includes $200 of amortization expense.

ii. During the year, Simple sold equipment originally costing $310 for net proceeds of $130.

The cash flow statement that can be derived from the information in Exhibit 5-3 is shown in Exhibit 5-4. (The letters in the "key" column refer to the explanations below.) In order to explain the flows that resulted in the net decrease of $35, we analyze all of the changes in the *non-cash* accounts, starting with information from the statement of income and retained earnings and with the *additional information*, as follows:

a. Net income of $330 is the basis for determining cash flow from operations. Therefore, the amount of net income is placed first in the operating activities section of the cash flow statement. Net income, of course, includes all revenues and expenses, so using net income on the cash flow statement places all revenues in operating activities, as inflows, and all expenses in operating activities, as outflows. It is then reconciled to the real cash inflow and outflow for revenue and expenses.

b. Dividends of $225 were declared (and paid) during the year. This amount is placed in the financing section. Note that net income and dividends completely explain the change in retained earnings during the year.

c. *Additional information* reveals that operating expenses includes $200 in amortization. Since amortization is an interperiod allocation of previous years' investment cash flows, its impact must be removed from net income. The $200 amortization is *added back* to net income to eliminate the effect of this interperiod allocation.

d. *Additional information* reveals that equipment that originally cost $310 was sold for $130. The income statement also shows a gain from the sale of equipment amounting to $70. The following entry must have been made when the equipment was sold:

Cash	130	
Accumulated amortization	250	
Plant and equipment		310
Gain on sale of equipment		70

On the cash flow statement, we will show the $130 cash received as an investing activity, and we need to eliminate the $70 gain from our operating cash flow. The gain is eliminated for two reasons:

1. The sale of assets is not an operating activity but reflects a change in asset structure; the disposal of assets must be reported as an investing activity.
2. The gain does not measure the actual cash flow during the period, but instead it is the difference between the proceeds of the sale and the net book value of the asset. The net book value is the original expenditure for the asset, reduced by the amortization to date.

e. Accounts receivable decreased by $15 during the year. This means that customers paid more than the amount reported as sales. The $15 is added to net income in the operations section, in order to restate the sales from an accrual to a cash basis.

f. Inventory decreased by $35. The change in inventory is a component of cost of goods sold. By definition, the beginning of year inventory was acquired in a previous period and not the current period. Therefore, a decrease in inventory indicates that less cash was paid for the goods than were sold during the year.

g. Accounts payable decreased by $25. This indicates that suppliers were paid more cash for goods and services than the company accrued during the period. The $25 decrease reduces the amount of cash from operations. The accounts payable adjustment is related to the inventory adjustment, since trade accounts payable relate largely to inventory purchases. This will be further explained later in the chapter.

h. Plant and equipment increased by $100 during the year. However, this amount is the net result of both new investment and retirement of old equipment. We know from (d) (above) that equipment with a historical cost of $310 was written off during the year. We can compute the amount of the 20X5 purchases as follows:

Beginning balance	$ 1,000
Cost of equipment sold during the year	−310
Amount invested in equipment during the year	+ ???
Ending balance	$ 1,100

The amount that makes the account balance is $410.

i. Accumulated amortization decreased by $50. Since we know that amortization expense of $200 for 20X5 was added to this account, the net decrease must be attributable to the $250 write-off of accumulated amortization on the equipment sold. This can be verified by referring to the reconstructed entry for the equipment sale shown in (d), above.

j. The current bank loan increased by $15. This is a loan, and not an overdraft; therefore, the loan will *not* be included as a component of cash and cash equivalents. The increase in the loan is a source of financing, and will go into the financing section of the cash flow statement.

k. Long-term note payable decreased by $30. This represents a financing activity.

l. Common shares did not change during the period. Therefore, in the absence of any information that shares were purchased and new shares were issued (that is, in offsetting amounts), there will be no impact on the cash flow statement relating to common shares.

The net result of entering all of these amounts in the cash flow statement is that we have explained the net decrease in cash of $35.

EXHIBIT 5-4

SIMPLE LIMITED
CASH FLOW STATEMENT

Year ended 31 December 20X5	Key		
Operating activities:			
Net income (from income statement)	(a)	$330	
Add (deduct) to reconcile net income to net operating cash flows:			
Amortization expense	(c)	200	
Gain on sale of equipment	(d)	(70)	
Decrease in accounts receivable	(e)	15	
Decrease in inventory	(f)	35	
Decrease in accounts payable	(g)	(25)	$485
Investing activities:			
Proceeds from sale of equipment	(d)	130	
Purchase of new equipment	(h)	(410)	(280)
Financing activities:			
Increase in current bank loan	(j)	15	
Dividends paid	(b)	(225)	
Reduction of long-term notes payable	(k)	(30)	(240)
Increase (decrease) in cash and cash equivalents			(35)
Cash and cash equivalents, 1 January			90
Cash and cash equivalents, 31 December			$ 55

Presentation of Operating Activities

There are two approaches for presenting the operating activities section:

- *Direct presentation:* The revenues and expenses are adjusted to a cash basis of reporting and shown directly in deriving cash provided by (or used by) operations on the cash flow section.
- *Indirect presentation:* Operations begins with net income, and all interperiod allocations and accruals are reversed out of net income to derive the cash from operations.

In Exhibit 5-4, the indirect method of presentation was used. Operating activities began with net income of $330 and then was adjusted for amortization, the accounting gain on sale of equipment, and for changes in the balances of the other current assets and current liabilities *except* for those included in the definition of "cash."

Exhibit 5-5 shows the operating activities section of Simple Limited's cash flow statement, using the direct approach of presentation. The amounts are obtained as follows:

1. To convert from accrual-basis sales to cash received from customers, we have to add the decrease in accounts receivable during the year ($15). This converts sales ($2,000) to cash received from customers ($2,015). This $15 adjustment is the same as adding the amount that customers owed at the beginning of the year ($125 opening balance) and subtracting the amount owing at the end of the year ($110 ending balance):

Sales, accrual basis (per income statement)	$2,000
Plus cash collected on opening accounts receivable	+125
Minus cash *not* collected at year-end	− 110
Cash received from sales during 20X5	$ 2,015

Therefore, the adjustment is to *increase* sales by the $15 net *decrease* in accounts receivable.

2. Cost of goods sold requires two adjustments. The first adjustment is for the decrease in inventory of $35 during the year. Since inventory purchased in the previous year was used this year, the cash flow requirements for buying inventory were $35 less than the expense shown for cost of goods sold. Therefore, we subtract the $35 decrease from the $1,100 expense to arrive at cash flow. Partially offsetting the decline in inventory is the decrease in accounts payable. The decrease in accounts payable of $25 indicates that more cash was expended to pay creditors (presumably, for inventory purchases and other expense components that comprise cost of goods sold). We must increase the expense by $25 to portray cash flow accurately. Therefore, the $1,090 cash flow for the components of cost of goods sold is lower than the expense by $10.
3. Other operating expenses are decreased by the $200 amortization.

Other items, such as amortization and the gain on sale of equipment are not cash flows and have no place in the statement under the direct presentation approach.

DIRECT OR INDIRECT? The AcSB permits either the direct or indirect method of reporting cash flows from operations, but enterprises are "encouraged" to report cash flows from operating activities using the direct method (*CICA* 1540.21). Regardless of any possible advantages in clarity of using the direct approach, the indirect method of presentation has been by far the more popular approach among accountants. *Financial Reporting in Canada 2002* reports that 99.5% of the surveyed companies use the indirect method of reporting.

It can be argued that the direct approach is clearer to financial statement users, because they do not have to untangle the adjustments that are made under the indirect approach. In particular, there is the concern that the indirect method encourages the idea that amortization is a source of funds. The addback of amortization is usually a large positive element in the operations section, and business people have often been heard to remark that they will be using their "amortization funds" for certain projects.

Of course, this is a mistaken impression, but the indirect presentation method certainly strengthens the myth. In most cash flow statements, as in the RIM statement in Exhibit 5-2, the amortization addback is labelled as an adjustment. But sometimes there is no such explanatory label.

TWO-STEP INDIRECT PRESENTATION A common refinement of the indirect method of presentation is a two-step approach. First, the net income is adjusted for interperiod allocations, and then it is adjusted for changes in other working capital accounts (usually as a single, summary amount rather than in detail). The operations section of Simple Limited's cash flow statement is illustrated in Exhibit 5-6 by using the two-step approach.

The RIM cash flow statement shows two distinct sections in the operating adjustments, with a subtotal following the "items not requiring an outlay of cash." This subtotal may pose a problem by implying that there is some special significance to that amount, which does *not* equal cash flow from operating activities.

EXHIBIT 5-5

SIMPLE LIMITED
CASH FLOW STATEMENT
SAMPLE OF DIRECT PRESENTATION OF OPERATIONS

Year ended 31 December 20X5

Operating Activities:		
Cash received from customers ($2,000 + $15)	**(1)**	$ 2,015
Operating expenses:		
Cash paid to suppliers ($1,100 – $35 + $25)	**(2)**	(1,090)
Cash paid for other operating expenses ($640 – $200)	**(3)**	(440)
Cash provided by operations		$ 485

EXHIBIT 5-6

SIMPLE LIMITED
OPERATING ACTIVITIES, CFS
TWO-STEP INDIRECT OPERATING ACTIVITIES

Year ended 31 December 20X5	
Operating Activities:	
Net income	$330
Plus (less) items not affecting cash:	
Amortization	200
Gain on sale of equipment	(70)
	460
Changes in other working capital items:	
Decrease in accounts receivable	15
Decrease in inventory	35
Decrease in accounts payable	(25)
Cash provided by operations	$485

Offsetting Transactions

A basic objective of the cash flow statement is to explain the investing and financing activities of the enterprise. Within each of those two categories, there often are transactions that, overall, have the effect of offsetting each other. For example, if a company refinances its debt by retiring an outstanding bond issue and issuing new bonds, the *net* impact on the balance sheet may be relatively minor. However, these activities do demonstrate the company's ability to renew its capital structure. The flows associated with the refinancing should be disclosed separately and not offset, or netted.

Section 1540 emphasizes that offsetting should not occur. In general, "an enterprise should report *separately* major classes of *gross* cash receipts and *gross* cash payments arising from investing and financing activities" (*CICA* 1540.23). The two key words are "separately" and "gross." Both words emphasize that transactions relating to similar items of asset or equity structure should not be netted.

CONDITIONS FOR OFFSETTING There are some exceptions to the general rule against offsetting, but they are narrowly defined and relate more to financial institutions than to other types of enterprise. In essence, offsetting (or netting) is permitted for:

- Cash receipts and payments that are on behalf of customers rather than for the reporting enterprise itself (*CICA* 1540.25(a)). An example is the cash flows of a rental agent who collects rents for landlords and passes those rents on to the property owners. The agent may keep a commission, which is the reported *net* cash flow to the agent.
- Cash receipts and payments for items where the volume of activity is high and the holding period is short (i.e., the *turnover* is quick) (*CICA* 1540.25(b)). An example is the investing and liquidating of investments by an investment dealer or by a company that is not an investment dealer but that engages in active market transactions. A cereal manufacturer may, for instance, routinely buy and sell a large volume of grain futures on the commodity market.

Section 1540 also contains recommendations for netting the cash flows relating to specific types of activities for financial institutions, but those activities fit the two general guidelines above.

Non-Cash Transactions

Some transactions have a significant effect on the asset or equity structure of an entity without involving any direct cash flow at all. These non-cash transactions are economically similar to cash transactions. For example, settling a debt by issuing shares directly to the debt holder has the same effect as issuing the shares for cash and using the proceeds to settle the debt. Or, an asset may be acquired without cash by entering into a mortgage or a long-term capital lease; the effect is the same as borrowing money to buy the asset. Common types of non-cash transactions include

- Retiring bonds through share issuance;
- Converting bonds to common shares;
- Converting preferred shares to common shares;
- Settling debt by transferring non-cash assets;
- Bond refinancing;
- Incurring capital lease obligations in exchange for leased assets;
- Acquiring shares in another company in exchange for shares of the reporting enterprise; and
- Distributing assets other than cash as dividends (e.g., a spinoff of a subsidiary company).

At one point, non-cash transactions such as those listed above were required to be included in the cash flow statement. However, current reporting standards specifically exclude non-cash transactions from the cash flow statement on the grounds that such transactions are not cash flows (*CICA* 1540.46). For example, the acquisition of a building (an investing activity) that is financed through a capital lease (a financing activity) would not be shown on the face of the cash flow statement because there was no cash involved. Instead, the transaction would be reported in the disclosure notes.

PARTIAL CASH TRANSACTIONS For an acquisition in which part of the consideration is in cash and the remainder is in another asset (or a debt instrument or shares), the cash part of the transaction would be reported in the cash flow statement while the non-cash portion would not. For example, suppose that a building costing $4,000,000 is acquired by paying $1,000,000 cash and issuing a $3,000,000 long-term note. The cash flow statement would disclose only the $1,000,000 cash paid (as an investing activity), although the entry on the cash flow statement should be referenced to the note that contains the details of the transaction.

EVALUATION In one sense, the exclusion of non-cash transactions is an additional step away from the old concept of the funds flow statement as a summary of changes in non-current assets and equities. However, the total exclusion of non-cash transactions from the cash flow statement seems to give precedence to form over substance. The purchase of another company (i.e., a *business combination*) through an issue of shares would not be reported in the cash flow statement, while the issuance of shares for cash and the use of the proceeds to buy the company would be reported in the cash flow statement.

Extraordinary Items

As we have demonstrated, the cash flow statement begins with net income in the operating activities section, and gains and losses from such things as the sale of capital assets are added back as non-cash items. Proceeds from the sale of these assets are included in investing activities. The same treatment applies to gains and losses classified as extraordinary items. That is, the operating activities section begins with bottom-line net income, and any extraordinary gain or loss, to the extent it does not reflect cash flow, is adjusted as a non-cash item. The cash inflows or outflows are then classified according to their nature. In addition, cash flows are shown on a before-tax basis. *The tax related to the extraordinary item remains in the operating activities section* (CICA 1540.32 and Appendix A to Section 1540).

For example, assume that a company reported $3.5 million as net income, after a (gross) extraordinary gain of $210,000, reported on the income statement as $180,000 after a tax provision of $30,000. The extraordinary item was the gain on the expropriation of a piece of land, with a cost of $50,000 and expropriation proceeds of $260,000. The cash flow statement would reflect the following:

Operating activities:	
Net income	$3,500,000
Less: items not affecting cash:	
Extraordinary item (pre-tax)	(210,000)
Cash from operating activities	$3,290,000
Investing activities	
Cash proceeds on expropriation of land	$260,000

PRIOR DISCLOSURE NORMS In the past, the operating activities section would have begun with income before the extraordinary item of $3,320,000 ($3.5 million, less the $180,000 gain), and the net proceeds on the sale, $230,000 ($260,000, less tax of $30,000) would have been reported in the investing section. The AcSB has changed the preferred reporting presentation to that illustrated above.

Income Tax

In general, income tax should be shown in the operating activities section. (*CICA* 1540.38). This presents no problem if income tax is reported on the income statement. Occasionally, however, income tax is reported on other statements. For example, if an error correction, reported on the retained earnings statement, were to be shown net of $20,000 of tax currently payable, this $20,000 should be reported on the cash flow statement as a reduction to the cash provided by operations.

There are times when tax is specifically related to investing or financing activities. In these cases, tax may be classified as investing or financing (*CICA* 1540.39). The AcSB provides no examples of these situations, and this requirement seems to contradict the requirement that cash flows from extraordinary items be shown on a before-tax basis in the appropriate section. However, there are times when capital transactions, such as dividend distributions, attract specific taxes. It seems logical that the related tax be shown with the cash flow.

Cash Flow for/from Interest, Dividends, and Tax

Companies are required to separately disclose cash flows from or for the following items, if they are included on the income statement:

- interest received
- interest paid
- dividends received
- dividends paid
- tax paid

Dividends paid, of course, are usually on the retained earnings statement and would appear as a financing outflow. Occasionally, though, equity instruments are reclassified as debt if they are in substance a liability. If this happens, dividends paid are in substance an interest, or financing, expense and are placed on the income statement.

Separate classification of these cash flows can be accomplished through supplementary disclosure, or the information can be included on the bottom of the cash flow statement. For example, assume that Gerard Company reported $123,400 of interest expense and $21,600 of interest revenue. There were no dividends paid or received on the income statement. Interest payable increased by $5,700 during the year, and interest expense included $3,500 of bond discount amortization. Finally, interest receivable decreased by $2,300 during the year. Supplementary disclosure would appear as follows:

Cash paid for interest ($123,400 – $5,700 – $3,500)	($114,200)
Cash received for interest ($21,600 + $2,300)	$23,900

RIM includes the following in a disclosure note:

Note 17 Supplemental information

	March 1 2003	March 2 2002	Feb.28 2001
Interest paid during the year	$ 852	$779	$456
Income tax paid during the year	$1,070	$967	$897

Note that if the direct method of presentation is used, then these cash flows are included on the face of the cash flow statement, and no supplementary disclosure is required.

SUMMARY OF DISCLOSURE RECOMMENDATIONS

The *CICA Handbook* recommends the following disclosures relating to the cash flow statement:

- The cash flow statement should report the changes in cash and cash equivalents, net of bank overdrafts, resulting from the activities of the enterprise during the period.
- The components of cash, cash overdrafts, and cash equivalents should be disclosed and reconciled with the balance sheet.
- The statement should include only cash flows; non-cash transactions should not be reported on the cash flow statement, but should be disclosed elsewhere in the financial statements as appropriate.
- Cash flows during the period should be classified by *operating*, *investing*, and *financing* activities.
- Reporting enterprises are *encouraged* to report cash flows from operations by the direct method.
- Cash flows from investing and financing activities should not be netted or offset; the *gross* amount of inflows and outflows should be reported.
- Cash flows relating to extraordinary items should be classified according to their nature as operating, investing, or financing activities, and should be separately disclosed on a before-tax basis.
- Cash flows from interest and dividends that have been included in net income (both received and paid) should be disclosed separately. This may be accomplished in a disclosure note.
- Cash flows arising from income tax on operating income should be separately disclosed as an operating activity. *If* income tax cash flows can be specifically identified with investing or financing activities, they should be classified as investing or financing activities.
- The cash flows arising from acquisitions and disposals of subsidiaries or other business units should be presented separately and classified as investing activities. Non-cash exchanges involving such acquisitions or disposals would *not* be reported on the cash flow statement (but would be disclosed in a note). Disposals are not netted against acquisitions.[1]

[1] This aspect of cash flow reporting is discussed in Chapter 11.

CONCEPT REVIEW

1. Why is amortization added in deriving cash flow from operations from a starting point of net operating income? Is amortization a source of cash?
2. Explain why a gain on the sale of equipment is subtracted in the reconciliation of income and operating cash flows.
3. Why are changes in the balance of accounts receivable included in the cash flow statement under the indirect presentation approach, but not disclosed under the direct presentation approach?
4. If salaries payable increases during the year, why does this imply that salary expense exceeds salary payments?
5. How are extraordinary items shown on the cash flow statement?
6. What special disclosure is needed for cash paid for interest?

INTERPRETATION ISSUES

Cash Flow per Share

Financial analysts and other users often compute cash flow per share, which is defined in many different ways. One common measure of cash flow per share is net operating cash flow divided by common shares outstanding. Another common measure is net income plus non-cash charges, divided by common shares outstanding. Following the U.S. lead, the *CICA Handbook* prohibits disclosure of statistics labelled "cash flow per share" in financial statements, except for contractually determined cash flow per share values. (*CICA*, 1540.53) The AcSB believes that cash flow per share numbers have caused confusion. Of course, financial statement users are free to compute any statistic from published information.

Quality of Earnings

earnings quality
the relationship between net income and cash flow; high earnings quality from operations is highly positively correlated with cash flow, low earnings quality is not

Investment analysts sometimes refer to the **earnings quality** of a company that they are analyzing. This concept relates the amount of net income to the amount of cash flow from operations. A company is said to have high earnings quality when there is a close correspondence between *net income* and *cash flow from operations*, especially if the close relationship between earnings and cash flow persists over several years and moves in the same direction.

In contrast, a company that reports earnings that are not closely related to cash flows is said to have low earnings quality. In some companies, cash flows and earnings are actually counter-indicative. That is, a company can have high earnings but a negative cash flow from operations because of soaring receivables or expanding inventories; this situation often makes analysts a bit nervous, especially if it continues for more than one year.

On the other hand, a company can have low earnings (or even a loss) and still have positive cash flows from operations. For example, this can happen when net income includes a large amount of amortization of capitalized costs. Lenders may be quite willing to lend to such a company on the strength of the cash flow, despite the existence of losses, because they are convinced that there is adequate cash flow to service the loan (that is, to pay the interest and repay the principal).

Effect of Accounting Policy Choices on the Cash Flow Statement

One of the reasons that users like to see the cash flow statement is that "cash doesn't lie." A perception exists among many users that while managers and accountants can adopt accounting policies that can have a significant and substantial effect on the measurement of net income, they have little room to manipulate cash flows.

To a considerable extent, this perception is correct. For example, management of almost every type of enterprise makes accounting estimates and policy decisions about revenue recognition, operating expense recognition, and amortization policy (i.e., method, life, and salvage value).

In addition, there are many accounting estimates made by management regarding almost every asset on the balance sheet (such as year-end accruals, bad debt provisions, inventory obsolescence writedowns, and investment write-offs). These estimates are influenced by external events and are not entirely under the control of management, but management is responsible for making those estimates and certainly can influence their amount and timing of recognition.

Accounting policy decisions and management's measurement estimates can significantly affect net income, but they will have no impact on the underlying cash flow. It is true, therefore, that the overall net cash flow for an accounting period is unaffected by accounting policy choices.

capitalize

to record a transaction such that a balance sheet element, usually an asset, is created

POLICY AND CASH FLOW However, there is a certain type of accounting policy decision that affects the cash flow statement by changing the *classification* of items on the cash flow statement, and that is whether to expense or **capitalize** one or more types of cost. If expenditures of a certain category (i.e., start-up costs) are charged to expense, they will be included as a deduction in net income and be included in operating cash flow.

On the other hand, if those expenditures are capitalized, they will appear on the cash flow statement as an *investing* activity. In subsequent years, amortization of capitalized costs is deducted in determining net income, but is then added back to net income to derive cash flow from operations.

The result is that capitalized costs *never* enter into operating cash flow but will appear only as an investing activity. For example, a retail chain that capitalizes and amortizes its new store start-up costs will show a consistently higher cash flow from operations than one that charges start-up costs to expense, all other things being equal.

Interpreting the Cash Flow Statement

Interpretation involves examining the cash flow statement for the major sources and uses of cash. The following questions must be considered, with professional judgement:

- Has operations provided cash or used cash?
- Why is net income different than cash from operating activities? What are the major adjustments?
- What evidence is there of the quality of earnings?
- What are the major investing activities?
- What are the major financing activities?
- How are these activities interrelated?
- How do the company's cash activities compare to prior years? To competitors?
- What accounting policy choice might affect classification of cash flows?

Refer back to the RIM cash flow statement in Exhibit 5-2. RIM reported a loss of $148,664 (all amounts are in thousands of U.S. dollars) in 2003, but the cash flow from operating activities is actually a positive $2,790. This is because many expenses were non-cash items, and added back—notice the large amortization and future income tax add-backs. In addition, there were expenses reported on the income statement that were not yet paid. This adjustment appears in the net changes to working capital—notice the large increases in accounts payable and accrued litigation costs. These payables will have to be paid in future periods. In the current year, cash from operations is positive primarily because cash outflows have been delayed.

Over the three years presented, there is no correlation between net income and cash from operating activities; in 2003, a large loss became a positive cash flow, in 2002, a reported loss remained a negative cash flow, and in 2001, a loss became a positive cash flow. The statement shows large non-cash losses for the writedown of investments in both 2002 and 2001.

RIM, in financing activities, spent $24,502 to buy back shares. In investing activities, there was a $345,983 sale of marketable securities and a stream of acquisitions: long-term investments, capital assets, intangible assets, subsidiaries, and so on. Notice the large investments and disposals of marketable securities over the prior two years.

Overall, the cash balances increased by a modest $205 this year, and the company ended the year in a highly liquid position, with $340,681 in cash. The level of cash balances is largely dictated by the nature of the business: RIM operates in a relatively risky business and has cash reserves to finance future operations. The cash flow statement of RIM demonstrates its relatively fragile operating position, and its history of financing and acquisitions.

CONCEPT REVIEW

1. If cash from operating activities increases as net income increases, and declines when net income declines, what does this imply about the quality of earnings?
2. If development costs are deferred and amortized, how will they be reflected on the cash flow statement? If they are expensed?

ANALYZING MORE COMPLEX SITUATIONS

Using a Spreadsheet

When preparing the cash flow statement for Simple Limited, we used an informal, *ad hoc* approach. We went down the balance sheet and filled in the appropriate amounts in the cash flow statement. In the process, we explained all of the changes in the non-cash accounts, and thus indirectly explained all of the changes in the cash accounts.

This approach works because the net change in non-cash accounts must be equal to the change in cash accounts in order for the balance sheet to balance. Furthermore, the transactions we are interested in are those that took place between the cash accounts and the non-cash accounts (if there are non-cash transactions that directly affected the asset/equity structure of the company they are identified but excluded from the cash flow statement of facts). For the cash flow statement, we have no interest in the transactions that took place solely within the cash accounts themselves, such as investment in or liquidation of temporary investments that are cash equivalents.

While the simple approach is completely acceptable, in complex situations it is easy to lose track. Therefore, it is common to use some form of worksheet or spreadsheet to force some discipline on the process and to help ensure that we don't overlook any relevant transactions. The spreadsheet approach is useful because it

- Provides an organized format for documenting the preparation process.
- Facilitates review and evaluation by others.
- Provides proofs of accuracy.
- Formally keeps track of the changes in balance sheet accounts and ensures that all accounts are explained.

There are several different analytical methods in addition to the spreadsheet approach. The method does not affect the final cash flow statement. We will illustrate a spreadsheet approach in the main body of the chapter and present the T-account method in the appendix to this chapter. The T-account method is useful for understanding the relationships between accounts, but is cumbersome in a realistic setting when there is a large number of accounts.

The comparative balance sheet and the income statement for Accrue Corporation are shown in Exhibit 5-7, along with some important supplementary information. From the balance sheet, we can see that cash increased by $14,000 during the year. (The most recent year is shown in the first numerical column, as is standard practice in Canadian financial statements.) Short-term liquid investments, however, decreased by $24,000. Short-term liquid investments are *cash equivalents*, and thus the actual change in cash is really a decrease of $10,000.

	Ending	Beginning	Change	
Cash balance	$50,000	$36,000	$ 14,000	increase
Short-term investments	10,000	34,000	(24,000)	decrease
Total	$60,000	$70,000		
Net increase (decrease) in cash			$(10,000)	decrease

The task of the cash flow statement is to explain the transactions that caused this decrease of $10,000 in cash and cash equivalents. On the cash flow statement worksheet, the change in cash is explained by reconciling the change in cash and cash equivalents with the changes in all of the other accounts.

To set up the spreadsheet, we must transfer the accounts and account balances from the balance sheet to a four-column spreadsheet. Exhibit 5-8 demonstrates the set-up for Accrue Corporation, based on the information in Exhibit 5-7. The 20X4 account balances are entered into the first column, and the 20X5 balances are entered into the last column. In the two intervening columns, we will recreate the transactions that caused the changes in the non-cash and cash equivalents accounts. Once all of the changes in the account balances from 20X4 to 20X5 have been explained by reconstructing the entries, we will have all of the data that we need to construct the cash flow statement.

The intent is to identify the cash flows. But instead of debiting and crediting all of the cash flows directly to the cash account, we will classify the "cash" part of the transactions in another section of the spreadsheet. Below the balance sheet accounts, we create a section of the spreadsheet in which to record the cash flow effects. Within this lower section, a subsection is labelled for each type of cash activity: operating, investing, and financing. As cash flows are identified by reconciling the individual balance sheet accounts in the upper four-column part of the spreadsheet, the offsetting cash effect is entered into the appropriate lower subsection of the spreadsheet.

EXHIBIT 5-7

ACCRUE CORPORATION

BALANCE SHEET

31 December	20X5	20X4
Assets		
Current assets:		
Cash	$ 50,000	$ 36,000
Short-term liquid investments	10,000	34,000
Accounts receivable	84,000	70,000
Inventories	42,000	30,000
Prepaid expenses	15,000	11,000
	201,000	181,000
Fixed assets:		
Land	50,000	50,000
Plant and equipment	740,000	615,000
Accumulated amortization	(260,000)	(215,000)
	530,000	450,000
Deferred development costs	82,000	76,000
Long-term investments	92,000	70,000
Total assets	$905,000	$777,000
Liabilities and shareholders' equity		
Current liabilities:		
Bank loan	$ 20,000	$ 5,000
Accounts payable	36,000	45,000
Wages payable	10,000	5,000
	66,000	55,000
Long-term liabilities:		
Bonds payable	146,000	133,000
Future income tax	27,000	24,000
Total liabilities	239,000	212,000
Shareholders' equity:		
Preferred shares	142,000	120,000
Common shares	230,000	180,000
Retained earnings	294,000	265,000
	666,000	565,000
Total liabilities and shareholders' equity	$905,000	$777,000

Spreadsheet Procedures

Once the beginning and ending account balances have been entered into the spreadsheet, we can begin to make the necessary adjustments. Generally speaking, the place to start is with the reconciliation of retained earnings, because it is where the net income for the year has been transferred. Net income is the top line in the operating activities section. Starting with net income also focuses our attention on the income statement and on the adjustments that are necessary to remove the effects of interperiod allocations.

EXHIBIT 5-7 (cont'd)

ACCRUE CORPORATION
STATEMENT OF INCOME AND RETAINED EARNINGS

Year ended 31 December 20X5

Sales revenue	$960,000	
Gain on sale of equipment	4,000	
Operating expenses		$964,000
Cost of goods sold	597,000	
Interest expense	18,000	
Provision for income taxes	54,000	
Wages expense	100,000	
Other operating expenses	131,000	900,000
Net income		64,000
Dividends declared		(35,000)
Retained earnings, 1 January		265,000
Retained earnings, 31 December		$294,000

Additional information:

1. Cost of goods sold includes amortization of $65,000.
2. Other operating expenses includes amortization of deferred development of $5,000.
3. During 20X5, the corporation issued preferred shares with a market value of $22,000 for 1,000 common shares of THB Corporation. The THB shares are being held as a long-term investment. Market value and cost are identical for long-term investments.
4. Old equipment was sold for $9,000; the original cost was $25,000.
5. Bonds with a face value of $20,000 were repurchased at par and retired.
6. Other operating expenses includes a loss of $2,000 from liquidating the short-term investments (for net proceeds of $22,000).

Accrue Corporation's statement of income and retained earnings reveals that the change in retained earnings consists of two items: (1) net income, and (2) dividends paid. The net $29,000 increase in the retained earnings balance came about as the result of $64,000 in net income and $35,000 in dividends paid. Therefore, the first reconciling entry on the worksheet is to disaggregate the net income into its separately reported components:

a.

Cash: operating activities, net income	64,000	
Retained earnings		64,000

The second reconciling entry is to record the dividends declared:

b.

Retained earnings	35,000	
Cash: financing activities, dividends declared		35,000

Observe that these entries are recreations of the original entries to (a) transfer net income into the retained earnings account and (b) to record the declaration and payment of dividends. Dividends, for example, are debited to the balance sheet account in the upper section of the worksheet and credited to cash in the lower section.

The rest of the reconciliations are as follows, considering first the list of items of *additional information* in Exhibit 5-7:

c. Amortization of $65,000 was expensed during the period. The original entry was as follows:

Amortization expense (*Operating*)	65,000	
Accumulated amortization		65,000

This entry is reproduced in the spreadsheet, with the debit placed under *operating activities.*

d. Amortization of deferred development costs amounting to $5,000 was recorded during the year. The entry is entered on the worksheet:

Amortization of development costs (*Operating*)	5,000	
Deferred development costs		5,000

e. The company entered into an exchange of shares that was worth $22,000. That is, it acquired a long-term investment in another company's shares in exchange for Accrue's own preferred shares. No cash changed hands. This is an example of a non-cash transaction. Even though the transaction resulted in a material change in the asset and equity structure of the company, it will be disclosed in a note to the financial statements and will not be reported on the cash flow statement. Therefore, the effects of the increase of $22,000 on long-term investments and on preferred shares are offset against each other on the spreadsheet, with no corresponding entry in the lower section:

Long-term investments	22,000	
Preferred shares		22,000

f. Old equipment was sold for $9,000; the original cost was $25,000. Since the income statement shows a gain of $4,000, the net book value at the time of sale must have been $5,000. (The gain is the amount by which the proceeds exceed the net book value; since the gain was $4,000 and the proceeds were $9,000, the net book value must have been $5,000.) Accumulated amortization on the asset sold must therefore have been $20,000. That is

Proceeds from sale		$9,000
Net book value of the asset sold:		
Historical cost	$25,000	
Accumulated amortization	?	5,000
Gain on sale		$4,000

The "?" must be $20,000. The entry for the sale is as follows:

Cash: investing activities, sale of equipment	9,000	
Accumulated amortization	20,000	
Plant and equipment		25,000
Gain on sale (*Operating*)		4,000

g. Bonds with a face value of $20,000 were repurchased and retired (at face value, since there is no gain or loss on the income statement).

Bonds payable	20,000	
Cash: financing activities, bonds retired		20,000

The only other piece of additional information in Exhibit 5-7 is that other operating expenses includes a loss of $2,000 on liquidation of short-term investments. The initial reaction may be to eliminate this by adding it back to operating and to record $22,000 as an investing activity inflow. However, the catch here is that the loss relates to a component of cash. Since short-term liquid investments are a cash equivalent and included within our definition of cash, the loss really did cause cash and cash equivalents to decrease by $2,000. This amount is appropriately included in net income. Therefore, *there is no adjustment for gains and losses that are incurred within the cash and cash equivalent accounts*, including foreign currency exchange gains and losses.

h. The reconciliation entries that have been described above are those that result from the information provided in Exhibit 5-7. However, there obviously have been other transactions during the year that caused as-yet unexplained changes in the asset and equity accounts. An example is that of bonds payable. The bonds payable account grew from $133,000 to $146,000 during the year, a net increase of $13,000. However, to have a net increase of $13,000 after the $20,000 retirement, the company must have issued $33,000 in new bonds during the year:

Cash: financing activities, bonds issued	33,000	
Bonds payable		33,000

Reconciliations such as this one for the bond issuance sometimes are referred to as *hidden entries*, because they become apparent only as the result of reconciling those changes that are known beforehand. Once the known elements are entered, as above, the remaining reconciliation entries are all balancing entries that simply record the change in each account that is required to explain the net change, after taking into consideration the reconciliation entries already made. Starting with the first non-cash account, accounts receivable, they are as follows:

i.

Accounts receivable	14,000	
Cash: operating		14,000

j.

Inventories	12,000	
Cash: operating		12,000

k.

Prepaid expenses	4,000	
Cash: operating		4,000

l.

Plant and equipment	150,000	
Cash: investing activities, purchase of equipment		150,000

The *net* increase of $125,000 in plant and equipment is due to acquisitions of $150,000 and the retirement of equipment that originally cost $25,000.

m.

Deferred development costs	11,000	
Cash: investing activities, investment in development costs		11,000

Since the net account increase was $6,000 *after* amortization, costs of $11,000 must have been capitalized during the year.

n.

Cash: financing activities, increase in bank loan	15,000	
Bank loan		15,000

o.

Accounts payable	9,000	
Cash: operating		9,000

p.

Cash: operating	5,000	
Wages payable		5,000

q.

Cash: operating	3,000	
Future income tax		3,000

The $3,000 increase in the balance sheet account for future income tax represents the part of income tax expense that was not paid in cash.

r.

Cash: financing activities, common shares issued	50,000	
Common shares		50,000

Once we enter all of these reconciliation entries onto the spreadsheet, we can check for completeness by cross-adding (or cross-footing) each line to verify that the beginning balance plus the reconciliation equals the ending balance. Totalling the inflows and outflows in the lower section of the spreadsheet reveals that total cash inflows during the year were $249,000; total outflows equalled $259,000.

s. The final reconciliation is to transfer the change in cash and cash equivalents to the lower section. The $14,000 increase in cash and the $24,000 decrease in short-term investments are reconciled as follows:

Cash	14,000	
Change in cash and cash equivalents	10,000	
Short-term liquid investments		24,000

Entering the net change into the lower part of the statement balances the inflows and outflows. Totalling the debit and credit columns in the upper part of the worksheet reveals that they are in balance (at $311,000). The total of the debit and credit columns is meaningless *except* for the important fact that they balance. Any imbalance would indicate a debit-credit imbalance in the reconciliation entries.

The lower section of Exhibit 5-8 now contains all of the information that is necessary for preparing a cash flow statement. It is important to remember that Exhibit 5-8 is *not* a cash flow statement in itself; it is only a working paper.

EXHIBIT 5-8

ACCRUE CORPORATION
CASH FLOW STATEMENT WORKSHEET

Year ended 31 December 20X2	31 December 20X4	Key	Reconciliation Debit	Reconciliation Credit	Key	31 December 20X5
Assets:						
Cash	$ 36,000	(s)	$ 14,000			$ 50,000
Short-term liquid investments	34,000			$ 24,000	(s)	10,000
Accounts receivable	70,000	(i)	14,000			84,000
Inventories	30,000	(j)	12,000			42,000
Prepaid expenses	11,000	(k)	4,000			15,000
Land	50,000					50,000
Plant and equipment	615,000	(l)	150,000	25,000	(f)	740,000
Accumulated amortization	(215,000)	(f)	20,000	65,000	(c)	(260,000)
Deferred development costs	76,000	(m)	11,000	5,000	(d)	82,000
Long-term investments	70,000	(e)	22,000			92,000
Total assets	$ 777,000					$905,000
Liabilities and shareholders' equity:						
Bank loan	$ 5,000			$ 15,000	(n)	$ 20,000
Accounts payable	45,000	(o)	9,000			36,000
Wages payable	5,000			5,000	(p)	10,000
Bonds payable	133,000	(g)	20,000	33,000	(h)	146,000
Future income tax	24,000			3,000	(q)	27,000
Preferred shares	120,000			22,000	(e)	142,000
Common shares	180,000			50,000	(r)	230,000
Retained earnings	265,000	(b)	35,000	64,000	(a)	294,000
Total equities	$777,000		$ 311,000	$ 311,000		$905,000

Components of the Cash Flow Statement	Key	Debit	Credit	Key	Totals
Operating activities:					
Net Income	(a)	$ 64,000			
Non-cash items					
Amortization expense	(c)	65,000			
Amortization of development costs	(d)	5,000			
Gain on sale of equipment			4,000	(f)	
Working capital changes					
Increase in accounts receivable			14,000	(i)	
Increase in inventory			12,000	(j)	
Increase in prepaid expenses			4,000	(k)	
Decrease in accounts payable			9,000	(o)	
Increase in wages payable	(p)	5,000			
Increase in future income tax	(q)	3,000			99,000
Investing activities:					
Proceeds from equipment sold	(f)	9,000			
Purchase of plant and equipment			150,000	(l)	
Development costs			11,000	(m)	(152,000)
Financing activities:					
Dividends paid			35,000	(b)	
Bonds retired			20,000	(g)	
Increase in short-term bank loan	(n)	15,000			
Bonds issued	(h)	33,000			
Common shares issued	(r)	50,000			43,000
Subtotal		249,000	259,000		
Change in cash and cash equivalents:	(s)	10,000			$(10,000)
		$259,000	$259,000		

Cash Flow Statement—Indirect Method

The cash flow statement using the indirect approach for operating activities is shown in Exhibit 5-9. The indirect approach starts with net income, and makes all of the adjustments that are necessary to convert from the accrual basis to the cash basis. The two-step approach shown in Exhibit 5-9 is the most common format.

The "non-cash" items are usually shown first. The "non-cash" adjustments represent the expenses and/or revenues that result from interperiod allocations, such as capital asset amortization, future income tax, and deferred revenues. The second set of adjustments reflects the changes in the working capital balances. There is no reason to show the two sets of adjustments separately; it is simply traditional to do it that way because of the way the statement has evolved.

The cash flow for income tax, investment revenue, and interest expense may be shown at the bottom of the cash flow statement or in a disclosure note. In Exhibit 5-9, the disclosures are at the bottom of the statement.

Cash paid for income tax is the $54,000 expense, less the $3,000 increase in the long-term liability, income tax. Interest expense of $18,000, part of other operating expense, has no related balance sheet accounts and therefore is assumed to be equal to cash paid.

Cash Flow Statement—Direct Method

The operating activities section of the cash flow statement can be presented using the direct method, as we have seen. The direct method may be prepared through the following steps:

1. Begin with the analysis of operating activities under the indirect method. Specifically, refer to the journal entry analysis (or the summary of adjustments to operating activities in the spreadsheet in Exhibit 5-8.)

2. Prepare a schedule to support your calculations for the direct method. This schedule should have three columns. In the first column, copy the income statement amounts, with all expenses in brackets. This column should add to net income (See Exhibit 5-10, first column.)

3. Copy all the adjustments to arrive at cash flow from operations into the second column. Make sure the credit adjustments are in brackets. (See Exhibit 5-10.)

   Sort the adjustments to the line of the income statement to which they pertain. For example, accounts receivable is copied onto the revenue line, the adjustment for amortization on the cost of goods sold line (since we are told amortization is part of COGS), and so on.

4. Cross-add the schedule, entering cash flows in the third column (See Exhibit 5-10.) Notice that non-cash items, such as amortization and gains and losses, disappear as they are adjusted to zero.

5. Prepare the operating activities section of the cash flow statement, using the numeric data from your schedule, but changing the captions to appropriate cash flow descriptions, and group cash flows as is considered desirable.

The final product is shown at the bottom of Exhibit 5-10. Note that the investing and financing sections of the cash flow statement are not dependent on the format chosen for the operating section. Therefore, the investing and financing sections would appear as shown in Exhibit 5-9.

EXHIBIT 5-9

ACCRUE CORPORATION
CASH FLOW STATEMENT (INDIRECT APPROACH)

Year ended 31 December 20X5

Operating activities:		
Net income (per income statement)	$ 64,000	
Adjustments for items not affecting cash:		
Amortization of plant and equipment	65,000	
Amortization of development costs	5,000	
Gain on sale of equipment	(4,000)	
Future income tax	3,000	
	133,000	
Changes in working capital amounts:		
Increase in accounts receivable	(14,000)	
Increase in inventory	(12,000)	
Increase in prepaid expenses	(4,000)	
Decrease in accounts payable	(9,000)	
Increase in wages payable	5,000	
Cash provided (used) by operating activities		99,000
Investing activities:		
Acquisition of new plant and equipment	(150,000)	
Investment in development costs	(11,000)	
Proceeds from sale of equipment	9,000	
Cash provided (used) by investing activities		(152,000)
Financing activities:		
Increase in short-term bank loan	15,000	
Issuance of bonds	33,000	
Retirement of bonds	(20,000)	
New common shares issued	50,000	
Dividends paid	(35,000)	
Cash provided (used) by financing activities		43,000
Increase (decrease) in cash and cash equivalents during 20X5		$ (10,000)
Reconciliation of cash and cash equivalents:		
Increase in cash		$ 14,000
Decrease in short-term investments		(24,000)
Increase (decrease) in cash and cash equivalents		$ (10,000)
Supplemental disclosures:		
Cash payment for interest included in operations		$ 18,000
Cash payments for income tax included in operations		$ 51,000

EXHIBIT 5-10

ACCRUE CORPORATION
CASH FLOW STATEMENT (DIRECT METHOD)

Year ended 31 December 20X5	Income statement	Adjustments (refer to journal entries)	Cash flow
Sales revenue	$960,000	i. (14,000)	$946,000
Gain on sale of equipment	4,000	f. (4,000)	0
Cost of goods sold	(597,000)	c. 65,000 j. (12,000) o. (9,000)	(553,000)
Interest expense	(18,000)		(18,000)
Provision for income tax	(54,000)	q. 3,000	(51,000)
Wages expense	(100,000)	p. 5,000	(95,000)
Other operating expenses	(131,000)	d. 5,000 k. (4,000)	(130,000)
Net income and cash flow from operations	$64,000		$99,000

ACCRUE CORPORATION
CASH FLOW STATEMENT

Year ended 31 December 20X5	
Operating activities	
Cash received from customers	$946,000
Cash paid to suppliers ($553,000 + $130,000)	(683,000)
Cash paid to employees	(95,000)
Cash paid for interest	(18,000)
Cash paid for income tax	(51,000)
Cash from operating activities	$ 99,000

CONCEPT REVIEW

1. If cash increases by $40,000, cash equivalents increase by $16,000, and the bank overdraft declines from $20,000 to zero, what is the change in cash during the period?
2. What sections of the cash flow statement will be identical if the direct or indirect methods are chosen?
3. Under the direct method for operating activities, if cost of goods sold is $40,000, inventories have increased by $10,000 and accounts payable have decreased by $25,000, what was the cash paid to suppliers?

SUMMARY OF ADJUSTMENTS

To prepare the cash flow statement, we must convert the accrual-basis earnings to the cash-basis, and trace other cash flows that caused changes in the asset and equity structure of the reporting enterprise. Basically, there are three types of adjustments that must be made to the accrual-basis accounts:

1. The effects of interperiod allocations of costs and revenues must be reversed.
2. Accruals must be "backed out" of the monetary asset and liability accounts to determine the cash inflows and outflows for operations during the period.
3. Certain transactions, the net effects of which are included in net income, must be reclassified as investing or financing activities.

Common items of all three types that usually are needed to convert from the accrual basis to cash flows include the following:

1. Reverse interperiod allocations of costs and revenues. Specific examples are as follows:
   - Amortization of capital assets, including depreciation of plant, depletion of natural resources, and amortization of intangibles. These are added to net income because they do not cause cash to decrease. Net income is reduced by these expenses and thus understates operating cash flow, and so they must be added back.
   - Allocation of costs associated with liability measurement, including future income tax, amortization of bond discount and premium, and estimated liabilities associated with pension obligations.
   - Writedowns of assets must be added back to net income because they do not reflect a cash flow. Examples include writedowns of inventories (to lower of cost or market), investments, and losses from equity-method investments.
   - Non-cash revenues, including investment revenue from equity-method investments, are subtracted from income because they do not cause cash to increase. Net income is increased by these revenues and thus overstates operating cash flow.
   - Revenues received but deferred until the following period must be added to net income, and revenues received in a previous period but not recognized in income until the current period are deducted from net income because the cash was not received in the current period.

2. Adjustments must be made for changes in working capital accounts related to operations, such as accounts receivable, inventory, prepaid expenses, interest receivable, accounts payable, interest payable, income tax payable, and short-term payables to suppliers and others.

CHANGE IN ACCOUNT BALANCE DURING THE YEAR

	Increase	Decrease
Current asset	*Subtract* increase from net income	*Add* decrease to net income
Current liability	*Add* increase to net income	*Subtract* decrease from net income

Long-term payables to suppliers for inventory purchases and other operating activities and long-term receivables from customers are included in this type of adjustment.

The following working capital accounts are *excluded* from this category of adjustments because they are included in the definition of "cash":

- cash
- short-term investments considered to be cash equivalents
- bank overdrafts

3. Gains and losses must be eliminated, and the related cash flows reclassified as financing or investing activities, depending on the nature of the transaction that gave rise to the gain or loss. Gains are subtracted from net income, and losses are added back to net income. Examples are gains and losses on disposals of capital assets, investments, and bond retirements. Related cash flows must be properly classified as investing or financing flows.

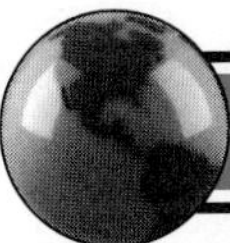

International Perspective

Internationally, a trend toward cash flow reporting has developed, similar to the experience of Canada over the 1980s and 1990s. Canada's recommended approach is in line with the recommendations of the International Accounting Standards Committee in IAS 7. The AcSB's change to Section 1540 was a move toward international harmonization, but it also is the final step toward a true cash flow statement instead of a broader and less focused reporting on balance sheet changes. Other countries have moved in this direction also, including the United Kingdom, New Zealand, South Africa, Hong Kong, and the United States.

While the trend clearly is toward cash flow reporting, a variety of fund definitions continue to be found in international settings. Many countries have not followed IAS 7, at least not yet. In France, for example, the statement of changes in financial position is not required; when it is provided, it continues to use a working capital approach rather than a true cash approach. Funds flow statements of any kind are rare in Germany.

Despite the absence of a cash flow reporting requirement in most industrialized countries, those companies that are listed on stock exchanges outside their home country may (except in the United States and Canada) report on the basis of international accounting standards. In that case, the companies will have to prepare and present a cash flow statement in accordance with the requirements of IAS 7.

CONCEPT REVIEW

1. What is the effect on the cash flow statement of selling a short-term investment, classified as a cash equivalent, at a $3,000 loss?
2. A company acquires a substantial amount of capital assets by issuing its own common shares to the seller. What is the impact of this transaction on the cash flow statement?

SUMMARY OF KEY POINTS

1. The cash flow statement is one of the three major financial statements. It is structured to report cash flows in meaningful categories.
2. The basic objective of the cash flow statement is to reveal the cash inflows and outflows of the reporting period, segregated between cash flows from operating activities, cash flows relating to investing activities, and cash flows relating to financing activities. In each category, *cash flows* includes both inflows and outflows.
3. Cash flow information is used to predict future cash flows and to assess liquidity, the ability of a firm to pay dividends and obligations, the ability of a firm to adapt to changes in the business environment, the quality of earnings, and for other purposes.
4. The reporting basis for the cash flow statement is the net cash position. The net cash position includes cash and cash equivalents, less bank overdrafts.
5. Cash equivalents include all short-term liquid investments that are readily convertible into cash and that bear little risk of change in value (maximum three-month term).
6. The components of cash and cash equivalents should be disclosed and should be reconciled to the balance sheet.
7. Operating flows are related to the main activities of the business and are connected to the earnings process.
8. Investing flows describe long-term asset acquisitions and the proceeds from sale of long-term assets. Interest and dividend income from investments is a component of operations but separate disclosure is required.
9. Financing flows describe the sources of debt and equity financing and repayments of liabilities and equities, excluding liabilities directly relating to operations such as accounts payable. Interest paid on debt and included in net income is reported as a component of operations, but separate disclosure is required.
10. Dividend payments to shareholders are reported as a financing outflow.
11. There are two allowable methods of reporting cash from operations—the direct and the indirect presentation methods. The direct method reports the cash inflows from the main classifications of revenues and cash outflows from the main classifications of expenses. In contrast, the indirect method reports operating activities by showing a reconciliation of net income with net cash flow from operating activities. Examples of adjustments are amortization and changes in operating working capital accounts. The AcSB "encourages" companies to use the direct method but few Canadian companies use this disclosure option.
12. The operating activity sections of both the direct and indirect cash flow statements convert accrual income to cash-basis income, the net cash flow from operations. The indirect method uses a series of add-backs to negate the effects of accruals and interperiod allocations.
13. In the investing and financing sections, gross cash flows are reported. Transactions are not netted against other flows in the same category.
14. Significant non-cash transactions (e.g., acquiring plant assets by issuing a long-term note) are not shown as outflows and inflows on the cash flow statement. However, they should be disclosed elsewhere in the financial statements, normally in a note.
15. Extraordinary items are an add-back in the operating activities section. Cash generated or used by/for extraordinary items is disclosed in the investing or financing section as appropriate. Cash flows are disclosed at the pre-tax amount.
16. Income tax is generally disclosed in the operating activities section.
17. Cash flows for interest paid, interest received, dividends paid, and dividends received all must be disclosed separately.

18. There are many approaches to preparing the cash flow statement. The same objectives apply to all—analyze transactions to identify all cash flows, reconciling items, and non-cash transactions.

19. The format-free approach to preparing the cash flow statement emphasizes transaction analysis and uses no particular format. Search for transactions in the following order: income statement, additional information, and comparative balance sheets.

20. The spreadsheet approach is an organized format that allows substantiation of the preparation process and provides many accuracy checks.

21. Net cash flow is not affected by accounting policy choices or by management's accounting estimates. However, the reported cash flow from operations can be increased by capitalizing certain types of costs (e.g., development costs or start-up costs), because the costs are reclassified as investing activities and amortization has no effect on operating cash flows in future periods.

KEY TERMS

REVIEW PROBLEM

The Phillies Corporation assembled the following information relevant when preparing its 20X7 cash flow statement:

Balance sheet accounts 31 December

	20X6	20X7
Cash	$ 50,000	$ 62,000
Temporary investments	150,000	—
Accounts receivable, net	60,000	80,000
Inventory	12,000	20,000
Prepaid expenses	6,000	10,000
Equipment, net of accumulated amortization	300,000	500,000
Goodwill	90,000	70,000
Total assets	$ 668,000	$ 742,000
Accounts payable	$ 40,000	$ 60,000
Salaries payable	60,000	50,000
Interest payable	6,000	9,000
Income tax payable	12,000	22,000
Mortgage payable	120,000	110,000
Bonds payable	200,000	100,000
Premium on bonds payable	8,000	3,000
Common shares	150,000	170,000
Retained earnings	72,000	218,000
Total liabilities and shareholders' equity	$ 668,000	$ 742,000

Income statement accounts, year ended 31 December 20X7	
Sales	$820,000
Cost of goods sold	(380,000)
Amortization expense	(100,000)
Write-off of goodwill	(20,000)
Other expenses	(46,000)
Loss on bond retirement	(3,000)
Interest expense	(22,000)
Income tax expense	(72,000)
Extraordinary gain—excess of insurance proceeds over book value of equipment destroyed by fire, net of $1,000 income tax	9,000
Net income	$186,000

Additional information:

1. Phillies declared $40,000 in dividends in 20X7.
2. Equipment (cost $100,000, accumulated amortization, $60,000) was destroyed by fire. Proceeds from insurance, $50,000. Applicable income taxes, $1,000 currently payable.
3. Bonds were retired on 1 January 20X7 for $107,000. The net book value of the bonds was $104,000: $100,000 at par value plus $4,000 premium.
4. The temporary investments are short-term money-market certificates.
5. Goodwill was written down by $20,000 because of impairment.

Required:

Prepare the 20X7 cash flow statement for Phillies Corporation. Use the indirect method of presentation for the operating activities section. Use whichever method of preparation you feel most comfortable with (i.e., choose from among the free-form, spreadsheet, or T-account (see appendix) methods). The suggested solution uses a spreadsheet.

REVIEW PROBLEM—SOLUTION

The spreadsheet solution appears on the following page. Other approaches are equally valid—it's the result that matters. The actual cash flow statement is shown at the end of this solution. Explanations for spreadsheet entries are as follows:

a. Net income is $186,000 income. In summary, the income statement is

Total revenues		$820,000
Total operating expenses, before interest and tax	$549,000	
Interest expense	22,000	
Income tax expense	72,000	
Total expenses		643,000
Net income from continuing operations		177,000
Extraordinary gain, net of tax		9,000
Net income		$186,000

The spreadsheet entry records net income.

b. Increase in accounts receivable; less cash was received from customers than was recognized as revenue.

	31 December 20X6	Key	Reconciliation Debit	Reconciliation Credit	Key	31 December 20X7
Assets						
Cash and cash equivalents	$200,000			$138,000	(q)	$ 62,000
Accounts receivable, net	60,000	(b)	$ 20,000			80,000
Inventory	12,000	(c)	8,000			20,000
Prepaid expenses	6,000	(g)	4,000			10,000
Equipment, net	300,000	(h)	60,000	100,000	(e)	500,000
		(n)	340,000	100,000	(h)	
Goodwill, net	90,000			20,000	(f)	70,000
Total assets	$668,000					$742,000
Liabilities and equity						
Accounts payable	$ 40,000			20,000	(d)	$ 60,000
Salaries payable	60,000	(g)	10,000			50,000
Interest payable	6,000			3,000	(i)	9,000
Income tax payable	12,000			10,000	(l)	22,000
Mortgage payable	120,000	(o)	10,000			110,000
Bonds payable	200,000	(j)	100,000			100,000
Premium on bonds payable	8,000	(j)	4,000			3,000
		(k)	1,000			
Common shares	150,000			20,000	(p)	170,000
Retained earnings	72,000	(m)	40,000	186,000	(a)	218,000
Total liabilities and equity	$668,000					$742,000

Components of the Cash Flow Statement		Key	Inflow — dr.	Outflows — cr.	Key	Totals
Operating activities:						
Net income from continuing operations		(a)	$186,000			
Increase in accounts receivable				$ 20,000	(b)	
Increase in accounts payable		(d)	20,000			
Increase in inventories				8,000	(c)	
Amortization expense		(e)	100,000			
Write-off of goodwill		(f)	20,000			
Extraordinary gain				10,000	(h)	
Accrued and prepaid expenses				14,000	(g)	
Loss on bond retirement		(j)	3,000			
Interest accrued, but not paid		(i)	3,000			
Interest expense, premium amortization				1,000	(k)	
Increase in income tax payable		(l)	10,000			289,000
Investing activities:						
Insurance proceeds, equipment	(h)		50,000			
Purchase of equipment				340,000	(n)	(290,000)
Financing activities:						
Retirement of bonds				107,000	(j)	
Dividends paid				40,000	(m)	
Mortgage principal payment				10,000	(o)	
Common shares issued		(p)	20,000			(137,000)
			412,000			
Net decrease in cash and cash equivalents		(q)	138,000	—		$(138,000)
			$550,000	$550,000		

c. Increase in inventories; more cash paid for inventories than recognized as cost of goods sold.

d. Increase in accounts payable; less paid to trade creditors than recognized as expenses.

e. Amortization expense removed from operating expenses—a non-cash expense.

f. Goodwill write-off removed from operating expenses—another non-cash expense.

g. Prepaid expenses increased, requiring more cash, and salaries payable decreased, also requiring more cash.

h. Adjustment to write off destroyed equipment and to record the insurance proceeds; $10,000 pre-tax gain removed from operating earnings, and proceeds recorded as an inflow in the investing activities section. Proceeds of $50,000 are shown on the cash flow statement. The tax amount is left in operating activities.

i. Increase in interest payable, indicating that less cash was paid for interest than the amount of interest expense accrued.

j. Entry to record the bond retirement on 1 January 20X7:

Bonds payable	100,000	
Bond premium (1/2 of $8,000 beginning balance)	4,000	
Loss on bond retirement	3,000	
Cash: financing activities, bond repayment (given)		107,000

k. Amortization of bond premium on those bonds not retired in 20X7: total reduction in bond premium account was from $8,000 to $3,000; bond retirement accounted for $4,000 of the reduction; remaining $1,000 must be due to amortization, which would have been charged to interest expense.

l. Increase in income taxes payable; less taxes paid than accrued.

m. Dividends declared *and paid* (i.e., there is no dividends payable account, so all must have been paid).

n. "Plug" entry to account for the otherwise unexplained change in the balance of the equipment account; the increase must have been due to the purchase of new equipment.

o. Decrease in mortgage payable implies repayment of mortgage, in the absence of other information.

p. Increase in common shares implies issuance of additional shares, in the absence of evidence to the contrary.

q. Net decrease in cash and cash equivalents:

Increase in cash account	$ 12,000
Decrease in temporary investment (cash equivalent)	(150,000)
Net decrease in cash and cash equivalents	$(138,000)

PHILLIES CORPORATION
CASH FLOW STATEMENT

Year ended 31 December 20X7		
Operating activities:		
Net Income		$186,000
Plus (less) items not affecting cash:		
Amortization expense	100,000	
Write-off of goodwill	20,000	
Loss on bond retirement	3,000	
Premium amortization	(1,000)	
Extraordinary gain	(10,000)	112,000
		298,000
Plus (less) changes in non-cash working capital		
Increase in accounts receivable	(20,000)	
Increase in accounts payable	20,000	
Increase in inventories	(8,000)	
Accrued and prepaid expenses	(14,000)	
Interest accrued, but not paid	3,000	
Increase in income tax payable	10,000	(9,000)
		290,000
Investing activities:		
Insurance proceeds from equipment destroyed by fire	50,000	
New equipment purchased	(340,000)	(290,000)
Financing activities:		
Retirement of bonds	(107,000)	
Dividends paid	(40,000)	
Reduction of mortgage principal	(10,000)	
Issuance of common shares	20,000	(137,000)
Net increase (decrease) in cash		$(138,000)
Reconciliation of cash and cash equivalents:		
Cash		$ 12,000
Temporary investments		(150,000)
Net change		$(138,000)

APPENDIX

T-Account Method

The main body of the chapter pointed out that the analytical method used to derive the cash flow statement is not important; what matters is the result. This chapter has illustrated two approaches—the *ad hoc* approach and a spreadsheet approach. Another method that is popular, especially with students who may be struggling with the rigours of a spreadsheet approach, is to reconstruct the balance sheet T-accounts. In essence, the T-account approach puts the spreadsheet data and analysis into individual T-accounts rather than into columnar format.

The T-account method is somewhat more flexible and less formal than the spreadsheet method. The T-account approach is particularly efficient for shorter and less involved problems, or when there is no need to review or retain working papers. However, location of errors and review of the preparation process may be more difficult under the T-account approach.

The T-accounts used in this approach are not actual ledger accounts. Rather, they are workspaces in account format used to accumulate the information necessary to prepare the cash flow statement and to explain all account balance changes. The cash T-account accumulates all changes in cash (and cash equivalents) and is divided into three sections, corresponding to the three cash flow categories.

T-accounts may be set up using both the beginning and ending balances for all accounts, just as we did in the spreadsheet approach used in the chapter. Alternatively, only the net *change* in the account may be used. In the illustration to follow, we will use the beginning and ending balances, and we will illustrate the T-account method using the indirect presentation approach to reporting operating cash flow.

T-Account Method: Simple Limited

To illustrate the T-account method, we will use the data for Simple Limited, Exhibit 5-3. The starting point is to sketch a simple T-account for each balance sheet account, including a single T-account for *cash and cash equivalents.* We will assume that Simple's short-term investments are cash equivalents, and therefore we will set up only one T-account for cash plus short-term investments. Leave lots of space in the cash T-account; it is where all the information necessary for preparing the cash flow statement will be accumulated.

The second step is to insert the beginning balance of each account at the top, and the ending balance at the bottom. Don't forget to check your transcribed balances, to make sure that the balance sheet accounts all balance after you set up the T-accounts.

The third step is to make entries directly in the T-accounts to duplicate (in summary form, of course) the entries that were made during the year, including those made to cash. As always, it is essential to *key* the entries, so that we can tell which debits belong with which credits, especially if we get something wrong and have to go back and re-evaluate what we've done. In more complex situations, it also helps to keep a side record of what each entry means, although it's not necessary.

Exhibit 5-A1 shows the balance sheet T-accounts for Simple Limited. The beginning and ending balances are shown in bold-face coloured type, to set them apart from the intervening entries. Remember that the beginning and ending balances (or, alternatively, just the net change) is the starting point for the analysis. Bear in mind that all revenues and expenses are summarized in the net income figure, which is part of the retained earnings account. Therefore, we don't need to set up T-accounts for the income statement accounts.

To begin, we should start with the statement of income and retained earnings, and with the additional information. After recording the relevant information from these sources, we then can make entries to explain the remaining changes in the balance sheet account balances.

The income statement shows net income of $330 and this is entered as the first entry in operating activities. It is also recorded as an increase to retained earnings.

EXHIBIT 5-A1

T-ACCOUNTS FOR SIMPLE LIMITED

Cash (including Short-Term Investments)

Beginning balance	**90**		
Operating activities:			
a. Net income	330		
d. amortization expense	200		
		b. gain in sale of equipment	70
e. decrease in accounts receivable	15	**g.** decrease in accounts payable	25
f. decrease in inventory	35		
Investing activities:			
b. proceeds from sale of equipment	130	**h.** purchase of plant and equipment	410
Financing activities:			
i. increase in bank loan	15	**c.** dividends paid	225
		j. reduction in long-term note payable	30
Ending balance	**55**		

Accounts Receivable

Beginning balance	**125**		
		e. net customer collections	15
Ending balance	**110**		

Inventory

Beginning balance	**135**		
		f. inventory decreased	35
Ending balance	**100**		

Plant and Equipment

Beginning balance	**1,000**		
h. assets acquired	410	**b.** cost of equipment sold	310
Ending balance	**1,100**		

Accumulated Amortization

		Beginning balance	**300**
b. accumulated amortization on assets sold	250	**d.** amortization expense	200
		Ending balance	**250**

EXHIBIT 5-A1 (cont'd)

T-ACCOUNTS FOR SIMPLE LIMITED

Bank Loan

		Beginning balance	50
		i. additional bank loan	15
		Ending balance	65

Accounts Payable

		Beginning balance	125
g. payment to suppliers	25		
		Ending balance	100

Long-Term Note Payable

		Beginning balance	330
j. partial payment on note payable	30		
		Ending balance	300

Common Shares

		Beginning balance	100
		Ending balance	100

Retained Earnings

		Beginning balance	445
		a. net income	330
c. dividends paid	225		
		Ending balance	550

Posting (b) is to record the transaction for the sale of equipment:

Cash—investing activities	130	
Accumulated amortization	250	
Plant and equipment		310
Operating activities—gain on sale of equipment		70

The gain is an adjustment to operating activities on the cash flow statement.

Posting (c) recognizes the dividends paid. The credit is to the financing activities section of the cash account. Amortization expense is eliminated by posting (d), which reduces the expenses (in cash—operating activities) for this non-cash expense. Postings (e) through (g) adjust the operating cash flow for the changes in working capital accounts. The remaining postings reconcile the balance sheet accounts by recognizing either investing (h) or financing activities (i) and (j).

Once all of the accounts have been reconciled, the cash flow statement can be prepared by using the information that has been summarized in the cash T-account. The cash flow statement is shown in Exhibit 5-A2, using the indirect method of presenting operating cash flows. It is identical to that shown in the chapter. Remember, the T accounts do not change the data—they just help organize it.

EXHIBIT 5-A2

SIMPLE LIMITED

Cash Flow Statement

Year ended 31 December 20X5		
Operating activities		
Net income (from income statement)	$ 330	
Add (deduct) to reconcile net income to net operating cash flows:		
Amortization expense	200	
Gain on sale of equipment	(70)	
Decrease in accounts receivable	15	
Decrease in inventory	35	
Decrease in accounts payable	(25)	$ 485
Investing activities		
Proceeds from sale of equipment	130	
Purchase of new equipment	(410)	(280)
Financing activities		
Increase in current bank loan	15	
Dividends paid	(225)	
Reduction of long-term note payable	(30)	(240)
Increase (decrease) in cash and cash equivalents		$(35)
Cash and cash equivalents, 1 January 20X5		90
Cash and cash equivalents, 31 December 20X5		$ 55

SUMMARY OF KEY POINTS

1. The T-account method is an alternative way to analyze information prior to preparing the cash flow statement. The T-account method is an analytical approach; it is *not* a method of presentation.
2. A T-account for *cash* (and *cash equivalents*) is used to accumulate all of the information needed to prepare the cash flow statement
3. The T-account method may be convenient for relatively small companies with limited numbers of accounts and few complex transactions.
4. It is more difficult to find errors when the T-account method is used, because the debits and credits are not as easily added and checked, compared to a spreadsheet approach.

QUESTIONS

Q5-1 Compare the purposes of the balance sheet, income statement, and cash flow statement (CFS).

Q5-2 During the year, a company records $100,000 in cash sales and $160,000 in credit sales, of which $40,000 was collected from customers. Also during the year, $80,000 was collected from last year's credit sales. Use this data to explain the difference between the accrual and cash basis. Which is reflected on the CFS?

Q5-3 A company pays $80,000 cash for a piece of machinery. On the date of acquisition, is the expenditure an expense? A cash disbursement? Will it become an expense?

Q5-4 Explain the basic difference between the three activities reported on the CFS: operating, investing, and financing.

Q5-5 For each category, list three major cash inflows and three major cash outflows properly classified under (a) operating activities, (b) investing activities, and (c) financing activities.

Q5-6 How is cash defined for CFS purposes? Why is disclosure of the definition so important?

Q5-7 What is the classification problem in assigning interest on the CFS?

Q5-8 Where are dividends paid classified on the CFS?

Q5-9 Assume that a company reported net income of $5,000, which included sales revenue of $100,000; the balance sheet shows an increase in accounts receivable of $10,000. What will the operations section of the CFS include, assuming that the indirect presentation approach is used?

Q5-10 During the year, a capital asset with an original cost of $750,000 and accumulated amortization on the date of sale of $560,000 was sold for $216,000. What will appear on the CFS as a result of this transaction? Assume the indirect presentation approach.

Q5-11 Explain why cash paid during the period for purchases and salaries is not specifically reported on the CFS as a cash outflow if the indirect presentation approach is used for operating activities.

Q5-12 Explain why a $50,000 increase in inventory during the year must be considered when developing disclosures for operating activities on the CFS.

Q5-13 Explain why an adjustment must be made for amortization to compute cash flow from operating activities if the indirect presentation approach is used.

Q5-14 Foley Corporation's records showed the following: Net income, $60,000; increase in accounts payable, $15,000; decrease in inventory, $20,000. What items would appear in the operating activities section of the CFS if the indirect presentation approach is used?

Q5-15 During 20X5, FRM Company recorded a decrease of $12,000 in the unearned revenue account, and a net increase of $50,000 in accounts receivable. Sales were $500,000. How much cash was collected from customers?

Q5-16 Why would the gain on sale of temporary investments classified as cash equivalents not be reflected on a CFS?

Q5-17 Explain the difference between the direct and indirect presentation approaches to the operating activities section of the CFS. Use the following data to illustrate the difference: a company reports $116,000 of net income, which includes sales of $750,000. During the year, accounts receivable increased by $47,000.

Q5-18 Why might the direct method of disclosing cash flows from operations be preferable to the indirect method? Which one dominates current practice?

Q5-19 Describe the two-step method to disclose cash flow from operations using the indirect method.

Q5-20 Explain offsetting. Is it ever allowable to offset cash flows in the CFS?

Q5-21 Give three examples of significant non-cash transactions. Are these items included in the CFS?

Q5-22 Barnum Company reported net income of $40,000, after an extraordinary loss of $140,000 on the destruction of capital assets caused by a hurricane. The assets had a book value of $80,000 and insurance proceeds were $220,000. What would appear on the CFS?

Q5-23 What special disclosure is required for investment income, interest, and tax? Explain.

Q5-24 Explain three types of reconciling items used to adjust from net income to cash flow from operating activities using the indirect method.

CASE 5-1
Barnard Developments Limited

Barnard Developments Ltd (BDL) is a public company that operates as a diversified Canadian communications company. Its core business is providing cable television services, high-speed Internet access, Internet infrastructure services, and, recently, telephone service. The company has a large investment in capital assets, and a high debt load. It has a history of operating losses, but positive cash flow from operations after material amortization charges are added back. Cash flows for investing activities, representing the purchase of capital assets, are negative. BDL is gradually building the volume that it needs to break even in this high–fixed cost business.

BDL reports the following in the 20X2 financial statements:

Note 1 Significant Accounting Policies
Marketing costs incurred to launch new specialty services and to launch data transmission services are deferred and amortized on a straight-line basis over a twenty-four-month period commencing with the commercial offering of the service.

Equipment subsidies granted to customers are deferred and amortized straight line over a twenty-four-month period. These costs are incurred in order to expand the Company's customer base, and represent the cost of equipment provided to subscription cable customers.

Note 7 Deferred Charges

	20X2		20X1	
(amounts in thousands)	Cost	Accumulated Amortization	Cost	Accumulated Amortization
Marketing costs	$ 15,702	$ 9,508	$ 11,300	$ 3,177
Equipment subsidies	403,040	261,400	280,300	114,100
	$418,742	$270,908	$291,600	$117,277

There were no disposals or write-offs of these assets during the year.

Cash flow statement (excerpts) (amounts in thousands)

Operating activities		
Cash flow from operations	$335,400	$289,100
Investing activities		
Cash flow for investing	($825,100)	($1,107,200)

You have been asked to prepare a report that evaluates BDL's accounting policy for marketing costs and equipment subsidies. This should include an analysis of the impact of the policy on the cash flow statement.

In talking with the senior management of BDL, you understand that management feels marketing costs have significant future value, as they establish the customer base for a particular service product. Once a customer is signed on, there is little turnover. The equipment subsidies are the result of BDL's policy, common in the industry, of providing needed hardware to a customer far below cost. Again, once a customer is established, there is very low turnover, and the future revenue steam from the customer is secure. In fact, BDL's management is convinced that the twenty-four-month amortization stream is very conservative, since the average customer stays for at least 10 years.

Required:
Prepare the report.

CASE 5-2
National Jeans Depot Incorporated

"Y'know, Joe, every time I look at one of these cash flow statements, it raises more questions than it answers! I've got some money to invest in the stock market right now, and I'm thinking about buying shares in a retail chain of casual clothing stores, called National Jeans Depot Limited. But look at their cash flow statement! I know you've been studying accounting, so maybe you can explain a few things to me.

"First, what major policy decisions does a company have to make in determining groupings and presentation on this statement? I'd like a general answer to that question, so I know what to look for in other companies' financial statements, but I'd also like you to be specific in relation to National Jeans Depot.

"Second, what would you conclude about National Jeans Depot as a result of the information in the cash flow statement? In other words, are there any strategic decisions or trends apparent?

"Thanks Joe, I knew I could count on you!"

Required:
Adopt the role of Joe and respond to the request.

NATIONAL JEANS DEPOT LIMITED
CASH FLOW STATEMENT

Year ended 31 December	20X4	20X3
Cash provided by (used in) operating activities:		
Net income	$ 620,784	$ 696,753
Add (deduct) items not involving a current cash flow		
Amortization	315,542	362,281
Future income tax	86,000	65,000
Net decrease in non-cash working capital balances	(3,642,864)	(479,230)
Cash provided by (used in) operating activities	(2,620,538)	644,804
Cash provided by (used in) investing activities:		
Purchase of capital assets	(1,343,283)	(1,010,601)
Related investment tax credits	404,015	322,008
Purchase of investment	(10,000)	—
Cash provided by (used in) investing activities	(949,268)	(688,593)
Cash provided by (used in) financing activities:		
Increase (reduction) in long-term debt	440,000	(60,000)
Payment of dividends	(196,000)	(212,667)
Cash provided by (used in) financing activities	244,000	(272,667)
(Decrease) in cash during the year	(3,325,806)	(316,456)
Bank lines of credit at beginning of year	1,861,341	1,544,885
Bank lines of credit at end of year	$ 5,187,147	$ 1,861,341

continued on next page

Year ended 31 December	20X4	20X3
Changes in non-cash working capital balances comprise the following:		
Cash provided by (used in)		
(Increase) in accounts receivable	$(2,093,157)	$(1,474,328)
(Increase) in income taxes recoverable	(94,854)	—
(Increase) decrease in inventories	(1,165,065)	623,095
(Increase) in prepaid expenses	(158,300)	(21,525)
Increase in accounts payable	76,492	198,696
Increase (decrease) in income taxes payable	(207,980)	194,832
Net cash (used)	$(3,642,864)	$ (479,230)

CASE 5-3
Federated Films Limited

Federated Films Limited (FFL) is a film production company located in Vancouver. It acquires, develops, and produces film productions (movies and series work) that are then sold to TV networks. It has had several highly successful comedy series over the last 10 years.

As a check on the accuracy of FFL's 20X4 cash flow statement, you have been asked to recreate the FFL 31 20X4 October balance sheet from the 20X3 balance sheet and the 20X4 cash flow statement (see Exhibit 1). In addition to the cash flow items listed, you are also aware that a film library, valued at $550,000, was acquired for common shares during the period. Finally, you must analyze and discuss the major sources and uses of cash during the period, as disclosed on the cash flow statement.

Required:
Prepare the 20X4 balance sheet and analysis of the cash flow statement, as requested.

EXHIBIT 1

FEDERATED FILMS LIMITED
BALANCE SHEET AS OF 31 OCTOBER 20X3

Assets	
Cash and cash equivalents	$ 3,733,118
Accounts receivable	39,576,516
Marketable securities	3,284,161
Investment in film and television program	12,705,267
Capital assets	4,508,250
Future income tax asset	2,497,209
Long-term investment, at equity	2,211,214
	$ 68,515,735
Liabilities	
Accounts payable and accrued liabilities	$ 8,238,491
Deferred revenue and government assistance	1,439,238
Income taxes payable	3,738,784
Interim production financing	23,552,530
Long-term debt	2,525,023
	$ 39,494,066
Shareholders' equity	
Capital stock	25,676,395
Retained earnings	3,345,274
	29,021,669
	$ 68,515,735

EXHIBIT 1 (cont'd)

FEDERATED FILMS LIMITED
CONSOLIDATED CASH FLOW STATEMENT

Year ended 31 October 20X4	
Cash provided by (used in):	
Operating activities	
Net income	$ 4,647,071
Items not involving cash	
Amortization of capital assets	837,360
Amortization of investment in film and television program	40,625,070
Gain on sale of marketable securities	(4,957,983)
Loss from equity investments	228,474
(Gain) on disposal of capital assets	(4,363)
Future income tax	(633,475)
	40,742,154
Net changes in other non-cash balances related to operations:	
Accounts receivable	(3,106,456)
Accounts payable	932,606
Deferred revenue and government assistance	236,429
Income tax payable	2,397,642
	$ 41,202,375
Financing activities	
Proceeds of interim production financing	9,775,319
Repayment of interim production financing	(9,272,595)
Repayment of long-term debt	(293,052)
Shares purchased and cancelled under normal course issuer bid (Note 1)	(579,653)
	$ (369,981)
Investing activities	
Advances to equity investee	(1,030,783)
Marketable securities—proceeds	6,427,812
Marketable securities—acquisitions	(491,739)
Investment in film and television program	(40,686,080)
Sale of capital assets	50,000
Acquisition of capital assets	(1,042,917)
Acquisition of a film library	(120,000)
	$(36,893,707)
Increase in cash and cash equivalents during the year	$ 3,938,687

Note 1: The shares retired had an average original issuance price of $812,644. The difference between the cancellation price and the original issuance price is credited to contributed capital.

CASE 5-4
Compuco Limtied

You have just started work with a firm of public accountants. You've been given a partially completed set of financial statements for a client, Compuco Ltd. You have been asked to prepare a cash flow statement for Compuco Limited, using the balance sheet provided in Exhibit 1, the statement of income and retained earnings provided in Exhibit 2, and the selected notes provided in Exhibit 3. Use indirect disclosure for the operating activities section. (Include separate disclosure of cash paid/received in regards to interest and tax in the disclosure notes.) Based on your cash flow statement, you've also been asked to draft an analysis of the strategic operating, financing, and investing strategies of the company that are apparent from the cash flow statement.

EXHIBIT 1

COMPUCO LIMITED
EXTRACTS FROM CONSOLIDATED BALANCE SHEET

(in $ thousands)

As at 31 December	20X5	20X4
Assets		
Current		
Cash and term deposits	$ 3,265	$ 3,739
Accounts receivable	23,744	18,399
Inventories	26,083	21,561
Income taxes recoverable	145	—
Prepaid expenses	1,402	1,613
	54,639	45,312
Loans receivable (Note 1)	5,960	6,962
Capital assets (Note 2)	37,332	45,700
Future income taxes	4,875	2,245
Goodwill	—	12,737
Development costs (Note 3)	4,391	1,911
	$ 107,197	$114,867
Liabilities		
Current		
Bank overdraft	$ 6,844	$ 6,280
Accounts payable	3,243	4,712
Current portion of long-term debt	1,800	1,200
	11,887	12,192
Long-term debt (Note 4)	14,900	14,500
Shareholders' equity		
Share capital (Note 5)	79,257	62,965
Retained earnings	1,153	25,210
	80,410	88,175
	$ 107,197	$114,867

EXHIBIT 2

COMPUCO LIMITED

EXTRACTS FROM CONSOLIDATED STATEMENT OF INCOME AND RETAINED EARNINGS

(in $ thousands)

For the years ended 31 December	20X5	20X4
Revenue		
Operating	$89,821	$68,820
Interest and other	1,310	446
	91,131	69,266
Expenses		
Operating	76,766	62,355
General and administrative	13,039	12,482
Amortization	10,220	11,709
Goodwill write-off	12,737	—
Interest	1,289	1,521
Loss on sale of capital assets	394	—
	114,445	88,067
Loss before writedown and income taxes	(23,314)	(18,801)
Writedown of loans receivable to recoverable amounts (Note 1)	(2,518)	—
Loss before income taxes	(25,832)	(18,801)
Income taxes	2,775	5,161
Net loss	(23,057)	(13,640)
Retained earnings, beginning of year	25,210	38,850
	2,153	25,210
Stock dividend	(1,000)	—
Retained earnings, end of year	$ 1,153	$25,210

EXHIBIT 3

COMPUCO LIMITED

EXTRACTS FROM SELECTED NOTES TO FINANCIAL STATEMENTS FOR THE YEAR ENDED 31 DECEMBER

1. Loans receivable
   The company's loans receivable at 31 December are due from related parties. Amounts as follows:

($ thousands)

	20X5	20X4
XYZ Inc.	$5,962	$5,962
Writedown to recoverable amount	(2,518)	—
	3,444	5,962
Other investments	2,516	1,000
	$5,960	$6,962

2. Capital assets
   Additions to capital assets for the current year amounted to $2,290 and proceeds from the disposal of capital assets amounted to $250.

3. Development costs
   Development costs for a product are amortized once the product is ready for market. The rate depends on the expected life of the product. In 20X5, $206 of amortization was expensed.

4. Long-term debt

	($ thousands)	
	20X5	**20X4**
Debentures	$12,500	$12,500
Bank term loans, due 31 December 20X2; Principal repayable $150 a month (20X4, $100 a month)	4,200	3,200
	16,700	15,700
Current maturities	(1,800)	(1,200)
	$14,900	$14,500

Debentures bear interest at 12% per annum and are due in 20X8. Bank term loans bear interest at 8% and the bank advanced $2.2 million during the year.

5. Share capital
   On 14 May 20X5, Compuco Limited issued 3.8 million shares. Net proceeds amounted to $15.292 million. On 31 December 20X5, a stock dividend of $1 million was issued.

Required:

Respond to the request.

(CICA, adapted)

ASSIGNMENTS

A5-1 Cash and Cash Equivalents: The following amounts appear on Williams Corporation's trial balance at 31 December 20X5:

Account	Dr(Cr)
Cash on hand	$ 5,400
Current account—Royal Bank of Montreal	110,600
Current account—Scotia Dominion Bank (overdraft)	(34,000)
Short-term money market certificates	200,000
Investment in Shou Limited shares	150,000
Short-term bank borrowings (line of credit)	(300,000)
Cash held in trust for pension plan	50,000

Required:

Determine the amount of cash and cash equivalents held by Williams Corporation at the end of 20X5, as defined by the *CICA Handbook*.

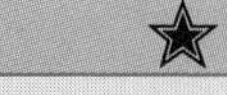

A5-2 Cash Flow Analysis of Sales: The records of JMV Company showed sales revenue of $800,000 on the income statement and a change in the balance of accounts receivable and unearned revenue. To demonstrate the effect of changes on cash, five independent cases are used. Complete the following tabulation for each independent case:

Case	Sales Revenue	Accounts Receivable Increase (Decrease)	Unearned Revenue** Increase (Decrease)	Cash Flow Amount*
A	$800,000	$ 80,000	$ 0	
B	800,000	(80,000)	0	
C	800,000	72,000	40,000	
D	800,000	(72,000)	(40,000)	
E	800,000	80,000	(40,000)	

* *Amount of cash collected from customers*

** *Cash received but unearned*

A5-3 Cash Flow Analysis of Cost of Goods Sold: The records of Van Company showed cost of goods sold on the income statement of $480,000 and a change in the inventory and accounts payable balances. To demonstrate the effect of these changes on cash outflow for cost of goods sold (i.e., payments to suppliers), five independent cases are used. Complete the following tabulation for each case:

Case	Cost of Goods Sold	Inventory Increase (Decrease)	Accounts Payable Increase (Decrease)	Cash Outflow Amount*
A	$480,000	$ (8,000)	$ 0	
B	480,000	8,000	16,000	
C	480,000	(48,000)	(16,000)	
D	480,000	48,000	(32,000)	
E	480,000	32,000	32,000	

* *This is the amount of cash paid during the current period for past and current purchases.*

A5-4 Cash Flow Statement—Item Analysis: The records of Easie Company provided the following data:

a. Sales revenue, $190,000; accounts receivable increased, $10,000.
b. Cost of goods sold, $86,000; inventory decreased, $4,000; accounts payable, no change.
c. Wages expense, $32,000; wages payable decreased, $3,000.
d. Amortization expense, $8,000.
e. Purchased productive asset for $36,000; paid one-third down and gave a two-year, interest-bearing note for the balance.
f. Borrowed $40,000 cash on a note payable.
g. Sold an old operational asset for $6,000 cash; original cost, $20,000, accumulated amortization, $18,000.
h. Paid a $5,500 note payable, $5,000 principal plus $500 interest.
i. Paid a cash dividend, $8,000.

Required:

For each of the above items give:

1. The cash flow statement category (operating, investing, financing).
2. The item that would appear on the cash flow statement (indirect presentation method for operating activities).
3. The item that would appear on the cash flow statement (direct presentation method for operating activities).

A5-5 Transaction Analysis, Indirect Method: You are requested by the controller of a large company to determine the appropriate disclosure of the following transactions in the cash flow statement. Assume all adjusting entries have been recorded.

a. Accounts receivable increased $50,000 during the year.
b. Pension expense is $50,000; the balance of the long-term accrued pension cost liability increased $12,000.
c. Future income tax (long term, credit balance) increased $40,000; income tax payable decreased $10,000.
d. Interest of $10,000 was capitalized to a building under construction, now completed and in use. There is no change in interest payable.
e. The company sold short-term investments (cash equivalents) at a $2,000 gain; cash proceeds, $8,000.
f. The company sold short-term investments (not cash equivalents) at a $4,000 loss; cash proceeds, $4,000.

Required:
Indicate the complete disclosure of each item in the cash flow statement under the indirect method of presentation for operating activities.

A5-6 Cash Flow Statement Classification: The main parts of a cash flow statement are shown below with letter identification. Next, several transactions are given. Match the transactions with the cash flow statement statement parts by entering a letter in each blank space. Assume loans and notes receivable are long-term investments not related to operating activities. State other assumptions or explanations if needed.

Cash flow statement:

A. Cash inflows (outflows) from operating activities (indirect method of presentation)
B. Cash inflows (outflows) from investing activities
C. Cash inflows (outflows) from financing activities
D. Not a cash flow

Transactions:

_____ 1. Acquisition of operational assets; paid cash
_____ 2. Cash dividends declared but not paid
_____ 3. Proceeds from note payable
_____ 4. Sale of operational assets
_____ 5. Issue a loan (loan receivable)
_____ 6. Purchase of a long-term security as an investment
_____ 7. Collections on notes receivable (principal only)
_____ 8. Change in inventory
_____ 9. Amortization expense
_____ 10. Payment of debt, 60% cash and 40% common shares issued
_____ 11. Issuance of the company's common shares, for cash
_____ 12. Sales revenue, cash
_____ 13. Repurchase and retirement of common shares
_____ 14. Payment on notes payable
_____ 15. Paid cash dividend

A5-7 Transaction Analysis, Indirect Method: The major classifications used in the cash flow statement are operating, investing, and financing. Assume that the indirect method is used for the operating sections. Classify each of the transactions that follow according to these groupings. An item may affect more than one grouping.

Cash flow statement

1. Operating—add to net income
2. Operating—deduct from net income
3. Investing activity
4. Financing activity
5. Not disclosed on the cash flow statement

Transactions

_____ a. Issuance of company's own common shares
_____ b. Purchase of land and building
_____ c. Redemption of bonds payable
_____ d. Decrease in accounts payable
_____ e. Increase in prepaid expenses
_____ f. Sale of equipment at a loss
_____ g. Cumulative effect of a change in amortization methods that increases retained earnings
_____ h. Increase in future income tax liability
_____ i. Amortization of patent
_____ j. Issuance of bonds in full payment for capital assets
_____ k. Sale of long-term investments at a gain
_____ l. Payment of cash dividends

A5-8 Prepare a Cash Flow Statement: The records of Rangler Paper Company provided the selected data given below for the reporting period ended 31 December 20X5.

Balance sheet data	
Paid cash dividend	$ 10,000
Established restricted construction cash fund (a long-term investment) to build a new building at 8% interest	60,000
Increased inventory of merchandise	14,000
Borrowed on a long-term note	25,000
Acquired five acres of land for a future site for the company; paid in full by issuing 3,000 shares of Rangler common shares, no-par, when the quoted market price per share was $15	45,000
Increase in prepaid expenses	3,000
Decrease in accounts receivable	7,000
Payment of bonds payable in full at book value	97,000
Increase in accounts payable	5,000
Cash from disposal of old operational assets (sold at book value)	12,000
Decrease in rent receivable	2,000
Income statement	
Sales revenue	$400,000
Rent revenue	10,000
Cost of goods sold	(190,000)
Amortization expense	(20,000)
Remaining expenses	(97,000)
Net income	$103,000

Required:

Prepare a cash flow statement. Use the indirect method for operations. Assume a beginning cash balance of $62,000.

A5-9 Cash Flow Categories—Transaction Analysis: Denton Corporation's balance sheet accounts as of 31 December 20X4 and 20X5, and information relating to 20X5 activities, are presented below.

31 December	20X5	20X4
Assets		
Cash	$ 230,000	$ 100,000
Short-term investments	300,000	—
Accounts receivable	510,000	510,000
Inventory	680,000	600,000
Long-term investments	200,000	300,000
Plant assets	1,700,000	1,000,000
Accumulated depreciation	(450,000)	(450,000)
Patent	90,000	100,000
Total assets	$3,260,000	$2,160,000
Liabilities and shareholders' equity		
Accounts payable and accrued liabilities	$ 825,000	$ 720,000
Short-term bank debt	325,000	—
Common shares	1,170,000	950,000
Retained earnings	940,000	490,000
Total liabilities and shareholders' equity	$3,260,000	$2,160,000

Information relating to 20X5 activities:

- Net income for 20X5 was $690,000.
- Cash dividends of $240,000 were declared and paid in 20X5.
- Equipment costing $400,000 and having a carrying amount of $150,000 was sold for $150,000.
- A long-term investment was sold for $135,000. There were no other transactions affecting long-term investments in the year.
- Ten thousand common shares were issued for $22 per share.
- Short-term investments consist of treasury bills maturing on 15 February 20X6.

Required:

Determine the following amounts for Denton for the year 20X5:

1. Net cash from operating activities (indirect method)
2. Net cash from investing activities
3. Net cash from financing activities (AICPA, adapted)

A5-10 Cash Flow Statement, Operations Section: The data given below were provided from the accounting records of Trent Company. Prepare the operations section of the cash flow statement using the indirect method.

Net income (accrual basis) $400,000, including interest expense of $70,000 and income tax expense of $270,000
Amortization expense, buildings and equipment, $80,000
Increase in interest payable, $12,000
Increase in trade accounts receivable, $18,000
Decrease in merchandise inventory, $40,000
Amortization of patent, $10,000

Purchase of equipment, $410,000
Increase in long-term liabilities, $10,000
Sale of common shares for cash, $25,000
Accounts payable decrease, $50,000
Increase in future income tax liability, $20,000

A5-11 Cash Flow Statement, Indirect Method—Individual Transactions: For each of the following independent transactions for Morrison Corporation, discuss how the transaction would be disclosed and classified in the 20X5 CFS, indirect method.

a. On 31 July 20X5, the corporation issued 1,000 common shares in exchange for a $100,000 debenture issued by Morrison Corporation five years ago.
b. On 31 December 20X5, the corporation sold a piece of machinery with an original cost of $239,000, and accumulated amortization of $164,000, for $110,000. The resulting gain of $35,000 was recorded on the income statement.
c. On 30 June 20X5, Morrison sold short-term investments with a net book value of $46,000, for $52,000. The resulting gain was recorded on the income statement.
d. On 31 October 20X5, the corporation paid a $50,000 income tax reassessment relating to the 20X1 fiscal period.
e. On 31 December 20X5, Morrison Corporation had inventory levels that were $20,000 higher than the previous year.

A5-12 Cash Flow Statement: Analysis of Cash Flows and Reporting: Selected transactions from the records of Dover Company are given below. The annual reporting period ends 31 December 20X2. The company uses the indirect method to present cash flows in the operating activities section. Analyze each transaction and give the following:

1. Classification of the transaction on the cash flow statement (operating, investing, financing, or none of these).
2. How the amount would be reported on the cash flow statement.

Example:
Declared and paid a cash dividend, $10,000.

Response:
Financing activity. Cash outflow, dividends paid, $10,000.

a. Purchased operational asset (machine) for $40,000; gave a one-year interest-bearing note for $25,000 and paid cash for the difference.
b. Sold long-term investment, at book value. Received cash of $12,000 and a three-year interest-bearing note for $13,000.
c. Net income, $60,000.
d. Inventory increased $20,000 during the year.
e. Declared a cash dividend of $8,000 and set up a short-term dividends payable account for $6,000 (to be paid in 20X3).
f. Repurchased and retired common shares for $17,000.
g. Amortization expense, $12,000.
h. Paid a loan payable in full, $5,000.
i. Sold an old capital asset for $5,000 cash; original recorded cost, $20,000; accumulated amortization to date, $16,000.
j. Issued a stock dividend that was debited to retained earnings and credited to common shares, $12,000.
k. Sold an investment in land for $35,000; received $10,000 cash and a one-year interest-bearing note for the remainder. The land was originally recorded in the accounts at $13,000; therefore, a $22,000 gain on sale of land was recorded.
l. Received a cash dividend of $6,000 on a long-term investment in the common shares of Harken Corporation.
m. Interest payable decreased $3,000.
n. Income tax payable increased $6,000.

A5-13 Partial Cash Flow Statement; Missing Data: A partial trial balance for Wellco:

	20X2	20X1
Debits:		
Accounts receivable	$ 140,000	$ 99,000
Inventory	244,600	302,900
Capital assets	988,500	326,800
Credits:		
Accumulated amortization	$ 487,600	$ 371,000
Accounts payable	187,000	104,000
Bank overdraft	45,800	–
Bonds payable	400,000	200,000
Preferred shares	10,000	50,000
Common shares	275,000	200,000
Retained earnings	345,000	217,000

Other information:

1. Cash dividends were $100,000.
2. Capital assets were acquired for $200,000 of bonds.
3. Preferred shares of $40,000 were converted to common shares.
4. Capital assets with an original cost of $80,000 and a book value of $30,000 were sold for a gain of $16,000.

Required:

Prepare the cash flow statement for 20X2, in good form, as far as possible. Note that only a partial trial balance is provided. It is not possible to do a complete cash flow statement, or have the cash flow statement balance, with the information given. Use the indirect method for operating activities. Assume that unexplained differences in balance sheet accounts flow from logical sources.

A5-14 Partial Cash Flow Statement; Missing Data: A *partial* trial balance for Rankin Limited:

As of 31 December	20X4	20X3
Temporary investments, 2-month term	$ 20,000	$ –
Accounts receivable	17,000	27,000
Inventory	138,500	123,200
Capital assets	614,000	455,000
Accumulated amortization	312,400	266,000
Accounts payable	116,000	84,000
Income tax payable	10,600	19,500
Bonds payable	400,000	–
Preferred shares	95,000	95,000
Common shares	113,000	84,000
Retained earnings	23,100	31,000

INCOME STATEMENT

For the year ended 31 December 20X4

Sales		$ 592,000
Cost of goods sold	$ 266,000	
Selling expenses	40,000	
Amortization expense	111,600	
Loss on sale of capital asset	4,300	
Interest expense	10,500	
Income tax expense	16,000	
		448,400
Net income		$ 143,600

Other information:

1. Stock dividends of $29,000 were declared and distributed, reducing retained earnings and increase of common shares.
2. Capital assets were acquired for $100,000 of bonds.
3. Capital assets with an original cost of $80,000 were sold for cash during the period.

Required:

1. Prepare the operating and investing sections (only) of the cash flow statement for 20X4, in good form. Use the indirect method for operating activities. Assume that unexplained differences in balance sheet accounts flow from logical sources.
2. Calculate cash dividends paid.

A5-15 Partial Cash Flow Statement; Missing Data: Shukla Corporation has the following balances:

	20X3	20X2
Inventory	125,000	136,200
Prepaid expenses	12,700	9,500
Buildings	998,000	1,206,000
Accumulated amortization, buildings	545,000	654,200
Dividends payable	21,000	15,000
Accounts payable	78,700	35,300
Bonds payable	–	300,000
Premium on bonds payable	–	44,200
Common shares	600,000	400,000
Retained earnings	870,600	637,900

Additional information:

Net income was $376,500. This included a $2,000 loss on the bond retirement, $1,000 of premium amortization, and a gain on sale of building for $51,000. Amortization expense was $74,200 on the building.

There was a $500,000 addition to the building account, financed through the issuance of common shares in the amount of $100,000; the balance was paid in cash.

Any other unexplained change in the above accounts should be assumed to be from the most logical underlying transaction.

Required:

Prepare the *investing* and *financing* (only) sections of the cash flow statement.

A5-16 Cash Flow Statement; Indirect Method: The following data were provided by the accounting records of Smiley Company at year-end, 31 December 20X1:

INCOME STATEMENT

Year ended 31 December 20X1	
Sales	$320,000
Cost of goods sold	(180,000)
Amortization expense	(24,000)
Remaining expenses	(80,000)
Loss on sale of operational assets	(4,000)
Gain on sale of investments	12,000
Net income	$ 44,000

COMPARATIVE BALANCE SHEETS

31 December	20X1	20X0
Debits		
Cash	$180,000	$ 116,000
Accounts receivable	68,000	48,000
Inventory	56,000	64,000
Long-term investments	—	24,000
Operational assets	392,000	320,000
Total debits	$696,000	$572,000
Credits		
Accumulated amortization	$160,000	$ 192,000
Accounts payable	48,000	76,000
Bonds payable	120,000	40,000
Common shares	260,000	200,000
Retained earnings	108,000	64,000
Total credits	$696,000	$572,000

Analysis of selected accounts and transactions:

a. Sold operational assets for $24,000 cash; cost, $84,000; two-thirds depreciated.
b. Purchased operational assets for cash, $36,000.
c. Purchased operational assets and exchanged unissued bonds payable of $120,000 in payment.
d. Sold the long-term investments for $36,000 cash.
e. Retired bonds payable at maturity date by issuing common shares, $40,000.
f. Issued unissued common shares for cash, $20,000.

Required:
Prepare the CFS. Use the two-step indirect method to present the operations section.

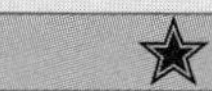

A5-17 Cash Flow Statement; Direct Method: Repeat A5-16, operations section, using the direct method to disclose the operations section.

A5-18 Prepare a Cash Flow Statement: The accounting records of Pall-Mall Company provided the following data:

INCOME STATEMENT

For year ended 31 December 20X1	
Sales	$300,000
Cost of goods sold	(180,000)
Depreciation expense	(4,000)
Remaining expenses	(64,000)
Net income	$ 52,000

COMPARATIVE BALANCE SHEETS

At 31 December	20X1	20X0
Debits		
Cash	$ 34,000	$ —
Accounts receivable	18,000	19,000
Inventory	25,000	20,000
Investment, long term	—	3,000
Capital assets	93,000	60,000
Total debits	$170,000	$102,000
Credits		
Bank overdraft	$ —	$ 5,000
Accumulated depreciation	14,000	10,000
Accounts payable	12,000	6,000
Short-term bank loan	4,000	3,000
Notes payable, long term	36,000	20,000
Common shares	80,000	50,000
Retained earnings	24,000	8,000
Total credits	$170,000	$102,000

Analysis of selected accounts and transactions:

a. Sold the long-term investment at cost, for cash.
b. Declared and paid a cash dividend of $36,000.
c. Purchased capital assets that cost $33,000; gave a $24,000 long-term note payable and paid $9,000 cash.
d. Paid an $8,000 long-term note payable by issuing common shares; market value, $8,000.
e. Sold common shares for cash.

Required:
Prepare the cash flow statement, using the two-step indirect method of presentation for the operations section.

A5-19 Prepare a Cash Flow Statement; Direct Method: Repeat A5-18, using the direct method to disclose the operations section.

A5-20 Cash Flow Statement, Indirect and Direct Method (Optional Spreadsheet): Todd Corporation reported the following on its 20X4 income statement:

TODD CORPORATION
INCOME STATEMENT
For the year ended 31 December 20X4

Sales	$624,000
Cost of goods sold	(330,000)
Depreciation expense	(48,000)
Patent amortization	(1,800)
Remaining expenses	(106,200)
Net income	$138,000

TODD CORPORATION
BALANCE SHEET

As of 31 December	20X4	20X3
Cash	$129,000	$ 90,000
Investments, short term	18,000	—
Accounts receivable	126,000	102,000
Inventory	90,000	60,000
Investments, long term	60,000	—
Property, plant, and equipment (net)	354,000	360,000
Patent (net)	16,200	18,000
Other assets	42,000	42,000
Total	$835,200	$672,000
Accounts payable	132,000	72,000
Accrued expenses payable	52,200	—
Bonds payable	120,000	240,000
Common shares	267,000	210,000
Retained earnings	264,000	150,000
Total	$835,200	$672,000

Analysis of accounts:

a. Retired bonds, paid $120,000 cash.
b. Bought long-term investment in common shares, $60,000 cash.
c. Purchased equipment, $42,000 cash.
d. Purchased short-term investment, $18,000 cash.
e. Paid cash dividend, $24,000.
f. Issued common shares, 3,000 shares at $19 cash per share.

Required:

1. Prepare the cash flow statement, using the indirect method. The solution to this assignment features an optional spreadsheet.
2. Prepare the operations section of the cash flow statement using the direct method.

A5-21 Cash Flow Statement: The following financial information is available for Buffalo Incorporated for the 20X3 fiscal year:

BUFFALO INCORPORATED
BALANCE SHEET

As at 31 December	20X3	20X2
Cash	$ 5,000	$ 20,000
Receivables	220,000	180,000
Marketable securities	190,000	230,000
Inventory	731,000	632,000
Land	330,000	410,000
Building	1,040,000	1,120,000
Accumulated amortization, building	(470,000)	(380,000)
Machinery	1,080,000	875,000
Accumulated amortization, machinery	(219,000)	(212,000)
Goodwill	110,000	110,000
	$3,017,000	$2,985,000
Current liabilities	$ 76,000	$ 146,000
Bonds payable	1,000,000	1,000,000
Premium on bonds	180,000	185,000
Preferred shares	1,048,000	843,000
Common shares	565,000	500,000
Retained earnings	148,000	311,000
	$3,017,000	$2,985,000

BUFFALO INCORPORATED
INCOME STATEMENT

For the year ended 31 December 20X3	
Sales	$1,684,000
Cost of goods sold	(1,103,000)
Gross profit	581,000
Amortization	
Building	110,000
Machinery	75,000
Interest	115,000
Other expenses	361,000
Loss on writedown of marketable securities	40,000
Gain on sale of land	(22,000)
Loss on sale of machine	27,000
	706,000
Net income (loss) before income tax	(125,000)
Income tax	54,000
Net income (loss)	$(71,000)

Additional information:

1. Marketable securities were sold at their carrying value. The marketable securities are not cash equivalents.
2. A partially amortized building was sold for an amount equal to its net book value.
3. Cash of $40,000 was received on the sale of a machine.

4. Preferred shares were issued for cash on 1 March 20X3. Dividends of $50,000 were paid on the non-cumulative preferred shares.
5. On 1 September 20X3, 25,000 common shares were purchased and retired for $55,000, their original issuance price. On 1 November 20X3, 65,000 common shares were issued in exchange for machinery.
6. Because of its loss, the company received a refund of taxes paid in prior years of $54,000.

The company has a 31 December year-end.

Required:
Prepare a cash flow statement, in good form. Use the indirect method for cash flows from operations.

A5-22 Cash Flow Statement, Indirect Method (Optional Spreadsheet): Shown below are the income statement, comparative balance sheets, and additional information useful in preparing the 20X5 CFS for Sells Company.

INCOME STATEMENT

For the year ended 31 December 20X5	
Net sales	$300,000
Cost of goods sold	80,000
Gross margin	220,000
Depreciation expense	45,000
Amortization of intangibles	2,000
Other expenses	44,000
Interest expense	3,000
Income tax expense	65,000
Net income	$ 61,000

COMPARATIVE BALANCE SHEETS

As of 31 December	20X5	20X4
Cash	$ 32,000	$ 16,000
Accounts receivable	47,000	50,000
Other receivables	2,000	3,000
Inventory	32,000	30,000
Equipment	77,000	80,000
Accumulated depreciation	(5,000)	(6,000)
Intangibles, net	53,000	55,000
Total assets	$238,000	$228,000
Accounts payable	$ 60,000	$ 50,000
Income taxes payable	50,000	70,000
Interest payable	1,000	2,000
Bonds payable	—	32,000
Discount on bonds payable	—	(2,000)
Common shares	80,000	70,000
Retained earnings	47,000	6,000
Total liabilities and owners' equity	$238,000	$228,000

Additional information:

a. Dividends of $20,000 were declared and paid in 20X5.
b. Equipment costing $66,000 with a book value of $20,000 was sold at book value. New equipment was also purchased; common shares were issued in partial payment.
c. The bonds were retired at net book value; $500 of bond discount had been amortized in 20X5.

Required:
Prepare the 20X5 cash flow statement, indirect method, for Sells Company. (The solution to this assignment features an optional spreadsheet.)

A5-23 Cash Flow Statement (Optional Spreadsheet): The records of Alberta Company provided the following data for the accounting year ended 31 December 20X5:

COMPARATIVE BALANCE SHEETS

At 31 December	20X5	20X4
Debits		
Cash	$ 75,000	$ 30,000
Investment, short term (cash equivalent)	8,000	10,000
Accounts receivable	86,000	56,000
Inventory	30,000	20,000
Prepaid interest	2,000	—
Land	25,000	60,000
Machinery	90,000	80,000
Other assets	39,000	29,000
Discount on bonds payable	900	1,000
Total debits	$355,900	$286,000
Credits		
Accumulated depreciation	26,900	20,000
Accounts payable	54,000	39,000
Salaries payable	2,000	5,000
Income taxes payable	8,000	2,000
Bonds payable	55,000	70,000
Common shares	130,000	100,000
Preferred shares	30,000	20,000
Retained earnings	50,000	30,000
Total credits	$355,900	$286,000

INCOME STATEMENT

For the year ended 31 December 20X5	
Sales revenue	$180,000
Cost of goods sold	(90,000)
Depreciation expense	(6,900)
Salaries	(33,900)
Interest expense	(6,100)
Remaining expenses	(4,000)
Gain on sale of land	18,000
Income tax expense	(12,100)
Net income	$ 45,000

Analysis of selected accounts and transactions:

a. Issued bonds payable for cash, $5,000.
b. Sold land for $53,000 cash; book value, $35,000.
c. Purchased machinery for cash, $10,000.
d. Sold short-term investments for cash, $2,000.
e. Retired $20,000 bonds payable by issuing common shares; the common shares had a market value of $20,000.
f. Acquired other assets by issuing preferred shares with a market value of $10,000.

g. Statement of retained earnings:

Balance, 1 January 20X5	$30,000
Net income for 20X5	45,000
Cash dividends	(15,000)
Stock dividend issued	(10,000)
Balance, 31 December 20X5	$50,000

Required:

1. Prepare the cash flow statement, using the two-step indirect method.
2. Prepare the operations section of the cash flow statement using the direct method of presentation. (The solution to this assignment features an optional spreadsheet.)

A5-24 Derive Balance Sheet from Cash Flow Data: Bewards Limited's balance sheet for 1 January 20X8, its income statement for the year ended 31 December 20X8, and the cash flow statement for the year ended 31 December 20X8 are presented below.

BEWARDS LIMITED
BALANCE SHEET

1 January 20X8	
Assets	
Cash	$ 24,000
Accounts receivable	200,000
Inventory	160,000
Prepaid insurance	4,000
Capital assets (net)	620,000
Total assets	1,008,000
Liabilities and shareholders' equity	
Salaries payable	8,000
Notes payable	100,000
Common shares	150,000
Retained earnings	750,000
Total liabilities and shareholders' equity	$1,008,000

BEWARDS LIMITED
INCOME STATEMENT

Year ended 31 December 20X8		
Sales revenue		$2,300,000
Expenses:		
Cost of goods sold	$1,600,000	
Salaries expense	200,000	
Amortization expense	40,000	
Insurance expense	24,000	
Other expenses	336,000	2,200,000
Net income		$ 100,000

BEWARDS LIMITED
CASH FLOW STATEMENT

Year ended 31 December 20X8

Cash flows from operating activities:		
Cash receipts from customers	$2,200,000	
Cash paid to suppliers	(1,700,000)	
Cash paid to employees	(202,000)	
Cash paid to insurers	(22,000)	
Cash paid for other expenses	(336,000)	
Net cash used in operating activities		$ (60,000)
Cash flows from financing activities:		
Proceeds from increase in note payable	$ 46,000	
Proceeds from issue of common shares	50,000	
Net cash provided by financing activities		96,000
Net increase in cash		36,000
Cash, 1 January 20X8		24,000
Cash, 31 December 20X8		$ 60,000

Additional information:

a. All inventory was purchased for cash.
b. The company did not purchase or sell any capital assets during the period.
c. During the year, all transactions related to notes payable and common shares were conducted for cash.

Required:

Based on the financial statements and other information, prepare the balance sheet at 31 December 20X8. Show all supporting calculations.

(CGA-Canada)

A5-25 Prepare Cash Flow Statement, Indirect Method: Linda Ray, the president of Zabron Electric Corporation, has asked the company controller for a cash flow statement for the reporting year ended 31 December 20X1. The following balance sheet data has been obtained from the accounting records:

a. Cash account balances: 1 January 20X1, $43,000; 31 December 20X1, $18,000.
b. The balance in accounts receivable decreased by $10,000 during the year. Wages payable decreased by $5,000.
c. Inventory increased $9,000, and accounts payable increased $3,000 during the year.
d. Income tax payable increased $4,000 during the year.
e. During December 20X1, the company settled a $10,000 note payable by issuing its own common shares with equivalent value.
f. Cash expenditures during 20X1 included (1) payment of long-term debts, $64,000; (2) purchase of new capital assets, $74,000; (3) payment of a cash dividend, $16,000; and (4) purchase of land as an investment, $25,000.
g. In 20X1, shares were issued for $20,000 cash.
h. In 20X1, Zabron issued a long-term mortgage note, $30,000.
i. Some capital assets were sold; the following entry was made:

Cash	5,000	
Accumulated amortization	12,000	
Capital assets		15,000
Gain on sale of capital assets		2,000

Income statement data:	
Sales revenue	$ 295,000
Cost of goods sold	(140,000)
Amortization expense, capital assets	(14,000)
Patent amortization	(1,000)
Income tax expense	(17,000)
Remaining expenses	(42,000)
Gain on sale of capital assets	2,000
Net income	$ 83,000

Required:

Prepare a CFS using the indirect method.

A5-26 Cash Flow Statement: The items from the 31 December 20X2 cash flow statement for Moon Limited are given below, in no particular order.

Closing cash	?
Repayment of long-term debt	$594,800
Amortization expense	372,000
Decrease in inventories	196,000
Capital expenditures	573,600
Proceeds from issuance of common shares	42,400
Decrease in accounts payable	180,000
Net income	76,600
Dividends paid	96,500
Proceeds from expropriation of land (a $12,500 extraordinary gain was recorded after tax of $5,000)	181,000
Opening cash	233,000
Decrease in prepaid expenses	1,000
Increase in future income tax liability	64,800
Proceeds from the sale of a long-term investment (no gain or loss)	560,000
Increase in long-term borrowings	61,300
Depletion	120,100
Increase in accounts receivable	134,000

Required:

1. Using the above information, prepare a cash flow statement in good form, using the two-step indirect method.
2. Based on this statement, what would you conclude about the company's cash flows for 20X2?

A5-27 Prepare Cash Flow Statement Showing a Net Loss: At the end of the current reporting year, 31 December 20X2, Felch Construction Company's executives were very concerned about the ending cash balance of $4,000; the beginning cash balance of $34,000 had been considered seriously low the year before.

During 20X2, management had taken numerous actions to attain a better cash position. In view of the decreased cash balance, management asked the chief accountant to prepare a cash flow statement. The following information was developed from the accounting records:

a. Debt:
   1. Borrowing on long-term note, $10,000.
   2. Payments on maturing long-term debt, $110,000.
   3. Settled short-term debt of $50,000 by issuing Felch common shares.

b. Cash payments:
   1. Regular cash dividends, $18,000.
   2. Purchase of new operational assets, $22,000.

c. Cash received:
   1. Sold and issued Felch common shares, $11,000.
   2. Sold old capital assets at their book value, $1,000.
   3. Sold investment (long term) in shares of Tech Corporation purchased this year and made the following entry:

Cash	90,000	
Loss on sale of investment	30,000	
Investment in Tech Corporation shares		120,000

d. Relevant balance sheet accounts:
   1. Increase in income tax payable, $10,000.
   2. Decrease in inventory, $38,000.
   3. Increase in accounts receivable, $5,000.

e. Income statement data:

Sales	$ 160,000
Cost of goods sold	(150,000)
Amortization expense	(58,000)
Amortization of patent	(2,000)
Income tax expense	(14,000)
Remaining expenses	(31,000)
Loss on sale of investment	(30,000)
Net income (loss)	$(125,000)

Required:

Based on the above data, prepare a cash flow statement. Use the indirect method.

A5-28 Cash Flow Statement, Direct Method: The balance sheet, income statement, and additional information are given below for Supreme Company.

COMPARATIVE BALANCE SHEETS

31 December	20X5	20X4
Debits		
Cash	$ 44,900	$ 40,000
Accounts receivable	52,500	60,000
Merchandise inventory	141,600	180,000
Prepaid insurance	1,200	2,400
Investments, long term	—	30,000
Land	38,400	10,000
Capital assets	259,000	250,000
Patent (net)	1,400	1,600
	$539,000	$574,000
Credits		
Accumulated depreciation	$ 79,000	$ 65,000
Accounts payable	53,000	50,000
Wages payable	1,500	2,000
Income taxes payable	13,400	9,000
Bonds payable	50,000	100,000
Premium on bonds payable	1,700	5,000
Common shares	324,000	315,000
Retained earnings	16,400	28,000
	$539,000	$574,000

INCOME STATEMENT

For the year ended 31 December 20X5	20X5
Sales revenue	$399,100
Cost of goods sold	(224,400)
Depreciation expense	(14,000)
Patent amortization	(200)
Salary expense	(80,000)
Interest expense	(4,400)
Other expenses	(44,000)
Investment revenue	900
Gain on sale of investments	10,000
Income tax expense	(24,600)
Net income	$ 18,400

Analysis of selected accounts and transactions:

a. Purchased capital asset, $9,000; payment by issuing 600 common shares.
b. Payment at maturity date to retire bonds payable, $50,000.
c. Sold the long-term investments for $40,000.
d. Reassessment for prior years' income taxes; paid during 20X5 and added to 20X5 tax expense, $6,600.
e. Purchased land, $28,400; paid cash.
f. Cash dividends declared and paid, $30,000.

Required:

Prepare the cash flow statement, using the direct method.

A5-29 Cash Flow Statement, Indirect Method: The records of Easy Trading Company provided the following information for the year ended 31 December 20X5:

INCOME STATEMENT

For the year ended 31 December 20X5	
Sales revenue	$80,000
Cost of goods sold	(36,000)
Depreciation expense	(5,000)
Insurance expense	(1,000)
Interest expense	(2,000)
Salaries and wages expense	(12,000)
Remaining expenses	(13,000)
Loss on sale of capital assets	(2,000)
Income tax expense	(3,000)
Net income	$ 6,000

BALANCE SHEET

At 31 December	20X5	20X4
Cash	$ 31,000	$ 15,000
Accounts receivable	26,500	28,500
Inventory	15,000	10,000
Prepaid insurance	1,400	2,400
Buildings and equipment	81,000	80,000
Accumulated depreciation	(16,000)	(20,000)
Land	81,100	40,100
Total	$220,000	$156,000

At 31 December	20X5	20X4
Accounts payable	$ 11,000	$ 10,000
Wages payable	1,000	2,000
Interest payable	1,000	—
Notes payable, long-term	46,000	20,000
Common shares	136,000	100,000
Retained earnings	25,000	24,000
Total	$220,000	$156,000

Analysis of transactions during the year:

a. Sold equipment for $4,000 cash (cost, $15,000; accumulated depreciation, $9,000).
b. Issued common shares for $5,000 cash.
c. Declared and paid a cash dividend, $5,000.
d. Purchased land, $20,000 cash.
e. Acquired land for $21,000 and issued common shares as payment in full.
f. Acquired equipment, cost $16,000; issued a $16,000, three-year, interest-bearing note payable.
g. Paid a $10,000 long-term note by issuing common shares to the creditor.
h. Borrowed cash on long-term note, $20,000.

Required:

Prepare the cash flow statement, using the two-step indirect method. Also prepare supplementary disclosure of cash paid for interest and taxes.

A5-30 Cash Flow Statement, Direct Method: Using the data given in A5-29, prepare the operations section of the cash flow statement using the direct method.

A5-31 Cash Flow Statement, Direct and Indirect Method: The income statement and balance sheet of Kenwood Company and related analysis are given below.

KENWOOD COMPANY
INCOME STATEMENT

For the year ended 31 December 20X4		
Sales revenue		$1,000,000
Less expenses:		
Cost of goods sold	560,000	
Salaries and wages	190,000	
Depreciation	20,000	
Patent amortization	3,000	
Interest expense	16,000	
Miscellaneous expenses	8,000	
Total expenses		797,000
Plus other:		
Loss on sale of equipment	(4,000)	
Gain on bond retirement	12,000	8,000
Income before income tax		211,000
Income tax expense		82,000
Net income		$ 129,000

KENWOOD COMPANY
COMPARATIVE BALANCE SHEETS

As of 31 December	20X4	20X3
Assets		
Current assets:		
Cash	$ 100,000	$ 90,000
Accounts receivable	210,000	140,000
Inventory	260,000	220,000
Total current assets	570,000	450,000
Land	325,000	200,000
Plant and equipment	580,000	633,000
Less: Accumulated depreciation	(90,000)	(100,000)
Patents	30,000	33,000
Total assets	$1,415,000	$1,216,000
Liabilities and shareholders' equity		
Liabilities:		
Current liabilities:		
Accounts payable	$ 260,000	$ 200,000
Salaries and wages payable	200,000	210,000
Income tax payable	140,000	100,000
Total current liabilities	600,000	510,000
Bonds payable (due 15 December 20X14)	130,000	180,000
Total liabilities	730,000	690,000
Shareholders' equity:		
Common shares, no par; authorized 100,000 shares, issued and outstanding 50,000 and 42,000 shares, respectively	483,000	380,000
Retained earnings	202,000	146,000
Total shareholders' equity	685,000	526,000
Total liabilities and shareholders' equity	$1,415,000	$1,216,000

Analysis of selected accounts and transactions:

a. On 2 February 20X4, Kenwood issued a 10% stock dividend to shareholders of record on 15 January 20X4. This increased common shares, and decreased retained earnings, by $63,000.

b. On 1 March 20X4, Kenwood issued 3,800 common shares for land. The common shares had a current market value of approximately $40,000.

c. On 15 April 20X4, Kenwood repurchased long-term bonds payable with a face value of $50,000 for cash. The gain of $12,000 was correctly reported on the income statement.

d. On 30 June 20X4, Kenwood sold equipment that cost $53,000, with a book value of $23,000, for $19,000 cash.

e. On 30 September 20X4, Kenwood declared and paid a cash dividend.

f. On 10 October 20X4, Kenwood purchased land for $85,000 cash.

Required:

1. Prepare the cash flow statement, using the indirect method. Use the two-step method for operations. Prepare supplementary disclosure for the cash flows for interest and income tax.
2. Prepare the cash flow statement, using the direct method, to disclose cash flows in the operating activities section.

(AICPA, adapted)

A5-32 Cash Flow Statement, Indirect Method: The differences between the Boole Incorporated balance sheet accounts of 31 December 20X4 and 20X5, are presented below:

	Increase (decrease)
Assets	
Cash	$ 120,000
Short-term investments (cash equivalents)	300,000
Accounts receivable	—
Inventory	80,000
Long-term investments	(100,000)
Capital assets	700,000
Accumulated amortization	—
	$1,100,000
Liabilities and shareholders' equity	
Accounts payable and accrued liabilities	$ (5,000)
Dividends payable	160,000
Bank overdraft (part of net cash position on CFS)	325,000
Long-term debt	110,000
Common shares, no par, an additional 10,000 shares	220,000
Retained earnings	290,000
	$1,100,000

Additional information for 20X5:

1. A building costing $600,000 and having a carrying amount of $350,000 was sold for $350,000.
2. Equipment costing $110,000 was acquired through issuance of long-term debt.
3. A long-term investment was sold for $135,000. There were no other transactions affecting long-term investments.
4. Common shares were issued for $22 a share.
5. Net income was $790,000.

Required:

Prepare Boole's cash flow statement in as much detail as possible, using the indirect method for the operating activities section.

(AICPA, adapted)

A5-33 Convert Operations from Direct to Indirect: The management of Crystal Corporation is reviewing the financial statements for the year ended 31 December 20X9. Management is pleased with the earnings performance of the company during the year, but is having difficulty understanding the operating activities section of the cash flow statement. The accountant explains that the operating activities are disclosed using the direct approach. In previous years, Crystal had used the indirect approach.

Management has asked you to prepare the operating activities section of the cash flow statement by using the indirect approach. The income statement for Crystal and the schedule used to prepare the operating activities section by the direct method are as follows:

INCOME STATEMENT

For the year ended 31 December 20X9

Sales	$1,230,000
Cost of goods sold	(870,000)
Gross profit	360,000
Loss on disposal of capital asset	(11,000)
Amortization expense	(41,000)
Operating expenses	(199,000)
Interest expense	(17,000)
Income tax expense	(31,000)
Net income	$ 61,000

CASH FLOW STATEMENT
OPERATING ACTIVITIES

Year ended 31 December 20X9	
Cash received from customers ($1,230,000 sales + $19,000 decrease in accounts receivable)	$1,249,000
Cash paid for goods and services ($870,000 cost of goods sold + $199,000 operating expenses − $27,000 decrease in inventory + $22,000 decrease in accounts payable)	(1,064,000)
Cash paid for interest ($17,000 interest expense − $4,000 increase in interest payable)	(13,000)
Cash paid for income taxes ($31,000 income tax expense + $6,000 decrease in income tax payable	(37,000)
Cash provided by operating activities	$ 135,000

Required:

Prepare the operating activities section of the cash flow statement using the indirect approach.

(CGA-Canada)

A5-34 Operations, Indirect Method, from Incorrect Format: The following schedule of cash receipts and disbursements was prepared by the bookkeeper of J. Ong Limited:

J. ONG LIMITED
SCHEDULE OF CASH RECEIPTS AND DISBURSEMENTS

Year ended 31 December 20X8		
Cash receipts:		
Net income		$ 600,000
Amortization—equipment		70,000
Amortization—patent		11,200
Accounts receivable decrease		40,000
Accounts payable increase		80,000
Bond discount amortization		6,400
Proceeds from sale of land		140,000
Proceeds from sale of long-term investments		80,000
Issuance of common shares for cash		200,000
Change in cash		18,400
Total		$1,246,000
Cash disbursements:		
Dividends		$ 80,000
Inventory increase		44,000
Repayment of long-term note		240,000
Gain on sale of land	$68,000	
Less: loss on sale of investment	26,000	42,000
New buildings		600,000
New equipment		240,000
Total		$1,246,000

Required:

Prepare, in good form, a cash flow statement assuming the cash balance on 1 January 20X8 was $82,000. The cash flows from operating activities should be presented using the indirect method.

(CGA-Canada)

A5-35 Integrative Problem, Chapters 1–5: Account balances, taken from the ledger of Argot Flooring Limited as of 31 December 20X5, appear below.

Accounts payable	$280,000	Inventory, 1 Jan. 20X5**	$344,000
Accounts receivable	632,000	Land	398,000
Accumulated amortization,		General operating expenses	338,000
building equipment	42,000	Notes payable	232,000
Allowance for doubtful		Notes receivable	120,000
accounts	3,000	Property tax expense	3,200
Building and equipment	198,000	Purchases	1,218,000
Cash	?	Purchase discounts	8,000
Common shares	204,100	Purchase returns and	
Extraordinary loss	71,000	allowances	32,000
Dividends declared	80,000	Retained earnings,	
Error correction (credit)	29,400	1 Jan. 20X5	806,400
Future income taxes		Revenue	2,632,000
(credit)	116,700	Salaries expense	232,000
Income tax expense*	334,600	Store supplies inventory	12,400
Interest revenue	5,000	Unearned revenue	32,000

* *Assume this amount is properly stated after all subsequent adjustments are considered. Tax expense includes $28,400 of tax reduction caused by the extraordinary loss, and a $12,000 expense related to the error correction.*

** *Inventory at 31 December is $480,000.*

Additional information:

1. Store supplies were counted at 31 December and found to be valued at $5,600.
2. Amortization of building and equipment is over eight years with an expected salvage value of $10,000.
3. Property taxes of $3,200 were paid on 1 October 20X5, and relate to the year 1 October 20X5 to 30 September 20X6.
4. The note payable was issued on 1 November 20X5 and has an annual interest rate of 12%. Interest must be paid each 30 October along with $30,000 of principal.
5. The note receivable has been outstanding all year. Interest at 10% is collected each 1 June. The note is due 1 June 20X11.
6. The allowance for doubtful accounts now has a $3,000 credit balance. Aging of accounts receivable indicates that $76,000 of the accounts are doubtful.
7. Unearned revenue represents an advance payment from a customer; 75% was still unearned at year-end.
8. At year-end, $10,000 (at retail value) of goods were shipped to customers but the sale was not yet recorded. Correctly, the goods were not included in closing inventory. Only the revenue must be recorded.

Required:

1. Explain the meaning of GAAP and compare GAAP to TAP.
2. Identify common objectives of financial reporting.
3. Prepare adjusting journal entries to reflect the additional information provided above.
4. Explain the following (a) through (e) and give an example of an adjusting journal entry in requirement (3) caused by each.

a. time-period assumption
b. continuity assumption
c. accrual concept
d. revenue recognition convention
e. matching convention

5. Prepare a multiple-step classified income statement, retained earnings statement, and a classified balance sheet based on the adjusted accounts.
6. Assume that accounts have changed (after the entries made in requirement (3)) as follows over the period:

Accounts receivable (net)	$41,900	decrease
Interest receivable	no change	
Inventory	136,000	increase
Store supplies inventory	8,000	decrease
Prepaid property tax	no change	
Buildings and equipment	40,000	increase
Accounts payable	75,000	increase
Interest payable	4,640	increase
Notes payable	232,000	increase
Future (deferred) income tax	26,400	increase
Unearned revenue	24,000	increase

Prepare the operations section of the cash flow statement using the indirect method of presentation.
7. What criteria must be met before an item can be considered extraordinary?
8. List the major areas of choice that are present in the format of the income statement and balance sheet.
9. List six functions of disclosure notes and give an example of each.

CHAPTER 6

Revenue and Expense Recognition

INTRODUCTION

Financial statement users place considerable reliance on a company's net income. Net income is a measure of company performance, management performance, cash flow (indirectly), and future earnings ability. However, the measurement of revenues and expenses is far from precise. Revenue and expense recognition both require a great deal of professional judgement and involve many accounting estimates. Recognition is affected by many factors, including an individual company's financial reporting objectives.

Revenue recognition is probably the most difficult single issue in accounting, because many modern business activities are very complex. Much economic activity in Canada (and in other developed countries) involves long-term earnings processes, including the broad resource and service sectors. In complex and long-term earnings processes, it is not at all obvious just when revenue should be recognized.

Similarly, expense recognition can be very challenging. The basic underlying concept of expense recognition is *matching*. The matching concept is simple and elegant, but how should it be applied in practice? There are different ways to treat a cost—as an asset or as an expense. If a cost is recorded as an asset (that is, if the cost is capitalized), we have to decide when and how the cost should be transferred from asset to expense. When is an asset impaired, giving rise to a loss? How (and when) should the lower-of-cost-or-market principle be applied? What is the role of conservatism in expense recognition? How should capital costs be amortized? When should accounting estimates be revised? What flexibility exists for managers to control the timing of expense recognition?

All of the issues in revenue and expense recognition have a direct impact on net income measurement; a relatively small change in revenue or expense recognition can have a major impact on net income.

This chapter will examine the conceptual guidelines for determining when revenue should be recognized. We will discuss several accounting approaches that have been developed to help resolve revenue recognition problems.

Then we will discuss the basic concepts of expense recognition. This chapter examines the general area of expense policy—the standards, practices, and policies that govern this crucial area of accounting policy choice and accounting estimates. Later chapters will discuss detailed expense recognition policies that are appropriate for specific types of expenditures.

DEFINITIONS

REVENUE What is revenue? It's *not* defined on its own as, for example "the value of goods and services delivered during the period." Revenue is the increase in net assets (that is, assets minus liabilities) that occurs through normal business activities. Revenue is reported on the income statement, but its creation is really the result of changes that occur on the balance sheet.

For example, suppose that a company sells merchandise on credit. The sale results in an account receivable. Creation of the account receivable increases assets. The increase in assets from this normal business activity is revenue, barring other complications such as a very liberal return policy.

To recognize and report revenue, a company must be entitled to the full benefits of the increase in net assets. For example, what should the online auction website eBay Inc. report as revenue—the total amount of sales that are transacted through its website? To do so would imply that the total sales value will increase eBay's net assets. But eBay has no control over the transaction prices. The company sets the commission and other fees that it charges, but the price of the goods is set between the buyer and the seller. eBay is not entitled to the full benefits of the negotiated price—only to the commission—even if the company collects the purchase price from the buyer and then passes on the proceeds, net of commission, to the seller.

Section 1000 of the *CICA Handbook* formally defines revenues as *increases in economic resources*, either through increases to assets or reductions to liabilities. These increases in resources must be the result of delivering or producing goods, rendering services, or performing other activities that constitute the entity's normal business.

EXPENSE When merchandise is sold, inventory is reduced, resulting in a decrease in assets. A decrease in net assets is an expense when the decrease is the result of normal business activities. In general, expenses are *decreases in economic resources*, either through outflows or the using up of assets or incurrence of liabilities from delivering or producing goods, rendering services, or carrying out other activities that constitute the entity's normal business.

ASSETS AND LIABILITIES The definitions of revenue and expense are derivative definitions in that they are based on the terms "assets" and "liabilities." Therefore, clear understanding of assets and liabilities is needed in order to understand revenues and expenses.

As we pointed out in Chapter 2, assets are economic resources controlled by an entity as a result of past transactions or events and from which future economic benefits can be obtained. Liabilities are present obligations of an entity arising from past transactions or events, the settlement of which may result in the transfer or use of assets, provision of services, or other yielding of economic benefits in the future.[1]

Although our attention in this chapter is focused on recognition and measurement of revenue and expense, this discussion cannot be separated from the issues of asset and liability recognition and measurement.

THE EARNINGS PROCESS

At a conceptual level, a firm earns revenue as it engages in activities that increase the value (or *utility*, in economic terms) of an item or service. For example, an automobile parts manufacturer increases the value of sheet metal when it undertakes activities to cut, shape, and weld the sheet metal into automobile fenders. Transporting completed fenders to a regional wholesale warehouse also adds value because it makes the fenders readily available for purchase and use by automobile repair shops. The earnings process is fully completed when the fenders are sold and delivered to a customer in return for cash or a promise to pay cash: finally, assets actually increase. All of these activities, and many more, are part of the earnings process.

[1] These definitions are from Section 1000 of the *CICA Handbook*, "Financial Statement Concepts."

Illustration of the Earnings Process

Exhibit 6-1 graphically illustrates the concept of the earnings process in a highly simplified setting. It focuses on the process of earning revenue; costs are not included. A firm undertakes many different activities, over the five periods shown, for the purpose of earning a profit. The top graph illustrates that revenue is earned throughout the earnings process as the different activities are performed. The graph also assumes that we know what the total amount of revenue will be when the earnings process is complete. Usually there is considerable uncertainty at the earlier stages of the earnings process (for example, during the design of a new product) as to whether the product will sell, and for what amount. This uncertainty is removed only when a price is agreed to, and the product is delivered to a customer.

The bottom graph in Exhibit 6-1 shows the amount of revenue that could *conceptually* be recognized in each accounting period as activities in the earnings process are completed. Because we assume that a constant rate of revenue is earned at each stage in the earnings process, the amount of revenue is the same for each period. The shaded area in the bottom graph equals the total amount of revenue earned over the completed earnings process, which is represented in the top graph by the height of the cumulative revenue earned at the end of the fifth period.

Recognizing Revenue

Do not confuse the conceptual notion that *economic value is added* (i.e., revenue is created) at each stage along the way in the production and sale process, with the *accounting revenue recognition* issue. The issue in accounting is *when* during that earnings process should revenue be recognized by recording the increase in value on the books?

The earnings process for most companies involves incurring costs to increase the value of an in-process product. Sometimes the process is very long. The design and development process for a new commercial airplane can take 5 to 10 years from initial design efforts to the delivery of the first airplane to a customer. *Economically, revenue is being earned as each of the many activities is completed,* assuming that the activity brings the company closer to having a saleable product. Companies are required to provide periodic reports on earnings even when the earnings process extends over several accounting periods. In these situations, the question of how much revenue (and expense) to recognize and report in each period must be carefully assessed.

FINANCIAL REPORTING OBJECTIVES

Companies do not necessarily pick their accounting policies with "good accounting" as their first objective. As we saw in Chapters 1 and 2, companies bring a variety of motives to the decision, and may wish to maximize or minimize reported net income and net assets, or affect other key financial statement data in support of their specific financial reporting objectives.

Revenue recognition is an area where firms that are anxious to show increasing sales and profits have followed a number of questionable and sometimes even improper accounting procedures. A relatively innocent-looking example occurs when a firm records as a sale goods that have been ordered for a later delivery. Suppose a firm receives an order in December for goods that the customer desires to receive in mid-January. Should the sale be recorded in December or January? Even more problematic would be a transaction in which goods are shipped (and recorded as a revenue) to a customer who regularly purchases such goods in approximately the amounts shipped, but who has not yet ordered the goods! There have also been cases where the invoices for goods shipped after the fiscal year-end are back-dated to the current fiscal year in order to record them as sales in the earlier period. Yes, this really happens, but it's not acceptable, either ethically or under GAAP. Such actions are deliberate attempts to mislead users, and are tantamount to fraud.

Choice of Method

The choice of method used to record revenues is an area where ethical questions are sometimes raised. An operator of campgrounds, Thousand Trails, used the point-of-sale method to recognize revenue on its membership rights transactions. Most of these transactions were

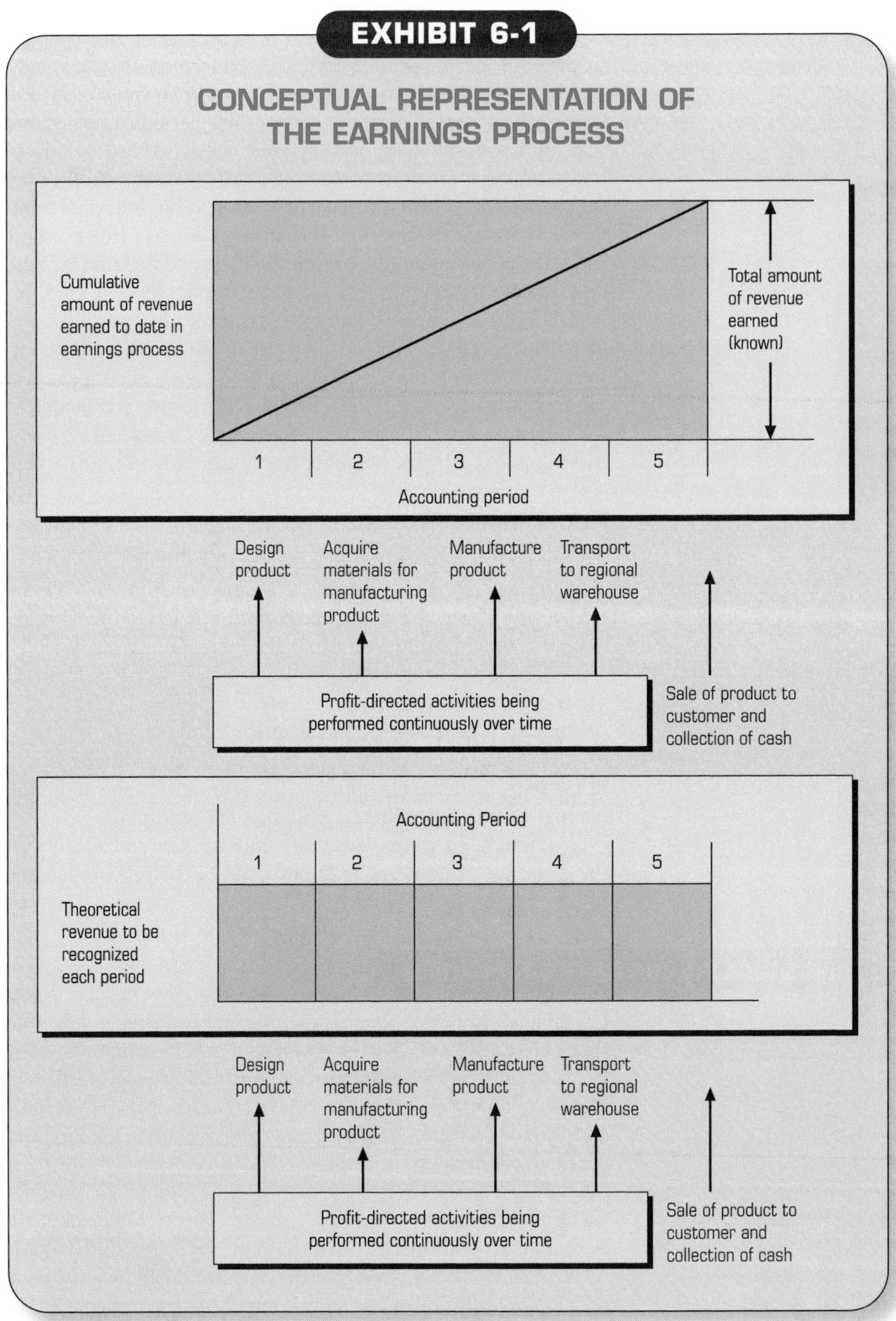

instalment sales and the default rate was high. Since the default rate may be very difficult to estimate with reasonable accuracy, the instalment sales method may have been a more appropriate choice for revenue recognition.

The company and its auditor maintained, however, that the point-of-sale method was appropriate because they felt they could estimate the future default amounts on the instalment receivables with reasonable accuracy. By using the point-of-sale method, the company reported rapid growth in sales and profits even though the company had received only a very small portion of the reported revenue in cash. Again, this is appropriate so long as the receivables do eventually convert into estimated amounts of cash. The fact that the company eventually got into severe financial difficulty, in part because of an unexpectedly large number of defaults on the receivables, reinforced concerns about whether the point-of-sale method was appropriate in the first place.

Choice of method and implementation of accounting procedures for revenue recognition must be done with a careful consideration of what is ethical and appropriate for the circumstances.

REVENUE RECOGNITION CRITERIA

When an item is recognized in the financial statements, it is assigned a value and recorded as an element in the appropriate financial statement(s) with an appropriate offset to another element (e.g., cash or accounts payable). Recognized items must meet the definition of a financial statement element, and have a measurement basis and amount. We know that financial statement elements are based on future economic benefits or sacrifices; these must be *probable* and *measurable* for recognition to be appropriate.

Revenue Recognition Principle

revenue recognition principle
the recognition and reporting of revenues that have met the recognition criteria; revenues typically must be earned, measurable, and realizable before recognition

The **revenue recognition principle** is that revenue should be recognized in the financial statements when

1. Performance has been achieved, and
2. There is reasonable assurance regarding the measurement and collectibility of the consideration.

Performance is achieved when the company has accomplished what it must do to be entitled to receive the associated benefits of the revenue. In a normal sales transaction, this occurs *when the vendor has transferred all the risks and rewards of ownership to the customer* and has no ongoing managerial control over the item.

When the earnings process spans more than one accounting period, revenue can sometimes be recognized even though the earnings process is not completed. This is acceptable when both (1) the total potential revenue and (2) the costs required to complete the earnings process can be reliably estimated.

The criteria of measurability and collectibility do not completely address the issue of timing of recognition. For example, gold can be sold at any time at a known price—gold is a commodity that is traded worldwide and can be sold instantly at a known price by a single telephone call. For gold (and for other commodities, such as wheat) both measurability and collectibility are assured. Should a gold-producing company record revenue when the gold is ready for sale, or only when it actually is sold? As we shall see later in this chapter, both options are feasible.

REVENUE MEASUREMENT

According to the recognition criteria, there are two issues in measuring revenue:

- when to recognize, and
- how much to recognize.

How much revenue to recognize is usually less of an issue than *when* to recognize it. The revenue amount is part of the contract between the buyer and the seller. Nevertheless, measuring the amount can sometimes be problematic.

For example, an agreement to sell computer software may include staff training and free upgrades. How much of the price is really for the initial software and how much is for future services?

Another example is a sale agreement that sets a price but allows the purchaser to pay over two or more fiscal periods with no interest charges. Since money is never interest-free, part of the agreement's contract price really is hidden interest.

Non-Monetary Transactions

barter transaction
an exchange involving non-monetary consideration

Measurement issues also are significant if the sale transaction is a **barter transaction**; that is, if the exchange involves only non-monetary goods. For example, an accountant may prepare a tax return for an innkeeper in exchange for a three-day weekend vacation at the innkeeper's facility. At what amount should this transaction be valued? The accountant could keep track of her time, multiply by her charge-out rate, and determine the amount she would have billed the client. Alternatively, she could ascertain the value of the weekend vacation to which she is entitled.

The recommendations in the *CICA Handbook* (Section 3830, "Non-monetary Transactions") indicate that the transaction should be valued at the fair value of the asset or service given up. The *value* of the asset given up is the *cost* of the asset acquired. However, if the value of the asset or service received is more reliable, it should be used to value the transaction.

For our accountant, this means that she'll look at the value of her time, then look at the value of the weekend trip, and ask which value she's more confident about. Likely she'll use the value of her time, but a comparison of the two values is always informative. If they're close, there's a high degree of comfort with the decision. It's not as easy as it seems: she may have been using otherwise-idle time to do this job, which implies that her time may not have been "worth" the full charge-out rate. She may be able to use the vacation weekend only in shoulder periods, when the room would otherwise have been vacant at the inn—implying that it may not be "worth" the advertised price. Judgement is pivotal to the measurement process.

The non-monetary transaction rules have one more twist. If the barter transaction does not have "commercial substance," the barter transaction is valued at the book value of the resource given up. "Commercial substance" is a term introduced by the revision of Section 3830, effective in 2005. Commercial substance exists when (1) there is a change in the configuration of the company's cash flows or (2) the net present value of the after-tax cash flows is changed by the non-monetary transaction (*CICA ED* 3830.10).

For example, suppose that a vendor "sells" a product to a customer, and in return takes a second product, which the vendor plans to sell to yet another company for cash. The non-monetary transaction has no commercial substance because the configuration of the company's cash flows does not really change. Therefore, the second product should be recorded at the book value of the first product. With no change in the expected cash flow configuration or net present value, there is no commercial substance to the transaction to warrant revenue recognition. Only when the second product is sold for cash is revenue recognition appropriate.

It also is not appropriate to record a gain on sale if two similar *capital* assets are exchanged. For example, if two real estate development firms swap apartment buildings, the asset acquired is recorded at the book value of the asset given up.

Measurement may also be a problem if the consideration is contingent on another transaction. For example, a customer may agree to pay a vendor on a sliding scale, based on the amount that the customer, in turn, can get by selling the product to another firm. If the customer does not have to pay the vendor at all unless the item is resold, the sale is a consignment sale, and is not recorded by the vendor until resale by the customer. However, there are other versions of a sale contract where a base price is agreed to, with further price adjustments based on the terms of eventual resale. If these arrangements create uncertainty that is material and unquantifiable, revenue recognition must wait until the item has been resold.

CONCEPT REVIEW

1. What is the difference between the concepts of revenue creation and revenue recognition?
2. In general, what two criteria must be satisfied before revenue can be recognized in the financial statements?
3. How should revenue be measured in a barter transaction?

APPROACHES TO REVENUE RECOGNITION

Essentially, there are two approaches to revenue recognition. Revenue can be recognized at one *critical event* in the chain of activities, for example, production, delivery, or cash collection. Alternatively, revenue can be recognized on a basis consistent with *effort expended*, a plan that will result in some revenue being recognized with every activity in the chain.

REVENUE RECOGNITION AT A CRITICAL EVENT

critical event

one point in a series of economic activities that is chosen for revenue recognition

What happens if a **critical event** is chosen to trigger revenue recognition? All costs incurred before the critical event *that can be specifically identified as relating to each individual earnings event* are deferred (usually as inventory costs). These expenditures qualify as assets because they will generate resources/sales revenue at the critical event. When revenue is recognized, deferred costs are expensed, and identifiable costs that *have not yet been incurred* must be accrued as estimated liabilities. *Revenues and expenses are all recognized at the critical event, regardless of when they are incurred.* This is the magic of an accrual-based accounting system.

Types of Critical Event

What events could be chosen as the critical event? Potentially, any activity in the earnings process could be so designated, but the key is that, following the critical event, the remaining aspects of the earnings process should unfold predictably in the normal course of business with no major uncertainties or immeasurables. Once the critical event has occurred, it's all downhill from there! The most commonly used critical events can be grouped by reference to the delivery of goods or services:

1. at delivery
2. before delivery
3. after delivery

Exhibit 6-2 illustrates revenue recognition associated with specific critical events in the context of production and sale of a manufactured product. Although this figure uses manufactured goods as the reference point, a similar chart could be drawn for other earnings cycles, such as for resource extraction, life insurance, or auditing. Not all possible methods are shown in Exhibit 6-2, even for manufacturing.

For most companies and for most goods and services, revenue is recognized at the time of delivery of the goods or services to the customer. Revenue is considered both earned and realized or realizable when the product or service is delivered.

An earlier critical event—production—may be appropriate if the selling and shipping functions are trivial, such as when the product is a commodity for which there is an organized market (e.g., wheat, copper, gold). A critical event *after* delivery is appropriate when there are measurement problems surrounding the amount of revenue actually generated, collection uncertainties, and/or when it is not possible to accurately estimate all the costs associated with the earnings process, which must be fully accrued at the critical event. In the face of any of these problems, revenue recognition should wait until major uncertainties are resolved.

REVENUE RECOGNIZED AT DELIVERY

The two conditions for revenue recognition, (1) performance is achieved and (2) the amount is measurable and collectible, are usually met at the time goods or services are delivered. Thus, revenue from the sale of products is usually recognized at the date of sale, meaning the date the product is delivered to the customer. Revenue from services rendered is likewise recognized when the services have been completed and accepted by the client.

Some transactions do not result in a one-time delivery of a product or service, but rather in continual "delivery" or fulfilment of a contractual arrangement. For example, revenue from contractual arrangements allowing others to use company assets (such as revenues

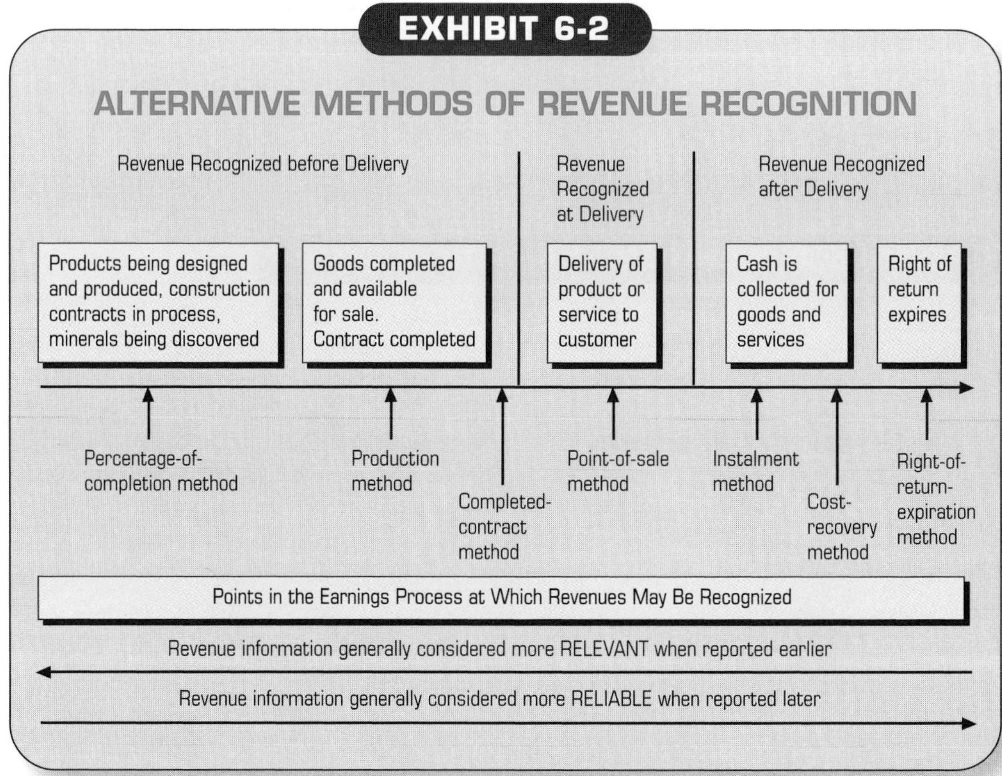

from rent, interest, lease payments, and royalties) is recognized as time passes or as the asset is used. Revenue is earned with the passage of time and is recognized accordingly.[2]

Separately identifiable costs incurred prior to the critical event are deferred in inventory or other deferred asset accounts. These costs are recognized as expenses at delivery, and thus are recognized at the same time as revenue. All other costs associated with the sale must be recognized in the same period as the revenue; this may include a reasonable estimate of bad debts, and a provision for guarantee or warranty costs.

Exhibit 6-3 illustrates a situation in which a company buys inventory, customizes it, and then holds it until sale. It is sold, on account, subject to a four-month warranty. Subsequently, the customer pays, some warranty costs are incurred, and, finally, the warranty expires.

The first column of Exhibit 6-3 traces the entries appropriate if delivery is considered to be the critical event. Product costs are deferred in the inventory account until delivery. When the item is delivered, the sales price is accrued, inventory is expensed to cost of goods sold, and warranty costs are estimated. In this example, collection is assumed to be certain, and no bad debt accrual is appropriate. Subsequent cash transactions—cash collection and payment of warranty costs—reduce receivables and payables established at the critical event. *Net assets (i.e., assets minus liabilities) are increased only at the critical event. Other transactions change the composition but not the total of net assets.* The remaining columns of Exhibit 6-3 will be analyzed in later sections.

For companies that sell services rather than products, revenue recognition policies are similar to the policies of companies selling tangible goods. Service revenue is usually recognized when performance is complete. Of course, the revenue is really earned by performing a series of acts, but recognition may be considered appropriate only after the final act occurs. This final act is essentially the same as delivery of a tangible good, and signifies that the customer accepts the service. For example, a consultant recognizes revenue only when an assignment has been completed. A trucking firm recognizes service revenue only after delivery of freight, even though packing, loading, and transporting preceded delivery. A laundry recognizes revenue when items are picked up by the customer.

---

[2] If, however, the contract is a lease and is essentially a non-cancellable transfer of all the risks and rights of ownership of the asset, the transaction qualifies as a sale. Such transactions, called capital leases, are considered in Chapter 17.

EXHIBIT 6-3

CRITICAL EVENTS AND IMPACT ON NET ASSETS

Data:

January 15	Inventory purchased, $14,500
January 17	Inventory repackaged and customized, labour and materials cost, $2,250. Now ready for sale.
March 6	Inventory delivered to customer on account. Agreed-upon price, $27,500. Collection is assured; there is a four-month warranty.
April 30	Customer paid.
June 14	Warranty work done, at a cost of $3,900.
July 6	Warranty expired.

Date	Revenue Recognized on Delivery	Pre-delivery: Revenue Recognized on Production	Post-delivery: Revenue Recognized on Warranty Expiration
Jan. 15	Inventory 14,500 Cash, A/P, etc. 14,500	Inventory 14,500 Cash, A/P, etc. 14,500	Inventory 14,500 Cash, A/P, etc. 14,500
Effect on net assets	None	None	None
Jan. 17	Inventory 2,250 Cash, A/P, etc. 2,250	Inventory 2,250 Cash, A/P, etc. 2,250 Cost of goods sold 16,750 Inventory 10,750 Revenue 27,500 Warranty expense 3,900 Estimated warranty liability 3,900	Inventory 2,250 Cash, A/P, etc. 2,250
Effect on net assets	None	Increase $6,850	None
March 6	Accounts receivable 27,500 Revenue 27,500 Cost of goods sold 16,750 Inventory 16,750 Warranty expense 3,900 Estimated warranty liability 3,900	Accounts receivable 27,500 Inventory 27,500	Accounts receivable 27,500 Deferred gross margin 10,750 Inventory 16,750
Effect on net assets	Increase $6,850	None	None
April 30	Cash 27,500 Accounts receivable 27,500	Cash 27,500 Accounts receivable 27,500	Cash 27,500 Accounts receivable 27,500
Effect on net assets	None	None	None
June 14	Estimated warranty liability 3,900 Cash 3,900	Estimated warranty liability 3,900 Cash 3,900	Deferred warranty costs 3,900 Cash 3,900
Effect on net assets	None	None	None
July 6	No entry	No entry	Cost of goods sold 16,750 Deferred gross margin 10,750 Revenue 27,500 Warranty expense 3,900 Deferred warranty costs 3,900
Effect on net assets	None	None	Increase $6,850

An Example: Franchise Fee Revenue

Accounting for franchise fee revenue provides an example of the problems that arise when trying to identify when "delivery" has occurred in a service transaction. Franchisees usually agree to pay a substantial fee to the franchisor. For revenue recognition purposes, it often is difficult to determine when performance is achieved and the franchisor's service has been delivered.

One common problem with franchise fee revenue recognition is that of evaluating the collectibility of the initial fee. If the franchisee pays the fee up front, this is less of a concern; if the franchisee plans to pay it over time with profits from the franchise operation, then collection is contingent on profitable operations, and careful assessment of business risk is necessary. A franchisor with no track history, or franchisees who are financially unsound, may have to delay revenue recognition due to collection concerns.

Another problem is that the franchisor may have significant ongoing obligations to the franchisee. If this is the case, and if the franchisee does not have to pay extra for these services (that is, they are part of the services encompassed by the initial franchise fee) recognition of all or part of the initial franchise fee might be delayed.

To help franchisors (and their auditors) deal with the problems of franchise fee revenue recognition, the CICA issued an Accounting Guideline many years ago.[3] The guideline suggests that "substantial performance" has occurred only when

a. The franchisor has performed substantially all of the initial services required by the franchise agreement or volunteered by the franchisor as a result of normal business practice.

b. The franchisor has no remaining obligation or intent to refund amounts received or forgive unpaid amounts owing.

c. There are no other material unfulfilled conditions affecting completion of the sale.

Thus, "delivery" has occurred only when the franchisor has done what is expected and gets to keep the money.

REVENUE RECOGNITION BEFORE DELIVERY

Completion of Production

In certain situations, revenue can be recognized at the completion of production but prior to delivery. The key criterion for using this method is that the sale will take place *without any doubt.* The normal criteria for recognizing revenue before delivery are

- The sale and collection of proceeds must be assured;
- The product must be marketable immediately at quoted prices that cannot be influenced by the producer;
- Units of the product must be interchangeable; and
- There must be no significant costs involved in product sale or distribution.

commodity
any article of commerce, often used to describe homogeneous goods, for example, minerals or agricultural products

Essentially, these criteria define a **commodity**. Examples include agricultural products, precious metals, and other goods that are traded on commodities markets such as orange juice concentrate, crude oil, and pork bellies. Commodities can be sold at any time simply by telephoning a broker or clicking a computer mouse; no significant effort is required. When this approach to revenue recognition is used, the increase in net asset value is recorded immediately upon the completion of production, and *requires valuing inventory at market value.*

While commodities that are traded on a public market are the most obvious candidates for pre-delivery revenue recognition, some companies may use this method if their product is in such strong demand that sale is virtually assured. It is a bit dangerous, however, because if demand suddenly falls off, the company is left with a lot of inventory carried at market value but no ready buyers. Substantial effort is then required to sell the product, which means that performance is not achieved and the criteria for revenue recognition have not been met.

---

[3] "Franchise Fee Revenue," Accounting Guidelines, *CICA Handbook,* July 1984.

The second column of Exhibit 6-3 demonstrates the sequence of entries that would be appropriate for revenue recognition at the completion of production. When inventory is customized and ready for sale, revenue is recognized in full by increasing the inventory value from its cost of $16,750 (that is, $14,500 plus $2,250) to market value ($27,500), a difference of $10,750. On the income statement, the gross margin will be disaggregated and will be presented as sales of $27,500 and cost of sales of $16,750.[4]

At the same time the inventory is revalued, warranty costs are accrued, to include all costs of the sale in the same accounting period. Note that the overall change in net assets is $6,850, the same that was recorded under the "delivery" alternative. *All that has changed is the point at which the increase in net assets is recognized.* After the critical event (i.e., production), all transactions change the allocation of the net asset balances but do not increase or decrease total net assets.

Completion of production for a service company is the completion of the service, also called specific performance. Is this any different than "delivery"? For many service activities, services are completed and delivered simultaneously (consider haircuts, tooth extractions, music lessons, and so on).

But what if the service is performed and only later accepted by the customer? For example, a consulting report could be written but not presented to the client for a month. Would it make sense to recognize revenue when the work is completed, prior to delivery? As in tangible products, this would be aggressive, as the risks and rewards have not yet passed to the client; there is no assurance that the consultant has fulfilled her or his mandate.

As a result, revenue recognition at production for service sales is not normally appropriate. In many cases, the lag between production and delivery is likely to be non-existent or very short, and so this isn't much of an issue for most short-term service sales. But long-term service contracts may result in partial recognition of revenue, period by period, as work is performed. This process will be discussed in a later section.

Initiation of Contract

To achieve matching, it is necessary to recognize revenue and related expenses in the same period. However, GAAP does not approve of the deferral of many types of cost that cannot be specifically identified with a unit of product or service. Promotional expenses, for example, can be deferred to a later period if they relate specifically to that later period, such as the cost of preparing television advertisements that will be aired in the next period, or the cost of publishing a printed catalogue for next year's product line. General advertising and promotional costs cannot be deferred, however, because it is impossible to have reasonable assurance that revenues will arise in the future as the result of this year's promotion.

On rare occasions, a large part of an enterprise's cost is in its promotional activities or in other non-deferrable costs. An example is a company that provides self-improvement home study courses by correspondence or via the Internet. The costs for developing the courses are incurred early, followed by a major TV and print media blitz to sign up customers. The course development costs can be deferred, of course, but the cost of the promotional campaign cannot.

Therefore, such a company may choose to recognize revenue *when it signs up the customer and receives the cash.* The costs of actually delivering the course may be relatively trivial (e.g., printing and mailing costs, and perhaps grading costs that are tightly budgeted and controlled) and are quite predictable; the future costs of delivering the course can be accrued at the time of revenue recognition. Therefore, the *critical event* is perceived to be the sale.

Recognizing revenue at the inception of a contract is usually regarded as *aggressive* accounting policy. Companies that use an aggressive policy and later get into financial difficulty usually find themselves the brunt of aggressive analysts and lawyers. Loewen Group Incorporated, a very large funeral services company, used early recognition of revenue on the sale of cemetery plots. The sales contracts were usually instalment sales, and the customer paid little or nothing at inception. The revenue for the entire contract was booked in the period that the

---

[4] Bear in mind that Canadian GAAP requires the amount of *revenue recognized* to be disclosed on the income statement (*CICA* 1520.03(a)).

sale was made, which is industry practice. Getting the sale is the critical event. This practice was used by Loewen for years without raising the concerns of analysts, but once the company got into difficulty (for largely unrelated reasons), it was accused of aggressive accounting.[5]

REVENUE RECOGNITION AFTER DELIVERY

In certain circumstances, revenue recognition must be delayed until after delivery. Typically, this is appropriate when there are uncertainties over the costs associated with the remaining activities in the earnings process, revenue collection, or measurement.

Revenue from the sale of goods should be recognized only when the risks and rewards of ownership pass from the vendor to the customer; substantially all of the elements of the earnings process must be complete before this condition is met. What if there is a major warranty associated with the sale? This may preclude revenue recognition until the task—the risk—is over. Refer to the third column of entries in Exhibit 6-3. This alternative is appropriate if the cost of the warranty cannot be estimated at the point of sale, or at any point up to its expiration, and is expected to be material.

Notice that product costs are capitalized in inventory, and therefore even delivery does not cause a change in net assets. Accounts receivable are recognized, inventory is reduced, but the gross margin is deferred; the deferred gross margin account is shown as deferred revenue in the liabilities section of the balance sheet. Warranty costs actually incurred are deferred charges on the balance sheet. *None of the transactions prior to the critical event—the expiration of the warranty period—triggers a change in net asset value.*

As previously discussed, if the amount of consideration (the sales amount) cannot be ascertained, revenue is recognized when those uncertainties are resolved. In a contract that involves a sliding scale of payment to the vendor based on the price the customer receives on the resale of the item, the critical event will be the resale of the goods for an ascertainable price.

In several industries, such as book publishing and equipment manufacturing, the sales terms allow customers the right to return goods under certain circumstances and over long periods of time. Thus, on delivery, the amount that will ultimately become realizable is not known.

The revenue section of the *CICA Handbook* states the following:

> Revenue would not be recognized when an enterprise is subject to significant and unpredictable amounts of goods being returned, for example, when the market for a returnable good is untested. If an enterprise is exposed to significant and predictable amounts of goods being returned, it may be sufficient to provide therefore. (*CICA* 3400.18(b))

This latter point deserves special emphasis; *if the risk can be quantified, then the sale can be recorded on delivery and the contingency accrued.*

Resale of Product

consignment
a sale of goods in which the customer pays only if the goods are resold to a final customer

No revenue should be recognized if the buyer's obligation to pay the seller is contingent on the resale of the product. If payment is contingent, this is a **consignment**: a marketing arrangement in which the owner of the product (the *consignor*) ships the product to another party (the *consignee*) who acts as a sales agent. The consignee does not purchase the goods, but assumes responsibility only for their care and resale. Upon sale, the consignee remits the proceeds (less specified expenses and commission) to the consignor. Goods on consignment are part of the inventory of the consignor until sold by the consignee. They are not a sale of the consignor when shipped to the consignee, but only when they are sold by the consignee.

Product-financing arrangements include agreements in which a sponsoring company sells a product to another company and in a related transaction agrees to repurchase the product at some future point in time if the customer has been unable to resell the product. This is consignment selling in a different legal form, and it is clear that the risks and rewards of ownership have not passed to the customer.

[5] "A Deathwatch for Loewen Group," *The Globe and Mail*, 1 August 1998, p. B1.

In these kinds of product-financing agreements, the sponsoring company must record a liability at the time the proceeds are received. It can neither record a sale nor remove the product from its inventory account. Only when the product is sold to an outside party without a related repurchase agreement can the sponsoring company record a sale.

Cash Collection

It is not appropriate to recognize revenue if it is not realized or realizable. A company must expect to be able to collect accounts receivable in order to record an entry that recognizes revenue. If there is no way to quantify collection risk, the critical event becomes cash collection.

However, there is usually some degree of collection risk in every credit sale, and delayed revenue recognition is not the norm. Instead, the risk is quantified by estimating an allowance for doubtful accounts and associated bad debt expense. As long as there is some objective basis for the allowance, such as past history, credit reports, etc., revenue recognition prior to cash collection can be justified.

When the eventual collection of cash is uncertain, companies usually delay revenue recognition until the cash is actually collected. This is common in certain types of retail stores, where credit terms are extended to customers who have very shaky credit records. The company compensates for its high default rate on bad credit by charging high interest to those who do pay and by having a well-organized repossession service.

If revenue is recognized on cash collection, the sequence of entries is similar to those in the third column of Exhibit 6-3. Cost will be deferred and delivery will result only in recognition of a deferred margin. On cash collection, warranty costs will be accrued, and the cash collection will trigger recognition of the gross margin. Net assets will increase accordingly.

Recognizing revenue on cash collection does not mean that it is appropriate to recognize revenue *prior* to delivery, if cash is received prior to delivery and there are major costs to be incurred to fulfill the contract with the customer. For example, when a publisher sells a magazine subscription or an airline sells a ticket for future air travel, cash is received before delivery of the product or service. Since significant effort and cost must be incurred before the earnings process is substantially complete, the earnings process is not completed until the product is delivered.

In this case, cash inflow does not result in revenue but in an obligation to produce and deliver the product: a liability. This liability is called "deferred revenue" or "unearned revenue." The revenue is not recognized until the product or service is delivered.

The example in Exhibit 6-3 is relatively straightforward, since the customer has paid in one complete lump sum. However, when cash collection is uncertain, the sale agreement often involves a series of payments for the customer. Then, the company must determine which of two revenue recognition approaches fits its risk profile: the instalment sales method or the cost recovery method.

Instalment Sales Method

Many consumer products are sold on an instalment or deferred payment plan, in which a purchaser makes payments in accordance with a periodic payment plan. If the company has a reasonable basis for estimating an allowance for uncollectible accounts, the company can choose to recognize revenue immediately, at the time of the sale.

However, a company that sells its products on an instalment plan may choose to use the **instalment sales method** of accounting. Revenue under the instalment sales method is recognized *when cash is collected* rather than at the time of sale. Under this method, revenue (and the related cost of goods sold) is recognized only when *realized.* For instance, the instalment method may be used to account for sales of real estate when the down payment is relatively small and ultimate collection of the sales price is not reasonably assured.

instalment sales method
a system that recognizes proportionate revenue at each instalment payment date rather than at the time of delivery

For example, assume that Truro Limited makes $80,000 of instalment sales in 20X2. The cost of goods sold is $60,000, and thus the gross margin is $20,000, or 25% of sales. The sale is recorded with a *deferred* gross margin.

Instalment accounts receivable	80,000	
Inventory		60,000
Deferred gross margin		20,000

The deferred gross margin will appear as a liability on the balance sheet, as deferred revenue. Notice that the entry to record the sale does not result in an increase in the company's net assets, because the increase of $20,000 in assets (that is, the increase from $60,000 inventory to $80,000 accounts receivable) is completely offset by the $20,000 increase in the liability.

If $10,000 is subsequently collected, the entries to record the collection and to recognize a proportionate part of the deferred revenue are as follows:

Cash	10,000	
Instalment accounts receivable		10,000
Deferred gross margin ($10,000 × 25%)	2,500	
Cost of goods sold	7,500	
Sales revenue		10,000

It is the last entry that records the increase to net assets that is the sign of revenue recognition. The increase in net assets is accomplished by reducing the amount of the liability for deferred gross margin. Note that the revenue recognition is recorded by disaggregating the realized gross margin of $2,500 into its two components of sales and cost of goods sold. This is in accordance with the *CICA Handbook* recommendation to disclose the gross amount of revenue on the income statement.

The Cost Recovery Method

cost recovery method
used normally in high-risk transactions; revenue offsets all costs incurred before any profit is recognized

The **cost recovery method** is sometimes called the *sunk cost method.* A company must recover all the related costs incurred (the sunk costs) before it recognizes any profit. The cost recovery method is used for highly speculative transactions when the ultimate realization of revenue or profit is unpredictable.

The method makes an even match of revenue and expense until all of the deferred cost has been recovered. Only then is any profit recognized. It is common only under extreme uncertainty about collection of the receivables or ultimate recovery of capitalized production start-up costs.

An example is Lockheed Corporation's use of the cost recovery method when it faced great uncertainty regarding the ultimate profitability of its TriStar Jet Transport program. Lockheed had invested more than $500 million in initial planning, tooling, and production start-up costs. These costs were to be amortized over the production and sale of the first 300 planes, but there was considerable uncertainty about how many airplanes might ultimately be sold: the TriStar program might not generate enough sales to recover the development costs. Therefore, the company decided to use the cost recovery method for revenue recognition for its TriStar program.

The cost recovery method is also justified when there is significant uncertainty regarding the ultimate collectibility of a string of customer payments. Cost recovery accounting is not uncommon in the real estate industry.

For example, suppose that Truro Limited sells $80,000 of product to a customer whose financial stability is uncertain. The cost of the goods sold is $60,000. Suppose that the customer makes one payment of $45,000, followed by another payment of $35,000. If Truro uses the cost recovery method, the entry at the time of sale will be exactly the same as under the instalment sales method:

Accounts receivable	80,000	
Inventory		60,000
Deferred gross margin		20,000

When the first cash payment is received, the receivable is reduced and the entire amount is recognized as revenue, but the offset is entirely to cost of goods sold. None of the gross margin is recognized yet:

Cash	45,000	
Accounts receivable		45,000
Cost of goods sold	45,000	
Revenue		45,000

When the second payment is received, the remaining revenue of $35,000 is recognized, as is the remaining $15,000 of cost of goods sold. The residual $20,000 reflects recognition of the deferred gross margin:

Cash	35,000	
Accounts receivable		35,000
Cost of goods sold	15,000	
Deferred gross margin	20,000	
Revenue		35,000

This revenue recognition method is highly skewed toward later revenue recognition and does a poor job of reflecting performance and cash flows. Its use is justified *only* in the face of significant uncertainties.

CONCEPT REVIEW

1. What is meant by the "critical event" in revenue recognition?
2. What effect does revenue recognition have on the balance sheet?
3. What criteria must ordinarily be satisfied in order for revenue to be recognized on production, prior to delivery?
4. When would revenue recognition be delayed to a point later than production and delivery?

REVENUE RECOGNITION BY EFFORT EXPENDED

So far, our discussion has examined the *critical event approach* to revenue recognition: identify one event in the earnings process, and recognize revenue and related costs at that event (which could involve multiple events for a single revenue-generating transaction, if the critical event is cash receipt).

An alternative to the critical event approach is to recognize revenue as *effort is expended* along each step in the earnings process. Think about the increase in value resulting from natural causes such as the growth of timberland or the aging of wines and liquors. As the product's value increases, revenue is being earned in an economic sense, and some accountants believe that it should be recognized. Recognition may be important when the natural process is very long, and knowing the change in value is relevant information for decision-making. Could you measure the change in value?

This approach to revenue recognition is not practical in the vast majority of situations: imagine trying to figure out how much a forest grew in a year, or trying to allocate the gross profit associated with a sale of manufactured goods to each activity in the process. Which of the tasks (getting the order, procuring raw materials, manufacturing, shipping, providing after-sales support, etc.) is the most valuable? The allocation problem would be a nightmare!

But accountants can and have solved allocation problems before. The more serious problem is that the revenue recognition principle is not satisfied at any time prior to delivery. Risks and rewards of ownership have not passed to the customer, and therefore the increase in net asset value is not reasonably assured. Remember, revenue recognition prior to delivery is aggressive, and is rare except in special industries. Notwithstanding this fact, there are a few cases where it is not only acceptable, but even desirable, to take the required leap of faith and recognize revenue as effort is expended.

Long-Term Contracts

In some instances the earnings process extends over several accounting periods. Delivery of the final product may occur years after the initiation of the project. Examples are construction of large ships and office buildings, development of space-exploration equipment, and development of large-scale custom software. Contracts for these projects often provide for progress billings at various points in the earnings process.

If the seller waits until the project or contract is completed to recognize revenue, the information on revenue and expense included in the financial statements will be reliable, but it may not be relevant for decision-making because the information is not timely.

For example, the financial reporting objective of performance evaluation is reasonably well served only if the financial statements report on the results of the enterprise's economic activity during the period. Delaying revenue recognition on long-term projects until the project is complete tells the financial statement reader nothing about economic activity (i.e., performance) during the period.

The cash flow reporting objective also is not well served by delaying revenue recognition, because the cash is flowing out (and usually in, as well) as the project is performed, not at the end. Therefore, it often is worthwhile to trade off reliability in order to provide more timely, relevant earnings information. There are two general methods of accounting for revenue on long-term contracts:

1. *Completed-contract method.* Revenues, expenses, and resulting gross profit are recognized only when the contract is completed. As costs are incurred, they are accumulated in an inventory account called *projects in progress, work in progress,* or some similar title. Progress billings are not recorded as revenues, but are accumulated in a *billings on contracts* or *progress billings* account that is deducted from the inventory account (i.e., a *contra* account to inventory). At the completion of the contract, all the accounts are closed, and the entire gross profit from the project is recognized.
2. *Percentage-of-completion method.* The percentage-of-completion method recognizes revenue on a long-term project as work progresses so that timely information is provided. Revenues, expenses, and gross profit are recognized each accounting period based on an estimate of the percentage of completion of the project. Project costs and gross profit to date are accumulated in the inventory account (projects in progress). Progress billings are accumulated in a contra inventory account (billings on projects in progress).

The *CICA Handbook* recommends that revenue from long-term contracts should be recognized by whichever method "relates the revenue to the work accomplished":

> Such performance should be regarded as having been achieved when reasonable assurance exists regarding the measurement of the consideration that will be derived from rendering the service or performing the long-term contract. (*CICA* 3400.08)

The percentage-of-completion and completed-contract methods are not intended to be free choice alternatives for the same circumstances. Is there a contract that establishes the contract price with a high degree of reliability? Is collection reasonably assured? These conditions would be met by the standard provisions of a long-term contract that involves a creditworthy customer expected to make regular progress payments.

The critical criteria are whether the seller can estimate with reasonable assurance (1) the progress toward completion of the contractual obligation, (2) the costs to complete the project, and (3) the total revenue. If these criteria are met, percentage of completion is the method that very clearly *relates the revenue to the work performed.* If the criteria are not met, the completed-contract method should be used. Of course, judgement plays a role in determining whether the criteria are met, and specific reporting objectives usually influence the selection of method.

Measuring Progress toward Completion

Measuring progress toward completion of a long-term project can be accomplished by using either input measures or output measures:

1. *Input measures.* The effort devoted to a project to date is compared with the total effort expected to be required in order to complete the project. Examples are (1) costs incurred to date compared with total estimated costs for the project and (2) labour hours worked compared with total estimated labour hours required to complete the project.
2. *Output measures.* Results to date are compared with total results when the project is completed. Examples are the number of kilometres of highway completed compared with total kilometres to be completed, or progress milestones established in a software development contract.

An expert, such as an engineer or architect, is often hired to assess percentage of completion or achievement of milestones. This is an art as much as a science.

The goal is to have a realistic measure of progress made toward completion of the project. Neither input nor output measures are always ideal. Input measures are often used when it is difficult to measure progress using output measures. However, input measures can be misleading when a constant relationship between the input measure and productivity does not exist. Cost overruns on projects would cause erroneous levels of completion to be estimated. Costs incurred also may be misleading as a measure of progress if costs include one-time, up-front expenditures for quantities of materials and supplies to be used during the construction period.

Despite their shortcomings, input measures are most frequently used because they are the most readily available. Among input measures, the cost-to-cost method is the most common. The cost-to-cost method measures the percentage completed by the ratio of costs incurred to date to the current estimate of the total costs required to complete the project:

$$\text{Percentage complete} = \frac{\text{Total costs incurred to date}}{\text{Most recent estimate of total costs of project (past and future)}}$$

The most recent estimate of total project costs is the sum of the total costs incurred to date plus the estimated costs yet to be incurred to complete the project. Once the percentage completed has been computed, the amount of revenue to recognize in the current period is determined as:

$$\text{Current period's revenue} = (\text{Percentage complete} \times \text{Total contract revenue}) - \text{Revenue previously recognized}$$

Example

There can be dramatic differences between the revenue and income effects of the completed-contract and percentage-of-completion methods. The completed-contract method is the simplest and most straightforward and it is discussed first.

To demonstrate the two methods, assume that the Ace Construction Corporation has contracted to erect a building for $1.5 million, starting construction on 1 February 20X1, with a planned completion date of 1 August 20X3. Total costs to complete the contract are estimated at $1.35 million, so the estimated gross profit is expected to be $150,000. Progress billings payable within 10 days after billing will be made on a predetermined schedule. Assume that the data shown in the upper portion of Exhibit 6-4 pertain to the three-year construction period. The facts for each of the three years will be ascertained as each year goes by. That is, in 20X1 the contractor does not know the information that is shown in the columns for 20X2 and 20X3.

The total construction costs were originally estimated at $1,350,000, of which $350,000 were incurred in 20X1. In 20X2, another $550,000 in costs were incurred, but the estimated total costs rose by $10,000 in 20X2, to $1,360,000. In 20X3, the total costs rose by another $5,000, and the total cost to complete the project turns out to be $1,365,000. Contract profit therefore drops from the original estimate of $150,000 to an actual amount of $135,000.

As costs are incurred, they are debited to an inventory account called "construction in progress." This inventory account is a current asset even for a multi-year project because the operating cycle of the contractor is the length of the longest project (rather than one year).

Construction companies do not wait until the end of the project to collect their money. Instead, **progress billings** are made throughout the duration of the project. The amount of progress billings is based on the amount of work accomplished to the date of the billing, as verified by an independent facilitator.

progress billings

in a long-term project, the amounts that are invoiced to the client or customer for work accomplished to date on the project

Progress billings are debited to *accounts receivable* and credited to *billings on contracts*, which is subtracted from the construction-in-progress inventory on the balance sheet. If the net of the construction-in-progress inventory (inventory less billings on contract) results in a debit balance, it is reported as a current asset. This account balance represents the contractor's net ownership interest in the construction project; it is sometimes referred to as the "contractor's draw."

If the net amount in the construction-in-progress inventory is a credit balance, it represents the developer's (buyer's) interest in the project and is referred to as the *developer's draw*. A credit balance is reported as a current liability in the contractor's financial statements.

Completed-Contract Method

Under the completed-contract method, there is no recognition of the project *in the income statement* until the project is completed and has been legally accepted by the customer.

The journal entries to record the construction-in-progress inventory, progress billings, and collections of progress billings for each year for Ace Construction are shown in the lower portion of Exhibit 6-4.

At the completion of the contact, income is recognized as the difference between the accumulated credit balance in the billings on contracts account and the debit balance in the construction-in-progress inventory account, assuming that the total price of the contract has been billed. The accumulated amount of billings on contracts is recognized as sales revenue, and the accumulated amount of construction-in-progress inventory on completion of the contract is recognized as cost of goods sold. It is this series of entries that increases net assets:

Billings on contracts	1,500,000	
Revenue from long-term contracts		1,500,000
Costs of construction	1,365,000	
Construction-in-progress inventory		1,365,000

On balance sheets during the construction period, the construction-in-progress inventory is reported as total accumulated costs to date less the total progress billings to date.

EXHIBIT 6-4

ACE CONSTRUCTION CORPORATION
EXAMPLE OF COMPLETED CONTRACT ACCOUNTING

Construction Project Fact Sheet Three-Year Summary Schedule

Contract Price: $1,500,000	**20X1**	**20X2**	**20X3**
1. Estimated total costs for project	$1,350,000	$1,360,000	$1,365,000
2. Costs incurred during current year	350,000	550,000	465,000
3. Cumulative costs incurred to date	350,000	900,000	1,365,000
4. Estimated costs to complete at year-end	1,000,000	460,000	0
5. Progress billings during year	300,000	575,000	625,000
6. Cumulative billings to date	300,000	875,000	1,500,000
7. Collections on billings during year	270,000	555,000	675,000
8. Cumulative collections to date	270,000	825,000	1,500,000

	20X1		**20X2**		**20X3**	
Construction-in-progress inventory	350,000		550,000		465,000	
Cash, payables, etc.		350,000		550,000		465,000
Accounts receivable	300,000		575,000		625,000	
Billings on contracts		300,000		575,000		625,000
Cash	270,000		555,000		675,000	
Accounts receivable		270,000		555,000		675,000

ADVANTAGES OF COMPLETED-CONTRACT METHOD The completed contract method has the advantage of delaying profit measurement until substantially all of the costs and revenues are known. There may be some remaining costs that are roughly similar to warranty costs; these can be estimated and accrued. Although the costs and revenues are known with a high degree of assurance, the *timing* of their recognition in the income statement is a matter for some manipulation. Contractors have been known to informally suggest to customers that they may want to delay formal acceptance of the project until after the contractor's year-end, usually in order to delay taxation. Taxation officials are aware of this practice, however, and often reach into the next year and claim tax on the profits generated on projects "closed" during the first two months of the contractor's next fiscal year.

The completed-contract method ranks high on the qualitative characteristic of objectivity because there is so little estimation involved. On the other hand, the method is perceived as lacking in the qualitative attributes of relevance and timeliness because the benefit of the contractor's economic activity during the year is not reflected on the income statement as long as the project is underway. Therefore, the completed-contract method is not very helpful if the dominant reporting objective is performance evaluation. The method is very useful for income tax minimization, however, since there is no taxation until the project is complete (even if there may be dispute about which period it was completed in).

Percentage-of-Completion Method

The objective of the percentage-of-completion method is to provide an estimate of the earnings of the company that will arise as the result of its economic activity (i.e., working on construction projects) during the year. Since the contractor spent a lot of time, effort, and money working on projects in progress, performance evaluation is better served if periodic profit (or loss) is measured on the basis of *effort expended* rather than contracts completed.

Under the percentage-of-completion method, a portion of revenue and expense (and thus income) is recognized as it is earned in each accounting period. The amount of income that is recognized is *added to the construction-in-progress inventory.* By adding the income earned to date to the inventory, the inventory is being increased to its net realizable value. Total actual income on the contract will not be known until the project is completed; what is recognized each period is an *estimate* of income that is based on many other estimates, as we discuss shortly.

Using the data shown in the upper portion of Exhibit 6-4, the relative proportion of the total costs that have been incurred to date can be used to determine percentage completed.

	20X1	20X2	20X3
Costs incurred to date	$ 350,000	$ 900,000	$1,365,000
Estimated total costs	1,350,000	1,360,000	1,365,000
Percent completed	26%	66%	100%

The percentage completed is computed by dividing the estimate of *costs incurred to date* by the *estimated total costs.* For example, estimated total costs at the end of 20X1 ($1,350,000) equals costs incurred to date ($350,000) plus estimated costs to complete at the end of 20X1 ($1,000,000). The percentages shown above have been rounded to the nearest full percentage point. The "exact" percentage for 20X2, to be precise, is 66.17647...%. But there is no point in calculating the percentage of completion to more than two digits (or, at the most, three). We are working with estimates here, and it is silly to be "precise" in calculating percentages that are based on approximations.

The next step is to compute the total amount of revenue recognizable up to each year-end by multiplying the total contract revenue by the percentage completed for each year. Then, revenue previously recognized is subtracted. The result is the revenue that is recognized in each specific year.

	20X1	20X2	20X3
20X1: $1.5 million × 26%	$390,000	—	—
20X2: $1.5 million × 66%	—	$990,000	—
20X3: $1.5 million × 100%	—	—	$1,500,000
Less: revenue previously recognized	—	(390,000)	(990,000)
Recognized revenue for the year	$390,000	$600,000	$ 510,000

The gross profit to be recognized is the difference between revenue and costs incurred in the period:

	20X1	20X2	20X3	Total
Revenue for the current year	$390,000	$600,000	$510,000	$1,500,000
Costs incurred in the current year	350,000	550,000	465,000	1,365,000
Gross profit for the year	$ 40,000	$ 50,000	$ 45,000	$ 135,000

The journal entries to record the costs incurred on the construction, the progress billings, and the collections of progress billings are the same as those for the completed-contract method. An additional entry is needed to record the recognition of revenue and expense each year. The gross profit is debited to the construction-in-progress inventory:

	20X1		20X2		20X3	
Construction-in-progress inventory (B/S)	40,000		50,000		45,000	
Costs of construction (I/S)	350,000		550,000		465,000	
Revenue from long-term contracts (I/S)		390,000		600,000		510,000

The construction-in-progress inventory account is greater under the percentage-of-completion method than under the completed-contract method by the amount of gross margin recognized to date. *This is the increase in net assets that always accompanies revenue recognition.*

Notice that the balance of the construction-in-progress inventory account is *not* reduced each year as the revenue and related costs are recognized in the income statement. On the income statement, the recognized gross profit is disaggregated into revenue less costs of construction. The offset to the inventory account is the billings on contracts account, just as for the completed-contract method.

When the project is completed, the billings on contracts will completely offset the construction-in-progress inventory. A journal entry is needed to remove both accounts of Ace Construction:

Billings on contracts	1,500,000	
Construction-in-progress inventory		1,500,000

Comparison of Results

Exhibit 6-5 compares the financial statement presentations for the completed-contract method and the percentage-of-completion method. Under the completed-contract method, inventory is carried at cost. Under the percentage-of-completion method, inventory is carried at cost plus recognized gross profit.

The difference between year-end inventory amounts under the two methods is the accumulated gross margin recognized under the percentage-of-completion method. Exhibit 6-5 also shows the dramatic difference in gross profit between the two methods on a year-to-year basis. However, *total gross profit over the three years is the same for each method.* This is another of the allocation games of which accountants are so fond.

Accounting for Losses on Long-Term Contracts

When the costs necessary to complete a contract result in losses, two situations are possible:

1. *The loss results in an unprofitable contract.* In this situation, the loss is recognized in full in the year it becomes estimable. For example, assume that, at the end of 20X2, Ace's costs incurred are as shown ($350,000 in 20X1 and $550,000 in 20X2), but the estimate of the costs to complete the contract in 20X3 increases to $625,000 from $465,000, an increase of $160,000.

   Since costs incurred through 20X2 total $900,000, the total estimated cost of the contract becomes $1,525,000 (instead of $1,365,000), and there is now an expected loss on the contract of $25,000.

EXHIBIT 6-5

FINANCIAL STATEMENT PRESENTATION OF ACCOUNTING FOR LONG-TERM CONSTRUCTION CONTRACTS

COMPLETED-CONTRACT METHOD

	20X1	20X2	20X3
Balance Sheet:			
Current Assets:			
Accounts Receivable	$ 30,000	$ 50,000	
Inventory:			
Construction in progress	350,000	900,000	
Less: Billings on contracts	300,000	875,000	
Construction in progress in excess of billings	$ 50,000	$ 25,000	
Income Statement:			
Revenue from long-term contracts	$ 0	$ 0	$1,500,000
Costs of construction	0	0	1,365,000
Gross profit	0	0	$ 135,000

Note 1: Summary of significant accounting policies.
Long-term construction contracts: Revenues and income from long-term construction contracts are recognized under the completed-contract method. Such contracts are generally for a duration in excess of one year. Construction costs and progress billings are accumulated during the periods of construction. Only when the project is completed are revenue, expense, and income recognized on the project.

PERCENTAGE-OF-COMPLETION METHOD

	20X1	20X2	20X3
Balance Sheet:			
Current Assets:			
Accounts Receivable	$ 30,000	$ 50,000	
Inventory:			
Construction in progress	390,000	990,000	
Less: Billings on contracts	300,000	875,000	
Construction in progress in excess of billings	$ 90,000	$ 115,000	
Income Statement:			
Revenue from long-term contracts	$390,000	$600,000	$510,000
Costs of construction	350,000	550,000	465,000
Gross Profit	$ 40,000	$ 50,000	$ 45,000

Note 1: Summary of significant accounting policies.
Long-term construction contracts: Revenues and income from long-term construction contracts are recognized under the percentage-of-completion method. Such contracts are generally for a duration in excess of one year. Construction costs and progress billings are accumulated during the periods of construction. The amount of revenue recognized each year is based on the ratio of the costs incurred to the estimated total costs of completion of the construction contract.

The $25,000 loss would be recognized in 20X2 under both methods of accounting for long-term construction contracts. A simple accrual entry is made for the completed-contract method, and the percentage-of-completion would record a gross loss of $65,000 ($25,000 + $40,000), which records the loss and reverses the profit recorded in prior years:

	20X1	20X2
Total estimated revenue	$1,500,000	$1,500,000
Cumulative costs to date	350,000	900,000
Estimated costs to complete	1,000,000	625,000
Estimated total costs	1,350,000	1,525,000
Estimated total profit (loss)	$ 150,000	$ (25,000)
Profit previously recognized	–	40,000
Profit (loss) recognized in current year	$ 40,000	$ (65,000)

The journal entry for 20X2, using the percentage-of-completion method, will be as follows:

Costs of construction (I/S)	550,000	
Construction-in-progress inventory (B/S)		65,000
Revenue from long-term contracts (I/S)		485,000

The loss is credited to the inventory account, which reduces the inventory to lower-of-cost-or market—not all of the costs can now be recovered.

2. *The contract remains profitable, but there is a current-year loss.* Suppose Ace's costs incurred to the end of 20X2 are as shown, but the estimate to complete the contract has increased to $550,000. Total costs of $900,000 have already been incurred; thus, the total estimated cost of completing the contract has risen to $1,450,000. The contract will still generate a gross margin of $50,000.

   Under the completed-contract method, all items are deferred until 20X3, and no entry is needed in 20X2. For the percentage-of-completion method, the 20X2 completion percentage is reworked (now 62%; $900,000 ÷ $1,450,000). This decreases the amount of revenue that will be reported, and results in a reported gross loss in 20X2.

Estimating Costs and Revenues

It is important to understand the extent of the estimates and approximations that underlie the percentage-of-completion method. Obviously, the *cost to complete* is an estimate. It may be wildly off the mark, because large-scale projects are often begun before the final design is even completed.

As well, the "costs incurred to date" is an estimate! How much of the contractor's overhead is to be included in the costs assigned to the project, and how much is charged as a period cost? What proportion of purchased and/or contracted materials should be included in cost to date? If the contractor has ordered and delivered 5,000 tonnes of bricks for exterior sheathing, should the cost of those bricks be included in the cost to date when the bricks are purchased or should the cost be excluded until the bricks are actually used in construction of the building?

ESTIMATING REVENUE A commonly overlooked estimate is that of the *revenue.* True, any long-term construction contract starts out with a contract price, but the initial price hardly ever ends up being the real revenue figure. Indeed, contractors often bid on jobs at zero profit or even at a loss in order to get the job. The reason is that every construction job involves *change orders*, which is a change in the original design of the building (or of whatever is being constructed). Change orders require additional revenue, and the contractor often bids low on the original contract because he knows that he will make his money on the change orders (which can hardly be submitted to a competitive bidding process!). So, in the course of a construction project

- The estimated cost to complete will change each period;
- The cost incurred in the current period (to be used in the percentage calculation) is an estimate; and
- The estimated total revenue will change from period to period.

It is safe to say that the percentage-of-completion method is an approximation! It represents a trade-off between conflicting qualitative criteria; objectivity is sacrificed for timeliness and relevance.

Proportional-Performance Method for Service Companies

The proportional-performance method is used to recognize service revenue that is earned by more than a single act, when the service extends beyond one accounting period. In fact, recording interest revenue or rental revenue as time passes are really applications of proportional-performance methods. Revenue is recognized based on the proportional performance of each act.

The proportional-performance method of accounting for service revenue is similar to the percentage-of-completion method and has to meet the same criteria as a long-term construction contract:

- A fixed or estimable amount of revenue with reasonable assurance of collection;
- A way to measure extent of performance; and
- An ability to estimate the remaining costs to completion.

Many service contracts are subject to at least as many uncertainties as are construction contracts. In particular, it is not unusual for the revenue to change as the client changes the scope of the assignment or the specifications of the task. Software contracts, for example, can double or triple in price if the client keeps changing his mind about what he wants the software to do.

Proportional measurement takes different forms depending on the type of service transaction:

1. *Similar performance acts.* An equal amount of service revenue is recognized for each such act (for example, processing of monthly mortgage payments by a mortgage banker).
2. *Dissimilar performance acts.* Service revenue is recognized in proportion to the seller's direct costs to perform each act (for example, providing examinations, and grading by a correspondence or Internet-based school). If the direct cost of each act cannot be measured reliably, the total service sales revenue should be prorated to the various acts by the relative sales value method. If sales value cannot be identified with each act, the straight-line method to measure proportional performance can be used.
3. *Similar acts with a fixed period for performance.* Service revenue is allocated and recognized by the straight-line method over the fixed period, unless another allocation method is more appropriate (for example, providing maintenance services on equipment for a fixed periodic fee).

CHOOSING A REVENUE RECOGNITION POLICY

This chapter has illustrated many different ways in which revenue can be recognized. Revenue recognition is the most pervasive and most difficult single accounting policy choice that many companies must face. With such a plentiful supply of alternatives, how can a company choose an appropriate policy?

Although there are many theoretical alternatives, the choice of policy is not a free game. The revenue recognition policy is, first and foremost, a function of the revenue-generating activity of the enterprise. When there is more than one revenue-generating activity, then there *may* be a different policy for each. For example, a retail company that engages in straightforward sales activity for cash or credit will probably recognize sales revenue at the point of delivery, while for interest revenue on its outstanding credit card balances the company will likely recognize interest revenue as time elapses.

A chosen revenue recognition policy must satisfy the general recognition criteria of *measurability* and *probability of collection*. Revenue must be measurable with reasonable assurance, and its eventual realization (in cash) must be highly probable. It is important to bear in mind that the act of revenue recognition *increases the net assets of the company*. The increase may be through an increase in cash, accounts receivable, or the value of inventories, but ultimately the amount must be realizable in cash.

Measurability and probability are essential requirements for revenue recognition, but those are relative terms. There is a trade-off between those two qualitative characteristics and those of relevance and timeliness. The earlier revenue is recognized, the more difficult it is to measure and the less certain it is of eventual realization. But the later revenue is recognized, the less useful it is for predicting cash flows and for evaluating management's performance.

Often, there are several different points in a single revenue-generating activity at which revenue can be recognized. This is especially true if the activity involves a sustained effort to earn the revenue or to collect it. The choice of revenue recognition policies depends very heavily on the financial reporting objectives of the company and on the motivations of its managers. An objective of income tax minimization will lead to a much different revenue recognition policy than will an objective of maximizing net income. Revenue recognition policy is, very often, the supreme test of an accountant's professional judgement.

CONCEPT REVIEW

1. What qualitative characteristics are better served by completed-contract reporting than by percentage-of-completion reporting?
2. Which financial reporting objectives are satisfied more by the percentage-of-completion method than by the completed-contract method?
3. What estimates are required in order to use the percentage-of-completion method?
4. How does the construction-in-progress inventory balance differ between the percentage-of-completion method and the completed-contract method?

RECOGNITION OF GAINS AND LOSSES

Gains and losses are distinguished from revenues and expenses in that they usually result from peripheral or incidental transactions, events, or circumstances. Whether an item is a gain or loss or an ordinary revenue or expense depends in part on the reporting company's primary activities or businesses.

For example, when a company that is primarily involved in manufacturing and marketing products sells some of its land, the transaction is accounted for as a net gain or loss because this is not the primary business of the company. When a real estate sales company sells land, however, the transaction gives rise to revenues and expenses.

A gain or loss may result from purely internal transactions, such as a writedown related to a plant closing. Such gains and losses are recognized in the period when the transaction occurs.

Most gains and losses are recognized when the transaction is completed. Thus, gains and losses from disposal of capital assets, sale of investments, and early extinguishment of debt are recognized only when the final transaction is recorded. However, estimated losses are recognized before their ultimate realization if they both (1) are probable and (2) can reasonably be estimated.

Examples are losses on disposal of a segment of the business, pending litigation, and expropriation of assets. If both conditions are not met, the nature and possible amount of the possible loss must be disclosed in a note to the financial statements. In contrast, gains are almost never recognized before the completion of a transaction that establishes the existence and amount of the gain. A gain should be recognized only when realized, except as explained in the following paragraph. This reflects an appropriate degree of skepticism about whether the gain will actually be realized.

There are circumstances in which gains and losses are recognized when there has been a *change in value* rather than a transaction. This happens when inventory items are reported at market value instead of cost. Examples of such inventory items include

- *Commodities that are carried at market value.* If a company produces commodities that are readily saleable on an open public market or to a marketing board, as described above for *recognition prior to delivery*, the act of revenue recognition means that the inventories are revalued from the cost of production to their market price. If the company holds the inventory from one period to another, changes in market value are recognized as gains or losses for the period. Examples include farm products (e.g., hogs, cattle, wheat, eggs) and many natural resources (e.g., gold, silver, copper, oil).
- *Trading securities held by a financial institution.* Securities dealers must report their inventory of securities held for sale at market. Investment companies (such as mutual funds) must carry their investment portfolio at market value so that investors can be informed of the net asset value of the company's holdings. Banks must carry the securities held in their trading account at market value. Life insurance companies report their investments on a five-year moving average of market prices. Companies such as these will recognize gains or losses on their investment portfolios. In some industries the *realized* gains and losses are segregated from the *unrealized*, but both realized and unrealized are *recognized.*
- *Available-for-sale assets.* Companies often hold assets that are intended for sale. The most common available-for-sale assets are temporary investments in debt or equity instruments that the company does not intend to hold to maturity. Available-for-sale assets can also be excess capital assets awaiting disposal or sale, including the assets of discontinued operations.

  Available-for-sale assets are shown on the balance sheet at fair value (effective October 2005). Fair value is market value for publicly traded securities. The company will have an *unrealized* gain or loss at the end of each reporting period for securities still held in the investment portfolio.

  Unrealized gains and losses are reported as a component of *other comprehensive income.* When the available-for-sale asset is sold, the full amount of gain or loss is recognized in net income. The previously unrealized portion is removed from other comprehensive income and recognized on the income statement as part of the overall gain or loss. We cover available-for-sale securities in more detail later, in Chapter 11.

It should be noted that changes in the market value of these types of items are referred to as gains and losses even though they are a part of the normal business activities of the enterprise. There is nothing peripheral about gains and losses on securities held by a bank!

Losses may also be recognized when the recoverable value of an asset falls below its historical cost. Common examples are inventory (discussed in Chapter 8), capital assets (discussed in Chapter 10), and long-term investments (discussed in Chapter 11).

REVENUE ON THE CASH FLOW STATEMENT

This chapter discussed the concept that economic revenue grows or is earned over time—sometimes in a brief time span, but often over quite a long period of time. Accounting, on the other hand, tends to recognize revenue at a particular *point* in a more continuous earning cycle. On occasion, revenue recognition also coincides with the cash inflow, but that circumstance is quite rare. Usually, a company recognizes revenue prior to receiving the cash.

In order to report cash flow from operations, the accruals relating to revenue recognition must be removed. Assuming that the *indirect* method is used for reporting cash from operations, the primary adjustments are

- Any increase in accounts receivable or notes receivable from customers must be deducted from net income (or from revenue); a decrease in receivables would be added.
- Expenses that have been accrued (but not expended) must similarly be added back to net income (or deducted from total operating expenses, if the direct method is used); examples include warranty provisions and bad debt expense.
- Unearned revenue must be added to revenue; the cash has been received but revenue has not yet been recognized.

Revenue can be recognized only if the cash flow is highly probable. The reporting problem is that revenue recognition and cash flow often do not occur in the same accounting period.

DISCLOSURE

The choice of revenue recognition method can have enormous impact on a company's reported earnings. As we have seen, most methods require some accounting estimates, and some methods require a great deal of estimation.

The *CICA Handbook* contains no explicit requirement for disclosure of revenue recognition policies, except for the general requirement that a company disclose its policies when there is a choice of policy. In practice, a substantial majority of public companies make some disclosure of their revenue recognition policies.[6]

An example of a detailed disclosure that adequately describes revenue recognition policies is that of DataMirror Corporation:

> Revenue is recognized in accordance with Statement of Position (SOP) 97-2, "Software Revenue Recognition" issued by the American Institute of Certified Public Accountants (AICPA) in October 1997 and amended by SOP 98-4, issued in March 1998. Software licence revenue is recognized when persuasive evidence of an arrangement exists, the related products are shipped, there are no significant uncertainties surrounding product acceptance, the fees are fixed and determinable, and collection is considered probable. Revenue from software maintenance and support agreements is recognized on a straight-line basis over the term of the related agreements. Revenue from services comprises consulting, training, and installation fees and is recognized at the time the services are performed. Deferred revenue comprises software maintenance and support fees and consulting revenue for which services have yet to be provided.

Other disclosures are less informative. For example, Celestica Inc. is a major company in electronics manufacturing services. The company operates a global manufacturing network, providing a broad range of services such as quality, technology, and supply chain management services to leading electronics equipment manufacturers. In its annual report, the company reports its revenue recognition policies as follows:

> Revenue is comprised of product sales and service revenue earned from engineering, design and repair services. Revenue from product sales is recognized upon shipment of the goods. Service revenue is recognized as services are performed.

Celestica's disclosure raises several questions. For example, what exchange and return policies are in effect for goods that have been shipped? For long-term contracts, what policy is used for allocating costs and revenues? How is performance measured? These are questions that cannot be answered from the meagre information provided in Celestica's note.

The Ontario Securities Commission issued a report in February 2001 on the revenue recognition policy disclosures of a sample of 75 public companies. Most of the sample companies (87%) were in computer technology industries, including software providers, service providers, and hardware products.

[6] *Financial Reporting in Canada 2003.*

The OSC staff felt that only 5% of the companies provided adequate disclosure in the notes. The report states,

> When revenue recognition policies were disclosed, they were often limited to vague or boilerplate language that provided little information relevant to the issuer's specific circumstances. For example, the disclosure stated merely that revenue is recognized when earned. It is staff's view that such disclosure provides no useful information and does not meet the requirements of *CICA* 1505.[7]

The OSC is requiring companies "to provide significantly more detailed disclosure in their financial statement notes or MD&A" (Section 3, page 5). Since the OSC cannot be ignored by public companies, we can hope to see much better reporting of revenue recognition policies in the future.

Looking Ahead

Change is in the air. Many financial statement users and securities regulators are concerned about the perceived ability of companies to "manage" their earnings. One target of this concern is revenue recognition—is there too much flexibility in current standards?

To deal with this perception of standards inadequacy, standard-setters are examining new and different approaches to revenue recognition. The difficulty with establishing more explicit revenue recognition policies is that the range of business activities is so very broad. How can standard-setters devise policies that will adequately address not only the huge range of current earnings activities, but also revenue strategies that will be developed by imaginative business corporations in the future?

The AcSB, jointly with the FASB and the IASB, has publicly issued tentative positions on concepts of revenue recognition. The tentative conclusions focus on contractual rights and obligations. For example, one of the current positions is that

> unconditional rights and obligations can give rise to assets and liabilities [that is, revenue recognition] if they are enforceable and have future economic consequences for the reporting entity.[8]

In general, the trend seems to be toward relying on the definitions of assets and liabilities in order to decide when revenue should be recognized. This approach is in contrast with the current (and past) practice of looking at the revenue-earning process itself.

CONCEPT REVIEW

1. What basic recognition criteria must be satisfied before a particular revenue recognition policy can be used?
2. What is the relationship between revenue recognition and a company's net asset value?
3. When there is more than one feasible revenue recognition policy that a company could use for a revenue-generating activity, how is a single policy chosen from the feasible set of policies?
4. When might a company recognize a gain due to an event rather than a transaction?
5. What adjustments must be made to revenue when the cash flow statement is prepared?

---

[7] Ontario Securities Commission, OSC Continuous Disclosure Team, Corporate Finance Branch, *Staff Notice 52-701—Initial Report on Staff's Review of Revenue Recognition*, Section 4.1, page 8 (published February 2001 on the OSC website at http://www.osc.gov.on.ca).

[8] *FYI: Activities of the CICA Accounting Standards Board and Staff*, September 2003, page 3.

EXPENSE RECOGNITION

We have discussed the principles of revenue recognition quite extensively in the preceding sections. In order to keep the discussion within reasonable length, we have intentionally omitted many details and complicating factors.

Now, what about expense recognition? One of the most basic concepts in all of accounting is the matching principle. When we recognize revenue, we must also recognize the expenses that relate to that revenue. But how do we measure the expense?

Much of the remainder of this book is devoted to many individual types of expenses and the timing of their recognition, such as cost of sales, amortization of capital assets, lease expense, pension expense, income tax expense, and so forth. However, there are some broad principles underlying all of the expense recognition principles that are discussed in the following chapters. To set the stage, we will conclude this chapter with an overview of the basic principles of expense recognition.

Cost, Expenditure, and Expense

Before embarking on an extended discussion of expense recognition, we should firmly establish the terminology:

- When we agree to pay out cash (or other assets) for goods or services received, we have incurred a **cost**.
- When we actually pay the cash, we have an **expenditure**.
- When the benefits of the cost have been used and we put that cost (or a portion thereof) on the income statement, we have recognized an expense.

cost
the amount, measured in money, to obtain goods or services

expenditure
payment of cash (or other asset) to acquire a good or service

Often, all three occur at the same time, or at least in the same accounting period. For example, when we pay salaries to administrative employees, we incur a cost for labour, make an *expenditure*, and recognize the full amount on the income statement as an *expense*. This sort of simultaneous occurrence is common for many routine transactions.

EXPENSE OR NOT? There are many expenditures that result in a cost that is not recognized immediately as an expense. A purchase of equipment is an obvious example. Equipment is recorded as an asset, and is gradually amortized to expense as the equipment is used. Furthermore, the cost assigned to the equipment may comprise several expenditures rather than just one; expenditures for shipping, installation, set up, and testing may be included in the cost of the equipment (or they may be expensed separately—this accounting policy choice is discussed in Chapter 9). Even expenditures for labour may not be an expense; for example, factory labour is added to the cost of manufactured inventory.

An expenditure may *follow* recognition of an expense. For example, think of a common year-end adjustment:

Income tax expense	176,000	
Income tax payable		176,000

This adjustment is made in order to recognize the income tax expense for the period, even if the company has not yet made the *expenditure* to pay the tax.

Thus, we must be very careful not to use the word "expense" when we really mean "cost" or "expenditure"—terminology does matter, especially when it comes to other people's understanding of what we are doing.

General Recognition Criteria

In order for an item to be recorded in the financial statements, it must meet the general recognition criteria that were outlined in Chapter 2. Recognized items must

- Meet the definition of a financial statement element, and
- Have a valid measurement basis and amount.

We know that the financial statement elements are based on future economic benefits or sacrifices; these must be *probable* for recognition to be appropriate.

How do the recognition criteria apply to expenses? Like revenues, expenses are not defined on their own. Their derivative definition rests on reduction of assets or increases in liabilities. That is,

> Expenses are decreases in economic resources, either by way of outflows or reductions of assets or incurrences of liabilities, resulting from an entity's ordinary revenue generating or service delivery activities. (CICA 1000.38)

Expenses are costs that are charged against revenue and that are related to the entity's ordinary or core business. The business may be the sale of a consumer or industrial product, design or management services, natural resource exploration, or any one of hundreds of other activities that represent core activities. The enterprise must incur expenses in order to generate revenue from these normal business activities. The expense is *matched* to the revenue, but never *netted* against the revenue.

For example, suppose that a land developer sells a parcel of land for $250,000. The developer originally paid $300,000 for the land. Since land sales are a normal part of the business, the developer will report revenue of $250,000 and will report cost of sales of $300,000, for a gross margin of $–50,000.

Activities that are not a part of normal business operations are treated somewhat differently. Losses are defined as decreases in net assets "from peripheral or incidental transactions and events" (*CICA* 1000.40). The costs of peripheral activities are netted against the related revenue to report a net gain or loss, which is reported as a single amount in the income statement. For example, suppose that a manufacturer of auto parts has idle land costing $300,000. The company decides that it will never use the land and sells it for $250,000. On its income statement, the manufacturer will report only a net loss of $–50,000 rather than separate revenue and expense.

The distinction between an expense and a loss depends only on whether the decrease in net assets is the result of normal business activities or of peripheral transactions and events. In either case, the cost results in a decrease in net assets. The basic recognition criteria are identical.

Asset or Expense?

An entity spends cash (or incurs a liability) to acquire a good or a service. The offset to that expenditure or liability will be a debit. Is the debit an *expense* or an *asset*? The definitions tell us that an entity has an asset if there is future economic benefit (that is, a cash flow, either direct or indirect) that will come from the item. If there is no such benefit, then the entry involves a debit to an expense because the item has no intrinsic value or future cash flow. If there is no future benefit that is both probable and measurable, then the item is treated as an expense.

IMPACT ON FINANCIAL STATEMENTS Exhibit 6-6 identifies the impact that these two alternatives will have on the financial statements. In one, the *distribution of assets* is changed; in the other, *net assets and shareholder wealth goes down.* The decision about what to debit is not a free choice: if the asset recognition criteria are met, an asset is recorded. If not, an expense is recorded.

Think about a transaction that involves buying goods for resale in a cash exchange. Cash goes down; what goes up? The goods are for resale, so they can be sold to a customer for at least their cost; the goods clearly represent a future cash flow to the entity and are an asset, *inventory.* Inventory becomes an expense, called "cost of goods sold," when it's sold. At this point, inventory is converted into cash, a financial instrument, or some other benefit to the entity.

When might goods bought for resale *not* be an asset? If the goods were bought and became unsaleable due to their physical condition or because they were obsolete, then the entity has no future cash flowing from the ownership of the items and the purchase would be reported as an expense. Inventory is an asset only if it can be resold for at least its carrying value. Unsaleable inventory must be written down, a common occurrence.

Earlier in this chapter, we emphasized that the point of revenue recognition is accompanied by an increase in net assets. When expenses are recognized, net assets go down. When

EXHIBIT 6-6

IMPACT OF AN EXPENDITURE: ASSET VERSUS EXPENSE

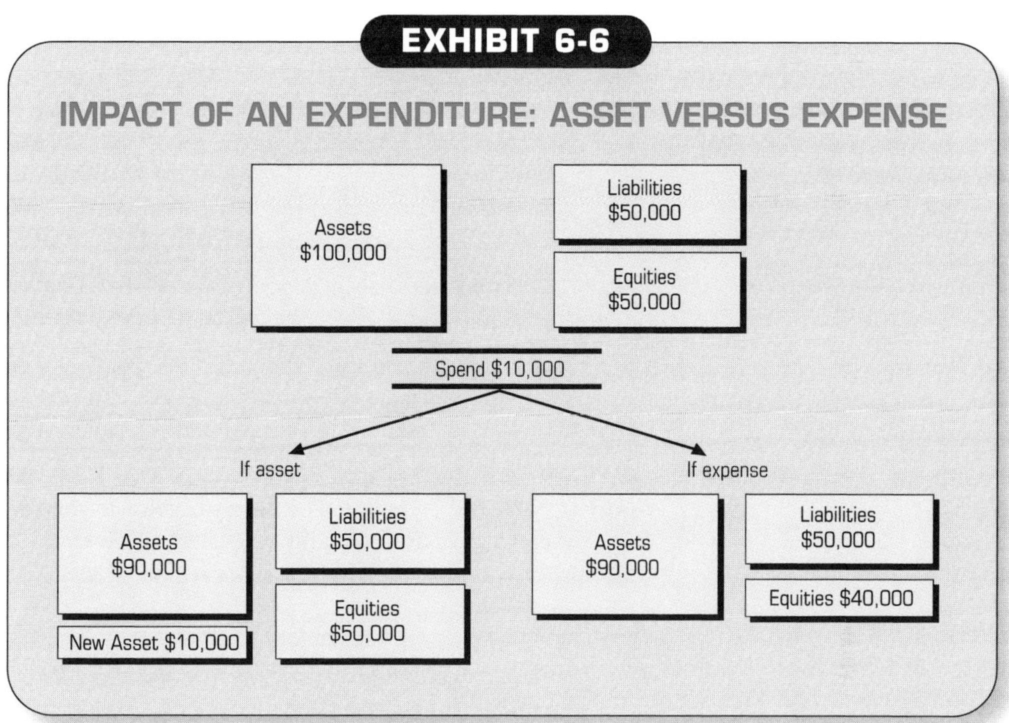

revenues and expenses are recognized simultaneously, one expects that revenues will exceed expenses and the combined impact on net assets will be positive.

Expense recognition is highly dependent on the revenue recognition point chosen by a company. If a company buys an item that will later be sold, its cost is deferred. If the revenue recognition point comes and goes but not all costs are yet incurred, then they must be accrued. Refer again to Exhibit 6-1, and observe how and when expenses (versus assets) were created. Remember that deferred costs are assets, and the future sale transaction is the future cash flow that backs up the asset value.

Approaches to Expense Recognition

What have you learned about expense recognition?

1. The debit to offset an outflow of cash (i.e., the credit) is either an expense or an asset. Criteria must be met to justify recognizing an asset.
2. The activity must be central to the core operations of the entity in order to classify the item as an expense.

Given these two initial requirements, we can identify two general approaches to deciding whether an expenditure results in an asset or an expense.

DEFINITIONAL APPROACH In this approach, expenses are determined in relation to the definition of assets and liabilities that is included in Section 1000 of the *CICA Handbook.* Expenses are created either through the reduction of an asset or the increase in a liability. We'll call this, for lack of a better term, the "definitional approach" to expense recognition. The "definitional approach" is oriented towards the balance sheet.

MATCHING APPROACH In this approach, expense recognition policy is justified using the doctrine of *matching.* Matching requires that once revenues are determined in conformity with the revenue principle for any reporting period, the expenses incurred in generating the revenue should be recognized in that period. The essence of the matching principle is that as revenues are earned, expenses are incurred to generate those revenues. These expenses must be recognized and reported as expenses of the period during which the related revenue is recognized. Matching typically involves the primacy of revenue and expense recognition and accurate net income measurement, not an analysis of changes in asset and liability balances.

To illustrate how expense recognition is explained by each of these two approaches, consider the following two examples of accounting policy and how they are justified under the definitional approach versus the matching approach.

Policy 1. Defer expenditures related to revenue generation activities incurred prior to the revenue recognition point. Expense these items when revenue is recognized.

Definitional: Up to the revenue recognition point, these items have probable future benefit arising from the revenue transaction: the cash flow, etc., that will be provided by the customer. As long as the revenue transaction is probable, the expenditure meets the recognition criteria for an asset. After revenue recognition, the asset becomes an expense.

Matching: The expenses must be deferred prior to the revenue recognition point so that they can be matched with the associated revenue.

Policy 2. Accrue expenses incurred but not yet substantiated by a transaction if they relate to revenue recognized on the income statement.

Definitional: The entity has incurred an obligation for the expenditures by virtue of the revenue transaction. The element (the liability) exists and must now be recognized.

Matching: The expenses must be accrued at the revenue recognition point to properly match revenues and all expenses.

Both lines of reasoning appear to support the same types of policies. So what's the big deal?

HISTORICAL PERSPECTIVE Matching has been with us for a long time. It was central in an influential monograph that was sponsored by the American Accounting Association in the 1960s. It dominated accounting thought for decades. Matching involves deferring expenditures as assets on the balance sheet if projected revenues are still on the horizon. Criteria for such deferral were not well developed through this period, and there were problematic cases of assets—cost deferrals—that had, in the end, no associated cash flow. Application of matching sometimes led to recording an expense even though no real liability was created. For example, an amount debited to expense might be credited to an account called "deferred credits." Deferred credits were often not true liabilities, at least not in conformity with the definition of liabilities that is presented in the *CICA Handbook.*

Many accountants feel that the balance sheet has to have integrity. That is, only "real" assets and liabilities can be properly included on the balance sheet. Thus, revenues and expenses are recognized only when balance sheet accounts, with real integrity, are created. This is the basis of the definitional approach. However, the continued devotion of accounting standards to interperiod allocations calls into question the real impact of the definitional approach.

Where does that leave us? The habit of talking about matching is firmly entrenched, but it takes a different perspective than the definitional approach. The safest thing to say is that we are, as a profession, in transition! Many of our customs and established accounting policies are justified with reference to matching. New rules may be based on the definitional approach. It is considered theoretically superior by those who subscribe to the balance sheet view of the financial statements. At this stage, it would be helpful for you to orient your thinking about accounting policy toward the definitional approach.

Measurement

Recognition is not possible unless there is a reliable amount to record. When is measurement an issue for expenses? Obviously, if the item is one where the cost transaction precedes the revenue recognition point, there's likely an invoice sitting around and measurement isn't much of an issue. The more complicated problem arises when the expense has to be accrued at the revenue recognition point, prior to settlement. Accurate measurement of the liability, and, by inference, the expense, is a major concern.

Consider the issue of environmental liabilities and cleanup costs associated with certain operations. In the mining industry, provincial legislation generally requires mining companies to restore mine sites to their original condition (minus the extracted resources, of course) after mining operations have ceased. The extent of restoration varies from province to province, and is subject to change—sometimes retroactively—by legislative action. Therefore, mining activities clearly create an obligation for site restoration. The only problem is: how much will the obligation amount to? To answer this question, a mining company will have to estimate the extent and cost of the restoration activities that will happen many years in the future—a highly uncertain amount.

For decades, mining companies responded to this situation by refusing to accrue any cost on the basis that the recognition criteria for measurement failed. That is, without the existence of a definitive estimate, no recognition was appropriate. Over the past 10 years, there has been a steady increase in the number of firms that choose to accrue an estimate. Has their ability to estimate improved? Perhaps, but another plausible explanation is that shareholders and other stakeholder groups now have higher expectations. They want to see indications that the company accepts its responsibilities for site restoration, and intends to honour its obligations. Recording a liability is one way to signal the company's intentions.

Recently, the AcSB began to require companies to record the liability at the time that an asset is acquired, if the company has a legal obligation relating to the retirement of tangible capital assets. This new requirement (*CICA Handbook* Section 3110) is at least partially in response to investor concerns that retirement or restoration obligations were understated.

Clearly, reporting entities must make an effort to measure costs. Both the matching approach and the definitional approach require that best efforts be made in cost measurement. The *CICA Handbook*, Section 1508, "Measurement Uncertainty," requires that entities disclose the nature and extent of a measurement uncertainty, in a disclosure note to the financial statements. This encourages firms to record items despite any lack of precision in the numbers. It should also help financial statement users understand the "soft spots" in the financial statements themselves.

Another major issue in expense measurement deals with the issue of *interperiod allocation*: what amortization policies are appropriate? How much amortization should be booked in a given period? We will return frequently to this issue in subsequent chapters.

CONCEPT REVIEW

1. What is the difference between an expenditure, an expense, and a cost?
2. What are the general recognition criteria for financial statement elements?
3. How do we decide whether a cost should be reported as an asset or as an expense?

SUMMARY OF KEY POINTS

1. For most companies, the earnings process is continuous. That is, the profit-directed activities of the company continually generate inflows or enhancements of the assets of the company.
2. Revenue recognition policies must be chosen carefully because of their profound effect on key financial results.
3. Before the results of the earnings process are recognized in the accounting records, revenue must meet the recognition criteria of *measurability* and *collectibility*.
4. A sale transaction is usually measured at the sales invoice price. When there are long-term, interest-free payment terms, discounting may be appropriate.
5. Barter transactions are typically recognized at the value of the asset or service given in the exchange.
6. Revenue can be recognized at a *critical event* or on the basis of *effort expended*. Critical events can be at delivery, prior to delivery (e.g., on production, if there are no uncertainties regarding the sale transaction), or after delivery (if there are significant uncertainties about measurement, collection, or remaining costs). *Delivery* is the normal critical event that triggers revenue recognition.
7. The recognition of revenue results in an increase in net assets, which is recognized at the critical event. Costs incurred prior to the critical event are deferred. When revenue is recognized, deferred costs are expensed, and future costs are accrued.
8. The instalment sales method of revenue recognition delays recognition of gross profit until cash is collected.
9. The cost recovery method is a conservative method in which no profit is recognized until all costs associated with the sale item have been recovered in cash. All subsequent cash collections are profit.
10. Long-term contracts can be accounted for using the percentage-of-completion method, or the completed-contract method. If a long-term, fixed-price contract with a credit-worthy customer is accompanied by reasonably reliable estimates of (a) total revenue, (b) cost to complete, and (c) percentage of completion, based either on output or input, then percentage-of-completion is appropriate.
11. Under the completed-contract method, revenues and expenses are recognized when the contract obligations are completed. Costs incurred in completing the contract are accrued in an inventory account, and any progress billings are accrued in a contra-inventory account.
12. Long-term contracts are often accounted for on the basis of effort expended. Under the percentage-of-completion method, revenues and expenses are recognized each accounting period based on an estimate of the percentage of completion. Costs incurred in completing the contract and recognized gross profit are accrued in an inventory account.
13. Revenue recognition policies are chosen in accordance with the financial reporting objectives of the enterprise, constrained by the general recognition criteria of probability and measurability. The choice of a revenue recognition policy involves a trade-off between qualitative criteria, such as between verifiability and timeliness.
14. Cash flow from operations must be computed by adjusting revenue (or net income) for changes in accounts and notes receivable, for changes in unearned revenue, and for accrued expenses that do not represent cash expenditures during the period.
15. An expenditure may be either an asset or an expense. Items that meet the recognition criteria for assets are capitalized as assets; other expenditures are expensed. Of key importance in establishing an asset is the presence of future economic benefits, essentially cash flow. This is the definitional approach to expense recognition.

16. An expenditure that results in asset recognition simply reorganizes the asset section of the balance sheet but does not affect net assets, assets less liabilities. In contrast, expense recognition reduces net assets.

17. Expense policy has traditionally been described as a matching process, where expenses are matched to revenues recognized on the income statement. Matching may result in questionable deferred asset and liability items recognized on the balance sheet; the definitional approach avoids this, which many accountants regard as preferable.

18. Measurement of an expense is usually an issue only when the expense is to be incurred at some future point in time, but must be accrued in the current period. Expenses may be estimated, and the presence of measurement uncertainty should be disclosed.

KEY TERMS

barter transaction, 270
commodity, 274
consignment, 276
cost, 293
cost recovery method, 278
critical event, 271
expenditure, 293
instalment sales method, 277
progress billings, 282
revenue recognition principle, 269

REVIEW PROBLEM 1

Precision Punctual Construction Company (PPCC) has agreed to build a 10-storey office building for Mountain Bank Limited. The contract calls for a contract price of $15,000,000 for the building, with progress payments being made by Mountain as the construction proceeds. The period of construction is estimated to be 30 months. The contract is signed on 1 February 20X5, and construction begins immediately. The building is completed and turned over to Mountain Bank on 1 December 20X7.

Data on cost incurred, estimated costs to complete, progress billings, and progress payments over the period of construction are as follows:

($ thousands)

	20X5	20X6	20X7
Costs incurred this period	$ 1,500	$ 7,875	$ 3,825
Costs incurred to date	1,500	9,375	13,200
Estimated costs to complete at year-end	10,500	3,125	0
Estimated total costs of project	12,000	12,500	13,200
Progress billings this period	1,200	6,000	7,800
Progress payments received this period	825	6,300	7,875

Required:

1. Show the entries to account for this project over the period of construction, assuming that PPCC uses
   a. the completed-contract method of recognizing revenue
   b. the percentage-of-completion method of recognizing revenue
2. Show the relevant balance sheet and income statement items for 20X5, 20X6, and 20X7 for PPCC, assuming that the company uses
   a. the completed-contract method
   b. the percentage-of-completion method

REVIEW PROBLEM 1—SOLUTION

1. The entries to record the construction of the building for both the completed-contract method and the percentage-of-completion method are as follows (in $ thousands):

Entries for 20X5:	Completed-Contract Method		Percentage-of-Completion Method	
a. *To record incurrence of construction costs:*				
Construction-in-progress inventory	1,500		1,500	
Cash, payables, etc.		1,500		1,500
b. *To record progress billings:*				
Accounts receivable	1,200		1,200	
Billings on contract		1,200		1,200
c. *To record billing collections:*				
Cash	825		825	
Accounts receivable		825		825
d. *To recognize revenue for percentage of completion:**				
Construction-in-progress inventory			375	
Cost of construction			1,500	
Revenue from long-term contract				1,875

* The percentage of completion is the cost incurred to date divided by total estimated project costs, or $1,500 ÷ $12,000 = 12.5%. The total amount of revenue recognizable to this point is $15,000 × 12.5% = $1,875.

Entries for 20X6:	Completed-Contract Method		Percentage-of-Completion Method	
a. *To record incurrence of construction costs:*				
Construction-in-progress inventory	7,875		7,875	
Cash, payables, etc.		7,875		7,875
b. *To record progress billings:*				
Accounts receivable	6,000		6,000	
Billings on contract		6,000		6,000
c. *To record billing collections:*				
Cash	6,300		6,300	
Accounts receivable		6,300		6,300
d. *To recognize revenue for percentage of completion:**				
Construction-in-progress inventory			1,500	
Cost of construction			7,875	
Revenue from long-term contract				9,375

* The percentage of completion is the cost incurred to date divided by total estimated project costs, or $9,375 ÷ $12,500 = 75%. The total amount of revenue recognizable to this point is $15,000 × 75% = $11,250. Since $1,875 was recognized in 20X5, the amount recognizable in 20X6 is $11,250 − $1,875 = $9,375.

Entries for 20X7:	Completed-Contract Method		Percentage-of-Completion Method	
a. *To record incurrence of construction costs:*				
Construction-in-progress inventory	3,825		3,825	
Cash, payables, etc.		3,825		3,825
b. *To record progress billings:*				
Accounts receivable	7,800		7,800	
Billings on contract		7,800		7,800
c. *To record billing collections:*				
Cash	7,875		7,875	
Accounts receivable		7,875		7,875
d. *To recognize revenue for percentage of completion:**				
Cost of construction			3,825	
Revenue from long-term contract				3,750
Construction-in-progress inventory				75

* The project is completed; any remaining portion of the contract price not previously recognized as revenue should be recognized this period. In prior years, $1,875 + $9,375 = $11,250 was recognized, thus $3,750 (i.e., $15,000 − $11,250) is recognized in 20X7.

	Completed-Contract Method		Percentage-of-Completion Method	
e. *To record elimination of contract costs from inventory:*				
Billings on contract			15,000	
Construction-in-progress inventory				15,000
f. *To recognize revenue for completed contract:*				
Billings on contract	15,000			
Cost of earned construction revenue	13,200			
Revenue from long-term contracts		15,000		
Construction-in-progress inventory		13,200		

2. Financial statement items:

	31 Dec. 20X5		31 Dec. 20X6		31 Dec. 20X7	
	Completed Contract	Percentage of Completion	Completed Contract	Percentage of Completion	Completed Contract	Percentage of Completion
Balance sheet:						
Accounts receivable	$ 375	$ 375	$ 75	$ 75	0	0
Inventory:						
Construction in progress	$ 1,500	$ 1,875	$ 9,375	$ 11,250	0	0
Less: Billings on contract	(1,200)	(1,200)	(7,200)	(7,200)	0	0
Construction in progress in excess of billings	$ 300	$ 675	$ 2,175	$ 4,050	0	0
Income statement:						
Revenue from long-term contracts	$___	$ 1,875	$___	$ 9,375	$ 15,000	$ 3,750
Cost of construction	$___	(1,500)	$___	(7,875)	(13,200)	(3,825)
Gross profit	$___	$ 375	$___	$ 1,500	$ 1,800	$ (75)*

* This is an example of a current year loss on a contract that is profitable overall.

REVIEW PROBLEM 2

Cromax Corporation is a Canadian public company whose shares are listed on the TSE. The following transactions and events occurred in 20X5. For each item, indicate the preferred accounting treatment. Assume all amounts are material.

1. Cromax paid $700,000 to a firm of engineers who undertook a study to determine more energy-efficient practices in Cromax's production facilities.
2. Cromax diverted workers and equipment to help prepare for government-sponsored public celebrations revolving around the Tall Ships festival in Halifax; the out-of-pocket cost was approximately $127,000; depreciation on equipment was $40,000. Cromax does a great deal of business with governments at all levels, and regards the expenditures as relationship-building that will have future benefit.
3. Cromax has recently signed a four-year contract with a new customer. As part of the terms of the contract, Cromax paid $500,000 up front to the customer to defray expenses the customer will incur as a result of changing suppliers. The contract involves substantial volumes of sales over the next four years between Cromax and the customer.
4. Cromax spent $4.2 million defending itself against an unfair competition lawsuit launched by six smaller firms. The lawsuit has been settled out of court. Of the $4.2 million, $3 million is the settlement, $800,000 is legal fees, and $400,000 is public relations spending to counteract the negative publicity surrounding the dispute. Cromax's future markets are secure as a result of the terms of the settlement.
5. Cromax has just set up a $20 million line of credit with its bank, which allows Cromax to borrow these funds on 24-hours' notice at any time over the next five years. The interest rate will be prime plus 1%. By year-end, Cromax had not borrowed any money under the lending arrangement, but expects to in the next fiscal year as a result of some planned capital expansion. Cromax paid an up-front fee of $125,000 to the bank in order to obtain the agreement.

(ASCA, adapted)

REVIEW PROBLEM—SOLUTION 2

1. Items are recognized if they meet the recognition criteria. This $700,000 payment may be an asset, if it has future benefits that are probable. Can the energy savings be documented? (That is, are they probable?) If sufficient appropriate evidence exists, the expenditure may be deferred, to be amortized on a basis consistent with the projected savings. Otherwise, the item is an expense.
2. An amount of $167,000 can be directly attributed to the activities, which may be an "asset" if it has future benefit. While demonstrating that Cromax is a good corporate citizen may help solidify relationships with governments that are major customers, is there *probable* future cash flow that will validate the asset? It would be difficult to quantify the benefits, and this is most likely an expense of the period.
3. Cromax has future economic benefit associated with the long-term contract with the customer, and, as long as the contract is firm, it is acceptable to defer this payment and amortize it in some fashion over the life of the contract.
4. Should the $4.2 million be recognized as an expense or as an asset, amortized to earnings over some future period of (now secure) profitable operations? All the items are incremental expenditures related to one event and should be accounted for the same way.

   The expenditures can be viewed as an asset if they have future benefits that are probable. Cromax's future operations in this line should be evaluated (cash flow projections) for sufficient appropriate evidence to support the asset value. Analogies can be drawn to pre-operating costs and legal fees spent to defend patents, both of which may be deferred and amortized.

   On the other hand, asset treatment may be inappropriate. Future operations are not enhanced by the expenditures; the *status quo* has only been preserved. Patents have finite legal lives, but operations in this case might be weakened by the precedent of the lawsuit settlement. Are they better off because of this payment? Would they be even "more" better off (i.e., have higher assets) if the settlement were higher? Under the definitions, in Section 1000, assets are *not* expenses deferred, but rather items with associated future cash flow. An appropriate analogy might be repairing a machine damaged in transportation, or fixing fire damage: the *status quo* is preserved by subsequent repairs, but no asset is created.

The arguments for expensing appear stronger; the amount should not be capitalized.

5. Cromax has incurred a cost that is analogous to prepaid interest expense. It can be deferred but should be amortized over the life of the agreement, five years. It does not simply relate to the period of time in which funds are actually borrowed under the facility, as Cromax is benefiting from the flexibility and locked-in interest rate for the entire five years. Deferred financing charges are a common deferred charge in Canada.

QUESTIONS

Q6-1 Explain the relationship between the definition of revenue and the definitions of assets and liabilities.

Q6-2 When is revenue earned in economic terms? How does this relate to typical accounting revenue recognition?

Q6-3 What impact do individual corporate reporting objectives have on revenue recognition policies?

Q6-4 What are the fundamental criteria for recognizing any element in the financial statements? Explain the additional criteria that revenue must meet before being recognized.

Q6-5 Under the revenue recognition principle, when is performance achieved?

Q6-6 Give two typical examples of revenues for which recognition occurs on the basis of the passage of time.

Q6-7 How is revenue measured in a barter transaction?

Q6-8 What is meant by revenue recognition at a critical event? Give examples of at least three critical events.

Q6-9 Why is revenue typically recognized on delivery?

Q6-10 Under what circumstances is revenue recognized at a critical event before delivery? After delivery?

Q6-11 What is a consignment? How is revenue recognized on a consignment transaction?

Q6-12 What conditions must be met in order for revenue to be recognized when a customer has the right to return purchased products? What accounting procedures are used until all conditions are met?

Q6-13 Describe the instalment sales method of recognizing revenue and when it is appropriately used.

Q6-14 Describe the cost recovery method of recognizing revenue. When is it appropriate?

Q6-15 Identify and explain two different approaches for determining the extent of progress toward completion of a construction project.

Q6-16 Why is the ending inventory of construction in progress different in amount when the percentage-of-completion method is used compared with the completed-contract method? Explain the amount of the difference.

Q6-17 When a loss is projected on an unprofitable long-term construction contract, in what period(s) is the loss recognized under (a) percentage-of-completion and (b) completed-contract methods?

Q6-18 Under what circumstances do gains and losses reflect changes in value, rather than realized transactions?

Q6-19 A company spends cash to acquire a service, such as legal fees. Describe the impact on the financial statements if the expenditure is classified as an asset compared to its impact when classified as an expense.

Q6-20 When does a cash expenditure result in recognition of an asset? An expense?

Q6-21 At what point in time will the purchase of a capital asset for cash result in a decline in net assets?

Q6-22 Contrast the definitional and matching approaches to explaining expense recognition policies.

Q6-23 Assume that a company has an expense recognition policy for bad debts that requires bad debt expense to be recognized, and an allowance for doubtful accounts established, as sales occur. The amount is measured as a percentage of sales. This accrual is to take place even though the actual amount of bad debt expense will not be known until specific customers actually default over the following 12 to 24 months. Justify this policy using the definitional approach, and then using the matching approach.

Q6-24 Give two examples of expenses for which measurement is an issue.

CASE 6-1
John and Mike

John and Mike set up a partnership early this year in order to speculate in real estate. They specialize in the acquisition of small, rundown apartment buildings, which they then renovate, rent out to improve occupancy rates, and resell. Mike works at this enterprise full-time, overseeing the renovation and rental process. John continues to work at a full-time salaried job in an unrelated business.

Annual profits are allocated as follows:

1. "Salary" of $50,000 to Mike.
2. Interest to both partners of 10% per annum, based on monthly average capital balances.
3. Remainder equally.

The partners have agreed on a schedule of monthly drawings, to be charged against each partner's capital accounts. Drawings may not exceed profit allocations.

In their first year, the partners successfully "flipped" three apartment buildings, and owned four more at year-end, awaiting resale. It is now the end of their first year, and accounting policies have yet to be finalized. The following are areas of contention:

1. Revenue recognition, rental income

Mike has proposed that revenue be recognized as rent is collected from tenants. John has proposed that rent revenue be recognized on the first day of the month, when it is due, whether collected or not. Typically, most rent is collected within a week, but there are always some problem tenants, especially in newly bought buildings, which need extensive renovations and often have undesirable tenants.

2. Depreciation policy, rental buildings

John reasons that rental buildings are all for resale, and are thus "inventory." As such, he claims that no depreciation should be charged as long as net book value is less than market value. Mike is not convinced that this reasoning is valid, as he thinks depreciation is always incurred and must be recorded.

3. Revenue recognition, building sale
Often, there is a time lag between the sale of a building (that is, the date upon which the sale agreement is signed), the date on which title passes, and the date that the partnership receives all the sale proceeds. For example, in a recent sale, the agreement was signed on 1 November, and title passed on 15 December, at which time half of the proceeds were paid. The other half is due on 15 December in three years' time, with accrued interest, since the partnership took back a long-term note as part of the sale financing. John favours revenue recognition when the sale agreement is signed; Mike prefers to wait until the cash is collected.

Both partners have agreed that statements will primarily be used for profit allocation and need not necessarily follow GAAP. They are more concerned about cash flow, and in particular, making sure there is enough cash flow for partners' withdrawals.

Required:
Analyze the issues and present your recommendations to the partnership.

(CGA-Canada, adapted)

Case 6-2
Tempus Fugit

Tempus Fugit is a large conglomerate of 30 subsidiary companies with plants and branches throughout the world. The company has been in the business of manufacturing and distributing clocks, watches, and other timepieces for over 50 years. Recently, the company experienced a change in management when the original founder retired and sold his controlling interest.

On 1 May 20X5, Smith & Smith, a publicly traded international consulting firm, was awarded the contract to design and install a computerized management information system in each of Tempus Fugit's subsidiaries. The project was projected to take four years to complete. Michael Smith, the founder and managing partner of Smith & Smith, and his staff, worked exclusively on this project from May to October. Currently, one-half of the company's workforce is working on the job. Smith & Smith obtained this project after submitting a bid on 1 March 20X5, which took most of February to prepare; the bid price was $45,000,000.

It is January 20X6, and annual financial statements for Smith & Smith are being prepared. Michael Smith has come to you, the controller of the company, to discuss how the contract will be reported. He is anxious to present the contract as favourably as possible under the limitations of GAAP. His comments to you are:

"I know this is the first long-term contract that we have entered into, and I have heard that we can recognize revenue based on the percentage of the project that is complete. That percentage should be based on management's best estimates, as are so many things under GAAP. In my opinion, even though we are behind in the installation, we should recognize revenue according to the percentage that we estimated would be done in our contract bid. If we don't, Tempus Fugit's management will be on our backs, wondering what is going on and slowing us down even more. I sure don't need that with all of the problems we are experiencing on this project!"

You ask Smith about the problems that are being experienced on the project. He responds that they are of a highly technical nature. He urges you to complete the financial statements as soon as possible, since Smith & Smith is experiencing a cash flow shortage and Tempus Fugit will not release the first payment on the contract until the year-end statements have been received.

You are aware of the following facts about Smith & Smith and Tempus Fugit:

- Smith & Smith has been in business for five years. This is the first time the company has landed a contract of this magnitude. Previous contracts have all been completed within a one-year time frame.

- The contract provides for Tempus Fugit to pay in four equal annual instalments on receipt of audited statements from Smith & Smith. One-quarter of the project should be completed each year.
- Much of the contract involves design and testing of computer programs, and it is difficult to determine the degree of completion of the project at any time. Few external experts in the area exist, since Smith & Smith is in a new industry and a specialized field. The company has never been too concerned about estimating completion before because all of its contracts have been short term.
- The auditor has no way of determining the percentage of completion of the project, since the work is so subjective. Because the same audit firm has been engaged by Smith & Smith for the past five years and has found the partners to be reputable, the auditor is generally able to rely on management's best estimates.

After your conversation with Michael Smith, you find yourself in the coffee room with Rachel Harris, the chief programmer on the Tempus Fugit project. You have always had a good relationship with Rachel. Out of curiosity, you ask her how much of the project she believes is done and about the problems the company is experiencing. Her response is: "You know, the partners bid on this one to get us into the big leagues, and let me tell you, the big leagues are tough! We have never handled a project this large, and it is taking us a lot longer to get some of the basic systems developed than we ever imagined. Although it's hard to tell, I would say we are only about 10% done at this time. We are in the process of hiring more staff and establishing supplier relationships, and all of this takes time. I am still confident that we will complete the project in four years, but I don't think we will catch up to our original estimates until the third year. By then, the staff will be trained and we will be much more effective."

After coffee, you run into Michael Smith again. He asks that you meet him in his office Monday morning, ready to discuss the accounting options available for the project and your recommended accounting treatment. He is rushing out the door to a meeting with the banker, who called with some concerns about the company's cash flow problems.

Required:

Identify and analyze the alternative treatments available to account for the timing of the revenues and expenses that will be recognized in the contract with Tempus Fugit. What are the ethical issues you must consider before making your recommendation to Michael Smith? What should you say during the Monday morning meeting with Smith?

(CGA-Canada, adapted)

Case 6-3
Kryton Corporation

Kryton Corporation is a property development company, with expertise in larger, multiple-unit apartment buildings. Kryton must comply with GAAP to satisfy bank lenders who provide project and working capital financing. Typically, the company finds a site, arranges for interim and mortgage financing, and then constructs the building through subcontractors. As the building is being built, Kryton looks for an investor to take over ownership of the building; often life insurance companies are interested, as are individuals through limited partnerships. Kryton has a property management division that runs such large apartment buildings.

It is now the end of 20X3; Kryton's latest project, a 255-unit apartment building, has been harder to sell. A deal is finally in place. An agreement has been signed with a group of individual investors, who have formed a limited partnership. When the project is completed, in July 20X5, the building will be sold to the partners, who will pay Kryton as follows:

Cash, provided by first mortgage from Confidential Insurance	$11,000,000
Cash, payments by the partners to Kryton	1,000,000
4% notes receivable to Kryton from the investors, payable in four equal instalments on the anniversary of the turnover date	2,000,000
Five-year, 18% second mortgage provided by Kryton	1,500,000
	$15,500,000

The estimated costs of the project are $12,300,000, of which $6,500,000 have been incurred to the end of 20X3. Kryton intends to record the profit ($3,200,000) in July 20X5, when the building is completed. The assets received in consideration (listed above) would be recorded at that time. Further details on the purchase agreement are below.

Required:

Explain how Kryton should recognize revenue for the project.

KRYTON CORPORATION LIMITED
INFORMATION ON PURCHASE AGREEMENT

The project differs from previous projects in both the manner of financing and in the number of indemnities and covenants that Kryton must provide. The turnover date, referred to below, is the date that the partnership assumes ownership of the project. It occurs when the project is 90% leased to occupants. Extracts from the offering memorandum:

Kryton second mortgage

The Kryton second mortgage will be in the principal amount of $1.5 million and will bear interest at the rate of 18% after the turnover date.

The mortgage will include the following terms:

1. The mortgage will be without recourse to the partners' personal assets.
2. Payments of principal and accrued interest at the maturity date are required only to the extent that proceeds are available from the refinancing of the first mortgage; the second mortgage is to be renewed for any unpaid balance for a further term, without interest.
3. The partnership will have the right to set off any amount owing by it under the second mortgage agreement against amounts by which Kryton is in default under the cash flow guarantee (see below).

Initial leasing period indemnity

The agreement provides that Kryton will operate the project on behalf of the partnership and will indemnify the partnership for all losses incurred in operating the project during the initial leasing period, which ends on the turnover date.

Cash flow guarantee

Kryton has agreed to provide interest-free loans to the partnership for the following purposes:

1. To fund, as required, for a period of 10 years from the turnover date, the amount, if any, by which the total operating expenses of the project (including payments on account of principal and interest due on the first mortgage, but excluding non-cash items such as depreciation and reserves for replacement of equipment and chattels) exceed the aggregate gross income receipts from the project.
2. To fund, during the period commencing on the turnover date and ending on 31 December 20X5, the amount (the "Guaranteed Amount"), if any, by which the actual net cash flow is less than the Kryton-prepared forecast of net cash flow (this forecast is not reproduced here).

Management of the project
Kryton will be appointed manager of the project for a term of 10 years, and will be paid 5% of monthly gross cash receipts. Kryton will be responsible for the ongoing leasing of apartment units comprising the project, maintenance and repairs, collection of rents, payment of all expenses properly incurred in connection with such duties out of revenues received from the project including all amounts payable under the mortgages, the maintenance of fire and liability insurance on the project, the preparation of a cash budget for each year, and the annual remittance of cash surpluses to the partners.

CASE 6-4
Acme Construction Limited

Bob Bothwell started Acme Construction Limited early in 20X2 after working for several years as a supervisor for a local construction company. An inheritance from his parents provided the start-up capital. Bob's wife, Susan, did all of the bookkeeping on weekends without pay to help conserve cash.

For the 20X2 and 20X3 year-ends, the firm where you are employed as a student-in-accounts had performed a review of the financial statements and prepared the tax returns for the company. In late December 20X4, Bob Bothwell phoned the partner in charge of the engagement to arrange a meeting in Bob's office on 30 December 20X4.

The partner asked George Cathcart, the senior field auditor on the engagement in 20X2 and 20X3, to represent him at the meeting and asked that you accompany George.

At the meeting, Bob explained that business was booming, and that he was considering privately raising additional equity capital to undertake some very large projects. He wanted to retain control of the company but was willing to relinquish sole ownership instead of increasing his bank loan. However, the preliminary draft statements for 20X4 did not look as impressive as he had expected.

He handed George and you a copy of the income statement (Exhibit 1), along with a summary of contracts undertaken (Exhibit 2). He shook his head and said, "I didn't bring the balance sheet because I don't think it is correct. The materials in inventory are worth $200,000 now, not the $150,000 I paid for them. The same thing applies to the temporary investments. My broker assures me that they are worth twice what I paid. I also don't see anything reflected in the financial statements about the lawsuit that I'm involved in. My lawyer says that, when we go to court next week, I'll be sure to win $27,000 from the subcontractor who delayed the curling rink project."

EXHIBIT 1

ACME CONSTRUCTION LIMITED
INCOME STATEMENT (DRAFT)

For the year ended 31 December	20X4	20X3
Net revenue from completed contracts	$365,000	$136,000
General and administrative expenses	172,000	100,000
Income before taxes	193,000	36,000
Income taxes	48,250	9,000
Net income for the year	$144,750	$ 27,000

"My biggest problem is with the income figure," he continued. "I don't seem to get credit for the projects that are in progress, even though my costs are usually in line, and I know I'm making money. Is there any way to improve my net income without paying any additional income tax?"

Required:

Prepare a memo to George Cathcart. The memo is to include a revised net income figure for both 20X4 and 20X3 assuming that the company changes its revenue recognition policy from completed-contract to percentage-of-completion, but continues to calculate taxes on the completed-contract basis. You should also include your thoughts on the best way to deal with the problems Bob raised. Cathcart will be using your work as a basis for his report to the partner.

(ICAO, adapted)

Significant Accounting Policies

Revenue recognition: the company follows the completed-contract method of recognizing revenue from construction projects.

EXHIBIT 2

ACME CONSTRUCTION LIMITED
SUMMARY OF CONTRACTS UNDERTAKEN

Started in 20X2

Mainline Apartments

The contract price was $600,000, and costs were estimated at $450,000. The project was one-half completed at the end of 20X2, and costs were on target at $225,000. In 20X3, the project was completed but costs were $14,000 higher than estimated. The customer was billed $600,000 and all but $90,000 was received in 20X3. The balance was collected in 20X4.

Started in 20X3

Harbour View Apartments

The contract price was $940,000 and costs were originally estimated at $800,000. At the end of 20X3, the project was 80% completed, but price declines on materials resulted in costs of only $600,000. Progress billings were sent out for $470,000, of which $310,000 had been received at the year-end.

In 20X4, the project was completed with additional costs of $150,000. The customer paid the full contract price by November 20X4.

Sunnyside Curling Rink

The contract was awarded at $1,425,000 and costs were estimated at $1,250,000. At the end of 20X3, the project was 20% completed, and costs were on target at $250,000. Progress billings had been sent for $200,000 and one half had been received by 31 December 20X3.

The contract was completed in 20X4. Costs were higher than estimated because of a subcontractor who delayed the project. Completed contract income of $148,000 is included in income, and all of the contract price was received from the customer before 31 December 20X4.

Started in 20X4

Victoria Mall

This contract for a three-unit mall was completed in 20X4. The contract price of $450,000 has been billed, but $70,000 has not been received. Total costs of $423,000 were incurred.

DaVinci Apartments
The contract price was $1,825,000 and costs were estimated at $1,500,000. At the end of 20X4, the project was 15% completed and actual costs included in construction in progress were $225,000. Although progress billings were sent out for $150,000, nothing had been received by 31 December 20X4.

Discount Don's Department Store
The contract was awarded in November 20X4, but no construction has started. The cost of preparing the bid was $9,000 and this has been included in general and administrative expenses.

CASE 6-5
Mitchum Office Corporation

Mitchum Office Corporation (Mitchum) is an organization of franchised companies with its head office in Oshawa, Ontario. Mitchum is the franchise owner and licenses the franchises to individual operators, each of whom is established as a separate corporation. Each franchise sells office supplies and equipment as its primary source of revenue. Franchises mainly serve business markets in smaller cities and towns throughout Canada.

Every third year, Mitchum's head office administers a contest among all franchises, whereby the franchise showing the greatest improvement in overall performance from one year to the next receives a $90,000 award. Overall performance is measured by net income. Out of the 12 franchises in 20X3, the winner was the Lethbridge franchise, Mitchum Lethbridge Ltd. (Lethbridge).

Head office does not normally demand audited financial statements from its individual franchises for the contest. However, each franchise owner and the controller must certify that the financial statements submitted conform to generally accepted accounting principles (GAAP). Head office believes that GAAP-based financial statements are fair and comparable. Also, the franchise agreement specifies that head office reserves the right to require audited financial statements from the winner, with the auditor selected by head office. The cost of the audit is shared between head office and the winning franchise.

The selection of Lethbridge as the winner for 20X3 has been contested by another franchise, Mitchum Halifax Ltd. (Halifax). Halifax contends that the dramatic improvement reported by Lethbridge suggests manipulation of the financial statements in violation of the competition rules (see Exhibit I). Halifax was the runner-up for 20X3, with an increase in net income of 60%.

It is now March 20X4. Head office has engaged your firm, Harrison & Ford, Chartered Accountants, to assess the validity of Halifax's claim and determine whether an audit is needed. Head office would like to see how Lethbridge's income statement would appear after having been corrected for manipulations, if any. Head office also wants to know how it could improve the measurement of overall performance.

The partner in charge of the engagement has asked you to do a preliminary investigation to determine whether there are sufficient indications of financial statement manipulation to warrant a full audit. He would like you to prepare a memo for him to use in an upcoming meeting with the client. The memo should provide the results of your preliminary investigation and discuss any audit issues that could arise if an audit is found necessary. In addition, it should address the client's performance-measurement concern and any other concerns relevant to the client.

You have visited Lethbridge and have recorded notes on your discussions with Lethbridge franchise president and sole shareholder, Lisa McGovern (Exhibit II), and Lethbridge controller Jeff Fisher (Exhibit III). You have also reviewed Lethbridge's financial statements for 20X3 and 20X2, together with some additional information provided by the controller (Exhibit IV) and Lethbridge's sales by month (Exhibit V).

Required:
Prepare the memo.

EXHIBIT I

COMPETITION RULES

1. Each franchise will submit annual financial statements that have been prepared according to generally accepted accounting principles (GAAP), as attested to by the signatures of the franchise owner and controller.
2. An award of $90,000 will be given to the franchise showing the highest percentage improvement in net income, calculated as:

$$\frac{\text{Current Year Net Income} - \text{Prior Year Net Income}}{\text{Prior Year Net Income}}$$

3. If net income in the prior year is less than $60,000, net income for the prior year will be deemed to be $60,000.
4. The financial statements of the winning franchise are subject to audit, if so requested by head office. The cost of the audit will be shared between head office and the audited franchise.

EXHIBIT II

EXCERPTS FROM DISCUSSION WITH MITCHUM LETHBRIDGE PRESIDENT AND SOLE SHAREHOLDER, LISA MCGOVERN

"I'm not impressed with Halifax protesting our victory," Lisa began. "We won fair and square, and I'm sure you'll find that we have followed the rules completely. I really don't see why we should bear any part of the cost of an audit that we don't need or want.

"I attribute Lethbridge's success in 20X3 to aggressive sales promotions. Most customers are regular, repeat customers who tend to buy enough supplies for about two months at a time. In late 20X2, though, I felt that we could win the 20X3 competition based on projections for economic growth in the city and confidence in my sales staff.

"Accordingly, I began planning for Lethbridge's first big sales promotion, 'Buy in Bulk and Save a Bundle,' which ran for about two weeks in early January 20X3. If customers were willing to buy larger amounts of supplies, typically enough to last them for three to four months, they would receive a 15% discount. Because I ordered my sales staff to give the event a lot of coverage with their regular clients, and purchased a few spots on local radio stations, the January promotion was a success.

"The success of the January 20X3 promotion led to a similar promotion in December 20X3. The extra boost in sales helped put Lethbridge 'over the top' for the competition.

"While I attribute our victory to aggressive marketing and planning, I am also proud of the fact that our accounting policies have, in fact, been quite conservative."

EXHIBIT III

NOTES FROM DISCUSSION WITH MITCHUM LETHBRIDGE CONTROLLER, JEFF FISHER

"I think you will find that our accounting policies have not been in the least bit aggressive," Jeff asserted. "I've always taken a conservative stance, and I'm pleased that Lisa has supported me in doing so."

Other notes from your discussion:

1. Jeff notes that 20X2 was a bad year for the franchise. The entire town had been suffering an economic recession, and it showed in the lower sales figures. Lower sales persisted, even in the latter part of the year when the recession lifted.

2. In light of the poor 20X2 sales, Jeff felt it prudent to carefully examine the valuation of the franchise's assets. Because sales had not picked up at year-end in 20X2 as they normally did, the company was left with an abnormally high level of inventory. Jeff was not sure that Lethbridge would be able to sell the extra inventory. In case the inventory had to be liquidated on short notice, he wrote it down to a conservative estimate of its market value.
3. In addition, Lethbridge considered moving in 20X2. Doing so would have meant breaking its five-year lease, of which three years remained at the end of 20X2. Negotiations for the new property fell through in early 20X3, and the company decided to stay put for the remainder of its existing lease. Jeff had accrued the penalty on the 20X2 financial statements because, at the time, it seemed likely that the lease would be cancelled and Lethbridge would have to pay the penalty. The accrual was reversed in 20X3 when the likelihood of its payment became remote. In addition, Jeff had written off the remaining $30,000 of the company's capitalized leasehold improvements in 20X2. The write-off was charged to amortization expense.
4. Lethbridge's poor performance in 20X2 led to a reported loss on its 20X2 corporate tax return. A loss of $24,000 was carried forward, and it was used up entirely on the 20X3 return. Jeff did not believe that the benefit of the tax loss should be recorded in 20X2, and therefore the benefit of the loss-carryforward was recognized in 20X3 when it was realized.
5. To help improve the bottom line, Lisa reduced her own salary by $45,000 in 20X3.
6. Lethbridge's sales history shows that monthly sales have generally remained constant from month to month, with only minor seasonal fluctuations.

EXHIBIT IV

MITCHUM LETHBRIDGE LIMITED
BALANCE SHEET

As at December 31 (unaudited)	20X3	20X2
Cash	$ 7,500	$ 9,600
Accounts receivable	64,500	36,000
Income taxes recoverable	0	13,200
Inventory	114,000	39,000
Prepaid expenses	16,080	15,900
Long-term investment	64,500	64,500
Capital assets	234,000	271,500
Land	54,000	54,000
	$554,580	$503,700
Accounts payable	$ 26,580	$ 50,085
Salary and commissions payable	52,500	33,000
Income taxes payable	21,960	0
Lease cancellation penalty	0	15,000
Future income taxes	12,000	9,000
Due to owner	120,000	120,000
Other long-term debt	189,000	210,000
Share capital	30,000	30,000
Retained earnings	102,540	36,615
	$554,580	$503,700

EXHIBIT IV

MITCHUM LETHBRIDGE LIMITED
STATEMENTS OF INCOME AND RETAINED EARNINGS

For the years ended December 31 (unaudited)	20X3	20X2
Sales revenue	$1,306,500	$1,125,000
Cost of goods sold	723,900	675,000
Gross profit	582,600	450,000
General and administration	105,000	103,200
Salary	150,000	195,000
Commissions	80,955	89,250
Franchise fee	88,260	75,000
Amortization	46,500	75,600
Inventory writedown	0	60,000
Loss—lease cancellation	0	15,000
Investment income from shares	(18,000)	0
Investment income from land	(6,000)	0
Net income (loss) before income taxes	135,885	(163,050)
Current income tax (benefit)	21,960	(13,200)
Future income tax (benefit)	3,000	(15,000)
Net income (loss)	110,925	(134,850)
Retained earnings, beginning of year	36,615	171,465
Dividends	(45,000)	0
Retained earnings, end of year	$ 102,540	$ 36,615

Because of the poor sales at the end of 20X2, Lisa agreed to pay expected commissions for January 20X3 in December 20X2. At the end of December, sales were projected to be $150,000 for January. Accordingly, an additional $10,500 was recognized as commission expense in 20X2. Commissions are approximately 7% of gross sales.

Except for investment income, Lethbridge is subject to tax at the Canadian-controlled private corporation rate of 20%. Investment income is taxed at 44%. The annual franchise fee is $30,000 plus 10% of gross profit.

(*CICA*, adapted)

EXHIBIT V

LETHBRIDGE'S SALES BY MONTH

October 20X2	$102,000
November	97,500
December 20X2	90,000
January 20X3	114,000
February	90,000
March	87,000
April	102,000
May	105,000
June	99,000
July	107,500
August	113,000
September	114,000
October	112,000
November	90,000
December 20X3	158,000
January 20X4	75,000

(CICA)

CASE 6-6
Ceramic Protection Company Limited

Ceramic Protection Company Limited (CP) is experiencing financial difficulties. Earnings have never been strong in the six-year history of the company and CP will record operating losses in 20X6. A tax loss will also be reported. A group of key executives, primarily in the production and technology areas, is compensated by cash bonuses based on operating income before financing charges and income tax. This group will earn no bonuses in 20X6.

CP manufactures ceramic ballistic armour products that are used in personal, vehicular, and structural armour systems (e.g., bulletproof vests, armour on tanks, etc.). While its ceramic production methods were well recognized for quality, CP experienced significant technical difficulties in the early stages of a 70-unit order for tank armour from NATO for use in Kosovo. The order was produced on time and 24 additional units were ordered and delivered. However, cost overruns in the initial stages were a major driving force behind 20X6 operating losses.

To make matters worse, CP discovered in 20X6 that a procurement manager had been involved in unauthorized speculation in a commodity used in ceramic production. Significant losses were incurred in 20X4, 20X5, and 20X6 and were hidden in fictitious inventory records. Inventory and other accounts turned out to be overstated by $1,500,000.

In mid-year, one of the shareholders of CP took advantage of the weak financial position of the company and purchased all of the other shares from the remaining shareholders. Mark Fortin, a multi-millionaire from investments in the technology industry, was convinced of the long-term potential for the company. Thus, the company ended 20X6 with only one shareholder. Mr. Fortin is managing the company with an eye on cash flow, his major concern. Lenders, fully secured with company assets and Fortin's guarantees, are primarily interested in cash flow reporting and performance evaluation. Although GAAP is not a constraint, all users of the financial statements are concerned with the representational faithfulness of the financial information.

In order to stem losses, Mr. Fortin is streamlining several areas of the company. He has made, or is about to make, several decisions that will reduce the level of management personnel and reduce the diversity of manufacturing operations to specialize in certain lines of ceramics. The area of chosen emphasis will be tank armour. Certain ceramic manufacturing facilities are understood to be for sale, although no offers have yet been received.

Employee labour groups have agreed to layoffs where necessary, with the following terms:

- Severance pay equal to one month's salary for each year worked, paid monthly after severance until the entitlement is extinguished.
- In addition to the above item, bonus payment of six months' salary paid monthly over 12 months after severance.
- Pension benefits automatically vest for any severed employee, even if vesting had not legally taken place.

CP has received orders for tank armour from Australia and Israel, and production is in full gear for these orders. These orders, started in 20X6, will not be completed until 20X7, as they will take nine to 14 months to complete. The orders are paid for 50% on receipt of the signed contract for the order, 40% on delivery, and 10% one month after delivery. This latter 10% is in the nature of a holdback to ensure completion of minor fitting adjustments by CP. Management anticipates no cost overruns on these projects as the technology used is identical to that used for the NATO project.

Significantly more speculative, however, is the contract entered into with the Egyptian army. Thirty sets of armour will be produced, again over nine to 14 months of production. Each unit will cost CP approximately $95,000 to manufacture. The revenue generated will be in the range of $100,000 to $220,000 per unit, based on the customer's experience with the armour over the first 12 months of operation. Egyptian officials will run tests on the armour at the 6- and 12-month milestones, with CP's help. The better the armour performs, the higher the price paid (in essence, a bonus of up to $120,000 per unit). CP will receive the minimum price per unit ($100,000) when the order is placed with the "bonus" paid after entitlement is established (on testing) after 12 months. CP is extremely confident that it will be entitled to the maximum price, although new production operations will have to be established to meet the specifications. This will involve investing at least $200,000 to $300,000 in activities to research and develop improved production methodologies.

It is now one month before the fiscal 20X6 year-end. You are the recently hired manager of accounting. The vice-president, Finance has asked you to draft a memo to her discussing the accounting issues that CP is facing, including an analysis of alternative accounting treatments and your supported recommendations.

Required:

Prepare the memo.

(ASCA, adapted)

CASE 6-7
Jaded Jeans Limited

Jaded Jeans Limited operates a nation-wide chain of clothing stores that caters to young men and women. Jaded Jeans has been trying to obtain space in a new downtown shopping development that is extremely popular with young people. The management of Jaded Jeans feels that it is important for Jaded Jeans to have a presence in this development, even if the cost of obtaining a sublease partially offsets the potential profits for this location.

Recently, Jaded Jeans was able to negotiate a sublease with Pencil & Paper Ltd. (PP), an office supply firm that had leased a 2,000 square foot store in the development. To induce PP to sublet, Jaded Jeans agreed to pay $500,000 to PP immediately. Jaded Jeans is to make lease payments directly to the mall owner. None of the $500,000 paid to PP will go to the mall owner; the money will be retained by PP.

Jaded Jeans accounted for the $500,000 payment by charging it directly to expense for the current period. CA, the auditor of Jaded Jeans, objected to Jaded Jeans's treatment of the item and insisted that the payment be capitalized and allocated to the remaining five years of the sublease, preferably by the declining-balance method. CA argued that treating the payment as a current expense would result in mismatching revenue and expense.

The vice-president, Finance (VP) has countered by arguing that although Jaded Jeans made the payment in expectation of large future revenues and profits from the new location, there was no way that the profits could reliably be predicted (if, indeed, they materialized at all). The VP felt that just as the *CICA Handbook*, Section 3450 prescribes that research costs be charged to expense due to the uncertainty of future benefits, so should Jaded Jeans's payment be charged to expense. The VP also stated that this payment could be written off immediately for income tax purposes and wondered why he could not do the same for accounting purposes.

In addition, the VP cited arguments from accounting literature that financial accounting allocations are inherently arbitrary. Since allocations are arbitrary, he argues, they must therefore be useless at best and misleading at worst.

The VP indicated that he had just finished cleaning up his balance sheet last year by writing off the balance of intangibles and he was not anxious to introduce a major intangible amount again. He indicated that bankers and financial analysts "discount" intangibles anyway.

Required:

Discuss the arguments presented and state your conclusion as to the appropriate accounting policy for this expenditure.

(CICA, adapted)

CASE 6-8
Ottawa Orioles Limited

The Ottawa Orioles Limited (OOL) operates a professional baseball club, which won the Canadian Baseball League title in October 20X4.

The club's owners are two brothers, wealthy financiers who live in Vancouver. The club is financed about 50/50 through debt and equity. The brothers' financial goal for the club is to have it break even with its total cash flows (that is, not require infusions of operating capital from the brothers). They also wish to be associated with the glamour and excitement of major league baseball.

The following accounting issues must be addressed for the year ended 30 November 20X4.

1. OOL moved into Big Top, a newly built stadium with a retractable roof, on 1 August 20X4. Seating capacity is 70,000. The new stadium is a great improvement over the 30,000-seat NoWay Park stadium used for the preceding seven years. On 24 July 20X4, OOL signed a 10-year lease with the new stadium's owners. However, OOL's lease on the old premises was not due to expire until 1 January 20X8. OOL therefore paid $3.6 million to terminate its lease.
2. Immediately before the start of the 20X4 baseball season in April, three of the club's top players were signed to long-term contracts. Amounts of the contracts are as follows:

	Term	Salary
Frank Ferter	3 years	$1,500,000 per year
Hugh G. Blast	5 years	900,000 per year
Bill Board	4 years	1,200,000 per year

The contracts of Ferter and Blast specify that if they suffer a career-ending injury, their contracts will become null and void. Board's contract is guaranteed for the full term.

On 27 April 20X4, Board was injured, forcing him to retire from playing baseball. As required by his contract, he has since been moved to the front office and is performing public relations and administrative services. Other equivalent PR staff are paid $50,000–$60,000 per annum.

Ferter has a bonus clause in his contract under which he will be paid $50,000 if he is selected to play for the All Star Team. Although he is favoured to capture this honour in 20X4, the selections will not be announced until after the financial statements will have been issued.

Because of Ferter's exceptional ability and the fact that he is considered a "player who will increase the popularity of the sport in this city for many years to come," management proposes to amortize the total cost of his contract ($4,500,000) over a 10-year period.

3. On 3 October 20X4, the day before the last playoff game, a wind storm caused the roof at Big Top to collapse, resulting in structural damage of $4,500,000 to the stadium. This damage will be paid for by OOL, under the terms of their lease agreement. This unforeseen event forced OOL's last playoff game to be played at NoWay Park. Hence, the club announced that some of the 70,000 tickets sold for Big Top could be used at NoWay Park and that the $35 cost of the remaining tickets could either be refunded or applied toward the cost of tickets for any of OOL's pre-season games next year. Also, the 40,000 fans who could not attend the game at NoWay were given $10 gift certificates that could be used toward purchasing tickets for any future OOL game. The rate and the extent to which these gift certificates will be redeemed is uncertain at 30 November 20X4. What is certain is that the fans who were left seatless were very upset, and talked about a boycott of the 20X5 season.

Required:

Write a report that evaluates the accounting issues raised and includes your recommendations.

(CICA, adapted)

CASE 6-9
Triple B Security

Triple B Security (TripleB) is a general partnership that was formed and is operating in a Canadian city. TripleB is owned and operated by three brothers, George, Henry, and Gordon Bishop. The brothers started TripleB 15 years ago, when they opened a centre to monitor security systems. TripleB provides the initial response when an alarm goes off at customers' business premises or homes, throughout the city.

TripleB follows an aggressive expansion strategy that includes acquiring customer contracts from competing monitoring services. The customers are immediately converted to TripleB's trademark and operating name.

As a condition of a refinancing agreement, TripleB is required to provide annual audited financial statements within 60 days of its fiscal year-end. TripleB has never previously been audited. Its prior year financial statements were prepared by TripleB's accountant, Todd Cook, for tax purposes only.

You are an audit senior with Stavness and Folk Chartered Accountants (SF). You and a partner in your firm recently met with the three Bishop brothers and Todd Cook to discuss the changes to TripleB's financial reporting requirements in light of the recent developments. George provided you with the unaudited financial statements for the year ended 31 January, 20X2, and for the nine months ended 31 October, 20X2. These statements are shown in Exhibit I, and notes related to financial statement items are in Exhibit II.

The partner has asked you to prepare a draft report for the client outlining accounting issues relevant to the 2003 audit engagement.

Required.
Prepare the report.

EXHIBIT I

TRIPLE B SECURITY
BALANCE SHEET

(unaudited)	October 31, 20X2	January 31, 20X2
Assets		
Current assets		
Cash	$ 395,427	$ –
Trade accounts receivable	254,148	271,976
Current portion of notes and advances	76,000	30,148
Prepaid expenses	51,810	47,713
	777,385	349,837
Notes and advances	–	76,000
Investment in customer contracts	2,675,356	2,447,126
Capital assets	851,159	558,466
	$4,303,900	$3,431,429
Liabilities		
Current liabilities		
Bank advance	$ –	$ 87,433
Accounts payable and accrued liabilities	252,002	283,504
Current portion of obligations under capital lease	11,014	106,814
Current portion of long-term debt	536,000	505,990
	898,150	983,741
Obligations under capital leases	248,399	334,014
Long-term debt	1,081,524	1,066,996
	2,228,073	2,384,751
Partners' equity		
Partners' equity	2,075,827	1,046,678
	$4,303,900	$3,431,429

TRIPLE B SECURITY

Income and Partners' Equity Statement

(unaudited)	9 Months Ended October 31, 20X2	Year Ended January 31, 20X2
Revenue	$2,992,466	$ 2,627,227
Direct expenses		
Monitoring costs	1,737,953	1,497,699
Amortization of investment in customer contracts	112,630	136,520
	1,141,883	993,008
Administrative and general expenses	630,826	514,417
Interest on long-term debt	106,763	65,397
Amortization of capital assets	65,145	42,552
Net income	339,149	370,642
Partners' equity, beginning of period	1,046,678	676,036
Partners' contributions	690,000	–
Partners' equity, end of period	$2,075,827	$1,046,678

EXHIBIT II

NOTES RELATED TO FINANCIAL STATEMENT ITEMS

Lawsuits
TripleB is being sued by several of its larger customers because of a system failure that occurred on 28 April, 20X1. TripleB's customers are claiming that other private security services were required during the period when TripleB's security systems failed. Management's position is that the system failure was caused by a lightning storm and therefore TripleB is not responsible. TripleB has not accrued any amount for these lawsuits because management believes it can defend its position.

Revenue
Large business and wholesale customers are billed in advance monthly or quarterly for monitoring services. Revenue is recognized when billed. Experience has shown that bad debt expense is low for these customers because they view security monitoring as an essential service.

TripleB's residential customers pay by one of two methods: pre-authorized monthly debit from their bank account or prepayment of an annual amount. When customers prepay their annual fee, TripleB allows a 5% discount from the fee. Upon receiving payment, TripleB recognizes revenue for the amount received. The contract terms range from one to three years.

TripleB issues a refund cheque to customers who cancel their monitoring service partway through the prepaid period. These payments are debited to revenue when paid. Customer refunds are approximately $375,000 for the nine months ended October 31, 20X2.

Investment in customer contracts
TripleB's aggressive expansion strategy has led management to acquire competing security-monitoring customer contracts at a premium. The purchase amount is booked to the "investment in customer contracts" account. TripleB commissioned a market research study that concluded that the average customer stays with TripleB for seven years.

(CICA, adapted)

ASSIGNMENTS

A6-1 Revenue Recognition: For each of the following independent items, indicate when revenue should be recognized.

a. Interest on loans made by a financial institution, receivable in annual payments.
b. Interest on loans made by a financial institution, receivable in three years when the customer, who has an excellent credit rating, will make payment.
c. Interest on loans made by a financial institution, where the loans are in default and payment of principal and interest is highly uncertain.
d. Recognition of revenue from the cash sale of airline tickets, where the travel purchased will occur in the next fiscal period.
e. Transportation of freight by a trucking company for a customer; the customer is expected to make payment in accordance with the terms of the invoice in 60 days.
f. Growing, harvesting, and marketing of Christmas trees; the production cycle is 10 years.
g. Building houses in a subdivision, where the project will take two years to complete and each house must be individually sold by the contractor.
h. Building houses in a subdivision, where the project will take two years to complete and the contractor is building the houses under a contract from the local government.
i. Selling undeveloped lots for future retirement homes in a western province, with very low down payment and long-term contracts.
j. Sale of a two-year parking permit by a parking garage, with one-half the sale price received on the sale, and the remainder to be received in equal monthly payments over the period of the permit.
k. A fixed-price contract with the government to design and build a prototype of a space arm; the costs to complete the project cannot be reliably estimated.
l. A silver-mining company produces one million ounces of silver but stores the silver in a vault and waits for silver prices to increase.

A6-2 Revenue Recognition—Four Cases: The York Lumber Company had been involved in the following transactions:

a. The value of goods delivered to customers was $600,000, of which two-thirds was collected by the end of 20X5; the balance will be collected in 20X6.
b. Regular services were rendered on credit amounting to $500,000, of which three-fifths will be collected in 20X6.
c. On 1 January 20X4, the company purchased a $10,000 note as a speculative investment. Because the collectibility of the note was highly speculative, the company was able to acquire it for $1,000 cash. The note specifies 8% simple interest payable each year (disregard interest prior to 20X4). The first collection on the note was $1,500 cash on 31 December 20X5. Further collections continue to be highly speculative.
d. An item that had been repossessed from the first purchaser and carried in inventory at $8,000 was sold again for $10,000 in 20X5. A $5,000 cash down payment was received in 20X5. The balance is to be paid on a quarterly basis during 20X6 and 20X7. Repossession again would not be a surprise.

Required:

For each of the following 20X5 transactions, write a brief one- or two-paragraph explanation, stating

1. The amount of revenue that you believe should be recognized during 20X5, and
2. An explanation of the basis for revenue recognition.

A6-3 Revenue Recognition—Three Cases: Three independent cases are given below for 20X5. The accounting period ends 31 December.

Case A. On 31 December 20X5, Zulu Sales Company sold a machine for $100,000 and collected $40,000 cash. The remainder plus 10% interest is payable 31 December 20X6. Zulu will deliver the machine on 5 January 20X6. The buyer has an excellent credit rating.

Case B. On 15 November 20X5, Victor Cement Company sold a tonne of its product for $500. The cement was delivered on that date. The buyer will pay for the product with two units of its own merchandise that are commonly sold for $250 each. The buyer promised to deliver the merchandise around 31 January 20X6.

Case C. On 2 January 20X5, Remer Publishing Company collected $900 cash for a three-year subscription to a monthly magazine, *Investor's Stock and Bond Advisory*. The March 20X5 issue will be the first one mailed.

Required:
Write a brief report covering the following:

1. The revenue recognition method that should be used.
2. Any entry that should be made on the transaction date.
3. An explanation of the reasoning for your responses to requirements (1) and (2).

A6-4 Revenue Recognition—Accounting Estimates: TaCheng Building Systems Incorporated is a construction contractor that specializes in high-tech building projects, that is, buildings that must incorporate a high level of technology such as hospitals, interactive learning centres, and chemical processing plants. The company has considerable experience in constructing buildings that must incorporate cutting-edge technology. The contracts usually are turn-key applications, in which the building and its technology must be ready for use the day that the tenant moves in. TaCheng works closely with the client throughout design and the construction process. The contract provides for incorporating changes during construction due to technological improvements that arise while construction is underway. Any changes in specifications or updating normally will require a change in the value of the contract. TaCheng uses the percentage-of-completion method of accounting.

Required:
Explain what accounting estimates TaCheng managers must make at the end of each reporting period in order to apply the percentage-of-completion method.

A6-5 Revenue Recognition—Accounting Estimates: As we perform a specific task, we get better and more efficient at that task (even at solving accounting problems!). This basic principle was quantified in the aircraft industry many decades ago, and is known as a learning curve. Learning curves also have been applied extensively in other industries such as automobile manufacturing.

A learning curve is a downward-sloping curve that is based on a prediction of constantly increasing efficiency. (For those students who are mathematically inclined, a learning curve is a logarithmic straight line.) Learning curves are used to predict the costs of aircraft production for planning and cost control purposes.

The notes to the 2003 financial statements of Bombardier Incorporated disclose the following information regarding accounting policies for revenue and expense recognition:

> Average unit cost for commercial and business aircraft is determined based on the estimated total production costs for a predetermined program quantity. Program quantities are established based on Management's assessment of market conditions and foreseeable demand at the beginning of the production stage for each program, taking into consideration, among other factors, existing firm orders and options. The average unit cost is recorded to cost of sales at the time of each aircraft delivery. Under the learning curve concept, which anticipates a

predictable decrease in unit costs as tasks and production techniques become more efficient through repetition and management action, excess over-average production costs during the early stages of a program are deferred and recovered from sales of aircraft anticipated to be produced later at lower-than-average costs.

Required:

Explain what estimates management must make in order to use the accounting policies described in Bombardier's notes. Note that while a particular type of airplane has a list price, the actual sales price is separately negotiated with each individual buyer.

A6-6 Revenue Recognition: Assume that in 20X5, the Public Utilities Board (PUB) issued a ruling raising the ceiling price on regulated gas, but with a "vintaging" system: gas suppliers could charge $1.42 per thousand cubic feet on "new gas" drilled after 1 January 20X5, and $1.01 on gas (now in inventory) drilled between 1 January 20X3 and 31 December 20X4. The old price had been 52 cents per thousand cubic feet and remained at this for all "old" gas (i.e., pre-20X3 gas). The PUB soon reduced the $1.01 rate to 93 cents but retained the $1.42 rate. As a result of a lawsuit by consumers against the PUB seeking a rollback to the old 52-cent rate, a court of appeal decided that gas suppliers should go ahead and collect the higher prices provided they would agree to refund the money if the final decision went against the PUB.

Required:

1. If you were part of the management of a gas supplier at the time of the court decision, what position would you take with respect to recognition of the extra amounts of revenue from the sale of new gas? Give reasons for whatever position you take.
2. Disregard the answer you gave to (1) above. If the revenue is deferred, explain how the deferral would affect the financial statements until a final court decision is rendered. How would the deferred revenue be recognized if the final court decision is delayed until a new accounting year and then is favourable?

A6-7 Magazine Subscription Revenue: At a meeting of the Board of Directors of Vanguard Publishing Company, where you are the controller, a new director expressed surprise that the company's income statement indicates that an equal proportion of revenue is earned with the publication of each issue of the magazines the company publishes. This director believes that the most important event in the sale of magazines is the collection of cash on the subscriptions and expresses the view that the company's practice smoothes its income. He has suggested that subscription revenue should be recognized as subscriptions are collected.

Required:

Discuss the propriety of timing the recognition of revenue on the basis of

1. Cash collections on subscriptions.
2. Publication of issues, concurrent with delivery to customers.
3. Both events, by recognizing part of the revenue with cash collections of subscriptions and part with delivery of the magazines to subscribers.

(AICPA, adapted)

A6-8 Revenue Recognition: Shawinegan Development Company (SDC) conducts research and development on specific projects under contract for clients; SDC also conducts basic research and attempts to market any new products or technologies it develops.

In January 20X4, scientists at SDC began research to develop a new industrial cleaner. During 20X4, $2,340,000 of costs were incurred in this effort. Late in July 20X5, potentially promising results emerged in the form of a substance the company called Scourge. Costs incurred through the end of July 20X5 were $1,260,000. At this point, SDC attempted to sell the formula of and rights to Scourge to Pride and Glory Industries Limited (P&G), for $15,000,000.

P&G, however, was reluctant to sign before further testing was done. It did wish, though, to have the first option to acquire the rights and formulas to Scourge if future testing showed the product to be profitable. SDC was very confident that Scourge would pass further testing with flying colours. Accordingly, the two companies signed an option agreement that allowed P&G to acquire the formulas and rights to Scourge any time before 31 December 20X6. Testing costs on the product incurred by SDC for the remainder of 20X5 amounted to $1,620,000.

In early 20X6, P&G exercised its option and agreed to purchase the formulas and rights to Scourge for $15,000,000. P&G paid $750,000 immediately with the balance payable in five equal annual instalments on 31 December 20X6 to 20X10. The formula was to be completed and delivered within 18 months.

In April 20X7, SDC delivered the formulas and samples of Scourge to P&G Industries. Additional costs incurred by SDC during 20X6 amounted to $540,000; in 20X7, $180,000.

Required:

1. When should revenue be recognized by SDC from its work on Scourge? Why?
2. Assume that the total costs of $5,940,000 actually incurred by SDC over the years 20X4 to 20X6 were accurately estimated in 20X4. Determine the amount of revenue and expense that should be recognized each year from 20X4 to 20X10, assuming revenue is to be recognized:
   a. At the time the option is signed.
   b. At the time the option is exercised.
   c. At the time the formulas are delivered.
   d. As cash is collected (use the instalment method).

Note that the $1,560,000 of research costs must be expensed in all alternatives to comply with accounting standards for research costs. Other costs may be deferred if appropriate. Do not attempt to do journal entries; your solution should focus on income statement presentation.

★★★

A6-9 Entries for Critical Events: Maypole Industries imports goods from Taiwan and resells them to domestic Canadian markets. Maypole uses a perpetual inventory system. A typical transaction stream follows:

18 July	Purchased goods for $456,000 (Canadian dollars)
24 August	Goods repackaged and ready for sale. Cost incurred, $60,000
10 September	Goods delivered to customer. Agreed-on price, $712,000
22 November	Customer paid

Required:

1. Prepare journal entries assuming the following critical events:
   a. Delivery to customer.
   b. Cash receipt.
   c. Preparation of goods for resale.
2. Explain the circumstances under which each of these methods would be appropriate.

A6-10 Entries for Critical Events: Dominum Corporation is a mining company that mines, produces, and markets teledine, a common mineral substance. The mineral is mined and produced in one large batch per year, as the mine is accessible only for a brief period in the summer due to severe weather conditions at the mine site. Transactions in 20X6:

30 August	186,000 tonnes of ore removed from mine, at a cost of $4,300,000
30 September	Ore refined to 95,000 tonnes of teledine, at a cost of $530,000
15 October	Teledine delivered to 25 customers, total contract price, $11,050,000

25 October	Teledine returned for full credit; ore improperly refined and teledine unusable; customer given full credit for $475,000 and unusable product scrapped. No other returns are anticipated.
30 November	Customers all paid except one that went bankrupt still owing $96,000

Required:

1. Prepare journal entries for
   a. 30 September
   b. 15 October
   c. 25 October

   Assume at each of these dates that the company can make appropriate, accurate accruals for future events such as sales returns and bad debts, if needed.
2. Explain the point at which net assets change for each alternative in requirement (1).
3. Explain the circumstances under which revenue recognition at each of these dates would be appropriate.

A6-11 Critical Event; Financial Statements: In each case below, several balance sheet accounts are presented. Determine, based on this information, the likely point at which revenue has been recognized.

Case A	
Inventory, at market value	$ 367,300
Accrued selling costs	31,900
Allowance for estimated sales returns	16,400
Case B	
Inventory, at cost	$ 566,300
Accounts receivable	1,040,000
Allowance for doubtful accounts	119,600
Deferred gross margin	249,700
Case C	
Accounts receivable	$ 2,567,700
Allowance for doubtful accounts	359,100
Inventory, at cost	1,876,400
Warranty liability	341,100

A6-12 Unconditional Right of Return: In 20X5, Balla Shoe Corporation developed a new product, an electric shoe tree. To increase acceptance by retailers, Balla sold the product to retailers with an unconditional right of return, which expires on 1 February 20X6. Balla has no basis for estimating returns on the new product. The following information is available regarding the product:

Sales—20X5	$360,000	
Cost of goods sold—20X5	240,000	
Returns—20X5	24,000	(cost, $16,000)
Returns—January 20X6	30,000	(cost, $20,000)

All sales are on credit. Cash collections related to the sales were $80,000 in 20X5 and $226,000 in 20X6. Balla uses a perpetual inventory system.

Required:

Give journal entries for sales, returns, and collections related to the new product. Include the entry made on 1 February 20X6 when the right of return expires. How much sales revenue should Balla recognize in 20X5?

A6-13 Unconditional Right of Return: McLaughlin Novelty Corporation developed an unusual product, electric clip-on eyeglass wipers. McLaughlin felt the product would appeal to hikers, joggers, and cyclists who engaged in their sports in rainy climates. Because retail establishments were skeptical about the market appeal of the product, McLaughlin sold the product with a declining unconditional right of return for up to 10 months, with 10% of the right-of-return amount of the purchase expiring each month for 10 months. Thus, after the retailer had the product for one month, only 90% could be returned. After two months, only 80% could be returned, and after 10 months, the right of return was fully expired.

McLaughlin had no basis for estimating the amount of returns. Consistent with the terms McLaughlin offered its customers, all retailers paid cash when purchasing the clip-on eyeglass wipers but received cash refunds if goods were returned. McLaughlin had its first sales of the product in September 20X5. Sales for the remainder of the year, and returns prior to 31 December 20X5, were as follows:

Month of Sale	Units Sold	Sales Price	Monthly Sales	Units Returned
September	10,000	$10	$100,000	2,500
October	12,000	10	120,000	1,000
November	15,000	12	180,000	1,000
December	11,000	12	132,000	0
Totals	48,000		$532,000	4,500

Each unit of product costs McLaughlin $6 to produce.

Required:

1. Show the journal entries to record the four months of sales transactions, including the deferral of gross margin. Prepare one summary entry.
2. Show a summary entry to record the returns in 20X5.
3. Compute the amount that McLaughlin can record as (realized) sales for 20X5. How much is gross margin? Record the revenue recognition entry.
4. For the above transactions, total returns in all of 20X6 were as follows:

Month of Sale	Units Returned
September	1,000
October	2,000
November	2,500
December	4,000

Show the entries to record the returns in 20X6 and to record sales revenue and cost of sales from the 20X5 shipments of this product.

A6-14 Revenue Recognition: Fly and Mattox, a professional corporation, contracted to provide, as required, all legal services for Brown Company until the end of 20X5. The contract specified a lump-sum payment of $60,000 on 15 November 20X4. Assume that Fly and Mattox can reliably estimate future direct costs associated with the contract. The following services were performed based on the estimate by Fly and Mattox:

	Direct Costs	Date Completed
Research potential lawsuit	$ 5,000	15 December 20X4
Prepare and file documents	15,000	1 March 20X5
Serve as Brown's counsel during legal proceedings	15,000	15 October 20X5

Required:

1. When should Fly and Mattox recognize revenue in this situation? Explain.
2. Give entries to recognize revenues related to this contract for Fly and Mattox.

A6-15 Critical Event: BC Corporation sells large pieces of construction equipment. The company had the following three sales in 20X5:

	Sales Amount	Cost of Goods Sold	Other Information
Byron Foods	$345,700	$210,000	Unlimited right of return until 30 June 20X6. Extent of returns is not estimable.
Addison Roads	$?	$166,800	Price to be determined after Addison has use of the equipment for six months: to be determined based on revenue generated and operating costs. BC believes that the sales price will likely be in the range of $200,000 to $230,000, but has no previous experience with this kind of contract.
Carson Construction	$567,000	$399,000	Collection contingent on Carson's continued operations; company close to bankruptcy. Title to equipment still in BC's name so that assets would not be lost in bankruptcy; Carson paid $50,000 up front as security. Balance to be paid within 12 months.

Required:

1. At what point should BC recognize revenue for each of the above sales transactions?
2. Show how the transactions would be reflected in the 20X5 balance sheet and income statement.

A6-16 Critical Event: Manzer Manufacturing had transactions in 20X6 as follows:

30 June	Purchased inventory, $378,000.
17 July	Sale to customer, $271,000, on account. Cost of goods sold, $164,500.
15 September	Warranty work of $20,000 was performed.
30 November	Customer returns $29,000 of goods for full credit; goods were spoiled and worthless.
15 December	Customer paid all outstanding amounts.

All goods were sold with unlimited right of return for 60 days and a one-year warranty. Manzer's year-end is 31 December.

Required:

1. Prepare 20X6 entries to record the above transactions assuming that the critical event is deemed to be
   a. The date of delivery.
   b. The date that the warranty expires.
   c. The date that the return privilege expires.

   If necessary, assume that total warranty cost can be estimated to be $41,000, and returns, $29,000.
2. Show how the income statement and balance sheet would reflect each of the alternatives in (1).
3. Comment on the relative timing of the increase in net assets.

A6-17 Instalment Sales Method: Bernice Corporation had credit sales of $60,000 in 20X5 that required use of the instalment method. Bernice's cost of merchandise sold was $45,000. Barr collected cash related to the instalment sales of $24,000 in 20X5 and $30,000 in 20X6. A perpetual inventory system is used.

Required:

1. What circumstances would dictate use of the instalment sales method?
2. Give journal entries related to the instalment sales for 20X5 and 20X6.
3. Give the ending 20X5 balances in the following accounts: instalment accounts receivable, instalment sales revenue, cost of instalment sales, and deferred gross margin on instalment sales.

A6-18 Instalment Sales: Baxter Land Corporation made a number of sales in 20X4 and 20X5 that required use of the instalment method. The following information regarding the sales is available:

	20X4	20X5	20X6
Instalment sales	$200,000	$150,000	$ 0
Cost of instalment sales	160,000	112,500	0
Collections on 20X4 sales	40,000	50,000	60,000
Collections on 20X5 sales		30,000	75,000

Baxter uses a perpetual inventory system.

Required:

1. Give journal entries relating to instalment sales for the years 20X4 to 20X6.
2. What is the year-end balance in instalment accounts receivable (net of any deferred gross margin) for 20X4, 20X5, and 20X6?
3. If the sales qualified for revenue recognition on the date of sale (i.e., delivery), what amounts of gross margin would Baxter report in 20X4, 20X5, and 20X6?

A6-19 Instalment Sales Method: Ontario Retail Company sells goods for cash, and on normal credit terms of 30 days. However, on 1 July 20X4, the company sold a used computer for $2,200; the inventory carrying value was $440. The company collected $200 cash and agreed to let the customer make payments on the $2,000 whenever possible during the next 12 months. The company management stated that it had no reliable basis for estimating the probability of default. The following additional data are available: (a) collections on the instalment receivable during 20X4 were $300 and during 20X5 were $200, and (b) on 1 December 20X5, Ontario Retail repossessed the computer (estimated net realizable value, $700).

Required:

1. Give the required entries for 20X4 and 20X5; assume that the instalment method is used.
2. Give the balances in the following accounts that would be reported on the 20X4 and 20X5 income statements and balance sheets: instalment sales revenue and cost of sales, instalment accounts receivable, and inventory of used computers.
3. How much profit would be recognized in 20X4 and 20X5 if the cost recovery method is used?

A6-20 Cost Recovery Method: The Trusett Merchandising Company has an inventory of obsolete products that it formerly stocked for sale. Efforts to dispose of this inventory by selling the products at low prices have not been successful. At the end of the prior year (20X4), the company reduced the value to a conservative estimate of net realizable value of $22,000. On 1 March 20X6, Watson Trading Company purchased this entire inventory for $10,000 cash as a speculative investment. Watson hopes to be able to dispose of it in some foreign markets for approximately $30,000. However, prior to purchase, Watson concluded that there was no reliable way to estimate the probable profitability of the venture. Therefore, Watson decided to use the cost recovery method. Subsequent cash sales have been as follows: 20X6, $4,000; 20X7, $5,000; and 20X8, $8,000. Approximately 12% of the inventory remains on hand at the start of 20X9.

Required:

Give the 20X6, 20X7, and 20X8 entries for Watson Trading Company to record revenues and cost of sales.

A6-21 Cost Recovery Method: Slatt Department Store has accumulated a stock of obsolete merchandise. Routine efforts have been made to dispose of it at a low price. This merchandise originally cost $60,000 and was marked to sell for $132,000. Management decided to set up a special location in the basement to display and (it was hoped) sell this stock starting in January 20X5. All items will be marked to sell at a cash price that is 30% of the original marked selling price. On 31 December 20X4, the company accountant transferred the purchase cost to a perpetual inventory account called "inventory, obsolete merchandise," at 30% of its purchase cost, which approximates estimated net realizable value. Management knows that a reliable estimate of the probable sales cannot be made. Therefore, the cost recovery method will be used. Subsequent sales were $9,000 in 20X5 and $7,000 in 20X6, and in 20X7 the remaining merchandise was sold for $8,000.

Required:

Give the entries that Slatt should make for 20X4 through 20X7.

A6-22 Instalment and Cost Recovery Methods: Beaver Limited is a retail company that sells goods for cash and on normal credit terms of 30 days. On 1 March 20X0, the company sold merchandise for $1,500 that cost $900. Management has stated it has no reliable basis on which to determine the collectibility of the account. The company collected $500 when the sale was made and agreed to allow the customer to make payments whenever possible over the next 12 months. On 14 September 20X0, the customer made a payment of $300.

Required:

1. Prepare the entries for the above transactions assuming the instalment sales method is used.
2. If the sale qualified for revenue recognition on the date of delivery, what amount of gross profit would be recognized in the year 20X2?
3. If the sale is accounted for by the cost recovery method, what amount of gross profit would be recognized in the year 20X2?

(CGA-Canada)

A6-23 Instalment, Delivery, and Cost Recovery Methods: Purple Limited uses the instalment sales method to recognize revenue on its sales to its customers. During August, instalment sales of $160,000 were recorded. The gross profit margin on instalment sales is 20%. During the month of September, $45,000 is collected on the previous month's instalment sales.

Required:

1. Prepare the entries to record the transactions for the instalment sales of $160,000 and the subsequent collection of $45,000.
2. Explain the impact on Purple's financial statements for the two months ending 30 September, assuming revenue is earned at delivery instead of on an instalment basis.
3. Explain the impact on Purple's financial statements for the two months ending 30 September, assuming revenue is reported by the cost recovery method instead of on an instalment basis.

(CGA-Canada, adapted)

A6-24 Recognition at Production, Delivery, and Cash Receipt: Korea Limited produces briefcases at a cost of $80 each. In June 20X7, Korea signed a contract with Seoul Incorporated to manufacture 10,000 briefcases for delivery to Seoul between July 20X7 and 31 December 20X9. The value of the contract is $1,500,000 (that is, $150 per briefcase) and is payable at the rate of $500,000 on 31 December for each of the next three years, beginning on 31 December 20X7.

A summary of the number of briefcases manufactured and delivered under this contract is as follows:

	Manufactured	Delivered
20X7	2,000	1,500
20X8	5,000	4,500
20X9	3,000	4,000

Required:

Calculate the amount of gross profit to be recognized in each of 20X7, 20X8, and 20X9 under each of the following three independent revenue recognition policies:

1. Revenue is recognized as production is completed.
2. Revenue is recognized as goods are delivered.
3. Revenue is recognized as cash is received.

Which of the three methods of revenue recognition would you recommend for Korea to use for its contract with Seoul? Explain why, and state any assumptions that you make.

(CGA-Canada)

A6-25 Completed-Contract and Percentage-of-Completion Methods Compared: Watson Construction Company contracted to build a plant for $500,000. Construction started in January 20X4 and was completed in November 20X5. Data relating to the contract are summarized below:

	20X4	20X5
Costs incurred during year	$290,000	$120,000
Estimated additional costs to complete	125,000	—
Billings during year	270,000	230,000
Cash collections during year	250,000	250,000

Required:

1. Give the journal entries for Watson in parallel columns, assuming (a) the completed-contract method and (b) the percentage-of-completion method. Use costs incurred to date divided by total estimated construction costs to measure percentage completed.

2. Complete the following table:

	Completed-Contract Method	Percentage-of-Completion Method
Income statement:		
Income:		
20X4	$	$
20X5	$	$
Balance sheet:		
Receivables:		
20X4	$	$
20X5	$	$
Inventory—construction in progress, net of billings:		
20X4	$	$
20X5	$	$

★★

A6-26 Completed-Contract and Percentage-of-Completion Methods Compared: Mullen Construction Company contracted to build a municipal warehouse for the city of Moncton for $750,000. The contract specified that the city would pay Mullen each month the progress billings, less 10%, which was to be held as a retention reserve. At the end of the construction, the final payment would include the reserve. Each billing, less the 10% reserve, must be paid 10 days after submission of a billing to the city. Transactions relating to the contract are summarized below:

20X4 Construction costs incurred during the year, $210,000; estimated costs to complete, $390,000; progress billing, $190,000; and collections per the contract.

20X5 Construction costs incurred during the year, $342,000; estimated costs to complete, $138,000; progress billings, $280,000; and collections per the contract. A contract change during 20X5 increased the total contract revenue to $800,000.

20X6 Construction costs incurred during the year, $148,000. The remaining billings were submitted by 1 October and final collections completed on 30 November.

Required:

1. Complete the following table:

Year	Method	Net Income Recognized	Contract Receivables, Ending Balance	Construction-in-Progress Inventory, Ending Balance
20X4	Completed contact	$	$	$
	Percentage of completion*			
20X5	Completed contract			
	Percentage of completion*			
20X6	Completed contract			
	Percentage of completion*			

* Use costs incurred to date divided by total estimated construction costs to measure percentage of completion.

2. Explain what causes the ending balance in construction-in-progress to be different for the two methods.
3. Which method would you recommend for this contractor? Why?

A6-27 Completed-Contract and Percentage-of-Completion Methods Compared: Pedlar Construction Company contracted to build an apartment building for $2,800,000. Construction began in October 20X4 and was scheduled to be completed in April 20X6. Pedlar has a 31 December year-end. Data related to the contract are summarized below:

($ thousands)

	20X4	20X5	20X6
Costs incurred during year	$ 400	$1,500	$ 700
Estimated additional costs to complete	2,200	400	—
Billings during year	350	1,450	1,000
Cash collections during year	325	1,300	1,175

Required:

1. Prepare the journal entries for Pedlar, assuming the completed-contract method.
2. Prepare the journal entries for Pedlar, assuming the percentage-of-completion method. Use costs incurred to date divided by total estimated construction costs to measure percentage complete. Round your estimate of revenue to the nearest thousand.

A6-28 Completed-Contract and Percentage-of-Completion Methods Compared: Star Construction Corporation has a contract to construct a building for $7,300,000. Total costs to complete the building were originally estimated at $5,900,000. Construction commenced on 4 February 20X5. Total construction costs incurred in each year were as follows:

20X5	$1,700,000
20X6	$3,100,000
20X7	$1,200,000

Actual costs were in line with estimated costs until 20X7, when actual costs exceeded estimated costs by $100,000. The additional costs reduced the total gross profit on the project from an estimated $1,400,000 to $1,300,000. Progress billings based on the amount of work completed were collected each year. The percentage of completion is based on costs incurred compared to estimated total costs of the project.

Required:

1. Calculate the revenues and gross profit for the construction project for each of the three years, assuming:
   a. Star Construction uses the percentage-of-completion method.
   b. Star Construction uses the completed-contract method.
2. Prepare the journal entry for 20X6 for recognition of revenue, using the percentage-of-completion method.

(CGA-Canada)

A6-29 Long-Term Construction—Percentage-of-Completion Method: Thrasher Construction Company contracted to construct a building for $975,000. The contract provided for progress payments. Thrasher's accounting year ends 31 December. Work began under the contract on 1 July 20X5, and was completed on 30 September 20X7. Construction activities are summarized below by year:

20X5 Construction costs incurred during the year, $180,000; estimated costs to complete, $630,000; progress billings during the year, $153,000; and collections, $140,000.

20X6 Construction costs incurred during the year, $450,000; estimated costs to complete, $190,000; progress billing during the year, $382,500; and collections, $380,000.

20X7 Construction costs incurred during the year, $195,000. Because the contract was completed, the remaining balance was billed and later collected in full per the contract.

Required:

1. Give Thrasher's entries assuming that the percentage-of-completion method is used. Assume that percentage of completion is measured by the ratio of costs incurred to date divided by total estimated construction costs.
2. Prepare income statement and balance sheet presentation for this contract by year; assume that the percentage-of-completion method is used.
3. Prepare income statement and balance sheet presentation by year; assume that the completed-contract method is used. For each amount that is different from the corresponding amount in (2), explain why it is different.
4. Which method would you recommend to this contractor? Why?

A6-30 Long-Term Construction: Methods Compared: Wallen Corporation contracted to construct an office building for Ragee Company for $1,000,000. Construction began on 15 January 20X4, and was completed on 1 December 20X5. Wallen's accounting year ends 31 December. Transactions by Wallen relating to the contract are summarized below:

	20X4	20X5
Costs incurred to date	$400,000	$ 850,000
Estimated costs to complete	420,000	—
Progress billings to date	410,000	1,000,000
Progress collections to date	375,000	1,000,000

Required:

1. In parallel columns, give the entries on the contractor's books. Assume
   a. The completed contract method, and
   b. The percentage-of-completion method.

   Assume that percentage of completion is measured by the ratio of costs incurred to date divided by total estimated construction costs.
2. For each method, prepare the income statement and balance sheet presentation for this contract by year.
3. What is the nature of the item "costs in excess of billings" that would appear on the balance sheet?
4. Which method would you recommend that the contractor use? Why?

A6-31 Percentage-of-Completion and Completed-Contract Methods: Banks Construction Company contracted to build an office block for $3,200,000. Construction began in September 20X4 and was scheduled to be completed in May 20X6. Banks has a 31 December year-end. Data related to the contract are summarized below:

($ thousands)	20X4	20X5	20X6
Costs incurred during year	$ 500	$1,800	$ 850
Estimated additional costs to complete	2,500	800	0
Billings during year	450	1,300	1,450
Cash collections during year	400	1,100	1,700

Required:

1. Prepare the journal entries for Banks, assuming the completed-contract method.
2. Prepare the balance sheet and income presentation for this contract by year, assuming the completed-contract method is used.
3. Prepare the journal entries for Banks, assuming the percentage-of-completion method. Use costs incurred to date divided by total estimated construction costs to measure percentage complete.
4. Prepare the balance sheet and income presentation for this contract by year, assuming the percentage-of-completion method is used.

A6-32 Expense Recognition: XYZ Company recorded a series of recent transactions, in chronological order, as follows:

Date	Entry #			
2 June	1	Inventory	165,000	
		Accounts payable		165,000
	2	Prepaid insurance	3,600	
		Cash		3,600
	3	Inventory	56,000	
		Cost of goods sold	60,000	
		Sales		116,000
	4	Warranty expense	9,000	
		Estimated liability for warranty		9,000
2 June	5	Commissions expense	11,600	
		Commissions payable		11,600
20 June	6	Accounts receivable	116,000	
		Inventory		116,000
30 June	7	Cash	116,000	
		Accounts receivable		116,000
	8	Insurance expense	400	
		Prepaid insurance		400
	9	Accounts payable	165,000	
		Cash		165,000
	10	Estimated liability for warranty	3,000	
		Cash		3,000

Required:

1. Explain the effect that each entry has on net assets. What is the revenue recognition point?
2. For each asset recognized above, explain how the asset meets the definition of an asset.
3. For each expense recognized above, explain whether the expense is a direct or indirect expense, and how the expense meets the expense definition.

A6-33 Expense Recognition: Kwik-Bild Corporation sells and erects shell houses. These are frame structures completely finished on the outside but unfinished on the inside except for flooring, partition studding, and ceiling joists. Shell houses are sold chiefly to customers who are handy with tools and who will do the interior wiring, plumbing, wall completion, finishing, and other work necessary to make the shell houses liveable dwellings.

Kwik-Bild buys shell houses from a manufacturer in unassembled packages consisting of all lumber, roofing, doors, windows, and similar materials necessary to complete a shell house. Upon commencing operations in a new area, Kwik-Bild buys or leases a site for its local warehouse, field office, and display houses. Sample display houses are erected at a total cost of $13,000 to $17,000, including the cost of the unassembled package. The chief element of cost of the display houses is the unassembled package, since construction is a short, low-cost operation. Old sample display houses have little net salvage value because dismantling and moving costs amount to nearly as much as the salvage value.

A choice must be made between expensing the costs of sample display houses in the period in which the expenditure is made, or capitalizing the cost and spreading it through amortization, over more than one period. (AICPA, adapted)

Required:

1. Discuss the merits of the two possible accounting policies, referring to the definitions of financial statement elements.
2. Discuss the merits of the two possible accounting policies, referring to matching.

A6-34 Expense Recognition: The general ledger of Airtime Incorporated, a corporation engaged in the development and production of television programs for commercial sponsorship, contains the following asset accounts (before amortization) at the end of 20X5:

Account	Balance
"Sealing Wax and Kings"	$75,000
"The Messenger"	36,000
"The Desperado"	19,000
"Shin Bone"	8,000
Studio rearrangement	7,000

An examination of contracts and records revealed the following information:

a. The first two accounts listed above represent the total cost of completed programs that were televised during 20X5. Under the terms of an existing contract, "Sealing Wax and Kings" will be rerun during 20X6 at a fee equal to 60% of the fee for the first televising of the program. The contract for the first run produced $300,000 of revenue. The contract with the sponsor of "The Messenger" provides that, at the sponsor's option, the program can be rerun during the 20X6 season at a fee of 75% of the fee for the first televising of the program. There are no present indications that it will be rerun.

b. The balance in "The Desperado" account is the cost of a new program that has just been completed and is being considered by several companies for commercial sponsorship.

c. The balance in the "Shin Bone" account represents the cost of a partially completed program for a projected series that has been abandoned.

d. The balance of the studio rearrangement account consists of payments made to a firm of engineers that prepared a report about a more efficient utilization of existing studio space and equipment.

Required:

Write a brief report addressed to the chief executive officer of Airtime Incorporated, responding to the following:

1. State the general principle (or principles) of accounting that are applicable to recognizing revenue and expense for the first four accounts.
2. How would you report each of the first four accounts in the financial statements of Airtime? Explain.
3. In what way, if at all, does the studio rearrangement account differ from the first four? Explain. Suggest an appropriate accounting policy.

(AICPA, adapted)

A6-35 Revenue and Expense Recognition: Pepper Publishing Company (PPC) prepares and publishes a monthly newsletter for an industry in which potential circulation is limited. Because information provided by the newsletter is available only piecemeal from other sources and because no advertising is carried, the subscription price for the newsletter is relatively high. PPC recently engaged in a campaign to increase circulation that involved extensive use of person-to-person long-distance telephone calls to research directors of non-subscriber companies in the industry. The telephone cost of the campaign was $38,000, plus salary payments to persons who made the calls amounting to $51,000.

As a direct result of the campaign, new one-year subscriptions at $175 each generated revenue of $164,500. New three-year subscriptions at $450 each generated revenue of $324,000, and new five-year subscriptions at $625 each generated $157,500. Cancellations are rare, but when they occur, refunds are made on a half-rate basis (e.g., if a subscriber has yet to receive $100 worth of newsletters, $50 is refunded).

Aside from the two direct costs of the campaign cited above, indirect costs, consisting of such items as allocated office space, fringe benefit costs for employees making telephone calls, and supervision, amounted to $21,000.

Required:

1. Identify the specific accounting issues involved in recognizing revenue and expense for PPC.
2. Assume that the campaign was begun and concluded in November of Year 0, new subscriptions begin with the Year 1 January issue of the monthly newsletter, and the company's accounting year ends 31 December. How should costs of the campaign be allocated from years one to five? Show calculations.

A6-36 Expense Policy: Computer Training Limited (CTL) is owned by a small group of investors, but plans to go public in five years' time. The company delivers an eight-month computer training program. While CTL is a new operation, the president has a successful history in the business, and has been successful in other training ventures over the last 10 years. He is paid a healthy salary, and will also receive common stock options based on his performance.

Management has prepared an operating cash flow forecast for the first six years of operation. These show an excess of cash disbursements for operating costs over cash receipts from tuition revenue for the first three years. In Years 4 and 5, the combination of additional student enrolment and projected tuition fee increases is expected to turn the tide: cash receipts and cash disbursements are expected to be equal. In Year 6, it is expected that cash receipts will exceed cash disbursements. The major costs fall into three categories: (1) costs for marketing and administration, (2) direct operating costs, primarily instructor salaries and occupancy costs, and (3) expenditures for capital assets (computer equipment), leasehold improvements, and similar long-lived assets.

The president has told you, the controller, that he wishes to use the following accounting policies:

a. Marketing and administration costs are to be capitalized and, commencing in Year 6, amortized over five years.
b. Direct operating costs in excess of tuition revenue in years 1 to 3 are to be capitalized and amortized in years 6 and 7.
c. Capital assets are to be capitalized and amortized on a sinking-fund basis.

Required:

Are the proposed accounting policies acceptable? Your answer must use the definitional approach (as distinct from the matching approach) to analyze policy.

CHAPTER 7

Current Monetary Balances

INTRODUCTION

One objective of financial reporting is to help users assess the amounts, timing, and uncertainty of future cash flows. Current monetary balances—receivables and payables—have the most immediate impact on the current position, so it's important to get them right! For example, consider Fun Key Studios Incorporated, a Canadian public company whose mission is to design, manufacture, and operate themed interactive entertainment centres, and to develop and distribute related software. For the year ended 30 April 2002, the balance sheet reports $659,000 in cash, and $37,000 in accounts receivable, out of total assets of about $3.8 million. Current liabilities are over $5.3 million, including current (about $3.2 million), and accounts payable ($1.6 million). Fun Key Studios is obviously in a position where its current monetary assets fall far short of current monetary obligations. This is potentially a high-risk situation.

Levels of current monetary items are critical when assessing the liquidity and viability of an operation. Their accurate treatment in the financial statements will help financial statement readers understand the business cycle of the operation, and the results of past transactions and decisions. Fun Key Studios states, in the disclosure notes, that its ability to continue in the normal course of business is dependent on the success of its efforts to raise financing. Obviously, current liquidity is a major issue for this company.

This chapter develops accounting principles for the recognition, measurement, and reporting of the primary categories of liquid resources: cash, accounts receivable and notes receivable, and the primary short-term claims to cash—the various types of payables. These financial statement elements are all financial instruments, cash, or claims to cash. The emphasis in this chapter is on short-term monetary balances. Long-term balances are discussed at length in Chapter 12.

When valuing receivables and payables, face value is not always the correct value to report. The value of money changes over time; a dollar to be received in the year 2015 does not have same value as a dollar today. There is a time value to money, and therefore monetary balances often must be discounted to their present value, or the implicit interest in a stream of payments must be taken into account.

Most students will already be familiar with the principles of compound interest—present value and future value—but, just in case you're out of practice, the Online Learning Centre for this text contains a brief review of compound interest calculations. Since there are several different types of notation for compound interest functions, all readers should consult the Summary of Compound Interest Tables and Formulae, found at the back of each volume, to acquaint themselves with the notation that is used throughout this book.

DEFINITION OF MONETARY ITEMS

The *CICA Handbook* defines *monetary items* as follows:

> Monetary financial assets and financial liabilities (also referred to as monetary financial instruments) are financial assets and financial liabilities to be received or paid in fixed or determinable amounts of money. (*CICA* 3860.05)

There are two key aspects of this definition:

1. The asset or liability must be settled by means of cash.
2. The amount of asset or obligation must be fixed (or determinable) by the transaction that gave rise to the balance.

Monetary items (i.e., monetary assets or liabilities) include

- Cash and cash equivalents;
- Contractual claims to receive a predetermined amount of cash (or a cash equivalent); and
- Contractual agreements to pay a predetermined amount of cash (or cash equivalent).

Chapter 5 discussed the definition of cash and cash equivalents; these obviously are monetary assets. Accounts and notes receivable and payable also are monetary items; their amount has been fixed or predetermined by means of a transaction, such as the sale of goods or services, the purchase of goods or services, or the borrowing of a fixed sum of money. In contrast, balances such as inventories and equity investments are not monetary items, even though they eventually will be converted into cash, because their cash value is not fixed in advance. The amount of cash to be obtained from such items will depend on future market conditions.

The definition includes balances that represent assets and obligations to be received or paid in a *determinable* amount of cash. An example of a *determinable* amount is a cash deposit held in foreign currency. The foreign currency deposit represents a claim to a fixed amount of cash, but its value in Canadian dollars is determinable from the exchange rate in effect at the balance sheet date. Similarly, the contracts underlying monetary balances such as accounts receivable, accounts payable, and bank loans payable may be expressed in a foreign currency. Despite the fact that their amount is not fixed in terms of Canadian currency, these balances are monetary items.

ACCOUNTING FOR CASH

Characteristics of Cash and Cash Equivalents

The cash account includes only those items immediately available to pay obligations. *Cash* includes balances on deposit with financial institutions, coins and currency, petty cash, and certain negotiable instruments accepted by financial institutions for immediate deposit and withdrawal, like cashier's cheques, certified cheques, and money orders.

T-bill
treasury bill; a short-term government security issued at a discount in lieu of interest

guaranteed investment certificate (GIC)
a certificate showing that a deposit of a specified amount has been made at a financial institution for a specific period of time, at a specified interest rate

CASH EQUIVALENTS Cash equivalents are items that can readily be converted to cash. They are limited to temporary investments that are highly liquid and have little risk of price fluctuation—**money market instruments**—but not equity investments such as common or preferred share investments. The most common examples of cash equivalents are treasury bills (widely known as **T-bills**), guaranteed investment certificates (**GICs**), commercial paper (short-term notes receivable from other companies), and money market funds. To be classified as a *cash equivalent*, the term of these investments must be short—three months is suggested—to minimize possible price fluctuations caused by interest rate changes. In Chapter 5, you learned that cash is defined as cash plus cash equivalents (and less bank overdrafts) on the cash flow statement. On the balance sheet, cash and cash equivalents are often lumped together, appropriately described.

BANK BALANCE An overdraft is a negative bank account balance. Overdrafts occur when the dollar amount of cheques honoured by the bank exceeds the account balance. It is reported as a separate current liability on the balance sheet, regardless of its inclusion as a cash equivalent on the cash flow statement. However, if a depositor overdraws an account but has positive balances in other accounts *with that bank*, it is appropriate to offset the negative and positive balances on the balance sheet as long as

- The bank has the legal right to offset, which is usual, *and*
- The company plans to settle the overdraft in this way—by a transfer from one of the other accounts.

Accounts with different financial institutions may not be offset against each other, since they fail the first condition, above.

For example, Loblaw Companies, in the disclosure notes to its 1 January 2002 financial statements, says that

> Cash balances which the company has the ability and intent to offset are used to reduce reported bank indebtedness.

A **compensating balance** is a minimum balance that must be maintained in a depositor's account as support for funds borrowed by the depositor. Technically, compensating balances are long term, and should not be included in the current cash account because they are not currently available for use. Many companies include these balances in cash and disclose the restrictions in notes to the financial statements. Either disclosure option avoids overstating the firm's liquidity position.

FOREIGN CURRENCY Items properly included in cash generally do not present valuation problems because they are recorded at cash value. That is, they are worth their face value in terms of Canadian dollars. On the other hand, the Canadian dollar value of cash holdings in foreign currency fluctuates with changes in the relevant exchange rate. To get the Canadian dollar equivalent, it is necessary to multiply the amount of foreign currency by the current exchange rate.

For example, assume that DGF Group Limited has a U.S. bank account, with U.S.$4,500 on deposit at year-end. The money was received as a result of a cash sale that took place when the exchange rate was U.S.$1.00 = Cdn.$1.34, and was recorded at a Canadian dollar amount of $6,030:

Cash, U.S. dollars [$4,500 × $1.34]	6,030	
Sales		6,030

At the end of the year, the exchange rate is U.S. $1.00 = Cdn. $1.38. The current Canadian dollar equivalency must be established:

Cash, U.S. dollars [$4,500 × ($1.38 – $1.34)]	180	
Exchange gain		180

The cash is included on the balance sheet at the 31 December exchange rate, $1.38, or $6,210. Of course, foreign cash holdings can be converted to the current exchange rate every time the rate changes, but this is a lot of extra work, and valuation is usually important only at reporting dates.

Only foreign currencies convertible to Canadian dollars without restriction are included in cash. Restricted currency balances are reported as other assets because they cannot be readily accessed.

Internal Controls for Cash

The need to safeguard cash is crucial. Cash is easy to conceal and transport, carries no mark of ownership, and is universally valued. Cash can be stolen in a lot of creative ways in addition to simply being physically picked up. The accounting system can be used and abused to put cash into the hands of a felon. For example, cheques can be issued to a fictitious company, and cashed by a dishonest employee.

internal control system

system of organizational design meant to safeguard assets and the integrity of the accounting system

INTERNAL CONTROL FUNDAMENTALS The risk of theft is directly related to the ability of individuals to access the accounting system and obtain custody of cash. Firms address this problem through an **internal control system**, designed to protect all assets and the integrity of the information system. A sound internal control system for cash increases the likelihood that the reported values for cash and cash equivalents are accurate and may be relied on by financial statement users. There are two internal control issues for cash: (1) ensuring that cash is not stolen, and (2) making sure that cash is wisely managed to maximize returns.

You'll learn all about internal controls if you ever study auditing; for now, the important things to remember *vis-à-vis* safeguarding cash are to

- Keep cash where it's hard to steal (common sense should tell you this!).
- Make sure that *no one person is in a position to misappropriate cash* ***and*** *cover up the theft.*

The most fundamental principle of internal control is that of *division of duties*—the person who handles cash must not keep the books. This is also called "segregation of duties." When the bookkeeper handles cash, it is both possible and occasionally tempting for him or her to set cash aside for personal use and cover up the cash shortage by making a fictitious entry in the books. In a large enterprise, quite a large amount of cash (in personal terms) can go missing before anyone starts to notice. Modest embezzlement may go undetected for many years, particularly if the enterprise is not audited.

If the functions of cash-handling and record-keeping are separated, it will be very difficult to embezzle cash in this fashion unless two people agree together (or *collude*) to take the money. Internal control is built largely on the principle that dishonest collusion is significantly less likely than individual action.

Internal Control and Bank Accounts

Obviously, bank accounts provide one means to physically safeguard cash balances, but they're also integral to proper cash management. For example, advanced electronic fund transfer schemes will transfer funds directly from a customer's bank account to the company's. Cash management is a function of the treasury department of large companies, whose task is to minimize idle cash and maximize returns to shareholders. It's a complex area.

The principles of internal control apply just as well to cash held in bank accounts as they do to currency. The record-keeper must not have the authority to sign cheques, or at least not the authority to sign cheques without someone else's signature also being required. Few legitimate companies have much real cash lying around; more money can be stolen by signing cheques and then creating fictitious bookkeeping entries to make the cheques look like they were for legitimate purposes.

CHECKING THE RECORDS We're mostly interested in the bank account because it provides a wonderful opportunity to *check the accuracy of the accounting records.* It's the *only* general ledger account that another company (the bank) completely runs in parallel. If the company has a deposit recorded, so should the bank. If the company has written a cheque, it should also go through the bank account. Now, there are timing problems—it takes a while for cheques and deposits to clear, and banks record some things, such as bank charges, before the company—but you get the picture.

By comparing the bank account to the cash general ledger account, the company can ensure that the books are being kept accurately, and that all expenditures and receipts are appropriate. The bank reconciliation provides the correct cash balance for the balance sheet and information for adjusting entries. Since cash forms a part of so many transactions, the accuracy of the cash account is usually a good surrogate for the accuracy of other accounts. Of course, it's crucial that the individual who's in charge of cheques and/or deposits is not also in charge of the bank statement reconciliation—it would be too easy to cover up something. You don't get to check your own work; that's division of duties.

Reconciliation of Bank and Book Cash Balances

Banks send monthly statements showing beginning and ending balances and transactions occurring during the month: cheques clearing the account, deposits received, and service charges. Every month, the bank's records and the company's records have to be compared, and the differences reconciled.

Usually, some items listed in the bank statement have not yet been recorded by the firm. These show up on the bank statement as debit and credit memos, and include items such as interest earned, cash collected by the bank from customers, and service charges. The company usually becomes aware of the exact amount of these items only when the company receives its bank statement. The company must record the bank's extra charges and credits as reconciling items.

debit memo
a memo issued by a bank that reports a decrease in the company's cash account

credit memo
a memo issued by a bank that reports an increase in the company's cash account

bank reconciliation
a schedule that analyzes the firm's cash account versus the bank's reported cash amount to ensure that transaction recording is complete and accurate; one means of internal control

BANK DEBITS AND CREDITS For a bank, a depositor's cash balance is a liability, the amount the bank owes to the company. A bank **debit memo** describes a transaction from the bank's point of view—a decrease in liability to the account holder. Therefore, a debit memo reports the amount and nature of a *decrease* in the company's cash account. A **credit memo** indicates an *increase* in the cash account. Since this debit-credit memo terminology is derived from the bank's point of view, it seems backward to the debit and credit convention in the company's cash account. This tends to create a little confusion.

A **bank reconciliation** begins with the two cash balances (bank and book), lists the differences between those balances, and ends with the true cash balance. Review the information in Exhibit 7-1 for West Company. The bank statement reported an ending $38,630 balance, and the cash account reflects an ending $34,870 cash balance. Of course, if they were the same amount, the reconciliation would be over before it even began! These figures are reconciled to $35,630, as shown in Exhibit 7-2. Here are the steps to follow:

Step 1 Compare all deposits made in the bank account with those in the books. If there are differences, determine why. If the bank has processed something that should be on the books, adjust the book balance. If the bank has made errors, or if deposits are in transit, adjust the bank balance. If the company has made errors, adjust the balance per the books. A careful bank reconciliation includes a comparison of the dates of deposits—there should be no delays in getting money to the bank. Deposits in transit from the prior month should clear in the first few days of the next month, and this month's deposits in transit should relate only to the last day or two.

Step 2 Compare all cheques and charges that went through the bank account to the cash disbursements journal. All cheques that the bank paid should be in the cash disbursements journal this month, or have been outstanding last month. If the bank has made errors, or cheques are still outstanding, adjust the bank balance. If the bank has processed something that should be on the books, adjust the book balance. If the company has made errors, adjust the balance per the books. Again, keep an eye out for irregularities; cheques are usually cashed after only a short delay.

Step 3 Make journal entries for all adjustments *to the book balance*, and inform the bank of any errors made by the bank, so they can be corrected before the end of next month.

EXHIBIT 7-1

WEST COMPANY
INFORMATION FOR BANK RECONCILIATION

31 August 20X2

Bank statement		
1 August balance		$32,000
Deposits recorded in August	$ 77,300	
Cheques cleared in August	(71,240)	
Accounts receivable collected (including $100 interest)	1,100	
NSF cheque, J. Fox, $300 plus $30 fee	(330)	
August service charges	(200)	6,630
31 August balance		$38,630
West Company's cash account		
1 August balance		$29,990
August deposits*	75,300	
August disbursements**	(70,420)	4,880
31 August balance		$34,870

* Per cash receipts journal
** Per cash disbursements journal

Additional data, end of July:
Deposits in transit, $5,000, and cheques outstanding, $8,000 (these two amounts were taken from the July bank reconciliation).

Additional data, end of August:
Cash on hand (undeposited), $990. This amount will be deposited 1 September. A cheque written by West in the amount of $240 for a repair bill in August is included in the cleared cheques. West recorded the cheque for $420, the correct amount, debiting repair expense. The cheque was issued for the wrong amount. The payee will bill West for the remaining $180 due. The service charges of $200 include a $10 charge to a company named "Weston Company" that was charged to West Company in error.

Take a look at the bank reconciliation in Exhibit 7-2 in detail:

ADJUSTMENTS TO THE BANK BALANCE What transactions are recorded in the books but have not yet gone through the bank account because of timing delays? What errors has the bank made? Adjust these things to the bank account.

A. *Cash on hand.* This is the cash recorded as a debit to the company's cash account, but not deposited at month-end. Cash or cheques are being held—in a safe, one hopes—by the company at 31 August. This amount is added to the bank balance.

B. *Deposits in transit.* These are deposits made too late to be reflected in the bank statement. This amount is determined by comparing the firm's record of deposits with the deposits listed in the bank statement or by using a schedule.

EXHIBIT 7-2

WEST COMPANY
BANK RECONCILIATION

31 August 20X2

Bank statement		
Ending bank balance, 31 August		$38,630
Additions:		
Cash on hand (undeposited)	$ 990	
Deposits in transit, 31 August ($5,000 + $75,300 − $77,300)	3,000	
Bank error re: service charge	10	
Deductions:		
Cheques outstanding 31 August ($8,000 + $70,420 − $180 − $71,240)	(7,000)	(3,000)
Adjusted balance		$35,630
Book balance		
Ending book balance, 1 August		$34,870
Additions:		
Accounts receivable collected by bank	1,000	
Interest	100	
Error in recording repair repayment	180	
Deductions:		
NSF cheque, J. Fox, $300, plus $30 NSF fee	(330)	
Bank service charges	(190)	760
Adjusted balance		$35,630

Deposits in transit at end of prior period	$ 5,000
Deposits for the current period (per books)	75,300
Total amount that could have been deposited	80,300
Deposits shown in bank statement	(77,300)
Deposits in transit at end of current period	$ 3,000

It's important to pin down the $3,000 deposit—in the schedule, it's an arithmetic result, but it has to be real. Was there a deposit made late in the month that did not clear? Or was some money lost or deposited in the wrong account? This is the time to find it!

C. *Outstanding cheques.* This amount is determined by comparing cheques written with cheques cleared or by using a schedule.

Outstanding cheques at end of prior period	$ 8,000
Cheques written during the current period (per cash payments journal, as corrected: $70,420 − $180 payment overstatement)	70,240
Total cheques that could have cleared	78,240
Cheques cleared shown in bank statement	(71,240)
Outstanding cheques at end of current period	$ 7,000

Again, this amount has to be real—there must be a list of cheques that have not cleared the bank, but are recorded on the books, in the amount of $7,000.

D. *Bank errors.* The bank charged the company $10 too much service charge. The bank will have to be informed of the error, and appropriate documentation provided so that the bank will put the $10 back in the account by reversing the charge.

After all appropriate entries are made, the adjusted bank balance is $35,630.

ADJUSTMENTS TO THE BOOK BALANCE Items needed to reconcile the firm's cash ledger account to the correct cash balance are amounts the firm did not know about at 31 August; none would have been necessary had the bank informed the company of entries in its bank account in enough time for the company to have recorded the entries in its cash receipts or disbursements journals prior to the end of the month. Each of these items now requires an adjusting journal entry to correct the cash balance. *Notice that there are no entries in West's books for anything that is a reconciling item to the bank balance.*

A. *Account receivable collected by bank.* An account receivable for $1,000 plus $100 accrued interest was collected by the bank but was not recorded by West. Customers sometimes do this at the company's request to speed up collection and/or to minimize the risk that the customer's cheque will not clear. Usually, the bank informs the company immediately, but if the item has not been recorded by month-end, it shows up as a reconciling item and is recorded at that time.

Cash	1,100	
Accounts receivable		1,000
Interest revenue		100

B. *Not sufficient funds (NSF) cheque.* A $300 cheque from customer J. Fox, which was not supported by sufficient funds in Fox's chequing account, was returned to West by the bank. West had deposited the cheque, increased cash, and decreased accounts receivable, but the bank was unable to get any money from Fox's account. Again, the company is usually informed immediately, so it can pursue its delinquent customer. However, if there are delays, or the NSF cheque occurs late in the month, it is a reconciling item, and will be recorded now. Note that the company will try to recover the bank fee charged as well as the original receivable.

Accounts receivable, J. Fox	330	
Cash		330

Is this really a bad debt? Fox might be delinquent, but no company will give up after only one try—it will create a receivable when an NSF cheque is received. The receivable may end up as part of the amount included in the allowance for doubtful accounts—but that's the next section in this chapter!

C. *Bank service charges.* The bank debited West's account for $190 of bank charges in August for cheque printing, chequing account privileges, and collection of customer cheques. West deducts this amount from the cash account as a reconciling item and records an entry:

Miscellaneous expense (or Bank service charge expense)	190	
Cash		190

D. *Error in recording.* West recorded a $240 cheque in the cash disbursements journal as $420, debiting accounts payable and crediting cash for too much. The book balance of cash and accounts payable is now understated by $180 ($420 – $240). West corrects the recording error as a reconciling item, and makes an entry.

Cash	180	
Accounts payable		180

This entry corrects the cash disbursement amount and establishes a payable for the remaining amount due. Correction entries of this kind always either debit or credit the cash account, and the other side of the entry is made to whatever the first cheque was charged to: in this case, accounts payable. It helps to reconstruct the original (incorrect) entry.

Book and bank balances are now reconciled to the same value, $35,630.

BALANCING But what if the two amounts are *not* equal? What if it didn't work? Then, the reconciler gets to do it again ... and again ... until it does work! Everyone's nightmare is that a $10 difference is really a $10,000 error in one direction, and a $10,010 error in the other direction! So the bank reconciliation really is expected to "work." Here are a couple of "tricks" to help find the most common errors:

- If a reconciling item is deducted when it should have been added (or vice versa), the amount will be *double* the item. Therefore, try dividing the unreconciled amount by 2, then look for an item of that amount. That, if $170 is the reconciled amount, look for a $85 item that is added when it should be subtracted, or *vice versa.*
- Transposition errors are *always* divisible by 9. For example, if $5,012 was written as $5,102, the unreconciled amount will be $90. If $5,012 was written as $5,210, the error will be $198, which also is divisible by 9.

Of course, if there are multiple errors, these tricks won't help much. In practice, after things have been very carefully reviewed a few times to make sure there is no possibility of large counterbalancing errors, small differences are written off to miscellaneous expense.

CASH ON THE BALANCE SHEET Cash and cash equivalents are reported as the first asset on the balance sheet. Companies are required to show the components of cash, which they often do in conjunction with the cash flow statement. Others provide a breakdown in the disclosure notes. For instance, Petro-Canada, in its 31 December 2002 financial statements, provides interesting disclosure of the components of its cash account, including the amount of outstanding cheques; this may be provided to explain the apparently negative cash position:

NOTE 11 CASH AND SHORT-TERM INVESTMENTS

Short-term investments are considered to be cash equivalents and are recorded at cost, which approximates market value.

	2002	2001
Cash	$ 139	$ 94
Less: outstanding cheques	(167)	(100)
	(28)	(6)
Short-term investments	262	787
	$ 234	$ 781

CONCEPT REVIEW

1. What is the definition of monetary assets and liabilities?
2. What is the most basic principle of internal control?
3. Why is it necessary to perform a bank reconciliation each month?
4. What are the major adjustments to the book balance in a bank reconciliation? The bank balance?

ACCOUNTING FOR RECEIVABLES

non-trade receivable

cash due to a corporation from transactions other than the sale of goods and services

Receivables represent claims for money, goods, services, and other non-cash assets from other firms. Receivables may be current or non-current, depending on the expected collection date. Accounts receivable, also called **trade account receivables**, are amounts owed by customers for goods and services sold in the firm's normal course of business. These receivables are supported by sales invoices or other documents rather than by formal written promises, and they include amounts expected to be collected either during the year following the balance sheet date or within the firm's operating cycle. Notes receivable are also amounts receivable but are usually supported by formal promissory notes. **Non-trade receivables** arise from many other sources, such as tax refunds, contracts, investments, finance receivables, instalment notes, sale of assets, and advances to employees. The main accounting issues pertaining to receivables are *recognition* and *measurement.* Both are affected by collectibility.

Recognition and Measurement of Accounts Receivable

Accounts receivable are recognized only when the criteria for recognition are fulfilled. Accounts receivable are typically valued at the original exchange price between the firm and an outside party. Generally, a 30- to 60-day period is allowed for payment, beyond which the account is considered past due, and interest may begin to accrue.

Individual accounts receivable for customers with *credit balances* (from prepayments or overpayments) are reclassified and reported as *liabilities* on the balance sheet if they are material. Credit balances should not be netted against other accounts receivable, but netting is a common practice if the amounts are small (i.e., immaterial).

The receivables are meant to be an approximation of the cash that will be collected. Say a company has $2,000,000 in accounts receivable at the end of 20X5. This may not be the amount of money it will actually collect. Usually adjustments have to be made at year-end to reduce receivables to net realizable value, for things like

- cash discounts
- sales returns and allowances
- allowances for uncollectible accounts

CASH DISCOUNTS Companies frequently offer a cash discount, or sales discount, for payment received within a designated period. Cash discounts are used to increase sales, to encourage early payment by the customer, and to increase the likelihood of collection. Sales terms might be 2/10, n/30, which means that the customer is given a 2% cash discount if payment is made within 10 days from sale; otherwise, the full amount net of any returns or allowances is due in 30 days. Theoretically, the sale and the receivable should be recorded at the lowest cash price, or the net amount after deducting the discount. This would be $980 for a $1,000 sale, if the discount for prompt payment is 2%.

In practice, though, sales are usually recorded *gross*, because it is easier to reconcile the balances of individual accounts receivable to the general ledger control account if the receivables are recorded at their gross amount. The subsidiary accounts may be a listing of outstanding invoices (either on paper or in a computer file) rather than a formal "ledger," and it is much easier to simply add up the total (gross) amount of outstanding invoices to reconcile to the control account, instead of figuring out the net amount if the customer takes the discount.

Under the gross method, if a material amount of cash discounts is expected to be taken on outstanding accounts receivable at year-end, and if this amount is reasonably estimable, an adjusting entry is required to decrease net sales and to reduce accounts receivable to the estimated amount collectible. To illustrate, assume that our $2 million of accounts receivable all have terms of 2/10, n/30, and are recorded gross. Management expects 60% of these accounts to be collected within the discount period. There is no balance in an allowance account. The adjusting entry on 31 December 20X5:

Sales discounts [$2,000,000 × 2% × 60%]	24,000	
Allowance for sales discounts		24,000

The sales discounts account is a contra account to sales. The allowance account is a contra account to accounts receivable, and reduces accounts receivable to their net cash value. If there had been a $3,000 credit balance in the allowance account prior to this entry, the entry would have been made for $21,000 ($24,000 − $3,000).

During 20X6, assuming that the estimates were correct, a summary entry reflects the receipts.

Allowance for sales discounts	24,000	
Cash	1,176,000	
Accounts receivable [$2,000,000 × 60%]		1,200,000

Alternatively, and more commonly, the sales discounts account can be directly debited when customers use cash discounts during the year, and the allowance can be adjusted at the end of each reporting period.

SALES RETURNS AND ALLOWANCES Return privileges are frequently part of a comprehensive marketing program required to maintain competitiveness. Sales *returns* occur when merchandise is returned by the customer; sales *allowances* occur when a company gives a price reduction to a customer who is not completely satisfied with purchased merchandise but does not actually return it.

Sales returns and allowances are significant amounts in some industries, including retailing and book publishing. Of course, if returns are material and unestimable, sales revenue cannot be recorded until after the uncertainty is resolved. This issue was discussed in Chapter 6. This chapter deals with the more likely case, *estimable returns*, and the problem again is to reduce receivables to their probable cash flow or *net realizable value*, which is net of returns. Sales returns and allowances reduce both net accounts receivable and net sales.

The company must estimate and recognize the returns and allowances expected for the accounts receivable outstanding at the end of 20X5. Assume that total estimated sales returns and allowances relating to the closing receivables balance is $9,000, and there is no balance in the allowance for sales returns account. The company records an adjusting entry on 31 December 20X5:

Sales returns and allowances	9,000	
Allowance for sales returns and allowances		9,000

If there had been a $5,000 credit balance in the allowance account prior to this entry, the entry would have been made for $4,000 ($9,000 – $5,000). Note that the sales returns and allowances account is a contra account to sales and the allowance is a contra account to accounts receivable.

As goods sold in 20X5 are returned in 20X6, they can be charged to the allowance account. It's usually easier, though, to charge the returns directly to a sales returns and allowances account and adjust the balance in the allowance account at the end of each reporting period.

ALLOWANCE FOR DOUBTFUL ACCOUNTS When credit is extended, some amount of uncollectible receivables is generally inevitable. Firms attempt to develop a credit policy that is neither too conservative (leading to excessive lost sales) nor too liberal (leading to excessive uncollectible accounts). Past records of payment and the financial condition and income of customers are key inputs to the credit-granting decision.

If uncollectible receivables are both likely and estimable, an estimate of uncollectible accounts must be recognized, so that accounts receivable and net income are not overstated. This is a form of asset valuation that is a common theme in accounting for assets: at the end of the accounting period, you must ensure that they're not overvalued. Are they representative of probable cash flow? If so, fine. If not, a writedown is made.

Because accounting recognition criteria require companies to anticipate a writedown before actually giving up on a particular account, the writedown is made to an allowance account, called the **allowance for doubtful accounts**. That is, individual accounts are not credited at this point because the company doesn't know which accounts will turn out to be uncollectible—if the company knew which accounts would go bad, it wouldn't have sold to those customers in the first place! Estimated uncollectibles are recorded in *bad debt expense*, an operating expense usually classified as a selling expense.

allowance for doubtful accounts
a contra account to accounts receivable that represents the portion of outstanding receivables whose collection is doubtful

If uncollectible accounts are likely to arise and are estimable, an adjusting entry is needed at the end of an accounting period. For example, if our company estimates that $120,000 of the $2,000,000 in receivables will not be collected, and the existing credit balance in the allowance account is $12,000, the adjusting entry is as follows:

Bad debt expense	108,000	
Allowance for doubtful accounts		108,000

Notice that both net income and net assets decline on this entry: this is expense recognition, after all.

This estimate of uncollectible amounts is made after the end of the year, but takes into consideration all facts known at the date of the review. For example, if a customer went into bankruptcy in January, the allowance established for the 31 December accounts receivable, estimated in January as the financial statements are finalized, would include the customer's balance, which will certainly be uncollectible. This is an example of a subsequent event that must be recorded in the current year.

Two other events must be considered: (1) the write-off of a specific receivable and (2) the collection of an account previously written off. The adjusting entry for bad debt expense creates the allowance for doubtful accounts for future uncollectible accounts. When specific accounts are determined to be uncollectible, they are removed from the accounts receivable and that part of the allowance is no longer needed. The bad debt estimation entry previously recognized the estimated economic effect of future uncollectible accounts. Thus, write-offs of specific accounts do not further reduce total assets unless they exceed the estimate.

For example, the following entry is recorded by a company deciding not to pursue collection of R. Knox's $1,000 account:

Allowance for doubtful accounts	1,000	
Accounts receivable, R. Knox		1,000

This write-off entry affects neither income nor the net amount of accounts receivable outstanding. Instead, it is the culmination of the process that began with the adjusting entry to estimate bad debt expense. The write-off entry changes only the components of net accounts receivable, not the net amount itself (amounts assumed):

	Before Knox Write-Off	After Knox Write-Off
Accounts receivable	$2,000,000	$1,999,000
Allowance for doubtful accounts	(120,000)	(119,000)
Net accounts receivable	$1,880,000	$1,880,000

When amounts are received on account after a write-off, the write-off entry is reversed to reinstate the receivable and cash collection is recorded. Assume that R. Knox is able to pay $600 on account some time after the above write-off entry was recorded. These entries are required:

Accounts receivable, R. Knox	600	
Allowance for doubtful accounts		600
Cash	600	
Accounts receivable, R. Knox		600

The net effect of these two entries is to increase cash and *reinstate* the allowance for doubtful accounts to the extent of the cash recovery. The reason for reinstating the allowance is that, since $600 cash was collected, the writedown of $1,000 was excessive; the write-down should have been for only $400. Another way of looking at it is that the only other place to put the credit (to offset the debit to cash) is to a revenue account. But the revenue was already fully recognized when the sale transaction was recorded. Crediting the $600 to a revenue account would be double-counting.

DISCLOSURE The balance sheet presentation of net accounts receivable provides focus on the realizable cash amount.

Accounts receivable, net	$1,847,000

The net balance is $2,000,000 less the $24,000 allowance for cash discounts, less the $9,000 allowance for sales returns and less the $120,000 allowance for doubtful accounts.

The *CICA Handbook* recommends, in Section 3020, that accounts receivable be segregated between

- ordinary trade accounts
- amounts owing by related parties
- other unusual items of substantial amount

However, the amount of any allowances need not be disclosed. Furthermore, amounts and maturity dates of instalment receivables should be disclosed. Accounts receivable are *financial instruments*, and information on terms and conditions, credit risk and fair values of financial instruments should be disclosed. For most companies, this is not difficult to measure. Receivables are stated at their cash equivalencies, which is fair value, the amount of receivables represents the maximum credit risk, and terms and conditions are so standard that separate disclosure is not warranted. In some cases, concentration of credit risk in certain geographic locations or with certain customers might be appropriate. For instance, the following disclosure note to the 2003 Bombardier Incorporated financial statements discusses such concentrations:

> The receivables were concentrated in the transportation and aerospace segments, 77% and 19% respectively, as at January 31, 2003 (86% and 9% respectively, as at January 31, 2002). They were mainly located in Europe and in North America, 56% and 34% respectively, as at January 31, 2003 (72% and 19% respectively, as at January 31, 2002).

Calculation of the Allowance for Doubtful Accounts

The previous section illustrated how the allowance is established, in an entry that increased the bad debt expense and increased the allowance. There are two approaches to determining how to get the amount of the entry: the "TO" and the "BY" methods.

Aging Method (*TO a calculated balance*): Accounts receivables can be examined item by item, or aged, or analyzed statistically, category by category, to determine net realizable value and the size of an appropriate allowance. The allowance is then increased TO this amount, which involves a consideration of the opening balance. This is formally called the **aging method**.

aging method
a method of estimating uncollectible accounts receivable and bad debt expenses by applying probability estimates of non-collection to specific balances that have been classified by age

Credit Sales Method (*BY a calculated balance*): Bad debt experience over time can be correlated to credit sales, to establish a percentage of sales that is normally uncollectible. The allowance is then increased BY this amount, irrespective of the opening balance. This is formally called the **credit sales method**.

credit sales method
a method of estimating uncollectible accounts receivable by establishing the percentage of sales that are historically uncollectible; the allowance for doubtful accounts is increased by this amount

Exhibit 7-3 presents background information for several examples. The current $500 debit balance in Rally's allowance account does not necessarily indicate that past estimates of bad debt losses were too low, although this is one explanation. Alternatively, it is possible that some receivables originating in 20X2 were written off and the debit balance does not yet reflect the estimate for bad debts based on 20X2 sales.

EXHIBIT 7-3

RALLY COMPANY
INFORMATION FOR BAD DEBT ESTIMATION EXAMPLES

1 January 20X2 balances:	
Accounts receivable (debit)	$101,300
Allowance for doubtful accounts (credit)	3,300
Transactions during 20X2:	
Credit sales	500,000
Cash sales	700,000
Collections on accounts receivable	420,000
Accounts written off as uncollectible during 20X2	3,800

After posting of sales, collections, and write-offs, accounts receivable and the allowance for doubtful accounts appear as follows:

Accounts Receivable

1 Jan. 20X2 balance	101,300	Collections	420,000
Credit sales	500,000	Write-offs	3,800
31 Dec. 20X2 balance	177,500		

Allowance for Doubtful Accounts

Write-offs	3,800	1 Jan. 20X2 balance	3,300
31 Dec. 20X2 balance *before* adjustments	500		

AGING METHOD This method emphasizes the net realizable value of net accounts receivable and uses historical data to estimate the percentage of accounts receivable expected to become uncollectible. Exhibit 7-4 illustrates Rally's aging schedule and the application of the collection loss percentages. The $177,500 receivable balance is divided into four age classifications with a collection loss percentage applied to each age category. This percentage is usually based on past experience. Rally's collection loss percentages increase with the age of the accounts. As accounts are collected and good accounts are removed from each category, the proportion represented by uncollectible accounts increases.

EXHIBIT 7-4

RALLY COMPANY

ACCOUNTS RECEIVABLE AGING SCHEDULE

31 December 20X2

Customer account	Balance 31 Dec. 20X2	Age of account balance			
		Current	31–60 days	61–90 days	Over 90 days
Denk	$ 500	$ 400	$ 100		
Evans	900	900			
Field	1,650		1,350	$ 300	
Harris	90			30	$ 60
King	800	700	60	40	
Zabot	250	250			
Total	$177,500	$110,000	$31,000	$29,500	$ 7,000
Percent estimated uncollectible		0.2%	1.0%	8.0%	40.0%
Amount estimated uncollectible		$ 220	$ 310	$ 2,360	$2,800

Total amount to include in allowance: $220 + $310 + $2,360 + $2,800 = $5,690

The age categories are based on the extent to which accounts are past due. An account is past due if it is not collected by the end of the period specified in the credit terms. For example, an account arising from a 1 November sale with terms 2/10, n/30, is due 1 December. If the account remains unpaid at 31 December, the aging analysis classifies the account as 30 days past due.

The computation in Exhibit 7-4 yields a required ending balance in the allowance account at 31 December 20X2, of $5,690 (credit). The allowance is increased to $5,690. Because the allowance balance is $500 (debit) before adjustment, the entry is for $6,190, yielding an ending $5,690 balance.

Bad debt expense [$5,690 + $500]	6,190	
Allowance for doubtful accounts		6,190

Had the allowance balance been a $500 credit before adjustment, bad debt expense would have been $5,190 ($5,690 – $500). Since the allowance is $5,690, net accounts receivable will be shown on the balance sheet at $171,810 ($177,500 – $5,690).

composite rate
a rate to estimate uncollectible receivables based on the percentage of historical bad debts and total accounts receivable

Aging may be more cumbersome than is warranted, and a **composite rate**, based on the accounts receivable total may be used. Assume that experience leads Rally Company (Exhibit 7-3) to use a single 3% composite rate. Therefore, the required ending allowance credit balance is $5,325 (3% × $177,500). The allowance account currently reflects a $500 debit balance, so the adjusting entry increases the allowance account *to* $5,325 through an entry for $5,825 ($5,325 + $500).

Bad debt expense	5,825	
Allowance for doubtful accounts		5,825

The estimated net realizable value of accounts receivable is $172,175 in this case.

CREDIT SALES METHOD This method emphasizes the matching principle and the income statement. The average percentage relationship between actual bad debt losses and net credit sales is estimated on the basis of experience. This percentage is then applied to a period's net credit sales to determine bad debt expense.

Assume that in the past, 1.2% of Rally's credit sales have not been collected. Barring changes in Rally's credit policies or major changes in the economy, Rally expects this rate to continue. Under this method, the following is the required 20X2 adjusting entry, which increases the allowance by a percentage of credit sales.

Bad debt expense [$500,000 × 1.2%]	6,000	
Allowance for doubtful accounts		6,000

After this entry is posted, the balance in the allowance account is $5,500 ($6,000 from the adjusting entry less the prior $500 debit balance). This method directly computes bad debt expense *without regard to the prior balance in the allowance account.* Rally would disclose $172,000 ($177,500 – $5,500) of net accounts receivable in the 20X2 balance sheet.

The percentage applied to credit sales should be updated periodically to approximate the rate of actual write-offs.

WHICH METHOD TO USE? Either method of estimation is acceptable for financial reporting as long as the resulting allowance is reasonable. Statistical support for the rates used to establish the allowance under either method helps establish this reasonableness. It is also fairly standard to evaluate the allowance with reference to major accounts receivable in various categories, in conjunction with the year-end audit or review. This evaluation uses all known facts at the date of the review including subsequent payments and defaults.

The credit sales and aging methods may be used together. Each is used to validate the other, although only one may be used in the accounts. For interim financial statements, many companies base monthly or quarterly adjusting entries on the credit sales method because of its low cost. At the end of the year, they may age their accounts receivable to check the reasonableness of the allowance balance.

Computerization has reduced costs of implementing the aging method, and increasing cash flow problems prompt companies to monitor the age of their receivables more closely to reduce losses.

The general condition of the economy, the economic health of specific customers, and the seller's credit policy and collection effort affect the rate of account write-offs. Over time, this rate changes, necessitating adjustment to the percentages applied to credit sales or receivables. If the balance in allowance for doubtful accounts is found to increase each year, the estimate of uncollectibles is decreased to reflect actual experience. Alternatively, if the allowance is inadequate, future estimates will increase.

Direct Write-Off of Uncollectible Accounts

Companies in the first year of operation or in a new line of business may have no basis for estimating uncollectibles. In such cases, and when uncollectible accounts are immaterial, receivables must be written off directly as they become uncollectible. The entry for the direct write-off of a $2,000 account receivable from M. Lynx is as follows:

Bad debt expense	2,000	
Accounts receivable, M. Lynx		2,000

No adjusting entry is made at the end of an accounting period under the direct write-off method.

The inability to estimate uncollectible accounts creates several unavoidable problems:

- Receivables are reported at more than their net realizable value, because it is virtually certain that not all receivables are collectible.
- The period of write-off is often after the period of sale, violating the matching principle. At the extreme, if bad debts are material and inestimable, revenue cannot be recognized until the uncertainty is cleared up—usually on collection.
- Direct write-off opens the potential for income manipulation by arbitrary selection of the write-off period.

Only new operations or very small companies may use the direct write-off method for these reasons.

SPEEDING UP CASH FLOW FROM RECEIVABLES

Credit Card Operations

At one point in time, many retail stores offered credit to customers—in fact, some built a business primarily on offering credit. (For example, consider People's Credit Jewellers, now usually just called People's.) Now, most retailers prefer to get their money up front, and let the customers owe the credit card company. Retailers are charged a fee, a percentage of the total sale, for the privilege, but prefer this charge because they avoid bad debts, there is no delay in receiving cash, and they hope that customers will spend more when they can charge their purchases. Except for the corner variety store and some coffee shops, there aren't many cash-only businesses around these days. Retail customers expect to be able to use credit cards.

Other retailers have expanded their credit-granting operations into their own credit card companies. These operations, usually separate subsidiaries, make money by charging interest on overdue accounts. Their largest expenses are the cost of money and bad debts.

VISA and Mastercard are the two primary independent credit card companies. Merchants enter into contracts with these companies, agreeing on fees and payment arrangements. When automated point-of-sale systems are used, the merchant receives money, through direct deposit to the company's bank account, the same day.

Assume that a merchant has $2,000 in credit card sales. The credit card company deducts a commission of a contracted amount for its services and the money is electronically transferred. Assuming that the fee is 6% in this example, the appropriate entry is as follows:

Cash	1,880	
Credit card fees expense [$2,000 × 6%]	120	
Sales		2,000

Alternatively, a merchant will accumulate credit card sales in batches, for low volume cards. Credit card vouchers are submitted by mail or deposited with a bank acting as agent for the credit card company. The company receives its money by cheque or direct deposit, after the request is reviewed and processed.

DEBIT CARDS Many merchants also accept debit cards. The primary difference between a debit card and a credit card is from the point of view of the customer: a debit card will remove the transaction amount immediately from the customer's bank account. The merchant has to go through the same motions as with credit cards: an agreement must be negotiated with the sponsoring financial institution for a fee (again a percentage of the transaction amount) and payment terms. All transactions are authorized through automated point-of-sale systems, and the merchant receives the cash immediately. No receivables are created; this is like a cash sale with a fee attached.

Loans Secured by Account Receivable

If a company has a $100,000 account receivable from a creditworthy customer who will not pay for 45 days, how can the company get cash sooner? Well, it would be nice if the customer would pay sooner, and a variety of policies are usually explored to speed up collection. Then what? The most common course of action is to go to a bank and borrow money using the account receivable as collateral.

This isn't very complicated on the books: a loan is recorded, and interest expense will be accrued as time passes. When the account is collected, the bank is repaid. Assets pledged as collateral are disclosed in the financial statements. Of course, it's less common to make credit arrangements for one receivable at a time: the overall balance of accounts receivable, and usually inventory, too, are used to secure working capital loans. These loans are a relatively permanent part of most companies' financial structure.

Transfer of Accounts Receivable

Accounts receivable can also be transferred to a financial institution to speed up cash flow. A transfer of accounts receivable can be recorded as a sale or a borrowing. These two arrangements are described as follows:

1. *A sale.* The accounts receivable come off the books of the selling company, and a financing fee is recognized.
2. *A borrowing.* The accounts receivable are left on the books of the selling company, and the amount received from the finance company is recorded as a loan until the customer actually pays.

To illustrate a transfer recorded as a sale, consider the following case. Largo Incorporated sells $200,000 of accounts receivable on 15 August 20X2. The buyer is a finance company. The finance company charges a 12% financing fee. The entry to record the transfer/sale is

Largo Incorporated			**Finance Company**		
Cash	176,000*		Accounts receivable	200,000	
Financing fee	24,000**		Deferred financing revenue***		24,000
Accounts receivable		200,000	Cash		176,000

* $200,000 − (12% × $200,000)
** 12% × $200,000; expensed immediately
*** Deferred and recognized over the collection period.

It looks pretty straightforward, doesn't it? Accounts receivable can be sold, like any other asset! To simplify this, and the following examples, no consideration is given to the likely sales discounts or returns that are inherent in the receivables balance. In a real situation, the finance company would hold back an allowance for this cause, and settle up with the company at the end of the arrangement. It doesn't change the substance of the transaction, though.

Now, what if an identical transaction was recorded as a transfer/borrowing?

Largo Incorporated			**Finance Company**		
Cash	176,000		Note receivable	200,000	
Discount on note payable	24,000		Discount on note receivable		24,000
Note payable		200,000	Cash		176,000

Both the accounts receivable and the loan are reported on Largo's books. The discount is amortized to finance/interest expense and revenue over the life of the note. When the receivables are collected, the money is remitted to the finance company, and the note is repaid:

Largo Incorporated			**Finance Company**		
Cash	200,000				
Accounts receivable		200,000			
Notes payable	200,000		Cash	200,000	
Cash		200,000	Notes receivable		200,000
Financing expense*	24,000		Discount on notes receivable	24,000	
Discount on notes payable		24,000	Finance revenue*		24,000

* recognized as time passes

recourse
in the assignment of accounts receivable, the right of a third-party financer to demand reimbursement from the transferor of receivables if they prove uncollectible

notification
in the transfer of accounts receivable to a third party, the original customer is informed of the transfer and makes payment to the third party

This is a very specialized type of financing, and the contracts can be very complicated. Receivables can be transferred with recourse, or without recourse. **Recourse** means that the finance company can come back to the company that sold the account receivable for payment if the account turns out to be uncollectible. Recourse arrangements often allow the company to replace defaulted receivables with "good ones" in the event of default. This may be part of a removal of accounts provision (ROAP).

Agreements to sell receivables are made either on a **notification basis** (customers are directed to remit to the new party holding the receivables, the finance company) or a **non-notification basis** (customers continue to remit to the original seller, who then, in turn, remits to the finance company). The Largo example above was an example of a non-notification arrangement since the customer paid Largo.

CRITERIA FOR CLASSIFICATION Sale versus borrowing accounting represent radically different views of the substance of the transaction, and will significantly change financial statement relationships, such as the current ratio. How is the substance of the transaction determined? The CICA's AcSB provides guidance, but not required standards, in the Accounting Guideline, "Transfers of Receivables." This Guideline states that a transfer of receivables should be accounted for as a sale as long as

transferee
in the transfer of accounts receivable to a third party, the third-party entity that receives the accounts receivable; the finance company

transferor
in the transfer of accounts receivable to a third party, the entity that delivers the accounts receivable; the company that has the accrued receivable

1. Measurable consideration changes hands.
2. The company (deemed the **transferor**) has surrendered control over the receivables to the finance company (the **transferee**). Control has transferred if
   a. Transferred receivables are beyond the legal control of the transferor, even if the transferor becomes bankrupt,
   b. The transferee (the finance company, in our example) has the unrestricted right to pledge the assets in other loan transactions as it sees fit without conditions attached by the transferor, and
   c. The transferor doesn't have access to the receivables, through a repurchase arrangement or a clause that would force the transferee to return the receivables under certain conditions.

What does all this mean?

- Initial transfer of consideration, $176,000 in the Largo case, must be established so that the consideration is measurable. If the consideration is contingent on the finance company's collection experience or other variables, condition (1) is not met.
- If the transfer is with recourse (in the event the customer defaults), and the cost of recourse cannot be estimated, then condition (1) is not met.

- If the sale is with recourse, but the cost of recourse can be estimated, then this cost is recorded and condition (1) is met.
- A recourse obligation can also be met through replacement of receivables, (a ROAP clause) and a sale may still be recorded if other conditions are met. Of course, Largo has to have other receivables to use as replacements.
- If a transfer results in transfer of title to the receivable, condition 2 is met.
- Once the receivables are transferred, they must be beyond the legal control of the transferor. For instance, if the transferor were to go into bankruptcy, and the trustee could regain control over the receivables for the benefit of creditors, condition (2a) is not met. Legislation governing legal control after transfer varies between provincial jurisdictions.
- Common clauses in transfer arrangements preclude the finance company from using the receivables as collateral for other loans (pledging the receivables) or reselling them. If the rights of the finance company are restricted, a sale has not taken place according to condition (2b).
- If the transferee (the finance company) can force the transferor to repurchase the receivables, condition (2c) is not met and a borrowing is recorded.
- If the transferor retains the right to repurchase the accounts receivable, again, control condition (2c) is not met and a borrowing results.

You should understand that the complexity of these arrangements, with their extensive call and put options, makes accounting in this area very specialized. We're going to only scratch the surface. A few examples follow.

Case 1 Transfer Recorded as a Sale. Assume that Largo sells $200,000 of accounts receivable with recourse on 15 August 20X2, to a finance company on a notification basis. The finance company estimates that uncollectible accounts will amount to $3,000. The financing fee is 6% (financing costs are lower when there is recourse). A ROAP clause is included in the agreement. That is, recourse means that if a customer that owes $6,800 does not pay on time, the finance company has recourse to Largo, and Largo has to provide $6,800 to the finance company, Largo can then try to collect from the customer. The ROAP clause allows Largo to assign a different $6,800 receivable to the finance company, avoiding the need to pay out $6,800. (This $6,800 default is over and above the expected uncollectible amount of $3,000.)

The arrangement is recorded as a sale; we assume that the cost of recourse is estimable and both conditions are met. The difference between the book value of receivables transferred and assets received from the finance company is recognized immediately as an expense.

Cash {$200,000 − $3,000 − [6% × ($200,000 − $3,000)]}	185,180	
Bad debt expense*	3,000	
Financing fee** [6% × ($200,000 − $3,000)]	11,820	
Accounts receivable		200,000

* May also be charged to allowance for doubtful accounts.
** Also called "a loss on sale of receivables."

Largo receives $197,000, the net "good" receivables balance, less the $11,820 financing fee on $197,000. Bad debts are recorded. Again, the impact of expected sales discounts and returns is ignored in this example.

In this example, *there will be final reckoning with the finance company.* If the finance company collects exactly $197,000, the transaction is over. If the finance company collects less, Largo will have to provide new receivables for the deficit, because the ROAP clause is in effect. If the finance company collects more than $197,000, Largo will get a cheque. If arrangements met the criteria for a sale, collection estimates should have been accurate enough so that the final reckoning is immaterial; otherwise, someone's judgement was at fault when the transaction was recorded!

Largo's contingent obligation under this arrangement, and the details of the arrangement itself, must be fully disclosed in the financial statements.

Case 2 Transfer Recorded as a Borrowing. In a transfer recorded as a borrowing, receivables stay on the books, and a loan is recorded. The transferor recognizes the difference between the assets received from the finance company and the book value of the receivables as interest *over the term of the loan.* This is in contrast to the sale example, in which the financing fee was immediately recognized as an expense. Assume the same facts as Case 1, except that Largo retains the option to repurchase the receivables. This means that the transaction is recorded as a borrowing. Entries to record the borrowing and estimated uncollectible accounts are

Cash {$200,000 – $3,000 – [6% × ($200,000 – $3,000)]}	185,180	
Discount on payable to finance company		
[6% × ($200,000 – $3,000)]	11,820	
Payable to finance company		197,000
Bad debt expense*	3,000	
Allowance for doubtful accounts		3,000

* Entry made if existing allowance is inadequate.

The discount account is a contra account to the payable to finance company account and represents the total interest to be paid by Largo. This contra account is amortized as interest expense over the loan term. Largo records sales adjustments, such as sales discounts and returns, as they occur and reduces the receivable from the customer and payable to the finance company as customers remit cash. At the end of the arrangement, Largo must pay any outstanding balance on the payable, whether or not customers have remitted on time.

It is worth noting that the payable to the finance company must be shown as a current liability on the balance sheet, and may not be netted with the related accounts receivable. Netting is appropriate only when there is a legal right to net, *and* intent to net; while intent is present in this case, there is no legal right to net and the balances must be shown as the separate elements they really are.

An example of disclosure of sale of accounts receivable is shown in Exhibit 7-5. Receivables are often transferred to a company subsidiary, and rules are quite stringent regarding the activities of this unit in order to ensure that the transfer constitutes a change in control.

NOTES RECEIVABLE AND PAYABLE

A note receivable is a written promise to pay a specified amount at a specified future date (or a series of amounts over a series of payment dates). Notes receivable are a current asset if the term is a year or an operating cycle; notes payable are a current liability and are the mirror image of receivables. Notes payable are also called "short-term commercial paper," issued by large companies with excellent credit ratings, and bought by other companies as temporary investments. Some notes formalize **collateral security** for the lender: assets of the borrower that the lender can take if the note is not repaid.

collateral security

assets of the borrower that the secured lender can seize if the note goes into default

Notes may be non-current assets or liabilities if their term exceeds the cut-off for current classification. Accounting for non-current notes is no different than that explained here; only the classification changes! Remember that classification is as much a function of intent as of term—how long does management mean to hang on to the note?

Notes usually provide

- extended payment terms
- more security than sales invoices and other commercial trade documents
- a formal basis for charging interest
- negotiability

EXHIBIT 7-5

IMPERIAL TOBACCO CANADA LIMITED
SALE OF ACCOUNTS RECEIVABLE DISCLOSURE

December 31 2002

From Note 2, Significant Accounting Policies:

Transfer of receivables

A wholly-owned subsidiary of the Corporation entered into an agreement under which it sells, on a revolving basis, an interest in a pool of eligible accounts receivable to a securitization trust. These transactions are accounted for as sales when the subsidiary is considered to have surrendered control over the transferred accounts receivable and receives proceeds from the trust, other than a beneficial interest in the assets sold. Accordingly, the related accounts receivable are removed from the consolidated balance sheets. Gains or losses on these transactions are dependent in part on the previous carrying amount of the accounts receivable transferred, which is allocated between the accounts receivable sold and the retained interest, based on their relative fair value at the date of the transfer. Due to the short-term nature of the receivables, the subsidiary's interest in the pool during the year is valued at historical cost, which approximates fair value. The accounts receivable are transferred on a fully-serviced basis.

We'll look at notes receivable and payable together in the material that follows.

TYPES OF NOTES Most notes represent loans from financial institutions. Notes also arise from normal sales, extension of the payment period of accounts receivable, exchanges of long-term assets, and advances to employees. The borrower is the *maker* of the note and the lender is the *payee.*

The **face value**, or **maturity value**, is the dollar amount stated on the note. The face value is the amount, excluding interest, payable at the end of the note term, unless the note requires that principal repayments be made according to an instalment schedule. The principal value equals the maturity value if the stated interest rate equals the market interest rate. The total interest over the life of the note equals the total cash receipts less the principal amount.

Notes may be categorized as **interest-bearing** or non-interest-bearing notes. Interest-bearing notes specify the interest rate to be applied to the face amount in computing interest payments. **Non-interest-bearing** notes do not state an interest rate but command interest through face values that exceed the principal amount.

Interest-bearing notes in turn can be divided into two categories according to the type of cash payment required: (1) notes whose cash payments are interest only, except for final maturity payment and (2) notes whose cash payments are *blended,* and include both interest and principal. Actually, there are an unlimited number of principal and repayment options. Payment schedules are not limited to those used in the examples.

Example 1: Blended payments. A 10%, $4,000, two-year note issued by Vancouver Sealines that requires interest to be paid on its face value, is an interest-bearing note. The annual interest of $400 ($4,000 × 10%) is payable at the end of each year of the note term. The $4,000 face amount is paid at the end of the second year. In total, $800 of interest is required over the term of the note. In notes of this type, the original principal is not decreased by the yearly payment.

Now assume that Vancouver's note is instead a note that requires blended payments, involving two equal annual amounts payable at the end of each year. These payments each contain interest and principal in the amount necessary to discharge the debt at 10% in two payments. The payment is computed as follows:

$4,000 = Present value of an annuity = Payment × (P/A, 10%, 2)
$4,000 ÷ (P/A, 10%, 2) = Payment
$4,000 ÷ 1.73554 = $2,304.76 = Payment

Payment	Interest Component	Principal Component
1	$400.00 ($4,000 × 10%)	$1,904.76 ($2,304.76 − $400)
2	$209.52 ($4,000 − $1,904.76) × 10%	$2,095.24 ($2,304.76 − $209.52)
	$609.52	$4,000.00

Total interest for the second type of note ($609.52) is less than for the first note because part of the first payment is a principal payment, which reduces the principal on which interest is paid in the second period.

Vancouver would record the note and its payments as follows:

Initial entry:		
Cash	4,000	
Note payable		4,000
First payment:		
Interest expense	400	
Note payable	1,905	
Cash (rounded)		2,305
Second payment:		
Interest expense	210	
Note payable	2,095	
Cash		2,305

Example 2: Interest-Bearing Note. On 1 April 20X2, Lionel Company loaned $12,000 cash to Baylor Company and received a three-year, 10% note. Interest is payable each 31 March, and the principal is payable at the end of the third year. The stated and market interest rates are equal. The entry to record the note is as follows:

Lionel			Baylor		
1 April 20X2			*1 April 20X2*		
Note receivable	12,000		Cash	12,000	
Cash		12,000	Note payable		12,000

Accounting for this note is very simple because the 12% interest rate charged is also the market rate. Cash interest received equals interest revenue recognized over the terms of the note, as indicated in the remaining entries. The computation for interest assumes months of equal length; in real life, interest is accrued by days if it is material.

Lionel			Baylor		
31 December 20X2, 20X3, 20X4—Adjusting entries					
Interest receivable	900*		Interest expense	900	
Interest revenue		900	Interest payable		900
* $12,000 × 10% × 9/12					
31 March 20X3 and 20X4—Interest payments					
Cash	1,200		Interest payable	900	
Interest receivable		900	Interest expense	300	
Interest revenue		300*	Cash		1,200
* $12,000 × 10% × 3/12					

Lionel			Baylor		
31 March 20X5—Payment at maturity					
Cash	13,200		Interest payable	900	
Note receivable		12,000	Interest expense	300	
Interest receivable		900	Note payable	12,000	
Interest revenue		300	Cash		13,200

Interest Rate

The interest rate stated in a note may not equal the market rate prevailing on obligations involving similar credit rating or risk, although the stated rate is always used to determine the cash interest payments. If the stated and market rates are different, the *market rate is used to value the note and to measure interest revenue or expense.*

market (interest) rate
the prevailing or last quoted interest rate for borrowing or lending identical amounts, with identical credit risk, terms, and conditions

The **market rate** is the rate accepted by two parties with opposing interests engaged in an arm's-length transaction. If the value of the consideration given is known, the rate can be determined by equating the present value of the cash flows called for in the note to the market value of the consideration. The rate can be determined with a computer program or calculator that determines the correct rate iteratively—that is, by trial and error.

For example, assume that on 30 June 20X5, a firm sells equipment with a cash price of $10,000 and receives in exchange a note that requires a payment of $6,000 on 30 June 20X6, and another $6,000 on 30 June 20X7. The note does not explicitly mention interest, but $2,000 of interest is implicit in the note ($6,000 × 2) − $10,000. The interest rate is computed using the present value of an annuity as follows:

$$\$10{,}000 = \$6{,}000 \times (P/A, i, 2)$$
$$\$10{,}000 \div \$6{,}000 = 1.66667 = (P/A, i, 2)$$

The value 1.66667 does not appear in the table for the present value of an ordinary annuity, but is almost halfway between the 12% and 14% values; a calculator equipped for present value tells us that i = 13.066%. This rate must at least equal the rate incurred by the debtor on similar financing.

Principal Amount of Note

For accounting purposes, the principal amount of a note is measured by the fair market value or cash equivalent value of goods or services provided in exchange for the note, if this value is known, or the present (discounted) value of all cash payments required under the note using the market rate. The principal is also the amount initially subject to interest. The principal represents the sacrifice by the payee, and therefore the present value of the future payments, at the date of the transaction. Any amount paid in excess of the principal is interest.

Example 3: Different Market and Stated Rates. Fox Company, which sells specialized machinery and equipment, sold equipment on 1 January 20X3, and received a two-year, $10,000 note with a 3% stated interest rate from its customer, Hound Limited. Interest is payable each 31 December and the entire principal is payable 31 December 20X4. The equipment does not have a ready market value. The market rate of interest appropriate for this note is 10%. The present value (and principal) of the note is computed as follows (amounts are rounded to the nearest dollar):

Present value of maturity amount:	
$10,000(P/F, 10%, 2) = $10,000(.82645) =	$8,265
Present value of the nominal interest payments:	
$10,000(3%)(P/A, 10%, 2) = $300(1.73554) =	521
Present value of the note at 10%	$8,786

Notes with stated interest rates below market may be used by companies to increase sales. The Fox Company note, for example, uses a low nominal (stated) interest rate offset by an increased face value. Many buyers of big-ticket items, including automobiles, home appliances, and even houses, are more concerned about the monthly payment than the final maturity payment—the balloon payment, as a large final payment is called. A note with an $8,786 face value and a 10% stated rate achieves the same present value to Fox, but a 3% interest payment on $10,000 ($300) may be more attractive than a 10% payment on $8,786 ($879) for Hound, the customer. Accounting for these arrangements involves appropriate recognition of the principal as the proceeds on sale, and interest as time passes.

Typically, if notes are for less than a year, low interest rates are ignored, because the effect of interest is immaterial. The stated interest would be recorded as interest revenue, and the stated amount of the note would be recorded as a sale. However, when low-interest loans have a term beyond a year, they must be valued with respect to the time value of money.

As the Fox Company example illustrates, when the stated and market interest rates are different, the *face value* and *principal* differ. Notes are recorded at gross (face) value plus a premium or minus a discount amount (the gross method), or at the net principal value (the net method). The two methods are illustrated below.

1 January 20X3:	**Gross**		**Net**	
For Fox Company				
Note receivable	10,000		8,786	
Discount on note receivable		1,214		—
Sales		8,786		8,786
For Hound Ltd.				
Equipment	8,786		8,786	
Discount on note payable	1,214		—	
Note payable		10,000		8,786

Under either method, the net book value of the note is $8,786, the principal value. The discount account is a contra account to notes receivable or payable. The gross method discloses both the note's face value and the implicit interest that is included in the face value of the note. Since the note is disclosed net of its discount on any balance sheet, the two methods are identical in presentation. In the remaining parts of the example, only the gross method will be illustrated, as it is more comparable with accounting for bonds payable, which you will see in Chapter 12.

The entries at the end of the fiscal year are as follows:

31 December 20X3:

Fox			Hound		
Cash ($10,000 × 3%)	300		Interest expense	878	
Discount on note receivable	578		Discount on note payable		578
Interest revenue ($8,786 × 10%)		878	Cash		300

The balance sheet dated 31 December 20X3 discloses net notes receivable and payable of $9,364 [$10,000 − ($1,214 − $578)]. This amount is also the present value of the payment on 1 January 20X4.

$10,300(P/F, 10%, 1) = $10,300(.90909) = $9,364 (rounded)

effective interest method

a measure of interest expense or revenue over the life of a financial instrument not issued at par; measures expense or revenue as a constant rate over the term of the financial instrument

The market rate of interest is applied to the beginning balance of the net note receivable to compute interest. This approach, called the **effective interest method**, results in a constant rate of interest throughout the life of the note. Another approach, the straight-line method, amortizes a constant amount of discount each period. The straight-line method produces a varying *rate* of interest period by period (that is, "interest ÷ note" will vary), but it is much simpler and may yield results that are not materially different from the effective interest method. In this example, the straight-line method results in discount amortization of $607 ($1,214 ÷ 2 years) and interest revenue or expense of $907 ($607 + $300) in both years.

Continuing with the effective interest method, the entry at the end of 20X4 is the following:

31 December 20X4:

Fox			Hound		
Cash ($10,000 × 3%)	300		Interest expense	936	
Discount on note receivable	636		Discount on note payable		636
Interest revenue ($9,364 × 10%)		936	Cash		300

After the 31 December 20X4 entry, the net notes receivable and payable balance is $10,000, the present value at that date. The discount account balance is zero, and the note is paid.

31 December 20X4:

Fox			Hound		
Cash	10,000		Note payable	10,000	
Note receivable		10,000	Cash		10,000

Example 4: Note Issued for Non-Cash Consideration. Siever Company sold specialized equipment originally costing $20,000 with a net book value of $16,000 on 1 January 20X2 to Bellow. The market value of the equipment was not readily determinable.

Siever received a $5,000 down payment and a $10,000, 4% note payable in four equal annual instalments starting 31 December 20X2. The current market rate on notes of a similar nature and risk is 10%. With the stated rate of 4%, the payment (A) is determined as follows:

$10,000 = A × (P/A, 4%, 4) = A × (3.62990)
$10,000 ÷ 3.62990 = $2,755 = P

Therefore, the note's principal (P) equals the present value of four $2,755 payments at 10%, plus the $5,000 down payment.

P = $2,755 × (P/A, 10%, 4) + $5,000 = $2,755 × (3.16987) + $5,000
= $8,733 + $5,000 = $13,733

The present value of the consideration received is $13,733, which is the assigned value of the equipment. The entry to record the sale (gross method) is:

1 January 20X2 (gross method)

Siever			Bellow		
Cash	5,000		Equipment	13,733	
Note receivable	10,000		Discount on note payable	1,267	
Accum. amortization	4,000*		Cash		5,000
Loss on sale	2,267		Note payable		10,000
Discount on note receivable		1,267**			
Equipment		20,000			

* ($20,000 − $16,000)
** ($10,000 − $8,733)

The loss on sale equals the net book value of the equipment ($16,000) less the present value of consideration received ($13,733). The discount on the note is its face value minus its present value, $1,267 (that is, $10,000 − $8,733). Interest is accrued on the note receivable at year-end using the 10% market rate.

Impairment

Notes receivable will be an asset only if the maker of the note pays—both the principal and interest are to be considered in this regard. After all, revenue cannot be recognized, i.e., interest cannot be accrued, unless it is supported by an increase in an asset, the receivable. An allowance for doubtful notes receivable must be established if value is impaired.

In calculating the extent of such an allowance, two things must be assessed:

1. *The present value of the cash flows expected from the maker of the note over its remaining life.* While some customers will pay nothing, it's quite common to get partial payment, or even complete payment, several months or years late. To assess the fair value of this cash flow, the time value of money must be taken into consideration by calculating the present value of the cash flow.

2. *The fair value of any collateral security (assets)* that the *lender can legally repossess*; this collateral has to be valued at its fair market value.

For example, assume that a note receivable was on the books for $4,800, including both principal and interest, and the customer has encountered financial difficulties. As a result, the cash flows associated with the note are expected to have a present value of $1,200. Some of this will come from a cash payment from the customer, and some from selling repossessed collateral. A $3,600 loan loss or bad debt expense is recognized, and an allowance for doubtful accounts is established.

Section 3025 of the *CICA Handbook*, "Impaired Loans," governs this area; it contains very technical rules over an area that is vastly complicated by the difficulty of making accurate predictions of cash flows to be received from a party in financial difficulty, and by the need to recognize interest revenue on balances as time passes. There is some room to be pessimistic, take large loan losses, and then watch income bounce back with loan loss recoveries.

Discounting Notes Receivable

discounting notes receivable
the transfer of notes receivable, usually to a financial institution; the purchasing institution reduces the face value of the note plus required interest payments by the interest fee charged to arrive at proceeds

Rather than hold a note receivable to maturity, payees may **discount** (transfer) the note with a bank or financial institution. Notes can be discounted by any holder, as well as by the original payee, at any time before the note's maturity date. Discounting notes receivable may be done with or without recourse, and is very similar to the transfer of accounts receivable. The criteria for accounting treatment are the same: the transaction can be recorded as a sale or a borrowing.

The most common outcome for notes receivable is that the transaction is recorded as a sale—the company records a gain or loss equal to the difference between the proceeds and book value of the note, including accrued interest, and has a contingent liability until the note is paid by the maker. If the note is discounted without recourse, the payee has no contingent liability.

A common version of this is an arrangement whereby a retail store's sales are immediately financed by a consumer loan company. It's like discounting a note, but they skip a step—the note is taken out by the customer directly with the finance company. Here's how it works: the customer goes to a store and decides on a purchase. The customer fills in a finance company loan application right in the retail store, and credit is granted, or not, usually on the spot. The payment scheme may start immediately, or may be deferred for some time (e.g., "Don't Pay a Cent!"). The store receives the present value of the loan agreement from the finance company, less some kind of financing fee, which is usually built into the discount rate. Since the finance company has approved the credit application, it has no recourse to the retail store, whose relationship with the customer is over as soon as the goods are delivered.

Disclosure

Disclosure of notes receivable and payable must satisfy the requirements of the Financial Instruments section of the *CICA Handbook*. *Terms and conditions* of notes must be disclosed, including maturity dates, amount and timing of all future cash flows, collateral, and so on. *Interest rates*, both stated and effective, are also required disclosure.

For notes receivable, *exposure to credit risk* must be disclosed, along with information about significant concentrations of credit risk. *Fair value* for this class of financial asset or financial liability must be disclosed. Fair value would be different than book value if interest rates had shifted from the time that the notes were issued, since fair value would be established through present value techniques using current market interest rates.

CONCEPT REVIEW

1. Which basic accounting concepts underlie the practice of establishing an allowance for doubtful accounts?
2. What is the purpose of an aging schedule?
3. Explain the difference between recording the transfer of accounts receivable as a sale or a borrowing.
4. What is the basic approach to measuring the value of notes receivable and notes payable?

CURRENT LIABILITIES

Current (short-term) liabilities are amounts payable within one year from the date of the balance sheet or within the normal operating cycle, where this is longer than a year. The time dimension (year versus operating cycle) that applies to current assets also generally applies to current liabilities. Liabilities that are not due within this current time frame are called long-term, or non-current, liabilities. Long-term liabilities are discussed in Chapter 12.

Most current liabilities are monetary items; they obligate the reporting enterprise to pay a fixed sum of cash in the future, sometimes with interest added. Common monetary current liabilities are

- accounts payable
- short-term notes payable
- cash dividends payable
- advances and returnable deposits
- monetary accrued liabilities
- estimated monetary liabilities, including:
  - taxes (sales, property, and payroll)
  - conditional payments (income taxes and bonuses)
  - compensated-absence liabilities (e.g., vacation pay)
- current loans payable
- current portion of long-term debt

Current liabilities also may include some non-monetary items. Most common non-monetary items are

- Non-monetary accrued liabilities, such as an airline's obligation to provide free flights under its frequent-flier reward plans, or a manufacturer's obligation to honour warranties on its products; and
- Unearned revenues, which are liabilities to provide goods and/or services in the future as the result of cash already received, such as magazine subscription revenue or pre-payment for goods on order.

Special accounting problems related to monetary current liabilities are discussed in the following sections. Accounting for non-monetary liabilities is discussed in Chapter 12.

Accounts Payable

trade accounts payable
amounts owed to suppliers for goods and services purchased on credit

Accounts payable—more descriptively, **trade accounts payable**—are obligations arising from the firm's ongoing operations, including the acquisition of merchandise, materials, supplies, and services used in the production and sale of goods or services. Current payables that are not trade accounts (such as income tax and the current portion of long-term debt) should be reported separately from accounts payable. In determining the amount of the liability, the accountant must adjust for purchase discounts, allowances, and returns, exactly as discussed for accounts receivable. Of course, a company never accrues an allowance for non-payment, since it is the payer!

Cash Dividends Payable

Cash dividends declared but not yet paid are reported as a current liability if they are to be paid within the coming year or operating cycle. Declared dividends are reported as a liability between the date of declaration and payment because declaration gives rise to an enforceable contract.

Liabilities are not recognized for undeclared dividends in arrears on preferred shares or for any other dividends not formally declared by the Board of Directors. Dividends in arrears on cumulative preferred shares should be disclosed in the notes to the financial statements. These dividends must be paid before any common dividends can be paid.

Monetary Accrued Liabilities

Examples of monetary accrued liabilities include wages and benefits earned by employees, interest earned by creditors but not yet paid, and the costs of goods and services received but not yet invoiced by the supplier. Monetary accrued liabilities are recorded in the accounts by making adjusting entries at the end of the accounting period. For example, any wages that have not yet been recorded or paid at the end of the accounting period must be recorded by debiting wage expense and crediting accrued wages payable. Recognition of accrued liabilities is consistent with the definition of a liability and the matching principle.

Advances and Returnable Deposits

A company may receive advances or cash deposits from customers as guarantees for payment of future obligations or to guarantee performance on a contract or service. For example, when an order is taken, a company may require an advance payment to cover losses that would be incurred if the order is cancelled. Such advances create liabilities for the company receiving the payment until the underlying earnings process is completed. Advances are recorded by debiting cash and crediting a liability account such as customer deposits.

Deposits may also be made as guarantees in case of non-collection or for possible damage to property. For example, deposits required from customers by gas, water, electricity, and other public utilities are liabilities of such companies to their customers. Employees may also make returnable deposits to ensure the return of keys and other company property, for locker privileges, and for club memberships. Deposits should be reported as current or long-term liabilities depending on the time involved between date of deposit and expected termination of the relationship. If the advances or deposits are interest-bearing, an annual adjusting entry is required to accrue interest expense and to increase the related liability.

Taxes

Provincial and federal laws require businesses to collect certain taxes from customers and employees for remittance to governmental agencies. These taxes include sales taxes, income tax withheld from employee paycheques, property taxes, and payroll taxes. Similar collections are made on behalf of unions, insurance companies, and employee-sponsored activities. Collections made for third parties increase both cash and current liabilities. The collections represent liabilities that are settled when the funds are remitted to the designated parties. Common examples of such taxes follow.

SALES TAXES Retail businesses are required to collect sales taxes from customers and remit them to the appropriate government agency. Taxes include the goods and services tax (GST) and, in most provinces, provincial sales taxes (PST), or both together, the harmonized sales tax (HST). The Emerging Issues Committee of the CICA has indicated that revenues should be recorded net of GST collected. Purchases of goods and services should be recorded net of any GST recoverable. GST is remitted periodically, net of GST paid on purchases. The net amount of the GST payable or receivable should be carried as a liability or asset, as appropriate.

Any GST that is not recoverable should be accounted for as a component of the cost of the goods or services to which it relates. If it is paid and is not recoverable in relation to a capital asset, GST is included in the asset's capital cost.

PST paid is part of the cost of whatever was bought: capital assets or inventory, for example.

Typical entries, with 7% GST and assuming 9% provincial sales tax and $500,000 of sales, are as follows:

1. At date the tax is assessed (point of sale):

Cash and accounts receivable	580,000	
Sales revenue		500,000
GST payable ($500,000 × 7%)		35,000
PST payable ($500,000 × 9%)		45,000

In some provinces, the PST is charged on the subtotal of sales plus GST. However, GST is never charged on the subtotal of sales plus PST. It probably goes without saying that companies need to become expert in the rules and regulations that govern sales tax application. Governments perform sales tax audits to encourage compliance.

Assume that $300,000 of inventory was purchased, subject to GST and PST:

2. At inventory purchase:		
Inventory ($300,000 × 1.09)	327,000	
GST payable ($300,000 × .07)	21,000	
Cash or accounts payable ($300,000 × 1.16)		348,000

Taxes are remitted:

3. At date of remittance to taxing authority:		
GST payable ($35,000 − $21,000)*	14,000	
Cash		14,000
PST payable	45,000	
Cash		45,000

* The GST remitted is reduced by the amount of GST paid on purchased goods and services.

PAYROLL TAXES Employers act as a collection agent for certain taxes and payments. They withhold appropriate amounts from their employees and send the money off to the appropriate party shortly thereafter; a liability exists in the meantime. Common withholdings include

- *Personal income tax.* An employee's personal federal and provincial tax are deducted at source and remitted regularly (at least monthly) to the federal government. At the end of the year, the employee receives a record of deductions, and determines, on his or her annual tax return, who owes whom and how much.
- *Canada pension plan (CPP).* Employees have to pay a percentage of their salary to the CPP; employers have to match this amount dollar for dollar.
- *Employment insurance (EI).* Employees have to pay a percentage of their salary to secure EI benefits; the employer must pay 1.4 times the employees' contributions as its share.
- *Union dues.* If stipulated in labour agreements, union dues are deducted at source and remitted to the union monthly.
- *Insurance premiums.* A variety of employee benefits, such as group insurance and medical insurance, require that employees pay all or a portion of the premiums; these are deducted at source.
- *Pension plan payments.* If employees are required to pay a portion of their salary to secure a pension, these amounts are deducted at source and remitted to the pension plan trustee.
- *Other deductions.* What else does the employee wish to have taken off his or her paycheque? Examples include certain charitable donations and parking fees. All of these are remitted to the appropriate party after deduction.

Payroll deduction accounting is illustrated in Exhibit 7-6.

PROPERTY TAXES Property taxes paid directly by the company are based on the assessed value of real property, and are used to support city, municipality, and other designated activities. Unpaid taxes constitute a lien on the assessed property. Property taxes are based on the assessed value of the property, which may or may not correspond to market value, and the mill rate (tax rate per thousand dollars of assessed value).

Property taxes are usually set by the taxing authority partway through the fiscal year, which means that the company must use last year's tax bill as an estimate to accrue monthly expenses until the final assessment and tax rate are known. Estimates are corrected when the real tax rate

EXHIBIT 7-6

ILLUSTRATION OF PAYROLL DEDUCTIONS

Thor Company reported the following information relating to payroll for January 20X5:

Gross wages		$100,000
Deductions:		
Income tax	$20,000	
Canada Pension Plan	2,250	
Employment insurance	2,100	
Union dues	1,400	
Charitable contributions	1,600	27,350
Net pay		$ 72,650

To record salaries and employee deductions:

Salary expense	100,000	
Employee income tax payable		20,000
CPP payable		2,250
EI payable		2,100
Union dues payable		1,400
Charitable contributions payable		1,600
Cash		72,650

To record payroll expenses payable by the employer:

Salary expense	5,190	
CPP payable (matching payment)		2,250
EI payable ($2,100 × 1.4)		2,940

To record remittance of payroll deductions (composite entry):

Employee income tax payable	20,000	
CPP payable	4,500	
EI payable	5,040	
Union dues payable	1,400	
Charitable contributions payable	1,600	
Cash		32,540

is known, but corrections to estimates affect only the current and future periods; retroactive corrections to prior fiscal years are not made for estimates. Taxes are also paid for a 12-month period that reflects the city or municipality fiscal year, which may or may not correspond to the company's; accruals or pre-payments typically result due to these timing problems.

Conditional Payments

Some liabilities are established on the basis of a firm's periodic income. Two examples are bonuses or profit-sharing payments to employees and corporate income tax based on taxable income. These items can be established at year-end, but the liability must be estimated whenever interim statements are prepared throughout the year—monthly or quarterly. Until paid, they represent current liabilities of the organization.

INCOME TAX PAYABLE Interim reports require a provision for both federal and provincial tax liabilities, so estimates are required. The estimated liability should be reported as a current liability based on the firm's best estimates. After year-end, the tax return is prepared and the estimate is adjusted for the year-end financial statements before the books are finally closed. Periodic instalment payments are required. Accounting for corporate income tax is reviewed in Chapters 15 and 16.

BONUSES Many companies pay cash bonuses, which depend on earnings. These are estimated at interim periods, but calculated "for real" at the end of the fiscal year. Calculations must be made in accordance with established formula or the authorization of the Board of Directors. Bonuses can be material—both to the company and to the employee, so it's important that they're properly approved.

Compensated-Absence Liabilities

The Canada Labour Code requires that employees receive paid vacations and holidays. The expense for salaries and wages paid during these absences from work is recognized in the current year. When employees can carry over unused time to future years, GAAP requires that any expense due to compensated absences must be recognized (accrued) in the year in which it is earned, provided that certain criteria are met. Compensated absence liabilities may also be recorded if there are sick days or parental leaves that are earned but not used in a given year (that is, carry over) or if employees have sabbatical entitlements. The criteria

- The absence from work relates to services already rendered.
- The benefits accumulate (carry over) or *vest.*
- The payment is probable (the absence will occur).
- The amount (i.e., cost) can be reliably estimated.

These should look like fairly standard recognition criteria by now!

Implementing the accrual of compensated absences requires an adjusting entry at the end of each fiscal year to accrue all of the compensation cost for the vacation and medical leave time that is carried over. An expense and a current liability are recorded. When the time is taken, the liability account may be debited at the time the employee is paid. Alternatively, the liability may be adjusted only at year-end. Either approach will recognize the cost of the compensated absences as an expense in the period earned rather than when taken.

For example, consider the carryover of vacation time of the Conway Company, which has 500 employees. Each employee is granted three weeks paid vacation time each year. Vacation time, up to a maximum accumulation of four weeks, may be carried over to subsequent years prior to termination of employment. At the end of 20X5, the end of the annual accounting period, personnel records revealed the following information concerning carryover vacation amounts:

CARRYOVERS FROM 20X5*

Number of Employees	Weeks per Employee	Total Weeks	Salary per Week	Total Accrual
10	2	20	$1,500	$30,000
3	1	3	2,000	6,000
				$36,000

* These are carryovers from 20X5 to future years.

Disregarding payroll taxes, which are excluded here to simplify the analysis, the indicated entries are as follows:

31 December 20X5—adjusting entry to accrue vacation salaries not yet taken or paid

	Dr.	Cr.
Salary expense	36,000	
Liability for compensated absences		36,000

During 20X6—vacation time carryover taken and salaries paid (all employees took their carried-over vacation time, except for one person who still carried over two weeks, valued at $1,500 per week)

Liability for compensated absences	33,000	
Cash ($36,000 – $3,000)		33,000

The balance remaining in the liability account is $3,000: 2 weeks @ $1,500 per week.

This illustration assumes that there was no change in the rate of pay from 20X5 to 20X6 (when the carryover was used) for those employees who had the carryover. If there were rate changes, the pay difference would be debited (if an increase) or credited (if a decrease) to salary expense during 20X6. The change is considered a change in estimate.

This item is a liability only if a company allows employees to carry over vacation entitlements: many do not, and no liability exists. Most financial institutions, for example, require employees to take all their vacation entitlements before the end of each calendar year; it's important to their internal control systems to have someone else go in and do the employee's job regularly, so that the employee can't hide suspicious activities indefinitely.

Loans as Current Liabilities

Loans may be long-term liabilities or current liabilities. These amounts are material, and must be carefully classified. Loans are current liabilities if

1. *Loans are due on demand.* Demand loans are payable on demand, or after a short delay of 7 to 30 business days to arrange alternate financing. These loans are legally current liabilities, and must be classified as such, even though a demand for payment within the current year is not expected.
2. *Loans are due within the next year.* If the loan has a due date within the next year, it is a current liability, even if the company expects to renegotiate the loan. If debt is partially due within the next year, the current portion must be reclassified. For example, consider the classification of this $500,000 liability:

Current liabilities:	
Current portion of bonds payable	$100,000
Long-term liabilities:	
Bonds payable (50,000 less current portion: $100,000)	$400,000

3. *Long-term debt is in violation of covenants and thus can be called by the lender at any time.* For example, a company might be in arrears on interest payments, or has exceeded the maximum debt-to-equity ratio on the balance sheet date. The company may not yet have had the opportunity to negotiate with the lender. Often all that happens in these circumstances is that the lender increases the interest rate. But the lender could call the loan, and thus the current classification is required.

SHORT-TERM OBLIGATIONS EXPECTED TO BE REFINANCED A company may want to reclassify liabilities from current to long term to improve the reported working capital position. This reclassification is not to be taken lightly—a large reclassification has a material impact on the financial statements.

Intention to restructure a short-term loan as a long-term loan is not enough to justify reclassification. It's common to enter into an agreement to restructure debt, prior to actually doing it. A financing agreement may be relied on to support classification of short-term obligations as long-term debt, if it meets the following criteria:

- The agreement must be non-cancellable by all parties and extend beyond one year from the balance sheet date or from the start of the operating cycle, whichever is longer.
- At the balance sheet date and the issue date, the company must not be in violation of the agreement.
- The lender must be financially capable of honouring the agreement.

If a short-term obligation is to be excluded from current liabilities under a future financing agreement, note disclosure is required and should include

- A general description of the financing agreement;
- The terms of any new obligation to be incurred, and
- The terms of any equity security to be issued.

Disclosure of Monetary Current Liabilities

Need we say it? Current liabilities are *financial instruments*, and must satisfy disclosure requirements for terms and conditions, interest rate risk, and fair value. Disclosure is most likely required for loans and notes payable, as the circumstances surrounding accounts payable render disclosure trivial.

Foreign Currency Receivables and Payables

Early in this chapter, we pointed out that if a company has a bank account in a currency other than Canadian dollars, the cash account on the balance sheet must include the *Canadian dollar equivalent* of that foreign currency. Obviously, we cannot simply add Canadian dollars, U.S. dollars, Hong Kong dollars, and Australian dollars together to derive the total for cash.

The same principle applies to receivables and payables. If a company has accounts or notes that are receivable or payable in foreign currencies, they must be restated to Canadian dollars at the current exchange rate at the balance sheet date.

Monetary items that are denominated in a foreign currency always arise from a transaction, of course. The transaction may be sales to a foreign customer, purchases from a foreign supplier, investments in foreign currency financial instruments, or foreign currency loans from a foreign bank (or from a Canadian bank but in a foreign currency). When the transaction occurs, it is recorded at the exchange rate in effect at the date of the transaction. For example, suppose that Talud Limited has a sale to a customer in England for 10,000 euros when the exchange rate was 1 euro = $2.20. The sale would be recorded as follows:

Accounts receivable (10,000 euros)	22,000	
Sales (10,000 euros × $2.20)		22,000

The receivable is stated (or *denominated*) in euros, not in dollars. The sale is recorded at the Canadian dollar equivalent of the British sales price. However, when the British company pays the account, it will pay 10,000 euros, not $22,000. If payment is made before the end of a fiscal period, the cash receipt must be recorded at the current exchange rate. Suppose that the customer pays the 10,000 euros when the exchange rate is 1 euro = $2.10. Talud will receive only $21,000 in Canadian currency when it converts the cash. The loss is recognized in the current period's income statement.

Cash (10,000 euros × $2.10)	21,000	
Foreign exchange gains and losses	1,000	
Accounts receivable		22,000

If the exchange rate had appreciated instead of depreciated, Talud would record a gain instead of a loss.

EXCHANGE GAIN OR LOSS The difference between the Canadian equivalent of the receivable and of the cash receipt is charged to a *gain or loss* account; this is a normal part of doing business abroad, and the use of the terms "gain"and "loss" for this routine revenue or expense is simply an accounting convention. Companies that do business outside Canada in one or more foreign currencies (which is very common) maintain a regular income statement account entitled "foreign exchange gains and losses." The net balance of the account at the end of each accounting period is reported in the income statement.

Assume now that at Talud's balance sheet date, the receivable is still outstanding. The receivable must be translated to the then-current exchange rate. If the exchange rate at the balance sheet date is 1 euro = $2.25, the value of the account receivable will be $22,500 (10,000 euros × $2.25). The increase of $500 in the Canadian equivalent of the 10,000 euros balance would be recorded as follows:

Accounts receivable ($22,500 – $22,000)	500	
Foreign exchange gains and losses		500

It is important to understand that changes in the exchange rate following the initial transaction affect only the monetary balance (receivable or payable). The change in exchange rates *does not affect the amount initially charged or credited to the non-monetary account.* In the Talud Limited example above, the sales account is not affected by the subsequent change in exchange rate.

Similarly, if inventory or capital assets (such as equipment) are purchased in a foreign currency, changes in the exchange rate between the date of purchase and the date of payment will not affect the originally recorded value of the asset. *Historical cost is determined by the exchange rate at the date of the purchase transaction.* Subsequent gains and losses on the outstanding monetary balance are recognized directly and immediately in the income statement, provided that the balance is classified as current.

CONCEPT REVIEW

1. What are the major categories of current liabilities?
2. Are all current liabilities also monetary liabilities? Explain.
3. How should monetary items that are denominated in a foreign currency be reported at each balance sheet date?

SUMMARY OF KEY POINTS

1. Monetary items are those that will be paid or received in fixed or determinable amounts of money.
2. Cash includes only those items immediately available to pay obligations.
3. The bank reconciliation is an internal control mechanism. The reconciliation of the book balance to the correct cash balance provides the data for end-of-month adjusting entries for cash.
4. In a bank reconciliation, adjustments to the bank are made for outstanding cheques and deposits, and bank errors. The book balance is adjusted for unrecorded items and errors.
5. Doubtful accounts, cash discounts, and sales returns and allowances represent adjustments to the recorded value of receivables, which are necessary to provide an estimate of net realizable value.

6. The allowance for doubtful accounts can be estimated through aging or a percentage-of-sales method.

7. Accounts receivable can be used as collateral for a loan to speed up the cash cycle. Alternatively, accounts receivable can be transferred to a finance company to obtain immediate cash. The key accounting issue is whether the transfer of accounts receivable is treated as a sale or borrowing. When the consideration is known and control is transferred, the transfer is accounted for as a sale. Otherwise, it is treated as a borrowing.

8. Long-term notes are recorded at the present value of all cash payments to be received using the appropriate market rate of interest. Interest is based on that market interest rate and the outstanding principal balance at the beginning of the period. Impaired notes are reduced to the present value of future cash flows.

9. Current liabilities are obligations that are payable within one year or within the normal operating cycle, whichever is longer.

10. Current liabilities commonly include accounts, notes, accruals, property taxes, cash dividends, taxes, bonuses, and other payables.

11. Loans are a current liability if due on demand. Also current liabilities are the current portion of long-term debt and long-term debt in default. Current debt that is to be refinanced as long term may be reclassified as long term only if certain specific conditions are met.

12. Transactions that are denominated in a foreign currency are recorded at the exchange rate that exists at the transaction date. Monetary balances (i.e., receivables and payables) are restated to the exchange rate that exists on the balance sheet date. Gains and losses are recognized in income.

KEY TERMS

aging method, 350
allowance for doubtful accounts, 348
bank reconciliation, 341
collateral security, 357
compensating balance, 339
composite rate, 351
credit memo, 341
credit sales method, 350
debit memo, 341
discounting notes receivable, 364
effective interest rate, 362
face value, 358
guaranteed investment certificate (GIC), 338
interest-bearing, 358
internal control system, 340
market (interest) rate, 360
money market instruments, 338
non-interest-bearing, 358
non-notification basis, 355
non-trade receivable, 346
notification, 355
recourse, 355
T-bill, 338
trade accounts payable, 365
trade accounts receivable, 346
transferee, 355
transferor, 355

REVIEW PROBLEM

At the end of 20X5, three companies ask you to record journal entries in three different areas associated with receivables. The fiscal year of each company ends on 31 December.

1. *Mandalay Company—uncollectible accounts receivable.* Mandalay Company requests that you record journal entries for its bad debt expense and uncollectible accounts receivable in 20X5. Mandalay's 1 January 20X5 balances relevant to accounts receivable are as follows:

Accounts receivable	$400,000 (dr.)
Allowance for doubtful accounts	20,000 (cr.)

During 20X5, $45,000 of accounts receivable are judged to be uncollectible, and no more effort to collect these accounts will be made. Total sales for 20X5 are $1,200,000, of which $200,000 are cash sales; $900,000 was collected on account during 20X5.

a. Assuming that Mandalay uses the credit sales method to estimate bad debt expense and uses 4% of credit sales as its estimate of bad debts, provide the journal entries to record write-offs and bad debt expense for 20X5. Also, provide the 31 December 20X5 balance sheet amount for net accounts receivable.
b. Assuming that Mandalay uses the aging method to estimate net accounts receivable and uses 9% of accounts receivable as its estimate of uncollectibles, provide the journal entries to record write-offs and bad debt expense for 20X5. Also, provide the 31 December 20X5 balance sheet amount for net accounts receivable.

2. *Berkshire Company—transfer of accounts receivable.* Berkshire Company requests that you record journal entries for accounts receivable transferred in 20X5:

On 1 January 20X5, Berkshire transferred $45,000 of accounts receivable with recourse to a finance company, on a notification basis. Bad debts are estimated to be $2,500. The financing fee is 10%. Criteria for sale are met.

3. *White Mountain Company—accounting for long-term notes:* White Mountain Company requests that you record journal entries for a note it received in 20X5. On 1 January 20X5, White Mountain Company sold merchandise for $12,000 and received a $12,000, three-year, 6% note; 12% was the current market rate of interest at that time. Interest is paid annually at the end of each year and the principal is due at the end of the third year. Provide journal entries from inception to final payment. Use the gross method to record the note.

REVIEW PROBLEM—SOLUTION

1. *Mandalay Company*

a. *Summary entry for write-offs during 20X5:*

Allowance for doubtful accounts	45,000	
Accounts receivable		45,000

Adjustment on 31 December 20X5:

Bad debt expense ($1,000,000 × 4%)	40,000	
Allowance for doubtful accounts		40,000

Balance sheet amounts at 31 December 20X5:

Accounts receivable	$455,000*
Allowance for doubtful accounts	(15,000)**
Net accounts receivable	$440,000

* $400,000 + $1,000,000 − $900,000 − $45,000
** $20,000 − $45,000 + $40,000

b. *Summary entry for write-offs during 20X5:*

Allowance for doubtful accounts	45,000	
Accounts receivable		45,000

Adjustment on 31 December 20X5:

Bad debt expense	65,950*	
Allowance for doubtful accounts		65,950

* *Calculation of adjustment:*		
Ending gross accounts receivable		$455,000
Required allowance balance ($455,000 × 9%)		$ 40,950
Allowance balance before adjustment for 20X5:		
Beginning balance, 1 January 20X5	$(20,000)	
Write-offs during 20X5	45,000	25,000
Increase necessary to adjust balance		$ 65,950

Balance sheet amounts at 31 December 20X5:

Accounts receivable	$455,000
Allowance for doubtful accounts	(40,950)
Net accounts receivable	$414,050

2. ***Berkshire Company***

Cash ($45,000 – $2,500 – (10% × $42,500))	38,250	
Bad debt expense	2,500	
Financing fee (10% × $42,500)	4,250	
Accounts receivable		45,000

3. ***White Mountain Company***

Present value of note	
$12,000 (P/F, 12%, 3) = $12,000 (.71178)	$ 8,541
$720 (P/A, 12%, 3) = $720 (2.40183)	1,729
	$ 10,270

a. *1 January 20X5:*

Note receivable	12,000	
Sales revenue		10,270
Discount on note receivable		1,730

b. *31 December 20X5:*

Cash	720	
Discount on note receivable ($1,232 – $720)	512	
Interest revenue ($10,270 × .12)		1,232

c. *31 December 20X6:*

Cash	720	
Discount on note receivable ($1,294 – $720)	574	
Interest revenue ($10,270 + $512) × .12		1,294

d. *31 December 20X7:*

Cash	720	
Discount on note receivable	644	
Interest revenue ($10,270 + $512 + $574) × .12		1,364

e. *31 December 20X7:*

Cash	12,000	
Note receivable		12,000

SUMMARY OF KEY POINTS

1. The compounding of interest is a function of the interest rate per period and the number of periods.
2. Annual interest rates are usually stated as the nominal interest rate, which is the interest rate per period multiplied by the number of periods in a year; the nominal rate understates the effective annual interest rate if compounding is present.
3. The factor for determining the present value of a future amount is the reciprocal of the factor for finding the future value of a present amount.
4. A series of equal periodic payments is known as an annuity.
5. To use an annuity interest factor, the number of payments must correspond with the number of interest periods. If some interest periods have no payment, then an annuity factor cannot be used.
6. When the annuity payments are made at the end of each period, the annuity is called an ordinary annuity or an annuity in arrears.
7. When annuity payments are made at the beginning of each period, the annuity is an annuity due.
8. Unless specifically stated otherwise, annuities are assumed to be ordinary annuities (i.e., with equal payments at the end of each period).
9. The relationship between the factor for an ordinary annuity and the factor for an annuity due is one period's interest.
10. The present or future value of a series of payments cannot be calculated by using an annuity interest factor if the payments are not equal in amount, not equally spaced, or don't correspond to the interest periods. Instead, the present or future value of each payment must be calculated individually. Computer spreadsheet programs can help in such calculations.

QUESTIONS

Q7-1 Define cash as it is used for accounting purposes. What is a cash equivalent?

Q7-2 ABC Company has U.S.$160,000 in a U.S. bank account. It received the money from a customer, for a cash sale, when the exchange rate was U.S.$1 = Cdn.$1.30. At year-end, the exchange rate is U.S.$1 = Cdn.$1.35. At what amount is the sale recorded? What amount of cash is reported on the end-of-year balance sheet?

Q7-3 Why is internal control over cash so important? What are its major components?

Q7-4 Briefly explain the basic purposes of a bank reconciliation. Who should perform the reconciliation?

Q7-5 Define the following terms related to accounting for cash: (a) deposits in transit, (b) cheques outstanding, (c) NSF cheque, and (d) service charge.

Q7-6 At the end of an accounting period, a company has $4,000,000 recorded in accounts receivable, all from sales. It's likely that the company won't collect all of the $4,000,000, even though all the sales really took place. Give three reasons collections might not equal $4,000,000.

Q7-7 Briefly describe the different methods of estimating bad debt expense and the allowance for doubtful accounts for trade receivables.

Q7-8 It sometimes happens that a receivable that has been written off as uncollectible is subsequently collected. Describe the accounting entries in such an event.

Q7-9 Under what circumstances should the direct write-off method for bad debts be used?

Q7-10 A company has a credit balance of $700 in its allowance for doubtful accounts. The amount of credit sales for the period is $80,000, and the balance in accounts receivable is $15,000. Assume that the bad debt estimates are as follows: (a) related to accounts receivable, 8%, or (b) related to credit sales, 0.4%. What would be the balance of the allowance for doubtful accounts and the bad debt expense, if (a) the credit sales method and (b) the aging method were used?

Q7-11 Describe several different ways a company could speed cash flow associated with accounts receivable.

Q7-12 A company with $200,000 in receivables could sell them for $169,000 without recourse, or for $195,000 with recourse. What do the terms "with recourse" and "without recourse" mean? Why is the "without recourse" alternative more expensive? How could the transfer be recognized?

Q7-13 Under what conditions will a transfer of receivables be recognized as a sale? As a borrowing?

Q7-14 A company transferred accounts receivable of $10,000 for $8,500, with recourse. Uncollectible accounts are estimated at $700. Give the required entry, assuming that the transaction is recorded as (a) a borrowing and (b) a sale. What conditions attached to the transfer arrangement would make it likely that the transaction would be recorded as a sale? As a borrowing?

Q7-15 Why is a note receivable sometimes preferred to an account receivable?

Q7-16 How is a note receivable valued if it is (a) a no-interest note and (b) a low-interest note? Assume in all cases that the note had a term of two years. How would your answer change if the note had a term of two months?

Q7-17 Compute the present value of a $20,000, one-year note payable that specifies no interest, although 10% would be a realistic rate. What is the true amount of the principal and interest?

Q7-18 Distinguish between the stated rate of interest and the market rate of interest (yield).

Q7-19 Assume that $6,000 cash is borrowed on a $6,000, 10%, one-year note payable that is interest-bearing and that another $6,000 cash is borrowed on a $6,600 one-year note that is non-interest-bearing. For each note, give the following: (a) face amount of the note, (b) principal amount, (c) maturity amount, and (d) total interest paid. The market interest rate is 10%.

Q7-20 Define a current liability.

Q7-21 Are undeclared dividends on cumulative preferred shares a liability? Explain.

Q7-22 What is a compensated absence? When should the expense related to compensated absences be recognized?

Q7-23 A company has a short-term bank loan outstanding, due on demand. The loan has been outstanding for several years, and will not be repaid in the coming year. Can it be classified as a long-term loan?

Q7-24 A company has an account receivable from a U.S. customer, for U.S.$100,000. It also is payable to another U.S. company, a supplier, in the amount of U.S.$75,000. The payable was incurred when the exchange rate was U.S.$1 = Cdn.$1.42; the receivable, when the rate was $1.38. At year-end, the rate is $1.43. What amount of total exchange gain or loss will the company report for the year? Can the receivable and payable be offset in the financial statements?

CASE 7-1
Network Tools Incorporated

Network Tools Incorporated (NTI) is a public company with revenues of over $40 million. The company is a leading producer of network testing and measurement products, and also network storage and application servers. The company has a strategy to design, market, and sell network server appliance products that provide users with easy-to-operate, scalable, reliable, and cost-effective solutions. Its products are characterized by rapidly changing technology, short product life cycles, and evolving industry standards. NTI has a current stable of approximately 24 products, but recent sales have been concentrated in seven products.

NTI has experienced considerable volatility in its stock price. This volatility has been fuelled by fluctuations in quarterly financial results, conditions in the computer network markets, technological change that has made some NTI products obsolete, and business conditions in general.

NTI depends on third-party distributors for product sales. These distributors support sales teams across North America and internationally. Sales teams must develop long-term relationships with customers, and have an in-depth understanding of customers' information network and needs. That is, effective distributors must devote considerable technical and sales resources to an often-long sales cycle. The distributors carry a variety of competitors' products, and help make decisions on the best fit. NTI's success depends on being that best fit within their primary markets.

NTI is occasionally vulnerable to changes in distributors' inventory strategies. Distributors will usually carry a certain level of inventory, but other times will place an order with NTI only when a customer order has been confirmed.

NTI has particularly close relationships with five dealers, one of whom accounted for 12% of 20X2 sales; all five together accounted for 28% of worldwide 20X2 sales.

Selected data from NTI's draft 20X2 financial statements are shown in Exhibit 1. NTI management is pleased with the draft 20X2 financial statements, which show a return to profitability after several challenging years. The improved results reflect increased sales to the five critical dealers. In the fourth quarter, when it was clear that revenue targets would not be met, senior executives met individually with these five dealers, and learned that all were carrying what they considered to be adequate inventory of NTI products. To encourage sales, special terms were offered:

1. Payment terms were changed from the current 45 days to 110 or 150 days, depending on the distributor. Two distributors were also allowed an additional 90 days to pay for inventory not sold at the end of the 110- or 150-day period.
2. Return rights, normally any goods to a total of 10% of the yearly sales value with a distributor, were increased. Three distributors received (in addition to 10% returns) the right to return up to 100% of the initial orders in exchange for other products within 180 days of delivery. NTI referred to this as "stock rotation rights"—that is, alternate stock would replace unsalable items at the distributor's warehouse. One distributor was permitted, with no restrictions on time, to return all products made obsolete by new NTI products.

Total sales to these five distributors under this program in the fourth quarter totalled $4,104,000. No allowance for doubtful accounts was set up for the resulting receivables, as the five distributors all have excellent payment histories with NTI. Sales returns were accrued at the 10% rate, normal on prior sales.

Another initiative undertaken in the fourth quarter was a special direct marketing program, which used a telephone sales team. The terms listed on the sales order form indicated that the sales were made "at absolutely no risk with a 30-day money-back guarantee." The customer was usually permitted to try the product with no money down for 30 days, and pay for it only after the 30 days were up and the customer had decided to buy the product. Direct marketing sales were $1,316,000 in the fourth quarter, primarily in the last two months. These sales were recognized on delivery, with a 10% allowance for doubtful accounts and a 10% allowance for sales returns accrued on the balance still owing at year-end.

These revenue recognition policies are under discussion as part of the annual audit. You, an analyst in NTI's accounting group, have been asked to quantify the impact of three alternatives:

1. The current policy, as reflected in the financial statements,
2. Recognition of sales only upon payment, and
3. Recognition of sales on delivery with allowances for return of 25% established for distributor sales, and allowances of 20% for return and 25% for non-payment for direct marketing sales.

Your analysis must include the likely impact of these alternatives on accounts receivable, current assets, net income, and the components of net income. Various estimates, assumptions, and approximations will be needed to quantify the alternatives. Your report should also analyze the original policies with respect to appropriate revenue recognition criteria.

Required:
Prepare the report.

EXHIBIT 1

NETWORK TOOLS INCORPORATED
SELECTED FINANCIAL DATA
CONSOLIDATED BALANCE SHEET

Year ended 31 December (in thousands)	20X2	20X1
Assets		
Current Assets		
Cash and cash equivalents	$10,431	$ 9,618
Restricted investments	293	1,124
Accounts receivable (net) (Note 1)	7,828	8,171
Inventories	4,289	6,572
Prepaid expenses	864	1,148
Income tax receivable	2,777	2,897
Future income tax	1,030	1,556
	$27,512	$31,086

Note 1: Accounts receivable are net of allowances for doubtful accounts of $871 (20X2) and $637 (20X1), and allowances for sales returns of $422 (20X2) and $392 (20X1).

CONSOLIDATED INCOME STATEMENT

Year ended 31 December (in thousands)	20X2	20X1
Net revenue	$45,759	$41,650
Cost of revenue	20,020	17,903
Gross profit	25,739	23,747
Operating expenses		
Sales and marketing (including bad debt expense)	12,791	12,720
Research and development	5,432	7,912
General and administrative	5,829	5,605
Total	24,052	26,237
Income (loss) before income tax	1,687	(2,490)
Income tax (recovery)	32	522
Net income	$ 1,655	$ (1,968)

CASE 7-2
Capital Projects Limited

Capital Projects Limited (Capital) is a major Canadian real estate company. It owns large parcels of land around major urban centres, notably Toronto and Calgary. It develops its own properties, and buys and sells land and other real estate properties as the opportunity arises. Because of the economy, recent sales have been slow, and planned activities have been scaled down. To ride out real estate slumps, the company has gone into hibernation in the past and is willing to do so again. The financial position of Capital Projects is such that it can afford this luxury. It has over $8 million in equity and access to a $15 million line of credit at market interest rates, now in the range of 8%.

Early in this fiscal year, Capital sold a parcel of land to PPL Partners (PPL), a smaller developer, who planned a housing project. The sales price was $4,432,000. Capital received $675,000 in cash, and took the rest as a note receivable. The note carried an annual interest rate of 12%, and principal was repayable when individual lots were sold to the final customer, after construction of a PPL home. Interest was to be paid annually. The land was held as collateral for the note, which had a maximum term of 10 years irrespective of sales. Capital recorded a gross profit of $2,900,000 on the sale transaction, all in the current fiscal period.

As the end of the year approached, Capital became aware that PPL had not committed any funds to the construction of its project, and indeed demand for such housing had weakened. There was some talk about interest payment default. Accordingly, Capital called a meeting with PPL to discuss the situation. Three alternatives emerged, as PPL confirmed that it was unwilling to begin construction until housing prices recovered, and it did not have current resources to commit to the interest payments.

The alternatives

1. PPL suggested that interest on the note be permanently waived. PPL would commence the construction project when the housing market recovered. Both parties agreed that this would be five years at most. After five years, the project would likely be up and running and Capital would receive the principal by the end of the sixth year. That is, PPL agreed that the final repayment date be moved from 10 to 6 years. No interest would be paid at any time.
2. PPL has received an offer of $2,100,000 for the land. After legal and transaction costs, about $1,900,000 would be left, and this amount would be turned over to Capital in full payment for the note.
3. Capital could let the default of interest payments happen, and step in and repossess the land. It would then wait for the housing market to rebound and either develop the project at that time or seek another buyer.

Ralph Yuang, the Capital controller, has asked you, a staff accountant, to outline the likely financial accounting treatment for each alternative as the business decision is mulled over by the executive committee.

Required:

Prepare a report that evaluates appropriate financial reporting for each alternative. Also comment on the business risk issues for each alternative.

CASE 7-3
New Design Limited

New Design Limited (NDL) is a jewellery wholesaler that plans to sign an agreement with Canadian Financial Company, in which Canadian will commit to purchase up to $10 million of NDL foreign customer accounts receivable. Under the terms of the agreement, Canadian receives the rights to all collections on the accounts sold, directly from the customer. All these customer accounts are for export sales, and all receivables are denominated in Canadian dollars. Two options are being considered:

Option 1

1. Canadian purchases accounts from NDL within six days of the transaction. Only transactions that are EDC-guaranteed are eligible. EDC is the Canadian federal government's Export Development Corporation, which guarantees collection of accounts receivable with specific foreign countries or companies, as long as there are no legal deficiencies in them. For example, if the customer claimed that it did not receive all the goods, or that the goods received were not those ordered, EDC insurance would not be effective. However, if the buyer could simply not pay, EDC insurance would be effective. EDC insurance has to be purchased by NDL and is based on country and company risk.
2. NDL receives, from Canadian, cash equal to the face value of the receivable, less a financing charge, based on the term of the receivable. There is no bad debt allowance because of the EDC guarantee. NDL cannot be forced to repurchase the receivables.

This agreement would cover approximately $6 million of the total $10 million foreign receivables of NDL; the remainder are not EDC-insured (due to country of origin or identity of specific customer) and would not be eligible.

Option 2

All foreign receivables are eligible for this option, which has the following key features:

- NDL is responsible for all bad debts. NDL has been in business for more than 20 years and is able to accurately forecast bad debt losses. Thus, its liability under this recourse provision can be reasonably estimated.
- Accounts are transferred to Canadian at the beginning of each month. This date is called the "settlement date."
- Interest on the outstanding amount is determined monthly. The interest rate charged will change regularly based on prime interest rates and risk of the portfolio.
- NDL can be required to repurchase or replace receivables if there are legal deficiencies in them. See the above discussion for an explanation of legal deficiencies.
- NDL may repurchase the receivables on the first settlement date subsequent to transfer of the receivables (i.e., monthly) if NDL and Canadian cannot agree on an interest rate for purposes of calculating the monthly payment (principal less interest) that Canadian pays to NDL. This repurchase option must be exercised within one week of the settlement date.
- NDL has the right to repurchase the receivables when the balances fall to a low level. The repurchase price will be the total forecasted collections less the actual collections to date.

Joe Basinger, the vice president, Finance for NDL, has asked you, the company's independent auditor, how each option would be accounted for. He's aware that some transfers of accounts receivable are treated as borrowings, while others are treated as sales, and he needs to know which treatment is appropriate.

The first option is more expensive for the company (because of the requirement to arrange EDC insurance) and involves a lower dollar value of receivables than the second option. Joe knows that another alternative is to arrange a loan secured by accounts receivable, and he's wondering if this arrangement would be any different on the balance sheet. He's particularly concerned about the key debt-to-total-assets ratio that is the subject of a loan covenant.

Required:

Respond to the request.

ASSIGNMENTS

A7-1 Define Cash: Podro Company is preparing its 20X5 financial statements; the accounting period ends 31 December. The following items, related to cash, are under consideration. You have been asked to indicate how each item should be reported on the balance sheet and to explain the basis for your responses.

a. A $1,600 cheque received from a customer, dated 1 February 20X6, is on hand.

b. A customer's cheque was included in the 20 December deposit. It was returned by the bank stamped NSF. No entry has yet been made by Podro to reflect the return.

c. Podro has a $40,000 three-month GIC. Interest accrued to 31 December of $800 has just been recorded by debiting interest receivable and crediting interest revenue. The chief accountant proposes to report the $40,800 as part of cash on the balance sheet.

d. Podro has a $300 petty cash fund. This is cash held in a strong box for miscellaneous disbursements.

e. Postage stamps that cost $30 are in the strong box.

f. A money order of $175 payable to Podro Company is in the strong box; it is dated 29 December.

g. Three cheques, dated 31 December 20X5, totalling $665, payable to vendors who have sold merchandise to Podro Company on account, were not mailed by 31 December 20X5. They have not been entered as payments in the cheque register and ledger.

h. Podro has two chequing accounts: one with a balance of $86,000, and another with a different bank that has an overdraft of $900. The company plans to show the two balances net, since it could easily pay off the overdraft with available cash.

A7-2 Bank Reconciliation: Jones Company shows the following 30 June bank statement:

Statement Summary:

Opening balance, 1 June	$23,000
Deposits	11,600
Cheques	(12,120)
Interest earned	100
Ending balance, 30 June	$22,580

Deposits and cheques:

Deposits		Cheques			
1 June	$ 2,000	2 June #61	$1,000	17 June #65	$ 400
8 June	3,000	7 June #63	2,000	23 June #60	1,100
17 June	4,500	9 June #66	3,000	27 June #67	2,100
22 June	2,100	14 June #64	1,420	28 June #59	1,100
Total	$ 11,600				$ 12,120

Transactions recorded in the cash account in the general ledger:

Balance, 1 June	$23,900
Cheques	(13,220)
Deposits	12,300

Deposits and cheques:

Deposits		Cheques			
		60	$1,100	65	$ 400
June 8	$3,000	61	1,000	66	3,000
June 17	4,500	62	900	67	2,100
June 22	2,100	63	2,000	68	1,300
June 30	2,700	64	1,420		
	$12,300				$13,220

The bank reconciliation at 31 May showed the following items:

Bank balance, $23,000, add deposit outstanding, $2,000,
Deduct cheque #59 outstanding, $1,100,
Book balance, $23,900.

Required:

Prepare the June bank reconciliation and give any entries required.

A7-3 Bank Reconciliation: The August bank reconciliation for Sour Patch Limited:

Balance per bank	$31,570
Plus: outstanding deposits	6,900
Less: Outstanding cheques ($1,245, $650, $570, $890, $120)	(3,475)
Cash, per general ledger	$34,995

September information, per books:

Cash receipts journal Deposits:		Cash disbursements journal: Cheques:	
7 Sept.	$ 4,600	1030	$ 9,000
11 Sept.	22,500	1031	4,650
14 Sept.	7,800	1032	4,780
22 Sept.	3,400	1033	75
25 Sept.	11,600	1034	165
30 Sept.	3,210	1035	15,700
30 Sept.	1,750	1036	10,420
	$ 54,860		$ 44,790

September information, per bank:

Opening balance: $31,570

Deposits:	Cheques:
$ 6,900	$ 570
4,600	890
22,500	175 (Cheque of Patch (Co.)*
7,800	90 (service charges)
1,750 (direct deposit by customer on account)	9,000
3,400	4,780
11,600	120
$ 58,550	19,700**
	4,650
	$ 39,975

* Charged to this account in error

** For automobile; incorrectly recorded as $15,700 by company.

Required:

1. Prepare a bank reconciliation in good form at the end of September.
2. Prepare any adjusting journal entries required as a result of the reconciliation.

A7-4 Bank Reconciliation: Ample Company carries its chequing account with Commerce Bank. The company is ready to prepare its 31 December bank reconciliation. The following information is available:

a. *The 30 November bank reconciliation showed the following:*

(1) cash on hand (held back each day by Ample Company for change), $400 (included in Ample's Cash account);
(2) deposit in transit, #51, $2,000; and
(3) cheques outstanding, #121, $1,000; #130, $2,000; and #142, $3,000.

b. *Ample Company cash account for December*

Balance, 1 December	$ 64,000
Deposits: #52—#55, $186,500; #56, $3,500	190,000
Cheques: #143—#176, $191,000; #177, $2,500; #178, $3,000; and #179, $1,500	(198,000)
Balance, 31 December (includes $400 cash held for change)	$ 56,000

c. *Bank statement, 31 December*

Balance, 1 December	$ 67,600
Deposits: #51—#55	188,500
Cheques: #130, $2,000; #142, $3,000; #143—#176, $191,000	(196,000)
Account receivable collected for Ample Co.	6,720
Cash received from foreign customer: prepayment on order; not yet recorded by Ample Co.	10,000
NSF cheque, Customer Belinda	(200)
United Fund (automatic charitable donation per transfer authorization signed by Ample Co.)	(50)
Bank service charges	(20)
Balance, 31 December	$ 76,550

Required:

1. Identify by number and dollars the 31 December deposits in transit and cheques outstanding.
2. Prepare the 31 December bank reconciliation.
3. Give all journal entries that should be made at 31 December, based on your bank reconciliation.

A7-5 Classification of Balances: For each of the items listed below, identify the correct balance sheet classification by using one of the following classifications:

Cash
Short-term cash equivalent
Investments (specify long- or short-term)
Accounts receivable, trade
Contra account to accounts receivable
Other accounts receivable
Accounts payable, trade
Other accounts payable
Other (identify)

The first item is completed for you.

Item	Classification
1. Chequing account	Cash
2. Allowance for sales returns	
3. Accounts receivable—officers (current collection expected)	
4. Accounts payable for merchandise	
5. Savings account	
6. Rare coins kept for long-term speculation	
7. Accounts receivable—customers	
8. Post-dated cheques received	
9. Allowance for doubtful accounts	
10. Expense advances to salespersons	
11. Treasury bills; two months remain in term	
12. Compensating balance for a short-term loan	
13. Short-term loan payable	
14. Sinking fund to retire a bond in five years	
15. Canada Savings Bond (10-year term; immediately liquid)	
16. Short-term investment in marketable equity securities	
17. Debit balances in supplier accounts	
18. Unpaid salaries	
19. Credit balances in customer accounts	

Required:

Classify the above accounts, as indicated.

A7-6 Net Accounts Receivable: At 31 December 20X5, Chester Company reported gross accounts receivable of $9,725,300. Investigation showed the following:

a. Terms of 2/10, n/30 were granted to all customers. Accounts receivable were recorded gross, and the discounts taken were recorded when taken by the customers in a discounts account, reported contra to the sales account. Estimated discounts inherent in the closing accounts receivable balance were $72,420. The allowance for sales discounts account was established at $62,900 last year, and has not been adjusted since.

b. Customers are permitted to return 8% of annual sales for full credit, as long as goods are returned in good condition within 60 days of delivery. Based on past years experience, $45,100 of goods might be returned. As returns are received during the year, the sales returns account, a contra account to sales, is increased. An allowance for sales returns exists, at $67,800, unchanged from the previous year-end.

c. The credit balance in the allowance for doubtful accounts of the Master Company was $492,300 after write-offs for the year but before any bad debt adjustment. Bad debt expense is based on a percentage of net credit sales. Net sales revenue for 20X5 amounted to $175 million, of which three-quarters was on credit. Based on the latest available facts, one-fifth of 1% of credit sales will not be collected.

Required:

1. Prepare year-end adjusting entries with respect to accounts receivable.
2. How would the net accounts receivable appear on the balance sheet on 31 December 20X5?

A7-7 Recognizing Cash Discounts: The annual reports of the following two companies provided information about cash discounts:

1. K&V Manufacturing:

Income statement	
Sales	$ 65,438,800
Less Sales discounts	865,432

Balance sheet	
Current assets:	
Accounts receivable, less allowance of $297,000 for doubtful accounts and sales discounts	$ 16,938,624

2. GenCo, Inc.:

Income statement	
Sales	$ 167,435,890
Finance revenue; discounts lost	1,576,320
Balance sheet	
Accounts receivable	$ 61,781,000
Allowance for bad debts	(3,173,000)
Net receivables	$ 58,608,000

Required:

1. Briefly comment on which method (gross versus net) you believe was used to account for cash discounts by these two companies. Assume they offered similar credit and payment terms.
2. How would an allowance for cash discounts be measured?

A7-8 Estimating Bad Debt Expense: The accounts of Long Company provided the following 20X5 information at 31 December 20X5 (end of the annual period):

Accounts receivable balance, 1 January 20X5	$ 51,000
Allowance for doubtful accounts balance, 1 January 20X5	3,000
Total sales revenue during 20X5 (on credit)	160,000
Uncollectible account to be written off during 20X5 (ex-customer Slo)	1,000
Cash collected on accounts receivable during 20X5	170,000

Estimates of bad debt losses

a. Based on credit sales, 1%.
b. Based on ending balance of accounts receivable, 8%.
c. Based on aging schedule (excludes Slo's account):

Age	Accounts Receivable	Probability of Non-Collection
Less than 30 days	$28,000	2%
31–90 days	7,000	10
91–120 days	3,000	30
More than 120 days	2,000	60

Required:

1. Give the entry to write off customer Slo's long-overdue account.
2. Give all entries related to accounts receivable and the allowance account for the following three cases:

   Case A—Bad debt expense is based on credit sales.

   Case B—Bad debt expense is based on the ending balance of accounts receivable.

   Case C—Bad debt expense is based on aging.
3. Show how the results of applying each case above should be reported on the 20X5 income statement and balance sheet.
4. Briefly explain and evaluate each of the three methods used in Cases A, B, and C.
5. On 1 August 20X6, customer Slo paid his long-overdue account in full. Give the required entries.

A7-9 Alternatives for Estimation—Allowance for Doubtful Accounts: At 31 December 20X5, the end of the annual reporting period, the accounts of Accurate Company showed the following:

a. Sales revenue for 20X5, $950,000, of which one-sixth was on credit.
b. Allowance for doubtful accounts, balance 1 January 20X5, $5,400 credit.
c. Accounts receivable, balance 31 December 20X5 (prior to any write-offs of uncollectible accounts during 20X5), $91,300.
d. Uncollectible accounts to be written off, 31 December 20X5, $4,700. These accounts are all in the "past due over 90 days" category.
e. Aging schedule at 31 December 20X5, showing the following breakdown of accounts receivable:

Status	Amount
Not past due	$50,200
Past due 1–60 days	14,300
Past due over 60 days	21,200
Past due over 90 days	5,600

Required:

1. Give the 20X5 entry to write off the uncollectible accounts.
2. Give the 20X5 adjusting entry to record bad debt expense for each of the following independent assumptions concerning bad debt loss rates:
   a. On credit sales, 1.9%.
   b. On total receivables at year-end (after write-off), 4.1%.
   c. On aging schedule: not past due, 0.4%; past due 1–60 days, 1.9%; past due over 60 days, 10%, and past due over 90 days, 70%.
3. Show what would be reported on the 20X5 balance sheet relating to accounts receivable for each assumption.

A7-10 Accounts Receivable and Bad Debts: Given below is the history of a sale on credit by Airport Company to J. Doe.

a. 24 December 20X1—Sold merchandise to J. Doe, $2,000, terms 2/10, n/30.
b. 2 January 20X2—Doe paid half of the receivable and was allowed the discount.
c. 31 December 20X4—Because of the disappearance of Doe, Airport Company wrote Doe's account off as uncollectible.
d. 31 December 20X6—Doe reappeared and paid the debt in full, plus 6% annual interest (not compounded, compute annually).

Required:

Give the entry(s) that Airport Company should make at each of the above dates. Record the receivable initially at its gross amount.

A7-11 Allowance for Doubtful Accounts: Simplex Company has been in business since January 20X4. The company has been growing rapidly and is unable to finance the growth internally. Consequently, Simplex has applied for a significant bank loan. Prior to considering the application, the bank asks you to conduct an audit for the past three years. In reviewing accounts receivable, you find that the company wrote off receivables, as they proved uncollectible, that is, bad debt expense was recognized at the time of write-off.

Your analysis indicated that losses from uncollectible accounts approximated 1% of credit sales. You compiled the following data:

		Accounts written off in each year		
Year	**Credit Sales**	**20X4**	**20X5**	**20X6**
20X4	$200,000	$500	$1,000	$ 600
20X5	300,000	—	800	2,000
20X6	400,000	—	—	1,100

Required:

1. Determine the amount by which net income was understated or overstated each year resulting from not using the generally accepted allowance method. Ignore income tax considerations.
2. Prepare all journal entries (recognition of bad debt expense and write-off accounts) for each of the three years, assuming the percent of credit sales method of estimation is used.
3. Why is the allowance method generally accepted?

(CGA-Canada, adapted)

A7-12 Allowance for Doubtful Accounts: The accounting records of Sine.Com Limited provided the following for 20X9:

Balance in accounts receivable, 1 January 20X9	$ 90,000
Balance in accounts receivable, 31 December 20X9	120,000
Balance in allowance for doubtful accounts, 1 January 20X9	3,000 (cr)
Accounts written off as uncollectible during 20X9	5,500

Cash sales were $900,000, while credit sales were $650,000. Recently, Sine.Com's management has become concerned about various estimates used in its accounting system, including those relating to receivables and uncollectible accounts. The company is considering various alternatives with a view to selecting the most appropriate approach and related estimates.

For analytical purposes, the following 20X9 alternative estimates have been developed for consideration:

a. Bad debts approximate 0.75% of credit sales.
b. Bad debts approximate 0.4% of total sales.
c. Six percent of the uncollected accounts receivable at year-end will be uncollectible.
d. Aging of the accounts receivable at the end of the period indicated that 80% would incur a 2% loss, while the remaining 20% would incur a 10% loss.

Required:

1. For each of the four alternatives listed above, give the following:
   a. 20X9 adjusting entry,
   b. Ending 20X9 balance in the allowance account, and
   c. An evaluation of the alternative.
2. Explain which of the four you would recommend.

(ASCA, adapted)

A7-13 Allowance for Doubtful Accounts: Technical Armour Company has $5,471,100 of accounts receivable at 30 September 20X7. Sales for the year had been $29,461,400.

These accounts are categorized as follows:

Age	Percentage of Total	Probability of Collection
0–30 days	60*	98
30–45 days	14	90**
45–60 days	8	80
60–90 days	6	60
over 90 days	12	55**

* round receivable to the nearest hundred

** percentage applies to remainder after write-off

Additional information:

a. Before any adjustments, the allowance for doubtful accounts has a credit balance of $67,900.
b. Write-offs are required for $138,700 of existing accounts receivable in the 30–45 day category, and $291,700 in the over-90-day category. The probability of collection provided above relates to the remaining accounts receivable in these categories.

Required:

1. Calculate bad debt expense, and the net balance of accounts receivable, as shown on the balance sheet, for the period ended 30 September 20X7.
2. Repeat requirement (1) assuming that the company uses the percentage-of-sales method and that 2.95% of sales are expected to be uncollectible. All other information is unchanged.

A7-14 Transfer of Accounts Receivable: On 1 April 20X5, XCourt Company transferred $75,000 of accounts receivable to Prima Finance Company to obtain immediate cash. There was no allowance for doubtful accounts set up on XCourt's books in relation to the $75,000.

Consider the two following independent circumstances.

Required:

1. The transfer agreement specified a price of $64,200 on a without-recourse, notification basis that effectively transferred control to Prima. Give the entry(s) that XCourt Company should make. The $10,800 reduction from face value represents a $6,800 financing fee and $4,000 of expected bad debts. Explain the basis for your response.
2. The transfer agreement specified a price of $70,000 on a with-recourse, notification basis. The $5,000 reduction from face value is related to expected bad debts, $2,000, and a $3,000 financing fee. XCourt retained the right to repurchase the receivables. Give the entry(s) that XCourt should make.
3. Explain the difference to the balance sheet between (1) versus (2).

A7-15 Transfer of Accounts Receivable—Sale or Borrowing? The following two cases are independent.

Case A. Appa Apparel manufactures fine sportswear for many national retailers and frequently sells its receivables to financing companies as a means of accelerating cash collections. Appa transferred $600,000 of receivables from retailers to a financing company and has no control over, or continuing interest in, the accounts receivable. The receivables were transferred without recourse on a notification basis. The financing company charged 12% of the receivables total.

Required:

1. Should Appa record the transfer of receivables as a sale or as a borrowing? Why?
2. Record all entries related to the transfer for Appa.

Case B. Bappa Apparel manufactures fine sportswear for many national retailers and frequently sells its receivables to financing companies as a means of accelerating cash collections. Bappa transferred $600,000 of receivables from retailers to a financing company. The receivables were transferred with recourse on a notification basis. The financing company charged 8%. Bappa has no obligation to the financing company other than to pay the account of a retailer in the event of a default. However, Bappa retains legal control over the receivables, and the financing company may not use the receivables as collateral in any other financing arrangement.

Required:

1. Should Bappa record the transfer of receivables as a sale or as a borrowing? Why?
2. Record Bappa's entries related to the transfer.

A7-16 Receivable Transfer—Sale or Borrowing? The following situations involve transactions that should be classified as either a sale or a borrowing:

a. Sherman Company pledges $400,000 of accounts receivable as collateral for a loan (notification basis). Interest is charged on the monthly outstanding loan balance, and a 2% finance fee is charged immediately on the accounts assigned.
b. Hopper Company transfers $50,000 of accounts receivable on a non-recourse basis. The finance company charges an 8% fee and withholds 10% to cover sales adjustments. The finance company obtains full title to the receivables and assumes collection responsibilities.
c. Pineapple Company transfers $40,000 of accounts receivable on a recourse basis. Pineapple assumes the cost of all sales adjustments. The receivables are part of a much larger group of receivables. Pineapple's business is stable, and sales adjustments are readily estimable. Pineapple is compelled under the ROAP clause of the transfer agreement to replace any defaulting receivables with others from its portfolio.
d. Helms Company transfers $80,000 of accounts receivable on a recourse basis. At the finance company's option, if it appears that the receivables are not collected as quickly as expected, Helms must repurchase the receivables.
e. Franklin Company transfers a $10,000 note received in a sale, on a recourse basis. Franklin must reimburse the bank in the event of default by the original maker of the note. The risk of default is negligible.
f. Puget Company transfers on a recourse basis a $30,000 note received in a sale. The bank allows repurchase of discounted notes at face value for a small fee. The risk of default is not determinable.
g. Pobedy Company pledges all of its accounts receivable as collateral for a loan. Pobedy must use the proceeds from the accounts receivable to service the loan. Pobedy retains title to the receivables. In the event of default by Pobedy on the loan, the finance company has a claim against any of these receivables for payment of the loan.

Required:

1. For each of the preceding situations, explain whether the financing of the receivables should most likely be recorded as a sale or a borrowing.
2. Explain, in general, the impact that the sale versus borrowing policy decision will have on the financial statements.

A7-17 Transfer of Accounts Receivable: GXR Computers Limited transferred $3,400,000 of its $12,000,000 accounts receivable portfolio from customers to the National Financing Company. There is an allowance for doubtful accounts of $645,700 for the whole portfolio. Two alternative independent arrangements are described:

Case A. The receivables were sold with recourse, on a notification basis. Expected bad debts, $125,000. The financing fee is 7% of the expected collectible amount. The bad debts are already allowed for in the allowance for doubtful accounts. Title to the receivable passes to the National Financial Company.

Case B. The receivables were sold with recourse, on a notification basis. Expected bad debts, $107,000. The financing fee is 8% of the expected collectible amount. The bad debts are not already allowed for in the allowance for doubtful accounts. GXR may repurchase the receivables at any time.

Required:

1. Prepare journal entries to record Case A and Case B.
2. List the balance sheet amounts and accounts, reflecting the entries made in requirement (1) for each case.

3. Assume that customers paid as expected. Prepare entries for both Cases A and B to reflect cash received from customers and payments to the financing company, if any. Assume that the estimates of bad debts are correct and uncollectable accounts are written off.

A7-18 Note Receivable: The following cases are independent. For each case

1. Give all entries related to the transactions. The company uses the gross method to account for accounts and notes receivable.
2. Show the items that will be reported on the 20X5 income statement and balance sheet.

Case A. On 15 April 20X5, Cumby Company sold merchandise to Customer Richards for $390,000, terms 2/10, n/EOM (i.e., end of month). Because of non-payment by Richards, Cumby received a $390,000, 15%, 12-month note on 1 May 20X5. The annual reporting period ends 30 September. Customer Richards paid the note in full on its maturity date.

Case B. On 1 May 20X5, Dickson Company sold merchandise to Customer Franks and received a $75,000 (face amount), one-year, non-interest-bearing note. The going (i.e., market) rate of interest is 10%. The annual reporting period for Dickson Company ends on 31 December. Customer Smith paid the note in full on its maturity date.

A7-19 Note Receivable: MacDonald Company sells large construction equipment. On 1 January 20X5, the company sold Chowdury Company a machine at a quoted price of $60,000. MacDonald collected $20,000 cash and received a two-year note payable for the balance.

Required:

1. Give MacDonald's required entries for the two years, assuming an interest-bearing note, face value $40,000. (8% interest, simple interest payable each 31 December.)
2. Assume that the market interest rate is still 8%. Give MacDonald's required entries for the two years, assuming a 2% interest-bearing note, face value $40,000. Prepare the entries based on the
   a. net basis
   b. gross basis
3. Compare the interest revenue and sales revenue under requirements (1) and (2).

A7-20 Non-Interest-bearing and Low-Interest Notes:

a. On 1 January 20X5, a heavy-duty truck was purchased with a list price of $35,500. Payment included $5,500 cash and a two-year, non-interest-bearing note of $30,000 (maturity date, 31 December 20X6). A realistic interest rate for this level of risk is 12%.
b. On 1 January 20X5, a small truck was purchased and payment was made as follows: cash, $5,000, and a two-year, 6%, interest-bearing note of $15,000, maturity date 31 December 20X6. A realistic interest rate for this level of risk is 12%.

Required:

Give all entries for each case from purchase date through maturity date of each note. Disregard depreciation. Round to the nearest dollar. Use the net method to record the note. The accounting period ends on 31 December.

A7-21 Notes Payable: Sable Corporation signed a $125,000 four-year note payable. The note required annual blended payments, to be paid at the end of each year. The market interest rate is 6%.

Required:

1. Calculate the required blended payment. Round to the nearest dollar.
2. Prepare a schedule that shows annual interest and principal portion of the four payments. Adjust interest expense in the last period to balance.
3. Prepare journal entries to record the initial loan and each payment.

A7-22 Notes Payable: Mercury Limited reports the following transactions in 20X3:

1. Mercury bought goods from NTY Limited, signing a note payable in return. The note was a $65,000, three-year note that required annual end-of-period payments in the amount of $24,768. The interest charged was the market interest rate at the time.
2. Mercury borrowed money from the Bank of Toronto, signing a $50,000, four-year, 8% note payable.
3. Mercury bought a piece of equipment, paying $5,000 in cash and signing a $50,000, two-year, 2% note. Interest is paid at the end of each year. Market interest rates are in the range of 8%.

Required:

1. What interest rate is implicit in the $65,000 note?
2. Record each note at its inception. Use the gross method, where appropriate.
3. How much interest expense will be recorded on the income statement with respect to the three notes in year one? Year two? Assume that these notes were issued at the beginning of the fiscal year.
4. What is the balance in each (net) note payable at the end of the first fiscal year? Again, assume that these notes were issued at the beginning of the fiscal year.

A7-23 Analysis and Comparison of Notes: On 1 September 20X5, Dyer Company borrowed an amount of cash on a $100,000 note payable due in one year. That is, Dyer agreed to repay $100,000 in one year, plus interest if specified in the loan contract. Assume the going rate of interest was 12% per year for this particular level of risk. The accounting period ends 31 December.

Required:

Complete the following tabulation; round to the nearest dollar:

	Assuming the Note Was	
	Interest-Bearing	**Non-Interest-Bearing**
1. Cash received	$	$
2. Cash paid at maturity date	$	$
3. Total interest paid (cash)	$	$
4. Interest expense in 20X5	$	$
5. Interest expense in 20X6	$	$
6. Amount of liabilities reported on 20X5 balance sheet:		
Note payable (net)	$	$
Interest payable	$	$
7. Principal amount	$	$
8. Face amount	$	$
9. Maturity value	$	$
10. Stated interest rate	%	%
11. Yield or effective interest rate	%	%

A7-24 Overview of Notes Payable: On 1 October 20X5, Dennis Company purchased computer equipment. It paid $10,000 cash and signed a two-year note payable, with a face value of $75,000, due on 30 September 20X7. The going rate of interest for this level of risk was 8%. The accounting period ends on 31 December.

Required:

1. Compute the cost of the computer equipment assuming:
   Case A—an 8% interest-bearing note. Interest is due each 30 September.
   Case B—a non-interest-bearing note.
   Case C—a 2% interest-bearing note. Interest is due each 30 September.
2. Give entries for each case from 1 October 20X5, through maturity date (assume that reversing entries were not made). Use the net method to record the note, and disregard amortization on the computer equipment.
3. Complete a tabulation as follows:

	Case A	Case B	Case C
a. Principal amount			
b. Amount received			
c. Stated interest rate			
d. Effective interest rate			
e. Cash interest paid, total			
f. Principal less amount received			
g. Interest expense, total			
h. Amount of liabilities reported			
• on the 20X5 balance sheet			
• on the 20X6 balance sheet			
• on the 20X7 balance sheet			

A7-25 Cash Flow and Doubtful Accounts: Excerpts from Marston's income statement, balance sheet, and statement of cash flows follow:

	($ millions)	
	20X1	**20X0**
Income statement:		
Revenues	$29,600	$29,300
Balance sheet:		
Current assets:		
Receivables, less allowance for uncollectibles of $220 and $270, respectively	$ 3,700	$ 3,440
Statement of cash flows:		
Cash flows from operating activities:		
Net income	$ 2,580	$ 2,740
Add back non-cash expenses: Bad debts	344	280

Required:

Answer the following questions assuming that (a) Marston uses the allowance method to estimate bad debts (provision for uncollectibles) and (b) all revenues are credit sales.

1. Are estimated uncollectible accounts increasing or decreasing as a percentage of revenues?
2. How much were net write-offs of accounts receivable during 20X1?
3. How much cash was collected on receivables during 20X1?
4. Why is the provision for uncollectibles added to net income in the operating activities section of the statement of cash flows, and why was the amount of cash collections from receivables not disclosed?

A7-26 Impairment; Change in Present Value: On 1 January 20X5, Robertson Inc. sold merchandise (cost, $8,000; sales value, $14,000) to Russell, Inc., and received a non-interest-bearing note in return. The note requires $17,636 to be paid in a lump sum on 31 December 20X7.

On 1 January 20X6, Russell requested that the terms of the loan be modified as follows: $7,000 to be paid in five years (at the end of 20X10), $10,636 due in six years (at the end of 20X11). Robertson refused Russell's request.

During 20X6, however, news of Russell's deteriorating financial condition prompted Robertson to reevaluate the collectibility of the note. Consequently, the modified terms requested by Russell were accepted and used to estimate the future cash flows to be received, as of 31 December 20X6.

Required:

1. Prepare the entry to record the sale by Robertson, assuming a perpetual inventory system. Also prepare the 31 December 20X5 adjusting entry. Use the net method. You will need to establish the interest rate implicit in the original note.
2. Prepare the entry to record the impairment on 31 December 20X6. Compare the book value of the note at 31 December to the present value of the newly acknowledged cash flow stream. Assume that no interest revenue is accrued in 20X6.
3. Prepare the entry to record interest revenue at 31 December 20X7.

A7-27 Compensated Absences: Tunacliff Mowers allows each employee to earn 15 fully paid vacation days each year. Unused vacation time can be carried over to the next year; if not taken during the next year, it is lost. By the end of 20X5, all but 3 of the 30 employees had taken their earned vacation time; these 3 carried over to 20X6 a total of 20 vacation days, which represented 20X5 salary of $6,000. During 20X6, each of these three used their 20X5 vacation carryover; none of them had received a pay rate change from 20X5 to the time they used their carryover. Total cash wages paid: 20X5, $700,000; 20X6, $740,000.

Required:

1. Give the entries for Tunacliff related to vacations during 20X5 and 20X6. Disregard payroll taxes.
2. Compute the total amount of wage expense for 20X5 and 20X6. How would the vacation time carried over from 20X5 affect the 20X5 balance sheet?

A7-28 Entries to Record Sales Taxes, Payroll, and Related Entries: Dornan Limited had the following transactions in February 20X6:

a. Recorded sales of $1,300,000, plus GST of 7%.
b. Recorded sales of $6,700,000, plus GST of 7%.
c. Bought capital assets of $675,000, plus GST of 7%.
d. Recorded the bi-monthly payroll of $85,900. CPP deductions were $1,200, EI deductions were $1,500, and income tax withheld amounted to $7,200. (Employer portions are recorded only at the end of the month.)
e. Recorded sales of $1,500,000, plus GST of 7%.
f. Bought inventory for $7,800,000, plus GST of 7%.
g. Recorded the bi-monthly payroll. The amounts were identical to the prior bi-monthly payroll.
h. Recorded the employer portion of payroll expenses for the entire month.
i. Remitted payroll taxes for the month.
j. Remitted net GST for the month.

Required:

Provide journal entries to record all transactions. Assume all transactions were for cash.

A7-29 Foreign Exchange: Golden Limited had the following transactions in 20X5:

a. Sold goods on 1 June to a British company for 70,000 euros with payment to be in four month's time.

b. Bought goods from a U.S. supplier on 15 June for U.S.$150,000; payment was due in one month's time.

c. Bought goods from a British supplier on 15 July for 20,000 euros; settlement was to be in two month's time.

d. Paid the U.S. supplier on 15 July.

e. Paid the British supplier on 15 September.

f. Received payment from the British customer on 1 October.

Exchange rates:

	Canadian Equivalencies	
	Euros	**U.S.$**
1 June	2.11	1.37
15 June	2.19	1.41
15 July	2.13	1.47
15 September	2.20	1.43
1 October	2.17	1.46

Required:

Prepare journal entries for the above transactions.

A7-30 Comprehensive: The following situations are independent:

1. YST Company sold goods to a U.S. company, for U.S.$125,000. The goods were carried in inventory at Cdn.$97,600. On the date of sale, the exchange rate was U.S.$1 = Cdn.$1.55. Thirty days later, when the exchange rate was $1.48, the customer paid. YST uses a perpetual system to account for inventory. Record all entries associated with the sale and the collection of cash.

2. Mirabella Company uses an allowance system for bad debts. At the beginning of the year, the allowance had a balance of $45,000 credit. The following transactions and events took place during the year:
   a. Accounts receivable of $34,000 were written off.
   b. GTT Company, which owed $1,000, was one of the accounts written off in (a). GTT subsequently paid $300. The balance of this account is now expected to be paid in the next six months.
   c. Aging of outstanding accounts receivable at the end of the year showed that an allowance of $60,000 is needed.

   Record all entries for (a), (b), and (c).

3. RRR Limited has $350,000 of accounts receivable. These are transferred to a financial institution at a discount rate of 8%. Of the total, $12,250 of the accounts are expected to be bad. The 8% financing fee relates to the net balance. The transaction is to be recorded as a sale of receivables.
   a. Record the transaction.
   b. Why is recording the transaction as a sale sometimes criticized?

Required:

Answer the questions as indicated in each of the above situations.

A7-31 Recording and Reporting Transactions: The following selected transactions of Mattingly Company were completed during the accounting year just ended, 31 December 20X5:

a. Merchandise was purchased on account; a $10,000, one-year, 16% interest-bearing note, dated 1 April 20X5, was given to the creditor. Assume a perpetual inventory system.
b. A customer paid for merchandise on 1 February 20X5, with a two-year, $16,000, 3% note. The going interest rate for this term and risk was 15%. Cost of goods sold was $8,320.
c. A supplier delivered goods costing U.S.$13,580. The Canadian dollar was worth U.S.$0.725 on this day.
d. On July 1, the company borrowed $25,000 in cash from the bank on a demand basis. The interest rate was 15%, to be paid on the anniversary date of the loan.
e. Payroll records showed the following:

Employee					Employer	
Gross Wages	Income Tax	EI	CPP	Union Dues	EI	CPP
$50,000	$15,000	$3,100	$2,900	$500	$4,340	$2,900

f. Remittances were income tax, $14,350; EI, $7,250; CPP, $5,720; union dues, $480.
g. The company sold goods to a foreign customer and charged U.S.$23,790. On this day, the Canadian dollar was worth U.S.$0.714. Cost of goods sold was $11,110.
h. Cash dividends declared but not yet paid were $14,000.
i. Accrued appropriate interest at 31 December, and adjusted foreign-denominated receivables and payables to the year-end rate, Cdn.$1 = U.S.$0.713.

Required:

1. Give the entry or entries for each of the above transactions and events.
2. Prepare a list (title and amount) of the balance sheet receivables and payables at 31 December 20X5.

A7-32 Comprehensive: Odyssey 2000 reported various selected balances in its 31 December 20X7 unadjusted trial balance:

Accounts receivable	$1,800,000 dr.
Accounts receivable under recourse arrangement	225,000 dr.
Note receivable	250,000 dr.
Accounts receivable—U.S.	116,000 dr.
Allowance for doubtful accounts	158,050 cr.
Cash deposits from customers	45,000 cr.
Compensated absence liability	221,600 cr.
Miscellaneous credits	216,000 cr.

The following additional information is available:

1. An analysis of accounts receivable indicated that $198,700 of accounts receivable should be written off. Of the remaining balance, 80% was current, and approximately 5% was deemed doubtful. Of the 20% that was non-current, 75% was doubtful.
2. The U.S. account receivable was recorded when the exchange rate was $1.45. The exchange rate at year-end was $1.42.

3. The account receivable under recourse arrangement was a single account receivable from a customer with an excellent credit rating that was transferred to a financial institution at a discount rate of 4% during the period. The transfer met the sale criteria. The cash collected from the financial institution was credited to an account called "Miscellaneous credits."
4. The note receivable is a payment arrangement with a customer, entered into on 30 June 20X7. The customer agreed to pay $50,000 per year for five years. The first payment is due 30 June 20X8. Sales was credited when the arrangement was recorded. Market interest rates are 8%.
5. The compensated absence liability is unadjusted from last year. All employees from last year's accrual have taken their vacation, as per company policy. At the end of this year, 45 employees have vacation entitlements; 30 for 1.5 weeks, and 15 for 2 weeks. Salary per week is an average of $2,200 for all employees. In addition, four executives have three weeks' vacation entitlement each at $3,500 per week.

Required:
Prepare journal entries to properly reflect the additional information. Use the gross method to adjust the note receivable.

A7-33 Comprehensive: Data regarding Farley Limited in October 20X7:

Selected opening balances:	GST payable	$68,400 cr.
	CPP payable	2,950 cr.
	EI payable	4,600 cr.
	Income tax deductions payable	16,360 cr.

Transactions, in chronological order:

a. Cash sales for the period, $890,000 plus 7% GST.
b. Credit card sales for the period, $1,200,000, plus 7% GST. The credit card fee is 4%, and is taken from the gross amount, including GST.
c. Inventory purchases on account, $1,780,000 plus 7% GST.
d. Monthly payroll, $128,000; less EI, $2,800; CPP, $2,200; income tax, $13,400. The employer portion of payroll taxes was also recorded.
e. Sales to U.S. customer on account, U.S.$107,000. There was no GST on the sale. The U.S. dollar was worth Cdn.$1.47 on this date.
f. The U.S. customer paid U.S.$50,000 on account, when the U.S. dollar was worth $1.50. The remaining amount will be paid in November.
g. A sale was made on account at the end of the month. The customer gave a $150,000, three-year, 4% note in exchange for the goods. Interest will be paid annually. The market interest rate was 9% on this date. For the sake of simplicity, assume that this sale is not subject to GST. Record the note using the gross method.
h. GST owing was remitted.
i. 75% of the amount owing to suppliers was paid.
j. At the end of the month, the U.S. exchange rate was Cdn.$1.49

Required:
1. Journalize all transactions listed above.
2. List the accounts and amounts that would appear on the 31 October balance sheet. Exclude cash and inventory.

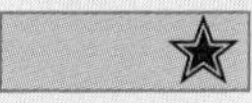

A7-34 Cash Flow Statement: Selected accounts from the Finch Company balance sheet at 31 December:

FINCH COMPANY
BALANCE SHEET

31 December	20X5	20X4
Cash	$172,000	$110,000
Receivables, net	150,000	170,000
Marketable securities	140,000	190,000
Inventory	575,000	498,000
Current liabilities	193,000	186,000
Bank overdraft	130,000	168,000

Other information:

a. Net income for the year was $59,100.

b. There was a bad debt expense of $27,500 for the year. The allowance of doubtful accounts was $34,500 at the end of 20X5, and had been $24,600 at the end of 20X4.

c. Marketable securities were short-term interest-bearing securities, considered to be cash equivalents.

Required:

1. Calculate the opening and closing cash figure that would appear on the cash flow statement.
2. Calculate cash from operations for the year based on the information given, using the indirect method of presentation.

(CGA-Canada, adapted)

CHAPTER 8

Inventories and Cost of Sales

INTRODUCTION

Inventories are an important asset for most businesses and typically represent the largest current asset of manufacturing and retail firms. In today's competitive economic climate, inventory accounting methods and management practices have become profit-enhancing tools. Better inventory systems can increase profitability; poorly conceived systems can drain profits and put businesses at a competitive disadvantage.

Inventory effects on profits are more noticeable when business activity fluctuates. During prosperous times, sales are high and inventory moves quickly from purchase to sale. But when economic conditions decline, sales levels retreat, and inventories accumulate and may be sold at a loss. Management must monitor inventory types and levels continuously if profits are to be maintained.

Inventory is a high-risk asset. For example, the bookstore chain Chapters Incorporated reported a $14.7 million loss from "inventory shrinkage" at its troubled distribution centre in July 2001. The company said this represented the difference between what the new management (Indigo Books) thought it had in stock and what it actually found when it did an inventory count.

There are lots of examples of fraud perpetrated through inventory schemes—creating fictitious inventory to boost assets, and so on. The use of fictitious inventories for fraud has a long and dishonourable history. In 2003, a huge international dairy company (Parmalat) was found to have overstated assets and net income by many billions of dollars over several years. A large part of the misstatement was inventory. Parmalat executives allegedly used essentially the same fraudulent techniques as were used 70 years earlier by the president of the largest U.S. pharmaceutical wholesaler (McKesson Robbins). Basically the technique is to record fictitious purchases of inventory, followed by fictitious sales to customers. In the intervening years, many other companies also have found their inventory accounts used for fraudulent purposes. The inventory accounts eventually are discovered to be false or overstated, but sometimes only many years after the fraud began.[1]

[1] You may wonder why auditors did not detect the fraud earlier. One of the basic postulates of auditing is that top management is not lying to the auditors. Senior executives have the ability to cover their tracks, often for extended periods of time. If top management is deliberately misleading auditors or hiding parts of the business, it is not easy for an auditor to uncover these systemic frauds.

This chapter covers the various accounting methods used to value and report inventories on the balance sheet and simultaneously measure the cost of sales required to determine income. We will begin with a discussion of the types of inventory that may exist (including those of manufacturing companies, resource companies, and service companies) and the types of costs that are included in inventory. Then we review the basic cost flow assumptions, including the popular average cost and first-in, first-out methods. A brief discussion of standard cost and just-in-time methods is also included.

Most inventories are carried at historical cost, although if revenue is recognized before delivery, inventory is valued at market value. Inventory will also be carried at market value if market value is lower than cost. Application of LCM (lower of cost or market) valuation will be examined.

Finally, the chapter reviews inventory estimation methods. Inventory amounts often must be estimated, particularly for interim statements and as a check on the reasonableness of physical inventory counts—to test for possible "missing" inventory, for example.

TYPES OF INVENTORY

Inventories consist of costs that have been incurred in an earnings process that are held as an asset until the earnings process is complete. We typically think of inventories as tangible goods and materials such as raw materials, work in process, finished goods, or merchandise held by retailers. But, depending on the nature of the company's business, inventory may include a wider range of costs incurred and held in an inventory account for matching against revenue that will be recognized later.

For example, a professional service firm such as a software development company or a law firm may accumulate the costs of fulfilling a particular contract as "inventory" until the contract has been substantially completed and the criteria for revenue recognition have been met. Even in companies that deal with physical goods, "inventory" is likely to consist more of costs such as labour and overhead than of the costs of tangible materials.

The term "inventory," therefore, must be viewed more broadly than simply the cost of goods purchased for resale. Most companies have some kind of inventory, even though the mercantile business (i.e., retailing and wholesaling) accounts for only about 15% of the Canadian economy.

Items that may be capital assets for one company may be inventory for another. Machinery and equipment, for example, are considered capital assets by the company that buys them, but before sale they are part of the inventory of the manufacturer that made them. Even a building, during its construction period, is an inventory item for the builder.

CLASSIFICATION OF INVENTORY The major classifications of inventories depend on the operations of the business. A wholesale or retail trading entity acquires merchandise for resale. A manufacturing entity acquires raw materials and component parts, manufactures finished products, and then sells them. A service company has no raw materials or finished goods but does have work in progress. Inventories are classified as follows:

1. *Merchandise inventory.* Goods on hand purchased by a retailer or a trading company such as an importer or exporter for resale. Generally, goods acquired for resale are not physically altered by the purchaser company; the goods are in finished form when they leave the manufacturer's plant. In some instances, however, parts are acquired and then further assembled into finished products. A bicycle dealer may assemble bicycles from frames, wheels, gears, and so on, prior to selling them at retail, for example.

2. *Production inventory.* The combined inventories of a manufacturing or resource entity, consisting of

   a. *Raw materials inventory.* Tangible goods purchased or obtained in other ways (e.g., by mining) and on hand for direct use in the manufacture or further processing of goods for resale. Parts or subassemblies manufactured before use are sometimes classified as *component parts inventory.*

   b. *Work-in-process inventory.* Goods or natural resources requiring further processing before completion and sale. Work-in-process inventory includes the cost of direct material and direct labour incurred to date, and usually some allocation of overhead costs.

   c. *Finished goods inventory.* Manufactured or fully processed items completed and held for sale. Finished goods inventory cost includes the cost of direct material, direct labour, and allocated manufacturing overhead related to its manufacture.

   d. *Production supplies inventory.* Items on hand, such as lubrication oils for the machinery, cleaning materials, and small items, such as bolts or glue, that make up an insignificant part of the finished product.

3. *Contracts in progress.* The accumulated costs of performing services required under contract. The costs of performing contract services are charged to a work-in-progress or contracts-in-progress account. The inventory will include the *direct* costs (mostly allocated salaries and wages) of working on the contract, and may include an allocation of overhead or *indirect* costs as well, including amortization on production facilities and depletion of natural resources. Construction companies will also include the costs of raw materials and of equipment purchased for use exclusively on a particular contract.

4. *Supplies inventories.* Items such as office, janitorial, and shipping supplies. Inventories of this type are typically used in the near future and may be recorded as selling or general expense when purchased instead of being accounted for as inventory.

INVENTORY POLICY ISSUES

Since cost of sales is often the largest single expense category on the income statement, and since inventory is an integral part of current and total assets, it makes sense that accounting policies in this area can cause income and net assets to change significantly. In what areas can policies be set? We'll look at

1. Items and costs to include in inventory;
2. Cost flow assumptions for measuring cost of sales (cost of goods sold); and
3. Application of LCM (lower of cost or market) valuations.

ITEMS AND COSTS INCLUDED IN INVENTORY

Items Included in Inventory

All goods for resale or use owned by the company on the balance sheet date should be included in inventory, regardless of their location. At any time, a business may hold goods that it does not own or own goods that it does not hold. Therefore, care must be taken to identify the goods properly includable in inventory.

Goods purchased and in transit should be included in the purchaser's inventory provided ownership has passed to the purchaser. Passage of title for goods in transit depends on the terms of the shipping contract. In some cases, title transfers to the buyer when the goods are passed to the carrier (e.g., a trucking company or railroad). This is sometimes described as FOB (free on board) shipping point. In other cases, the seller has title until the carrier delivers the goods to the final customer. This is sometimes described as FOB destination. There are at least a dozen common shipping arrangements, so contracts must be carefully scrutinized to establish ownership of goods in transit.

Goods that are owned by a company but are out on *consignment* (that is, held by agents) should be included in inventory. Goods should be *excluded* from inventory if they (1) are held for sale on commission or on consignment (but owned by someone else) or (2) have been received from a vendor but rejected and awaiting return to the vendor for credit.

REPURCHASE AGREEMENTS Some companies enter into repurchase agreements to sell and buy back inventory items at prearranged prices if they are not resold by a certain date. This practice has several advantages. Inventory is, in effect, "parked" outside the company, so the selling company may be able to avoid finance and storage expenses that would be incurred if the inventory stayed in-house. The buyer usually pays all or most of the retail value of the inventory covered in the repurchase agreement until the goods are reacquired by the seller, again at a prearranged price. However, when a repurchase is likely, the inventory must remain on the seller's books. In effect, repurchase agreements may be loans from customers rather than sales because the vendor has an obligation to pay back the customer if the goods are not resold.

Special sales agreements exist in some industries, including those selling items to retailers; sporting goods manufacturers and book publishers provide examples. These agreements permit goods to be returned if not sold. Should such goods be considered sold when delivered to the retailer? Revenue recognition rules suggest that these goods should be considered as sales only if returns can be reasonably estimated or if the return privilege has expired. Otherwise, the items remain in the seller's inventory account.

Although legal ownership is a useful starting point to identify items that should be included in inventory, a strict legal determination is often impractical. In such cases, the sales agreement, industry practices, and other evidence of intent should be considered.

Elements of Inventory Cost

GOODS PURCHASED FOR RESALE In general, inventory cost is measured by the total cash equivalent outlay made to acquire the goods and to prepare them for sale. These costs include materials purchase cost and incidental costs incurred until the goods are ready for sale to the customer. Cost also includes customs and excise duties. The total of these costs is known as the *laid-down* cost.

Freight charges and other incidental costs incurred in connection with the purchase of tangible inventory are additions to inventory cost. When these costs can be attributed to specific goods, they should be added to the cost of such goods. However, in some cases, specific identification is impractical. Therefore, freight costs are often recorded in a special account, such as freight-in, which is reported as an addition to the cost of goods available for sale.

Certain incidental costs, although theoretically a cost of tangible goods purchased, are often not included in inventory valuation but are reported as separate expenses. Examples include insurance costs on goods in transit, material handling expenses, and import brokerage fees. These expenditures are usually not included in determining inventory costs because the cost of allocating them to specific purchased goods is not worth the benefit.

Companies in some industries regularly offer *cash discounts* on purchases to encourage timely payment from buyers (which speeds up cash flow and may save on borrowing costs). Terms of 2/10, n/30, for example, mean that if the invoice is paid within 10 days, a discount of 2% can be taken. Alternatively, the full balance, n, is due in 30 days. Most buyers make timely payments and take advantage of cash discounts because the savings are normally quite substantial.[2] In fact, some companies borrow money in order to take advantage of cash dis-

[2] Discounts for prompt payment are very expensive for the vendor. If a 2% discount speeds up customers' payments by 20 days, on average, then the annual interest rate is equivalent to 43%. The vendor is better off to not give a discount and to borrow from the bank to finance the receivables (or sell the receivables). An annoying aspect of discounts is that some large customers will blithely deduct the discount from their payment even if they pay late; the discount is viewed as a price reduction rather than a reward for quick payment.

counts. Inventory should be recorded at the lowest available cash price, which is 98% of the invoice price in this case. Lost discounts are a cost of financing and should not be included in inventory amounts.

General and administrative (G&A) expenses are normally treated as period expenses because they are not solely or directly related to purchase or manufacture of inventory. Distribution and selling costs are also considered to be period operating expenses and are not allocated to inventories.

SERVICE CONTRACTS When a company enters into a contract to deliver services, there are two elements of cost:

- *Direct costs.* These are the costs of fulfilling the service obligations for each specific contract, such as direct labour and any material or equipment (e.g., special computer equipment or software) that is necessary to complete a particular service contract. Direct labour normally includes the costs of the service company's employees, such as the staff of an accounting or law firm who are working directly on an assignment for a particular client.
- *Overhead costs.* Overhead consists of costs that are necessary to complete service contracts but that cannot be attributed specifically to individual contracts. Overhead includes general items such as office rental, amortization of general office and computer equipment, and supervision. It also includes supplies and other small costs that are theoretically assignable to specific contracts, but are not worth the effort to assign.

For a service company, inventory consists of the accumulated costs of contract work performed to date but not yet completed. This inventory is called *work in progress* or *work in process*, and is shown on the balance sheet as a current asset.

When service contracts are short-term contracts, only the direct costs are normally inventoried; overhead costs usually are treated as period costs. When the contract is complete and the revenue is recognized, the inventoried costs are transferred from *work in process* on the balance sheet to *cost of services* provided (or some similar title) on the income statement.

For long-term service contracts, the *CICA Handbook* requires that some element of overhead should be included in work-in-process inventory, as we will explain in the next section. There are several different methods of recognizing revenue for long-term contracts. We will explain these methods later in this chapter.

MANUFACTURED GOODS In a retail or wholesale business, there is just one type of inventory—the laid-down cost of goods available for sale. In a service company, we also will see just one inventory type—work in progress. In contrast, a manufacturing or producing company will normally have three types of inventory:

- *Raw materials*—the laid-down cost of raw materials and purchased parts that will be used in production.
- *Work in progress*—the costs incurred on goods that are in production, but not yet finished; work in progress consists of raw materials, direct labour, and some component of overhead.
- *Finished goods*—the cost of goods manufactured and ready for sale.

Costs move through the different levels of inventory and finally into cost of sales:

- The cost of purchased raw materials and parts starts out in raw materials inventory.
- When raw materials enter production, their cost is transferred to work in progress, with direct labour and overhead costs added to work in progress.
- When production is complete, the accumulated costs are transferred to finished goods.
- When the goods are sold, the cost is transferred from finished-goods inventory to cost of sales.

A particular issue arises with the allocation of overhead cost. The *CICA Handbook* recommends that manufacturers' inventories include an allocation of overhead:

> In the case of inventories of work in process and finished goods, cost should include the laid-down cost of material plus the cost of direct labour applied to the product and the *applicable share of overhead expense properly chargeable to production.*
> (*CICA* 3030.06, italics added)

There is a great deal of judgement inherent in this recommendation. The implication is that *some* overhead should be included in inventory, but management could decide that the "applicable" share "properly chargeable" is only the variable overhead.

The decision on which elements of overhead to include in inventory and which to treat as period costs will be determined with reference to the enterprise's financial reporting objectives and to the qualitative criteria of materiality, cost-benefit relationship, relevance, and fairness. Timeliness enters the picture because variable costing eliminates the time-consuming task of allocating overhead.

SUPPLIES INVENTORY In addition to the inventory types described above, most companies also will have an inventory of supplies. *Supplies* are items that are used in the productive activities of the company but that either (1) are used during production (such as lubricant for machinery) or (2) are too small to try to keep track of individually, even though they may enter the product directly (such as screws and nails). Supplies inventories seldom appear directly on the face of a balance sheet. Instead, they usually are combined with other miscellaneous current assets such as prepaid expenses.

CONCEPT REVIEW

1. Identify three policy issues to be considered when accounting for inventory.
2. What categories of inventory does a manufacturer have?
3. What are the three elements of cost that should be included in a manufacturer's finished-goods inventory cost?

PERIODIC VERSUS PERPETUAL RECORDING METHODS

Inventory cost may be measured by either a periodic inventory system or a perpetual inventory system. The essential difference between these two systems from an accounting point of view is the *frequency with which the cost flows are calculated.*

Periodic Inventory

In a periodic inventory system, the quantity of the ending inventory is established at the end of the accounting period. The unit costs are then applied to derive the ending inventory valuation by using a particular cost flow assumption (e.g., FIFO, LIFO, or average cost). Cost of goods sold (or cost used in production or in a service contract) is determined by subtracting the ending inventory value from the cost of goods available for sale.

In a periodic system, purchases are debited to a purchases account, and end-of-period entries are made to close the purchases account, to close out beginning inventory, and to record the ending inventory as an asset (i.e., the ending inventory replaces the beginning inventory in the accounts). Additional accounts, for costs tracked separately (e.g., freight-in or customs duties) are also closed at this time. Finally, any contra accounts to purchases, such as accounts for purchase returns and allowances or purchase discounts, must also be closed.

Under a periodic system, cost of sales (also commonly called cost of goods sold) is computed as a residual amount (beginning inventory plus net purchases less ending inventory) and for all practical purposes cannot be verified independently from an inventory count. The lack of verifiability is one reason that estimation methods may be used as a check; estimation methods are discussed at the end of this chapter.

Perpetual Inventory

perpetual inventory system

an inventory record-keeping system that continuously updates the quantity of inventory on hand and cost of goods sold on the basis of transaction records that report units acquired and sold

In a **perpetual inventory system**, each receipt and each issue of an inventory item is recorded in the inventory records to maintain an up-to-date perpetual inventory balance at all times. The result of the perpetual system is verified at least once a year by physically counting the inventory and matching the count to the accounting records. Thus, the perpetual inventory records provide the units and costs of inventory and cost of goods sold at any time. The unit costs applied to each issue or sale are determined by the cost flow assumption used.

Exhibit 8-1 compares these two systems and the typical entries that accompany each. It is important to make a distinction between tracking the *physical flow* of goods and the *costing* of the goods. Many companies maintain an ongoing record of physical flows as quantity information only. A continuous tracking of physical flows does not constitute a perpetual inventory system (from an accounting standpoint) unless the costs associated with those flows are simultaneously tracked. A good example is provided by supermarkets that use automated scanners at checkout stations to keep track of physical inventory levels but place accounting values on the physical flows only periodically.

Periodic versus Perpetual—Illustration

To illustrate the periodic versus the perpetual systems, consider the following data for the Lea Company:

	Units	Unit Cost	Total
Beginning inventory	500	$4.00	$2,000
Purchases	1,000	4.00	4,000
Goods available for sale	1,500		$6,000
Less: Sales	900		
Ending inventory, as calculated	600		
Ending inventory, based on physical count	580		

Note that there should have been 600 units on hand, not 580; 20 must have been damaged and discarded or stolen. The amount by which the physical count falls short of the expected level of inventory is generally (and euphemistically) referred to as "shrinkage." However, it also is possible that the sales records are not completely accurate.

Based on the prior data, the computation of the cost of sales yields the following amounts:

Beginning inventory (carried forward from the prior period): 500 × $4	$2,000
Merchandise purchases (accumulated in the purchases account): 1,000 × $4	4,000
Total goods available for sale during the period	6,000
Less: Ending inventory (quantity determined by a physical count): 580 × $4	2,320
Equals: Cost of sales (a residual amount)	$3,680

EXHIBIT 8-1

COMPARISON OF THE PERIODIC AND PERPETUAL INVENTORY SYSTEMS

Transaction—Routine Purchases of Various Inventory Items

Periodic system All inventory item values are debited to the purchases account regardless of the particular items acquired. That is,

Purchases	xx	
Cash, accounts payable, etc.		xx

Perpetual system Inventory items are debited to the inventory control account. A subsidiary ledger is kept for control purposes. That is,

Inventory	xx	
Cash, accounts payable, etc.		xx

Transaction—Goods Are Sold or Used

Periodic system No accounting entries are made.

Perpetual system Goods are moved from the inventory account and debited to cost of sales, or whatever debit is appropriate. Some goods may leave one inventory, raw materials, to move to another inventory, work in process, or to an appropriate expense, such as cleaning or maintenance. That is,

Cost of sales, etc.	xx	
Inventory		xx

Transaction—End-of-Period Accounting Entries

Periodic system Physical count of the ending inventory is taken and dollar values are assigned. This activity is a prerequisite to computing the cost of sales (COS) for the period. Adjusting entries are made to compute the cost of sales (COS) using the following formula: *COS = Beginning inventory + Purchases − Ending inventory.*

Cost of sales	xx	
Inventory (closing, per count)	xx	
Inventory (opening)		xx
Purchases		xx

This process is also frequently accomplished through the closing entries, rather than in an adjusting entry.

Perpetual system Physical count of inventory is not needed for calculation of cost of sales for the period, but such inventory counts are made in order to verify the accuracy of the perpetual system and to identify inventory overages and shortages. Shortages are most common. An entry is needed to adjust the inventory account on the books to the actual balance.

Cost of sales	xx	
Inventory (actual less accounting balance)		xx

Cost of sales is automatically determined from the sum of the daily postings to the cost of sales expense account.

PERIODIC RECORDING At the beginning of the year, the balance of the inventory account will be the $2,000 cost of the 500 units that were on hand. The entries to record the purchases and cost of sales under a periodic inventory system are as follows:

To record the purchases		
Purchases	4,000	
Accounts payable		4,000
To re-allocate the cost of opening inventory and purchases		
Cost of sales	3,680	
Inventory (closing, per count)	2,320	
Inventory (opening)		2,000
Purchases		4,000

A slight variation on the second entry above is to explicitly recognize the shrinkage of 20 units as an expense, instead of lumping it in with cost of goods sold.

Cost of sales (900 × $4)	3,600	
Inventory shrinkage expense (20 × $4)	80	
Inventory (closing, per count: 580 × $4)	2,320	
Inventory (opening)		2,000
Purchases		4,000

The inventory shrinkage expense will appear as an expense on the income statement.[3]

Under a periodic inventory system, the inventory is counted at least once a year. For interim financial statements, however, the amount of inventory may be estimated. If a perpetual record of only the *physical units* of inventory is maintained, then only the cost of that inventory needs to be estimated. If the company maintains no perpetual inventory count, then both the quantity and unit cost must be estimated. Later in the chapter, we will discuss the two most common methods of inventory estimation.

PERPETUAL RECORDING When a perpetual inventory system is used, detailed perpetual inventory records, in addition to the usual ledger accounts, are maintained for each inventory item, and an inventory control account is maintained in the general ledger. The perpetual inventory record for each item must provide information for recording receipts, issues, and balances on hand, both in units and in dollar amounts. With this information, the physical quantity and the valuation of goods on hand at any time are available from the accounting records. Therefore, a physical inventory count is still necessary but only to verify the accuracy of the perpetual inventory records. A physical count is made annually to compare the inventory on hand with the perpetual record and to provide data for any adjusting entries needed (errors and losses, for example).

When a difference is found between the perpetual inventory records and the physical count, the perpetual inventory records are adjusted to the physical count. In such cases, the inventory account is debited or credited as necessary for the correction, and cost of sales is increased or decreased. The loss may be accumulated in a separate account such as inventory shortages, to keep track of inventory shrinkage for internal purposes.

[3] It may be shown as a separate expense line on an income statement prepared for management use. It will not be found on published income statements, however. In public financial statements, management usually prefers not to indicate that there is any "shrinkage," and the amount is usually buried in the total amount shown for cost of sales.

In the Lea Company example above, the company began the year with 500 units in inventory, at a cost of $4 per unit. The purchase of 1,000 additional units is recorded as a debit to the inventory account (not to a purchases account).

Inventory (1,000 × $4)	4,000	
Accounts payable		4,000

When goods are sold, two entries are made; one to record the sale and the other to transfer their cost to COS. Assuming that Lea sells 900 units at a price of $10:

Accounts receivable (900 × $10)	9,000	
Sales revenue		9,000
Cost of sales (900 × $4)	3,600	
Inventory		3,600

The company will end the accounting period with an inventory balance of $2,400 (600 × $4). At the end of the year, a physical count would reveal only 580 units, and the additional expense would be recorded (it may also be recorded in a separate expense account):

Cost of sales	80	
Inventory ($2,320 − $2,400)		80

Thus at the end of the period, both the perpetual and periodic systems report identical inventory ($2,320) and cost of sales ($3,680) amounts.

Choosing a Recording Method

The choice of a periodic or perpetual system is not really an accounting policy choice, although modest differences in inventory and cost of sales amounts can arise under the average cost assumption and under LIFO, depending on which recording method is used. Instead, the choice of recording method is one of practicality—which method gives the best cost-benefit relationship?

PERPETUAL VERSUS PERIODIC A perpetual inventory system is especially useful when inventory consists of items with high unit values or when it is important to have adequate but not excessive inventory levels. Perpetual inventory systems require detailed accounting records and therefore tend to be more costly to implement and maintain than periodic systems. Computer technology has made perpetual inventory systems more popular today than ever before. Thanks to robotics and computer technology, there are automated inventory systems that not only account for the inventory but also manage the stocking and handling of inventory goods and materials. For example, a store may have a point-of-sale perpetual inventory system (using bar codes) to keep track of its merchandise and to facilitate prompt reordering of popular items. This is information that a periodic system could not possibly provide on a timely basis.

However, even with automated systems, certain aspects of physical inventory management and control are problematic. Theft and pilferage, breakage and other physical damage, mis-orders and mis-fills, and inadequate inventory supervision practices must be dealt with regardless of the type of inventory accounting system used.

The choice of method depends on whether the company really needs to have *both* quantity information and cost information at its fingertips for control purposes:

- Does the company need to know exactly how many units it has at any point in time? If so, then it needs a perpetual system *for quantities* but not necessarily for costs. Point-of-sale computer terminals that read bar codes are very useful for maintaining quantity flow information, but need not necessarily be tied to the accounting records.
- Does the company to know exactly how many units it has on hand, how old they are, *and how much they cost* on a regular basis (such as weekly or monthly)? The need for frequent interim financial statements will make perpetual tracking of costs more useful.

Bank operating lines of credit are often tied to the carrying value of receivables and inventory. If, for example, a company's bank is willing to lend up to 60% of the carrying value of the inventory, it is necessary to know at least monthly (and to report to the bank) the value of the inventory. In this case, a perpetual system makes sense. Also, full information on quantities and costs may be needed for insurance purposes.

The basic question is whether the additional cost of a perpetual accounting inventory system is worth the cost. If a company doesn't need the full capabilities of a perpetual system, it's likely that the company will use the cheaper, less complicated, periodic system.

Remember that a company may have a sophisticated perpetual inventory system for quantities and still use the periodic system for its accounting records. The perpetual system may not be integrated into the accounting system. For quarterly reporting, the company may still take a physical inventory or use an estimation method (which will be discussed later in this chapter).

Even with the most sophisticated perpetual system, it still is necessary to take a physical inventory at or near each fiscal year-end. A physical inventory is necessary not only to satisfy the auditors (if any), but also to verify the integrity of the perpetual system. If there is a significant difference between the count revealed by the physical inventory and the quantity of inventory that the perpetual system says should be there, there can be only two reasons: (1) there is a problem with the perpetual system or (2) someone is stealing the merchandise. Prompt investigation and remedial action is required in either case.

COST FLOW ASSUMPTIONS

At date of acquisition, inventory items are recorded at their cash equivalent cost. Subsequently, when an item is sold, net assets decline and expenses increase as a result of the transfer of the item's cost from inventory to cost of sales. The cost value assigned to the end-of-period inventory of merchandise and finished goods is an allocation of the total cost of goods available for sale between that portion sold (cost of sales) and that portion held as an asset for subsequent sale (ending inventory). This isn't a problem when costs are stable over the period, but when costs change, the allocation issue rears its ugly head: Which item was sold? The central issue is the *order* in which the actual unit costs incurred are assigned to the ending inventory and to cost of sales.

COST OF SALES

Underlying Concepts of Cost Flow

Cost of sales (COS) is often the most significant expense category on the income statement. A small percentage shift in COS will have a material impact on net income. Therefore, any accounting policy choice in this area is very important. The important issue in this area is the cost flow policy. This allocates the total cost of goods available for sale during each period between (1) the cost of sales and (2) the cost of ending inventory. If inventory unit acquisition or production costs are constant over time, the choice of an allocation process will not affect the result. However, inventory item costs—both acquisition and manufacturing costs—typically vary over time, changing up or down in response to prevailing conditions in the economy.

The physical movement of goods is nearly always on a first-in, first-out basis, especially if the product is perishable or subject to obsolescence. But the cost flow method used to account for the value of both the inventory used up during the period and the inventory on hand at the end of the period can be quite different from the actual flow of goods. *Inventory accounting policy determines the flow of costs through the accounting system, not the flow of goods physically in and out of a stockroom.* The *CICA Handbook* states that

> The method selected for determining cost should be one which results in the fairest matching of costs against revenues regardless of whether or not the method corresponds to the physical flow of goods. (*CICA* 3030.09)

Notice the way matching is invoked: this section of the *CICA Handbook* is dated 1973, and predates the work on the definitional approach to expense recognition. It's one of many inconsistencies in the *CICA Handbook* in this regard.

The central issue in cost flow policy is the order in which the actual unit costs incurred are assigned to the ending inventory and to cost of sales. Selection of an inventory flow method determines the cost of sales, which is deducted from sales revenue for the period. Four inventory cost flow methods are discussed in this section. Which cost flow assumption results in the "fairest" matching? The AcSB does not provide guidance in this regard, but indicates only that the decision depends on the circumstances of the enterprise and industry. The selection of an inventory cost flow assumption depends on the financial reporting objectives of each individual enterprise. The two methods in common use in Canada are FIFO and average cost; you'll understand why as this section progresses.

Each cost flow assumption changes the income statement and the balance sheet, since both cost of sales and inventory change. There is no difference in reporting the cash flow from operating activities, however.

Cost Flow Alternatives

The major cost flow methods are:

- specific cost identification
- average cost
- first-in, first-out (FIFO)
- last-in, first-out (LIFO)

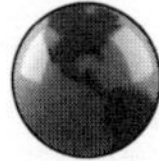

LIFO is not a common method in Canada (nor in most other countries), due largely to the fact that it is not acceptable for income tax purposes. Specific identification is used mainly for large, unique items, such as custom-built equipment, or in accounting for service contracts. For other types of business, average cost and FIFO are the popular methods.

The example that follows is a numeric example of the methods applied to both a perpetual and periodic system.

Specific Identification

This method is, in theory, the most straightforward of all the methods. At the end of the year (periodic method) or on each sale (perpetual method) the specific units sold, and their specific cost, are identified to determine inventory and cost of sales. In the example in Exhibit 8-2, there are 300 units left in closing inventory. **Specific identification** under a periodic system reveals that, at the end of January, there are 100 units from the 9 January purchase, 100 units from the 15 January purchase, and 100 units from the 24 January purchase. Ending inventory is then valued at \$352, and cost of sales at \$768 (\$1,120 − \$352).

In practice, specific identification may not be so simple for most businesses because it is inconvenient and difficult to establish just which items were sold and what their specific initial cost was. However, it is the method used when each product or service is unique (and substantial), such as for shipbuilding, special-order heavy equipment, custom software, construction contracts, consulting operations, and so forth.

EXHIBIT 8-2

CHASE CONTAINER CORPORATION
INVENTORY DATA

Transaction Date	Purchased	Units Sold	On Hand
1 January—Inventory @ $1.00			200
9 January—Purchase @ $1.10	300		500
10 January—Sales		400	100
15 January—Purchase @ $1.16	400		500
18 January—Sale		300	200
24 January—Purchase @ $1.26	100		300

The costs to be allocated; goods available for sale:

Beginning inventory	200 × $1.00 =		$ 200
Purchases	300 × $1.10 =	$330	
	400 × $1.16 =	464	
	100 × $1.26 =	126	920
Cost of goods available for sale			$1,120

The $1,120 is allocated between ending inventory and cost of sales, using one of the cost flow assumptions described.

Average Cost

When the average cost method is used in a periodic system, it is called a **weighted-average system**. *A weighted-average unit cost is computed by dividing the sum of the beginning inventory cost plus total current period purchase costs by the number of units in the beginning inventory plus units purchased during the period.* That is,

$$\text{Average cost} = \frac{\text{Opening inventory} + \text{Purchases}}{\text{Units in opening inventory} + \text{Units purchased}}$$

Exhibit 8-3 illustrates application of the weighted-average method under a periodic system using the data given in Exhibit 8-2 for the Chase Container Corporation.

When the average cost method is used in a perpetual inventory system, a **moving-average** unit cost is used. *The moving average provides a new unit cost after each purchase.* When goods are sold or issued, the moving-average unit cost at the time is used. Application of the moving-average concept in a perpetual inventory system is shown in Exhibit 8-4, based on Exhibit 8-2. For example, on 9 January, the $1.06 moving-average cost is derived by dividing the total cost ($530) by the total units (500). The January ending inventory of 300 units is costed at the latest moving-average unit cost of $1.18 ($354 ÷ 300). The cost of sales for the period is the sum of the sales in the total cost column, $766. There's a lot of calculating involved!

First-In, First-Out

The **first-in, first-out (FIFO)** method treats the first goods purchased or manufactured as the first units costed out on sale or issuance. *Goods sold (or issued) are valued at the oldest unit costs, and goods remaining in inventory are valued at the most recent unit cost amounts.* Exhibit 8-5 demonstrates FIFO for the periodic system. Exhibit 8-6 demonstrates the perpetual system. Using the perpetual system, a sale is costed out either currently throughout the period or each time there is a withdrawal. In Exhibit 8-6, issues from inventory on 10 and 18 January (FIFO basis) are costed out as they occur. FIFO always produces the same numeric results whether a periodic or perpetual system is used.

EXHIBIT 8-3

CHASE CONTAINER CORPORATION
WEIGHTED-AVERAGE INVENTORY COST METHOD, PERIODIC INVENTORY SYSTEM

Goods Available	Units	Unit Price	Total Cost
1 January—Beginning inventory	200	$1.00	$ 200
9 January—Purchase	300	1.10	330
15 January—Purchase	400	1.16	464
24 January—Purchase	100	1.26	126
January—Total available	1,000		$1,120
Weighted-average unit cost ($1,120 ÷ 1,000)		1.12	
Ending inventory at weighted-average cost:			
31 January	300	1.12	336
Cost of sales at weighted-average cost:			
Sales during January	700*	1.12	784
Total cost allocated			$1,120

* 400 units on 10 January plus 300 units on 18 January.

EXHIBIT 8-4

CHASE CONTAINER CORPORATION
MOVING-AVERAGE INVENTORY COST, PERPETUAL INVENTORY SYSTEM

	Purchases			Sales			Inventory Balance		
Dates	Units	Unit Cost	Total Cost	Units	Unit Cost	Total Cost	Units	Unit Cost	Total Cost
1 January							200	$1.00	$ 200
9 January	300	$1.10	$330				500	1.06(a)	530
10 January				400	$1.06	$424	100	1.06	106
15 January	400	1.16	464				500	1.14(b)	570
18 January				300	1.14	342	200	1.14	228
24 January	100	1.26	126				300	1.18(c)	354
Ending inventory									$ 354
Cost of sales						$766			766
Total cost allocated									$1,120

(a) $530 ÷ 500 = $1.06
(b) $570 ÷ 500 = $1.14
(c) $354 ÷ 300 = $1.18

EXHIBIT 8-5

CHASE CONTAINER CORPORATION
FIFO INVENTORY COSTING, PERIODIC INVENTORY SYSTEM

Beginning inventory (200 units at $1)		$ 200
Add purchases during period (computed as in Exhibit 8-2)		920
Cost of goods available for sale		1,120
Deduct ending inventory (300 units per physical inventory count):		
100 units at $1.26 (most recent purchase—24 January)	$ 126	
200 units at $1.16 (next most recent purchase—15 January)	232	
Total ending inventory cost		358
Cost of sales		$ 762*

* Can also be calculated as 200 units on hand 1 January at $1 plus 300 units purchased 9 January at $1.10, plus 200 units purchased 15 January at $1.16.

EXHIBIT 8-6

CHASE CONTAINER CORPORATION
FIFO INVENTORY COSTING, PERPETUAL INVENTORY SYSTEM

	Purchases			Sales			Inventory Balance		
Dates	Units	Unit Cost	Total Cost	Units	Unit Cost	Total Cost	Units	Unit Cost	Total Cost
1 January	200	$1.00	$ 200						
9 January	300	$1.10	$330				200	1.00	200
							300	1.10	330
10 January				200	$1.00	$200			
				200	1.10	220	100	1.10	110
15 January	400	1.16	464				100	1.10	110
							400	1.16	464
18 January				100	1.10	110			
				200	1.16	232	200	1.16	232
24 January	100	1.26	126				200	1.16	232
							100	1.26	126
Ending inventory ($232 + $126)									$ 358
Cost of sales						$762			762
Total cost allocated									$ 1,120

ACCOUNTING ENTRIES—ILLUSTRATION To illustrate the accounting entries typical in a periodic and perpetual system, the data for the FIFO example will be used. The entries are those described in Exhibit 8-1. Both methods begin the period with 200 units in inventory at a cost of $200.

		Periodic		Perpetual	
9 Jan.	Purchases	330		—	
	Inventory	—		330	
	Cash, etc.		330		330
10 Jan.	Cost of sales	—		420	
	Inventory		—		420
15 Jan.	Purchases	464		—	
	Inventory	—		464	
	Cash, etc.		464		464
18 Jan.	Cost of sales	—		342	
	Inventory		—		342
24 Jan.	Purchases	126		—	
	Inventory	—		126	
	Cash, etc.		126		126
31 Jan.	Cost of sales	762		—	
	Inventory (closing)	358		—	
	Inventory (opening)		200		—
	Purchases		920		—

Last-In, First-Out

The **last-in, first-out (LIFO)** method of inventory costing matches inventory valued at the most recent unit acquisition cost with current sales revenue. The units remaining in ending inventory are costed at the oldest unit costs incurred, and the units included in cost of sales are costed at the newest unit costs incurred, the exact opposite of the FIFO cost assumption. Like FIFO, application of LIFO requires the use of inventory cost layers for different unit costs.

When LIFO is used, the ending inventory is costed at the oldest unit costs. Cost of sales is determined by deducting ending inventory from the cost of goods available for sale. The periodic LIFO system permits the cost of purchases occurring after the last sale to be included in cost of sales, which cannot occur in the perpetual system. This method is illustrated in Exhibit 8-7. For the current example, the LIFO cost of the 18 January sale includes the cost of the 24 January purchase! The ending inventory therefore consists of two layers, one at $1.00 and one at $1.10.

Exhibits 8-6 and 8-8 illustrate the rather tedious nature of the perpetual inventory system under both FIFO and LIFO. Thanks to computers, some degree of relief from the burdensome nature of this work has been made possible, but extensive record-keeping is still required.

INCOME TAX FACTORS CRA will not accept LIFO for tax purposes. Companies must use either the FIFO or the average cost method when they compute their taxes payable. If a company uses LIFO for financial reporting, it must maintain two different inventory costing systems—one for financial reporting (LIFO) and another for income tax (FIFO or average). Since there is a substantial additional work load to maintaining two different systems, Canadian companies rarely use LIFO. *Financial Reporting in Canada 2003* reported that only 3 of the 2003 sample companies use LIFO for any part of their inventory.

LIFO is most likely to be used by a Canadian subsidiary of a U.S. parent corporation. LIFO is acceptable for computing U.S. income tax, if the same method is also used for U.S. financial reporting. A Canadian subsidiary may then maintain LIFO inventory accounts in order to facilitate the parent's consolidation process. However LIFO still would not be acceptable for the subsidiary's Canadian tax return.

EXHIBIT 8-7

CHASE CONTAINER CORPORATION
LIFO INVENTORY COSTING, PERIODIC INVENTORY SYSTEM

Cost of goods available (see Exhibit 8-2)		$1,120
Deduct ending inventory (300 units per physical inventory count):		
200 units at $1 (oldest costs available, from 1 January inventory)	$200	
100 units at $1.10 (next oldest costs available; from 9 January purchase)	110	
Ending inventory		310
Cost of sales		$ 810*

* Can also be calculated as 100 units at $1.26 plus 400 units at $1.16 plus 200 units at $1.10

EXHIBIT 8-8

CHASE CONTAINER CORPORATION
LIFO INVENTORY COSTING, PERPETUAL INVENTORY SYSTEM

	Purchases			Sales			Inventory Balance		
Dates	**Units**	**Unit Cost**	**Total Cost**	**Units**	**Unit Cost**	**Total Cost**	**Units**	**Unit Cost**	**Total Cost**
1 January*							200	$1.00	$ 200
9 January	300	$1.10	$330				200	1.00	200
							300	1.10	330
10 January				300	$1.10	$330			
				100	1.00	100	100	1.00	100
15 January	400	1.16	464				100	1.00	100
							400	1.16	464
18 January				300	1.16	348	100	1.00	100
							100	1.16	116
24 January	100	1.26	126				100	1.00	100
							100	1.16	116
							100	1.26	126
Ending inventory ($100 + $116 + $126)									$ 342
Cost of sales						$778			778
Total cost allocated									$1,120

* Beginning inventory.

SUMMARY Let's review the basics of the cost flow assumption again. This is an accounting policy choice. When prices are rising, as they often are, FIFO will produce higher inventory, lower cost of sales, and higher income. It's probably popular with firms that would like to see higher income and net assets in their financial statements. LIFO has the opposite effect: lower inventories, higher cost of sales, and lower incomes. It would likely be very popular among those firms trying to minimize income tax payments except for the fact that it can't be used for income tax reporting in Canada. Average cost methods provide inventory and cost of sales amounts between the LIFO and FIFO extremes, and are the next best thing to LIFO for income and tax minimization when inventory costs are rising. Canadian practice is about evenly divided between FIFO and average cost. LIFO is very seldom used in Canada, except by Canadian subsidiaries of U.S. companies which mandate its use in order to be consistent with the parent's accounting policies.

The impacts of FIFO versus LIFO are illustrated in Exhibit 8-9.

EXHIBIT 8-9

COMPARISON OF THE EFFECTS OF FIFO VERSUS LIFO

If purchase prices are:	The impact on ending inventory is:	The impact on cost of sales is:	The impact on net income and retained earnings is:
Rising	FIFO > LIFO	FIFO < LIFO	FIFO > LIFO
Falling	FIFO < LIFO	FIFO > LIFO	FIFO < LIFO

Effect of Changing Methods

What if a company were to change inventory costing methods, say, to switch from FIFO to average cost, or *vice versa*? What will change in the financial statements? Obviously, closing inventory will change, and cumulative income to date will also change by this amount. However, the individual effect in any one year will be determined by the change in closing inventory and the change in opening inventory, since both opening and closing inventories change cost of sales on the income statement. Tax amounts will also change, but we're going to ignore income tax in the example that follows, for simplicity. Consider the following situation:

	Opening Inventory	Closing Inventory	Net Income
20X4 FIFO	$157,000	$189,000	$642,900
20X4 average	157,000	170,000	
20X5 FIFO	189,000	162,000	450,000
20X5 average	170,000	158,000	

What will be the effect if the company changes to the average cost method? At the end of 20X5, the difference in inventory is $4,000 ($158,000 − $162,000). Both inventory and retained earnings on the balance sheet will be reduced by this amount.

On the income statement, both opening and closing inventories will be affected, and COS will change. This amount is calculated as follows:

	20X5	20X4
Existing net income, FIFO	$450,000	$642,900
Opening inventory differential		
20X5 ($170,000 − $189,000)	19,000	
20X4 ($157,000 − $157,000)		0
Closing inventory differential		
20X5 ($158,000 − $162,000)	(4,000)	
20X4 ($170,000 − $189,000)		(19,000)
Revised net income	$465,000	$623,900

In 20X5, there is $19,000 less opening inventory under the average cost method. This means that goods available for sale is $19,000 lower than under FIFO, COS is lower, and net income is higher. On the other hand, closing inventory, a deduction from COS, is $4,000 lower. This means that COS will be $4,000 higher, and net income lower. Remember, inventory changes an *expense*, which is a deduction in calculating net income. For the 20X4 comparative year, opening inventories are identical for the two policies. The closing inventory is $19,000 lower under average cost, increasing COS and decreasing income.

Note that the total effect over two complete years balances out—$19,000 is added in one place and subtracted in the other. Notice also that the total change to income over the two years is the $4,000 difference that relates only to the 20X5 closing inventory.

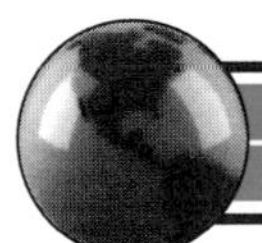

International Perspective

Accounting for inventories, called *stocks* in the United Kingdom and in some other English-speaking countries, is similar throughout the world, with one exception: the use of LIFO. LIFO is used in the United States (largely because it is acceptable for U.S. income tax purposes), but is not generally acceptable in the rest of the world, including Australia, France, the Netherlands, and the United Kingdom.

Germany does permit LIFO, but average cost is the most frequently used method because that is the method used for tax purposes. Belgium permits LIFO, but only if it is used on an item-by-item basis. Italy does not formally permit LIFO, but a pricing method acceptable for tax purposes is basically a LIFO approach. In Japan, like Canada, LIFO can be used for financial reporting but not for tax reporting.

The International Accounting Standards Board revised IAS 2, *Inventories*, in 2003, effective 1 January 2005. The revised standard has dropped LIFO as a permissible cost flow assumption, after several earlier attempts to ban LIFO were defeated. As of 1 January 2005, companies that prepare their statements on the basis of international standards are permitted to use only FIFO or average cost.

In its revised IAS 2, the Board dropped references to "matching" that had existed in earlier versions of IAS 2. This change reflects the trend of accounting standards away from the matching approach and toward a definitional approach. The definitional approach is based on definitions of assets (and other financial statement elements), and LIFO was deemed not to yield an appropriate measure of inventory assets.

CONCEPT REVIEW

1. Explain the essential differences in accounting for inventories under the periodic and perpetual inventory systems.
2. If the price to acquire inventory is rising, and the company is pursuing an income maximization reporting strategy over the long term, which inventory cost flow assumption is management most likely to choose?
3. Why is LIFO unlikely to be used by Canadian companies?

SPECIAL APPROACHES TO INVENTORY COSTING

Standard Costs

For manufacturing entities using a standard cost system, the inventories are valued, recorded, and reported for internal purposes on the basis of a standard unit cost. Standard cost, which approximates an ideal or expected cost, prevents the overstatement of inventory values because it excludes from inventory all expenditures that are due to inefficiency, waste, and abnormal conditions. Actual historical cost is used only once, on acquisition. Standard cost is used thereafter, which simplifies record-keeping significantly!

Under this method, the differences between actual cost (which includes losses due to inefficiencies, etc.) and standard cost (which excludes losses due to inefficiencies, etc.) are recorded in separate variance accounts. These accounts are usually written off as a current period loss rather than capitalized in inventory. To illustrate, assume that a manufacturing company has just adopted standard cost procedures and that the beginning inventory is zero. During the current period, the company makes two purchases and one issuance and records them as follows:

1. *To record the purchase of 10,000 units of raw material at $1.10 actual cost; standard cost has been established at $1:*

Raw materials (10,000 units × $1)	10,000	
Raw materials purchase price variance (10,000 units × $.10)	1,000	
Accounts payable (10,000 units × $1.10)		11,000

2. *To record issuance of 8,000 units of raw material to the factory for processing:*

Work in progress	8,000	
Raw materials (8,000 × $1)		8,000

3. *To record the purchase of 2,000 units of raw materials at $0.95:*

Raw materials (2,000 × $1)	2,000	
Raw materials purchase price variance (2,000 × $.05)		100
Accounts payable (2,000 × $0.95)		1,900

Under standard cost procedures there would be no need to consider inventory cost flow methods (such as LIFO, FIFO, and average) because only one cost—standard cost—appears in the records. In addition, perpetual inventory records can be maintained in units because all issues and inventory valuations are at the same standard cost. Because standard cost represents a departure from the cost principle, it is acceptable for external reporting under GAAP only if results are not materially different than actual costs. However, standard costs can easily be adjusted to actual cost for external reporting by simply pro-rating (i.e., allocating) the variances to inventory and cost of sales. Pretty tempting, isn't it? The size of the variances indicates the differences between actual and standard and can be used to assess materiality.

Just-in-Time Inventory Systems

Just-in-time (JIT) inventory systems are a response to the high costs associated with stockpiling inventories of raw materials, parts, supplies, and finished goods. Rather than keeping ample quantities on hand awaiting use, the idea is to reduce inventories to the lowest levels possible and thus save costs. As the name suggests, the ultimate goal is to see goods and materials arrive at the company's receiving dock *just in time* to be moved directly to the plant's production floor for immediate use in the manufacturing or assembly process. Then, taking the concept one step further, finished goods roll off the production floor and move directly to the shipping dock just in time for shipment to the customers. The ideal result is low inventory levels and low inventory costs.

JIT systems tend to result in simplified inventory accounting procedures, primarily because inventory levels are kept low, but also because raw materials and work-in-process inventories are in many cases combined. At Hewlett-Packard, for example, raw materials are charged to a combined account and then transferred to finished goods upon completion of production.[4]

JIT systems also affect the way companies account for production costs. Conversion costs (labour and direct overhead costs) are charged directly to the cost of sales account as a matter of expediency. The working premise is that almost everything being produced is in response to orders from customers. Therefore, all conversion costs are charged to the cost of sales account and charge-backs are made (finished items not sold or unfinished items still in production as of the end of the accounting period) to finished goods or work-in-process inventories, respectively. In effect, JIT systems work backward in comparison with traditional inventory accounting systems, which put everything first into inventory.

OTHER ISSUES

Damaged and Obsolete Inventory

Special inventory categories are created for items that are damaged, shopworn, obsolete, defective, or are trade-ins or repossessions. These inventory items are valued at **current replacement cost**, defined as the price for which the items can be purchased in their present condition.

To illustrate a situation in which the current replacement cost can be determined reliably, assume that Allied Appliance Company has on hand a repossessed TV set that had an original cost of $650 when new. The set, which originally sold for $995, was repossessed when $500 was owed by the customer. Similar used TV sets can be purchased in the wholesale market for $240. $240 is the replacement cost. The repossessed item should be recorded as follows:

Inventory, repossessed merchandise*	240	
Loss on repossession	260	
Accounts receivable		500

* Note that the inventory is placed in a separate category and not included with normal goods.

Subsequent resale of the TV at a price greater or less than $240 triggers a gain or loss on sale.

When the replacement cost cannot be determined reliably, such items should be valued at their estimated net realizable value (NRV), defined as the estimated sale price less all

[4] B. Newmann and P. Jaouan, "Kanban, Zips and Cost Accounting: A Case Study," *Journal of Accountancy* (August 1986), pp. 132–141.

costs expected to be incurred in preparing the item for sale. Replacement cost is preferred over NRV because it is typically a more objective value, established by existing market forces rather than by managerial estimates.

To illustrate accounting for inventory at NRV when replacement cost cannot be determined reliably, assume that Allied suffers fire damage to 100 units of its regular inventory. The item, which originally cost $10 per unit (as reflected in the perpetual inventory records), was marked to sell before the fire for $18 per unit. No established used market exists. The company should value the item for inventory purposes at its NRV. Allied estimates that after cleaning and making repairs, the items would sell for $7 per unit; the estimated cost of the repairs for all the units is $150, and the estimated selling cost is 20% of the new selling price. Given this data, the total inventory valuation for the items is as follows:

Estimated sale price (100 × $7)		$700
Less: Estimated cost to repair	$150	
Estimated selling costs ($700 × 20%)	140	(290)
NRV for inventory		$410

Damaged inventory is segregated in a separate account as part of the writedown entry:

Inventory, damaged goods	410	
Loss from fire damage	590	
Inventory (100 × $10)		1,000

Losses on Purchase Commitments

To lock in prices and ensure sufficient quantities, companies often contract with suppliers to purchase a specified quantity of materials during a future period at an agreed unit cost. Some purchase commitments (contracts) are subject to revision or cancellation before the end of the contract period; others are not. Each case requires different accounting and reporting procedures. A loss must be accrued on a purchase contract when

- The purchase contract is not subject to revision or cancellation; and
- When a loss is likely and material, and
- The loss can be reasonably estimated.

Assume that the Bayshore Company enters into a non-cancellable purchase contract during October 20X2 that states, "During 20X3, 50,000 tanks of compressed chlorine will be purchased at $5 each," a total commitment of $250,000. Suppose that the current replacement cost of the chlorine is $240,000 by year-end. Thus, a $10,000 loss is likely.[5] The loss on the purchase commitment should be recorded at the end of 20X2 as follows:

Estimated loss on purchase commitment ($250,000 – $240,000)	10,000	
Estimated liability on non-cancellable purchase commitment		10,000

[5] This is known as an *opportunity cost*, because the company missed the opportunity to buy the chlorine at a lower price.

The estimated loss is reported on the 20X2 income statement, and the liability is reported on the balance sheet. When the goods are acquired in 20X3, merchandise inventory (or purchases) is debited at the current replacement cost, and the estimated liability account is debited. Assume that the above materials have a replacement cost at date of delivery of $235,000. The purchase entry would be as follows:

Materials inventory (or purchases)	235,000	
Estimated liability on non-cancellable purchase commitment	10,000	
Loss on purchase commitment	5,000	
Cash		250,000

This treatment records the loss in the period when it became likely. Note that inventory is never recorded for more than its replacement cost—so, if the actual historical cost is higher than the replacement cost, historical cost is not used.

If there were a full or partial recovery of the purchase price, the recovery would be recognized (only as a loss recovery; gains are not recognized) in the period during which the recovery took place. Thus, if in 20X3 the materials had a replacement cost at date of delivery of $255,000, the purchase entry would be as follows:

Materials inventory (or purchases)	250,000	
Estimated liability on non-cancellable purchase commitment	10,000	
Recovery of loss on purchase commitment		10,000
Cash		250,000

Review the three criteria for accounting recognition of a loss listed above. What if the contract were cancellable? Then the loss is no longer likely, and the amount would not be accrued. What if the loss were not estimable? Recognition criteria are not met, and again no entry can be made. What if commodity prices are going up, not down? Then a loss is not likely and no entry is appropriate. Gains are not recognized. Disclosure of the contracts and terms is appropriate when the contracts are significant, or out of the ordinary, or when an inestimable loss is present.

Inventory Errors

In our discussion so far, we have focused mainly on the relationship between inventory and cost of sales. Obviously, we won't get the correct cost of sales if we have problems with our inventory calculations.

But inventory interacts with more than just cost of sales. Incoming inventory relates directly to accounts payable and purchases, while outgoing inventory relates directly to accounts receivable and to revenue. Because of the sheer volume of transactions involving inventory, it takes special vigilance to ensure that there are no errors.

There may be some estimation errors in inventory, especially in lower-of-cost-or-market estimates, in work-in-process inventories relating to long-term contracts, and in estimation techniques such as the retail inventory method (which we will discuss shortly). However, estimates are a fact of life in accounting. They may turn out to be wrong, but they are not errors—we just do the best we can with the information that we have at the time we exercise our professional judgement.

The errors that we are primarily concerned about are *cut-off errors*. "Cut-off" refers to the closing of the books. When we reach the end of a fiscal period, we must draw a line between transactions at (1) the period just ending and (2) the start of the next period. In theory, this is a simple exercise. But in practice, accurate cut-offs are both difficult and crucial.

Think of an ongoing factory. New inventory is delivered almost continuously during every day, and finished goods are shipped to customers all day long. If the factory operates 24 hours a day, when do we stop counting for last year and start counting for next year? Consistency is crucial. If we say that the year-end inventory is the amount in our factories, warehouses, and offices at midnight on 31 December, we must use that same cut-off time each year. The physical count of inventory must be taken as of that specific time, even though inventory is flowing in and out of our factory while the physical count is taking place over the following days.

Counting inventory is only part of the problem. We must be sure that goods shipped on the closing days of the year have also been invoiced to the customers—revenue and accounts receivable must include last-minute shipments. Goods and raw materials flowing into the factory in the final days must be included in purchases and accounts payable. Similarly, we must make sure that revenue has not been recorded for shipments that won't be made until the early days of the next year.

Assuring proper cut-off is a major accounting (and auditing) control issue due to the sheer volume of activity and the need to coordinate all of the accounting activities that involve inventory. As well, unethical managers may be tempted to delay or accelerate shipments around year-end in order to manipulate income. As a result, one of the most common types of accounting error is inventory cut-off error.

Suppose that a company discovers in 20X7 that its 20X6 year-end inventory was overstated by $750,000. The error is discovered after its 20X6 financial statements were issued. An overstatement of ending inventory leads to an (1) understatement of cost of sales, (2) overstatement of income, and (3) overstatement of retained earnings. Therefore, the correction in 20X7 will be recorded as follows:

Retained earnings	750,000	
Inventory (1 January 20X7)		750,000

When the 20X7 financial statements are prepared, the comparative 20X6 financial statements will be restated to show the correct inventory and income amounts. Errors are always corrected by restatement, and never by showing special charges or credits in the income statement.

Later in the book, we devote a full chapter (Chapter 20) to accounting changes, including error correction. Therefore, we will not elaborate further at this point in the text.

LOWER-OF-COST-OR-MARKET VALUATION

GAAP requires that inventories be valued either at cost or at current market value, whichever is lower. While the GAAP model relies on historic cost, it also establishes a lower-of-cost-or-market (LCM) test of some type for every asset—overstatement of assets is not permitted! Assets should always be substantiated by some kind of future economic benefit. For inventory, it's clear that if you can't use it or sell it, then inventory can't really be called an asset. The LCM test recognizes an impairment of value for inventory.

To illustrate the basic operation of LCM inventory valuation, assume that a retailer has an inventory consisting of a single line of office electronics products, all purchased during 20X2 at a cost of $165 per unit, the going wholesale price at the time the merchandise was acquired. Late in the year, stiff competition in the electronics and office products market causes wholesale prices for the retailer's products in inventory to drop substantially, with retail prices following suit. As of the end of the year, manufacturers are quoting wholesale prices of $125 per unit. Assume that none of the retailer's inventory has been sold. The retailer's ending inventory for 20X2 should be valued and reported at $125 per unit, which represents a $40 loss per unit based on the $165 original purchase cost. This $40-per-unit loss must be reported in the retailer's 20X2 financial statements, the period during which the market price decline took place.

Assume that the retailer's inventory is sold in 20X3. For each unit sold, the cost of sales is now $125, not $165. Assuming that retail selling prices dropped commensurate with last year's decline in wholesale prices, the lower cost of sales provides the retailer with approximately the same gross margin on sales as would have been available in 20X2, when both wholesale and retail prices were higher. The net effect of the LCM application in this instance is to (appropriately) shift the $40-per-unit loss from the period when the inventory was sold to the period in which the replacement cost decreased.

LCM tests are complicated by a couple of policy choices:

1. What is the definition of market value?
2. Should the LCM test be applied to individual inventory items, to categories, or to totals? The question of aggregation is not trivial.

Definition of Market Value

net realizable value (NRV)

the amount of funds expected to be received upon the sale or liquidation of an asset net of incremental expenses

The basic difficulty with determining market value is that there are two markets: (1) the supplier market or **replacement cost** and (2) the customer market (sales price). Sales price is called **net realizable value (NRV)** when costs expected to be incurred in preparing the item for sale are deducted. Net realizable value can be taken further, deducting expected costs and also a normal gross profit margin; use of net realizable value less a normal profit margin will preserve normal profits when the item is finally sold. Take a look at Exhibit 8-10 for an example of calculations.

Which one is "market"? If you're looking for a measure of future cash flow, NRV is very attractive, but can be very subjective. Will the sales price hold? Replacement cost is more objective, and chances are that if replacement cost goes down, sales price will, too. It's more onerous to compile, though.

Canadian standard-setters have provided no recommendations as to the meaning of "market" in the term "lower of cost or market." The *CICA Handbook* provides the following comment:

> In view of the lack of precision in meaning, it is desirable that the term "market" not be used in describing the basis of valuation. A term more descriptive of the method of determining market, such as "replacement cost," "net realizable value" or "net realizable value less normal profit margin," would be preferable.
> (*CICA* 3030.11)

In the absence of authoritative guidance, Canadian companies are free to choose the definition of market value that is most appropriate in the circumstances—a judgement call by management. Industry practice undoubtedly plays a role: *the majority of Canadian companies use net realizable value as the determination of market value.* However, companies use various methods and it's important to check the disclosure notes to pin down the valuation rule in use.

EXHIBIT 8-10

NET REALIZABLE VALUE AND NET REALIZABLE VALUE LESS A NORMAL PROFIT MARGIN

Inventory item A, at original **cost**	$ 70
Inventory item A, at estimated current selling price in completed condition	$ 100
Less: Estimated costs to complete and sell	− 40
Net realizable value	$ 60
Less: Allowance for normal profit (10% of sales price)	− 10
Net realizable value less normal profit	$ 50

The net realizable value for raw materials and work in process is more difficult to determine because the costs to complete and ultimate selling prices are more uncertain. Therefore, replacement costs for raw materials, plus manufacturing costs to date for work in process, is often used on the expectation that selling prices tend to move in step with replacement costs. Nevertheless, a writedown may still be required if realizable values have declined despite the absence of a decline in replacement costs.

In the United States, there is a different approach to the determination of market value. To apply this approach, one must determine three definitions of market value (replacement cost, net realizable value, and net realizable value less a normal profit margin) and then use the *middle* value. Some Canadian firms may follow this approach, but it certainly requires a lot of data collection!

Extent of Grouping

Application of LCM can follow one of three approaches:

1. Comparison of cost and market separately for each item of inventory;
2. Comparison of cost and market separately for each classification of inventory; and
3. Comparison of total cost with total market for the total inventory.

Exhibit 8-11 shows the application of each approach. Inventory is valued at $67,500, a loss of $3,500, if the individual approach is used. If valued as a whole, inventory is reported at $69,500, a loss of $1,500.

Consistency in application over time is essential. *The individual unit basis produces the most conservative inventory value because units whose market value exceeds cost are not allowed to offset items whose market value is less than cost. This offsetting occurs to some extent in the other approaches.* The more you aggregate, the less you write down. The less you aggregate, the more you write down.

What level of offsetting is appropriate? There is no easy answer to this question. Most people find it uncomfortable to think that a loss in market value say, of the new car inventory of a car dealer would be avoided because the used-car inventory has strong resale values. On the other hand, some degree of offsetting, especially within categories, seems appropriate given the nature of estimates in general and the fact that sales markets can be hard to predict.

EXHIBIT 8-11

APPLICATION OF LCM TO INVENTORY CATEGORIES

			LCM Applied to		
Inventory Types	**Cost**	**Market**	**Individual Items**	**Classifications**	**Total**
Classification A:					
Item 1	$10,000	$ 9,500	$ 9,500		
Item 2	8,000	9,000	8,000		
	18,000	18,500		$18,000	
Classification B:					
Item 3	21,000	22,000	21,000		
Item 4	32,000	29,000	29,000		
	53,000	51,000		51,000	
Total	$71,000	$69,500			
Inventory valuation under different approaches			$67,500	$69,000	$69,500

LCM Recording and Reporting

Two methods of recording and reporting the effects of the application of LCM are used in practice:

1. *Direct inventory reduction method.* The inventory holding loss is not separately recorded and reported. Instead, the LCM amount, if it is less than the original cost of the inventory, is recorded and reported each period. Thus, the inventory holding loss is automatically included in cost of sales, and ending inventory is reported at LCM. This method is feasible only when LCM is applied to each item of inventory separately.
2. *Inventory allowance method.* The inventory holding loss is separately recorded using a contra inventory account, allowance to reduce inventory to LCM. Thus, the inventory and cost of sales amounts are recorded and reported at original cost, while any inventory holding loss is recognized separately. Assume that the company illustrated in Exhibit 8-11 had an existing allowance of $2,500, and decided to do LCM by individual items. The entry would be as follows:

Holding loss on inventory	1,000	
Allowance to reduce inventory to LCM		
($2,500 − $3,500)		1,000

The major difference between the two methods is the detail in the entries and disclosures on the income statement and balance sheet. The allowance method captures more detail. However, writedowns recognized through the allowance method can reverse in subsequent years, as is true for other allowances, such as the allowance for doubtful accounts and the allowance used to reduce temporary investments to market value. In contrast, writedown made directly to inventory is permanent.

The Impact of Inventory Writedowns

We began this LCM discussion with an example of an inventory item that was purchased for $165, and then written down to $125 in 20X2. The inventory was sold in 20X3. Let's extend the example by considering the reported profit in both years. Assume that the item was sold for $175 in 20X3. The income statement will reflect the following:

	20X2	20X3
Holding loss on inventory ($165 – $125)	$(40)	
Gross profit on inventory sale ($175 – $125)		$50

Overall, the company has made $10 on this transaction (that is, $175 − $165), but that $10 has been reported as a loss of $40 in 20X2, and a gain of $50 in 20X3. The writedown was based on replacement cost.

Some would argue that as long as the net realizable value was above $165, no writedown was needed. If net realizable value is used as the definition of market value, and the $175 was foreseeable in 20X2, then no writedown might have been recorded:

	20X2	20X3
Holding loss on inventory	—	
Gross profit on inventory sale ($175 – $165)		$10

However, the writedown in 20X2 allowed a "normal profit" to be recorded in 20X3; if no writedown is made, the $10 profit in 20X3 is probably not typical of normal sales.

You should notice, though, that LCM valuations provide substantial room to manipulate profit. Inventory can be written down in one year, and sold at a substantial profit in a later year. Sometimes this happens with no intent to mislead if weak market conditions and poor selling prices dictate writedowns. A recovery in later years may be unexpected. In other cases, unethical decisions may drive high write-offs in a big bath scenario. Managers who receive bonuses based on net income may be particularly motivated if the first year, or write-down year, results are below the level needed to trigger a bonus anyway.

MARKET VALUE BASIS

In Chapter 6, we discussed the use of market values for certain types of inventory. Revenue may be recognized when commodities are produced—if a public auction market exists for the commodities and a sale can be completed at any time with minimal effort. Once revenue is recognized, net assets increase. The increase is reflected in the carrying value of the related inventory. That is, *inventory is carried at market value when revenue is recognized on production.*

Market value really means net realizable value. Companies that use (or can use) market values include

- Agricultural producers;
- Other commodities, such as oil and certain metals;
- Investment companies, whose activity consists of holding and trading publicly traded securities; and
- Companies that record revenue on the percentage-of-completion basis; the recognition of revenue has the effect of increasing the carrying value of the work-in-process inventory to net realizable value.

Companies that deal in commodities are not *required* to report their inventories by market value; market valuation is a choice, not a requirement.

In contrast, inventories of financial instruments are treated differently. The inventory of trading securities held by a broker or an investment banker must be recorded at fair value (*CICA* 3855.59). Similarly, the investments of a mutual fund are required by law to be reported at market value so that the holders of mutual fund shares can see the underlying asset value of their holdings.

Companies that deal in commodities or financial instruments often try to offset the risk of price change by *hedging.* If a company holds 1,000 tonnes of wheat, the company is vulnerable to a fall in the market price of wheat. To protect its investment, the company usually will enter into a contract to deliver the grain in the future at a fixed price. That contact is a *hedge.* Hedging contracts can be sold at any time prior to maturity; it is not necessary to actually deliver the wheat. The value of the hedge contract fluctuates along with changes in the price of wheat. Canadian, U.S., and international accounting standards all require that gains or losses on a hedge contract be reported in net income. Therefore, to offset the gain or loss from the hedge, the company is likely to value the wheat at market value as well.

These issues are discussed more fully later in the book, in Chapter 13, so don't worry about them now. The point to remember is that since financial instruments must be reported at market value, any hedged assets should also be reported at market value even though GAAP does not require market value for commodities. For example, the 2003 annual report of Goderich Elevators Limited explains its carrying value of grain as follows:

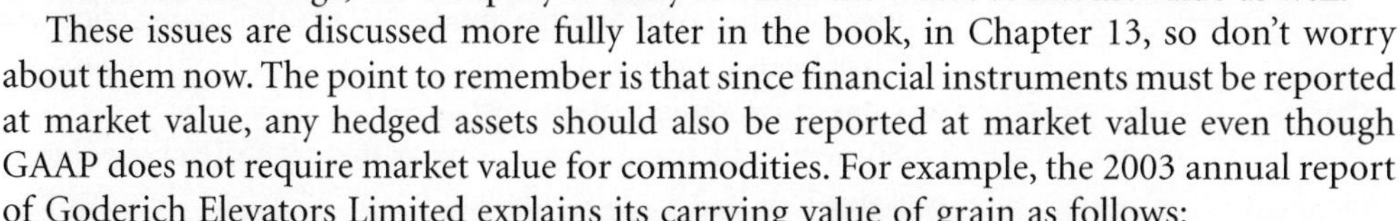

Inventories

Grain inventories include both hedged and non-hedged commodities. Hedgeable grain inventories are valued on the basis of closing market quotations less handling costs and also reflect gains and losses on open grain purchase and sale contracts to the extent these positions have been hedged. Non-hedgeable grains are valued at the lower of cost or market. Farm supply, seed, feed and livestock inventories are valued at the lower of cost or net realizable value.

Some managers may prefer to use historical cost (or LCM) to value commodity inventories even if they are not bound by fixed price contracts and have not hedged the inventory. While we might be tempted to praise their choice of a "conservative" accounting policy, we must bear in mind that historical cost inventory valuation gives the manager an opportunity to manipulate reported earnings by deciding when to engage in transactions that trigger an accounting gain or loss. Commodity prices (and real economic value) change regardless of whether or not the changes are recognized in the books.

CONCEPT REVIEW

1. Why are cost flow methods irrelevant when standard costs are used?
2. What is the definition of net realizable value?
3. What does "market" mean in "lower of cost or market"?
4. What is the difference in reporting holding losses under the direct inventory reduction method and the inventory allowance method?
5. When may inventories be valued at net realizable value, even if it is higher than historical cost?

INVENTORY ESTIMATION METHODS

Many large companies rely on the periodic inventory method. Does this mean that they can't prepare monthly or quarterly statements without also taking a physical inventory? Generally, inventory counts are very expensive and therefore may be done only once each fiscal year. So what can be done when statements are needed?

The answer is quite simple: inventory can be estimated. In a small business, the owner or inventory manager might be able to provide an accurate estimate. Alternatively, a more formal calculation can be made, using methods such as the gross margin method or the retail inventory method. It's important to understand that these methods *estimate* inventory levels, and thus introduce some level of unreliability to the financial results, while increasing their timeliness.

Estimation methods are also useful for providing a cross-check on the results of accounting inventory systems. It should be possible to reconcile the estimated inventory (or, more importantly, cost of sales) to a physical inventory count or to the accounting records of perpetual inventory. Obviously the reconciliation will not be exact, but there should be a rough similarity between the results of the accounting inventory system (periodic or perpetual) and the estimated inventory. Large discrepancies raise questions of the accuracy of the accounting system, the effectiveness of the system of internal control, or the possibility of theft.

For example, a local manufacturer of fruit juices and soft drinks also distributed Coca-Cola syrup to restaurants and bars. The Coca-Cola syrup was, in fact, the company's biggest single seller and was also the most profitable product. Despite high sales, the company was only marginally profitable. A gross profit analysis revealed that the recorded cost of sales was much too high, given the level of sales. A closer examination revealed that the inventory of syrup was too low for the amount that was actually recorded as being sold. It finally was discovered that, due to a supervisory lack of vigilance in reconciling each driver's sales with the inventory loaded onto the truck, it was possible for unethical truck drivers to sell jugs of syrup "on their own account," pocketing the money.

Estimation methods are used primarily in mercantile firms: retailing and wholesaling. They are of more limited usefulness in manufacturing but still are useful for finished goods inventories. Estimates of inventory cannot be used for audited annual financial statements—a physical count is required.

Gross Margin Method

gross margin method

a method of estimating inventories based on historical gross profit margins

The **gross margin method** (also known as the *gross profit method*) assumes that a constant gross margin estimated on recent sales can be used to estimate inventory values from current sales. That is, the gross margin rate (gross margin ÷ sales), based on recent past performance, is assumed to be reasonably constant in the short run. The gross margin method has two basic characteristics, (1) it requires the development of an estimated gross margin rate for different lines or products and (2) it applies the rate to relevant groups of items.

Is the method accurate? Well, it depends on whether gross margins are really "reasonably constant in the short run" or not! If retail prices are slashed this year to spur consumer demand, or theft has increased, the gross margin method will overstate earnings and inventory, perhaps materially. Similarly, if the product mix changes a lot in the current period, the results will not be accurate.

For example, if a company has traditionally sold about half its volume in a high-profit category, and half in a low-profit category, the historical gross profit margin will reflect this mix. In the current year, if volumes fall off in the high-profit side, the estimation method will produce inaccurate results. It's better to do separate estimates for each different product line. Mis-estimates will be uncovered at the end of the year, when inventory is actually counted—an unpleasant "surprise" for those who relied on the interim statements.

ESTIMATING BY GROSS MARGIN METHOD Estimating the ending inventory by the gross margin method requires five steps, as illustrated in Exhibit 8-12:

Step 1 Estimate the gross margin rate on the basis of prior years' sales: gross margin rate = (sales − cost of sales) ÷ sales.

Step 2 Compute total cost of goods available for sale in the usual manner (beginning inventory plus purchases), based on actual data provided by the accounts.

Step 3 Compute the estimated gross margin amount by multiplying sales by the estimated gross margin rate.

Step 4 Compute cost of sales by subtracting the computed gross margin amount from sales.

Step 5 Compute ending inventory by subtracting the computed cost of sales from the cost of goods available for sale.

USES OF THE GROSS MARGIN METHOD The gross margin method is used to

- Test the reasonableness of an inventory valuation determined by some other means such as a physical inventory count or from perpetual inventory records. For example, assume the company in Exhibit 8-12 counted inventory, and got a figure of $10,000. The gross margin method provides an approximation of $7,000, which suggests that the physical count may be overvalued and should be examined.
- Estimate the ending inventory for interim financial reports prepared during the year when it is impractical to count the inventory physically and a perpetual inventory system is not used.
- Estimate the cost of inventory destroyed by an accident such as fire or storm. Valuation of inventory lost is necessary to account for the accident and to establish a basis for insurance claims and income taxes. This is an example of a case where it would be helpful to know the markup on cost (i.e., gross profit ÷ cost of sales) since cost is used for the insurance claim and to establish the loss.
- Develop budget estimates of cost of sales, gross margin, and inventory for budgets.

EXHIBIT 8-12

GROSS MARGIN METHOD

	Known Data		Following Computations:* Estimated Results	
Net sales revenue (base amount)		$10,000		$10,000
Cost of goods sold:				
Beginning inventory	$ 5,000		$ 5,000	
Add: Purchases	8,000		8,000	
Goods available for sale	13,000		13,000	
Less: Ending inventory			7,000	
Cost of sales				6,000
Gross margin				$ 4,000

***Steps:**
1. Gross margin rate (estimated as percent of sales based on last year's results) = 40%
2. Goods available for sale, above: $13,000
3. Gross margin: $4,000 (i.e., $10,000 × 40%)
4. Cost of sales: $6,000, ($10,000 − $4,000)
5. Ending inventory $7,000, ($13,000 − $6,000)

Retail Inventory Method

retail inventory method a method of estimating inventories based on actual markups and markdowns during the period; the organization calculates its inventory and retail and then converts to cost using a cost-to-retail ratio

cost ratio ratio derived from relative costs of a group of assets; denominator is the total cost of the group of assets; numerator is the cost of each item in the group, in turn

The **retail inventory method** is often used by retail stores, especially stores that sell a wide variety of items. In such situations, perpetual inventory procedures may be impractical, and a complete physical inventory count is usually taken only once, annually. The retail inventory method is appropriate when items sold within a department have essentially the same markup rate and articles purchased for resale are priced immediately. Two major advantages of the retail inventory method are its ease of use and reduced record-keeping requirements, compared to perpetual inventory systems.

The retail inventory method uses both retail value and actual cost data to

1. Compute a ratio of cost to retail (referred to as the **cost ratio**);
2. Calculate the ending inventory at *retail value*, and
3. Convert that retail value to a cost value by applying the computed cost ratio to the ending retail value.

Application of the retail inventory method requires that internal records be kept to provide data on

- Sales revenue;
- Beginning inventory valued at both cost and retail;
- Purchases during the period valued at both cost and retail;
- Adjustments to the original retail price, such as additional markups, markup cancellations, markdowns, markdown cancellations, and employee discounts; and
- Other adjustments, such as interdepartmental transfers, returns, breakage, and damaged goods.

The retail inventory method differs from the gross margin method in that it uses a computed cost ratio based on the actual relationship between cost and retail for the current period, rather than an historical ratio. The computed cost ratio is often an average across several different kinds of goods sold.

ESTIMATING BY RETAIL INVENTORY METHOD The retail inventory method is illustrated in Exhibit 8-13. The steps are as follows:

Step 1 Determine cost of goods available for sale at cost and retail.
The total cost of goods available for sale during January 20X2 is determined to be $210,000 at cost and $300,000 at retail, as shown in Exhibit 8-13.

Step 2 Compute the cost ratio (ratio of cost to sales).
This is done by dividing the total cost of goods available for sale at cost ($210,000) by the same items at retail ($300,000). In this instance, the cost ratio is ($210,000 ÷ $300,000) = .70, or 70%, as shown in Exhibit 8-13. This is an *average cost* application of the retail method, because both beginning inventory and purchases are included in determining the cost ratio.

Step 3 Compute closing inventory at retail (goods available for sale at retail, less sales.)
This is done by taking the total cost of goods available for sale at retail ($300,000) less the goods that were sold in January ($260,000), resulting in the value of the ending inventory at retail ($40,000), as shown in Exhibit 8-13.

Step 4 Compute ending inventory at cost.
This is done by applying the cost ratio (70%), derived in (2), to the ending inventory at retail ($40,000), derived in (3). The result is an ending inventory of $28,000 at cost ($40,000 × 70%).

MARKUPS AND MARKDOWNS The data used for Exhibit 8-13 assumed no changes in the sales price of the merchandise as originally set. Frequently, however, the original sales price on merchandise is changed, particularly at the end of the selling season or when replacement costs are changing. The retail inventory method requires that a careful record be kept of all changes to the original sales price because these changes affect the inventory cost computation. To apply the retail inventory method, it is important to distinguish among the following terms:

- **Original sales price.** Sale price first marked on the merchandise.
- **Markup.** The original or initial amount that the merchandise is marked up above cost. It is the difference between the purchase cost and the original sales price, and it may be expressed either as a dollar amount or a percentage of either cost or sales price. Sometimes this markup is called "initial markup" or "markon."
- **Additional markup.** Any increase in the sales price above the original sales price. The original sales price is the base from which additional markup is measured.

EXHIBIT 8-13

RETAIL INVENTORY METHOD, AVERAGE COST

	At Cost	At Retail
Goods available for sale:		
Beginning inventory	$ 15,000	$ 25,000
Purchases	195,000	275,000
Total goods available for sale	$210,000	300,000
Cost ratio:		
$210,000 ÷ $300,000 = 70%; average, January 20X2		
Deduct January sales at retail		260,000
Ending inventory:		
At retail		$ 40,000
At cost ($40,000 × 70%)	$ 28,000	

- **Additional markup cancellation.** Cancellation of all, or some, of an additional markup. Additional markup less additional markup cancellations is usually called *net additional markup.*
- **Markdown.** A reduction in the original sales price.
- **Markdown cancellation.** An increase in the sales price (that does not exceed the original sales price) after a reduction in the original sales price markdown.

The definitions are illustrated in Exhibit 8-14. An item that cost $8 is originally marked to sell at $10. This item is subsequently marked up $1 to sell at $11, then marked down to a sales price of $7.

In the application of the retail method, additional markups and markup cancellations, markdowns and markdown cancellations are all included in the early calculations that determine goods available for sale at cost and at retail. However, in order to provide a conservative cost ratio that will approximate lower of cost or market (LCM), the denominator of the cost ratio *excludes net markdowns.* See the example in Exhibit 8-15.

The retail inventory method can be applied in different ways to estimate the cost of ending inventory under alternative inventory cost flow assumptions such as FIFO and LIFO. In each case, the cost flow assumption will dictate the items (markups and markdowns) to be included in the cost ratio.

USES OF THE RETAIL INVENTORY METHOD Like the gross margin method, the retail inventory method is used only to estimate the amount of the ending inventory and cost of goods sold. A physical inventory count must be taken at least annually as a check on the accuracy of the estimated inventory amounts. This method provides a test of the overall reasonableness of a physical inventory.

The retail inventory method is also useful if the entity counts its inventory and then extends the inventory sheets *at retail.* Remember, retail prices are much easier to determine on the selling floor than cost! The retail value then is converted to cost by applying the retail inventory method without reference to the costs of individual items. This value may be used for external reporting if sufficient evidence is accumulated to support the accuracy of the cost percentages.

Perhaps even more than the gross margin method, though, the retail inventory method is subject to estimation errors. A lot of its accuracy depends on how carefully the company keeps track of markups and markdowns and other data needed to develop an accurate cost ratio.

EXHIBIT 8-14

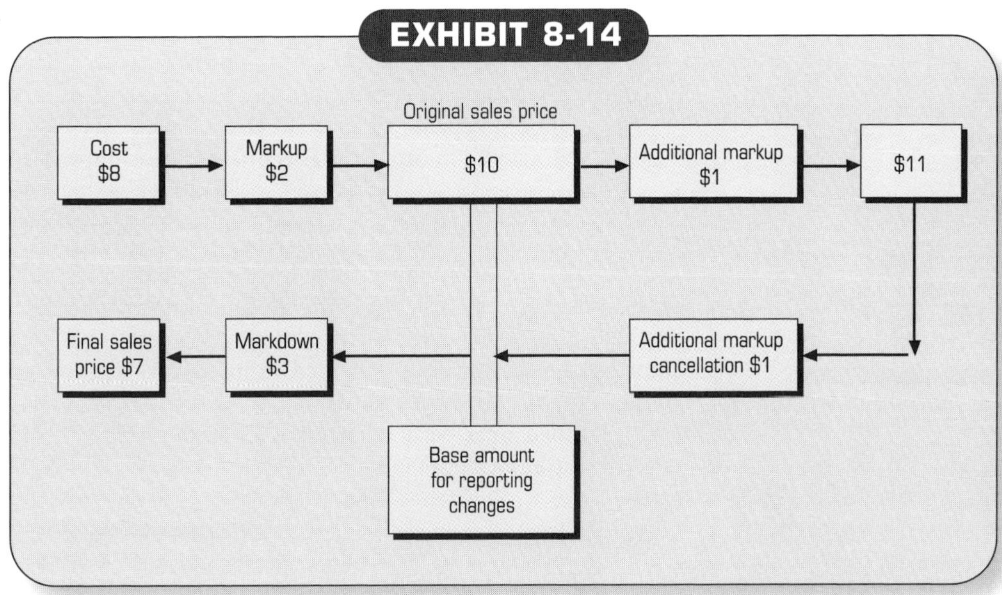

EXHIBIT 8-15

RETAIL INVENTORY METHOD, LCM

	At Cost	At Retail
Goods available for sale:		
Beginning inventory	$ 550	$ 900
Purchases during period	6,290	8,900
Plus: additional markups during period		225
Less: additional markup cancellations		(25)
		$10,000
Less: markdowns		(600)
Plus: markdown cancellations		100
Total goods available for sale	$6,840	$ 9,500
Cost ratio:		
$6,840 ÷ $10,000 = 68.4%		
Deduct:		
Sales		(8,500)
Ending inventory:		
At retail		$ 1,000
At cost, approximating LCM ($1,000 × 68.4%)	$ 684	

REPORTING ISSUES

Cash Flow Statement

Inventory costs represent expenditures. However, the expenditures do not make their way to the income statement until the inventory is sold. Therefore, the amount of inventory expenditures that are included in cost of goods sold in any accounting period will be different from the amount that was spent to acquire inventory. The cash flow statement must show the amount of inventory *paid for*, not the amount *sold*.

To determine the amount of cash provided by operations using the indirect method, net income must be adjusted by the change in inventory during the period:

- An *increase* in inventory means that the cash flow to purchase inventory was higher than the amount of expense reported as cost of goods sold—the increase must be subtracted from net income in order to reflect higher cash outflow.
- A *decrease* in inventory means that the cash flow to acquire inventory was less than the amount of expense reported as cost of goods sold—the decrease must be added to net income.

A further adjustment must be made for a manufacturing, resource, or service company. The cost of sales (or cost of services provided) of such companies almost always includes amortization (e.g., depreciation on facilities or depletion on resources). Any depreciation or amortization that has been charged to inventory, whether to work in process or finished goods, must be added back to net income when determining the cash flow from operations.

Finally, there must be an adjustment for accounts payable, since accounts payable primarily relates to inventory purchases.

Disclosure

According to the inventory section of the *CICA Handbook*, recommended disclosures are as follows:

- The basis for valuation (e.g., historical cost, lower of cost or market, market value) (*CICA* 3030.10);

- Major categories of inventory (desirable, not required) (*CICA* 3030.10);
- Method of determining cost (e.g., FIFO, LIFO, average cost) (*CICA* 3030.11);
- A definition of market value (desirable, not required), *if* "market" is used in some aspect of inventory valuation (*CICA* 3030.11); and
- Any change in valuation from that used in the prior period, and the effect of a change on net income (*CICA* 3030.13).

Recall (from Chapter 3) that companies are not required to disclose their cost of sales under Canadian GAAP—only disclosure of inventory amounts are required by the *CICA Handbook*. Similarly, cost of sales is not included in the list of required disclosures in IAS 1, *Presentation of Financial Statements*. However, IAS 1 does show cost of sales in one of its two sample illustrations of styles of presentation, and states that companies "shall disclose additional information on the nature of expenses" [para. 93].

An example of inventory disclosure is that of Le Château Incorporated, a Montreal-based manufacturer and retailer of women's and men's fashions. Le Château's accounting policy note contains the following statement about inventory valuation:

> Raw materials and work-in-process are valued at the lower of specific cost and net realizable value. Finished goods are valued, using the retail inventory method, at the lower of cost and net realizable value less normal profit margin.

Notice that the company uses "specific cost" as its inventory method. Since the company deals in fashion merchandise, it keeps each style separate for cost purposes. The company uses LCM, with net realizable value as the measure of "market" for raw materials and work in process. For finished-goods inventory, the company uses the retail inventory method for estimating the net realizable value.

In Note 3, Le Château shows the breakdown of the total inventory amounts that are shown on the balance sheet:

	January 31, 2004	January 25, 2003
Raw materials	$ 4,246	$ 4,800
Work-in-process	1,119	1,234
Finished goods	20,710	19,448
	$26,075	$25,482

CONCEPT REVIEW

1. Why would a company use an inventory estimation method?
2. What is the basic difference between the gross profit method and the retail inventory method?
3. Why are markdowns excluded from the cost ratio when the retail inventory method is used?

SUMMARY OF KEY POINTS

1. Inventories are assets consisting of goods owned by the business and held either for future sale or for consumption in manufacture or service provision.
2. Cost at acquisition, including all costs to obtain the inventory, such as freight, is the valuation basis of inventory.
3. Work in process and finished-goods inventories of manufacturers should include raw materials, direct labour, and at least the variable portion of manufacturing overhead.
4. All goods owned at the inventory date, including those out on consignment, should be counted and valued.
5. Either a periodic or a perpetual inventory system may be used to track inventory. Computer technology now makes it easier and less costly to use a perpetual system, which also provides up-to-date inventory records.
6. Several cost flow assumptions are in current use, including specific identification, average cost, FIFO, and LIFO. LIFO is very rarely used in Canada, except by Canadian subsidiaries of U.S. parent companies that also use that method.
7. The lower-of-cost-or-market (LCM) method of estimating inventory recognizes declines in market value in the period of decline. The lower-of-cost-or-market method values inventories at market if market is below cost. Market may be interpreted to be net realizable value, net realizable value less a normal profit margin, or replacement cost. Use of net realizable value is most common.
8. The cash flow from operations is affected by (1) changes in inventory levels and (2) amortization that has been included in the inventory. Cash flow must be adjusted to reflect the amount of inventory *purchased* rather than sold, and must be adjusted by adding back any amortization.
9. Market value may be used as the inventory valuation basis if the inventories are commodities, such as traded securities, precious metals, and agricultural commodities.
10. The gross margin method is used to estimate inventory values when it is difficult or impractical to take a physical count of the goods. The method is most accurate when profit margins are stable.
11. The retail inventory method of estimating inventory applies the ratio of actual cost to sales value to the ending inventory at sales value to estimate the inventory value.

KEY TERMS

additional markup, 430
additional markup cancellation, 431
cost ratio, 429
current replacement cost, 419
first-in, first-out (FIFO), 411
gross margin method, 428
just-in-time inventory system, 419
last-in, first-out (LIFO), 414
markdown, 431
markdown cancellation, 431
markup, 430
moving-average markup, 411
net realizable value (NRV), 423
original sales price, 430
perpetual inventory system, 405
replacement cost, 423
retail inventory method, 429
specific identification, 410
weighted average, 411

REVIEW PROBLEM

The inventory data for the Black Eagle Lounge for the beginning of June is shown below. Compute the inventory value at 30 June, using both perpetual inventory and periodic inventory approaches, under each of the following methods:

1. Specific cost identification
2. Average cost
3. FIFO
4. LIFO

1 June—no inventory on hand
2 June—bought one case of Red Hook Ale @ $10
13 June—bought one case of Red Hook Ale @ $16
24 June—sold one case of Red Hook Ale @ $20*
28 June—bought one case of Red Hook Ale @ $18

* This case of Red Hook Ale was purchased on 13 June.

REVIEW PROBLEM—SOLUTION

At 30 June, there are two cases of ale on hand. The carrying value of the 30 June inventory is shown below under each method:

1. Specific cost identification:

   Periodic (1 × $10) + (1 × $18) = $28
   Perpetual (1 × $10) + (1 × $18) = $28

2. Average cost:

   Periodic [[(1 × $10) + (1 × $16) + (1 × $18)] ÷ 3] × 2 remaining
   = $14.67 × 2 = $29.34

   Perpetual (moving average):

		Units		Total Inventory
Average Bought (Sold)	**@ Cost**	**Cost**	**Units**	**Cost**
1	$10	$10	1	$10.00
1	16	26	2	13.00
(1)	(13)	13	1	13.00
1	18	31	2	15.50

3. FIFO:

   Periodic (1 × $16) + (1 × $18) = $34
   Perpetual (1 × $16) + (1 × $18) = $34

4. LIFO:

   Periodic (1 × $10) + (1 × $16) = $26
   Perpetual (1 × $10) + (1 × $18) = $28

Comments:

- Under specific identification, *periodic* and *perpetual* always give the same result, because the cost of each specific item sold is identified. Therefore, the same inventory amount is shown for both.
- Average cost yields different results under the periodic and perpetual methods, because the numbers of items and their costs are averaged together differently under a moving average (perpetual) than under a historical tabulation of purchases (periodic).
- FIFO always yields the same result under both periodic and perpetual methods.
- LIFO almost always yields different results under periodic and perpetual methods, unless the purchase cost per unit is constant.

QUESTIONS

Q8-1 In general, why should financial statement users and preparers be especially concerned with inventories?

Q8-2 List and briefly explain the usual inventory classifications for a trading entity and a manufacturing entity.

Q8-3 Which of the following items should be included in inventory?

a. Goods held by our agents for us.
b. Goods held by us for sale on commission.
c. Goods held by us but awaiting return to vendor because of damaged condition.
d. Goods returned to us from buyer, reason unknown to date.
e. Goods out on consignment.
f. Goods sold under conditional resale agreements, where we have agreed to repurchase the items that our customer does not resell, and reimburse the customer for carrying costs incurred.
g. Merchandise at our branch for sale.
h. Merchandise at a convention for display purposes.

Q8-4 What is variable costing? What impact would it have on the inventory account on the balance sheet?

Q8-5 Briefly explain the differences between periodic and perpetual inventory systems. Under what circumstances is each generally used?

Q8-6 Does the adoption of a perpetual inventory system eliminate the need for a physical count or measurement of inventories? Explain.

Q8-7 Explain four different cost flow assumptions that can be used to measure cost of sales. Which alternative will always result in the highest net income when prices are rising?

Q8-8 What cost flow assumptions used to measure cost of sales are most common in Canada? What factors have likely led to these choices of policy?

Q8-9 Explain the specific identification inventory costing method and explain when the method is appropriate.

Q8-10 Distinguish between a weighted average and a moving average in determining inventory unit cost. When is each generally used? Explain.

Q8-11 Explain the essential features of first-in, first-out (FIFO). Explain the difference in the application of FIFO under a periodic and perpetual inventory system.

Q8-12 Compare the balance sheet and income statement effects of FIFO with those of LIFO when prices are rising and when prices are falling.

Q8-13 Can standard cost be used to value an inventory for external reporting? Explain.

Q8-14 What types of inventory are most frequently measured at selling price or net realizable value in excess of cost?

Q8-15 Define replacement cost, net realizable value, and net realizable value less a normal profit margin as approaches used to estimate market values of inventory. Which is GAAP in Canada?

Q8-16 Why is the LCM rule applied to inventory valuation?

Q8-17 What is the holding loss (gain) recognized using the LCM, inventory allowance method, for each of the years 20X4 through 20X8?

	Cost	Market
20X3 Ending inventory	$ 0	$ 0
20X4 Ending inventory	12,000	14,000
20X5 Ending inventory	15,000	13,000
20X6 Ending inventory	18,000	17,000
20X7 Ending inventory	20,000	16,000
20X8 Ending inventory	22,000	23,000

Q8-18 Explain why it is important to decide whether to apply the LCM test to individual inventory items, categories, or totals.

Q8-19 List the required financial statement disclosures for inventory.

Q8-20 Approximate the value of ending inventory, assuming the following data:

Cost of goods available for sale	$170,000
Sales	150,000
Gross margin (on sales)	25%

Q8-21 Explain the gross margin method. What basic assumption is implicit in the gross margin method?

Q8-22 Explain the approach of the retail method for estimating inventories. What data must be accumulated in order to apply the retail method?

Q8-23 Why is the year-end inventory cut-off so important? What are the complexities inherent in assuring that the year-end inventory cut-off is correct?

CASE 8-1
Traders International Limited

Traders International Limited (TIL) has recently been awarded a monopoly to export four different agricultural products grown on a Caribbean island. That is, Traders is the only enterprise allowed to buy the goods from local farming enterprises and market the products on the international market. TIL is incorporated in the Caribbean island, which has no tax on corporate earnings. TIL is interested in attracting debt or equity investment from multinational companies in the future, as aggressive expansion is planned.

Inventory of the four agricultural products is the major asset of TIL; the products can be stored for several years. TIL acquires the inventory from local farmers for "current market value less 10%." Market value is quite volatile. TIL is expected to earn profits by timing the sale of these products, and selling during periods of high prices. Government equity and private bank loans finance inventory that accumulates when low world prices dominate. Profits of TIL, after bonuses and interest are paid, are distributed to the government, as a shareholder, and finally to the farmers, in relation to their volume with TIL.

It is now the end of the first fiscal year, and you, the accountant, have been asked to comment on issues surrounding the choice of an inventory costing method: FIFO, LIFO, or average cost. Domestic accounting rules allow any of the three.

The company president has asked the following questions:

1. In general, how are "generally accepted accounting principles" chosen?
2. Why would an intelligent and informed reader care about the inventory costing method? It is, after all, just an accounting allocation problem. Cash flow for purchases and inventory carrying costs are not affected by the choice of method.

3. What method do you recommend for TIL? You must evaluate the three alternatives.
4. Will there be any particular concerns about valuation at lower of cost or market, with any alternative?

The president has reminded you that managers' bonuses are a function of reported net income. There continues to be some pressure to create a competitor to TIL, in the hopes that competition would inspire best operating results.

Required:
Write a report responding to the president's questions.

(CGA-Canada, adapted)

CASE 8-2
HighQ BOOKS

HighQ Books Limited (HighQ)is a small book publishing company located in Kingston, Ontario. HighQ specializes in history and biography titles, and currently has 76 titles in print. Each year, 10 to 15 titles are added.

On 2 September, there was a fire in the company premises, which destroyed a large quantity of inventory and printing equipment. Smoke and water damaged the physical premises.

The company has prepared an insurance claim (Exhibit 1), and has asked you, the external accounting advisor, to review the claim for reasonableness. HighQ expects the claim to be paid 30 days from the submission date, and needs the cash flow as the cleanup expenses and loss of revenue have created a cash flow crunch. Fortunately, HighQ has had an excellent relationship with its banker, who has provided interim funding. However, the insurance money is sorely needed, and HighQ is aware that a contested claim would be delayed. Thus, your review is considered advisable to ensure that the claim is appropriate.

Based on your prior experience with this company, you know that its internal cost system has proven reliable. Perpetual inventory records are kept, but are not relied on for external reporting, since a physical count is always taken. For external reporting, HighQ establishes an allowance for inventory obsolescence based on the age of the books in inventory. Titles printed in the current year are written down 5% at year-end; one-year-old books, 10%, two-year-old books, 15%, and books three or more years old, 25%.

Approximately 75% of HighQ's sales occur in the fall season, as retailers deal with the Christmas rush. HighQ has and is struggling to meet its delivery requirements this year, largely successfully, although some sales have been lost due to inventory shortages.

HighQ's insurance policy specifies that capital assets will be covered based on replacement cost, but limited to the amount that would be needed to repair the damaged asset (if repairs are possible). Replacement cost is based on replacement with an asset of like kind. Inventory is insured for replacement cost or net realizable value, whichever is lower. All cleanup work is covered; cleanup work done by outsiders is covered with no limit, but cleanup/repair work performed internally may not include any allocation for overhead or profit. Furthermore, only 50% of internal labour for cleanup is covered. Business interruption insurance covers lost profits caused by the insured event. Your notes on the various elements of the insurance claim are in Exhibit II.

Required:
Prepare a report evaluating the statement of claim, including a revised claim and additional information needed, as appropriate.

(CICA, adapted)

EXHIBIT I

HIGHQ STATEMENT OF CLAIM

Building repairs and cleaning	$ 53,067
Printing equipment	485,000
Inventory-books	512,850
Inventory-materials	115,985
Display books	15,000
Promotion costs	7,500
Profit on lost sales	512,850
	$1,702,252

EXHIBIT II

NOTES ON STATEMENT OF CLAIM

- Display books are signed first editions of all company books. The 150-book collection is displayed in glass cabinets in the HighQ administrative office. Smoke damage was repaired by Restorers'R'Us at a cost of $15,000.
- The normal markup on books is 100% of cost. Profit on lost sales is calculated as equal to the cost of inventory lost. HighQ had expected to operate at capacity all fall.
- Building repairs and cleaning included $23,500 of labour, done internally to save time and money. All other costs in this category were for external services.
- Damaged equipment, which was approximately one-third depreciated, was not repairable. The equipment lost in the fire, an XT100 printing press, is no longer available. One alternative was an XP550, at a cost of $475,000. This machine has enhanced features as compared to the XT100 that allow a wider range of print styles. The other alternative was an XP750, also with a broader range of print styles, but faster and with higher capacity, lowering operating costs by 10%. The XP750 costs $485,000. HighQ purchased the XP750, reasoning that the operating efficiencies and capacity improvements were well worth the additional cost.
- Inventory of materials included paper of $72,700, inks of $34,040, and other items of $9,245. This represents cost, although the replacement cost of paper was approximately 5% less than cost, and the replacement cost of ink was approximately 10% above cost on 2 September.
- Estimates of books and materials lost have been based on the quantities recorded in the perpetual inventory system, less the quantity of inventory salvaged after the fire and counted at that time.

The claim for book inventory is summarized as follows:

Year Printed	Number of Books	Average Cost	Total Cost
Current year	26,827	$7.50	$ 201,200
1 year prior	5,329	7.60	40,500
2 years prior	16,350	7.75	126,710
3 or more years prior	18,284	7.90	144,440
	66,790		$ 512,850

HighQ spent $15,000 promoting books for the new season. Because of the fire, HighQ anticipates not being able to produce enough copies to meet demand and has included 50% of this cost in the statement of claim.

CASE 8-3
Mountain Mines Lubricant Limited

Mountain Mines Lubricant Limited (MML) supplies lubricant to mining operations in northern British Columbia (B.C.) and the Northwest Territories (N.W.T.). MML has two products: "Slip Coat" and "Maximum Guard." MML's lubricants are used in large, expensive mining machines and are crucial to the operation of the machines. Without good lubrication, the machines will overheat and break down. Given the remote location of its customers, MML minimizes its costs by shipping enough lubricant to customers to last them a year.

In recent years, the mining industry as a whole performed poorly due to low world prices. Some mines experienced cash flow problems. However, in the last six months prices have begun to improve, and industry experts predicted that volumes and profitability should improve.

MML was affected by the problems in the industry, and also experienced cash flow pressures. To resolve this problem, MML decided to be more flexible in its dealings with customers. Instead of charging customers for product as they put it into their machines, MML arranged to have meters installed to read the number of hours a machine is in use. Customers were charged based on hours of usage.

If a machine is running at peak capacity, it takes about four weeks before it needs to have its lubricant tanks refilled. At the time lubricant is transferred to the mine's machine, MML sends the customer a "no charge" invoice, and at the same time, charges the cost of lubricant to cost of goods sold. When the mine workers pour lubricant into the tank of one of their machines, they let MML know by fax. Each week, the mines fax in their meter readings and MML records revenue based on the hours of operation of the machine. Customers are billed at this time. This system has worked well for MML, which has seen an increase in volume of sales over the past year (see Exhibit 1).

MML has three customers in B.C. Two of these, Moon Crater Mine and Dead Fish Mine, are owned by Broken Wing Properties, which has been financially squeezed. Dead Fish is the only one of MML's four customers that is billed for product when it is poured in the tank. All others are billed based on meter readings of hourly machine usage. The third B.C. customer, Scorched Earth Mine, was eager to switch to MML's new hourly usage billing because its cash flow was tight. MML's fourth customer, Big Scar Mine, is a new mine operating in the N.W.T. Big Scar Mine is owned and operated by North Canadian Developments Limited, a subsidiary of Broken Wing Properties.

Exhibit 2 presents details related to the capacity of the various mine machines and, where relevant, the dates the machines were last filled. You have been hired by MML's bank to prepare a report on the company's inventory policies. Specifically, the bank is interested in your opinion on the decline in MML's gross margin.

Required:

Prepare the report. (CICA, adapted)

EXHIBIT 1

DRAFT FINANCIAL STATEMENT INFORMATION

	Slip Coat	Maximum Guard	Total
Current year, as of 31 August			
Sales	$136,000	$200,250	$336,250
Cost of goods sold	117,933	168,358	286,291
Gross margin	$ 18,067	$ 31,892	$ 49,959
Kilograms sold	8,500	8,900	17,400

Previous year			
Sales	$111,750	$164,640	$276,390
Cost of goods sold	96,850	135,240	232,090
Gross margin	$ 14,900	$ 29,400	$ 44,300
Kilograms sold	7,450	7,840	15,290

EXHIBIT 2

CURRENT INVENTORY DATA

As of 31 August	Slip Coat	Maximum Guard
Current year		
Average price per kg.	$16.00	$22.50
Average cost per kg.	$13.50	$18.25
Previous year		
Average price per kg.	$15.00	$21.00
Average cost per kg.	$13.00	$17.25
Scorched Earth Mine (B.C.)		
Mining machine capacity	50 kg.	50 kg.
Date of last top-up	August 25	August 25
Moon Crater Mine (B.C.)		
Mining machine capacity	50 kg.	50 kg.
Date of last top-up	August 13	August 13
Dead Fish Mine (B.C.)		
Mining machine capacity	20 kg.	20 kg.
Date of last top-up	Not applicable	Not applicable
Big Scar Mine (N.W.T.)		
Mining machine capacity	200 kg.	300 kg.
Date of last top-up	August 28	August 28

CASE 8-4
Michael Metals Limited

Michael Metals Limited (MML) has been a private company since it was incorporated under federal legislation over 40 years ago. At the present time (September 20X5), ownership is divided among four cousins, each of whom holds 25% of the 100 outstanding common shares of MML. Each shareholder obtained the shares from his or her parents, who formed and operated the company for many years.

The owners have decided to offer the business for sale over a period of years. Laser Investments Limited (LIL), an investment firm holding shares of companies in a number of other businesses, has been given the opportunity to acquire 46.67% of MML immediately and the balance over the next five years. The proposal is as follows:

	Shares	Percentage
Obtain 33.33% by purchasing 50 new shares of MML	50	33.33%
Acquire one-fifth of the shares held by each cousin, reducing their shares from 25 to 20 each	20	13.34
	70	46.67%

The other 80 shares would be acquired at a rate of four per year from each cousin for five years. The purchase price of the 80 shares would be tied to MML's profitability as measured by generally accepted accounting principles (GAAP).

The Board of Directors of LIL is interested in pursuing the investment in MML. The proposed purchase price of the initial 70 shares is to be partially based on the financial statements for fiscal 20X5 and for future years. The Board of Directors of LIL has asked its auditors, Bouchard and Co., Chartered Accountants, to assist it in evaluating the proposed purchase. Jules Bouchard, the partner in charge of the engagement, has asked you to prepare a memo discussing all relevant considerations pertaining to the purchase so that he can discuss the issues with the Board of Directors.

MML is a scrap metal dealer, primarily dealing in iron and copper. In recent years it has also dealt in lead, brass, aluminum, and other metals. Scrap iron is acquired from a variety of sources (e.g., old automobiles, appliances, and spoilage during manufacturing processes) and is sorted, compacted, and sold to steel mills. Much of the scrap copper is coated electrical wiring, which has to be stripped of the insulation coating and then chopped into pieces. The copper wire pieces are stored in barrels, which are about one metre high. In summary, a limited amount of processing is needed to convert the purchased scrap into saleable products.

Most of the scrap arrives at MML's storage yards on trucks, which are weighed both loaded and empty in order to determine the physical quantities of scrap on the truck. Some of the scrap is kept indoors, but most is kept outdoors in several large piles in different yard locations. MML's property is protected by tall wire fences and monitored by security cameras 24 hours a day. Trucks are similarly weighed by MML when metal is sold.

To be successful in this industry, a scrap dealer has to buy at low prices and store the processed or unprocessed scrap until metal prices are high. Sometimes, quantities of some grades of metal have to be stored for several years. When selling prices are stable, the purchase price has to be sufficiently low that a profit can be made after processing costs have been incurred.

MML tends to operate at its maximum bank line of credit, as it is generally short of cash. MML's maximum line of credit is 70% of its receivables and 50% of its inventory.

Your client arranged for you to have access to all of MML's accounting records and the auditors' working papers. MML's fiscal year-end is 30 June.

From the accounting records and auditors' working papers, you and your staff have assembled the information provided in Exhibit 1.

Required:
Prepare the memo.

EXHIBIT 1

MICHAEL METALS LIMITED
INFORMATION GATHERED BY CA

1. From audit working paper reviews:

a. Most of the processing equipment and the buildings are old and almost fully depreciated. The company's land was purchased many years ago. As a result, inventory often represents two-thirds of the balance sheet assets, and receivables are close to one-fifth of assets in most years. Total assets vary between $25 and $32 million from year to year. Accounts receivable turnover can be anywhere between 1.5 and 4.0 times per year. Inventory is $19 million at the end of 20X5.

b. Perpetual records are limited to estimates of quantity because the quality of the scrap, the amount of insulation on wires, and a variety of other factors affect how much saleable metal will result from a bulk purchase of scrap.

c. A seller of scrap (to MML) seldom knows how much it weighs. MML usually quotes a price per unit but does not inform the seller of the weight until the delivery truck has been weighed at MML's yard. MML's auditors are suspicious that MML reduces weights before calculating the amount payable.

2. The truck weigh scales produce weigh tickets that can be attached to receivable and payable invoices. However, no numerical ticket sequence exists to account for all tickets that have been printed. Receiving records are handwritten in a looseleaf book.
3. Approximately 15% of sales invoices have to be adjusted for weight discrepancies between what was shipped and what the customer claims to have received. On average, the reductions are approximately 20% of the invoice amount.
4. The perpetual inventory weight records appear to have been adjusted each year, sometimes in material amounts, to whatever the physical inventory count indicated.
5. In recent years, the after-tax profits of MML have ranged between $1.2 and $3 million, after management bonuses.
6. MML maintains two corporate vacation homes, one in Florida and one in Barbados. These homes are usually occupied by suppliers and customers of MML free of charge.
7. Accounts receivable and inventory are pledged as security to MML's bank. In addition, the bank has a general security agreement against all other assets and has limited personal guarantees from the shareholders. The bank loan is now at its maximum level, $13.5 million.
8. Revenue is usually recognized on shipment of the metal. Adjustments for weight discrepancies are made as they become known to MML.
9. MML's management has been considering expansion because one competitor is nearing retirement and wants to sell his company. In recent years, MML has purchased from, and sold to, this competitor. MML has also borrowed inventory from and loaned inventory to this competitor to meet sales requests.
10. Some purchases of scrap are acquired on a conditional basis. MML pays the supplier only after it has determined the quality of metal that the scrap yielded when processed.

(CICA, adapted)

ASSIGNMENTS

A8-1 Inventory Cost—Items to Include in Inventory: On 31 December 20X5, Patco computed an ending inventory valuation of $500,000 based on a periodic inventory system. The accounts for 20X5 have been adjusted and closed. Subsequently, the accountant prepared a schedule that showed that the inventory should be $573,000, not $500,000.

a. Merchandise in store (at 50% above cost)	$500,000
b. Goods purchased, in transit (shipped FOB shipping point, estimated freight, not included, $800), invoice price	9,000
c. Goods held on consignment from Davis Electronics at sales price (sales commission, 20% of sales price, included)	14,000
d. Merchandise out on consignment at sales price (including markup of 60% on selling price)	25,000
e. Goods (office equipment) removed from the warehouse and now used in company marketing office (at cost)	20,000
f. Goods out on approval, sales price, $5,000, cost, $2,000	5,000
Total inventory as corrected	$573,000

Average income tax rate = 40%

Required:

1. Review the items making up the list of inventory. Compute the correct ending inventory amount.
2. The income statement and balance sheet now reflect a closing inventory of $500,000. List the items on the income statement and balance sheet for 20X5 that should be corrected for the above errors; give the amount of the error for each item affected, if possible.

A8-2 Inventory Cost: Majestic Stores Incorporated, a dealer in radio and television sets, buys large quantities of a television model that costs $500. The contract reads that if 200 or more sets are purchased during the year, a rebate of $20 per set will be made. On 15 December, the records showed that 150 sets had been purchased; purchases are recorded at $75,000 (150 × $500). All these units were sold. Fifty more sets were ordered FOB destination. The sets were received on 22 December, and a request for the rebate was made. The rebate cheque was received on 20 January, after Majestic's books were closed. Furthermore, the supplier provides terms of 2/10, n/30. Majestic has a policy of always paying invoices within the discount period. Discounts are recorded as a credit to an interest income account. Further investigation reveals that a total of $1,760 of freight was paid to acquire the sets purchased this year, including $375 on the last order of 50 sets.

Required:

1. Calculate the ending inventory value at 31 December.
2. What entry should be made relative to the rebate on 31 December? Why?
3. What entry would be made on 20 January?

A8-3 Inventory Cost—Items to Include in Inventory: Gerard Limited reported inventory of $689,600 and accounts payable to suppliers of $456,300 for the year ended 31 December 20X6. The company has a periodic inventory system, and the inventory value given is the result of the physical count.

Additional information:

a. The inventory count took place on 31 December. Late in the day on 31 December, goods with a cost of $54,300 and a retail price of $98,500 were delivered to a customer. These goods had been counted earlier in the day, and were included in the inventory count. The company did not record the sale until 3 January, due to the New Year's break.
b. On 4 January 20X7, a $6,000 bill for freight for the month of December was received. The freight was for goods bought from a supplier and delivered to the Gerard warehouse. None of these goods have been resold.
c. Goods received from a supplier on 30 December were counted and included in inventory, but the invoice was not recorded as a purchase or accounts payable by the end of December. The invoice was for $41,100.
d. The inventory count was subsequently determined to include $21,900 of goods on consignment from a supplier; the goods have to be paid for only if they are sold to Gerard's customers.
e. Goods from a supplier, in transit on 31 December, were neither counted nor recorded as a purchase and account payable as of 31 December. The goods, with a cost of $35,700, legally belonged to Gerard while they were in transit over the year-end.
f. Gerard had goods with a recorded cost of $12,700 that were properly recorded as a purchase and account payable, and counted in inventory. However, the goods were damaged and Gerard entered into negotiations with the supplier that resulted in a discount of $4,000 off the price. The negotiations were completed in early January 20X7.
g. Market value of remaining inventory *after* any adjustments appropriate for items (a)–(f), at replacement cost, was determined to be $598,000. The allowance to reduce inventory to LCM, unchanged for the end of the last fiscal period, was $31,200.

Required:

1. Calculate the correct balances for inventory (net) and accounts payable, as of 31 December 20X6.
2. Calculate the holding loss on inventory that will appear on the income statement for the year ended 31 December 20X6.
3. Assume that cost of goods sold had been calculated to be $2,211,400 based on the original physical count. What is the new cost of goods sold? Assume that the holding loss on inventory is not reported as part of cost of goods sold.

A8-4 Inventory Issues: Consider each of the following independent situations. In each, describe the accounting policy decision. Describe the impact that the chosen policy has had on the income statement and balance sheet. If the company's policy is not correct, or if there is an alternate policy that should be considered, explain the alternative.

Case A. Inventory was bought for $675,000 in 20X6 and was recorded at cost. The inventory was bought under the terms of a purchase agreement signed in 20X4; the market value of these goods had been $695,000 at the end of 20X4, $640,000 at the end of 20X5, and was $660,000 on the date of acquisition.

Case B. Inventory was received and recorded at the invoice price of $56,000. The goods had not been sold at year-end. Subsequently, a discount of $5,000 was received on the goods. This discount was recorded as other revenue.

Case C. In the lower-of-cost-or-market valuation at year-end, replacement cost was used as the definition of market value. The evaluation resulted in a writedown of $135,500. The company reports that, although its supplier's prices were lower for certain products at year-end, thus causing the writedown, its prices to its own customers had remained at constant levels.

Case D. Inventories, costing $56,000, with a sales price of $79,000, were with a customer on consignment. These goods were excluded from the physical inventory count, and the $79,000 sale was recorded in the current fiscal year, because in the past this customer has always been able to sell all the goods sent on consignment.

A8-5 Inventory Cost—Four Methods: The records of Johnson Brothers showed the following data about one raw material used in the manufacturing process. The transactions occurred in the order given.

	Units	Unit Cost
1. Inventory	4,000	$7.00
2. Purchase 1	3,000	7.70
3. Issue 1	5,000	
4. Purchase 2	8,000	8.00
5. Issue 2	7,000	
6. Purchase 3	3,000	8.40

Required:

1. Compute cost of materials issued (to work in process) and the valuation of raw materials ending inventory for each of the following independent assumptions (round unit costs to the nearest cent for inventory; show computations).
   a. FIFO
   b. LIFO, periodic inventory system
   c. Weighted average, periodic inventory system
   d. Moving average, perpetual inventory system
2. In parallel columns, give all entries indicated for an average cost system, transaction by transaction. Assume a count of the raw material on hand at the end of the period showed 6,000 units. Remember that goods used are debited to work in process, not cost of sales.

   Case A—periodic inventory system; weighted average used.

   Case B—perpetual inventory system; moving average used.

A8-6 Inventory Cost and Cost of Sales-Periodic Inventory: Anson Xu Limited had the following inventory transactions for the six months ended 30 June 20X8. 20X8 is the company's first year of operations:

Date	Transaction	Number of Units	Unit Cost
13 January	Purchase	40,000	$ 40
31 January	Shipments to customers	−30,000	
4 February	Purchase	50,000	38
28 February	Shipments to customers	−45,000	
5 March	Purchase	15,000	37
17 March	Purchase	25,000	36
25 April	Shipments to customers	−22,000	
13 May	Shipments to customers	− 8,000	
25 May	Purchase	27,000	32
5 June	Shipments to customers	−24,000	
17 June	Purchase	18,000	33
28 June	Shipments to customers	−20,000	
30 June	Purchase	12,000	30
	Ending inventory	38,000	

Required:

Anson Xu Limited has not yet installed a perpetual inventory system. Compute the ending inventory and the cost of sales for Anson Xu Limited using each of the following periodic inventory costing methods:

a. FIFO
b. Weighted average
c. LIFO (periodic)

A8-7 Inventory Cost Flow: FIFO has been used as a cost flow assumption by the Hwan Company since it was first organized in 20X0. Results have been as follows (in $ thousands):

	20X0	20X1	20X2	20X3
Reported net income (FIFO)	$ 26,250	$ 45,000	$ 48,750	$ 67,500
Reported ending inventories—FIFO	82,250	142,000	164,000	173,000
Ending inventory —average cost	78,500	101,650	117,500	135,500

Required:

1. Restate net income assuming use of the average cost method.
2. Explain the likely trend in net income if LIFO were to be used.
3. What inventory cost flow policy would you expect this company to adopt if it was trying to:
   a. Match the most recent cost of acquisition with sales revenue.
   b. Minimize income tax payments.
   c. Report maximum inventory values on the balance sheet.

A8-8 Inventory Cost Flow: Brian Rogers, a local businessman, is contemplating investing in a business. He has narrowed his choice to two firms in the same industry and would like you to take a look at their income statements:

	Company A	Company B
	($ thousands)	
Sales	$476,000	$420,000
Cost of goods sold:		
Opening inventory	16,000	14,000
Purchases	360,000	340,000
	376,000	354,000
Less: Closing inventory	40,000	34,000
Cost of goods sold	336,000	320,000
Gross profit	140,000	100,000
Operating expenses	70,000	72,000
Net income	$ 70,000	$ 28,000

Brian has determined that each firm held the same physical amount of inventory at year-end. However, one firm uses the average cost method and one uses FIFO. Prices have been rising over the last year.

Required:

1. Compare the gross profit margins of the two firms. Which firm uses FIFO? Redraft both income statements to use average cost. Assume opening inventory is not affected.
2. Explain the reasons that a company may prefer either FIFO or average cost as a cost flow assumption.
3. Use of a different cost flow assumption reduces the comparability of financial statements. Why is choice allowed?

A8-9 Periodic and Perpetual Inventory—Journal Entries: The records for Cummings Company at 31 December 20X5 reflected the following:

	Units	Unit Price
Sales during period (for cash)	10,000	$10 (sales price)
Inventory at beginning of period	2,000	6 (cost)
Merchandise purchased during period (for cash)	16,000	6 (cost)
Purchase returns during period (cash refund)	100	6 (cost)
Inventory at end of period	?	6 (cost)
Total expenses (excluding cost of goods sold) = $30,000		

Required:

Give entries for the above transactions, including adjusting entries to correct inventory levels, as needed, at the end of the period. Repeat the entries twice in parallel columns: assume a periodic inventory system for Case A and a perpetual inventory system for Case B.

A8-10 Perpetual Inventory—FIFO: Berzo Company maintains perpetual inventory records on a FIFO basis for the three main products distributed by the company. A physical inventory is taken at the end of each year in order to check the perpetual inventory records.

The following information relating to one of the products, blenders, for the year 20X5, was taken from the records of the company:

	Units	Unit Cost
Beginning inventory	7,200	$6.60
Purchases and sales (in order given):		
Purchase 1	4,000	6.65
Sale 1	8,000	
Purchase 2	12,800	6.70
Sale 2	8,800	
Purchase 3	3,200	7.00
Purchase 4	5,600	6.75
Sale 3	11,200	
Purchase 5	4,000	6.60

Ending inventory (per count), 8,300

Replacement cost (per unit) at year-end, $6.60; sales price was constant all year at $19.00. Replacement cost is used for LCM valuation.

Required:

1. Reconstruct the perpetual inventory record for blenders.
2. Give all entries indicated by the above data. Similar transactions can be summarized into one entry.
3. Prepare the income statement through gross margin for this product.
4. Comment on the possible need for a LCM writedown of the inventory.

A8-11 Inventory Cost Methods: The inventory records of Acme Appliances showed the following data relative to a food processor in inventory (the transactions occurred in the order given):

Transaction	Units	Unit Cost
1. Inventory	30	$19.00
2. Purchase	45	20.00
3. Sale	50	
4. Purchase	50	20.80
5. Sale	50	
6. Purchase	50	21.60

Required:

Compute the cost of goods sold for the period and the ending inventory, assuming the following (round unit costs to nearest cent):

a. Weighted average (periodic inventory system)
b. Moving-average (perpetual inventory system)
c. FIFO
d. LIFO (periodic inventory system)
e. LIFO (perpetual inventory system)

A8-12 Inventory Cost Methods: The inventory records of Gilman Company provided the following data for one item of merchandise for sale (the six transactions occurred in the order given):

	Units	Unit Cost	Total Amount
Beginning inventory	600	$6.00	$ 3,600
1. Purchase	700	6.10	4,270
2. Sales	(1,000)		
3. Purchase	700	6.20	4,340
4. Sales	(600)		
5. Purchase	500	6.30	3,150
6. Sales	(400)		
Total	500		$ 15,360 (for 2,100 units)

Required:

1. Complete the following schedule (round unit costs to nearest cent and total amounts to nearest dollar):

	Valuation	
Costing Method	**Ending Inventory**	**Cost of Goods Sold**
a. FIFO	$	$
b. LIFO (periodic inventory system)	$	$
c. Weighted average	$	$
d. LIFO (perpetual inventory system)	$	$

2. Compute the amount of pre-tax income and rank the methods in order of the amount of pre-tax income (highest first), assuming that FIFO pre-tax income is $50,000.
3. Which method is preferable? Explain your choice.

A8-13 Inventory Cost Methods: The College Store inventory records showed the following data relative to a particular item sold regularly (transactions occurred in the order given):

Transaction	Units	Unit Cost
1. Inventory	2,000	$5.00
2. Purchase	18,000	5.20
3. Sales (at $13 per unit)	7,000	
4. Purchase	6,000	5.50
5. Sales (at $13.50 per unit)	16,000	
6. Purchase	3,000	6.00

Required:

1. Complete the following schedule (round unit costs to nearest cent and total costs of inventory to the nearest $10):

	Ending Inventory	Cost of Goods Sold	Gross Margin
a. FIFO			
b. Weighted average			
c. Moving average			

2. Prepare journal entries, including year-end adjusting entries to establish ending inventory, if needed, for the two average calculations (b) and (c) above). Assume that the weighted-average method is used with a periodic system and the moving-average method with a perpetual system.
3. Explain how your entries in (2) would be different if a standard cost system were used, with the standard cost established at $5.50.

A8-14 Expense Policy: The president of Aggressive Limited has come to you for advice. Aggressive Limited is a newly established company with prospects for high growth. Decisions must soon be made concerning accounting policies for external financial reporting. The following information pertains to the company's first year of operations (in $ thousands):

Revenue	$48,000
Purchases	18,000
Closing inventory—FIFO	6,000
Closing inventory—average cost	4,800
Depreciation—straight line	2,400
Depreciation—declining balance	4,800
Advertising and promotion expense	2,400
Amortization of advertising and promotion over five years	480
Other expenses	5,000
Common shares outstanding (in thousands)	1,200
Income tax rate	30%

Note: Regardless of the depreciation method chosen on the books, CCA on capital assets will be claimed for tax purposes. For tax purposes, advertising and promotion expenses may be expensed as incurred, again, regardless of accounting policy.

Required:

1. Prepare a columnar income statement. In column 1, show net income assuming the use of FIFO, declining-balance depreciation and expensing of advertising and promotion. Also calculate earnings per share. In successive columns, show the separate effects of the following on net income and earnings per share: in column 2, average cost; in column 3, straight-line depreciation; and in column 4, amortization of advertising and promotion. In column 5, show all effects of choosing the alternatives presented separately in columns 2 through 4.
2. As president, which accounting policies would you choose? Explain.

A8-15 Inventory Policy Comparison: Carlyon and Dennis are North American manufacturers of auto parts. The two firms use different inventory cost flow accounting policies. This question asks you to determine some of the differences due to the reporting. The two firms report the following selected information for 20X1:

	($ thousands)	
	Carlyon	**Dennis**
Earnings from continuing operations	$ (538)	$ (3,432)
Cost of sales	24,803	71,826
Net earnings per share (continuing operations)	(2.22)	(7.21)
Assets (total)	43,076	174,429
Inventories	3,571	6,215
Total shareholders' equity	6,109	22,690
Comparative units sold: U.S. and Canada (millions)	1.661 units	3.114 units
Comparative units sold: World-wide (millions)	1.866 units	5.346 units

Carlyon Corporation
Note 1: *Summary of Significant Accounting Policies*
Inventories are valued at the lower of cost or market. The cost of approximately 41% and 49% of inventories at 31 December 20X1 and 20X0, respectively, is determined on a last-in, first-out (LIFO) basis. The balance of inventory cost is determined on a first-in, first-out (FIFO) basis.

Note 2: *Inventories and Cost of Sales*
Inventories are summarized by major classification as follows (in $ thousands):

	31 December	
	20X1	**20X0**
Finished products, including service parts	$1,192	$1,114
Raw materials, finished, production parts, and supplies	873	1,100
Work-in-process	1,476	911
Other	30	25
Total	$3,571	$3,150

Inventories valued on the LIFO basis would have been $239 million and $208 million higher than reported had they been valued on the FIFO basis at 31 December 20X1 and 20X0, respectively (see Note 1). Total manufacturing cost of sales aggregated $24.81 million, and $24.13 million for 20X1 and 20X0, respectively.

Dennis Motor Company
Note 1: *Accounting Policies (Inventory Valuation)*
Inventories are stated at the lower of cost or market. The cost of substantially all North American inventories is determined by the last-in, first-out (LIFO) method. The cost of the remaining inventories is determined substantially by the first-in, first-out (FIFO) method.

If FIFO were the only method of inventory accounting used by the company, inventories would have been $1,323 and $1,331 higher than reported at 31 December 20X1 and 20X0, respectively. The major classes of inventory at 31 December were as follows (in $ thousands):

	20X1	**20X0**
Finished products	$2,979.2	$3,628.2
Raw materials and work-in-process	2,800.9	3,025.7
Supplies	435.2	461.5
Total	$6,215.3	$ 7,115.4

Required:

1. Are prices rising or falling in the 20X1 supplier markets in which Dennis (and Carlyon) buys? How do you know?
2. Compare Dennis's and Carlyon's inventory levels and comment on the comparison.
3. Is it desirable to have similar companies using different inventory cost flow policies? If not, why do accounting standard-setters not require uniformity?

A8-16 Cost Flow Assumptions: The records of Egypt Company showed the following data relative to one of the major items held in inventory. Assume that the transactions occurred in the order given.

	Units	**Unit Cost**
Beginning inventory	6,000	$7.95
Purchase No. 1	7,000	8.40
Sale No. 1 (at $24)	6,500	
Purchase No. 2	8,000	9.00
Sale No. 2 (at $26)	5,500	

Required:

For each independent assumption given, calculate the total dollar amount for ending inventory and cost of goods sold.

a. Weighted-average cost, periodic inventory system
b. FIFO, perpetual inventory system
c. LIFO, periodic inventory system (CGA-Canada, adapted)

A8-17 Inventory Cost and Cost of Sales—Two Methods: The following data relates to Sirshi Corporation for the month of March:

	Units	Cost per Unit
Opening inventory	180	$14.00
Sale 3 March	75	
Purchase, 5 March	2,700	14.40
Purchase, 13 March	1,050	15.20
Sale, 15 March	2,000	
Sale, 18 March	500	
Purchase, 21 March	4,700	15.80
Purchase, 25 March	2,800	16.00
Sale, 26 March	5,000	

Required:

1. Calculate the inventory cost and cost of goods sold under the following cost flow assumptions:
   a. FIFO
   b. Weighted average, periodic inventory system
2. Give all entries to record purchases and sales using a FIFO cost system and perpetual inventory costing. Assume all sales were for $22 per unit, and were on credit. All inventory purchases were also on credit.
3. Repeat requirement (2) using a weighted-average cost system and periodic inventory. The inventory was counted on 31 March and cost of sales was recorded on that date.
4. Prepare the entry that would be made if FIFO was used and the actual physical count revealed that 3,800 units were on hand.

A8-18 Inventory Cost Methods: The records of Clayton Company showed the following transactions, in the order given, relating to the major inventory item:

	Units	Unit Cost
1. Inventory	3,000	$6.90
2. Purchase	6,000	7.20
3. Sale (at $15)	4,000	
4. Purchase	5,000	7.50
5. Sale (at $15)	9,000	
6. Purchase	11,000	7.66
7. Sale (at $18)	9,000	
8. Purchase	6,000	7.80

Required:

Complete the following schedule for each independent assumption (round unit costs to the nearest cent; show computations):

Independent Assumptions	Units and Amounts		
	Ending Inventory	Cost of Goods Sold	Gross Margin
a. FIFO			
b. LIFO, periodic inventory system			
c. LIFO, perpetual inventory system			
d. Weighted average, periodic inventory system			
e. Moving average, perpetual inventory system			

A8-19 Match Inventory Cost Methods: Stigler and Sons sells two main products. The records of the company showed the following information relating to one of the products:

	Units	Unit Cost
Beginning inventory	500	$6.00
Purchases and sales (in order given):		
Purchase 1	400	6.20
Purchase 2	600	6.30
Sale 1	1,000	
Purchase 3	800	6.50
Sale 2	700	
Sale 3	500	
Purchase 4	700	6.60

In considering a change in inventory policy, the following summary was prepared:

	Case			
	(1)	(2)	(3)	(4)
Sales	$32,000	$32,000	$32,000	$32,000
Cost of goods sold	14,220	13,992	13,810	13,860
Gross margin	$ 17,780	$18,008	$18,190	$ 18,140

Required:

Identify the inventory flow method used for each of the four cases, assuming that only the ending inventory was affected. Show computations.

(AICPA, adapted)

A8-20 Inventory Error: When the accounting staff of Nicodemus Limited was preparing the first quarter 20X5 interim financial statements, they discovered an error in the 31 December 20X4 financial statements. Inventory costing $225,000 had been in transit and was not received until 4 January 20X5. The accounts payable department had recorded the purchase as an account payable on 28 December 20X4. Title to the inventory had passed to Nicodemus on 27 December, the date that the supplier had loaded the shipment onto the shipping company's trucks.

Nicodemus uses a periodic inventory method.

Required:

1. What impact did the error have on Nicodemus's 20X4 financial statements?
2. When the error is discovered in the first quarter of 20X5, what correcting entry should Nicodemus make?

A8-21 Inventory-Related Errors: Swamy Systems Incorporated prepared its draft 20X4 financial statements in February 20X5. The draft income statement showed a tentative net income of $550,000. After the draft statements were prepared, but prior to their approval and release, the auditors discovered several errors:

a. The company had made a calculation error in the worksheets used for the year-end 20X5 physical inventory. Inventory actually should have been $50,000 greater than recorded.
b. Inventory of $40,000 that was received on 29 December 20X4 (and included in the 31 December 20X4 physical inventory count) had not been recorded as an account payable until well into January 20X5.
c. The company had shipped goods worth $150,000 to a distant customer on 28 December 20X4. The revenue (and account receivable) was recorded by Nicodemus on 4 January 20X5.

Required:

1. What effect will correction of these errors have on the tentative net income of $550,000? What will the revised net income be?
2. Suppose that these errors were not discovered until *after* the 20X4 statements were released. What adjustment(s), if any, should the company make on its books in 20X5?

A8-22 Net Realizable Value of Damaged Goods: A fire damaged some of the merchandise held for sale by Adams Appliance Company. Eight television sets and 12 DVD players sets were damaged. They were not covered by insurance. The appliances will be repaired and sold "as is." Data follows:

	Per Appliance	
	Television	**DVD**
Inventory (at cost)	$800	$300
Estimated cost to repair	70	90
Estimated cost to sell	30	30
Estimated sales price	450	160

Required:

1. Compute net realizable value for each appliance and for the inventory in total.
2. Give the separate entries to record the damaged merchandise inventory for the televisions and DVDs. Assume a perpetual inventory system.
3. Give the entries to record the subsequent repair of the televisions and the DVDs (credit cash).
4. Give the entries to record sale for cash of two televisions and one DVD. It will be necessary to record payment of the sales costs in a separate entry. Credit sales costs in the entry to record the sale. Assume that actual sales prices equalled the estimated sales prices.

A8-23 Net Realizable Value: During shipping, merchandise purchased by the Atlantic Trading Company was damaged. The original total invoice price of this material was $50,000. Atlantic, which was responsible for shipping, has no insurance covering this type of damage. The company has decided to repair and resell the damaged items.

Item	**1**	**2**	**3**
Volume	500 units	300 units	100 units
Cost (per unit)	$55	$17	$250
Estimated cost to rebuild (per unit)	15	6	110
Estimated sales price (per unit)	45	19	180
Estimated cost to sell (per unit)	5	2	18

Required:

1. Calculate the net realizable value for each item and for the inventory as a whole. Also calculate total cost and the required writedown.
2. Prepare the entry to write the inventory down to net realizable value. The inventory account should be reduced directly; an allowance should not be used. The damaged inventory should be transferred to a separate damaged inventory account.
3. Prepare entries to record rebuilding, sales, and selling expenses. Assume all estimates are accurate. Prepare summary entries for the three products together. A perpetual inventory is kept.
4. Explain which of the entries recorded in requirements (2) and (3) have an impact on net income.

A8-24 Loss on Purchase Commitment: During 20X5, Mossback Company signed a contract with Alpha Corporation to "purchase 15,000 subassemblies at $30 each during 20X6."

Required:

1. On 31 December 20X5, the end of the annual accounting period, the financial statements are to be prepared. Assume that the cost of the subassemblies is dropping and the total estimated current replacement cost is $425,000. Under what additional contractual and economic conditions would note disclosure only be required? Prepare an appropriate note.
2. What contractual and economic conditions would require accrual of a loss? Give the accrual entry.
3. Assume that the subassemblies are received in 20X5 when their replacement cost was $410,000. The contract was paid in full. Give the required entry, assuming the entry in requirement (2) was made, and a periodic inventory system is used.

A8-25 LCM: The management of Tarry Hardware Company has collected some information regarding the LCM valuation of a lawnmower:

Handyman deluxe gas mower: 150 on hand; cost $460 each; replacement cost, $390 each; estimated sales price, $610; estimated distribution cost, $40; and normal profit, 30% of the sales price.

Required:

1. Present alternate values for "market." Which is to be used for the LCM test?
2. What amount of writedown is required, assuming use of the following definitions of market value:
   a. Replacement cost
   b. Net realizable value
   c. Net realizable value less a normal profit margin.
3. Assume that all the mowers subsequently resold for $100,000. How much gross profit would be recorded after the writedown in (a), (b), and (c)? In retrospect, which do you think portrays reality most accurately?

★

A8-26 LCM—Compute the Allowance: The records of Loren Moving Company showed the following inventory data:

		Cost	Market
Category 1			
	Item A	$10,000	$ 9,000
	Item B	40,000	35,000
	Item C	25,000	33,000

Category 2		
Item D	$18,000	$ 16,500
Item E	20,000	4,000
Item F	42,000	42,000

Required:

1. Calculate three different amounts that could justifiably be recorded as the allowance to reduce inventory to the lower of cost or market.
2. Which of the above approaches do you prefer? Explain.

A8-27 LCM: Halloo Lighting Limited applies LCM valuation to inventory annually, by category, using an allowance system. The company has collected the following information regarding two categories of inventory at the end of the current fiscal period:

Floor lamps: Cost, $344,750. Replacement cost, $295,100. Estimated sales value, $425,000. Commission rate on sales, 10%. Normal gross profit, before sales commissions, 28%.

Outdoor floodlights: Cost, $167,900. Replacement cost, $100,500. Estimated sales value, $250,000. Commission on sales, 15%. Normal gross profit, before sales commissions, 20%.

Required:

1. List the three alternative values, for each category, that could be used for market value in the LCM test. Determine the amount of the writedown, if any, that would result from each valuation.
2. Assume that the inventory was subsequently sold for the estimated sales value given. How much gross profit would be recorded under each alternative definition of market value? What pattern appears?
3. Explain what measure of market value you think would be appropriate in this case.
4. Explain the factors that companies must consider in choosing a measurement base for market values.

A8-28 Lower of Cost or Market: Hanlon Company purchased a significant amount of raw materials inventory for a new product it is manufacturing. Hanlon purchased insurance on these raw materials while they were in transit from the supplier.

Hanlon uses the lower-of-cost-or-market rule for these raw materials. The company applies the test to each individual inventory item. The replacement cost of the raw materials is above the net realizable value, but both are below the original cost.

Hanlon uses the average cost method for these raw materials. In the last two years, each purchase has been at a lower price than the previous purchase, and the ending inventory quantity for each period has been higher than the beginning inventory quantity for that period.

Required:

1. What is the appropriate method that Hanlon should use to account for the insurance costs on the raw materials incurred while they were in transit from the supplier? Why?
2. At what amount should Hanlon's raw materials inventory be reported on the balance sheet? Why?
3. In general, why is the lower-of-cost-or-market rule used to report inventory?
4. What would have been the effect on ending inventory and cost of goods sold had Hanlon used the LIFO inventory method instead of the average cost inventory method for the raw materials? Why?

(AICPA, adapted)

A8-29 LCM—Three Ways to Apply: The information shown below relating to the ending inventory was taken from the records of Components Company.

Inventory Classification	Quantity	Per Unit Cost	Market
Zip drives			
Stock X	200	$200	$230
Stock Y	60	150	130
CD burners			
Stock D	20	240	270
Stock E	10	270	255
Keyboards			
Stock A	9	75	70
Stock B	5	95	80
Stock C	8	100	110

Required:

1. Explain three different ways that the market value listed above could be defined.
2. Determine the valuation of the above inventory at cost and at LCM, assuming application of LCM by (a) individual items, (b) classifications, and (c) total inventory.
3. Give the entry to record the writedown, if any, to reduce ending inventory to LCM. Assume periodic inventory and the allowance method.
4. Of the three applications described in (2) above, which one appears preferable in this situation? Explain.

A8-30 Gross Margin Method: You are auditing the records of Yu Sun Coldridge Corporation. A physical inventory has been taken by the company under your observation. However, the valuations have not been completed. The records of the company provide the following data: sales, $378,000 (gross); returned sales, $20,000 (returned to stock); purchases (gross), $186,000; beginning inventory, $120,000; freight-in, $8,400; and purchase returns and allowances, $2,200. The gross margin last period was 35% of net sales; you anticipate that it will be 30% for the year under audit.

Required:

Estimate the cost of the ending inventory using the gross margin method. Show computations.

A8-31 Retail Inventory Method: Dan's Clothing Store values its inventory using the retail inventory method at the lower of average cost or market. The following data are available for the month of June 20X5:

	Cost	Selling Price
Inventory, 1 June	$ 107,600	$160,000
Markdowns		42,000
Markups		58,000
Markdown cancellations		20,000

	Cost	Selling Price
Markup cancellations		18,000
Purchases	346,400	447,200
Sales		500,000
Purchase returns and allowances	6,000	7,200
Sales returns and allowances		20,000

Required:
Prepare a schedule to compute the estimated inventory at 30 June, using the retail inventory method to approximate LCM.

(AICPA, adapted)

Ex

A8-32 Gross Margin and Retail Inventory Methods: The records of Diskount Department Store provided the following data for 20X5:

Sales (gross)	$800,000
Sales returns	2,000
Additional markups	9,000
Additional markup cancellations	5,000
Markdowns	7,000
Purchases:	
At retail	850,000
At cost	459,500
Purchase returns:	
At retail	4,000
At cost	2,200
Freight on purchases	7,000
Beginning inventory:	
At retail	80,000
At cost	45,000
Markdown cancellations	3,000

Required:

1. Estimate the valuation of the ending inventory and cost of goods sold using the gross margin method. Last year's gross margin percentage was 51%.
2. Estimate the valuation of the ending inventory and cost of goods sold using the retail sales method, which approximates LCM.
3. Which method is likely to be more accurate? Comment.

A8-33 Gross Margin Method: The manager of Seton Book Company, a book retailer, requires an estimate of the inventory cost for a quarterly financial report to the owner on 31 March 20X5. In the past, the gross margin method was used because of the difficulty and expense of taking a physical inventory at interim dates. The company sells both fiction and non-fiction books. Due to their lower turnover rate, non-fiction books are typically marked up to produce a gross profit of 37.5%. Fiction, on the other hand, generates a 28.6% gross profit. The manager has used the average gross profit of 33.333% to estimate interim inventories.

You have been asked by the manager to estimate the book inventory cost as of 31 March 20X5. The following data are available from Seton's accounting records:

	Fiction	Non-Fiction	Total
Inventory, 1 January 20X5	$100,000	$ 40,000	$140,000
Purchases	600,000	200,000	800,000
Freight-in	5,000	2,000	7,000
Sales	590,000	160,000	750,000

Required:
Round gross margin ratios to three decimal places.

1. Using the average gross profit margin of 33.333%, compute the estimate of inventory as of 31 March 20X5, based on the method applied to combined fiction and non-fiction books.

2. Compute the estimate of ending inventory as of 31 March 20X5, based on the gross margin method applied separately to fiction and non-fiction books.
3. Which method is preferable in this situation? Explain.

A8-34 Retail Inventory Method: Auditors are examining the accounts of Acton Retail Corporation. They were present when Acton's personnel physically counted the Acton inventory; however, the auditors made their own tests. Acton's records provided the following data for the current year:

	At Retail	At Cost
Inventory, 1 January	$ 300,000	$180,500
Net purchases	1,453,000	955,000
Freight-in		15,000
Additional markups	31,000	
Additional markup cancellations	14,000	
Markdowns	8,000	
Employee discounts	2,000	
Sales	1,300,000	

Inventory at 31 December (per physical count valued at retail) = $475,000

Required:

1. Compute the ending inventory at LCM as an audit test of the overall reasonableness of the physical inventory count.
2. Note any discrepancies indicated. What factors should the auditors consider in reconciling any difference in results from the analysis?
3. What accounting treatment (if any) should be accorded the discrepancy?

A8-35 Inventory Estimation: Banff Mountain Equipment Limited (Banff) sells skiing and hiking equipment to retailers. After a very successful ski season and just as it was about to commence shipping its hiking equipment for the upcoming season, Banff lost all of its hiking equipment in a fire in March 20X8. Fortunately, the company's insurance policy will cover 80% of the loss suffered in this fire. The loss is to be determined based on the cost of the inventory. Corporate records disclose the following:

Inventory—1 January 20X8	$150,000
Purchases (all on credit) during 20X8	480,000
Purchase returns	30,000
Payments to suppliers for purchases	440,000
Customs and duty on purchases	8,000
Sales (all on credit) at retail price	615,000
Sales returns at retail price	15,000
Cash collected from accounts receivable	580,000

Banff normally realizes a gross profit of 30% on its sales. It accounts for its inventory using a periodic inventory system. The net loss from the fire is deductible for income tax purposes. Banff's tax rate is 40%.

Required:

1. Calculate the net loss from the fire.
2. Should the loss from the fire be reported as an extraordinary item? Why or why not?

(CGA-Canada, adapted)

A8-36 Inventory Concepts—Recording, Adjusting, Closing, Reporting: Gamit Company completed the following selected (and summarized) transactions during 20X5:

a. Merchandise inventory on hand 1 January 20X5, $105,000 (at cost, which was the same as LCM).
b. During the year, purchased merchandise for resale at cost of $200,000 on credit, terms 2/10, n/30. Immediately paid 85% of the cash cost.
c. Paid freight on merchandise purchased, $10,000 cash.
d. Paid 40% of the accounts payable within the discount period. The remaining payables were unpaid at the end of 20X5 and were still within the discount period.
e. Merchandise that had a quoted price of $3,000 (terms 2/10, n/30) was returned to a supplier. A cash refund of $2,940 was received because the items were unsatisfactory.
f. During the year, sold merchandise for $370,000, of which 10% was on credit.
g. A television set caught fire and was damaged internally; it was returned by the customer. The set was originally sold for $600, of which $400 cash was refunded. The set originally cost the company $420. Estimates are that the set, when repaired, can be sold for $240. Estimated repair costs are $50, and selling costs are estimated to be $10.
h. Operating expenses (administrative and distribution) paid in cash, $120,000; includes the $10 in (k).
i. Excluded from the purchase given in (b) and from the ending inventory was a shipment for $7,000 (net of discount). This shipment was in transit, FOB shipping point at 31 December 20X5. The invoice had arrived.
j. Paid $50 cash to repair the damaged television set; see (g) above.
k. Sold the damaged television set for $245; selling costs allocated, $10.
l. The ending inventory (as counted) was $110,000 at cost, and $107,000 at market. Assume an average income tax rate of 40%.

Accounting policies followed by the company are:

(1) The annual accounting period ends 31 December.
(2) A periodic inventory system is used.
(3) Purchases and accounts payable are recorded net of cash discounts.
(4) Freight charges are allocated to merchandise when purchased.
(5) All cash discounts are taken.
(6) Used and damaged merchandise is carried in a separate inventory account.
(7) Inventories are reported at LCM and the allowance method is used.

Required:

1. Give the entries for transactions (b) through (k).
2. Give the end-of-period adjusting entries.
3. Prepare a multiple-step income statement for 20X5. Assume that 20,000 common shares are outstanding.
4. Show how the ending inventory should be reported on the balance sheet at 31 December 20X5.

A8-37 Inventory Issues—Overview and Explanation: HHL Limited has significant investment in inventory of retail goods. It has a periodic inventory system, but uses the gross profit method to estimate inventory for its monthly statements. At the end of the current fiscal period, 31 December 20X5, the following issues have arisen:

a. In October 20X5, HHL bought goods for $355,600. This amount was recorded as the cost of purchases. The goods were purchased under a contract that had guaranteed the price for 12 months; prices have been volatile. When the goods were delivered, their replacement cost was $321,000. Replacement cost had rebounded to the price paid by the end of the year. All of the goods were still in inventory at the end of the period. If any adjustment is needed, prepare the entry.

b. The gross profit method, by category, is used to estimate inventory amounts and cost of goods sold during the period. The gross profit method produced an estimate of $2,456,000 of inventory that should have been present on 31 December. The actual count showed that $2,009,100 of goods was present. Explain at least three reasons why this discrepancy could occur. What impact will the discrepancy have on the balance sheet and the income statement as compared to the preliminary numbers, based on the actual count?

c. The company is wondering whether the retail method would produce more accurate numbers for inventory. In the past year, opening inventory was $1,788,900 at cost and $2,500,000 at retail. Freight-in was $66,800. Purchases were $11,300,000 at cost and $19,710,000 at retail. There were no additional markups, but there were $544,200 of markdowns. Sales were $17,750,000. What estimated inventory value would the retail sales method have produced?

d. In light of the discrepancies discovered this year, the company is considering switching to a perpetual inventory system. Explain what would be required and how the company's information would change or not change as compared to its existing information system.

e. The actual physical count was $2,009,100. This inventory was categorized as follows:

	Cost	Market
Type A	$322,000	$260,000
Type B	540,000	575,000
Type C	675,900	650,000
Type D	471,200	475,000

Market value is defined as replacement cost. The allowance to reduce inventory to LCM has a balance of $45,000, unchanged from the last fiscal year-end. Prepare any needed entry to adjust the allowance, and justify your decision.

f. All inventories are now carried at weighted-average cost. Management would like to know how inventory, cost of sales, and net income would be affected if the FIFO inventory method were to be used.

Required:

Respond to each request, (a)–(f), above.

A8-38 Cash Flow Statement: Therot Corporation reported the following items in its 20X5 financial statements:

	20X5	20X4
From the balance sheet:		
Inventories (net)		
Finished goods	$ 477,226	$ 404,477
Work in progress	197,368	166,193
Materials and supplies	269,974	271,374
	944,568	842,044
Accounts payable	615,904	597,211
Estimated liability on non-cancellable purchase commitments	7,943	—
From the income statement:		
Cost of goods sold*	$ 4,919,316	$ 4,101,564
Loss on purchase commitment	7,943	—

* Includes loss due to decline in market value

From the notes:

Inventories are carried at FIFO cost, net of an allowance to reduce finished goods inventory to the lower of cost or market of $64,816 (20X4, $45,719). Market value is defined as net realizable value.

At year-end, the company has outstanding purchase commitments in the amount of $13,299 (20X4, $6,587). The market value of these goods is equal to, or exceeds, the purchase commitment cost except as accrued in the financial statements.

Required:

1. What items would appear on the cash flow statement as a result of the inventory transactions of the year? Assume the use of the indirect method of presentation in the operating activities section.
2. How much did the company pay for inventory during the period?
3. Assume that inventory values as reflected above were standard cost. The income statement reflected unfavourable price variances of $43,110, and favourable usage variances of $19,850. These variances were considered immaterial, so inventory could be reported at standard cost for external reporting. Other facts are unchanged. How much money did the company pay for inventory during the period?
4. Would the LCM writedown have been the same, greater than, or less than that recorded if the company had used (a) average cost or (b) LIFO as a cost flow assumption? Assume that prices have generally been rising in these markets over the last several years.

CHAPTER 9

Capital Assets, Goodwill, and Deferred Charges

INTRODUCTION

In Chapter 6, we established that expenditures often are classified as assets first, and then become expenses later as the asset is consumed. To qualify as assets, expenditures must meet the definition of an asset and must also satisfy all recognition criteria. Chapter 8 examined inventories, the primary current asset that arises from expenditures. In this chapter we look at a broad range of long-lived assets—assets that have a useful life of longer than one year (or one operating cycle, whichever is longer).

The main focus of this chapter is on the very broad category of long-lived assets known generally as capital assets—both tangible and intangible. For example, IMAX Corporation, the large-screen movie operation, reports film assets (the company makes its own movies), projection equipment, motion simulation equipment, and camera equipment, in addition to the more classic tangible capital assets such as land, buildings, office equipment, production equipment, and leasehold improvements. Its intangible assets include patents, trademarks, and capitalized computer software. IMAX also reports goodwill from acquired businesses. Quite a collection, all necessary to operate in this industry!

In this chapter, we will examine the issues surrounding the measurement and recording of capital assets and goodwill. We also will examine a type of long-lived asset that is closely related to intangible capital assets—long-term deferred charges. In Chapter 10, we will discuss accounting following acquisition, including amortization, impairment, and revaluation.

OVERVIEW OF LONG-LIVED ASSETS

In Chapter 6, we discussed the fact that many expenditures become assets before they become expenses. Tangible capital assets are the most obvious example. First they are assets, then they are amortized to expense over their useful life (except land). Expenditures give rise to costs, and expense recognition of many of those costs is deferred until future years. Therefore, broadly speaking, all long-lived assets are really *deferred costs*, even though we give them different names on the balance sheet.

When we account for long-lived assets, we normally separate them into four categories:

1. tangible capital assets
2. deferred charges
3. intangible capital assets
4. goodwill

In this chapter, we will discuss deferred charges and intangible assets together, since there is no clear distinction between them.

You probably are most familiar with tangible capital assets, from your study of introductory accounting. There are many issues surrounding capital assets, besides depreciation and amortization (which we discuss in Chapter 10). In particular, we will examine the issues surrounding valuation and the measurement of acquisition cost. Acquisition cost may seem to be a minor issue, but there are many ways to acquire an asset that do not involve a clear and unambiguous payment of cash in return for a physical asset.

DEFINITION OF CAPITAL ASSETS

A **capital asset** can be defined as an *identifiable long-lived asset, acquired for use in the revenue-producing activities of the enterprise.* There are three important aspects of this definition:

1. Capital assets are held for use in the production or supply of goods and services or for rental to others. Capital assets may also be used for administrative purposes or for maintenance of other capital assets.
2. Capital assets have been acquired to be used on a continued basis.
3. Capital assets are not intended for sale in the ordinary course of business.

It is important to distinguish between capital assets and inventory. A computer is a *capital asset* to the company that buys and uses it, but it was *inventory* to the manufacturer that made it and to the dealer that sold it. It is not the asset itself that governs classification as a capital asset; it is the intended *use* of the asset that matters. If an asset is held for sale, it is not a capital asset.

Long-lived assets that were originally acquired for use in generating revenue but that no longer are intended for that purpose cease to be capital assets. Instead, they become investment assets or assets held for sale, and are reported in the long-term other assets classification on the balance sheet.

TANGIBLE AND INTANGIBLE ASSETS Capital assets can be described as *tangible* or *intangible.* Tangible capital assets are items of property, plant, and equipment. These assets have a physical presence; the word "tangible" means, literally, that the asset can be touched. Tangible assets include land, buildings, equipment, furniture, leasehold improvements, and other such touchable assets. Tangible assets also include long-lived property held to generate revenue through rental, such as office buildings, apartments, cars and trucks, industrial property, furniture, computers, airplanes, etc.

Intangible capital assets are long-lived assets that do *not* have a physical substance. They often arise from legal or contractual rights. These assets are held to generate revenue, and are not intended for sale in the ordinary course of business. Examples include copyrights, patents, subscription lists, mineral rights, franchises, computer software, licences, and trademarks.

Goodwill is also an *intangible* asset, but it is excluded from the general term "capital assets." It merits separate classification because it is not an *identifiable* asset; goodwill arises as a residual in the purchase of other assets. The superior earning potential of the entity is assumed be the reason that goodwill exists.

Tangible and intangible capital assets with finite lives are amortized. Amortization is a "rational and systematic" allocation of the cost of an asset over its useful life. Amortization is essentially arbitrary, especially for intangible assets where the useful life is not really predictable. Land is *not* amortized, since it is assumed to hold its intrinsic value forever.[1] Goodwill is also exempted from the amortization requirement. Like land, goodwill is assumed to hold its intrinsic value. Finally, if there is a specific intangible asset with an indefinite life, amortization is not required. Goodwill and indefinite-life intangibles must be regularly evaluated to see if value is impaired.

Deferred Charges and Intangible Assets

There is a fine line between deferred charges and intangible capital assets. For example, *CICA Handbook* Section 3070 mentions development costs as an example of a long-term deferred charge. A deferred charge is really just a long-term prepaid expense. On the other hand, deferred development costs become intangible assets when they lead to new or improved products.

The AcSB's definition of an intangible asset is not much help in deciding whether a deferred cost should be treated as a deferred charge or as an intangible capital asset:

> An intangible asset is an asset, other than a financial asset, that lacks physical substance (*CICA* 3062.05(c)).

If that is the case, then it would seem that all deferred charges automatically are intangible assets.

Not quite true. A useful way of distinguishing between a deferred charge and an intangible asset is to ask whether the deferred cost gives rise to a *separable asset*. A separable asset is one that can be separated from the company that currently owns it. If a company develops a new or improved product, and if the rights to produce that product can be sold or licensed to another company, then the development costs are an intangible asset.

In contrast, suppose that a company spends a lot of money to develop a corporate website. The website is an integral part of the company. No one else has a use for a website that is dedicated to a specific company. Nevertheless, the initial cost of developing the website may be expected to benefit the company in future periods and might be capitalized. It is not a separable asset, and therefore website development costs would be classified as a deferred charge rather than as an intangible asset.

The distinction between deferred charges and intangible assets is fuzzy, and frankly is not of much concern as long as the company clearly discloses the nature of the deferred costs and the accounting policies relating to them. Since there is a close relationship between these two categories of deferred cost, we will discuss them together in later sections of this chapter.

VALUATION OF CAPITAL ASSETS

Initial Acquisition

Capital assets are normally recorded at cost, defined as follows:

> Cost is the amount of consideration given up to acquire, construct, develop, or better [an asset] ... and includes all costs directly attributable to the acquisition, construction, development or betterment of the asset including installing it in the location and in the condition necessary for its intended use. (*CICA* 3061.05)

Cost is usually the *fair value* at the date of purchase. That is, the asset is bought for its fair value as of the date of acquisition. As time passes, the fair value of the asset will change as the price for a comparable asset changes in the market, due to changes in technology and supply and demand forces. Also, the asset itself becomes used; consumed in operations. Historical cost financial statements do not attempt to reflect the current value of capital assets, just the sacrifice made to acquire them.

---

[1] Land may lose its value, however, and may then be written down. An example of the loss of value of land arises when land has been heavily polluted. This is called an *impairment of value*, and will be discussed in the next chapter.

DEVELOPED ASSETS Many capital assets are not purchased, *per se*, but are constructed (for tangible assets) or developed (for intangible assets) by the enterprise. The cost of a constructed or developed asset is the sum of the expenditures relating to its construction or development. These costs may not reflect the fair value of the asset, even at the time of its creation. A tangible asset may be constructed at a lower cost than its purchase price, and an intangible asset may be developed for far less than it would cost to buy it from someone else if it were fully developed.

Indeed, developed assets may not be available for purchase at any price; they often are unique, which is what gives them their revenue-generating value. Examples include software applications and natural resource deposits. The capitalized value for these assets is not, was not, and was never intended to be, fair value at acquisition. Again, this is not the purpose of historical cost financial statements. It is undeniably difficult to interpret the earnings potential of companies with significant assets of this nature, without detailed knowledge of the assets beyond that provided in the financial statements.

Constructed and developed assets may not be recorded at costs that *exceed* fair value. Fair value may be determined with reference to future benefits; future cash flow. This can be hard to establish! Alternatively, for tangible assets, it usually is feasible to compare the capitalized cost with a hypothetical purchase price (for example, what it would have cost to pay a commercial contractor to construct a building). For other capital assets, however, such a comparison may not be feasible. It may be impossible to determine whether an intangible asset is worth what was spent to develop it, until its development is complete. For example, the costs of developing a mining site are capitalized until it is known whether the value of the mineral resources is worth continued development of the mine site.

capital expenditures

expenditures expected to yield benefits beyond the current period, to be added to an asset account

POST-ACQUISITION EXPENDITURES Expenditures related to capital assets subsequent to their acquisition are either capitalized or expensed. **Capital expenditures** are expenditures expected to yield benefits beyond the current accounting period; that is, have future cash flows, and thus should be added to the capital asset account. The cost of a capital asset is recognized as an expense in current and future periods through amortization.

Other expenditures, such as ordinary repairs, are expected to yield benefits only in the current accounting period. These are costs incurred for maintenance. They are recorded in expense accounts and matched against the revenue of the period.

Policy Choice

Accounting practice has developed steadily in this area, and much time and energy has gone into studying the typical kinds of costs that should be capitalized versus expensed in each category. Common practices are summarized in Exhibit 9-1. Read it carefully, and make sure you understand why each capitalized item creates some sort of future enhancement of cash flows. Often, it is because the expenditure is inescapable in order to get the capital asset into operation.

Exhibit 9-1 is fairly comprehensive. No such list can really be complete, but this list includes a wide range of deferred charges, tangible capital assets, intangible capital assets, and goodwill.

Is there any room for choice or manipulation? You'll find that some firms are quick to disclaim any future benefit associated with a variety of expenditures related to capital assets. For whatever reason, these companies seem to be attempting to minimize current net income and net assets, and enjoy lower future amortization expenses. A company may also prefer to expense rather than capitalize if it has cash flow prediction as a primary reporting objective. By including the expenditures in current expenses, a company achieves a net income figure that is closer to the actual cash flow.

At the other end of the spectrum, some companies are very aggressive in their capitalization policies, seeking higher current income and capital assets, and accepting higher future amortization. For example, a regulated public utility will generally capitalize as many costs as possible because the enterprise's permitted (i.e., regulated) profit is based on its regulated rate of return multiplied by the asset base. The higher the asset base, the larger the profit it is entitled to earn.

Another effect of capitalizing rather than expensing is that the expenditures are classified as investing activities in the cash flow statement, and therefore never have an impact on *reported* cash flow from operations.

That's the trade-off. If you don't expense now, you will expense later. That is, capitalized costs, in almost all cases, are carried to income through amortization. The two approaches will provide different income and asset values throughout the life of the asset. As we progress through this chapter discussion, policy choices will be pointed out.

Materiality plays a role in this area, as well. Small capital expenditures are often expensed on the basis that the more correct capitalization and amortization would not produce results different enough to cause investors to make different decisions.

EXHIBIT 9-1

COMMON CAPITALIZATION PRACTICES

Capital Asset	Capitalize
Buildings, purchased	• purchase price • cost of modifications
Buildings, constructed	• architectural fees • payments to contractors • cost of permits • excavation costs • legal fees, closing costs
Buildings, self-constructed	• direct construction costs • excavation costs • reasonable apportionment of overhead • legal costs, permits, etc. • interest on *specific* construction loans
Machinery and equipment	• invoice cost, net of discounts, whether taken or not • taxes, freight, and duty • special platforms, foundations, other required installation costs • costs of building modifications necessary for installation • cost of preparing asset for use, including testing
Land	• purchase price • back taxes on acquisition, paid in order to release title • legal fees, closing costs • general land preparation costs, including grading, filling, draining, and surveying • cost of removing structures and other obstructions, if land is acquired for development (proceeds from salvaged materials reduce the cost capitalized) • special assessments for local government-maintained improvements, including streets, sidewalks, sewers, and streetlights • property taxes, insurance, and other holding costs incurred on land not in current productive use (may be expensed on grounds of expedience and conservatism) • landscaping and other property enhancements, if permanent
Land improvements	• driveways, parking lots, fencing • streets and sidewalks that the company must maintain • landscaping, if not permanent
Resource exploration and development costs	• resource exploration and development costs incurred • under full costing, all sites deferred • under successful efforts, only productive sites deferred

EXHIBIT 9-1

COMMON CAPITALIZATION PRACTICES (continued)

Capital Asset	Capitalize
Patents	• purchase price, transfer and legal fees if bought from another entity • development costs to internally develop a patented item; research costs are expensed • legal and other necessary documentation costs to register the patent, if self-developed • costs of a successful court defence (unsuccessful defenses are expensed, along with the now-worthless patent)
Industrial design registrations (i.e., a five-year renewable registration of the shape, pattern, or ornamentation of a manufactured item)	• acquisition and registration cost, as per patents • successful defence costs, as per patents
Copyrights	• acquisition and registration cost, as per patents • successful defence costs, as per patents
Trademarks and trade names	• legal and other necessary documentation costs to register the trademark, if self-developed • acquisition cost, as per patents • successful defence costs, as per patents
Franchise rights	• initial franchise fees, not related to annual volumes • legal fees, closing costs
Leasehold improvements (alterations, improvements, or refurbishing of leased space)	• invoice, installation costs
Development costs	• costs involved in translation of research findings into new products, etc., prior to commercial production • five criteria must be met to justify capitalization
Pre-operating costs	• established companies may defer costs related to putting a new business into service • expenditures must be incremental and recoverable from future operations
Computer software costs	• for self-developed software, costs that meet development criteria • for software for resale, capitalize costs after technical feasibility is established, if markets ensure recoverability
Website development costs	• application and infrastructure costs deferred • graphics costs deferred • some content development, depending on longevity and nature
Organization costs	• legal, accounting, promotional, and clerical activities associated with creating a new company
Share issuance costs	• printing share certificates and related items, professional fees, commissions paid for selling capital stock, and the costs of filing with securities commissions

CONCEPT REVIEW

1. What is the difference between tangible and intangible capital assets?
2. What are the characteristics of an intangible capital asset?
3. Define a capital expenditure.
4. What difference does it make to a company's reported financial results if the company is highly aggressive in its capitalization policies?

DETERMINING THE COST OF CAPITAL ASSETS

Basket Purchase of Several Assets

Occasionally, several assets are acquired for a single lump-sum price that may be lower than the sum of the individual asset prices, to encourage the sale. In other cases, the assets are attached, for example, land and building. This type of acquisition is called a **basket purchase**, **group purchase**, or lump-sum purchase. A portion of the single lump-sum price must be allocated to each asset acquired.

Any portions of the lump-sum price directly attributable to particular assets in the group are assigned in full to those assets. Land appraisal costs are assigned only to the land account, for example. Allocation of the remaining lump-sum price to each asset is necessary. Under the cost principle, the sum of the individual asset account balances at acquisition is limited to the lump-sum price.

Allocation is based on the relative fair values of the several assets involved (*CICA* 3061.18). Possible indicators include

1. Market prices for similar assets;
2. Current appraised value;
3. Assessed value for property tax purposes; and
4. The present value of estimated future net cash flows, including manufacturing cost savings.

The seller's book values are not relevant because they do not reflect the current value of the assets.

Each asset is valued according to the ratio of its value to the total value of the group; this valuation is called the *proportional method*. If the value of only the first asset(s) in a group is determinable, the second (or remaining) asset is valued at the cost remaining to be allocated. This less desirable procedure is called the *incremental method*.

To illustrate the proportional method, assume that $90,000 is the negotiated acquisition price paid for land, a building, and machinery. These assets are appraised individually, as the best available indication of value in this case: land, $30,000; building, $50,000; and machinery, $20,000. The cost apportionment of the single lump-sum price and the entry to record the transaction are as follows:

	Appraised Asset Value	Apportionment of Cost	Apportioned Cost
Land	$ 30,000	30%* × $ 90,000	$ 27,000
Building	50,000	50% × $ 90,000	45,000
Machinery	20,000	20% × $ 90,000	18,000
Total	$100,000		$90,000

* 30% = $30,000 ÷ $100,000

To record the basket purchase		
Land	27,000	
Building	45,000	
Machinery	18,000	
Cash		90,000

Assume, instead, that the building was worth $48,000, and the machinery, $17,000, but it was not possible to determine an objective value for the land. In this case, land would be assigned the residual $25,000, using the incremental method.

Capital Assets Purchased with Long-Term Debt

Sometimes, payment terms for an asset stretch out over a long period. In such a case, the asset is recorded at the most objective amount, considering

1. The cash equivalent price, or fair value, versus
2. The present value of the future cash payments required by the debt agreement discounted at the prevailing (market) interest rate for that type of debt.

If the debt instrument does not bear interest and the current cash price of the asset can be determined, the excess of the face value of the debt instrument over the cash price is viewed as interest expense. When the debt instrument is issued, the normal procedure is to record its face value as a liability. The difference between the face value and the cash price of the asset is debited to a contra-liability account as *discount on note payable.* The discount is amortized over the term of the debt, thereby increasing interest expense each period. If the cash price is not determinable, the current market interest rate is used to determine total interest cost and to compute the asset's present value for recording purposes.

To illustrate the purchase of a capital asset on credit, assume that Cobb Corporation purchases equipment on 1 January 20X2, with a $600 cash down payment and a $1,000, one-year note payable on 31 December 20X2 plus 12% interest. The stated interest rate is equal to the current market rate, so the note's present value equals its face value.

$$
\begin{aligned}
P &= (\$1,000 + \$120) \times (P/F, 12\%, 1) \\
&= \$1,120 \times .89286 \\
&= \$1,000
\end{aligned}
$$

The asset is recorded at the sum of the cash down payment plus the present value of the note because the cash equivalent price of the asset is not available. The recorded amount is

$$
\begin{aligned}
\text{Equipment value} &= \text{Cash down payment} + \text{Present value of note} \\
&= \$600 + \$1,000 = \$1,600
\end{aligned}
$$

Assume instead that Feller Company acquires a machine on 1 January 20X2, with a non-interest-bearing note that requires $8,615 to be paid on 31 December 20X2, 20X3, and 20X4. The note has no explicit interest, but the prevailing interest rate is 14% on liabilities of similar risk and duration. The face amount of the note is $25,845 ($8,615 × 3). The cash equivalent cost of the machine is unknown, so the asset is recorded at the present value of the three payments discounted at 14%.

$$
\begin{aligned}
\text{Recorded cost} &= \$8,615 \times (P/A, 14\%, 3) \\
&= \$8,615 \times 2.32163 \\
&= \$20,000 \text{ (rounded)}
\end{aligned}
$$

Feller's entries to record the asset and the note are as follows:

1 January 20X2	Gross Method	Net Method
Equipment	20,000	20,000
Discount on note payable	5,845	—
Note payable	25,845*	20,000

* $8,615 × 3

The discount on note payable is a contra note payable account. It reduces the net note payable balance to the present value of the future cash flows ($20,000). The discount is amortized to interest expense over the life of the liability.

Capital Assets Acquired in Exchange for Equity Securities

When equity securities (e.g., common shares) are issued to acquire capital assets, the assets are recorded at the fair market value of the securities issued, or, if more objectively determinable, at the fair market value of the asset.

The market value of the shares issued provides a reliable fair market value for publicly traded securities if the number of shares in the exchange is below the typical daily trading volume. Assume that Medford Corporation purchases used equipment in 20X5. The equipment is in reasonable condition but is not normally sold before the end of its useful life. Thus, it has no reliable market value. In payment for this equipment, Medford issues 2,000 common shares. Medford's common shares are listed on the Toronto Stock Exchange and currently trade at $10 per share. Medford has 10 million common shares outstanding. The proper value for the equipment is 2,000 × $10, or $20,000.

COMPLICATING FACTORS Several factors can complicate the situation, however. The effect of a substantial share offering on the market price of the shares is often not known until after issuance. Also, the shares of many companies are not traded with sufficient frequency to establish a daily market price. In other cases, organizers of a newly formed corporation may issue a substantial number of shares for capital assets when there is no established fair value for the shares.

If the market value of the securities (in the volume exchanged) cannot be determined reliably, the market value of the assets acquired is used if it can be reliably determined. In the absence of recent cash sale evidence, an independent appraisal can be used to value the assets. This may be easier said than done: unexplored or unproven mineral deposits, manufacturing rights, patents, chemical formulas, and mining claims are all difficult to value.

If no reliable market value can be determined for either the securities issued or the assets acquired, the Board of Directors of the corporation must establish a reasonable valuation. The directors have considerable discretion in establishing values, and firms experiencing financial difficulty may be tempted to overstate asset values, overstating owners' equity as well. A disincentive to overvaluation, however, is the increased amortization expense in future years.

Donated Assets

Shareholders and other parties occasionally donate assets and services to corporations. For example, shareholders may donate valuable paintings to adorn the corporate boardroom.

The assets cost the company nothing; that is, they are obtained in a *non-reciprocal transfer*, meaning that the company gives nothing in return. Does that mean that the assets need not be recognized? If the balance sheet is to provide a record of assets controlled by the entity, and the income statement is to record the costs of doing business, then it seems logical to include these assets at fair value. But the entity sacrificed no resources to obtain the assets. If the assets are depreciable, they will create an expense in future years, as they are used. Should future years' income be reduced because of a charge created in such a way? Is the return on shareholders' investment understated in such circumstances? It's a thorny issue.

Current practice in Canada is often to record the asset at its fair value, and increase a shareholders' equity contributed capital account. Depreciation based on the market value of the donated asset is matched against future revenue presumably generated by the assets.

However, an additional procedure that sometimes is used is to also amortize the balance of the contributed capital account using the same pattern as the depreciation of the related asset. The credit may be either directly to a revenue or expense account. The net effect is to remove the impact of the depreciation from net income. There is no Canadian standard on this issue but such amortization is suggested for donations to not-for-profit enterprises (*CICA* 4410.33).

If the donor imposes restrictions on the use of the asset donated, the expected cost of complying with those restrictions should be estimated and deducted from the market value of the asset in determining the valuation to be recorded.

Example To illustrate accounting for a donated asset, assume a building (fair market value $400,000), and the land on which it is located (fair market value $100,000) are donated to Sui Limited. A $5,000 legal and deed transfer cost is borne by Sui, which records the donation as follows:

Building	400,000	
Land	105,000	
Cash		5,000
Contributed capital—donated assets		500,000

It's interesting to note that this is an area where Canadian and U.S. practices are significantly different: U.S. standards require that the credit for donated assets be *included in income* in the year of donation rather than in contributed capital.

Self-Constructed Assets

Companies sometimes construct plant assets for their own use. For example, a utility employs its personnel to extend transmission lines and construct pipelines. All costs directly associated with the construction are capitalized to the constructed asset. These costs include incremental material, labour, and overhead costs. Overhead includes general costs not directly related to production, such as utility costs, maintenance on equipment, and supervision.

OVERHEAD COST Some of the overhead incurred during construction is included in the cost of self-constructed assets. The *CICA Handbook* specifies that "overhead costs directly attributable to the construction or development activity" should be capitalized (*CICA* 3061.20). What does this mean?

One view is that self-constructed assets should bear the incremental overhead cost and the portion of general overhead cost that would be assigned to any regular production displaced by the special project. According to this view, if general overhead is allocated on the basis of labour-hours, and 8% of labour-hours are associated with self-construction, then 8% of total general overhead during construction should be included as a cost of the self-constructed asset.

Many accountants contend that failure to allocate some portion of the general overhead to self-construction projects causes an undervaluation of self-constructed assets. On the other hand, others argue that assets are often self-constructed during slack periods when the production facility and workers would otherwise be idle. Using this line of reasoning, no general overhead should be capitalized because of the income-manipulation potential associated with this "make-work" project.

The amount of overhead to be included in self-constructed assets is quite nebulous. "Overhead" can be interpreted narrowly to include only identifiable and incremental costs, or broadly to include many items of general production costs. Accounting practice in a particular situation will be affected by the financial reporting objectives of the enterprise. The more overhead that is allocated to a self-constructed asset, the greater will be the carrying value of the asset. Companies that want to show high asset values will tend to interpret "overhead" quite broadly and will allocate significant amounts of overhead cost to the project.

INTEREST COST The period required for construction of capital assets can be lengthy. There is general agreement that time-related costs, including property taxes and insurance during construction, should be capitalized to the asset under construction. Consistent logic supports capitalization of interest during the construction period. After all, if the asset were purchased rather than self-constructed, the purchase price would normally include a cost component to cover the seller's financing expenses. Also, many firms would be unable to construct assets without debt financing.

Interest is usually a period cost, not eligible for capitalization. The *CICA Handbook* states that interest can be capitalized "when the enterprise's accounting policy is to capitalize interest costs" (*CICA* 3061.23). This does not provide much guidance! Current practice in Canada is to allow cash paid for interest costs on loans related to a construction project to be capitalized, if the company wishes. The interest has to have actually been paid; imputed interest, or opportunity cost, on equity investment is not eligible for capitalization. Furthermore, the loans should be specifically related to construction. Finally, the company can set its own policy in this regard; it is not forced to capitalize interest. It may also be more aggressive in interest capitalization policy.

The *CICA Handbook* provides for interest capitalization but does not contain detailed guidelines to implement the policy. Variety in practice is thus expected. (In the United States, on the other hand, there are excruciatingly detailed rules establishing procedures to be followed.) Section 3850 of the *CICA Handbook* requires disclosure of interest capitalized, allowing financial statement users to determine the effect of capitalized interest on earnings and assets.

FAIR MARKET VALUE CAP The actual cost of a self-constructed asset does not necessarily equal fair market value at the point of acquisition, as is also the case for natural resources and intangible assets. Using the higher market value would result in recording a gain on construction. A company cannot record a gain as the result of expenditures! The lower construction cost is ultimately reflected in higher net income through lower depreciation expense in future years.

Consistent with the valuation of other assets, the maximum valuation allowed by GAAP for self-constructed assets is fair market value. If total capitalized cost exceeds the market value of a similar asset of equal capacity and quality, the excess is recognized as a loss. Failure to do so carries forward cost elements that have no future benefit and causes overstated depreciation in future years.

To illustrate the accounting for a self-constructed asset, assume that Kelvin Corporation completes a project with total construction costs as follows:

Material	$200,000
Labour	500,000
Incremental overhead	60,000
Applied general overhead	40,000
Capitalized interest	100,000
Total	$900,000

Kelvin has recorded costs in the equipment under construction account. If the asset's market value at completion equals or exceeds $900,000, the summary entry is:

Equipment	900,000	
Equipment under construction		900,000

If the asset's market value is only $880,000, the entry is

Equipment	880,000	
Loss on construction of equipment	20,000	
Equipment under construction		900,000

It is important to watch capitalization very carefully—many firms, with a desire to maximize earnings or assets by deferring costs, seize on self-construction as an opportunity to try to defer lots of interesting things! Others wish to capitalize as little as possible. Remember, though, that the higher asset value generated is a base for future depreciation.

Asset Retirement Obligations

Some companies may have a legal requirement to incur costs when an asset (or group of assets) is retired. For example,

- Mining companies often are required by law to restore land to its original condition.
- Land fills must be covered, capped (e.g., with concrete), and perhaps landscaped when they are full.
- Companies that use rooftops for billboard advertising or for relay antennas usually are required by contract to repair physically remove billboards or antennas at the end of the contract, and to repair the roofs as well.

These legal requirements are known as *asset retirement obligations*:

> An *asset retirement obligation* is a legal obligation associated with the retirement of a tangible long-lived asset that an entity is required to settle as a result of an existing or enacted law, statute, ordinance, or written or oral contract....
>
> (*CICA* 3110.03(a))

A legal obligation may arise even though no asset has been recorded on the books (*CICA* 3110.A17). For example, if the asset is being used by means of an operating lease, the asset will not be capitalized, but the retirement obligation will be recognized.

Asset retirement obligations are recognized *only* when there is a legal commitment. Companies often will incur costs to remove or retire major physical assets. Machinery has to be disassembled and removed, buildings have to be demolished, etc. These costs sometimes are called *negative salvage values*; instead of receiving a residual value when an asset is retired, the company must incur a cost. But unless there is a legal obligation, future costs are not recognized until they are incurred at retirement.

INITIAL RECOGNITION When a legal retirement obligation exists, the cost of fulfilling that obligation must be recognized when the asset is acquired. The process is as follows:

- Estimate the amount at which the liability could be settled in a *current* transaction;
- Discount the cash flow at the company's *credit-adjusted* risk-free interest rate;
- Credit a liability account for the present value of the estimated liability; and
- Offset the liability by increasing the acquisition cost of the asset by the amount of the liability.

For example, suppose that on 2 January 20X0 Firkin Limited purchased equipment for $500,000 to install in a leased building. The company is required by the building lease to remove the equipment at the end of 10 years. The estimated *current* cost of removal is $70,000.

To recognize the liability, the $70,000 must be discounted at Firkin's credit-adjusted risk-free interest rate. Suppose that the risk-free rate is 3.5%, and that Firkin pays a premium of 1.5% above the risk-free rate. The future obligation must be discounted at 5.0% for 10 years:

$$P = \$70,000 \times (P/F, 5\%, 10) = \$70,000 \times 0.61391 = \$42,974$$

The asset purchase and the retirement obligation are recorded as follows:

Equipment	500,000	
Account payable (to equipment vendor)		500,000
[To record the purchase of equipment]		
Equipment	42,974	
Asset retirement obligation		42,974
[To record the legal obligation to remove the equipment in the future]		

The asset's beginning book value will be $542,974.

SUBSEQUENT AMORTIZATION AND ACCRUAL Once the asset and the retirement obligation have been recorded, the combined book value must be amortized. If we assume that Firkin uses straight-line amortization with zero residual value, the initial book value will be amortized at $54,297 per year. The amortization is recorded exactly the same way as any other amortization expense. For 20X0, the entry will be

Amortization expense—equipment	54,297	
Accumulated amortization—equipment		54,297

In addition to amortization expense, interest expense must also be recorded. The retirement obligation was recorded at its *present value.* By the end of 10 years, the obligation must be $70,000 on Firkin's books, not $42,974. Therefore, Firkin must accrue interest each year in order to build up the total obligation to $70,000. Interest is accrued by using the same interest rate as was used in the initial measurement, which was 5% in our example. For 20X0, the accrual will be

Interest expense [$42,974 × 5%]	2,149	
Asset retirement obligation		2,149

At the end of 20X0, the book value of the obligation will be $42,974 + $2,149 = $45,123. For 20X1, the interest accrual will be $45,123 × 5% = $2,256. Each year's accrual is based on the accumulated obligation at the end of the preceding year.

REMEASUREMENT In addition to amortizing the cost and accruing interest on the obligation, Firkin must also adjust the amount of the obligation if there is a change in the amount or timing of the expected retirement obligation cash flows. In Firkin's case, the timing could change if the lease term is extended. As well, the estimate of the future amount could change quite easily. The amount of the future obligation is based on the current cost of satisfying that obligation at each measurement date (i.e., each fiscal year-end). The current cost is quite likely to change from year to year as legislation changes, technology changes, and cost components change due to increasing or decreasing prices.

Suppose that at the end of 20X1, Firkin decides that the cost of fulfilling the retirement obligation has gone up to $80,000, but that the timing has not changed (that is, the asset still must be retired at the end of 20X9). The increase of $10,000 must be recognized, again by using the company's current credit-adjusted risk-free borrowing rate. At the beginning of 20X2, the risk-free rate has gone down to 2.5% but Firkin still pays 1.5% above the risk-free rate. The discount rate for the *additional* obligation is 4.0%. The increment to the retirement obligation is

$10,000 × (P/F, 4%, 8) = $10,000 × 0.73069 = $7,307

The additional obligation will be recorded as follows:

Equipment	7,307	
Asset retirement obligation		7,307

At the end of 20X1, Firkin's balance sheet will show the following amount for the obligation:

Initial recognition, 2 January 20X0	$42,974
Interest accrual, 31 December 20X0	2,149
Interest accrual, 31 December 20X1	2,256
Balance of original estimated obligation	47,379
Additional obligation estimate, 31 December 20X1	7,307
Balance, 31 December 20X1	$54,686

Notice that the interest is computed first, and then any increase (or decrease) in the expected future retirement cost is recognized:

> An entity should measure and incorporate changes due to the passage to time [that is, interest] into the carrying amount of the liability before measuring changes resulting from a revision to either the timing or the amount of estimated cash flows.
>
> (*CICA* 3110.16)

On 31 December 20X2, the revised amount in the asset account will be amortized over the remaining eight years before retirement. The amortization for 20X2 will be

($542,974 ÷ 10) + ($7,307 ÷ 8) = $55,210 (rounded)

Amortization expense—equipment	55,210	
Accumulated amortization—equipment		55,210

The 20X2 interest accrual on the retirement obligation will have two layers: (1) the original estimate, accrued at 5%, and (2) the additional amount from the 20X1 remeasurement, accrued at 4%. The interest on each remeasurement obligation must be accrued at the same rate used to calculate that specific present value. The interest accrual on 31 December 20X2 will be

Interest on the initial 2 January 20X0 estimate:	
$47,379 x 5%	$2,369
Interest on the 31 December 20X1 remeasurement:	
$7,307 x 4%	292
Total interest accrual for 20X2	$2,661

Exhibit 9-2 shows the derivation of the balances in both the asset account and the liability account through 31 December 20X2.

OTHER ASPECTS In the above example, the remeasurement resulted in an increase in the liabilities. Increases are discounted at the company's then-existing credit-adjusted risk-free borrowing rate. If the remeasurement results in a *decrease* in the liability, the decrease is accounted for by using the interest rate that was used earlier for determining the present value of the obligation—the historical rate. Otherwise, increases and decreases are accounted for similarly.

In our example, we assumed that Firkin could estimate the cost of fulfilling the obligation with some precision. However, Section 3110 requires the use of *expected values* for the predicted cash flows, rather than the *most likely* cash flow. For example, if there is a 70% probability (using *current* settlement costs) that the cost will be $90,000 and a 30% probability that the cost will be $60,000, the expected value (EV) to be discounted will be $81,000:

EV = ($90,000 × 70%) + ($60,000 × 30%) = $63,000 + $18,000 = $81,000

EXHIBIT 9-2

ASSET RETIREMENT OBLIGATION

Asset account:	
Acquisition cost, 2 January 20X0	$ 500,000
Present value of expected asset retirement cost	42,974
Balance, 2 January 20X0	542,974
Amortization for 20X0 ($542,974 ÷ 10)	(54,297)
Balance, 31 December 20X0	488,677
Amortization for 20X1 ($542,974 ÷ 10)	(54,297)
Increase in expected asset retirement cost	7,307
Balance, 31 December 20X1	441,687
Amortization of initial cost ($542,974 ÷ 10)	(54,297)
Amortization of 20X1 increase in asset retirement cost ($7,307 ÷ 8)	(913)
Balance, 31 December 20X2	$ 386,477
Liability account:	
Present value of expected asset retirement cost, 2 January 20X0	$ 42,974
Interest at 5% ($42,974 × 5%)	2,149
Balance, 31 December 20X0	45,123
Interest at 5% ($45,123 × 5%)	2,256
Balance before cost increase	47,379
Present value of increase in expected asset retirement cost, 31 December 20X1	7,307
Balance, 31 December 20X1	54,686
Interest on initial estimate ($47,379 × 5%)	2,369
Interest on 20X1 increase ($7,307 × 4%)	292
Balance, 31 December 20X2	$ 57,347

Sometimes, there will not be adequate information to assess the probabilities or the future cash flows at the time the asset is acquired. In that case, no accrual is made until "the period in which sufficient information exists to estimate a range of potential settlement dates" and the related cash flows (*CICA* 3110.A18). The *CICA Handbook* asserts that

> Uncertainties about the amount and timing of future cash flows can usually be accommodated by using the expected cash flow technique and therefore will not prevent the determination of a reasonable estimate of fair value. (*CICA* 3110.A24)

This is a very broad statement. It remains to be seen whether it is a valid assertion. The statement appears to confuse *risk* with *uncertainty*. Expected values are based on risk assessment—the quantification of measurable risk. Risk is the knowable probability distribution for a set of outcomes. For example, we can know with certainty the probabilities of the various possible winning and losing outcomes when we buy a lottery ticket, even though we have no foreknowledge of whether or not we will actually win something in the lottery. Uncertainty, in contrast, means that we just don't know what the outcomes will be. Probabilities attached to uncertainties are just guesses.

Section 3110 was the result of an FASB effort that began as a project on decommissioning nuclear power plants. Appendix A to Section 3110 contains several references to nuclear power plants, even though decommissioning of a nuclear power plant is a very rare event in Canada. The FASB's highly limited focus eventually was expanded to cover all legal obligations relating to asset retirements. The AcSB followed the FASB's lead. In Canada, resource industries are most likely to be affected, due to legislative requirements on site reclamation and restoration.

CONCEPT REVIEW

1. Why is it necessary to allocate the overall cost of a basket purchase of assets to the individual assets in the basket?
2. What amount would be recorded for a capital asset purchased for common shares, if the asset does not have a ready market value?
3. Under what circumstances can a company capitalize interest cost?
4. When must a company record the present value of the costs of future asset retirement? How is the present value calculated?

DEFERRED CHARGES AND INTANGIBLE ASSETS

Deferred Charges and Prepaid Expenses

Deferred charges are costs that are deferred for more than one year. The distinction between deferred charges and prepaid expenses is quite simple. Prepaid expenses are current assets, while deferred charges are long-term assets. As we discussed early in this chapter, deferred charges are long-term deferred costs that do not fall into the other categories of tangible capital assets, intangible capital assets, or goodwill. Deferred charges will be recognized as expenses in future periods.

In following sections, we will look at accounting for a few of the more common types of deferred charges.

Specific Intangible Assets

Specific intangibles are recognized when they result from contractual or other legal rights. Patents and trademarks are examples. Specific intangibles are also recognized when the asset exists, and is capable of being separated or divided from the rest of a business operation. Customer lists are an example.

Intangible assets are similar to tangible capital assets in that their cost is capitalized, and they are later subject to systematic and rational amortization. Refer to Exhibit 9-1, and reread the capitalizable costs for specific intangibles such as copyrights, trademarks, franchise fees, and the like.

Specific intangibles can be quite significant. For example, the 2003 financial statements for Shaw Communications Incorporated show an intangible asset of $4.6 billion for "broadcast licenses." This one intangible asset is 61% of Shaw's total assets of $7.6 billion. Shaw does not amortize the broadcast licenses because they are assumed to have an indefinite life. We will discuss amortization in the next chapter.

Like tangible capital assets, intangibles can be acquired either by developing them internally or by purchasing them. For self-developed intangibles, legal fees can be a major component of cost. It can be a long and expensive process to register and protect some of these intangibles. It's interesting to note that legal fees for successful defence of these assets are to be capitalized. These lawsuits clearly establish property rights over the intangible asset. Conversely, unsuccessful lawsuits result in expense recognition and usually mean that any remaining balance in the intangible asset account must be written off. The asset isn't worth anything if it can't be defended!

Organization Costs

Organization costs are expenditures incurred in organizing a business. Costs directly related to the organizing activities, such as expenditures for legal, accounting, promotional, and clerical activities, are capitalizable as organization costs. The rationale for capitalizing organization costs is that they benefit future years' operations. To expense the total amount in the first year of operation would result in a mismatching of expense with revenue.

Because the life of a business is usually indefinite, the length of the period receiving the benefits of these costs usually is indeterminate. No amortization is required for an intangible asset with an indefinite life, although annual impairment tests are required.

Share Issue Costs

Expenditures associated with issuing capital stock are called **share issuance costs**. Such costs include printing share certificates and related items, professional fees, commissions paid for selling shares, and the costs of filing with securities commissions. Share issuance costs, as opposed to organizational costs, are often accounted for as an offset to the issuance price of the shares to which they relate, or as a reduction to retained earnings. Sometimes, though, they appear as an intangible asset, although they aren't used in production or operations and are technically a deferred charge. Fortunately, they're rarely material in amount.

Pre-Operating Costs

What would you recommend in this scenario?

Samatron Corporation has been in business for 15 years, and manufactures automobile subassemblies for one of the Big Six auto manufacturers. In June of the current year, Samatron's Board of Directors approved the development of a new division, selling a product unrelated to automobile parts. The new product will be an underwater mobile device capable of deep-water recognizance and salvage activities. It cost $2.1 million to develop a working prototype of the product. Between October and December, the end of the fiscal year, Samatron spent an additional $1.4 million in connection with the new venture. Manufacturing equipment was rented, employees were hired and relocated to Kitchener, Ontario, where the production facility is located. Money was spent on promotional activities, marketing plans, administrative salaries, and a wide range of other activities. By the end of December, the division was, in management's view, still six months away from commercial production. The $2.1 million spent to develop the prototype is classified as development and expensed. But, how should Samatron account for the $1.4 million of other expenditures to date?

If you agree with the premise that the operation is viable, then there will be future cash flows when the operation goes into commercial production; cash flows that will recoup the pre-operating period expenditures. Clearly, there must be reasonable grounds to assume that this is the most likely scenario, or the Board of Directors would never have approved the project in the first place.

On the other hand, new businesses are risky things. There is no precedent for the operation, and no guarantee that there will be future profitable operations. If the company defers the expenditures as assets, then it, in some respects, implies a guarantee about the success of future operations. Is this appropriate?

CRITERIA FOR DEFERRAL The CICA's Emerging Issues Committee considered appropriate accounting policy in this area, and suggested that an *established company* can defer (and amortize) expenditures in the pre-operating period to the extent that

- The expenditure is related directly to placing the new business into service;
- The expenditure is incremental in nature (i.e., a cost that would not have been incurred in the absence of the new business); and
- It is probable that the expenditure is recoverable from the future operation of the new business. (*EIC* 27)

Notice especially the last criterion: the asset (deferred pre-operating costs) *must be related to future economic benefits (cash flow in the operating period)*. This is the definitional approach; matching is not invoked as a criterion. However, deferral of these expenditures, to be later amortized when revenue is reported on the income statement, will achieve matching.

EVIDENCE OF RECOVERABLE EXPENDITURE What kind of evidence would establish whether the expenditure is recoverable from the future operation of the business? This is obviously the critical issue; in the absence of appropriate evidence, these expenditures must be expensed. At a minimum, one would expect market research and detailed cash flow projections; some orders would be nice, too. In the end, it's always a judgement call.

The EIC opinion applies only to established businesses with a record of profitability; this stable base and successful history is clearly important in establishing a track record. The EIC suggests that the duration of the pre-operating period should be finite, ending when the operation is ready to commence commercial production. Any incidental revenue recognized in the pre-operating period is netted with (deferred) expenditures. Once in commercial operation, the pre-operating expenditures should be amortized; the EIC indicated that this amortization period should not normally exceed five years, although it did not explain the rationale for this arbitrary cut-off. Choice of amortization pattern is left to the discretion of management.

EIC recommendations are non-binding even for public companies. Therefore, the capitalization of pre-operating costs and start-up costs is a common practice, especially among firms that are attempting to maximize their reported net income. The rationale is usually one of matching, rather than one of asset definition.

Research and Development Costs

Broadly defined, research and development (R&D) includes the activities undertaken by firms to create new products and processes, or to improve old ones, and to discover new knowledge that may be of value in the future. For many firms, R&D is a very important part of ongoing activities and can be a large and significant expenditure. These expenditures are undertaken because the R&D effort is expected to more than pay for itself in the future by providing the firm with competitive, profitable products and processes.

Once upon a time, the reporting and accounting for R&D costs varied greatly. Different firms included the costs of different activities in R&D. R&D costs were sometimes capitalized as intangible assets, and amortized over time. At other times they were expensed immediately.

Due to these variations in accounting for R&D costs, financial statements were not comparable among firms, and firms could potentially manipulate income by expensing or capitalizing R&D costs as needed to obtain the desired amount of income. *CICA Handbook* Section 3450 was issued by the AcSB to provide guidance both in defining research and development costs and in recommending how to report R&D costs.

To distinguish between costs to be included in R&D and similar costs to be excluded from R&D, Section 3450 defines both research and development:

> *Research* is planned investigation undertaken with the hope of gaining new scientific or technical knowledge and understanding. Such investigation may or may not be directed toward a specific practical aim or application.
>
> *Development* is the translation of research findings or other knowledge into a plan or design for new or substantially improved materials, devices, products, processes, systems, or services prior to the commencement of commercial productions or use. (*CICA* 3450.02)

CICA Handbook Section 3450 provides many examples of costs that should be (1) included in research, (2) included in development, or (3) excluded from both research and development. The classification matters because the accounting treatment is different for research costs and development costs.

R&D ACCOUNTING REQUIREMENTS *CICA Handbook* Section 3450 recommends that all research costs should be charged to expense when incurred.

In contrast, development costs should be capitalized and amortized if *all* of the following criteria are met:

(a) the product or process is clearly defined and the costs attributable thereto can be identified,

(b) the technical feasibility of the product or process has been established,

(c) the management of the enterprise has indicated its intention to produce and market, or use, the product or process,

(d) the future market for the product or process is clearly defined or, if it is to be used internally rather than sold, its usefulness to the enterprise has been established, and

(e) adequate resources exist, or are expected to be available, to complete the project.

(*CICA* 3450.21)

Development costs that do not meet all of these five criteria should be charged to expense.

These five criteria are often regarded as being clear and relatively unambiguous. But who makes the estimates that are involved?

a. The first criterion simply says that the costs relating to specific development projects can be separately identified—it is not sufficient just to arbitrarily allocate part of the research budget to a new product development and call it "development cost." Fair enough.

b. The second criterion says only that the product can be produced. This means that the cost of dead-end projects that are not technically feasible should not be capitalized. But technical feasibility is essentially assessed by *management.*

c. *Management* must decide whether it intends to market the product or process. There is no external validation or verification needed; it's a management call.

d. Who is to say that the future market for the product is clearly defined? Clearly, *management* does, although auditors may demand reasonable evidence.

e. If *management* is intending to go ahead with the development, and if management wishes to capitalize the costs, it most certainly will assert that there are or will be adequate resources to proceed.

These apparently iron-clad criteria are almost completely subject to management determination. If management wishes to capitalize identifiable development costs for products or processes that the company is undertaking, it will be a brave auditor who tries a challenge.

THE DEFINITIONAL APPROACH TO DEVELOPMENT Nevertheless, these criteria do represent an effort by the AcSB to recognize that some development efforts do have future benefit, and that they qualify as assets. Thus, this section of the *CICA Handbook* is an example of the *definitional* approach to expense recognition.

Research and development programs are undertaken by entities with a clear expectation of future profitable results. Their future benefits establish them as assets. Why do accounting standards recommend that all research and some development costs be expensed? Typically, research costs fail the recognition criteria of "probability." That is, one cannot be certain that future cash flows will accrue. Unfortunately, for some firms, the expensing of research costs means that an item that some consider the firm's most valuable asset is not shown at all on its balance sheet and that current period expenses are overstated.

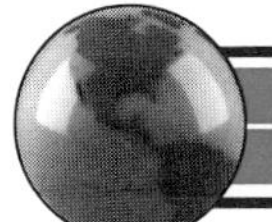

International Perspective

There is considerable variation in accounting for research and development costs around the world. In the United States, for example, all research and development costs must be expensed. There, FASB found no direct causal link between research and development spending and eventual benefits. That is, spending might result in new revenue streams, or it might not. Furthermore, FASB's research indicated that capitalization did not improve the ability of financial statement users to predict the future rate of return or its variability. Thus, there seemed no support for capitalization.

However, the refusal to capitalize research and development seems counter-intuitive. It's hard to understand why a company would fund R&D programs if no value were being created!

The IASB includes development costs in IAS 38, *Intangible Assets.* The recommendations in IAS 38 relating to development costs are quite consistent with the Canadian approach. IAS 38 allows capitalization and amortization as long as the product or process is technically and commercially feasible and management intends to market the product or process.

Country by country around the world, there is a great deal of diversity in standards. Reading the disclosure notes is critical!

Computer Software Costs

One type of research and development cost that has become increasingly important is that of computer software development. Accounting issues concerning the costs of developing computer software arise in two different contexts:

1. Many companies develop computer software systems for their internal use, either by developing the software with their own staff or by contracting with an outside developer.
2. Other companies develop software as a product, to be sold to outsiders.

There is no specific Canadian accounting standard that applies to computer software costs, and companies in these two contexts tend to approach the issue in somewhat different ways.

SOFTWARE DEVELOPED FOR INTERNAL USE The first category of companies, those that develop software for their own use, generally apply the AcSB's development deferral criteria as outlined in the previous section. The guidelines are applicable because they quite specifically refer to *internal use* of the product or process being developed. Bear in mind that we are not talking about small software programs that can be stored on a floppy disk and be easily pirated; instead, we are referring to large-scale systems and program development that is the life blood of many modern corporations.

Think, for example, of the massive systems financial institutions must use (and of the extensive security precautions that must be built in) or of the many interrelated systems that an airline must use to keep its planes in the air and to get its customers into their seats. Banks routinely talk about annual development costs in billions of dollars.

Companies that develop large-scale systems normally will capitalize their software development costs and amortize them over three to five years. The accounting policy is the same whether the software is developed internally or under contract from a consultant or specialist.

When software is developed internally, two questions arise about which costs to capitalize:

1. Should all costs be capitalized, from the very beginning of the project, or should early feasibility and systems development studies be expensed?
2. Should only direct costs be capitalized, or should indirect and overhead costs also be capitalized?

A lot of different measures of cost could be used and there is significant variation in practice. The costs must be written down if the software is no longer used.

SOFTWARE DEVELOPED AS A PRODUCT Companies that develop software as a product may have a somewhat different approach. Software product development, like most other types of product development activities, has an initial period of feasibility testing to determine whether a proposed product is technically and financially feasible. Costs incurred during this period are viewed as research costs rather than as development costs and are written off. Only costs incurred after a working model exists are considered development and deferred. A market must exist to ensure these deferred costs are recoverable.

In the Canadian software industry, this approach is often used by public companies that wish to report on a basis that is consistent with their U.S. competitors, with whom they also are competing for capital. FASB issued a special standard regarding computer software costs in this industry.[2] As usual, the FASB standard is very detailed, but the essence is that the costs are accounted for in two phases:

1. All costs incurred to establish the technological feasibility of a computer software product are treated as research and are expensed as incurred.
2. Once the technological feasibility of the software product is established, subsequent costs incurred to obtain product masters are capitalized as an intangible asset.

---

[2] *SFAS No. 86*, "Accounting for the Costs of Computer Software to be Sold, Leased, or Otherwise Marketed," FASB, Stanford, Conn., August 1985.

The FASB standard is widely adopted by Canadian software companies in theory. However, a scan of software companies' annual reports on www.sedar.com shows that very few companies are actually capitalizing software development costs, even when they are selling functioning software products. The following accounting policy statement from the 2003 annual report of Absolute Software Corporation is typical:

> (e) Research and development costs:
> Research costs are charged to expense in the year in which they are incurred. Development costs are deferred if they meet specific criteria, otherwise they are expensed as incurred. At June 30, 2003 and 2002 no development costs have been deferred.

Remember that there is a lot of judgement involved in deciding whether the capitalization criteria have been met. Financial reporting objectives play a big role in the selection *and application* of accounting policies. The financial analyst community has tended to look unfavourably on software companies that capitalize a lot of their development costs. Therefore, to please the investment community, software companies tend to be conservative when applying capitalization policies.

Website Development Costs

Another type of software development cost is the sometimes material amount that companies spend to create websites. The companies may be traditional enterprises with more traditional marketing channels, or they may base their business model on electronic transactions or a blend of both strategies. That is, websites may be used to promote or advertise products or services, replace traditional products or services, and/or sell things.

How should the costs of website development be accounted for? EIC 118 deals with this issue. The approach is to break down website development costs into five areas, presented below along with the EIC conclusion:

1. Cost incurred in the planning stage—*Expense as incurred.*
2. Costs incurred for website application and infrastructure—*Capitalize and amortize.*
3. Costs incurred to develop graphics—*Capitalize and amortize.*
4. Costs incurred to develop content—*No conclusion.* There are a lot of case-specific factors involved in this area, and generalizations are not possible.
5. Operating costs—*Expense as incurred.*

So, what's the overall theme? If amounts are very early in the process, (planning) then there is nothing tangible to pin the asset flag on, and the costs must be expensed. After that, the question is always whether there is a long-term benefit from the expenditure. Future benefits support asset treatment, otherwise, the expense category wins.

Exploration and Development Costs

Exploration and development (ED) costs are the costs that oil and gas companies and mining companies incur in exploring and developing their resource properties. *Exploration* is the process of seeking mineral deposits, while *development* is the process of turning a found deposit into a productive mine site or oil field. Much exploration is fruitless; that is the nature of the business. Most development does work out, since development is not undertaken unless there is reasonable assurance of generating enough revenue from the site to recover the development costs. It can take years to develop a mine site or an oil field. How should the costs of exploration and development be accounted for?

full cost method
all costs associated with the exploration for and development of a natural resource, whether successful or not, are capitalized to the natural resources account on the balance sheet, to be subsequently amortized

ACCOUNTING FOR ED COSTS The accounting for exploration and development costs varies widely but there are two major approaches. These approaches are

1. the **full cost method**, in which ED costs for the company's entire sphere of operations are accumulated as a deferred charge and amortized on the basis of global production; or

successful efforts method
the costs associated with successful exploration and development activities of a natural resource are capitalized to a balance sheet natural resource account to be subsequently amortized; the costs of unsuccessful exploration activities are expensed

2. the **successful efforts method**, in which the ED costs are accumulated by site. If a site has been determined to be unproductive, ED costs are expensed. The ED costs of successful sites are segregated as a deferred charge and amortized usually by geographic region.

In the *full cost method*, the assumption is that unsuccessful efforts are a part of doing business; not every attempt to find mineral deposits or oil and gas reserves will be successful. Unless it is extraordinarily lucky, a resource company not will hit "pay dirt" every time it tries to find natural resources.

Under the *successful efforts method*, unsuccessful efforts are written off *once they are determined to be unsuccessful.* The costs are initially capitalized, since the effort may last more than one reporting period, but the accumulated costs relating to that site are charged to the income statement when management gives up the effort. Note that this is a management decision; timing of that decision will determine which accounting period's earnings bear the cost.

The successful efforts method requires management to segregate its ED costs by geographic area. There is a great deal of flexibility in this regard. One company may decide to segregate its successful sites on the basis of geological formation, while another may choose to use national boundaries as the definition of area. Some may view the United States and Canada as a single area, while others may view Oklahoma as one area, Alberta as another, and the Atlantic Provinces' offshore fields as yet another. Management choice is at the core of the successful efforts method.

The choice of accounting policy does not change the cash flow patterns of the company. The monies are spent when they are spent, usually upfront. The question is, will they be *expensed* upfront, with low subsequent amortization (successful efforts) or will they be *deferred*, with higher subsequent amortization (full cost). Allocation methods are inherently arbitrary; there are good arguments that support both full cost and successful efforts.

There are no accounting standards in North America on this topic, and companies have free choice between the two. Since the choice of policy will make a big difference to income patterns, there is clearly an urgent need to check the disclosure notes.

In practice, large integrated companies use successful efforts. Large companies engage in a more or less constant search for new assets, and there is no undue strain on profitability as a result of immediately expensing this regular cost. Obviously, expensing is also the least complicated accounting method.

Junior resource companies typically have only one site under exploration, or a small number of sites. They do not engage in perpetual, worldwide exploration. Junior resource companies in Canada tend to use the full cost method. They have no revenue when their one site is under development, and expensing would result in a huge deficit in retained earnings, perhaps increasing the anxiety of investors and the cost of capital. Capitalization looks pretty good under these circumstances.

Take a look at Exhibit 9-3 for disclosure notes that describe the two policies. Bonavista Petroleum Limited uses full cost, and Petro-Canada uses successful efforts.

CAPITALIZATION AND AMORTIZATION Capitalized ED costs consist of two components: (1) structures and (2) other costs. Structures (that is, buildings and equipment) are tangible capital assets that are depreciated once production begins. The other costs are an intangible capital asset that is subject to *depletion*, which is the name traditionally given to amortization of natural resources.

Depletion is usually calculated on a unit-of-production basis, using the estimated reserves as the denominator in the per-unit calculation. The *estimated reserves* are the quantity of minerals or oil and gas that the geologists and engineers estimate can be profitably extracted and processed. The rate of depletion is adjusted for major changes in estimated reserves during a period.

Notice that there are a lot of estimates in the depletion calculation, perhaps even more than are present in amortization calculations. The degree of estimation is even more pronounced because the depletion should, according to a CICA accounting guideline, include "estimated future costs to be incurred in developing proved undeveloped reserves."[3] In other

[3] "Full Cost Accounting in the Oil and Gas Industry," CICA Accounting Guideline (October 1990), para. 34.

EXHIBIT 9-3

BONAVISTA PETROLEUM LIMITED
EXAMPLES OF ACCOUNTING POLICY DISCLOSURE FOR ED COSTS

For the year ended 31 December 2003

(b) Oil and natural gas operations
The Company follows the full cost method of accounting, whereby all costs associated with the exploration for and development of oil and natural gas reserves are capitalized in cost centres on a country-by-country basis. Such costs include land acquisitions, drilling, well equipment, and geological and geophysical activities. General and administrative costs are not capitalized. Gains or losses are not recognized upon disposition of oil and natural gas properties unless crediting the proceeds against accumulated costs would result in a change in the rate of depletion of 20 percent or more.

PETRO-CANADA

For the year ended 31 December 2003

Property, plant and equipment
Investments in exploration and development activities are accounted for on the successful efforts method. Under this method the acquisition cost of unproven acreage is capitalized. Costs of exploratory wells are initially capitalized pending determination of proven reserves and costs of wells which are assigned proven reserves remain capitalized while costs of unsuccessful wells are charged to earnings. All other exploration costs are charged to earnings as incurred.

words, the depletion (for oil and gas companies) should be based not only on the costs incurred to date, but also on the *future* costs that will be incurred for further development of the field. This is done so that later production will not be burdened by higher amortization than early production.

One hazard of capitalizing ED costs is that the total capitalized amount may exceed the net post-production value of the resources being mined. ED costs are *sunk costs*, of course, and therefore the fact that ED costs have exceeded the value of the resource does not necessarily mean that development should cease. Whether or not development continues depends on the relationship between *future* costs and *future* revenue.

If amortization of past costs (i.e., depletion) plus the costs of extracting the resource from the ground would result in an accounting loss, then the capitalized costs are in excess of their *future benefit* (which is part of the definition of an asset) and should be written down. This process is called the ceiling test. Of course, the projected future benefits and future costs consist of a vast array of estimates and assumptions, including the future price of the resource on the open market, and therefore the test is a rather subjective one.

Costs for Enterprises in the Development Stage

In the Pre-Operating Costs section, earlier in this chapter, we gave an example of an existing company starting a new product line. As we saw, certain costs could be deferred if future revenues were assured. What happens if the whole company is just starting up? There will be operating expenses but no revenue, perhaps for years. What accounting principles are appropriate in this case?

In March 2000, the AcSB issued Accounting Guideline 11 (not a *CICA Handbook* standard) entitled "Enterprises in the Development Stage." This Guideline covers enterprises whose primary efforts are devoted to establishing a new business. Principal operations have not yet commenced. That is, major activities are perhaps raising capital; exploring for natural resources; acquiring property, plant or equipment; developing markets; starting up production; and so on.

TYPES OF COSTS INCURRED The Guideline states that accounting treatment is dictated by the kind of cost incurred, not the degree of maturity of the enterprise. Thus, capital assets are capitalized and amortized in a rational and systematic manner. Research and development costs are accounted for in accordance with the appropriate rules (that is, research is expensed and development may be deferred if the criteria are met). Resource exploration costs are accounted for using either successful efforts or full cost method.

Many of the activities of an enterprise in the development stage, not surprisingly, would be classed as development; appropriate judgement of the deferral criteria is very important. Especially contentious is the estimate of future markets, since future cash flow from revenue is necessary to justify asset creation. A development-stage company has no track record to provide credibility for estimates, so judgement calls are often difficult. Another consideration is the going-concern concept, as historic cost is not useful if the enterprise won't survive. In the development stage, one of the most important questions in this regard is whether adequate cash exists to tide the enterprise over until revenue begins.

As always, when assets are created, they must be regularly evaluated for potential impairment. If capitalization has been too aggressive, and future revenue will not recoup all deferred costs, then assets must be written down. Undiscounted net revenue (that is, net of expenses) is used as the ceiling, or maximum, value. For development stage companies, the issue is particularly problematic as estimates of uncertain future revenue can swing significantly.

The Guideline calls for extensive disclosure of the nature of the enterprise's principal operations and plans, including cumulative expenditures to date in all major areas. Disclosure about projects underway, including full description, costs, and any contractual rights and obligations, is particularly relevant to financial statement users.

THE END OF THE DEVELOPMENT STAGE An enterprise is considered to be past the development stage and into normal operations when significant revenue has been earned, significant funding is directed toward operations rather than start-up activities, and employees' attention shifts to operating activities. Sometimes, there is a pre-determined "line in the sand"—either a specific date, or a specific level of sales, that signals the end of the development stage. No enterprise can stay in the development stage forever.

As with any guideline, the provisions are not binding, but provide input to the accounting policy decisions that must be made. This area is very judgemental, with high risk, and perhaps high return, for investors and creditors.

Other Deferred Charges

Deferred charges can include a variety of other items in addition to the few that we have discussed above. Examples include

- Debt financing costs, such as bond issue costs and upfront payments to obtain long-term financing (covered in Chapter 12);
- Future income tax assets (Chapters 15 and 16);
- Advance payments on operating leases (Chapter 17); and
- Deferred pension costs (Chapter 18).

None of these items can be considered to be intangible assets, despite the *CICA Handbook's* broad definition of intangible assets (i.e., any asset that lacks physical substance). They really are the result of interperiod allocations of costs such as long-term financing, income taxes, leases, and pensions. If a cost is incurred before the expense recognition criteria are met, then the cost must be deferred as either a current prepaid or as a long-term deferred charge.

EXHIBIT 9-4

MAGNA INTERNATIONAL INCORPORATED
"OTHER ASSETS" DISCLOSURE

15. OTHER ASSETS

Other assets consist of:	2003	2002
Long-term receivables	$ 48	$ 101
Preproduction costs related to long-term supply agreements with contractual guarantee for reimbursement	175	136
Restricted cash	45	—
Other	66	33
	$334	$270

Reporting Requirements for Deferred Charges

CICA Handbook Section 3470 deals with deferred charges. This is a very short section. The reporting requirements are quite simple:

- Long-term deferred charges should not be classified as current assets (*CICA* 3070.01);
- Major items should be shown separately (*CICA* 3070.02);
- When amortization has been deducted, this fact should be disclosed (CICA 3070.03); and
- The amount of amortization should be disclosed, with separate disclosure of amortization of deferred development costs (*CICA* 3070.04).

On the balance sheet, deferred charges may be shown as a separate classification. More commonly, deferred charges are lumped into the miscellaneous "other assets" category. Exhibit 9-4 shows the other assets note for Magna International Incorporated, a major producer of automobile parts. The only deferred charge is preproduction cost relating to long-term supply contracts. The other two items in *other assets* are both financial assets (plus the ubiquitous "other").

Cash Flow Reporting of Capitalized Costs

An interesting wrinkle to the issue of capitalizing instead of expensing certain costs is the impact that the capitalization policy has on the reporting of cash flows. In Chapter 5, we pointed out that the cash flow statement is the only one of the primary financial statements that has an AcSB-mandated format. The cash flow statement must include three sections (1) operating activities, (2) investing activities, and (3) financing activities.

It is obvious that the accounting policy decision to capitalize or expense a cost will not affect actual cash flows. The cost has been incurred and either has been or will be paid in cash. The accounting policy choice is only of whether to put the cost on the balance sheet (as an asset) or on the income statement (as an expense). Consider these differences in *cash flow reporting*, however:

- Costs that are accounted for as expenses are included in the cash flow from *operations.*
- Costs that are capitalized as assets are included in the *investing activities* section of the cash flow statement.
- Amortization on capitalized assets is deducted in determining net income but is removed from cash flow from operations either by adding it back in the indirect approach, or leaving it out in the direct approach.

For example, assume that Lorimer Limited spends $100,000 on development costs during 20X2, and that net income before deducting the development costs is $300,000. If the development costs are capitalized, they will be amortized straight line over the five years *following* their incurrence (that is, from 20X3 through 20X7).

If Lorimer's management decides to expense the development costs (that is, decides that not all of the criteria in *CICA Handbook* Section 3450 have been met), the net income for 20X2 is $200,000, and that amount is shown in the cash flow statement as the cash flow from operations (ignoring the many other adjustments that may be made to net income to convert it to cash flow).

If the 20X2 costs are capitalized and amortized, however, an interesting thing occurs. Because the costs are not charged as an expense, that $100,000 is shown as an investing activity outflow rather than being included in operations. Cash flow from operations therefore is reported as $300,000. In 20X3, $20,000 of the development costs (i.e., one-fifth) are amortized and are charged against net income. In the operations section, however, amortization is added back to net income, and therefore the effect of the amortization is removed. The result is that *if costs are capitalized, they will never affect reported cash flow from operations.*

A company that follows a policy of capitalizing as many expenses as possible will, over time, show a consistently higher cash flow from operations than one that expenses those costs. While this may not fool a sophisticated user of the financial statements, management may choose to follow the capitalize-and-amortize approach consistently in an attempt to improve cash flow per share calculations (made by some analysts) or to increase the company's apparent operating cash flow used to evaluate some debt covenants.

CONCEPT REVIEW

1. What is the difference between research and development?
2. In general, when is it appropriate to capitalize development costs?
3. What is the difference between deferred charges and intangible assets?
4. Explain the two general methods for accounting for exploration and development costs.

DISPOSALS OF CAPITAL ASSETS

The disposal of capital assets may be *voluntary*, as a result of a sale, exchange, or abandonment, or *involuntary*, as a result of a *casualty* such as a fire, storm, or by government action, such as expropriation.

If the asset to be disposed of is subject to depreciation, it is depreciated up to the date of disposal in order to update the recorded book value. Applicable property taxes, insurance premium costs, and similar costs are also accrued up to the date of disposal. At the date of disposal, the original cost of the asset and its related accumulated depreciation are removed from the accounts.

The difference between the book value of a capital asset and the amount received on disposal is recorded as a *gain or loss*. Ideally, the gain or loss is segregated from ordinary income and reported in the income statement as part of income from continuing operations. Occasionally, the gain or loss is an extraordinary item, and thus is shown separately on the income statement, net of tax, after income from continuing operations.

involuntary conversions (disposition)

conversion (loss or sale) of an asset that takes place unintentionally; for example, as the result of a casualty or government action

Extraordinary item treatment is applied when a company loses a major asset or group of assets through a natural disaster, or is forced to dispose of an asset by outside authority (such as by a government or a court order). Disposals that are not the choice of the company are called **involuntary conversions.**

To illustrate the disposal of a capital asset, assume that on 1 February 20X1, Brown Company paid $32,000 for office equipment with an estimated service life of five years and an estimated residual value of $2,000. Brown uses straight-line depreciation and sells the asset on 1 July 20X5, for $8,000. The entries for Brown, a calendar-year company, at date of disposal are as follows:

Depreciation expense	3,000*	
Accumulated depreciation—equipment		3,000

* ($32,000 − $2,000) × (1/5) × (6/12)

Cash	8,000	
Accumulated depreciation—equipment	26,500**	
Equipment		32,000
Gain from disposal of equipment		2,500

** ($32,000 − $2,000) × (53 months used) ÷ (60 months total useful life)

However, the economic value of Brown Company is unaffected by the disposal. Brown received an asset worth $8,000 (cash) for an asset worth $8,000. Why is a gain recognized? Brown depreciated the equipment faster than it declined in value. The book value ($5,500) is less than market value ($8,000) at date of disposal. If depreciation reflected market value changes, there would be no gain or loss from disposal. *The accounting gain in this example is a correction for excessive depreciation charges recognized before disposal.* In effect, the gain records a change in estimate.

If the asset is destroyed in an accident, and was insured, then the entry will mirror the one recorded above. That is, the insurance proceeds will produce a certain amount of cash, and the difference between cash and net book value will determine the gain or loss.

This approach is also used when an asset is abandoned or destroyed without insurance, when there are no proceeds. The loss recognized equals the book value of the asset at disposal. For the Brown Company example, the loss recognized would be $5,500.

The costs of dismantling, removing, and disposing of plant assets are treated as reductions of any proceeds obtained from disposal. Therefore, the resulting gain is reduced, or the resulting loss is increased by these costs. If Brown Company incurs $500 in disposal costs, the net cash debit is $8,000 − $500, or $7,500, reducing the gain to $2,000 in the original example.

When the decision to sell or abandon plant assets is made near the end of a fiscal year, an estimated loss from disposal is recognized in that year if the loss is estimable according to Section 3290, "Contingencies." Gains are not recognized before disposal, however.

CONCEPT REVIEW

1. What is an involuntary conversion?
2. Why would a company dispose of a capital asset at a loss? Is the company necessarily in a worse position economically after doing so?
3. How would you interpret the gain on the disposal of a capital asset?

EXCHANGES OF NON-MONETARY ASSETS

Capital assets are often exchanged for other non-monetary assets. Remember that monetary assets are those whose value is fixed in terms of dollars, like cash and receivables. Non-monetary assets, such as inventory and capital assets, *do not have a value fixed in terms of dollars.* Valuation of the acquired asset is the substantive issue in non-monetary asset exchanges. This valuation determines whether a gain or loss is recognized. Non-monetary transactions are

> … exchanges of non-monetary assets, liabilities or services for other non-monetary assets, liabilities or services with little or no monetary consideration involved.
> (*CICA* ED3830.06)[3]

Valuation Alternatives

When a capital asset is given in exchange for another asset, how should the transaction be valued? There are two general approaches to valuation of a non-monetary exchange transaction:

- Measure the transaction at the fair value of either the asset given up or the asset being received, *whichever is more reliably measurable* (*CICA* ED3830.06); or
- Record the acquired asset at the carrying value of the asset given up (*CICA* ED3830.07).

Consider the following example of an exchange:

	Co. 1	Co. 2
Asset original cost	$76,400	$91,600
Asset accumulated depreciation	58,000	61,900
Net book value of asset	$18,400	$29,700
Fair value of asset	$40,000	$45,000
Cash to change hands: $5,000, paid by Co. 1 to Co. 2		

Here are the two alternative ways to record the transaction on Company 1's books:

At Fair Value			At Book Value		
New asset	45,000		New asset**	23,400	
Accumulated depreciation, old	58,000		Accumulated depreciation, old	58,000	
Gain on exchange*		21,600	Cash		5,000
Cash		5,000	Old asset		76,400
Old asset		76,400			

* $40,000 − $18,400
** $5,000 + $18,400

Both entries record the disposal of the old asset, removing original cost and accumulated depreciation from the books. Both record the $5,000 cash paid. But they differ significantly in the valuation of the new asset and recognition of a gain or loss. Under fair value treatment, the new asset is recorded at its $45,000 fair value, and a gain is recorded as the difference between the $18,400 book value of the old asset and the $40,000 fair value of the old asset. Under the book value alternative, the new asset is recorded at a deflated value—the book value of the old asset, $18,400, plus $5,000 cash paid. Quite a difference!

Which alternative could be used? The answer depends on the answers to sequential questions:

1. Does the transaction have *commercial substance*? If it does, then
2. Can the fair value of *either* the asset given up or the asset received be measured reliably?

[3] In March 2004, the AcSB issued an exposure draft (ED) on *Non-Monetary Transactions*. The ED is a substantial revision of *CICA Handbook* Section 3830. The intent is to harmonize Canadian standards with the U.S. and international standards. Paragraph references in this book are based on the ED; individual paragraph numbers may be slightly different in the final standard.

We can most easily approach the first question by posing a situation in which commercial substance does *not* exist. In our example just above, valuing the exchange at fair value enables Company 1 to recognize a substantial gain, even though the assets exchanged have similar fair values. Indeed, the two assets may be substantially similar and may perform the same function. By trading assets, the two companies can create a gain or loss that has little economic substance. In such a situation, accounting standards require that the acquired asset be recorded at the carrying value of the asset being given up.

COMMERCIAL SUBSTANCE To see what commercial substance is, we must turn to the *CICA Handbook*. Essentially, commercial substance exists if there is a significant change in the company's cash flows after the exchange. A transaction has **commercial substance** when

- The configuration (that is, the risk, timing, or amount) of the cash flows of the asset received differs significantly from the configuration of the cash flows of the asset given up; or
- The present value of the after-tax cash flow of the entity's operation is changed significantly as a result of the exchange.

Significance is measured relative to the fair value of the assets exchanged, not to the overall operations of the company. "The determination of significance requires the application of professional judgement."[4]

When similar assets are exchanged, there will not be a significant change in cash flows or present value—commercial substance does not exist. When commercial substance does not exist, the carrying value method must be used.

DETERMINING FAIR VALUE If the exchange does cause a significant change in cash flows or present value, then the second question becomes relevant. To record the transaction at fair value, we must be able to measure a fair value.

Generally, the cost of an asset is measured by the consideration given, whether payment is in cash or in other assets. In the case of a non-monetary exchange, however, Section 3830 specifies that the more reliable fair value be used, regardless of whether it is the asset being given up or the asset being received. Two arm's-length companies would not trade assets unless the fair value of each was similar. Therefore, we should use the more reliable measurement. Consider the following cases:

	Case 1	Case 2	Case 3
Fair value of (old) asset given up	$16,000	$100,000	$73,000
Fair value of (new) asset received	50,000	?	?
Cash paid	34,000	4,000	—
Cash received	—	—	50,000

In Case 1, the values are considered to be verifiable and the new asset may be recorded at its fair value, $50,000. In Case 2, the fair value of the new asset is unknown and its fair value must be implied by the value of the old asset, $100,000. However, the company also had to pay $4,000 to get the new asset, so the new one must have been worth $104,000. In Case 3, the fair value of the new asset is again unknown. The old asset was worth $73,000, but the company received $50,000 in the exchange. Therefore, the new asset must have been worth $23,000. To generalize, the fair value of the new asset is

1. Its appraised fair value, if reliably known, or, if not,
2. The fair value of the asset given up less cash received, or plus cash paid.

In all instances, the fair value of the new asset must be based on the more reliable estimate.

[4] CICA Accounting Standards Board, *Background Information and Basis for Conclusions-Non-Monetary Transactions*, paragraph 14.

SOURCES OF FAIR VALUES Where do fair value quotations come from? Sometimes they are quoted cash prices from suppliers of new and used assets. When a quoted cash price is unavailable, a company can invite bids for the asset to be exchanged. The highest bid for the asset in question is used as the market value. However, this approach is not always appreciated by the companies that invest time and energy submitting quotes, only to discover that the asset wasn't really to be sold! A less reliable but commonly used alternative is published information on the average price of specific used assets, such as the *Kelley Blue Book Auto Market Report* for automobiles. Appraisal is another commonly used approach, but appraisals are notoriously subjective. List prices are often unreliable, as they do not represent the lowest cash price the vendor will accept.

In the absence of a reasonably determinable market value for *either* asset, the valuation of the acquired asset is based on the book value of the asset transferred, adjusted for any cash paid or received.

Examples of Non-Monetary Asset Exchanges

The following information for Regina Corporation is used in the examples that follow:

Asset Transferred	Crane
Original cost	$90,000
Accumulated depreciation, updated to date of exchange	$60,000

1. **Transaction has commercial substance**

   a. *Fair values are determinable; no cash payment.* Assume that the crane has a fair value of $47,000 and is exchanged for a truck whose value is not more clearly measurable; no cash is paid or received. The book value of the crane is $30,000; therefore, a $17,000 gain is recognized. The entry is

Equipment—truck	47,000	
Accumulated depreciation—crane	60,000	
Equipment—crane		90,000
Gain on capital asset disposal		17,000

   b. *Fair values are determinable; with cash payment.* Assume that the crane's fair value is not easily determinable, but that the truck has a fair value of $33,000. In addition, Regina receives $12,000 cash. The acquired truck is recorded at its fair value. The entry is

Equipment—truck	33,000	
Cash	12,000	
Accumulated depreciation—crane	60,000	
Equipment—crane		90,000
Gain on capital asset disposal		15,000

   c. *Fair values are not determinable; no cash payment.* Assume that neither fair value is reliably measurable. The acquired truck is recorded at the book or carrying value of the crane. There can be no gain or loss recognized on the transaction:

Equipment—truck	30,000	
Accumulated depreciation—crane	60,000	
Equipment—crane		90,000

2. Transaction does not have commercial substance

a. *Fair values are determinable; no cash payment.* Assume that the crane has a fair value of $47,000 and is exchanged for another crane whose fair value is not more reliably measurable. There is no cash payment. Because the transaction does not significantly affect Regina's cash flows, the acquired crane is recorded at the book value of the crane being given up. There can be no gain or loss recognized on the transaction:

Equipment—crane 2	30,000	
Accumulated depreciation—crane 1	60,000	
Equipment—crane 1		90,000

b. Fair values are determinable; with cash payment. Assume that the old crane's fair value is not easily determinable, but that the new crane has a fair value of $33,000. In addition, Regina receives $12,000 cash. Since there is no commercial substance to the transaction, the acquired crane is recorded at the old crane's book value minus the cash received. The entry is

Equipment—crane 2	18,000	
Cash	12,000	
Accumulated depreciation—crane 1	60,000	
Equipment—crane 1		90,000

Whenever cash is involved in a transaction without commercial substance, the new asset always is recorded at the book value of the old asset, *plus any cash received or minus any cash paid* (*CICA ED* 3830.07). Fair values are irrelevant. No gain or loss may be recognized.

POST-ACQUISITION EXPENDITURES

After acquisition, many costs related to capital assets are incurred. Examples include repairs, maintenance, betterments, and replacements.

Expenditures that increase service potential are capitalized. Such expenditures are called capital expenditures. Service potential is enhanced when the useful life of the asset is extended, operating costs are decreased, or quality or quantity of output is increased. A capitalized post-acquisition expenditure is depreciated over the number of periods benefited, which can be less than the remaining useful life of the original asset.

The service potential of assets and their estimated useful life at acquisition assume a certain minimum level of maintenance and repair. Costs for maintenance are expensed in the period incurred. Some companies expense all post-acquisition expenditures less than a certain dollar amount (for example, $1,000). This policy is acceptable because the amounts are not material.

Expenditures that result from accident, neglect, intentional abuse, or theft are recognized as losses. For example, if a computer workstation is damaged during installation, the repair cost is recognized as a loss. After repair, the asset is no more valuable than it was before the mishap. Outlays made to restore uninsured assets damaged through *casualty*, or accident, are also recorded as losses. They do not enhance the utility of the asset beyond the value before the casualty. Such losses may or may not be extraordinary.

Significant post-acquisition expenditures fall into four major categories:

1. maintenance and ordinary repairs
2. betterments
3. additions
4. rearrangements and other adjustments

Maintenance and Ordinary Repairs

Maintenance expenditures include lubrication, cleaning, adjustment, and painting, incurred on a continuous basis to keep plant assets in usable condition. Ordinary repair costs include outlays for parts, labour, and related supplies that are necessary to keep assets in operating condition but neither add materially to the use of assets nor prolong their useful life significantly. Ordinary repairs usually involve relatively small expenditures. *Most expenditures made on capital assets are repairs, and expensing is the norm.* Keep this in mind as a rule of thumb—capitalization may look too tempting at times!

Many firms accrue repairs each month, and charge actual repairs to the accrued repair liability account, in order to report smooth monthly expenses. This seems to make some sense, especially in a business where regular repairs and maintenance are all done in a regular slack season. At the end of the year, any remaining balance in the liability account is reversed, so that repair expense represents the amount actually spent during the year.

Betterments

A betterment is the cost incurred to enhance the service potential of a capital asset. It often involves the replacement of a major component of a capital asset with a significantly improved component. Examples include the replacement of an old shingle roof with a modern fireproof tile roof, installation of a more powerful engine in a ship, and significant improvement of the electrical system in a building.

But, as the name implies, the result should be *better* than the old—not just more attractive, but *better* from an asset sense. That is, the asset should be able to deliver enhanced cash flows to the firm, either through more revenue (higher quality or quantity of output, more service hours per day, or a longer life) or through reduced operating costs. Then, the betterment has status as an asset and capitalization is warranted. Otherwise, the expenditure is a repair. Repairs are the norm, betterments are the exception.

Betterments may be replacements or renewals. A *replacement* is the substitution of a major component of a plant asset with one of comparable quality. *Renewals* involve large expenditures, are not recurring in nature, and usually increase the utility or the service life of the asset beyond the original estimate. Major overhauls of equipment and strengthening of a building foundation are examples.

Two different approaches have evolved to account for these expenditures: substitution and an increase to the asset account.

1. *Substitution* This approach removes the cost of the old component and related accumulated depreciation, recognizes a loss equal to the remaining book value, and increases the original asset account in the amount of the expenditure. To illustrate, assume that a shingle roof with an original cost of $20,000 and now 80% depreciated is replaced by a fireproof tile roof costing $60,000. The two entries to record the betterment are as follows:

To remove old component accounts		
Accumulated depreciation (old roof, $20,000 × 80%)	16,000	
Loss on asset improvement	4,000	
Building (old roof)		20,000
To record cost of new component		
Building (new roof)	60,000	
Cash		60,000

This approach works well in theory. The only problem is that, by the time the building needs a new roof, the portion of the cost of the building that relates to the old roof is virtually impossible to figure out.

2. *Increase Asset Account* This approach is used when the costs and depreciation amounts of the old component are not known and when the primary effect is to increase efficiency rather than the economic life of the basic asset. The cost of the betterment is simply debited to the original asset account. It may also be used when economic life is lengthened, if substitution is not practical.

   One result of this treatment is an overstatement of the basic asset's book value and subsequent depreciation, although this value is usually relatively minor at time of replacement. For example, simply capitalizing the new roof in the previous example means that the building would have two roofs in its capital cost. The net effect is only to *overstate* net book value by $4,000 (the net book value of the old roof).

Sometimes, replacements are required by law to ensure public safety or to meet environmental standards. For example, many localities require removal of asbestos insulation for health reasons. Is asbestos removal and replacement capitalizable, or should it be expensed? A case can be made either way. The useful life of the building is likely to remain unchanged as will the overall productivity of the building. On the other hand, employee safety is increased, and the firm has less exposure to health-related lawsuits.

Additions

Additions are extensions, enlargements, or expansions of an existing asset. An extra wing or room added to a building is an example. Additions represent capital expenditures and are recorded in the capital asset accounts at cost. Related work on the existing structure, such as shoring up the foundation for the addition or cutting an entranceway through an existing wall, is a part of the cost of the addition and is capitalized. If the addition is an integral part of the older asset, its cost (less any estimated residual value) is normally depreciated over the shorter of its own service life or the remaining life of the original asset. If the addition is not an integral part, it is depreciated over its own useful life.

Rearrangements and Other Adjustments

The costs of reinstallation, rerouting, or rearrangements of factory machinery to increase efficiency are capital expenditures if the benefits of the rearrangement are tangible cash flows that extend beyond the current accounting period. Such costs are capitalized as a deferred charge, or a specific plant asset, and amortized over the periods benefiting from the rearrangement.

CAPITAL ASSETS ON THE CASH FLOW STATEMENT

Investments in capital assets are shown as *investing activities* on the cash flow statement, provided that the acquisition is for cash. If a capital asset is acquired in a non-cash transaction, the investment will be reported in the notes to the financial statements, but it would not be reported as part of the cash flow statement because no cash was involved. If cash was only part of the consideration to acquire a capital asset, then only the cash portion will be shown.

For self-constructed or self-developed capital assets (e.g., buildings or product development costs), expenditures that otherwise would have been reflected in the operating cash flow end up being shown instead as investing activities. When companies aggressively capitalize expenditures as capital assets, they increase their *reported* cash flow from operations. The actual cash flow doesn't change, of course, but the classification of capitalized expenditures as investing activities changes the *apparent* cash flow from operating activities. Financial statement readers should be careful about comparing operating cash flow across companies. However, there is no way that the financial statement reader can know, for example, how much overhead has been capitalized as part of capital assets. A company's accounting policy disclosure may state that capitalized costs include some portion of overhead, but the amount is never disclosed.

Gains and Losses

Gains and losses on the sale of capital assets are non-cash items, from the viewpoint of operating activities. These are excluded from cash flow operations either through their omission (direct presentation) or adjustment (indirect presentation). When an asset is sold for cash, what appears on the cash flow statement is the amount of the proceeds (i.e., the cash actually received) for the asset. The proceeds are shown in the investing activities section as a cash *inflow*.

If a capital asset is disposed of through a non-cash transaction or exchange, the transaction will not appear on the cash flow statement.

CONCEPT REVIEW

1. If an asset is acquired in an exchange transaction, how do we determine the amount at which the asset is recorded in the books?
2. When should expenditures made on a capital asset after its acquisition be capitalized instead of expensed?
3. What is the difference between maintenance and betterment? What accounting treatment is given to expenditures for each?
4. Suppose that a company is very aggressive at capitalizing expenditures related to intangible assets. How will the capitalization of large amounts of expenditures affect the cash flow statement, compared to a company that expenses many of the same types of expenditures?

GOODWILL

Goodwill is a common intangible asset. It represents the value associated with favourable characteristics of a firm that result in earnings in excess of those expected from identifiable assets of the firm. Goodwill is *internally generated*, but is recorded only when *purchased*, along with identifiable tangible and intangible assets that constitute an operating unit. Goodwill typically cannot be separated from those identifiable assets. In the absence of an arm's-length transaction, it is difficult to measure the value of goodwill that a firm creates as it engages in business activities.

Essentially, goodwill represents the expected value of future above-normal financial performance, which is the enhancement of assets or cash flow required of the asset definition. The expectation of enhanced performance arises because intangible, favourable characteristics or factors make it likely that the firm will produce higher than average earnings from its tangible assets. A few examples of such factors are

- A superior management team;
- An outstanding sales organization;
- Especially effective advertising;
- Exceptionally good labour relations;
- An unusually good reputation in the industry for total quality; or
- A highly advantageous strategic location.

For accounting purposes, **goodwill** is the difference between the actual purchase price of an acquired firm or operation and the estimated fair market value of the identifiable net assets acquired. That is, goodwill is "the excess of the cost of an acquired enterprise over the net of the amounts assigned to assets acquired and liabilities assumed" (*CICA* 3062.05).

MEASURING GOODWILL The value of goodwill is computed only indirectly in an acquisition of a business unit. The total cost of the purchase is the value of whatever the purchaser gives up to acquire the business unit. The cost is measured as the cash payment plus the fair value of shares or assets given to the seller. Once the cost is determined, that cost must be allocated. Earlier in this chapter, we explained that the cost of a lump-sum purchase of assets is allocated on the basis of the *fair values of the net assets acquired*. The same principle holds when we buy an ongoing business unit.

To measure goodwill, we first need to estimate the fair values of each tangible and identifiable intangible asset, as well as the fair value of the liabilities that we acquired along with the assets. The fair value of the *net* assets acquired is the total fair value of the assets minus the total fair values of the liabilities:

Fair value of tangible and identifiable intangible assets − Fair value of liabilities = Fair value of the net assets acquired

We then compare the total fair value of the net assets to the total cost of the purchase. The difference is *goodwill*:

Purchase price − Fair value of the net assets acquired = Goodwill

In essence, goodwill is simply the amount of the purchase cost that is left over after the buying company allocates the cost to the fair values of all the identifiable assets and liabilities. Goodwill is the purchase cost residual that cannot otherwise be assigned to specific assets or liabilities.

EXAMPLE Assume that Hotel Company is considering the acquisition of the net assets of Cafe Corporation. Hotel Company obtains financial statements and other financial data on Cafe and estimates the fair value of Cafe's identifiable assets at $530,000 and the fair value of the liabilities at $400,000. (See Exhibit 9-5.)

EXHIBIT 9-5

CAFE CORPORATION
BALANCE SHEET
BOOK VALUE AND FAIR VALUE

As of 31 December 20X4	Book Value	Fair Value
Assets		
Cash	$ 30,000	$ 30,000
Receivables	90,000	85,000
Inventory	60,000	60,000
Other current assets	33,000	30,000
Plant and equipment (net)	220,000	235,000
Other assets	85,000	90,000
Total assets	$518,000	$530,000
Liabilities		
Short-term notes payable	$ 85,000	$ 85,000
Accounts payable	45,000	45,000
Other current liabilities	30,000	30,000
Long-term debt	250,000	240,000
Total liabilities	410,000	400,000
Shareholders' equity	108,000	
Total liabilities and equities	$518,000	
Net assets at fair market value		$130,000

The fair value column in Exhibit 9-5 shows that several assets have an estimated fair value different from their book value as reported in the published historic cost financial statements.

The total fair value of Cafe's identifiable net assets is determined to be $130,000 ($530,000 total assets less liabilities of $400,000). Assume that Hotel negotiates a purchase price with the owners to acquire Cafe as of 31 December 20X4, for $202,000. Goodwill inherent in this price is $72,000, that is, the purchase price of $202,000, less current market value of the identifiable net assets of $130,000. The entry Hotel Company makes to reflect the acquisition of Cafe's operations, at their *fair values*, is as follows:

Cash	30,000	
Receivables	85,000	
Inventory	60,000	
Other current assets	30,000	
Plant and equipment	235,000	
Other assets	90,000	
Goodwill	72,000	
Short-term notes payable		85,000
Accounts payable		45,000
Other current liabilities		30,000
Long-term debt		240,000
Cash		202,000

Recording this $72,000 goodwill asset implicitly means that Hotel was willing to pay for anticipated superior earnings/cash flow from Cafe's operations. These superior results could be caused by a superior location, reputation for service or quality, and so on.

Do you *know* that goodwill is present, just because Hotel paid more than the fair value of the net assets? After all, Hotel may have been outbargained by the old owners of Cafe. The $72,000 could be the result of an inflated price. Just because the price is arm's length doesn't mean it can't be stupid. Accountants, however, don't account for stupidity (think of the arguments with clients!) and always make the comfortable assumption that goodwill explains excess purchase price. But beware—the assets acquired are supposed to provide a return consistent with the existence of goodwill, or the goodwill does not, in substance, exist.

In the 1990s, many companies purchased Internet-based developing enterprises (the so-called "dot-com" companies) at prices that turned out to be exorbitant. There were very few identifiable assets in the acquired businesses, and therefore almost all of the purchase price was accounted for as goodwill. When the stock market for dot-coms collapsed, any prospect of future earnings collapsed as well. Goodwill is supposed to indicate superior future earnings ability. If it becomes apparent that superior earnings ability doesn't really exist, the goodwill does not meet the definition of an asset, and its carrying value must be written down. The moral of this story is that goodwill must be regularly reviewed with reference to profit performance to make sure continued recognition of goodwill is appropriate. We'll discuss this issue again in Chapter 10.

Negative Goodwill

When the fair market value of the identifiable net assets acquired is greater than the purchase price, the acquiring firm has made what is sometimes called a bargain purchase. The amount of goodwill (the difference between the purchase price and fair value of assets acquired) is negative, that is, **negative goodwill** has been created. Even though it would seem that the seller could benefit from selling the assets individually rather than selling the firm as a whole, such situations do occasionally occur. For example, the seller may be in financial difficulty and have an immediate cash need. Alternatively, the seller may not have the time or resources to take on the risks of selling the assets separately.

negative goodwill

in a purchase of a business unit, when the purchase price is less than fair value of acquired net assets.

Any negative goodwill should be allocated to reduce the values assigned to *identifiable non-monetary assets* to the extent that the negative amount is eliminated.

Assume now that Hotel Company purchases Cafe Corp. for $91,500, which is $38,500 less than the fair value of the net assets acquired. The negative goodwill of $38,500 must be allocated *proportionally* to reduce the recorded values for plant, equipment, inventory, and most other non-monetary assets (*CICA* 1581.50). In the rather unlikely case that negative goodwill is larger than identifiable non-monetary assets, the non-monetary assets would be reduced to zero and the excess recorded as an extraordinary item (*CICA* 1581.50).

Form of Acquisition

In the previous example, one company bought the net assets of another company, and goodwill was directly recorded on the purchaser's books. In many acquisition transactions, the acquiring company buys the shares of the target company, which is then left to operate as before, only with new shareholders.

At *reporting dates*, the two sets of financial statements are combined, or *consolidated*, to produce a report of the economic activity of the combined entity. In consolidation, the assets of the target company are recorded at fair value at the date of acquisition, and the goodwill inherent in the purchase price is recorded. The nature of goodwill is identical, but the form of the transaction is different. We'll take a brief look at consolidation in Chapter 11.

PRESENTATION AND DISCLOSURE

The AcSB recommends disclosure of the cost of each major category of property, plant, and equipment and specific intangible assets, and the related accumulated amortization (*CICA* 3061.54 and 3062.51). Goodwill is presented as a separate line item on the balance sheet (*CICA* 3062.48).

Segregation by major asset category is important, as the various categories of capital assets are associated with different levels of business risk and may have dissimilar useful lives and amortization policies. Typically, capital assets are shown as one net amount on the balance sheet, or perhaps two net amounts, one for tangible assets and one for intangibles. The required detailed breakdown is usually shown in the notes.

For example, the 2003 balance sheet of Mediagrif Interactive Technologies Incorporated shows four separate amounts for capital assets—i.e., tangible, intangible assets, goodwill, and deferred charges ("other assets"). The amounts for 31 March 2003 are

Capital assets	$ 6,900,383
Intangible assets	44,653,710
Goodwill	3,456,490
Other assets	1,107,349

The notes reveal that the fourth category, other assets, includes "Deferred start-up and organizational costs." Exhibit 9-6 contains excerpts from Mediagrif's accounting policy note. Exhibit 9-7 shows most of the detail that is disclosed in other notes relating to capital assets. There are several things to observe in these disclosures:

1. In both intangible assets and goodwill, the company refers to "impairment." Public companies are now required to conduct an annual impairment test for these types of assets. We will discuss impairment tests in the next chapter.
2. The company discloses amortization amounts (in Exhibit 9-7) for *both* tangible and intangible capital assets. Many companies, however, do not show amortization amounts for intangible assets, even though such disclosure is recommended by the *CICA Handbook.*
3. The company classifies "software" as a tangible capital asset rather than as an intangible asset. This is rather unusual—most people would consider software to be intangible, in the same way that a brand name or trademark is intangible. However, the classification doesn't really matter; the company could have put both tangible and intangible assets into the same "capital assets" classification.

EXHIBIT 9-6

MEDIAGRIF INTERACTIVE TECHNOLOGIES INCORPORATED
ACCOUNTING POLICIES FOR CAPITAL ASSETS

Capital assets

Capital assets are recorded at cost less accumulated amortization. Amortization is provided for based on the estimated useful lives of the related assets using the following methods and periods or annual rates:

	Method	Period/rate
Office furniture	Declining balance	20%
Computer and other equipment	Straight-line	3 years
Software	Straight-line	3 years
Leasehold improvements	Straight-line	5 years

Intangible assets

Intangible assets, which consist of exclusive contracts, customer base, acquired technology and brand name, are recorded at cost less accumulated amortization. Intangible assets are amortized on a straight-line basis over the estimated useful lives of the related assets, which do not exceed five years. The Company evaluates the carrying value of intangible assets in each reporting period to determine if there has been an impairment in value that would result in an inability to recover the carrying amount. Such evaluation is based on estimated discounted future cash flows. When it is determined that the carrying value of an asset exceeds the recoverable amount, the asset is written down to the net recoverable amount with a charge to earnings in the period that such a determination is made.

Goodwill

Effective April 1, 2002, goodwill is not amortized but instead the Company assesses periodically whether a provision for impairment in the value of goodwill should be recorded to earnings. This is accomplished mainly by determining whether projected discounted future cash flows exceed the net book value of goodwill of the respective business units. Goodwill is tested for impairment annually on March 31, or when an event or circumstance occurs that could potentially result in a permanent decline in value.

Until the implementation of the new recommendation on April 1, 2002, as described in note 2(a), goodwill previously recorded was amortized on a straight-line basis over periods not exceeding three years. However, goodwill arising from business combinations initiated on or after July 1, 2001 is not amortized in accordance with the transitional provisions of the new recommendation of the CICA dealing with goodwill and other intangible assets.

Other assets

Deferred start-up and organizational costs are amortized on a straight-line basis over their estimated useful lives of three years commencing once commercial operations have begun. These costs, which relate to the launch of electronic networks and consist mainly of consulting fees, salaries, and technology support costs, are deferred when it is probable that they will be recovered from future operations. When the expected recovery through future revenues less related costs is less than the unamortized balance of such costs, the excess is charged to earnings in the period.

4. Intangible assets includes a "brand name." It is important to understand that this most likely is a purchased brand name. A company cannot impute a value to its own brand name and capitalize that value. Also, the company specifically lists "acquired technology," which tells us that this amount does not represent capitalized costs for technology that the company developed itself.

EXHIBIT 9-7

MEDIAGRIF INTERACTIVE TECHNOLOGIES INCORPORATED
NOTE DISCLOSURES FOR CAPITAL ASSETS

(all amounts for 31 March 2003)

7. CAPITAL ASSETS

a) Capital assets comprise the following:

	Cost	Accumulated Amortization	Net
Office furniture	$ 771,195	$ 316,448	$ 454,747
Computer and other equipment	6,627,714	4,764,720	1,862,994
Software	6,441,635	2,513,982	3,927,653
Leasehold improvements	1,104,448	449,459	654,989
	$ 14,944,992	$ 8,044,609	$ 6,900,383

b) Computer and other equipment include assets under capital lease with a cost and accumulated amortization of $1,104,312.

c) Amortization of capital assets amounts to $3,867,297 for the year ended 31 March 2003.

8. INTANGIBLE ASSETS

Intangible assets comprise:

Exclusive contracts, net of accumulated amortization of $969,441	$ 3,696,751
Customer base, net of accumulated amortization of $85,208	616,346
Existing technology, net of accumulated amortization of $68,724	269,871
Brand name, net of accumulated amortization of $30,661	100,742
	$ 4,653,710

9 (b) OTHER ASSETS

Deferred start-up and organizational costs, net of accumulated amortization of $391,655	$ 179,872
Loans to employees	927,477
	$ 1,107,349

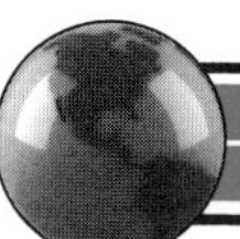

International Perspective

Accounting for acquisition costs of tangible capital assets is similar around the world. In general, accounting practice in all countries is to capitalize the initial cost of the asset and any expenses necessary to prepare it for use.

There is substantial variation in practice relating to intangible assets, however. The United States, Australia, and Germany (to name a few) prohibit the capitalization of any research and development costs, while Spain and Switzerland permit capitalization of all types of such costs. Capitalization of the cost of other self-generated intangibles, such as patents, is *forbidden* in Austria, France, Germany, Switzerland, and the United Kingdom; it is *required* in the United States and Japan; and it is *allowed* by the IASB. Exhibit 9-8 summarizes intangible asset practices in several countries. The guidelines to determine which costs are to be capitalized are also varied, even among those countries that allow or require the capitalization of internal costs for self-generated intangible assets.

Goodwill is also subject to widely varying practice. Recognition of purchased goodwill is usually permitted, but is *required* only in Argentina, Canada, Spain, Sweden, the United Kingdom, and the United States (although only in certain circumstances). It is also required by IASB standards. Recognition of self-generated goodwill is universally forbidden.

EXHIBIT 9-8

COMPARISON OF INTERNATIONAL PRACTICE CAPITALIZATION OF INTANGIBLE CAPITAL ASSETS

	Patents		Goodwill		Research & Development			Reorgani-
Country	**Acquired**	**Self-generated**	**Acquired**	**Self-generated**	**Basic research**	**Applied research**	**Develop-ment**	**zation costs**
Argentina	R	F	R	F	A	A	A	A
Australia	R	A	A	F	F	A	A	R
Austria	R	F	A	F	F	F	F	A
Belgium	R	A	A	F	F	A	A	A
Canada	**R**	**A**	**R**	**F**	**F**	**F**	**A**	**A**
Denmark	A	F	A	F	A	A	A	A
France	R	F	A	F	F	A	A	—
Germany	R	F	A	F	F	F	F	A
IASC	R	A	R	F	F	F	R	R
Japan	R	R	A	F	F	F	F	F
Netherlands	R	A	A	F	F	A	A	F
Spain	R	R	R	F	A	A	A	R
Sweden	R	A	R	F	F	A	A	A
Switzerland	R	F	A	F	A	A	A	A
U.K.	R	F	R	F	F	F	A	F
U.S.	R	R	R	F	F	F	F	F

Legend:
F = forbidden
A = allowed
R = required

Source: Adapted from *Transnational Accounting: A Reference Matrix* by Anne d'Arcy and Dieter Ordelheide (London: Palgrave Publishers Ltd., 2001).

SUMMARY OF KEY POINTS

1. Capital assets include tangible property, plant, and equipment. Specific identifiable intangible properties and goodwill are also discussed. All the assets contribute to future net cash flows of the entity by contributing to operating activities.

2. The cost and accumulated amortization of capital assets and identifiable intangibles must be disclosed by major category.

3. Capital assets are recorded at cost, including cost to install the asset and prepare it for use. Specific guidelines exist to aid in classification of expenditure for various asset cat-

egories including buildings, self-constructed assets, machinery and equipment, land, land improvements, resource exploration and development costs, patents, industrial copyrights, trademarks, software costs, website development costs, and other intangibles.

4. Cost less accumulated amortization equals net book value, which is not meant to reflect fair value after acquisition.
5. Assets acquired in a basket purchase should be valued using the proportional method, although the incremental method is used when information is not complete.
6. Capital assets purchased on credit are valued at the cash equivalent price, or at the present value of the debt issued. Assets acquired for share capital are valued at the fair value of the share capital issued, unless that value is less reliable than the fair value of the asset received. Donated assets are valued at fair value, and give rise to contributed capital.
7. When assets are sold or otherwise retired or disposed, the difference between proceeds, if any, and book value is the gain or loss on disposal. The gain or loss is, in substance, a correction of the recorded amortization over the period that the asset was used.
8. When non-monetary assets are exchanged, the transaction is valued at fair market value and a gain or loss on the exchange is recorded when there is commercial substance to the transaction. If there is no commercial substance, the new asset is recorded at the book value of the asset given in exchange.
9. Post-acquisition expenditures are typically repairs, which are expensed. If the expenditure results in enhanced cash flows for the asset, it is classified as a betterment and is capitalized and amortized over the asset's remaining useful life.
10. Pre-operating costs can be deferred, and later amortized, if certain criteria are met. The criteria include an assessment of whether it is probable that expenditures will be recovered from future profitable operations; the asset definition must be met through future cash flow.
11. All research and many development costs must be expensed as incurred.
12. If certain criteria are met, development costs can be deferred and amortized. Since the criteria are based on management estimates; substantial variation in practice can arise.
13. Resource companies may use either the full cost method or the successful efforts method of accounting for ED costs. The full cost method combines the costs of all exploration and development activities for purposes of amortization; the successful efforts method capitalizes the costs of successful wells and writes off the costs of exploration in unsuccessful wells. Costs are segregated by geographic region for amortization purposes.
14. Goodwill is recognized on the purchase of another business unit. It is measured as the excess of purchase price over the fair value of identifiable net assets acquired.
15. On the cash flow statement, cash expenditures to acquire capital assets are reported as investing activities. Capital assets acquired in a non-cash exchange are not included on the cash flow statement.

KEY TERMS

basket purchase, 469
capital assets, 464
capital expenditures, 466
commercial substance, 491
full cost method, 483
goodwill, 496
group purchase, 469
intangible capital assets, 464
involuntary conversions, 488
negative goodwill, 498
organization costs, 478
share issuance costs, 479
successful efforts method, 484

REVIEW PROBLEM

The following four episodes are independent.

1. *Plant asset cost classification.* Maldive Company completes the construction of a building. The following independent items are the costs and other aspects relevant to the purchase of the lot and construction:

Cash payments to contractor	$100,000
Total sales tax on materials used in construction in addition to payments made to contractor	3,000
Cost of land (building site)	50,000
Gross cost to demolish old building on land	20,000
Proceeds from old building salvage	5,000
Power bill for electricity used in construction	2,000
Interest on loans to finance construction	3,000

What is the final recorded cost (i.e., carrying value) for *each* of the land and building?

2. *Accounting for debt incurred on acquisition.* The Round Wheel Barn Company purchases a tractor by making a down payment of $10,000. In addition, Round Wheel Barn signs a note requiring monthly payments of $2,000, starting one month after purchase and continuing for a total of 20 months. The contract calls for no interest, yet the prevailing interest rate is 24% per annum on similar debts. What is the cost (and initial carrying value) of the asset? What is the interest expense that should be recognized for the month following purchase?

3. *Accounting for exchange of plant asset.* Ocular Company trades an electron microscope for new optical equipment (a similar asset) and receives $30,000 cash as well. The old microscope had an original cost of $200,000 and has accumulated depreciation of $80,000 at the time of the trade. The old microscope has a fair market value of $160,000 at trade-in time. What entry should be made to record the exchange?

4. *Post-acquisition costs.* After one-quarter of the useful life had expired on equipment with an original cost of $100,000 and no salvage value, a major component of the equipment is unexpectedly replaced. The old component was expected to last as long as the equipment itself. Company records indicate that the component originally cost $20,000 and had no expected salvage value. The replacement component cost $30,000 and has no usefulness beyond that of the equipment. What is the entry to record the replacement? Assume straight-line depreciation.

REVIEW PROBLEM—SOLUTION

1. Cost components of the land and building:

Land		**Building**	
Land cost	$50,000	Cash payments to contractor	$ 100,000
Demolition	20,000	Sales tax on materials	3,000
Salvage proceeds	(5,000)	Power bill	2,000
		Capitalized loan interest	3,000
Total land cost	$65,000	Total building cost	$ 108,000

2. The cost of the tractor is the present value of the monthly payment annuity:

$$P = \$10{,}000 + \$2{,}000(P/A, 2\%, 20) = \$42{,}703$$

Interest cost for the first month is the present value times the monthly interest rate:

$32,703 × 2% = $654

3. An exchange of similar assets implies that there is no commercial substance to the transaction. The new equipment is recorded at the book value of the old equipment, minus the cash received:

Equipment ($162,000 – $30,000)	90,000	
Accumulated depreciation	80,000	
Cash	30,000	
Equipment		200,000

4. The new component is a replacement of an old component, and such is a *substitution.* It is not a betterment, because it does not improve or extend the functioning of the asset. The entries to remove the old component and substitute the new are as follows:

Loss on asset replacement	15,000	
Accumulated depreciation ($20,000 ÷ 4)	5,000	
Equipment		20,000
Equipment	30,000	
Cash		30,000

APPENDIX

Government Assistance

Assets sometimes are acquired with monetary assistance from various levels of governments. This may be in the form of a cash grant. The terms of the grant may require the firm to maintain certain employment levels or pollution-control levels. If the conditions are not met, the firm may be required to refund the amounts received.

One common program is in the form of an investment tax credit, which reduces the amount of income tax otherwise payable based on a set percentage of eligible capital expenditures for a period. For example, assume that a company had a tax bill of $675,000. During the year, it spent $750,000 on new manufacturing machinery, which qualifies for a 10% investment tax credit. The company can reduce its tax bill by $75,000, to $600,000. Taxes payable go down, and are debited, for $75,000. What account is credited?

This question has been very controversial. There are three alternatives.

1. Capital could be credited.
2. Tax expense, or another current income statement account could be credited, reflecting cash flow and the impact on current taxes.
3. The capital asset could be credited, or a related deferred credit established. This would reduce the amount of future depreciation charged: that is, only depreciation on the *firm-financed* portion of the capital asset would be expensed over time. Thus, the income statement will reflect the benefit of the government assistance, but only over the useful life of the asset.

Through lobbying behaviour, some firms have demonstrated their clear preference for the second alternative, which has the happy effect of increasing current earnings. The first alternative is consistent with the treatment given to donated assets. However, the third alternative is very firmly entrenched in Canadian practice.

> Government assistance toward the acquisition of fixed assets should be either
>
> (a) Deducted from the related fixed assets with any depreciation calculated on the net amount; or

(**b**) Deferred and amortized to income on the same basis as the related depreciable fixed assets are depreciated. (*CICA* 3800.26)

This choice reflects a policy decision on the part of standard-setters to reflect capital assets subject to government assistance, and their related depreciation expense, at the amount that the shareholders have financed. Given that this policy is inconsistent with the choice for donated assets, it is perhaps just as well that donations are relatively rare, and often involve fine art donations, which do not depreciate.

Example To illustrate accounting for a government grant, assume that machinery costing $100,000 was eligible for assistance of 30%. The machinery has a 10-year life with no salvage value. Because both the *net method* and *deferral method* of accounting are acceptable, both sets of journal entries are provided.

	Net Method		Deferral Method	
Record purchase				
Machinery	100,000		100,000	
Cash		100,000		100,000
Record receipt of government assistance				
Cash*	30,000		30,000	
Machinery		30,000		—
Deferred government grant		—		30,000

* Cash is debited if government assistance is in the form of money. If assistance was investment tax credit, taxes payable would be debited.

	Net Method		Deferral Method	
Record straight-line depreciation expense at the end of years 1 to 10				
Depreciation expense	7,000		10,000	
Accumulated depreciation		7,000		10,000
Deferred government grant	—		3,000	
Depreciation expense		—		3,000

The effect on income is the same under either method. The difference is on the balance sheet where with the deferral method, the gross amount of the capital asset would appear. The credit may be a contra account to the asset, or shown on the opposite side of the balance sheet. Which method would you choose if you were trying to maximize assets to reassure creditors? Companies often prefer higher asset values.

This is another area where Canadian and U.S. accounting practices diverge. In the United States, practice allows government assistance received in the form of investment tax credits to be included in income in the year in which they arise—that is, alternative (2), above. U.S. standard-setters have tried to switch to alternative (3) a few times, but political action by firms, who obviously appreciate the potential to increase income by the use of this accounting policy, has prevented any change to accounting standards. We'll take another look at the investment tax credit in the Appendix to Chapter 15—stay tuned!

OTHER GOVERNMENT ASSISTANCE Before we leave government assistance, perhaps it's worth mentioning that government assistance can be obtained for a wide variety of purposes, not just capital asset acquisition. The purpose of the government assistance governs its accounting. For example, if the assistance is to offset current expenses, then accounting for government assistance must reflect that fact, and recognize government assistance on the income statement when the related expenses appear. If assistance is for future expenses, then assistance should be deferred and recognized when the expenses are recognized.

Finally, government assistance is sometimes in the form of **forgivable loans**. The loans are forgiven when certain conditions are met, such as maintenance of a stated level of employment or volume levels for specific periods of time. In these circumstances, management must assess the conditions that are attached to the "loan." If the conditions are deemed likely to be met, the "loan" is recorded as assistance, and the conditions and unforgiven balance are disclosed in the notes. Should management's expectations prove to be wrong and the loan becomes repayable in the future, this event should be accounted for in the period that conditions change. But the future is fraught with uncertainties. Therefore, forgivable loans are typically classified as loans payable until the conditions have been satisfied. The conditions are disclosed in the notes.

QUESTIONS

Q9-1 To determine the cost of a capital asset, how should the following items be treated: (a) invoice price, (b) freight, (c) discounts, (d) title verification costs, (e) installation costs, (f) testing costs, and (g) cost of a major overhaul before operational use?

Q9-2 A machine was purchased on the following terms: cash, $100,000, plus five annual payments of $5,000 each. How should the acquisition cost of the machine be determined? Explain.

Q9-3 When several capital assets are purchased for a single lump-sum consideration, cost apportionment is usually employed. Explain the alternatives. Why is apportionment necessary?

Q9-4 How is an asset's acquisition cost determined when the consideration given consists of equity securities?

Q9-5 Some businesses construct capital assets for their own use. What costs should be capitalized for these assets? Explain what policy to follow for (a) general company overhead, (b) costs of construction in excess of the purchase price of an equivalent asset from an outsider, and (c) interest on construction loans.

Q9-6 Does cost necessarily equal fair value on the date of acquisition for self-constructed assets, and intangibles? Explain.

Q9-7 What outlays are properly considered part of the cost of an intangible asset?

Q9-8 When are post-acquisition costs capitalized rather than expensed?

Q9-9 Explain two approaches used when recording a betterment. Which is preferable?

Q9-10 Under what circumstances must a company record a liability for future costs of retiring an asset? What judgements are necessary to record a retirement obligation? What is the offsetting debit?

Q9-11 Suppose that an asset retirement liability is recorded, and that the original estimates are not changed in subsequent years. Is any accounting treatment required for the liability in the intervening years until retirement? Explain.

Q9-12 How are assets recorded when they are acquired by exchanging another asset? Explain when fair value versus book value recording would be appropriate.

Q9-13 An asset with a book value of $12,000 and a fair value of $25,000 is exchanged for another asset with a book value of $17,000. No cash is exchanged. What is the value of the transaction?

Q9-14 Return to the facts of question 9-13. Assume that $5,000 cash is also included with the asset, in order to obtain the second asset. What is the value of the transaction?

Q9-15 Explain the impact on income and net assets, over an asset's life, of a decision to capitalize or write off certain expenditures made at the time of purchase.

Q9-16 What items commonly are reported on the cash flow statement in relation to capital assets?

Q9-17 Under what circumstances can pre-operating costs be deferred and amortized? How do these costs meet the asset definition when they qualify for deferral?

Q9-18 What is the difference between research and development? How must a company account for research? For development?

Q9-19 Computer software development costs present a particular challenge for policy-makers. What is the basic problem?

Q9-20 Describe two different policies to account for exploration and development costs incurred by oil and gas companies.

Q9-21 If a company wished to pick accounting policies that are closer to actual cash flows, would you expect the company to use full cost or successful efforts for exploration and development costs?

Q9-22 When is an enterprise considered to be in the development stage? What impact does the development stage have on accounting policy choice?

Q9-23 Under what circumstances will a cash flow for development expenses appear in the investing activities section of the cash flow statement? Explain.

Q9-24 Define goodwill and describe how it is calculated.

Q9-25 What is negative goodwill? How does it arise? How is it treated for accounting purposes?

CASE 9-1
Penguins in Paradise

"The thing you have to understand is how these stage plays work. You start out with just an idea, but generally no cash. That's where promoters like me come in. We find ways of raising the money necessary to get the play written and the actors trained. If the play is a success, we hope to recover all those costs and a whole lot more, but cash flow is the problem. Since less than half of all plays make money, you cannot get very much money from banks.

"Take my current project, Penguins in Paradise (PIP). You only have to look at the cash inflows to see how many sources I had to approach to get the cash. As you can see, most of the initial funding comes from the investors in the limited partnership. They put up their money to buy a percentage of the future profits of the play.

"The money that the investors put up is not enough to fund all the start-up costs, so you have to be creative. Take reservation fees, for example. You know how tough it is to get good seats for a really hot play. Well, PIP sold the right to buy great seats to some dedicated theatregoers this year for next year's performance. These amounts are non-refundable, and the great thing is that the buyers still have to pay full price for the tickets when they buy them.

"Consider the sale of movie rights. Lots of good plays get turned into movies. Once the stage play is a success, the movie rights are incredibly expensive. My idea was to sell the movie rights in advance. PIP got a lot less money, but at least we got it upfront when we needed it.

"The other sources are much the same. We received the government grant by agreeing to have at least 50% Canadian content. We also negotiated a bank loan with an interest rate of 5% a year plus 1% of the gross revenue of the play, instead of the usual 16% annual interest a year. Even my fee for putting the deal together was taken as a percentage of the profit, so just about everybody has a strong interest in the play's performance."

Required:

Prepare a memo addressing the major financial accounting issues to be established by PIP. Include your recommendations. Do not prepare financial statements.

(CICA, adapted)

SUMMARY OF CASH FLOWS

for the period ended 31 December 20X4

($ thousands)

Cash inflows:	
Investor contributions to limited partnership	$6,000
Bank loan	2,000
Sale of movie rights	500
Government grant	50
Reservation fees	20
	8,570
Cash outflows:	
Salaries and fees	3,500
Costumes and sets	1,000
Miscellaneous costs	1,260
	5,760
Net cash inflows	$2,810

CASE 9-2
Biotech Wonders Incorporated

Biotech Wonders Incorporated (BWI) was founded by Dr. Sam Hickey six years ago. Hickey has a PhD in organic chemistry and is guiding his team of scientists as they develop all-natural products to help deal with the damage caused by repetitive stress injuries. The demand for this type of product is expected to grow as baby boomers age and continue their active lifestyles.

Initially, all the capital came from Hickey and government grants. Several venture capital funds became investors two years ago. As a result, 40% of the common shares are held by three venture capital funds and Hickey owns 60%. The venture capital investors are looking forward to a public offering of BWI shares, likely when the company has at least one more product in commercial development.

Biotechnology companies have significant hurdles to clear before a product can be commercially marketed. These products are subject to significant government regulation, in three phases. Phase I testing must establish product safety with animals. Phase II testing must establish product safety with humans, and Phase III clinical trials, the most expensive and risky, must establish that the product is effective for treating the condition for which it is designed. Fewer than 3% of Phase I compounds reach commercial production. The major risks are that the product will not be safe or effective, or that another treatment, a competitor product, will be developed that is more effective. However, once product approval is received, profit margins are very high—80 to 90%.

BWI has two products in commercial production, one in Phase III testing, and two in Phase II testing. A number of other compounds are "in the lab" and are being considered for Phase I testing. The two products in commercial production have been modest successes, but not blockbusters.

BWI hired a reputable marketing research company, which reported that there is significant demand for BWI's proposed products, that is, those still being developed. There is significant interest in the product now in Phase III testing, as the condition that it will treat is widespread.

You have been approached by one of the venture capital companies with a common share investment in BWI. The BWI balance sheet and some additional information has been provided to you (Exhibit 1). However, the income statement, cash flow statement, and disclosure notes have not been completed. You understand that BWI will report a loss of about $2,300,000 this year, which is largely the result of expenditures of $2,100,000 for the product in Phase III testing. Hickey has described the loss as "a good thing, because it demonstrates our commitment to Phase III testing of a product with significant commercial potential." Hickey is unhappy that these costs have not been deferred, as they represent a major investment in a future revenue-producing product.

The venture capital investor is interested in any financial statement adjustments that you feel are necessary. You must provide the dollar amount, where possible, and rationale for any suggested changes to BWI's financial information. Furthermore, you have been asked to suggest any qualitative factors or other performance measures that the venture capital investor should consider as part of its evaluation of BWI.

Required:
Prepare the report.

(ASCA, adapted)

EXHIBIT 1

BIOTECH WONDERS INCORPORATED
BALANCE SHEET (UNAUDITED)

31 March 20X1

Assets		
Current assets:		
Cash		$ 549,059
Inventory		11,651
Total current assets		560,710
Long-term assets:		
Investment in Ocean Growers (Note 1)		60,000
Deferred development costs (Note 2)		112,250
Leasehold improvements (Note 3)	$ 103,445	
Less: accumulated amortization	(31,034)	
Net book value	72,411	72,411
Equipment (Note 3)	50,876	
Less: accumulated amortization	(15,088)	
Net book value	35,788	35,788
Total long-term assets		280,449
Total Assets		**$ 841,159**
Liabilities		
Current liabilities:		
Accounts payable		$ 34,075
Wages payable		1,750
Rent payable		800
Total liabilities		36,625
Shareholders' equity		
Common shares		6,400,000
Deficit		(5,595,466)
Total shareholders' equity		804,534
Total Liabilities and Equities		**$ 841,159**

Notes:

1. BWI owns 18% of the common shares of Ocean Growers (OG) and accounts for its investment in OG using the cost method. Sam Hickey owns the other 82% of OG's common shares. OG has incurred losses of $220,000 since BWI purchased its investment. OG's losses are due to its extensive research activities in dietary supplements designed to enhance bone density.
2. Deferred development costs relate to products in commercial production. All additional costs of development are deferred once Phase III approval is obtained. The costs are amortized straight line over 10 years.
3. The leasehold improvements were made three years ago and are being amortized over the current lease term of five years plus the time of an estimated new lease of five years (total life of 10 years). BWI has not negotiated the new lease. Equipment is amortized on a straight-line basis over the useful life of five years. On 1 October 20X0, BWI transferred to Lincoln Therapeutics, another biotechnology company, certain equipment that BWI had carried on its books for $108,000. BWI accepted other laboratory equipment in exchange. This equipment had a net book value of $125,000 on Lincoln's books. The equipment was appraised at $126,400, and BWI recorded a gain on the trade of $18,400.

CASE 9-3
Multi-Communications Limited

Multi-Communications Limited (MCL) is a Canadian-owned public company operating throughout North America. Its core business is communications media, including newspapers, radio, television, and cable. The company's year-end is 31 December.

You have recently joined MCL's corporate office as a finance director, reporting to the chief financial officer, Robert Allen. It is October 20X2. Mr Allen has asked you to prepare a report that discusses the accounting issues that might arise when the auditors visit in November.

MCL's growth in 20X2 was achieved through expansion into the United States. MCL acquired a conglomerate, Peters Holdings (PH), which had substantial assets in the communications business, including a number of newspapers, and television and cable operations. Since the U.S. side of MCL's operations is now significant, management will begin reporting its financial statements in U.S. dollars in 20X2.

Over the past three months, MCL has sold off 80% of PH's non-communication-related businesses. The remaining 20% are also for sale, and are reported as long-term investments in the MCL statements.

To date, the sale of these non-communications assets has generated proceeds of $175 million, while their cost on the date of acquisition was $153 million. The proceeds have been treated as a reduction of the cost of acquiring PH, and no gain on sale has been reported on income statements prepared to date.

Overall, the cost of PH was $498 million, which MCL has reduced by $175 million, to $323 million. The tangible assets acquired have a value in the range of $240–$280 million, depending on the appraiser's report used (three were obtained). The major variation between the appraiser's reports is the interest rate used in the valuation; interest rates have been volatile.

In MCL's major newspaper markets, newspaper readership has peaked and there is little or no room for expansion. To increase its readership in one major urban market, MCL bought all the assets of a competing newspaper for $10 million in 20X2, which represented $4 million for tangible assets and $6 million for customer lists and goodwill. Later in the year, MCL ceased publication of the competing paper—publicly billed as a merger of the two papers—and liquidated the tangible assets for $3.2 million. MCL has classified the $.8 million loss on sale of these capital assets as an increase in goodwill, bringing the total goodwill from the acquisition to $6.8 million. This is based on the underlying rationale for acquiring the newspaper: to increase MCL's own readership by restricting choice in this particular urban market. While MCL has not kept the entire customer group, readership in MCL's "merged" newspaper is higher than the single paper circulation before. MCL feels that this enhanced readership clearly justifies the capitalization of goodwill.

MCL estimates the value of its entire intangibles at $250 million. Included as intangibles are newspaper and magazine publication lists, cable subscriber lists, and broadcast licences. Some of these have been acquired through the purchase of existing businesses; others have been generated internally by operations that have been part of MCL for some time.

Amounts paid for acquired intangibles are not hard to determine, but the cost of internally generated intangibles is much more difficult to ascertain. Subscription lists are built through advertising campaigns, cold calls, and product giveaways. MCL estimates that it has expensed $35 million because of such activities over the last 10 years. Independent appraisers have determined the fair value of these internally generated assets to be in the range of $60 to $80 million. Because management feels that accurate portrayal of these assets is crucial to fairly present MCL's financial position, management has included these assets at $60 million on the balance sheet.

Required:

Prepare the report for Mr. Allen.

(CICA, adapted)

Case 9-4
Nova Scotia Timber Resources Limited

Nova Scotia Timber Resources Limited (NSTR) is a privately held company incorporated under the companies legislation of Nova Scotia. It is owned by a family syndicate based in Bonn, Germany. The syndicate has been actively involved in acquiring timberland in Nova Scotia for the past five years. Early in 20X3, the decision was made to roll the assets into a corporation and harvest timber for the first time. Previously, land acquired had been left idle.

While the immediate objective is to profit from the timber resource, the syndicate's long-term goals include profit on the land itself. Germany has high-density population, and recreational land is scarce. Nova Scotia waterfront properties represent attractive acquisition targets. Regular market value appraisals are obtained on both the land value, and, separately, the timber resource.

The syndicate members have borrowed money to pay for the land in their personal names; the land, not the debt, has been transferred to NSTR, although the land is often collateral for the debt. In addition, though, the syndicate members provided personal guarantees on an operating line of credit for NSTR of up to $4 million with the Chartered Bank of Canada. This loan is also secured by a floating charge on inventory and receivables.

NSTR, in its first year of production, leased a building (for 10 years) which housed sawmill operations, administrative offices, and a warehouse. It also acquired about $1,400,000 of processing equipment, trucks, tools, and other necessary assets. There are many incidental costs associated with these acquisitions: transportation costs, installation costs, (approximately $114,000) and renovations to the leased facility ($178,000).

As trees are harvested, the decision must be made whether to sell the logs to other sawmills or users of timber, or to process the logs in NSTR's own facilities. The quality of logs varies. A five-year contract was signed with a plant in Nova Scotia that used low-quality logs to produce chipboard and panelling. The price agreed on was "fair market value," determined monthly, and minimum delivery quantities were established for each month.

Higher-quality logs, processed internally, become lumber of various dimensions, sold to both building supply companies and independent contractors in the Maritimes and in the Quebec and Ontario markets. Transportation costs make it difficult to compete strongly in the Quebec and Ontario markets. Terms are usually cash payment within 60 days of delivery.

Prices of these finished products are a function of supply and demand at the date of sale. Inventory is stored in NSTR's warehouses, incurring interest and storage costs, if the current market price is deemed unacceptably low by management. Management has refused to accept prices below cost, and lumber prices were quite volatile in 20X3.

Management has the responsibility for making these decisions as well as decisions concerning how much lumber to harvest in any one year, based on market predictions.

The syndicate has set a policy of reforestation of harvested land, consistent with its long-term goals of land appreciation. The costs to fulfil this policy, while not large in 20X3, are expected to be material in future years.

The company's first year-end has just passed. The syndicate has not indicated how net income is to be computed, nor has Canadian management spent much time considering financial accounting policies. There has been some indication that the syndicate wishes to be able to draw funds, in the form of dividends, to meet debt service charges and principal repayments. In addition, some consideration has been given to awarding senior management a bonus on net income, although details have yet to be worked out.

Syndicate members are very anxious to keep an eye on the market value of the land, as this was a primary financial incentive for the acquisition in the first place.

Required:

Assume the role of an accounting advisor to the company and explain the financial accounting policies and principles the company should adopt.

[ASCA, adapted]

Case 9-5
Blue River Gold Company

In 20X3, the Blue River Gold Company Limited (BRGCL) commenced development activities in northern Alberta. The company is in the process of developing a gold mining property called Castle Mountain, and management is of the opinion that this property contains economically recoverable ore reserves. The recoverability of the amounts spent for resource properties and capital assets is dependent on the ability of the company to complete development of the property and upon future profitable operation.

Mineral exploration costs (acquisition, exploration, and development expenditures) are being capitalized until commercial production is established. These amounts do not necessarily represent present or future values of the ore, just costs incurred to date.

Commercial production is contingent on government approval, which is expected early in 20X4. As a result, construction of mine buildings is in the final planning stage and commercial production is expected to start during the coming fiscal year (20X4).

You have been called to advise the company on the accounting policies it should adopt once it goes into commercial production. As a junior mining company listed on the TSE, the Board of Directors has indicated that members wish to adopt accounting policies that will "keep them out of trouble with the auditors and regulatory bodies."

Required:

Prepare an appropriate report to the Board of Directors.

BLUE RIVER GOLD COMPANY INCORPORATED
SCHEDULE OF CASH RECEIPTS AND DISBURSEMENTS TO 31 DECEMBER 20X3

Cash receipts:	
Issuance of common shares (Note 1)	$29,433,000
Gold loan (Note 2)	10,714,000
Interest revenue (Note 3)	566,400
	$40,713,400
Cash disbursements:	
Cost of mining properties (Note 4)	18,784,000
Administrative expenses (Note 5)	2,309,000
Acquisition of marketable securities (Note 6)	4,000,000
	$25,093,000
Excess of receipts over expenditures	$15,620,400

Note 1: Common shares were issued on the TSE on 31 January 20X3, for net proceeds of $29,433,000.

Note 2: On 30 November 20X3 BRGCL entered into a loan agreement with a bank consortium to borrow up to 95,000 ounces of gold to finance the development of the Castle Mountain gold mine. The loan will bear interest, payable in gold, at prime rates (7% on 30 November 20X3) plus 2%. The loan is secured by all assets of the company. The lender may elect to be paid cash for any or all principal and interest payments at a fixed conversion rate of $350 per gold ounce. The company has agreed not to incur additional indebtedness and not to create any additional security interests in any of its assets. BRGCL is also restricted from distributing dividends during the term of the loan.

The loan is repayable by delivery of gold in semi-annual instalments, beginning in 20X4 and covering five years. At 31 December 20X3, the loan had been drawn to the amount of $10,714,000, or 30,611 ounces of gold at the conversion price of $350.

BRGCL would like to consider two alternatives to account for this loan.

1. Treat the contract as a deferred sales contract. The loan proceeds, net of the finance charges and interest over the contract term, would be treated as deferred revenue, to be recognized on delivery of gold per the agreement.
2. Treat the contract as a loan. Gold deliveries would be recorded partially as principal repayment, and partially as interest.

Note 3: Interest revenue was earned throughout the year on cash raised through the sale of common shares.

Note 4: Cost of mining properties can be broken down as follows:

Mining properties	
Acquisition costs	$ 2,420,000
Exploration and development expenditures	16,364,000
	$18,784,000

Next year, as construction and mining commence, costs will be incurred for the following capital assets:

Capital Asset	*Useful Life*
Roads	Indefinite; roads assigned to the province once the mine is depleted
Mine buildings and structures	15 years, no salvage value
Equipment	2 years, minor salvage values

Note 5: Administrative expenses include salaries of executives and the costs of the rented head office facilities located in Vancouver, B.C., as well as other operating costs.

Note 6: In 20X3, BRGCL acquired shares in Brascorp, at a cost of $4,000,000. The current market value of these shares is $2,500,000. BRGCL does not plan to sell these shares until market value recovers.

Note 7: BRGCL has two options for revenue recognition of its gold production:

1. Revenue recognition on production, with inventory carried at net realizable value (sales price).
2. Revenue recognition on delivery to customers, with inventory carried at cost.

Surveys of industry practice show that both alternatives are found in Canadian gold mining companies.

(ASCA, adapted)

CASE 9-6
Speed Technology Incorporated

Speed Technology Incorporated (STI), based in Edmonton, offers high-speed Internet access services to residential and commercial customers throughout the western provinces. It is owned, in part, by the provincial telephone companies in these provinces. Approximately 35% of SRI common shares are publicly traded. The equity base is $60 million. The company was formed in early 20X3, and by 30 September, 20X3, the initial $60 million had been spent on the following:

(in millions of dollars)	
Customer sales and marketing	$15
Fibre-optic lines	35
Administration costs	10

The company has lines of credit with two chartered banks for operational funding.

All costs were capitalized for the first nine months of 20X3. Customer sales and marketing costs were incurred primarily to recruit customers. It is anticipated that such costs will decrease over time, as STI's services become more widely known. Most of the costs related to advertisements on local television and radio. The administrative costs include $5 million of salaries and wages for administrative personnel and $5 million of payments made to attract and relocate senior management to Edmonton. Managers who have relocated have signed three-year contracts; if these contracts are broken, relocation bonuses must be repaid.

The $35 million payment for fibre-optic cables was for the acquisition, from an unrelated party, of the right to use lines, which connect customers to the Internet. Ownership of the fibre-optic lines remains with the unrelated company, which is also responsible for maintenance. If properly maintained, the lines will last for 20 years.

The $35 million payment was made on 1 September 20X3. Under the terms of the agreement, STI has the exclusive right to use two fibre-optic lines over a five-year period beginning 1 September 20X3. The right-to-use agreement can be extended for another five years on 1 September 20X8, for an additional payment of $30 million.

STI began to provide customer Internet access on 1 September 20X3. To attract subscribers, any customer who signed up before 1 September 20X3 was given one month of free service. Accordingly, no revenue was recorded in September. As of 1 October 20X3, STI had signed 12,000 residential customers to one-year contracts at an average rate of $25 per month. In addition, approximately 150 commercial contracts were in place on 1 October at an average rate of $2,250 per month. The commercial rate allows an entire office unlimited Internet access.

As of 1 October, only one of the fibre-optic lines was in use because there were not enough customers to justify use of the second line. STI has capitalized the $35 million cost and allocated $17.5 million to each line. For September, amortization was charged only for the line in use. STI plans to amortize each line over five years commencing on the date when it is first used, to the extent that capacity is used. For example, the existing customers represent 65% of the capacity of the first line. The amortization charge for September was therefore 65% of the monthly charge.

STI's business plan required aggressive promotion for the first two years of operation, building to 60% of total capacity at the end of the first operating year, and 80% at the end of the second year. Volume targets were not achieved in the start-up period, although management is optimistic that, now that service is available, the operation will catch up to targets in the next 12 months.

STI is approaching its first year-end, and must establish accounting policies for its major operational costs. You have been asked to review existing accounting policy choices, and identify and evaluate other areas of choice.

Required:

Prepare a report dealing with STI's accounting policy alternatives.

(CICA, adapted)

ASSIGNMENTS

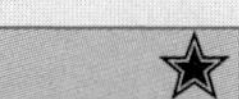

A9-1 Asset Cost: The following cases are independent.

Case A. CST Company purchased a $325,000 tract of land for a factory site. CST razed an old building on the property and sold the materials it salvaged from the demolition. CST incurred additional costs and realized salvage proceeds as follows:

Demolition of old building	$50,000
Legal fees for purchase contract and recording ownership	10,000
Title guarantee insurance	8,000
Routine maintenance (mowing) done on purchase	4,000
Proceeds from sale of salvaged materials	8,000

Case B. Mirax Limited bought a building for $943,400. Before using the building, the following expenditures were made:

Repair and renovation of building	$32,000
Construction of new driveway	6,000
Repair of existing driveways	2,200
Installation of 220-volt electrical wiring	8,000
Deposits with utilities for connections	600
Painting company name on two sides of building	3,800
Installation of wire fence around property	7,000

Required:

a. What balance should CST report in the land account?
b. What balance would Mirax report in the building account? If any items in the list above are excluded from the building account, indicate the appropriate classification.

A9-2 Acquisition Cost: An examination of the property, plant, and equipment accounts of James Company on 31 December 20X5, disclosed the following transactions:

a. On 1 January 20X4, a new machine was purchased having a list price of $45,000. The company did not take advantage of a 2% cash discount available upon full payment of the invoice within 30 days. Shipping cost paid by the vendor was $200. Installation cost was $600, including $200 that represented 10% of the monthly salary of the factory superintendent (installation period, two days). A wall was moved two feet at a cost of $1,000 to make room for the machine.

b. On 1 January 20X4, the company bought plant fixtures with a list price of $4,500; paid $1,500 cash and gave a one-year, non-interest-bearing note payable for the balance. The current interest rate for this type of note was 15%.
c. During January 20X4, the first month of operations, the newly purchased machine became inoperative due to a defect in manufacture. The vendor repaired the machine at no cost to James; however, the specially trained operator was idle during the two weeks the machine was inoperative. The operator was paid regular wages ($850) during the period, although the only work performed was to observe the repair by the factory representative.
d. On 1 July 20X4, a contractor completed construction of a building for the company. The company paid the contractor by transferring $400,000 face value, 20-year, 8% James Company bonds payable. Financial consultants advised that the bonds would sell at 96 (i.e., $384,000).
e. During January 20X5, the company exchanged the electric motor on the machine in part (a) for a heavier motor and gave up the old motor and $600 cash. The market value of the new motor was $1,250. The parts list showed a $900 cost for the original motor (estimated life, 10 years).
f. On 1 January 20X4, the company purchased an automatic counter to be attached to a machine in use, cost $700. The estimated useful life of the counter was 7 years, and the estimated life of the machine was 10 years.

Required:

1. Prepare the journal entries to record each of the above transactions as of the date of occurrence. Explain and justify your decisions on questionable items. James Company uses straight-line depreciation.
2. Record depreciation at the end of 20X4. None of the assets is expected to have a residual value except the fixtures (residual value is $500). Estimated useful lives: fixtures, 5 years; machinery, 10 years; and building, 40 years. Give a separate entry for each asset.

A9-3 Asset Cost and Related Expenditures: The following transactions relate to capital assets:

a. A company purchased land and buildings for $157,800 cash. The purchaser agreed to pay $1,800 for land property taxes already assessed. The purchaser borrowed $100,000 at 15% interest (principal and interest due in one year) from the bank to help make the cash payment. The property was assessed for taxes as follows: land, $50,000; and building, $100,000.
b. The building was recarpeted and painted at a cost of $20,000. Landscaping, costing $2,200, was completed.
c. The company purchased a tract of land for $64,000; assumed taxes already assessed amounting to $360. Paid title fees of $100 and legal fees of $600 in connection with the purchase. Payments were in cash except for the tax balance, which is still owing. The property is being held as a future plant site.
d. The land purchased in (c) above was levelled, and two retaining walls were built to stop erosion that had created two rather large gulleys across the property. Total cash cost of the work was $6,000.
e. Purchased a used machine at a cash cost of $17,000. Subsequent to purchase, the following expenditures were made:

General overhaul prior to use	$2,400
Installation of machine	600
Cost of moving machine	300
Cost of removing two small machines to make way for larger machine purchased	200
Cost of reinforcing floor prior to installation	800
Testing costs prior to operation	120
Cost of tool kit (new) essential to adjustment of machine for various types of work	440

Required:

Prepare journal entries to record the above transactions. Justify your position on doubtful items.

A9-4 Expenditure Classification: Consider each of the following items:

a. Surveyor's fees.
b. Cost to demolish an old building that is on a piece of land where a new building will be constructed.
c. Architect's fees.
d. Cost of routine testing of food products in the company's lab.
e. Cost of installing a new roof on the company's building.
f. Lawyer's fees associated with an unsuccessful patent application.
g. An impairment in value of the company's building from its net book value.
h. Cost of a grease and oil change on the company's truck.
i. Lawyer's fees associated with a successful patent application.
j. Excess of the book value of an old asset over the fair market value of the new asset in a trade of similar assets.

Required:

For each of the above items, give the name of the account to which the expenditure should be charged; that is, what account should be debited? Be specific.

A9-5 Acquisition of Land—Non-Cash Consideration: Under the cost principle, what amount should be used to record land acquired in each of the following independent cases? Give reasons in support of your answer.

a. At the middle of the current year, a cheque was given for $40,000 for land, and the buyer assumed the liability for unpaid taxes in arrears at the end of last year, $1,000, and those assessed for the current year, $900.
b. A company issued 14,000 shares of capital stock with a market value of $6 per share (based on a recent sale of 100 shares) for land. The land was recently appraised at $80,000 by independent and competent appraisers.
c. A company rejected an offer to purchase land for $8,000 cash two years ago. Instead, the company issued 1,000 shares of capital stock for the land (market value of the shares, $7.80 per share based on several recent large transactions and normal weekly share trading volume).
d. A company issued 1,000 shares of capital stock for land. The market value (shares sell daily with an average daily volume of 5,000 shares) was $60 per share at time of purchase of the land. The vendor earlier offered to sell the land for $59,000 cash. Competent appraisers valued the land at $61,000.

A9-6 Asset Acquisition—Non-Cash Consideration: Machinery with a fair value of $45,000 is acquired in a non-cash exchange. Below are five independent assumptions (a) to (e) as to the consideration given in the non-cash exchange:

a. Bonds held as a long-term investment, which originally cost $84,000 and had been written down 50% because of a perceived permanent loss of their value.
b. Land with a book value of $25,000 and a market value of $45,000.
c. A similar type of used machinery with a book value of $18,000 and a fair value of $21,000, plus cash of $24,900. When new, the used machinery cost $26,400. There will be no charge in cash flows as the result of this exchange.
d. Inventory carried at $28,500 on the most recent balance sheet as part of a perpetual inventory carried at LCM. When originally acquired, the goods had cost $42,750.
e. A non-interest-bearing note for $51,750 maturing in one year. Notes of similar risk required 15% interest at the date of the exchange.

Required:
Give the journal entry required for each of the above independent assumptions.

A9-7 Expense Recognition Examples: Respond to each of the following situations:

Case A. CSI develops and markets specialized diagnostic equipment for the medical profession. During 20X0, CSI spent $200,000 on a study to help identify the needs of users. As a result of this study, CSI started work on a new diagnostic product to be used by the medical profession. Approximately $1 million was spent on creating prototypes, only one of which has turned out to be usable.

CSI's financial statements are prepared in accordance with generally accepted accounting principles. How should CSI account for these costs in its 20X0 financial statements? Support your recommendations.

Case B. The Boring Drilling Company operates in the oil and gas exploration business, and uses successful efforts to account for its exploration and development expenditures. The company began drilling a well on Acre 313 in September 20X5. By the end of December 20X5, $1,250,000 of costs had been incurred on this well. Efforts have been unsuccessful and the company is planning to abandon the well in 20X6. However, there are a few more activities to perform (such as cleaning up the site) before the well is formally abandoned.

The controller wants to leave the costs capitalized on the 31 December balance sheet on the basis that the exploration activities were not complete and that a final determination of success had not been made at the end of the year. Is this policy acceptable?

(CGA-Canada, adapted)

Case C. Fox is a new computer software company. In 20X4, the firm incurred the following costs in the process of designing, developing, and producing its first new software package, which it expects to begin marketing in 20X5:

Designing and planning costs	$150,000
Production of product masters	400,000
Cost of developing code	240,000
Testing	60,000
Production of final product	500,000

The costs of designing and planning, code development, and testing were all incurred before the technological feasibility of the product had been established. Fox estimates that total revenues over the four-year life of the product will be $2,000,000, with $800,000 in revenues expected in 20X5.

Calculate the amount of expenditures capitalized versus expensed in 20X4. Assuming 20X5 revenue is on target, how much will be expensed in 20X5?

A9-8 Cost Determination: The following three cases are unrelated:

Case A. Brushy Machine Shop purchased the following used equipment at a special auction sale for $60,000 cash: a drill press, a lathe, and a heavy-duty air compressor. The equipment was in excellent condition except for the electric motor on the lathe, which will cost $1,200 to replace with a new motor. Brushy has determined that the selling prices for the used items in local outlets are approximately as follows: drill press, $12,600; lathe, with a good motor, $36,000; and air compressor, $21,000. The electric motor was immediately replaced.

Case B. A large company, upon abandoning its operations at a particular site, donated a building and the land on which it was located to another company that was to hire two-thirds of the old company's workforce. The property was reliably appraised at a value of $160,000 (one-quarter related to the land). The recipient company paid transfer costs of $4,000 related to the land.

Case C. Fairview Forestry Limited (FFL) leased a large tract of land from the provincial government for $4 million per year for six years. The present value of the lease payments is $20.4 million. FFL will log the land over the six-year period. Before returning the land to the government at the end of the lease, FFL is obligated to remove its entire infrastructure (e.g., roads and buildings) and reforest the land with mixed vegetation, at an estimated cost (present value) of $2.5 million.

Required:
Determine the cost of the assets acquired in each case. Explain your reasoning, if choices must be made.

A9-9 Asset Acquisition: At 31 December 20X4, certain accounts included in the property, plant, and equipment section of Hint Corporation's balance sheet had the following balances:

Land	$ 600,000
Buildings	1,300,000
Leasehold improvements	800,000
Machinery and equipment	1,600,000

During 20X5, the following transactions occurred:

a. Land site number 101 was acquired for $3,000,000. Additionally, to acquire the land, Hint paid a $180,000 commission to a real estate agent. Costs of $30,000 were incurred to clear the land. During the course of clearing the land, timber, and gravel were recovered and sold for $16,000.

b. A second tract of land (site number 102) with a building was acquired for $600,000. The closing statement indicated that the land value was $400,000 and the building value was $200,000. Shortly after acquisition, the building was demolished at a cost of $40,000. A new building was constructed for $300,000 plus the following costs:

Excavation fees	$12,000
Architectural design fees	16,000
Building permit fee	4,000

The building was completed and occupied on 30 September 20X5.

c. A third tract of land (site number 103) was acquired for $1,500,000 and was put on the market for resale.

d. Extensive work was done to a building occupied by Hint under a lease agreement that expires on 31 December 20X14. The total cost of the work was $250,000, as follows:

Item	Cost	Useful Life (Years)
Painting of ceilings	$ 10,000	1
Electrical work	90,000	10
Construction of extension to current working area	150,000	25
	$250,000	

The lessor paid half the costs incurred for the extension to the current working area.

e. During December 20X5, $120,000 was spent to improve leased office space.

f. A group of new machines was purchased subject to a royalty agreement, which requires payment of royalties based on units of production for the machines. The invoice price of the machines was $270,000, freight costs were $2,000, unloading costs were $3,000, and royalty payments for 20X5 were $44,000.

Required:
Disregard the related accumulated depreciation accounts.

1. Prepare a detailed analysis of the changes in each of the following balance sheet accounts for 20X5:

a. Land.
b. Buildings.
c. Leasehold improvements.
d. Machinery and equipment.

2. What items would appear on the cash flow statement in relation to the accounts in part (1)?
3. List the amounts in the items (a) to (f) that were not used to determine the answer to (1) above, and indicate where, or whether, these items should be included in Hint's financial statements.

(AICPA, adapted)

A9-10 Asset Acquisition: During the current year, Candle Soap Company began a project to construct its new corporate headquarters. Candle purchased land with an old building for $375,000. The land was valued at $350,000 and the building at $25,000. Candle plans to demolish the building. Additional expenditures on the project include

a. Interest of $107,000 on construction financing paid during construction of the headquarters building.
b. Payment of $12,250 for delinquent real estate taxes assumed by Candle on purchase of the land and building.
c. Liability insurance premium of $9,000 covering the construction period.
d. Cost of $35,000 for razing the existing building.
e. Costs of $875,000 for construction of the building.
f. Costs of $68,000 to move into new headquarters.

Required:

Determine Candle's ending balance in all relevant capital asset accounts given the above information. Also note the total amount of expense, if any, to be recognized.

(AICPA, adapted)

A9-11 Donated Assets: Markus Company received a vacant building as a donation. The building has a 25-year estimated remaining useful life ($40,000 residual value), which was recognized in the donation agreement at the time that the company was guaranteed occupancy. Transfer costs of $25,000 were paid by the company. The building originally cost $700,000, 10 years earlier. The building was recently appraised at $410,000 market value by the city's tax assessor. Anticipating occupancy within the next 10 days, the company spent $84,000 for repairs and internal rearrangements, expected to have value for 8 years. There are no unresolved contingencies about the building and Markus Company's permanent occupancy.

Required:

1. Give all entries for Markus Company related to (a) the donation, (b) the renovation, and (c) any amortization at the end of the first year of occupancy, assuming that Markus uses straight-line amortization and that the assets have no residual value.
2. What would appear on the CFS in relation to the transactions recorded in part (1)? Assume that the direct method is used to present cash flow from operations.
3. What objections are raised concerning the accounting policy of capitalizing and depreciating a donated asset? Explain.

A9-12 Lump-Sum Purchase: Freeman Company purchased a tract of land on which a warehouse and an office building were located. The cash purchase price was $140,000 plus $10,000 in fees connected with the purchase. The following data was collected concerning the property:

	Tax Assessment	Vendor's Book Value	Original Cost
Land	$20,000	$10,000	$10,000
Warehouse	40,000	20,000	60,000
Office building	60,000	50,000	80,000

Required:
Give the entry to record the purchase; show computations.

A9-13 Capital Asset Accounting: Moray Capital reported various transactions in 20X7:

a. Equipment with an original cost of $40,000 and accumulated depreciation of $34,000 was deemed to be unusable and was sold for $400 scrap value.
b. A new moulding system was acquired for $35,700. The invoice was marked 2/10, n/30, but Moray did not pay in time to take advantage of the 2% discount for early payment and thus paid the gross amount of $35,700. Wiring was improved to accommodate the needs of the system at a cost of $800. Related software upgrades were purchased for $2,500. Installation and testing cost $4,000.
c. Regular machine maintenance was carried out for $23,000.
d. A piece of machinery with an original cost of $77,400 and accumulated depreciation of $56,000 was traded, along with cash of $50,900, for a similar new machine with a fair market value of $62,700.
e. The building roof was replaced during the period at a cost of $22,800 to improve the insulation in the building and save on heating costs. The old roof had a cost of $13,500 and was three-quarters depreciated.
f. Two machines were acquired for a lump-sum amount of $53,800. One machine had an appraised value of $40,000; the other, $20,000.
g. A piece of land was acquired, adjacent to the company's existing manufacturing site. The land was acquired for $40,000 cash plus a zero-interest note payable in the amount of $200,000. The note is due in 10 years' time. Market interest rates are 6%.
h. Land and building were acquired from a member of the Board of Directors in exchange for 325,000 of the company's own common shares. The land was appraised at $75,000, and the building, $400,000. The facility will be used for long-term storage. The market value of common shares has been around $1.25 per share this year, with weekly highs and lows ranging from $1.80 to $0.95, respectively.
i. The company spent $430,000 in a research lab program this year. It was successful in developing three new commercial projects, which represented $157,000 of the expenditures budget. Legal fees associated with the three successful projects amount to $89,600.
j. Moray paved its factory parking lot, previously a dirt lot, at a cost of $112,100.

Required:
Prepare journal entries to record the transactions listed above. State any assumptions made. Use the gross method to record the note payable.

A9-14 Capital Asset Transactions: Vizard Limited began the year with modest capital asset balances; it had a $40,000 organization cost asset, and machinery for which the company had paid $345,000 three years ago. Most capital assets are rented. Net balances are as follows:

Organization costs (cost of $40,000, less amortization of $8,000)	$ 32,000
Machinery (cost of $345,000 less depreciation of $129,375)	215,625

In the current year, Vizard expanded rapidly and recorded the following:

a. In January, Vizard bought the assets of a small manufacturing facility in order to achieve vertical integration. Vizard used this company's main product in its operation, and the other company was going out of business. At market values, Vizard bought accounts receivable, $45,000; prepaid expenses, $5,800; inventory of $111,400; patents worth $55,000; machinery of $344,000; a building worth $678,000; and land worth $44,800. Vizard paid $2,200,000 for the assets; cash of $500,000 and a 10-year, 10% note payable for the balance. Ten percent represented market interest rates.

b. Vizard spent $35,000 in legal fees during an unsuccessful patent infringement case on the patent acquired in (a). Subsequently, the patent was considered worthless.

c. Vizard sold the land and building acquired in (a) for a total of $1,000,000. It accepted a $1,000,000 three-year zero-interest note receivable in full payment.

d. Vizard spent $40,000 refurbishing and repairing machinery acquired in the purchase.

e. Vizard rents its production facilities at an annual rental of $45,600. During the year, Vizard spent $11,000 painting and cleaning this space. It also spent $5,000 upgrading the wiring.

f. The company discovered that some of the equipment bought would replace, more effectively, some of its own machinery. Accordingly, Vizard disposed of its redundant assets. One machine, with an original cost of $38,000, and accumulated depreciation of $26,000, was sold for $11,500. Another, with an original cost of $25,000 and accumulated depreciation of $17,500, was traded for a new, but smaller, piece of machinery with a different function. The second piece of machinery had a fair value of $14,000. No cash changed hands in this transaction. Finally, a piece of machinery with an original cost of $17,000 and accumulated depreciation of $11,000 was exchanged, along with $500 cash, for a new machine with a similar but more efficient function. The old equipment had a fair value of $8,000.

g. Vizard bought new trucks this year, for product delivery. Three vehicles, with appraised values of $15,000, $30,000, and $17,000, respectively, were purchased for $10,000 cash and a note payable that required payment of $20,000 at the end of each year for three years.

Required:

1. Determine the balance in each capital asset account, after reflecting the transactions listed above. If expenditures are not capitalized, explain. Do not calculate the balance of the accumulated depreciation account for capital assets.
2. Calculate the gain or loss on sale or disposal of capital assets during the year. Show your calculations.

A9-15 Self-Constructed Asset: Amethyst Corporation needed an extension to its factory building. Amethyst obtained a construction contract bid from a major construction company for $3,200,000. However, the Amethyst general manager recommended to senior management that Amethyst construct the building itself, using the company's own work force, as a way to keep the work force fully employed. Amethyst approved the general manager's recommendation. Construction of the extension began on 27 July 20X3. The building will be used as additional production facilities. During 20X3, the company incurred the following costs:

Materials	$ 650,000
Direct labour	1,750,000
Supervision and other indirect labour	80,000
Interest on general corporate debt, allocated on basis of material costs	10,000
Overhead cost, allocated on basis of direct labour costs	30,000
Total	$ 2,520,000

At 31 December 20X3, the company's general manager estimated that the building was about 70% complete. The construction engineers estimated that it would cost an additional $1,000,000 to complete the building.

Required:

1. Is it appropriate for Amethyst to include interest and overhead in the capitalized cost of the building extension? Discuss.
2. How should Amethyst show these costs in its 20X3 year-end financial statements?

A9-16 Self-Constructed Asset: Brazilia Corporation had need of a warehouse and maintenance facility on its company site, which already housed three manufacturing/storage facilities and the company head office. The lowest outside bid for the facility was $3,200,000. Brazilia was of the opinion that it could successfully construct the facility, and have more control over the construction process. Accordingly, it began construction on company-owned land in 20X5. The facility was completed in 20X6. Costs related to the project have been accumulated in one account, "manufacturing facility":

Materials	$1,066,200
Subcontracted work (primarily electrical and plumbing)	345,900
Direct labour; plant workers assigned to construction tasks	455,800
Direct labour; construction workers hired specifically for this project	123,600
Plant foreman used for construction supervision; salary and benefits	34,900
Direct labour; plant maintenance workers assigned to construction tasks	53,200
Engineering and architectural services	216,700

Additional information:

a. Overhead is assigned in the plant to cover supplies used, electricity, occupation costs, maintenance, etc. in the production environment at a rate of $0.57 for every dollar of direct plant labour.
b. A loan was negotiated to cover the cash flow needed for construction. Interest of $75,900 was paid on this loan. When the building was completed, a 10-year commercial mortgage was arranged on the property for $2,000,000, at an interest rate of 8%.
c. Of the $455,800 of plant workers' time assigned to construction tasks, 70% or $319,060, relates to time that would otherwise have been idle.
d. The administrative office handled the planning and paperwork related to the construction. The staff worked full time on this for approximately six months, representing salary and benefit costs of $57,000.
e. The executive team (chief executive officer and chief financial officer of the company, primarily) devoted approximately 10% of their time to this project during construction. The compensation package for these two individuals was $320,000 for this period.

Required:

1. Prepare a schedule showing the costs that can be capitalized for the building. If any items are not capitalized, explain why not.
2. What, if anything, would change in your answer if the outside bid on this project had been $2,400,000? Explain.
3. Under what circumstances can loan interest be capitalized as part of the cost of self-constructed assets? Explain.

A9-17 Self-Constructed Asset and Interest Capitalization: Mannheim Company begins construction of a factory facility on 4 January of the current year. Mannheim uses its own employees and subcontractors to complete the facility. The following list provides information relevant to the construction. The facility is completed 27 December of the current year.

a. At the beginning of January, Mannheim obtains construction financing: a 10%, $12,000,000 loan with principal payable at the end of construction provides significant financing for the project. Interest on the loan is payable semi-annually. Mannheim pays the interest and principal when due.

b. Mannheim owns the land site (cost, $4,000,000). In January, a subcontractor is employed to raze the building on the site, which was used by Mannheim for a number of years (cost, $800,000; accumulated depreciation, $600,000) for $80,000. Mannheim received $10,000 from salvaged materials.
c. Also in January, subcontractors survey, grade, and prepare the land for construction at a cost of $200,000 and excavate the foundation of the new facility for $1,000,000.
d. In January, a subcontractor poured and finished the foundation for $1,500,000. This work is financed separately through a one-year, 9% loan. Mannheim secured the financing at the beginning of January. The principal and interest were paid on 30 December.
e. The total material cost for construction, excluding other items in this list, is $8,000,000.
f. Payments to subcontractors, excluding others in this list, amount to $2,000,000.
g. Payments to Mannheim employees for work on construction are $9,000,000.
h. General overhead is assigned to all work done for customers on the basis of labour costs. If company-wide rates are used, the share of general overhead applicable to the job would be $7,000,000. The company uses a factory overhead applied account. Of the $7,000,000, $1,250,000 relates to amortization of capital assets.
i. In October, a subcontractor constructed a parking lot and fences for $300,000.
j. Incidental fees and other costs associated with facility construction were $150,000.
k. For purposes of interest capitalization, assume the company records interest to an expense and capitalizes interest once per year as an adjusting entry. Since construction costs were incurred fairly evenly over the year, the company has decided to capitalize one-half of the interest expense related to the general construction loans outstanding during the year (see (a)).
l. The market value of the building upon completion is $25,000,000.

Required:

1. Provide general journal entries to account for all aspects of construction and related events. Construction costs are accumulated in Mannheim's facility under construction account. Your entries should lead to the correct total cost to record for the building. You may record the events in any order you feel is easiest for you.
2. What disclosures would appear on the CFS in relation to the constructed asset? Assume the company uses the indirect method to present cash flows from operations.

A9-18 Asset Retirement Obligation: Broadcast Systems Incorporated (BSI) has a 10-year renewable lease contract with CBE Limited (CBEL), the owner of Metropolis's tallest building, to erect a transmission tower on the top of the building. Broadcast's contract with CBEL requires BSI to dismantle the tower if and when BSI discontinues its use. BSI expects to use the tower for only 10 years, due to the rapid advance in transmission technology that is likely to render the tower obsolete in 10 years. The lease payments to CBEL are $60,000 per year.

BSI constructed the tower at the beginning of 20X6 at a cost of $750,000. BSI estimates that dismantling and removal of the tower will cost $100,000, at 20X6 current prices. The risk-free interest rate is 4%; BSI's risk premium is 2%. BSI plans to use straight-line amortization; the company's policy is to take a full year's amortization in the year of acquisition but none in the year of disposal.

Required:

1. Prepare the journal entry to record construction of the tower and the retirement obligation.
2. Prepare the necessary adjusting entries pertaining to the tower and the retirement obligation for each of the years ending 31 December 20X6 and 20X7. Assume that there is no change in interest rates or in the estimated cost of the tower's removal.

A9-19 Asset Retirement Obligation: At the end of 20X1, Garrulous Garbage Systems Incorporated (GGSI) leased an abandoned mine in northern Ontario as a landfill site for non-industrial garbage from Detroit, Michigan. GGSI has a five-year contract with Detroit, renewable at Detroit's option. The lease with the mine owner requires GGSI to cover and plug the mine shafts used for the garbage. GGSI must comply with all Ontario environmental regulations. GGSI will begin with one mine shaft. At 20X1 prices, the estimated cost of plugging that shaft is $70,000. If Detroit does not renew the contract, the shaft will have to be plugged in 20X6. Even if the city does renew, that first shaft will probably be full by 20X6. GGSI's risk-adjusted interest rate is 8% in 20X1. GGSI uses straight-line amortization; amortization will begin in 20X2.

Required:

1. Prepare the journal entries to record the above information for 20X1.
2. In 20X2, the estimated cost to plug the shaft increased to $90,000 due to increased environmental requirements imposed by the Province of Ontario. GGSI's 20X2 risk-adjusted interest rate is 7%. Prepare the journal entries to record this additional information.
3. Assume instead that, in 20X2, the estimated plugging cost decreased to $60,000 due to technological advancements. GGSI's 20X2 risk-adjusted interest rate is 7%. Prepare the necessary journal entries for 20X2.

Required:

Prepare the necessary journal entries to record the above information for each of 20X6, 20X7, and 20X8. Assume that GGSI uses straight-line amortization and uses the half-year convention.

A9-20 Asset Retirement Obligation—Remeasurement: At the beginning of 20X1, Timber Lake Corporation (TLC) leased a tract of forest land from the provincial government for a period of four years, during which period TLC expects to harvest all of the timber. At the end of the lease (on December 20X4) or at termination of the harvest (whichever happens first), TLC is obligated to reforest the land. TLC will not do any reforesting as the lease progresses, because cleared land must continue to be used for roads and other operations.

a. At the end of 20X1, TLC has harvested about one-third of the land. The company estimates that the cost of reforestation of the land harvested so far will be $350,000 (at the end of the lease, three years hence), in current costs. TLC's risk-adjusted interest rate is 6%.
b. At the end of 20X2, TLC has harvested an additional 40% of the crop. The current cost of that part of the reforestation is estimated to be $400,000. TLC's risk-adjusted interest rate is 5%.
c. Also, at the end of 20X2, TLC realizes that the entire site will be fully harvested by the end of 20X3. Reforestation will begin at that time.

Required:

Prepare the journal entries that are necessary to record this information in each of 20X1 and 20X2.

A9-21 Research and Development Costs: Airfield Answers Corporation had several expenditures in 20X5:

a. Testing new plastic prior to use in commercial production.
b. Redesign of prototype to improve performance.
c. Testing electronic instrument components during their production.
d. Study of the possible uses of a newly developed fuel.
e. Start-up activities for the production of a newly developed jet.
f. Construction of a prototype for a new jet model.
g. Design of a new, more efficient wing for an existing airplane.
h. Portion of vice-president's salary, related to the time spent managing the research lab.
i. Experimentation to establish the properties of a new plastic just discovered.
j. Current period amortization taken on the company's laboratory research facilities.
k. Salary of lab technician working on clinical trials of new drug.

Required:

1. Explain the accounting policies required by the *CICA Handbook* for research and development expenditures.
2. Which of the above expenditures are considered research? Development? Neither?

A9-22 Research and Development; Start-Up: Cameras Limited is a new company, whose only operation is the development of a new kind of camera that will link to home computers and easily allow image transferring. The camera will come with a program to allow editing, so customers can edit their home movies and, for example, airbrush pictures and alter backgrounds. The camera and software are protected by several patents and copyrights, but technology in the area is moving quickly and competition is fierce from competing products with different technology.

By the end of 20X6, a prototype existed and was being used to solicit orders. The product itself is due out in the third quarter of 20X7, in time for the Christmas season, which represents the vast majority of the annual camera-buying volume.

In 20X6, various costs were incurred: design costs ($675,800), engineering costs ($244,600), software development costs ($397,500), and market research costs ($68,900). Administration costs amounted to $670,000. Interest on bank loans was $62,500. Legal costs to register patents and copyrights amounted to $82,200. In addition, manufacturing equipment costing $450,000 was purchased and installed. It was used briefly to manufacture the prototype in the second quarter of 20X6, but is primarily idle and will continue to be idle until the second quarter of 20X7. At that time, production will begin in earnest.

Required:

Discuss classification of the various costs listed above. As part of your response, include a list of any additional information you would like to have.

A9-23 Research and Development: In 20X1, Chiltoe Company purchased a building site for its proposed research and development laboratory at a cost of $140,000 plus legal fees of $8,000. The building was constructed during 20X2 at a cost of $500,000. The building was put into use on 2 January 20X3 and has been used exclusively for research and development activities ever since. The building has an estimated useful life of 25 years and a salvage value of $100,000 at the end of its useful life. The building is being amortized on a declining-balance basis at the rate of 6% per year.

Management estimates that about 60% of the 20X4 projects are development activities that meet the criteria for capitalization of costs. The remaining projects either benefit the current period only or are abandoned before completion. Capitalized development costs are amortized over a six-year period with a full year of amortization provided in the year the project is completed. A summary of the number of projects and the direct costs incurred in conjunction with the research and development activities for 20X4 appears below.

	Number of Projects	Salaries and Benefits	Materials, Supplies, Other
Completed projects with long-term benefits	48	$470,000	$ 80,000
Abandoned projects or projects that benefit current period only	25	280,000	110,000
Projects in process results indeterminate	7	60,000	50,000
Total	80	$810,000	$240,000

Required:

1. On the basis of the above information, prepare the capital asset and development costs sections of the balance sheet for Chiltoe Company at 31 December 20X4.
2. Determine the research and development-related items that will appear on the income statement for Chiltoe Company for the year ended 31 December 20X4. Assume an appropriate amount of building depreciation is included in "other" expenses above.

(CGA-Canada, adapted)

A9-24 Software Development Costs: GEE Software Limited is an established software development and marketing company. The following transactions were entered into in 20X5 with respect to software:

a. GEE bought the prototype of a software game from its developer, who had worked on it as a school project. GEE paid $35,000 for the prototype, and agreed to pay the creator a 15% royalty on net sales. After acquisition, costs were as follows: Design and planning, $65,000; code development, $38,200; testing, $17,100; and production cost, $356,800. The company then spent $113,400 in promotion and advertising, and launched the game. GEE has spent another $21,700 on a website to support the game. So far, sales have been encouraging.
b. GEE paid $350,000 for the rights to another software game and agreed to pay the creator 10% of net revenues as a royalty. This game has been on the market for several years, and has been a modest success. GEE is in the redesign stage now, having spent $114,000 upgrading the game, and providing an expansion pack. Redesign work will be complete within the next few months. In the meantime, GEE has begun a promotion campaign, at a cost of $54,400, to boost future sales.
c. GEE has been working on a security software program, which will be useful to business websites. Costs to date, for design and planning, $88,700; code development, $156,000; and testing, $65,000. The company had a working prototype after 65% of the code development and 10% of the testing was complete. All the design and planning work preceded the prototype. Market research, part of the planning stage, indicates a strong market for this product.

Required:
Establish appropriate accounting treatment for each of the expenditures explained above. State any assumptions made.

A9-25 Website Development: Lexicon Corporation established a new division in 20X5. The mandate of this new division is to establish a presence in the growing travel business. This division will offer, through a sophisticated website, on-line quotes for travel packages, primarily cruises. The website will include ratings of the various boats and cruise lines, including video clips of past cruises and interviews with passengers. Lowest prices will be guaranteed. Lexicon will act as a booking agent for the cruise lines and will be paid a commission. Initial market research indicates that there is a demand for objective information about travel opportunities, and increased purchasing over the Internet.

In 20X5, Lexicon incurred costs in relation to the operation:

Manager salaries (half planning)	$123,000
Rented space	24,500
Software purchased	45,800
Consultant's fees—graphics design	235,900
Computer equipment purchased; three-year life	47,800
Operating costs—heat, power, etc.	26,100
Travel and research costs re: travel packages	104,200
Preparation of content	23,100
Promotion of website to customers	67,700

The website is just recently up and running at the end of 20X5. The winter months of 20X6 will be the first real test of the viability of the service.

Required:
Provide recommendations as to how to account for the expenditures listed above. Be specific.

A9-26 Exploration and Development Costs: Resource extraction companies, including those involved in the oil and gas sector, incur a variety of exploration costs prior to the point in time when it is known whether the site is viable or not. Such costs include direct acquisition costs of property, or the mining rights thereto, geological surveys, test drilling, and mining activities and related activities. These expenditures are generally significant for each site, and often for each test drill on a site.

There are two ways to determine depletion for such costs, both acceptable under generally accepted accounting principles, and both frequently encountered in actual practice. These methods are

1. *Full Cost Method.* Exploration costs are capitalized on a global basis. For example, if an oil company was carrying out exploration activities in three areas: the Beaufort Sea, Texas, and off the coast of Ireland, the cost of all exploration activities would be included in one pool. A ceiling test is employed annually to ensure costs accumulated by cost centre do not exceed estimated cash flows from proven mineral reserves and the cost of undeveloped properties. Exploration costs are subject to depletion, or amortization, based on successful sites, usually on a units-of-production basis.

   The full cost method results in the cost of unsuccessful exploration activities being deferred, and recognized as an expense against the revenue generated by successful sites. Its proponents argue that all exploration activities are not expected to be successful, but are based on probabilities. Exploration of one site or test drill is part of a certain capital commitment to an exploration program. It is this program that represents the cost of exploration that must be expensed with revenue from successful programs. Opponents of full cost point out that this policy results in capitalization of unsuccessful sites and tests. How can a "dry hole" off the Atlantic Coast of Canada be an asset, even backed by a "gusher" in Texas? It may also result in over-capitalization, as the ceiling is difficult to determine.
2. *Successful Efforts.* Exploration expenditures are deferred on a project basis until the viability of the project is established. If the project is not viable, the costs are immediately expensed. If viable, the capitalized cost is usually grouped with other successful sites and is then subject to depletion, usually on a units-of-production basis. Successful efforts results in less cost deferred, as all unsuccessful projects are written off versus deferred. Depletion charged to subsequent mining revenues is also correspondingly lower. However, over time, both methods result in the same total expense charged to income.

   Proponents of successful efforts claim that assets are more representative of future cash flows, and therefore are less likely to be overstated. Opponents argue that assets are often materially understated, as it is often not possible to locate a viable site without extensive exploration of several areas. Subsequent depletion is also understated, in their view.

Three companies are currently considering the appropriate accounting policy choice in this area. All know that tax rules are different from both successful efforts and full cost, and thus either method may be chosen for external reporting without jeopardizing tax status. All wish to comply with GAAP.

Company 1 is a small, independent oil exploration company. It is financed 60% through equity and 40% by debt, and there are restrictive debt covenants on debt-to-equity, return on equity, dividends, and executive compensation.

Company 2 is a large, diversified mining company involved in exploration, production, and transportation of a wide range of minerals. The bulk (80%) of its financing is through a wide range of equity instruments.

Company 3 is a small mining company specializing in exploration activities. Successful properties are usually sold to the highest bidder for commercial production. The shares are closely held by a small group of investors who provide the bulk of the financing. Only one of these investors is actively involved in the business. The financial statements are used to measure performance. Cash flow is carefully monitored and is critical to survival.

Required:

After assessing the corporate reporting objectives of each company, evaluate the GAAP alternatives and recommend an accounting policy that would be most appropriate for each.

A9-27 Development Stage Company: GTX Company was formed in July 20X5. It is now the end of the 20X5 fiscal year, and accounting policies have to be set. The company has spent 20X5 raising capital and setting up its production process. Monies have been spent as follows:

Purchase of production facilities	$3,280,000
Purchase of equipment	1,789,900
Salaries of skilled workers during training	435,000
Development costs; fine-tuning specifications of major products	688,000
President and other operating staff salaries	134,700
Other operating expenses	75,000

Skilled workers have been hired and are being trained. Although orders have been received, there have been no major orders delivered. Commercial production is expected to begin in the first quarter of 20X6.

Required:

1. How would you classify this company in 20X5? Explain.
2. Suggest appropriate accounting treatment for the costs listed above.
3. What evidence would be needed to establish the need for a writedown of deferred costs recorded as assets?
4. When will this company begin principal operations? What accounting policies will be relevant at that time?

A9-28 Intangible Assets: Transactions during 20X5, the first year of the newly organized Jenny's Discount Foods Corporation, included the following:

2 Jan. Paid $8,000 lawyer's fees and other related costs for assistance in obtaining the articles of incorporation, drafting bylaws, and advising on operating in other provinces.

31 Jan. Paid $2,000 for television commercials advertising the grand opening. This advertising increased customers' awareness of the company name and location.

1 Feb. Paid $4,000 to the financial institution that assisted in the private placement of $400,000 of the company's no-par value shares. Under the contract, the underwriter charged 1% of the gross proceeds from the stock sale. The stock issuance has already been recorded. The $4,000 must be recorded.

1 May Acquired a patent from an existing patent holder for $10,200. The patent will not be used in the operations of the corporation but rather will be held as a long-term investment to produce royalty revenue.

1 July Paid consultants $6,400 for services in securing a trademark enabling the company to market under the now protected name "Jenny's Recipe."

1 Oct. Obtained a licence from the city to conduct operations in a specific location. The licence, which cost $600, runs for one year and is renewable.

1 Nov. Acquired another business and paid, after analysis, $36,000 cash for its goodwill. Recorded only the goodwill.

31 Dec. Paid $5,000 in legal fees in an unsuccessful patent defence related to the patent acquired on 1 May, which, as a result of the lawsuit, now appears to be questionable in its revenue-generating capacity.

Required:

Give the journal entry that Jenny should make for each of the above transactions.

A9-29 Disposal of Capital Assets—Interpretation of Resulting Gain or Loss: Electronic Solutions Company (ESC) sells a machine on 1 June 20X5, for $208,500. ESC incurred $3,000 of removal and selling costs on disposal. The machine cost $430,000

when it was purchased on 2 January 20X2. Its estimated residual value and useful life were $60,000 and eight years, respectively. ESC uses straight-line depreciation and records annual depreciation on 31 December. ESC takes a half-year of depreciation in the year of aquisition.

Required:

1. Provide the journal entries needed to record the disposal. Depreciation for 20X5 has not yet been recorded.
2. How would the gain or loss in (1) be affected if the machine were scrapped (zero market value)?
3. Provide an interpretation of the gain or loss in (1) for someone with little or no background in accounting.
4. Would the gain or loss affect the cash flow statement? Explain.

A9-30 Disposals: Equipment that cost $18,000 on 1 January 20X1 was sold for $10,000 on 30 June 20X6. It was being depreciated over a 10-year life by the straight-line method, assuming its residual value would be $1,500.

A warehouse that cost $150,000, residual value $15,000, was being depreciated over 20 years by the straight-line method. At the beginning of 20X6, when the structure was 15 years old, an additional wing was constructed at a cost of $90,000. The estimated life of the wing considered separately was 15 years, and its residual value was expected to be $10,000.

The accounting period ends 31 December.

Required:

1. Give all required entries to record:
   a. Sale of the equipment, including depreciation to the date of sale.
   b. The addition to the warehouse: cash was paid.
   c. Depreciation on the warehouse and its addition after the latter has been in use for one year.
2. Show how the building and attached wing would be reported on a balance sheet prepared immediately after entry 1(c) was recorded.

A9-31 Disposals: VestCo recorded the following asset disposals during the year:

a. A computer system with an original cost of $35,700, 80% depreciated, was judged obsolete during the period and scrapped.

b. Automotive equipment, a large truck with an original cost of $50,800, 60% depreciated, was exchanged for a smaller truck. The smaller truck had a fair value of $25,000. The smaller truck will be used for the same general functions, but it is hoped that it will be more efficient. The larger used truck had a fair value of $23,000, and VestCo paid $2,000 in the exchange.

c. Vestco sold machinery with an original cost of $50,000 for $45,000 cash at the end of the year. It had held the machinery for three years. Originally, Vestco had planned to hold the machinery for eight years, and charged straight-line depreciation, with an estimate of a $10,000 salvage value. At the beginning of the second year, Vestco had spent $2,000 on routine maintenance of this machine, and another $7,000 to build a special base for it in the plant that improved its efficiency. The base is now worthless.

d. A trademark, with an amortized cost of $12,000, representing primarily unamortized legal fees, was sold for $86,500 cash.

e. Vestco sold a piece of land with an original cost of $180,000 during the period. It accepted 20,000 common shares of the purchasing company, $30,000 in cash, and a five-year note that requires end-of-year payments of $50,000 per year for five years. The market interest rate is 7%. The purchaser's shares are widely traded in the stock market, and have had a market value of about $2 per share in the last 12 months, but have ranged from $1.10 to $5 in a volatile market. The land has been appraised a number of times over the years, with values ranging from $220,000 to $310,000.

Required:

1. Provide journal entries to record the disposal transactions listed above. Record the note receivable using the net method.
2. What would appear in the investing activities section of the cash flow statement as a result of each of these transactions?

A9-32 Capital Asset Exchanges—Four Situations: Pasquale Construction Company Limited has some heavy equipment that cost $480,000; accumulated amortization is $320,000. Pasquale traded the equipment with another construction company. The fair value of Pasquale's old equipment is estimated to be $250,000, and the fair value of the equipment being acquired is estimated to be $280,000. Four different possible scenarios are presented below:

a. The new equipment will perform essentially the same tasks as the new equipment, but will be more useful in tight spaces. The estimate of the fair value of the new equipment is the more reliable of the two estimates.
b. The new equipment has very different functions than the old equipment. The new equipment will permit Pasquale to attract new business that it had previously been unable to obtain. The fair value estimate of the old equipment is the more reliable of the two estimates.
c. In addition to exchanging its old equipment, Pasquale pays $40,000 cash. The characteristics of Pasquale's operating cash flow will change as a result of the exchange. The fair value of the old equipment is the more reliable estimate.
d. Assume the same facts as in (c) above, except that the exchange will not significantly alter Pasquale's cash flows.

Required:

For each scenario, prepare the journal entry to record the exchange.

A9-33 Asset Exchange: Cadillac Corporation has spare land that it no longer needs. The land cost $300,000; its appraised value of the land is $500,000. The company has exchanged the land for new computer equipment that has a list price of $600,000. If Cadillac negotiated a purchase of the equipment, it is likely that a 10% price reduction could be obtained. In addition, Cadillac would have to pay sales-related taxes of 15%. Cadillac will have to pay $40,000 in transportation costs to get the new equipment to its headquarters building. The new computer equipment is expected to significantly affect the administrative costs of Cadillac.

Required:

Prepare the journal entry that Cadillac should make to record the exchange. Explain briefly.

A9-34 Asset Exchange—Two Transactions:

a. A large truck, which cost Company A $100,000 ($60,000 accumulated depreciation), has a market resale value of $70,000. The truck is traded to a dealer, plus a cash payment of $20,000, for a new truck that will perform essentially the same services as the old truck, but will look a lot nicer to the customers. The new truck has a list price of $95,000, although discounts of 3% to 4% may be negotiable.
b. Rochester Shipping Company received a new ferry that has a normal purchase price of $1.30 million. In exchange, the company gave the vendor a parcel of land and a building located on the waterfront. The market value of the land and building is $1.15 million. The land cost $300,000; the building cost $700,000 and is 30% depreciated. The vendor will use the land and building to operate a maintenance facility. The new ferry will enable Rochester Shipping to launch a new ferry service across Lake Ontario. The ferry was available because the buyer for whom it had been built went bankrupt and was unable to take delivery. The boat remained unsold for two years before Rochester was able to negotiate the exchange. Because the boat had been dormant for so long, it needed some upgrading and maintenance. Rochester agreed to pay for the necessary work, which was estimated to cost $350,000.

Required:
Prepare the journal entry to record each of these two independent transactions.

A9-35 Repairs and Other Expenditures: Orion Corporation has various transactions in 20X6:

a. Bought a piece of machinery at an auction for $40,000, cash. The machinery had an appraised value of $57,000, so Orion was pleased to get this bargain. The company knew that the machine had to be painted and tuned up. Sales tax of 15% was paid.
b. The machine was delivered to Orion's manufacturing facility. The freight bill was $1,000.
c. The machine was painted and tuned up, at a cost of $4,000. In the process of the tune-up, it was discovered that the machine needed additional repairs that were done at a cost of $9,000.
d. Plant rearrangement, including building a new platform, was undertaken to install the new machine, at a cost of $2,200.
e. The entire manufacturing facility was repainted at a cost of $24,800.
f. The roof on the manufacturing facility was replaced at a cost of $46,700. At the same time, various upgrades were done to the electrical systems at a cost of $33,200. Neither of these transactions increased the life of the manufacturing facility, although the safety of the facility was enhanced. The cost of the original roof and the replaced wiring is not known.

Required:
Provide journal entries to record the transactions listed above. Justify your decisions. All items were acquired for cash.

A9-36 Replacements and Repairs: The plant asset records of Stavros Company reflected the following at the beginning of the current year:

Plant building (residual value, $60,000; estimated useful life, 20 years)	$300,000
Accumulated depreciation, plant building	(180,000)
Machinery (residual value, $60,000; estimated useful life, 10 years)	360,000
Accumulated depreciation, machinery	(180,000)

During the current year ending 31 December the following transactions (summarized) relating to the above accounts were completed:

1. Expenditures for non-recurring, relatively large repairs that tend to increase economic utility but not the economic lives of assets:

Plant building	$90,000
Machinery	30,000

2. Replacement of original electrical wiring system of plant building (original cost, $36,000; 75% amortized), $58,000.
3. Additions:

Plant building—added small wing to plant building to accommodate new equipment acquired; wing has useful life of 18 years and no residual value	108,000
Machinery—added special protection devices to 10 machines; devices are attached to the machines and will have to be replaced every three years (no residual value)	20,000

4. Outlays for maintenance parts, labour, and so on to keep assets in normal working condition:

Plant	55,600
Building	31,000
Machinery	29,600

Required:

Give appropriate entries to record transactions (1) through (4). Explain the basis underlying your decisions. Indicate the amortization period, when appropriate.

A9-37 Goodwill: On 1 January 20X5, the balance sheet of Nance Automotive Company was as follows:

Assets:	
Cash	$ 60,000
Accounts receivable (net)	90,000
Inventories	120,000
Plant and equipment (net)	580,000
Deferred charges (long term)	30,000
Total assets	$ 880,000
Liabilities and shareholders' equity:	
Current liabilities	$ 130,000
Long-term liability	270,000
	400,000
Shareholders' equity:	
Common shares	100,000
Retained earnings	380,000
	480,000
Total liabilities and shareholders' equity	$ 880,000

The long-term liability is bank financing, which is secured by liens on the plant and equipment. On 1 January 20X5, Magda International Incorporated purchased all of the assets except cash and deferred charges, and assumed all of the liabilities. Magda paid $780,000 cash. On the date of the sale, the fair values of the assets and liabilities of Nance were similar to their book values with two exceptions. The fair value of plant and equipment was $400,000, and the value of the long-term liability was $260,000 (due to an increase in market rates of interest).

Required:

1. Compute the amount of goodwill included in the purchase price.
2. Prepare the general journal entry that would appear on Magda's books to record the purchase.

A9-38 Goodwill: On 30 June 20X5, Backlog Software Limited purchased the net assets of Sigma Software Incorporated for cash. Sigma had been operating at a loss. Sigma's balance sheet on 30 June 20X5 was quite simple:

Accounts receivable (net)	$ 105,000
Computer equipment (net)	235,000
Total assets	$ 340,000
Bank overdraft	$ 165,000
Accounts payable and accrued liabilities	205,000
Common shares	100,000
Retained earnings (deficit)	(130,000)
Total liabilities and shareholders' equity	$ 340,000

Backlog's net assets changed by the following amounts as the result of the purchase:

	Dr./(Cr.)
Cash	$ (1,185,000)
Accounts receivable (net)	105,000
Computer equipment (net)	115,000
Software acquisition cost	870,000
Goodwill	300,000
Accounts payable and accrued liabilities	(205,000)

Required:

1. What were the fair values of Sigma's assets and liabilities at the date of the purchase? How much did Backlog pay for Sigma's net assets?
2. Why would a purchaser record some of the purchase price as goodwill when the purchased company had been losing money?

A9-39 Goodwill Calculation: During 20X4, the Evergreen Corporation entered into negotiations to buy Pine Company. During December 20X4, a final cash purchase price of $267,000 was agreed on. Evergreen will acquire all assets and liabilities of Pine Company, except for the existing cash balances of Pine.

The 31 December 20X4 balance sheet prepared by Pine Company is shown below in column (a), and the revised market values added later by Evergreen Corporation are shown in column (b).

PINE COMPANY

BALANCE SHEET

At 31 December 20X4	(a) Book Values of Pine Co.	(b) Market Values Developed by Evergreen Corp.
Assets		
Cash	$ 20,000	not applicable
Accounts receivable (net)	58,000	$ 54,000
Inventory	160,000	90,000
Property, plant, and equipment (net)	309,000	285,000
Land	11,000	40,000
Franchise (unamortized balance)	19,000	21,000
Total	$577,000	
Liabilities and shareholders' equity		
Current liabilities	$ 37,000	37,000
Bonds payable	200,000	200,000
Shareholders' equity	340,000	not applicable
Total	$577,000	

Required:

1. Compute the amount of goodwill purchased by Evergreen Corporation.
2. Give the entry for Evergreen Corporation to record the purchase of Pine Company.

A9-40 Cash Flow Statement: The following items have been extracted from the 20X3 financial statements of MC Limited:

From the balance sheet

	20X3	20X2
Machinery	$ 172,600	$145,600
Accumulated amortization, machinery	65,000	58,000
Equipment	350,000	124,000
Accumulated amortization, equipment	71,200	84,600
Buildings	276,800	246,000
Accumulated amortization, buildings	104,600	134,000
From the 20X3 income statement		
Loss on disposal of equipment	$ 3,500	
Loss on write-off of building components	6,700	
Amortization ($25,000 on machinery, $10,400 on equipment, and $9,600 on the building)	45,000	

Additional information:

1. Equipment with a market value of $36,500 was donated by a local business to encourage manufacturing activity.
2. Equipment costing $200,000 was purchased. It was eligible for a $30,000 government grant that was credited directly to the equipment account.
3. Equipment with a cost of $58,800 and a net book value of $35,000 was sold at a loss during the year.
4. Machinery with a cost of $38,000 and a net book value of $20,000 was traded for similar equipment that had a market value of $22,000. No cash was exchanged in the transaction.
5. Buildings were renovated during the year. The old roof and electrical work, with a cost of $45,700, and accumulated depreciation of $39,000, were written off and replaced at a cost of $76,500. Further repairs of $12,500 were expensed.
6. Machinery with a fair market value of $45,000 was acquired in exchange for common shares.
7. Additional equipment was acquired for cash.

Required:

Prepare cash flow statement disclosures based on the above information. The company uses the indirect method to present cash flows from operations.

A9-41 Government Assistance (Appendix): On 1 July 20X4, Theriout Corporation acquired a manufacturing plant in Cape Breton for $1,750,000. The plant, employing 50 workers, began operation immediately, and is expected to be in operation for 16 years with no residual value. In connection with the purchase, the following government assistance was received:

a. Theriout received an investment tax credit of 20% of the purchase price. The company has sufficient taxable income from other sources to use the tax credit in 20X4.

b. Theriout received a loan from the provincial government to help buy the capital assets, in the amount of $1,200,000. The loan need not be repaid as long as the plant operates for at least 10 years, and employs an average of 25 people each year. Theriout is optimistic about the prospects for the plant, but is mindful of the high rate of business failure in Cape Breton.

Required:

1. Provide two acceptable ways to record the investment tax credit. Explain the reporting ramifications of the alternatives—that is, what is the difference between the financial statement presentations?
2. Provide the entry to record the loan. Explain your choice of entry.
3. How much net depreciation expense on the manufacturing plant would be recorded in the year ended 31 December 20X4? Provide calculations.

A9-42 Government Assistance (Appendix): The Gysbers Company Limited has embarked on a two-year pollution-control program that will require the purchase of two smoke stack scrubbers costing a total of $600,000. One scrubber will be bought in 20X5, and one in 20X6. These scrubbers qualify for an investment tax credit of 20%. In addition, the federal government will lend Gysbers $100,000 for each scrubber installed. Provided that emissions are reduced 95% by the end of 20X8, the loans will be forgiven. The federal funds are received as the expenditures are made. If the emission standards are not met, the loan will have to be repaid. In 20X5, it was impossible to predict the success that the company would have with the scrubbers.

Gysbers will depreciate the devices over 20 years, straight line (no residual value), and will take a full year's depreciation in the year installed. The purchase and installation schedule is as follows:

		Cost
January 20X5	Scrubber 1	$300,000
January 20X6	Scrubber 2	300,000
Total		$600,000

Required:

1. Prepare journal entries to record the purchase of Scrubber 1 and Scrubber 2, and the receipt of the federal loans and investment tax credits. The company wishes to record the investment tax credits in a separate deferred credit account, and has enough taxable income in 20X5 and 20X6 to utilize the tax credits.
2. Prepare journal entries to record depreciation and amortization for the year ending 31 December 20X6.
3. Prepare a partial balance sheet showing the relevant information regarding the pollution-control devices as at 31 December 20X6.
4. Assume that after testing in early 20X9, it is found that the emissions have been reduced only 85%. After negotiations, it was agreed that 45% of the loans will be repaid to the government in February 20X9. The balance of the loan will be forgiven. Prepare the journal entries to record the repayment and reclassification in 20X9.

CHAPTER 10

Amortization and Impairment

INTRODUCTION

You already know that there are several acceptable methods of amortization. All methods result in allocation of the amortizable capital cost over an asset's life. Calculations involve lots of dividing and multiplying. It's really not complicated.

The emphasis in this chapter, other than a review of basic calculations, is to remind you that this is a significant area of accounting policy *choice*, since companies have the freedom to choose amortization methods. We'll look at the financial reporting objectives, and the more theoretical factors that influence choice.

Another area that is fraught with judgement issues, and choice, is the issue of writing down capital assets and goodwill when there has been an impairment in value. Lower of cost or market assessments are nothing new—all assets have to be assessed to ensure that book value does not overstate future value to the firm. However, this process is very complicated for capital assets because "market value" is not relevant. The appropriate reference point is a projection of future cash flows, which is subjective at best. There's lots of room for uncertainty to rule, and for the motivations of management to be reflected in the financial statements.

In January 2002, AOL Time Warner, the world's largest media and Internet company, announced goodwill writedowns of up to U.S. $60 billion. The goodwill had been recorded on the acquisition of Time Warner in the prior year. The impairment loss followed revision of earnings forecasts. Original forecasts had promised earnings growth of 20 to 30%; the revised figures were in the 8 to 12% range. At the time of the writedown, there was speculation in the financial press that AOL's incoming chief executive officer might prefer more conservative reporting to "promise a lot less and deliver more."

This chapter will focus on the many facets of amortization and impairment of tangible and intangible capital assets.

There also are occasions when assets (and liabilities) of a company may be restated *up* to fair values, thereby establishing a new basis of accounting for those assets. For companies that are bound by the limitations imposed by the *CICA Handbook*, the occasions when upward revaluation is acceptable are highly restricted. Since assets may be revalued upward only in very limited circumstances, we will discuss asset revaluation in an Appendix rather than in the main body of the chapter.

REVIEW OF DEFINITIONS

A review of terminology is probably the best place to start. *Capital assets*, both tangible and intangible, produce revenue through use rather than through resale. They can be viewed as quantities of *economic service potential* to be consumed over time in the earning of revenues.

Accounting principles call for *matching* the costs of all types of capital assets against revenue over their useful lives. **Amortization** allows for the periodic allocation of the cost of capital assets against revenue earned. Amortization is also called **depreciation** when it is associated with tangible capital assets, and **depletion** when associated with natural resources. Amortization is a broad term that includes both depreciation and depletion as well as the amortization of intangibles and of long-term deferred charges.

Depreciation (i.e., on tangible capital assets) is recorded in an **accumulated depreciation** account, which is a *contra account* that is deducted from the related asset account for balance sheet presentation. Amortization of intangible assets has generally been recorded as a direct credit to the asset account. It would be better to use a contra account for intangible assets, because the *CICA Handbook* requires separate disclosure of both cost and accumulated amortization. This disclosure recommendation is not well followed in practice, as we pointed out in Chapter 9.

The **net book value** (carrying value) of an asset is its original cost plus any capitalized post-acquisition cost less accumulated amortization to date. **Amortizable cost** is total capitalized asset cost less estimated residual value, the total amount of amortization to be recognized over the useful life of the asset. *Residual value* is the estimated net recoverable amount from disposal or trade-in of the asset at the end of its estimated useful life. It is the portion of an asset's acquisition cost not consumed through use, and it is not matched against revenues through amortization. The minimum net book value is residual value.

NATURE OF AMORTIZATION

What is amortization? Simply put, *it is an allocation of capital cost, expensed over the useful life of the asset.* Amortization applies to all items of limited life that appear on the balance sheet, including long-term deferred charges and credits as well as both tangible and intangible capital assets.

"Amortization" is the general term that applies to the interperiod allocation of the cost of any capital asset. What is amortization *not*? Misconceptions abound. For example,

- Accumulated amortization does not represent cash set aside for replacement of assets.
- Amortization does not imply the creation of a separate cash fund for asset replacement.
- Amortization does not measure the decline in market value during the period, and net book value does not equal market value.

Depreciation is commonly used to describe a decline in market value; for example, "A new car will depreciate by $3,000 as soon as you drive it off the dealer's lot." The accounting meaning of the term "depreciate" is different. Historical cost financial statements track cost, not market value.

The Conceptual Basis of Amortization

The amount of amortization recognized is not linked to the decline in an asset's utility or market value in a given period. However, the *inevitable eventual* decline in value justifies periodic recognition of amortization. The decline in utility of capital assets is caused by

- physical factors, mainly usage (wear and tear from operations, action of time and the elements, and deterioration and decay) and
- obsolescence (the result of new technology).

Assets rendered obsolete are often in good condition and still capable of supplying the service originally expected of them. Technological advances may have rendered their operating costs uneconomic. Obsolescence also occurs when facility expansion renders certain assets unusable under new operating conditions or when demand for the product or service supplied by the asset declines.

Technological change does not automatically mean that older equipment is obsolete, however. If the older equipment meets the *present needs* of the company, obsolescence is not a factor. For example, in the computer industry, new computer chips substantially increase computer speeds and capabilities. For many companies, continual upgrades to state-of-the art hardware are not cost effective. Older computers will still run required software and they are not obsolete. Of course, software upgrades often require hardware upgrades, and this is the point at which obsolesence becomes a factor.

The Requirement to Recognize Amortization Expense

Do companies have to charge amortization expense for all capital assets? The answer, generally, is yes. Amortization is now a well-entrenched practice, but such was not always the case. For example, in the early days of the railroads, the nature of obsolescence was not well understood, and there were those who claimed that the assets would physically last forever if well maintained. Alas, the steam locomotive is with us no more.

Generally, capital assets must be amortized. Why?

- Amortization is an allocation of capital cost. Operations must bear this cost as a cost of assets used during the period. The general requirement for amortization is based on the matching concept and on the underlying assumption that financial reporting will match the costs of providing services to the revenue generated.
- Amortization is justifiable based on an *eventual* decline in market value, often caused by obsolescence.

There are three asset categories that do not have to be amortized:

1. LAND Land is not at risk due to obsolescence nor does it suffer from wear and tear. Therefore, land is not amortized. We hope you find this intuitively appealing! Of course, if the land is a mining site, then the situation is far different and depletion would be recorded.

2. INTANGIBLE CAPITAL ASSETS WITH AN INDEFINITE LIFE When an intangible asset is determined to have an indefinite useful life, it should not be amortized (*CICA* 3062.10). What is indefinite life? The *CICA Handbook* defines it as follows:

> When no legal, regulatory, contractual, competitive, economic or other factors limit the life of an intangible asset to the enterprise, the useful life of the asset is considered to be indefinite. The term "indefinite" does not mean infinite.
> (*CICA* 3062.15)

How often will this happen? Many intangibles have limited legal or contractual life, and competitive and economic factors are important. These intangibles will be amortized. The standard that exempts indefinite life intangibles from amortization is entirely logical, just as the land exemption was logical. For example, a trademark can be legally protected for an infinite period. If the product associated with the trademark has indefinite sales potential, the trademark would not be amortized.

However, indefinite existence of a trademark does not necessarily mean that its useful life will continue forever. Trademarks are occasionally updated. CBC and Air Canada both have updated or replaced their trademark designs in recent years. The old designs obviously have no more useful economic life. Many companies amortize the costs of acquiring or designing a trademark (which can be quite expensive) even though the trademark has an endless legal life.

Useful lives have to be reviewed regularly, and if the useful life becomes finite, amortization of these assets must commence (*CICA* 3062.17). Intangible assets that are not amortized must be reviewed for impairment on an annual basis.

3. GOODWILL Goodwill does not have to be amortized, but is subject to an annual review for impairment. The useful life of goodwill is assumed to be indefinite (*CICA* 3062.23).

Standard-setters have gone back and forth on this issue. Before 1974, goodwill was not amortized. Between 1974 and mid-2001, all goodwill had to amortized, over periods not to exceed 40 years. Effective 30 June 2001, goodwill amortization is not permitted in the United States or Canada.

Such a general exemption seems aggressive, since competitive and economic forces are such that much goodwill cannot be considered to be permanent. On the other hand, if operations are successful, goodwill could be increasing, not decreasing. Useful life is very hard to assess in this area.

CONCEPT REVIEW

1. What are the main causes of the decline in value or usefulness of plant assets over time?
2. Why is amortization expense not necessarily an accurate measure of the decline in value of capital assets?
3. What assets are not amortized? Why?

ACCOUNTING POLICY CHOICE

The *CICA Handbook* requires that the method of amortization chosen be *rational and systematic*, appropriate to the nature of the capital asset and its use (*CICA* 3061.28). The choices are

1. Based on equal allocation to each time period—the straight-line (SL) method.
2. Based on inputs and outputs (variable charge).
   a. Service-hours (SH) method.
   b. Productive output (PO), or units-of-production, method.
3. Accelerated methods (decreasing charge).
   a. Declining-balance (DB) methods.
   b. Sum-of-the-years'-digits (SYD) method.
4. Sinking-fund methods (increasing charge).

The *CICA Handbook* provides some commentary on usage patterns:

> A straight-line method reflects a constant charge for the service as a function of time. A variable charge method reflects service as a function of usage. Other methods may be appropriate in certain situations. For example, an increasing charge method may be used when an enterprise can price its goods or services so as to obtain a constant rate of return on the investment in the asset; a decreasing charge method may be appropriate when the operating efficiency of the asset declines over time.
>
> (*CICA* 3061.31)

For intangible assets, when the pattern of economic benefits cannot be reliably determined, a straight-line amortization method should be used (*CICA* 3062.14).

Conceptual Analysis

In theory, at least, the amortization method should describe the nature and use of the asset. For example, assume that a delivery truck has an estimated useful life of five years or 300,000 kilometres. Amortization based on distance driven might yield a more accurate matching of expense and revenue than amortization based on useful life in years. Based on this reasoning, the methods based on usage appear to be the most logical, unless obsolescence is a major factor, in which case straight line is appealing.

However, GAAP allows choice with few guidelines: all methods are rational and systematic, and an evaluation of the nature of use of an asset can be subjective. Why aren't amortization methods narrowed down? The reason is that there is a lack of one "correct method," really. The amount of revenue or cash produced by the use of one specific capital asset is usually impossible to determine clearly. Revenues are not generated by assets used in isolation. Rather, they are produced by a number of assets and people working together. It is impossible to associate specific revenues (benefits) to specific assets, and thus impossible to allocate the cost of most operational assets on the basis of benefits or revenues.

As an allocation, amortization is *incorrigible*—it cannot be supported or refuted without question.[1] If you can't establish one right way, then all rational and systematic methods are equally acceptable. Companies tend to let corporate reporting objectives, rather than pattern of use, dictate policy choice. This does not do wonders for comparability.

Studies of the U.S. stock market have suggested that investors are not fooled by accounting policy choices that do not have any impact on cash flows. That is, investors are smart enough to see the fundamental equivalency between two identical firms, earning identical return but reporting different incomes only because of different amortization policies, at least in the short run. However, that's just one group of users. Most Canadian companies are not traded on large, well-disciplined, stock exchanges.

Policy Choice in Practice

Financial Reporting in Canada 2003 reports the following about choice of amortization policy:

Amortization Policy	Number	Proportion
Straight-line	182	64%
Declining balance	53	19
Units-of-production	44	16
Sinking fund	4	1
	283	100%

There are two points of interest here. First is the fact that 200 companies report use of 283 methods. This isn't a misprint; many companies use more than one method! For example, a company may use straight-line amortization for intangible assets and declining-balance for tangible assets, and so on. Second, of the 200 sample companies, 182 use straight-line for at least some of their capital assets—64% of the observations, and 91% of the companies. Simple is often best!

Factors Influencing Choice

How do companies pick an accounting amortization policy? Here is a summary of factors considered:

- *Nature and use of asset.* To promote matching, the pattern of usage—and thus the pattern of revenue generated—is evaluated to establish the most logical amortization pattern.
- *Corporate reporting objectives.* On a situation-by-situation basis, it is important to analyze the various elements that drive reporting objectives. Is there a bonus based on net income? Is the entity regulated? Is it held under restrictive loan covenants governing debt-to-equity ratios, profitability, etc? These factors have a powerful impact on the accounting policies chosen.

[1] The *incorrigibility* of accounting allocations was definitively demonstrated by Professor Arthur L. Thomas (McMaster University) in two research studies published by the American Accounting Association in the series *Studies in Accounting Research: #3: The Allocation Problem in Financial Accounting Theory* (1969), and *#9: The Allocation Problem: Part Two* (1974). The conclusions of these studies were not greeted warmly by many accountants who preferred to believe in the "truth" of their allocations, but no one has ever been able to demonstrate that allocations are not inherently arbitrary.

- *Industry norms.* Comparability is an important qualitative characteristic of financial reporting. Companies' financial statements are used by investors, creditors, and others to assess their performance relative to their competition. Using the same amortization method helps. Amortization methods—such as sinking-fund amortization for rental properties and units of production for natural resources—become generally accepted within an industry.
- *Parent company preferences.* Is the company a subsidiary of another company (the parent)? If so, its financial statements will be combined, or *consolidated*, at the end of the fiscal year. These consolidated financial statements are more meaningful if all constituents follow the same accounting policies, and thus the parent company often dictates key policies to its subsidiaries. A lot of Canadian companies that are wholly owned subsidiaries of foreign parents (usually American) do what their parents tell them, which may include accounting methods not widely used by Canadian-owned enterprises.
- *Minimize future (deferred) income taxes.* Many smaller firms don't really care what amount of amortization is booked, but are interested in keeping their financial statements simple. Therefore, it seems logical to use an accounting policy that results in amortization that coincides with the required tax treatment (which generally is a form of declining-balance amortization, as we'll see in the Appendix to this chapter).
- *Accounting information system costs.* Notwithstanding the computer revolution, detailed information about acquisition costs, post-acquisition costs, useful life, residual value, and accumulated amortization must be maintained. Which system is the least complex?

The latitude in adoption of amortization methods and the variety of estimates of useful life and residual value are at odds with the uniformity and consistency objectives of financial reporting. The large dollar amount of amortization expense reported combined with the inherently approximate nature of amortization results in a potentially difficult comparison problem for financial statement users.

Estimates Required

Amortization methods require that the preparer make the following estimates:

1. acquisition cost
2. residual value
3. useful life

ACQUISITION COST Acquisition cost may not appear to be an estimate. In some cases, the cost of an asset is readily determinable. Acquisition cost is particularly "fuzzy" for intangible assets; many of the acquisition or development costs may have been expensed, and only a portion capitalized. However, acquisition cost often is a bit of an approximation even for tangible capital assets because ancillary acquisition costs such as excise taxes, shipping costs, installation, and start-up training costs either are estimated or ignored. Thus, the measurement of "historical cost" is governed by various policies concerning capitalization (versus expensing), as we discussed in the previous chapter.

RESIDUAL VALUE To estimate residual value, consideration is given to the costs of dismantling, restoring, and disposing of the retired asset. Future removal and site restoration costs also reduce residual value and can be material. These include all costs to dismantle and restore a property. These costs are particularly important for natural resources. For example, if the estimated realizable value upon retirement of an asset is $2,500 and estimated dismantling and selling costs are $500, the net residual value is $2,000.

In practice, residual values for tangible assets are often assumed to be zero. This is logical when assets are held almost until the end of their useful lives and restoration or removal costs are low.

An *intangible* asset would usually have a residual value of zero. There would have to be an established market for similar intangible assets, or a specific sale agreement, to justify a residual value higher than zero (*CICA* 3062.13).

USEFUL LIFE The useful life (economic life) generally has a much greater impact on amortization than estimated residual value. The useful life of an asset must be finite to justify amortization recognition. An estimate of useful life for a tangible asset requires assumptions about potential obsolescence, severity of use, and adequate maintenance. It is even more difficult to estimate the useful life of an *intangible asset.* Often, the real question is how long the intangible asset will be used or can generate revenue. It's important to take a hard look at many factors:

1. The expected use of the asset.
2. The legal life of an intangible asset (see Exhibit 10-1) plus any renewal provisions.
3. The effects of economic factors, along with demand and competition.
4. Potential obsolescence.
5. The level of maintenance expenditures required (high maintenance implies an end to useful life).
6. The expected use of another asset or process that is related to the intangible asset (for instance, a patent for a process versus the machinery that runs the process).

Amortization is not recognized (that is, useful life does not begin) until the asset is in its intended condition and location and is contributing to revenue. When facilities are temporarily idle, recognition of amortization continues when the method used is based on the passage of time, reflecting increased obsolescence and the reduced economic usefulness of the asset.

When a company permanently stops using a capital asset, the asset is reclassified as *held for sale* and amortization stops. If the asset's fair value is less than its carrying value, the asset is written down to its fair value. The loss is recognized in income. We will discuss the accounting for held-for-sale capital assets in a separate section at the end of this chapter.

Assets should not be amortized below residual value under any method or system. Although declining-balance methods do not use residual value in calculating periodic amortization expense, a determination should, in theory, be made at the end of each accounting period to ensure that book value is higher than residual value. Where the residual value of individual assets is relatively small, however, this test often is not performed and the assets are amortized to zero.

EXHIBIT 10-1

LEGAL LIFE OF CERTAIN INTANGIBLE ASSETS

Patent	20 years from date granted but registration period is also covered
Industrial Design Registration	Five years; renewable for a further five years
Trademark	20 years; renewable for infinite successive periods
Franchise	Unlimited unless specified in contract with franchisor
Copyright	Life of the author plus 50 years

CONCEPT REVIEW

1. What is the most popular method of amortization in Canada?
2. Name three factors that influence management's choice of amortization policy.
3. What estimates must be made before a capital asset can be amortized?

AMORTIZATION METHODS

Exhibit 10-2 summarizes the amortization formulas for six common amortization methods. Each of the six amortization methods will be illustrated in the following sections, using the data shown in Exhibit 10-3. Exhibit 10-4 shows amortization schedules for the four most common methods.

Straight-Line Method

The **straight-line (SL) method** is based on the assumption that an asset provides equivalent service, or value in use, each year of its life. The SL method relates amortization directly to the passage of time rather than to the asset's use, resulting in a constant amount of amortization recognized per time period. The formula for computing periodic SL amortization, with its application to the asset in Exhibit 10-3, is

Yearly SL amortization
= (Acquisition cost − Residual value) ÷ Estimated useful life in years
= ($6,600 − $600) ÷ 5
= $1,200 per year

The SL method is logically appealing as well as rational and systematic. It is especially appropriate for a tangible asset when the use of the asset is essentially the same each period, and repairs and maintenance expenditures are constant over the useful life. The method is less appropriate for assets whose decline in service potential or benefits produced relates not to the passage of time but rather to other variables, such as units produced or hours in service.

The SL method is the most popular method in use in Canada, by far. Ease of use partially explains the method's popularity. It is also popular because it provides a stable, smooth amortization pattern, and expenses a relatively low amount in its initial year, popular with firms trying to maximize earnings and net assets in the short run. For intangible assets, SL amortization must be used if the pattern of economic benefits cannot be determined.

Methods Based on Inputs and Outputs

Amortization methods that associate periodic amortization with measurable use of capital assets include the service-hours method and productive output method (also called the units-of-production method). The input-output methods are rational and systematic and logically match expense and revenue if the asset's utility is measurable in terms of service time or units of output.

These methods do not relate amortization to the passage of time, as the other individually applied methods do. Hence, amortization expense under these methods is not recorded when assets are idle, and thus they are appropriate when obsolescence is not as much of a factor in determining useful life as wear and tear. If obsolescence is a factor, an asset's utility decreases whether used or not, and these methods will not portray this reality.

EXHIBIT 10-2

AMORTIZATION FORMULAS

Straight line (SL):

Annual SL amortization = (Acquisition cost − Residual value)
÷ Estimated useful life in years

Service hours:

Amortization rate per service hour = (Acquisition cost − Residual value)
÷ Estimated service life in hours

Annual service hour amortization = Amortization rate per service hour
× Hours of usage

Productive output:

Amortization rate per unit of output = (Acquisition cost − Residual value)
÷ Estimated productive output in units

Annual productive output amortization = Amortization rate per unit of
output × Units produced

Declining balance (DB):

Annual DB amortization = (Acquisition cost − Accumulated amortization)
× DB rate

Sum of the years digits (SYD):

Annual SYD amortization = (Acquisition cost − Residual value)
× SYD Fraction

Sinking fund:

Annual sinking fund amortization = [(Acquisition cost − Residual value)
÷ (F/A, i%, # of periods)]
+ annual compound interest to date

EXHIBIT 10-3

DATA USED TO ILLUSTRATE AMORTIZATION METHODS

Acquisition cost, 1 January 20X1	$ 6,600
Residual value	600
Estimated useful life:	
Years	5
Service hours	20,000
Productive output in units	10,000

Activity	Service Hours	Units Produced
20X1	3,800	1,800
20X2	4,000	2,000
20X3	4,500	2,400
20X4	4,200	1,800
20X5	3,500	2,000
	20,000	10,000

service-hours amortization

a method of calculating amortization expense that bases amortization expense on current service hours used as related to total service hours expected

SERVICE-HOURS METHOD The **service-hours (SH) method** is based on the assumption that the appropriate amortization is directly related to the amount of time the asset is in use.

Amortization rate per service-hour	= (Acquisition cost − Residual value) ÷ Estimated service life in hours
	= ($6,600 − $600) ÷ 20,000 = $0.30
Yearly SH amortization, 20X1	= Amortization rate per service hour × Hours used
	= $0.30 × 3,800 = $1,140

Exhibit 10-4 illustrates the service-hours method for the life of the asset.

productive output (PO) amortization

a method of calculating amortization expense that bases amortization on current production output as related to expected productive output

PRODUCTIVE OUTPUT METHOD The **productive output (PO) method** is similar except that the number of units of output is used to measure asset use. A constant amount of amortizable cost is allocated to each unit of output as a cost of production, so annual amortization amounts fluctuate with changes in the volume of output:

Amortization rate per unit of output	= (Acquisition cost − Residual value) ÷ Estimated productive output in units
	= ($6,600 − $600) ÷ 10,000 = $0.60
Yearly PO amortization, 20X1	= Amortization rate per unit of output × Units produced
	= $0.60 × 1,800 = $1,080

Exhibit 10-4 illustrates the PO method over the life of this asset.

The service-hours and productive output methods can produce different results, depending on the ratio of machine-hours to units produced. For the asset under study, 2.11 machine-hours were required to produce one unit in 20X1 (3,800 ÷ 1,800), while in 20X2 that figure was reduced to 2.00 (4,000 ÷ 2,000), indicating a greater efficiency. The SH method, therefore, yielded slightly higher amortization per unit of output in 20X1 than in 20X2. If the yield ratio is constant, the two methods would produce identical results and the firm would choose the one that is easier to implement.

The productive output method is commonly used to measure depletion of natural resources. For example, assume that a company incurs costs of $4,000,000 to lease, explore, and develop a mine site that is expected to produce two million tonnes of coal. The land can be sold for $500,000 after mining is finished. The depletion per tonne is $1.75, [($4,000,000 − $500,000) ÷ 2,000,000]. Annual depletion is based on the actual production level. For these companies, mining equipment and even buildings are often also amortized on a units of production basis.

ESTIMATES A significant difficulty in input and output methods is an *accurate* estimate of total projected activity. Annual usage data is also needed to apply the method. Often, the extra cost of this data is not worth the effort. Remember, too, that if usage is relatively constant, the result will not be materially different from the straight-line method. Another problem arises when the running time of an asset varies without a corresponding effect in the output of service. For example, the increasingly heavy traffic in urban areas causes vehicles to run many more hours per week with no increase in their productive service.

Accelerated Amortization Methods

Accelerated amortization methods recognize greater amounts of amortization early in the useful life of capital assets and lesser amounts later. Thus, they accelerate the recognition of amortization.

Accelerated methods are based on the assumption that newer assets produce more benefits per period because they are more productive and require less maintenance and repair. Accelerated methods match more of the acquisition cost against the revenue of these earlier periods when greater benefits are obtained. A smoother pattern of total annual operating expense is often the result, with the sum of annual amortization and maintenance expense more constant than is likely with SL amortization. The one accelerated method that is in wide use in Canada is the declining-balance method.

declining-balance amortization
a method of accelerated amortization in which amortization is calculated as cost less accumulated amortization multiplied by a given constant percentage until net book value declines to residual value

DECLINING-BALANCE METHOD **Declining-balance (DB) methods** are significantly different from other methods in two ways:

1. Residual value is not subtracted from cost when computing amortization. Instead, declining-balance amortization stops when the net book value of the asset is equal to residual value.
2. The amortization rate is applied to a declining (*net*) balance rather than to a constant cost.

How do companies arrive at an amortization rate? There is a formula that can be used to find the rate that will reduce the book value of the asset to its estimated salvage value at the end of its estimated useful life, but the formula is never used in practice! Instead, firms may pick a fairly arbitrary rate, based on their assessment of useful life, on industry norms, or perhaps based on corporate reporting objectives.

Another approach is to use the rates established by income tax regulations for Capital Cost Allowance (CCA). CCA is mostly a declining-balance method, but uses straight line for some kinds of assets. CCA doesn't work exactly the same as declining-balance amortization, but, if the same rates are used (and a half-year's depreciation is charged in the year of acquisition), the tax and book amortization are often identical and future (deferred) income tax balances are minimized as a result. The CCA system is briefly described in the Appendix to this chapter. Tax-based rates are commonly used by private companies.

Another approach to determining the rate is called double-declining balance amortization (DDB), which uses a rate equal to twice the straight-line rate. For example, the asset in Exhibit 10-3 has a 20% straight-line rate (the reciprocal of the years of life; 1/5 = 20%), and so the DDB rate would be 40%. This is a fairly aggressive amortization rate—40% of the capital cost would be written off in the first year. If this capital asset is a piece of machinery, its CCA rate is set, in Class 8, at 20%. Amortization rates, which must be disclosed, should be reviewed by financial statement users to see if they are aggressive or not.

For our example, assume that the firm has chosen a 40% DB rate.

Annual DB amortization = (Acquisition cost − Accumulated amortization) × DB rate
20X1 DB amortization = $6,600 × 40% = $2,640
20X2 DB amortization = ($6,600 − $2,640) × 40% = $1,584

See Exhibit 10-4 for the complete set of calculations. Notice in particular the last line, where amortization expense *stops* when accumulated amortization equals the $6,000 amortizable cost, leaving the $600 residual value intact. Thus, the maximum amortization for 20X5 is $256 ($6,000 − $5,744) rather than $342 (40% of $856).

sum-of-the-years' digits (SYD) amortization
a method of accelerated amortization where amortization is calculated by multiplying the amortizable cost by a fraction whose denominator is the sum of the years' digits

SUM-OF-THE-YEARS'-DIGITS METHOD The **sum-of-the-years'-digits (SYD) method** computes annual amortization as follows:

Annual SYD amortization = (Acquisition cost − Residual value) × SYD Fraction

EXHIBIT 10-4

AMORTIZATION SCHEDULES—Four Common Methods

Straight-Line Method

Year	Amortization Expense	Accumulated Amortization	Cost	Net Book Value
1 January 20X1			$6,600	$6,600
31 December 20X1	$1,200	$1,200	6,600	5,400
31 December 20X2	1,200	2,400	6,600	4,200
31 December 20X3	1,200	3,600	6,600	3,000
31 December 20X4	1,200	4,800	6,600	1,800
31 December 20X5	1,200	6,000	6,600	600 (residual)
Total	$6,000			

Service-Hours Method

Year	Service Hours	Amortization Expense	Accumulated Amortization	Cost	Net Book Value
1 January 20X1				$6,600	$6,600
31 December 20X1	3,800	(3,800 × $.30) = $1,140	$1,140	6,600	5,460
31 December 20X2	4,000	(4,000 × $.30) = 1,200	2,340	6,600	4,260
31 December 20X3	4,500	(4,500 × $.30) = 1,350	3,690	6,600	2,910
31 December 20X4	4,200	(4,200 × $.30) = 1,260	4,950	6,600	1,650
31 December 20X5	3,500	(3,500 × $.30) = 1,050	6,000	6,600	600 (residual)
Total	20,000	$ 6,000			

Productive Output Method

Year	Units Produced	Amortization Expense	Accumulated Amortization	Cost	Net Book Value
1 January 20X1				$6,600	$6,600
31 December 20X1	1,800	(1,800 × $.60) = $1,080	$1,080	6,600	5,520
31 December 20X2	2,000	(2,000 × $.60) = 1,200	2,280	6,600	4,320
31 December 20X3	2,400	(2,400 × $.60) = 1,440	3,720	6,600	2,880
31 December 20X4	1,800	(1,800 × $.60) = 1,080	4,800	6,600	1,800
31 December 20X5	2,000	(2,000 × $.60) = 1,200	6,000	6,600	600 (residual)
Total	10,000	$6,000			

Declining-Balance Method

Year	Amortization Expense	Accumulated Amortization	Cost	Net Book Value
1 January 20X1			$6,600	$6,600
31 December 20X1	(40% × $6,600) = $2,640	$2,640	6,600	3,960
31 December 20X2	(40% × $3,960) = 1,584	4,224	6,600	2,376
31 December 20X3	(40% × $2,376) = 950	5,174	6,600	1,426
31 December 20X4	(40% × $1,426) = 570	5,744	6,600	856
31 December 20X5	256*	6,000	6,600	600 (residual)
Total	$6,000			

* Should be 40% of $856, or $342, but limited to $256 so that net book value does not go below residual.

The SYD fraction is calculated with a numerator and a denominator:

- *Numerator.* The number of years remaining in the useful life at the beginning of the period. The first year for the asset in Exhibit 10-3 will have a numerator of 5; the second year, 4; the third year, 3; and so on. The numerator always declines with each year of asset use.
- *Denominator.* The name of the method tells it all: the denominator is the sum of the years' digits. For our asset, with a five-year life, this is 15, (1 + 2 + 3 + 4 + 5).

Amortization expense in 20X1 in our example:

20X1 SYD amortization = ($6,600 − $600) × (5/15) = $2,000
20X2 SYD amortization = ($6,600 − $600) × (4/15) = $1,600

Hardly any Canadian companies use this method. It's a lot more popular in the United States, where it may also be used for tax reporting. Canadian adopters are almost always subsidiaries of U.S. parents.

Sinking Fund Amortization

So far, we've seen amortization methods that produce level amounts of annual amortization, decreasing amounts of annual amortization, and amortization that will go up and down based on output or usage. The last amortization method we'll talk about produces a pattern of *increasing* amortization—less in the initial years, and more in later years.

This amortization method has gained a toehold in real estate companies that hold apartment buildings, office buildings, and shopping complexes. These properties are usually highly levered, meaning lots of debt, which translates into lots of interest, especially in the early years. The combination of high interest expense and straight-line—or especially declining-balance—amortization would destroy the profit picture for one of these operations. Highly levered companies are often saddled with debt covenants that specify debt-to-equity ratios, and the like, and thus they have a motive for wishing to maximize income. Subsequently, when interest declines because the mortgage is paid down later in the building's life, there's more "room" for amortization expense.

There is probably some energetic theoretical basis for this method, too, but it's primarily popular because of the profit pattern it produces when combined with interest expense. And, of course, it's rational and systematic, and that's all we require!

Any method that provides for increasing amortization is risky in some sense, because it leaves a material amount of cost unamortized until the latter part of an asset's life. What if the estimate of useful life was optimistic? A large write-off would result. Also, repair costs can escalate in later years, which, combined with higher amortization expenses, would have an unfortunate impact on earnings.

sinking fund amortization
a method of allocating costs in which amortization expense is lowest in an asset's early years but increases over time

There are several methods of increasing amortization, but the most popular is called **sinking fund amortization.** It is calculated as though there was a sinking fund being accumulated for asset replacement. Each year, amortization is equal to the increase in the sinking fund, both "principal" and "interest." *All these amounts are purely notional, as no sinking fund exists*; the numbers are just used to provide the amortization expense calculation.

If a $5,500,000 building with no residual value was to be amortized over 20 years, using an interest rate of 8%, the principal portion of the amortization would be equal to $120,187 [$5,500,000 ÷ (F/A, 8%, 20)].

	Principal Payment	Interest @ 8%	Increase in Fund	Balance
1	$120,187	—	$120,187	$120,187
2	120,187	$9,615	129,802	249,989
3	120,187	19,999	140,186	390,175
etc. ...				

By the end of the 20th year, the balance in the "fund" will be the $5,500,000 amortizable cost. Annual amortization expense is equal to the increase in the "fund"—$120,187 the first year, $129,802 the next, and so on. If you worked the table all the way through you'd discover that the amortization in year 20 was $518,691, which is a hefty increase from the $120,187 booked in the first year!

CONCEPT REVIEW

1. When is a company most likely to use an output-based amortization method?
2. What is double about double-declining balance amortization?
3. Why might a company want to use an amortization method that coincides with tax-basis capital cost allowance?

ADDITIONAL AMORTIZATION ISSUES

Additional amortization issues include a minimum amortization test, fractional-year amortization, site restoration costs, and amortization systems.

Minimum Amortization Test

Capital assets are not held for sale, but sometimes their fair market values are apparent, and recording amortization seems counter-intuitive. For example, assume that you're in the following situation:

Asset	Apartment building
Expected life	An additional 20 years
Original cost	$3,750,000
Net book value	$3,150,000
Salvage at the end of 20 years	nominal; structure would have to be dismantled
Market value of similar buildings now, excluding land value	$4,350,000

Market values may be responding to increased demand for rental properties, but more likely to interest rate shifts. Why should any amortization be claimed on this property, whose current fair value exceeds its book value by a significant margin? Again, refer to the rationale for amortization at the beginning of the chapter: amortization is an *allocation* of capital cost, and is still appropriate in these circumstances.

However, there's another angle on the game: what if the company announces that it plans to hold the building for only another five years, and then sell it? The amortization formulas mostly start by taking cost and subtracting the residual value, the fair value on the expected sale date. Now, it's quite possible that the fair value five years' hence might still be higher than the existing net book value.

Assume that several appraisals of the real estate market, and this building in particular, conclude that the building could be sold for something in the range of $4,400,000 in five years time, excluding a land value. If the company used straight-line amortization, the calculation would go as follows:

($3,150,000 − $4,400,000) ÷ 5 = −$1,250,000 ÷ 5 = −$250,000

(Note that the calculation starts with net book value as an amortizable cost, because the company is in the process of changing the estimate of useful life; we'll take another look at these accounting changes in Chapter 20.) The amortization number produced by the formula is *negative*, but negative amortization is never recorded. Assets are not written *up*.

Can the company avoid amortization on these grounds? Remember that the company is not committed to the sale; it can easily avoid the sale when the time comes if management doesn't like market conditions, or if management really wasn't on the level in the first place. The accountant is relatively powerless to prevent the manipulation of "intention." Fortunately, there is a solution. In these circumstances, the *CICA Handbook* recommends

> that the amount of amortization should be the larger of:
> (a) the cost less scrap value over the life of the asset; and
> (b) the cost less resale value over the useful life of the asset.
> (*CICA* 3061.28)

salvage value
an asset's fair value at the end of its life; often zero or scrap only

residual value
the estimated net recoverable amount from disposal or trade-in of an asset at the end of its estimated useful life

Salvage value is defined as the asset's fair value *at the end of its life*; scrap value, for our building. **Residual value** is the asset's fair value when the company is done with it; the $4,400,000 appraisal. Assuming scrap value is negligible, this company would have to do a second calculation, under (a): ($3,150,000 − $0) ÷ 20, or $157,500. The calculation under (b) produced zero amortization, because the result was negative. The greater amount of amortization, $157,500, would have to be recorded.

This situation is not really common—it's not often that a second-hand asset is worth a lot more than its net book value. But it does sometimes happen, and the rule acts to prevent an end-run around the amortization requirements.

Fractional-Year Amortization

The calculations illustrated in Exhibit 10-4 assume that the company takes a full year of amortization in the year that the asset was acquired. This seems logical in the specific example, because the asset was assumed to have been purchased on 1 January. However, most capital assets are not placed in service at the beginning of a reporting period, nor do disposals occur neatly at the end of a year. Firms adjust for fractional periods in two different ways. Some compute the exact amount of amortization for each fractional period, and others apply an accounting policy **convention.** A *convention* is a standardized short cut.

convention
an accepted practice adopted to simplify calculations

EXACT CALCULATION APPROACH This approach computes the "precise" amount of amortization for each fractional period. For example, assume that an asset costing $20,000 with a residual value of $2,000 and useful life of four years is placed into service on 1 April 20X1. The firm has a calendar-year reporting cycle. The asset in question is used only 9/12 of a year in 20X1. Under SL amortization, the asset's fractional service period is applied to the annual amortization amount, as illustrated:

Amortization expense for 20X1 = ($20,000 − $2,000) × (1/4) × (9/12) = $3,375
Amortization expense for 20X2 through 20X4 = ($20,000 − $2,000) × (1/4)
= $4,500 per year
Amortization expense for 20X5 = ($20,000 − $2,000) × (1/4) × (3/12) = $1,125

The service-hours and productive output methods automatically adjust for fractions of a year. The number of hours used or units produced in the partial-year period is applied to the amortization rate in the normal manner.

Using declining balance, the rate for the first year is simply the assumed annual rate times the fraction of the year during which the asset was owned. For an annual amortization rate of 40%, the first year's amortization will be 40% × 9/12 = 30%. For the following years, the rate will be the normal 40% applied to the asset's net book value at the beginning of each year:

Recognized amortization expense
20X1 amortization = $20,000 × 40% × 9\12 = $6,000
20X2 amortization = ($20,000 − $6,000) × .40 = $5,600, etc.

The word "exact" should not be interpreted too literally. The "exact" approach usually means that amortization is calculated only to the nearest month. Seldom will a company try to figure out depreciation to the exact day—what would be the benefit? Amortization involves selecting one from among many possible policies and applying it to amounts that are estimates. There is nothing less "precise" in accounting than amortization, and therefore it makes no sense at all to try to be highly precise about a highly arbitrary number!

ACCOUNTING POLICY CONVENTION APPROACH To avoid tedious fractional-year amortization, many firms adopt a policy convention. Examples of conventions in current use are

1. *Half-year convention.* Under this approach, a half-year's amortization is charged on all assets acquired or disposed of during the year. The implicit assumption is that assets are acquired throughout the year and as a result are, on average, acquired in the middle of the year. Given that amortization is an approximation at best, this assumption is as good as any. This method also has the added convenience that it coincides with the convention used for income tax purposes in the year of acquisition.
2. *Full first-year convention.* A full year's amortization is charged to all assets that exist at the end of the year, including those acquired throughout the year. No amortization is taken on assets disposed of during the year. This is particularly popular in group depreciation methods, which generally are based on the asset account balance at the end of the year.
3. *Final year convention.* Annual amortization is determined solely on the basis of the balance in the capital asset accounts at the beginning of the period. Assets disposed of during a period are depreciated for a full period, and assets purchased during a period are not depreciated that period. When a company has high capital expenditures and increasing asset bases, this method tends to lower the amount of depreciation taken each period, thereby enhancing net income.

When a company reports on an interim basis, such as quarterly, these conventions may be applied to the *quarter* instead of to the *year.* For example, the half-year convention becomes the *half-quarter* convention—one-half quarter's amortization is taken on all assets acquired or disposed of during the quarter.

Regardless of the convention chosen, the same policy should be used consistently. The exact approach to fractional-year amortization should be used only if the information advantages justify the added cost.

Amortization Systems

Unique features of certain capital assets, as well as practical considerations, may cause firms to modify the application of standard amortization methods. We call these adaptations "amortization systems" because they apply amortization computations to *groups* of assets.

1. group and composite systems
2. "inventory" appraisal systems
3. retirement and replacement systems

Amortization systems reduce accounting costs because fewer amortization calculations are required and accumulated amortization records are not maintained on individual assets.

GROUP AND COMPOSITE SYSTEMS Capital assets are sometimes grouped together for application of an average amortization rate that reflects the characteristics of the group. There are two approaches:

group amortization

the amortization of a set of similar assets on average rates designed to be statistically valid for the group as a whole

composite amortization

the amortization of a set of related but similar assets using one composite rate

1. **Group amortization** is used for homogeneous assets. For example, a company may group all of its delivery trucks together in a single account, or may account for all of its computers as a group.
2. **Composite amortization** is used for heterogeneous assets that form a working whole. For example, a pipeline pumping station functions as a single unit, but comprises a variety of different components that have different costs, useful lives, and residual values. Individual components must be replaced as they fail or wear out in order to protect the functioning of the pumping station as a whole.

Although there is a difference in the underlying rationale between group accounts and composite accounts, the calculations are identical.

Group accounts work on the principle of averaging. For each individual asset, the estimates of salvage value and useful life are almost certain to be incorrect. For a group of assets as a whole, however, the law of averages can be applied. As long as the estimates are correct *on average*, the amortization will be correct.

Composite accounts work on the principle that it is meaningless to account individually for assets that function together as a cohesive and mutually dependent group. An assembly line can function only as long as all of its component parts are functioning properly. Even at acquisition, it may be difficult to isolate the cost of each individual part of the assembly line. To amortize each part as though it were an independent asset is to ignore the economic reality of the process. Therefore, the assembly line is accounted for (and amortized) as a single unit.

Group and composite systems are not only theoretically sound, but also easier for accounting purposes. When a company is accounting for many similar assets (which can easily involve thousands of units for asset like desks and laptops), the record-keeping for individual-asset accounting is an enormous burden. Group accounts do away with the need to maintain that level of detail and reflect an apt application of the cost/benefit constraint.

Of course, the company must still maintain adequate *physical* control over the assets.

Although the original cost for each asset acquired is maintained, only one control account for capital assets and accumulated amortization is used. As with the inventory appraisal method, gains and losses are not recognized on disposal. Instead, the asset control account is credited for the original cost of the item, and the accumulated amortization account is debited for the difference between cash received and the original cost of the item.

For example, assume that in 20X8 a company sells a filing system that it had acquired in 20X2 for $10,000. The company received $1,200 from the sale of the asset. The asset is part of a group account that is depreciated at the rate of 10% per year, straight line. When the asset is disposed of, only two pieces of information are needed in order to record the sale: (1) the original cost of the asset, and (2) the proceeds from the sale. The sale is recorded as follows:

Cash	1,200	
Accumulated depreciation—filing systems	8,800	
Capital assets—filing systems		10,000

Notice that the debit to accumulated depreciation is the plug figure for this entry. There is no attempt to calculate the book value for the asset, nor any gain or loss.

Effectively, what happens is that the full cost of the asset is removed from both the capital asset account and the accumulated depreciation account, and the disposal proceeds are credited to the accumulated depreciation account. Another way to book the disposal is as follows:

Accumulated depreciation—filing systems	10,000	
Capital assets—filing systems		10,000
Cash	1,200	
Accumulated depreciation—filing systems		1,200

Some companies simplify this system even further by not attempting to identify the actual cost of the asset retired. Instead, a FIFO approach is often used (oldest unit is sold, just as with inventory).

Amortization Expense Exhibit 10-5 presents information and calculations for an example that uses *composite* amortization. Annual amortization expense is the product of an average amortization rate and the balance in the asset control account. The composite amortization rate is the percentage of total cost amortized each year.

Annual group SL amortization ÷ Total group acquisition cost = Composite rate

Residual value is taken into account because the numerator used in determining the composite rate reflects the SL method. It also is possible to apply declining-balance amortization methods.

Calculation of annual depreciation expense in a group system involves averaging the data for the group of assets. Calculations are exactly like those for composite systems, illustrated in Exhibit 10-5. Of course, in a group system the assets are homogeneous and there will be less dispersion around the mean.

If no changes occur in the makeup of the group during the entire composite life, annual amortization does not change. When assets are added or disposed of before the end of their useful life, the original amortization rate is maintained if the changes are not significant to the overall amortizable cost and useful life composition of the group. Amortization is computed with the old rate and the new balance in the group asset control account, which reflects the addition or deletion of assets. Material changes in the makeup of composite groups may require changes in amortization rates because these assets are heterogeneous.

INVENTORY APPRAISAL SYSTEM Although this method is called an "inventory" system, it applies to tangible capital assets, not to inventory! Under the **inventory appraisal system**, capital assets are appraised at the end of each accounting period in their present condition through application of a deterioration percentage to the cost of the assets in place or through an outside assessment of replacement cost. This system is especially suitable for firms with numerous low-cost capital assets. The word "inventory" is not used in the sense of goods available for sale, but rather in the sense of an ongoing supply of capital assets, usually of small individual value.

The decline in the total appraisal value during the period is recorded directly in the asset account as amortization expense. Cash received on disposal is recorded as a credit to amortization expense. The book value (appraisal value) of the assets at the end of the period is an estimate of current acquisition cost that takes into account current condition and usefulness.

To illustrate how this system works, assume the following information on the hand tools capital asset account of Miller Company, which began operations in 20X1:

Purchases of hand tools in 20X1	\$ 1,900
Appraisal value of tools at the end of 20X1	\$ 1,080
Proceeds from disposal of tools in 20X1	\$ 70

The value of tools on hand decreased $820, but the $70 received on disposal offsets that decline, resulting in $750 of net amortization expense.

Accounting cost savings are evident from the elimination of individual subsidiary accounts, with amortization recorded only for the group. Disposals do not require retrieval of accumulated amortization information, and no gain or loss is recorded when an individual asset is sold or scrapped. Furthermore, the appraisal is made for the entire group rather than for each individual asset.

Although inventory appraisal systems appear to be a departure from the historical cost principle, assets are not written up in value, and the resulting amortization expense must be consistent with results obtained with historical cost-based amortization methods. The method is open to criticism, however, because appraisals can be quite subjective.

RETIREMENT AND REPLACEMENT SYSTEMS **Retirement and replacement systems** are used by public utilities and railroads to reduce record-keeping costs. Such companies typically own large numbers of items dispersed over extensive geographic areas, including rolling stock, track, wire, utility poles, and telephone equipment. The bookkeeping cost to amortize these items individually is prohibitive.

Under both the retirement system and the replacement system, amortization is not recorded for individual assets, no gain or loss is recognized on disposal, and an accumulated amortization account is not used. The total original cost of acquisitions is maintained although often not on an individual asset basis. Residual value is treated as a reduction of amortization expense in the disposal period. Amortization expense under both systems is based on assets *retired* during the period.

The key difference between the two systems is the assumed cost of the retired assets, which can be substantial. *Amortization under the retirement system equals the original cost of the item retired less residual value.* If the cost of acquisition cannot be associated with specific physical units, the oldest remaining cost of the type of asset retired less residual value is used for amortization purposes. This is essentially a FIFO system.

Amortization under the replacement system equals the cost of the most recent acquisition of the type of item retired less residual value. This is essentially a LIFO system. The most recent acquisition is considered the replacement for the item retired.

EXHIBIT 10-5

DATA FOR COMPOSITE AMORTIZATION
COMPONENTS OF OPERATING ASSEMBLY ACQUIRED EARLY 20X1

Component	Quantity	Original Unit Cost	Residual Value	Useful Life	Annual SL Amortization
A	10	$50,000	$5,000	15 years	$3,000
B	4	20,000	4,000	10 years	1,600
C	6	7,000	600	8 years	800
D	20	3,000	0	3 years	1,000

Total annual amortization: 10($3,000) + 4($1,600) + 6($800) + 20($1,000) = $61,200
Total asset acquisition cost: 10($50,000) + 4($20,000) + 6($7,000) + 20($3,000) = $682,000
Total amortizable cost: $682,000 − 10($5,000) − 4($4,000) − 6($600) = $612,400
Composite annual amortization rate = $61,200 ÷ $682,000 = 0.0897
Composite group useful life = $612,400 ÷ $61,200 = 10 years
Annual amortization expense = Composite rate × Acquisition cost = (.0897)($682,000) = $61,200

Retirement and replacement systems can result in amortization amounts that bear no relationship to those of individually applied methods. For example, if no retirements are made, no amortization would be recorded. Furthermore, the asset balances under both systems can be distorted to the point that the balances are meaningless if there are a large number of early retirements, or a large number of delayed retirements. Only if a firm replaces assets on a regular basis will amortization results approximate those of one of the more traditional methods; neither system meets the requirement of being rational and systematic. Perhaps the most important point is that the only companies that use this approach are very, very large, with tremendous volumes in capital assets and regular replacement. This minimizes the chance that error is material.

CONCEPT REVIEW

1. Why is it pointless to calculate and record amortization to the exact number of days that a capital asset was owned during its year of acquisition?
2. Explain the half-year convention for capital asset amortization. Why do companies use a convention like the half-year convention for amortizing capital assets?
3. Why are group and composite systems of amortization useful for large companies?
4. How is annual depreciation calculated for a replacement system? Retirement system?

IMPAIRMENT OF CAPITAL ASSETS AND GOODWILL

Capital assets and goodwill are subject to the same sort of "lower of cost or market value" assessment as other assets—overvaluation of any asset is a major issue in our GAAP model. Therefore, one has to critically examine capital assets and goodwill periodically and ask, "Do these assets still have the ability to generate revenue commensurate with their net book value?" The question is not, "What is market value?", since these assets are not for sale. These assets provide value to the operation through their ability to *increase net assets through profitable operation.* Capital assets and goodwill that lose a significant portion of utility or value suffer an **impairment of value**.

impairment of value
the loss of a portion of the asset's utility or value; a permanent reduction in value necessitating loss recognition

When is value impaired? What is the extent of the impairment? There are no easy answers to these questions. In practice, accounting for impairment losses has not been uniform. The amount and timing of recognized impairment losses have varied depending on the particular situation. However, it seems obvious that if an asset will not generate value for the entity, then it should be written down.

Impairment of Long-Lived Assets with Limited Lives

The recommendations on recognition of impairments are in *CICA Handbook* Section 3063, which came into effect on 1 April 2003. This section applies to tangible capital assets (property, plant, and equipment), to intangible assets with finite useful lives, to deferred preoperating costs, and to other long-term prepaid assets. This section takes a definitional approach—if the asset's carrying value is not recoverable, then it does not meet the definition of an asset and must be written down.

The basic recommendation is that

> An impairment loss should be recognized when the carrying value of a long-lived asset is not recoverable and exceeds its fair value. (*CICA 3063.04*)

As this recommendation implies, the amount of an impairment loss is the excess of an asset's carrying value over its fair value (*CICA 3063.06*).

WHEN TO TEST FOR IMPAIRMENT Sometimes asset impairment is as plain as day, such as when a building is destroyed in a fire. In such a case, the asset is written off and the insurance proceeds (if any) reduce the loss (and can even create a reported *gain* if the insurance proceeds are greater than the asset's net book value).

Assets should be subjected to an impairment test whenever events or changes in circumstances indicate that their carrying value may not be recoverable (CICA 3063.09). Examples of such circumstances include

- A significant change in the business environment, such as a new product from a competitor that makes the company's product or processes obsolete;
- A history of operating and/or cash flow losses that indicate that the company isn't able to recover the cost of the asset;
- A probability of greater than 50% that the company will retire or dispose of the asset significantly earlier than planned; or
- Loss of a patent infringement lawsuit that has a significant effect on overall operations.

GROUPING An impairment test should not necessarily be applied to an individual asset, either tangible or intangible. An impairment test is applied only to assets "for which identifiable cash flows are largely independent of the cash flows of other assets or groups of assets and liabilities" (*CICA* 3063.03(a)). Assets function together, as a group, to generate revenue. Patents, equipment, trademarks, and software all may function together as an *asset group*:

> For purposes of recognition and measurement of an impairment loss, a long-lived asset should be grouped with other assets and liabilities to form an asset group, *at the lowest level for which identifiable cash flows are largely independent of the cash flows of other assets and liabilities.* (*CICA* 3063.12; italics added)

From a practical point of view, this means that individual assets seldom will be subjected to an impairment test. Impairment is most likely to be applied to assets at an operating division level. For example, a company may have patents on several products and processes, all of which use the same facilities for production and administrative support. If sales of one product are killed by a new product from a competitor, there has not necessarily been an impairment—the impairment test is applied to the cash flows from the assets used in production. The cash flow from the asset group is generated by all of the assets working together to produce several products.

Liabilities will be included in the group only when the sole source of cash to satisfy the liability is the asset or asset group being tested for impairment (CICA 3063.08; 3063.14). If there are other cash sources to pay liabilities, the liabilities are not included in the group because they are general liabilities of the enterprise. Examples include mortgage debt and asset retirement obligations.

MEASURING THE IMPAIRMENT LOSS The impairment loss is the amount by which the carrying value of an asset (or asset group) exceeds its *fair value*. The difficult part is to measure fair value. The *CICA Handbook* states that "quoted market prices in active markets are the best evidence of fair value" (CICA 3063.A2). If quoted market prices are not available, then the prices for similar items or "other valuation techniques" can be used (*CICA* 3063.A3).

Market prices may well exist for a company's land and buildings. But for equipment and other long-lived assets (such as pre-operating costs), there may not be an active market and/or a readily determinable market price.

Fortunately, the concept of an asset group can help. Although individual assets in an operating unit may not have observable market values, the group as a whole may have a measurable fair value. A group of assets can be sold to another company as an operating unit, similar to a discontinued operation. The price that a buyer would pay will be based on the discounted present value of the asset group's estimated future cash flows.

Estimating future cash flows (and the probabilities attached to those cash flows) is not the job of the accountant. That is the task of management, with the assistance of professional business evaluators. But once management estimates the fair value, the accountant must assure that the impairment is properly recorded. Since assets may be revealed upward only in very limited circumstances, we will discuss asset revaluation in an Appendix rather than in the main body in the chapter.

ALLOCATING THE IMPAIRMENT LOSS As we have just seen, impairment losses are normally applied to asset groups. But the assets are recorded individually on the books, not in groups. So how should the overall impairment loss be allocated to the assets? The rule is that impairment losses are allocated only to the long-lived assets of the group. If the group includes other assets, such as inventories or accounts receivable, the impairment loss is not allocated to those assets. Of course, inventories and accounts receivable are still subject to the usual LCM valuation practices.

An allocation of impairment loss should not reduce the carrying amount of an asset below its fair value if "the fair value is determinable without undue cost and effort" (*CICA* 3063.17). For example, suppose that an Internet service provider (ISP) has a historical cost for a subscriber base that it purchased from another company. An ISP subscriber list has a fairly readily determinable value. If the ISP is consistently losing money, it is probable that the company's assets are impaired. If an impairment loss is recognized, the carrying value of the subscription base should not be reduced below its fair market value. Instead, a greater portion of the impairment loss should be allocated to the other long-lived assets, such as equipment and limited-life intangibles.

EXAMPLE Suppose that Justus Limited has the following assets in its recreational products group:

	Carrying Value (thousands)
Inventory	$ 300
Land	400
Building	640
Equipment	560
	$ 1,900

A change in the competitive environment suggests that the fair value of this division may be less than its carrying value. Management conducts an impairment test, and estimates that the fair value of the asset group is $1,300. The impairment loss is $600—the excess of $1,900 carrying value over $1,300 fair value.

The impairment loss must be allocated to the long-lived assets. The inventory is excluded from the allocation, but may be revalued on its own by the lower-of-cost-or-market rule. The $600 impairment loss will be allocated to the other three assets in proportion to their carrying value:

Asset	Carrying Value	Proportion	Allocation of Impairment Loss	Adjusted Carrying Value
Inventory	$300	–	–	$300
Land	400	25%	$150	250
Building	640	40%	240	400
Equipment	560	35%	210	350
	$ 1,900	100%	$600	$1.300

Now, suppose that the fair value of the land is $320. Assets should not be written down below their fair value. In that case, the allocation must be first to reduce the land's carrying value by $80 (from $400 to $320), and then the remaining $520 impairment loss is allocated to the remaining assets:

Asset	Carrying Value	Proportion	Allocation of Impairment Loss	Adjusted Carrying Value
Inventory	$300	–	–	$300
Land	400	–	$80	320
Building	640	53%	276	364
Equipment	560	47%	244	316
	$ 1,900	100%	$600	$ 1.300

DISCLOSURE Disclosure requirements for impairment losses are straightforward. The basic requirements are (*CICA* 3063.24):

- A description of the impaired asset or asset group, and the facts and circumstances leading to the impairment;
- The amount of the impairment loss, and an indication of where it appears in the income statement if it is not presented separately on the face of the income statement; and
- The method used for determining fair value.

EXHIBIT 10-6

IMPAIRMENT DISCLOSURE
CHC HELICOPTER CORPORATION

Excerpts from disclosure notes:

2. *Accounting estimates and measurement uncertainty*

(i) *Recoverability of pre-operating expenses*

The ability to defer pre-operating expenses is dependent on the future recoverability of the amounts from cash flows generated by the related commercial operations. If operations perform below anticipated recoverable levels the portion of pre-operating expenses that cannot be recovered is expensed immediately when known. At April 30, 2003 management evaluated the recoverability from cash flows of future operations of the carrying value of pre-operating expenses. Management determined that all $12.8 million of such costs related to the composites manufacturing business carried on by its wholly-owned subsidiary, CHC Composites Inc. ("Composites"), should be written off and recorded as an asset impairment charge (Note 8). At April 30, 2003, $3.4 million in unamortized pre-operating expenses related to new contract awards remained in other assets on the balance sheet.

8. *Other assets*

April 30 (thousands)	2003	2002
Pre-operating expenses *(ii)*	3,412	15,947

(ii) The pre-operating expense balance as of April 30, 2003 consists primarily of costs incurred in the start-up phase of new contract awards. These costs are being amortized over the term of the contract. The Company has determined that the pre-operating expenses are recoverable from future cash flows to be generated from the contracts.

During the year, the Company expensed $2.5 million (2002 – $0.9 million) related to the amortization of pre-operating expenses. In addition, the Company recorded a $12.8 million asset impairment charge related to pre-operating expenses in Composites (Note 2).

An example of an asset impairment charge is that of CHC Helicopter Corporation, which showed a $12.8 million impairment charge on its 2003 income statement. CHC provides helicopter services to other corporations worldwide, particularly in the offshore oil and gas industry. CHC performed an impairment test on its long-term pre-operating costs relating to the airframe component manufacturing part ("Composites") of the company's business. CHC concluded that the asset was impaired. The company's MD&A contained the following paragraph:

> At April 30, 2003, the Company evaluated the recoverability from cash flows of future operations of the carrying value of Composites' pre-operating expenses, which had been previously deferred and recorded in other assets on the Company's balance sheet. The Company determined it appropriate to write off the entire $12.8 million book value of such pre-operating expenses at April 30, 2003 as an asset impairment charge.

The total pre-operating costs on the balance declined from $15.9 million in 2002 to $3.4 million in 2003. The disclosure notes contained two explanations for this charge, shown in Exhibit 10-6.

SUBSEQUENT RECOVERY IN VALUE In Canada and the United States, restoring or reversing an impairment loss is not permitted. Once an asset has been written down, the reduced carrying value cannot be written back up if the recoverable amount increases.

International accounting standards, as well as the national standards in many countries, take a different approach. IAS 36 recommends that impairment losses be reinstated if the fair value of the asset has recovered: "a reversal of an impairment loss for an asset should be recognised as income immediately in the income statement" (IAS 36.104).

The problem with reversing an impairment loss is that this provides yet another method by which management may be tempted to "manage" or smooth earnings—take an impairment loss in a high-income year, and restore it in a low-income year. Of course, IAS 36 provides guidelines on how to ascertain that an impairment loss has occurred and when the value has recovered.

OTHER INTANGIBLE ASSETS Note that only intangible assets *that are amortized* are tested for impairment using the process described above. For intangible assets that have an indefinite life, and for goodwill, read on!

Impairment of Goodwill and Intangible Assets Not Subject to Amortization

There are separate standards in the *CICA Handbook* governing recognition of impairment of goodwill and intangible assets not subject to amortization. These rules are explained in Section 3062, "Goodwill and Other Intangible Assets."

Since goodwill and intangibles with indefinite lives are not amortized, it makes sense to examine these assets carefully for impairment. Regular impairment writedowns would have the same effect as amortization, although impairment is more likely to be infrequent. Infrequent, large write-offs will create "bumpy" earnings patterns.

In the discussion that follows, we'll refer only to goodwill, but these rules apply to all intangibles that are not amortized.

The requirement is that

> A goodwill impairment loss should be recognized when the carrying amount of the goodwill of a reporting unit exceeds the fair value of the goodwill. An impairment loss should not be reversed if the fair value subsequently increases.
>
> (*CICA* 3062.25)

Presentation of an impairment loss follows the pattern set by capital assets: the item is not extraordinary. It is shown separately on the income statement. It may well be part of a restructuring charge or discontinued operations, if circumstances warrant.

CONDITIONS FOR IMPAIRMENT As we saw in Chapter 9, goodwill is measured as a residual—the excess of the purchase price paid for a unit over the fair value of its net assets on the acquisition date. To establish the potential for impairment, a two-step impairment test is done (*CICA* 3062.27):

Step 1. The fair value of a unit is compared with its total net book value. As long as the fair value of *the unit* is higher than the net book value of all assets and liabilities, the impairment test stops here and no impairment loss is needed.

The relevant fair value here is the fair value of the *unit as a whole.* This fair value may be based on multiples of earnings or revenues, or on *discounted* cash flow projections. All these valuation models are highly sensitive to assumptions regarding sales volumes and prices, and to the discount rates or multiples used. (Discounting is used here, unlike the valuation of amortized capital assets.) Business valuation is an art! If the fair value of the reporting unit is lower than net book value, it is necessary to go to Step 2.

Step 2. The goodwill calculation that was done on acquisition is repeated, using current fair values and current book values. In Step 2, the fair values used are those for each asset and liability, not for the unit as a whole. The process is identical to that illustrated in Chapter 9, and it results in a residual value assigned to goodwill. That is, goodwill is calculated as the purchase price less the current fair value of net assets acquired. If this is a lower goodwill figure than that recorded on the books, an impairment loss is recorded.

Consider the following examples:

Example 1. The fair value of a unit is $6,400,000. The net book value of assets less liabilities, including unamortized goodwill of $1,000,000, is $5,175,000. Fair value exceeds net book value, and the impairment test is over, with no loss recorded.

Example 2. The fair value of the unit is $ 4,300,000. The net book value of net assets is $5,175,000, including $1,000,000 of goodwill. A Step 2 valuation must be done because fair value is less than net book value.

The fair value of all assets and liabilities must be established. Some fair values will be higher than book value, and some are lower. Those with lower book value will be evaluated for a potential writedown of their own. A writedown may or may not be needed, depending on the circumstances. Capital assets subject to amortization will be written down only if the decline is permanent. Then, goodwill is recalculated.

In this example, assume that, in addition to knowing that the unit has a fair value of $4,300,000, we determine that individual assets and liabilities have a fair value of $4,100,000. Goodwill as recalculated amounts to $200,000. An impairment loss of $800,000 must be recorded.

This impairment loss is *not* equal to the original differential between net book value and fair value of the unit. This original differential was $875,000 (that is, $5,175,000 − $4,300,000) The original differential can be caused by various items, not just goodwill.

There are many technical elements to this valuation and many judgemental elements as well. For instance, goodwill must be evaluated for each reporting unit. But is "a reporting unit" each division of an acquired business, or the business as a whole? What valuation model is most relevant for the unit acquired? What degree of optimism about future revenues is most appropriate? How should fair values be determined when there is no intermediate market for assets?

There are answers, or at least approaches to answers for all these questions, and more. However, the technical aspects of this impairment test are beyond the scope of this book. Our focus is on the criteria for the impairment loss, and its subsequent presentation in the financial statements.

TIMING Goodwill must be evaluated for impairment annually. The only exception to this is if there has been no real change to net assets or events and circumstances since the last valuation, and the last valuation showed a comfortable excess fair value over net book value (*CICA* 3062.39). There has to be some margin for error. The test may be done more frequently if events take place that suggest impairment.

EXAMPLES OF GOODWILL IMPAIRMENT One of the interesting aspects of the goodwill impairment requirements is that the test is performed at the level of the *reporting unit.* A segment or component of a business is a reporting unit when it

> ... constitutes a business for which discrete financial information is available and ... management regularly reviews the operating results of that component.
> (*CICA* 3062.05(d))

This definition raises an interesting question. Consider the following explanation from the 2003 financial statements of eNGENUITY Technologies Incorporated:

> The Company determined that at December 1, 2001, it had two reporting units, Xtend, Inc. and Loox Software S.A., and that the goodwill related to Xtend, Inc. was impaired. As a result, an amount of $1,869,000 was charged to opening deficit, in accordance with the transition provisions of the accounting standard (see Note 7). The Company performs the annual impairment test on June 30 of each year.
>
> During the third quarter of 2003, following a review by management of the Company's operations, the organizational and corporate structure was changed. The new structure operates all companies in the consolidated group as one component under a single management. Accordingly, as of April 1, 2003, the Company had one reporting unit, and goodwill is tested for impairment by comparing the carrying value of the Company to its fair value.

Did the company change its reporting structure in order to minimize the likelihood of future goodwill impairment charges? We can only guess at the company's motivation. However, having fewer reporting units will certainly reduce the amount of effort that goes into the annual impairment review.

Another example of goodwill impairment is contained in the 2003 income statement of Gemcom Software International Incorporated. Gemcom charged $31,215 against earnings as "write-off of impaired value, Peru." The disclosure note explains the impairment as follows:

> The Company completed its annual impairment test of goodwill on March 31, 2003. The goodwill allocated to the company in Peru, Gemcom Peru S.A., was determined impaired as operations in Peru have been combined with those in Chile and Brazil to form the Latin American segment. The Company in Peru is no longer being used to manage these operations and therefore the $31,215 in goodwill associated with it has been written off at year-end.

In other words, the goodwill is impaired because the company no longer uses the Peru unit to manage its Peruvian operations. The amount that was allocated to goodwill when Gemcom first purchased this subsidiary is completely written off.

THE ROLE OF JUDGEMENT It would be impossible to over-emphasize the role of judgement when evaluating the need for an impairment writedown. Since fair values are estimates, often based on future revenue projections, the optimism and pessimism of management will have a profound effect on the end result. There is significant temptation to take a bath in poor years, and record large writedowns. Recall the AOL Time Warner goodwill writeoff that was described in the introduction to this chapter.

International Perspective

The current Canadian requirement to *not* amortize goodwill is the result of harmonization with FASB standards. Prior to 2002, goodwill was subject to amortization over a period not to exceed 40 years. In 1999, the FASB began a politically difficult project to revise its accounting for business combinations. The goal was to eliminate a widely used accounting approach known as pooling-of-interest accounting. In this method, acquired assets are carried forward on the buyer's financial statements at the seller's book value. No goodwill is recognized, and therefore no amortization is needed. The United States was the only country to permit pooling-of-interests accounting on a broad basis.

The AcSB and the IASB both supported the FASB's attempt. The idea was to go forward in unison so that the FASB could argue "international harmonization" as a reason to force this change. Pooling-of-interests accounting was seldom used in Canada (or elsewhere), and there was no real reason to change the Canadian standard except as a way of supporting the FASB.

As the battle raged in the United States, it became politically necessary for the FASB to compromise. In order to require companies to use fair values when they acquired other business units, the FASB had to agree not to amortize goodwill. Thus, the Canadian standard changed from *requiring* goodwill amortization to *prohibiting* goodwill amortization. The impairment test was required instead.

In the international standard (*IAS* 22), goodwill still must be amortized. The maximum amortization period is 20 years: "There is a rebuttable presumption that the useful life of goodwill not exceed twenty years from initial recognition" (*IAS* 22.44). An impairment test is required as well. The view of the IASB is that goodwill is a cost of the purchase, but the goodwill does not last forever. Remember that goodwill represents the superior earnings ability of the acquired business unit. As the acquired unit becomes integrated into the buyer's business, continuing goodwill is really internally generated. Therefore, the purchased goodwill should be amortized.

The international standard requires an impairment test as well as amortization. The impairment test is essentially identical to the Canadian standard.

As with other capital assets, *IAS* 36 permits impairment losses to be reversed. However, reversal of a goodwill impairment loss can be reversed only if the original impairment was due to an extraordinary external event and "subsequent external events have occurred that reverse the effect of that event" (*IAS* 36.109).

More broadly, goodwill is treated in many different ways in various nations' accounting standards. Some countries permit goodwill to remain on the balance sheet forever. At the opposite end of the spectrum, some countries permit goodwill to be written off to retained earnings immediately. Others require amortization, usually over no more than 20 years.

Returning to the Canadian standards, it is worthwhile to remember that the prohibition against amortization of goodwill was the result of a political compromise—in this case, a compromise arranged to accommodate a standard-setting goal in the United States. It is impossible to eliminate political influences in accounting standard-setting. "Political" doesn't just mean influence by governments, although that definitely is one important source. Political influence also originates from the companies affected by accounting standards and from audit firms.

DISCLOSURE REQUIREMENTS

Not surprisingly, the requirement to disclose amortization policy is front and centre in the disclosure requirements. If you're going to let companies pick a policy, it is crucial that financial statement readers be told about the choice. Thus, "for each major category of property, plant and equipment there should be disclosure of ... the amortization method used, including the amortization period or rate" (*CICA* 3061.54). There is an identical requirement for intangible assets subject to amortization (*CICA* 3062.51). Other recommended disclosures relating to capital asset amortization are

- The amount of any impairment loss or writedown during the period (*CICA* 3061.57 and 3062.51);
- The amount of amortization charged to income for the period (*CICA* 3061.56 and 3062.51);
- The accumulated amortization of each major category (*CICA* 3061.54 and 3062.51); and
- Details about comprehensive revaluations (see Appendix 2) (*CICA* 1625.50 to 1625.52).

The amount of amortization expense is a recommended disclosure not only in the capital assets sections, but also in the income statement section of the *CICA Handbook*. In practice, however, the amount may not be reported directly on the face of the income statement. Amortization may be included in various components of the income statement, such as cost of goods sold, cost of goods produced, cost of contracts completed, and general and administrative expense. If the amount of amortization is not shown on the face of the income statement, the disclosure is usually either in a note to the financial statements or in the cash flow statement (i.e., as an add-back to net income in the operating activities section). A fairly comprehensive disclosure example was shown in the previous chapter, Exhibits 9-6 and 9-7.

CASH FLOW STATEMENT

Amortization expense is an add-back to the operations section of the cash flow statement, if the common indirect form of presentation is used. It's important to remember that amortization is a little different from other expenses, because amortization is a non-cash expense. Clearly, the company has to pay out cash or other resources to obtain the capital asset, but the timing of the cash paid is likely to be a lot different than the timing of the expense recognition.

Any writedowns of capital assets, including impairment of goodwill, are a non-cash charge to income. Like amortization, they are added back to net income.

CAPITAL ASSETS HELD FOR SALE

Definition

Eventually, a capital asset ceases to be used in a company's operations. If the asset is taken out of service only temporarily, there is no change in the accounting. Idle assets continue to be amortized. But if an asset is taken out of service permanently, one of three things will usually happen to it:

- It will be disposed of or scrapped as having no further use.
- It will be exchanged for another asset.
- It will be put up for sale.

We already have discussed the first two options. Now we will examine the accounting when the asset is being disposed of by sale.

A long-lived asset that is taken out of service and put up for sale is classified as *held for sale*. That's a rather obvious statement, but "held for sale" now has a specific meaning in the *CICA Handbook*. As you will see in the next chapter, there are held-for-sale financial instruments that get one treatment, and held-for-sale long-lived assets that get a somewhat different treatment.

In order for a long-lived asset (or an asset group) to be classified as held for sale, *all* of six criteria must be met (*CICA* 3475.08). In brief, these criteria are

- Management must have committed to sell the asset.
- It is available for sale in its present condition.
- The company is actively seeking a buyer.
- It is being marketed at a reasonable price.
- A sale is expected to be completed within one year.
- It is unlikely that management will change its plan to sell the asset.

The point of these criteria is to reduce the possibility of income manipulation. Management may be tempted to declare assets as held for sale when there actually may be little probability that management will actually sell them. The temptation exists because amortization stops when assets are classified as held for sale. Without the criteria, it would be possible to classify temporarily idle assets as held for sale in slow economic times so that the amortization expense is reduced.

If an idle asset does not meet all of these six criteria, it should not be classified as held for sale—amortization will continue on the asset.

Accounting Treatment

When an asset (or asset group) qualifies as held for sale, there are three accounting consequences:

1. Amortization ceases, as we have already pointed out.
2. The asset (or asset group) is written down to its fair value less cost to sell *if* its fair value is less than its carrying value.
3. The asset is separately classified on the balance sheet as a long-term held-for-sale asset.

Fair value is the market value for assets that have an active secondary market. If there is no active or observable market for an asset (or asset group), fair value may be measured by discounting the asset's potential future cash flows, similar to the techniques used for an asset impairment test. The estimated fair value is reduced by the estimated costs to sell the asset, such as commissions, legal fees, and closing costs.

The loss from the asset writedown should be included in net income in the period in which the asset was classified as held for sale. When the sale transaction has been completed, a gain or loss is recognized for the difference between the net sales price and the carrying value (after any writedown) of the asset.

Both the loss from a writedown and the gain/loss on the final sale are recognized in net income. If the asset is part of a discontinued operation, then gains and losses should be included in discontinued operations. Otherwise, the loss will be reported within continuing operating earnings.

If financial statements are prepared prior to completion of a sale, the carrying value of the asset is again evaluated. Any additional decline in fair value should be recognized. However, in a departure from the usual rules pertaining to written-down assets, the *CICA Handbook* recommends that

> A gain should be recognized for any subsequent increase in fair value less cost to sell, but not in excess of the cumulative loss previously recognized for a write-down to fair value less cost to sell. (*CICA* 3475.19)

Since the asset is held for sale, it should be shown on the balance sheet at its fair value, provided that the fair value does not exceed the original carrying value. This recommendation is more or less consistent with valuation of available-for-sale financial instruments, as we shall see in the next chapter. Therefore, the rule against writing impaired long-lived assets back up is relaxed if the assets are held for sale.

Assets held for sale should be presented separately on the company's balance sheet as long-term assets (*CICA* 3475.33). They are not reclassified as current assets even though the intent is to sell them within the next year.

Assuming that the asset is material within the context of the financial statements, additional information should be provided in a disclosure note (*CICA* 3475.36):

- A description of the asset and the facts and circumstances leading to its disposal; and
- The amount of gain or loss, and where it is included in the income statement.

Example

In July 20X5, Schumacher Incorporated shut down the company's Alberta distribution centre and put the centre up for sale. The facility met all of the criteria for held-for-sale classification. The historical cost of the building was $4,300,000. At the time of abandonment, accumulated amortization was $1,850,000, resulting in a net book value of $2,450,000.

After contacting several industrial brokers, Schumacher management had obtained evidence that the fair market value of the building was $2,200,000. Commission, closing costs, and transfer taxes are estimated to be 10% of the sales price. The entry to record the reclassification of the asset is

Accumulated amortization—Alberta distribution centre	1,850,000	
Long-lived assets held for sale (net of 10% costs to sell)	1,980,000	
Loss on building held for sale	470,000	
Buildings—Alberta distribution centre		4,300,000

This entry (1) offsets the accumulated amortization against the building cost, (2) reclassifies the asset as held for sale at fair value less costs to sell, and (3) records the loss of $470,000, which will be charged against earnings.

On 31 December 20X5, Schumacher is making good progress on the sale. Indeed, due to a sharp increase in economic activity in Alberta, the estimated market value of the building has risen sharply, to $2,600,000. At year-end, Schumacher must write the asset up to fair value, limited to the pre-abandonment carrying value of $2,450,000. At first glance, it would appear that fair value is higher than the old book value. However, the 10% selling cost must be subtracted to find the net fair value: $2,600,000 × 90% = $2,340,000. Schumacher will increase the held-for-sale asset value and decrease the previously recorded loss:

Long-lived assets held for sale ($2,340,000 – $1,980,000)	360,000	
Loss on building held for sale		360,000

The 31 December 20X5 carrying value is not higher than the $2,450,000 carrying value in July 20X5, the date of abandonment.

On 17 March 20X6, Schumacher closes the sale. The final selling price is $2,650,000. The net proceeds are 90% of that amount or $2,385,000. The entry to record the sale is

Cash	2,385,000	
Long-lived assets held for sale		2,340,000
Gain on sale of building		45,000

CONCEPT REVIEW

1. In general, when is it necessary to write down property, plant, and equipment? How can we determine the value to which it should be written down?
2. Describe the two steps followed to determine whether there has been an impairment of goodwill.
3. How do Canada's practices regarding the restoration of writedowns and the revaluation of individual assets differ from the most common international practice?

SUMMARY OF KEY POINTS

1. Amortization is a rational and systematic process of allocating amortizable cost (acquisition cost less residual value) to the periods in which capital assets are used. Amortization expense for a period does not represent the change in market value of assets, nor does it necessarily equal the portion of the asset's utility consumed in the period. Amortization is justified on the basis of eventual decline in value, through physical wear and tear and obsolescence.
2. Goodwill, land, and intangible assets with an indefinite life are not amortized.
3. Several methods of amortization are rational and systematic and acceptable under GAAP: the straight-line, service-hours, productive output, accelerated, and sinking-fund methods. Factors affecting choice include individual corporate reporting objectives, information processing costs, a desire to minimize income tax temporary differences, industry norms, and parent company preferences.
4. Three factors contribute to the determination of periodic amortization expense: original acquisition cost and any capitalized post-acquisition costs, estimated residual value, and estimated useful life or productivity measured either in service-hours or units of output.
5. For all methods, the estimated residual value is the minimum book value. Except for the declining-balance methods, amortizable cost (cost-residual value) is multiplied by a rate or

fraction to determine periodic amortization. Declining-balance amortization is based on cost less accumulated amortization and ceases when net book value equals residual value.

6. For assets acquired during an accounting period, an accounting convention such as the half-year convention is usually used in practice.
7. Three amortization systems (appraisal, composite and group, and replacement/retirement) are alternatives to amortization methods applied individually to assets. These systems save accounting costs and are justified under cost-benefit and materiality constraints.
8. Capital assets subject to amortization must be reviewed for potential writedown on a regular basis. A loss is recognized when the sum of undiscounted expected future net cash inflows from use and disposal of the asset is less than carrying value. The loss equals the difference between the asset's carrying value and the asset's fair value.
9. Goodwill and other intangible assets not subject to amortization must be evaluated annually, and written down if their value is impaired. This is done in a two-step process. First, the fair value of the business unit is compared to book value. If fair value is lower, Step (2) is done, which recalculates the residual goodwill figure based on current fair value and book values for all net assets of the business unit.
10. Reversal of an impairment charge is not permitted within Canadian GAAP, but is permitted in international GAAP.
11. Amortization is not a cash flow; the cash flow occurred when the capital asset was acquired. Amortization and impairment writedowns are added back to net income when cash flow from operations is determined on the cash flow statement.
12. Companies should disclose the amortization method chosen for major categories of capital assets, the amortization period or rate, and the amount of amortization charged to income for the period.

KEY TERMS

accumulated depreciation, 539
amortizable cost, 539
amortization, 539
composite amortization, 554
convention, 552
declining-balance (DB) amortization, 548
depletion, 539
depreciation, 539
group amortization, 554
impairment of value, 557
inventory appraisal system, 555
net book value, 539
productive output (PO) amortization, 547
residual value, 552
retirement and replacement systems, 556
salvage value, 552
service-hours (SH) amortization, 547
sinking fund amortization, 550
straight-line (SL) amortization, 545
sum-of-the-years' digits (SYD) amortization, 548

REVIEW PROBLEM

The following cases are independent.

1. *Partial-year depreciation.* Whitney Corporation purchased equipment on 1 April 20X4 for $34,000. The equipment has a useful life of five years and a residual value of $4,000. What is depreciation for 20X4 and 20X5, using declining-balance depreciation at a 40% rate?
2. *Asset impairment.* Rancho Company purchases equipment on 1 April 20X3 for $34,000. The equipment has a useful life of five years, a residual value of $4,000, and is depreciated using the straight-line method and the half-year convention. At the end of 20X5, Rancho suspects that the original investment in the asset will not be realized; the total remaining future cash inflows expected to be produced by the equipment, including the original residual value, are $10,000. The equipment's fair value at 31 December 20X5 is $7,000. Determine whether the asset is impaired and, if so, the impairment loss at 31 December 20X5.

EXHIBIT 10A-2

EXAMPLE OF CALCULATING CAPITAL COST ALLOWANCE

20X1 UCC opening balance		0
Additions (4 × $5,000)		$20,000
CCA for 20X1; ($20,000 × 20% × 1/2 year)		(2,000)
20X2 UCC opening balance		$18,000
Additions		5,700
CCA for 20X2; ($18,000 × 20%) + ($5,700 × 20% × 1/2)		(4,170)
20X3 UCC opening balance		$19,530
Additions	$6,500	
Proceeds on disposal	(1,200)	
Net additions		5,300
CCA for 20X3; ($19,530 × 20%) + ($5,300 × 20% × 1/2)		(4,436)
20X4 UCC opening balance		$20,394
Proceeds on disposal		(1,100)
CCA for 20X4; [($20,394 − $1,100) × 20%]		(3,859)
20X4 UCC closing balance		$15,435

The basic rules for the capital cost allowance system can be explained for most classes as follows:

1. When assets are purchased, their purchase price (capital cost) is added to the balance (unamortized capital cost, or UCC) of the appropriate asset class.
2. When assets are sold, the lesser of the proceeds or the capital cost is deducted from the balance in that asset's class.
3. Assets are considered to be purchased in the middle of the taxation year (half-year rule).
4. The maximum capital cost allowance deductible for a particular class is the balance of unamortized capital cost (UCC), *after adjusting for the half-year rule in the year of purchase*, multiplied by the CCA rate for that class.

Exhibit 10A-2 provides an example of a calculation for capital cost allowance. Iles Machine Shop begins business in January 20X1 and purchases four lathes (class 8) for $5,000 each. A fifth lathe is purchased in 20X2 for $5,700. In 20X3, one of the original lathes is sold for $1,200 and is replaced with another lathe costing $6,500. In 20X4 one of the lathes was sold for $1,100.

When net asset additions take place, *the net addition is subject to the half-year rule* (see 20X2 and 20X3 in Exhibit 10A-2). However, when there is a net asset disposal, the entire amount is deducted prior to determining the CCA for the year (see 20X4 in Exhibit 10A-2).

The amount deducted on an asset disposal is the lesser of the proceeds and the asset's capital cost. Any proceeds on disposal in excess of the capital cost are treated, for tax purposes, as a capital gain. Proceeds up to the original capital cost are credited to the pool. This may drive the pool into a negative balance. The negative unamortized capital cost (UCC) is reported as taxable income. More likely, though, proceeds up to capital cost just reduce the positive balance of UCC and reduce the future CCA claimable in that class.

When *all* of the assets in a class are disposed of, any remaining balances are treated as follows:

- A positive UCC balance is deducted as a terminal loss in determining taxable income.
- A negative UCC balance is added to taxable income as *recaptured* CCA.

In effect, this treatment is similar to the gain or loss on disposal of plant assets on the assumption that either too little or too much amortization (i.e., CCA) was taken over the lives of the assets. Any proceeds received in excess of the assets' capital (original) cost are treated as a capital gain for tax purposes.

SUMMARY OF KEY POINTS

1. Accounting amortization has no tax impact; amortization of capital assets for tax purposes is governed by the *Income Tax Act* and Regulations, and is completely independent of accounting amortization.
2. Income tax amortization is called the *capital cost allowance (CCA)* system.
3. The CCA system groups capital assets into *classes* of assets of similar types. Except for certain buildings, assets are not amortized individually.
4. The regulations specify an amortization *rate* to be used for each class of asset; the rate is a maximum—a company can claim less CCA in any year if management so chooses, without losing the maximum deduction in future years.
5. The half-year rule is applied to assets acquired during a taxation year.
6. Gains and losses are not recognized on the disposal of capital assets in a class, unless all of the assets in the class are disposed of. Proceeds on disposal of individual assets are credited to the asset class.

APPENDIX 2

Revaluation of Capital Assets

Historical cost has long been the generally accepted basis for reporting capital assets in Canada. On rare occasions, however, a company may restate one or more of its capital assets upward, generally by using appraisal values. Sometimes, a company will establish an entirely new basis of accountability, not only for its assets but also for its liabilities. This is known as a comprehensive revaluation.

Revaluation of Individual Assets

In the high-inflation period of the 1980s, some companies experimented with writing up their assets, using appraised values, in an attempt to show more relevant asset balances and restate depreciation on a current cost basis. This was an instance in which companies (including public companies) decided that the nominal dollar capital maintenance assumption (see Chapter 2) was no longer valid and attempted to move toward a productive capacity capital maintenance basis.

Another situation in which it makes sense to revalue individual assets (or groups of assets) arises primarily in private companies. Bankers grant mortgage loans (and other secured loans) on the basis of assets' values; recorded historical costs are irrelevant. Private corporations sometimes end up with a balance sheet in which total liabilities exceed total assets, simply because loans have been granted on the basis of fair values while the balance sheet shows assets at their depreciated historical cost. Consequently, the corporation appears to have negative net worth, which is a condition of technical insolvency. Since corporations dislike showing negative net assets, a logical response is to restate the assets to the market values by which the loans are secured, thereby reinstating a positive net worth.

Prior to 1990, there was no specific recommendation in the *CICA Handbook* that historical cost should be used as the carrying value for capital assets. While historical cost clearly was an important aspect of GAAP, it was possible to depart from historical cost and to record appraised values when circumstances warranted, without necessarily deviating from GAAP. Practice recognized that sometimes the trade-off between relevance and reliability was better served by recording appraisals, as long as they were based on arm's-length professional valuations (usually, two or three independent appraisals were solicited).

The permissibility of appraisal revaluations changed when the capital asset section of the *CICA Handbook* was introduced in 1990. The flat statement that "a capital asset should be recorded at cost" (*CICA* 3061.16) effectively limits the ability of companies to revalue (upward) specific assets, regardless of their motivation to do so and regardless of the company's situation-specific financial reporting objectives. The *CICA Handbook*'s insistence on historical cost effectively prevents public companies (and any other companies constrained by GAAP) from restating individual assets. Asset revaluation may still be encountered in some financial statements, although it would be a non-GAAP situation. Let's see how it works.

When assets are restated on the basis of appraisal values, there is no gain recorded. Instead, the asset value is written up to the appraised value and the offsetting credit is to a separate component of shareholders' equity. Future amortization of the asset is then based on the new carrying value. As the asset is amortized, an amount equal to the increase in amortization is transferred from the appraisal increment account (in shareholders' equity) to the retained earnings account. When the asset has been fully amortized, the appraisal increment account also will have disappeared from the balance sheet. Alternatively, if the asset is sold, the appraisal increase credit is eliminated at that time.

For example, suppose that Yvan Limited has land purchased for $50,000 and a building that was purchased for $100,000 in 20X1. Yvan began depreciating the building in 20X1 on a straight-line basis over 25 years. The area in which the building is located has increased substantially in value, and in 20X6 the company decides to restate the property. Yvan obtains two independent professional appraisals but decides to use the lower of the two: $250,000 for the building and $325,000 for the land. Yvan will continue to use the original estimate of useful life for the building: 25 years from 20X1; 20 years more from 20X6. The revalued building will be depreciated at a straight-line rate of 5%.

EXHIBIT 10A-3

EXAMPLE OF CAPITAL ASSET REVALUATION

	Land	Building
Carrying value at date of appraisal		
Historical cost (20X1)	$ 50,000	$100,000
Accumulated depreciation ($100,000 × 4% × 5 years)	—	20,000
Net book value at date of revaluation (20X5)	$ 50,000	$ 80,000
Fair market value; appraisal value	$325,000	$250,000
Recording the appraisal		
Capital asset—land ($325,000 – $50,000)	275,000	
Shareholders' equity—appraisal increment		275,000
Capital asset—building ($250,000 – $100,000)	150,000	
Accumulated depreciation	20,000	
Shareholders' equity—appraisal increment		170,000
Annual depreciation subsequent to the revaluation		
Depreciation expense ($250,000 × 5%)	12,500	
Accumulated depreciation		12,500
Shareholders' equity—appraisal increment	8,500	
Retained earnings ($170,000 × 5%)		8,500

Exhibit 10A-3 illustrates the accounting for Yvan Limited for this revaluation. Land is written up by $275,000. For the building, the undepreciated book value after four years of depreciation was $80,000. The appraisal requires an increase in the net book value of $170,000. Since a new basis of accounting is being established for the asset, the accumulated depreciation account is eliminated in the entry to record the revaluation. Subsequent depreciation is based on the fair value of the building but is partially offset by amortization of the equity account.

This treatment of asset revaluation prevents artificial income boosting that would occur if a gain was recorded. It also prevents retained earnings, if not net income, from being dragged down by higher depreciation on the revalued assets. Remember, though, that this policy is not GAAP.

Comprehensive Revaluation

Capital assets may be recorded at market value as part of a *financial reorganization*. In a *financial reorganization*, the standings of shareholders and unsecured (or inadequately secured) creditors are altered because the company is not able to meet its debt obligations. Financial reorganizations can be voluntary, but they also can be triggered by creditors. A financial reorganization results in a new basis of accountability for the assets, liabilities, and share equity. A key element of this procedure is that it must be *comprehensive. All assets and liabilities,* not just a selected few, must be revalued at fair market value.

comprehensive revaluation restating the carrying value of a company's assets and liabilities to market value; permitted only when there has been a change in ownership of virtually all of a company's equity interests

In 1992, the AcSB issued Section 1625, "Comprehensive Revaluation of Assets and Liabilities." In this section, the AcSB allows **comprehensive revaluation** only when one of two conditions has been satisfied. Either

a. All or virtually all of the equity interests in the enterprise have been acquired, in one or more transactions between non-related parties, by an acquirer who controls the enterprise after the transaction or transactions; or

b. The enterprise has been subject to a financial reorganization, and the same party does not control the enterprise both before and after the reorganization;

and in either situation new costs are reasonably determinable.

The crucial element in this recommendation is *that there is a change in control.* All assets and liabilities are recorded at market value to reflect this fresh start. Fair value must be determinable.

In a comprehensive revaluation, accumulated amortization accounts are eliminated, and all assets and liabilities are adjusted to appropriate fair market values. As part of the financial reorganization, equity accounts are likely shuffled around, too. For instance, the preferred shareholders might become common shareholders, or bondholders might become shareholders. Retained earnings, often a deficit, might be wiped out by reducing share capital. The gains and losses from revaluation are part of this equity reshuffling.

No gains or losses from a comprehensive revaluation are recognized on the income statement. The section specifically states that gains and losses "should be accounted for as a capital transaction and recorded as share capital, contributed surplus, or a separately identified account within shareholders' equity" (*CICA* 1625.44). Anything goes, as long as shareholders' equity is the catchall.

We'll take a look at accounting for reorganization in Chapter 13. For now, the focus is on this specific instance where capital assets can be written up to market value.

CIRCUMSTANCES WHERE REVALUATION IS PROHIBITED The AcSB rejected revaluation in other situations where revaluation might seem to provide more useful or relevant information for the users of the financial statements. Those situations explicitly considered and rejected by the AcSB are when

(a) an enterprise issues shares to the public;
(b) an enterprise issues debt based on asset appraisals;
(c) an enterprise results from a spin-off transaction to shareholders;
(d) an enterprise undergoes a change in its operations or line of business; and
(e) transactions in the equity interests when an enterprise is a joint venture.

(*CICA* 1625.17)

Of particular note are the first two. The AcSB refuses to recognize that when a company has an initial public offering (IPO), its financial reporting objectives are likely to change because there is an important new group of stakeholders. For debt-based appraisals, the AcSB seems to believe that it is more important to preserve historical cost than to permit a consistent basis of asset and liability presentation, even for private companies where there are no external stakeholders other than the bank that issued the debt.

Revaluation of all assets and liabilities *is* also allowed when there has been a change of control resulting from a business combination, e.g., a company has a new parent. If that parent owns more than 90% of the shares, then it is clearly the dominant shareholder and the acquired company is a subsidiary. The financial statements of the subsidiary are consolidated with those of the parent under GAAP. This involves adjusting all the subsidiary's assets to market value—a tedious process in annual consolidation. To reduce bookkeeping costs, the AcSB allows the subsidiary to record its assets and liabilities at fair value after such an acquisition (*CICA* 1625.04(a)). This is called *push-down accounting*, because fair market values are *pushed down* from the parent to the subsidiary. You'll encounter this in advanced accounting courses.

The common thread that you should keep in mind is that revaluation is allowed only in very limited circumstances that always involve new controlling shareholders. Secondly, revaluation is never permitted for only a few items—all assets and liabilities must be revalued together. Finally, revaluation of specific assets may be encountered in non-GAAP situations.

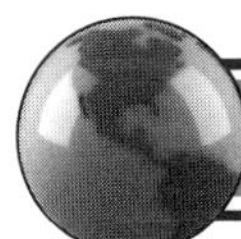

International Perspective

Canada is clearly out of step with international accounting standards on capital asset valuation. We already have discussed the fact that Canada's refusal to permit the restoration of written-down costs is at variance with widespread practice (and with the IASB standards). Canada's refusal to permit revaluations of individual assets also is unusually strict. Austria and Germany also forbid revaluations, while Japan, Spain, and the United States permit it only under special circumstances. On the other side are Australia, Belgium, Denmark, France, the Netherlands, Sweden, Switzerland, and the United Kingdom, all of which permit revaluations of tangible capital assets. If Canada is going to achieve international harmonization of its capital asset accounting standards, we will have to drop our rigid stance against revaluations of individual assets.

SUMMARY OF KEY POINTS

1. Upward revaluation of individual capital assets is not permitted in Canadian GAAP. Capital assets must be recorded at cost.
2. Capital assets may be written up to market value as part of a financial reorganization because a financial reorganization creates a new basis of accounting for the enterprise.
3. Financial reorganizations can either be voluntary or forced by creditors. To qualify for comprehensive revaluation in Canadian GAAP, control of the enterprise must pass from the pre-reorganization shareholders to a new shareholder group.
4. Comprehensive revaluations are not permitted in anticipation of an initial public offering of shares. They also are not permitted when new debt is issued on the basis of asset market or appraised values.
5. Comprehensive revaluation is also permitted for the acquired company in a business combination, provided that at least 90% of the acquired company's shares have been purchased by the parent company.

QUESTIONS

Q10-1 Explain and compare the words "amortization," "depletion," and "depreciation."

Q10-2 What are the primary causes of amortization? What effect do changes in the current market value of the asset being amortized have on amortization estimates?

Q10-3 Explain why land need not be amortized, with reference to the causes of amortization.

Q10-4 What items must be estimated before amortization can be calculated? Explain each item.

Q10-5 Explain the difference in meaning between the balances in the following two accounts: (a) accumulated amortization and (b) allowance to reduce inventory to the lower of cost or market.

Q10-6 Why is disclosure of amortization methods and rates so important?

Q10-7 List several factors a firm would consider in choosing an amortization method.

Q10-8 Under what circumstances would an asset with a 30-year physical life be amortized over a period shorter than 30 years?

Q10-9 Compare the effect of straight-line and productive output methods of depreciation on the per unit cost of output for a manufacturing company.

Q10-10 Why is straight-line amortization so popular in practice?

Q10-11 What are accelerated methods of amortization? Under what circumstances would these methods generally be appropriate?

Q10-12 Explain the minimum amortization test, and the circumstances under which it is important. Your response should include an explanation of the difference between residual value and salvage value.

Q10-13 Explain the accounting policy alternatives that exist with respect to depreciation when a firm's reporting year and the "asset year" do not coincide.

Q10-14 Explain the inventory appraisal system of depreciation. Under what circumstances is such a system appropriate?

Q10-15 Compare retirement and replacement depreciation systems. Explain when each of these systems would be appropriate.

Q10-16 How do the composite and group depreciation systems differ?

Q10-17 What is an impairment in the value of property, plant, and equipment? How is it measured and reported?

Q10-18 Assume that the fair value of an acquired business unit was estimated at $17,000,000, while recorded assets had a net book value of $22,000,000. What is the problem? What is the next step?

Q10-19 What estimates have to be made when recording an impairment of value? Can a writedown of a capital asset be reversed?

Q10-20 What accounting treatment is required when a company permanently stops using a capital asset?

Q10-21 What is the criterion for defining an asset group for held-for-sale accounting?

Q10-22 If a held-for-sale asset increases its value at a balance sheet date prior to its disposal, can the carrying value be written up? Explain.

Q10-23 Is it possible to revalue a specific asset to market value when market value is higher than net book value? Explain.

Q10-24 What is a comprehensive revaluation, and when can it be recorded?

CASE 10-1
Good Quality Auto Parts

Good Quality Auto Parts Limited (GQAP) is a medium-sized, privately owned producer of auto parts, which are sold to car manufacturers, repair shops, and retail outlets. In March 20X0, the union negotiated a new three-year contract with the company for the 200 shop-floor employees. At the time, GQAP was in financial difficulty and management felt unable to meet the contract demands of the union. Management also believed that a strike of any length would force the company into bankruptcy.

The company proposed that, in exchange for wage concessions, the company would implement a profit-sharing plan whereby the shop-floor employees would receive 10% of the company's annual after-tax profit as a bonus in each year of the contract. Although the union generally finds this type of contract undesirable, it believed that insisting on the prevailing industry settlement would jeopardize GQAP's survival. As a result, the contract terms were accepted.

The contract specifies that no major changes in accounting policies may be made without the change being approved by GQAP's auditor. Another clause in the contract allows the union to engage a chartered accountant to examine the books of the company and meet with GQAP's management and auditor to discuss any issues. Under the terms of the contract, any controversial accounting issues are to be negotiated by the union and management to arrive at a mutual agreement. If the parties cannot agree, the positions of the parties are to be presented to an independent arbitrator for resolution.

GQAP presented to the union its annual financial statements and the unqualified audit report for the year ended 28 February 20X1, the first year during which the profit-sharing plan was in effect. The union engaged you to analyze these financial statements and determine whether there are any controversial accounting issues. As a result of your examination, you identified a number of issues that are of concern to you. You met with the controller of the company and obtained the following information:

1. GQAP wrote off $250,000 of inventory manufactured five to eight years previously. There have been no sales from this inventory in over two years. The controller explained that up until this year she had some hope that the inventory could be sold as replacement parts. However, she now believes that the parts cannot be sold.
2. The contracts GQAP has with the large auto manufacturers allow the purchaser to return items for any reason. The company has increased the allowance for returned items by 10% in the year just ended. The controller contends that, because of the weak economy and stiff competition faced by the auto manufacturers with whom GQAP does business, there will likely be a significant increase in the parts returned.
3. In April 20X0, GQAP purchased $500,000 of new manufacturing equipment. To reduce the financial strain of the acquisition, the company negotiated a six-year payment schedule. Management believed that the company would be at a serious competitive disadvantage if it did not emerge from the current downturn with updated equipment. GQAP decided to use accelerated depreciation at a rate of 40% for the new equipment. The controller argued that because of the rapid technological changes occurring in the industry, equipment purchased now is more likely to become technologically, rather than operationally, obsolete. The straight-line depreciation method applied to the existing equipment has not been changed.
4. Six years ago, GQAP purchased a small auto parts manufacturer and merged it into its own operation. At the time of acquisition, $35,000 of goodwill was recorded. It was not amortized. The company has written off the goodwill in the year just ended. The controller explained that the poor performance of the auto parts industry, and of GQAP in particular, has made the goodwill worthless.

The union has asked you to prepare a report on the position it should take on the issues identified when discussing them with management.

Required:

Prepare the report. (CICA, adapted)

CASE 10-2
Canadian Wilderness Wonders Incorporated

Canadian Wilderness Wonders Incorporated (CWW) is a privately owned company that operates a safari-style wildlife park in southern Ontario. Until late last year, CWW was owned and managed by John Blake, founder and CEO. Following his death, his heirs (all family members), not wishing to run the park themselves, unanimously agreed to sell all the shares to David Winters, the CFO of CWW, on 30 September 20X4. Because CWW is a private company, a market price for the shares was not available and it was agreed that the purchase and sale price would be "three times earnings from continuing operations for the year ended 30 June 20X4, measured in accordance with Canadian GAAP."

In past years, CWW's financial statements were prepared by Winters without review or audit. Under the terms of the purchase and sale agreement, the Blake family, at its own expense, may request an independent audit of the financial statements.

Similar to wildlife safari parks in Africa, visitors drive through CWW's 1,300-hectare park, which is home to over 100 species of native animals, birds, and fish. Although hunting is not allowed in the park, fishing is permitted from man-made lakes that CWW constructed and began stocking with fish two years ago. Vehicular traffic through the park increased from 56,000 in 20X3 to 62,000 in 20X4. Revenues are from park admissions and from a hotel located on the park grounds. Admission to the park has been $20 per vehicle for the past three years, and hotel nightly rates average $110. There is a 60% occupancy rate.

It is now August 20X4. You are a close personal friend of Bill Blake, one of the Blake family members. During a lunch meeting, he expresses his concerns about the financial statements prepared by Winters. "I thought that, by using GAAP as a solid benchmark, the financial statements would be a perfect tool for setting the purchase and sale price. But I'm concerned that Winters has manipulated the accounting for his personal benefit and to the detriment of the Blake family. I'd like you to look at the statements and tell me if any of the numbers look suspicious. Also, I'd like to know if Winters has followed GAAP. Based on the preliminary conclusions in your report, I'll decide whether I should have a full audit done in accordance with the terms of the agreement. Until I have confirmation of my concerns, I don't want to tarnish my family's relationship with Winters or incur any audit fees unnecessarily."

The financial statements that were prepared by Winters are included in Exhibit 1.

Required:
Prepare an appropriate report for the Blake family.

(ASCA, adapted)

EXHIBIT 1

CANADIAN WILDERNESS WONDERS INCORPORATED
BALANCE SHEET (UNAUDITED)

(in thousands of dollars)

As at 30 June	20X4	20X3
Assets		
Cash	$244	$113
Hotel customer accounts receivable	403	460
Less: Allowance for doubtful accounts	(110)	(40)
Animal and fish stock	699	714
Capital assets	1,956	1,942
Less: Accumulated amortization	(271)	(235)
	$2,921	$2,954

Liabilities and shareholders' equity		
Accounts payable	$537	$629
Accrued liabilities	308	155
Long-term debt	1,802	1,911
	2,647	2,695
Share capital	2	2
Retained earnings	272	257
	274	259
	$2,921	$2,954

CANADIAN WILDERNESS WONDERS INCORPORATED
STATEMENT OF INCOME AND RETAINED EARNINGS (UNAUDITED)

(in thousands of dollars)

Year ended 30 June	**20X4**	**20X3**
Revenues—park admission	$1,184	$1,120
—hotel	2,123	2,080
	3,307	3,200
Hotel operating costs	1,628	1,451
Animal feed and care	1,064	1,129
Interest expense	198	96
Depreciation and fish write-offs	71	29
Environmental restoration and other costs	162	10
	3,123	2,715
Income before income tax	184	485
Income tax paid	120	167
Income before discontinued operations	64	318
Discontinued operations		
Animal sales revenue	156	102
Cost of animal sales	72	31
	84	71
Net income	148	389
Dividends	(133)	(280)
Retained earnings, beginning of year	257	148
Retained earnings, end of year	$272	$257

CANADIAN WILDERNESS WONDERS INCORPORATED
NOTES TO UNAUDITED FINANCIAL STATEMENTS

30 June 20X4

1. Significant accounting policies

Revenue

Partway through the year, the Company started a loyalty program to encourage return visits. The driver of each vehicle visiting the park was given a coupon worth $5 off the price of the next visit. Revenue was reduced by the $5 fair market value of all coupons issued, and a corresponding accrual was established to allow for future coupon redemptions.

Animal and fish stock

In accordance with industry practice, the stock of animals and fish is reported at the lower of cost and market value. Market values are estimated using current replacement costs.

A perpetual inventory system was implemented in the 20X3 fiscal year to track quantities of fish and animal stock present on the CWW park grounds. CWW personnel track the number of fish released into the man-made lakes, as well as the number of fish caught and removed. Since the number of fish births and mortalities are more difficult to track, CWW estimates these numbers based on its prior experience, allowing for possible changes in environmental conditions.

December 20X3 marked the start of an unusually harsh winter and, accordingly, management had to write off 20% of the December 20X3 fish stock that was presumed dead. This write-off is included in the 20X4 results.

Capital assets

Capital assets include land, man-made lakes, hotel buildings, and equipment. Hotel buildings and equipment are amortized on a straight-line basis over their estimated useful lives. In 20X4, the remaining estimated useful life of hotel buildings was reduced from 25 years to 18 years. Land and man-made lakes are not amortized.

Hotel repair costs are expensed as incurred. In 20X4, repairs included a $90,000 upgrade to replace aging meeting rooms with a state-of-the art, multimedia presentation room, intended to attract more group business to CWW.

Contingent liabilities

CWW does not routinely collect the scientific data needed to evaluate the ecological health of its park, yet significant growth in visitors over the past five years is thought to be damaging park ecology. In 20X4 CWW started a policy of accruing a liability each year in the amount of $150,000 for possible future environmental restoration costs that may be incurred as a result of deteriorating park ecology.

2. **Discontinued operations**

   Animal stock apparently survived the harsh weather with much greater success than the fish. Thirty newborn animals survived in 20X4, as compared to only 20 in each of the prior three years. Prices for animals have increased significantly over the past two years, as live capture in the wild becomes more difficult each year due to legislation. CWW normally sells at least half of its newborn animals to private zoos and other animal parks annually. Management has decided that this practice will cease in 20X4, as management plans to keep all animals to build inventory. Accordingly, discontinued operations accounting has been adopted for this aspect of the business.

3. **Interest expense**

   Long-term debt outstanding at the end of 20X3 was retired in 20X4, at a loss of $96,000 when the debt had a remaining term of six years. New long-term debt, with a six-year term but a lower interest rate, was negotiated to replace the retired debt. The loss on debt retirement is included in interest expense on the income statement.

4. **Income tax**

   CWW did not claim capital cost allowance in 20X4. Management anticipates that corporate income tax rates will increase, and plans to preserve this discretionary deduction for use in a future year when it may have greater benefit.

CASE 10-3
Provincial Hydro

Provincial Hydro (PH) is an electric utility that generates, supplies, and delivers electric power throughout a small Canadian province. It is incorporated as a Crown corporation and operates as a cooperative partnership with the relevant municipalities and the provincial government. It is a financially self-sustaining company without share capital, regulated by the provincial government. Its primary customers are the municipal utilities (which serve about 600,000 end users), 40 large industrial companies (direct service), and 100,000 rural retail customers. PH operates various generating stations, including both nuclear and fossil fuel–fired plants. As a result, it is very capital intensive. This, in turn, makes PH sensitive to the cost of money.

PH plays a major role in attracting industry to the province by maintaining competitive rates for electricity. It is profoundly affected by various pieces of provincial legislation.

The financial statement results are used to set utility rates, although there are specific rules about which expenses are permissible and at what time. Many accounting policies are chosen based on the rules for rate recovery. Profits of the corporation are to be applied toward the reduction of the cost of power for the municipalities with which the utility has a cooperative partnership.

Management and the municipalities are very sensitive to political pressures. PH is in the public spotlight, and financial results and policies can generate considerable publicity.

A major component of the cost of electricity is fuel cost, which includes the following components: fuel (quantity and price), interest on funds tied up in inventory, transportation, and overheads.

PH has two mothballed generating stations, which are not producing energy at present but may be used during peak demand periods when needed. The plants, all oil-fired, were mothballed as more efficient generation methods were developed.

PH has chosen to reflect the situation by accelerating the rate of depreciation to "reflect the reduced economic value" of the assets. PH has produced demand forecasts (which are regularly updated) that predict when and how much energy will have to come from the mothballed plants. Based on these probability factors, PH establishes an amortization rate, higher than the original rate, which takes the change of circumstances into account. Depreciation is charged only when the plant is used. Care is taken to avoid premature write-off while the plant may still be useful.

PH uses the CANDU reactor in its nuclear stations. This reactor has relatively low fuel cost but must use "heavy water," H_2O_2 (versus "light water," H_2O, which other reactors use). Heavy water is not consumed in the fissioning process but acts as a moderator of the process. With periodic in-station upgrading to remove impurities, heavy water has an indefinite life.

Heavy water costs, plus interest on inventories of heavy water designated for future use, are capitalized. These capital costs are being written off over 60 years, which is the date PH estimates heavy water will be replaced by new technology. However, the last committed CANDU nuclear unit is due to be retired in 40 years. Management has indicated that nuclear units are regularly upgraded by replacing pressure tubes, which extends their useful life. In addition, the useful life of heavy water does not depend on the life of the station since it can be transferred to another station.

Inventories of fossil fuels are expensed based on an average costs system where the average is calculated monthly on a rolling basis. Average cost was chosen as it seemed the most fair to current and future customers and had a smoothing effect on price fluctuations. Recently, however, with significant declines in fossil fuel prices, there has been considerable public comment as electricity prices did not fall accordingly. Management is beginning to consider the alternatives and their advantages and disadvantages.

Management has reminded you that one-time writedowns are not permissible costs in utility rate-setting formulas, nor is it possible to make retroactive changes to the rate structure.

Required:

PH has asked you, an external adviser, to consider accounting issues raised. and to provide a report incorporating your recommendations.

(ASCA, adapted)

CASE 10-4
May Company

May Company owns a chain of eight small hotels in the western provinces. The chain specializes in family vacations, promoting "free family breakfasts," reduced rates for children, and a variety of activity packages for special weekends in off-peak seasons and during the busy summer months.

Two hotels, a 75-room unit and a 100-room unit, have had marginal cash flow over the past three years. Management pursued aggressive promotion campaigns to improve business, but the only way to increase occupancy at these locations proved to be deep discounting of room rates, and cash flow has remained unacceptably low. Management concluded that these locations were poor for tourist and holiday business. Both hotels were in line for expensive refurbishing, which was not economically justifiable.

Rather than close the buildings, however, the company investigated the alternative of converting the hotels to residential apartment units. Low residential vacancy rates in the respective towns has convinced management that the plan is feasible. There would be expensive conversion costs upfront, basically to install kitchens in each apartment unit. However, thorough marketing, engineering, and construction investigation has provided a level of comfort with the project, which was recently approved by the May Company Board of Directors. Discussions have been held with lenders, and mortgage financing will be arranged that pays out existing loans secured by these two properties. This financing provides 80% of the funds needed for renovation. The company will arrange short-term construction loans, which will be replaced by the new mortgage funding when the renovation work is substantially complete. Lenders will require audited financial statements, and pay particular attention to cash flow and the times-interest-earned ratio (net income before tax and interest expense divided by interest expense).

The hotels will be closed at the end of the summer, and will then be vacant for six to eight months while renovations take place. Studies indicate that it will then take 6 to 14 months to rent the buildings to a target occupancy level, which is around the 80% level.

The company believes that it need not record depreciation expense during the period it takes to convert and rent the buildings. That is, depreciation would cease as soon as the hotels were closed, and recommence when the target rental level is achieved. The company believes that continuation of past depreciation policies during the conversion and rent-up period does not make sense for the following reasons:

- The nature of the business is changing for these two properties, and they are essentially "construction in progress" for the period. New operations will emerge out the other end.
- The properties are currently recorded at amounts lower than their current market values.
- The properties have remaining useful lives as apartment buildings in excess of their current accounting lives estimated for hotels.

The company believes that it makes more sense to match depreciation with revenues achieved at full rent-up so that future periods are not unduly enhanced by charges made to operations in prior years.

Another issue being considered is the method of depreciation to be used for the apartment buildings. The hotel properties are all depreciated using the straight-line method over their useful lives, which are relatively long. The company wonders if this method will be the most appropriate for the apartment buildings.

Required:
Advise the company on appropriate accounting policies with respect to the conversion.

CASE 10-5
Canadian Energy Corporation

Canadian Energy Corporation (CEC) is a large, privately owned corporation that provides electricity to customers in western Canada and the United States. CEC operates 12 nuclear plants and five fossil fuel plants located throughout British Columbia, Alberta, and Manitoba. It was federally incorporated in Canada in 1968.

On 1 January 20X4, the media leaked details of a report stating that CEC had dumped thousands of tonnes of pollutants in major waterways, the source of drinking water for millions of people. The President of CEC blamed employees for "a lot of poor judgement" for not becoming alarmed at the amount of pollutants being poured into major waterways over the past 20 years without proper disclosure to federal and provincial environmental agencies. The problem originated in the failure to replace old and inadequate pipes used to carry cooling water when they clearly should have been replaced. The report was based on the findings of two CEC staff members, a medical health official, and a university professor. The two CEC staff members thought it was about time to "speak out and let the truth be known."

The newspaper article included an interview with a former executive who had recently resigned from CEC. He stated that the current problem stems from the fact that CEC is "basically out of control." The article reported that there is a weak system of accountability. The Board of Directors and senior management have no means of holding each operating unit accountable for its actions. When proposals went to the Board, they were signed by four or five vice-presidents, making it virtually impossible to pinpoint responsibility. The newspaper article went on to say, "The Board kept getting good reports stating that everything was going as planned. But, as we know now, that has not proven to be the case."

Within days of this article, the president announced that CEC will close five of its 12 nuclear plants and downsize its staff. These plants no longer meet minimum federal safety standards and must be shut down under Canadian environmental laws. They will be shut down immediately and decommissioned over the next five years. Decommissioning refers to the work required to take a plant out of service and close it down permanently.

CEC will also engage in an intensive refitting program that will bring the utility up to federal standards. The company will invest millions of dollars in four of the five fossil fuel plants, on employee retraining, on upgrading capital equipment, and on generating replacement power. Exhibit I provides notes from your discussions with CEC's controller concerning decommissioning.

CEC officials are trying to persuade their American energy customers to give CEC relief from the demands of binding export contracts. Its U.S. contracts run for another three years. These contracts, signed when CEC had plenty of excess energy-generating capacity, required CEC to supply a minimum of 35,000 megawatts in 20X3 to utilities in the United States. CEC charges $3,000 per megawatt to each U.S. customer. Each year, CEC is compelled under its contracts to supply 10% more than the previous year. The contracts stipulate that a $1,500 penalty must be paid by CEC for each megawatt not delivered. All contracts with U.S. customers are in Canadian dollars.

With the shutdown of its nuclear plants, CEC will have to rely more heavily on its fossil fuel plants, which use coal and oil to generate energy. Air emission restrictions limit the extent to which CEC can rely on its fossil fuel plants without fines or penalties. If a fossil fuel plant exceeds its annual limit of 7,000 megawatts, governmental regulatory agencies will impose fines of $1,000 for each additional megawatt produced. In addition, CEC is required under Canadian law to meet all domestic energy demands first before any energy can be exported. The Canadian government requires CEC to supply 110,000 megawatts to Canadian customers each year. Demand is not expected to increase in the near future.

The chair of CEC's Board of Directors, Gord Roper, has come to the engagement partner for advice. He wants a report discussing the implications of these recent developments on CEC's operations and financial reporting. This should include projected cash flows from operations for the next three years.

You are the audit manager on the CEC engagement. The partner has asked you to draft the report to CEC's Board of Directors. It is the middle of January 20X4. Exhibit II contains the draft financial statements. Exhibit III contains other information regarding CEC.

Required:
Prepare the draft report to the Board.

(CICA, adapted)

EXHIBIT 1

NOTES FROM DISCUSSIONS WITH CEC'S CONTROLLER CONCERNING DECOMMISSIONING

1. Provincial legislation requires that all nuclear plants be decommissioned and dismantled so as to restore the site to its original condition once operations have ceased.
2. The five nuclear generating plants will be shut down immediately and decommissioned over the next five years. Their staff will receive lay-off notices within the week. Currently, these five plants employ 500 employees at a payroll cost of $20 million each year. Severance payments will be $5 million. Employees are bound by a collective agreement that expires in 20X5.
3. As a result of the nuclear plant shutdowns, a major program will be undertaken to refit four of the five fossil fuel plants. Refitting activities will continue until 2001 and are estimated to cost $15 million over the next three years. Once the refitting work has been completed, fossil fuel plants will be able to increase their efficiency and reduce emissions. CEC will retrain staff for the refitted fossil fuel plants.
4. At the end of 20X2 CEC estimated that the total cost of decommissioning its 12 nuclear plants would be $1 billion. CEC accrues a portion of the total cost each year over the estimated lives of the plants. At the end of 20X2 one half of the useful lives of the nuclear plants had expired and accordingly $500 million had been accrued for decommissioning. Fossil fuel plants are not subject to mandatory decommissioning standards and laws.
5. On 31 December 20X3, the federal government approved the development of new technology that is expected to reduce decommissioning costs by 20%. Government officials are reasonably certain that this technology will be available in the near future. The total amount accrued on the 20X3 balance sheet for decommissioning is being reduced by $100 million to account for the change in technology. The annual accrual for decommissioning is now $20 million.
6. CEC received a report in late December 20X3 from an independent consultant that estimates the cost of decommissioning the five nuclear plants to be shut down. The current cost of decommissioning ranges from $120 million to $150 million per nuclear plant being shut down, depending on the extent of the damage caused by the corroded pipes.
7. The controller has never discounted any of the decommissioning liabilities in the past but feels that it would be the right thing to do now.

EXHIBIT II

CANADIAN ENERGY CORPORATION
EXTRACTS FROM DRAFT BALANCE SHEET

(in thousands of dollars)

	As at December 31, 20X3 (unaudited)	As at December 31, 20X2 (audited)
Assets		
Current		
Cash and short-term investments	$7,256	$56,834
Accounts receivable	53,300	42,155
Inventory	39,889	38,911
Other	10,794	9,873
	111,239	147,773
Non-current		
Capital assets (net)	1,030,256	967,027
Investments (Government of Canada bonds—market approximately equal to cost)	5,000	5,000
	$1,146,495	$1,119,800
Liabilities and Shareholders' Equity		
Current		
Accounts payable and accrued liabilities	$56,444	40,800
Bank loan (Note 1)	30,000	30,000
	86,444	70,800
Non-current		
Debentures (Note 1)	350,000	350,000
Decommissioning provision	420,000	500,000
Common shares	25,000	25,000
Retained earnings	265,051	174,000
	$1,146,495	$1,119,800

Note 1:
Bank loan bears interest at 8%, is due on demand, and is secured by accounts receivable. The debentures are unsecured; principal is repayable in 20X8 and interest is payable annually at an average rate of 8%.

CANADIAN ENERGY CORPORATION
EXTRACTS FROM DRAFT INCOME STATEMENT

(in thousands of dollars)

	For the Year Ended December 31, 20X3 (unaudited)	For the Year Ended December 31, 20X2 (audited)
Revenue		
Canadian sales	$289,000	$286,000
US exports	105,000	95,455
Other revenue	5,545	8,771
	399,545	390,226
Expenses		
Operating, maintenance, and administration	256,083	225,922
Cost of energy	57,782	56,384
Amortization	44,229	41,353
Decommissioning expenses	20,000	25,000
Adjustment due to reduction in the decommissioning provision	(100,000)	–
Financing charges	30,400	30,400
	308,494	379,059
Net income	$91,051	$11,167

EXHIBIT III

OTHER INFORMATION

1. As a result of the recent newspaper article, a class action has been launched against CEC by the towns that use the drinking water in the areas where the pipes are damaged. These parties claim $10 million in damages. CEC says that there is no evidence that the drinking water is not fit for human consumption, although more tests are required. CEC estimates that these tests and preliminary studies would cost at least $1 million, and it is not willing to incur the cost at this time. Management will not record any liability due to its inability to reasonably estimate cleanup costs, if any.
2. The internal audit function consists of one full-time staff member who hires temporary staff when needed during peak audit periods.
3. The controller has been too busy to prepare revised budgets for future years that reflect the impact of the plant shutdowns. He expects that the balance sheet and income statement will not differ significantly from the current year's financial statements, as there is a freeze on spending except for expenditures relating to the plant shutdowns.
4. Audited financial statements of prior years indicate that CEC has experienced positive cash flows since 20X0.
5. CEC is currently in a short-term federal tax shelter program whereby companies are not required to pay taxes if certain criteria are met. The objective of this program is to boost activity in the energy sector.
6. Currently, each nuclear plant produces 10,000 megawatts per year, which is 67% of capacity. Each fossil fuel generating plant produces 5,000 megawatts annually, which is 70% of capacity.
7. The Board's environmental committee met twice in the past year.

(CICA)

ASSIGNMENTS

A10-1 Amortization Policy: Everett MacLaughlin, the president of MacLaughlin Enterprises, is proposing the following amortization policy for the capital assets of the company:

> "Since most companies use the rates in the *Income Tax Act*, we'll do the same. Buildings will be amortized at a rate of 4%, declining balance, equipment at a rate of 20%, and automobiles and manufacturing equipment at 30%, still declining balance. Those are the tax rules! I know that the manufacturing equipment will last for at least six years, but I prefer the fast write-off to be conservative."

Required:

Is this amortization policy acceptable? Write a brief memo to the president explaining your position.

A10-2 Amortization Policy: Five different methods of amortization have been described in the chapter:

1. straight line
2. units of production
3. declining balance
4. sum of the years' digits
5. sinking fund

Required:

Indicate the likely choice of amortization method expected to be chosen if

a. The firm is a real estate property developer and the asset to be amortized is a highly levered apartment building.
b. The firm has a lot of debt on its balance sheet and is trying to meet minimum net income levels specified in debt covenants.
c. The firm is a mining company and assets to be amortized are mine development costs.
d. The firm wishes to minimize the amount of future (deferred) tax recognized in the financial statements.
e. The firm wishes to portray stable income patterns over time.
f. The firm wants to be comparable to other firms in its industry that commonly use declining balance. However, usage patterns are level over time.
g. The firm has a parent company that uses SYD.
h. The firm wants to minimize bookkeeping costs by keeping allocation methods simple.
i. The firm expects to use the asset heavily in initial years, and less as it grows older.
j. The firm expects to use the asset sporadically, but the asset will not wear out unless used.
k. Technological obsolescence is a significant factor in estimating the useful life of the asset.

A10-3 Amortization Computation: To demonstrate the computations involved in several methods of amortizing a capital asset, the following information is used:

Acquisition cost	$18,500
Residual value	500
Estimated service life:	
Years	6
Service-hours	12,000
Productive output (units)	36,000

Required:

Give the formula and compute the annual amortization amount using each of the following methods (show computations and round to the nearest dollar):

1. Straight-line amortization.
2. Service-hours method; compute the amortization rate and amount for the first year, assuming 3,200 service-hours of actual operation.
3. Productive output method of amortization; compute the amortization rate and amount for the first year, assuming 9,000 units of output. Is all of the amortization amount (computed in your answer) expensed during the current period?
4. Declining-balance method; compute the amortization amount for five years assuming a rate of 50% is used and the residual value is $1,000.

A10-4 Amortization Computation: Mace Company acquired equipment that cost $18,000, which will be amortized on the assumption that it will last six years and have a $1,200 residual value. Several possible methods of amortization are under consideration.

Required:

1. Prepare a schedule that shows annual amortization expense for the first two years, assuming the following (show computations and round to the nearest dollar):
   a. Declining-balance method, using a rate of 30%.
   b. Productive output method. Estimated output is a total of 105,000 units, of which 12,000 will be produced the first year; 18,000 in each of the next two years; 15,000 the fourth year; and 21,000 the fifth and sixth years.
   c. Straight-line method.
   d. Sum-of-the-years'-digits.
2. Repeat your calculations for part (1), assuming a useful life of 10 years, a DB rate of 20% that reflects the longer life, but the same number of units of production. The residual value is unchanged. What conclusion can you reach by comparing the results of (1) and (2)?
3. What criteria would you consider important in selecting an amortization method?

A10-5 Amortization Schedule: Quick Producers acquired factory equipment on 1 January 20X5, costing $39,000. In view of pending technological developments, it is estimated that the machine will have a resale value upon disposal in four years of $8,000 and that disposal costs will be $500. Quick has a fiscal year-end that ends on 31 December. Data relating to the equipment follow:

Estimated service life:

Years	4
Service-hours	20,000

Actual operations:

Calendar Year	Service Hours
20X5	5,700
20X6	5,000
20X7	4,800
20X8	4,400

Required:

Round to the nearest dollar and show computations.

1. Prepare an amortization schedule for the asset, using
   a. Straight-line amortization.
   b. Declining-balance amortization, using a 50% rate.

c. Sum-of-the-years'-digits amortization.
d. Service-hours amortization.

2. Express straight-line amortization as a percentage of original cost.
3. Explain whether
   a. the rate of 50% was a good choice for DB amortization, and
   b. the 20,000 estimate of total service hours was accurate.

A10-6 Analysis of Four Amortization Methods—Maximize Income: On 1 January 20X5, Vello Company, a tool manufacturer, acquired new industrial equipment for $2 million. The new equipment had a useful life of four years, and the residual value was estimated to be $200,000. Vello estimates that the new equipment can produce 14,000 tools in its first year. Production is then estimated to decline by 1,000 units per year over the remaining useful life of the equipment.

The following amortization methods are under consideration:

a. declining balance (50% rate)
b. straight line
c. sum of the years' digits
d. units of output

Required:
Which amortization method would result in maximum income for financial statement reporting for the three-year period ending 31 December 20X7? Prepare a schedule showing the amount of accumulated amortization at 31 December 20X7, under each method selected. Show supporting computations in good form. Ignore present value, income tax, and future (deferred) income tax considerations in your answer.

(AICPA, adapted)

A10-7 Interpreting Amortization Disclosures: Portions of the 20X0 financial statements of William's Company, a paint manufacturer, are reproduced below ($ thousands):

Partial Income Statement for the year ended 31 December 20X0

Net sales	$2,266,732
Total expenses	2,079,455
Income before income tax	187,277
Income tax	64,611
Net income	$122,666

Note 1: Significant Accounting Policies

Property, Plant, and Equipment. Property, plant, and equipment are stated on the basis of cost. Amortization is provided principally by the straight-line method. The major classes of assets and ranges of amortization rates are as follows:

Buildings	2%–6%
Machinery	4%–20%
Furniture and fixtures	5%–20%
Automobiles and trucks	10%–33%

Note 16: Property, Plant, and Equipment Schedules

Cost	Beginning	Additions	Retirements	Other	Ending
Buildings	$ 191,540	$ 11,574	$ (960)	($7,185)	$ 194,969
Machinery	404,156	43,968	(16,319)	466	432,271

Total accumulated amortization

	Beginning	Additions	Retirements	Other	Ending
Buildings	$ 62,843	$ 7,422	$ (769)	($4,951)	$ 64,545
Machinery	211,662	37,085	(12,302)	(845)	235,600

Required:

1. What method of amortization is used by Williams?
2. What are the average estimated useful lives of buildings owned by Williams?
3. What percentage of the useful life of buildings remains, on average, at the end of the year?
4. What is the book value of machinery retired in the year?
5. Amortization on buildings and machinery was what percentage of (a) total expenses and (b) pretax earnings?

A10-8 Identify Amortization Methods—Amortization Schedules: Veto Company bought equipment on 1 January 20X5 for $60,000. The expected life is 10 years, and the residual value is $10,000. Based on two acceptable amortization methods, the annual amortization expense and cumulative balance of accumulated amortization at the end of 20X5 and 20X6 are shown below.

	Case A		Case B	
Year	Annual Expense	Accumulated Amount	Annual Expense	Accumulated Amount
20X5	$12,000	$12,000	$5,000	$5,000
20X6	9,600	21,600	5,000	10,000

Required:

1. Identify the amortization method used in each case.
2. Based on your answer to part (1), prepare an amortization schedule for each case for 20X5 through 20X8.

A10-9 Identify, Recalculate Amortization: Beans Company purchased a special machine at a cost of $81,000 plus provincial sales tax of $6,480. The machine is expected to have a residual value of $6,000 at the end of its service life.

To assist in preparing the journal entries for amortization of this machine, your assistant prepared the following spreadsheet:

BEANS COMPANY

Cost of Asset			$ 87,480
Asset's Residual Value			6,000
Years of Service Life			4
Output in units	Year 1	1,400	
	Year 2	1,300	
	Year 3	1,000	
	Year 4	1,100	
Total expected output			4,800

Year	Method 1 Amortization Expense	Method 1 Accumulated Amortization	Method 2 Amortization Expense	Method 2 Accumulated Amortization	Method 3 Amortization Expense	Method 3 Accumulated Amortization
1	$21,870	$21,870	$27,265	$27,265	$21,870	$21,870
2	21,870	43,740	25,318	52,583	16,403	38,273
3	21,870	65,610	19,475	72,058	12,302	50,575
4	21,870	87,480	21,422	93,480	36,905	87,480
Total	$87,480		$93,480		$87,480	

The spreadsheet includes statistics relating to the machine, and calculates amortization using three different methods—productive output, straight line, and declining balance at a 50% rate. However, due to some carelessness, your assistant made at least one error in the calculations for each method.

Required:

1. Identify which method is the
   a. productive method
   b. straight-line method
   c. declining-balance method (50% rate)
2. Describe the error(s) made in the calculations for each method.
3. Recalculate amortization expense for Year 2 under each method.

(CGA-Canada, adapted)

A10-10 Amortization and Sale: Gentry Hair Salons opened in April 20X4. It spent $96,000 on leasehold improvements on a property for which it signed a five-year lease on 1 April 20X4. The lease was renewable at Gentry's option for another five years. Equipment was purchased at a cost of $49,600. The equipment was expected to last for 20,000 service hours, or approximately eight years. Service hours consumed in 20X4 were 2,400, 4,900 in 20X5, and 3,700 in 20X6. Equipment will have a $2,000 salvage value at the end of its life, but the leasehold improvements will be worthless if the leased property is vacated. Gentry has a 31 December year-end.

Required:

1. Calculate total amortization for 20X4, 20X5, and 20X6, assuming:
   a. Straight-line amortization for both assets. Assume Gentry claims a half-year of amortization in the year of acquisition and a half-year in the year of disposal.
   b. Declining-balance depreciation at a 40% rate for equipment and 30% for leaseholds. Assume Gentry claims a full year of amortization in the year of acquisition and none in the year of disposal.
   c. Service life amortization for equipment and straight-line amortization for leaseholds. For straight-line amortization, assume Gentry claims a half-year of amortization in the year of acquisition and a half-year in the year of disposal.
2. At the end of 20X6, Gentry ceases operations. It pays a $30,000 fee to the landlord and quits the leased property, abandoning the leasehold improvements. Equipment is sold for $9,000. Provide the entry to record the payment, the write-off of the leasehold improvements, and the sale of the equipment under each of the three amortization methods in part (1).
3. Comment on the pattern of losses recorded in part (2).

A10-11 Amortization and Sale: On 31 December 20X5, Soccer Limited reported the following capital assets:

Machinery	$375,000	
Less: Accumulated amortization	(191,250)	$183,750
Buildings	400,000	
Less: Accumulated amortization	(105,000)	295,000

Machinery is amortized at a 30% declining-balance rate and has a residual value of $125,000. A full year of amortization is charged in the year of acquisition for assets, but none in the year of sale. Buildings are amortized straight line over 20 years with a salvage value of $50,000.

Required:

1. Calculate amortization expense for the machinery in 20X6 and 20X7.
2. How many years has the company owned the building?
3. Assume that the building was re-appraised on 5 January 20X6, and was estimated to be now worth $400,000. It was expected to last another 25 years, after which time it would have a salvage value of $100,000. How much amortization would be recorded in 20X6?
4. Assume instead that the machinery is sold on 25 May 20X6 for $160,000. Provide the journal entry to record the sale. No amortization is charged in the year of sale.
5. In 20X6, a bulldozer was acquired at a cost of $91,200, plus tax and duty of $13,680. Delivery costs amounted to $9,100, and it cost $4,700 to adjust the machine to ready it for use. The bulldozer was expected to last for 10 years, and have a salvage value of $7,000 at that time. It was expected to be run for 16,000 hours over its life. In 20X6, it was used for 1,200 hours. Using the service-hours method, how much was amortization in 20X6?

(CGA-Canada, adapted)

A10-12 Comprehensive Intangibles—Accounting and Amortization: Beta Designs Limited began operations in 20X5, and, at the end of its first year of operations, reported a balance of $1,376,950 in an account called "intangibles." Upon further investigation, it is discovered that the account had been debited throughout the year as follows:

5 Jan.	Organization costs; legal fees. Economic life is indefinite.	$ 25,800
1 Feb.	Patent registration; legal fees re: patent with 17-year life to be used in research activities.	10,750
1 July	Operating expenses, first six months.	509,700
1 Aug.	Goodwill; excess of purchase price of an advertising company paid over tangible assets acquired.	345,000
10 Nov.	Copyright acquired; remaining legal life is 29 years but economic life is 10 years.	37,600
30 Nov.	Trademark registration; legal fees. The trademark is expected to have an indefinite economic life.	13,400
5 Dec.	Staff training costs; staff is expected to stay with the company for an average of three years.	45,200
31 Dec.	Research costs incurred over the year; 40% of all research costs are properly classified as development. The product developed will begin commercial production next year.	389,500
		$1,376,950

Required:

1. Prepare a correcting entry that reallocates all amounts charged to intangibles to the appropriate accounts. State any assumptions made.
2. Calculate amortization expense on intangible assets for 20X5. Straight-line amortization, to the exact month of purchase, is used. All salvage values are expected to be zero.

A10-13 Sinking-Fund Amortization: Brexel Properties Limited owns apartment buildings in an urban centre. At the beginning of 20X4, Brexel acquired a new building for $14,350,000. The building is expected to last 25 years, and have no salvage value at the end of its life. Brexel uses sinking-fund amortization, at a rate of 9%, on similar buildings. Brexel has borrowed $13,500,000 to finance this building, at an interest rate of 10%. Interest is paid at the end of each year, along with a principal payment in the amount of $500,000. Remaining principal is due at the end of the loan term.

Required:

1. Calculate the annual amortization for the first five years.
2. Calculate the amount of interest expense for the first five years.
3. Comment on the expense patterns demonstrated in parts (1) and (2). What factors explain the choice of sinking-fund amortization in the real estate industry?

A10-14 Cost, Minimum Amortization, Sale: German Limited purchased Machine No. 103 on 2 January 20X8. The following information relates to this machine:

Invoice price	$ 70,000
Credit terms 2/10, n/30	
Customs and duty costs	2,000
Preparation and installation costs	7,400

The company borrowed $75,000 to pay for the machine promptly and take advantage of the cash discount. It incurred interest costs of $600 on this loan during 20X8. Machine No. 103 has a physical life expectancy of 12 years with a salvage value of zero. However, German intends to use the machine for 10 years and hopes to sell it for $20,000 at that time. The president of German tells you to record a relatively high amount of amortization in 20X8 in order to minimize 20X8 income.

Required:

1. What amortization method could be used to abide by the president's request? Is this method acceptable under generally accepted accounting principles? Explain.
2. Compute amortization expense for 20X8 using the straight-line method.
3. Assume that the machine is sold on 1 January 20X11, for $50,000 cash. Prepare the journal entry to record the sale assuming the straight-line method of amortization was used.

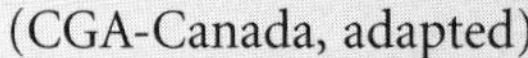
(CGA-Canada, adapted)

A10-15 Minimum Amortization Test: AC Metals bought a piece of manufacturing equipment at the beginning of 20X5.

- The equipment had an original cost of $750,000.
- AC expects to use the equipment for 10 years, and then sell it. The equipment will likely have a five-year useful life remaining at that time.
- Expected residual value at the end of 10 years is $300,000.
- Expected salvage value at the end of 15 years is nil—scrap value only.
- AC Metals uses straight-line amortization on all manufacturing assets.

Required:

1. Explain the difference between the terms "residual" and "salvage values," as used above.
2. How much amortization on the equipment should AC recognize in 20X5? Explain the circumstances that cause this result.

A10-16 Fractional Year Amortization: Jackson Company's records show the following machinery acquisitions and retirements during the first two years of operations:

	Acquisition		Retirement	
Date	Cost of Machinery	Estimated Useful Life (years)	Acquisition Date	Original Cost
1 January 20X5	$50,000	10		
1 April 20X5	40,000	5		
1 December 20X6	20,000	10		
31 December 20X6			20X5*	$7,000

* part of machinery acquired on 1 January 20X5

Required:

1. Compute amortization expense for 20X5 and for 20X6 and the balances of the machinery and related accumulated amortization accounts at the end of each year, using straight-line amortization. Machinery is depreciated according to the number of months of ownership in the year of acquisition or retirement. Assume no residual values. There are no sale proceeds upon retirement. Show computations and round to the nearest dollar. Set up separate columns in a schedule for machinery and for accumulated amortization.
2. Compute amortization expense for 20X5 and for 20X6 and the balances of the machinery and related accumulated amortization accounts at the end of each year using straight-line amortization. Machinery is depreciated for one-half year in the year of acquisition. Machinery retired is amortized for one-half year in its year of retirement. Assume no residual values. There are no sale proceeds upon retirement. Show computations and round to the nearest dollar. Set up separate columns in a schedule for machinery and for accumulated amortization.
3. Comment on the differences between parts (1) and (2).

(AICPA, adapted)

A10-17 Analyze Accounts, Cash Flow Statement: Selected accounts included under property, plant, and equipment on Abel Company's balance sheet at 31 December 20X5, had the following balances (at original cost):

Land	$220,000
Land improvements	75,000
Buildings (acquired 30 October 20X0)	600,000
Machinery and equipment (acquired 30 April 20X3 and 1 April 20X5)	650,000
Accumulated amortization, building	102,857
Accumulated amortization, machinery and equipment	317,200
Accumulated amortization, land improvements	12,857

- Building and existing land improvements amortization is based on the straight-line method over 35 years.
- Machinery and equipment amortization is based on the declining-balance method, using a rate of 20%.
- Residual values are immaterial and are not included in amortization calculations.
- The company claims a full year of amortization in the year of acquisition and none in the year of disposal.

During 20X6, the following transactions occurred:

a. A plant facility consisting of land and building was acquired from Club Company in exchange for 10,000 of Abel's common shares. On the acquisition date, Abel's shares had a closing market price of $32 per share on a national stock exchange. The plant facility was carried on Club's accounts at $95,000 for land and $130,000 for the building at the exchange date. Current appraised values for the land and building, respectively, are $120,000 and $240,000.

b. A tract of land was acquired for $85,000 as a potential future building site.

c. Machinery was purchased at a total cost of $250,000. Additional costs were incurred as follows:

Freight and unloading	$ 5,000
Sales taxes	10,000
Installation	25,000

d. Expenditures totalling $90,000 were made for new parking lots, streets, and sidewalks at the corporation's various plant locations. These items had an estimated useful life of 15 years.

e. A machine that cost $50,000 on 1 April 20X5 was scrapped on 30 June 20X6. DB amortization, at a 20% rate, has been recorded in 20X5.

f. A machine was sold for $25,000 on 1 July 20X6. Original cost of the machine was $37,000 at 1 January 20X3, and it had been amortized from 20X3 to 20X5 using the DB method.

Required:

1. Prepare a detailed analysis of the changes in each balance sheet account for 20X6.
2. Show how the transactions in requirement (1) would be shown in the cash flow statement. The indirect method is used in the operating activities section.
3. List the information items in the problem that were not used to determine the answer to part (1) above, showing the relevant amounts and supporting computations for each item. In addition, indicate where, or if, these items should be included in Abel's financial statements.

A10-18 Inventory Appraisal System: Mite Engineering Company acquired a large number of small tools at the beginning of operations on 1 January 20X5, for $10,000. During 20X5 and 20X6, Mite disposed of several used tools, receiving cash salvage value of $800 in 20X5 and $1,000 in 20X6. During 20X6, Mite acquired additional tools at a cost of $3,000. Inventories of tools on hand, valued at current acquisition cost adjusted for the present condition of the tools, indicated a value of $6,500 on 31 December 20X5, and $7,500 on 31 December 20X6. Mite uses the inventory appraisal system of depreciation for small tools.

Required:

How much amortization expense will be recognized on the small tools in 20X5 and 20X6? Show calculations.

A10-19 Composite Amortization System: WIT Company owned the following machines, all acquired on 1 January 20X5:

Machine	Original Cost	Estimated Residual Value	Estimated Life (years)
A	$20,000	None	5
B	15,000	$1,700	7
C	27,000	3,000	10
D	33,500	3,500	12

Required:

1. Prepare a schedule calculating individual straight-line depreciation for each machine that shows the following: cost, residual value, depreciable cost, life in years, and annual depreciation.
2. Compute the composite depreciation rate (based on cost), composite life, and 20X5 depreciation expense if the machines are depreciated using the composite system.

A10-20 Composite Amortization System: Capital assets acquired on 1 January 20X5 by Sculley Company are to be amortized under the composite system. Details regarding each asset are given in the schedule below.

Component	Cost	Estimated Residual Value	Estimated Life (Years)
A	$90,000	$10,000	10
B	30,000	0	6
C	76,000	16,000	15
D	12,400	400	8

Required:

1. Calculate the composite life and annual composite amortization rate (based on cost) for the asset components listed above. Give the entry to record amortization after one full year of use. Round the amortization rate to the nearest two decimal places.
2. During 20X6, it was necessary to replace component B, which was sold for $16,000. The replacement component cost $36,000 and will have an estimated residual value of $3,000 at the end of its estimated six-year useful life. Record the disposal and substitution, which was a cash acquisition.
3. Record amortization at the end of 20X6, assuming that the company does not change the composite rate determined in part (1).

A10-21 Amortization Systems: Answer each of the following questions.

1. Information relevant to the assets designated as small equipment for a corporation follows:

Beginning balance	$64,000
Acquisitions this year	12,000
Cash from disposals	400
Ending inventory at appraisal value	$58,000

   Assuming that the inventory appraisal system is used, what is amortization expense for this year?
2. Slaunwhite Corporation began 20X5 with 100 railroad cars each with a $16,000 unit book value. During 20X5, Slaunwhite purchased 50 cars for $24,000 each and retired 60 cars. Slaunwhite received $240,000 in total from the disposal of the railroad cars. What is the balance in the ledger account for railroad cars on 1 January 20X6, using the retirement system? Replacement system?
3. At the beginning of 20X5, Tyrou had 300 trucks (cost $16,000 each) in use. During 20X5, Tyrou sold 75 trucks and received $2,000 each and purchased 120 more at $20,000 each. What is amortization expense for 20X5 using the retirement system? Using the replacement system?
4. X Imports purchased the following assets 1 January 20X5:

Quantity	Type	Unit Cost	Salvage Value	Estimated Useful Life
10	Truck	$12,000	$1,000	5 years
5	Bus	24,000	2,000	8 years

   Under the composite system of amortization, what is the composite rate based on cost?
5. Assume that the composite rate for the assets in part (4) is 20% and that in 20X6, X Imports sold two trucks for $6,000 salvage each and replaced them with trucks costing $14,000 each, with $2,000 estimated salvage value each. The new vehicles are considered representative of the group. What is amortization for 20X6?

A10-22 Accounting for Capital Assets: Brannen Manufacturing Corporation was incorporated on 3 January 20X4. The corporation's financial statements for its first year's operations were not examined by a public accountant. You have been engaged to examine the financial statements for the year ended 31 December 20X5, and your examination is substantially completed. The corporation's adjusted trial balance appears as follows:

BRANNEN MANUFACTURING CORPORATION
ADJUSTED TRIAL BALANCE

31 December 20X5	Debit	Credit
Cash	$ 11,000	
Accounts receivable	68,500	
Allowance for doubtful accounts		$ 500
Inventories	38,500	
Prepaid expenses	10,500	
Machinery	75,000	
Equipment	29,000	
Accumulated amortization		12,100
Patents	102,000	
Organization costs	29,000	
Goodwill	24,000	
Licensing agreement 1, net	48,750	
Licensing agreement 2, net	59,000	
Accounts payable		152,400
Unearned revenue		12,500
Share capital		317,000
Retained earnings deficit, opening	17,000	
Sales revenue		661,500
Cost of goods sold	466,000	
Selling and general expenses	173,000	
Amortization expense	0	
Interest expense	4,750	
Totals	$1,156,000	$1,156,000

The following information relates to accounts that may still require adjustment:

a. Patents for Brannen's manufacturing process were acquired 2 January 20X5, for $68,000. An additional $34,000 was spent in late December 20X5 to improve machinery covered by the patents and was debited to the patents account.

b. The balance in the organization costs account properly includes costs incurred during the organization period. Brannen had decided to amortize organization costs over a five-year period beginning 1 January 20X4. No amortization has yet been recorded for 20X4 or 20X5.

c. During the second week of January 20X5, an explosion caused a permanent 60% reduction in the expected revenue-producing value of licensing agreement 1. No entry was made to reflect the explosion in 20X5. The agreement is expected to have an unlimited life at this lower amount.

d. On 1 January 20X5, Brannen bought licensing agreement 2, which has a life expectancy of 10 years. The balance in the licensing agreement 2 account includes the $58,000 purchase price and $2,000 in acquisition costs, but it has been reduced by a credit of $1,000 for the advance collection of 20X6 revenue from the agreement. No amortization on agreement 2 has been recorded.

e. The balance in the goodwill account includes (1) $8,000 paid 30 April 20X5, for an advertising program that management believes will assist in increasing Brannen's sales over a period of three to five years following the disbursement, and (2) legal expenses of $16,000 incurred for Brannen's incorporation on 3 January 20X4. No amortization has been recorded on the goodwill.

f. All machinery is being amortized on a straight-line basis, assuming a 10% residual value, over its expected life of eight years. There were no acquisitions in 20X5 other than that mentioned in (a).

g. Brannen's practice is to provide a full year's amortization in the year of acquisition and no amortization in the year of disposal.

h. Equipment is amortized using the declining-balance method, at a rate of 20%, and assuming a residual value of $4,000. Of the accumulated amortization at the end of 20X4, $5,800 relates to equipment. On 1 October 20X5, a piece of equipment had been bought for $9,000, and properly debited to the equipment account.

Required:

1. Prepare journal entries as of 31 December 20X5, as required by the information given above, including correcting entries. State any assumptions made. Ignore income taxes
2. What items would appear on the cash flow statement as a result of the 20X5 capital asset transactions? Assume that the indirect method is used for the operating activities section.
3. What accounting policy information does the company have to disclose? Be specific.

(AICPA, adapted)

★★

A10-23 Depreciation and Depletion—Schedule, Entries: Gaspe Mining Corporation bought mineral-bearing land for $150,000 that engineers estimate will yield 200,000 kilograms of economically removable ore. The land will have a value of $30,000 after the ore is removed.

To work the property, Gaspe built structures and sheds on the site that cost $40,000; these will last 10 years, and because their use is confined to mining and it would be expensive to dismantle and move them, they will have no residual value. Machinery that cost $29,000 was installed at the mine, and the added cost for installation was $7,000. This machinery should last 15 years; like that of the structures, the usefulness of the machinery is confined to these mining operations. Dismantling and removal costs when the property has been fully worked will approximately equal the value of the machinery at that time; therefore, Gaspe does not plan to use the structures or the machinery after the minerals have been removed.

In the first year, Gaspe removed only 15,000 kilograms of ore; however, production was doubled in the second year. It is expected that all of the removable ore will be extracted within eight years from the start of operations.

Required:

Prepare a schedule showing (1) unit and total depletion and amortization and (2) net book value of the capital assets for the first and second years of operation. Use the units-of-production method of depreciation for all assets.

A10-24 Asset Impairment—Five Situations: Each of the following five cases is independent.

a. Marlene Incorporated produces several lines of office furniture. All of the furniture is sold through sales agents who sell the full array of lines. Each line is developed by the company internally, and the development costs are capitalized and amortized over 12 years. After several years of high revenue, one of Marlene's lines has recently suffered a significant decline. Marlene is considering shutting down production and discontinuing the line. About 40% of the development cost has not yet been amortized.
b. Antigonish Actuators Limited (AAL) has a production and sales division in northern Ontario. The divisional vice-president reports directly to the AAL CEO. AAL is decentralized, and the Northern Ontario division is one of several such divisions. The Northern Ontario division has operated at a loss for the past two years, and future prospects seem dim. The division has substantial tangible capital assets.
c. Canadian Wheels Corporation operates hardware and automotive stores throughout Canada. A few years ago, the company opened a series of stores in the northwestern United States. The new stores have not been doing well, and the company is thinking of selling them or shutting them down.
d. Capital Helicopter Services Corporation (CHSC) provides helicopter services for other corporations, mainly those in the resource industry that need extensive helicopter services for offshore oil and gas platforms, forestry operations, and otherwise inaccessible

field operations. In addition, the company operates a separate division within Canada that manufactures airframe parts for manufacturers. This division is completely separate from the company's other operations and has a separate reporting line directly to the company's senior management. The division generates more than 10% of the company's overall revenues. However, the division has become only marginally profitable, and CHSC management has decided to sell the division and has put a plan for disposition in place.

e. Several years ago, Robertson Connectors Corporation (RCC) purchased the patents for a new type of connector. The new connector has enjoyed great success until recently. A competitor introduced a new product that is almost the same as RCC's product and that can be used interchangeably. RCC launched a patent infringement suit against the competitor, and RCC management was confident of success. In 20X4, however, the court ruled against RCC, thereby leaving the competitor free to continue its product. RCC management is considering whether to appeal the decision.

Required:

For each situation, explain whether an impairment test is necessary. If you need more information, explain what information you need and why you need it.

A10-25 Asset Impairment: BetaInc has conducted an impairment test on an industrial site that the company has abandoned. The site consists of land and one building. The building has been emptied of all usable equipment. At 31 December 20X1, the land is shown on BetaInc's balance sheet at its historical cost of $800,000. The building originally cost $3 million to construct, but its carrying value now is $1.2 million. A professional valuation has determined that the fair value of the land is now only $700,000, provided that BetaInc cleans the land of toxins prior to its sale. Cleaning up the land will cost an estimated $500,000. Once the land is cleaned, the building will have a fair value of $800,000 in its current condition. It will take approximately eight months to clean the land. The estimated cost to sell the land and building is $80,000 plus 5% of the sales price.

Required:

Prepare an adjusting journal entry to record the impairment.

A10-26 Asset Impairment: Softsweat Incorporated is a software development company. It has several products on the market, including the widely used PlayMark animation software. The cash flows from PlayMark are clearly distinguishable within Softsweat. The company has recorded development costs of $1.4 million relating to PlayMark, which is being amortized on a straight-line basis over seven years. At the end of 20X5, the carrying value was $980,000. Softsweat maintains a separate account for accumulated amortization on PlayMark.

In 20X5, a large U.S. company, Macrosoftie, released a competing product that has been hailed as a substantial improvement over PlayMark. However, the competing product requires installation of a great deal of additional Macrosoftie software to make the new product run efficiently. In addition, the high price may delay its acceptance by some users.

Because of the new competition, Softsweat management decided that an impairment test should be made. In January 20X6, as the 20X5 financial statements were being prepared, the company hired a professional business valuator. The valuator's appraisal was that the fair value of PlayMark at the end of 20X5 was $500,000.

Required:

1. Prepare the necessary adjusting journal entry to record the results of the impairment test.
2. Suppose that in 20X6, the Macrosoftie product was found to be unreliable, and sales of PlayMark returned to almost their 20X4 level. The fair value of PlayMark therefore was $800,000 at the end of 20X6. How (if at all) would this change be recorded in Softsweat's financial statements for 20X6?

A10-27 Asset Group Impairment: On 2 July 20X6, the Board of Directors of Joshi Limited approved the sale of the assets of its northern Ontario operations and began action to negotiate a sale. A sale is expected within the next year. The operation is one part of Joshi's overall operations, and therefore does not qualify as a discontinued operation. The assets were shown on Joshi's 30 June 20X6 balance sheet as follows:

	Carrying Value (thousands)
Inventory	$ 600
Building	750
Equipment	1,200
Furniture and fixtures	250
	$2,800

An impairment test indicated that the fair value of the northern Ontario operations as a group is $2,000. Brokerage costs will be 10% of the selling price. The fair value of the building as a separate asset is $650.

Required:

How will the impairment test affect the carrying value of the assets? Be specific, and show calculations.

A10-28 Asset Group Impairment: The abrasives group of Sarnia Chemical Products Incorporated (SCPI) has been suffering a decline in its business, due to new product introductions by competitors. At 31 December 20X5, the assets of the abrasives group are shown as follows (in millions) on the company's balance sheet:

	Cost	Accumulated Amortization	Net Book Value
Inventory	$60	–	$60
Equipment	300	$120	180
Fixtures	180	50	130
Patent rights	90	60	30
	$630	$230	$400

An impairment test indicates that the fair value of the abrasives group's assets is $300 million. The assets are not separable—they must be operated or sold together as a group.

Required:

Prepare an adjusting journal entry to record the impairment.

A10-29 Capital Asset Impairment: Timmons Limited built a plant facility in 20X4, and opened for commercial production in 20X5. The plant facility had a capital cost of $4,600,000, and equipment in the plant had a cost of $3,875,000. Both these capital assets were depreciated, beginning in 20X5, on a straight-line basis assuming a 10% salvage value, a 20-year life for the plant facility, and an eight-year life for the equipment. The company uses the half-year convention.

Late in 20X9, the market for Timmons' products declined precipitously, because of a competing product offered at a lower price. Operations in the plant were temporarily suspended while inventory was reduced, but are expected to restart on a more modest level in 20X10.

Required:

1. Explain the conditions that would lead to a writedown of capital assets. What factors would be examined in this case to ascertain whether a writedown was needed?
2. Calculate the net book value of the plant and equipment at the end of 20X9. Timmons charges a half-year of amortization in the year of acquisition.

3. Assume that an impairment should be recognized at the end of 20X9. Describe how the value of the capital assets, for the impairment test, would be calculated.
4. Assume that an impairment should be recognized in 20X9, and that the assets are to be written down to 60% of their net book value prior to the writedown. Provide the entry to record the writedown.

A10-30 Goodwill Impairment: Information has been collected regarding Black Company's acquired business units:

	Unit 1	Unit 2	Unit 3	Unit 4
Book values, 31 December 20X5				
Book value, assets other than goodwill	$3,200,000	$17,900,000	$20,400,000	$3,900,000
Book value, goodwill	500,000	6,000,000	3,000,000	5,600,000
Book value, liabilities	2,100,000	11,700,000	6,900,000	1,700,000
Fair values, 31 December 20X5				
Fair value, net assets acquired	2,200,000	7,900,000	13,700,000	2,600,000
Fair value, unit as a whole	3,000,000	16,000,000	14,000,000	6,000,000

Required:

For each unit, perform the two-step test to determine the need to record an impairment of goodwill. Calculate the impairment loss, if any.

A10-31 Cash Flow Statement: Idea Limited reflected the following items in the 20X5 financial statements:

Income statement	
Amortization expense, machinery	$300,000
Amortization expense, patent	60,000
Loss on sale of machinery	25,000
Gain on sale of land	30,000
Balance sheet	
Decrease in land account	$400,000
Increase in net patent account	65,000
Decrease in net machinery account	456,000

The only entry through the land account was a sale of land. The other accounts may reflect more than one transaction.

Required:

List the items that would appear on the cash flow statement as a result of the above items. Indicate in which section each item would appear. Assume that the indirect method is used for the operating activities section. State any assumptions that you make.

A10-32 Comparative Analysis, Amortization: The amortization policy disclosure notes for the 31 December 20X3 annual reports of Company A, Company B, and Company C are reproduced below, along with summary information from their annual reports. These companies all operate in the same business, mining and smelting operations, which are very capital intensive.

Company A

Amortization—Amortization is calculated on the straight-line method using rates based on the estimated useful lives of the respective assets. The principal rates are 2% for buildings and range from 1% to 4% for power assets, and 3% to 6% for chemical and fabricating assets.

Company B

Fixed Assets—Fixed assets are recorded at their historical cost. Amortization is computed generally by the straight-line method applied to the cost of assets in service at annual rates based on their estimated useful lives, as follows:

Buildings	2.5%–5%
Equipment	5%–7.5%
Mobile equipment	20%–25%
Mine and quarry	
Processing facilities	4.5%–5%
Mobile equipment	4.5%–20%

Company C

Fixed Assets and Amortization—Fixed assets are recorded at historical cost less investment tax credits realized and include construction in progress. Amortization is provided using the straight-line method applied to the cost of the assets at rates based on their estimated useful life and beginning from the point when production commences.

The following annual amortization rates are in effect:

Buildings	2%–5%
Equipment	6%–7%
Automotive and mobile equipment	10%–20%
Plants and properties	4%–5%

Financial data (amounts in $ millions)

	Co. A	Co. B	Co. C
Total assets, 31 December 20X3	$ 9,810	$3,218	$2,364
Average owners' equity, 20X3	4,181	1,426	948
Earnings from continuing operations:			
20X3	(104)	66	(36)
20X2	(112)	(38)	(127)
Amortization, 20X3	443	180	122
Gross plant assets, 1 January 20X3	11,015	3,732	3,332
Gross plant assets, 31 December 20X3	11,092	3,618	3,353
Accumulated amortization, 31 December 20X3	5,087	1,769	2,179
Capital expenditures, 20X3	25	17	58

Required:

Discuss the amortization policy of the three firms relative to their financial results. Make an analysis of the relevant summary financial statement information to support your comments.

A10-33 Comprehensive Capital Asset Transactions and Amortization: MH Plumbing Incorporated (MH) is the largest plumbing contractor in Moncton. Information on selected transactions/events is given below:

a. On 15 January 20X2, MH purchased land and warehouse building for $455,000. The land was appraised at $175,000, while the building was appraised at $375,000.

b. During January and February 20X2, MH spent $53,200 on the warehouse building, renovating it for its expected use as a storage and shipping facility.

c. MH used the warehouse building from February 20X2 until August 20X7. The building was expected to have a 20-year life and a salvage value of $11,000.

d. In late August 20X7, MH traded the warehouse and land for another facility on the other side of town. The second facility was slightly larger. MH paid $33,750 to the vendor, and $19,800 in legal fees as a result of the transaction. The new warehouse was appraised at $425,000, and the new land at $180,000. This warehouse facility was expected to have a useful life of 18 years, and a salvage value of $7,800.

e. MH used the new warehouse facility from August 20X7 until February 20X9. At that time, a fire destroyed the warehouse. MH received $356,800 from the insurance company.

f. MH called for tenders for construction of a new warehouse building in March 20X9, but the lowest bid was $788,000. The company decided to self-construct, and began in May 20X9. Monies spent were as follows:

Architect fees	$ 80,000
Removing debris from building site	13,400
Material cost for construction	245,800
Labour cost for construction	199,600
Parking lot	45,200
General overhead assigned to construction	24,800
Interest on loans related to construction	34,100

g. MH received a $100,000 investment tax credit in 20X9 as a result of the building activities, which reduced 20X9 taxes payable.

h. MH occupied its new warehouse in September 20X9. It was appraised at $650,000. It was expected to last for 25 years, and have a salvage value of $20,000.

Required:

Prepare journal entries to record all transactions listed above, including annual amortization to the end of 20X9. Record annual amortization using a declining-balance method of 10% for buildings, and 5% for parking lots. MH records a full year of amortization in the year of acquisition and no amortization in the year of disposal. Justify any decisions made with respect to accounting policy or application.

(CGA-Canada, adapted)

A10-34 Comprehensive Accounting for Capital Assets: At the end of 20X4, Merriweather Limited had the following balances in capital asset accounts:

Equipment	$ 316,000	
Accumulated depreciation, equipment	(284,000)	$ 32,000
Copyright, net		31,000
Leasehold improvements, net		91,800
Building	786,000	
Accumulated amortization, building	(146,000)	640,000
Land		880,000

Assets are depreciated as follows:

Equipment—declining balance, 10%. Salvage value is estimated to be $32,000.

Building—declining balance, 5%. Salvage value is estimated to be $23,500.

Copyright—straight line over 17 years with no salvage value; the copyright had been held for 12 years to the end of 20X4.

Leasehold improvements—straight line over 20 years with no salvage value; the leaseholds had been held for three years to the end of 20X4.

Land—The land included mineral rights. The original price of the land was $1,200,000, of which $800,000 was appropriately assigned to mineral rights. Expected mining will last for 10 years, and the deposit was 40% exhausted at the end of 20X4. The land will be sold, likely for $500,000, net of restoration costs.

For all assets except the mineral rights, a full year of depreciation is claimed in the year of purchase, but none in the year of sale. Mineral rights are depreciated as used.

Transactions in 20X5:

a. Equipment was traded in August for new equipment with a fair value of $257,800. Merriweather paid $216,000 and the old equipment. It also spent $12,300 having the new equipment transported and installed. During installation the equipment was slightly damaged, but repaired quickly at a cost of $4,900.

b. A competing product was introduced by a competitor that rendered the copyright worthless.
c. Monies were spent this year on a new product, a computer game. Costs were as follows: Designing and planning, $200,000; code development, $116,000; testing, $45,100; and production costs for units sold, $345,600. The product is expected to generate volumes of 50,000 units, of which 12,000 were sold in 20X5.
d. Another 15% of the mineral rights were mined and sold during the year.

Required:

1. Based on the closing balance as of 31 December 20X4, what was the original cost of the copyright and leasehold improvements? Also prove the balance in the land account.
2. Prepare the capital asset section of the balance sheet as at 31 December 20X5. Justify any accounting policy or application decisions made.
3. List the amounts and accounts that would appear on the income statement for the year ended 31 December 20X5. Include 20X5 amortization for all assets, as appropriate.

A10-35 Asset Held for Sale: In July 20X4, the Bank of P.E.I. negotiated an outsourcing agreement with Hamlet-Packard (HP), a major computer services company. Under the agreement, HP will provide full computing services for a major segment of the bank's business, effective 16 August 20X4. As a result, the bank declared one of its own computing centres to be redundant, and asked for tender offers from other major corporations. The bank will sell the equipment only—all software will be removed prior to sale. The redundant computer installation is quite new, having been purchased by the bank only nine months previously (in November 20X3) for $2,000,000. The bank takes 7.5% declining-balance amortization per quarter, with full amortization in the quarter of acquisition.

A dealer in used computer equipment was retained on 27 July 20X4. The dealer estimates that the equipment can be sold for approximately $1,300,000. For security reasons, the bank will undertake the physical removal of the equipment. The cost of removal is estimated at $100,000. The dealer will receive a commission of 8% on the sales price.

By the end of 20X4, the dealer had received several expressions of interest from prospective buyers. As a result, the dealer revised the estimated sales price to $1,450,000. On 29 February 20X5 (after the 31 December 20X4 statements had been issued), the bank signed a sales agreement with a purchaser for $1,400,000. The Bank of P.E.I. prepares financial statements quarterly.

Required:

Prepare all journal entries necessary to record the above information, in accordance with *CICA Handbook* Section 3063.

A10-36 Assets Held for Sale: On 30 September 20X7, Renége Corporation closed a "big box" retail store on the outskirts of Edmonton. The merchandise is being moved to Renége's other stores in Alberta. The interior fixtures have been sold to a disposal company for $200,000. The disposal company will dismantle and remove the fixtures.

Renége has retained a commercial real property sales agent to find a buyer for the building and land. The agent has posted an asking price of $1,200,000 for the building and land. The agent estimates that the land is worth about one-third of that amount. The agent will receive a commission of 5% when a sale closes, and transfer taxes and fees will be 2%. The agent is confident that a buyer can be found within the next 12 months. The store property is shown on Renége's books as follows, with amortization (depreciation) updated to 30 September 20X7:

	Land	*Building*	*Fixtures*
Cost	$ 250,000	$ 3,000,000	$ 500,000
Accumulated depreciation	–	1,600,000	350,000
	$ 250,000	$ 1,400,000	$ 150,000

In March 20X8, Renége reaches agreement with a buyer to sell the land and building for $1,100,000. The sale closes on 1 April 20X8. Renége's fiscal year ends on 31 December.

Required:

1. Prepare the necessary journal entries in 20X7 to record Renége's abandonment of the Edmonton store and its sale in 20X8.
2. What amounts relating to this property will appear on Renége's income statement, balance sheet, and cash flow statement on 31 December 20X7? How will each amount be classified? Renége uses the indirect method of reporting cash flows from operations.

A10-37 Asset Held for Sale: On 17 August 20X2, the board of Hellinger Incorporated voted unanimously to sell the CEO's corporate jet. The plane had cost $20 million three years earlier and was being depreciated at 20% declining balance per year, with no amortization in the year of acquisition. At the end of 20X2, the accumulated depreciation is $7.2 million. Additional information is as follows:

- An airplane broker was retained in late August 20X2. The broker's fee is 5% of the eventual sales price.
- Due to a weak market for corporate jets, the broker estimated a potential price of $13 million, even though the plane is fairly new and is in excellent condition.
- Transportation to the eventual buyer will be the responsibility of the buyer.
- In early January 20X3, as Hellinger's 20X4 financial statements were being prepared, the broker informed the Board that the market had improved significantly; the broker now expected to be able to get about $15 million.
- The plane was sold on 17 March 20X5 for $12.4 million.

Required:
Prepare the appropriate journal entries to record the preceding information.

A10-38 Integrative Problem, Chapters 6–10: Hyperium Computers Limited is a small producer and marketer of software for personal computers. The company is owned by a group of about 20 shareholders, including two venture capitalists who own preferred shares that must be redeemed in 10 years' time. Bank debt, used to finance inventory and accounts receivable, allows borrowing of up to 40% of the book value of inventory and 70% of the book value of accounts receivable. The company picks many accounting policies to minimize tax payments.

Accounting policy issues facing the company this year are given below.

1. Hyperium began selling products to large discount retailers under the retailer's "house brand" for the first time in 20X5. Agreements with the retailers specify that 80% of products not sold to final customers within six months may be returned to Hyperium for a refund. Data with respect to the sales:

	January–June	July–December
Sales at retail	$401,000	$798,600
Cash collected	199,000	362,000
Returns to date (at retail)	76,000	172,500*

* $110,000 relate to sales made in the January–June period.

Hyperium has recorded the sales as cash has been collected. Regardless of the accounting policy chosen, taxable income must include revenue equal to cash collected.

When should revenue be recognized? Analyze the accounting policy choices and make a recommendation. Evaluate point of sale, cash collection, and the end of the return period.

2. Hyperium incurred $657,000 of costs to advertise a new software program this year. The program is expected to sell strongly in the lucrative 10-to-16-year-old age bracket over

the next three years. Should the costs be deferred and amortized or immediately expensed? Provide an analysis and recommendation.

3. Hyperium incurred $340,000 of costs to revise existing software products (goods for resale) so that they utilize the more sophisticated graphics that are available on newer personal computers.

   Should the costs be deferred and amortized or immediately expensed? Provide an analysis and recommendation.

4. Hyperium accrues bad debt expense in the year of sale. An aging of accounts receivable at year-end reveals the following:

	Accounts Receivable	Percentage Expected to Be Non-Collectible
Current	$613,200	2%
30–60 days	114,900	20
60–90 days	70,700	40
Over 90 days	54,300	60

   The allowance has a debit balance of $47,900 prior to adjustment. Provide the adjusting journal entry to record bad debt expense.

5. Hyperium sold $400,000 of accounts receivable to a finance company the day before the end of the fiscal year. The finance company charged $6,960 in interest. All the receivables were expected to be collected. The cash received was debited to cash, and credited to an account called "suspense."

   Provide the adjusting journal entry to correct the suspense account and record the sale. Indicate the circumstances under which the sale would be recorded as a loan.

6. Hyperium has a U.S.$40,000 account receivable, recorded at Cdn.$54,000. The year-end exchange rate is U.S. $1 = Cdn.$1.41. Hyperium has a U.S.$98,000 account payable recorded at Cdn.$132,900.

   Provide adjusting journal entries.

7. Hyperium uses a FIFO cost flow assumption for inventory. In general, prices of raw materials have increased 10% over the period. While inventories include thousands of items, a database is available that could be used to reconstruct inventory and cost of sales using LIFO or weighted average.

   The company wishes to understand the financial statement impact of using a different cost flow assumption.

8. Hyperium counted its finished-goods inventory and obtained a dollar value, at cost, of $4,413,000. However, it is wondering what level of inventory shrinkage has been experienced. The following data has been provided:

Opening inventory, as counted, at cost	$ 4,691,400
Closing inventory, as counted, at cost	4,413,000
Purchases, at invoice price	16,924,300
Sales and excise taxes	2,030,900
Freight-in	712,800
Purchase discounts and returns	419,100

   Gross profit margins have been stable at 32%. Net sales during the year were $28,200,000. Note that amounts appropriately exclude inventory and sales related to house brand sales described in part (1).

   Provide an estimate of inventory losses due to shrinkage.

9. Hyperium acquired new computer equipment, nine months into the year, part of a regular upgrade program to keep the company on the cutting edge of technology. These computers have an expected useful life of five years, although Hyperium has had to upgrade its computers about every two years to stay abreast of technology. Costs associated with the upgrade were

Computer invoice price	$6,450,000
Sales tax	967,500
Delivery charges	57,000
Improvement to wiring necessary to connect computers to network	116,000
Training course for employees to upgrade skills	40,900

The company wishes you to evaluate use of straight-line and declining-balance amortization (50%) methods. Your analysis should include calculation of amortization expense for each of the first two fiscal years. Salvage values would be 40% of cost after 24 months and 5% of cost after five years. Be sure to separately calculate the cost of the equipment, and indicate how other (non-capitalized) expenditures should be accounted for.

Required:

Address the accounting policy issues listed above, providing appropriate analysis and entries, as required.

A10-39 CCA Calculations (Appendix 1): Dixon Company purchased several small pieces of equipment in May 20X5 for $300,000, which qualifies as a Class 8 asset for tax purposes. The equipment has a useful life of six years. Subsequent transactions were

30 September 20X6	Sold equipment bought in 20X5 for $20,000; proceeds, $11,200
1 February 20X7	Sold equipment bought in 20X5 for $40,000; proceeds, $19,800
31 August 20X7	Bought Class 8 equipment for $25,000
16 November 20X8	Bought Class 8 equipment for $36,000

Required:

Calculate CCA and the closing UCC balance for 20X5 to 20X8.

A10-40 Asset Revaluation (Appendix 2): Grand Corporation is a privately held corporation. The majority of the shares are held by Ed Grand, and financial statements are prepared primarily to satisfy the needs of the bankers and to keep Mr. Grand up to date on how well his company is performing. The company has a block of commercial real estate in the downtown core of a small city; this real estate was acquired in 20X1 and has appreciated significantly since then. Mr. Grand wished to reflect the current appraised value of this investment in his financial statements, as the banker continually asks for market value information when assessing loan security.

At the beginning of 20X4, the asset accounts are as follows:

Land	$2,100,000
Buildings, net	810,000

The buildings are being amortized over 30 years, in the amount of $30,000 per year.

Appraisals indicate that land values are in the range of $5,000,000, while the buildings were worth, at the beginning of 20X4, $1,500,000. The estimate of useful life has not changed.

Required:

1. Record the revaluation of assets as of the beginning of 20X4. Note that the accumulated amortization account for the building is eliminated when the building is revalued.
2. How much amortization would be recorded on the 20X4 income statement after the write-up in requirement (1)? Explain.
3. Are the statements reflecting the revaluation in accordance with GAAP? Explain.
4. Assume that appraisals indicated a value of $1,600,000 for land and $700,000 for the buildings. How would the picture change?

CHAPTER 11

Investments in Debt and Equity Securities

INTRODUCTION

The cash flow associated with an investment in the securities of another company can be straightforward. Such an investment is usually purchased for cash, produces an annual cash flow of interest or dividends that can be recorded as revenue, and is sold for cash. What can be so complicated?

First, the cost and market value of an investment will be different over the period for which it is held. If the investments can or will be sold, market value information is likely far more relevant to the financial statement user, and it is objectively determinable in securities markets. It stands to reason that market value should be recorded. The related issue is what to do with any gain or loss on the value of the investment while it is held. It hasn't been realized though a sale transaction. Is it income or not?

Accounting for investments is further complicated by the fact that investments in voting securities can represent more than just a passive investment undertaken to generate investment income. Long-term investments in voting shares may be used to establish an intercompany relationship through which the investor corporation can control or significantly influence the operating, investing, and financing strategies of the investee corporation. If the investor can control or influence the dividend policy of the investee, dividends received from the investee are not the result of an arm's-length transaction. If investment revenue was measured as dividends declared, the amount could easily be manipulated. Furthermore, if a control relationship exists, it may not be possible to grasp the activities of the economic entity—both the investor and investee corporations—unless their records are consolidated, or added together.

In accounting for investments in the shares of other corporations, the accounting problem is twofold:

1. What is the nature of the investment?
2. How can the investment, and the investment revenue, be reported to reveal the economic impact of the investment rather than just its legal form?

We'll explore these questions in this chapter, and provide an overview of this complex area. Keep in mind, though, that many accounting programs devote an entire course to this issue, so what we're doing here is only the tip of the proverbial iceberg!

CLASSIFICATION OF INTERCORPORATE INVESTMENTS

Investment Objectives

passive investment

an intercorporate investment in which the investor cannot significantly influence or control the operations of the investee company

strategic investment

an investment in another company for strategic purposes; usually conveys control or significant influence or is a joint venture

Companies invest in the securities of other enterprises for a variety of reasons. The investment can be a **passive investment**, meant primarily to increase investment income, or a **strategic investment**, meant to enhance operations in some way:

- *Investment of Idle Cash.* Companies often have cash on hand that is not needed at present but will be needed in the future. Rather than allow the idle cash to remain in a low-interest bank account, companies find temporary investments with short terms that provide a higher return. These investments typically have low risk and are easily converted to cash.

  Cash on hand can be invested in investments that may generate return through interest or dividends and also may be sold when market price has increased. These investments will likely be of higher risk and/or a longer term, but the intent is to sell the investment when money is needed for other activities and/or when the price is attractive.
- *Active Trading Investment Portfolio.* Some companies, primarily financial institutions, invest in trading portfolios. Securities in the portfolio are actively traded as part of the normal course of business, generally yielding a return because of price fluctuations or a dealer's margin.
- *Long-Term Investments to Generate Earnings.* Cash on hand can be invested in less liquid securities in order to increase investment income. These investments are usually money market instruments (for example, bonds), and the intent is to keep the investment until maturity.
- *Strategic Alliances.* An investment, especially in voting shares, may establish or cement a beneficial intercompany relationship that will increase the profitability of the investing company, both directly and indirectly. Strategic decisions may be made to invest in suppliers, customers, and even competitors.
- *Legal Frameworks.* Companies may choose to establish operations in one large company with numerous branches, or organize activities in a set of smaller companies, all or partially controlled by a central holding company. This may be done for tax reasons, to allow outside shareholders a small stake in particular operations, to satisfy legal requirements in particular jurisdictions, and/or to limit potential liability claims to particular portions of the enterprise.

CLASSIFICATION OF INVESTMENTS

Many securities are **financial instruments** under the definitions established in Section 3860 of the *CICA Handbook*. A financial instrument is any contract that gives rise to both a financial asset of one party and a financial liability or equity instrument of another party. In the context of intercorporate investments, financial assets are defined as any contractual right to receive cash or another financial asset from another company. Bonds and share investment meet this definition.

Investments that are financial instruments are classified according to the rules in propsosed Section 3855, "Financial Instruments—Recognition and Measurement." These classifications and rules are brand new, effective in any fiscal year beginning after 1 October 2006—that is, in the 2007 fiscal year. This chapter is based on the 2003 exposure draft in this area; *strategic investments* in shares are specifically excluded from the financial instruments sections of the *CICA Handbook*, but are accorded specific attention in other sections. For those interested in the rules in place up to 2006, refer to the superceded investments chapter available on the Online Learning Centre.

This section explores the classification rules in depth. The classifications that follow are summarized in Exhibit 11-1.

DEBT VERSUS EQUITY INVESTMENTS An investment in a debt instrument of another entity can be classified as available for sale, held to maturity, or a trading investment. An investment in common shares may be available for sale, held to maturity, or a trading investment, or, if strategic, a control investment, a significant influence investment, or a joint venture. It depends on intent and circumstances. We'll define these terms in the sections that follow.

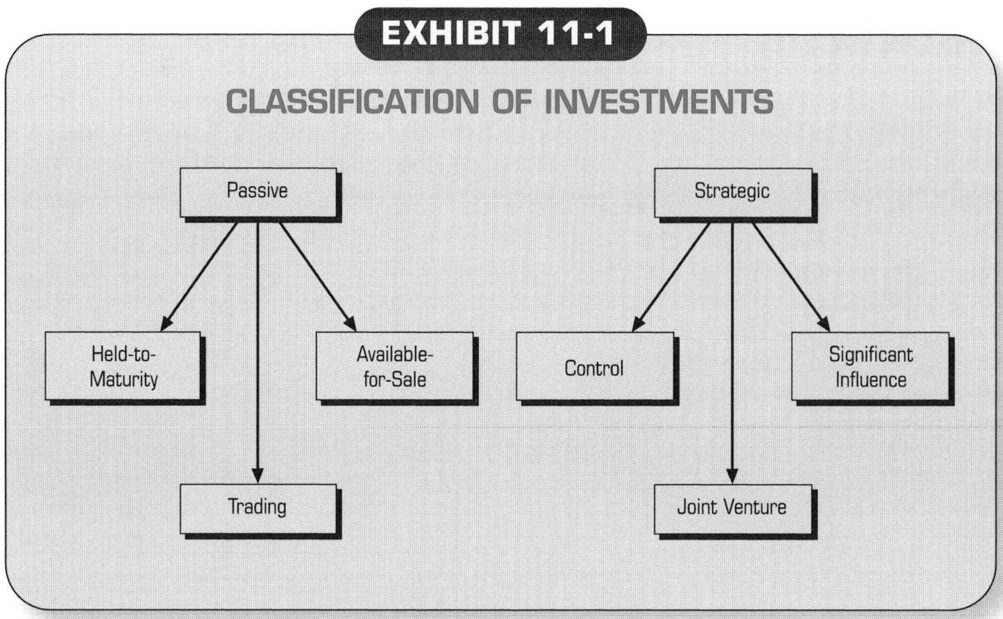

Held-to-Maturity Investments

held-to-maturity investments those investments that have a defined maturity date, fixed or determinable payments, and for which there is positive intent to hold to maturity

Held-to-maturity investments must meet three tests:

- First, rather obviously, the securities must have a maturity date. This includes bonds and other money market instruments, but excludes common shares and any other investment with an indeterminate length.
- The securities must have fixed or determinable payments: set amounts at set points in time.
- Management must have the positive intent to hold the investments to their maturity dates.

For example, if a company buys a bond with a 10-year maturity date, and management plans to hold it until maturity, it is classified as a held-to-maturity security. On the other hand, if management stands ready to sell the investment if the price is appealing or if the company needs cash, then the bond is an available-for-sale investment. If management plans for the investment are *undecided,* the investment is available for sale. This is the meaning of positive intent—there must be an *active will* to hold to maturity.

MANAGEMENT INTENT Management intent can be a slippery classification tool. Management can change its intentions, or even misrepresent its intentions. This reduces the credibility of the financial statements, and future management representations.

RECLASSIFICATION OR SALE Reclassification, or sale, of a held-to-maturity investment calls the integrity of the original classification into question. Therefore,

> [If the company] ... has sold or reclassified more than an insignificant amount of held-to-maturity investments in the past two years, then no securities can be classified as held-to-maturity. (*CICA* ED 3855)

Of course, there are a few exceptions to this sweeping prohibition—for example, if there was

- an isolated event (e.g., a change in tax law or a major business combination) that caused the reclassification or sale;

- a significant decline in the credit rating of the issuer of the investment and sale is the only appropriate response; or
- a sale of securities on a date very close to the original maturity date,

then the sale is not "held against" the integrity of the initial classification. In any of these circumstances, the held-to-maturity classification is still open for future use.

Available-for-Sale Investments

available-for-sale investment

any investment that is not classified as a control, joint venture, significant influence, held-to-maturity, or trading investment; the catch-all category of investment

Any investment that is available for sale if the company needs cash, or if the market value is appealing, is considered an **available-for-sale investment**. This category includes short-term money-market investments, such as Treasury bills, but also bonds and shares of other companies that could be sold. While the investments are held, they will generate investment and dividend income. When they are sold, they will yield a realized gain or loss on sale. Market value will fluctuate during the time that the investments are held.

The *CICA Handbook* definition of this category is negatively put: investments that are not in the other categories are classified here. The available-for-sale category is the catch-all. To understand what this involves, we must proceed on to the other categories.

Trading Investments

trading investment

an investment designated by management as held for trading; part of a portfolio managed for short-term profit or acquired principally for resale. Financial institutions are the major holders of trading investments.

The **trading investment** category is determined primarily by management intent. That is, when the investment is bought, the investment must be designated as a trading investment. This means that it is

1. held principally for the purpose of selling, or
2. is part of a portfolio of investments managed together for short-term profit.

For the most part, trading investments are held by financial institutions, which engage in trading activities as part of the normal course of business. Any marketable financial instrument can be designated as a trading investment when purchased. Even if there is no plan to sell the investment in the near future, the investment can still be a trading investment, as long as intent to trade is present.

Controlled Investments

controlled investment

the investment in a controlled subsidiary; normally consolidated for financial reporting

What are **controlled investments**? The *CICA Handbook* defines **control** as

> the continuing power to determine ... strategic operating, investing and financing policies [of the other enterprise] without the cooperation of others.
>
> (*CICA* 1590.03)

control

the continuing power to determine the strategic policies of an investee without the cooperation of other shareholders

Since strategic policies of the enterprise are typically established by the Board of Directors, the right to elect a majority of the Board of Directors would normally constitute control. Of course, percentage share ownership is still the primary input to this decision. If a company owns more than 50% of the voting shares of a company, it must establish why it does not have control; if it owns 50% or less, it must establish why it does have control.

An important phrase in the AcSB's definition of control is "without the cooperation of others." This means that, for control to be deemed to exist, the investor has to be able to withstand hostile takeover attempts. If an opponent can gather enough shares (or the support of enough voting shareholders) to take over control, then control does not exist in fact. Many corporations are "controlled" by a major shareholder who owns the largest single block of shares, but if this is less than 50%, then control does not really exist in an accounting sense.

An investor can control a corporation while holding less than a majority of the corporation's voting shares through any of several methods:

- The investee corporation may have two or more classes of shares that have different voting rights, in which case control can be maintained by holding a majority of the votes but not necessarily a majority of voting shares. Examples are given in Chapter 13.
- The investor may hold convertible securities or stock options and, if control is challenged, securities could be converted or exercised. Afterward, the investor has an absolute majority of the votes.
- A shareholders' agreement may exist that gives control to a shareholder who owns less than 50% of the shares (or, to look at the reverse side, restricts the voting power of other investors). This device is common in private corporations, but can exist in public corporations as well.
- An investor with a minority of the shares may also be a major source of debt financing, and the debt agreement gives the investor the right to select a majority of the investee's Board of Directors.

If the investee is controlled by the investor corporation, the investor corporation is called a **parent company** and the investee corporation is known as a **subsidiary**.

parent company
a corporation that controls one or more other corporations through ownership of a majority of the shares, carrying the right to elect at least a majority of the Board of Directors

subsidiary company
an investee company in which the investor company (the parent) controls the investee, usually by having the right to appoint a majority of the Board of Directors and/or holding in excess of 50% of the voting shares

Significant Influence Investments

Significant influence investments exist when an investor has the ability to exert influence over the strategic operating, investing, and financing policies of the investee corporation even though the investor does not control the investee. Significant influence can be exerted through several means, and not just by equity investment. The *CICA Handbook* cites the following possible evidence of significant influence:

> The ability to exercise significant influence may be indicated by, for example, representation on the board of directors, participation in policy-making processes, material intercompany transactions, interchange of managerial personnel or provision of technical information. (*CICA* 3050.04)

Normally, ownership of 20% or more of an investee corporation's shares is deemed to indicate that significant influence exists. But this is a guideline, not a rule.

> If the investor holds less than 20% of the voting interest in the investee, it is presumed that the investor does not have the ability to exercise significant influence, unless such influence is clearly demonstrated. On the other hand, the holding of 20% or more of the voting interest in the investee does not in itself confirm the ability to exercise significant influence. (*CICA* 3050.04)

significant influence investment
an investment representing ownership interest to the extent that the investor can affect strategic operating, investing, and/or financing policies of the investee

It's important to not put too much weight on the percentage of share ownership, though; a great deal depends on who owns the other shares, as well as on the other (non-ownership) financial and operating relationships between the investor and the investee corporations. For example, ownership of 30% of an investee corporation may not give the investee significant influence (or any influence) if the other 70% is held by a single shareholder who will not tolerate any influence. Conversely, an ownership interest of 15% may give the investor virtually unchallenged influence if ownership of the other 85% is widely dispersed.

It is worth noting that, in the United States, the 20% ownership guideline is a firm rule; if 20% or more but less than a majority of the shares is owned by an investor, then significant influence is automatically deemed to exist. Therefore, an investor corporation may avoid the presumption of significant influence (and the accounting requirements that significant influence entails) by holding only 19.9%. In Canadian GAAP, however, it is the substance that matters, not a fraction of a percentage.

Joint Ventures

joint venture
an investment resulting in a contractual arrangement whereby two or more venturers jointly control an economic activity; the joint venture is subject to joint control by the joint venturers

Another type of strategic equity investment is a **joint venture**.

> A joint venture is an economic activity resulting from a contractual arrangement whereby two or more venturers jointly control the economic activity.
> (*CICA* 3055.03(c))

Joint ventures are distinct in that they are subject to *joint control*, regardless of share ownership percentage. That is, the investors must unanimously agree on key operating, investing, and financing decisions before they are implemented. This feature of joint control means that majority ownership does not confer control, nor does the right to appoint the majority of the Board of Directors.

Joint ventures are quite common in mining operations and in oil and gas ventures. The joint venturers all contribute something to exploration activities, and all share in any wealth generated. For example, a small mining company may have exploration rights over a property, and agree to explore the property with a larger joint venture partner, who provides management, working capital, and capital assets in exchange for a certain percentage of the profits. However, key decisions over when and where to explore, or when to put the property into commercial production, etc. are subject to common control of both venturers.

Change in Classification

Intent and ability to hold must be assessed at every balance sheet date. If intent changes, and the investment is still unsold, then its balance sheet classification and accounting treatment will change.

CONCEPT REVIEW

1. Under what circumstances is an investment in bonds classified as a held-to-maturity investment? As an available-for-sale investment?
2. Can an investment in common shares be classified as a held-to-maturity investment? Explain.
3. In the current year, a company sells all its held-to-maturity investments because the market values had appreciated significantly. Can other investments now be classified as held to maturity?
4. An investor owns 40% of the shares of another company. Is this evidence enough to conclude that significant influence exists?
5. An investor owns 60% of the voting shares of another corporation, but has never become heavily involved in the management or governance of the company, although they could if they wished. Does control exist?

ACCOUNTING FOR INVESTMENTS

There are six ways to account for investments, depending on how the investment is classified. For a summary of the application of accounting methods, refer to Exhibit 11-2. The highlights of the accounting methods themselves are summarized in Exhibit 11-3. This section is an overview; we'll look at some more detail, and examples, in later sections of this chapter.

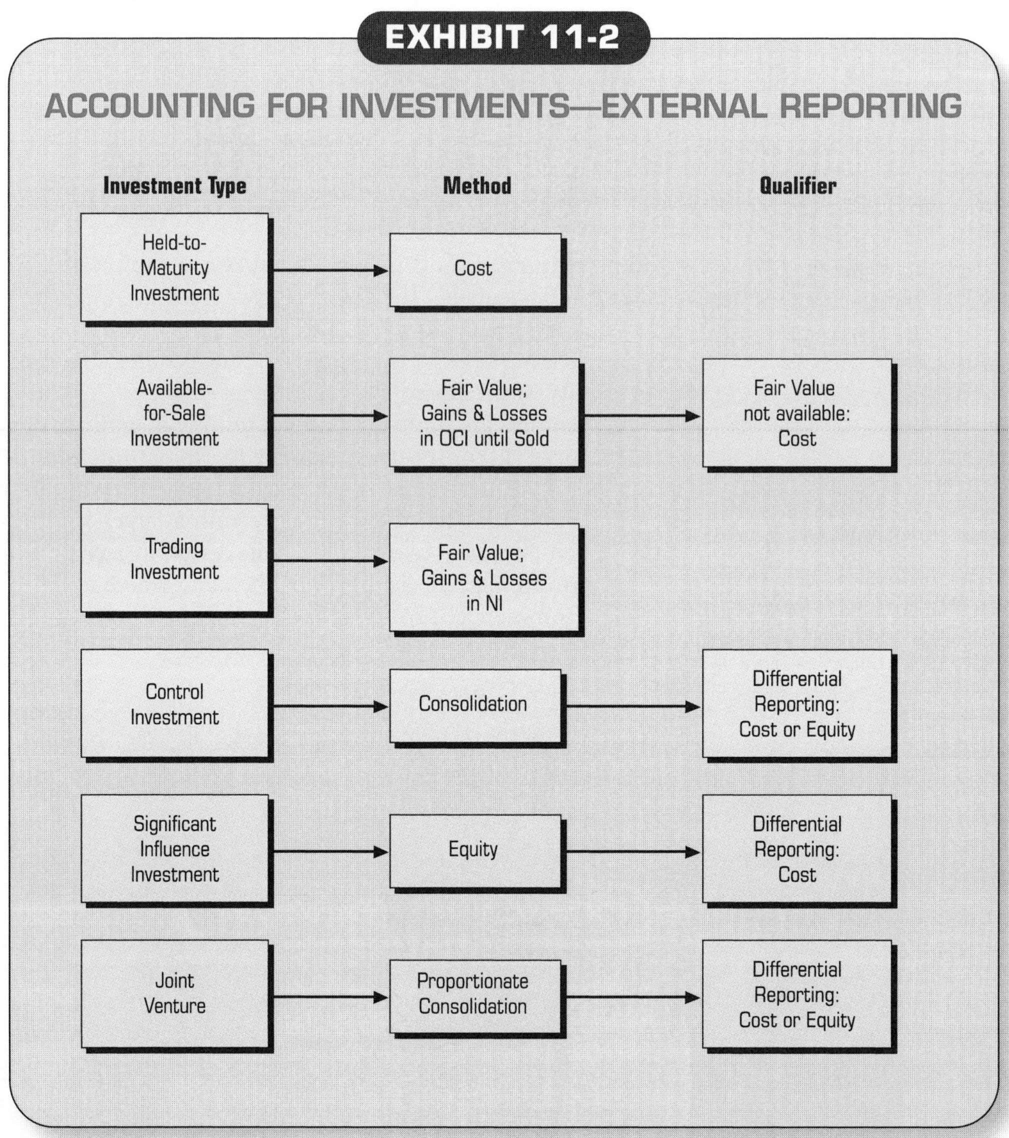

Cost Method

cost method of accounting for investments
investments are recorded at cost and revenue is recorded as time passes (interest) or as declared (dividends); interest income includes premium or discount amortization

The **cost method** is used to account for held-to-maturity investments. In the cost method

- The original investment is recorded at its investment cost. This is book value or carrying value, but it also represents fair value on the purchase date. It excludes any accrued interest.
- Transaction costs, such as brokerage fees, may be included in acquisition cost and capitalized, or immediately expensed. *(CICA* ED *3855.56.)*
- Interest or dividends declared are recorded as investment income.
- If the investment is a long-term investment in debt securities, any premium or discount is amortized to income over the life of the investment. This will change book value. Book value will be move toward maturity value, and be equal to maturity value on the maturity date.
- When an investment is sold before maturity (which should be a rare event), the difference between proceeds and book value is recorded as a gain or loss on sale.
- When an investment matures, cash increases and the investment decreases. There is no gain or loss on the maturation of debt securities, because cash received is equal to the recorded maturity amount.

Fair Value Method; Unrealized Gains and Losses Recognized in Other Comprehensive Income (OCI)

fair value method of accounting for investments
investments are initially recorded at cost, but adjusted to fair value at each reporting date. Realized gains and losses are included in income; unrealized amounts are included in income (trading investments) or in other comprehensive income (available-for-sale investments)

The **fair value method**, with unrealized gains and losses included in *other comprehensive income*, is used to account for available-for-sale investments. In this method

- The original investment is recorded at its investment cost. This is fair value on the purchase date.
- Transaction costs, such as brokerage fees, may be included in acquisition cost and capitalized, or immediately expensed.
- Interest or dividends declared are recorded as investment income. Interest income includes amortization of any premium or discount inherent in the initial purchase price
- At the end of each reporting period, the investments are revalued to fair value (market value), whether this is higher or lower than the existing balance in the investment account.
- **Unrealized holding gains**, defined as the difference between the existing balance in the investment account (the new fair value) and the old fair value, are recorded in *other comprehensive income*. Such gains and losses are not included in net income, but are segregated in a special shareholders' equity account, called other comprehensive income (OCI).
- When an investment is sold, the total cumulative **realized holding gain** or loss is reported in net income; related *cumulative* unrealized holding gains are eliminated from other comprehensive income in shareholders' equity when the sale is recorded.

unrealized holding gains
increase in fair value of an asset while held; unrealized because asset is not yet sold

realized holding gain
increase in fair value of an asset while held, realized through sale

The investment is reported at fair value on the balance sheet.

Fair Value Method; Unrealized Gains and Losses Recognized in Net Income

The fair value method, with unrealized gains and losses included in net income, is used to account for trading investments. In this method

- The original investment is recorded at its investment cost. This is fair value on the purchase date.
- Transaction costs, such as brokerage fees, may be included in acquisition cost and capitalized, or immediately expensed.
- Interest or dividends declared are recorded as investment income.
- At the end of each reporting period, the investments are revalued to fair value, whether this is higher or lower than the existing balance in the investment account.
- Holding gains, defined as the difference between the existing balance in the investment account (the new fair value) and the old fair value, are recorded in *net income*. That is, net income includes the change in value of the investment each year, whether realized through sale or unrealized because the investment is still held.

The investment is reported at fair value on the balance sheet.

VOLATILITY The difference between the two applications of the fair value method obviously relates to holding gain and loss recognition. For trading investments, unrealized holding gains and losses are included on the income statement. For available-for-sale investments, unrealized gains are collected in other comprehensive income until realized. *Realization* is a primary test for revenue recognition. For trading investments, realization is not considered necessary because of their rapid turnover. Remember, though, that if investment prices are volatile, inclusion of holding gains introduces volatility to net income.

Companies with trading portfolios have registered concern about this volatility, because they are often using their trading portfolios to hedge, or offset, fluctuations caused by similar portfolios of financial liabilities, which are carried at cost, and not adjusted to fair value. Standard-setters continue to grapple with these issues.

ESTIMATING FAIR VALUE Since financial statements will reflect **fair value** for some investments, it stands to reason that fair value must be carefully estimated. After all, fair value is not substantiated by the objective evidence of a transaction of the reporting entity. Fair value is defined as

> The amount of the consideration that would be agreed upon in an arm's length transaction between knowledgeable, willing parties who are under no compulsion to act. (*CICA* ED 3855.17(j))

Many equity investments have a quoted market price in an active market, which is used as fair value. These market prices reflect normal market transactions and are readily available from brokers or in the financial press. When trading is light, recent bid prices are acceptable, although light trading may indicate that estimating fair value is problematic. For example, a recent price might not be relevant if significant events had taken place after the bid date (*CICA* ED 3855.A26).

What if there are no recent transactions? The AcSB suggests that fair value can be estimated, through judicious use of valuation techniques. These valuation techniques must incorporate all factors that market participants consider when establishing prices. Fair value can be estimated through well-recognized valuation alternatives such as discounted cash flow models and option pricing models. In other cases, fair value can be inferred by referring to the current value of similar financial instruments, adjusting the market price for differences in terms and risk. Estimates are needed, and the reasonableness of any result must be carefully considered before the value can be used in the financial statements. It makes sense to disclose the method used to assess fair value, and any assumptions made.

FAIR VALUE NOT AVAILABLE In some cases, it may not be possible to obtain fair value. In these cases, the investments must be carried at cost (*CICA* ED 3855.59c). However, if investments are classified as available for sale, and there is no apparent market value, the classification is somewhat suspect. Fair values should be ascertainable in most situations.

Equity Method

equity method of accounting for investments
investments are initially recorded at cost, and revenue is recorded as the investor's appropriate share of earnings, increasing the investment account; dividends received reduce the investment account

The **equity method** is used for significant influence investments. Under the equity method:

- The original investment is recorded at its acquisition cost; this is initial book value.
- The investor's proportionate share of the investee's net income (subject to certain adjustments) is recognized on the investor's income statement as revenue and on the balance sheet as an increase in book value.
- Dividends are recorded as a decrease in the investment account rather than as investment revenue. This reduces book value.
- When the investment is sold, the difference between proceeds and book value is recorded as a gain or loss on sale.

unremitted earnings
when accounting for a significant influence investment, the difference between the investor's cumulative share of an investee's net income and the cumulative dividends actually received

At any point in time, the equity method investment account consists of

1. the investment's cumulative historical cost, plus
2. the investor's cumulative share of the investee's adjusted earnings since the investment was made, minus
3. the investor's share of dividends paid by the investee since the shares were purchased.

The difference between the investor's share of the investee's net income and the dividends actually received is called **unremitted earnings** and increases book value above cost.

The Consolidation Method

consolidation
combining the financial statements of a parent company and its subsidiary(ies); fair value on acquisition is established, and intercompany transactions are eliminated

When an investor controls an investee, **consolidation** is required. The parent investor must prepare consolidated statements, to enable investors (and others) to see the assets, liabilities, revenues, and expenses of the entire economic entity, consisting of the parent and all of its subsidiaries.

When consolidated statements are prepared, the investment account relating to a controlled subsidiary disappears entirely from the balance sheet. Instead, the subsidiary's assets and liabilities are added to those of the parent and reported together as a single economic entity. If the parent owns less than 100% of the subsidiary's shares, the interest of the non-controlling (i.e., minority) shareholders is shown as a separate account on the parent's consolidated balance sheet and income statement.

Proportionate Consolidation Method

proportionate consolidation
combining the financial statements of an investor company and a joint venture enterprise; only the investor's proportionate share of the financial elements of the joint venture are included

Joint ventures are reported by means of **proportionate consolidation**. Such a consolidated statement again involves adding the investor and investee financial statements together. This time, though, a *pro-rata* share of the investee's assets, liabilities, revenues, and expenses is calculated and added to the investor's own financial results. (This differs from a regular consolidation, where *all* the subsidiary's assets, etc., are included regardless of the ownership interest, partially offset by the non-controlling interest accounts.) Proportionate consolidation is considered in depth in advanced accounting courses, and will not be further explored in this chapter.

Differential Reporting

We discussed *differential reporting* in Chapter 1. Essentially, if an organization has no public accountability and all owners consent, including those not otherwise entitled to vote, simpler accounting rules may be adopted in certain areas.

Remember that the entities that are eligible for this GAAP treatment are private companies—those with no shares or debt traded on public markets. Usually, this is the smaller business sector, but not always. There are some large private companies in Canada. For these companies, if the equity holders all agree, the cost of more complex accounting standards can be avoided. The benefit of information provided is not worth the effort. Accounting for long-term investments is one of those areas.

For investments, the following policies would be GAAP under **differential reporting**.

Significant influence investments	—	Cost
Controlled ivestments	—	Cost or Equity
Joint ventures	—	Cost or Equity

GAAP is responsive to user needs in this area.

Recording versus Reporting

It is very important to make a distinction between the way that an investor records investments in its books and the way that the investment is reported in the investor's financial statements. We're already seen that reporting may involve cost, fair value, equity, consolidation, or proportionate consolidation. Often, an investor will account for a strategic investment by using the cost method during the year simply because it is the easiest method; this is the investor's *recording method.* When financial statements are prepared, a different *reporting method* may be more appropriate for the financial reporting objectives of the company. In that case, the accounts relating to the investment are adjusted by means of a worksheet and adjusting entries.

Public companies may prepare non-consolidated (or separate entity) statements for specific users, such as for their bankers, as well as consolidated general purpose statements. Indeed, knowledgeable bankers will insist on seeing a corporation's non-consolidated statements because they have immediate recourse only to the assets and cash flows of the specific legal entity to which they are making the loan. Business history is full of instances in which a bank has lent money to a parent company only to discover later that all of the cash flow is in an operating subsidiary that is out of reach of the bank (sometimes, in a foreign country). If the lender does not have the shares or assets of the operating subsidiary as collateral for the loan, the lender has no recourse. As well, non-consolidated statements are essential for income tax purposes, because every corporation is taxed separately (with some exceptions) and the corporation's separate entity financial statements must be attached to the tax return.

Private companies often do not prepare consolidated statements, because they don't really have "general purpose" financial statements; their range of users is limited. The *CICA Handbook* provides an explicit exemption for private companies through differential disclosure.

CONCEPT REVIEW

1. Where are unrealized holding gains and losses recognized in the financial statements when using the fair value method? Give two alternatives.
2. Under the equity method, if an investee declares no dividends, there may still be investment income. Why is this the case?
3. Will an investment in subsidiary account appear on a set of consolidated financial statements? Explain.
4. What is the difference between consolidation and proportional consolidation?
5. If a company adopts differential reporting, how may a subsidiary be accounted for?

EXHIBIT 11-3

SUMMARY OF ACCOUNTING METHODS ACCOUNTING FOR INVESTMENTS

Method	Carrying Value	Investment Income	Unrealized Holding Gains and Losses	Realized Gains and Losses
Cost	Cost or amortized cost	Interest or dividends; effective interest method	N/A	Included in net income
Fair value; Unrealized G/L included in other comprehensive income	Fair value	Interest or dividends; effective interest method	Included in other comprehensive income; part of shareholders' equity	Cumulative amount included in net income when realized
Fair value; Unrealized G/L included in net income	Fair value	Interest or dividends; effective interest method	Included in net income	Included in net income; the annual change in value
Equity	Cost plus unremitted earnings to date	Share of investee earnings adjusted for amortizations and intercompany profits	N/A	Included in net income; sale unlikely
Consolidation	Investment account replaced with financial statements elements of investee in reporting	Investment revenue represented through inclusion of investee income statement elements; adjusted for amortizations and intercompany profits	N/A	Included in net income; sale unlikely
Proportional consolidation	Investment account replaced with fractional financial statements elements of investee in reporting	Investment revenue represented through inclusion of *fractional* investee income statement elements; adjusted for amortizations and intercompany profits	N/A	Included in net income; Sale unlikely

THE COST METHOD

The cost method presents no special complications. Interest-bearing debt securities that are purchased between interest dates are recorded at cost, which is market value on the date of acquisition. Accrued interest since the last interest payment date is recorded as interest receivable. Accrued interest is added to the cash paid because, at each interest date, the interest is paid to whomever holds the securities regardless of when they actually purchased them. When debt securities are sold between interest dates, the seller collects accrued interest, which is recorded as interest revenue. When the debt securities are purchased, the accrued interest must be recorded separately from the cost of the security itself.

Example—Debt Investment

To illustrate the cost-basis accounting for investment in debt, assume that on 1 November 20X1, Able Company purchases face amount of $30,000 of Charlie Corporation 8% coupon bonds that mature on 31 December 20X7, at 100, plus accrued interest. Interest is paid semi-annually on 30 June and 31 December. Able classifies this investment as a held-to-maturity investment. Able includes transaction costs, if any, in acquisition cost and nets commissions on sale with proceeds received.

Notice that bond prices are quoted as percentages of the face value of the bond. A quote of 98 implies that a $30,000 face amount bond has a market price of $29,400. Able paid par, or 100, and so paid $30,000. The quoted price does not include accrued interest, which also must be paid to the seller of the bond. The bond price is based on the present value of the cash flows, discounted at the market interest rate.

ACQUISITION The entries to record the acquisition is as follows:

Investment in Charlie Corporation bonds	30,000	
Accrued interest receivable ($30,000 × 8% × 4/12)	800	
Cash		30,800

REVENUE When interest is received on 31 December, a portion of it represents the accrued interest recorded at the acquisition date.

To record receipt of interest on 31 December:

Cash ($30,000 × 8% × 6/12)	1,200	
Investment income: Interest		400
Accrued interest receivable		800

MATURITY When a held-to-maturity investment comes due, the investor receives the face value, or principal, plus interest, since maturity occurs on an interest date.

To record receipt of face value plus interest:

Cash	31,200	
Investment income: Interest		1,200
Investment in Charlie Corporation bonds		30,000

In the unlikely event that the held-to-maturity security is sold before maturity, the difference between book value and the selling price (net of accrued interest), less commissions and other expenses, is recorded as a gain or loss. Suppose that on 31 March 20X2 Able Company sells its Charlie Corporation bonds at 105 plus accrued interest, and incurs commissions and other expenses of $550. The cash generated includes the accrued interest of $600 ($30,000 × 8% × 3/12) plus the net proceeds from the bond itself, $30,950 (($30,000 × 105%), less $550 commissions.) The gain on the sale is $950; the proceeds of $30,950 are greater than the cost of $30,000.

The entry to record the sale is as follows:

Cash	31,550	
Investment income: Interest		600
Investment in Charlie Corporation bonds		30,000
Gain on sale of investment		950

Gains and losses on disposal are recognized on the income statement as part of income from continuing operations.

Amortization of Premium or Discount

premium

a difference between the issuance price (or cost) and the maturity value of a debt security where the maturity value is lower

discount

a difference between the issance price (or cost) and the maturity value of a debt security where the maturity value is higher

What happens if debt securities are bought for an amount other than par value, for example, at 98 or 104? The investment is recorded at its cost, which is greater or less than the face amount of the debt. Any **premium** or **discount** should be amortized in order to bring the carrying value up (or down) to par value at maturity. Otherwise, a substantial gain or loss will be recognized at maturity. This is particularly true when the investment is a so-called "zero coupon" bond that carries little or no annual cash interest payment. These bonds are purchased at a very low price relative to their face value. The implicit interest must then be recognized by amortizing the discount.

ISSUANCE PRICE To ascertain market value, the present value of the cash flows associated with the debt is calculated using the market interest rate as the discount rate. For example, assume that Marcus Corp purchased Baker Company bonds when the market interest rate was 6%. The Baker bonds had a $500,000 maturity value, paid 5.5% interest semi-annually, and had a five-year life. The market value is calculated as follows:

Principal $500,000 × (P/F, 3%, 10) (.74409) =	$ 372,045
Interest $13,750 (P/A, 3%, 10) (8.53020) =	117,290
Market value	$ 489,335

Both the principal of $500,000 and the semi-annual interest payments of $500,000 × (5.5% × 6/12), or $13,750, must be included in the present value calculation. Notice that the discount rate used is 3%. This is the 6% market rate multiplied by 6/12, as payments and compounding are semi-annual. The number of periods is 10, which is the five-year life multiplied by two payments per year. Principal is a lump sum, and the interest amount is an ordinary annuity.

The market value on this investment is $489,335, which is .97867 of face value ($489,335/$500,000). This investment would therefore be quoted at 97.867. Acquisition would be recorded as follows, assuming that the investment is to be held to maturity:

Investment in debt securities: Baker bonds	489,335	
Cash		489,335

Since the bond will mature at $500,000, the $10,665 ($500,000 − $489,335) discount must be amortized to interest income over the life of the investment.

effective interest method

a measure of interest expense or revenue over the life of a financial instrument not issued at par; measure expense or revenue as a constant rate over the term of the financial instrument

METHODS There are two methods of amortization, the **straight-line** and **effective interest** methods. Straight line is simpler and is much more common in practice, but the effective interest method is preferable because it provides a constant yield on the recorded value of the investment. Both methods will be illustrated in this chapter. The effective interest method must be used whenever the premium or discount is material. However, straight line may be used when the results are not materially different than the effective interest method. Fortunately, this is a common outcome!

EXAMPLE: EFFECTIVE INTEREST AMORTIZATION Using the effective interest amortization method, interest income is measured as a constant percentage of the bond investment. Interest income is measured using the market interest rate when the bonds were issued. The investment carrying value is multiplied by the market interest rate to obtain interest income. The difference between cash received and interest income is the premium or discount amortization. The investment value changes by the amortization, and the investment book value climbs to face value at maturity.

Effective interest method calculations are illustrated in Exhibit 11-4. Notice that

- The cash payment amount is constant each period, consistent with the terms of the bond. This is the stated interest rate of 2.75% each six months, or 5.5% × 6/12.
- Interest revenue is a constant percentage of the bond carrying amount. To obtain interest revenue, multiply the bond carrying value by the market interest rate. For example, the first amount is $14,680 or 3% of $489,335.
- Amortization is the difference between the cash payment and interest revenue. On the first line, this is $930, or $14,680 − $13,750.
- The bond carrying value grows each period by the amortization amount. On the first line, this is $489,335 plus $930, to equal $490,265.
- The bond carrying value is increased to face value by the end of the 10-period amortization process.

EXHIBIT 11-4

EFFECTIVE INTEREST AMORTIZATION

Period	Cash Payment	3% Interest Revenue	Amortization	Bond Carrying Value
0				$489,335
1	$13,750	$14,680	$ 930	490,265
2	13,750	14,708	958	491,223
3	13,750	14,737	987	492,210
4	13,750	14,766	1,016	493,226
5	13,750	14,797	1,047	494,273
6	13,750	14,828	1,078	495,351
7	13,750	14,861	1,111	496,462
8	13,750	14,894	1,144	497,606
9	13,750	14,928	1,178	498,784
10	13,750	14,966*	1,216	500,000

* $14,964 + $2 rounding error

Interest income is recorded for the first period as follows:

Cash	13,750	
Investment in debt securities: Baker bonds	930	
Investment income: Interest		14,680

EXAMPLE: STRAIGHT-LINE AMORTIZATION Using the straight-line method, interest income is measured as a constant amount each period, cash received plus a discount amortization, or less premium amortization. The investment value changes by the amortization amount, and the investment book value approaches face value at maturity.

The straight-line amortization method calculations are illustrated in Exhibit 11-5. Notice that

- The cash payment, interest revenue, and amortization are constant each period.
- Amortization is obtained by dividing the discount of $10,665 ($500,000 − $489,335) by 10 (the number of interest payments).
- Interest revenue is the sum of cash payment plus amortization, or $13,750 plus $1,067 or $1,066.
- The bond carrying value is increased to face value by the end of the 10-period amortization process.

EXHIBIT 11-5

EFFECTIVE INTEREST AMORTIZATION

Period	Cash Payment	Interest Revenue	Amortization	Bond Carrying Value
0				$489,335
1	$13,750	$14,817	$1,067*	490,402
2	13,750	14,817	1,067	491,469
3	13,750	14,817	1,067	492,536
4	13,750	14,817	1,067	493,603
5	13,750	14,817	1,067	494,670
6	13,750	14,816	1,066	495,736
7	13,750	14,816	1,066	496,802
8	13,750	14,816	1,066	497,868
9	13,750	14,816	1,066	498,934
10	13,750	14,816	1,066	500,000

* $10,665/10; rounded

PURCHASE AT PREMIUM Suppose Marcus paid more than the face of the bonds, because the market interest rate was 4% when the bonds were purchased. In this case, the market value would be

Principal $500,000 × (P/F, 2%, 10) (.82035) =	$ 410,175
Interest $13,750 (P/A, 2%, 20) (8.98259) =	123,511
Market value	$ 533,686

The excess paid over the face amount is a premium. At acquisition, the bonds would be recorded at $533,686, but over the period to their maturity the $33,686 premium would be amortized, reducing the carrying amount (and reducing investment income) each year.

Using the effective interest method, the amortization table would appear as follows:

EXHIBIT 11-6

EFFECTIVE INTEREST AMORTIZATION

Period	Cash Payment	2% Interest Revenue	Amortization	Bond Carrying Value
0				$533,686
1	$13,750	$10,674	$3,076	530,610
2	13,750	10,612	3,138	527,472
3	13,750	10,550	3,200	524,272
etc.				

Only the first three interest periods have been included here; the table is constructed as for a discount situation, except that the carrying value begins at a value *higher* than face value, the cash received is *reduced* by premium amortization to arrive at interest income, and the investment carrying value is *reduced* to face value over the life of the investment.

The first interest payment would be recorded as follows:

Cash	13,750	
Investment in debt securities: Baker bonds		3,076
Investment income: Interest		10,674

EXAMPLE: SHARE INVESTMENT To illustrate the cost-basis accounting for investment in shares, assume that on 1 November 20X1, Able Company purchases 50,000 shares of Phillips Company common shares for $20 per share. Commissions and legal fees with respect to the purchase are $50,000; Able includes these expenditures in the acquisition cost. This investment gives Able control of Phillips, and Able will consolidate at year-end. During the year, however, Able will record the investment using the cost method.

ACQUISITION The entries to record the purchase are as follows:

Investment in Phillips Company common shares	1,050,000	
Cash [(50,000 shares × $20) + $50,000 fees]		1,050,000

REVENUE On 31 December, Phillips declares a dividend of $0.50 per share. The dividend is recorded when declared:

Dividends receivable (50,000 × $0.50)	25,000	
Investment income: Dividends		25,000

The dividend is paid on January 13 and the cash receipt is recorded:

Cash	25,000	
Dividend receivable		25,000

SALE If the investment is sold, the difference between book value and the selling price, less commissions and other expenses, is recorded as a gain or loss. Assume that the shares of Phillips Company common shares were sold for $2,300,000, less $61,000 of fees and commissions.

Cash ($2,300,000 – $61,000)	2,239,000	
Investment in Phillips Company common shares		1,050,000
Gain on sale of investment		1,189,000

Impairment

The market value of a held-to-maturity debt security will fluctuate, based on market interest rates. Also, if the credit rating of the borrower changes, the market value of the investment will fluctuate, as the risk attached to future cash flow is changed. This, again, changes the risk premium appropriately included in the discount rate. When the value of an investment falls below its acquisition cost, assets may be overstated. Conservatism might dictate loss recognition. However, since the security is not held for sale, and its maturity value is assured, market value is not a relevant measurement attribute. Therefore, the loss is not recognized in net income.

Impairment is a different situation. At each year-end, every investment must be reviewed to see if value is *permanently impaired.* If such an impairment exists, the investment must be written down (*CICA* ED 3855.66)

The following evidence about the issuer (the investee) would suggest impairment:

1. Significant financial difficulty;
2. A breach of contract, such as failure to pay required interest or principal on outstanding debt;
3. Concessions granted because of financial difficulties;
4. High probability of bankruptcy or financial reorganization;
5. Prior impairment losses;
6. Disappearance of an active market for the investment because of financial difficulties; or
7. An historical pattern of financial difficulties. (*CICA* ED 3855.A44)

These situations must be evaluated to see if there is real impairment. So, for instance, if an active market for an investment disappears because a once-public company has gone private, but the company is still in good financial position, there is no impairment. Similarly, a downgrade in credit rating does not mean impairment unless it is accompanied by one of the above conditions.

When an impairment loss must be recorded, it is measured as the difference between the investment's carrying value and fair value. The carrying value of the investment is reduced to fair value either directly or indirectly through an allowance. Impairment losses are not reversed as long as the asset is held.

EXAMPLE Review the facts of the Baker bond given above, originally purchased for $489,335. After three years, if the effective interest amortization method is used, the carrying value of the bond is $495,351. Assume that the value of this investment has become impaired. Baker is in financial reorganization, and the fair value of the bond was $213,500, because interest and principal payments have been reduced significantly as part of the financial reorganization.

The impairment is recognized:

Impairment loss ($495,351 – $213,500)	281,851	
Investment in debt securities: Baker bonds		281,851

Alternatively, the impairment can be recorded in a valuation allowance:

Impairment loss ($495,351 – $213,500)	281,851	
Allowance for impairment loss: Baker bonds		281,851

The allowance is shown as a contra account to the investment on the balance sheet. The loss would be reported on the income statement. The investment account now has a balance of $213,500, which cannot be written back up to original cost if fair value subsequently recovers. Note that, for tax purposes, such losses are deductible only when realized, so the impairment loss is tax deductible only when the (reduced) payments are actually accepted.

CONCEPT REVIEW

1. A debt security is bought for $14,700, including $700 of accrued interest, and sold for $14,900, including $900 of accrued interest. Why is there no gain or loss on sale?
2. How is the market value of a bond determined?
3. Is interest revenue on a held-to-maturity investment necessarily just the cash entitlement? Explain.
4. Suppose that the value of a company's held-to-maturity investment falls below its cost. Would the carrying value of the investment necessarily be impaired? Explain.

THE FAIR VALUE METHOD; UNREALIZED GAINS AND LOSSES RECOGNIZED IN OTHER COMPREHENSIVE INCOME

The fair value method recognizes that the most relevant attribute for reporting investments is fair value. Therefore, at reporting dates, investments are adjusted to fair value. Gains and losses are excluded from net income until the investment is sold. This is an attempt to avoid recognition of gains and losses that have not been realized through sale.

EXAMPLE As an example of the fair value method, assume that on 1 December 20X5, YZone Manufacturing Limited purchased two investments, both designated as available-for-sale investments. YZone bought 5,000 shares of Gerome Limited, a public company, for $26.75 per share plus $1,200 in broker's fees. YZone also purchased a $100,000, 9%, ten-year Provincial Hydro bond that pays interest each 31 October and 30 April, at 100 plus accrued interest. YZone includes broker's fees in the cost of the investment, and nets proceeds on sale with fees charged.

To record purchase of investments:

Investment in Provincial Hydro bonds	100,000	
Accrued interest receivable ($100,000 × 9% × 1/12)	750	
Investment in Gerome Ltd. shares ((5,000 × $26.75) + $1,200)	134,950	
Cash ($107,750 + $134,950)		235,700

REVENUE Bond interest is accrued on 31 December.

To record accrual of interest:

Accrued interest receivable ($100,000 × 9% × 1/12)	750	
Investment income: Interest		750

FAIR VALUE ADJUSTMENT At year-end, fair value is determined through reference to stock market quotations. The Gerome shares are trading for $24.75 and the bonds are trading at 100.5. This means that the shares must be reflected in the financial statements at $123,750 (5,000 shares at $24.75) and the bonds at $100,500.

To record changes in fair value:

Investment in Provincial Hydro bonds ($100,500 − $100,000)	500	
Unrealized holding gain: Provincial Hydro Bond		500
Unrealized holding loss: Gerome Ltd. shares ($123,750 − $134,950)	11,200	
Investment in Gerome Ltd. shares		11,200

The 100.5 bond price is quoted exclusive of accrued interest. Notice that the unrealized loss on the Gerome Limited shares includes the write-off of the broker's fees.

REPORTING Unrealized gains and losses are not recorded as income, but rather as unrealized holding gains, part of other comprehensive income in shareholders' equity.

Common shares (assumed)	$500,000
Retained earnings (assumed)	897,300
Other comprehensive income:	
Unrealized holding losses, net ($11,200 − $500)	(10,700)
Total shareholders' equity	$1,386,600

Other comprehensive income includes the *changes* in unrealized holding gains and losses during the year. *Cumulative* unrealized holding gains are a special component of shareholders' equity on the balance sheet. At this point, the balance sheet reflects a net unrealized holding loss (a debit) of $10,700.

In the 20X5 income statement, YZone reported interest income of $750. The balance sheet reflects investments at their fair value of $224,250, or $100,500 plus $123,750. The cumulative unrealized losses are disclosed as a debit balance in shareholders' equity.

SECOND YEAR In 20X6, YZone has further transactions with respect to its available-for-sale investments. Interest on the Provincial Hydro bonds is paid on 30 April and 31 October:

To record receipt of interest on 30 April:

Cash ($100,000 × 9% × 6/12)	4,500	
Investment income: Interest		3,000
Accrued interest receivable		1,500

To record receipt of interest on 31 October:

Cash ($100,000 × 9% × 6/12)	4,500	
Investment income: Interest		4,500

The bond is sold on 30 November for 103 plus accrued interest. A broker's fee of $300 is charged.

To record the sale:

Cash (($100,000 × 103%) + $750 − $300))	103,450	
Unrealized holding gain: Provincial Hydro Bond	500	
Investment income: Interest		750
Investment in Provincial Hydro bonds		100,500
Gain on sale of investment		2,700

When an available-for-sale investment is sold, *cumulative* unrealized holding gains or losses, a $500 gain in this case, are eliminated. The recorded $2,700 gain on sale is included in net income.

Gerome Limited paid a $0.43 per share dividend in 20X6:

Cash (5,000 × $0.43)	2,150	
Investment revenue: Dividend revenue		2,150

The Gerome shares are still unsold at year-end. Their quoted share price is now $31.50 or a total of $157,500. Since the shares are now recorded at $123,750, an unrealized holding gain is recorded:

Investment in Gerome Ltd. shares ($157,500 − $123,750)	33,750	
Unrealized holding gain: Gerome Ltd. shares		33,750

SECOND YEAR REPORTING At the end of 20X6 the financial statement will reflect:

On the income statement:

Investment revenue ($3,000 + $4,500 + $2,700 + $2,150)	$12,350

Y Zone may choose to disclose the various sources on investment income together on the income statement, as illustrated, or break down the various components.

In other comprehensive income:

Opening balance (debit)	$10,700
Changes in unrealized holding gains and losses ($33,750 − $500)	(33,250)
Closing balance (credit)	$22,550

Other comprehensive income includes the changes in unrealized holding gains during the year. The change in unrealized amounts comes from two sources: first, the $33,750 new unrealized holding gain on Gerome Limited shares and, second, the $500 realization of a previously recorded unrealized gain on the Provincial Hydro bonds. The realization of a gain is a *decrease* in other comprehensive income.

On the balance sheet:

Available for sale investments, Gerome Ltd. shares	$157,500
Shareholders' equity	
Other comprehensive income:	
Unrealized holding gains	22,550

As a proof of the cumulative amount, compare the $157,500 carrying value of the Gerome shares with their original cost, $134,950. The result is $22,550.

THIRD YEAR In 20X7, the Gerome Limited shares are sold for $30.50, less $1,700 in broker's fees:

To record the sale of shares:

Cash ((5,000 × $30.50) − $1,700)	150,800	
Unrealized holding gain: Gerome Ltd. shares (cumulative balance)	22,550	
Investment in Gerome Ltd. shares		157,500
Gain on sale on investment		15,850

At this point, there are no unrealized amounts remaining, and all realized gains and losses have been included in net income.

Impairment

The above example reflected an unrealized holding loss for the Gerome Limited shares at the end of 20X5. This loss is assumed to be the result of market fluctuations and not a permanent impairment. Of course, the shares, since they are recorded at market value, are not overvalued on the balance sheet. Notice, though, that the loss is excluded from income. If, on the other hand, the decline in market value reflected a permanent impairment, *the loss must be included in net income.* The impairment test is identical to that described under the cost method—the key element is to look for conditions that indicate a permanent decline in value.

If value of the Gerome Limited shares had been impaired at the end of 20X5, the entry would have been as follows:

Impairment loss	11,200	
Investment in Gerome Ltd. shares		11,200

When an impairment loss is recorded, any cumulative holding gains and losses in other comprehensive income are reversed out. An impairment loss cannot be reversed, through gain recognition, until the investment is sold (*CICA* ED 3855.A51). Of course, these Gerome Limited shares recovered their value, in our example, in 20X6. This would not have happened if the investment was truly impaired.

Other Issues

BASKET PURCHASES OF SECURITIES A purchase of two or more classes of securities for a single lump sum is a basket purchase. The total purchase price must be allocated to the different types of securities. The general principles are as follows:

- When the market price of each class of security is known, the proportional method of allocation is used, wherein the total cost is allocated in proportion to the market values of the various securities in the basket.
- If the market price is not known for one class of security, the incremental method can be used, wherein the purchase price is allocated first to the securities with known prices, and then the remainder of the lump-sum purchase price is attributed to the class of investment that does not have a market price.

The incremental method is not a lot of help when more than one security in the basket does not have a market price. In this case, recourse had best be made to pricing models offered in finance literature and practice. Since few accountants are expert at the pricing of financial instruments, valuations may be obtained from independent financial consultants in order to allocate the total purchase price.

INVESTMENTS MADE IN A FOREIGN CURRENCY It is not unusual for an enterprise to purchase equity or debt instruments that are priced in a foreign currency. The purchase price must be converted into Canadian dollars for recording on the Canadian investor's books and reporting in the investor's financial statements. To record the purchase, the exchange rate on or about the date of purchase is used.

For example, assume that LeBlanc Limited purchases 20,000 shares of AllAm Incorporated, a U.S. corporation. The purchase price is U.S.$65 per share, for a total of U.S.$1,300,000. At the time of the purchase, the U.S. dollar is worth Cdn.$1.35. The purchase would be recorded in Canadian dollars as follows:

Investment in AllAm Inc.	1,755,000	
Cash (U.S.$1,300,000 × Cdn.$1.35)		1,755,000

This entry establishes the cost of the investment to LeBlanc, and will be the carrying value of the investment. Changes in the value of the U.S. dollar in subsequent reporting periods are irrelevant to the cost of an equity investment.

For debt instruments, the issue is a bit more complicated. Debt instruments, by definition, are payable in a given amount of currency. When the debt is stated or denominated in a currency other than the investor's reporting currency, the equivalent value of the instrument in the reporting currency changes as the exchange rate changes. Therefore, an investment in foreign currency–denominated bonds must be restated on every balance sheet date to the equivalent amount in Canadian dollars, using the exchange rate at the balance sheet date (known as the spot rate). The change in Canadian dollar equivalents between balance sheet dates is an exchange gain or loss, and is reported on the income statement.

THE FAIR VALUE METHOD; GAINS AND LOSSES RECOGNIZED IN NET INCOME

The fair value method, with gains and losses recognized in net income as they arise, is similar in structure to our previous example. The difference lies in the entries to record changes in value, and the entries on sale. Balance sheet values represent fair values, a highly relevant measurement for financial statement users.

EXAMPLE Return to the example of YZone Manufacturing above. YZone now classifies its investments as trading investments. The fair value method is unchanged except for the treatment of the changes in value.

At the end of 20X5, YZone would record holding gains and losses on the income statement:

Investment in Provincial Hydro bonds	500	
Investment revenue; unrealized holding gain: Provincial Hydro Bond		500
Gerome Ltd. shares	11,200	
Investment in Gerome Ltd. shares		11,200

Investment revenue: unrealized holding loss

The investment revenue accounts, even though unrealized, would be reported on the income statement. Therefore, there would be no special equity accounts recorded on the balance sheet.

Entries in 20X6 would be identical for interest and dividends, but the sale of the Provincial Hydro bond would be recorded as follows:

Cash	103,450	
Investment income: Interest		750
Investment in Provincial Hydro bonds		100,500
Gain on sale of investment		2,200

A $2,700 gain was recorded in 20X6 in the available-for-sale example, versus $2,200 in this trading investment example. YZone has still earned $2,700 on the bond. In the trading investment example, $500 is included in net income in 20X5 and $2,200 in 20X6. *Timing* of gain and loss recognition has changed.

At the end of 20X6

Investment in Gerome Ltd. shares ($157,500 – $123,750)	33,750	
Investment income: unrealized holding gain: Gerome Ltd. shares		33,750

When the Gerome shares are sold in 20X7

Cash	150,800	
Loss on sale of investment	6,700	
Investment in Gerome Ltd. shares		157,500

Recognizing the gain or loss caused by the change in value in net income immediately has again changed the timing, but not the amount, of the net gain. When unrealized holding gains and losses were deferred, in the prior example, a net gain of $15,850 was recognized in 20X7. When gains and losses are recognized as they occur, there is a loss of $11,200 in 20X5, a gain of $33,750 in 20X6, and a loss of $6,700 in 20X7. The total is still $15,850.

IMPAIRMENT Since losses on declines in fair value are included in income immediately, there are no impairment rules applied to this method. Declines in market value may reverse if market value recovers.

CONCEPT REVIEW

1. An available-for-sale investment is bought for $10,000, and has a fair value of $14,000 at the end of the first year, $16,000 at the end of the second year, and is sold for $21,000 in the third year. What amount of gain is recorded in net income in the third year?
2. Assume that the same investment is classified as a trading investment. What gain is included in income in the third year?
3. An available-for-sale investment had a carrying value of $50,000 and a fair value of $40,000. If the decline in value is considered a normal fluctuation in market value, what amount will be recorded in net income? What if the decline was considered an impairment?

THE EQUITY METHOD

Conceptually, the equity method treats the investee company as if it were condensed into one balance sheet item and one income statement item and then merged into the investor company at the proportion owned by the investor. The equity method is sometimes called "one-line consolidation" because it results in the same effect on the investor's earnings and retained earnings as would result from consolidating the financial statements of the investor and investee companies. It does so without combining both companies' financial statements.

ILLUSTRATION In its simplest form, the equity method requires that the investment account represent the investor's proportionate share of the book value of the investee and that the investment income represent the investor's proportionate share of the investee's income. Assume, for initial simplicity, that Teck Computer Company (TCC) makes an initial investment of $100,000 for 40% of the voting shares of RPP Software on 1 January 20X1. In 20X1, RPP has earnings of $30,000 and pays dividends totalling $10,000. If the investment is accounted for by the equity method, TCC will make the following two entries at the end of 20X1:

To record TCC's share of RPP's net income:

Investment in RPP Software	12,000	
Investment income ($30,000 × 40%)		12,000

To record receipt of dividends from RPP:

Cash ($10,000 × 40%)	4,000	
Investment in RPP Software		4,000

Note that dividends from the investee are not recorded as investment income. Under the equity method, the investor company records its proportionate share of the investee earnings as investment income and increases its investment account by this amount. When the investee pays dividends, its net worth is reduced, and thus the investment account of the investor is reduced. Dividends are viewed as a dis-investment, that is, a return of the investment to the investor, rather than a return on the investment.

Following the two entries for 20X1, the investment account for RPP will reflect the following:

Investment in RPP Software, at equity	
Original investment	$100,000
Proportionate share of earnings of investee ($30,000 × 40%)	12,000
Dividends received from investee ($10,000 × 40%)	(4,000)
Ending balance	$108,000

The difference between investee earnings and investee dividends is the amount of earnings accruing to the investor that the investee retained, or the unremitted earnings of the investee. Thus, the equity-based investment account is equal to the original investment plus the investor's proportionate share of the investee's cumulative retained earnings since the investment was made. In this sense, the equity method represents an extension of accrual accounting to investments in common shares. However, the balance sheet doesn't reflect the cost of the investment anymore. This number isn't market value, either, and is hard to interpret.

EXTRAORDINARY ITEMS AND DISCONTINUED OPERATIONS When the investee reports extraordinary items, or discontinued operations, the investor company must report its proportionate share of these items on its income statement separately, in the same way it would if they were incurred by the investor company. However, separate disclosure is needed if they remain material items on the income statement of the investor, which usually is larger than the investee.

NECESSARY ADJUSTMENTS The equity method is typically more complicated than this simple example. It is usually necessary to make certain adjustments to the amount of annual income that is recorded on the investor's books. Two factors must be considered:

1. When an investor company acquires the equity securities of an investee company, it may pay more for the securities than their book value. In this situation, the investor's proportionate share of the investee's net income must be adjusted. The adjustment is needed to amortize the underlying fair value of the net assets acquired.

   When there is an investment to be accounted for under the equity method, it is necessary to

   a. Measure the fair value of net assets acquired;
   b. Compare the proportionate fair value to the price paid; and
   c. Determine the amount of goodwill, if any.

   The fair values of assets and goodwill are not explicitly recognized under the equity method, but the investor's share of income must be decreased by appropriate amortization on the fair values of depreciable assets and any writedown caused by an impairment of goodwill.

2. If the investor and the investee have transactions with each other during the year, either company, or both companies, will have the profits from these transactions recorded in income. For example, assume that the investor sold inventory to the investee at a profit of $25,000. If the investee subsequently sold these goods to a third party, then the intercompany sales price is validated, or realized, in this subsequent transaction and no particular accounting concerns arise. However, if the inventory is still on the investee's balance sheet, then the profit is unrealized as far as the investor is concerned. It is not acceptable to recognize an increase in net income if all that's happened is a sale to a "customer" that the vendor can significantly influence. Therefore, the equity method, properly applied, involves adjustments for unrealized intercompany profits of both companies.

Example: Equity Method

On 2 January 20X1, Giant Company purchased 3,600 shares of the 18,000 outstanding common shares of Small Corporation for $300,000 cash. Two Giant Company senior executives were elected to the Small Corporation Board of Directors. Giant is deemed to be able to exercise significant influence over Small's operating and financial policies, so the equity method of accounting for the investment is appropriate.

ACQUISITION Giant records its investment as follows:

Investment in Small, at equity	300,000	
Cash		300,000

FAIR VALUE INCREMENTS AND GOODWILL The balance sheet for Small at 2 January 20X1, and estimated market values of its assets and liabilities are as follows:

	Book Value	Market Value	Difference
Cash and receivables	$ 100,000	$ 100,000	$ 0
Inventory (FIFO basis)	400,000	405,000	5,000
Plant and equipment, net (10-year remaining life)	500,000	700,000	200,000
Land	150,000	165,000	15,000
Total assets	$1,150,000	$1,370,000	
Less: liabilities	(150,000)	(150,000)	0
Net assets	$1,000,000	$1,220,000	$220,000

Giant bought 20% of Small's shareholders' equity, which has a book value of $200,000 ($1,000,000 × 20%); $200,000 is the proportion of Small book value purchased by Giant. Giant paid $300,000 for its 20% interest in Small. The amount above book value that Giant paid, $100,000, is called the *purchase price discrepancy*. The accounting problem is to determine why Giant paid that much, and then to account for the acquisition price accordingly.

First, each asset and liability is examined to see if book value understates fair market value. To the extent this is true, the $100,000 excess is explained. If there is a remaining unexplained residual, it is attributed to goodwill. This is based on the assumption that intangible assets, which promise future cash flow, explain the purchase price.

The "difference" column shows the specific assets whose market value exceeds book value. Giant acquired a portion (20%) of each of these items, including the amount by which market value exceeds book value.

	Book Value	Market Value	Difference	20% of Difference
Inventory	$400,000	$405,000	$ 5,000	$ 1,000
Plant & equipment (10-year remaining life)	500,000	700,000	200,000	40,000
Land	150,000	165,000	15,000	3,000
Totals			$220,000	$44,000

Thus, $44,000 of the $100,000 purchase price premium over book value that Giant paid can be identified with these specific assets. The remaining difference, $56,000, cannot be specifically identified with any asset and therefore represents goodwill. Goodwill is defined as the excess of the amount invested in acquiring all or a portion of another firm over the fair value of the net identifiable assets acquired. Goodwill can also be computed as follows:

Computation of Goodwill Purchased by Giant Company		
Purchase price (of 20% interest)		$300,000
Market value of identifiable assets	$1,370,000	
Less: Market value of liabilities	(150,000)	
Total	$1,220,000	
Market value of 20% of identifiable net assets acquired: ($1,220,000 × 20%)		(244,000)
Goodwill		$ 56,000

Giant, then, has acquired a 20% interest in Small at a cost of $300,000, and the items acquired can be represented as follows:

20% of the net book value of Small ($1,000,000 × .20)		$200,000
20% of excess of market value over book value for:		
Inventory (20% × $5,000)	$ 1,000	
Plant and equipment (20% × $200,000)	40,000	
Land (20% × $15,000)	3,000	44,000
Goodwill		56,000
Total		$300,000

SUBSEQUENT AMORTIZATION The equity method requires that Giant record its initial $300,000 investment in Small in one investment account, despite the fact that it has many components. No formal recognition is given to the various component parts of the investment. However, the amount of income recognized annually will be changed as a result of these components.

When Small disposes of any of the above items, either in the normal course of business or by asset sales, Giant must record appropriate adjustments to its investment account, through the annual entry that recognizes investment income.

For example, since Small uses FIFO to cost its inventory, the beginning inventory is treated as sold first during the coming year. Likewise, its plant and equipment is used and depreciated each year for 10 years. Since the valuation of these items from Giant's investment perspective is different from that recorded by Small, Giant will adjust annual investment income to reflect the using up of the difference between the market value and the book value of these assets.

Assuming that all of Small's beginning inventory is sold during 20X1, Small's cost of goods sold for 20X1 is understated by $1,000 from the single-entity (Giant) perspective. Also, amortization is understated. If the plant and equipment have a remaining useful life of 10 years and Small uses straight-line amortization, Giant needs to increase the amortization expense for Small by $40,000 divided by 10 years, or $4,000 each year for the next 10 years.

Next, goodwill must be considered. Goodwill is not amortized, but must be evaluated for possible impairment. If there is an impairment, investment income must be decreased accordingly.

No annual adjustments need be made for the excess of market value over book value for the land. Only if Small disposes of the land would an adjustment need to be made, showing that the cost of 20% of the land from the Giant perspective is understated by $3,000 on Small's books. Giant's proportionate share of any gain (loss) on disposal of the land would be decreased (increased) by $3,000.

INVESTMENT REVENUE Giant's income from its investment in Small requires adjusting to reflect the above analysis. Suppose that for the fiscal year ending 31 December 20X1, Small reports the following:

Income before discontinued operations	$ 73,000
Net earnings from discontinued operations	30,000
Net income	$103,000
Cash dividends, paid on 31 December	$ 50,000

Goodwill has been evaluated for potential impairment, but no writedown is required. In 20X1, Small sold goods to Giant for $46,000 during the year, and none have been resold by Giant at year-end. The goods originally cost Small $38,000, and thus Small has recorded an $8,000 increase in income that has not been confirmed by a transaction with an outside party. Since Giant owns 20% of Small, and records only 20% of Small's income, it must eliminate 20% of the gain, or $1,600 of the $8,000 unrealized gain.

Investment income is a combination of Giant's share of a variety of items.

Small's net income before discontinued operations ($73,000 × 20%)	$14,600
Cost of goods sold adjustment for the fair value of inventory purchased ($5,000 × 20%)	(1,000)
Additional amortization on plant and equipment fair value ($40,000 ÷ 10)	(4,000)
Elimination of unrealized inter-company profit in inventory ($8,000 × 20%)	(1,600)
Net investment income, ordinary income	$ 8,000
Small's net earnings from discontinued operations ($30,000 × 20%)	$ 6,000

The investment revenue for 20X1, after all the adjustments, is $8,000 of ordinary income and a gain from discontinued operations of $6,000. These two items would be shown separately on the income statement. If no adjustments had been made, Giant would have recorded a total of $20,600 of income ($103,000 × 20%). This result of the equity method is quite common; less income than you might expect is recorded. This happens because the investor very often pays more than book value for its interest in the investee, and resulting amortizations reduce income. Then, too, intercompany transactions are quite common, and elimination of unrealized profits can also reduce income.

ENTRIES At 31 December Giant would make the following entries to reflect its interest in the earnings of Small:

Investment in Small, at equity	14,000	
Investment income (as above)		8,000
Earnings from discontinued operations ($30,000 × 20%)		6,000

To record the receipt of cash dividends paid by Small:

Cash ($50,000 × 20%)	10,000	
Investment in Small, at equity		10,000

BALANCE IN INVESTMENT ACCOUNT After these entries are posted, the balance in the investment in account is $304,000.

Beginning balance (acquisition price)	$300,000
Proportionate share of Small's net income	14,000
Dividends received	(10,000)
Investment account balance, 31 December 20X1	$304,000

The total investment income Giant reports from its investment in Small is $14,000. Since Giant received $10,000 of this in the form of cash dividends, the net increase of its investment is $4,000.

Unrealized Profit Elimination

The example shown above involved an intercompany unrealized profit that had been recorded by the investee. This is called an **upstream profit**, because the transaction went from the bottom of the investment river (the investee) to the top (the investor). Since the investor picks up only its share of the investee's income, its also picks up only a partial, or 20%, elimination of the profit.

upstream profits intercompany profits on transactions between an investor company and investee where the investee records the profit

downstream profits intercompany profits on transactions between an investor company and investee where the parent records the profit

Assume instead that the transaction in the Giant example is **downstream**, a sale from the investor to the investee. Again, none of the inventory is sold at year-end. In this case, Giant has recorded, as part of gross profit, an $8,000 sale that has not been confirmed by a sale to an outside party. No adjustment is made to the investor's sales or gross profit. Instead, investment income is reduced by the *full $8,000 intercompany downstream unrealized profit.* Thus, the bottom line net income for the investor company will reflect the elimination of the gross profit, but through a reduction of investment income rather than a reduction of reported gross profit.

The rule is that upstream unrealized profits are fractionally eliminated (the investor's share only) but downstream unrealized profits are eliminated in their entirety, because the full amount is in the investor's accounts.

Goodwill Impairment

The procedures for evaluating goodwill for potential impairment were explained in Chapter 10. If goodwill had to be written down, investment income is reduced by the amount of the writedown. This may well create an investment loss for the year, and the investment account on the balance sheet would be reduced as a result. This is the obvious result of a writedown: assets go down!

CONCEPT REVIEW

1. Why is the equity method sometimes called the one-line consolidation method?
2. Explain what is meant by unrealized profits. Why should they be eliminated when the investor's financial statements are being prepared?
3. What difference is there between the amounts reported as income from equity-reported investments and the cash flow from those investments?

CONSOLIDATION

A parent company is required to consolidate its financial statements with those of its subsidiaries when general purpose financial statements are issued. The parent company uses the cost or equity method to account for the investment during the year, but, at the end of the reporting period, must prepare consolidated financial statements for reporting to its shareholders and other financial statement users. Consolidated statements are prepared by combining the sets of financial statements into one, which is intended to portray the activities of the whole enterprise. This is an application of substance over form, as consolidated statements portray the economic entity that exists in substance, rather than relying on the legal form that has been used to organize the activities of an enterprise.

Consolidation is accomplished using the purchase method. That is, the parent company purchases the subsidiary, and the two companies are combined as of that date. Fair market values of the subsidiary's assets are recognized from this acquisition transaction, including goodwill. Prior results are not combined.

It is important to understand that consolidation does not happen on anyone's books; there's a spreadsheet that imports financial statements from the parent and the subsidiary as inputs. Then, certain adjustments are processed, and the consolidated financial statements are produced.

Consolidation is mostly an additive process; the financial statements are added together, line by line. Common adjustments include

1. The investment account must be eliminated from the parent company's financial statements, and the corresponding equity accounts must be eliminated from the subsidiary's financial statements.
2. If net assets' book values reflected on the subsidiary's books on the date of acquisition are different from their market values on that date, the difference, called a fair value increment, must be recognized on the consolidated financial statements, along with any goodwill inherent in the purchase price. This reflects the fact that the parent acquired assets, including intangible assets, at fair value.
3. If fair values (i.e., market values) were recognized, they must be amortized in subsequent years.
4. Goodwill is not amortized. Goodwill is written down if impaired. The impairment test must be done on an annual basis.

5. Any portion of the subsidiary that is consolidated but is owned by non-controlling, or minority, subsidiary shareholder must be recognized as a separate balance sheet and income statement account.
6. Intercompany receivables and payables, gains and losses, and revenues and expenses must be eliminated so that the financial statements will reflect only transactions with outsiders.
7. If there are any intercompany unrealized profits at year-end, these must be eliminated so that income is not misstated.

THE END RESULT OF CONSOLIDATION A whole course in consolidations is offered at the advanced accounting level in many accounting programs. We won't go into that much depth here! The Appendix to this chapter contains a basic consolidation example, along with brief explanations of the elimination entries. This example will give you a taste of the consolidation process. However, it is worthwhile to take a look at the end result for a few minutes, even if you're not covering the Appendix material. Look at Exhibit 11A-1 now. What should you notice about these consolidated results, as shown in the final column?

- Consolidated assets are higher than just the parent's alone, and also are different from just the parent and the subsidiary added together. The subsidiary's assets are written up (or down) to reflect their fair values on the date on acquisition. Goodwill inherent in the purchase price is recognized. Goodwill is shown with intangible assets.
- Assets and liabilities of the parent and the subsidiary are added together, and intercompany balances are eliminated.
- The parent's investment account and investment revenue are eliminated.
- The portion of the subsidiary that is not owned by the parent is included in consolidated totals, but the outside interests are reflected in consolidated financial statements via a balance sheet account and an income statement account that relate to the **non-controlling interests.**
- The consolidated income statement reflects higher expenses, because fair values recognized are amortized.
- The consolidated income statement reflects eliminations for intercompany unrealized profits.
- Dividends reported are only those dividends paid by the parent.
- Equity accounts of the subsidiary that existed on acquisition are eliminated.

non-controlling interest (minority interest)
when a company controls a subsidiary but does not own 100% of the voting shares, it still includes 100% of the net assets and net income in the consolidated financial statements; the non-controlling interest in earnings is the portion of the subsidiary's earnings that accrue to the other, minority shareholders; the non-controlling interest in net assets—a balance sheet credit—is the portion of net assets that represent the minority shareholders' share

COMPLICATIONS Consolidations can be very complicated. Many parent companies have more than one subsidiary, and all must be consolidated together, with all intercompany transactions eliminated. This can seem mind boggling when there are 200 subsidiaries, but it's no big challenge for consolidation computer software as long as all of the intercompany transactions and balances are coded correctly.

Profit eliminations are potentially complex, too, when the impact on future (deferred) income tax is considered. Then, too, intercompany unrealized profits usually have an impact for multiple years, and appropriate entries must be made. The parent's percentage ownership in the subsidiary can change, either up or down. There are also many subtleties associated with fair value amortizations. We could go on, but we're sure you get the picture.

DIFFERENTIAL ACCOUNTING Remember, though, that non-public companies can adopt differential reporting for controlled investments and use either the cost or the equity method for accounting.

RECLASSIFICATION

It happens that investment intent changes, and investments that were once available for sale become held to maturity, or significant influence investments are reclassified as available for sale. Trading investments, because of the specialized nature of the portfolio category, may not be reclassified (*CICA* ED 3855.71).

Sometimes, reclassifications are caused by the action of others—for example, significant influence may be lost if another shareholder becomes dominant. Most often, though, management intent is the driving factor in these changes. Granted, the financial position of the investor and the investee influences management intent. It may not be possible to hold investments to maturity if the investor is in need of funds. The investee might be struggling, or suddenly prosperous, and this may influence intent.

If investments are reclassified, the investment is transferred to the alternate portfolio, at an appropriate value. For example, if investments are transferred to the held-to-maturity or the significant influence category, the transfer takes place at carrying value, and the investment is then accounted for using the cost or equity method as appropriate. If the investments are transferred to available for sale, the transfer takes place at fair value and other comprehensive income is created. Future income is recognized based on the new classification rules. Refer to Exhibit 11-7 for a summary of the rules for reclassification. Note in particular that

- If held-to-maturity investments are transferred to available for sale, the transfer takes place at fair value and the difference between amortized cost (the carrying value) and fair value is included in other comprehensive income until realized through sale.
- If available-for-sale investments are reclassified as held to maturity, then the cumulative gain or loss in other comprehensive income is amortized to interest income over the remaining term of the investment.

Reclassifications are clearer if a formal entry is made to reclassify the investment. For example, if a held-to-maturity bond investment with a carrying value of $98,000 and a fair value of $105,000 is reclassified as available for sale, the following entry would be made:

Available-for-sale investment: bonds	105,000	
Held-to-maturity investment: bonds		98,000
Unrealized holding gain: bonds		7,000

Remember, such a reclassification out of the held-to-maturity classification means that this classification cannot be used for two years, as management intent has proven unreliable.

EXHIBIT 11-7

RECLASSIFICATION RULES

Transfer From	Transfer To	Transfer Value	Prior Gains and Losses
Any appropriate category	Available-for-sale	Fair value	Gain or loss at date of transfer recognized in other comprehensive income until sale
Any appropriate category	Equity	Carrying value	No gain or loss recorded; any cumulative amounts in other comprehensive income remain until sale
Available-for-sale	Held-to-maturity	Carrying value	Unrealized gain or loss to date amortized to interest income
Note: transfers to and from trading category **not permitted**			

CLASSIFICATION AND DISCLOSURE REQUIREMENTS

Temporary versus Long-Term Investments

Should investments be classified as temporary or long-term in the financial statements? The answer will have a large effect on the current liquidity picture portrayed. An investment is classified as a **temporary investment** if *both* of the following conditions are satisfied:

temporary investment
an investment in debt or equity securities that can be liquidated quickly and is intended by management as a short-term use of cash

1. The investment matures within the next year (or operating cycle) or is capable of reasonably prompt liquidation (either by sale on the open market or sale to a financial institution), and
2. The investment is intended by management to be a temporary use of cash.

If these two conditions are not satisfied, the investment is classified as long term.

Held-to-maturity investments are obviously classified as long-term investments, at least until the investment's maturity date falls within the one-year window. Available-for-sale investments may be either temporary or long term, depending on a careful assessment of the factors above. Trading investments would usually be temporary in nature, but again, specific circumstances must be carefully reviewed. If the trading window is over one year, the investments would be long term.

Disclosure of Financial Instruments

All held-to-maturity, available-for-sale, and trading investments are financial instruments, so disclosure must be made of

- *Significant terms and conditions.* Terms and conditions include due dates, interest rates, interest payment dates, and all major terms. This disclosure is meant to help financial statement users assess the amount, timing, and uncertainty of cash flows related to the investment.
- *Interest rate risk.* Financial statement readers must be informed of the effective interest rate that is embedded in the purchase price, and any maturity dates or contractual repricing dates prior to maturity.
- *Credit risk.* An investor assumes credit risk when lending money to another company, which is what investing in a debt instrument amounts to. What if the company doesn't pay? Collateral is often present to protect the investor. In any event, a company must disclose the maximum credit risk it has accepted, which would usually be limited to the face value of the investment.

Disclosure of Strategic Investments

Disclosures relating to strategic investments, that is, significant influence, control, and joint venture relationships, are generally more extensive than those recommended for financial instruments. There are two reasons for the more extensive disclosure:

1. By their nature, strategic investments are intended to extend the reach of the reporting enterprise and to increase the volume of non–arm's length transactions.
2. There are substantial differences between the income effects of strategic investments and their cash flow effects, as has been described in the preceding section.

The least extensive disclosure relates to controlled subsidiaries. When control exists, normal practice is to consolidate the subsidiaries and the parent, with the result that there is a single reporting entity that includes two or more separate legal entities. When the subsidiaries are consolidated, all intercompany transactions are eliminated and the several enterprises are reported as one. Little additional disclosure is required.

Some companies list their consolidated subsidiaries in their annual reports, but this is a voluntary disclosure. Most companies do not tell the readers who their subsidiaries are, perhaps because the subsidiaries are so thoroughly integrated into the parent's operations that their existence is irrelevant to most statement users.

If one company acquired another company during the accounting period—a business combination—the parent company must disclose the transaction and the amounts of the identifiable assets and liabilities that were acquired. The amount and form of consideration given for the purchase must also be disclosed, such as cash, common shares, preferred shares, long-term debt, etc. Only the amount of cash consideration is shown on the face of the cash flow statement, however.

Joint ventures are reported on the basis of proportionate consolidation. The notes to the consolidated statements should disclose summary financial amounts for interests in joint ventures, such as total current assets and long-term assets, current and long-term liabilities, major components of net income, and major categories of cash flow.[1]

The disclosures recommended by the *CICA Handbook* for investments in significantly influenced investees are quite extensive. They include disclosure of

- The amount of investment in significantly influenced companies.
- The basis of reporting each investment (i.e., cost or equity).
- The income from investments in significantly influenced investees, reported separately from other investment income.

In practice, compliance with these recommendations is uneven. Materiality undoubtedly plays a role, since a company may well have investments that confer significant influence but that constitute a small portion of the reporting enterprise's operations.

CASH FLOW STATEMENT

Companies often make short-term investments in highly liquid financial instruments such as certificates of deposit, guaranteed investment certificates, or treasury bills. This type of investment is a temporary use of cash in order to earn a return when the company has a temporary excess of cash. In Chapter 5, we pointed out that if such financial instruments are considered to be *cash equivalents*, they are included in the definition of cash when the cash flow statement is prepared. Consequently, investments in cash equivalents do not appear in the cash flow statement, but instead are included in the cash balance.

For other investments in debt and equity securities, the cash flow impacts occur in three ways:

1. There is a cash outflow when an investment is purchased.
2. Cash payments are received by the investor (dividends or interest).
3. Cash is received when the investment is sold or is redeemed at maturity.

For most investments, the initial cash outflow is reported as an investing activity on the cash flow statement in the period that the investment is made. If securities are held for trading, they are analogous to inventory, and related cash flows are classified as operating (*CICA* 1540.17).

When the recorded values of available-for-sale investments or trading investment changes because of changes in fair value, this is a non-cash event; it does not appear on the cash flow statement. For trading investments, gains and losses on the income statement are adjusted as non-cash amounts. For available-for-sale investments, other comprehensive income is affected, but no adjustments are needed on the cash flow statement.

On sale, the net cash proceeds that the company receives when it sells or redeems an investment security are reported as a positive (inflow) amount in the investing activities section of the cash flow statement. Any gain or loss on disposal must be removed from net income when computing the operating cash flow, since a gain or loss is merely the difference between the cash proceeds and the investment's carrying value at the time of the sale. Note also that premium or discount amortization in investment income if the investment is held to maturity are also non-cash items, and must be included as a reconciliation item in the operating activities section.

Reporting the periodic cash flows for dividends received on strategic investments presents a somewhat greater challenge. If the investment is being reported on the equity basis, then

1. Cash received in dividends must be reported on the cash flow statement, as cash flow from investment revenue.

[1] The difference between the price paid for the investment and the underlying net book value of the investee's net assets, and the accounting treatment (e.g., amortization policies) for the difference.

2. The investor's share of the investee's earnings must be removed from net income when calculating the operating cash flow.

If the strategic investment gives the investor control over the investee and the parent prepares consolidated statements, the cash flows between the parent and subsidiary are eliminated in consolidation and do not appear on the cash flow statement at all. A consolidated cash flow statement is prepared.

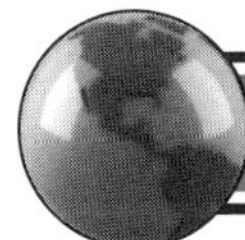

International Perspective

FAIR VALUE METHOD Both the United States and the IASC require that securities be remeasured to fair value at each balance sheet date, except for debt securities that are being held to maturity and for situations where there is significant influence or control. As with the new Canadian rules, unrealized holding gains and losses on available-for-sale investments are included in other comprehensive income until realization. Thus, the 2004 Canadian rules are a step toward international harmonization.

CONSOLIDATION Accounting for investments is an area where there are significant differences between Canadian accounting rules and those of many other countries. Many European companies do not consolidate or include the earnings of unconsolidated subsidiaries on an equity basis in their earnings. Moreover, when the operations of a business segment do not go as well as planned, many countries allow the parent to transfer those operations to an unconsolidated subsidiary. Thus, the income statements and balance sheets of many foreign companies will not provide the same kind of information as those of Canadian-based companies.

The European Union (E.U.) has a priority for standardizing the financial reporting among its member countries. In particular, the E.U.'s Seventh Directive requires firms to provide consolidated statements that include controlled subsidiaries. Consolidated statements are considered as supplementary statements; however; the unconsolidated, separate-entity statements are the primary statements. The E.U. is also moving toward requiring use of the equity method for investments in which the investor has a significant influence, where significant influence is defined similarly to Canadian GAAP.

SIGNIFICANT INFLUENCE Canadian standards for strategic investments are substantially in line with the recommendations of the IASC. The United States, however, has different classification standards. Significant influence is rigidly defined in the United States as ownership of between 20% and 50% of the outstanding equity of the investee; other factors that shape an investee's influence are ignored.

SUMMARY OF KEY POINTS

1. Companies invest in the securities of other entities for a variety of reasons, including increasing return on idle funds, active trading of an investment portfolio, long-term investments for earnings generation, creating strategic alliances, and creating appropriate legal vehicles for business activities.
2. Appropriate accounting for investments is determined by the substance of the investment vehicle, and also the intent of the investor. Differential reporting can be adopted by non-public organizations in this area.
3. Investments must be classified as held to maturity, available for sale, trading, control, significant influence, or joint ventures.
4. Held-to-maturity investments are accounted for using the cost method. The security is recorded at cost and interest revenue is accrued as time passes. If the investments are purchased at a premium or discount from face value, the premium or discount should is amortized to income over the life of the investment.

5. Available-for-sale investments are accounted for using the fair value method, where the investment is remeasured at current fair value at each balance sheet date. Gains or losses are recognized in other comprehensive income (shareholders' equity) until the investment is sold, when the cumulative realized amount is recorded in net income.
6. Trading investments are accounted for using the fair value method, where the investment is remeasured at current fair value at each balance sheet date. Gains or losses are recognized in net income immediately.
7. Held-to-maturity and available-for-sale investments are subject to impairment tests, where a permanent decline in value is recorded as a loss, which is not reversed.
8. Long-term investments in equity instruments are classified according to the power of the investor within the corporate governance structure of the investee. If the investor controls the investee, the investment is a subsidiary, and is consolidated. If the investor has power but does not have control without the cooperation of others, there is a significant influence investment that must be accounted for using the equity method
9. If a non-public organization adopts differential reporting, a significant influence investment may be reported at cost, and controlled investments and joint ventures accounted for with cost or equity methods.
10. Investments that are acquired in a foreign currency must be reported on the investor's books at their equivalent cost in Canadian dollars, using the exchange rate in effect at the time of the purchase. Investments in debt instruments that are denominated in a foreign currency must be restated to their current equivalent amount in Canadian dollars at each balance sheet date. Exchange gains and losses are recognized in income immediately.
11. In the equity method, the investment is first recorded at cost, but the balance of the investment account changes to reflect the investor's proportionate share of the investee's adjusted earnings, losses, and dividends. Investment revenue includes the investor's share of profits (or losses), less amortizations of fair values present at acquisition, goodwill writedowns, and elimination of unrealized intercompany profits.
12. Consolidation requires combining the financial statements of the parent and the subsidiary at reporting dates.
13. Under purchase accounting, the parent consolidates the fair values of identifiable assets and liabilities. Any excess of the purchase price above the fair values of the assets is recorded as goodwill.
14. When statements are consolidated, all intercompany transactions and any unrealized profits are eliminated. The portion of the subsidiary that is not owned by the parent is reflected in the consolidated statements as a non-controlling or minority interest.
15. Investments may be reclassified from one category to another. The reclassification generally takes place at the prior carrying value, and any gains and losses are subject to specific rules depending on the reclassification category.
16. Investments are classified as current assets on the balance sheet if they are temporary; otherwise, they are long term.
17. Significant disclosure is needed for investments. Exact disclosures vary depending on how the investment is classified.
18. The cash flow statement reflects cash paid for investments, cash received on sale, and cash received as investment income. Non-cash gains and losses, and premium and discount amortization, are adjusted in operations when the indirect method of presentation is used.
19. IASC, Canadian, and U.S. rules for investments to be carried at cost or fair value are generally harmonized.
20. There are radically different requirements governing consolidation around the world. This is an area that requires careful examination of reporting policies when analyzing financial statements.

KEY TERMS

available-for-sale investment, 611
consolidation, 617
control, 611
controlled investment, 611
cost method, 614
differential reporting, 617
discount, 621
downstream profits, 637
effective interest amortization method, 622
equity method, 616
fair value, 616
fair value method, 615
financial instruments, 609
held-to-maturity investments, 610
impairment, 625
joint venture, 613
non-controlling interest, 639
other comprehensive income, 629
parent company, 612
passive investment, 609
premium, 621
proportionate consolidation, 617
realized holding gain, 615
significant influence investment, 612
straight-line amortization, 622
strategic investment, 609
subsidiary company, 612
temporary investment, 641
trading investment, 611
unrealized holding gains, 615
unremitted earnings, 616
upstream profits, 637

REVIEW PROBLEM

On 1 January F20X5, Acme Fruit Company has the following investments:

	Net Carrying Value at 1 January 20X5
Available-for-sale investments:	
Apple (2,000 common shares)	$19,000
Quince (10,000 common shares)	50,000
Cherry (5,000 common shares)	40,000

Other comprehensive income, on the balance sheet, includes a $5,000 unrealized loss with respect to the Apple shares, a $5,000 unrealized gain with respect to the Quince shares, and a $2,000 unrealized gain with respect to the Cherry shares.

Assume that there are no income taxes.
The following transactions and reclassifications occur during the year:

a. On 1 February 20X5, Acme purchases $30,000 of face amount bonds issued by Plum Incorporated for $29,500 plus accrued interest. The bonds have a coupon rate of 8%, pay interest semi-annually on 30 June and 31 December, and mature on 31 December 20X9. The investment is classified as held to maturity. Straight-line amortization of the discount is appropriate.
b. Dividends of $0.75 per share are received on the Apple common shares on 30 May.
c. Interest on the Plum bonds is received on 30 June and 31 December.
d. On 1 July, the Quince shares are sold for $58,000. The proceeds are used to buy 1,000 Banana Company shares for $40 per share.
e. On 30 November, Apple shares are sold for $21,000.
f. At 31 December, the market values of the various investments are determined to be as follows:

ii. Cherry common	$ 57,500
ii. Banana common	23,000
iii. Plum bonds (excluding accrued interest)	31,000

The decline in value of the Banana Company shares is deemed to be an impairment.

g. The Cherry and Banana shares are temporary investments at year-end, while the Plum bonds are long term.

Required:

1. What amount of investment income or loss, from all sources, is shown on the income statement for 20X5?
2. Show the change in other comprehensive income for the year, and the equity balances within other comprehensive income that would be reported at the end of 20X5.
3. Show the accounts and amounts related to the investments that are reported in the assets section of the 20X5 balance sheet of Acme Fruit Company.

REVIEW PROBLEM—SOLUTION

1. Investment income

Plum bonds:		
Interest: $30,000 × 8% × 11/12	$2,200	
Discount amortization: $500 × 11/59	93	$2,293
Apple dividends: 2,000 shares × $0.75		1,500
Gain on sale of Quince shares ($8,000 + $5,000)		13,000
Loss on sale of Apple shares ($2,000 − $5,000)		(3,000)
Impairment loss on Banana shares ($23,000 − $40,000)		(17,000)
Total investment income (loss)		$ (3,207)

2. Change in other comprehensive income, 20X5:

Elimination of unrealized loss on Apple shares	$ 5,000
Elimination of unrealized gain on Quince shares	(5,000)
New unrealized gain on Cherry shares	17,500
Change in other comprehensive income in 20X5	$17,500
Other comprehensive income, balance sheet, 31 December, 20X5	
Unrealized gain on Cherry shares ($2,000 + $17,500)*	$19,500

3. Investment assets at 31 December 20X5

Temporary investments ($57,500 + $23,000)	$ 80,500
Long-term investments	$ 29,593

* Also, opening balance of $2,000, net, plus $17,500 increase in 20X5.

APPENDIX

Consolidation Illustration

The main body of this chapter explained the general principles underlying consolidation but did not demonstrate a consolidation because of the complexities that quickly arise. This Appendix, however, does provide a simple demonstration of a consolidation following a business combination for those readers who are interested in how the numbers fit together. The final section of the Appendix briefly addresses the issue of consolidating foreign subsidiaries.

BASIC ILLUSTRATION

P Company bought 80% of the voting shares of S Company one year ago for $4,700,000. The other 20% of S Company shares are owned by a small group of S Company top management. P Company controls S Company by virtue of its voting control and must consolidate its financial statements at the end of each fiscal period. Refer to the financial statements shown in the first two columns of Exhibit 11A-1, which are at the end of the first year of ownership.

During the year, P Company used the cost method of recording the investment, and thus the investment account is still recorded at $4,700,000. P Company shows $80,000 of other income on its income statement; S Company had declared $100,000 of dividends, which were paid $80,000 to P Company and $20,000 to the other shareholders.

As of the date of acquisition, S Company had net assets (that is, assets minus liabilities) of $3,782,000 at book value. By definition, this is equal to shareholders' equity on the date of acquisition. There was $140,000 in the common shares account, and $3,642,000 in retained earnings, to equal $3,782,000. P Company would determine the fair value of net assets on this date, through appraisal and other examination. Assume that fair values were equal to book values except for capital assets with a 10-year life, which were worth $1,000,000 more than book value. There was no impairment of goodwill by the end of the first year of acquisition.

During the year, S Company had sales of $4,000,000 to P Company All the goods had been resold to other customers, except goods for which P Company had paid $300,000, which were still in inventory. These items had cost S Company $200,000. Finally, P Company owed $175,000 to S Company at year-end.

GOODWILL The goodwill on acquisition is calculated as follows:

Purchase price		$4,700,000
Less: Market value acquired		
Book value	$3,782,000	
Market value increment	1,000,000	
Total	$4,782,000	
P Co. share	80%	(3,825,600)
Goodwill		$ 874,400

Notice that 80% of S Company was purchased and thus 80% is used in the calculation.

ELIMINATION ENTRIES Most of what happens in a consolidation is that the two sets of financial statements are added together. However, entries are needed for a variety of things.

1. **Investment elimination entry** This is a busy entry, as it eliminates the equity accounts of the subsidiary on the date of acquisition, eliminates the parent's investment account, sets up the non-controlling interest on the date of acquisition, and recognizes fair value differences and goodwill inherent in the purchase price.

Common shares (S Co.)	140,000	
Retained earnings (S Co.)	3,642,000	
Capital assets ($1,000,000 × 80%)	800,000	
Goodwill	874,400	
Investment in S Co.		4,700,000
Non-controlling interest ($3,782,000 × 20%)		756,400

The non-controlling interest account is a balance sheet account that is typically classified between long-term debt and shareholders' equity. It is the portion of the subsidiary's net assets—equity—owned by shareholders other than the parent. This account often is called "minority interest."

2. **Amortization entry** Next, accounts created in the investment elimination entry must be amortized to reflect the passage of time, one year in this case. Assuming amortization over 10 years for the capital assets:

Amortization expense	80,000	
Capital assets, net ($800,000 ÷ 10)		80,000

If any goodwill was impaired, it would be recorded in a similar manner: an expense would be debited and goodwill credited.

3. **Dividend entry** S Company paid dividends to its shareholders, and these are recorded in its books. Assuming that P Company uses the cost method for recording the investment, the dividend paid to the majority shareholder is recorded as dividend revenue on the parent's income statement, while the dividend paid to the non-controlling shareholders reduces their interest in remaining net assets on the subsidiary. After this elimination, the only dividends left are those paid to the shareholders of P Company.

Dividend revenue	80,000	
Non-controlling interest	20,000	
Dividends declared		100,000

4. **Intercompany balances and transactions elimination entries** These amounts are eliminated so that all that remains on the consolidated accounts are transactions that the consolidated entity has had with outside parties. Note that the entries do not change net income or net assets; they simply deflate offsetting components.

Sales	4,000,000	
Cost of sales		4,000,000
Accounts payable	175,000	
Accounts receivable		175,000

5. **Intercompany unrealized profit eliminations** Inventory on the books of the parent is recorded at $300,000, when it has a cost to the consolidated entity of $200,000. The $100,000 overstatement must be eliminated, and the corresponding overstatement of the subsidiary's net income must be corrected.

Cost of sales	100,000	
Inventory		100,000

The debit to cost of sales reduces income. This entry creates a temporary difference between accounting and taxable income, and should result in an adjustment to tax expense and the balance sheet tax future (deferred) income tax account; this tax entry has been omitted in the interests of simplicity.

6. **Non-controlling interest share of income** The non-controlling (or minority) interest has been allocated its share of equity and subsidiary dividends, but they also have an interest in the earnings of the subsidiary for the current period ($254,000), at least to the extent that these earnings have been confirmed by transactions with outside parties ($254,000 – $100,000). Thus, the non-controlling interest's share in confirmed subsidiary profits is allocated to them by creating an "expense" on the income statement that increases the non-controlling interest element on the balance sheet. This works much the same way as a debit to wages expense increases the wages payable account, if wages have not yet been paid.

Provision for non-controlling interest (I/S)	30,800	
Non-controlling interest (B/S) ($154,000 × 20%)		30,800

All these entries are posted to the worksheet. The final step in the consolidation worksheet is to cross-add each account line, giving effect to the adjustments and eliminations above, as is illustrated in the final column of Exhibit 11A-1. The final column provides the amounts that are used to prepare the consolidated financial statements.

Be sure to remember that all of the consolidation entries are worksheet entries only. The entries listed above do not get recorded on any company's books.

Foreign Subsidiaries

The procedure illustrated above is the same for all subsidiaries. However, an additional complication arises when the subsidiary is in a foreign country. The subsidiary's financial statements will be in a foreign currency, and must be restated to Canadian dollars before consolidation can occur. Because exchange rates change, the net asset value of the subsidiary will be different at each year-end, even if there has been no change in the assets and liabilities. Thus, a gain or loss will arise simply from the mechanics of the foreign currency translation and consolidation process. This cumulative gain or loss is a component of other comprehensive income, accumulated in shareholders' equity.

EXHIBIT 11A-1

CONSOLIDATION WORKSHEET

	P. Co.	S. Co.	Consolidation Elimination Entries	P. Co. + S. Co. Consolidated Results
Cash	$ 460,000	$ 64,000		$ 524,000
Accounts receivable	2,390,000	790,000	(4) 175,000 cr.	3,005,000
Inventory	4,910,000	1,700,000	(5) 100,000 cr.	6,510,000
Capital assets, net	8,224,000	4,622,000	(1) 800,000 dr.	
			(2) 80,000 cr.	13,566,000
Investment in S. Co.	4,700,000	–	(1) 4,700,000 cr.	0
Intangible assets	400,000	–	(1) 874,400 dr.	1,274,400
Totals	$21,084,000	$ 7,176,000		$24,879,400
Current liabilities	$ 5,320,000	$1,100,000	(4) 175,000 dr.	$ 6,245,000
Long-term debt	8,100,000	1,500,000		9,600,000
Future income taxes	1,050,000	640,000		1,690,000
Non-controlling interest	–	–	(1) 756,400 cr.	
			(3) 20,000 dr.	
			(6) 30,800 cr.	767,200
Common shares	2,600,000	140,000	(1) 140,000 dr.	2,600,000
Retained earnings	4,014,000	3,796,000	from below	3,977,200
Totals	$21,084,000	$ 7,176,000		$24,879,400
Sales	$16,800,000	$9,300,000	(4) 4,000,000 dr.	$22,100,000
Cost of sales	9,900,000	4,216,000	(4) 4,000,000 cr.	
			(5) 100,000 dr.	10,216,000
Operating expenses	5,650,000	4,590,000	(2) 80,000 dr.	10,320,000
Other income	80,000	–	(3) 80,000 dr.	0
Income tax expense	560,000	240,000		800,000
Non-controlling interest	–	–	(6) 30,800 dr.	30,800
Net income	$ 770,000	$ 254,000		$ 733,200
Opening retained earnings	3,454,000	$3,642,000	(1) 3,642,000 dr.	3,454,000
Dividends	210,000	100,000	(3) 100,000 cr.	210,000
Closing retained earnings	$ 4,014,000	$3,796,000	0	$ 3,977,200

SUMMARY OF KEY POINTS

1. Goodwill is measured as the amount by which the purchase price (of a purchased subsidiary) exceeds the fair value of the subsidiary's identifiable assets at the date of acquisition, for the portion of the shares purchased by the parent company.
2. Consolidation is performed on worksheets; there are no entries in either the parent's or the subsidiary's books.
3. When a subsidiary is purchased, the cost of the acquisition is recorded in an investment account on the parent's books.
4. When the subsidiary's financial statements are consolidated with those of the parent, the investment account is eliminated, and instead all of the assets and liabilities of the subsidiary are added to the parent's on the balance sheet. Any offsetting balances between the parent and the subsidiary are eliminated against the other.
5. Amortization of the subsidiary's assets is based on fair value. Goodwill is not amortized, but must be written down if its value is impaired.
6. All of the revenues and expenses of the subsidiary are added to those of the parent on the parent's consolidated income statement. Intercompany transactions are eliminated, to avoid double-counting, and any unrealized profits are eliminated.
7. If the parent does not own all of the subsidiary, the proportion of the subsidiary's net asset book value that is not owned by the parent is reported by the parent on its balance sheet as a credit, placed below liabilities but before shareholders' equity.
8. The minority interest's proportionate share of the subsidiary's net income is deducted on the parent's consolidated income statement, to offset the fact that all of the subsidiary's revenues and expenses have been combined with the parent's.
9. The account balances of foreign subsidiaries must be translated into Canadian dollars before they can be consolidated. Exchange rate movement causes translation gains and losses, which are accounted for differently depending on whether the subsidiary is integrated or self-sustaining.

QUESTIONS

Q11-1 Why do companies invest in the securities of other enterprises?

Q11-2 Distinguish between debt and equity securities.

Q11-3 How can a debt investment be classified? An equity investment? How should each category be accounted for?

Q11-4 What criteria must be met for an investment to be classified as held to maturity? Trading? Available for sale?

Q11-5 Why are held-to-maturity investments carried at amortized cost but available-for-sale and trading investments carried at fair value?

Q11-6 What is the difficulty encountered in relying on management intent as a classification criteria?

Q11-7 What factors indicate that significant influence may be present between an investor and an investee? How would such an investment be reported?

Q11-8 What factors indicate that control exists between an investor and an investee? How would such an investment be reported?

Q11-9 It is often said that an investor with 20% of the voting shares of another company has significant influence, and an investor with 50% has control. Is this always true?

Q11-10 What is the distinguishing feature of a joint venture? How are joint ventures accounted for?

Q11-11 How is fair value estimated?

Q11-12 On 1 August 20X4, Baker Company purchased $50,000 face amount of Sugar Company 6% coupon value bonds for $43,200. The market interest rate was 8% on this date. The bond pays interest semi-annually on 31 July and 31 January. At the fiscal year-end for Baker, the bonds have a market value of $45,000. Show the journal entries (a) to record the investment and (b) to record investment income and any other needed adjustments at 31 December. The investment is classified as held to maturity and the effective interest amortization method is used.

Q11-13 When is it permissible to use straight-line amortization of a discount or premium on a held-to-maturity investment? Explain.

Q11-14 Under what circumstances is it appropriate under GAAP to account for a significant influence investment using the cost method? Explain.

Q11-15 An investor purchased 100 shares of Zenics at $20 per share on 15 March 20X4. At the end of the 20X4 accounting period, 31 December 20X4, the stock was quoted at $19 per share. On 5 June 20X5, the investor sold the stock for $22 per share. Assuming this investment is available for sale, give the journal entry to be made at each of the following dates:

- 15 March 20X4
- 31 December 20X4
- 5 June 20X5

Q11-16 What conditions may indicate that the value of an investment has been impaired? How is an impairment accounted for if the investment is held to maturity? Available for sale? Trading?

Q11-17 On 31 December 20X1, ABC Company owned 10,000 shares of A Company, with a cost of $23 per share and a market value of $24 per share. The shares were purchased in 20X1. At the end of 20X2, the market value was $28 per share. The investment was sold in 20X3 at $30 per share. The investment is classified as available for sale. What would be included in other comprehensive income and net income in each of 20X1, 20X2, and 20X3?

Q11-18 On 31 December 20X1, XYZ Company owned 10,000 shares of B Company, with a cost of $21 per share and a market value of $26 per share. The shares were purchased in 20X1. At the end of 20X2, the market value was $29 per share. The investment was sold in 20X3 at $33 per share. The investment is classified as a trading investment. What would be included in other comprehensive income and net income in each of 20X1, 20X2, and 20X3?

Q11-19 The 31 December 20X3 balance sheet shows available-for-sale investments at $456,800, and cumulative other comprehensive income at $169,000. Interpret these two values. At what amount were the investments originally purchased?

Q11-20 An available-for-sale investment is carried at $550,000, and there is a cumulative gain of $35,000 recorded in other comprehensive income. The investment is sold for $520,000. What gain or loss is included in net income because of the sale? What amount is included in this year's other comprehensive income because of the sale? Explain.

Q11-21 On 1 July 20X2, a company bought an investment in IBM bonds for U.S.$50,000 when the exchange rate was U.S.$1 = Cdn.$1.32. The investment is classified as available for sale. The company paid cash on the acquisition date. At 31 December, the exchange rate was U.S.$1 = Cdn.$1.38. The market value was still U.S.$50,000. Prepare journal entries to record the purchase of bonds and any adjusting entries at year-end.

Q11-22 Assume that Company R acquired, as a long-term investment, 30% of the outstanding voting common shares of Company S at a cash cost of $100,000. At the date of acquisition, the balance sheet of Company S showed net assets and total shareholders' equity of $250,000. The market value of the depreciable assets of Company S was $20,000 greater than their net book value at date of R's acquisition. Compute goodwill purchased, if any.

Q11-23 Assume the same facts as in Q11-22, with the addition that net assets that were undervalued at acquisition have a remaining estimated life of 10 years (assume no residual value and straight-line depreciation). There is no goodwill impairment. How much investment revenue would Company R report using the equity method if Company S reported $80,000 of net income?

Q11-24 Investor Limited owns 35% of Machines Limited, and has significant influence. The investment was made five years ago, when Machine's fair values equalled book values; $40,000 of goodwill was inherent in the purchase price. Goodwill is not impaired. In the current fiscal year, Machines reported $225,000 in income. This includes a $50,000 profit on inventory sold to Investor Limited, which Investor has not yet resold. How much investment revenue will Investor report using the equity method? How would your answer change if Investor had reported the sale of inventory to Machines?

Q11-25 What accounts appear in the consolidated financial statements that are not present in either the parent's or the subsidiary's financial statements? Explain each item. What accounts always disappear from the unconsolidated financial statements?

Q11-26 Equity income, and consolidated income, is usually lower than one would predict by simply adding the investor's income and the pro-rata share of the investee's income. Why does this happen?

Q11-27 Under what circumstances is an investment reclassified from held to maturity to available for sale? What are the ramifications of the transfer? How is the transfer accounted for?

Q11-28 Under what circumstances is an investment reclassified from available for sale to held to maturity? How is the cumulative other comprehensive income amount accounted for?

Q11-29 Under what circumstances is an investment reclassified from significant influence to available for sale? How is the transfer accounted for?

Q11-30 In many European countries, companies are not required to consolidate subsidiaries. Why might this be the case?

CASE 11-1
MacKay Industries Limited

MacKay Industries Limited (MIL) is a Canadian company that manufactures leather furniture. Sales in 20X3 were $265 million, with strong exports to the United States. MIL is the leading Canadian manufacturer of leather furniture, and is ranked fourth in this category in the U.S. market. While MIL has, in the past, had manufacturing facilities in the United States, difficulties in quality control and logistics have recently convinced the owner to centralize all operations in Niagara Falls, Canada. The plant employs 250 workers.

MIL is a private company. The majority of shares are held by the president and CEO, Jeff MacKay, who inherited the business from his father. The firm was founded by Mr. MacKay's grandfather. The remainder of the shares are held by members of the MacKay family. MIL has substantial long-term bank financing in place, secured by company assets and the personal guarantees of Jeff MacKay and key family members.

MacKay himself is a graduate of Harvard Business School and is well regarded in the industry. He focuses on marketing and strategy, and usually leaves operations to his production managers, all of whom receive a bonus based on overall company profits.

You, a professional accountant in public practice, review the annual financial statements of the company, prepare the tax returns, and provide advice on a wide range of issues, including financing, tax, personnel, and accounting policy.

You have been asked to look at the investment portfolio of MIL, and comment on appropriate accounting. Mr. Mackay is aware that rules have recently changed in the investments area, and he'd like a summary of how his investments should be accounted for.

Investments can be summarized as follows:

1. *Short-term investments*
MIL has excess cash tied up in short-term investments at various times of the year. This money is often invested in Treasury bills, but may also be invested in common shares of public companies, if MacKay feels there is an opportunity to earn capital appreciation.

2. *Hyperion*
MIL bought 4,000 shares of Hyperion, an aircraft engine manufacturer, two years ago, for $43 per share. The investment is recorded at cost. Hyperion has 490,000 common shares outstanding, of which 20,000 to 40,000 change hands annually. Mr. MacKay is a personal friend of the president and CEO of this small public company. No dividends have been declared on the shares. The stock price quoted at the end of last year was $42. This year, market values have been in the $33–$35 range. Mr. MacKay has stated that he would not consider selling the investment unless market values return to $43. Mr. MacKay is confident that this will be the case sometime in the next five years.

3. *March Limited*
Mr. MacKay (personally) is the sole shareholder of March Limited, which he incorporated two years ago. The Boards of Directors for March Limited and MIL are almost identical. March is engaged in researching new imitation leather fabrics, and ways of chemically treating real leather to improve its quality. Throughout the last two years, March has spent $216,000 on these activities. All this amount is financed by MIL; Mr. MacKay himself has put no money into March Limited other than a token investment to create share capital. MIL reports the $216,000 as a long-term receivable. It has no stated interest rate or term, and will be repaid only when marketable fabrics are developed by March Limited.

4. *Kusak Limited*
MIL owns a $500,000, 10-year bond issued by Kusak Limited. Kusak is a public company and this bond is publicly traded. MIL bought the bond for $412,700, plus accrued interest. MIL will hold the bond until maturity, although if funds are needed for operating or capital purposes during that time, the bond would certainly be sold.

5. *DML Corporation*
MIL owns 19,975 (2%) of the voting common shares of DML Corporation, a French furniture manufacturer that MacKay may use to enter the European market sometime in the future. Five years ago, MIL bought notes payable and preferred shares in the company. This year, the notes and preferred shares were exchanged for the common shares pursuant to an agreement signed when the notes and preferred shares were acquired. On the exchange date, the notes and preferred shares had a book value of $175,000, and this value was used to record the common shares. Their market value was indeterminable on that date because the securities were never traded. Common shares, thinly traded over the counter, have sold for $7–$9 in the last 12 months.
MIL has one member on the 18-seat Board of Directors of DML Corporation. Mr. MacKay himself attends these meetings, and reports that he is well regarded in debate. Mr. MacKay usually takes a bilingual advisor with him, as proceedings take place in French, a language in which Mr. MacKay is not fluent. In the past year, DML reported a marginal net income; the company has never declared dividends.

Required:

Prepare a report summarizing investment accounting policies as they apply to MIL's investments.

CASE 11-2
Jackson Capital Incorporated

Jackson Capital Incorporated (JCI) is a new private investment company that provides capital to business ventures. JCI's business mission is to support companies to allow them to compete successfully in domestic and international markets. JCI aims to increase the value of its investments, thereby creating wealth for its shareholders.

Funds to finance the investments were obtained through a private offering of share capital, conventional long-term loans payable, and a bond issue that is indexed to the TSX Composite. Annual operating expenses are expected to be $1 million before bonuses, interest, and taxes.

Over the past year, JCI has accumulated a diversified investment portfolio. Depending on the needs of the borrower, JCI provides capital in many different forms, including demand loans, short-term equity investments, fixed-term loans, and loans convertible into share capital. JCI also purchases preferred and common shares in new business ventures where JCI management anticipates a significant return. Any excess funds not committed to a particular investment are held temporarily in money market funds.

JCI has hired three investment managers to review financing applications. These managers visit the applicants' premises to meet with management and review the operations and business plans. They then prepare a report stating their reasons for supporting or rejecting the application. JCI's senior executives review these reports at their monthly meetings and decide whether to invest and what types of investments to make.

Once the investments are made, the investment managers are expected to monitor the investments and review detailed monthly financial reports submitted by the investees. The investment managers' performance bonuses are based on the returns generated by the investments they have recommended.

It is 1 August 20X2. JCI's first fiscal year ended on 30 June 20X2. JCI's draft balance sheet and other financial information are provided in Exhibit I. An annual audit of the financial statements is required under the terms of the bond issue. Potter & Cook, Chartered Accountants, has been appointed auditor of JCI. The partner on the engagement is Richard Potter. You are the in-charge accountant on this engagement. Mr. Potter has asked you to prepare a memo discussing the significant accounting issues raised.

Required:
Prepare the memo requested by Mr. Potter.

JACKSON CAPITAL, INCORPORATED
DRAFT BALANCE SHEET

As of 30 June 20X2

(in thousands of dollars)	
Assets	
Cash and marketable securities	$ 1,670
Investments (at cost)	21,300
Interest receivable	60
Furniture and fixtures (net of accumulated amortization of $2)	50
	$23,080
Liabilities	
Accounts payable and accrued liabilities	$ 20
Accrued interest payable	180
Loans payable	12,000
	$12,200

Shareholders' equity	
Share capital	12,000
Deficit	(1,120)
	10,880
	$23,080

JACKSON CAPITAL INCORPORATED
SUMMARY OF INVESTMENT PORTFOLIO

As at 30 June 20X2

Investment	*Cost of Investment*
15% common share interest in Fairex Resource Inc., a company listed on the TSX Venture Exchange. Management intends to monitor the performance of this mining company over the next six months to make a hold/sell decision based on reported reserves and production costs.	$3.8 million
25% interest in common shares of Hellon Ltd., a private Canadian real estate company, plus 7.5% convertible debentures with a face value of $2 million, acquired at 98% of maturity value. The debentures are convertible into common shares at the option of the holder.	$6.2 million
5-year loan denominated in Brazilian currency (reals) to Ipanema Ltd., a Brazilian company formed to build a power generating station. Interest at 7% per annum is due semi-annually. 75% of the loan balance is secured by the power generating station under construction. The balance is unsecured. The Brazilian currency is unstable, as is the Brazilian political situation.	$8 million
50,000 stock warrants in Tornado Hydrocarbons Ltd., expiring 22 March 20X4. The underlying common shares trade publicly.	$1.3 million

JACKSON CAPITAL INCORPORATED
CAPITAL STRUCTURE

As at 30 June 20X2

Loans payable

The Company has $2 million in demand loans payable with floating interest rates, and $4 million in loans due 1 September 20X6, with fixed interest rates.

In addition, the Company has long-term 5% stock indexed bonds payable. Interest at the stated rate is to be paid semi-annually, commencing 1 September 20X2. The principal repayment on 1 March 20X7 is indexed to changes in the TSX Composite as follows: the $6 million original balance of the bonds at the issue date of 1 March 20X2 is to be multiplied by the stock index at 1 March 20X7, and then divided by the stock index as at 1 March 20X2. The stock-indexed bonds are secured by the Company's investments.

Share capital

Issued share capital consists of

• 1 million 8% Class A (non-voting) shares redeemable at the holder's option on or after 10 August 20X6	$7 million
• 10,000 common shares	$5 million

(CICA, adapted)

CASE 11-3
Major Developments Corporation

Major Developments Corporation (Major) is a publicly traded company operating primarily in the real estate sector. Major has a 31 March year-end. In 20X5, Major reported revenues of $704 million and after-tax income of $118 million. The company buys and sells commercial real estate properties, invests in various securities in the real estate industry, and manufactures commercial elevator components.

Major's common share price climbed steadily from its IPO, in 20X0, until 11 July 20X5. On that date, Bouchard Securities Incorporated. (BS) released a research report on Major that attracted considerable market attention. The report contained the following statements:

> It is our contention that in 20X5, Major clearly violated Canadian generally accepted accounting principles (GAAP), as set out in the *CICA Handbook*. We feel the accounting is wrong, not just aggressive.
>
> Major's accounting for two real estate loans violates GAAP. The company consolidates the assets and results of two corporations to whom it has granted loans when it does not own any shares in these companies.
>
> Also, Major owns 48% of the shares of Rely Holdings, a company that lost $750,000 in its most recent fiscal year. The investment is valued at over $29 million. This makes no sense, since Major bought about half of these shares for $5 million in 20X5. The investment is clearly overvalued.
>
> We feel that Major is overvalued and has poor prospects.

Major's stock had been trading in the $15–$16 range but immediately dropped to around $9. BS profited from the decline in the stock price because it held a significant short position in Major's stock. Within four days, lawyers working for Major launched a legal action against BS, claiming damages plus a full retraction of all statements made.

BS's legal counsel is now examining various courses of action. To help prepare for the case, BS's legal counsel has hired you to provide a report on the validity of each of the parties on the disagreements. They need to be briefed fully in order to properly advise BS. You have obtained some information from Major's 20X5 annual report (see Exhibit 1). Major's lawyers have provided the information in Exhibit 2.

Required:
Prepare a report for Bouchard Securities Incorporated's legal counsel.

EXHIBIT 1

EXTRACTS FROM MAJOR'S 20X5 ANNUAL REPORT

Note 1: Accounting Policies

The consolidated financial statements include the accounts of Major and its majority owned subsidiaries and commencing prospectively in 20X5, the accounts of companies in which Major has no common share ownership, but to which it has advanced loans that are currently in default. The equity method is used for investments in which there is significant influence, considered to be voting ownership of 20% to 50%.

Note 6: Loans in Default

Major granted loans to two related companies, Skyscraper Incorporated and Wenon Corporation, on 18 August 20X0 that are now in default, and have been in default since 20X2. These loans are secured by a first charge on residential real estate buildings, which Major has the legal right to repossess. Major has the intention of such legal action in 20X6. Accordingly, the operating results and net assets associated with these properties have been included in these financial statements.

Note 14: Investments	**20X5**	**20X4**
Rely Holdings Inc.	$29,640,000	$25,000,000

In 20X5, Major purchased an additional 25% interest in Rely Holdings Incorporation. for $5 million. Major now owns 48% of Rely Holdings Incorporated.

EXHIBIT 2

EXTRACTS FROM INFORMATION PROVIDED BY MAJOR'S LAWYERS

Major has a legal opinion that two loans are in default (see Item A below), and a third-party accounting opinion (see Item B below) that this default permits consolidation of those loans.

Item A

In my opinion, the loan to Skyscraper Incorporated and the loan to Wenon Corporation are in default as of 1 February 20X2, under the terms of default of the respective loan agreements, dated 12 August 20X0. The lender has the right under law and contract to repossess these properties, for the purposes of realization of the loans.

—Matthew Krebs, Q.C.

Item B

Based on the facts set out in the attached document, we concur that it is acceptable under Canadian generally accepted accounting principles to consolidate Skyscraper Incorporated and Wenon Corporation.

—Jesse and Mitchell,
Chartered Accountants

(CICA, adapted)

ASSIGNMENTS

A11-1 Investment Classification: Consider the following investment categories:

A. Held-to-maturity investment
B. Available-for-sale investment
C. Trading investment
D. Significant influence investment
E. Control investment
F. Joint venture

An investor company that is a public company has the following items:

1. Sixty-day treasury bill (T-bill).
2. Investment in Nortel common shares bought with idle cash in expectation that the price per share will rise.
3. Investment in Forman Company, a supplier. Forman is a supplier in some financial difficulties. The shares owned amount to 20% of the shares outstanding and allow the investor two seats on the 12-member Board of Directors. Forman will not be paying dividends in the near future. The company is currently recording losses.

4. Investment in Gotcha.com, a dot-com marketing company. The $600,000 investment gives the investor a 7.5% share of the company, and one seat on an 18-member Board. The shares are not publicly traded, but Gotcha has plans to go public. There are no buyers for these shares that could be quickly found, although Gotcha often buys back its own shares if pressured by unhappy shareholders. The investment is highly speculative. Gotcha has never paid dividends.
5. Investment of $6,000,000 in Power Corporation government-guaranteed bonds, 8%, bought at $6,135,000. The securities will be held until maturity.
6. Investment of $6,000,000 in Power Corporation government-guaranteed bonds, 8%, bought at $6,135,000. The securities will be held until the investor needs short-term cash, or until interest rates swing and increase the price of the bonds, whichever comes first.
7. Stratos preferred shares, paying a dividend of $6 per share. The shares are not intended to be sold in the near future
8. Cygnet common shares, representing 80% of outstanding voting shares. The remaining 20% are held by one other shareholder. The 80% investor receives 80% of the dividends declared, and can appoint eight of the 13-member Board of Directors, including the chair. All operating, investing, and financing decisions must be unanimously agreed to by the two shareholders.
9. Investment in bonds, held as part of a portfolio that is actively traded to match the duration of a loan portfolio held by the investor.

Required:

Classify the items above into one of the investment categories, as appropriate. State any assumptions made.

A11-2 Investment Classification: For each situation below, indicate how the investment would be classified, and how it would be accounted for. Assume the investor is a public company.

1. Strip bonds (that is, those sold without interest, or "stripped" of interest) are acquired as a temporary investment. Management expects interest rates to fall and the price of the strip bonds to increase significantly over the coming year.
2. Investment in $500,000 of 10-year bonds, intended to be held to maturity. Another investment in bonds, intended to be held to maturity, was sold last year because interest rate fluctuations made the market price attractive.
3. Common shares are bought in a small, family-owned business. The investor is the only non-family shareholder. The shares constitute 20% of the voting shares and the investor has one member on an eight-member Board of Directors, all of the rest of whom are members of the family investor group. Market values for the shares are not available as they are never sold.
4. A mining property is exchanged for 60% of the voting shares in a company formed to develop the mining property. The remaining 40% of the shares are held by a large mining company that will contribute equipment and expertise to physically mine the site. All decisions regarding operations and financing must be agreed to by both shareholders.
5. Common shares are bought in a large public company, whose shares are broadly held and widely traded. The investor owns 5% of the voting shares, sits on the Board, and is the largest single shareholder. The shares will be held for a long time period, awaiting favourable market price appreciation.
6. Common shares are bought in a large public company whose shares are broadly held and widely traded. The investor owns 45% of the voting shares, puts eight people on a 20-member Board of Directors, and generally has its way in operating, investing, and financing policy of the investee.
7. Common shares are bought in a small, family-owned business. The investor is the only non-family shareholder, but sits on the family-controlled Board. The investor also allows the company to use patented production processes for a fee, a right not previously granted to any other company, and provides $5,000,000 in long-term loans to the investee.

8. To invest idle cash, common shares are bought in a large, public company, a tiny fraction of the outstanding common shares. The share price appreciated after sale, but the investor is convinced that significant additional price appreciation is probable. Therefore, the shares were not sold when cash was needed; the company borrowed from the bank instead, using the shares as collateral.

A11-3 Investment Classification: As of 31 December 20X5, Austin Holdings Limited (a public company) holds a number of investments in the securities of other companies:

1. Austin holds $8,000,000 in bonds of RJR Limited. These bonds will mature in 20X10. Austin intends to hold these bonds to maturity.
2. Austin holds 15% of the voting shares of Broxit Manufacturing Limited. Austin has two members on the 10-member Board of Directors, and has extensive intercompany transactions with Broxit.
3. Austin holds a $1,000,000, 10% bond that matures in 20 years time. Austin will sell this bond if the market price is attractive, or if money is needed for planned expansion.
4. Austin owns 4% of the outstanding common shares of Development Corporation, a company whose shares are thinly traded on the over-the-counter market. Austin would like to sell its shares, but no buyer has been found at the price that Austin is determined to realize.
5. Austin owns .5% of the common shares of ABC Limited, public company, held for short-term capital appreciation.
6. Austin owns 30% of the common shares of Phone Sales Limited. The remaining shares are equally divided among three other investors. Each investor has two representatives on the eight-member Board of Directors. All strategic decisions to date appear to have been suggested and decided by the Austin representatives on the Board of Directors; other representatives are quite passive and often do not attend meetings.
7. Austin owns 60% of the common shares of Info Capital Corporation. The remaining shares are held by the founder, Bill Capital. The six-member Board of Directors consists of four members appointed by Austin, and two appointed by Mr. Capital. All decisions must be unanimously agreed to by the Board members.

Required:

How should Austin account for each of the above investments? Be specific, and explain your reasoning.

A11-4 Cost Method—Debt Investment: The Shepard Hydrant Company purchased $50,000 face amount of Beagle Bugler 9% bonds at a price of 98.5 on 1 January 20X5. The bonds mature on 31 December 20X7, and pay interest annually on 31 December. Shepard uses the straight-line method of amortizing any premium or discount on investments in bonds. At 31 December 20X5 and 20X6, the market value of the bonds is quoted at 98 and 99, respectively.

Required:

1. Show the entry to record the purchase of the bonds.
2. Show the entry(ies) to be made on 31 December 20X5.
3. Show the entry(ies) to be made on 31 December 20X6.
4. Show the income statement and balance sheet items and amounts related to the above investment that would be reported for 20X5 and 20X6.
5. Show any additional disclosure that would be required for this investment.

A11-5 Cost Method—Debt Investment: On 1 July 20X2, New Company purchased $600,000 of Old Corporation 5.5% bonds to be held to maturity. The bonds pay semi-annual interest each 30 June and 31 December. The market interest rate was 5% on the date of purchase. The bonds mature on 30 June 20X5.

Required:

1. Calculate the price paid by New Company.
2. Construct a table that shows interest revenue reported by New, and the carrying value of the investment, for each interest period to maturity. Use the effective interest method.
3. Give entries for the first three interest periods based on your calculations in requirement 2.
4. Construct a table that shows interest revenue reported by New, and the carrying value of the maturity, for each interest period to maturity. Use the straight-line method.
5. Give entries for the first three interest periods based on your calculations in requireement 4.

A11-6 Cost Method—Debt Investment: On 1 May 20X3, Amazon Limited purchased $5,000,000 of Price Limited 6.3% bonds to be held to maturity. The bonds pay semi-annual interest each 1 May and 1 November. The market interest rate was 8% on the date of purchase. The bonds mature on 1 November 20X7.

Required:

1. Calculate the price paid by Amazon Limited.
2. Construct a table that shows interest revenue reported by Amazon, and the carrying value of the investment, for each interest period to maturity. Use the effective interest method.
3. Give entries for 20X3 and 20X4 for Amazon Limited, including adjusting entries at the year-end, which is December 31.
4. Assume that Amazon sold the bonds on 1 February 20X5, for 99 plus accrued interest. Give the entry to record interest income to 1 February, and the entry for the sale.
5. What implications would the sale have on Amazon's ability to classify other bond investments as held-to-maturity investments? Explain.

A11-7 Cost Method—Debt Investment: On 1 July 20X4, Wyder Door Company acquired the following bonds, which Wyder intended to hold to maturity:

Bond	Price	Face Amount Purchased
Flakey Cement 10% bonds, maturity date 31 December 20X9	101.65	$30,000
Green Lawn 8% bonds, maturity date, 31 December 20X6	97.0	20,000

Both bonds pay interest annually on 31 December. Premium and discount will be amortized on a straight-line basis.

Required:

1. Prepare the entry to record acquisition of the investments. Accrued interest was paid on the acquisition dates, as appropriate.
2. Prepare the entries to be made at 31 December 20X4.
3. Show the items and amounts that would be reported in the 20X4 income statement and balance sheet related to these investments.
4. Prepare the entries to be made on 31 December 20X5.
5. Show the items and amounts that would be reported in the 20X5 income statement and balance sheet related to these investments.

A11-8 Cost Method—Debt Investment: On 1 December 20X4, the Chemical Company bought two bond investments, to be held to maturity:

Security	Par Value	Interest Rate	Interest Payable	Maturity Date
A Corp. bonds	$70,000	6%	1 Dec. 1 June	1 Dec. 20X7
B Corp. bonds	100,000	9%	1 Dec. (annual)	1 Dec. 20X12

Chemical's annual reporting period ends on 31 December. At 31 December 20X4, the A Corporation bonds were selling at 98.5 and the B Corporation bonds at 105.

Required:

1. Calculate the price that Chemical would pay for each bond, and record the acquisition. The market interest rate was 8% on 1 December 20X4.
2. Construct a table that shows interest revenue reported by Chemical, and the carrying value of the investment, each interest period to maturity. Use the effective interest method.
3. Show the items that would appear on the 20X5 income statement and balance sheet with respect to the investments.

A11-9 Fair Value Method—Comprehension: At the end of 20X8, CN Limited reported available-for-sale investments on the balance sheet as follows:

Temporary investments:	
First Co. common shares	$456,700
Second Co. common shares	144,900
Shareholders' equity; other comprehensive income:	
First Co. shares, unrealized gain	$ 50,100
Second Co. shares, unrealized loss	8,200

Required:

1. Why are the shares classified as temporary? Under what circumstances would they be classified as long term?
2. What criteria must be met for the shares to be classified as available for sale? Could they, in other circumstances, be classified as held to maturity? Under what circumstances would these shares be trading investments?
3. What price would originally have been paid for the First Co. shares? Second Co. shares?
4. If the decline in value of the Second Co. shares was classified as an impairment, what would change about balance sheet presentation at the end of 20X8?
5. Assume both shares are correctly classified as available for sale and the Second Co. loss was not an impairment. If the First Co. shares are sold for $500,000, and the Second Co. shares are sold for $145,000, what gain or loss is included in net income?

A11-10 Fair Value Method: On 1 November 20X2, Decker Company acquired the following available-for-sale investments:

- X Corporation—500 common shares at $60 cash per share
- Y Corporation—300 preferred shares at $20 cash per share

The annual reporting period ends 31 December.

Quoted market prices on 31 December 20X2 were as follows:

- X Corporation common, $52
- Y Corporation preferred, $24

The following information relates to 20X3:

2 March	Received cash dividends per share as follows:
	X Corporation, $1; and Y Corporation, $0.50.
1 October	Sold 100 shares of Y Corporation preferred at $25 per share.
31 December	Market values were as follows: X common, $46, and Y preferred, $26.

Required:

1. Give the entry for Decker Company to record the purchase of the securities.
2. Give the adjusting entry needed at the end of 20X2.
3. Give the items and amounts that would be reported on the 20X2 income statement, a calculation of the change in other comprehensive income, and asset and equity amounts on the balance sheet.
4. Give all entries required in 20X3.
5. Give the items and amounts that would be reported on the 20X3 income statement, a calculation of the change in other comprehensive income, and asset and equity amounts on the balance sheet.
6. Repeat requirement 5, assuming that the investments are trading investments.

A11-11 Fair Value Method: At 31 December 20X4, the available-for-sale investments of Bertha Company were as follows:

Security	Shares	Unit Cost	Unit Market Price
Preferred shares, $.80 dividend, Ping Corp.	900	$50	$47
Common shares, no-par value, Wilson Corp.	400	15	17

The fiscal year ends 31 December, and these securities were all purchased during 20X4. The transactions that follow all relate to the above equity investments and to those additional investments bought and sold during 20X5.

- 2 February—Received the annual cash dividend from Ping Corporation.
- 1 March—Sold 150 Wilson shares at $22 per share.
- 1 May—Sold 400 Ping shares at $49.50 per share.
- 1 June—Received a cash dividend on Wilson shares of $3.50 per share.
- 1 August—Purchased 6,000 common shares of Dunlop Corporation at $22 per share. This investment is classified as available for sale.

At 31 December 20X5, the quoted market prices were as follows: Ping preferred, $48; Wilson common, $28; and Dunlop common, $24.

Required:

1. Give the entries that Bertha Company should make on 31 December 20X4, to adjust the investments to fair value.
2. Give the entries for all transactions in 20X5.
3. Give the entries required at 31 December 20X5 to adjust investments to fair value.
4. List the items and amounts that should be reported on Bertha's 20X5 income statement and balance sheet. Also calculate the change in other comprehensive income for the year.
5. Repeat part 4, assuming that the investments are trading investments.

A11-12 Fair Value Method: Testco has the following securities classified as available-for-sale investments on 31 December 20X6:

- 3,000 shares of Y Co. common shares, with a fair value of $70,500 and a cumulative unrealized gain of $12,000 in other comprehensive income;
- 10,000 shares of Q Co. common stock, which have a fair value of $546,000 and a cumulative unrealized loss of $34,000 in other comprehensive income; and

- T Co. 8% bonds, $104,000 market value, purchased at par, with a $4,000 cumulative unrealized gain in other comprehensive income.

In 20X7, the following transactions occurred:

a. A dividend of $2 per share was received on the Y Co. shares.
b. 1,000 Y Co. shares were then sold for $ 34,000, less $2,000 in commissions.
c. The annual interest was received on the T Co. bond. ($3,500 of the amount received related to 20X6 and had been accrued at the end of 20X6 as interest receivable.)
d. Purchased 4,000 shares of Z Co. for $53.50 per share, including commission of $1 per share.
e. Late in the year, the T Co. bond was sold for $102,500 plus $3,000 of accrued interest. A $500 commission was paid on the sale.

Market values at the end of the year: Y Co., $15 per share: T Co., $103,000: Q Co., $59 per share; and Z Co., $55 per share.

Required:

1. List the amounts that would appear on the income statement, and the change in other comprehensive income, in 20X7 as a result of these transactions and events.
2. List the items that would appear on the balance sheet at the end of 20X7, including both the investments and the cumulative amount of other comprehensive income.
3. Repeat parts 1 and 2, assuming that the investments are trading investments.

A11-13 Fair Value Method: On 31 December 20X2, Martello Company's portfolio of available-for-sale investments in equity securities was as follows (all purchased on 1 September 20X2):

Security	Shares	Unit Cost	Unit Market
Parker Corp., common shares	50	$120	$70
Monty Corp., $2.40 preferred shares	200	30	32
Bekon Corp., common shares	400	70	73

Transactions relating to this portfolio during 20X3 were as follows:

- 25 January—Received a dividend cheque on the Monty shares.
- 15 April—Sold 30 Parker Corporation shares at $62 per share.
- 25 July—Received a $600 dividend cheque on the Parker shares.
- 31 July—Received a $5 per share dividend on Bekon Corporation shares.
- 1 October—Sold the remaining shares of Parker Corporation at $60 per share.
- 1 December—Purchased 100 Bisset Ltd. common shares at $23 per share plus a $300 brokerage fee. The fee is part of the cost of shares.
- 5 December—Purchased 400 Sanford Corporation common shares at $15 per share.

On 31 December 20X3, the following unit market prices were available: Parker stock, $55; Bekon Corp, $61.25; Monty stock, $38; Bisset stock, $3; and Sanford stock, $16. Martello has determined that the decline in value of the Bisset shares is a permanent impairment.

Required:

1. Give the entries that Martello Company should make on (1) 1 September 20X2, and (2) 31 December 20X2.
2. Give the investment items and amounts that should be reported on the 20X2 income statement, the change in other comprehensive income, and balance sheet accounts.
3. Give the journal entries for 20X3 related to the investments.
4. Give the investment items and amounts that should be reported on the 20X3 income statement, the change in other comprehensive income, and balance sheet accounts.

A11-14 Fair Value Method: During 20X2, Morran Company purchased shares in two corporations and debt securities of a third. The investments are classified as available for sale. Morran is a public company. Transactions in 20X2 include:

a. Purchased 3,000 of the 100,000 common shares outstanding of Front Corporation at $31 per share plus a 4% brokerage fee. The fee is part of the share cost.
b. Purchased 10,000 of 40,000 outstanding preferred shares (non-voting) of Ledrow Corporation at $78 per share plus a 3% brokerage fee. The fee is part of the share cost.
c. Purchased an additional 2,000 common shares of Front Corporation at $35 per share plus a 4% brokerage fee. The fee is part of the share cost.
d. Purchased $400,000 par value of Container Corporation, 9% bonds at 100 plus accrued interest. The purchase is made on 1 November; interest is paid semi-annually on 31 January and 31 July. The bond matures on 31 July 20X7.
e. Received $4 per share cash dividend on the Ledrow Corporation shares.
f. Interest is accrued at the end of 20X2.
g. Fair values at 31 December 20X2: Front shares, $34 per share; Ledrow, $82 per shares; Container Corporation bonds, 98.

Required:

1. Give the entries in the accounts of Morran Company for each transaction.
2. Show how the income statement and balance sheet (including the other comprehensive income account) for Morran Company would report relevant data concerning these investments for 20X2.
3. Repeat requirements 1 and 2, assuming that the investments are trading investments.

A11-15 Impairment: Snelgrove Corporation purchased a $567,800 investment in the common shares of Wood Corporation on 15 July 20X5. Snelgrove was speculating that the value of the Wood common shares might increase dramatically when a major contract bid was accepted. Unfortunately, the bid was rejected, and Wood shares declined in value to $350,400 by the end of 20X5. Snelgrove continued to hold the investment throughout 20X6 and 20X7, waiting for positive developments that would increase share value. The aggregate market value at the end of 20X6 was $360,500 and, for 20X7, $367,100. The shares were finally sold in 20X8 for $380,900.

Required:

1. Assume that the shares were available for sale, and the decline in value in 20X5 was considered an impairment. List the accounts and amounts that would appear on the income statement, the change in other comprehensive income, and account balances on the balance sheet for 20X5 to 20X8, inclusive.
2. Assume that the shares are trading investments, and list the accounts and amounts that would appear on the income statement and the balance sheet for 20X5 to 20X8, inclusive. Why is impairment not an issue for trading investments?
3. What criteria must be met for a decline in value of an available-for-sale investment to be considered permanent? What accounting treatment is given to an impairment?
4. When the market value of an investment, written down because of an impairment, subsequently increases, is the increase in value recorded? Explain.

A11-16 Reclassification: On 31 December 20X2, Woolfrey Company's investments were as follows:

	Carrying Value	Other Comprehensive Income (Cumulative)
Available-for-sale investments		
Logan Corp., common shares	$120,000	$ 44,700 gain
Norman Corp., $5.00 preferred shares	316,000	5,000 gain
Luciano Corp., 8% bonds, $275,000 par value	271,200	14,300 loss
Held-to-maturity investment		
Cashin Ltd. 9% bonds, $500,000 par value	511,000	
Significant influence investment		
Curtis Commercial Ltd.	896,000	

Woolfrey makes formal entries for reclassification.

Required:

1. On this date, the Cashin Ltd. bonds, with a current market value of $550,000, are reclassified as available-for-sale investments. Provide the entry for the reclassification. What are the ramifications of reclassification (and subsequent sale) of a held-to-maturity investment? Explain.
2. Woolfrey reclassifies the Luciano Corp. bonds as a held-to-maturity investment (assume that the transaction in requirement 1 has not taken place and this reclassification is permitted). Give the entry for the reclassification. What accounting is required for the other comprehensive income amount recognized to date?
3. Woolfrey reclassifies the Curtis Commercial Ltd. shares as available for sale. The market value of this investment is estimated to be $1,150,000. Record the reclassification. What accounting is required for the unrealized holding gain?

A11-17 Reclassification: On 31 December 20X6, Kirwan Company's investments in equity securities were as follows:

	Carrying Value	Other Comprehensive Income (Cumulative)
Available-for-sale investments		
Goldhar Corp., common shares	$920,000	$ 34,700 loss
McKinley Corp., common shares	669,700	113,500 gain
Held-to-maturity investment		
Walsh Ltd. 7% bonds, $300,000 par value	297,000	
Significant influence investment		
Orr Ltd.	$1,456,000	

Required:

1. Explain what the carrying value for each investment represents.
2. What was the original cost of each of the available-for-sale investments?
3. Kirwan reclassified the held-to-maturity investment to available for sale on this date, when its market value was $316,000. Explain how the reclassification will be reflected in the financial statements.
4. Kirwan reclassifies the Orr common shares as an available-for-sale investment when the market value is $1,568,500. What accounting is required for this reclassification?

A11-18 Basket Purchase of Securities: On 1 December 20X4, Voss Company purchased stock in the three different companies listed below for a lump sum of $114,000, including commissions. They will be held as long-term available-for-sale investments.

N Corporation, common shares, 300 shares.
O Corporation, preferred shares, 400 shares.
P Corporation, common shares, 500 shares.

At the time of purchase, the shares were quoted on the local over-the-counter stock market at the following prices per share: N common, $100; O preferred, $120; and P common, $84.

Required:

1. Give the entry to record the purchase of these investments. Record each stock in a separate account and show the cost per share.
2. How would your response to part 1 change if there was no market value available for the P Corporation common shares?

A11-19 Investments and Foreign Currency: On 14 June 20X4, Jackson Limited purchased 40,000 shares of Hardy Limited for U.S.$2.15 per share, plus U.S.$2,400 in commissions and fees. The shares were held as an available-for-sale investment. On this date, the exchange rate was U.S.$1 = Cdn.$1.34. The account was settled with the broker on 1 August 20X4, when U.S.$1 = Cdn.$1.29.

On 1 July 20X4, Jackson bought a U.S.$100,000 five-year bond at face value, when the exchange rate was U.S.$1 = Cdn.$1.31. It paid cash on the acquisition date. There was no accrued interest. Management plans to hold this bond until maturity.

At 31 December 20X4, Hardy shares had a quoted market value of US$3.04 per share, the bonds were still selling at par, and the exchange rate was U.S.$1 = Cdn.$1.28.

Required:

1. Provide journal entries to record the acquisition of the Hardy shares on 14 June, and payment to the broker in August. Brokerage fees are part of the investment cost.
2. Provide the journal entry to record purchase of the bond on 1 July.
3. Explain the 31 December 20X4 adjustment that must be made for the shares (for market value), and for bonds, because of the exchange rate change.

A11-20 Equity Method: On 1 January 20X4, JR Company purchased 400 of the 1,000 outstanding common shares of RV Corporation for $30,000. The equity method will be used to account for the investment. At that date, the balance sheet of RV showed the following book values:

Assets not subject to depreciation	$40,000 *
Assets subject to depreciation (net)	26,000 **
Liabilities	6,000 *
Common shares	50,000
Retained earnings	10,000

* Book value is the same as market value.
** Market value $30,000; the assets have a 10-year remaining life (straight-line depreciation).

Required:

1. Give the entry by JR Company to record the acquisition.
2. Show the computation of goodwill purchased at acquisition.
3. Assume that at 31 December 20X4 (end of the accounting period), RV Corporation reported a net income of $10,900, and paid dividends of $5,000. Goodwill has not been impaired. Prepare the entries JR Company would record.
4. Repeat requirement 3, assuming that there was an unconfirmed profit on a sale from JR Company to RV Corporation in the amount of $2,000.

A11-21 Long-Term Equity Investment, Cost and Equity Methods Compared, Entries: On 3 January 20X4, TA Company purchased 2,000 shares of the 10,000 outstanding shares of common stock of UK Corporation for $14,600 cash. TA has significant influence as a result of this acquisition. At that date, the balance sheet of UK Corporation reflected the following:

- Nondepreciable assets, $50,000 (book value is the same as market value);
- Depreciable assets (net), $30,000 (market value, $33,000);
- Total liabilities, $20,000 (book value equals market value); and
- Shareholders' equity, $60,000.

Assume a 10-year remaining life (straight-line method) for the depreciable assets. Goodwill is not been impaired over the time period in question.

Required:

1. Give the entries, if any are required, for TA's books for each item (a) through (d) below assuming that the cost method is appropriate.
   a. Entry at date of acquisition.
   b. Goodwill purchased—computation only.
   c. Entry on 31 December 20X4 to record $15,000 net income reported by UK.
   d. Entry on 31 March 20X5 for a cash dividend of $1 per share declared and paid by UK.
2. Repeat requirement 1 above, assuming that the equity method is appropriate.
3. Why might TA use the cost method if it has significant influence?

A11-22 Equity Method: ABC Company bought 40,000 of the available 100,000 voting common shares of Tiny Corporation. This acquisition provided ABC with significant influence. ABC paid $1,450,000 cash for the investment. At the time of acquisition, Tiny had assets of $3,000,000, and liabilities of $1,700,000. Asset values reflected fair market value, except for capital assets that had a net book value of $400,000 and a fair value of $625,000. These assets had a remaining useful life of five years. After 12 months of ownership, Tiny reported net income of $526,000 and paid cash dividends of $75,000.

Required:

1. At the end of the first year of ownership, what would appear on the (1) income statement and (2) balance sheet of ABC? Show supporting calculations, including a calculation of goodwill.
2. Repeat part 1, assuming that the cost method was used. Under what circumstances would this level of share ownership be accounted for under the cost method?

A11-23 Equity Method: On 1 January 20X8, Father Limited purchased 40% of the common shares of Son Incorporated for $120,000. On the date of acquisition, net assets were $170,000, and shareholders' equity for Son comprised the following:

Common shares	$100,000
Retained earnings	70,000
Total	$170,000

All of Son's assets and liabilities had a fair value equal to book value, except for land, which had a fair value in excess of book value of $20,000. During 20X8, Son reported net income of $72,500 and paid dividends of $60,000. Son sold goods to Father at a gain of $5,000 late in 20X8. Father has not yet resold the goods.

Required:

1. What criterion must be met in order to account for this investment using the equity method?
2. Calculate the amount of goodwill purchased by Father as part of its investment in Son.

3. Prepare the journal entry under the equity method for Father to record investment income, assuming that goodwill has not been impaired.
4. Determine the balance in the Investment in Son account at the end of 20X8, using the equity method.

(CGA-Canada, adapted)

A11-24 Equity Investment, Entries and Reporting: On 1 January 20X5, Redmond Company purchased 3,000 of the 15,000 outstanding common shares of Decca Computer (DC) Corporation for $80,000 cash. Redmond had significant influence as a result of the investment, and will use the equity method to account for the investment.

On 1 January 20X5, the balance sheet of DC showed the following book values (summarized):

Assets not subject to depreciation	$140,000 *
Assets subject to depreciation (net)	100,000 **
Liabilities	40,000
Common shares	150,000
Retained earnings	50,000

* Market value, $150,000; difference relates to land held for sale, which is sold in 20X5.

** Market value, $140,000, estimated remaining life, 10 years. Use straight-line depreciation with no residual value.

Assume there is no impairment of goodwill.

Additional subsequent data on DC:

	20X5	20X6
Net income	$25,000	$31,000
Cash dividends declared and paid	10,000	12,000
Market value per share	25	26

Required:

1. Provide the investor's entries or give the required information for
   a. Entry at date of acquisition.
   b. Amount of goodwill purchased.
   c. Entries at 31 Dec. 20X5 to recognize investment revenue and dividends.
   d. Entries at 31 Dec. 20X6 to recognize investment revenue and dividends.
2. Are any entries needed to recognize a writedown to fair value at the end of 20X5 or 20X6? Explain.
3. Reconstruct the investment account, showing the opening and closing balance and all changes in the account.
4. How much investment revenue would be reported each year if the cost method was used? What would be the balance in the investment account?

A11-25 Consolidation—Explanation: In 20X1, Pepper Company bought 75% of S Company's common shares, establishing control over the Board of Directors. Pepper Company used the cost method to account for its investment in S during the year, but prepared consolidated financial statements at the end of the fiscal year, which are shown in summary form:

	P Co.	S Co.	Consolidated
Cash	$ 11,000	$ 12,000	$ 23,000
Accounts receivable	22,000	19,000	37,000
Inventory	14,200	9,200	22,400
Capital assets	83,000	64,300	152,300
Investment in S Co.	74,000	—	—
Intangible assets	—	—	3,725
	$204,200	$104,500	$238,425
Current liabilities	$ 30,000	$ 9,000	$ 35,000
Long-term liabilities	4,000	2,500	6,500
Non-controlling interest	—	—	23,000
Common shares	100,000	60,000	100,000
Retained earnings	70,200	33,000	73,925
	$204,200	$104,500	$238,425
Sales and other revenue	$ 96,000	$ 63,000	$146,750
Cost of sales	80,500	49,000	120,500
Operating expenses	2,500	4,900	7,500
Non-controlling interest	—	—	2,025
Net income	$ 13,000	$ 9,100	$ 16,725
Opening retained earnings	67,200	26,900	67,200
Dividends	10,000	3,000	10,000
Closing retained earnings	$ 70,200	$ 33,000	$ 73,925

Required:

1. Why does the parent company use the cost method during the year?
2. Identify the accounts on the consolidated balance sheet that do not appear on either of the unconsolidated balance sheets. Explain their meaning.
3. Identify the accounts or amounts that appear on the unconsolidated financial statements that do not appear on the consolidated statements. Explain why they have been eliminated.
4. What is the most likely reason that the unconsolidated accounts receivables and current liabilities do not add to the balance shown on the consolidated balance sheet?

A11-26 Reporting a Subsidiary: Cohen Corporation, a public company, is contemplating investing in a supplier company, Abbott Metals Limited, in order to ensure a reliable source of supply. The controlling shareholder, who owns 147,000 shares, is willing to sell to Cohen for a price of $50 per share. Summarized financial statements and additional information related to Abbott, follow:

ABBOTT METALS

BALANCE SHEET

At 30 June 20X5	Book Value	Fair Value
Cash	$ 120,000	$ 120,000
Accounts receivable ($419,000 from Cohen)	849,000	800,000
Inventory	1,310,000	1,800,000
Capital assets	1,492,000	700,000
Mining properties	6,701,000	11,400,000
	$10,472,000	$14,820,000

Accounts payable	$ 1,375,000	$ 1,375,000
Long-term debt	4,990,000	5,219,000
Common shares (250,000 shares)	2,700,000	
Retained earnings	1,407,000	
	$10,472,000	

Required:

Assume Cohen buys 147,000 shares of Abbott at $50 per share. Describe the resulting reporting requirements, and describe the effect on the annual financial statements of Cohen. Include a calculation of goodwill in your response.

A11-27 Comprehensive Investments: Reston Suppliers is a public company. It reported the following at the end of 20X5:

Available-for-sale investments		
S Co., 20,000 shares	$448,000	
R Co., $50,000 par value, 10% bond, due 31 December 20X7	52,000	$ 500,000
Held-to-maturity investments		
T Co. bonds, $100,000 par value, 9% bond, due 30 June 20X8 (straight-line amortization of the discount)		$ 96,750
V Ltd., 45,000 shares, equity method		$2,578,900
Other comprehensive income		
Unrealized holding gains ($2,000 related to R Co. bonds and $13,000 related to S Co.)		$ 15,000

The following transactions and events took place in 20X6:

a. Dividends received, S Co., $1 per share, V Ltd., $3 per share.
b. Semi-annual interest was received on both bonds on 30 June.
c. Early in July, the S Co. shares were sold for $32 per share, less $3,000 in commissions.
d. 1,000 W Ltd. shares were acquired for a total of $67,000, including $500 of commissions. This is an available-for-sale investment.
e. Reston owns 30% of the voting shares of V Ltd. V Ltd. reported earnings of $450,000 for 20X6. There was $216,000 of goodwill inherent in the original purchase price, but no other fair value allocations that require adjustment. There were no intercompany transactions requiring adjustment. A goodwill impairment of $10,800 must be recorded in 20X6.
f. The R Co. bond was sold for $51,400 plus accrued interest on 1 October 20X6.
g. X Co. shares were acquired as an available-for-sale investment, 300,000 shares for a cost of $138,000, including $3,800 of commissions.
h. Semi-annual interest was received on the T Co. bond at the end of December.
i. W Co. paid a dividend of $0.40 per share.
j. Market values on 31 December 20X6: W Ltd., $25 per share; X Co., $0.65 per share; V Ltd., $62 per share; T Co., 95. The W Ltd. decline in value is considered to be an impairment.

Required:

1. List the accounts and amounts that would appear on the income statement. Also calculate the change in other comprehensive income for the year ended 31 December 20X6.
2. List the accounts and amounts that would appear on the balance sheet for the year ended 31 December 20X6. Available-for-sale investments are temporary investments.

A11-28 Comprehensive Investments: Fetch Company, a public company, had the following transactions in securities during 20X6:

a. Purchased $700,000 par value of 10% NS Power Ltd. bonds for 102.5 plus accrued interest, on 1 June 20X7. The bonds will mature on 31 December 20X11, and pay interest on 1 February and 1 August. The bonds will be held to maturity.
b. Purchased 300,000 common shares of Talcon Ltd., a publicly traded company, as an available-for-sale investment on 16 June. The price per share was $0.75, plus a $4,500 broker commission.
c. Received the semi-annual interest on the NS Power bonds on 1 August. Premium amortization is also recorded. Use straight-line amortization.
d. On 1 October, invested $3,000,000 in Ball Ltd., a customer that was experiencing financial difficulty but had great potential. Fetch received 25% of the common shares of Ball, and was given representation on the Board of Directors. Fetch felt that it had significant influence with Ball. On the date of acquisition, Ball had tangible assets with a book value of $14,700,000. Liabilities were $9,600,000. All book values represented fair values, except plant and equipment with a 10-year life. For plant and equipment, book value was $6,750,000 and fair values were $7,980,000. Goodwill was not impaired in 20X6.
e. Purchased $200,000 par value of 8% Ontario Electric Ltd. bonds for 100 plus accrued interest on 1 November 20X7. The bonds will mature on 31 December 20X9, and pay interest on 1 March and 1 September. The bonds are held as an available-for-sale investment.
f. Talcon Ltd. paid a cash dividend of $0.05 per share on 1 November.
g. Ball did not declare or pay any dividends in 20X6 but reported a loss, earned evenly over the year, of $475,000.
h. Interest was accrued on 31 December on bonds, and premium/discount amortized, as appropriate.
i. Market values on 31 December: NS Power bonds, 101.5; Talcon, $0.62 per share; Ball Ltd., undeterminable; Ontario Electric bonds, 98.5.

Fetch Company had the following transactions in 20X7 related to its investments:

a. Received the semi-annual interest on the NS Power bonds on 1 February. Premium amortization is also recorded.
b. Received the semi-annual interest on the Ontario Electric bonds on 1 March.
c. Sold the Talcon shares for $1.20 per share, less brokerage fees of $7,900.
d. Received the semi-annual interest on the NS Power bonds on 1 August. Premium amortization is also recorded.
e. Sold the Ontario Electric bonds for 99, plus accrued interest, on 1 August. There was a commission of $565 on the transaction.
f. On 1 November, purchased 16,000 shares of Vulture Corp for $5.50 per share, plus commissions of $1,650. The shares are being held as an available-for-sale investment.
g. Ball did not declare or pay any dividends in 20X7 but reported net income, earned evenly over the year, of $79,200. Goodwill was impaired in the amount of $200,000.
h. Interest was accrued on 31 December on bonds, as appropriate. Premium amortization is also recorded.
i. Market values on 31 December: NS Power bonds, 102; Talcon, $1.15 per share; Ball Ltd., undeterminable; Ontario Electric bonds, 98; Vulture Corp, $7 per share.

Required:

Provide entries for all transactions and adjustments related to investments. Broker commissions are included in original cost, and netted with the proceeds of disposition. Include a calculation of acquired goodwill on the acquisition of Ball.

A11-29 Cash Flow Statement: For each of the following transactions, identify the item(s) that would appear on the cash flow statement. Identify the appropriate section (i.e., operating, investing, financing) and whether the item is an inflow or an outflow, or an add-back or deduction in operating. Assume that the indirect method of presentation is used in the operating section.

1. ABC Company reported a held-to-maturity investment of $46,000, a $50,000, 10-year bond bought at a discount in previous years. The bond pays annual interest of 7%, and $1,000 of discount amortization had been recorded in the current year.
2. Common shares were purchased for $36,000, an available-for-sale investment.
3. The common shares in part 2 were revalued to $50,000 fair value at year-end, and $14,000 of other comprehensive income was recognized.
4. The common shares in parts 2 and 3 were sold for $60,000. A gain of $24,000 was recognized, and other comprehensive income was reduced by $14,000.
5. T-bills were purchased for $350,000, an available-for-sale investment that is considered a cash equivalent.
6. The T-bills in part 4 were sold for $365,000. A gain of $15,000 was recorded.
7. The company owns 460,000 shares of Therion Co., over which it has significant influence. In the current year, investment revenue of $57,000 was recorded, and cash dividends of $36,000 were received.

A11-30 Cash Flow Statement: The following comparative data is available from the 20X4 balance sheet of Investcorp:

	20X4	20X3
Available-for-sale investments	$ 2,950,000	$1,216,000
Long-term investments		
Investment in Tandor Ltd., at equity	1,071,200	950,000
Held-to-maturity investment in Byron bonds, at amortized cost	615,000	609,300
Shareholders' equity:		
Other comprehensive income		
Unrealized holding gains	75,900	52,100

In 20X4, the following transactions took place, and are properly reflected in the balance sheet accounts, above.

1. Dividends of $140,000 were received from Tandor Ltd. No shares of Tandor were bought or sold during the year.
2. Available-for-sale investments, with a carrying value of $56,200 and cumulative unrealized holding gains of $21,000, were sold for $87,500.
3. Available-for-sale investments were increased to fair value at year-end.

Other "typical" transactions and entries also occurred in 20X4 that are reflected in the balance sheet accounts. (You may find it helpful to reconstruct the transactions.)

Required:

What items would appear on the 20X4 cash flow statement? Assume the operating section is presented using the indirect method of presentation.

A11-31 Consolidation (Appendix): At the beginning of the current fiscal year, Poppa Company bought 90% of the common shares of Son Limited for $7,350,000 cash. At that time, the book value of Son's assets reflected fair value except for land, which was undervalued on the books by $1,200,000. Son reported $500,000 of common stock and $5,500,000 of retained earnings on this date. Financial results at the end of the current fiscal year (in thousands):

	Poppa	Son
Cash	$ 1,610	$ 480
Accounts receivable	8,920	1,410
Inventory	12,100	1,400
Capital assets	10,520	1,310
Investment in Son Co.	7,350	0
Mining properties	0	6,050
	$ 40,500	$ 10,650
Current liabilities	$ 8,060	$ 1,400
Long-term debt	20,900	3,102
Common shares	8,600	500
Retained earnings	2,940	5,648
	$ 40,500	$ 10,650
Sales	$ 49,700	$ 12,900
Cost of sales	36,200	8,100
Other expenses	12,925	4,552
Other revenues	665	0
Net income	$ 1,240	$ 248
Opening retained earnings	2,100	5,500
Dividends	400	100
Closing retained earnings	$ 2,940	$ 5,648

During the year, Poppa bought $1,000,000 of goods from Son. Three-quarters had been resold at year-end. Son had recorded a $120,000 gross profit on these sales. Poppa still owed Son $800,000 at year-end. Goodwill was not impaired during the year.

Required:

Prepare a consolidated balance sheet, income statement, and retained earnings statement for the current fiscal year. Round calculations to the nearest thousand.

A11-32 Consolidation (Appendix): P Company bought 90% of the voting shares of S Company on 1 January 20X2 for $19,500,000. On that date, S Company had shareholders' equity of $15,900,000, including $6,000,000 of common shares. On that date, fair values of net assets approximated market values, except land that was undervalued on the books in the amount of $500,000, and depreciable capital assets that were undervalued by $1,400,000. Goodwill was not impaired in 20X2; amortizable capital assets are to be amortized over 15 years.

During 20X2, P Company sold goods to S Company in the amount of $600,000. All these goods were resold by S Company by the end of 20X2. S Company sold $400,000 of products to P Company; one quarter had been resold by the end of the year. S Company had recorded a $220,000 profit on the sale. P Company still owed S Company $375,000 at year-end.

Unconsolidated financial statements follow:

Year Ended 31 December 20X2	P Co.	S. Co.
Cash	$ 1,450,000	$ 213,000
Accounts receivable	16,300,000	3,415,000
Inventory	28,900,000	5,900,000
Capital assets	114,300,000	11,100,000
Investment in S Co.	19,500,000	—
Intangible assets	7,916,000	—
	$188,366,000	$20,628,000
Current liabilities	$ 39,000,000	$ 2,100,000
Long-term debt	80,000,000	500,000
Future (deferred) income tax	10,195,000	1,400,000
Common shares	17,900,000	6,000,000
Retained earnings	41,271,000	10,628,000
	$188,366,000	$20,628,000
Sales	$240,350,000	$30,600,000
Cost of sales	170,700,000	18,900,000
Other expenses	42,900,000	10,522,000
Other revenue	405,000	—
Net income	$ 27,155,000	$ 1,178,000
Opening retained earnings	30,316,000	9,900,000
Dividends	16,200,000	450,000
Closing retained earnings	$ 41,271,000	$10,628,000

Required:

1. Prepare consolidated financial statements as of 31 December 20X2.
2. Under what circumstances would P Co. not have to consolidate its subsidiary?
3. In what way are the consolidated financial statements superior to unconsolidated statements? Why do some people believe that consolidated statements are inferior?

APPENDIX

Fundamentals: The Accounting Information Processing System

ACCOUNTS, TRANSACTION RECORDING, AND FINANCIAL STATEMENTS

Financial accounting information is recorded in accounts, which describe specific resources, obligations, and the changes in these items. There are seven major types of accounts, grouped under two headings: **permanent accounts** (assets, liabilities, and owners' equity accounts) and **temporary accounts** (revenues, expenses, gains, and losses). Permanent accounts are also called "real accounts," and temporary accounts are also called "nominal accounts." The permanent accounts are those appearing in the balance sheet. The descriptive term "permanent" means that balances in these accounts are carried over to future accounting periods. *Temporary* accounts are closed out at the end of each fiscal year. Other temporary accounts are used, including cash dividends declared, income summary, and various "holding" accounts that are used for a specific purpose but are not separately disclosed in financial statements.

The **accounting identity** states the relationship between the balances of the permanent accounts:

$$\text{Assets} = \text{Liabilities} + \text{Owners' Equity}$$

The temporary accounts report events related to income-generating activities and appear primarily on the income statement. For example, when rent is paid, the rent expense account describes the reason for the decrease in cash.

Economic events are recorded in an **accounting information system (AIS)** in such a way as to change at least two accounts. This practice, called the **double-entry system**, records the change in a resource or obligation and the reason for, or source of, the change. In the rent example above, if only the cash decrease was to be recorded, no record of the transaction's purpose would be maintained.

The double-entry system also ensures that the accounting equation remains in balance. For example, when a company acquires $10,000 worth of equipment by tendering a note payable to the seller for that amount, both assets and liabilities increase by $10,000. The accounting identity remains in balance.

Complementing the double-entry system, the **debit-credit convention** is used as a recording and balancing procedure. This convention divides accounts into two sides. In North

American bookkeeping, the debit (dr.) side is always the left side, and the credit (cr.) side is always the right side.[1] These terms carry no further meaning and can't be interpreted as "increases" or "decreases" since, depending on the account type, a debit or a credit can record an increase or decrease. This is illustrated in the T-accounts summarized in Exhibit A-1. The T-account is a form of account used for demonstrating transactions; its skeletal form takes the shape of the letter T. The T-account reflects the general format of general ledger accounts, as we will discuss later.

The debit-credit convention helps maintain the accounting identity. For example, increases in assets (debits) are often associated with increases in liabilities (credits). Asset decreases (credits) are often associated with expenses (debits). Salary payments are an example: the dollar amount of the salary expense debit equals the dollar amount of the cash credit.

The debit-credit convention is a convenient way to check for recording errors. When the sums of debits and credits are not equal, an error is evident. (The converse, however, is not true. Equality of total debits and total credits does not imply that no errors have been made.) Without the convention, only increases and decreases in accounts would be recorded. In general, the dollar value of account increases would not equal the dollar value of account decreases for a given group of transactions. For example, paying off a long-term liability results in two decreases: to cash and to long-term liabilities. Therefore, inequality of total increases and total decreases could not be used to signal errors.

At the end of a reporting period, after all transactions and events are recorded in accounts, **financial statements** are prepared. The financial statements report account balances, changes in account balances, and aggregations of account balances, such as net income and total assets. The financial statements include the *income statement*, the *balance sheet*, and the *cash flow statement*. The income statement reports the portion of the change in net assets (owners' equity) attributed to income-producing activities. The balance sheet reflects the financial position of the entity—the accounting identity. The cash flow statement reports sources and uses of cash. Two other statements, the retained earnings statement and the statement of shareholders' equity, are also commonly reported. The steps leading to these financial statements are discussed in the rest of this appendix.

THE AIS AND THE ACCOUNTING CYCLE

An accounting information system (AIS) is designed to record accurate financial data in a timely and chronological manner, facilitate retrieval of financial data in a form useful to management, and simplify periodic preparation of financial statements for external use. Design of the AIS, to meet the company's information requirements, depends on the firm's size, the nature of its operations, the volume of data, its organizational structure, and government regulation.

The accounting cycle, illustrated in Exhibit A-2, is a series of sequential steps leading to the financial statements. This cycle is repeated each reporting period, normally a year. Exhibit A-2 applies to the preparation of all financial statements except the cash flow statement, which requires additional input. Companies may combine some of these steps or change their order to suit their specific needs. Depending on the information-processing technology used, certain accounting cycle steps can be combined or in some cases omitted. Computerized systems increase the reliability of processing without compromising the relevance of the information. For example, general ledger software is used to perform much of the accounting cycle work. Worksheets may also be used to facilitate the process and are discussed later in this appendix. The fundamental nature of the process, however, is the same regardless of the technology used.

The first three steps in the accounting cycle require the most time and effort. The frequency of Step 3, posting, depends on the volume and nature of transactions, and the technology used. For example, firms with many cash transactions post to the cash account daily. Steps 4 through 9 generally occur at the end of the fiscal year. The last step, the posting of reversing entries, is optional and occurs at the beginning of the next accounting period.

[1] The debit-left and credit-right is reversed in the United Kingdom, where the debits appear on the right and the credits on the left. Why is debit abbreviated as "dr.," when the letter "r" does not appear in the word? It's because the abbreviations *dr.* and *cr.* were originally derived from the words *debtor* and *creditor.*

EXHIBIT A-1

DEBIT/CREDIT IMPACT ON T-ACCOUNTS

Permanent Accounts

Assets		=	Liabilities		+	Owners' Equity	
Debit entries *increase* assets	Credit entries *decrease* assets		Debit entries *decrease* liabilities	Credit entries *increase* liabilities		Debit entries *decrease* owners' equity	Credit entries *increase* owners' equity

Temporary Accounts

Expenses		Revenues	
Debit entries *increase* expenses	Credit entries *decrease* expenses	Debit entries *decrease* revenues	Credit entries *increase* revenues

Losses		Gains	
Debit entries *increase* losses	Credit entries *decrease* losses	Debit entries *decrease* gains	Credit entries *increase* gains

THE IMPACT OF COMPUTERIZATION

Few businesses keep manual records. The norm is to use a customized or off-the-shelf computer program that will facilitate the following steps in the accounting cycle (refer to Exhibit A-2):

- Journalizing transactions, adjustments, closing, and reversing entries;
- Posting entries;
- Preparing trial balances; and
- Preparing financial statements.

Such programs have many advantages, including speed and accuracy.

What is left for the accountant to do? First, identification and control of transactions and adjustments is crucial. The accountant manages the entire process, ensuring that information entered is accurate and complete. Second, many elements in financial reporting require the exercise of professional judgement—choice of accounting policy, composition of the notes to the financial statements, and so on. These tasks require qualified decision-makers.

Regardless of how the steps in the accounting cycle are performed, they accomplish the same task—posting is posting, manual or computerized. The accountant has to understand this process to manage it.

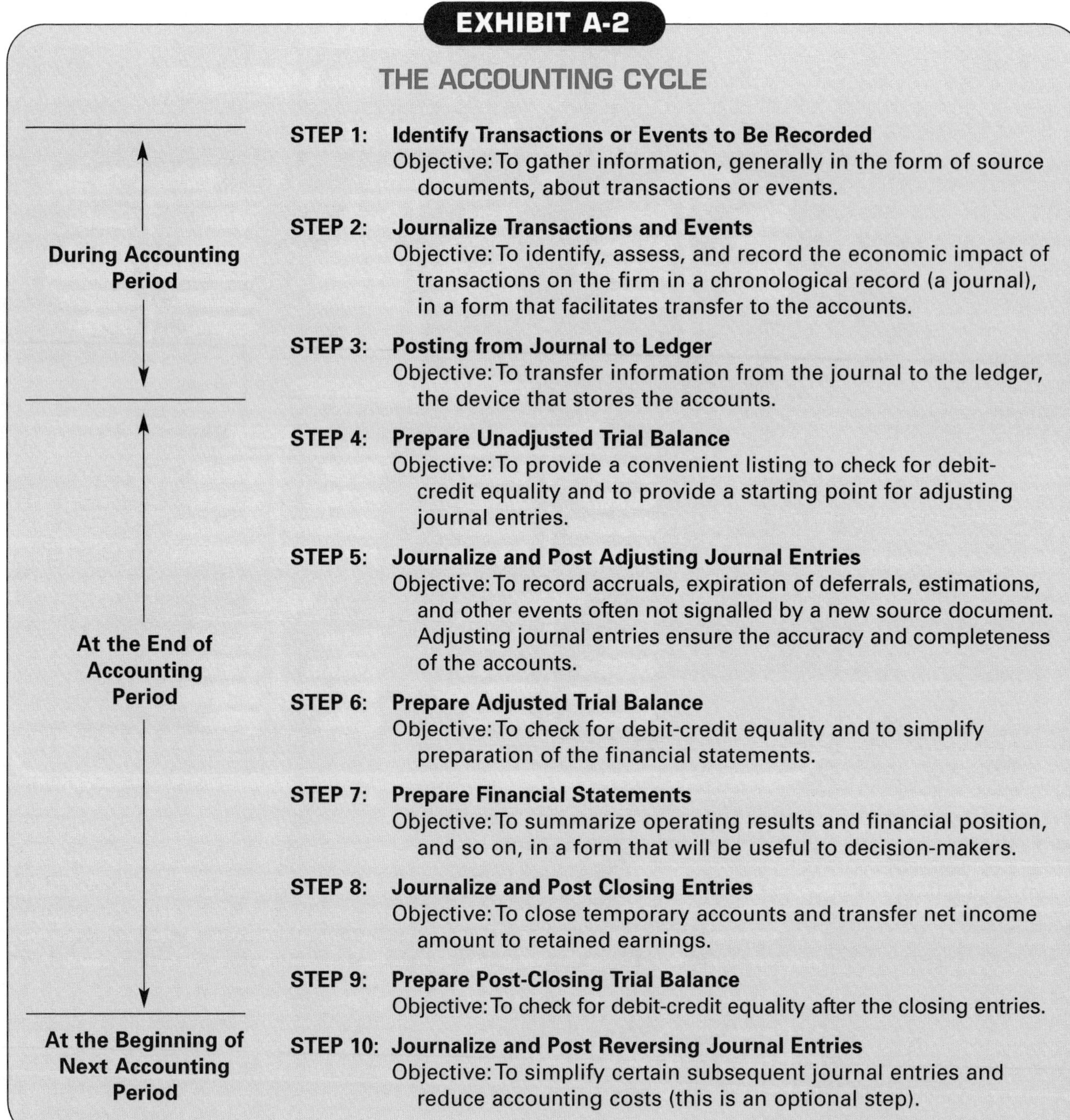

EXHIBIT A-2

THE ACCOUNTING CYCLE

During Accounting Period	**STEP 1: Identify Transactions or Events to Be Recorded** Objective: To gather information, generally in the form of source documents, about transactions or events.
	STEP 2: Journalize Transactions and Events Objective: To identify, assess, and record the economic impact of transactions on the firm in a chronological record (a journal), in a form that facilitates transfer to the accounts.
	STEP 3: Posting from Journal to Ledger Objective: To transfer information from the journal to the ledger, the device that stores the accounts.
At the End of Accounting Period	**STEP 4: Prepare Unadjusted Trial Balance** Objective: To provide a convenient listing to check for debit-credit equality and to provide a starting point for adjusting journal entries.
	STEP 5: Journalize and Post Adjusting Journal Entries Objective: To record accruals, expiration of deferrals, estimations, and other events often not signalled by a new source document. Adjusting journal entries ensure the accuracy and completeness of the accounts.
	STEP 6: Prepare Adjusted Trial Balance Objective: To check for debit-credit equality and to simplify preparation of the financial statements.
	STEP 7: Prepare Financial Statements Objective: To summarize operating results and financial position, and so on, in a form that will be useful to decision-makers.
	STEP 8: Journalize and Post Closing Entries Objective: To close temporary accounts and transfer net income amount to retained earnings.
	STEP 9: Prepare Post-Closing Trial Balance Objective: To check for debit-credit equality after the closing entries.
At the Beginning of Next Accounting Period	**STEP 10: Journalize and Post Reversing Journal Entries** Objective: To simplify certain subsequent journal entries and reduce accounting costs (this is an optional step).

THE ACCOUNTING CYCLE

The annual accounting cycle includes 10 steps, explained in the following section.

Step 1: Identify Transactions or Events to be Recorded

The first step will identify transactions and events that cause a change in the firm's resources or obligations and will collect relevant economic data about those transactions. Events that change a firm's resources or obligations are categorized into three types:

1. *Exchanges of resources and obligations between the reporting firm and outside parties.* These exchanges are either **reciprocal transfers** or **non-reciprocal transfers.** In a reciprocal transfer, the firm both transfers and receives resources (e.g., sale of goods for cash). In a non-reciprocal transfer, the firm either transfers *or* receives current or future resources (e.g., payment of cash dividends or receipt of a donation). All exchanges require a journal entry.
2. *Internal events within the firm that affect its resources or obligations but do not involve outside parties.* Examples are recognition of amortization of capital assets and the use of inventory for production. These events also generally require a journal entry. However, other events, such as increases in the value of assets resulting from superior management and similar factors, are not recorded.
3. *External economic and environmental events beyond the control of the company.* Examples include casualty losses and changes in the market value of most assets and liabilities. At the present time, accounting standards allow recording of market value changes for only a few types of assets.

Transactions are defined as all events requiring a journal entry. Transactions are often accompanied by a source document, generally a paper record that describes the exchange, the parties involved, the date, and the dollar amount. Examples are sales invoices, freight bills, and cash register receipts. Certain events, such as the accrual of interest, are not signalled by a separate source document. Recording these transactions requires reference to the underlying contract supporting the original exchange of resources. Source documents are essential for the initial recording of transactions in a journal and are also used for subsequent tracing and verification, for evidence in legal proceedings, and for audits of financial statements.

Step 2: Journalize Transactions and Events

This step measures and records the economic effect of transactions in a form that simplifies transfer to the accounts. Accounting principles that guide measurement, recognition, and classification of accounts are applied.

Transactions are recorded chronologically in a **journal**—an organized medium for recording transactions in debit-credit format. A journal entry is a debit-credit description of a transaction that includes the date, the accounts and amounts involved, and a brief description. A journal entry is a temporary recording, although journals are retained as part of the audit trail; account balances are not changed until the information is transferred to the ledger accounts in Step 3.

general journal
a journal with a flexible format in which any transaction can be recorded

special journal
a journal with a non-flexible, pre-determined format in which only specific transactions that fit the format can be recorded

Accounting systems usually have two types of journals: the **general journal** and **special journals.** Non-repetitive entries and entries involving infrequently used accounts are recorded in the general journal. Repetitive entries are recorded in special journals. If special journals are not used, all transactions are recorded in the general journal. Special journals are discussed later in this appendix. The general journal is used to illustrate most entries in this text.

The journal entry step is not absolutely essential; transaction data can be recorded directly into the accounts. However, the journal entry step has advantages, and it is standard practice to record all transactions first in a journal. Transaction processing is more efficient, and less costly, if transactions are grouped in a journal and processed together. By using journals, review and analysis of transactions is much simpler and the accounts consume less storage space. Also, a chronological list of transactions is provided. Transactions can be difficult to reconstruct without a journal because the debits and credits are located in different accounts. Journals are typically part of the paper trail relied on by auditors.

Some companies use computerized systems to bypass the traditional journal entry step. Retailers, for example, record relevant information about a transaction by using bar codes printed on product packages. Optical scanning equipment reads the bar code and transmits the information to a computer, which records the proper amount directly in the relevant ledger accounts. Accounting cost savings can be significant.

Exhibit A-3 illustrates an entry in a general journal. This entry records the purchase of equipment financed with cash and debt. Equipment is recorded at the value of the resources used to acquire it. The names of the accounts credited are listed below and to the right of the debited account.

EXHIBIT A-3

Page J-16

GENERAL JOURNAL

Date 20X5	Accounts and Explanation	Posting Ref.	Amount Debit	Amount Credit
2 Jan.	Equipment	150	15,000	
	Cash	101		5,000
	Notes payable	215		10,000
	Purchased equipment for use in the business. Paid $5,000 cash and gave a $10,000, one-year note with 15% interest payable at maturity.			

Step 3: Posting from Journal to Ledger

Transferring transaction data from the journal to the ledger is called **posting**. Posting reclassifies the data from the journal's chronological format to an account classification format in the ledger, which is a collection of the formal accounts. Computerized systems store ledger data until it is needed for processing in another step in the accounting cycle.

Accounting systems usually have two types of ledgers: the **general ledger** and **subsidiary ledgers**. The general ledger holds all the individual accounts, grouped according to the seven elements of financial statements. Subsidiary ledgers support general ledger accounts that comprise many separate individual accounts. For example, a firm with a substantial number of customer accounts receivable will maintain one ledger account per customer, stored in an accounts receivable subsidiary ledger. The individual customer account is called the "subsidiary account." The general ledger holds only the control account, the balance of which reflects the sum of all the individual customer account balances. Only the control accounts are used in compiling financial statements.

For example, assume that a firm's accounts receivable consists of two individual accounts with a combined balance of $6,000. The firm's general and subsidiary ledgers might show these balances:

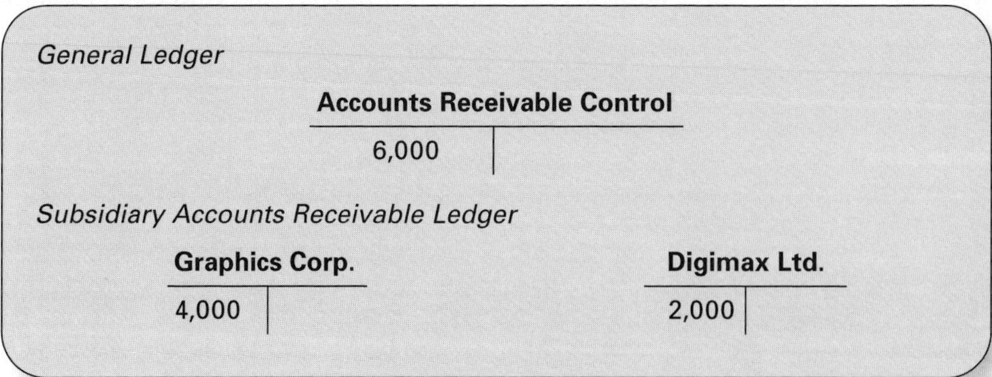

POSTING Exhibit A-4 illustrates a section of a general ledger in T-account form. This ledger depicts three general ledger accounts after posting the journal entry shown in Exhibit A-3. Posting references and page numbers are used in both the journal and the ledger to ensure that an audit trail exists—that is, to indicate where an item in the account ledger came from and to which account the item was posted. Posting references also serve to confirm that an entry was posted.

EXHIBIT A-4

GENERAL LEDGER (Excerpts)

Cash — Acct. 101

20X5			20X5		
1 Jan.	Balance	18,700	2 Jan.	J-16	5,000

Equipment — Acct. 150

20X5					
1 Jan.	Balance	62,000			
2	J-16	15,000			

Notes Payable — Acct. 215

			20X5		
			2 Jan.	J-16	10,000

When the $5,000 cash credit from the general journal entry of Exhibit A-3 is posted to the cash ledger account, "101" is listed in the journal to indicate the account number *to which* the credit is posted. Similarly, in the cash ledger account, "J-16" indicates the journal page number *from which* this amount is posted. Cross-referencing is especially important when posting large numbers of transactions, detecting and correcting errors, and maintaining an audit trail.

Step 4: Prepare Unadjusted Trial Balance

An unadjusted trial balance is prepared at the end of the reporting period, after all transaction entries are recorded in the journals and posted to the ledger. The unadjusted trial balance is a list of general ledger accounts and their account balances, in the following order: assets, liabilities, owners' equity, revenues, expenses, gains, and losses. For accounts with subsidiary ledgers, only the control account balances are entered into the trial balance, after reconciliation with the subsidiary ledger.

The unadjusted trial balance is the starting point for developing adjusting entries and for the worksheet, if used. Exhibit A-5 illustrates an unadjusted trial balance for Sonora Limited, a fictitious retailing company, at the end of the fiscal year. The trial balance reflects Sonora's transaction journal entries recorded during 20X5 and is the basis for the remainder of this accounting cycle illustration.

The unadjusted trial balance is a convenient means for checking that the sum of debit account balances equals the sum of credit account balances. If the sums of debit and credit balances are not equal, the error must be found and corrected. A reexamination of source documents and postings is one way to discover the source of an error. Equality of debits and credits does not, however, imply that the accounts are error free. A completely unposted journal entry, an incorrectly classified account, and an erroneous journal entry amount are errors that do not cause inequality of total debits and credits.

periodic inventory system
an inventory record-keeping system that determines the quantity of inventory on hand and related cost of goods sold only at the end of the fiscal period

As reported in Exhibit A-5, Sonora uses a **periodic inventory system**. Under this system, merchandise on hand is counted and costed at the end of each accounting period. The resulting inventory amount is used to update the inventory account balance. During the period, however, the inventory account balance remains at the 1 January amount and the cost of goods sold is not readily determinable. The unadjusted trial balance for Sonora at 31 December 20X5 reflects the 1 January 20X5 balance.

In a *perpetual inventory system*, the inventory account balance is constantly updated as merchandise is purchased and sold. Thus, the inventory account balance is correctly stated at the end of the accounting period, and there will be an up-to-date cost of goods sold account before any adjustments are made.

EXHIBIT A-5

SONORA LIMITED
UNADJUSTED TRIAL BALANCE

31 December 20X5

Account	Debit	Credit
Cash	$ 67,300	
Accounts receivable	45,000	
Allowance for doubtful accounts		$ 1,000
Notes receivable	8,000	
Inventory (1 January balance, periodic system)	75,000	
Prepaid insurance	600	
Land	8,000	
Building	160,000	
Accumulated amortization, building		90,000
Equipment	91,000	
Accumulated amortization, equipment		27,000
Accounts payable		29,000
Bonds payable, 6%		50,000
Common shares, no-par, 15,000 shares		170,000
Retained earnings (1 January balance)		41,500
Dividends declared	10,000	
Sales revenue		325,200
Interest revenue		500
Rent revenue		1,800
Purchases	130,000	
Freight on purchases	4,000	
Purchase returns		2,000
Selling expenses*	104,000	
General and administrative expenses*	23,600	
Interest expense	2,500	
Loss on discontinued operations	9,000	
Totals	$738,000	$738,000

* These broad categories of expenses are used to simplify presentation.

As shown in Exhibit A-5, Sonora's retained earnings account also reflects the 1 January 20X5 balance since no transactions affected this account during 20X5. Income tax expense is not listed in the unadjusted trial balance because the corporate income tax liability for the current year is not known until pre-tax income is computed, although companies that are required to pay quarterly estimated income taxes would have a balance in this account at this point. The loss from discontinued operations also does not yet reflect any tax effect.

Step 5: Journalize and Post Adjusting Journal Entries

Many changes in a firm's economic resources and obligations occur continuously. For example, interest accrues daily on debts, as does rent expense on an office building. Other resources and obligations, such as employee salaries, originate as service is rendered with payment to follow at specified dates. The end of the accounting period generally does not coincide with the receipt or payment of cash associated with these types of resource changes.

adjusting journal entries
entries used to record resource changes that occur continuously and must be recorded to accurately reflect the financial results and position of an entity; also prepared for corrections

Accrual-basis accounting requires the recording of these changes at the end of the accounting period so that financial statements are fairly stated. **Adjusting journal entries (AJEs)** are used to record such resource changes to ensure the accuracy of the financial statements.

Cash-basis accounting, which generally records a journal entry only upon an exchange of cash between firms, does not typically require many adjusting entries. For example, unpaid wages at the end of a fiscal year require an adjusting entry under accrual accounting but not under cash-basis accounting. Cash-basis accounting can be used if it meets the needs of the financial statements users, which it may if cash flow is the only key variable, or if almost all transactions are immediately cash-based. Cash-basis financial statements are rarely in accordance with generally accepted accounting principles, though, which typically focus on accrual measures of both financial performance and financial position.

CLASSIFICATION OF AJES AJEs generally record a resource or obligation change and usually involve both a permanent and a temporary account. AJEs are recorded and dated as of the last day of the fiscal period. They are recorded in the general journal and posted to the ledger accounts. Source documents from earlier transactions are the primary information sources for AJEs. AJEs may be classified into three categories: *deferrals*, *accruals*, and *other AJEs*.

Deferrals are recorded for cash flows that occur before expense and revenue recognition. These AJEs are recorded when cash is paid for expenses that apply to more than one accounting period or when cash is received for revenue that applies to more than one accounting period. The portion of the expense or revenue that applies to future periods is deferred as a prepaid expense (asset) or unearned revenue (liability).

The AJE required for a deferral depends on the method used for recording routine operational cash payments and receipts that precede expense and revenue recognition. One method, here called the **standard recording method**, records an asset upon payment of cash before goods or services are consumed and records a liability upon receipt of cash before goods or services are provided. For example, if two months' rent is prepaid on 1 July, the standard method debits prepaid rent for that amount. An adjustment later in the year recognizes rent expense and the expiration of prepaid rent.

A second method, here called the **expedient recording method**, records an expense upon payment of cash before goods or services are consumed and records a revenue upon receipt of cash before goods or services are provided. In the case of rent paid in advance, the expedient method debits rent expense for two months' rent. This method is expedient because many cash payments and receipts relate to expenses and revenues that apply only to the year in which the cash flow occurs. No AJE is required in this example because rent expense is correctly stated at year-end. If a portion of the expense or revenue applies to a future accounting period, however, an AJE is required.

Accruals are recorded for cash flows that occur after expense and revenue recognition. These AJEs are recorded when cash is to be paid or received in a future accounting period but all or a portion of the future cash flow applies to expenses or revenues of the current period. For example, unpaid wages accrued as wages payable at year-end represent wage costs matched against current-year revenues but not to be paid until next year. If the company is a landlord and rents space to tenants, uncollected rent accrued as rent receivable at year-end represents revenue earned in the current year but to be collected next year. In both cases, the expense or revenue is recognized before the cash flow occurs.

Other types of journal entries are often recorded at the end of the accounting period and are listed here as adjusting journal entries for completeness. These include

- reclassifications of permanent accounts
- estimation of expenses (bad debt expense, for example)
- cost allocations (amortization, for example)
- recognition of cost of goods sold and inventory losses
- correction of errors discovered at year-end

Cash generally is not involved in AJEs because of the purpose of AJEs. However, corrections of errors involving the cash account discovered at the end of the accounting period are recorded as AJEs. Also, the entry required to adjust the cash balance upon receipt of the end-of-year bank statement, which lists service charges and other items unknown until receipt, is recorded as an AJE.

In the following discussion, Sonora's 31 December 20X5 unadjusted trial balance (Exhibit A-5) and additional information are used to illustrate AJEs.

DEFERRAL EXAMPLE *Deferred Expenses.* On 1 November 20X5, Sonora paid a six-month insurance premium of $600 in advance. On that date, the $600 payment is recorded as a debit to prepaid insurance and a credit to cash (the standard method). On the unadjusted trial balance, the full $600 payment is reflected in prepaid insurance. One-third of this payment ($200) is applicable to 20X5. A $200 expense, indicating the partial expiration of the asset, must be recognized. Sonora records insurance expense and other similar expenses in the general and administrative expense account. AJE (a) adjusts prepaid insurance and recognizes the expense:

a. *31 December 20X5*		
General and administrative expenses	200	
Prepaid insurance		200

The credit to prepaid insurance records the reduction in the asset that took place during the last two months of 20X5 as insurance benefits were used up. No source document or transaction signals this entry, although the underlying insurance document was probably consulted. The remaining $400 of prepaid insurance reflects insurance coverage for the first four months of 20X6.

Deferred Revenue. Sonora leased a small office in its building to a tenant on 1 January 20X5. The lease required an initial payment of $1,800 for 18 months' rent, which is recorded as a debit to cash and a credit to rent revenue (the expedient method). On 31 December 20X5, the unadjusted trial balance reports $1,800 in rent revenue, which is overstated by the $600 (one-third) relating to 20X6. AJE (b) is required to reduce the revenue recognized in 20X5 from $1,800 to $1,200 and to create a liability equal to the amount of rent relating to 20X6 ($600).

b. *31 December 20X5*		
Rent revenue	600	
Rent collected in advance (liability)		600

The result of this adjustment is a liability equal to the resources received for future services.

ACCRUAL EXAMPLE *Accrued Expenses.* Sonora has issued, at face value, $50,000 of 6% bonds paying interest yearly each 31 October. For the current accounting period, a two-month interest obligation accrues between 31 October 20X5 and 31 December 20X5. Sonora must recognize the liability and the resulting expense. The amount for the two-month period is $500 ($50,000 × 6% × 2/12). Therefore, on 31 December 20X5, both the interest expense and the associated payable are recognized in AJE (c):

c. *31 December 20X5*		
Interest expense	500	
Interest payable		500

Accrued Revenue. Sonora's unadjusted trial balance lists $8,000 in notes receivable. The interest rate on these notes is 15%, payable each 30 November. As of 31 December 20X5, the maker of the notes is obligated to Sonora for one month's interest of $100 ($8,000 × 15% × 1/12). AJE (d) records the resulting receivable and revenue:

d. *31 December 20X5*		
Interest receivable	100	
Interest revenue		100

OTHER EXAMPLES *Amortization Expenses.* Property, plant, and equipment (capital assets) is the balance sheet category used to report many productive assets with a useful life exceeding one year. The cost of these assets is recognized as an expense over their period of use. *Amortization* or *depreciation* is a systematic and rational allocation of plant asset cost over a number of accounting periods. Throughout this text, the terms "depreciation" and "amortization" are used interchangeably. In practice, there is considerable diversity in the terminology used. The amount of amortization expense recognized depends on a number of factors:

- the original expenditure and subsequent capitalized expenditures
- the asset's useful life
- the method chosen for amortization measurement
- the asset's residual value

Amortization is similar to the recognition of an expense on a deferred item such as prepaid insurance in that the cash flow occurs before the expense is recognized. The main differences are the longer life and greater uncertainty of expected benefits of capital assets.

AJE (e) illustrates amortization recorded for Sonora at the end of 20X5 under the straight-line method. Sonora debits two expense accounts because the company uses the building and equipment assets both for selling and for general and administrative functions. Amortization is commonly allocated to several functions, including manufacturing operations. The adjusting entry for amortization is as follows:

e. 31 December 20X5		
Selling expense (amortization)	8,200	
General and administrative expense (amortization)	10,800	
Accumulated amortization, building		10,000
Accumulated amortization, equipment		9,000

				Proportionate Use by Function	
Asset	**Cost**	**Residual Value**	**Useful Life Years**	**Selling Function**	**G & A* Function**
Building	$160,000	$10,000	15	46%	54%
Equipment	91,000	1,000	10	40	60

Computation:

Building:						
[($160,000 − $10,000)/15 yrs.]	=	$10,000	× .46 =	$4,600	× .54 =	$ 5,400
Equipment:						
[($91,000 − $1,000)/10 yrs.]	=	9,000	× .40 =	3,600	× .60 =	5,400
Totals		$19,000		$8,200		$ 10,800

* General and administrative

contra account
general ledger account that is always reported on the financial statements with its "main" account; since two accounts will have opposite (debit versus credit) balances, the net amount will be reported

AJE (e) reduces the *net book value* of the building and equipment accounts. Accumulated amortization is a **contra account**. A contra account has the opposite balance of the related, main account. Thus, accumulated amortization is subtracted from the gross building and equipment accounts, leaving the net unamortized account balances (net book value). Sonora's balance sheet illustrates this offset. Contra accounts ensure that major assets are reported at original cost.

Many methods of amortization are permitted under GAAP. All entail systematic and rational allocation of capital asset cost to accounting periods. Amortization expense recognized in an accounting period does not generally equal the decline in market value during the year. Amortization expense recognition is an allocation process, not an asset valuation process, and the net book value of plant assets does not generally equal current value. However, amortization does spread the cost of an asset over its useful life.

BAD DEBT EXPENSE Goods and services are often sold on credit. Accounts that are never collected result in bad debt expense, which is a risk of doing business on credit terms. Most large firms use a bad debt estimate to reduce income and accounts receivable in the period of sale. This practice prevents overstatement of both income and assets and is required if bad debts are probable and estimable. Recognition of bad debt expense is accomplished with an AJE that debits bad debt expense and credits the allowance for doubtful accounts, a contra account to the accounts receivable account.

Estimates of uncollectible accounts may be based on credit sales for the period or the year-end accounts receivable balance. Assume that Sonora extends credit on $120,000 of sales during 20X5. Prior experience indicates an expected 1% average bad debt rate on credit sales. Sonora treats bad debt expense as a component of selling expenses and records AJE (f):

f. *31 December 20X5*		
Selling expense ($120,000 × .01)	1,200	
Allowance for doubtful accounts		1,200

The credit is made to the allowance account, rather than to accounts receivable, because the identities of the uncollectible accounts are not yet known. In addition, the use of the contra allowance account maintains agreement between the balance in accounts receivable control and the total of account balances in the accounts receivable subsidiary ledger.

The $1,200 allowance is the portion of 20X5 credit sales not expected to be collected. Net accounts receivable, the difference between the balance in accounts receivable and the allowance account, is an estimate of the cash ultimately expected to be received from sales on account. Bad debt expense is reported in the income statement, although often not as a separate line item.

COST OF GOODS SOLD The methodology used to determine cost of goods sold (a retailer's largest expense) depends on whether a perpetual or a periodic inventory system is used. In a perpetual system, no AJE is needed to establish cost of goods sold because cost of goods sold is recorded as each sale is made. However, an AJE might be needed to correct errors or to recognize inventory losses due to theft and economic factors. In a periodic system, cost of goods sold is determined either by an AJE or by closing entries, both of which update the inventory account and close inventory-related accounts.

A perpetual inventory system maintains an inventory record for each item stocked. This record contains data on each purchase and issue. An up-to-date balance is maintained in the inventory account. The cost of each item purchased is debited to the inventory account. Suppose an item that sells for $300 is carried in inventory at a cost of $180. A sale of this item requires two entries:

Cash (or accounts receivable)	300	
Sales revenue		300
Cost of goods sold	180	
Inventory		180

In a perpetual inventory system, the ending balance in the inventory account equals the correct ending inventory amount, assuming no errors or inventory losses. The cost of goods sold balance is also up to date, reflecting the recorded cost of all items sold during the period. Thus, no AJEs are needed unless the inventory account balance disagrees with the total of individual item costs determined by the annual physical count.

In contrast, a periodic system does not maintain a current balance in inventory or cost of goods sold. Instead, the physical inventory count at the end of the period is used to determine the balances of these two accounts. The purchases account, rather than the inventory account, is debited for all purchases during the period. In this case, the unadjusted trial balance at the end of an accounting period reflects the beginning inventory, and cost of goods sold does not yet exist as an account. An AJE can be used to set purchases, purchases returns, and other purchase-related accounts to zero (i.e., close these accounts), to replace the beginning inventory amount with the ending inventory amount in the inventory account, and to recognize cost of goods sold for the period.

To illustrate, Sonora determines its ending inventory to be $90,000. The company uses a periodic system, and computes cost of goods sold and records AJE (g) as follows:

g. *31 December 20X5*			
Inventory (ending)		90,000	
Purchase returns		2,000	
Cost of goods sold (see below)		117,000	
Inventory (beginning)			75,000
Purchases			130,000
Freight on purchases			4,000

Cost of Goods Sold Computation—
31 December 20X5

Beginning inventory		$ 75,000
Add (from the current-year accounts):		
Purchases	$130,000	
Freight on purchases	4,000	
Purchase returns	(2,000)	
Net purchases		132,000
Total goods available for sale		$207,000
Less: Ending inventory (from physical account)		90,000
Cost of goods sold		$117,000

Two sources of information contribute to entry (g): the unadjusted trial balance from which several account balances are taken, and the physical inventory count indicating $90,000 of inventory on hand. *Alternatively, the accounts related to cost of goods sold may be left in the adjusted trial balance, untouched, and used in detail to create the financial statements. They would then be eliminated in closing entries.* Both approaches are widely used in practice and result in the same reported income and financial position. It's really a question of which method is preferred by a particular accountant and/or computerized reporting package. The closing entry approach is illustrated below in the discussion of Step 9, closing entries.

INCOME TAX EXPENSE The recognition of income tax expense, an accrual item, is often the final AJE. Many firms pay estimated income taxes monthly, necessitating an AJE at the end of the accounting period to record any additional taxes due. For simplicity, assume that Sonora pays its income tax once each year after the end of the full accounting period.

A worksheet or partial adjusted trial balance (prior to income tax determination) simplifies the calculation of pre-tax income. The amounts in square brackets indicate the account balance in the unadjusted trial balance plus or minus the effects of AJEs, denoted by letter.

Assume that Sonora faces an average income tax rate of 40%, amortization expense equals tax amortization, and the loss from discontinued operations and all other expenses are fully tax deductible. AJE (h) recognizes the resulting $20,000 ($50,000 × 40%) income tax expense:

h. *31 December 20X5*		
Income tax expense	20,000	
Income tax payable		20,000

Calculation of Pre-tax Income		
For the Year Ended 31 December 20X5		
Revenues:		
Sales revenue	$325,200	
Interest revenue [$500 + $100 (d)]	600	
Rent revenue [$1,800 − $600 (b)]	1,200	$327,000
Expenses:		
Cost of goods sold (g)	117,000	
Selling expenses [$104,000 + $8,200 (e) + $1,200 (f)]	113,400	
General and administrative expenses [$23,600 + $200 (a) + $10,800 (e)]	34,600	
Interest expense [$2,500 + $500 (c)]	3,000	
Discontinued operations (pre-tax)	9,000	277,000
Pre-tax income		$ 50,000
Income tax expense ($50,000 × .4)		$ 20,000

For simplicity, the entire income tax expense is recorded in one account. Sonora's income statement (Exhibit A-7), however, separates the $3,600 income tax reduction associated with the loss from discontinued operations ($9,000 × 40%) from income tax on income before the discontinued operation. This practice is called *intraperiod tax allocation.*

Additional adjusting journal entries are illustrated throughout this text. In all cases, AJEs are posted to the appropriate ledger accounts.

Step 6: Prepare Adjusted Trial Balance

At this point in the cycle, the transaction journal entries and the AJEs have been journalized and posted and an adjusted trial balance is prepared. This trial balance lists all the account balances that will appear in the financial statements (with the exception of retained earnings, which does not reflect the current year's net income or dividends). The purpose of the adjusted trial balance is to confirm debit-credit equality, taking all AJEs into consideration. Exhibit A-6 presents the adjusted trial balance for Sonora.

The account balances in the adjusted trial balance reflect the effects of AJEs. For example, the $400 balance in prepaid insurance equals the $600 balance in the unadjusted trial balance less the reduction caused by AJE (a) for this year's coverage. New accounts not appearing in the unadjusted trial balance emerge from the adjustment process. For Sonora, several accounts are created as a result of an AJE: interest receivable, interest payable, rent collected in advance, income tax payable, cost of goods sold, and income tax expense. AJE (g) has the opposite effect: it eliminates purchases, freight on purchases, and purchase returns. Accounts with zero balances have not been listed, although some prefer to include these accounts to make the trial balance complete. The financial statements now can be prepared from the adjusted trial balance.

Step 7: Prepare Financial Statements

The financial statements are the culmination of the accounting cycle. Financial statements can be produced for a period of any duration. However, monthly, quarterly, and annual statements are the most common.

The income statement, retained earnings statement, and balance sheet are prepared directly from the adjusted trial balance. The income statement is prepared first because net income must be known before the retained earnings statement can be completed. The temporary account balances are transferred to the income statement (except for dividends), and the permanent account balances (except for retained earnings) are transferred to the balance sheet. Exhibit A-7 illustrates Sonora's 20X5 income and retained earnings statements.

Total income tax expense ($20,000) in the income statement is allocated as follows: $23,600 to income before discontinued operations and $3,600 tax savings to the loss from discontinued operations.

EXHIBIT A-6

SONORA LIMITED
ADJUSTED TRIAL BALANCE

31 December 20X5

Account	Debit	Credit
Cash	$ 67,300	
Accounts receivable	45,000	
Allowances for doubtful accounts		$ 2,200
Notes receivable	8,000	
Interest receivable	100	
Inventory (31 December balance)	90,000	
Prepaid insurance	400	
Land	8,000	
Building	160,000	
Accumulated amortization, building		100,000
Equipment	91,000	
Accumulated amortization, equipment		36,000
Accounts payable		29,000
Interest payable		500
Rent collected in advance		600
Income tax payable		20,000
Bonds payable, 6%		50,000
Common shares, no par, 15,000 shares		170,000
Retained earnings (1 January balance)		41,500
Dividends declared	10,000	
Sales revenue		325,200
Interest revenue		600
Rent revenue		1,200
Cost of goods sold	117,000	
Selling expenses	113,400	
General and administrative expenses	34,600	
Interest expense	3,000	
Income tax expense	20,000	
Loss on discontinued operations	9,000	
Totals	$776,800	$776,800

The retained earnings statement explains the change in retained earnings for the period. Sonora declared dividends during 20X5, and they are subtracted on the retained earnings statement. Dividends are a distribution of capital to shareholders. They are not an expense and do not belong on the income statement. A retained earnings statement (and a statement of shareholders' equity) generally are included in the complete set of financial statements. Sonora chose to report only a retained earnings statement because no changes occurred in the other equity accounts during 20X5.

Exhibit A-8 illustrates the 20X5 balance sheet. The ending retained earnings balance is taken from the retained earnings statement rather than from the adjusted trial balance.

EXHIBIT A-7

SONORA LIMITED
INCOME STATEMENT

For the year ended 31 December 20X5

Revenues:		
Sales	$325,200	
Interest	600	
Rent	1,200	
Total revenues		$327,000
Expenses:		
Cost of goods sold	117,000	
Selling	113,400	
General and administrative	34,600	
Interest	3,000	
Total expenses before income tax		268,000
Income before tax and discontinued operations		59,000
Income tax on income before discontinued operations ($59,000 × 40%)		23,600
Income before discontinued operations		35,400
Loss from discontinued operations	9,000	
Less tax savings ($9,000 × 40%)	3,600	5,400
Net income		$ 30,000

SONORA LIMITED
RETAINED EARNINGS STATEMENT

For the year ended 31 December 20X5

Retained earnings, 1 January 20X5	$ 41,500
Net income	30,000
	$ 71,500
Less: dividend declared	10,000
Retained earnings, 31 December 20X5	$ 61,500

Step 8: Journalize and Post Closing Entries

Closing entries

- Reduce to zero (close) the balances of temporary accounts related to earnings measurement and dividends;
- Are recorded in the general journal at the end of the accounting period; and
- Are posted to the ledger accounts.

Permanent accounts are not closed because they carry over to the next accounting period. The retained earnings account is the only permanent account involved in the closing process.

Because net income is measured for a specific interval of time, the balances of the income statement accounts are reduced to zero at the end of each accounting period. Otherwise, these accounts would contain data from previous periods.

EXHIBIT A-8

SONORA LIMITED
BALANCE SHEET

At 31 December 20X5			
Assets			
Current assets:			
Cash			$ 67,300
Accounts receivable		$ 45,000	
Allowance for doubtful accounts		(2,200)	42,800
Notes receivable			8,000
Interest receivable			100
Inventory			90,000
Prepaid insurance			400
Total current assets			208,600
Capital assets:			
Land		8,000	
Building	$ 160,000		
Accumulated amortization, building	(100,000)	60,000	
Equipment	91,000		
Accumulated amortization, equipment	(36,000)	55,000	
Total capital assets			123,000
Total assets			$331,600
Liabilities			
Current liabilities:			
Accounts payable			$ 29,000
Interest payable			500
Rent collected in advance			600
Income tax payable			20,000
Total current liabilities			50,100
Long-term liabilities:			
Bonds payable, 6%			50,000
Total liabilities			100,100
Shareholders' Equity			
Contributed capital:			
Common shares, no par, 15,000 shares issued and outstanding		$170,000	
Retained earnings		61,500	
Total shareholders' equity			231,500
Total liabilities and shareholders' equity			$331,600

While some accountants prefer to close temporary accounts directly to retained earnings, it is quite common to use an account called "income summary" to accumulate the balances of income statement accounts in the closing entry process. The income summary is a temporary clearing account—an account used on a short-term basis for a specific purpose. The balances in expenses and losses are reduced to zero and transferred to the income summary by crediting each of those accounts and debiting income summary for the total. Revenues and gains are debited to close them, and the income summary account is credited.

This process leaves a net balance in the income summary account equal to net income (credit balance) or net loss (debit balance) for the period. The income summary account is then closed by transferring the net income amount to retained earnings. Sonora makes three closing entries to transfer 20X5 net income to retained earnings:

31 December 20X5		
1. *To close the revenue and gain accounts to the income summary*		
Sales revenue	325,200	
Interest revenue	600	
Rent revenue	1,200	
Income summary		327,000
2. *To close the expense and loss accounts to the income summary*		
Income summary	297,000	
Cost of goods sold		117,000
Selling expenses		113,400
General and administrative expenses		34,600
Interest expense		3,000
Loss from discontinued operations		9,000
Income tax expense		20,000
3. *To close the income summary (i.e., transfer net income to retained earnings)*		
Income summary	30,000	
Retained earnings		30,000
4. *To close dividends to retained earnings*		
Retained earnings	10,000	
Dividends declared		10,000

After the first two closing entries are recorded and posted, the balance in the income summary equals net income ($30,000):

Income Summary			
(2)	297,000	(1)	327,000
		Balance	30,000

The temporary accounts now have zero balances and are ready for the next period's accounting cycle. The third entry closes the income summary account and transfers net income to retained earnings. Finally, dividends declared is closed to retained earnings. The retained earnings account in the ledger now has a balance of $61,500, per the balance sheet.

ALTERNATIVE APPROACH FOR INVENTORIES Inventory-related accounts can be adjusted and closed in the closing process as an alternative to the AJE approach illustrated previously in AJE (g). If the closing entry alternative is used, the following two closing entries replace AJE (g) and the first two closing entries illustrated above:

1. Inventory (ending)	90,000	
Sales revenue	325,200	
Interest revenue	600	
Rent revenue	1,200	
Purchase returns	2,000	
Income summary		419,000

2. Income summary	389,000	
Inventory (opening)		75,000
Purchases		130,000
Freight on purchases		4,000
Selling expenses		113,400
General and administrative expenses		34,600
Interest expense		3,000
Loss from discontinued operations		9,000
Income tax expense		20,000

Using this approach, inventory-related accounts are included with expenses and revenues for closing entry purposes. The net impact on the income summary account and, in turn, income and retained earnings are identical under both approaches. However, this approach does not isolate cost of goods sold in a separate account.

Step 9: Prepare Post-Closing Trial Balance

A post-closing trial balance lists only the balances of the permanent accounts after the closing process is finished. The temporary accounts have balances of zero. This step is taken to check for debit-credit equality after the closing entries are posted. Firms with a large number of accounts find this a valuable checking procedure because the chance of error increases with the number of accounts and postings. The retained earnings account is now stated at the correct ending balance and is the only permanent account with a balance different from the one shown in the adjusted trial balance. Exhibit A-9 illustrates the post-closing trial balance.

EXHIBIT A-9

SONORA LIMITED
POST-CLOSING TRIAL BALANCE

31 December 20X5

Account	Debit	Credit
Cash	$ 67,300	
Accounts receivable	45,000	
Allowance for doubtful accounts		$ 2,200
Notes receivable	8,000	
Interest receivable	100	
Inventory (31 December balance)	90,000	
Prepaid insurance	400	
Land	8,000	
Building	160,000	
Accumulated amortization, building		100,000
Equipment	91,000	
Accumulated amortization, equipment		36,000
Accounts payable		29,000
Interest payable		500
Rent collected in advance		600
Income tax payable		20,000
Bonds payable, 6%		50,000
Common shares, no par, 15,000 shares		170,000
Retained earnings (31 December balance)		61,500
Totals	$469,800	$469,800

Step 10: Journalize and Post Reversing Journal Entries

Depending on the firm's accounting system and its accounting policies, reversing journal entries (RJEs) may be used to simplify certain journal entries in the next accounting period. RJEs are optional entries that

- Are dated the first day of the next accounting period;
- Use the same accounts and amounts as an AJE but with the debits and credits reversed; and
- Are posted to the ledger.

RJEs are appropriate only for AJEs that

1. Defer the recognition of revenue or expense items recorded under the expedient method, or
2. Accrue revenue or expense items during the current period (for example, wages expense).

Thus, if a deferral or accrual AJE creates or increases an asset or liability, an RJE is appropriate. RJEs are inappropriate for AJEs that adjust assets and liabilities recorded for cash flows preceding the recognition of revenues and expenses (the standard method) and for some other AJEs, such as reclassifications, error corrections, and estimations.

In the following examples, assume a 31 December year-end.

Deferred Item—Expedient Method. Assume that on 1 November 20X5, $300 is paid in advance for three months' rent:

1 November 20X5—originating entry		
Rent expense	300	
Cash		300
31 December 20X5—adjusting entry		
Prepaid rent	100	
Rent expense		100

	With Reversing Entry			Without Reversing Entry		
1 January 20X6						
Reversing entry:	Rent expense	100				
	Prepaid rent		100			
20X6						
Subsequent entry:	(No entry needed)			Rent expense	100	
				Prepaid rent		100

With or without an RJE, rent expense recorded in 20X6 is $100. Use of the RJE, however, saves the cost and effort of reviewing the relevant accounts and source documents to determine the subsequent year's entry. The RJE makes the necessary adjustments to the accounts while the information used in making the AJE is available.

Now consider the standard method applied to the same example.

1 November 20X5—originating entry		
Prepaid rent	300	
Cash		300
31 December 20X5—adjusting entry		
Rent expense	200	
Prepaid rent		200

An RJE is not appropriate. No purpose is served by reinstating (debiting) prepaid rent $200 because that amount has expired.

Accrued Item. Assume that the last payroll for 20X5 is on 28 December. Wages earned through 28 December are included in this payroll. The next payroll period ends 4 January 20X6, at which time $2,800 of wages will be paid. Wages earned for the three-day period ending 31 December 20X5 are $1,500, which will be paid in 20X6. The following AJE is necessary to accrue these wages:

31 December 20X5—adjusting entry

Wages expense		1,500	
Wages payable			1,500

	With Reversing Entry			Without Reversing Entry		
1 January 20X6						
Reversing entry:	Wages payable	1,500				
	Wages expense		1,500			
4 January 20X6						
Subsequent entry:	Wages expense	2,800		Wages expense	1,300	
	Cash		2,800	Wages payable	1,500	
				Cash		2,800

In this example, the RJE simplifies the subsequent payroll entry, which can now be recorded in a manner identical to all other payrolls. With or without reversing entries, total 20X6 wage expense recognized through 4 January 20X6 is $1,300. RJEs often create abnormal short-term account balances. In the above 1 January 20X6 entry, the RJE creates a credit balance in wages expense. The subsequent entry changes the net balance of wages expense to a $1,300 debit.

Some of Sonora's AJEs could be reversed:

(b) Rent expense (expedient method—deferred item);

(c) Interest expense (accrual);

(d) Interest revenue (accrual); and

(h) Income tax expense (accrual).

SUBSIDIARY LEDGERS

Companies typically maintain both *control* and *subsidiary* ledger accounts. Subsidiary ledgers are often kept for accounts payable and accounts receivable, although any ledger account can be supported by a subsidiary ledger if size and complexity warrant.

The sum of all account balances in a subsidiary ledger must equal the related control account balance in the general ledger. To ensure that the control account and its subsidiary ledger are equal, frequent reconciliations are made. All posting must be complete, both to the control account and to the subsidiary ledger, before a reconciliation can be accomplished. Postings are made *in total* to the control account and *to individual accounts* in the subsidiary ledger. These postings are described in more depth in the next section.

To illustrate a reconciliation, refer ahead to the accounts receivable subsidiary ledger in Exhibit A-14. A reconciliation for accounts receivable control and the accounts receivable subsidiary ledger based on the information in Exhibit A-14 follows:

RECONCILIATION OF ACCOUNTS RECEIVABLE SUBSIDIARY LEDGER

At 31 January 20X5	**Amount**
Subsidiary ledger balances	
112.13 Adams Co.	$ 980
112.42 Miller, J. B.	196
112.91 XY Manufacturing Co.	1,960
Total	$ 3,136
General ledger balance	
Accounts receivable control ($5,000 + $9,360 − $11,224)	$ 3,136

Subsidiary ledgers contain information that helps the company operate efficiently—individual account receivable and payable balances are essential information. In smaller companies, subsidiary ledgers can be maintained through a simple filing system—for example, a copy of a sales invoice that is not paid can be kept in a special file until the money is received. At any time, the outstanding receivables are equal to the total of the invoices in the file. The same can be done with accounts payable, if all unpaid bills are kept in an accounts payable file. The point is that formal accounting systems are made necessary by size and complexity, but simple methods in simple situations can be just as effective if efficiently operated.

SPECIAL JOURNALS

Both *general journals* and *special journals* are used in many accounting systems. Even when extensive use is made of special journals, a need exists for a general journal to record the adjusting, closing, reversing, and correcting entries and those transactions that do not apply to any of the special journals. A general journal was illustrated in Exhibit A-3.

A special journal is designed to expedite the recording of similar transactions that occur frequently. Each special journal is constructed specifically to simplify the data-processing tasks involved in journalizing and posting those types of transactions. Special journals can be custom designed to meet the particular needs of the business. Commonly used special journals include

1. *Sales journal* for recording only sales of merchandise on credit.
2. *Purchases journal* for recording only purchases of merchandise on credit.
3. *Cash receipts journal* for recording only cash receipts, including cash sales.
4. *Cash disbursements journal* for recording only cash payments, including cash purchases.
5. *Voucher system*, designed to replace the purchases journal and cash payments journal, composed of:
   a. A *voucher register* for recording only vouchers payable. A voucher payable is prepared for each cash payment regardless of purpose.
   b. A *cheque register* for recording all cheques written in payment of approved vouchers.

The special journals illustrated in this appendix carry page numbers preceded by letters indicating the journal name. The S in the page number of Exhibit A-10 denotes the sales journal, for example.

SALES JOURNAL This special journal is designed to record sales on account, which otherwise would be recorded as follows in a general journal:

2 January 20X5		
Accounts receivable ($1,000 × 98%)	980	
Sales revenue		980
(Credit sale to Adams Company; invoice price, $1,000; terms 2/10, n/30)		

The sales journal can accommodate any entry that involves a debit to accounts receivable and a credit to sales. However, this is the *only* entry it can record. If the debit is to cash, or notes receivable, another journal must be used. Exhibit A-10 illustrates a typical sales journal for credit sales. The above entry is shown as the first entry in 20X5. The amount of sale is recorded only once. Each entry in the sales journal records the same information found in the traditional debit-credit format.

Terms 2/10, n/30 mean that if the account is paid within 10 days after date of sale, a 2% cash discount is granted. The cash discount encourages early payment. If the bill is not paid within the 10-day discount period, the full amount must be paid. The account is past due at the end of 30 days. Receipt of $1,000 after the 10-day discount period does not increase sales revenue but means that the seller has earned finance revenue of $20 ($1,000 − $980). Hence, it is correct to record net sales revenue of $980. However, many companies prefer to record the *gross* sale, $1,000 in this example, because it is easier to focus on the amount of the invoice. Sales discounts are then recorded when the customer pays the net amount.

The posting of amounts from the sales journal to the general and subsidiary ledgers is simplified. The two phases in posting a sales journal are the following:

1. Daily posting: The amount of each credit sale is posted daily to the appropriate individual account in the accounts receivable subsidiary ledger. Posting is indicated by entering the account number in the posting reference column. For example, the number 112.13 entered in the posting reference column in Exhibit A-10 is the account number assigned to Adams Company and shows that $980 is posted as a debit to Adams Company in the subsidiary ledger. The number 112 is the general number used for accounts receivable (see Exhibit A-14).

2. Monthly posting: At the end of each month, the receivable and sale amount column is totalled. This total is posted to two accounts in the general ledger. In Exhibit A-10, the $9,360 total is posted as a debit to account no. 112 (accounts receivable control) and as a credit to account no. 500 (sales revenue). The T-accounts shown in Exhibit A-14 illustrate how these postings are reflected in both the general ledger and the subsidiary ledger. The two ledgers show the journal page from which each amount is posted.

EXHIBIT A-10

Page S-23

SALES JOURNAL

Date 20X5	Sales Invoice No.	Accounts Receivable (name)	Terms	Post. Ref.	Receivable and Sale Amount
2 Jan.	93	Adams Co.	2/10, n/30	112.13	$ 980
3	94	Sayre Corp.	2/10, n/30	112.80	490
11	95	Cope & Day Co.	net	112.27	5,734
27	96	XY Mfg. Co.	2/10, n/30	112.91	1,960
30	97	Miller, J. B.	2/10, n/30	112.42	196
31	—	Total			$ 9,360
31	—	Posting			(112/500)

PURCHASES JOURNAL This special journal is designed to accommodate frequent purchases of merchandise on account. Again, there is only one entry that can go into this journal—a debit to purchases, and a credit to accounts payable. Other entries, including purchases for cash, go elsewhere. Consider the following entry, recorded in general journal format:

3 January 20X5		
Purchases ($1,000 × .99)	990	
Accounts payable (PT Mfg. Co.)		990
(terms 1/20, n/30)		

Again note the use of net recording. The invoice is recorded at its net amount, after the 1% discount. Some companies prefer to record purchase invoices gross, and record purchase discounts taken when they record payment. Notice also that the entry assumes a periodic inventory. Under a perpetual inventory system, the debit would always be to the inventory account.

This entry is recorded as the first 20X5 entry in the purchases journal illustrated in Exhibit A-11. The accounting simplifications found in the sales journal are present in the purchases journal as well. Each amount is posted daily as a credit to the account of an individual creditor in the accounts payable subsidiary ledger. At the end of the month, the total of the purchases and payable amount column ($6,760 in Exhibit A-11), is posted to the general ledger as a debit to the purchases account (no. 612) and as a credit to the accounts payable control account (no. 210).

EXHIBIT A-11

Page P-6

PURCHASES JOURNAL

Date 20X5	Purchase Order No.	Accounts Payable (Name)	Terms	Posting Ref.	Purchases and Payable Amount
3 Jan.	41	PT Mfg. Co.	1/20, n/30	210.61	$ 990
7	42	Able Suppliers Ltd.	net	210.12	150
31	—	Total	—	—	6,760
31	—	Postings	—	—	(612/210)

CASH RECEIPTS JOURNAL A special cash receipts journal is used to accommodate a large volume of cash receipts transactions. This journal can accommodate any entry that involves a debit to cash. Multiple sources of cash (the credits) are accommodated by designing several credit columns for recurring credits, and a miscellaneous accounts column for infrequent credits, as shown in Exhibit A-12. Space is also provided for the names of particular accounts receivable.

During the month, each amount in the accounts receivable column is posted daily as a credit to an individual customer account in the accounts receivable subsidiary ledger. At the end of the month, the individual amounts in the miscellaneous account column are posted as credits to the appropriate general ledger accounts, and the totals for the cash, accounts receivable, and sales revenue columns are posted to the general ledger as indicated by the posting reference. The total of the miscellaneous accounts column is not posted because it consists of changes in different accounts. However, this column is totalled to ascertain overall debit-credit equality.

CASH DISBURSEMENTS JOURNAL Most companies use some form of a cash disbursements journal, which is also sometimes called a cheque register. This journal can accommodate any entry that involves a credit to cash, and has columns for the common debits and a miscellaneous debits column to make it flexible. Exhibit A-13 illustrates a typical cash disbursements journal. Journalizing and posting follow the same procedures explained for the cash receipts journal.

EXHIBIT A-12

Page CR-19

CASH RECEIPTS JOURNAL

Date 20X5	Explanation	Debit Cash	Account Title	Credits Post. Ref.	Accounts Receivable	Sales Revenue	Misc. Accounts
4 Jan.	Cash sales	$ 11,200		—		$11,200	
7	On acct.	4,490	Sayre Corp.	112.80	$ 4,490		
8	Sale of land	10,000	Land	123			$ 4,000
			Gain on sale of land	510			6,000
10	On acct.	1,000	Adams Co.	112.13	1,000		
19	Cash sales	43,600		—		43,600	
20	On acct.	5,734	Cope & Day Co.	112.27	5,734		
31	Totals	$ 116,224		—	$ 11,224	$71,000	$34,000
31	Posting	(101)		—	(112)	(500)	(NP)*

* NP—not posted as one total because the individual amounts are posted as indicated in the posting reference column.

EXHIBIT A-13

Page CD-31

CASH DISBURSEMENTS JOURNAL

Date 20X5	Cheque No.	Explanation	Credit Cash	Account Name	Debits Post. Ref.	Accounts Payable	Purchases	Misc. Accounts
2 Jan.	141	Pur. mdse.	$ 3,000		—		$ 3,000	
10	142	On acct.	990	PT Mfg. Co.	210.61	$ 990		
15	143	Jan. rent	660	Rent exp.	1300			$ 660
16	144	Pur. mdse.	1,810				1,810	
31	—	Totals	$98,400		—	$ 5,820	$90,980	$1,600
31	—	Posting	(101)		—	(210)	(612)	(NP)

THE GENERAL JOURNAL Special journals can be used to record common entries, but there will always be entries that do not fit the format for any special journal and must be recorded in general journal format. Adjusting and reversing entries are prime examples, but unusual operating transactions will also be recorded in this format. The general journal is an essential element of accounting record-keeping.

VOUCHER SYSTEMS Voucher systems are designed to enhance internal control over cash disbursements. A voucher is a document that describes a liability and lists information about the creditor, a description of the good or service received, authorizing signatures, and other details of the transaction, including invoice number, terms, amount due,

EXHIBIT A-14

GENERAL LEDGER AND SUBSIDIARY LEDGER

GENERAL LEDGER (PARTIAL)

Cash Acct. 101

20X5			20X5		
1 Jan.	Balance	18,700	31 Jan.	CD-31	98,400
31	CR-19	116,224			

Accounts Receivable Control Acct. 112

20X5			20X5		
1 Jan.	Balance	5,000	31 Jan.	CR-19	11,224
31	S-23	9,360			

Sales Revenue Acct. 500

			20X5		
			31 Jan.	S-23	9,360
			31	CR-19	71,000

SUBSIDIARY LEDGER FOR ACCOUNTS RECEIVABLE (ACCT. NO. 112)

Date 20X5	Post Ref.	Explanation	Debit	Credit	Balance
		Adams Company—Acct. No. 112.13			
1 Jan.		Balance			1,000
2	S-23		980		1,980
10	CR-19			1,000	980
		Cope & Day Company—Acct. No. 112.27			
11 Jan.	S-23	Balance	5,734		5,734
20	CR-19			5,734	0
		Miller, J. B.—Acct. No. 112.42			
30 Jan.	S-23	Balance	196		196
		Sayre Corporation—Acct. No. 112.80			
1 Jan.		Balance			4,000
3	S-23		490		4,490
7	CR-19			4,490	0
		XY Manufacturing Company—Acct. No. 112.91			
27 Jan.	S-23		1,960		1,960

and due date. In a voucher system, every transaction requiring payment by cheque begins with an invoice or other document that supplies information for completing a voucher.

Together, the voucher, purchase order, receiving report, and invoice form a packet of information that must be complete before a cash disbursement can be made. All authori-

EXHIBIT A-15

Page V-64

VOUCHER REGISTER

Voucher Date 20X5	Voucher Number	Payee	(Entered Later) Date Paid	(Entered Later) Cheque No.	Voucher Payable Credit	Account Debited (Multiple Columns)
1 Jan.	1	Crowell Co.	2 Jan. 20X5	141	$3,000	Purchases
3	2	PT Mfg. Co.	10 Jan. 20X5	142	990	Purchases
9	3	Williams Co.	15 Jan. 20X5	143	660	Rent Expense

zations must be indicated. Verification of amounts and calculations are part of the payment authorization process. Often, several departments, including the internal audit and accounting departments, are required to authorize a large cash payment.

The completed voucher is the basis for an accounting entry in a special journal called the voucher register. The voucher register is not restricted to purchases. Before payment is made, the authorized voucher is recorded in the voucher register. Exhibit A-15 illustrates an abbreviated page from a voucher register.

A new account, vouchers payable, is used to record all routine liabilities. This new account replaces accounts payable and other payables used for routine payments. When a voucher is recorded in the voucher payable credit column, it reflects the amount of the liability. The account debited reflects the good or service received. Unlike the voucher register shown in Exhibit A-15, most voucher registers have several debit columns for speedy recording of repetitive cash payments of the same type. The total of the vouchers payable column is posted to the vouchers payable control. The cheque number and date paid do not appear in the voucher register until a cheque is issued and payment is made to the payee. Although a voucher is prepared for each item, one cheque can be issued for the payment of several vouchers to the same creditor.

Unpaid vouchers are placed into a file pending payment and are typically filed by due date. It is important that payments be initiated within cash discount periods to obtain the lowest possible price for merchandise purchases. The unpaid voucher file is the subsidiary ledger in a voucher system.

When a voucher becomes due, it is sent by the accounting department to a person authorized to issue cheques. After a review of the authorization on the voucher is made, a cheque is prepared for the correct amount. The paid voucher is sent back to the accounting department, which enters the cheque number and payment into the voucher register. Information from the voucher is also entered in the cheque register illustrated in Exhibit A-16.

The total of the amount column in the cheque register is posted to the vouchers payable control account (dr.) and to the cash account (cr.). The paid voucher is retained to substantiate cash payments and for audit trail purposes. The voucher register and cheque register replace the purchases and cash payments journals.

EXHIBIT A-16

CHEQUE REGISTER

Date	Payee	Voucher Number	Cheque Number	Vouchers Payable Dr. and Cash Cr.
2 Jan. 20X5	Crowell Co.	1	141	$3,000
10	PT Mfg. Co.	2	142	990
15	Williams Co.	3	143	660

WORKSHEETS

A worksheet is a multicolumn work space that provides an organized format for performing several end-of-period accounting cycle steps and for preparing financial statements before posting AJEs. It also provides evidence, or an audit trail, of an organized and structured accounting process that can be more easily reviewed than other methods of analysis.

In manual accounting systems, worksheet input is developed by transferring account name and balance information manually from the general ledger to the worksheet. With most computerized systems, this task is accomplished automatically. Computer spreadsheet and accounting software programs can be used to generate worksheets quickly and with relative ease. Computer spreadsheets also offer important labour and time savings in the planning and mechanical posting of AJEs on the worksheet. This software is a powerful tool for accomplishing several steps in the accounting cycle.

Use of a worksheet is always optional. The worksheet is not part of the basic accounting records. Worksheets assist with only a portion of the accounting cycle. Formal AJEs are recorded in the accounts in addition to those entered on the worksheet.

Illustration of the Worksheet Approach

Exhibit A-17 illustrates the completed worksheet for Sonora Limited, the company used in this appendix to present the accounting cycle. The worksheet has a debit and a credit column for each of the following: the unadjusted trial balance, the AJEs, the adjusted trial balance, the income statement, the retained earnings statement, and the balance sheet. The worksheet is prepared in four steps:

Step 1 *Enter the unadjusted trial balance in the first set of columns of the worksheet by inserting the year-end balances of all ledger accounts.*

- The inventory and retained earnings balances are the beginning-of-year balances because no transactions have affected these accounts. Confirm the debit-credit equality of the totals.

Step 2 *Enter the adjusting entries.*

- The lowercase letters refer to the same AJEs discussed in this appendix for Sonora Limited.
- The worksheet AJEs are facilitating entries only and are not formally recorded in the general journal at this point. If a new account is created by an AJE, it is inserted in its normal position or at the bottom of the worksheet. Confirm the debit-credit equality of the totals.
- Determine income tax expense and payable. (Sonora's tax computation was illustrated earlier.) Enter the accounts and the amounts in the AJE columns. Income tax expense (entry (h)) is positioned below the totals of the AJE columns because this reflects its sequence in the adjustment process.

Step 3 *Cross-add.*

- Enter the adjusted trial balance by adding or subtracting across the unadjusted trial balance sheet columns and AJE columns, for each account. For example, the adjusted balance of the allowance for doubtful accounts is the sum of its unadjusted balance ($1,000) and the $1,200 increase from AJE (f).
- The inventory account now displays ending inventory, purchases and related accounts no longer have balances, and cost of goods sold is present. Confirm the debit-credit equality of the totals.

Step 4 *Extend the adjusted trial balance amounts to the financial statements; complete the worksheet.*

- Each account in the adjusted trial balance is extended to one of the three sets of remaining debit-credit columns. Temporary accounts are sorted to the income statement columns (revenues to the credit column, expenses to the debit column). Permanent accounts are sorted to the balance sheet columns except for the beginning balance in retained earnings, which is extended to the retained earnings columns. Dividends go in the retained earnings columns.

EXHIBIT A-17

COMPLETED WORKSHEET FOR SONORA LTD.

	Unadjusted Trial Balance		Adjusting Entries		Adjusted Trial Balance		Income Statement		Retained Earnings Statement		Balance Sheet	
	Debit	Credit	Debit	Credit	Debit	Credit	Debit	Credit	Debit	Credit	Debit	Credit
Cash	67,300				67,300						67,300	
Notes receivable	8,000				8,000						8,000	
Accounts receivable	45,000				45,000						45,000	
Allowance for doubtful accounts		1,000		(f) 1,200		2,200						2,200
Interest receivable			(d) 100		100						100	
Inventory (periodic)	75,000		(g) 90,000	(g) 75,000	90,000						90,000	
Prepaid insurance	600			(a) 200	400						400	
Land	8,000				8,000						8,000	
Building	160,000				160,000						160,000	
Accumulated amortization, building		90,000		(e) 10,000		100,000						100,000
Equipment	91,000				91,000						91,000	
Accumulated amortization, equipment		27,000		(e) 9,000		36,000						36,000
Accounts payable		29,000				29,000						29,000
Interest payable				(c) 500		500						500
Rent collected in advance				(b) 600		600						600
Bonds payable, 6%		50,000				50,000						50,000
Common shares, no par, 15,000 shares		170,000				170,000						170,000
Retained earnings		41,500				41,500				41,500		
Dividends declared	10,000				10,000				10,000			
Sales revenue		325,200				325,200		325,200				
Interest revenue		500		(d) 100		600		600				
Rent revenue		1,800	(b) 600			1,200		1,200				
Purchases	130,000			(g) 130,000								
Freight on purchases	4,000			(g) 4,000								
Purchase returns		2,000	(g) 2,000									
Cost of goods sold			(g) 117,000		117,000		117,000					
Selling expenses	104,000		(e) 8,200									
			(f) 1,200		113,400		113,400					
General and administrative expenses	23,600		(a) 200									
			(e) 10,800		34,600		34,600					
Interest expense	2,500		(c) 500		3,000		3,000					
Loss on discontinued operations	9,000				9,000		9,000					
	738,000	738,000	230,600	230,600	756,800	756,800	277,000	327,000				
Income tax expense			(h) 20,000		20,000		20,000					20,000
Income tax payable				(h) 20,000		20,000	297,000	327,000				
					776,800	776,800						
Net income to retained earnings							30,000			30,000		
Retained earnings to balance sheet									61,500			61,500
Totals							327,000	327,000	71,500	71,500	469,800	469,800

- Total the income statement columns before income tax expense. Pre-tax income is the difference between the debit and credit column totals. A net credit represents income; a net debit represents a loss. For Sonora, pre-tax income is $50,000 ($327,000 − $277,000). Next, determine net income after taxes by extending the income tax expense amount ($20,000) into the debit column and again totalling the columns. Net income is the difference between the columns, equalling $30,000 for Sonora ($327,000 − $297,000).
- Next, add a line description (net income to retained earnings) and enter the $30,000 net income amount as a balancing value in the income statement columns: positive net income is a debit balancing value; negative income is a credit. Then complete this entry by recording $30,000 in the credit column under the retained earnings columns. (Positive net income is a credit entry, and negative income is a debit entry.)
- Total the retained earnings columns and enter a balancing amount (the ending retained earnings balance) in the appropriate column to achieve debit-credit equality. For Sonora, the balancing amount is a $61,500 debit. Add a line description (retained earnings to balance sheet) and enter the balancing amount into the appropriate balance sheet column.
- Total the balance sheet columns and confirm debit-credit equality.

The worksheet is now complete, and the financial statements are prepared directly from the last three sets of worksheet columns. The formal AJEs are then journalized and posted.

SUMMARY OF KEY POINTS

1. The AIS provides information for daily management information needs and for preparation of financial statements.
2. There are seven basic types of accounts. The balance sheet discloses the balances of the permanent accounts, which include assets, liabilities, and owners' equity accounts. The income statement discloses the pre-closing balances of most temporary accounts, which include revenues, gains, expenses, and losses. Debits to assets, expenses, and losses increase those accounts. Credits to liabilities, owners' equity, revenues, and gains increase those accounts.
3. There are 10 steps in the accounting cycle that culminate in the financial statements. Refer to Exhibit A-2.
4. The application of accounting principles generally occurs at the journal entry step. Journal entries record events and transactions. Account changes are posted to accounts, and accounts are used to create financial statements.
5. Companies may use the standard or the expedient method or both to record routine operating cash receipts and payments that precede revenue and expense recognition. The choice of methods affects some AJEs and the use of RJEs.
6. AJEs are required under accrual accounting to complete the measurement and recording of changes in resources and obligations.
7. RJEs are optional entries, dated at the beginning of the accounting period, that reverse certain AJEs from the previous period and are used to facilitate subsequent journal entries.
8. Subsidiary ledgers are used to maintain records on the component elements of ledger control accounts.
9. Special journals are used to record repetitive entries, such as sales, purchases, cash receipts, and cash disbursements. A general journal is used to record entries that do not fit into special journals. A voucher register may replace a purchases journal.
10. A worksheet may be used to organize the adjustment and financial statement preparation phases of the accounting cycle.

KEY TERMS

accounting identity, 675
accounting information system (AIS), 675
adjusting journal entries (AJEs), 683
cash-basis accounting, 683
contra account, 685
debit-credit convention, 675
double-entry system, 675
expedient recording method, 683
financial statement, 676
general journal, 679
general ledger, 680
journal, 679
non-reciprocal transfers, 679
periodic inventory system, 681
permanent accounts, 675
posting, 680
reciprocal transfer, 679
special journal, 679
standard recording method, 683
subsidiary ledger, 680
temporary accounts, 675
transactions, 679

REVIEW PROBLEM

Bucknell Company developed its unadjusted trial balance dated 31 December 20X5, which appears below. Bucknell uses the expedient recording method whenever possible, adjusts its accounts once per year, records all appropriate RJEs, and adjusts its periodic inventory-related accounts in an AJE. Ignore income taxes.

BUCKNELL COMPANY
UNADJUSTED TRIAL BALANCE

31 December 20X5	Debit	Credit
Cash	$ 40,000	
Accounts receivable	60,000	
Allowance for doubtful accounts		$ 6,000
Inventory	90,000	
Equipment	780,000	
Accumulated amortization		100,000
Land	150,000	
Accounts payable		22,000
Notes payable, 8%, due 1 April 20X10		200,000
Common shares, no-par, 60,000 shares		400,000
Retained earnings		50,000
Sales revenue (all on account)		900,000
Subscription revenue		24,000
Purchases	250,000	
Rent expense	60,000	
Interest expense	12,000	
Selling expense	40,000	
Insurance expense	30,000	
Wages expense	110,000	
General and administrative expense	80,000	
Totals	$1,702,000	$1,702,000

Additional information:

a. Ending inventory by physical count is $70,000.
b. The equipment has a total estimated useful life of 14 years and an estimated residual value of $80,000. Bucknell uses straight-line amortization and treats amortization expense as a general and administrative expense.
c. Bad debt expense for 20X5 is estimated to be 1% of sales.
d. The note payable requires interest to be paid semi-annually, every 1 October and 1 April.
e. $5,000 of wages were earned in December but not recorded or paid.
f. The rent expense represents a payment made on 2 January 20X5, for two years' rent (20X5 and 20X6).
g. The insurance expense represents payment made for a one-year policy, paid 30 June 20X5. Coverage began on that date.
h. The subscription revenue represents cash received from several university libraries for an 18-month subscription to a journal published by Bucknell. The subscription period began 1 July 20X5.

Required:

1. Record the required AJEs.
2. Prepare the adjusted trial balance.
3. Prepare the income statement and an unclassified balance sheet for 20X5.
4. Prepare closing entries.
5. Prepare RJEs.

REVIEW PROBLEM—SOLUTION

Requirement 1

a. Inventory (ending)	70,000	
Cost of goods sold	270,000	
Purchases		250,000
Inventory (beginning)		90,000
b. General and administrative expense ($780,000 − $80,000)/14	50,000	
Accumulated amortization		50,000
c. Bad debt expense (.01 × $900,000)	9,000	
Allowance for doubtful accounts		9,000
d. Interest expense ($200,000 × .08 × 3/12)	4,000	
Interest payable		4,000
e. Wages expense	5,000	
Wages payable		5,000
f. Prepaid rent ($60,000 × 1/2)	30,000	
Rent expense		30,000
g. Prepaid insurance ($30,000 × 6/12)	15,000	
Insurance expense		15,000
h. Subscription revenue ($24,000 × 12/18)	16,000	
Unearned subscriptions		16,000

Requirement 2

BUCKNELL COMPANY
ADJUSTED TRIAL BALANCE

31 December 20X5	Debit	Credit
Cash	$ 40,000	
Accounts receivable	60,000	
Allowance for doubtful accounts		$ 15,000
Prepaid rent	30,000	
Prepaid insurance	15,000	
Inventory	70,000	
Equipment	780,000	
Accumulated amortization		150,000
Land	150,000	
Accounts payable		22,000
Interest payable		4,000
Wages payable		5,000
Unearned subscriptions		16,000
Notes payable, 8%, due 1 April 20X10		200,000
Common shares, no-par, 60,000 shares		400,000
Retained earnings		50,000
Sales revenue		900,000
Subscription revenue		8,000
Cost of goods sold	270,000	
Rent expense	30,000	
Interest expense	16,000	
Selling expense	40,000	
Insurance expense	15,000	
Wages expense	115,000	
Bad debt expense	9,000	
General and administrative expense	130,000	
Totals	$1,770,000	$1,770,000

Requirement 3

BUCKNELL COMPANY
INCOME STATEMENT

For the year ended 31 December 20X5		
Revenues:		
Sales revenue	$900,000	
Subscription revenue	8,000	
Total revenue		$908,000
Expenses:		
Cost of goods sold	270,000	
Rent expense	30,000	
Interest expense	16,000	
Selling expense	40,000	
Insurance expense	15,000	
Wages expense	115,000	
Bad debt expense	9,000	
General and administrative expense	130,000	
Total expenses		625,000
Net income		$283,000

BUCKNELL COMPANY
BALANCE SHEET

31 December 20X5

Assets			
Cash		$ 40,000	
Accounts receivable	$ 60,000		
Allowance for doubtful accounts	(15,000)	45,000	
Prepaid rent		30,000	
Prepaid insurance		15,000	
Inventory		70,000	
Equipment	780,000		
Accumulated amortization	(150,000)	630,000	
Land		150,000	
Total assets			$980,000
Liabilities			
Accounts payable		$ 22,000	
Interest payable		4,000	
Wages payable		5,000	
Unearned subscriptions		16,000	
Notes payable, 8%, due 1 April 20X10		200,000	
Total liabilities			$247,000
Shareholders' Equity			
Common shares, no par, 60,000 shares outstanding		400,000	
Retained earnings		333,000*	
Total owners' equity			733,000
Total liabilities and owners' equity			$980,000

* $50,000 + $283,000

Requirement 4

Sales revenue	900,000	
Subscription revenue	8,000	
Income summary		908,000
Income summary	625,000	
Cost of goods sold		270,000
Rent expense		30,000
Interest expense		16,000
Selling expense		40,000
Insurance expense		15,000
Wages expense		115,000
Bad debt expense		9,000
General and administrative expense		130,000
Income summary	283,000	
Retained earnings		283,000

Requirement 5

Interest payable	4,000	
Interest expense		4,000
Wages payable	5,000	
Wages expense		5,000
Rent expense	30,000	
Prepaid rent		30,000
Insurance expense	15,000	
Prepaid insurance		15,000
Unearned subscriptions	16,000	
Subscription revenue		16,000

ASSIGNMENTS

A-1 Effect of Transactions: The following captions are totals or subtotals on the balance sheet for Cyber Corporation:

A. Total current assets.
B. Total capital assets (net of accumulated amortization).
C. Total current liabilities.
D. Total long-term liabilities.
E. Total contributed capital (or share capital).
F. Total retained earnings (including income effects).

Required:

For each event listed below, indicate which subtotal(s) increased or decreased as a result of the event. Indicate with an X if there has been no subtotal increase or decrease. Consider each event to be unrelated to the others.

Events	Increase	Decrease
Example: Issued shares for cash	A, E	X
1. Wrote off an uncollectible account receivable to the allowance for doubtful accounts.		
2. Sold temporary investments for cash, received less than the original cost.		
3. Recorded a cash sale.		
4. Recorded the cost of goods sold in a perpetual inventory system.		
5. Bought inventory on account in a perpetual inventory system.		
6. Increased the allowance for doubtful accounts.		
7. Converted long-term convertible bonds into common shares.		
8. Paid a previously recorded accounts payable.		
9. Decreased the supplies inventory as part of year-end adjustments; the company uses the expedient method during the year.		
10. Reduced the unearned revenue account as part of year-end adjustments; the company uses the standard method during the year.		
11. Recorded amortization on capital assets.		
12. Borrowed money and issued a long-term note payable.		

A-2 Journalize Transactions: RCV Company recorded the following transactions in the month of October:

a. Sold merchandise on account, $284,800.
b. Borrowed $300,000 from the bank.
c. Cash sales, $614,400.
d. Paid $108,800 for operating expenses.
e. Bought merchandise on credit, $365,600.
f. Collected $196,800 from customers on account.
g. Bought automotive equipment, $36,200; paid $10,000 in cash and borrowed the rest.
h. Returned $16,000 of the good purchased in (e) because of defects.
i. Paid for $172,800 of the goods bought on credit in (e), plus $133,600 from last month's outstanding bills.

j. Paid dividends to common shareholders, $29,000.
k. Paid wages of $24,800.
l. Paid $8,600 in interest to the bank.

Required:

1. Journalize each of the above transactions in general journal form.
2. Indicate in which special journal each transaction would normally be recorded, assuming that a company keeps purchases, sales, cash receipts, cash disbursements, and general journals.

A-3 Journalize Transactions and Adjustments; Valuation: Zfind Corporation reports the following in the month of April:

a. Issued 17,000 no-par common shares for cash, $68,000.
b. Issued 15,000 no-par common shares for a piece of used equipment with an appraised value of $52,000. The equipment had an original cost of $76,000 to the seller three years ago. The net book value (cost less accumulated depreciation) on the books of the seller was $42,900 on the date of sale.
c. Bought land with an appraised value of $70,000. An 8%, three-year note payable was issued in the amount of $50,000, and $20,000 was paid in cash.
d. Bought office supplies on account, $1,200. A balance sheet account is debited.
e. Hired three employees. All employees are paid on a monthly basis. Monthly salaries for the three will amount to $8,000. (Two will be paid $3,000 per month each, and one will be paid $2,000 per month.)
f. Three months' rent is paid in advance. The lease calls for $1,000 of rent per month. A balance sheet account is debited.
g. Goods for resale in the amount of $120,000 are bought. Twenty percent of the price is paid in cash, and the rest is on account. These goods are priced to sell at $266,000.
h. Received an order from a customer for goods worth $50,000. The goods will be shipped in the next week (see (j)).
i. Miscellaneous operating expenses are paid in the amount of $14,400, cash.
j. Goods are delivered to customers and they are billed, on account, $245,000. The order, in (h) above, is included in this total. The goods delivered to the customers cost $110,000. There are still goods that cost $10,000, with a retail value of $21,000, in inventory.
k. One month has gone by, and monthly rent expense is recorded.
l. Employee salaries for one month are paid.
m. The Board of Directors declares, but does not pay, a dividend in the amount of $13,600.
n. Office supplies on hand at year-end, per physical count, $400.
o. Goods purchased on account in (g) above are paid for in full.
p. Eighty percent of the accounts receivable from customers, as recorded in (j) above, are received.

Required:

1. Journalize the transactions and events listed above. If no journal entry is needed, write "no entry." If there is a choice of value to use, justify your choice.
2. Which entries recorded are transactions, and which are adjustments? Explain.

A-4 Journalize and Post; Unadjusted Trial Balance: The following selected transactions were completed during 20X5 by Marlon Corporation, a retailer of Scandinavian furniture:

a. Issued 60,000 shares of its own no-par common shares for $16.50 per share and received cash in full.
b. Borrowed $600,000 cash on a 9%, one-year note, interest payable at maturity on 30 April 20X6.

c. Purchased equipment for use in operating the business at a net cash cost of $588,000; paid in full.
d. Purchased merchandise for resale at a cash cost of $560,000; paid cash. Assume a periodic inventory system; therefore, debit purchases.
e. Purchased merchandise for resale on credit terms 2/10, n/60. The merchandise will cost $19,600 if paid within 10 days; after 10 days, the payment will be $20,000. The company plans to take the discount; therefore, this purchase is recorded net of discount.
f. Sold merchandise for $180,000; collected $110,000 cash, and the balance is due in one month.
g. Paid $120,000 cash for operating expenses.
h. Paid three-quarters of the balance for the merchandise purchased in (e) within five days; the balance remains unpaid and the discount has been lost.
i. Collected 50% of the balance due on the sale in (f); the remaining balance is uncollected.
j. Paid cash for an insurance premium, $3,600; the premium is for two years' coverage (debit prepaid insurance).
k. Purchased a tract of land for a future building for company operations, $196,000 cash.
l. Paid damages to a customer who was injured on the company premises, $80,000 cash.

Required:

1. Enter transactions in a general journal; use J1 for the first journal page number. Use the letter of the transaction in place of the date.
2. Set up appropriate T-accounts and post the journal entries. Use posting reference numbers in your posting. Assign each T account an appropriate title, and number each account in balance sheet order followed by the income statement accounts; start with Cash, No. 101.
3. Prepare an unadjusted trial balance.

A-5 Trial Balance Errors: The trial balance for Nguyen Repairs Limited as at 31 July 20X8 does not balance because of a number of errors. These errors include copying errors, posting errors, and so on, as described below.

NGUYEN REPAIRS LTD
TRIAL BALANCE AS OF 31 JULY 20X8

	Debit	*Credit*
Cash	$ 5,800	
Accounts receivable	12,376	
Supplies	3,520	
Prepaid insurance	896	
Equipment	27,720	
Notes payable		$ 6,000
Accounts payable		2,280
Common shares		10,200
Retained earnings		3,600
Dividends	800	
Sales		59,060
Wages expense	18,600	
Rent expense	4,400	
Advertising expense	324	
Utilities expense	980	
Totals	$75,416	$81,140

Errors noted:

a. As the result of a copying error when listing the trial balance, the balance of cash was overstated by $400.
b. A cash receipt of $1,280 was posted as a debit to cash $1,820.

c. A credit of $360 to accounts receivable was not posted.
d. A return of $840 of defective supplies was erroneously posted as a $480 credit to supplies.
e. An insurance policy, acquired at year-end for the next fiscal year, with a cost of $4,400 was posted as a credit to prepaid insurance.
f. The balance of notes payable was understated by $800.
g. A debit of $1,040 in accounts payable was overlooked when determining the balance of the account.
h. A debit of $800 for a dividend was posted as a credit to the common share account.
i. The balance of $1,324 in advertising expense was entered as $324 in the trial balance.
j. Miscellaneous expense, with a balance of $1,250, was omitted from the trial balance.
k. A credit to sales of $2,753 was posted as a debit.

Required:
Prepare a corrected trial balance.

A-6 Adjusting Entries: Rivers Corporation manufactures zippers in Quebec. It adjusts and closes its accounts each 31 December. The following situations require adjusting entries at the current year-end:

a. Machine A is to be depreciated for the full year. It cost $90,000, and the estimated useful life is five years, with an estimated residual value of $10,000. Use straight-line depreciation.
b. Credit sales for the current year amounted to $160,000. The estimated bad debt loss rate on credit sales is 0.5%.
c. Property taxes for the current year have not been recorded or paid. A statement for the calendar year was received near the end of December for $4,000; if paid after 1 February in the next year, a 10% penalty is assessed.
d. Office supplies that cost $800 were purchased during the year and debited to office supplies inventory. The inventories of these supplies on hand were $200 at the end of the prior year and $300 at the end of the current year.
e. Rivers rented an office in its building to a tenant for one year, starting on 1 September. Rent for one year amounting to $6,000 was collected at that date. The total amount collected was credited to rent revenue.
f. Rivers recorded a note receivable from a customer dated 1 November of the current year. It is a $12,000, 10% note, due in one year. At the maturity date, Rivers will collect the amount of the note plus interest for one year.

Required:
Prepare adjusting entries in the general journal for each situation. If no entry is required for an item, explain why.

A-7 Adjusting Entries: The following items are independent. Assume that the original transactions have been recorded correctly, or as described.

a. Carey Company has two notes payable outstanding. The first is a $445,000, 8% note, issued on 1 September. No interest has been paid to date. The second is a $350,000, 7% note issued on 1 April. Six months' interest was paid on 1 October. The notes payable themselves were properly recorded on issuance but interest must be accrued to 31 December, the year-end.
b. There is an unearned revenue account with a balance of $145,000. This includes a $10,000 security deposit from a tenant. This deposit will be returned when the tenant eventually vacates. The remaining $135,000 is six months' rent received, on a lease beginning 1 December, on commercial property.
c. Supplies inventory had a balance of $46,800 at the end of last year. During the year, $169,300 of supplies were purchased, and were debited directly to supplies expense. At year-end, an inventory count was conducted, and the balance was ascertained to be $34,750.
d. Advertising expense of $34,800 includes a $4,700 payment for an advertisement that will run in January of next year.

e. Prepaid insurance had a debit balance of $9,100 at the beginning of January. This represents the remaining 14 months in an insurance policy that was purchased in a prior year. On 1 April of the current year, a 30-month policy was bought for $25,200, which was debited to prepaid insurance. There were no other entries to the prepaid insurance account during the year. On 1 November, an 18-month policy was bought for $4,680. This policy was debited to insurance expense.

f. Certain invoices had not been recorded at 31 December: a $3,700 bill for power, a $460 phone bill, and a repair bill for $675. All these bills are due in January.

g. Salaries payable has a balance of $1,850, unadjusted from the last year-end. There are 14 employees. They were paid up to Friday, 27 December. There were two working days prior to the year-end. Three employees earn $300 per (five-day) week each, three earn $250 per week, and eight earn $400 per week.

Required:

1. Prepare adjusting journal entries to reflect the facts above.
2. Prepare reversing entries for adjusting journal entries that must be reversed.

A-8 Adjusting Entries: Voss Company, an accounting firm, adjusts and closes its accounts each 31 December.

1. On 31 December 20X5, the maintenance supplies inventory account showed a balance on hand amounting to $1,400. During 20X6, purchases of maintenance supplies amounted to $4,000. An inventory of maintenance supplies on hand at 31 December 20X6 reflected unused supplies amounting to $2,000. Give the adjusting journal entry that should be made on 31 December 20X6, under the following conditions:

   Case A: Purchases were debited to the maintenance supplies inventory account;

   Case B: Purchases were debited to maintenance supplies expense.

2. On 31 December 20X5, the prepaid insurance account showed a debit balance of $5,400, which was for coverage for the three months, January to March. On 1 April 20X6, the company obtained another policy covering a two-year period from that date. The two-year premium, amounting to $57,600, was paid on 1 April. Give the adjusting journal entry that should be made on 31 December 20X6.

   Case A: $57,600 was debited to prepaid insurance;

   Case B: $57,600 was debited to insurance expense.

3. On 1 June, the company collected cash, $25,200, which was for rent collected in advance from a tenant for the next 12 months. Give the adjusting journal entry assuming the following at the time of the collection:

   Case A: $25,200 was credited to rent revenue;

   Case B: $25,200 was credited to rent collected in advance.

Required:
Provide adjusting journal entries.

A-9 Adjusting Entries: Pacific Company adjusts and closes its books each 31 December. It is now 31 December 20X5, and the adjusting entries are to be made. You are requested to prepare, in general journal format, the adjusting entry that should be made for each of the following items:

a. Credit sales for the year amounted to $320,000. The estimated loss rate on bad debts is three-eighths of 1%.

b. Unpaid and unrecorded wages incurred at 31 December amounted to $4,800.

c. The company paid a two-year insurance premium in advance on 1 April 20X5, amounting to $9,600, which was debited to prepaid insurance.

d. Machine A, which cost $80,000, is to be depreciated for the full year. The estimated useful life is 10 years, and the residual value, $4,000. Use straight-line depreciation.

e. The company rented a warehouse on 1 June 20X5, for one year. It had to pay the full amount of rent one year in advance on 1 June, amounting to $9,600, which was debited to rent expense.

f. The company received from a customer a 9% note with a face amount of $12,000, in exchange for products purchased. The note was dated 1 September 20X5; the principal plus the interest is payable one year later. Notes receivable was debited, and sales revenue was credited on the date of sale, 1 September 20X5.

g. On 31 December 20X5, the property tax bill was received in the amount of $5,000. This amount applied only to 20X5 and had not been previously recorded or paid. The taxes are due, and will be paid, on 15 January 20X6.

h. On 1 April 20X5, the company signed a $60,000, 10% note payable. On that date, cash was debited and notes payable credited for $60,000. The note is payable on 31 March 20X6, for the face amount plus interest for one year.

i. The company purchased a patent on 1 January 20X5, at a cost of $11,900. On that date, the patent account was debited and cash credited for $11,900. The patent has an estimated useful life of 17 years and no residual value.

j. Pre-tax income has been computed to be $80,000 after all the above adjustments. Assume an average income tax rate of 30%.

A-10 Adjusting Entries: The following situations are unrelated:

a. On 1 January, ABC Corporation had a supplies inventory of $13,500. During the year, supplies of $65,700 were bought and recorded in temporary accounts. At the end of the year, inventory of $27,600 was on hand.

b. On 10 December, ABC Corporation received a deposit of $90,000 on a consulting project that was just beginning. This was accounted for as revenue. By the end of the year, the $150,000 job was 40% complete.

c. During the year, ABC Corporation sold 10,000 units of a product that was subject to a warranty. Past history indicates that 3% of units sold require repairs at an average cost of $120 per unit. The sales have been recorded; costs incurred for the warranty to date, totalling $26,100, were debited to warranty liability when paid. No warranty expense has been recognized.

d. The company uses the percent-of-sales method to calculate bad debt expense: 1% of credit sales of $18,750,000 is expected to be uncollectible.

e. In 20X3, a machine was purchased for $522,000. It had a useful life of 12 years and a $72,000 residual value. A full year's depreciation was charged in 20X3 and 20X4. In 20X5, the accountant discovered that she had forgotten to deduct the salvage value when calculating (straight-line) depreciation for these two years. Prepare a journal entry to correct the error (to retained earnings) and record 20X5 depreciation. Ignore income tax.

f. ABC Corporation wrote off a $48,000 bad debt. The allowance method is used.

g. ABC Corporation buys one-year insurance policies each 1 November. The year ends on 31 December. On 1 January 20X5, there was a balance of $28,320 in the prepaid insurance account; a cheque for $38,130 was issued on 1 November 20X5, for new one-year policies and debited to the prepaid insurance account.

Required:

Prepare adjusting journal entries.

A-11 Adjusting Entries: The following transactions and events for Stellar Manufacturing Corporation are under consideration for adjusting entries at 31 December 20X5 (the end of the accounting period):

a. Machine A used in the factory cost $450,000; it was purchased on 1 July 20X2. It has an estimated useful life of 12 years and a residual value of $30,000. Straight-line depreciation is used.

b. Sales for 20X5 amounted to $4,000,000, including $600,000 in credit sales. It is estimated, based on the experience of the company, that bad debt losses will be one quarter of 1% of credit sales.

c. At the beginning of 20X5, office supplies inventory amounted to $600. During 20X5, office supplies amounting to $8,800 were purchased; this amount was debited to office supplies expense. An inventory of office supplies at the end of 20X5 showed $400 on the shelves. The 1 January balance of $600 is still reflected in the office supplies inventory account.

d. On 1 July 20X5, the company paid a three-year insurance premium amounting to $2,160; this amount was debited to prepaid insurance.

e. On 1 October 20X5, the company paid rent on some leased office space. The payment of $7,200 cash was for the following six months. At the time of payment, rent expense was debited for the $7,200.

f. On 1 August 20X5, the company borrowed $120,000 from the Royal Bank. The loan was for 12 months at 9% interest payable at maturity date. The loan was properly recorded on 1 August.

g. Finished goods inventory on 1 January 20X5 was $200,000, and on 31 December 20X5 it was $260,000. The perpetual inventory record provided the cost of goods sold amount of $2,400,000.

h. The company owned some property (land) that was rented to B. R. Speir on 1 April 20X5, for 12 months for $8,400. On 1 April, the entire annual rental of $8,400 was credited to rent collected in advance, and cash was debited.

i. On 31 December 20X5, wages earned by employees but not yet paid (or recorded in the accounts) amounted to $18,000. Disregard payroll taxes.

j. On 1 September 20X5, the company loaned $60,000 to an outside party. The loan was at 10% per annum and was due in six months; interest is payable at maturity. Cash was credited for $60,000 and notes receivable debited on 1 September for the same amount.

k. On 1 January 20X5, factory supplies on hand amounted to $200. During 20X5, factory supplies that cost $4,000 were purchased and debited to factory supplies inventory. At the end of 20X5, a physical inventory count revealed that factory supplies on hand amounted to $800.

l. The company purchased a gravel pit on 1 January 20X3, at a cost of $60,000; it was estimated that approximately 60,000 tonnes of gravel could be removed prior to exhaustion. It was also estimated that the company would take five years to mine this natural resource. Tonnes of gravel removed and sold were 20X3, 3,000; 20X4, 7,000; and 20X5, 5,000. Hint: Deplete on an output basis; no residual value. Only 20X5 depletion should be recorded.

m. At the end of 20X5, it was found that postage stamps that cost $120 were on hand (in a "postage" box in the office). When the stamps were purchased, miscellaneous expense was debited and cash was credited.

n. At the end of 20X5, property taxes for 20X5 amounting to $59,000 were assessed on property owned by the company. The taxes are due no later than 1 February 20X6. The taxes have not been recorded on the books because payment has not been made.

o. The company borrowed $120,000 from the bank on 1 December 20X5. The loan is due in 60 days' time, along with interest at 9.5% per annum. On 1 December 20X5, cash was debited and loans payable credited for $120,000.

p. On 1 July 20X5, the company paid the city a $1,000 licence fee for the next 12 months. On that date, cash was credited and licence expense debited for $1,000.

q. On 1 March 20X5, the company made a loan to the company president and received a $30,000 note receivable. The loan was due in one year and called for 6% annual interest payable at maturity date.

r. The company owns three cars used by the executives. A six-month maintenance contract on them was signed on 1 October 20X5, whereby a local garage agreed to do "all the required maintenance." The payment was made for the following six months in advance. On 1 October 20X5, cash was credited and maintenance expense was debited for $9,600.

Required:
Give the adjusting entry (or entries) that should be made on 31 December 20X5, for each item. If an adjusting entry is not required, explain why. Assume all amounts are material.

A-12 Adjusting Entries: Selected account balances, taken from the ledger of PC Repairs Limited as of 31 December 20X4, appear below in alphabetical order:

Accounts payable	$25,200
Accounts receivable	6,200
Allowance for doubtful accounts	150
Cash	19,300
Dividends	6,600
Interest expense	480
Interest revenue	700
Note payable	8,000
Note receivable	4,000
Purchases	164,000
Purchase discounts	4,600
Purchase returns and allowances	3,300
Sales	170,000
Sales furniture	7,400
Sales salaries	16,510
Store supplies inventory	1,200
Tax expense (property)	1,200
Unearned revenue	4,000

Required:
Record adjusting entries, as needed, for the following facts and events:

1. Store supplies inventory at 31 December 20X4 was $480.
2. Depreciation of sales furniture is to be recorded straight line over 10 years. The furniture will have no salvage value.
3. Unpaid and unrecorded advertising bills at 31 December 20X4 totalled $790.
4. Property taxes paid (the tax expense of $1,200, above) in 20X4 were paid on 1 July 20X4 and were related to the period 1 April 20X4–31 March 20X5.
5. The note payable had an interest rate of 12% and was borrowed on 1 February 20X4. No interest was paid in 20X4.
6. There was $210 of outstanding accrued interest on the note receivable at 31 December 20X4.
7. Five percent of the outstanding accounts receivable are expected to prove uncollectible. The allowance for doubtful accounts is now in a credit balance but is inadequate.
8. Unearned revenue represented an advance payment from a customer; 75% was still unearned at year-end.
9. Closing merchandise inventory was $32,000. There was no opening inventory. Prepare an adjusting journal entry to record the change in the inventory account and cost of goods sold.

A-13 Entries and Statements: Set forth below is the adjusted trial balance of the Whitehead Company as of 31 October 20X5:

Account	Debit	Credit
Cash	$ 8,400	
Accounts receivable	45,000	
Merchandise inventory	150,000	
Prepaid rent	9,000	
Equipment	25,200	
Accumulated amortization		$ 3,600

Account	Debit	Credit
Accounts payable		60,000
Note payable		30,000
Accrued interest payable		750
Capital stock		75,000
Retained earnings		68,250
	$ 237,600	$ 237,600

The following information describes all of Whitehead's November transactions and provides all the data required for month-end adjustments:

- Whitehead had cash sales of $75,300.
- Whitehead had sales on account of $60,000.
- Whitehead collected $51,000 in cash from its customers on account.
- Whitehead acquired $90,000 of merchandise on account.
- The cost of merchandise sold during November was $75,000.
- Whitehead paid its suppliers $57,000 (cash) on account.
- Whitehead spent $6,000 for November's advertising.
- During November, Whitehead paid $16,500 in cash for wages.
- Miscellaneous expenses of $15,000 were paid in cash.
- $3,000 of wages earned by Whitehead's employees in November had not yet been paid.
- Whitehead had earlier paid its rent in advance to 31 December 20X5.
- The store equipment had been purchased by Whitehead for $25,200 on 1 November 20X4. This equipment is expected to last seven years and to have no salvage or residual value at that time.
- The note payable was dated 1 June 20X5 and the principal is due in two equal instalments on 1 June 20X6 and 20X7. Interest on the note is also to be paid on 1 June 20X6 and 20X7. The note bears an interest rate of 6% per year.

Required:

1. Journalize November transactions and adjusting journal entries. Include an adjusting journal entry for cost of goods sold.
2. Prepare an income statement and balance sheet for the month of November.

A-14 Adjustments and Income Statement: Dan Richards incorporated an appliance repair shop on 1 January 20X2, and has been quite pleased with the results of his first year. His cash receipts and disbursements:

Inflows:	
Repair revenue received	$49,000
Rent revenue received	6,000
Cash refunds from suppliers, for returned parts	1,200
Cash originally invested by Dan	3,000
Bank loan	18,000
	$77,200
Outflows:	
Wages paid	18,000
Dividends paid	3,400
Parts and supplies paid for	9,000
Insurance premiums paid	2,000
Rent paid	12,500
Equipment purchased	9,500
Other operating expenses paid	2,000
	$56,400

Notes:

- Equipment has a 10-year life, a $500 salvage value, and is to be depreciated using the declining-balance method, using a rate of 20%.
- Parts still on hand amount to $2,760.
- The insurance premium was paid on August 1 for an eight-month policy.
- Rental revenue is from a tenant who rents excess space. She paid 12 months rent on April 1 when she moved in.
- Dan owes his workers another $1,200 in wages, and customers owe him $ 7,560 for repair work done.
- Dan owes his suppliers $1,490 for parts.
- The bank loan was taken out on 1 March and has an interest rate of 12%.
- Bad debts are likely 4% of repair revenue.
- Rent paid was for the 12-month calendar year of 20X2. Dan must also pay 1% of repair revenue to his landlord but has not done this yet.
- For simplicity, assume that there are no income taxes.

Required:

1. Prepare an income statement for Dan for the year ended 31 December 20X2. Show all calculations.
2. Prepare a balance sheet as of 31 December 20X2.

A-15 Balance Sheet Preparation: Nicolette Corporation reported the following account balances on 31 December 20X3, which is the company's year-end.

Account	Debit	Credit
Cash	$ 17,200	
Accounts receivable, trade	38,000	
Short-term investment in marketable securities (cost, $52,000)	50,000	
Supplies inventory	5,000	
Prepaid insurance (short-term)	3,000	
Dividends (cash) declared during 20X3	12,000	
Rent receivable	11,000	
Investment in Public Co. shares (long term, at cost, which approximates market)	143,000	
Unamortized discount on bonds payable	5,000	
Loans to employees (company president; payment date uncertain)	105,000	
Land (building site, in use)	40,000	
Building	560,000	
Equipment	95,000	
Franchise (used in operations) (net)	20,000	
Mortgage payable (8%, maturity 20X20)		85,000
Accounts payable, trade		19,200
Dividends (cash) payable (payable 1 March 20X4)		12,000
Deferred rent revenue		7,000
Income tax payable		5,000
Accumulated depreciation, building		308,000
Accumulated depreciation, equipment		25,000
Allowance for doubtful accounts		4,000
Bonds payable (10%, maturity 20X14)		300,000
Common shares, no-par (25,000 shares outstanding)		100,000

Account	Debit	Credit
Preferred shares, no par (16,000 shares outstanding)		$ 72,000
Retained earnings, 1 January 20X3		69,000
Net income for 20X3		98,000
	$1,104,200	$1,104,200

Required:
Prepare a balance sheet.

(ASCA, adapted)

A-16 Prepare a Balance Sheet: Your assistant has prepared the following *partial* adjusted trial balance data for the Lopez Supply Corporation as of 31 December 20X8. The accounts are arranged in alphabetical order; unfortunately, the debit and credit balances have been listed in the same column.

Accounts payable	$ 72,000
Accounts receivable	134,400
Accumulated depreciation—buildings	39,600
Accumulated depreciation—equipment	20,000
Advertising expense	9,600
Bonds payable	80,000
Buildings	144,000
Capital stock	432,000
Cash	48,000
Depreciation expense—buildings	16,000
Depreciation expense—equipment	4,000
Dividends declared	28,800
Dividends payable	4,000
Equipment	108,560
Expired insurance	2,880
Interest earned	1,320
Interest receivable	600
Inventory (merchandise) (closing balance)	121,200
Land	139,200
Long-term investments	109,200
Mortgage payable	96,000
Notes payable—short term	30,000
Office expenses	32,160
Premium on bonds payable	4,000
Prepaid insurance	1,000
Property tax expense	15,960
Retained earnings—31 December 20X7	19,680
Sales	492,000
Supplies on hand	1,600
Unearned revenue	2,400

Required:
Prepare the 31 December 20X8 balance sheet. For the closing retained earnings, use the value that will make the balance sheet balance.

A-17 Income Statement: The following accounts for Blocker Company were selected from the ledger after adjustment at 31 May 20X8.

Accounts payable	$ 99,700
Accounts receivable	98,600

Accumulated amortization—office equipment	20,700
Accumulated amortization—store equipment	39,500
Administrative expense	125,200
Capital stock	100,000
Cash	38,500
Cost of merchandise sold	338,400
Dividends	20,000
Dividends payable	7,500
General expense	55,100
Interest payable	4,500
Merchandise inventory	144,600
Mortgage note payable (due in 20X14)	50,000
Office equipment	45,500
Prepaid insurance	3,700
Rent income	6,000
Retained earnings	74,650
Salaries payable	4,150
Sales	640,900
Selling expense	82,500
Store equipment	86,500

Required:
Based on the information provided, prepare an income statement in good form.

A-18 Prepare Financial Statements: The following trial balance for Falcon Corporation is in alphabetical order.

31 December 20X7	Debit	Credit
Accounts payable		235,900
Accounts receivable	344,000	
Accumulated amortization, building		200,700
Allowance for doubtful accounts		46,200
Bank loans payable, short-term		460,000
Building	456,000	
Cash	26,500	
Common shares		170,000
Cost of goods sold	933,100	
Dividends	24,000	
Income tax expense	116,000	
Interest expense	52,100	
Inventory, 31 December 20X7	291,700	
Land	36,000	
Long-term bonds payable		120,000
Long-term investments	230,000	
Notes receivable (short-term)	100,000	
Office supplies	3,600	
Operating expenses	458,000	
Operating expenses payable		48,900
Prepaid insurance	1,500	
Rent revenue		24,700
Retained earnings (1 January 20X7)		44,300
Sales		1,822,200
Selling expenses	107,800	
Unearned revenue		4,000
Wages payable		3,400
	$3,180,300	$3,180,300

Required:

1. Prepare an income statement from the information given.
2. Prepare a balance sheet and a statement of retained earnings.

A-19 The Accounting Cycle: The post-closing trial balance of the general ledger of Wilson Corporation, a retailer of home weight-training machines, at 31 December 20X4, reflects the following:

Acct. No.	Account	Debit	Credit
101	Cash	$ 27,000	
102	Accounts receivable	21,000	
103	Allowance for doubtful accounts		$ 1,000
104	Inventory (perpetual inventory system)*	35,000	
105	Prepaid insurance (20 months remaining at 1 January)	900	
200	Equipment (20-year estimated life, no residual value)	50,000	
201	Accumulated depreciation, equipment		22,500
300	Accounts payable		7,500
301	Wages payable		
302	Income taxes payable (for 20X4)		4,000
400	Common shares, no par, 80,000 shares		80,000
401	Retained earnings		18,900
500	Sales revenue		
600	Cost of goods sold		
601	Operating expenses		
602	Income tax expense		
700	Income summary		
		$133,900	$133,900

* Ending inventory on 31 December 20X5, by physical count, $45,000.

The following transactions occurred during 20X5 in the order given (use the letter at the left in place of date):

a. Sales revenue of $30,000, of which $10,000 was on credit; cost, provided by perpetual inventory record, $19,500. (*Hint*: When the perpetual system is used, make two entries to record a sale: *first*, debit cash or accounts receivable and credit sales revenue; *second*, debit cost of goods sold and credit inventory.)

b. Collected $17,000 on accounts receivable.

c. Paid income taxes payable (20X4), $4,000.

d. Purchased merchandise, $40,000, of which $8,000 was on credit.

e. Paid accounts payable, $6,000.

f. Sales revenue of $72,000 (in cash); cost, $46,800.

g. Paid operating expenses, $19,000.

h. On 1 January 20X5, issued 1,000 common shares for $1,000 cash.

i. Purchased merchandise, $100,000, of which $27,000 was on credit.

j. Sales revenue of $98,000, of which $30,000 was on credit; cost, $63,700.

k. Collected cash on accounts receivable, $26,000.

l. Paid accounts payable, $28,000.

m. Paid various operating expenses in cash, $18,000.

Required:

1. Journalize each of the transactions listed above for 20X5; use only a general journal.
2. Set up T-accounts in the general ledger for each of the accounts listed in the above trial balance and enter the account number and 31 December 20X4 balance.
3. Post the journal entries; use posting reference numbers.
4. Prepare an unadjusted trial balance.
5. Journalize the adjusting entries and post them to the ledger. Assume a bad debt rate of 0.5% of credit sales for the period at 31 December 20X5; accrued wages were $300. The average income tax rate was 40%. Use straight-line depreciation. Debit expenses to the operating expense account. (Check your work: Income tax expense is $11,784.)
6. Prepare an adjusted trial balance.
7. Prepare the income statement and balance sheet.
8. Journalize and post the closing entries.
9. Prepare a post-closing trial balance.

A-20 The Accounting Cycle: The post-closing trial balance of Gensing Enterprises, a farming operation, at 31 December 20X6, reflects the following:

Acct. No.	Account	Debit	Credit
101	Cash	$ 42,000	
102	Accounts receivable	35,800	
103	Allowance for doubtful accounts		$ 2,000
104	Inventory, 31 December 20X6	46,000	
105	Fertilizer and supplies inventory	6,700	
106	Prepaid insurance (expires at the end of November 20X7)	9,000	
200	Equipment	344,800	
201	Accumulated amortization, equipment		124,600
202	Land	682,000	
300	Accounts payable		67,500
301	Unearned revenue		32,000
302	Notes payable		75,000
400	Common shares		400,000
401	Retained earnings		465,200
500	Sales revenue		
600	Cost of goods sold		
601	Operating expenses		
700	Income summary		
		$1,166,300	$1,166,300

Various transactions occurred in 20X7:

a. Sales amounted to $767,000. Cash sales were 25% of the total, and the rest was on account.
b. At the beginning of the year, there was $32,000 of unearned revenue. This revenue was earned in 20X6, in addition to the sales transactions in (a).
c. Operating expenses of $67,200 were paid in cash.
d. Fertilizer and other supplies were bought for $46,900, on credit.
e. Harvesting costs of $244,200 were paid. Harvesting costs of the crop are debited to inventory.
f. The cost of all goods sold for the period was $281,400. This should be recorded as a journal entry that increases cost of goods sold and reduces the inventory account.
g. The opening accounts receivable were collected in the amount of $31,000. No accounts were written off. Seventy percent of the current year sales on account were also collected.
h. The opening balance of accounts payable were paid in full.
i. Ninety percent of the fertilizer and other supplies, bought on credit, were paid for.

j. Paid dividends of $22,000.
k. A $10,800, 12-month insurance policy was paid on 1 December. The amount was debited to prepaid insurance.
l. A contract was signed with a customer for a certain quantity of next year's crop. The customer paid the full $50,000 price in cash in advance.
m. The note payable was partially repaid at the end of November, in the amount of $50,000. Interest of $5,500 was also paid on the entire note, all pertaining to 20X7. The remaining $25,000 balance of the note payable has an interest rate of 12% per annum. Interest must be accrued for the month of December 20X7. The $25,000 balance is long term.

Required:

1. Journalize the transactions for 20X7. Use only a general journal. Debit all operating expenses to a general "operating expense" account, for simplicity. Add other accounts if needed. Interest expense is recorded in a separate account.
2. Set up T-accounts in the general ledger for each of the accounts listed in the above trial balance and enter the account number and the 31 December balance.
3. Post the journal entries; use posting reference numbers. Assign account numbers as needed.
4. Prepare an unadjusted trial balance.
5. Journalize and post the following adjusting journal entries:
   a. Depreciation for the year, $45,000.
   b. Bad debts are expected to be 2% of credit sales.
   c. Inventory of fertilizer and other supplies was $7,600 at year-end.
   d. Interest expense was accrued for December 20X7.
   e. Prepaid insurance expired.
   f. Wages earned but unpaid at year-end, $5,000.

   Debit expenses other than interest to operating expenses, and payables to accounts payable, for simplicity.
6. Prepare an adjusted trial balance.
7. Prepare the income statement and balance sheet. The remaining note payable is long term.
8. Journalize and post the closing entries.
9. Prepare a post-closing trial balance.
10. For which adjusting journal entries in requirement 5 above would reversing entries be appropriate? Explain.

A-21 Worksheet, Adjusting and Closing Entries, Statements: Darma Corporation is currently completing the end-of-the-period accounting process. At 31 December 20X5, the following unadjusted trial balance was developed from the general ledger:

Account	Debit	Credit
Cash	$ 120,520	
Accounts receivable	76,000	
Allowance for doubtful accounts		$ 4,000
Interest receivable	0	
Inventory (perpetual inventory system)	210,000	
Sales supplies inventory	1,800	
Long-term note receivable, 14%	24,000	
Equipment	360,000	
Accumulated depreciation, equipment		128,000
Patent (net)	16,800	
Accounts payable		46,000
Interest payable	0	
Income tax payable	0	
Property tax payable	0	

Account	Debit	Credit
Rent collected in advance		
Mortgage payable		120,000
Common shares, no par, 10,000 shares		230,000
Retained earnings		64,880
Sales revenue		1,400,000
Investment revenue		2,240
Rent revenue		6,000
Cost of goods sold	760,000	
Selling expenses	328,800	
General and administrative expenses	110,000	
Interest expense	13,200	
Extraordinary gain (pre-tax)		20,000
	$2,021,120	$2,021,120

Additional data for adjustments and other purposes:

a. Estimated bad debt loss rate is 0.25% of credit sales. Credit sales for the year amounted to $400,000; classify as a selling expense.
b. Interest on the long-term note receivable was last collected and recorded on 31 August 20X5.
c. Estimated useful life of the equipment is 10 years; residual value, $40,000. Allocate 10% of depreciation expense to general and administrative expense and the balance to selling expense to reflect proportionate use. Use straight-line depreciation.
d. Estimated remaining economic life of the patent is 14 years (from 1 January 20X5) with no residual value. Use straight-line amortization and classify as selling expense (used in sales promotion).
e. Interest on the mortgage payable was last paid and recorded on 30 November 20X5.
f. On 1 June 20X5, the company rented office space to a tenant for one year and collected $6,000 rent in advance for the year; the entire amount was credited to rent revenue on this date.
g. On 31 December 20X5, the company received a statement for calendar-year 20X5 property taxes amounting to $2,600. The payment is due 15 February 20X6. Classify the adjustment as a selling expense.
h. Sales supplies on hand at 31 December 20X5 amounted to $600; classify as a selling expense.
i. Assume an average 40% corporate income tax rate on all items including the extraordinary gain. (*Check your work:* Total income tax expense is $70,264.)

Required:

1. Enter the above unadjusted trial balance on a worksheet.
2. Complete the worksheet.
3. Prepare the income statement and balance sheet.
4. Journalize the closing entries.

A-22 Perform All Accounting Cycle Steps: YT Enterprises, a calendar-year firm, began operations as a retailer in January 20X5. You are to perform the 10 accounting cycle steps for YT for 20X5. Worksheets, special journals, and subsidiary ledgers are not required. Prepare journal entries in summary (for the year) form. Post to T-accounts. YT uses the expedient recording system and records reversing entries whenever appropriate. YT also uses a periodic inventory system and adjusts inventory in an adjusting entry.

Information about transactions in 20X5:

1. Investors contributed $400,000 in exchange for 10,000 shares of no-par common shares. On the advice of its underwriter, YT offered the shares at $40 per share.

2. YT obtained a 12%, $200,000 bank loan on 1 February. This loan is evidenced by a signed promissory note calling for interest payments every 1 February. The note is due in full on 31 January 20X9.
3. A rental contract for production and office facilities was signed 1 February, which required $8,000 immediate payment covering the first month's rent and a $4,000 deposit refundable in three years or upon termination of the contract, whichever occurs first. Monthly rent is $4,000. As an added incentive to pay rent in advance, YT accepted an offer to maintain rent at $4,000 per month for the first three years if YT paid the 2nd through the 13th (March 20X5 through February 20X6) months' rent immediately. In all, YT paid $56,000 for rent on 1 February. YT intends to occupy the facilities for at least three years.
4. Equipment costing $220,000 was purchased for cash in early February. It has an estimated residual value of $20,000 and a five-year useful life. YT uses the straight-line method of depreciation and treats depreciation as a separate period expense. A full year of depreciation is recorded in the year of acquisition.
5. YT recognized various cash operating expenses for the year, including the following:

Wages	$160,000
Utilities	60,000
Selling	50,000
General and administrative	125,000

6. Total merchandise purchases for the year amounted to $2,775,000. Ending inventory amounted to $300,000 at cost. YT uses a periodic inventory system.
7. Total payables relating to merchandise purchases and other operating expenses are $70,000 at year-end.
8. All sales are made on credit and totalled $3,500,000 in 20X5; $2,850,000 was collected on account during the year. YT estimates that 0.5% of total sales will be uncollectible and has written off $7,000 of accounts.
9. YT declared a cash dividend of $84,000, payable in January 20X6.
10. Income tax expense is $260,000. All taxes for a fiscal year are payable in April of the following year.

A-23 Worksheet: The accounts in the ledger of Huang Company with the unadjusted balances on 30 June, the end of the current year, are as follows:

Cash	$ 10,250	Sales	$ 842,500
Accounts receivable	270,685	Purchases	413,715
Merchandise inventory	93,800	Cost of goods sold	0
Prepaid insurance	12,510	Sales salaries	124,000
Store supplies	3,725	Advertising expense	32,825
Store equipment	178,100	Amortization expense—	
Accumulated amortization		Store equipment	0
—store equipment	24,400	Delivery expense	5,800
Accounts payable	57,210	Store supplies expense	0
Salaries payable	0	Tax expense	9,000
Common shares	200,000	Rent expense	35,400
Retained earnings	126,600	Office salaries	39,500
Dividends	7,500	Insurance expense	0
		Misc. general expense	12,650
		Loss on disposal of equip.	1,250

The data needed for year-end adjustments on 30 June are as follows:

Merchandise inventory on 30 June		$64,900
Insurance expired during the year		9,210
Store supplies inventory on 30 June		1,275
Amortization for the current year		5,950
Accrued salaries on 30 June:		
Sales salaries	$2,640	
Office salaries	1,170	3,810

Required:
Complete an eight-column work sheet for the fiscal year ended 30 June. This worksheet should have two columns each for the unadjusted trial balance, adjusting journal entries, income statement and balance sheet. Since there are no columns for the retained earnings statement, opening retained earnings, dividends, and current year net income are included in the balance sheet columns as separate accounts.

A-24 Worksheet: Following is the unadjusted trial balance for TRM Corporation as of 31 December 20X4:

Account	Debit	Credit
Cash	$ 1,335	
Accounts receivable	1,000	
Prepaid insurance	3,400	
Office supplies	365	
Prepaid rent	375	
Office equipment	3,140	
Accum. amortization, OE		$ 855
Delivery equipment	22,185	
Accum. amortization, DE		4,500
Accounts payable		3,845
Rent payable		0
Salaries and wages payable		0
Unearned revenue		1,050
Share capital		14,355
Retained earnings		20,000
Dividends	2,000	
Delivery service revenue		63,085
Rent expense	4,125	
Utilities expense	1,290	
Insurance expense	0	
Office supplies expense	0	
Amortization expense	0	
Salaries expense	30,715	
Delivery wages expense	30,480	
Gas, oil, and repairs expense	7,280	
	$ 107,690	$ 107,690

Other information:

a. In December 20X3, the company put a one-month deposit down on rental premises. This deposit will be returned when the company vacates. This amount appears as the balance of the prepaid rent account. Rents for January through November were paid each month and debited to the rent expense account. As of the trial balance date, the December rent had not been paid.

b. An examination of insurance policies showed $415 of unexpired insurance.

c. An inventory showed $165 of unused office supplies on hand.
d. Amortization on the office equipment was $450, and on delivery equipment, $3,625.
e. Several stores signed contracts with the delivery service in which they agreed to pay a fixed fee for the delivery of packages. Two of the stores made advance payments on their contracts, and the amounts paid were credited to the unearned revenue account. An examination of their contracts shows $600 of the $1,050 paid was earned by the end of the accounting period.
f. A $55 December power bill and a $90 bill for repairs to delivery equipment were unpaid and unrecorded at year-end.
g. Office salaries, $310, and delivery wages, $160, have accrued but are unpaid and unrecorded

Required:

1. Prepare adjusting journal entries to reflect the above information.
2. Enter the adjustments into a worksheet, and complete the worksheet columns.

A-25 Special Journals: THJ Limited incurred the following transactions in October 20X5:

Oct.	
4	Board of Directors declared a $160,000 dividend. The dividend was both recorded and paid on this date.
5	Purchased goods for resale on credit, $58,200.
5	Purchased goods for resale with cash, $12,350.
6	Borrowed $50,000 from the bank, and signed a 60-day, 8% note payable.
8	Bought office supplies on credit, $1,250.
9	Bought machinery, and issued a 120-day, 12% note payable for the full amount of $32,200.
9	Sold goods to customers on account, $35,600.
9	Sold goods to customers for cash, $68,400.
14	Paid for the goods bought on credit on 5 October.
16	Bought goods from a supplier on credit, $31,100.
17	Sold goods to customer on account, $100,700.
22	Paid wages and salaries, $33,700.
23	Paid electricity bill, $1,600.
25	Received payment from customers for 80% of 9 October sale.
27	Returned goods to supplier from order of 16 October and got a credit note of $3,600.
27	Repaid note payable of $50,000, borrowed and properly recorded in August, plus $1,000 interest.
30	Paid net amount due to supplier for goods purchased on 16 October.
30	Received goods back from customer of 17 October and issued a credit note for $5,200.
31	Recorded amortization expense on plant machinery of $7,400 for the month of October.

Required:

1. Draft special journals for cash receipts, cash disbursements, sales, and purchases. Also open a general journal.
2. Record the transactions in the appropriate journal. Leave the column blank if details (name or account number, for example) are not available. There are no discounts offered to or by THJ Limited, so all sales and purchases are recorded gross.

A-26 Special Journals: Next to each transaction place the letter of the journal in which that transaction would be recorded. Assume that the company uses special journals whenever appropriate.

Transactions:

1. Borrow money from the bank.
2. Collect cash on account.
3. Purchase merchandise on account.
4. Record adjusting entries.
5. Pay dividends.
6. Receive cash for cash sales.
7. Pay employee wages.
8. Record a completed but unpaid voucher.
9. Correct an erroneous journal entry.
10. Sell merchandise on credit.
11. Pay accounts payable.
12. Pay interest on bank loan.
13. Pay the voucher in (8).
14. Pay income tax instalment.

Journals:

A. General journal
B. Sales journal
C. Purchases journal
D. Cash receipts journal
E. Cash disbursements journal
F. Voucher register
G. Cheque register (for use with voucher register)

A-27 Special Journals: Marigold Corporation had transactions in June as follows:

June	
1	Received merchandise and an invoice dated 31 May, terms n/60, from Hollingsworth Company, $47,800.
2	Purchased office equipment on account from Dunlap Company, invoice dated 2 June, terms n/10 EOM, $14,625.
3	Sold merchandise on account to Tamara Smith, Invoice No. 902, $22,300. (Terms of all credit sales are 2/10, n/30.)
8	Issued cheque No. 548 to *The Monthly News* for advertising, $275.
10	Issued cheque No. 549 to Hollingsworth Company in payment of its 31 May invoice, previously recorded.
11	Sold unneeded office supplies at cost for cash, $940.
16	Sold merchandise on account to Mary Cortez, invoice No. 903, $9,735.
18	Received payment from Tamara Smith for the sale of 3 June.
20	Received merchandise and an invoice dated 18 June, terms n/60, from Riteway Company, $17,500.
21	Issued a credit memorandum to Mary Cortez for defective merchandise sold on 16 June and returned for credit, $1,835.
24	Received a $1,700 credit memorandum from Riteway Company for defective merchandise received on 20 June and returned for credit.
25	Purchased on account from The Store Depot, merchandise, $22,390, invoice dated 25 June, terms n/10 EOM.

26 Received payment from Mary Cortez for the 16 June sale. She paid the net amount due within the discount period, and deducted 2% from the amount owing.
28 Issued cheque No. 550 to Riteway Company in payment of its 18 June invoice, less the purchase return.
30 Cash sales for the month ended 30 June were $31,230.

Required:

1. Draft special journals for cash receipts, cash disbursements, sales, and purchases. The company also maintains a general journal.
2. Record the transactions in the appropriate journal. Leave columns blank if details (account numbers, for example) are not available. Sales are recorded at the gross amount.

A-28 Special Journals: Morra Limited incurred the following transactions in September:

Sept.

1 Invested $10,000 in the corporation.
2 Purchased $6,000 of automotive equipment for cash.
2 Purchased office equipment by issuing a note payable, $4,760.
5 Purchased inventory priced at $10,320 on account, terms 1/15, n/30.
10 Sold merchandise for $6,210 to a customer on account, terms 2/10, n/30.
12 Received a credit memo from the supplier re: the inventory acquired on 5 September, $1,320 gross ($1,306.80 net).
12 Borrowed $10,000 from the bank at an interest rate of 12%.
13 Paid the supplier for the net purchase of 5 September.
22 Received payment from the customer re: sale on 10 September. This cheque was issued within the discount period.
25 Paid salaries of $1,200.
29 Cash sales for the month of September amounted to $47,250.

Required:

1. Draft special journals for cash receipts, cash disbursements, sales, and purchases. The company also maintains a general journal.
2. Record the transactions in the appropriate journal. Leave columns blank if details (account numbers, for example) are not available. Purchases and sales are recorded at the net amount.

A-29 Financial Statements: Jean Dubois began operation of a hot dog stand on May 1 and has had a fairly successful summer. However, it is now 31 October, Jean is packing up her operation for the winter, and she needs to complete financial statements.

On 1 May, Jean invested $500 of her savings in the company bank account, which made her the sole shareholder of Halifax Hot Dogs Limited. On the same day, Jean borrowed $3,000 from the bank (at 12% interest) to buy her mobile hot dog cart, which cost $3,200. She estimates that this cart will last 10 years, but she will likely operate it herself for only two more years after this one, and then sell it. She hopes to get $2,000 for it at that time. At the end of October, Jean knows that similar one-year-old carts are selling for $2,500.

Jean initially bought $1,200 of food supplies, and has placed five $1,000 orders over the summer from the same supplier. She still owes her supplier $550. She has $400 of food left, which she will eat herself. In addition, Jane bought $425 of goods from the grocery store over the summer, bought in small orders when she ran out of things and needed to replace them quickly.

Jean paid no rent during the summer, but she did have to buy a vendor's license from the city for $750. This license is valid from 1 May to 31 December. She paid herself a salary of $1,500 a month. She hired her younger brother to work with her on busy weekend days, paying him a total of $450 over the summer, although she still owes him $100.

According to her bank book, Jean deposited $18,250 during the period. However, a customer still owes her $300 for hot dogs served at a company baseball game, which Jean catered.

Required:
Provide Jane with an income statement showing the results of her first summer of operation, and a balance sheet as of 31 October.

A-30 Financial Statements: When Darlene Gerroir, a university student, was unable to find a summer job, she decided to open a painting business for the summer. She took her last $500 and invested in the common shares of her company on 1 May.

Darlene borrowed $1,000 from the bank at 12%, and spent $750 on ladders, brushes, and scaffolding. She leased a small van for the four summer months at $400 per month. Darlene's $150 advertising campaign was so successful that she was able to employ another student as a part-time assistant for $550 a month.

Darlene spent cash of $450 for gas, $60 for oil, and $320 on repairs. At the end of the summer, she still owed $50 for gas. She calculated that it cost $500 per house for paint and supplies, and each homeowner was charged $1,050 for the job. Twenty-two houses had been painted, but three customers had not yet paid for the work. Additionally, Darlene still owed the hardware store $1,200 on account.

Darlene has paid herself monthly salary of $900. She has not repaid the bank loan or interest, although she has $2,520 in the company bank account and $1,200 in her personal account. She estimates that the ladders and scaffolding will be good for two more summers after the current summer.

Required:
Prepare an income statement to reflect the operation of Darlene's Painting Limited for the summer, and a balance sheet as of 31 August.

A-31 Transactions and Financial Statements: Multimedia Incorporated, a producer of graphics and artwork for movie theatres and other media distributors, provided the following information for 20X5:

Selected Accounts from the Balance Sheet, as of 1 January 20X5

Accounts receivable	$ 10,000
Prepaid insurance	20,000
Supplies	5,000
Equipment (net)	80,000
Accounts payable (suppliers)	40,000*
Unearned rent	13,000
Wages payable	7,000
Common shares (no par)	27,000
Retained earnings	50,000

* The 31 December 20X5 balance is $50,000.

Income Statement, year ended 31 December 20X5

Sales	$200,000
Insurance expense	(15,000)
Amortization expense	(10,000)
Supplies expense	(30,000)
Wages expense	(60,000)
Rent revenue	12,000
Net income	$ 97,000

Cash Flow Statement, year ended 31 December 20X5

Operating activities:	
Collections from customers	$ 90,000
Insurance payments	(25,000)
Payments to suppliers	(45,000)
Payments to employees	(52,000)
Rental receipts	19,000
Net operating cash flow	$ (13,000)
Cash balance, 1 January 20X5	22,000
Cash balance, 31 December 20X5*	$ 9,000

* No investing or financing cash flows.

Required:
Prepare the 31 December 20X5 balance sheet for Multimedia.

A-32 Transactions and Financial Statements: During the first week of January 20X8, Gary Benneford began an office design business, Efficient Interiors Limited. He kept no formal accounting records; however, his record of cash receipts and disbursements was accurate. The business was an instant success. In fact, it was so successful that he required additional financing to keep up. He approached his bank for a $10,000 loan and was "put on hold" until he brought a balance sheet and an income statement prepared on an accrual basis.

Knowing very little about accounting, he engages you to prepare statements requested by the bank. He supplies you with the following information:

	Receipts	Disbursements
Investment	$ 90,000	
Equipment		$ 55,200
Supplies		36,600
Rent payments		28,800
Insurance premium		5,400
Advertising—all ads complete		10,800
Wages of assistant		55,200
Telephone		2,940
Payments to Gary Benneford		57,000
Design revenue received	184,500	
Cash balance		22,560
	$274,500	$274,500

Additional information:

- The equipment has an estimated 10-year life and $1,200 salvage value.
- Supplies on hand 31 December 20X8 were $5,300.
- Rent payments included $2,250 per month rental and $1,800 deposit refundable at termination of the two-year lease.
- Insurance premium was for a two-year policy that expires on 31 December 20X9.
- Wages earned in the last week of December 20X8 to be paid in January 20X9 amounted to $1,600.
- Design revenue earned but not yet collected amounted to $11,400.
- The organization is set up as a company; the $57,000 withdrawn by Gary is $54,000 salary and $3,000 dividends.

Required:
Prepare the financial statements as requested.

(CGA-Canada, adapted)

A-33 Transactions and Financial Statements: Shirt Shack is a retail store operating in a downtown shopping mall. On 1 January 20X5, it reported the following:

SHIRT SHACK
BALANCE SHEET

As of 1 January 20X5	
Cash	$ 4,000
Accounts receivable (net of allowance of $2,000)	28,000
Prepaid rent (rental deposit)	1,000
Inventory	36,000
Leasehold improvements (net)	16,000
Total assets	$85,000
Accounts payable	$32,000
Accrued wages payable	3,500
Accrued interest payable	200
Accrued rent payable	0
Notes payable, 10%	14,800
Common shares	10,000
Retained earnings	24,500
Total liabilities plus equity	$85,000

During 20X5, the company reported the following:

a. Cash paid to employees (salaries and commissions), $67,000. Cash paid to suppliers, $90,000.
b. Cash collected from customers, $220,000.
c. On 31 December 20X5, a physical inventory count revealed that inventory was $42,000.
d. At 31 December 20X5, customers owed Shirt Shack $35,000, and the company owed its suppliers $14,000. Of the accounts receivable, aging analysis indicated that $4,000 was expected to be uncollectible. No accounts were written off in 20X5.
e. Cash paid to landlord, $12,000 ($1,000 per month for 12 months). Shirt Shack is required to pay monthly rent and, at year-end, make an additional payment to bring the total rent expense up to 10% of sales. This payment will be made in January 20X6.
f. Cash paid for miscellaneous operating expenses, $6,000.
g. Cash paid in dividends, $14,500; in interest, $1,680. No interest is owing at 31 December 20X5.
h. Shirt Shack owed employees $500 in wages and $1,000 in commissions at year-end.
i. The leasehold improvements were acquired on 1 January 20X4. They had an expected life of 10 years and were installed in leased premises that had a five-year lease on 1 January 20X4.

Required:

1. Prepare journal entries for all transactions and needed adjustments.
2. Prepare an income statement for the year ended 31 December 20X5. Ignore income tax. Show all calculations.

TABLE I-1: Present value of 1: (P/F, *i*, *n*)

$$P/F = \frac{1}{(1+i)^n}$$

n	2%	2.5%	3%	4%	5%	6%	7%	8%	9%	10%	11%	12%	14%	15%
1	0.98039	0.97561	0.97087	0.96154	0.95238	0.94340	0.93458	0.92593	0.91743	0.90909	0.90090	0.89286	0.87719	0.86957
2	0.96117	0.95181	0.94260	0.92456	0.90703	0.89000	0.87344	0.85734	0.84168	0.82645	0.81162	0.79719	0.76947	0.75614
3	0.94232	0.92860	0.91514	0.88900	0.86384	0.83962	0.81630	0.79383	0.77218	0.75131	0.73119	0.71178	0.67497	0.65752
4	0.92385	0.90595	0.88849	0.85480	0.82270	0.79209	0.76290	0.73503	0.70843	0.68301	0.65873	0.63552	0.59208	0.57175
5	0.90573	0.88385	0.86261	0.82193	0.78353	0.74726	0.71299	0.68058	0.64993	0.62092	0.59345	0.56743	0.51937	0.49718
6	0.88797	0.86230	0.83748	0.79031	0.74622	0.70496	0.66634	0.63017	0.59627	0.56447	0.53464	0.50663	0.45559	0.43233
7	0.87056	0.84127	0.81309	0.75992	0.71068	0.66506	0.62275	0.58349	0.54703	0.51316	0.48166	0.45235	0.39964	0.37594
8	0.85349	0.82075	0.78941	0.73069	0.67684	0.62741	0.58201	0.54027	0.50187	0.46651	0.43393	0.40388	0.35056	0.32690
9	0.83676	0.80073	0.76642	0.70259	0.64461	0.59190	0.54393	0.50025	0.46043	0.42410	0.39092	0.36061	0.30751	0.28426
10	0.82035	0.78120	0.74409	0.67556	0.61391	0.55839	0.50835	0.46319	0.42241	0.38554	0.35218	0.32197	0.26974	0.24718
11	0.80426	0.76214	0.72242	0.64958	0.58468	0.52679	0.47509	0.42888	0.38753	0.35049	0.31728	0.28748	0.23662	0.21494
12	0.78849	0.74356	0.70138	0.62460	0.55684	0.49697	0.44401	0.39711	0.35553	0.31863	0.28584	0.25668	0.20756	0.18691
13	0.77303	0.72542	0.68095	0.60057	0.53032	0.46884	0.41496	0.36770	0.32618	0.28966	0.25751	0.22917	0.18207	0.16253
14	0.75788	0.70773	0.66112	0.57748	0.50507	0.44230	0.38782	0.34046	0.29925	0.26333	0.23199	0.20462	0.15971	0.14133
15	0.74301	0.69047	0.64186	0.55526	0.48102	0.41727	0.36245	0.31524	0.27454	0.23939	0.20900	0.18270	0.14010	0.12289
16	0.72845	0.67362	0.62317	0.53391	0.45811	0.39365	0.33873	0.29189	0.25187	0.21763	0.18829	0.16312	0.12289	0.10686
17	0.71416	0.65720	0.60502	0.51337	0.43630	0.37136	0.31657	0.27027	0.23107	0.19784	0.16963	0.14564	0.10780	0.09293
18	0.70016	0.64117	0.58739	0.49363	0.41552	0.35034	0.29586	0.25025	0.21199	0.17986	0.15282	0.13004	0.09456	0.08081
19	0.68643	0.62553	0.57029	0.47464	0.39573	0.33051	0.27651	0.23171	0.19449	0.16351	0.13768	0.11611	0.08295	0.07027
20	0.67297	0.61027	0.55368	0.45639	0.37689	0.31180	0.25842	0.21455	0.17843	0.14864	0.12403	0.10367	0.07276	0.06110
21	0.65978	0.59539	0.53755	0.43883	0.35894	0.29416	0.24151	0.19866	0.16370	0.13513	0.11174	0.09256	0.06383	0.05313
22	0.64684	0.58086	0.52189	0.42196	0.34185	0.27751	0.22571	0.18394	0.15018	0.12285	0.10067	0.08264	0.05599	0.04620
23	0.63416	0.56670	0.50669	0.40573	0.32557	0.26180	0.21095	0.17032	0.13778	0.11168	0.09069	0.07379	0.04911	0.04017
24	0.62172	0.55288	0.49193	0.39012	0.31007	0.24698	0.19715	0.15770	0.12640	0.10153	0.08170	0.06588	0.04308	0.03493
25	0.60953	0.53939	0.47761	0.37512	0.29530	0.23300	0.18425	0.14602	0.11597	0.09230	0.07361	0.05882	0.03779	0.03038
26	0.59758	0.52623	0.46369	0.36069	0.28124	0.21981	0.17220	0.13520	0.10639	0.08391	0.06631	0.05252	0.03315	0.02642
27	0.58586	0.51340	0.45019	0.34682	0.26785	0.20737	0.16093	0.12519	0.09761	0.07628	0.05974	0.04689	0.02908	0.02297
28	0.57437	0.50088	0.43708	0.33348	0.25509	0.19563	0.15040	0.11591	0.08955	0.06934	0.05382	0.04187	0.02551	0.01997
29	0.56311	0.48866	0.42435	0.32065	0.24295	0.18456	0.14056	0.10733	0.08215	0.06304	0.04849	0.03738	0.02237	0.01737
30	0.55207	0.47674	0.41199	0.30832	0.23138	0.17411	0.13137	0.09938	0.07537	0.05731	0.04368	0.03338	0.01963	0.01510
31	0.54125	0.46511	0.39999	0.29646	0.22036	0.16425	0.12277	0.09202	0.06915	0.05210	0.03935	0.02980	0.01722	0.01313
32	0.53063	0.45377	0.38834	0.28506	0.20987	0.15496	0.11474	0.08520	0.06344	0.04736	0.03545	0.02661	0.01510	0.01142
33	0.52023	0.44270	0.37703	0.27409	0.19987	0.14619	0.10723	0.07889	0.05820	0.04306	0.03194	0.02376	0.01325	0.00993
34	0.51003	0.43191	0.36604	0.26355	0.19035	0.13791	0.10022	0.07305	0.05339	0.03914	0.02878	0.02121	0.01162	0.00864
35	0.50003	0.42137	0.35538	0.25342	0.18129	0.13011	0.09366	0.06763	0.04899	0.03558	0.02592	0.01894	0.01019	0.00751
36	0.49022	0.41109	0.34503	0.24367	0.17266	0.12274	0.08754	0.06262	0.04494	0.03235	0.02335	0.01691	0.00894	0.00653
37	0.48061	0.40107	0.33498	0.23430	0.16444	0.11579	0.08181	0.05799	0.04123	0.02941	0.02104	0.01510	0.00784	0.00568
38	0.47119	0.39128	0.32523	0.22529	0.15661	0.10924	0.07646	0.05369	0.03783	0.02673	0.01896	0.01348	0.00688	0.00494
39	0.46195	0.38174	0.31575	0.21662	0.14915	0.10306	0.07146	0.04971	0.03470	0.02430	0.01708	0.01204	0.00604	0.00429
40	0.45289	0.37243	0.30656	0.20829	0.14205	0.09722	0.06678	0.04603	0.03184	0.02209	0.01538	0.01075	0.00529	0.00373
45	0.41020	0.32917	0.26444	0.17120	0.11130	0.07265	0.04761	0.03133	0.02069	0.01372	0.00913	0.00610	0.00275	0.00186
50	0.37153	0.29094	0.22811	0.14071	0.08720	0.05429	0.03395	0.02132	0.01345	0.00852	0.00542	0.00346	0.00143	0.00092

TABLE I-2: Present value of an ordinary annuity of n payments of 1: (P/A, i, n)

$$P/A = \frac{1 - \dfrac{1}{(1+i)^n}}{i}$$

n	2%	2.5%	3%	4%	5%	6%	7%	8%	9%	10%	11%	12%	14%	15%
1	0.98039	0.97561	0.97087	0.96154	0.95238	0.94340	0.93458	0.92593	0.91743	0.90909	0.90090	0.89286	0.87719	0.86957
2	1.94156	1.92742	1.91347	1.88609	1.85941	1.83339	1.80802	1.78326	1.75911	1.73554	1.71252	1.69005	1.64666	1.62571
3	2.88388	2.85602	2.82861	2.77509	2.72325	2.67301	2.62432	2.57710	2.53129	2.48685	2.44371	2.40183	2.32163	2.28323
4	3.80773	3.76197	3.71710	3.62990	3.54595	3.46511	3.38721	3.31213	3.23972	3.16987	3.10245	3.03735	2.91371	2.85498
5	4.71346	4.64583	4.57971	4.45182	4.32948	4.21236	4.10020	3.99271	3.88965	3.79079	3.69590	3.60478	3.43308	3.35216
6	5.60143	5.50813	5.41719	5.24214	5.07569	4.91732	4.76654	4.62288	4.48592	4.35526	4.23054	4.11141	3.88867	3.78448
7	6.47199	6.34939	6.23028	6.00205	5.78637	5.58238	5.38929	5.20637	5.03295	4.86842	4.71220	4.56376	4.28830	4.16042
8	7.32548	7.17014	7.01969	6.73274	6.46321	6.20979	5.97130	5.74664	5.53482	5.33493	5.14612	4.96764	4.63886	4.48732
9	8.16224	7.97087	7.78611	7.43533	7.10782	6.80169	6.51523	6.24689	5.99525	5.75902	5.53705	5.32825	4.94637	4.77158
10	8.98259	8.75206	8.53020	8.11090	7.72173	7.36009	7.02358	6.71008	6.41766	6.14457	5.88923	5.65022	5.21612	5.01877
11	9.78685	9.51421	9.25262	8.76048	8.30641	7.88687	7.49867	7.13896	6.80519	6.49506	6.20652	5.93770	5.45273	5.23371
12	10.57534	10.25776	9.95400	9.38507	8.86325	8.38384	7.94269	7.53608	7.16073	6.81369	6.49236	6.19437	5.66029	5.42062
13	11.34837	10.98318	10.63496	9.98565	9.39357	8.85268	8.35765	7.90378	7.48690	7.10336	6.74987	6.42355	5.84236	5.58315
14	12.10625	11.69091	11.29607	10.56312	9.89864	9.29498	8.74547	8.24424	7.78615	7.36669	6.98187	6.62817	6.00207	5.72448
15	12.84926	12.38138	11.93794	11.11839	10.37966	9.71225	9.10791	8.55948	8.06069	7.60608	7.19087	6.81086	6.14217	5.84737
16	13.57771	13.05500	12.56110	11.65230	10.83777	10.10590	9.44665	8.85137	8.31256	7.82371	7.37916	6.97399	6.26506	5.95423
17	14.29187	13.71220	13.16612	12.16567	11.27407	10.47726	9.76322	9.12164	8.54363	8.02155	7.54879	7.11963	6.37286	6.04716
18	14.99203	14.35336	13.75351	12.65930	11.68959	10.82760	10.05909	9.37189	8.75563	8.20141	7.70162	7.24967	6.46742	6.12797
19	15.67846	14.97889	14.32380	13.13394	12.08532	11.15812	10.33560	9.60360	8.95011	8.36492	7.83929	7.36578	6.55037	6.19823
20	16.35143	15.58916	14.87747	13.59033	12.46221	11.46992	10.59401	9.81815	9.12855	8.51356	7.96333	7.46944	6.62313	6.25933
21	17.01121	16.18455	15.41502	14.02916	12.82115	11.76408	10.83553	10.01680	9.29224	8.64869	8.07507	7.56200	6.68696	6.31246
22	17.65805	16.76541	15.93692	14.45112	13.16300	12.04158	11.06124	10.20074	9.44243	8.77154	8.17574	7.64465	6.74294	6.35866
23	18.29220	17.33211	16.44361	14.85684	13.48857	12.30338	11.27219	10.37106	9.58021	8.88322	8.26643	7.71843	6.79206	6.39884
24	18.91393	17.88499	16.93554	15.24696	13.79864	12.55036	11.46933	10.52876	9.70661	8.98474	8.34814	7.78432	6.83514	6.43377
25	19.52346	18.42438	17.41315	15.62208	14.09394	12.78336	11.65358	10.67478	9.82258	9.07704	8.42174	7.84314	6.87293	6.46415
26	20.12104	18.95061	17.87684	15.98277	14.37519	13.00317	11.82578	10.80998	9.92897	9.16095	8.48806	7.89566	6.90608	6.49056
27	20.70690	19.46401	18.32703	16.32959	14.64303	13.21053	11.98671	10.93516	10.02658	9.23722	8.54780	7.94255	6.93515	6.51353
28	21.28127	19.96489	18.76411	16.66306	14.89813	13.40616	12.13711	11.05108	10.11613	9.30657	8.60162	7.98442	6.96066	6.53351
29	21.84438	20.45355	19.18845	16.98371	15.14107	13.59072	12.27767	11.15841	10.19828	9.36961	8.65011	8.02181	6.98304	6.55088
30	22.39646	20.93029	19.60044	17.29203	15.37245	13.76483	12.40904	11.25778	10.27365	9.42691	8.69379	8.05518	7.00266	6.56598
31	22.93770	21.39541	20.00043	17.58849	15.59281	13.92909	12.53181	11.34980	10.34280	9.47901	8.73315	8.08499	7.01988	6.57911
32	23.46833	21.84918	20.38877	17.87355	15.80268	14.08404	12.64656	11.43500	10.40624	9.52638	8.76860	8.11159	7.03498	6.59053
33	23.98856	22.29188	20.76579	18.14765	16.00255	14.23023	12.75379	11.51389	10.46444	9.56943	8.80054	8.13535	7.04823	6.60046
34	24.49859	22.72379	21.13184	18.41120	16.19290	14.36814	12.85401	11.58693	10.51784	9.60857	8.82932	8.15656	7.05985	6.60910
35	24.99862	23.14516	21.48722	18.66461	16.37419	14.49825	12.94767	11.65457	10.56682	9.64416	8.85524	8.17550	7.07005	6.61661
36	25.48884	23.55625	21.83225	18.90828	16.54685	14.62099	13.03521	11.71719	10.61176	9.67651	8.87859	8.19241	7.07899	6.62314
37	25.96945	23.95732	22.16724	19.14258	16.71129	14.73678	13.11702	11.77518	10.65299	9.70592	8.89963	8.20751	7.08683	6.62881
38	26.44064	24.34860	22.49246	19.36786	16.86789	14.84602	13.19347	11.82887	10.69082	9.73265	8.91859	8.22099	7.09371	6.63375
39	26.90259	24.73034	22.80822	19.58448	17.01704	14.94907	13.26493	11.87858	10.72552	9.75696	8.93567	8.23303	7.09975	6.63805
40	27.35548	25.10278	23.11477	19.79277	17.15909	15.04630	13.33171	11.92461	10.75736	9.77905	8.95105	8.24378	7.10504	6.64178
45	29.49016	26.83302	24.51871	20.72004	17.77407	15.45583	13.60552	12.10840	10.88120	9.86281	9.00791	8.28252	7.12322	6.65429
50	31.42361	28.36231	25.72976	21.48218	18.25593	15.76186	13.80075	12.23348	10.96168	9.91481	9.04165	8.30450	7.13266	6.66051

TABLE I-3: Present value of an annuity due of n payments of 1: (P/AD, i, n)

$$P/AD = \left[\frac{1 - \frac{1}{(1+i)^n}}{i}\right] \times (1+i)$$

n	2%	2.5%	3%	4%	5%	6%	7%	8%	9%	10%	11%	12%	14%	15%
1	1.00000	1.00000	1.00000	1.00000	1.00000	1.00000	1.00000	1.00000	1.00000	1.00000	1.00000	1.00000	1.00000	1.00000
2	1.98039	1.97561	1.97087	1.96154	1.95238	1.94340	1.93458	1.92593	1.91743	1.90909	1.90090	1.89286	1.87719	1.86957
3	2.94156	2.92742	2.91347	2.88609	2.85941	2.83339	2.80802	2.78326	2.75911	2.73554	2.71252	2.69005	2.64666	2.62571
4	3.88388	3.85602	3.82861	3.77509	3.72325	3.67301	3.62432	3.57710	3.53129	3.48685	3.44371	3.40183	3.32163	3.28323
5	4.80773	4.76197	4.71710	4.62990	4.54595	4.46511	4.38721	4.31213	4.23972	4.16987	4.10245	4.03735	3.91371	3.85498
6	5.71346	5.64583	5.57971	5.45182	5.32948	5.21236	5.10020	4.99271	4.88965	4.79079	4.69590	4.60478	4.43308	4.35216
7	6.60143	6.50813	6.41719	6.24214	6.07569	5.91732	5.76654	5.62288	5.48592	5.35526	5.23054	5.11141	4.88867	4.78448
8	7.47199	7.34939	7.23028	7.00205	6.78637	6.58238	6.38929	6.20637	6.03295	5.86842	5.71220	5.56376	5.28830	5.16042
9	8.32548	8.17014	8.01969	7.73274	7.46321	7.20979	6.97130	6.74664	6.53482	6.33493	6.14612	5.96764	5.63886	5.48732
10	9.16224	8.97087	8.78611	8.43533	8.10782	7.80169	7.51523	7.24689	6.99525	6.75902	6.53705	6.32825	5.94637	5.77158
11	9.98259	9.75206	9.53020	9.11090	8.72173	8.36009	8.02358	7.71008	7.41766	7.14457	6.88923	6.65022	6.21612	6.01877
12	10.78685	10.51421	10.25262	9.76048	9.30641	8.88687	8.49867	8.13896	7.80519	7.49506	7.20652	6.93770	6.45273	6.23371
13	11.57534	11.25776	10.95400	10.38507	9.86325	9.38384	8.94269	8.53608	8.16073	7.81369	7.49236	7.19437	6.66029	6.42062
14	12.34837	11.98318	11.63496	10.98565	10.39357	9.85268	9.35765	8.90378	8.48690	8.10336	7.74987	7.42355	6.84236	6.58315
15	13.10625	12.69091	12.29607	11.56312	10.89864	10.29498	9.74547	9.24424	8.78615	8.36669	7.98187	7.62817	7.00207	6.72448
16	13.84926	13.38138	12.93794	12.11839	11.37966	10.71225	10.10791	9.55948	9.06069	8.60608	8.19087	7.81086	7.14217	6.84737
17	14.57771	14.05500	13.56110	12.65230	11.83777	11.10590	10.44665	9.85137	9.31256	8.82371	8.37916	7.97399	7.26506	6.95423
18	15.29187	14.71220	14.16612	13.16567	12.27407	11.47726	10.76322	10.12164	9.54363	9.02155	8.54879	8.11963	7.37286	7.04716
19	15.99203	15.35336	14.75351	13.65930	12.68959	11.82760	11.05909	10.37189	9.75563	9.20141	8.70162	8.24967	7.46742	7.12797
20	16.67846	15.97889	15.32380	14.13394	13.08532	12.15812	11.33560	10.60360	9.95011	9.36492	8.83929	8.36578	7.55037	7.19823
21	17.35143	16.58916	15.87747	14.59033	13.46221	12.46992	11.59401	10.81815	10.12855	9.51356	8.96333	8.46944	7.62313	7.25933
22	18.01121	17.18455	16.41502	15.02916	13.82115	12.76408	11.83553	11.01680	10.29224	9.64869	9.07507	8.56200	7.68696	7.31246
23	18.65805	17.76541	16.93692	15.45112	14.16300	13.04158	12.06124	11.20074	10.44243	9.77154	9.17574	8.64465	7.74294	7.35866
24	19.29220	18.33211	17.44361	15.85684	14.48857	13.30338	12.27219	11.37106	10.58021	9.88322	9.26643	8.71843	7.79206	7.39884
25	19.91393	18.88499	17.93554	16.24696	14.79864	13.55036	12.46933	11.52876	10.70661	9.98474	9.34814	8.78432	7.83514	7.43377
26	20.52346	19.42438	18.41315	16.62208	15.09394	13.78336	12.65358	11.67478	10.82258	10.07704	9.42174	8.84314	7.87293	7.46415
27	21.12104	19.95061	18.87684	16.98277	15.37519	14.00317	12.82578	11.80998	10.92897	10.16095	9.48806	8.89566	7.90608	7.49056
28	21.70690	20.46401	19.32703	17.32959	15.64303	14.21053	12.98671	11.93516	11.02658	10.23722	9.54780	8.94255	7.93515	7.51353
29	22.28127	20.96489	19.76411	17.66306	15.89813	14.40616	13.13711	12.05108	11.11613	10.30657	9.60162	8.98442	7.96066	7.53351
30	22.84438	21.45355	20.18845	17.98371	16.14107	14.59072	13.27767	12.15841	11.19828	10.36961	9.65011	9.02181	7.98304	7.55088
31	23.39646	21.93029	20.60044	18.29203	16.37245	14.76483	13.40904	12.25778	11.27365	10.42691	9.69379	9.05518	8.00266	7.56598
32	23.93770	22.39541	21.00043	18.58849	16.59281	14.92909	13.53181	12.34980	11.34280	10.47901	9.73315	9.08499	8.01988	7.57911
33	24.46833	22.84918	21.38877	18.87355	16.80268	15.08404	13.64656	12.43500	11.40624	10.52638	9.76860	9.11159	8.03498	7.59053
34	24.98856	23.29188	21.76579	19.14765	17.00255	15.23023	13.75379	12.51389	11.46444	10.56943	9.80054	9.13535	8.04823	7.60046
35	25.49859	23.72379	22.13184	19.41120	17.19290	15.36814	13.85401	12.58693	11.51784	10.60857	9.82932	9.15656	8.05985	7.60910
36	25.99862	24.14516	22.48722	19.66461	17.37419	15.49825	13.94767	12.65457	11.56682	10.64416	9.85524	9.17550	8.07005	7.61661
37	26.48884	24.55625	22.83225	19.90828	17.54685	15.62099	14.03521	12.71719	11.61176	10.67651	9.87859	9.19241	8.07899	7.62314
38	26.96945	24.95732	23.16724	20.14258	17.71129	15.73678	14.11702	12.77518	11.65299	10.70592	9.89963	9.20751	8.08683	7.62881
39	27.44064	25.34860	23.49246	20.36786	17.86789	15.84602	14.19347	12.82887	11.69082	10.73265	9.91859	9.22099	8.09371	7.63375
40	27.90259	25.73034	23.80822	20.58448	18.01704	15.94907	14.26493	12.87858	11.72552	10.75696	9.93567	9.23303	8.09975	7.63805
45	30.07996	27.50385	25.25427	21.54884	18.66277	16.38318	14.55791	13.07707	11.86051	10.84909	9.99878	9.27642	8.12047	7.65244
50	32.05208	29.07137	26.50166	22.34147	19.16872	16.70757	14.76680	13.21216	11.94823	10.90630	10.03624	9.30104	8.13123	7.65959

Index